Lecture Notes in Artificial Intelligence 4701

Edited by J. G. Carbonell and J. Siekmann

Subseries of Lecture Notes in Computer Science

Joost N. Kok   Jacek Koronacki
Ramon Lopez de Mantaras   Stan Matwin
Dunja Mladenič   Andrzej Skowron (Eds.)

Machine Learning: ECML 2007

18th European Conference on Machine Learning
Warsaw, Poland, September 17-21, 2007
Proceedings

Springer

Series Editors

Jaime G. Carbonell, Carnegie Mellon University, Pittsburgh, PA, USA
Jörg Siekmann, University of Saarland, Saarbrücken, Germany

Volume Editors

Joost N. Kok
Leiden University, The Netherlands
E-mail: joost@liacs.nl

Jacek Koronacki
Polish Academy of Sciences, Warsaw, Poland
E-mail: korona@ipipan.waw.pl

Ramon Lopez de Mantaras
Spanish National Research Council (CSIC), Bellaterra, Spain
E-mail: mantaras@iiia.csic.es

Stan Matwin
University of Ottawa, Canada
E-mail: stan@site.uottawa.ca

Dunja Mladenič
Jožef Stefan Institute, Ljubljana, Slovenia
E-mail: Dunja.Mladenic@ihjs.si

Andrzej Skowron
Warsaw University, Poland
E-mail: skowron@mimuw.edu.pl

Library of Congress Control Number: 2007934766

CR Subject Classification (1998): I.2, F.2.2, F.4.1, H.2.8

LNCS Sublibrary: SL 7 – Artificial Intelligence

ISSN 0302-9743
ISBN-10 3-540-74957-8 Springer Berlin Heidelberg New York
ISBN-13 978-3-540-74957-8 Springer Berlin Heidelberg New York

Springer is a part of Springer Science+Business Media

springer.com

Printed in Germany

Typesetting: Camera-ready by author, data conversion by Scientific Publishing Services, Chennai, India
Printed on acid-free paper SPIN: 12124169 06/3180 5 4 3 2 1 0

Preface

The two premier annual European conferences in the areas of machine learning and data mining have been collocated ever since the first joint conference in Freiburg, 2001. The European Conference on Machine Learning (ECML) traces its origins to 1986, when the first European Working Session on Learning was held in Orsay, France. The European Conference on Principles and Practice of Knowledge Discovery in Databases (PKDD) was first held in 1997 in Trondheim, Norway. Over the years, the ECML/PKDD series has evolved into one of the largest and most selective international conferences in machine learning and data mining. In 2007, the seventh collocated ECML/PKDD took place during September 17–21 on the central campus of Warsaw University and in the nearby Staszic Palace of the Polish Academy of Sciences.

The conference for the third time used a hierarchical reviewing process. We nominated 30 Area Chairs, each of them responsible for one sub-field or several closely related research topics. Suitable areas were selected on the basis of the submission statistics for ECML/PKDD 2006 and for last year's International Conference on Machine Learning (ICML 2006) to ensure a proper load balance among the Area Chairs. A joint Program Committee (PC) was nominated for the two conferences, consisting of some 300 renowned researchers, mostly proposed by the Area Chairs. This joint PC, the largest of the series to date, allowed us to exploit synergies and deal competently with topic overlaps between ECML and PKDD.

ECML/PKDD 2007 received 592 abstract submissions. As in previous years, to assist the reviewers and the Area Chairs in their final recommendation authors had the opportunity to communicate their feedback after the reviewing phase. For a small number of conditionally accepted papers, authors were asked to carry out minor revisions subject to the final acceptance by the Area Chair responsible for their submission. With very few exceptions, every full submission was reviewed by three PC members. Based on these reviews, on feedback from the authors, and on discussions among the reviewers, the Area Chairs provided a recommendation for each paper. The four Program Chairs made the final program decisions following a 2-day meeting in Warsaw in June 2007. Continuing the tradition of previous events in the series, we accepted full papers with an oral presentation and short papers with a poster presentation. We selected 41 full papers and 37 short papers for ECML, and 28 full papers and 35 short papers for PKDD. The acceptance rate for full papers is 11.6% and the overall acceptance rate is 23.8%, in accordance with the high-quality standards of the conference series. Besides the paper and poster sessions, ECML/PKDD 2007 also featured 12 workshops, seven tutorials, the ECML/PKDD Discovery Challenge, and the Industrial Track.

An excellent slate of Invited Speakers is another strong point of the conference program. We are grateful to Ricardo Bazea-Yates (Yahoo! Research Barcelona), Peter Flach (University of Bristol), Tom Mitchell (Carnegie Mellon University), and Barry Smyth (University College Dublin) for their participation in ECML/PKDD 2007. The abstracts of their presentations are included in this volume.

We distinguished four outstanding contributions; the awards were generously sponsored by the *Machine Learning Journal* and the *KD-Ubiq network*.

ECML Best Paper: Angela Kimming, Luc De Raedt and Hannu Toivonen: "Probabilistic Explanation-Based Learning"

PKDD Best Paper: Toon Calders and Szymon Jaroszewicz: "Efficient AUC-Optimization for Classification"

ECML Best Student Paper: Daria Sorokina, Rich Caruana, and Mirek Riedewald: "Additive Groves of Regression Trees"

PKDD Best Student Paper: Dikan Xing, Wenyuan Dai, Gui-Rong Xue, and Yong Yu: "Bridged Refinement for Transfer Learning"

This year we introduced the Industrial Track chaired by Florence d'Alché-Buc (Université d'Evry-Val d'Essonne) and Marko Grobelnik (Jožef Stefan Institute, Slovenia) consisting of selected talks with a strong industrial component presenting research from the area covered by the ECML/PKDD conference.

For the first time in the history of ECML/PKDD, the conference proceedings were available on-line to conference participants during the conference. We are grateful to Springer for accommodating this new access channel for the proceedings. Inspired by some related conferences (ICML, KDD, ISWC) we introduced videorecording, as we would like to save at least the invited talks and presentations of award papers for the community and make them accessible at **http://videolectures.net/**.

This year's Discovery Challenge was devoted to three problems: user behavior prediction from Web traffic logs, HTTP traffic classification, and Sumerian literature understanding. The Challenge was co-organized by Piotr Ejdys (Gemius SA), Hung Son Nguyen (Warsaw University), Pascal Poncelet (EMA-LGI2P) and Jerzy Tyszkiewicz (Warsaw University); 122 teams participated. For the first task, the three finalists were:

Malik Tahir Hassan, Khurum Nazir Junejo and Asim Karim from Lahore University, Pakistan

Krzysztof Dembczyński and Wojciech Kotłowski from Poznań University of Technology, Poland and Marcin Sydow from Polish-Japanese Institute of Information Technology, Poland

Tung-Ying Lee from National Tsing Hua University, Taiwan

Results for the other Discovery Challenge tasks were not available at the time the proceedings were finalized, but were announced at the conference.

We are all indebted to the Area Chairs, Program Committee members and external reviewers for their commitment and hard work that resulted in a rich but selective scientific program for ECML/PKDD. We are particularly grateful to those reviewers who helped with additional reviews at very short notice to assist us in a small number of difficult decisions. We further thank our Workshop and Tutorial Chairs Marzena Kryszkiewicz (Warsaw Technical University) and Jan Rauch (University of Economics, Prague) for selecting and coordinating the 12 workshops and seven tutorial events that accompanied the conference; the workshop organizers, tutorial presenters, and the organizers of the Discovery Challenge and the Industrial track; Richard van de Stadt and CyberChairPRO for competent and flexible support; Warsaw University and the Polish Academy of Sciences (Institute of Computer Science) for their local and organizational support. Special thanks are due to the Local Chair, Marcin Szczuka, Warsaw University (assisted by Michal Ciesiołka from the Polish Academy of Sciences) for the many hours spent making sure that all the details came together to ensure the success of the conference. Finally, we are grateful to the Steering Committee and the ECML/PKDD community that entrusted us with the organization of the ECML/PKDD 2007.

Most of all, however, we would like to thank all the authors who trusted us with their submissions, thereby contributing to the one of the main yearly events in the life of our vibrant research community.

September 2007

Joost Kok (PKDD Program co-Chair)
Jacek Koronacki (General Chair)
Ramon Lopez de Mantaras (General Chair)
Stan Matwin (ECML Program co-Chair)
Dunja Mladenič (ECML Program co-Chair)
Andrzej Skowron (PKDD Program co-Chair)

Organization

General Chairs

Ramon Lopez de Mantaras (Spanish Council for Scientific Research)
Jacek Koronacki (Polish Academy of Sciences)

Program Chairs

Joost N. Kok (Leiden University)
Stan Matwin (University of Ottawa and Polish Academy of Sciences)
Dunja Mladenič (Jožef Stefan Institute)
Andrzej Skowron (Warsaw University)

Local Chairs

Michał Ciesiołka (Polish Academy of Sciences)
Marcin Szczuka (Warsaw University)

Tutorial Chair

Jan Rauch (University of Economics, Prague)

Workshop Chair

Marzena Kryszkiewicz (Warsaw University of Technology)

Discovery Challenge Chair

Hung Son Nguyen (Warsaw University)

Industrial Track Chairs

Florence d'Alché-Buc (Université d'Evry-Val d'Essonne)
Marko Grobelnik (Jozef Stefan Institute)

Steering Committee

Jean-François Boulicaut
Pavel Brazdil
Rui Camacho
Floriana Esposito
Johannes Fürnkranz
João Gama
Fosca Gianotti
Alípio Jorge
Dino Pedreschi
Tobias Scheffer
Myra Spiliopoulou
Luís Torgo

Area Chairs

Michael R. Berthold
Hendrik Blockeel
Olivier Chapelle
James Cussens
Kurt Driessens
Peter Flach
Eibe Frank
Johannes Fürnkranz
Thomas Gärtner
João Gama
Rayid Ghani
Jerzy Grzymala-Busse
Eamonn Keogh
Kristian Kersting
Mieczysław A. Kłopotek
Stefan Kramer
Pedro Larranaga
Claire Nedellec
Andreas Nürnberger
George Paliouras
Bernhard Pfahringer
Enric Plaza
Luc De Raedt
Tobias Scheffer
Giovanni Semeraro
Władysław Skarbek
Myra Spiliopoulou
Hannu Toivonen
Luís Torgo
Paul Utgoff

Program Committee

Charu C. Aggarwal
Concha Bielza
Jesús Aguilar-Ruiz
Mikhail Bilenko
David W. Aha
Francesco Bonchi
Nahla Ben Amor
Gianluca Bontempi
Sarabjot Singh Anand
Christian Borgelt
Annalisa Appice
Karsten M. Borgwardt
Josep-Lluis Arcos
Daniel Borrajo
Walid G. Aref
Antal van den Bosch
Eva Armengol
Henrik Boström
Anthony J. Bagnall
Marco Botta
Antonio Bahamonde
Jean-François Boulicaut
Sugato Basu
Janez Brank
Bettina Berendt
Thorsten Brants
Francesco Bergadano
Ulf Brefeld
Ralph Bergmann
Carla E. Brodley
Steffen Bickel
Paul Buitelaar

Toon Calders
Luis M. de Campos
Nicola Cancedda
Claudio Carpineto
Jesús Cerquides
Kaushik Chakrabarti
Chien-Chung Chan
Amanda Clare
Ira Cohen
Fabrizio Costa
Susan Craw
Bruno Crémilleux
Tom Croonenborghs
Juan Carlos Cubero
Pádraig Cunningham
Andrzej Czyżewski
Walter Daelemans
Ian Davidson
Marco Degemmis
Olivier Delalleau
Jitender S. Deogun
Marcin Detyniecki
Belén Diaz-Agudo
Chris H.Q. Ding
Carlotta Domeniconi
Marek J. Druzdzel
Sašo Džeroski
Tina Eliassi-Rad
Tapio Elomaa
Abolfazl Fazel Famili
Wei Fan
Ad Feelders
Alan Fern
George Forman
Linda C. van der Gaag
Patrick Gallinari
José A. Gámez
Alex Gammerman
Minos N. Garofalakis
Gemma C. Garriga
Eric Gaussier
Pierre Geurts
Fosca Gianotti
Attilio Giordana
Robert L. Givan
Bart Goethals
Elisabet Golobardes
Pedro A. González-Calero
Marko Grobelnik
Dimitrios Gunopulos
Maria Halkidi
Mark Hall
Matthias Hein
Jose Hernandez-Orallo
Colin de la Higuera
Melanie Hilario
Shoji Hirano
Tu-Bao Ho
Jaakko Hollmen
Geoffrey Holmes
Frank Höppner
Tamás Horváth
Andreas Hotho
Jiayuan Huang
Eyke Hüllemeier
Masahiro Inuiguchi
Inaki Inza
Manfred Jaeger
Szymon Jaroszewicz
Rosie Jones
Edwin D. de Jong
Alípio Mário Jorge
Tamer Kahveci
Alexandros Kalousis
Hillol Kargupta
Andreas Karwath
George Karypis
Samuel Kaski
Dimitar Kazakov
Ross D. King
Frank Klawonn
Ralf Klinkenberg
George Kollios
Igor Kononenko
Bożena Kostek
Walter A. Kosters
Miroslav Kubat
Halina Kwasnicka
James T. Kwok
Nicolas Lachiche

Michail G. Lagoudakis
Niels Landwehr
Pedro Larranaga
Pavel Laskov
Mark Last
Dominique Laurent
Nada Lavrac
Quoc V. Le
Guy Lebanon
Ulf Leser
Jure Leskovec
Jessica Lin
Francesca A. Lisi
Pasquale Lops
Jose A. Lozano
Peter Lucas
Richard Maclin
Donato Malerba
Nikos Mamoulis
Suresh Manandhar
Stéphane Marchand-Maillet
Elena Marchiori
Lluis Marquez
Yuji Matsumoto
Michael May
Mike Mayo
Thorsten Meinl
Prem Melville
Rosa Meo
Taneli Mielikäinen
Bamshad Mobasher
Serafín Moral
Katharina Morik
Hiroshi Motoda
Toshinori Munakata
Ion Muslea
Olfa Nasraoui
Jennifer Neville
Siegfried Nijssen
Joakim Nivre
Ann Nowe
Arlindo L. Oliveira
Santi Ontañón
Miles Osborne
Martijn van Otterlo
David Page
Spiros Papadimitriou
Srinivasan Parthasarathy
Andrea Passerini
Jose M. Peña
Lourdes Peña Castillo
José M. Peña Sánchez
James F. Peters
Johann Petrak
Lech Polkowski
Han La Poutre
Philippe Preux
Katharina Probst
Tapani Raiko
Ashwin Ram
Sheela Ramanna
Jan Ramon
Zbigniew W. Ras
Chotirat Ann Ratanamahatana
Francesco Ricci
John Riedl
Christophe Rigotti
Celine Robardet
Victor Robles
Marko Robnik-Sikonja
Juho Rousu
Céline Rouveirol
Ulrich Rückert (TU München)
Ulrich Rückert (Univ. Paderborn)
Stefan Rüping
Henryk Rybiński
Lorenza Saitta
Hiroshi Sakai
Roberto Santana
Martin Scholz
Matthias Schubert
Michele Sebag
Sandip Sen
Jouni K. Seppänen
Galit Shmueli
Arno Siebes
Alejandro Sierra
Vikas Sindhwani
Arul Siromoney
Dominik Ślęzak

Carlos Soares
Maarten van Someren
Alvaro Soto
Alessandro Sperduti
Jaideep Srivastava
Jerzy Stefanowski
David J. Stracuzzi
Jan Struyf
Gerd Stumme
Zbigniew Suraj
Einoshin Suzuki
Roman Swiniarski
Marcin Sydow
Piotr Synak
Marcin Szczuka
Luis Talavera
Matthew E. Taylor
Yannis Theodoridis
Kai Ming Ting
Ljupco Todorovski
Volker Tresp
Shusaku Tsumoto
Karl Tuyls
Michalis Vazirgiannis
Katja Verbeeck
Jean-Philippe Vert
Michail Vlachos
Haixun Wang
Jason Tsong-Li Wang
Takashi Washio
Gary M. Weiss
Sholom M. Weiss
Shimon Whiteson
Marco Wiering
Slawomir T. Wierzchoń
Graham J. Williams
Stefan Wrobel
Ying Yang
JingTao Yao
Yiyu Yao
François Yvon
Bianca Zadrozny
Mohammed J. Zaki
Gerson Zaverucha
Filip Zelezny
ChengXiang Zhai
Yi Zhang
Zhi-Hua Zhou
Jerry Zhu
Wojciech Ziarko
Albrecht Zimmermann

Additional Reviewers

Rezwan Ahmed
Fabio Aiolli
Dima Alberg
Vassilis Athitsos
Maurizio Atzori
Anne Auger
Paulo Azevedo
Pierpaolo Basile
Margherita Berardi
Andre Bergholz
Michele Berlingerio
Kanishka Bhaduri
Konstantin Biatov
Jerzy Błaszczyński
Gianluca Bontempi
Yann-ael Le Borgne
Zoran Bosnic
Remco Bouckaert
Agnès Braud
Bjoern Bringmann
Emma Byrne
Olivier Caelen
Rossella Cancelliere
Giovanna Castellano
Michelangelo Ceci
Hyuk Cho
Kamalika Das
Souptik Datta
Uwe Dick
Laura Dietz
Marcos Domingues
Haimonti Dutta

Marc Dymetman
Stefan Eickeler
Timm Euler
Tanja Falkowski
Fernando Fernandez
Francisco J. Ferrer-Troyano
Cèsar Ferri
Daan Fierens
Blaz Fortuna
Alexandre Francisco
Mingyan Gao
Fabián Güiza
Anna Lisa Gentile
Amol N. Ghoting
Arnaud Giacometti
Valentin Gjorgjioski
Robby Goetschalckx
Derek Greene
Perry Groot
Philip Groth
Daniele Gunetti
Bernd Gutmann
Sattar Hashemi
Yann-Michael De Hauwere
Vera Hollink
Yi Huang
Leo Iaquinta
Alexander Ilin
Tasadduq Imam
Tao-Yuan Jen
Felix Jungermann
Andrzej Kaczmarek
Benjamin Haibe Kains
Juha Karkkainen
Rohit Kate
Chris Kauffman
Arto Klami
Jiri Klema
Dragi Kocev
Christine Koerner
Kevin Kontos
Petra Kralj
Anita Krishnakumar
Matjaž Kukar
Brian Kulis
Arnd Christian König
Christine Körner
Fei Tony Liu
Antonio LaTorre
Anne Laurent
Baoli Li
Zi Lin
Bin Liu
Yan Liu
Corrado Loglisci
Rachel Lomasky
Carina Lopes
Chuan Lu
Pierre Mahé
Markus Maier
Giuseppe Manco
Irina Matveeva
Nicola Di Mauro
Dimitrios Mavroeidis
Stijn Meganck
Ingo Mierswa
Mirjam Minor
Abhilash Alexander Miranda
João Moreira
Sourav Mukherjee
Canh Hao Nguyen
Duc Dung Nguyen
Tuan Trung Nguyen
Janne Nikkilä
Xia Ning
Blaž Novak
Irene Ntoutsi
Riccardo Ortale
Stanisław Osiński
Kivanc Ozonat
Aline Paes
Pance Panov
Thomas Brochmann Pedersen
Maarten Peeters
Ruggero Pensa
Xuan-Hieu Phan
Benjarath Phoophakdee
Aloisio Carlos de Pina
Christian Plagemann
Jose M. Puerta

Aritz Pérez
Chedy Raissi
M. Jose Ramirez-Quintana
Umaa Rebbapragada
Stefan Reckow
Chiara Renso
Matthias Renz
Francois Rioult
Domingo Rodriguez-Baena
Sten Sagaert
Luka Šajn
Esin Saka
Saeed Salem
Antonio Salmeron
Eerika Savia
Anton Schaefer
Leander Schietgat
Gaetano Scioscia
Howard Scordio
Sven Van Segbroeck
Ivica Slavkov
Larisa Soldatova
Arnaud Soulet
Eduardo Spynosa
Volkmar Sterzing
Christof Stoermann
Jiang Su
Piotr Szczuko
Alexander Tartakovski
Olivier Teytaud
Marisa Thoma
Eufemia Tinelli
Ivan Titov
Roberto Trasarti
George Tsatsaronis
Katharina Tschumitschew
Duygu Ucar
Antonio Varlaro
Shankar Vembu
Celine Vens
Marcos Vieira
Peter Vrancx
Nikil Wale
Chao Wang
Dongrong Wen
Arkadiusz Wojna
Yuk Wah Wong
Adam Woźnica
Michael Wurst
Wei Xu
Xintian Yang
Monika Zakova
Luke Zettlemoyer
Xueyuan Zhou
Albrecht Zimmermann

Sponsors

We wish to express our gratitude to the sponsors of ECML/PKDD 2007 for their essential contribution to the conference. We wish to thank Warsaw University, Faculty of Mathematics, Informatics and Mechanics, and Institute of Computer Science, Polish Academy of Sciences for providing financial and organizational means for the conference; the European Office of Aerospace Research and Developement, Air Force Office of Scientific Research, United States Air Force Research Laboratory, for their generous financial support.[1] KDUbiq European Coordination Action for supporting Poster Reception, Student Travel Awards, and the Best Paper Awards; Pascal European Network of Excellence for sponsoring the Invited Speaker Program, the Industrial Track and the video-recording of the invited talks and presentations of the four Award Papers; Jožef Stefan Institute, Slovenia, SEKT European Integrated project and Unilever R & D for their financial support; the *Machine Learning Journal* for supporting the Student Best Paper Awards; Gemius S.A. for sponsoring and supporting the Discovery Challenge. We also wish to express our gratitude to the following companies and institutions that provided us with data and expertise which were essential components of the Discovery Challenge: Bee Ware, l'École des Mines d'Alès, LIRMM - The Montpellier Laboratory of Computer Science, Robotics, and Microelectronics, and Warsaw University, Faculty of Mathematics, Informatics and Mechanics. We also acknowledge the support of LOT Polish Airlines.

[1] AFOSR/EOARD support is not intended to express or imply endorsement by the U.S. Federal Government.

Table of Contents

Invited Talks

Long Papers

Short Papers

Learning, Information Extraction and the Web*

Tom M. Mitchell

Machine Learning Department
Carnegie Mellon University, USA
tom.mitchell@cs.cmu.edu

Abstract. Significant progress has been made recently in semi-supervised learning algorithms that require less labeled training data by utilizing unlabeled data. Much of this progress has been made in the context of natural language analysis (e.g., semi-supervised learning for named entity recognition and for relation extraction). This talk will overview progress in this area, present some of our own recent research, and explore the possibility that now is the right time to mount a community-wide effort to develop a never-ending natural language learning system.

---

* Invited speakers at ECML/PKDD are supported by the PASCAL European network of excellence.

J.N. Kok et al. (Eds.): ECML 2007, LNAI 4701, p. 1, 2007.

Putting Things in Order: On the Fundamental Role of Ranking in Classification and Probability Estimation*

Peter A. Flach

Department of Computer Science, University of Bristol, United Kingdom
Peter.Flach@bristol.ac.uk

Abstract. While a binary classifier aims to distinguish positives from negatives, a ranker orders instances from high to low expectation that the instance is positive. Most classification models in machine learning output some score of 'positiveness', and hence can be used as rankers. Conversely, any ranker can be turned into a classifier if we have some instance-independent means of splitting the ranking into positive and negative segments. This could be a fixed score threshold; a point obtained from fixing the slope on the ROC curve; the break-even point between true positive and true negative rates; to mention just a few possibilities.

These connections between ranking and classification notwithstanding, there are considerable differences as well. Classification performance on n examples is measured by accuracy, an $O(n)$ operation; ranking performance, on the other hand, is measured by the area under the ROC curve (AUC), an $O(n \log n)$ operation. The model with the highest AUC does not necessarily dominate all other models, and thus it is possible that another model would achieve a higher accuracy for certain operating conditions, even if its AUC is lower.

However, within certain model classes good ranking performance and good classification performance are more closely related than suggested by the previous remarks. For instance, there is evidence that certain classification models, while designed to optimise accuracy, in effect optimise an AUC-based loss function [1]. It has also been known for some time that decision tree yield convex training set ROC curves by construction [2], and thus optimising training set accuracy is likely to lead to good training set AUC. In this talk I will investigate the relation between ranking and classification more closely.

I will also consider the connection between ranking and probability estimation. The quality of probability estimates can be measured by, e.g., mean squared error in the probability estimates (the Brier score). However, like accuracy, this is an $O(n)$ operation that doesn't fully take ranking performance into account. I will show how a novel decomposition of the Brier score into calibration loss and refinement loss [3] sheds light on both ranking and probability estimation performance. While previous decompositions are approximate [4], our decomposition is an exact one based on the ROC convex hull. (The connection between the ROC convex hull and calibration was independently noted by [5]). In the case of decision trees, the analysis explains the empirical evidence that probability estimation trees produce well-calibrated probabilities [6].

* Invited speakers at ECML/PKDD are supported by the PASCAL European network of excellence.

J.N. Kok et al. (Eds.): ECML 2007, LNAI 4701, pp. 2–3, 2007.

References

1. Rudin, C., Cortes, C., Mohri, M., Schapire, R.E.: Margin-based ranking meets boosting in the middle. In: Auer, P., Meir, R. (eds.) COLT 2005. LNCS (LNAI), vol. 3559, pp. 63–78. Springer, Heidelberg (2005)
2. Ferri, C., Flach, P.A., Hernández-Orallo, J.: Learning decision trees using the area under the ROC curve. In: Proceedings of the Nineteenth International Conference on Machine Learning (ICML 2002), pp. 139–146. Morgan Kaufmann, San Francisco (2002)
3. Flach, P.A., Matsubara, E.T.: A simple lexicographic ranker and probability estimator. In: Kok, J.N., Koronacki, J., Lopez de Mantaras, R., Matwin, S., Mladenič, D., Skowron, A. (eds.) ECML 2007. LNCS, vol. 4701, Springer, Heidelberg (2007)
4. Cohen, I., Goldszmidt, M.: Properties and benefits of calibrated classifiers. In: Boulicaut, J.-F., Esposito, F., Giannotti, F., Pedreschi, D. (eds.) PKDD 2004. LNCS (LNAI), vol. 3202, pp. 125–136. Springer, Heidelberg (2004)
5. Fawcett, T., Niculescu-Mizil, A.: PAV and the ROC convex hull. Machine Learning 68(1), 97–106 (2007)
6. Niculescu-Mizil, A., Caruana, R.: Predicting good probabilities with supervised learning. In: Proceedings of the Twenty-Second International Conference on Machine Learning (ICML 2005), pp. 625–632. ACM, New York (2005)

Mining Queries*

Ricardo Baeza-Yates

Yahoo! Research, Barcelona, Spain
and Yahoo! Research Latin America, Santiago, Chile
ricardo.baeza@upf.edu

Abstract. User queries in search engines and Websites give valuable information on the interests of people. In addition, clicks after queries relate those interests to actual content. Even queries without clicks or answers imply important missing synonyms or content. In this talk we show several examples on how to use this information to improve the performance of search engines, to recommend better queries, to improve the information scent of the content of a Website and ultimately to capture knowledge, as Web queries are the largest wisdom of crowds in Internet.

* Invited speakers at ECML/PKDD are supported by the PASCAL European network of excellence.

J.N. Kok et al. (Eds.): ECML 2007, LNAI 4701, p. 4, 2007.

Adventures in Personalized Information Access*

Barry Smyth

Adaptive Information Cluster, School of Computer Science and Informatics,
University College Dublin, Ireland
barry.smyth@ucd.ie

Abstract. Access to information plays an increasingly important role in our everyday lives and we have come to rely more and more on a variety of information access services to bring us the right information at the right time. Recently the traditional one-size-fits-all approach, which has informed the development of the majority of today's information access services, from search engines to portals, has been brought in to question as researchers consider the advantages of more personalized services. Such services can respond to the learned needs and preferences of individuals and groups of like-minded users. They provide for a more proactive model of information supply in place of today's reactive models of information search. In this talk we will consider the key challenges that motivate the need for a new generation of personalized information services, as well as the pitfalls that lie in wait. We will focus on a number of different information access scenarios, from e-commerce recommender systems and personalized mobile portals to community-based web search. In each case we will describe how different machine learning and data mining ideas have been harnessed to take advantage of key domain constraints in order to deliver information access interfaces that are capable of adapting to the changing needs and preferences of their users. In addition, we will describe the results of a number of user studies that highlight the potential for such technologies to significantly enhance the user experience and the ability of users to locate relevant information quickly and reliably.

* Invited speakers at ECML/PKDD are supported by the PASCAL European network of excellence.

J.N. Kok et al. (Eds.): ECML 2007, LNAI 4701, p. 5, 2007.

Statistical Debugging Using Latent Topic Models*

David Andrzejewski, Anne Mulhern, Ben Liblit, and Xiaojin Zhu

Computer Sciences Department, University of Wisconsin, Madison WI 53706, USA

Abstract. Statistical debugging uses machine learning to model program failures and help identify root causes of bugs. We approach this task using a novel Delta-Latent-Dirichlet-Allocation model. We model execution traces attributed to failed runs of a program as being generated by two types of latent topics: normal usage topics and bug topics. Execution traces attributed to successful runs of the same program, however, are modeled by usage topics only. Joint modeling of both kinds of traces allows us to identify weak bug topics that would otherwise remain undetected. We perform model inference with collapsed Gibbs sampling. In quantitative evaluations on four real programs, our model produces bug topics highly correlated to the true bugs, as measured by the Rand index. Qualitative evaluation by domain experts suggests that our model outperforms existing statistical methods for bug cause identification, and may help support other software tasks not addressed by earlier models.

1 Introduction

We all depend on buggy software. Computers and computer failures are inescapable features of modern life. As software grows ever more complex and more dynamic, perfectly predicting the (mis)behavior of a software application becomes impossible both in theory and in practice. Therefore, we see increasing interest in *statistical debugging*: the use of statistical machine learning to support debugging. Statistical methods can cope with uncertain and incomplete information while still providing best-effort clues about the causes of software failure. In particular, one can collect examples of successful and failed (e.g., crashed) program runs, then use machine learning techniques to identify those software actions which are strongly associated with program failure. Our goal is *not* to predict whether a run succeeded or failed, but to identify potentially multiple types of bugs in the program.

In contrast with earlier work [1,2,3,4,5,6,7,8] we approach this task using *latent topic models*. These models, such as probabilistic Latent Semantic Analysis [9] and Latent Dirichlet Allocation (LDA [10]), have been successfully applied to model natural language documents [11], images [12] and so on. The contribution of the present work is two-fold:

1. To the best of our knowledge, our work is the first to apply latent topic models to debugging. We employ a novel variant of the LDA model. Each run of a program yields a record of its execution behavior. This record is our document; the words in the

* This research was supported in part by AFOSR Grant FA9550-07-1-0210, NSF Grant CCF-0621487, and NLM Training Grant 5T15LM07359.

J.N. Kok et al. (Eds.): ECML 2007, LNAI 4701, pp. 6–17, 2007.

document are the events that have been recorded. We describe these records in greater detail in section 2. We assume that there are multiple hidden *bug topics*, each with its own multinomial word distribution. The record for each failed run consists partly of words generated from a mixture of the bug topics. The task is to automatically infer the bug topics and mixing weights from multiple runs of the program. We would prefer that bug topics and bug causes had a one-to-one correspondence. This is not a property that our analysis guarantees, but we have found that in practice it is likely.

2. Our latent topic model, Delta Latent Dirichlet Allocation (ΔLDA), can identify weak bug topics from strong interference, while existing latent topic models cannot. In statistical debugging, our primary interest is in the bug topics. For example, a particular bug might trigger a specific segment of code, and produce the corresponding words. However, in a typical run such bug word patterns are overwhelmed by much stronger *usage* word patterns (e.g., code to open a file or to print a page), which are executed more frequently and produce more words. As shown in the literature [8] as well as in our experiments, many standard models are confused by usage patterns and cannot identify bug topics satisfactorily. We explicitly model both bug topics and usage topics on a collection of reports from both failed and successful runs. ΔLDA models successful runs using *only usage topics*, and failed runs with *both usage and bug topics*. Thus, the bug topics are forced to explain the differences between successful runs and failed runs, hence the name ΔLDA.

We review concepts of statistical debugging in section 2, present the ΔLDA model and its collapsed Gibbs sampling inference procedure in section 3, and demonstrate its effectiveness for debugging with both a synthetic example and four real programs, i.e., `exif`, `grep`, `gzip`, and `moss`, in section 4. For the task of helping humans identify root causes of bugs, our ΔLDA model performs as well or better than the best previously-proposed statistical methods. Furthermore, it supports related debugging tasks not contemplated by prior work. These benefits are all built upon a single integrated model with a coherent interpretation in both machine-learning and software-engineering terms.

2 Cooperative Bug Isolation

The Cooperative Bug Isolation Project (CBI) is an ongoing effort to enlist large user communities to isolate and ultimately repair the causes of software bugs [13]. Statistical debugging is a critical component of CBI as it allows us to cope with unreliable and incomplete information about failures in deployed software systems. In this section we briefly review the CBI approach and infrastructure to show how it maps software behavior into a document-and-word model suitable for latent topic analysis.

The data for CBI analysis consists of reports generated by instrumented versions of software applications. The code inserted by the CBI instrumentor passively logs many program-internal events of potential interest to bug-hunting software engineers while the software application is being executed. Interesting events may include the direction taken when a branch (`if` statement) is executed, whether a function call returns a negative, zero, or positive result, the presence of unusual floating-point values, and so forth. Via the instrumentation, each run of a program generates a sequence of recorded events. This sequence is the "document"; the recorded events are the "word tokens". The set of all possible events that can be recorded by the instrumentation code corresponds to the set of "word types".

Instrumentation code is distributed throughout the source code of a program. Even a medium-sized program can have hundreds of thousands of instrumentation points (word types); a single event (word token) may occur millions of times during a single run. For reasons of performance, scalability, and user privacy, we cannot record every event. Instead, events are sparsely sampled during each run. A typical sampling rate is $1/100$, meaning each event has only a $1/100$ chance of being observed and recorded each time it occurs. More sophisticated instrumentation can adapt the sampling rate to the expected number of occurrences of a given event, sampling rare events at a higher rate and common events at a lower rate, and thereby increasing the probability that a rare event will be recorded if it occurs. A second practical measure is to discard all event ordering information, and instead report the number of times an event was recorded. A single run, then, results in a single fixed-length vector of event counts, called a *feedback report*. The data in any single feedback report is an incomplete but unbiased random sample of the behavior during that run. In machine-learning terms, a feedback report is a "bag of words" representation of the document generated by a run.

Feedback reports are collected centrally for aggregation and analysis. Reports may come from real users participating in the ongoing CBI public deployment [14] or may be produced in-house with fixed or randomly-generated test suites. Each feedback report carries one additional piece of information: an *outcome flag* recording whether this run succeeded or failed. In the simplest case, all fatal software crashes might be considered "failures" and all non-crashing runs considered "successes." More sophisticated flagging strategies such as comparing program output against that of a known-good reference implementation may also be used.

For any program of non-trivial complexity, we must further assume that there are an unknown number of latent bugs. Because instrumentation is so broad, we must assume that the vast majority of program events are not directly connected to any given bug. Thus, the bug "signal" is both noisy due to sparse sampling and weak relative to the majority non-buggy behavior of the program.

The statistical debugging challenge, then, is as follows. **Given** a large collection of feedback reports of a program, where each report is flagged according to whether the run succeeded or failed, and where there may be a number of bugs, i.e., causes for failure, **distinguish** among these causes of failure, **identify** events that contributed to a failure and are connected with its underlying cause, and **use** this information to help support the debugging process in particular and software understanding more broadly.

3 The ΔLDA Model

Standard LDA [10] models a single document collection. For example, when applied to a collection of failed runs only, standard LDA is likely to recover stronger usage patterns rather than generally weaker bug patterns. In contrast, ΔLDA models a mixed collection of successful and failed runs. We reserve extra bug topics for failed runs in order to capture the weaker bug patterns. By explicitly modeling successful vs. failed

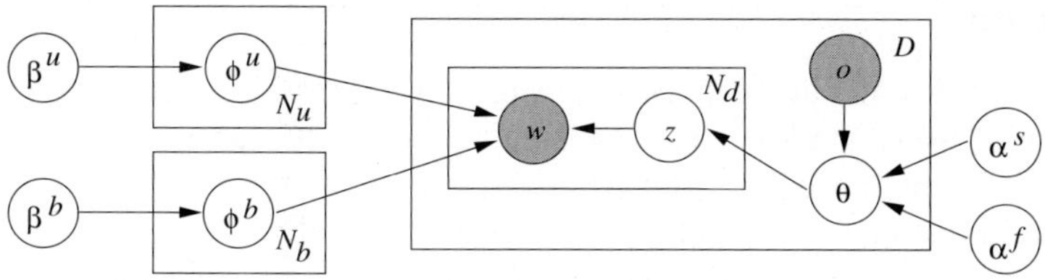

Fig. 1. The ΔLDA model

runs, and usage vs. bug topics, ΔLDA is able to recover the weak bug topics more clearly. The ΔLDA model (Figure 1) has the following major components:

(i) There are N_u usage topics ϕ^u, and N_b bug topics ϕ^b. These are sampled from two Dirichlet distributions: $\phi^u \sim \text{Dir}(\beta^u)$, $\phi^b \sim \text{Dir}(\beta^b)$. We distinguish β^u and β^b (instead of a single β) to facilitate the incorporation of certain types of domain knowledge. For example, if we believe that some parts of the software are more error-prone (e.g., less tested) than others, then the bug topics may focus more on the corresponding words.

(ii) There are a total of D documents. Each document has an observed outcome flag $o \in \{s, f\}$ for successful and failed run, respectively. These D documents constitute the mixed collection of successful and failed runs.

(iii) Each document is generated as a "bag of words" by a mixture of the $N_u + N_b$ topics. The mixing weight θ is sampled from one of two Dirichlet distributions α^s or α^f, depending on the outcome flag o: $\theta \sim \text{Dir}(\alpha^o)$. In the simplest case, the elements in α^s that correspond to bug topics are set to zero, ensuring that any successful run will not use any bug topic[1]. By contrast, all the elements of α^f are greater than zero, allowing failed runs to use both usage and bug topics.

(iv) The rest of the model is identical to LDA: for each of the N_d word positions in the document, one samples a topic index $z \sim \text{Multi}(\theta)$, $z \in \{1, \ldots, N_u + N_b\}$, and produces a word $w \sim \text{Multi}(\phi_z)$.

The ΔLDA model thus specifies the conditional probability $p(\mathbf{w}|\mathbf{o}, \beta^u, \beta^b, \alpha^s, \alpha^f)$, where we use bold face to denote sequences of variables. Omitting hyperparameters for notational simplicity, this can be computed as $p(\mathbf{w}|\mathbf{o}) = \sum_{\mathbf{z}} p(\mathbf{w}|\mathbf{z})p(\mathbf{z}|\mathbf{o})$, where

$$p(\mathbf{w}|\mathbf{z}) = \prod_{i}^{N_u+N_b} \int p(\phi_i|\beta^u, \beta^b) \prod_{j}^{W} \phi_{ij}{}^{n^i_j} \, d\phi_i \tag{1}$$

$$p(\mathbf{z}|\mathbf{o}) = \prod_{d}^{D} \int p(\theta_d|o_d, \alpha^s, \alpha^f) \prod_{i}^{N_u+N_b} \theta_{di}{}^{n^d_i} \, d\theta_d \,. \tag{2}$$

Here W is the vocabulary size, n^i_j is the number of times word-type j is assigned to topic i, and n^d_i is the number of times topic i occurs in document d. Also, ϕ_{ij} is the probability of word j being generated by topic i and θ_{di} is the probability of using topic i in document d.

[1] It is straightforward to allow small but non-zero bug topic weights for successful runs. This is useful if we believe some runs were affected by bugs but did not fail.

3.1 Inference

We are interested in the hidden variables $\mathbf{z}, \theta, \phi$. We can draw $\mathbf{z}$ samples from the posterior $p(\mathbf{z}|\mathbf{w}, \mathbf{o})$ using Markov Chain Monte Carlo (MCMC). In particular, we use collapsed Gibbs sampling [11], drawing from $p(z_k = i|\mathbf{z}_{-k}, \mathbf{w}, \mathbf{o})$ for each site k in sequence. This inference procedure is linear in the number of samples taken, the total number of topics used, and the size of the corpus. Since

$$p(z_k = i|\mathbf{z}_{-k}, \mathbf{w}, \mathbf{o}) = \frac{p(z_k = i, \mathbf{z}_{-k}, \mathbf{w}|\mathbf{o})}{\sum_{i'} p(z_k = i', \mathbf{z}_{-k}, \mathbf{w}|\mathbf{o})}, \tag{3}$$

the site conditionals can be computed from the joint $p(\mathbf{z}, \mathbf{w}|\mathbf{o}) = p(\mathbf{z}|\mathbf{o})p(\mathbf{w}|\mathbf{z})$, as given in (1) and (2). The Dirichlet priors can then be integrated out ("collapsed") in (1) and (2), resulting in the following multivariate Pólya distributions:

$$p(\mathbf{w}|\mathbf{z}) = \prod_{i}^{N_u+N_b} \left[\frac{\Gamma(\sum_{j'}^{W} \beta^i_{j'})}{\Gamma(\sum_{j'}^{W} \beta^i_{j'} + n^i_*)} \prod_{j}^{W} \frac{\Gamma(n^i_j + \beta^i_j)}{\Gamma(\beta^i_j)} \right] \tag{4}$$

$$p(\mathbf{z}|\mathbf{o}) = \prod_{d}^{D} \left[\frac{\Gamma(\sum_{i'}^{N_u+N_b} \alpha^{o_d}_{i'})}{\Gamma(\sum_{i'}^{N_u+N_b} \alpha^{o_d}_{i'} + n^d_*)} \prod_{i}^{N_u+N_b} \frac{\Gamma(n^d_i + \alpha^{o_d}_i)}{\Gamma(\alpha^{o_d}_i)} \right]. \tag{5}$$

Here n^i_* is the count of all words assigned to topic i, and n^d_* is the count of all words contained in document d. β^i_j is the hyperparameter associated with word j in topic i, where β^i is β^u if i is a usage topic and β^b if it is a bug topic. $\alpha^{o_d}_i$ is the hyperparameter associated with topic i for outcome flag value o_d. Rearranging (4) and (5) yields

$$p(z_k = i|\mathbf{z}_{-k}, \mathbf{w}, \mathbf{o}) \propto \left(\frac{n^i_{-k,j_k} + \beta^i_{j_k}}{n^i_{-k,*} + \sum_{j'}^{W} \beta^i_{j'}} \right) \left(\frac{n^{d_k}_{-k,i} + \alpha^{o_k}_i}{n^{d_k}_{-k,*} + \sum_{i'}^{N_u+N_b} \alpha^{o_k}_{i'}} \right). \tag{6}$$

In this equation, all "n_{-k}" are counts excluding the word or topic assignment at position k. Also, j_k is the word at position k, d_k is the document containing position k, and o_k is the outcome flag associated with d_k. This equation allows us to perform collapsed Gibbs sampling efficiently using easily obtainable count values. Note that for topics i such that $\alpha^{o_k}_i = 0$, the count $n^d_{-k,i}$ is also 0, meaning that topic i will never be assigned to this word.

After the MCMC chain mixes, we can use a single sample from the posterior $p(\mathbf{z}|\mathbf{w}, \mathbf{o})$ to estimate ϕ_i, the multinomial over words for topic i, and θ_d, the topic mixture weights for document d:

$$\hat{\phi}_{ij} = \frac{n^i_j + \beta^i_j}{n^i_* + \sum_{j'}^{W} \beta^i_{j'}} \tag{7}$$

$$\hat{\theta}_{di} = \frac{n^d_i + \alpha^{o_d}_i}{n^d_* + \sum_{i'}^{N_u+N_b} \alpha^{o_d}_{i'}}. \tag{8}$$

We use domain expert knowledge to set the hyperparameters $\alpha^s, \alpha^f, \beta^u, \beta^b$, as well as the number of usage and bug topics N_u, N_b. Hyperparameter values used are not specially fitted to our data and should perform well in a variety of situations. Alternatively, these values could be estimated from the data using Bayesian model evidence maximization. This involves finding the values which maximizes the evidence, $p(\mathbf{w}|\mathbf{o})$. In

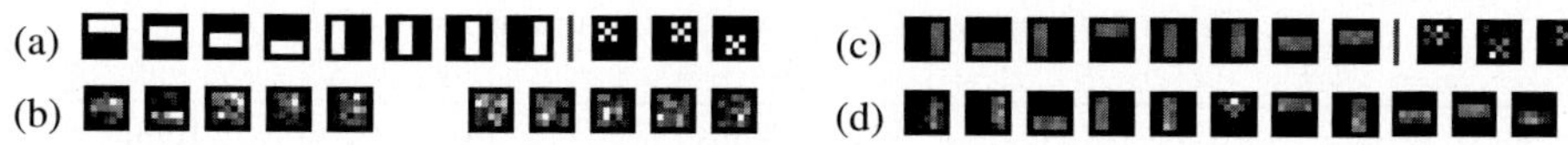

Fig. 2. A toy example showing ΔLDA's ability to recover weak bug topics. (a) Truth: 8 usage topics and 3 bug topics; (b) Example success (left) and failure (right) documents; (c) ΔLDA successfully recovers the usage and bug topics; (d) Standard LDA cannot recover or identify bug topics.

particular, the Gibbs sampling technique employed by our model allows the convenient estimation of the evidence by importance sampling, using **z** samples drawn from our MCMC chain [15].

4 Experiments

4.1 A Toy Example

We first use a toy dataset to demonstrate ΔLDA's ability to identify bug topics. The vocabulary consists of 25 pixels in a 5-by-5 grid. We use 8 usage topics and 3 bug topics as in Figure 2(a). Each of the 8 usage topics corresponds to a uniform distribution over a 2-pixel wide horizontal or vertical bar. Each of the 3 bug topics corresponds to a uniform distribution over the pixels in a small "x". In all diagrams, each image also has a 1-pixel black frame for visibility, which does not correspond to any vocabulary word. We generate 2000 documents of length 100 with these topics according to the procedure described in Section 3. Half of the documents are "successful runs" and the other half "failed runs." For the topic mixture hyperparameters, we use $\alpha^s = [1, 1, 1, 1, 1, 1, 1, 1, 0, 0, 0]$ and $\alpha^f = [1, 1, 1, 1, 1, 1, 1, 1, 0.1, 0.1, 0.1]$. This means that the bug topics are never present in the $o_d = s$ (successful) documents, and tend to be only weakly present in the $o_d = f$ (failed) documents. Some example documents from this generated corpus are shown in Figure 2(b).

We then run ΔLDA and standard LDA [11, using code at `http://psiexp.ss.uci.edu/research/programs_data/toolbox.htm`] on the toy dataset. In order to give standard LDA the best chance of identifying the bug topics, it is run on $o_d = f$ documents only[2], using 11 topics. ΔLDA is run on all documents, using 8 usage topics and 3 bug topics. ΔLDA is supplied with the true α vectors used to generate the data, but the standard LDA implementation used in this experiment only allows a symmetric α hyperparameter (where all values in the α vector have the same value). Therefore we supply the standard LDA model with the symmetric hyperparameter $\alpha = 1$. Further experiments (not shown here) using a different implementation of standard LDA and the true α^f vector achieve similar results. Both models use the same symmetric hyperparameter $\beta = 1$ (which is not actually used to generate the data because the topics are fixed). Both MCMC chains are run for 2000 full samples, after which ϕ and θ are estimated from the final sample as described above.

[2] Additional experiments (not shown here) validate the intuition that the inclusion of $o_d = s$ documents does not improve the recovery of bug topics with standard LDA.

Table 1. General information about test programs

Program	Lines of Code	Bugs	Runs		Word Types	Topics	
			Successful	Failing		Usage	Bug
`exif` [16]	10,611	2	352	30	20	7	2
`grep` [17,18]	15,721	2	609	200	2,071	5	2
`gzip` [17,18]	8,960	2	29	186	3,929	5	2
`moss` [19]	35,223	8	1,727	1,228	1,982	14	8

The estimated topics for ΔLDA are shown in Figure 2(c), and the estimated topics for standard LDA are shown in Figure 2(d). ΔLDA is able to recover the true underlying usage and bug topics quite cleanly. On the other hand, standard LDA is unable to separate and identify bug topics, either mixing them with usage topics or simply duplicating usage topics. The toy example clearly shows the superiority of ΔLDA over standard LDA in this setting.

4.2 Real Programs

While ΔLDA performs well on our toy example, real programs are orders of magnitude more complex. We have applied ΔLDA to CBI feedback reports from four buggy C programs, details of which appear in Table 1. Bugs are naturally-occurring (`exif`), hand-seeded (`grep`, `gzip`), or both (`moss`). All four programs are in use by real users or are directly derived from real-world code. Test inputs are randomly-generated among reasonable inputs for each program, and "failure" is defined as crashing or producing output different from a known-correct reference implementation. Hand-coded "bug oracles" provide ground truth as to which bugs were actually triggered in any given run. For our experiments on `grep` and `gzip` we used test suites supplied by the SIR repository developers [18]. For `exif` and `moss` tests were generated using randomly selected command line flags and inputs. Feedback data is non-uniformly sampled during program execution as in prior work [5].

For these experiments, all hyperparameters used are symmetric, and the same hyperparameter settings are used for all programs. We set $\beta^u = \beta^b = 0.1$, and nonzero entries of $\alpha^s = \alpha^f = 0.5$ to encourage sparsity. The number of topics for each program are chosen according to domain expert advice. The number of bug topics N_b for each program is set equal to the number of distinct bugs known to be manifested in our dataset, with the goal of characterizing each bug with a single topic. The number of usage topics N_u for each program is chosen to approximately correspond to the number of different program use cases. For example, `exif` uses seven different mutually-exclusive command line flags, each of which corresponds to a different program operation. Therefore, it is natural to model the program usage patterns with seven different usage topics. Table 1 gives the number of usage and bug topics used for each program. For all programs, the Gibbs chain is run for 2000 iterations before estimating ϕ and θ. For the largest dataset, `moss`, the inference step took less than one hour to run on a desktop workstation.

Where possible, we compare ΔLDA results with corresponding measures from two earlier statistical debugging techniques. *PLDI05* refers to earlier work by Liblit et al. [5] that uses an iterative process of selecting and eliminating top-ranked predicates until all failures are explained. The approach bears some resemblance to likelihood ratio testing and biased minimum-set cover problems, but is somewhat *ad hoc* and highly specialized for debugging. *ICML06* refers to earlier work by Zheng et al. [8] that takes inspiration from bi-clustering algorithms. This approach uses graphical models to estimate complete (non-sampled) counts, then applies an iterative collective voting scheme followed by a simple clustering pass to identify and report likely bug causes.

Bug Topic Analysis on θ. We show that ΔLDA is capable of recovering bug topics that correlates well with the underlying software bugs. Note that each failed run's N_b bug topic elements in θ, which we call θ^b, can be viewed as a low-dimensional bug representation of failed runs. We plot the failed runs in this θ^b space for the programs in Figure 3(a-d), where we use different symbols to mark the failed runs by their ground truth bug types. In the case of moss, we project the 8-dimensional θ^b space down to 3 dimensions for visualization using Principal Component Analysis. The plots show that actual bug types tend to cluster *along the axes* of θ^b, which means that often a ΔLDA bug topic maps to a unique actual bug type. Multi-bug runs exhibit multiple high-weight θ^b components, which is consistent with this mapping between bug topics and actual bugs. This observation could be used to focus debugging efforts on single-bug runs.

Figure 3(e) compares the quality of clusterings given by ΔLDA to those of the other analyses. For each analysis we compute the Rand index [20] of a clustering based on that analysis with respect to the ground truth (determined by our oracle). A Rand index of 1 indicates that the clustering is identical to the ground truth; lower indices indicate worse agreement. For ΔLDA, we assign a failed run to cluster i if its bug topic i has the largest θ_i among all bug topics. Other clustering methods are possible and may produce better clusters. No method dominates, but ΔLDA consistently performs well.

Bug Topic Analysis on ϕ. We now discuss how to extract ranked lists of suspect words (potentially buggy program behaviors) for each bug topic. We qualitatively evaluate the usefulness of these lists in finding root causes of bugs, both for ΔLDA and for PLDI05 and ICML06. Overall, we find that ΔLDA and PLDI05 perform equally well, with ΔLDA resting on a stronger mathematical foundation and potentially supporting a wider variety of other important tasks.

The parameter ϕ itself specifies $p(w|z)$. But a word w may have a large $p(w|z)$ simply because it is a frequent word in all topics. We instead examine $p(z|w)$ which is easily obtained from ϕ using Bayes rule. Furthermore, we define a confidence score $S_{ij} = \min_{k \neq i} p(z = i|w = j) - p(z = k|w = j)$. For each topic, $z = i$, we present words ranked by their score, S_{ij}. If S_{ij} is less than zero, indicating that word j is more predictive of some other topic, we do not present the word at all. On the other hand, if S_{ij} is high, then we consider that word j is a suspect word and a likely cause of the bug explained by topic i.

In lieu of formal human-subject studies, which are outside the scope of this paper, we informally assess the expected usefulness of these suspect-word lists to a bug-hunting programmer. We compare ΔLDA results with analogous lists built using the PLDI05 and ICML06 algorithms mentioned earlier.

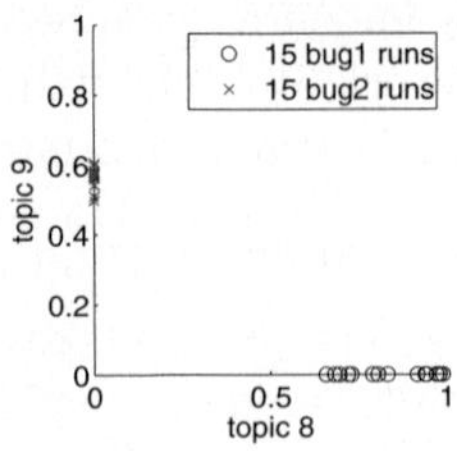

(a) `exif` bug topics

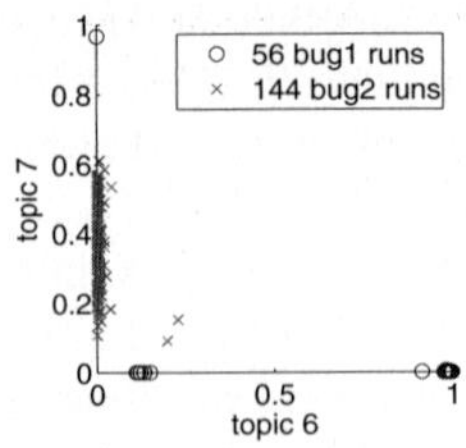

(b) `grep` bug topics

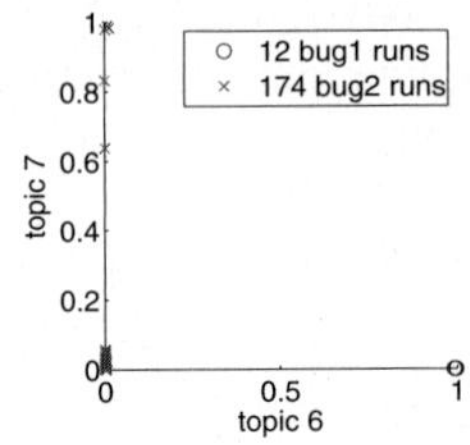

(c) `gzip` bug topics

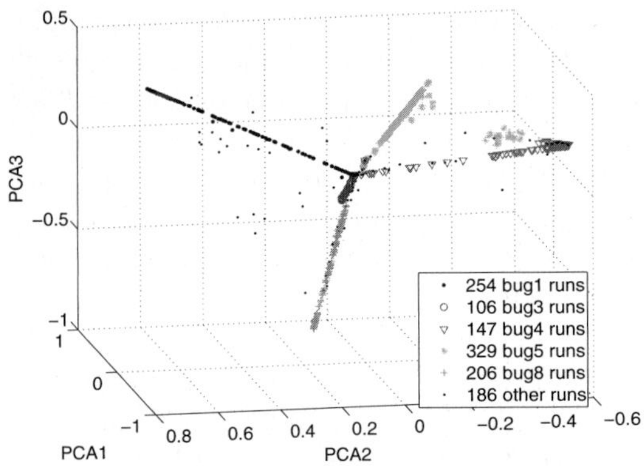

(d) `moss` bug topics (with PCA)

	ΔLDA	ICML06	PLDI05
`exif`	1.00	0.88	1.00
`grep`	0.97	0.71	0.77
`gzip`	0.89	1.00	1.00
`moss`	0.93	0.93	0.96

(e) Rand index

Fig. 3. ΔLDA recovers bug topics that highly correlate with actual software bugs

For `exif`, the two ΔLDA bug topics cleanly separate the two bugs. Each topic's list of suspect words is short (4 and 6 items) but relevant. For one of the bugs, this list includes a clear "smoking gun" that immediately reveals the root cause; the other bug topic includes less direct secondary effects of the root problem. PLDI05 performs well for both `exif` bugs. However, while ΔLDA's word list is naturally restricted to words for which $S_{ij} > 0$, PLDI05 has no intuitive cut-off point. Thus, PLDI05's lists include all words under analysis (19 for `exif`) and risk overwhelming programmers with irrelevant information. In our subjective experience, if the first five or ten items in a "suspect program behaviors" list are not immediately understandable, the programmer is unlikely to search further. ICML06 struggles with this as well. If clustering is not used, ICML06 reports all 19 words without good separation into bug-specific groups. If clustering is used, ICML06 offers a short 3-item list that describes one bug three times and omits the other bug entirely.

`moss` results vary in quality from bug to bug. Overall, we find that most ΔLDA bug topics correspond directly to individual `moss` bugs, and that highly-suspect words for each of these topics often identify either primary "smoking gun" causes for failure or else closely related secondary effects of the initial misbehavior. PLDI05 performs better than ΔLDA for some bugs and worse for others, with each analysis identifying at least one smoking gun that the other misses. ICML06 with clustering produces identifies the smoking gun for one bug that both ΔLDA and PLDI05 miss. However, ICML06 reports thirty clusters while there are only eight actual `moss` bugs: several bugs are split among multiple clusters and therefore presented redundantly.

`grep` and `gzip` results are equivocal. ICML06 identifies an informative precondition for one `grep` bug, though not the smoking gun. Otherwise, all three algorithms identify words that are strongly associated with bugs but which do not immediately reveal any bugs' root causes. These algorithms do not truly model causality, and therefore it is not surprising that root causes may be difficult to recover. Furthermore, in some cases, no smoking guns were actually among the words instrumented and considered by the models. We feel that all three models perform as well as can be reasonably expected given the less-than-ideal raw data.

Overall, we find that the PLDI05 and ΔLDA approaches perform roughly equally well in guiding humans to the root causes of bugs. However, PLDI05 is highly specialized and somewhat difficult to reason about formally. For example, whereas ΔLDA ranks words using conditional probabilities, PLDI05 computes multi-factor harmonic mean scores that, while about as effective, have no simple interpretation either in machine learning terms or as quantitative measures of expected program behavior. ΔLDA has, we assert, a stronger mathematical foundation and potentially broader applicability to problems in other domains (see section 5).

Furthermore, even within the domain of statistical debugging, components of an ΔLDA model can be used to support other important software engineering tasks not contemplated by earlier approaches. Suppose, for example, that one's task is to fix the bug associated with a particular bug topic, and that a repeatable test suite is available. In that case, one would prefer to investigate runs where the weight for that bug topic is very high compared to the weight for all other bug topics, as those runs would be likely to be the most pure embodiments of the bug. For another example, prior work has shown how to automatically construct extended paths through multiple suspect program points [21]; ΔLDA offers a model whereby the aggregate scores along such paths can be given a sensible probabilistic interpretation. While we have not yet explored these alternate uses in detail, they hint at the power of a statistical debugging approach that is both well-founded in theory and highly effective in practice.

Usage Topic Analysis. Information gleaned from usage topics might support a variety of software engineering tasks. To characterize a usage topic, we examine the words that have the highest probability conditioned on that topic. Each word is associated with the source code immediately adjacent to its instrumentation point. We find that in many cases usage topics correspond to distinct usage modes of the program.

We describe `gzip` in detail, since the DEFLATE algorithm which it implements is in the public domain and likely to be familiar to many in the machine learning community. Recall that the DEFLATE algorithm consists of two steps, duplicate string elimination and bit reduction using Huffman coding.

For each usage topic there is a small number of highly probable words and a much larger number that are significantly less probable. The most probable word by far in topic 1 is associated with an inner loop in `longest_match()`, the underlying procedure in the duplicate string elimination step of the algorithm. We infer that topic 1 is highly associated with this step. We expect runs with a high $p(z = 1|d)$ value to use the algorithm which finds the most redundant strings and does the best compression at the expense of running more slowly; this is the case. There are about twenty highly probable words in topic 2; all are associated with command line handling or exit clean-up code. In runs where $p(z = 2|d)$ is relatively high no compression occurred; instead, for example, a help message or version message was requested. Of the twenty most probable words in topic 3, several are associated with `longest_match()`, several with `compress_block()`, and several with `deflate_fast()`. We infer that this usage topic is associated with the fast deflation algorithm which does only very simple duplicate string elimination. In the runs where $p(z = 3|d)$ is highest, `gzip` was invoked with a flag explicitly calling for the fast algorithm. The modes associated with topics 4 and 5 are less pronounced. Topic 4 seems to capture output activity, as it includes a highly probable word in in `write_buf()` as well as a few highly probable words associated with the duplicate string elimination algorithm. Topic 5 seems to capture the bit reduction mode, as words in `updcrc()`, a utility function used for shifting bits, are by far the most probable.

5 Conclusions and Discussion

Software continues to be released with bugs, and end users suffer the consequences. However, statistical models applied to instrumented feedback data can help programmers repair problems. ΔLDA shows promise as a statistical model with both strong empirical results and a sound mathematical foundation. Some future directions have been suggested earlier, such as incorporating domain knowledge into the Dirichlet hyperparameters or automatically identifying the number of bugs. Another direction is to endow ΔLDA with more complex topic structure similar to Hierarchical LDA [22], which arranges topics in a tree. However, Hierarchical LDA provides no mechanism for document-level control (the outcome flag) on topic availability. Other modifications to the model could exploit some of the interesting structure inherent in this problem domain, such as the static program graph.

Note that ΔLDA need not be restricted to statistical debugging. For example, ΔLDA may be applied to text sentiment analysis [23] to distinguish "subjective sentiment topics" (e.g., positive or negative opinions, the equivalent of bug topics) from much stronger "objective content topics" (in the movie domain these are movie plots, actor biographies etc., the equivalent of usage topics). For the movie domain, the mixed document collection may consist of user-posted movie reviews (which contain both sentiment and content topics), and formal movie summaries (which contain mostly objective contents).

References

1. Arumuga Nainar, P., Chen, T., Rosin, J., Liblit, B.: Statistical debugging using compound boolean predicates. In: Elbaum, S. (ed.) International Symposium on Software Testing and Analysis, July 9–12, 2007, London, United Kingdom (2007)
2. Dickinson, W., Leon, D., Podgurski, A.: Finding failures by cluster analysis of execution profiles. In: Proceedings of the 23rd International Conference on Software Engeneering (ICSE-01), pp. 339–348. IEEE Computer Society, Los Alamitos (2001)

3. Hangal, S., Lam, M.S.: Tracking down software bugs using automatic anomaly detection. In: ICSE '02: Proceedings of the 24th International Conference on Software Engineering, pp. 291–301. ACM Press, New York (2002)
4. Jones, J.A., Harrold, M.J.: Empirical evaluation of the Tarantula automatic fault-localization technique. In: ASE '05: Proceedings of the 20th IEEE/ACM international Conference on Automated software engineering, pp. 273–282. ACM Press, New York (2005)
5. Liblit, B., Naik, M., Zheng, A.X., Aiken, A., Jordan, M.I.: Scalable statistical bug isolation. In: Proceedings of the ACM SIGPLAN 2005 Conference on Programming Language Design and Implementation, June 12–15 2005, Chicago, Illinois (2005)
6. Liu, C., Yan, X., Fei, L., Han, J., Midkiff, S.P.: SOBER: statistical model-based bug localization. In: Wermelinger, M., Gall, H. (eds.) ESEC/SIGSOFT FSE, pp. 286–295. ACM, New York (2005)
7. Zheng, A.X., Jordan, M.I., Liblit, B., Aiken, A.: Statistical debugging of sampled programs. In: Thrun, S., Saul, L., Schölkopf, B. (eds.) NIPS 16, MIT Press, Cambridge, MA (2004)
8. Zheng, A.X., Jordan, M.I., Liblit, B., Naik, M., Aiken, A.: Statistical debugging: Simultaneous identification of multiple bugs. In: ICML (2006)
9. Hofmann, T.: Probabilistic latent semantic analysis. In: Proc. of Uncertainty in Artificial Intelligence, UAI'99, Stockholm (1999)
10. Blei, D.M., Ng, A.Y., Jordan, M.I.: Latent Dirichlet allocation. Journal of Machine Learning Research 3, 993–1022 (2003)
11. Griffiths, T., Steyvers, M.: Finding scientific topics. Proceedings of the National Academy of Sciences 101(suppl. 1), 5228–5235 (2004)
12. Fei-Fei, L., Perona, P.: A Bayesian hierarchical model for learning natural scene categories. In: IEEE Conference on Computer Vision and Pattern Recognition (CVPR), IEEE Computer Society Press, Los Alamitos (2005)
13. Liblit, B.: Cooperative Bug Isolation: Winning Thesis of the 2005 ACM Doctoral Dissertation Competition. LNCS, vol. 4440. Springer, Heidelberg (2007)
14. Liblit, B.: The Cooperative Bug Isolation Project, `http://www.cs.wisc.edu/cbi/`
15. Kass, R., Raftery, A.: Bayes factors. Journal of the American Statistical Association 90, 773–795 (1995)
16. EXIF Tag Parsing Library, `http://libexif.sf.net/`
17. Do, H., Elbaum, S., Rothermel, G.: Supporting controlled experimentation with testing techniques: An infrastructure and its potential impact. Empirical Software Engineering: An International Journal 10(4), 405–435 (2005)
18. Rothermel, G., Elbaum, S., Kinneer, A., Do, H.: Software-artifact intrastructure repository (September 2006), `http://sir.unl.edu/portal/`
19. Schleimer, S., Wilkerson, D.S., Aiken, A.: Winnowing: local algorithms for document fingerprinting. In: Proceedings of the 2003 ACM SIGMOD International Conference on Management of Data 2003, San Diego, California, June 09–12, 2003, pp. 76–85. ACM Press, New York (2003)
20. Rand, W.M.: Objective criteria for the evaluation of clustering methods. Journal of the American Statistical Association 66, 846–850 (1971)
21. Lal, A., Lim, J., Polishchuk, M., Liblit, B.: Path optimization in programs and its application to debugging. In: Sestoft, P. (ed.) 15th European Symposium on Programming, Vienna, Austria, pp. 246–263. Springer, Heidelberg (2006)
22. Blei, D.M., Griffiths, T.L., Jordan, M.I., Tenenbaum, J.B.: Hierarchical topic models and the nested Chinese restaurant process. In: NIPS 16 (2003)
23. Pang, B., Lee, L.: A sentimental education: Sentiment analysis using subjectivity summarization based on minimum cuts. In: Proceedings of the Association for Computational Linguistics, pp. 271–278 (2004)

Learning Balls of Strings with Correction Queries*

Leonor Becerra Bonache[1], Colin de la Higuera[2], Jean-Christophe Janodet[2], and Frédéric Tantini[2]

[1] Research Group on Mathematical Linguistics, Rovira i Virgili University
Pl. Imperial Tárraco 1, 43005 Tarragona, Spain
leonor.becerra@urv.cat
[2] Laboratoire Hubert Curien, Université Jean Monnet
18 rue du Professeur Benoît Lauras, 42000 Saint-Étienne, France
{cdlh,janodet,frederic.tantini}@univ-st-etienne.fr

Abstract. During the 80's, Angluin introduced an active learning paradigm, using an Oracle, capable of answering both membership and equivalence queries. However, practical evidence tends to show that if the former are often available, this is usually not the case of the latter. We propose new queries, called correction queries, which we study in the framework of Grammatical Inference. When a string is submitted to the Oracle, either she validates it if it belongs to the target language, or she proposes a correction, *i.e.*, a string of the language close to the query with respect to the edit distance. We also introduce a non-standard class of languages: The topological balls of strings. We show that this class is not learnable in Angluin's MAT model, but is with a linear number of correction queries. We conduct several experiments with an Oracle simulating a human Expert, and show that our algorithm is resistant to approximate answers.

Keywords: Grammatical Inference, Oracle Learning, Correction Queries, Edit Distance, Balls of Strings.

1 Introduction

Do you know how many *Nabcodonosaur* were kings of Babylon? And do you know when *Arnold Shwartzeneger* was born? A few years ago, just 2 decades ago, you would have had to consult encyclopedias and Who's Who dictionaries in order to get answers to such questions. At that time, you may have needed this information in order to participate to quizzes and competitions organised by famous magazines during the summers, but because of *these* questions, you might possibly have missed the very first prize. Why?... Nowadays, everything has changed: You naturally use the Web, launch your favourite search engine,

* This work was supported in part by the IST Programme of the European Community, under the PASCAL Network of Excellence, IST-2002-506778. This publication only reflects the authors' views.

J.N. Kok et al. (Eds.): ECML 2007, LNAI 4701, pp. 18–29, 2007.

type 2 keywords, follow 3 links and note down the answers. In this particular case, you discover... that no king of Babylon was called *Nabcodonosaur* but 2 *Nab***uch***odonos***or**'s reigned there many centuries ago. Again, the day *Arnold Shwartzeneger* was born is not clear, but it is easy to check that *Arnold S***c***hw***arz***ene***gg***er* was born in 1947, July 30th.

So you would probably win today the great competitions of the past. Indeed, the actual search engines are able to propose *corrections* when a keyword is not frequent. Those corrections are most often reliable because the reference dictionary is built from the billions of web pages indexed all over the world. Hence, a search engine is playing the role of an imperfect but powerful oracle, able to validate a relevant query by returning relevant documents, but also to correct any suspect query. Such an oracle is able to answer to what we shall call *correction queries*.

The first goal of this paper is to show, from a theoretical standpoint, that correction queries allow to get new challenging results in the field of Active Learning. In this framework developed by Angluin in the 80's [1], a Learner (He) has access to an Oracle (She) that knows a concept he must discover; To this purpose, he submits different kinds of queries (*e.g.*, Correction Queries) and she has to answer without lying. The game ends when he guesses the concept. Query-based learners are often interesting from a practical viewpoint. For instance, instead of requiring a human expert to label huge quantities of data, this expert could be asked by the Learner, in an interactive situation, to provide a small amount of targeted information. The second goal of this paper is to provide evidence that correction queries are suitable for this kind of real-life applications. Assuming that the Oracle is a human expert, however, introduces new constraints. On the one hand, it is inconceivable to ask *a polynomial* number of queries: This may still be too much for a human. So the learning algorithm should aim at minimising the number of queries even if we must pay for it with a worse time complexity. On the other hand, a human being (or even the Web) is fallible. Therefore the learning algorithm should also aim at learning functions or languages from *approximate* corrections.

In the above Web example, the distance used by the search engine to find a closest string is a variant of the *edit distance* which measures the minimum number of deletion, insertion or substitution operations needed to transform one string into another [2,3]. This distance and variants where each elementary operation may have a different weight have been used in many fields including Computational Biology [4], Language Modelling [5] and Pattern Recognition [6]. Edit distance appears in specific Grammatical Inference problems, in particular when one wants to learn languages from noisy data [7]. The classes of languages studied there are not defined following the Chomsky Hierarchy. Indeed, even the easiest level of this hierarchy, the class of regular languages, is not at all robust to noise, since the parity functions (which can be defined as regular languages) are not learnable in the presence of noise [8]. In this paper also, in order to avoid this difficulty, we shall consider only special finite languages, that seem elementary to formal language theoreticians, but are relevant for topologists and complex for combinatorialists: the *balls of strings*.

Hence, we study the problem of identifying balls of strings from correction queries. After some preliminaries in Section 2, we prove that balls are not learnable with Angluin's membership and equivalence queries (Section 3). Then, we show in Section 4 that balls are learnable with a linear number of correction queries. In Section 5, we study the effectiveness of our algorithm from an experimental standpoint, showing that it is *robust* when the answers of the Oracle are approximate. We conclude in Section 6. Due to the lack of space, we have skipped most formal proofs. The interested reader may find them at `http://labh-curien.univ-st-etienne.fr/~tantini/pub/bhjt07Long.pdf`.

2 On Balls of Strings as Languages

An *alphabet* Σ is a finite nonempty set of symbols called *letters*. A *string* $w = a_1 \dots a_n$ is any finite sequence of letters. We write Σ^* for the set of all strings over Σ, and λ for the empty string. Let $|w|$ be the length of w and $|w|_a$ the number of occurrences of a in w.

The *edit distance* $d(w, w')$ is the minimum number of *edit operations* needed to transform w into w' [2]. The edit operations are either (1) *deletion*: $w = uav$ and $w' = uv$, or (2) *insertion*: $w = uv$ and $w' = uav$, or (3) *substitution*: $w = uav$ and $w' = ubv$, where $u, v \in \Sigma^*$, $a, b \in \Sigma$ and $a \neq b$. *E.g.*, $d(abaa, aab) = 2$ since $a\underline{b}aa \rightarrow aa\underline{a} \rightarrow aab$ and the rewriting of $abaa$ into aab cannot be achieved with less than 2 steps. Notice that $d(w, w')$ can be computed in $\mathcal{O}(|w| \cdot |w'|)$ time by dynamic programming [3].

It is well-known that the edit distance is a *metric* [9], so it conveys to Σ^* the structure of a *metric space*. The *ball of centre* $o \in \Sigma^*$ *and radius* $r \in \mathbb{N}$, denoted $B_r(o)$, is the set of all strings whose distance is at most r from o: $B_r(o) = \{w \in \Sigma^* : d(o, w) \leq r\}$. *E.g.*, if $\Sigma = \{a, b\}$, then $B_1(ba) = \{a, b, aa, ba, bb, aba, baa, bab, bba\}$ and $B_r(\lambda) = \Sigma^{\leq r}$ for all $r \in \mathbb{N}$.

The latter example illustrates the fact that the number of strings in a ball grows exponentially with the radius. This remark raises the problem of the representation scheme that we should use to learn the balls. Basically, we need representations whose size is reasonable, which is not the case of an exhaustive enumeration, nor of the *deterministic finite automata* (DFA) since experiments show that the corresponding minimum DFA is often exponential with r (but linear with $|o|$) [10], even if a formal proof of this property remains a challenging combinatorial problem.

On the other hand, why not represent the ball $B_r(o)$ by the pair (o, r) itself? Indeed, its size is $|o| + \log r$. Moreover, deciding whether $w \in B_r(o)$ or not is immediate: One only has to (1) compute $d(o, w)$ and (2) check whether this distance is $\leq r$, which is achievable in time $\mathcal{O}(|o| \cdot |w| + \log r)$. Finally, when the alphabet has at least 2 letters, (o, r) is a unique thus *canonical* representation of $B_r(o)$:

Theorem 1. *If* $|\Sigma| \geq 2$ *and* $B_{r_1}(o_1) = B_{r_2}(o_2)$, *then* $o_1 = o_2$ *and* $r_1 = r_2$.

Notice that if $\Sigma = \{a\}$, then $B_2(a) = B_3(\lambda) = \{\lambda, a, aa, aaa\}$ for instance.

Hence, representing the ball $B_r(o)$ by the pair (o, r) is reasonable. However, it is worth noticing that *huge* balls, whose radius is not polynomially related to the length of the centre (*e.g.*, $r > 2^{|o|}$), will pose tricky problems of complexity. For instance, to learn the ball $B_r(\lambda) = \Sigma^{\leq r}$, one needs to manipulate at least one string of length $r + 1$. Therefore, in the following, we will always consider *good* balls only:

Definition 1. *Given any fixed polynomial $q()$, we say that a ball $B_r(o)$ is q-good if $r \leq q(|o|)$.*

3 Learning Balls from Queries

Query learning is a paradigm introduced by Angluin [1]. Her model brings a Learner (he) and an Oracle (she) into play. The goal of the Learner is to identify the representation of an unknown language, by submitting queries to the Oracle. The latter knows the target language and answers properly to the queries (*i.e.*, she does not lie). Moreover, the Learner is bound by efficiency constraints: (1) He can only submit a polynomial number of queries (in the size of the target representation) and (2) the available overall time must be polynomial in the size of the target representation[1].

Between the different combinations of queries, one, called MAT (Minimally Adequate Teacher), is sufficient to learn DFA [11]. Two kinds of queries are used:

Definition 2. *Let Λ be a class of languages on Σ^* and $L \in \Lambda$ a target language known by the Oracle, that the Learner aims at guessing. In the case of membership queries, the Learner submits a string $w \in \Sigma^*$ to the Oracle; Her answer, denoted* MQ(w), *is either* YES *if $w \in L$, or* NO *if $w \notin L$. In the case of equivalence queries, the Learner submits (the representation of) a language $K \in \Lambda$ to the Oracle; Her answer, denoted* EQ(K), *is either* YES *if $K = L$, or a string belonging to the symmetric difference $\big((K \setminus L) \cup (L \setminus K)\big)$ if $K \neq L$.*

Although MQ and EQ have established themselves as a standard combination, there are real grounds to believe that EQ are too powerful to exist or even be simulated. As suggested in [11] we may be able to substitute them with a random draw of strings that are then submitted as MQ (*sampling*), but there are many cases where sampling is not possible as the relevant distribution is unknown and/or inaccessible [12]. Besides, we will not consider MQ and EQ because they do not help to learn balls:

Theorem 2. *Assume $|\Sigma| \geq 2$. Let $m, n \in \mathbb{N}$ and $\mathcal{B}_{\leq m,n} = \{B_r(o) : r \leq m, o \in \Sigma^*, |o| \leq n\}$. Any algorithm that identifies every ball of $\mathcal{B}_{\leq m,n}$ with* EQ *and* MQ *necessarily uses $\Omega(|\Sigma|^n)$ queries in the worst case.*

[1] The time complexity usually concerns the time spent after receiving each new example, and takes the length of the information returned by the Oracle into account; Thus, our constraint is stronger but not restrictive, if we focus on good balls only.

Proof. Following [13], we describe an Adversary who maintains a set S of all possible balls. At the beginning, $S = \mathcal{B}_{\leq m,n}$. Her answer to the equivalence query $L = B_r(o)$ is the counterexample o. Her answer to the membership query o is No. At each step, the Adversary eliminates many balls of S but only one of centre o and radius 0. As there are $\Omega(|\Sigma|^n)$ such balls in $\mathcal{B}_{\leq m,n}$, identifying them requires $\Omega(|\Sigma|^n)$ queries. □

It should be noted that if the Learner is given one string from the ball, he can learn using a polynomial number of MQ. We shall see that *correction queries* (CQ), introduced below, allow to get round these problems:

Definition 3. *Let L be a fixed language and w a string submitted by the Learner to the Oracle. Her answer, denoted* CQ(w)*, is either* YES *if $w \in L$, or a correction of w w.r.t. L if $w \notin L$, that is a string $w' \in L$ at minimum edit distance from w:* CQ(w) = *one string of $\{w' \in L : d(w, w')$ is minimum$\}$.*

Notice that the CQ can easily be simulated knowing the target language. Moreover, we have seen in the introduction that they naturally exist in real-world applications such as the search engines of the Web. Also, CQ are relevant from a cognitive point of view: There is growing evidence that corrective input for grammatical errors is widely available to children [14].

4 Identifying Balls Using Corrections

In this section, we propose an algorithm that learns balls using a *linear* number of CQ. First, when one submits a string outside of a ball to the Oracle, she answers with a string that belongs to the 'circle' delimiting the ball. However, a string often has a lot of different possible corrections, contrarily to what happens in the plane. *E.g.*, the possible corrections for the string $aaaa$ *w.r.t.* the ball $B_2(bb)$ are $\{aa, aab, aba, baa, aabb, abab, abba, baab, baba, bbaa\}$. By definition of the CQ, the Oracle will choose one of them arbitrarily, potentially the worst one *w.r.t.* the Learner's point of view. Nevertheless, the Oracle's potential malevolence is limited by the following result, that characterises the set of *all* the possible corrections for a string:

Theorem 3. *Let $B_r(o)$ be a ball and $m \notin B_r(o)$. Then the set of possible corrections of m is exactly $\{z \in \Sigma^* : d(o, z) = r$ and $d(z, m) = d(o, m) - r\}$.*

Here is a geometric interpretation of the result above. Let us define the *segment* $[o, m] = \{w \in \Sigma^* : d(o, w) + d(w, m) = d(o, m)\}$ and the *circle* $C_r(o) = \{w \in \Sigma^* : d(o, w) = r\}$. Theorem 3 states that a string z is a possible correction of m *iff* $z \in [o, m] \cap C_r(o)$. The fact that m has several possible corrections shows that the geometry of Σ^* is very different from that of $\mathbb{R}^2$.

Now, building the centre of a ball from strings on its periphery is difficult for at least 2 reasons. On the one hand, (Σ^*, d) is a metric space with no vector space as an underlying structure. This is the same story as if we were trying to learn the disks of the plane with just a compass but no ruler... On the other hand, the

```
Require: a string w = x_1 ... x_n ∈ B_r^max(o), the radius r
Ensure: the centre o of the ball B_r(o)
c ← 0; i ← 1; a ← x_n
while c < r do
    Assume w = x_1 ... x_n and let w' = a x_1 ... x_{i-1} x_{i+1} ... x_n
    if CQ(w') = YES then w ← w'; c ← c + 1 end if
    i ← i + 1
end while
Assume w = x_1 ... x_n and return x_{r+1} ... x_n
```

Fig. 1. Algorithm EXTRACT_CENTRE

problem is formally *hard*: Given a finite set of strings $W = \{w_1, \ldots, w_n\}$ and a constant K, deciding whether a string $z \in \Sigma^*$ exists such that $\sum_{w \in W} d(z, w) < K$ (*resp.* $\max_{w \in W} d(z, w) < K$) is $\mathcal{NP}$-hard [15].

Therefore, we must study the balls in more detail and make the best possible use of the CQ so as not to build the centres from scratch. We begin by distinguishing the longest strings of any ball:

Definition 4. *The upper border of a ball $B_r(o)$, denoted $B_r^{max}(o)$, is the set of all the strings that belong to $B_r(o)$ and are of maximum length: $B_r^{max}(o) = \{z \in B_r(o) : \forall w \in B_r(o), |w| \leq |z|\}$.*

E.g., let $\Sigma = \{a, b\}$, then $B_1^{max}(ba) = \{aba,\ baa,\ bab,\ bba\}$. The strings of $B_r^{max}(o)$ are remarkable because they are all built from the centre o by doing r insertions. So from a string $w \in B_r^{max}(o)$, one 'simply' has to guess the inserted letters and delete them to find o again. Some strings of $B_r^{max}(o)$ are even more informative. Indeed, let $a \in \Sigma$ be an arbitrary letter. Then $a^r o \in B_r^{max}(o)$. So, if we know r, we can easily deduce o. We claim that CQ allow us to get hold of $a^r o$ from any string $w \in B_r^{max}(o)$ by swapping the letters (see Algorithm EXTRACT_CENTRE in Figure 1).

Consider $B_2^{max}(bb) = \{aabb, abab, abba, abbb, baab, baba, babb, bbaa, bbab, bbba, bbbb\}$. Running EXTRACT_CENTRE on the string $w = baab$ and radius $r = 2$ transforms, at each loop, the ith letter of w to an a that is put at the beginning and then submits it to the Oracle. c counts the number of times this transformation is accepted. We get:

i	w	w'	CQ(w')	w changes	c
1	$\underline{b}aab$	$aaab$	$baab$	no	0
2	$b\underline{a}ab$	$abab$	YES	yes	1
3	$ab\underline{a}b$	$aabb$	YES	yes	2

When $c = 2 = r$, EXTRACT_CENTRE stops with $w = aabb$ and returns $o = bb$.

Lemma 1. *Given $w \in B_r^{max}(o)$ and r, Algorithm* EXTRACT_CENTRE *returns o using $\mathcal{O}(|o| + r)$* CQ *and a polynomial amount of time.*

Hence, we are now able to deduce the centre of a ball as soon as we know its radius and a string from its upper border. The following technical lemma is a step towards finding this string (although we have no information about r and $|o|$ yet):

Lemma 2. *Suppose $\Sigma = \{a_1, \dots, a_n\}$. Then every correction w of the string $m = (a_1 \dots a_n)^k$ where $k \geq |o| + r$ belongs to $B_r^{max}(o)$.*

Submitting $(a_1 \dots a_n)^k$ with a sufficiently large k is sure to be corrected by a string from $B_r^{max}(o)$. So all that remains is to find such an interesting k. The following lemma states that if one asks the Oracle to correct a string made of a lot of a's, then the correction contains precious informations on the radius and the number of occurrences of a's in the centre:

Lemma 3. *Consider the ball $B_r(o)$ and let $a \in \Sigma$ and an integer $j \in \mathbb{N}$ such that $a^j \notin B_r(o)$. Let $w = \text{CQ}(a^j)$. If $|w| < j$, then $|w|_a = |o|_a + r$.*

Now, let us assume that the alphabet is $\Sigma = \{a_1, \dots, a_n\}$ and let $j_1, \dots, j_n \in \mathbb{N}$ be large integers. Define $k = \sum_{i=1}^{n} |\text{CQ}(a_i^{j_i})|_{a_i}$. Then, Lemma 3 brings $k = \sum_{i=1}^{n}(|o|_{a_i} + r) = |o| + |\Sigma| \cdot r \geq |o| + r$. Thus we can plug k into Lemma 2 to get a string $w = \text{CQ}\left((a_1 \dots a_n)^k\right) \in B_r^{max}(o)$. Moreover, we have $|w| = |o| + r$ and $k = |o| + |\Sigma| \cdot r$. So, we deduce that the radius is $r = (k - |w|)/(|\Sigma| - 1)$.

Let us summarise, by assuming that $\Sigma = \{a_1, \dots, a_n\}$ and that the target is the ball $B_r(o)$. (1) For each letter a_i, the Learner asks for the correction of a_i^j where j is sufficiently large to get a correction whose length is smaller than j; (2) We define $k = \sum_{i=1}^{n} |\text{CQ}(a_i^{j_i})|_{a_i}$ and suppose the Learner gets the correction w for the string $m = (a_1 \dots a_n)^k$; (3) From k and $|w|$, we deduce r; (4) The Learner uses EXTRACT_CENTRE on w and r in order to find o. In other words, we are able to learn the balls with CQ (see Algorithm IDF_BALL in Figure 2).

Require: The alphabet $\Sigma = \{a_1, \dots, a_n\}$
Ensure: The representation (o, r) of the ball $B_r(o)$
$j \leftarrow 1; k \leftarrow 0$
for $i = 1$ **to** n **do**
  while $|\text{CQ}(a_i^j)| \geq j$ **do** $j \leftarrow 2 \cdot j$ **end while**
  $k \leftarrow k + |\text{CQ}(a_i^j)|_{a_i}$
end for
$w \leftarrow \text{CQ}((a_1 a_2 \dots a_n)^k)$
$r \leftarrow (k - |w|)/(|\Sigma| - 1)$
$o \leftarrow$ EXTRACT_CENTRE(w, r)
return (o, r)

Fig. 2. Algorithm IDF_BALL

For instance, consider the ball $B_2(bb)$ defined over $\Sigma = \{a, b\}$. IDF_BALL begins by looking for the corrections of a^j and b^j with a sufficiently large j. We might observe: $\text{CQ}(a) = $ YES, $\text{CQ}(a^2) = $ YES, $\text{CQ}(a^4) = aabb$, $\text{CQ}(a^8) = abba$,

$\text{CQ}(b^8) = bbbb$. So $k = |abba|_a + |bbbb|_b = 2 + 4 = 6$. Then $\text{CQ}\left((ab)^6\right) = \text{CQ}(abababababab) = baab$, for instance, so $r = (6-4)/(2-1) = 2$. Finally, EXTRACT_CENTRE$(baab, 2)$ returns bb. So the algorithm returns $(bb, 2)$.

Theorem 4. *Given any fixed polynomial $q()$, the set of all q-good balls $B_r(o)$ is identifiable with an algorithm using $\mathcal{O}(|\Sigma| + |o| + r)$ CQ and a polynomial amount of time.*

Proof. The identifiability is clear. Concerning the complexity, the corrections of the strings a_i^j requires $\mathcal{O}(|\Sigma| + \log(|o| + r))$ CQ (lines 2-5). EXTRACT_CENTRE needs $\mathcal{O}(|o| + r)$ CQ (line 8). □

Notice that the set of all the balls, that contains good balls but also *huge* ones such that $r > 2^{|o|}$ for instance, is not polynomially identifiable with IDF_BALL since $\mathcal{O}(|\Sigma| + |o| + r) > \mathcal{O}(2^{|o|})$ for some of them.

5 Experiments with a Human-Like Oracle

In this section, we would like to show the advantages of our approach. Therefore, we have made several experiments that aim at studying the responses of IDF_BALL faced with an Oracle that could be human. As we said in introduction, our algorithm should not believe unwisely the answers he gets since they can be approximate. We would like to show here that IDF_BALL withstands such approximate (*i.e.*, inaccurate, noisy) answers.

Designing the Approximate Oracle

We begin by modelling a human expert by an Approximate Oracle. Firstly, we assume that an expert can easily determine whether an example fulfils a concept or not, thus here, whether w belongs to $B_r(o)$ or not. Secondly, what is really hard for the expert is to *compute* the correction of w when $w \notin B_r(o)$, and more precisely, a string of the ball that is *as close to w as possible*.

Let $X = d\big(w, \text{CQ}_h(w)\big) - d\big(w, \text{CQ}(w)\big)$ measure how far an approximate correction is from a perfect one. Intuitively, an Approximate Oracle will often provide corrections such that $X = 0$, sometimes $X = 1$ and rarely $X \geq 2$... To formalise this idea, we introduce a confidence parameter $0 < p \leq 1$, called the *accuracy level of the Oracle*, that translates the quality of her answers, and use a geometric distribution: We assume that $Pr(X = k) = (1-p)^k p$, for all $k \in \mathbb{N}$. Therefore, with probability $(1-p)^k p$, the correction $\text{CQ}_h(w)$ of a string w will be in the target ball, at distance k of $\text{CQ}(w)$. Basically, we get $E(X) = (1/p) - 1$. So when the Oracle is very accurate, say $p = 0.8$, then the average distance between an approximate and a perfect correction is low (0.25). Conversely, an expert with limited computation capacities, say $p = 0.4$, will often provide inaccurate corrections, at distance $\simeq 1.5$.

Our model of Approximate Oracle is simple. For instance, we do not suppose that she has any memory, thus by submitting twice every string w, we would probably get 2 different corrections, that could be used to *correct the corrections*! However, we want here to study the resistance of IDF_BALL to approximate answers, not to design the best possible algorithm, so our model is sufficient.

Behaviour of the Algorithm faced with an Approximate Oracle
Following Theorem 4, IDF_BALL systematically guesses the target ball with the help of a Perfect Oracle. But of course, he is sometimes going to fail in front of an Approximate Oracle. So, in order to assess the resistance of IDF_BALL to approximate corrections, we conduct the following experiment. For every accuracy level $0.5 \leq p \leq 1$, we randomly choose a set of 100 balls $B_r(o)$ such that $|o| + r = 200$. More precisely, the radius r varies between 20 and 180 by step of 20, and we randomly choose 10 centres o of length $200 - r$ for each radius. Then we ask IDF_BALL to learn them and compute the percentage of balls he is able to retrieve, which we call the *precision of the algorithm*. We show the result in Figure 3. We notice that IDF_BALL is able to identify about 75% of the balls faced with an accuracy level of $p = 0.9$. Of course, as one can expect, with lower levels of accuracy, his performances quickly drop (15% for $p = 0.5$). We also show, in Figure 4, the average distances between the centres of the target balls and the centres of the learnt balls when he fails to retrieve them. We observe that these distances are not that important: Even with an accuracy level of $p = 0.5$, this distance is less than 4.

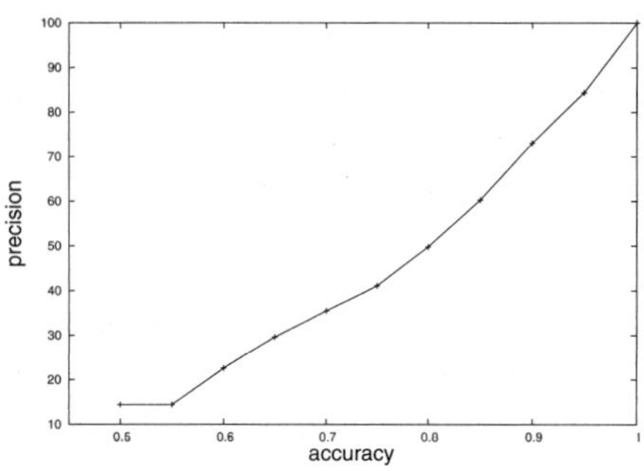

Fig. 3. Precision of IDF_BALL faced with an Approximate Oracle in function of the accuracy level p. Each point is assessed on 100 balls.

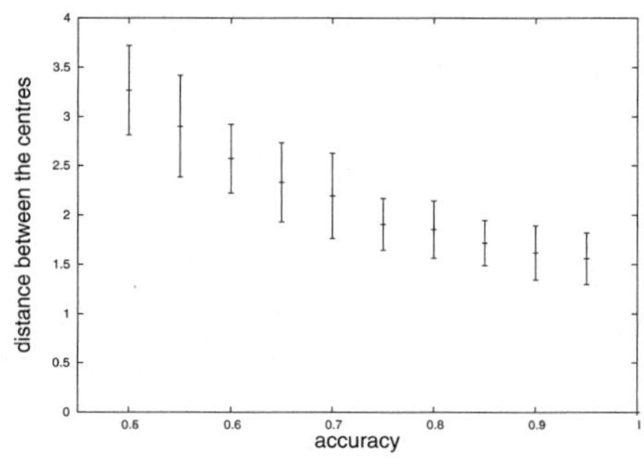

Fig. 4. Average distances (and standard deviation) between the centres of the target balls and the centres of the learnt balls, when IDF_BALL fails in retrieving them

Improving the Precision with a posteriori *Heuristics*
We have seen that IDF_BALL was able to assimilate the approximations of the Oracle up to a certain level of accuracy. Moreover, the centre returned by the algorithm is generally not far from the target one. Thus, it is reasonable to think that we could improve the precision by mining the neighbourhood of the learnt centre, using local edit modifications. This kind of approaches has been pioneered by Kohonen in [16] and is surveyed in [17].

Suppose that the learnt ball is $B_k(u)$. We test each neighbour (at distance 1) of u and examine if it is better (*i.e.* if k can be reduced) in such a way as to contain all the corrections given up to now. This heuristics will be very good each time u is at distance 1 from the target centre. But as soon as this distance grows,

IDF_BALL will fail again. In order to enhance the one-step heuristics, we can iterate the process and design a second until-convergence heuristics by repeating the local search until the size of the ball cannot be diminished anymore.

In order to show that the balls learnt by IDF_BALL can be corrected *a posteriori*, we compare, in a series of experiments, the precision of the algorithm without any post-treatment, with the one-step heuristics and with the until-convergence heuristics. We fix $|o| + r = 200$. The accuracy level varies from 0.5 to 1 and the radius, from 20 to 180. For each pair (accuracy, radius), we randomly draw 50 centres of length $200 - r$, and ask IDF_BALL to retrieve them. We plot the resulting precisions in Figure 5.

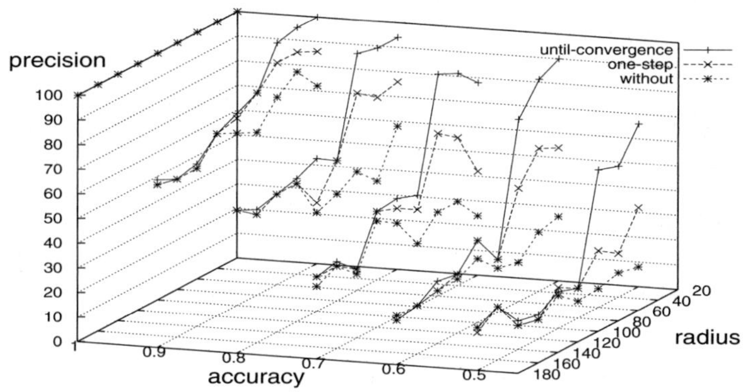

Fig. 5. Precision of IDF_BALL with and without heuristics in function of accuracy and radius when $|o| + r = 200$. For each pair (accuracy, radius), we compute the precision over 50 balls.

Firstly, we must explain the bumpiness of the graph. Actually, each point assesses the precision of IDF_BALL using a sample of 50 balls. However, the number of balls of radius 100, for instance, is greater that 10^{30}! So, whatever the sample, we will definitively not get any relevant estimate of the true precision, that explains the variance. On the other hand, this is not limiting since our experiments still allow to compare the heuristics themselves: We can remark that whatever the accuracy level, using the until-convergence heuristics is never worse than the one-step heuristics, which is never worse than no post-treatment at all. But it is also clear that our heuristics do not always improve the precision of the algorithm: This depends on the ratio between the radius of the target ball and the length of its centre. In order to detail this, we have extracted 2 transverse sections, shown in Figure 6, where we fix the radius.

The left curves of Figure 6 describe the precision of IDF_BALL for target balls such that $r = 120$ and $|o| = 80$. In this case, we gain little using the heuristics. Notice that these balls are not *good* for the identity polynomial. On the other hand, the right curves of Figure 6 describe the precision for target balls such

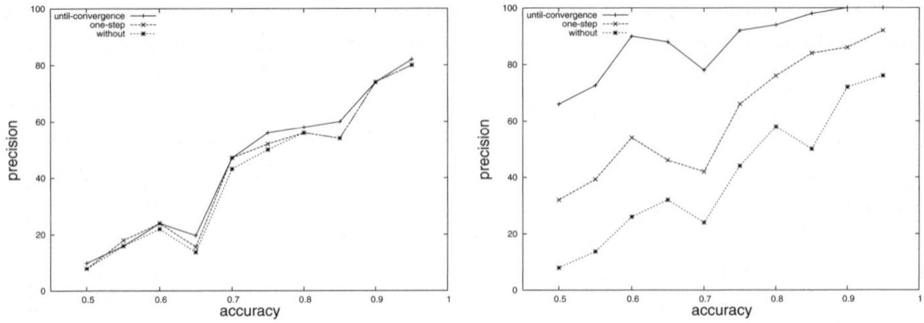

Fig. 6. Precision of IDF_BALL when $|o|+r = 200$ for $r = 120$ (left) and $r = 20$ (right). For each accuracy, we compute the average over 50 balls.

that $r = 20$ and $|o| = 180$. Basically, our heuristics outperform the precision *w.r.t.* the algorithm without any post-treatment, whatever the accuracy level of the Oracle. Moreover, the benefit is all the more important as the accuracy level is bad. For instance, when $p = 0.6$, the until-convergence heuristics is able to dramatically boost the precision from 26% to 90%. So in this setting, with no further enhancement, IDF_BALL produces balls that are so close to the targets that they can easily be improved using only basic local modifications.

6 Discussion and Conclusion

In this work, we have used correction queries to learn languages from an Oracle. The intended setting is that of an inexact Oracle, and experiments show that the algorithm we propose can learn a language sufficiently close to the target for simple local modifications (with no extra queries) to be possible. In order to do this, the languages we consider are balls of strings defined with the edit distance. Studying them allowed us to catch a glimpse of the geometry of sets of strings, which is very different from the Euclidean geometry. A number of questions and research directions are left open by this work.

A first question concerns the distance we use. We have chosen to work with the unitary edit distance, but in many applications, the edit operations can have different weights. Preliminary work has allowed us to notice that the geometry of sets of strings, thus the algorithmics, could change considerably depending on the sorts of weights we used. For instance, with the substitutions costing less than the insertions and the deletions, a much faster algorithm exists, requiring only a number of queries in $\mathcal{O}(\log(|o| + r))$ [18].

A second question concerns the inaccuracy model we are using: As noticed in Section 5, with the current model it would be possible to repeat the same CQ various times, getting different corrections, but possibly being able, through some majority vote scheme, to get the adequate correction with very little extra cost. Just asking for *persistent* corrections is not enough to solve this problem: A good model should require that if one queries from a close enough string (a^{999}

instead of a^{1000}) then the corrections should also remain close. Topologically, we would expect the Oracle to be k-Lipschitz continuous (with $0 < k < 1$).

Acknowledgement. The authors wish to thank the anonymous reviewers as well as Dana Angluin, Jose Oncina and Rémi Eyraud for their helpful comments.

References

1. Angluin, D.: Queries and concept learning. Machine Learning Journal 2, 319–342 (1987)
2. Levenshtein, V.I.: Binary codes capable of correcting deletions, insertions, and reversals. Doklady Akademii Nauk SSSR 163(4), 845–848 (1965)
3. Wagner, R., Fischer, M.: The string-to-string correction problem. Journal of the ACM 21, 168–178 (1974)
4. Durbin, R., Eddy, S., Krogh, A., Mitchison, G.: Biological sequence analysis. Cambridge University Press, Cambridge (1998)
5. Amengual, J.C., Sanchis, A., Vidal, E., Benedí, J.M.: Language simplification through error-correcting and grammatical inference techniques. Machine Learning Journal 44(1), 143–159 (2001)
6. Oncina, J., Sebban, M.: Learning stochastic edit distance: Application in handwritten character recognition. Pattern Recognition 39(9), 1575–1587 (2006)
7. Tantini, F., de la Higuera, C., Janodet, J.C.: Identification in the limit of systematic-noisy languages. In: Sakakibara, Y., Kobayashi, S., Sato, K., Nishino, T., Tomita, E. (eds.) ICGI 2006. LNCS (LNAI), vol. 4201, pp. 19–31. Springer, Heidelberg (2006)
8. Kearns, M.J., Li, M.: Learning in the presence of malicious errors. SIAM Journal of Computing 22(4), 807–837 (1993)
9. Crochemore, M., Hancart, C., Lecroq, T.: Algorithmique du texte, Vuibert (2001)
10. Schulz, K.U., Mihov, S.: Fast string correction with levenshtein automata. Int. Journal on Document Analysis and Recognition 5(1), 67–85 (2002)
11. Angluin, D.: Learning regular sets from queries and counterexamples. Information and Computation 75, 87–106 (1987)
12. de la Higuera, C.: Data complexity issues in grammatical inference. In: Data Complexity in Pattern Recognition, pp. 153–172. Springer, Heidelberg (2006)
13. Angluin, D.: Queries and concept learning. Machine Learning 2, 319–342 (1988)
14. Becerra-Bonache, L., Yokomori, T.: Learning mild context-sensitiveness: Towards understanding children's language learning. In: Paliouras, G., Sakakibara, Y. (eds.) ICGI 2004. LNCS (LNAI), vol. 3264, pp. 53–64. Springer, Heidelberg (2004)
15. de la Higuera, C., Casacuberta, F.: Topology of strings: median string is NP-complete. Theoretical Computer Science 230, 39–48 (2000)
16. Kohonen, T.: Median strings. Information Processing Letters 3, 309–313 (1985)
17. Martínez-Hinarejos, C.D., Juan, A., Casacuberta, F.: Use of median string for classification. In: Proc. of the 15th International Conference on Pattern Recognition, vol. 2, pp. 2903–2906 (2000)
18. Becerra-Bonache, L., de la Higuera, C., Janodet, J.C., Tantini, F.: Apprentissage des boules de mots avec des requêtes de correction (in french). In: Proc. of 9th Conférence en Apprentissage, Presses Universitaires de Grenoble (2007)

Neighborhood-Based Local Sensitivity

Paul N. Bennett

Microsoft Research, One Microsoft Way, Redmond WA 98052, USA
paul.n.bennett@microsoft.com

Abstract. We introduce a nonparametric model for sensitivity estimation which relies on generating points similar to the prediction point using its k nearest neighbors. Unlike most previous work, the sampled points differ simultaneously in multiple dimensions from the prediction point in a manner dependent on the local density. Our approach is based on an intuitive idea of locality which uses the Voronoi cell around the *prediction point*, *i.e.* all points whose nearest neighbor is the prediction point. We demonstrate how an implicit density over this neighborhood can be used in order to compute relative estimates of the local sensitivity. The resulting estimates demonstrate improved performance when used in classifier combination and classifier recalibration as well as being potentially useful in active learning and a variety of other problems.

1 Introduction

Consider the following tasks often faced during peer review: (1) Make a recommendation accept/reject; (2) Rate from 0 to 5, where 0 is definitely reject and 5 is definitely accept; (3) State your confidence on a 0 to 5 scale in your review. When a reviewer answers the first question, he is classifying the paper. The answer to the second question is an implicit measure of the posterior probability regarding "Accept/Reject". As with a posterior and a classification decision, a consistent reviewer can use the rating to provide information that both summarizes and subsumes the classification decision.

Next, the reviewer states his confidence — which intuitively is a self-assessment of his expertise (previous familiarity with topic, perceived completeness of study, *etc.*) and mathematically is a statement about how strongly he believes the posterior he gave is correct. In other words it is a second-order summary of the uncertainty the reviewer has about his classification.

Given only the feedback and rating from a single reviewer, we cannot use this secondary confidence information if immediately forced to make a decision. However, if one of our choices is to consult another expert, then suddenly we are faced with a *value of information* problem, and presumably, we will consult an additional expert when the confidence of the first expert is low. Likewise when combining the opinions of several reviewers, instead of directly averaging the acceptance ratings we could weight them by confidence or treat low confidence reviews as abstentions regardless of the rating.

Furthermore, given access to a past history of the reviewer's ratings and the final decisions regarding the papers, we might conclude this reviewer is either too

J.N. Kok et al. (Eds.): ECML 2007, LNAI 4701, pp. 30–41, 2007.

harsh or too lenient and opt to post-calibrate the reviewer's ratings. Additionally, the calibration function may vary depending on confidence; for example, the reviewer may be perfectly calibrated when his confidence is high but increasingly uncalibrated as his confidence decreases.

Finally, when attempting to improve his own ratings, the reviewer may opt to perform active learning by requesting what the decisions should be from an oracle. However, rather than simply requesting decisions on papers that have borderline ratings (some papers simply are borderline!) he could request decisions where his confidence is low to identify areas where his expertise could be improved.

Similarly, confidence information can be used in similar ways for value of information estimation, classifier combination, post-learning recalibration, and active learning when provided by automated systems. However, most previous work has targeted estimating only the posterior at a particular point rather than estimating both the posterior and confidence. This paper partially addresses that limitation by demonstrating the link between sensitivity estimates of the stability or rate of change of the learned posterior function and the confidence in the posterior. Rather than obtaining sensitivity estimates by tweaking a point in a single dimension or independently in several dimensions, we use the neighborhood around the prediction point and sample from this neighborhood in a way that exploits the local covariance of the input and is not constrained to relying on global estimates of the covariance. The resulting estimates are demonstrated to be of use in both post-learning recalibration over synthetic datasets and in combining classifiers over text classification corpora.

Before explaining our approach for sensitivity estimation, we first further distinguish the concepts of posterior and confidence in the posterior and demonstrate the latter's relationship to sensitivity. Next, we motivate and explain the use of neighbors to estimate the sensitivity and related terms of a learned model. Using several synthetic datasets, we demonstrate how these quantities can be used to improve post-learning recalibration of the estimates provided by the kNN classifier. We then summarize several ensemble learning experiments over text classification corpora where these quantities play a key role. Finally, we conclude with a discussion of related work and a summary of our contributions.

2 Variance and Sensitivity

Returning to our motivating example, consider if instead of making the reviewer specify his uncertainty, we allowed him to specify an entire distribution expressing his belief, $p(P(c \mid \boldsymbol{x}) = z \mid \boldsymbol{x})$, where $\boldsymbol{x}$ is the item being classified, c is a particular class, and z is a specific value of the random variable $P(c \mid \boldsymbol{x})$. Then when he is asked to summarize his uncertainty via a rating, the typical approach is to predict the expected value of the distribution: $\hat{P}(c \mid \boldsymbol{x}) = \int z\, p(P(c \mid \boldsymbol{x}) = z \mid \boldsymbol{x})\, dz$.

However, the mean of a distribution does not fully summarize the distribution. Presumably, as the reviewer receives more information or perceives he has all necessary information because of his expertise, his confidence that the expected value fully summarizes his uncertainty will become quite high. Therefore a reasonable measure for confidence is to treat it as an (inverse) measure of the variance of $p(P(c \mid \boldsymbol{x}) = z \mid \boldsymbol{x})$. Since "confidence" is often used in the literature to refer to the posterior distribution estimate, $\hat{P}(c \mid \boldsymbol{x})$, we will avoid this confusion for the remainder of the paper by referring to the "posterior distribution", $P(c \mid \boldsymbol{x})$, and the "confidence distribution", $p(P(c \mid \boldsymbol{x}) = z \mid \boldsymbol{x})$.

Rather than estimating the variance of the true posterior according to the confidence distribution, $p(P(c \mid \boldsymbol{x}) = z \mid \boldsymbol{x})$, we will instead consider the variance of the output of the classifier under the distribution $p(\hat{P}(c \mid \boldsymbol{x}) = z \mid \boldsymbol{x})$. The variance of this second distribution is the local *sensitivity* of the classifier, and we will demonstrate how it can be useful in several of the scenarios where we previously motivated the importance of the confidence distribution.

Consider again observing a past history of the reviewer's ratings and the final decisions on a set of papers in order to learn a recalibration function for the reviewer's ratings. For the remainder of the paper, it will be convenient to work with log-odds estimates, $\log \frac{\hat{P}(c|\boldsymbol{x})}{1-\hat{P}(c|\boldsymbol{x})}$. However, the derivation below holds for any function $\hat{\lambda}(\boldsymbol{x})$ such that $\mathrm{VAR}_{\Delta}\left[\hat{\lambda}\right] \neq 0$ and thus can be used for computing the sensitivity of a variety of functions. Now, given our reviewer's uncalibrated estimate of the acceptance rating $\hat{\lambda}$, we will attempt to recalibrate it with a locally weighted recalibration function:

$$\hat{\lambda}^*(\boldsymbol{x}) = W_0(\boldsymbol{x}) + W_1(\boldsymbol{x})\hat{\lambda}(\boldsymbol{x}). \tag{1}$$

We can determine the optimal weights in a simplified case by assuming we are given "true" log-odds values, λ, and a family of distributions $\Delta_{\boldsymbol{x}}$ such that $\Delta_{\boldsymbol{x}} = p(\boldsymbol{s} \mid \boldsymbol{x})$ encodes what is local to $\boldsymbol{x}$ by giving the probability of drawing a point $\boldsymbol{s}$ near to $\boldsymbol{x}$. We use Δ instead of $\Delta_{\boldsymbol{x}}$ for notational simplicity. Since Δ encodes the example-dependent nature of the weights, we can drop $\boldsymbol{x}$ from the weight functions. To find weights that minimize the squared difference between the true log-odds and the estimated log-odds in the Δ vicinity of $\boldsymbol{x}$, we can solve a standard regression problem, $\mathrm{argmin}_{w_0,w_1} E_{\Delta}\left[\left(w_1\,\hat{\lambda} + w_0 - \lambda\right)^2\right]$. Under the assumption $\mathrm{VAR}_{\Delta}\left[\hat{\lambda}\right] \neq 0$, this yields:

$$w_0 = E_{\Delta}[\lambda] - w_1 E_{\Delta}\left[\hat{\lambda}\right] \qquad w_1 = \frac{\mathrm{COV}_{\Delta}[\hat{\lambda},\lambda]}{\mathrm{VAR}_{\Delta}[\hat{\lambda}]} = \frac{\sigma_{\lambda}}{\sigma_{\hat{\lambda}}}\rho_{\lambda,\hat{\lambda}} \tag{2}$$

where σ and ρ are the standard deviation and correlation coefficient under Δ, respectively. The first parameter w_0 is a measure of calibration that addresses the question, "How far off on average is the estimated log-odds from the true log-odds in the local context?" The second parameter w_1 is a measure of correlation, "How closely does the estimated log-odds vary with the true log-odds?" Note that the second parameter depends on the local sensitivity of the base classifier, $\mathrm{VAR}_{\Delta}^{1/2}\left[\hat{\lambda}\right] = \sigma_{\hat{\lambda}}$. Although we do not have true log-odds, we *can* introduce local density models to estimate the local sensitivity of the model.

3 Neighborhood-Based Locality

To compute the local sensitivity, we define a simple nonparametric method based on the k nearest neighbors. Since we are concerned with how the decision function changes locally around the current prediction or *query* point, it is natural to use a neighborhood-based definition. In particular, consider all points in the input space whose nearest neighbor is the query (*i.e.* the Voronoi cell of the query).

Next, we can either explicitly define a density over the Voronoi cell of the query or implicitly do so by defining a procedure that allows us to draw S samples from the cell. We do the latter by finding k neighbors of the query $\boldsymbol{x}$ in the training set and then draw $S = k$ samples by using the difference vector between the query and its neighbor to interpolate a sample point where the vector intersects the boundary of the cell. This is illustrated in Figure 1.

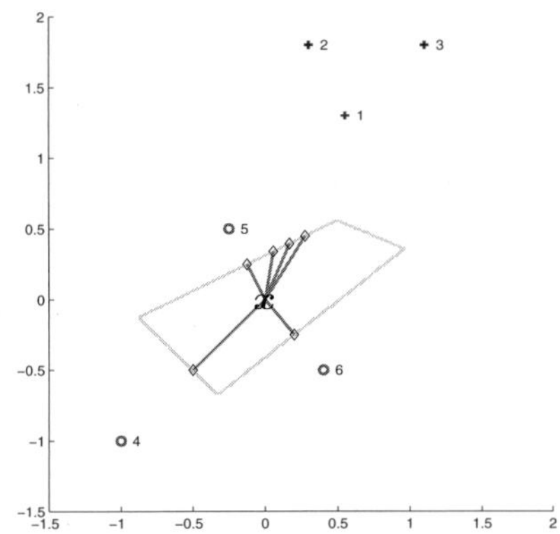

Fig. 1. Given the numbered points as the neighbors of the query point $\boldsymbol{x}$, the figure illustrates the points that would be sampled within the Voronoi cell of $\boldsymbol{x}$

There are multiple advantages to defining the points to sample within the Voronoi cell in terms of the neighbors of the query point. First, we need not explicitly compute the Voronoi cell of the query point. Instead after determining the k neighbors, we can directly compute the sample points. Second, by using the k neighbors to guide sampling, we sample in locally dense directions. For example in Figure 1 we do not sample by shifting the query point directly to the right because no data supports variance in this direction.

More formally, we can consider this as shifting $\boldsymbol{x}$ toward each one of k neighbors with equal probability. Let $\boldsymbol{x}_i$ denote the query after it has been shifted by a factor β_i toward its ith neighbor, $\boldsymbol{n}_i$. That is, $\boldsymbol{x}_i = \boldsymbol{x} + \beta_i(\boldsymbol{n}_i - \boldsymbol{x})$. To determine β_i we choose the largest β_i such that the closest neighbor to the new point is the original example. Thus, the new point cannot be more than halfway to the neighbor, and β_i will not exceed 0.5. Furthermore, we can find it within a small ϵ efficiently using a simple bisection algorithm.

In terms of computational cost, since every bisection step halves the remaining range of β_i, this will terminate in at most $\lceil \log_2 \frac{0.5}{\epsilon} \rceil$ iterations. Thus to find β_i within $\epsilon = 0.001$ for a given neighbor would require at most 9 iterations. Furthermore, for the standard Euclidean space, only neighbors closer than the neighbor we are currently interpolating between can have an insulating effect that reduces β_i. Thus, we need only check our candidate interpolation point against the closer neighbors to see if we must move the interpolated point. Therefore, after finding the k neighbors, the sample points can be computed relatively efficiently.

Returning to our quantities of interest, let Δ be a uniform point-mass distribution over the shifted points. Given this definition of Δ and an output function or classifier $\hat{\lambda}$, it is straightforward to compute $\mathrm{VAR}_\Delta\left[\hat{\lambda}\right]$ and $E_\Delta\left[\hat{\lambda}\right]$. Rather than computing exactly these quantities, for comparison to previous work we compute the closely related quantities $\mathrm{VAR}_\Delta\left[\hat{\lambda}(\boldsymbol{s}) - \hat{\lambda}(\boldsymbol{x})\right]$ and $E_\Delta\left[\hat{\lambda}(\boldsymbol{s}) - \hat{\lambda}(\boldsymbol{x})\right]$. Note, since $\hat{\lambda}(\boldsymbol{x})$ is constant with respect to Δ, $\mathrm{VAR}_\Delta\left[\hat{\lambda}\right] = \mathrm{VAR}_\Delta\left[\hat{\lambda}(\boldsymbol{s}) - \hat{\lambda}(\boldsymbol{x})\right]$ and $E_\Delta\left[\hat{\lambda}(\boldsymbol{s}) - \hat{\lambda}(\boldsymbol{x})\right] = E_\Delta\left[\hat{\lambda}(\boldsymbol{s})\right] - \hat{\lambda}(\boldsymbol{x})$.

Although based on the k nearest neighbors, the neighborhood-based sensitivity estimates can be used to estimate the sensitivity of any function. All that is required is an input space where interpolation is meaningful and a function $\hat{\lambda}$ that can be applied to any point in the input space. For example, the input space could be the bag-of-words representation of documents in a text corpus and $\hat{\lambda}$ could be the margin score using a linear model learned by an SVM algorithm.

4 Empirical Analysis

To understand the impact sensitivity estimates can have in practice, we studied the use of the estimates in two settings: post-learning recalibration of the output of the kNN classifier and combining classifiers for text classification. The bulk of our analysis focuses on the recalibration task to isolate the behavior of the neighborhood-based estimates. We then summarize the ensemble learning work which uses neighborhood-based estimates as well as other similar quantities to improve text classification — full details of the ensemble study are in [1].

4.1 Post-learning Recalibration

The post-learning recalibration problem attempts to take either poor probability estimates from a classifier or a more general rating and learn a function that will output good probability estimates or an improved thresholding [2,3,4,5]. In Platt recalibration [2], we perform nested cross-validation over the training set to collect a set of data for which we know both the class labels and model predictions. These collected pairs $\left\langle \hat{\lambda}(\boldsymbol{x}), c(\boldsymbol{x}) \right\rangle$, where $c(\cdot)$ denotes the actual class of the example, are then used as a training set by logistic regression to learn a and b such that our final recalibrated estimate is:

$$\hat{\lambda}^*(\boldsymbol{x}) = a\hat{\lambda} + b \qquad (3)$$

As noted above, we can compute neighborhood-based sensitivity estimates for a variety of classifiers, but for this study we will focus on the case where the classifier to be recalibrated is the *k*NN classifier. Our expectation is that a *k*NN classifier that is input to a local recalibration function should perform well in many sets where adaptive *k*NN methods work well.

Given the similarity between Equation 3 and Equation 1, an obvious experiment is one in which we compare the performance of three systems:

1. *k*NN — use the estimates from *k*NN directly;
2. Recalibrated *k*NN — Use the log-odds estimates from *k*NN obtained by nested cross-validation as inputs to logistic regression to produce improved estimates that depend only on the original *k*NN estimations;
3. Sensitivity Recalibrated — Use both the log-odds estimates from *k*NN and sensitivity-related estimates obtained by nested cross-validation as inputs to logistic regression to produce improved estimates that use both the original estimates and the sensitivity estimates.

Synthetic Datasets. Friedman [6] introduced a series of synthetic datasets to highlight the differences between various flexible *k*NN approaches and other adaptive methods. These datasets form an interesting case study since we expect a locally recalibrated *k*NN classifier to demonstrate many of the strengths of adaptive *k*NN methods. We note that Friedman's work and this work could complement each other by extending the work here to more general metric spaces and learning a metric before estimating the sensitivity using that metric.

We present results here for the first five synthetic problems in [6]. Each problem is binary classification and varies as to whether each dimension is equally informative. Because these are binary classification tasks, we refer to the positive and the negative class. We use the same number of training/testing points per problem as used in Friedman's original study. Ten train/test sets are drawn for each problem and the error averaged across the ten runs is computed. Since we expect the base *k*NN to produce poor log-odds estimates, we do not compare probability quality and instead compare improvement in error.

Problem 1. The number of input dimensions equals ten, $d = 10$. A class label is drawn with $P(c = +) = P(c = -) = 0.5$. For the negative class, the examples are drawn from a standard normal $\boldsymbol{x} \sim N(\mathbf{0}, \mathbf{1})$. For the positive class the examples are drawn from a normal $\boldsymbol{x} \sim N(\mu, \boldsymbol{\Sigma})$ where $\mu_i = \frac{\sqrt{i}}{2}$, $\boldsymbol{\Sigma}_{ii} = \frac{1}{\sqrt{i}}$, and $\boldsymbol{\Sigma}_{ij} = 0$ for $i \neq j$ and $i, j = 1, \ldots, d$. Thus the higher number dimensions have both means that are further separated and variances that are smaller and are generally more informative than the lower dimensions. For each run, 200 training and 2000 testing points are generated.

Problem 2. The number of input dimensions equals ten, $d = 10$. A class label is drawn with $P(c = +) = P(c = -) = 0.5$. For the negative class, the examples are drawn from a standard normal $\boldsymbol{x} \sim N(\mathbf{0}, \mathbf{1})$. For the positive class the examples are drawn from a normal $\boldsymbol{x} \sim N(\mu, \boldsymbol{\Sigma})$ where $\mu_i = \frac{\sqrt{d-i+1}}{2}$, $\boldsymbol{\Sigma}_{ii} = \frac{1}{\sqrt{i}}$, and $\mathbf{\Sigma}_{ij} = 0$ for $i \neq j$ and $i, j = 1, \ldots, d$. Thus the higher number dimensions have means that are closer together, but the variance binds the values more closely to the means. Whereas, the lower dimensions have means that are well separated but also have higher variances. Thus all dimensions are informative. For each run, 200 training and 2000 testing points are generated.

Problem 3. The number of input dimensions equals ten, $d = 10$. All examples are drawn from a standard normal $\boldsymbol{x} \sim N(\mathbf{0}, \mathbf{1})$ and are labeled with a class by the rule: if $\sum_{i=1}^{d} \frac{x_i^2}{i} \leq 2.5$ then negative else positive. The resulting class distribution marginalizes to approximately $P(c = +) = 0.51$. Unlike the previous two problems, the optimal error here is zero. Again, the dimensions contribute unequally to the final determination of the class label although the values of the features vary uniformly in the space. The decision surface is quadratic. For each run, 200 training and 2000 testing points are generated.

Problem 4. The number of input dimensions equals ten, $d = 10$. All examples are drawn from a standard normal $\boldsymbol{x} \sim N(\mathbf{0}, \mathbf{1})$ and are labeled by the rule: if $\sum_{i=1}^{d} x_i^2 \leq 9.8$ then negative else positive. The resulting class distribution marginalizes to approximately $P(c = +) = 0.46$. Again the optimal error here is zero, but now the dimensions contribute equally to the final determination of the class label. For each run, 500 training (instead of 200) and 2000 testing points are generated.

Problem 5. The number of input dimensions equals ten, $d = 10$. All examples are drawn from a standard normal $\boldsymbol{x} \sim N(\mathbf{0}, \mathbf{1})$ and are labeled with a class by the rule: if $\sum_{i=1}^{d} x_i \leq 0$ then negative else positive. The resulting class distribution is $P(c = +) = P(c = -) = 0.5$. Again the optimal error here is zero, and the dimensions contribute equally to the final determination of the class label. The decision surface is linear. For each run, 200 training and 2000 testing points are generated.

kNN Classifier. We use a standard way of performing a distance-weighted vote of the neighbors to compute the output for the kNN classifier [7]. k is set to be $2\lceil \log_2 N \rceil + 1$ where N is the number of training points.[1] The score used as the uncalibrated log-odds for being in a class y is:

$$\hat{\lambda}_{k\mathrm{NN}}(\boldsymbol{x}) = \sum_{\boldsymbol{n} \in k\mathrm{NN}(\boldsymbol{x}) | c(\boldsymbol{n}) = y} K(\boldsymbol{x}, \boldsymbol{n}) \quad - \sum_{\boldsymbol{n} \in k\mathrm{NN}(\boldsymbol{x}) | c(\boldsymbol{n}) \neq y} K(\boldsymbol{x}, \boldsymbol{n}). \tag{4}$$

where K is a kernel (similarity) function. For text classification, this is typically cosine similarity. For the synthetic datasets, we use a Gaussian RBF kernel with $\sigma = 1$ since the problems imply a translation invariant kernel is desirable. It is reasonable to expect this score to behave like an uncalibrated log-odds estimate

[1] This rule is motivated by theoretical results which show such a rule converges to the Bayes optimal classifier as the number of training points increases [8].

since it is similar to SVM's margin score, $\sum \alpha_i y_i K(\boldsymbol{s}_i, \boldsymbol{x})$, which has been shown to empirically behave like an uncalibrated log-odds estimate [2,4].

Efficient Approximation. Because identifying the k neighbors of a point in kNN is computationally expensive, we desire a more efficient approach than separate neighbor retrievals for the $k+1$ classifications. In this case, we perform a single retrieval around the query point to obtain a cache of size $K \geq k$ such that the k neighbors of a sample point are approximated by taking the k closest of the K. We use $K = 2k$ as a heuristic derived from the fact that retrieving K neighbors by finding all points within twice the *radius*, r, of the original example (the farthest neighbor of the k from the query) would guarantee that the k closest neighbors of a sample point are contained within the K. This is because the sample point is within $0.5r$ of the original example, and therefore the original query's k neighbors are within $1.5r$ of the sample. Thus, the sample has radius $\leq 1.5r$ and therefore $2r$ from the original will contain all its neighbors.

For benchmarking, we ran over a text classification corpus using a kNN algorithm with an inverted index, the same algorithm but retrieving $2k$ neighbors, and the version that computes both predictions and sensitivity estimates. The experiments were run on a machine with an Intel Pentium® 4 CPU, 3GHz clock speed, and 1 GB of RAM. As can be seen in Table 1, a slowdown of three times the baseline is experienced instead of the naïve slowdown of $k + 1 = 30$ times the baseline. For the synthetic experiments below, we do not use this caching approximation, but for the experiments over the text corpora we do.

Table 1. Effect on running time of computing the kNN sensitivity estimates for the Reuters 21578 corpus (9603 training examples, 3299 testing examples, 900 features)

Method	Total Run Time (s)	Ratio to Baseline
Sparse *(k)*	69.1	1
Sparse *(2k)*	80.07	1.16
Sparse w/Sensitivity *(2k)*	196.37	2.84

Recalibration Results and Discussion. Table 2 summarizes results over the synthetic datasets giving the average error for each method over the ten runs as well as the standard deviation across runs. Table 3 presents a summary of the two recalibration methods in terms of the relative reduction in error they yield over the baseline kNN method. When the best result is statistically significant according to a two-tailed paired t-test with p=0.01, it is underlined.

To ensure that our baseline error is not artificially poor, we list the average error reported by Friedman for his baseline kNN method. Our baseline performs either approximately the same or far better (Problems 1 and 2); the latter probably results from our use of a distance-weighted kNN vote rather than Friedman's unweighted vote.

Examining the performance of Recalibrated kNN, we see that simple recalibration gains large reduction in errors in all problems but one — Problem 5 where it loses slightly relative to the baseline. Examining the Sensitivity Recalibrated results, we see that not only does this method always achieve large wins over the baseline method, but it also yields large improvements over Recalibrated *k*NN in all but one case — Problem 4 where it improves over Recalibrated *k*NN by only a slight amount.

In the fifty different runs (10 runs * 5 problems), the Sensitivity Recalibrated method only has a worse error on 3/50 runs vs. Recalibrated *k*NN and on 4/50 runs vs. *k*NN; furthermore, no more than one of these runs occurs on the same Problem (explaining the paired *t*-test significance). Relative to the baseline, the Sensitivity Recalibrated method reduces the error anywhere from 13% to 65%. Altogether, the evidence argues that not only are the sensitivity estimates useful in recalibrating *k*NN, but they provide information beyond that which is captured in the original log-odds estimates.

Table 2. The average error of each method in the synthetic datasets as well as one standard deviation. The best result in each problem is in bold.

	Problem 1		Problem 2		Problem 3		Problem 4		Problem 5	
	Error	Stdev	Error	Stdev	Error	Stdev	Error	Stdev	Error	Stdev
Friedman kNN [6]	13.2	—	10.3	—	35.9	—	34.0	—	17.4	—
kNN	2.57	0.2973	2.81	0.5868	36.22	1.7335	38.16	0.6919	17.07	1.5592
Recalibrated kNN	2.23	0.6601	2.40	0.3752	21.81	0.9459	21.52	1.4870	18.00	1.9490
Sensitivity Recal.	**1.33**	0.2679	**1.81**	0.3354	**20.97**	1.0061	**13.19**	0.9562	**14.85**	1.6264

Table 3. Relative Reduction in Error, 1 - Error(Method) / Error(*k*NN)

	Problem 1	Problem 2	Problem 3	Problem 4	Problem 5
Recalibrated kNN	0.13	0.15	0.40	0.44	-0.05
Sensitivity Recal.	0.48	0.36	0.42	0.65	0.13

4.2 Local Classifier Combination

We have seen that sensitivity estimates can boost the performance of recalibration techniques. However, it seems likely that they should also be useful in classifier combination. Returning to our peer review problem, when faced with opinions from three reviewers, we might want the weight on a reviewer's acceptance rating to depend on the reviewer's confidence.

The STRIVE metaclassification approach [9] extended Wolpert's stacking framework [10] to use reliability indicators. In this framework a metaclassifier has access to both the outputs of base classifiers as well as some auxiliary reliability indicators. If each of the base classifiers outputs a log-odds like estimate, then a linear metaclassifier has a natural interpretation as both recalibrating and weighting each classifier according to its class-conditional information content [11,1]. Note that this is the direct extension of the recalibration paradigm in the previous section to multiple classifiers. A metaclassifier that recalibrates a single base classifier is now replaced by a stacking approach which applies a metaclassifier to the outputs of multiple base classifiers. Likewise recalibrating with the additional sensitivity information is now replaced by a striving approach which applies a metaclassifier to the outputs of multiple base classifiers and additional sensitivity information.

Our goal in this section is to illustrate that computing the neighborhood-based sensitivity estimates is both practical in "real-world" datasets and yields increased performance. To demonstrate this, we compare the performance of the base classifiers to both a stacked model of the base classifier outputs and to striving with the base classifier outputs and sensitivity information.

For the base classifier outputs, we obtain log-odds like estimates from five standard classifiers (kNN, linear SVM, decision trees, multivariate naïve Bayes, and multinomial naïve Bayes), and use a linear SVM as a metaclassifier to learn a stacked model. For the striving model, we apply a linear SVM metaclassifier to the base classifier outputs and the sensitivity estimates described above for kNN as well as a variety of other variables tied to sensitivity as motivated in [1]. Since an <u>**S**</u>VM is used as a metaclassifier in both cases, we refer to the stacking model as *Stack-S* and the striving model as *STRIVE-S*. Space prevents us from providing a full description of these experiments, but see [1].

We examined performance over several topic-classification corpora including: the *MSN Web Directory*; two corpora drawn from the *Reuters* newswire; and the *TREC-AP* corpus. We selected these corpora because they offer an array of topic classification problems from very broad topics over web pages to very narrow topics over financial news stories. In terms of scale, the number of training documents across these corpora varies from 9603 to 142791 while the number of testing documents varies from 3299 to 781265.

4.3 Results and Discussion

For space, only the base SVM — which typically performs best among the base classifiers — is explicitly listed. We note that our implementation of the base SVM is on par with the best results in previously reported literature [12,9]. In Figure 2, we display the changes in the three components that determine error and F1: false positives, false negatives, and correct positives. Not only does *STRIVE-S* achieve considerable reductions in error of 4-18% (*left*) and 3-16% (*right*), but it also nearly always improves beyond those gains achieved by *Stack-S*. Furthermore, *STRIVE-S* never hurts performance relative to the *SVM* on these performance measures as *Stack-S* does over RCV1-v2 on the far left. Examining a micro-sign, macro-sign, and macro t-test, *STRIVE-S* significantly improves ($p < 0.05$) over the base SVM classifier (except for one collection and one performance measure, F1 for RCV1-v2), and over *Stack-S* for the majority of collections and performance measures (see [1] for more detail).

Finally, the STRIVE model augmented with sensitivity information not only demonstrates improved and robust performance across a variety of corpora, but in post-analysis, backward selection reveals that the primary variables of interest are the neighborhood-based sensitivity related estimates [1].

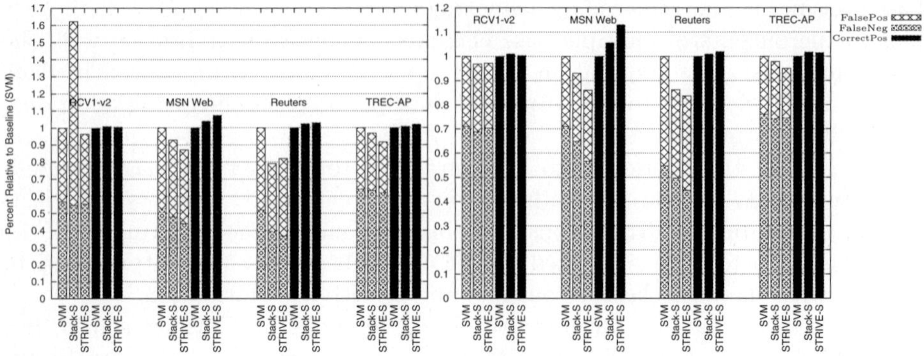

Fig. 2. For *Stack-S* and *STRIVE-S* change relative to the best base classifier — the *SVM* classifier — over all the topic classification corpora. On the *left*, we show the relative change using thresholds learned for F1, and on the *right*, we show the relative change using thresholds learned for error.

5 Related Work, Future Work, and Summary

In addition to the related work mentioned throughout the paper, several approaches merit mention. The STRIVE metaclassification approach [9] extended Wolpert's stacking framework [10] to use reliability indicators. In recent work, Lee *et al.* [13] derive variance estimates for naïve Bayes and tree-augmented naïve Bayes and use them in a combination model. Our work complements theirs by laying groundwork for how to compute variance estimates for models such as *k*NN that have no obvious probabilistic component in addition to being able to use the same framework to compute estimates for any classification models.

A variety of other work has examined stability and robustness related to sensitivity. Several researchers have attempted to obtain more robust classifiers by altering feature values [14] or training multiple classifiers over feature subsets [15]. Similarly, [16] compresses a more complex model into a simpler model by using the former to label instances generated by combining attributes of a point with its nearest neighbor. Finally, [17] contains a variety of related work that focuses on sensitivity analysis to determine the significance of input dimensions while [18] examines the stability of the algorithm with respect to small changes in the training set. Where much of the previous work focuses on change in a single dimension, we focus on characterizing the change around the current prediction point according to the local density across all dimensions.

There are a variety of interesting directions for future work. One of the most interesting directions is extending the neighborhood-based estimates for learned metrics. Additionally, exploring other methods of sampling from the Voronoi cell and characterizing how these methods differ in the quality of estimates they yield could be quite useful. Such a study could also analyze how critical staying within the Voronoi cell is. In our experiments, we found performance over the synthetic datasets was less sensitive to staying within the Voronoi cell while it was more important over the text datasets. Formally characterizing this dimension will be important in advancing the understanding of sensitivity estimators.

In conclusion, we motivated the use of sensitivity information in a variety of different scenarios including active learning, recalibration, and classifier combination. We then demonstrated how a neighborhood-based sensitivity estimator can sample efficiently from the points in the input space near the prediction point to estimate sensitivity. Finally, the resulting estimates were demonstrated to be useful in improving performance in both recalibration over synthetic data and classifier combination over standard text classification corpora.

References

1. Bennett, P.N.: Building Reliable Metaclassifiers for Text Learning. PhD thesis, CMU, CMU-CS-06-121 (2006)
2. Platt, J.C.: Probabilistic outputs for support vector machines and comparisons to regularized likelihood methods. In: Smola, A.J., Bartlett, P., Scholkopf, B., Schuurmans, D. (eds.) Advances in Large Margin Classifiers, MIT Press, Cambridge (1999)
3. Zadrozny, B., Elkan, C.: Reducing multiclass to binary by coupling probability estimates. In: KDD '02 (2002)
4. Bennett, P.N.: Using asymmetric distributions to improve text classifier probability estimates. In: SIGIR '03 (2003)
5. Zhang, J., Yang, Y.: Probabilistic score estimation with piecewise logistic regression. In: ICML '04 (2004)
6. Friedman, J.H.: Flexible metric nearest neighbor classification. Technical report, Department of Statistics, Stanford University (1994)
7. Yang, Y.: An evaluation of statistical approaches to text categorization. Information Retrieval 1, 67–88 (1999)
8. Devroye, L., Györfi, L., Lugosi, G.: A Probabilistic Theory of Pattern Recognition. Springer, New York (1996)
9. Bennett, P.N., Dumais, S.T., Horvitz, E.: The combination of text classifiers using reliability indicators. Information Retrieval 8, 67–100 (2005)
10. Wolpert, D.H.: Stacked generalization. Neural Networks 5, 241–259 (1992)
11. Kahn, J.M.: Bayesian Aggregation of Probability Forecasts on Categorical Events. PhD thesis, Stanford University (2004)
12. Lewis, D.D., Yang, Y., Rose, T.G., Li, F.: Rcv1: A new benchmark collection for text categorization research. Journal of Machine Learning Research 5, 361–397 (2004), `http://www.jmlr.org/papers/volume5/lewis04a/lewis04a.pdf`
13. Lee, C.H., Greiner, R., Wang, S.: Using query-specific variance estimates to combine bayesian classifiers. In: ICML '06 (2006)
14. O'Sullivan, J., Langford, J., Caruana, R., Blum, A.: Featureboost: A meta-learning algorithm that improves model robustness. In: ICML '00 (2000)
15. Bay, S.D.: Combining nearest neighbor classifiers through multiple feature subsets. In: ICML '98 (1998)
16. Bucila, C., Caruana, R., Niculescu-Mizil, A.: Model compression. In: KDD '06 (2006)
17. Saltelli, A., Tarantola, S., Campolongo, F., Ratto, M.: Sensitivity Analysis in Practice: A Guide to Assessing Scientific Models. John Wiley & Sons Ltd., Chichester (2004)
18. Bousquet, O., Elisseeff, A.: Stabilitiy and generalization. JMLR 2, 499–526 (2002)

Approximating Gaussian Processes with $\mathcal{H}^2$-Matrices

Steffen Börm[1] and Jochen Garcke[2]

[1] Max Planck Institute for Mathematics in the Sciences
Inselstraße 22–26, 04103 Leipzig, Germany
sbo@mis.mpg.de

[2] Technische Universität Berlin, Institut für Mathematik, MA 3-3
Straße des 17. Juni 136, 10623 Berlin
garcke@math.tu-berlin.de

Abstract. To compute the exact solution of Gaussian process regression one needs $\mathcal{O}(N^3)$ computations for direct and $\mathcal{O}(N^2)$ for iterative methods since it involves a densely populated kernel matrix of size $N \times N$, here N denotes the number of data. This makes large scale learning problems intractable by standard techniques.

We propose to use an alternative approach: the kernel matrix is replaced by a data-sparse approximation, called an $\mathcal{H}^2$-matrix. This matrix can be represented by only $\mathcal{O}(Nm)$ units of storage, where m is a parameter controlling the accuracy of the approximation, while the computation of the $\mathcal{H}^2$-matrix scales with $\mathcal{O}(Nm \log N)$.

Practical experiments demonstrate that our scheme leads to significant reductions in storage requirements and computing times for large data sets in lower dimensional spaces.

1 Introduction

In this paper we consider the regression problem arising in machine learning. A set of data points $\underline{x}_i$ in a d-dimensional feature space is given, together with an associated value y_i. We assume that a function f_* describes the relation between the predictor variables $\underline{x}$ and the (noisy) response variable y and want to (approximately) reconstruct the function f_* from the given data. This allows us to predict the function value for any newly given data point.

We apply Gaussian Process regression (GP) [1] for this task. In the direct application this method gives rise to a computational complexity of $\mathcal{O}(N^3)$; for iterative methods one has $\mathcal{O}(N^2)$ in each iteration. This makes large scale learning problems intractable for exact approaches.

One approximation approach for large problems is to use only a subset of the data for the iterative solver, i.e., to compute the inverse of a smaller matrix and extend that result in a suitable way to the whole data set, see [1] for an overview and further references. In [2] probabilistic sparse approximations are presented under a unified concept as “exact interference with an approximated prior”.

One can interpret the above approaches also as “approximated interference with the exact prior”, this view especially holds for recent approaches using

J.N. Kok et al. (Eds.): ECML 2007, LNAI 4701, pp. 42–53, 2007.

Krylov subspace iteration methods with an approximation of the matrix-vector product in the case of Gaussian kernels. In [3] this product is approximated using tree-type multiresolution data structures like *kd*-trees. [4,5] compare several multipole approaches, these can show speedups of an order of magnitude or more, but the results heavily depend on the parameters of the problem.

In this paper we use hierarchical matrices ($\mathcal{H}$-matrices) [6] to derive a data-sparse approximation of the full kernel matrix. $\mathcal{H}$-matrices are closely related to panel-clustering and multipole techniques for the treatment of integral operators in two or three spatial dimensions. They reduce the storage requirements for N-by-N matrices to $\mathcal{O}(Nm \log N)$ by applying local rank-m-approximations and allow us to evaluate matrix-vector products in $\mathcal{O}(Nm \log N)$ operations. Other operations like multiplication or inversion can also be accomplished in almost linear complexity [6,7].

For very large N it is a good idea to look for even more efficient techniques: $\mathcal{H}^2$-matrices [8] reduce the storage requirements to $\mathcal{O}(Nm)$, and using the recompression algorithm described in [9], the conversion of the original $\mathcal{H}$-matrix representation into the more efficient $\mathcal{H}^2$-matrix format can be accomplished with only a minor increase in run-time.

2 Gaussian Process Regression

Let us consider a given set of data (the training set) $S = \{(\underline{x}_i, y_i) \in \mathbb{R}^d \times \mathbb{R}\}_{i=1}^N$, with $\underline{x}_i$ representing data points in the feature space and y_i their associated response variable. Assume for now that these data have been obtained by sampling an unknown function f with additional independent Gaussian noise e_i of variance σ^2, i.e., $y_i = f(\underline{x}_i) + e_i$. The aim is now to recover the function f from the given data as well as possible. Following the Bayesian paradigm, we place a prior distribution on the function $f(\cdot)$ and use the posterior distribution to predict on new data points $\underline{x}$. In particular we assume a Gaussian process prior on the function $f(\underline{x})$, meaning that values $f(\underline{x})$ on points $\{\underline{x}_i\}_{i=1}^N$ are jointly Gaussian distributed with zero mean and covariance matrix $\mathcal{K}$. The kernel (or covariance) function $k(\cdot,\cdot)$ defines $\mathcal{K}$ via $\mathcal{K}_{i,j} = k(\underline{x}_i, \underline{x}_j)$.

It turns out that the solution $f(\underline{x})$ takes on the form of a weighted combination of kernel functions on training points $\underline{x}_i$ [1]

$$f(\underline{x}) = \sum_{i=1}^{N} \alpha_i k(\underline{x}_i, \underline{x}), \tag{1}$$

where the coefficient vector α is the solution of the linear equation system

$$(\mathcal{K} + \sigma^2 \mathcal{I})\alpha = y, \tag{2}$$

here $\mathcal{I}$ denotes the unit matrix. The variance σ^2 is in practice estimated via the marginal likelihood criterion, cross-validation, or similar techniques [1].

Directly solving this equation by inverting $\mathcal{K} + \sigma^2 \mathcal{I}$ involves in general $\mathcal{O}(N^3)$ operations. Furthermore, the storage requirement of the covariance matrix $\mathcal{K}$

exceeds the memory of current workstations even for the moderate dimension $N \geq 15000$. A common approach is to use a smaller subset of the data and the associated kernel functions to represent the solution f [1,2]. That way one can in principle achieve methods of order $\mathcal{O}(M^2 \cdot N + M^3)$ instead of $\mathcal{O}(N^3)$, but one loses the exact theoretical properties of the approach. Furthermore, these approximate methods are known to fail for some data sets or have costly subset selection strategies for competitive results, see [10] for results in the related case of regularised least squares classification. Note that these methods still scale with the square of M and therefore show a quadratic complexity in N if $M \geq \sqrt{N}$.

2.1 Iterative Solution with Krylov Subspace Methods

The use of conjugate gradients (CG) for the solution of the linear equation system (2) is for example described in [1]. In Krylov subspace iteration methods the k-th approximate solution x^k of $Ax = b$ is searched in the Krylov space $\mathrm{span}\{b, Ab, \dots, A^{k-1}b\}$, i.e., the history of the already computed approximation is used, see, e.g., [11]. For symmetric positive definite matrices, the CG algorithm ensures that x^k minimises the A-norm of the error, i.e., $\langle Ae^k, e^k\rangle^{1/2}$ with $e^k := x - x^k$. In the case of general matrices, the GMRES algorithm minimises the Euclidean norm of the residual, i.e., $\|b - Ax^k\|$. Note that in both cases only the action of the matrix A on a vector is needed in the actual computation. As long as the number of iterations is bounded by a constant independent of the matrix size and the problem parameters under consideration, these iterative approaches result in a computational complexity that is proportional to the complexity of one matrix-vector multiplication, i.e., $\mathcal{O}(N^2)$ operations are required for the solution of (2) in the standard case.

Since $\mathcal{O}(N^2)$ is still too costly for large problems, approaches using Krylov subspace iteration methods with a more efficient approximation of the matrix-vector product in the case of Gaussian kernels have been studied recently. In [3] the matrix-vector product is approximated using tree-type multiresolution data structures like *kd*-trees. [4,5] compare the fast Gauss transform, the improved fast Gauss transform (IFGT) and dual-tree approaches for fast Gauss transforms, see [3,4,5] for references with regard to the algorithms. In these articles empirical speedups of an order of magnitude or slightly more, in comparison with on-the-fly computation of the kernel matrix, are shown. The results heavily depend on the parameters, e.g., the number of dimensions, the width of the Gaussian kernel, the regularisation parameter, and the data distribution, see [5]. This is not always taken into proper account in experimental studies.

2.2 $\mathcal{H}$- and $\mathcal{H}^2$-Matrices

We propose to use a Krylov-based approach and rely on $\mathcal{H}$- (cf. [6,7]) and $\mathcal{H}^2$-matrices (cf. [8,9]) to speed up the computation of the matrix-vector multiplication by the full matrix $\mathcal{K}$. In order to reach this goal, we replace the matrix by a data-sparse approximation $\widetilde{\mathcal{K}}$ that allows us to perform matrix-vector multiplications (and other arithmetic operations) very efficiently.

$\mathcal{H}$- and $\mathcal{H}^2$-matrices have originally been developed for the approximation of matrices arising when treating elliptic partial differential equations. They require only $\mathcal{O}(Nm \log N)$ and $\mathcal{O}(Nm)$ units of storage, respectively, where m determines the accuracy. The matrix-vector multiplication is of the same order, since it requires not more than two operations per unit of storage.

In the following we will present the core ideas behind these matrix approximations and their computation. For more details we refer to the references, in particular the lecture notes [6].

The basic idea of $\mathcal{H}$- and $\mathcal{H}^2$-matrix techniques is to exploit the smoothness of the kernel function k: if k is sufficiently smooth in the first variable, it can be replaced by an interpolant

$$\tilde{k}(\underline{x}, \underline{z}) := \sum_{\nu=1}^{m} \mathcal{L}_\nu(\underline{x}) k(\underline{\xi}_\nu, \underline{z}),$$

where $(\underline{\xi}_\nu)_{\nu=1}^m$ are interpolation points and $(\mathcal{L}_\nu)_{\nu=1}^m$ are corresponding Lagrange polynomials. Replacing k by $\tilde{k}$ in the matrix $\mathcal{K}$ yields an approximation

$$\tilde{\mathcal{K}}_{ij} := \tilde{k}(\underline{x}_i, \underline{x}_j) = \sum_{\nu=1}^{m} \mathcal{L}_\nu(\underline{x}_i) k(\underline{\xi}_\nu, \underline{x}_j) = (AB^\top)_{ij} \tag{3}$$

with matrices $A, B \in \mathbb{R}^{N \times m}$ defined by $A_{i\nu} := \mathcal{L}_\nu(\underline{x}_i)$ and $B_{j\nu} := k(\underline{\xi}_\nu, \underline{x}_j)$. While the standard representation of $\mathcal{K}$ requires N^2 units of storage, only $2Nm$ units are sufficient for the factorised representation (3). If k is sufficiently smooth, m can be quite small, and the new representation will be far more efficient than the standard one.

Computing the factorised representation $\widetilde{\mathcal{K}} = AB^\top$ by interpolation will be relatively inefficient if the function k has special properties: if, e.g., k is a quadratic polynomial, interpolating it by seventh-order polynomials will lead to an unnecessary increase in computational complexity. In order to avoid this effect, we replace the interpolation by the heuristic *adaptive cross approximation* (ACA) algorithm [12]:

1: set $\widehat{\mathcal{K}} := \mathcal{K}$ and $\widetilde{\mathcal{K}} := 0$
2: estimate $\epsilon_0 := \|\widehat{\mathcal{K}}\|$
3: set $m := 0$
4: **while** $\epsilon_m > \epsilon_0 \epsilon_{\mathrm{ACA}}$ **do**
5:     set $m := m + 1$
6:     pick pivot indices $i^m, j^m \in \{1, \ldots, N\}$
7:     compute $a_i^m := \widehat{\mathcal{K}}_{ij^m}$ for $i = 1, \ldots, N$
8:     compute $b_j^m := \widehat{\mathcal{K}}_{i^m j} / a_{i^m}^m$ for $j = 1, \ldots, N$
9:     set $\widetilde{\mathcal{K}} := \widetilde{\mathcal{K}} + a^m (b^m)^\top$ and $\widehat{\mathcal{K}} := \widehat{\mathcal{K}} - a^m (b^m)^\top$
10:     estimate $\epsilon_m := \|\widehat{\mathcal{K}}\|$
11: **end while**

There are different strategies for picking the pivot indices in step 6 of the algorithm. A simple approach is to assume that j^m is given, compute a^m, pick i^m

such that $|a^m_{i^m}|$ is maximised, compute b^m, pick j^{m+1} such that $|b^m_{j^m}|$ is maximised, and repeat the procedure for $m+1$. In our experiments, we use the more refined strategies of the HLib package [13].

Since $a^m(b^m)^\top$ is a rough approximation of $\widehat{K}$, a reasonable strategy for estimating the remaining error in steps 2 and 10 of the algorithm is to use $\|\widehat{K}\|_2 \approx \|a^m(b^m)^\top\|_2 = \|a^m\|_2\|b^m\|_2$. Of course, problem-dependent norms can be used instead of the spectral norm, provided that they can be estimated efficiently.

The entries $\widehat{\mathcal{K}}_{ij^m}$ and $\widehat{\mathcal{K}}_{i^m j}$ used in steps 7 and 8 should not be computed explicitly, since this would require computing the entire matrix K. A more elegant approach is to use the definition of $\widehat{\mathcal{K}}$: due to

$$\widehat{\mathcal{K}}_{ij} = (\mathcal{K} - \widetilde{\mathcal{K}})_{ij} = \mathcal{K}_{ij} - \left(\sum_{\ell=1}^{m-1} a^\ell (b^\ell)^\top\right)_{ij} = \mathcal{K}_{ij} - \sum_{\ell=1}^{m-1} a^\ell_i b^\ell_j,$$

we can avoid storing $\widehat{\mathcal{K}}$ explicitly and reconstruct its entries as necessary.

At the end of each iteration of the inner loop, we have $\widehat{\mathcal{K}} + \widetilde{\mathcal{K}} = \mathcal{K}$, i.e., $\|\mathcal{K} - \widetilde{\mathcal{K}}\| = \|\widehat{\mathcal{K}}\|$, so the stopping criterion allows us to control the relative approximation error if the estimates for the norms of $\widehat{\mathcal{K}}$ are sufficiently accurate. The vectors $(a^\nu)_{\nu=1}^m$ and $(b^\nu)_{\nu=1}^m$ yield the desired representation $\widetilde{\mathcal{K}} = AB^\top$.

In many applications, e.g., if the function k is not globally smooth, the representation (3) will not be efficient for the global matrix $\mathcal{K}$. Typical functions k are *locally* smooth or decay rapidly, and the factorised representation can be applied for submatrices $\mathcal{K}|_{t\times s} = (\mathcal{K}_{ij})_{i\in t, j\in s}$ with suitable subsets $t, s \subseteq \{1, \ldots, N\}$.

The analysis in [14] shows that the approximation error will even decrease *exponentially* depending on m if k is locally analytic and if

$$\operatorname{diam}(B_t) \le \eta \operatorname{dist}(B_t, B_s) \tag{4}$$

holds for a parameter $\eta \in \mathbb{R}_{>0}$ and two axis-parallel boxes B_t and B_s satisfying $\underline{x}_i \in B_t$ for all $i \in t$ and $\underline{x}_j \in B_s$ for all $j \in s$. Here the Euclidean diameter and distance are used, which can be computed easily for axis-parallel boxes.

We are faced with the task of splitting $\mathcal{K}$ (up to a sparse remainder) into a collection of submatrices which satisfy a condition of the type (4), i.e., can be approximated in the form (3). Since the data points $(\underline{x}_i)_{i=1}^N$ are embedded in $\mathbb{R}^d$, a hierarchy of *clusters* of indices assigned to boxes B_t can be constructed by binary space partitioning. If a cluster t is "too large", its box B_t is split in two equal parts along its longest edge, and this induces a splitting of the cluster t. Starting with $t = \{1, \ldots, N\}$ in the whole domain and applying the procedure recursively yields a cluster tree.

The corresponding hierarchical matrix structure is also constructed by recursion: if a block $t \times s$ is admissible, it is represented by a low-rank matrix. If t or s are leaves, the block is considered "small" and stored in the standard format. Otherwise, the sons of t and s are tested until no untested blocks remain. This procedure requires $\mathcal{O}(N \log N)$ operations [7], but the complexity will grow exponentially in d: each cluster t can be expected to "touch" at least $3^d - 1$ other blocks s, these blocks will not satisfy the admissibility condition (4) and have to be examined by recursion. Therefore the current implementation of the $\mathcal{H}$-matrix approach is attractive for up to four spatial dimensions, but will suffer from the "curse of dimensionality" if d becomes larger due to the use of binary space partitioning.

The $\mathcal{H}$-matrix approximation based on ACA or interpolation will have an algorithmic complexity of $\mathcal{O}(Nm \log N)$ [6]. If N is very large, the logarithmic factor can have a significant impact regarding the total storage requirements, and some problems may even become intractable given a fixed amount of storage.

The situation is different for the $\mathcal{H}^2$-matrix representation [8,9], which relies on the same basic ideas as the $\mathcal{H}$-matrix approach: the matrix is split into blocks, and each block is approximated by a low-rank matrix. The main difference between the two methods is the choice of this low-rank matrix: for the $\mathcal{H}$-matrix, it is motivated by the interpolation in the x variable, for the $\mathcal{H}^2$-matrix, we interpolate in both variables and get

$$\tilde{k}(\underline{x}, \underline{z}) := \sum_{\nu=1}^{m} \sum_{\mu=1}^{m} \mathcal{L}_\nu(\underline{x}) k(\underline{\xi}_\nu, \underline{\zeta}_\mu) \mathcal{L}_\mu(\underline{z}),$$

which leads to the factorisation $\mathcal{K}|_{t \times s} \approx VSW^\top$ for a small *coupling matrix* $S \in \mathbb{R}^{m \times m}$ and *cluster bases* $V, W \in \mathbb{R}^{N \times m}$. If this approximation scheme is applied to submatrices of $\mathcal{K}$, the special structure of V and W, i.e., the fact that they are discretised Lagrange polynomials, can be used in order to reach a total complexity of $\mathcal{O}(Nm)$.

Using the quasi-optimal algorithm presented in [9], an $\mathcal{H}$-matrix can be converted into a more compact $\mathcal{H}^2$-matrix with only a minor run-time overhead while keeping the approximation error under close control.

2.3 Coarsening

The $\mathcal{H}$- and $\mathcal{H}^2$-matrix structures created by this procedure will suffer from the "curse of dimensionality", i.e., their complexity will grow exponentially in the spatial dimension d. In order to reduce this effect, the coarsening techniques described in [15] are employed to construct a far more efficient $\mathcal{H}$-matrix structure: even if t and s do not satisfy the admissibility condition, the block $\mathcal{K}|_{t \times s}$ may have an efficient low-rank approximation. Using the singular value decomposition of $\widetilde{\mathcal{K}}|_{t \times s}$, we can determine the *optimal* low-rank approximation for a given precision ϵ_{HC} and use it instead of the original one if it is more efficient.

repeat
  pick t and s in such a way that $\widetilde{\mathcal{K}}_{t' \times s'}$ is represented by a low-rank matrix for all subblocks $t' \times s'$ of $t \times s$.
  compute a low-rank approximation of $\widetilde{\mathcal{K}}_{t \times s}$ up to an error of ϵ_{HC}
  if the new approximation is more efficient than the original ones **then**
    replace the original low-rank representations by the new one
  end if
until all pairs t and s have been checked

In most practical situations, the algorithm is relatively inexpensive compared to the initial approximation and yields a very significant compression.

See Figure 1 for an example of the resulting structure and the local ranks of an $\mathcal{H}^2$-matrix for a typical data set (using a suitable permutation of the data).

The full algorithm to compute the $\mathcal{H}^2$-matrix approximation consists of the following steps:

build hierarchy of clusters t by binary space partitioning
build blocks $t \times s$ using the admissibility criterion (4)
for all admissible blocks $t \times s$ **do**
    use ACA to compute a low-rank approximation $\widetilde{\mathcal{K}}|_{t \times s} = AB^\top$
end for
for all remaining blocks $t \times s$ **do**
    compute standard representation $\widetilde{\mathcal{K}}|_{t \times s} = \mathcal{K}|_{t \times s}$
end for
coarsen the block structure adaptively
convert the $\mathcal{H}$-matrix into an $\mathcal{H}^2$-matrix

Note that the blockwise errors introduced by ACA can be estimated by a simple heuristic approach. A rigorous error estimate can be provided if the approximation is based on interpolation and the growth rate of the derivatives of the kernel function can be bounded [14]. The blockwise errors introduced by the coarsening algorithm can be computed and controlled directly based on the singular value decomposition [15]. Given a bound for the condition number of $\mathcal{K}$, error estimates for the solution vector are possible [16, Theorem 2.7.2].

3 Experimental Results

We employ the Gaussian RBF kernel $e^{-\|\underline{x}-\underline{y}\|^2/w}$ in the following experiments. The hyperparameters w and σ were found using a 2:1 split of the training data for each data set size. Note that many GP users prefer to use marginal likelihood as a criterion. Since we concentrate for now on the approximation properties of our approach we have not investigated in much detail how to (more) efficiently find good hyperparameters. Since one $\mathcal{H}^2$-matrix approximation can be used during the computation for several σ, this property, which allows the cheap solution for several σ, should be exploited, which we can by using the 2:1 split.

For the following experiments, we set both the tolerance for the cross approximation ϵ_{ACA} and the tolerance for the coarsening to ϵ_{HC} to 10^{-7}. The admissibility parameter in (4) is chosen as $\eta = 0.1$. In general these parameters should depend on the type of kernel function and its parameters. We choose these fixed values in this study to have a good approximation of the kernel matrix in all cases, they could be larger if chosen depending on the actual kernel and therefore result in less computation time. We aim to have a difference of less than 1% for the error on the test data from the 2:1 split of the training data due to the employed approximation.

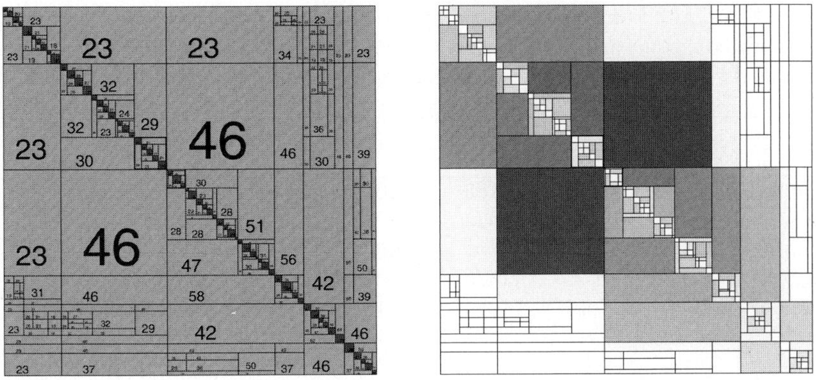

Fig. 1. Structure and rank of the $\mathcal{H}^2$-matrix approximation for the mote22 data set using 5000 data. On the right hand side error of the approximation, the darker the larger the error. The difference between the full matrix and the $\mathcal{H}^2$-matrix approximation is $3.79 \cdot 10^{-8}$ in the spectral norm for this example.

The computations are carried out with the HLib package [13] on an AMD Opteron 275 with about 4 GB of available memory. To solve the linear system (2) for the $\mathcal{H}$-matrix we use GMRES, since the use of the adaptive cross approximation algorithm disturbs the symmetry of the matrix $\widetilde{\mathcal{K}}$ slightly and gives somewhat unstable results with conjugate gradients. Note that we currently can not exploit the symmetry of the kernel matrix by only using the upper or lower half of the matrix due to limitations in the HLib, but the extension for this situation is in development. We also limit the number of iterations by 3000.

Two regression data sets are used, in the first one the data originates from a network of simple sensor motes[1] and the task is to predict the temperature at a mote from the measurements of neighbouring ones [17]. Mote22 consists of 30000 training / 2500 test data from two other motes and mote47 has 27000 training / 2000 test data from three nearby motes. The second data is from a helicopter flight project [18] and the task is to use the current state to predict subdynamics of the helicopter for one timestep later, in particular its yaw rate, forward velocity, and lateral velocity. We have 40000 training / 4000 test data in three dimensions in the case of the yaw rate, both velocities depend on two other measurements. For all these data sets we linearly transform the domain of the predictor variable $\underline{x}$ to $[0,1]^d, d = 2,3$.

In Table 1 we present results of our experiments on these data sets, we use the mean absolute error (MAE) on the test set as the quality criterion. We give in each case results for 20000 data, here the matrix $(\mathcal{K} + \sigma^2\mathcal{I})$ can still be stored in the available memory of 4 GB, and for the full data set. The times (in seconds) presented here and in the following are for the computation using the given hyperparameters, i.e., solution of the equation system (2) and the evaluation on the data. In the case of the $\mathcal{H}^2$-matrix this includes the computation of the

[1] Intel Lab Data `http://berkeley.intel-research.net/labdata/`

Table 1. MAE and runtime (in seconds) for different data sets using the matrix in memory (stored), computing the matrix action in every iteration (on-the-fly) and using the $\mathcal{H}^2$-matrix approximation. Also given are the w and σ used.

data set	#data	w/σ	stored time	on-the-fly time	error (for both)	$\mathcal{H}^2$-matrix time	error	KB/N
mote 22	20000	$2^{-9}/2^{-5}$	2183	21050	0.278530	230	0.278655	2.0
mote 22	30000	$2^{-11}/2^{-5}$	n/a	88033	0.257725	494	0.257682	3.7
mote 47	20000	$2^{-9}/2^{-5}$	3800	36674	0.132593	1022	0.132553	16.4
mote 47	27000	$2^{-9}/2^{-6}$	n/a	73000	0.128862	1625	0.128913	17.2
heliX	20000	$2^{-8}/2^{-6}$	4084	37439	0.015860	603	0.015860	2.9
heliX	40000	$2^{-10}/2^{-10}$	n/a	$> 50h$	n/a	1975	0.014748	9.5
heliY	20000	$2^{-7}/2^{-10}$	4053	37546	0.020373	724	0.020372	3.2
heliY	40000	$2^{-10}/2^{-10}$	n/a	$> 50h$	n/a	2303	0.018542	15.1
heliYaw	20000	$2^{-5}/2^{-6}$	1091	10781	0.009147	676	0.009154	2.3
heliYaw	40000	$2^{-7}/2^{-6}$	n/a	162789	0.008261	3454	0.008263	6.6

Table 2. Runtimes in seconds and MAE results for the mote22 data set for different data set sizes using 'optimal' parameters w / σ

N=#data	w / σ	stored	on-the-fly	error	$\mathcal{H}^2$-matrix	error	size KB/N
1000	$2^{-3}/2^{-6}$	0.3	1.1	0.34979	1.56	0.34987	0.8
5000	$2^{-7}/2^{-7}$	30	296	0.31834	22.8	0.31938	1.1
10000	$2^{-7}/2^{-8}$	811	8502	0.30380	76.2	0.30743	1.1
20000	$2^{-9}/2^{-5}$	2183	19525	0.27853	230.1	0.27865	2.0
30000	$2^{-11}/2^{-5}$	n/a	88033	0.25772	494.8	0.25768	3.7

approximation matrix, the largest part of the total time for this approach. We observe a speedup between 1.6 and 9.5 against the stored matrix and between 16 and 91 measured against on-the-fly computation of the matrix-vector-product.

On the full version of the data set the matrix cannot be stored anymore and we can only compare against the on-the-fly computation, the speedup here is between 44 and 178, going from hours to minutes. Note that the additional data always results in an improvement on the test data, the mean absolute error is reduced by 3% to 11%. One also observes that the bigger data sets use different parameters w and σ, using the ones obtained on a smaller version of the data set often results in no improvement at all. The amount of memory needed, measured in KB per data points, can be reduced for the large helicopter data set from 156.25 down to 6.6, or in total from about 6 GB to about 250 MB. Note that [3] observe for these data sets speedups of 3.3 to 88.2 against on-the-fly computation of the matrix-vector-product using an approach based on *kd*-trees, although no mention of the employed parameters w and σ is made, which heavily influences the runtime as we will see in the following.

In Table 2 we show the results for the mote22 data set using different training set sizes, but the same test data. One can observe the different 'optimal' w / σ found for each data set size, which shows the need for parameter tuning on

Table 3. Runtimes in seconds, number of iterations and time per iteration for the mote22 data set using $w = 2^{-9}$ and $\sigma = 2^{-5}$ for different data set sizes

		1000	5000	10000	20000	30000
$\mathcal{H}^2$-matrix	time (sec.)	1.43	22.64	75.0	230.0	427.5
	its	284	688	1111	1599	2025
	time/its	0.00504	0.0329	0.0675	0.144	0.211
stored matrix	time (sec.)	1.18	51.15	324.1	2183	
	its	284	689	1103	1596	n/a
	time/its	0.00415	0.0742	0.29383	1.368	
on-the-fly	time (sec.)	9.13	565.2	3620.2	21050	60990
	its	284	689	1103	1596	2005
	time/its	0.032	0.82	3.282	13.189	30.42

Table 4. Using the 30000 data of mote22, the shown test results are from the 2:1 split using $w = 2^{-8}$ and different σ. Observe how the number of iterations needed by the GMRES solver depends on σ.

σ	2^{-7}	2^{-6}	2^{-5}	2^{-4}	2^{-3}	2^{-2}	2^{-1}	2^{0}
MAE 2:1 test	0.26447	0.26311	0.26349	0.26472	0.26818	0.27506	0.28929	0.32003
its	3000	2375	597	179	91	70	55	41

the full data instead of employing parameters found on a subset. Note that the runtime of the $\mathcal{H}^2$-matrix starts to make an improvement against the stored matrix already for 5000 data points.

To study the scaling behaviour with regard to N, the number of data, we present in Table 3 runtime results for one set of parameters. Since the number of iterations grows with the data set size we compare the runtime per iteration for the different values of N. For the on-the-fly computation one observes the expected $\mathcal{O}(N^2)$ scaling behaviour. For the full matrix it actually is even worse than $\mathcal{O}(N^2)$ from 10000 to 20000 data, this may be due to changes in the efficiency of the memory access in the dual core system after certain memory requirements. In the case of the $\mathcal{H}^2$-matrix the scaling is nearly like $\mathcal{O}(Nm\log(N))$.

We study in Table 4 how the number of iterations depends on the σ employed, it grows with smaller σ. This is due to the fact that the smaller σ is, the larger the condition of the matrix $(\mathcal{K} + \sigma^2\mathcal{I})$ becomes. But the smallest mean absolute errors are often achieved for small σ and one therefore typically needs quite a large number of iterations. Note also that with smaller w the number of iterations usually grows as well.

In Table 1 we also observe that typically with more data the best results are achieved with both decreasing w and σ, both cases result in more iterations of the Krylov solver. Therefore efficient computation of the matrix-vector-product gets even more important for large data sets, not just due to the number of data, but also because of the growing number of iterations in the solution stage.

Finally we use the $\mathcal{H}^2$-matrix with a different kernel, we tried the Matérn family [1] of kernels which is given by $\phi_\nu(r) = \frac{2^{1-\nu}}{\Gamma(\nu)}(cr)^\nu K_\nu(cr)$, where K_ν is a modified Bessel function of the second kind of order $\nu > 0$ and $c > 0$. For $\nu = 1/2$ one obtains the 'random walk' Ornstein-Uhlenbeck kernel. We did experiments with the mote22 dataset for $\nu = 1/2, 1, 3/2$ and $5/2$ and achieved the best results with $\nu = 1/2$. Using all 30000 data the best parameters turn out to be $c = 8.0$ and $\sigma = 2^{-4}$. Computing the matrix-vector-product on-the-fly we need 5265 seconds, the approach with the $\mathcal{H}^2$-matrix is finished after 431 seconds using 3.3 KB/N. The result on the test data is 0.2004, a significant improvement over the use of the Gaussian kernel.

4 Conclusions and Outlook

We introduce the concept of hierarchical matrices for Gaussian Processes. Our approach scales with $\mathcal{O}(Nm \log(N))$, i.e., far less than quadratic in the number of data, which allows the efficient treatment of large data sets. On large data sets, where the kernel matrix cannot be stored, we observe speedups of up to two orders of magnitude compared to the on-the-fly computation of the matrix-vector-product during the iterative Krylov solution of the linear equation system.

Among the competing methods, in particular the probabilistic sparse approximations [2] are promising. These techniques have a complexity of $\mathcal{O}(NM^2)$, where the hyperparameter M, the number of data chosen for computational core, controls the accuracy of the approximation. Comparing this estimate to the estimate for our approach suggests that the latter will be preferable if $m \log N \leq M^2$. To our knowledge, the proper choice of M has not been investigated in detail up to now. Results in [1] suggest that even a choice of $M = 2000$ is not sufficient for a data set of size $N = 45000$ to achieve good accuracy.

The current implementation of the HLib is optimised for two and three spatial dimensions, the extension to higher dimensions is a topic of ongoing research. The basic structure of local rank-m- or more general tensor approximations should be usable in this case as well. In our case ideas like hierarchical clustering are most promising. It is also worthwhile to investigate if the ideas from probabilistic sparse approximations can be combined with the hierarchical matrix approach presented here.

In our experiments we use a simple 2:1 splitting of the training data for the hyperparameter fitting. For large data sets one advantage of the marginal likelihood criterion, that all data is employed in learning and fitting, is not as significant as for small data sets. Nevertheless we intend to adopt this criterion for hyperparameter fitting in the future. The goal is to use one approximation of the kernel matrix for several values of σ.

Till now we have not considered preconditioning at all. We could use a larger error tolerance ϵ_{HC} to compute a second but much coarser and therefore smaller $\mathcal{H}^2$-matrix. We then can cheaply compute its LU or Cholesky decomposition and use it as a preconditioner for GMRES [6]. In other application areas the number of iterations typically goes from hundreds or thousands down to ten or twenty, depending on how coarse the second $\mathcal{H}^2$-matrix is.

This is especially worthwhile for the computation of the predictive variance on the test data. In our case it seems that this would necessitate the solution of a linear equation system for each test data point [1]. Since the kernel matrix would be the same in every case, additional computation to obtain a good and cheap preconditioner is easily compensated, since the solution would then need only a few matrix-vector-multiplications.

References

1. Rasmussen, C.E., Williams, C.K.I.: Gaussian Processes for Machine Learning. MIT Press, Cambridge (2006)
2. Quiñonero-Candela, J., Rasmussen, C.E.: A unifying view of sparse approximate gaussian process regression. J. of Machine Learning Research 6, 1935–1959 (2005)
3. Shen, Y., Ng, A., Seeger, M.: Fast gaussian process regression using kd-trees. In: Weiss, Y., Schölkopf, B., Platt, J. (eds.) NIPS 18, MIT Press, Cambridge (2006)
4. Freitas, N.D., Wang, Y., Mahdaviani, M., Lang, D.: Fast krylov methods for n-body learning. In: Weiss, Y., Schölkopf, B., Platt, J. (eds.) Advances in Neural Information Processing Systems 18, MIT Press, Cambridge, MA (2006)
5. Lang, D., Klaas, M., de Freitas, N.: Empirical testing of fast kernel density estimation algorithms. Technical Report TR-2005-03, Department of Computer Science, University of British Columbia (2005)
6. Börm, S., Grasedyck, L., Hackbusch, W.: Hierarchical Matrices. Lecture Note 21 of the Max Planck Institute for Mathematics in the Sciences (2003)
7. Grasedyck, L., Hackbusch, W.: Construction and arithmetics of $\mathcal{H}$-matrices. Computing 70(4), 295–334 (2003)
8. Hackbusch, W., Khoromskij, B., Sauter, S.A.: On $\mathcal{H}^2$-matrices. In: Bungartz, H., Hoppe, R., Zenger, C. (eds.) Lect. on Applied Mathematics, pp. 9–29. Springer, Heidelberg (2000)
9. Börm, S., Hackbusch, W.: Data-sparse approximation by adaptive $\mathcal{H}^2$-matrices. Computing 69, 1–35 (2002)
10. Rifkin, R., Yeo, G., Poggio, T.: Regularized least-squares classification. In: Suykens, J., Horvath, G., Basu, S., Micchelli, C., Vandewalle, J. (eds.) Advances in Learning Theory: Methods, Models and Applications, pp. 131–153. IOS Press, Amsterdam (2003)
11. Greenbaum, A.: Iterative methods for solving linear systems, Philadelphia, PA, USA (1997)
12. Bebendorf, M.: Effiziente numerische Lösung von Randintegralgleichungen unter Verwendung von Niedrigrang-Matrizen. PhD thesis, Uni. Saarbrücken (2000)
13. Börm, S., Grasedyck, L.: HLib – a library for $\mathcal{H}$- and $\mathcal{H}^2$-matrices (1999), Available at `http://www.hlib.org/`
14. Börm, S., Grasedyck, L.: Low-rank approximation of integral operators by interpolation. Computing 72, 325–332 (2004)
15. Grasedyck, L.: Adaptive recompression of $\mathcal{H}$-matrices for BEM. Computing 74(3), 205–223 (2004)
16. Golub, G.H., Van Loan, C.F.: Matrix Computations. Johns Hopkins U. P. (1996)
17. Buonadonna, P., Hellerstein, J., Hong, W., Gay, D., Madden, S.: Task: Sensor network in a box. In: Proc. of European Workshop on Sensor Networks (2005)
18. Ng, A.Y., Coates, A., Diel, M., Ganapathi, V., Schulte, J., Tse, B., Berger, E., Liang, E.: Autonomous inverted helicopter flight via reinforcement learning. In: International Symposium on Experimental Robotics (2004)

Learning Metrics Between Tree Structured Data: Application to Image Recognition*

Laurent Boyer[2], Amaury Habrard[1], and Marc Sebban[2]

[1] Université de Provence, LIF, France
[2] Université de Saint-Etienne, Laboratoire Hubert Curien, France
{laurent.boyer,marc.sebban}@univ-st-etienne.fr,
amaury.habrard@lif.univ-mrs.fr

Abstract. The problem of learning metrics between structured data (strings, trees or graphs) has been the subject of various recent papers. With regard to the specific case of trees, some approaches focused on the learning of edit probabilities required to compute a so-called stochastic tree edit distance. However, to reduce the algorithmic and learning constraints, the deletion and insertion operations are achieved on entire subtrees rather than on single nodes. We aim in this article at filling the gap with the learning of a more general stochastic tree edit distance where node deletions and insertions are allowed. Our approach is based on an adaptation of the EM optimization algorithm to learn parameters of a tree model. We propose an original experimental approach aiming at representing images by a tree-structured representation and then at using our learned metric in an image recognition task. Comparisons with a non learned tree edit distance confirm the effectiveness of our approach.

1 Introduction

In many machine learning or pattern recognition tasks, the choice of metrics plays an essential role for computing similarity between objects. Some classification, clustering or learning techniques are even intrinsically based on a metric, that is the case for the nearest-neighbors-based algorithms or some kernel-based methods. So, the choice or the parametrization of a similarity measure can drastically influence the result of an algorithm. One way to improve the influence of a metric is to integrate domain knowledge about the objects. While calling on an expert seems to be reasonable for small amount of data in domains where the background knowledge does exist, it becomes clearly intractable with huge data sets, where the expertise is low. In this context, a solution is to automatically infer the metric while capturing domain knowledge from a learning sample.

The general problem of learning metrics received an increasing interest since the beginning of 2000. With regards to numerical data, Bilenko et al [1] proposed an EM-based algorithm that integrates constraints and metric learning in the domain of semi-supervised clustering. Schultz et al [2] use some SVM techniques

* This work is funded by the Marmota project and the Pascal Network of Excellence.

J.N. Kok et al. (Eds.): ECML 2007, LNAI 4701, pp. 54–66, 2007.

to learn a measure given a set of relative comparisons of the form *"x is closer to y than to z"*. Kummamuru et al in [3] improved these techniques providing the concept of Context-sensitive Learnable Asymmetric Dissimilarity (CLAD) measures. Bayoudh et al [4] proposed an approach for learning a measure by analogy in the form *"x is to y as z is to t"*. Concerning structured data, recent works have tried to tackle this learning problem with data represented by strings or trees. In the majority of the cases, they dealt with the edit distance (ED) [5] that handles three primitive edit operations (deletion, insertion, substitution) for changing an input instance into an output one. The resulting learned metrics lead to significant improvements on real world applications. For instance, Oncina et al. [6] introduced a string ED learning algorithm via the inference of a discriminative stochastic transducer. They showed a dramatic improvement on a handwritten digit recognition task, using Freeman codes for converting scanned digits to strings. In [7], Ristad and Yianilos provided a generative model of string ED, and illustrated its high utility on the difficult problem of learning the pronunciation of words in conversational speech. Recently, the Pascal network of excellence funded a pump priming project on the learning of a stochastic tree ED for musical recognition. A first learning algorithm, where deletions and insertions only concern entire subtrees, has been proposed in [8]. Although this type of tree ED is costless from an algorithmic standpoint (quadratic complexity [9] rather than a polynomial complexity of order 4 for a more general case [10]), it is not the most used in the literature because of a clear loss of generality. In this paper, we propose to overcome this restriction by allowing insertions and deletions of single nodes. However, this requires to define a new probabilistic learning framework. This is the main aim of this paper. Then, we propose to apply our learned metric on an image recognition task, whose novelty comes from the use of a structured representation of images. If much work has been done on images having high levels of definition, the question of recognizing small images for which the definition is too low to allow the application of numerical techniques (such as segmentation into regions) is still an open problem. Moreover, numerical vectors are, in general, not suited for expressing notions such as sequentiality or relationships between features. In this context, we think that a symbolic structural representation can provide a richer modeling of the object. Among the first approaches using a symbolic representation for image recognition, Jolion et al. [11] have proposed a method for encoding some relevant information of images in strings. The idea consists in extracting some characteristic points with a high level of contrast and to sort them in the form of a string. Despite of its interest, this representation does not include spatial knowledge, that implies a strong loss of information. In order to add this spatial information, one needs a two dimensional representation. In this paper, we propose an original representation of images in the form of trees, and we use our learned tree ED in an image recognition task.

The paper is organized as follows. We introduce in Section 2 some definitions and notations. Then, we recall the classic tree ED in Section 3. Section 4 deals

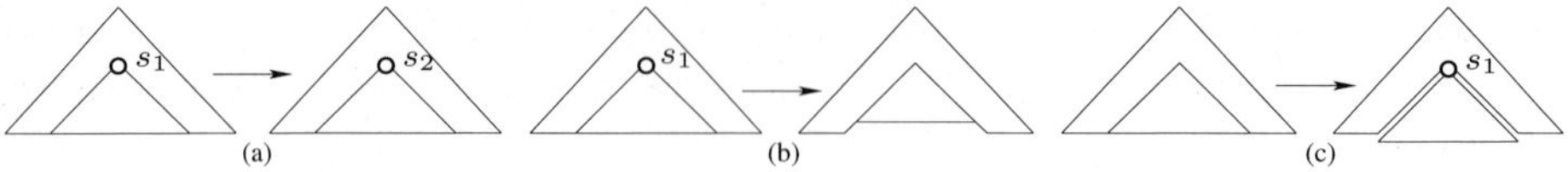

Fig. 1. (a) Substitution of $s_1 \in \mathcal{L}$ into s_2 (b) Deletion of s_1 (c) Insertion of s_1

with our stochastic model for learning tree edit probabilities. We finally present our application in image recognition in Section 5.

2 Definitions and Notations

We assume we handle ordered labeled trees of arbitrary arity. There is a left-to-right order among siblings of a tree and trees are labeled with elements of a set $\mathcal{L}$ of labels. We denote $\mathcal{T}(\mathcal{L})$ the set of all labeled trees buildable from $\mathcal{L}$.

Definition 1. *Let $\mathcal{V}$ be a set of nodes. We inductively define trees as follows: a node is a tree, and given T trees $a_1, .., a_T$ and a node $r \in \mathcal{V}$, $r(a_1, .., a_T)$ is a tree. r is the root of $r(a_1, .., a_T)$, and $a_1, .., a_T$ are subtrees.*

Definition 2. *Let $\mathcal{L}$ be a set of labels, and let $\lambda \notin \mathcal{L}$ be the empty label. Let $l : \mathcal{V} \rightarrow \mathcal{L}$ be a labeling function. $r(a_1, .., a_T)$ is a labeled tree if its nodes are labeled according to l.*

We assume that trees can be concerned by three edit operations (see Fig.1): The *substitution* operation which consists in changing the label $l(r)$ of a node r by another label of $\mathcal{L}$; the *deletion* operation which removes a node r of parent r', the children of r becoming a subsequence of those of r' according to a left-to-right order; the *insertion* operation adds a node r as a child of r' making r the parent of a subsequence of children of r' according to a left-to-right order.

Definition 3. *Assuming that a cost function assigns a cost to each edit operation, an edit script between two trees $r(a_1, .., a_T)$ and $r'(b_1, .., b_V)$ is a set of edit operations changing $r(a_1, .., a_T)$ into $r'(b_1, .., b_V)$. The cost of an edit script is the sum of the costs of its edit operations.*

Definition 4. *The edit distance (ED) between two trees $r(a_1, .., a_T)$ and $r'(b_1, .., b_V)$ is the cost of the minimum cost edit script.*

We are interested in the learning of a probabilistic tree ED. Roughly speaking, we aim at learning the probability of each edit operation used during a transformation process of an input tree into an output one. These probabilities are the parameters of a generative model describing a joint distribution over (input,output) pairs of trees. In [8], we proposed a first solution to this problem, in a restrictive case of tree edit distance, when a deletion (resp. an insertion) implies the removal (resp. the add) of an **entire subtree**. The objective of this paper is to fill the gap with a more general approach of the tree ED allowing the insertion/deletion of nodes. This case is more general because the deletion (or insertion) of an entire subtree can also be achieved by iteratively using the deletion (or insertion) operation on a single node. However, it implies to set a new probabilistic framework, intrinsically more difficult due to a larger size of the search space. To do that, we recall the principle of the algorithms computing such a tree ED. The interested reader can find more details in [10,12,13].

3 Tree ED Algorithm

To allow a larger spectrum of applications, the majority of the tree ED algorithms usually handled forests, a tree being a particular case of a forest.

Definition 5. *A forest $F = \{a_1, .., a_T\}$ is a set of trees. F is an ordered forest if there is a left-to-right order among the trees $a_1, .., a_T$ and if each tree is ordered.*

Definition 6. *Let F be a forest, and $\rho(a)$ be the root node of a tree $a \in F$. $F - \rho(a)$ is the forest obtained from F by the deletion of $\rho(a)$. Children of $\rho(a)$ becomes a sequence of trees of the forest $F - \rho(a)$. $f(\rho(a))$ is the forest composed of the children of $\rho(a)$. $F - a$ is the forest obtained by removing the tree a of F.*

Let F_1 and F_2 be two forests and a and b the rightmost trees of F_1 and F_2 respectively. Let δ be a cost function on pairs of labels, representing the edit operations. The ED $d(F_1, F_2)$ for the general case of forests is given by:

$$
\begin{aligned}
d(\lambda,\lambda) &= 0\\
d(F_1,\lambda) &= d(F_1-\rho(a),\lambda)+\delta(l(\rho(a)),\lambda)\\
d(\lambda,F_2) &= d(\lambda,F_2-\rho(b))+\delta(\lambda,l(\rho(b)))\\
d(F_1,F_2) &= min\begin{cases} d(F_1-\rho(a),F_2)+\delta(l(\rho(a)),\lambda) & \backslash * \mathit{deletion}\\ d(F_1,F_2-\rho(b))+\delta(\lambda,l(\rho(b))) & \backslash * \mathit{insertion}\\ d(F_1-a,F_2-b)+d(f(\rho(a)),f(\rho(b))) & \\ \quad +\delta(l(\rho(a)),l(\rho(b))) & \backslash * \mathit{substitution}\end{cases}
\end{aligned}
$$

where $l(\rho(x))$ is the label of the root of tree x.

This pseudo-code suggests a dynamic programming approach to compute the tree ED. In fact, we can note that $d(F_1, F_2)$ depends on a constant number of relevant subproblems of smaller size. Zhang and Shasha [10] defined these subproblems from the notion of *keyroots* of a given tree a:

$$keyroots(a) = \{\rho(a)\} \cup \{r \in \mathcal{V}(a) | r \ has \ a \ left \ sibling\}.$$

From this set of keyroots (see Fig 2.a), one can deduce the set of *special subforests* of a (see Fig 2.b), defined by the forests $f(u)$, where $u \in keyroots(a)$. Zhang and Shasha also defined the set of relevant subproblems that allows us to design a dynamic programming algorithm to compute the tree ED. These relevant subproblems are all the forests corresponding to the prefixes of the special subforests (see Fig 2.(b+c)). Then, to compute the tree ED $d(F_1, F_2)$, one can show that is it sufficient to compute $d(S_1, S_2)$ for all relevant subproblems S_1 and S_2 (for more details see [10]). So far, we assumed that we had a function δ

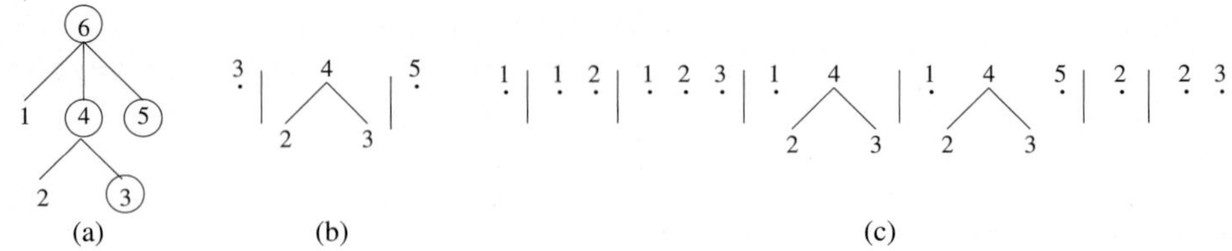

Fig. 2. (a) Example of keyroots represented by nodes with a circle, (a)+(b) the special subforests, and (a)+(b)+(c) the relevant subproblems

which returns the cost induced by an edit operation. In real world applications, these costs are often tuned by hand. We claim that machine learning techniques can efficiently be used to improve this task which can become tricky when the size of the alphabet is large. In the next section, we show how to automatically learn edit probabilities (rather than edit costs) from a learning set of tree pairs.

4 Learning Tree Edit Probabilities

4.1 Stochastic Tree ED

A *stochastic tree ED* supposes that edit operations occur according to a random process. We aim at learning the underlying distribution $\delta(s, s')$, $(s, s') \in (\{\mathcal{L} \cup \{\lambda\})^2$, in order to infer a generative model of all possible edit scripts. We will use a special symbol # to denote the end of an edit script. For sake of convenience, we will also denote the termination cost of a script $\delta(\#)$ by $\delta(\lambda, \lambda)$. To be a statistical distribution, the function δ must fulfill the following conditions:

$$\sum_{(s,s')\in(\mathcal{L}\cup\{\lambda\})^2} \delta(s, s') = 1 \;\; and \;\; \delta(s, s') \geq 0 \tag{1}$$

Let $e = e_1 \cdots e_n$ be an edit script with n edit operations ($e_i = (s, s') \neq (\lambda, \lambda)$), the probability of e is evaluated by: $p(e) = \prod_{i=1}^{n} \delta(e_i) \times \delta(\#)$. To model the distance between two trees, we propose to compute the probability of all ways to change a tree a into another one b (as described in [7] for the case of strings).

Definition 7. *Let two trees a and b, we denote by $E(a, b)$ the set of all possible edit scripts for transforming a in b. The stochastic tree ED between a and b is defined by: $d_s(a, b) = -\log \sum_{e\in E(a,b)} p(e)$.*

To learn the matrix δ, we propose to adapt the Expectation-Maximization (EM) algorithm [14] to this specific context of tree ED. Let us remind that EM estimates the hidden parameters of a probabilistic model by maximizing the likelihood of a learning sample. In our case, the parameters will correspond to the matrix δ of edit probabilities, and the learning sample will be composed of (input,output) tree pairs. In a pattern recognition task, these pairs can be either randomly generated from instances of the same class, or built by hand by an

Algorithm 1. $\boldsymbol{\alpha}(\{a_1,..,a_T\},\{b_1,..,b_V\})$

```
Input      : Two forests {a_1,..,a_T}, {b_1,..,b_V}
Let α be a matrix of dimension (T+1) × (V+1); α[{},{}] ← 1
for t de 0 à T do
    for v de 0 à V do
        if (t > 0) or (v > 0) then
            α[{a_1,..,a_t},{b_1,..,b_v}] = 0
        if t > 0 then
            α[{a_1,..,a_t},{b_1,..,b_v}]+ = δ(l(ρ(a_t)),λ).α[{a_1,..,f(ρ(a_t))},{b_1,..,b_v}]
        if v > 0 then
            α[{a_1,..,a_t},{b_1,..,b_v}]+ = δ(λ,l(ρ(b_v))).α[{a_1,..,a_t},{b_1,..,f(ρ(b_v))}]
        if (t > 0) and (v > 0) then
            α[{a_1,..,a_t},{b_1,..,b_v}]+ = 𝛂(f(ρ(a_t)),f(ρ(b_v))).δ(l(ρ(a_t)),l(ρ(b_v)))
                                             .α[{a_1,..,a_{t-1}},{b_1,..,b_{v-1}}]
return α[{a_1,..,a_T},{b_1,..,b_V}]
```

expert who judged them as being similar. EM achieves an expectation step followed by a maximization stage. During the first step, EM accumulates, from the training corpus, the expectation of each hidden event (edit operation) for transforming an input tree into an output one. In the maximization step, EM sets the parameter values (edit probabilities) in order to maximize the likelihood.

4.2 Forward and Backward Functions

To learn the matrix δ, EM uses two auxiliary functions, so-called *forward* (α) and *backward* (β), that are respectively described in Algorithms 1 and 2. The bold font is used for a recursive call of these algorithms ($\boldsymbol{\alpha}$ and $\boldsymbol{\beta}$), while the normal font (α and β) describes intermediate values stored in a local matrix. We can note that both functions α and β return the quantity $\sum_{e\in E(a,b)} p(e)$, *i.e* the sum of probabilities of all paths (described by a script e) changing an input forest into an output one. Beyond the fact that they allow to compute the tree ED (cf Def. 7), they are overall combined to achieve the expectation step in order to estimate the expectation of each edit operation (see Fig. 3 and details in the next section). What is important to note is that functions α and β are nothing else but an extension to the stochastic case of the original tree ED algorithm. Actually, they contain the three main instructions corresponding to the three edit operations. For instance, considering the substitution operation, $\boldsymbol{\alpha}(f(\rho(a_t)), f(\rho(b_v)))$ and $\alpha[\{a_1,..,a_{t-1}\},\{b_1,..,b_{v-1}\}]$ are the stochastic version of $d(f(\rho(a)), f(\rho(b)))$ and $d(F_1 - a, F_2 - b)$ respectively. The main difference is that in our probabilistic framework, we use all the paths transforming a forest into another one, while the classic ED only keeps the costless path.

4.3 Expectation

During the expectation step, we estimate the expectation of the hidden events, *i.e* the edit operations used to transform an input tree into an output one. These expectations are stored in an auxiliary matrix γ $(|\mathcal{L}|+1)\times(|\mathcal{L}|+1)$. This process

Algorithm 2. $\boldsymbol{\beta}(\{a_1,..,a_T\},\{b_1,..,b_V\})$

```
Input      : Two forests{a_1,..,a_T}, {b_1,..,b_V}
Let β be a matrix of dimension (T+1) × (V+1); β[{},{}] ← 1
for t de T à 0 do
    for v de V à 0 do
        if (t < T) or (v < V) then
            β[{a_t,..,a_T},{b_v,..,b_V}] = 0
        if t < T then
            β[{a_t,..,a_T},{b_v,..,b_V}]+ = δ(l(ρ(a_T)),λ).β[{a_t,..,f(ρ(a_T))},{b_v,..,b_V}]
        if v < V then
            β[{a_t,..,a_T},{b_v,..,b_V}]+ = δ(λ,l(ρ(b_V))).β[{a_t,..,a_T},{b_v,..,f(ρ(b_V))}]
        if (t < T) and (v < V) then
            β[{a_t,..,a_T},{b_v,..,b_V}]+ = δ(l(ρ(a_T)),l(ρ(b_V))).β(f(ρ(a_T)),f(ρ(b_V)))
                                            .β({a_t,..,a_{T-1}},{b_v,..,b_{V-1}})
return β[{a_1,..,a_T},{b_1,..,b_V}]
```

takes a training tree pair (x, y) in input. Then, for all the subtree pairs (a_t, b_v), where a_t is a subtree of x and b_v a subtree of y, it accumulates the expectations of the three edit operations consisting either in deleting $\rho(a_t)$, or inserting $\rho(b_v)$ or substituting $l(\rho(a_t))$ by $l(\rho(b_v))$. The pseudo-code of the expectation step is described in Algorithm 3, which requires the following definitions.

Definition 8. *A postorder traversal of a labeled tree $x = r(a_1,..,a_T)$ is obtained by first recursively visiting the subtrees $a_t, t = 1..T$ and then the root r. The postorder numbering assigns a number to each node of x according to a postorder traversal. Let $\phi_\alpha : \mathcal{V}(x) \to \mathcal{T}(\mathcal{L})^*$ be the function that takes a node r' and returns the ordered forest composed of the subtrees with root a node having a number strictly smaller than that of r' according to a postorder numbering.*

Definition 9. *Let $x = r(a_1,..,a_T)$ be an ordered tree. Let $\phi_\beta : \mathcal{V}(x) \to \mathcal{T}(\mathcal{L})^*$ be the function that takes a node r' and returns the ordered tree with root r and with the children of r having a number strictly smaller than that of r' according to a reverse postorder numbering.*

Fig. 3 shows an example of postorder (in arabic font) and reverse postorder numbering (in roman font). Considering the node labeled by `4|III` of the left tree, ϕ_α returns the forest composed of 3 subtrees with root the nodes labeled respectively by `1|VI`, `2|V` and `3|IV`, ϕ_β returning the subtree with root the node labeled by `6|I` and with the child `5|II`. Let us recall that this algorithm calculates the expectation of the number of times each edit operation is used for changing a tree x into another one y. To do this, for each edit operation (whose probability is given by δ), we consider not only all the ways leading to this operation (given by $\boldsymbol{\alpha}$) but also those allowing us to finish the transformation (given by $\boldsymbol{\beta}$) after the edit operation. While the deletion and insertion operations are quite understandable, the substitution one deserves some explanations. Fig. 3 graphically describes the substitution of the input node `4|III` into the output one `4|IV`. This requires to calculate the forward function $\boldsymbol{\alpha}(\phi_\alpha(\rho(a_t)) - f(\rho(a_t)), \phi_\alpha(\rho(b_v)) - f(\rho(b_v)))$, *i.e.* the probability of

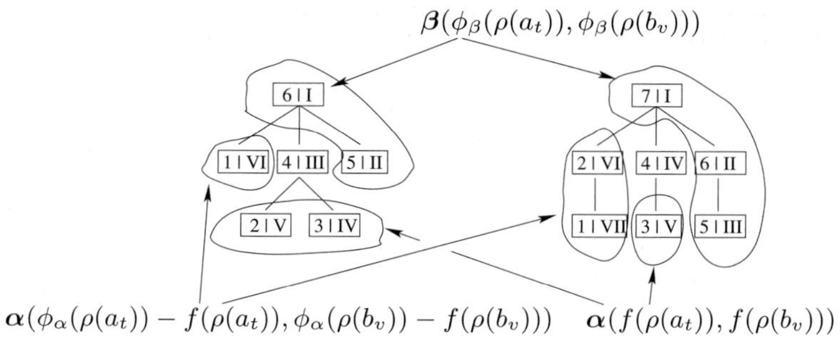

Fig. 3. Illustration of the Expectation step for a substitution operation

---

Algorithm 3. expectation(x, y)

Input : Two trees x and y

Let $\mathcal{E}$ be the empty tree;

foreach a_t *s.t.* $\rho(a_t) \in \mathcal{V}(x) \cup \mathcal{E}, b_v$ *s.t.* $\rho(b_v) \in \mathcal{V}(y) \cup \mathcal{E}$ **do**

  if $a_t \neq \mathcal{E}$ **then**

    $\gamma(l(\rho(a_t)), \lambda) += \frac{\boldsymbol{\alpha}(\phi_\alpha(\rho(a_t)), \phi_\alpha(\rho(b_v)) \cup \{b_v\}).\delta(l(\rho(a_t)), \lambda).\boldsymbol{\beta}(\phi_\beta(\rho(a_t)), \phi_\beta(\rho(b_v)))}{\boldsymbol{\alpha}(x,y)}$

  if $b_v \neq \mathcal{E}$ **then**

    $\gamma(\lambda, l(\rho(b_v))) += \frac{\boldsymbol{\alpha}(\phi_\alpha(\rho(a_t)) \cup \{a_t\}, \phi_\alpha(\rho(b_v))).\delta(\lambda, l(\rho(b_v))).\boldsymbol{\beta}(\phi_\beta(\rho(a_t)), \phi_\beta(\rho(b_v)))}{\boldsymbol{\alpha}(x,y)}$

  if $(a_t \neq \mathcal{E})$ *and* $(b_v \neq \mathcal{E})$ **then**

    $\gamma(l(\rho(a_t)), l(\rho(b_v))) += \frac{\boldsymbol{\alpha}(\phi_\alpha(\rho(a_t)) - f(\rho(a_t)), \phi_\alpha(\rho(b_v)) - f(\rho(b_v))).\boldsymbol{\alpha}(f(\rho(a_t)), f(\rho(b_v))).\delta(l(\rho(a_t)), l(\rho(b_v))).\boldsymbol{\beta}(\phi_\beta(\rho(a_t)), \phi_\beta(\rho(b_v)))}{\boldsymbol{\alpha}(x,y)}$

---

the forest pair $[\{$1|VI$\}, \{$2|VI(1|VII)$\}]$. This forest pair is constituted of subtrees with root node having a numbering smaller than 4 according to a postorder numbering (given by function ϕ_α), minus subtrees that are the children of 4|III and 4|IV (given by function f). We estimate, as well, the backward function $(\boldsymbol{\beta}(\phi_\beta(\rho(a_t)), \phi_\beta(\rho(b_v))))$ on the pair $[\{$6|I(5|II)$\}, \{$7|I(6|II(5|III))$\}]$, with nodes smaller than III for the input forest and IV for the output one, according to a reverse postorder numbering. We need also to compute the forward function $(\boldsymbol{\alpha}(f(\rho(a_t)), f(\rho(b_v))))$ on the pair $[\{$2|V, 3|IV$\}, \{$3|V$\}]$ corresponding to the children of the nodes involved in the substitution operation.

4.4 Maximization

The final step of the EM algorithm is achieved by the maximization procedure presented in Algorithm 4. This step is crucial since it ensures a convergence of the process under constraints thanks to the normalization of the expectations. For learning a stochastic tree ED in the form of a generative model, we must fulfill constraints of Eq.1. This implies a simple normalization consisting in dividing each expectation $\gamma(s, s')$ by the total accumulator $TA = \sum_{(s,s') \in (\mathcal{L} \cup \{\lambda\})^2} \gamma(s, s')$. With Algorithms 1,2,3 and 4, we can now present in Algorithm 5 the global procedure for learning a stochastic tree ED.

Algorithm 4. ***maximization***

Input: A matrix of accumulators γ
Output: A matrix of probabilistic edit costs δ
$TA \leftarrow 0$
foreach $(s, s') \in (\mathcal{L} \cup \{\lambda\})^2$ **do** $TA \leftarrow TA + \gamma(s, s')$
foreach $(s, s') \in (\mathcal{L} \cup \{\lambda\})^2$ **do** $\delta(s, s') \leftarrow \frac{\gamma(s,s')}{TA}$

Algorithm 5. ***tree edit distance − EM***

Input: LS a learning set of tree pairs
repeat
  foreach $(s, s') \in (\mathcal{L} \cup \{\lambda\})^2$ **do** $\gamma(s, s') \leftarrow 0$
  foreach $(x, y) \in LS$ **do** expectation(x, y)
  maximization(γ)
until *convergence*

4.5 Example of Learning

We present here the running of our algorithm on a simple example, with an input alphabet $\mathcal{L}_1 = \{a, b, c\}$, an output alphabet $\mathcal{L}_2 = \{a, b\}$ and a training set composed of only one tree pair $[a(b, c(a, b)); b(c, a(b), a, b)]$ (see Fig. 4(a)). The algorithm converges towards an optimum after only 4 iterations. The learned matrix δ (initialized with random values) is described in Fig. 4(b). We can note that our algorithm has correctly learned the target. Actually, on this example, one optimal solution consists in: (i) inserting the symbol a that becomes the father of the symbol b, (ii) keeping unchanged the symbol b, (iii) deleting the symbol c and (iv) changing one out of twice the symbol a by b or by itself.

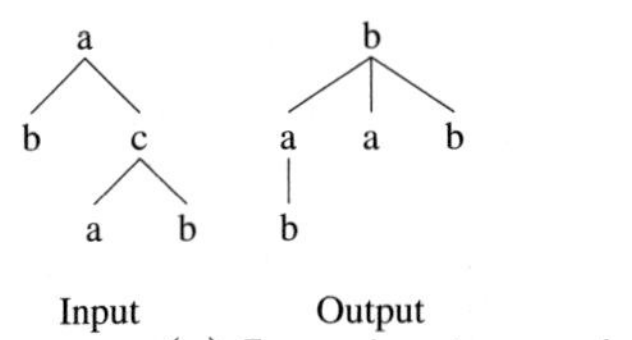

(a) Learning tree pair

δ	λ	a	b
λ	–	0.167	0
a	0	0.167	0.167
b	0	0	0.332
c	0.167	0	0

(b) Matrix δ after 4 EM iterations.

Fig. 4. Example of learning from a tree pair

5 Experiments in Image Recognition

5.1 From a Numerical to a Symbolic Representation of Images

In this section, we aim at verifying the interest of our learning algorithm on an image classification task. So far, the main trend in image recognition has mainly concerned numerical approaches based on color and texture [15,16,17]. However, many objects are poorly modeled with numerical values that can not express the relationships between attributes. Strings and trees are structured representations that allow us to take into account either the sequentiality or the

(a) Original image (b) Charact. points (c) Binary image

Fig. 5. Example of image represented by characteristic points

hierachization between attributes. A pioneer work has been recently achieved by Jolion et al. [11] with a string representation showing very interesting results on clustering and recognition tasks. The principle of this approach is first based on the extraction of characteristic points (see Fig. 5(b)) according to their contrast level in the original image (Fig. 5(a)). Then, to each of these points is assigned the symbol of the alphabet constituted of all the 512 binary masks 3×3, and that is applicable on that point in the binary version of the image (see Fig. 5(c)). Finally, these characteristic points are sorted according to their decreasing level of contrast, providing a sequence of masks labeled by a symbol $\in [0, 512]$.

5.2 Tree Representation of Images

This string representation outperformed numerical features in various classification and clustering tasks [11]. However, we can note that no spatial information is considered. One way to tackle this drawback is to consider a tree representation linking the depth of a tree with that information. To illustrate our approach, consider the example of Fig. 6(a). First, we propose to divide the image in four equal parts and we extract, for each of them, the characteristic point with the highest level of contrast. These four points constitute the first level of our tree. They are ordered from left-to-right according to their respective level of contrast. In a second step, we sub-divide each of the four original parts into four new sub-parts, and we extract again the characteristic points with the highest level of contrast in each sub-part. These points become the children of the node extracting during the first step. We recursively repeat this process until no more division can separate two points. To obtain a labeled tree, we assign to each node its corresponding mask applicable in the binary image. The main properties of this tree representation are the following: (i) We do not challenge the alphabet distribution observed in the sequence built with Jolion's approach; (ii) we keep the sequentiality between the characteristic points for each granularity level; and (iii) deep leaves represent a large local density of characteristic points.

5.3 Experimental Setup and Results

In order to assess the relevance of our model in a pattern recognition task, we applied it in handwritten digit classification. We used the NIST Special Database

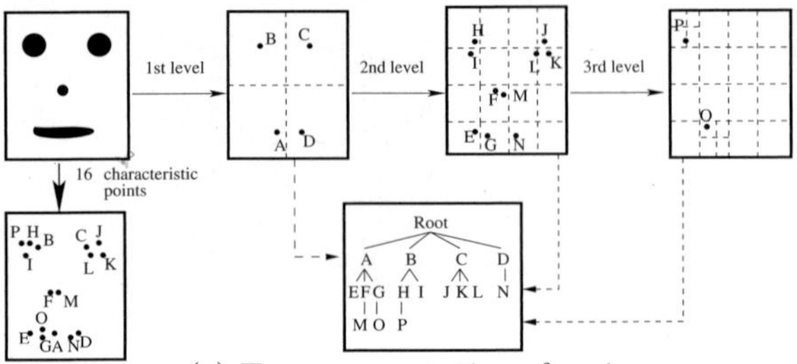

(a) Tree-representation of an image.

SWL-SNL	TNL-SNL	TWL-SNL
+6	+11	+32

(b) The 1st column shows the interest of learning a string ED, the 2nd the contribution of our tree representation and the 3th the relevance of learning a tree ED.

Fig. 6. (a) Tree representation and (b) experimental results

3 of the National Institute of Standards and Technology, already used in several articles such as [18,6]. A part of this database consists in 128×128 bitmap images of handwritten digits written by 100 different writers. Each class of digit (from 0 to 9) has about 1,000 instances. We divided these data in a learning set LS (6,000 digits) and a test set TS (4,000 digits). Since our model handles trees, we coded each digit as previously explained but we reduced the alphabet from 2^9 to 15 by removing small frequent masks. Then, to construct a learning set of tree pairs, we used an uniform matrix δ of tree edit probabilities and we associated to each input tree $x \in LS$ the output tree $y \in LS, y \neq x$ s.t. $p(x, y)$ is maximal and s.t. x and y belong to the same class. We then learned matrix δ with our EM algorithm. We classified each digit $t \in TS$ by the class i of the tree $x \in LS$ maximizing $p(t, x)$ (result `TWL`).

We compared our learning approach with a standard tree ED with a priori fixed edit costs (result `TNL`). Moreover, to assess the relevance of our tree-based image representation, we used the same protocol with images coded in strings (see Section 5.1) using non learned and learned stochastic **string** EDs as presented in [6] (results `SNL` and `SWL`). To compare all the results, we present in Table 6(b) the relative accuracy gain on TS of each approach (`SWL`, `TNL`, `TWL`) in comparison with the standard string ED `SNL`. We can make the following interesting remarks: First, the results confirm the relevance of our tree-based image representation in comparison with strings (+11 percentage points); second, they definitely prove the interest of our approach for learning a tree similarity measure. Actually, not only a learned tree distance outperforms a standard string ED (+32 percentage points) but also it outperforms a non learned tree ED (+21 percentage points).

6 Conclusion

In this paper, we extended the tree ED, in its more general form, to a stochastic context. From this new point of view, the probabilities of the primitive edit operations are seen as hidden parameters that an adapted EM-based algorithm is able to learn from a set of tree pairs. We think that this work opens the door to significant improvements in classification and clustering, that is confirmed by our first experimental results in digit recognition. However, some problems deserve further investigations. First, we think that the constitution of the learning tree pairs can be highly improved and still constitutes an open problem; second, the tree representation issued from characteristic points must be further studied to tackle a larger spectrum of image recognition tasks; moreover, our algorithm has to be adapted in a form of a discriminative model (rather than the presented generative one) to handle small datasets; finally, in front of the emergence of huge datasets of XML documents, we plan to use our model on web applications.

References

1. Bilenko, M., Basu, S., Mooney, R.J.: Integrating constraints and metric learning in semi-supervised clustering. In: 21th Int. Conf (ICML 2004), ACM Press, New York (2004)
2. Schultz, M., Joachims, T.: Learning a distance metric from relative comparisons. In: Advances in Neural Information Processing Systems 16 [Neural Information Processing Systems], NIPS 2003, MIT Press, Cambridge (2003)
3. Kummamuru, K., Krishnapuram, R., Agrawal, R.: On learning asymmetric dissimilarity measures. In: Proc. of the 5th IEEE Int. Conf. on Data Mining (ICDM 2005), pp. 697–700. IEEE Computer Society Press, Los Alamitos (2005)
4. Bayoudh, S., Miclet, L., Delhay, A.: Learning by analogy: A classification rule for binary and nominal data. In: IJCAI, pp. 678–683 (2007)
5. Wagner, R., Fisher, M.: The string to string correction problem. Journal of the ACM (1974)
6. Oncina, J., Sebban, M.: Learning stochastic edit distance: application in handwritten character recognition. Journal of Pattern Recognition (2006)
7. Ristad, S., Yianilos, P.: Learning string-edit distance. IEEE Transactions on Pattern Analysis and Machine Intelligence 20(5), 522–532 (1998)
8. Bernard, M., Habrard, A., Sebban, M.: Learning stochastic tree edit distance. In: Fürnkranz, J., Scheffer, T., Spiliopoulou, M. (eds.) ECML 2006. LNCS (LNAI), vol. 4212, pp. 42–53. Springer, Heidelberg (2006)
9. Selkow, S.: The tree-to-tree editing problem. Information Processing Letters 6(6), 184–186 (1977)
10. Zhang, K., Shasha, D.: Simple fast algorithms for the editing distance between trees and related problems. SIAM Journal of Computing, 1245–1262 (1989)
11. Jolion, J.: Some experiments on clustering a set of strings. In: Hancock, E.R., Vento, M. (eds.) GbRPR 2003. LNCS, vol. 2726, pp. 214–224. Springer, Heidelberg (2003)
12. Klein, P.: Computing the edit-distance between unrooted ordered trees. In: Proc. of the 6th European Symposium on Algorithms (ESA), pp. 91–102. Springer, Heidelberg (1998)
13. Bille, P.: A survey on tree edit distance and related problem. Theoretical Computer Science 337(1-3), 217–239 (2005)
14. Dempster, A., Laird, M., Rubin, D.: Maximum likelihood from incomplete data via the EM algorithm. J. R. Stat. Soc B(39), 1–38 (1977)
15. Pentland, A., Picard, R., Sclaroff, S.: Photobook: Tools for content-based manipulation of image databases. In: SPIE Storage and Retrieval of Image and Video Databases, vol. 2, pp. 18–32 (1995)
16. Wang, J., Li, J., Wiederhold, G.: Simplicity: Semantics-sensitive integrated matching for picture libraries. IEEE Trans. on Pat. Ana. Mach. Int. 23(9), 947–963 (2001)

17. Carson, C., Belongie, S., Greenspan, H., Malik, J.: Blobworld: Image segmentation using expectation-maximization and its application to image querying. IEEE Trans. on Pattern Analysis and Machine Intelligence 24(8), 1026–1038 (2002)
18. Gómez, E., Micó, L., Oncina, J.: Testing the linear approximating eliminating search algorithm in handwritten character recognition tasks. In: VI Symposium Nacional de reconocimiento de Formas y Análisis de Imágenes, pp. 212–217 (1995)

Shrinkage Estimator for Bayesian Network Parameters

John Burge and Terran Lane

University of New Mexico, New Mexico, USA
{lawnguy,terran}@cs.unm.edu

Abstract. Maximum likelihood estimates (MLEs) are commonly used to parameterize Bayesian networks. Unfortunately, these estimates frequently have unacceptably high variance and often overfit the training data. Laplacian correction can be used to smooth the MLEs towards a uniform distribution. However, the uniform distribution may represent an unrealistic relationships in the domain being modeled and can add an unreasonable bias. We present a shrinkage estimator for domains with hierarchically related random variables that smoothes MLEs towards other distributions found in the training data. Our methods are quick enough to be performed during Bayesian network structure searches. On both a simulated and a real-world neuroimaging domain, we empirically demonstrate that our estimator yields superior parameters in the presence of noise and greater likelihoods on left-out data.

Keywords: Bayesian networks, shrinkage, hierarchy, parameter estimation.

1 Introduction

Our primary contribution is a *shrinkage* parameter estimator that allows learned Bayesian networks (BNs) to be less affected by noisy data and to generalize more effectively to unseen data than maximum likelihood estimates (MLEs) with Laplace smoothing. We also demonstrate that the estimator operates quickly enough to be performed during Bayesian network structure searches.

The amount of data available to train a BN's parameters is often inadequate to train MLEs, resulting in high variance estimates that overfit the data and generalize poorly to left-out data. These effects can be lessened by smoothing the MLE towards distributions with lower variance. One widely employed method is Laplace smoothing [7] which smoothes MLEs towards a uniform distribution. While this has been shown to improve BN classification [7], the uniform distribution is an arbitrary choice that may represent an unrealistic bias in complex real-world domains.

We propose smoothing MLEs towards other distributions found in the data. To illustrate our method, we will start with an example in a neuroscience domain. Assume that the correlation between the visual cortex and the motor cortex is being modeled for some population of mentally-ill patients. For discrete BNs, this relationship can be parameterized with a series of multinomials. The MLEs for these multinomials will have a certain degree of variance and may overfit the data. Laplacian smoothing helps, but introduces a bias that is not observed in the data. Uniform distributions poorly model relationships between brain regions.

J.N. Kok et al. (Eds.): ECML 2007, LNAI 4701, pp. 67–78, 2007.

Instead, we can smooth towards other distributions in the data. In particular, we can take advantage of the anatomical placement of the cortices within larger regions of the brain. The visual cortex is encased in the occipital lobe and the motor cortex is encased in the frontal lobe. Since the lobes contain the cortices, the relationship between the lobes may be similar to the relationship between the cortices. Thus, we propose smoothing MLEs for the cortices towards MLEs for the lobes. There is more training data available for the lobes than for the cortices (they are larger structures) and thus, their MLEs will be lower in variance. This smoothing still introduces some bias, but it is more realistic than the bias added by Laplacian smoothing.

Smoothing MLEs towards other "similar" MLEs with lower variance is often referred to as *shrinkage* and has been successfully employed in Machine Learning applications (Section 1.2). What makes two MLEs "similar" depends on the domain. In the neuroscience domain, two MLEs are said to be "similar" if they are associated with correlations between brain regions that contain or are contained by each other. In previous applications [14], MLEs were "similar" if they were associated with the number of times a particular word appeared in different classes of text documents. We formalize the notion of "similarity" as a hierarchical arrangement of the random variables (RVs) in a domain. This hierarchy is then used to select distributions that are shrunk towards when computing MLEs.

We compare the performance of BNs trained with our shrinkage estimators versus BNs trained with MLEs plus Laplace smoothing (MLE+L) on two sets of data: a simulated data domain, where ground truth is known and controllable and a set of ten real-world neuroimaging datasets. On both the simulated and neuroimaging datasets, we find that shrinkage estimates are more robust to noisy data. On the neuroimaging datasets, we show that shrinkage estimates increase the likelihood of BNs on data left out of the training process. While classification is not the main focus of this work, we also demonstrate that shrinkage estimators do not degrade the classification performance of BN-based classifiers.

2 Background

2.1 Bayesian Networks

BNs [15] are graphical models that explicitly represent dependencies among RVs. A BN's topological structure, represented as a directed acyclic graph (DAG), contains nodes for RVs and directed links between correlated *parent* and *child* nodes. A *family* is composed of a single child and its parents. We assume fully observable discrete RVs so that a family's conditional probability, *P*(*child* | *parents*), can be represented with a conditional probability table (CPT).

Searching for a BN's topology is accomplished by proposing many hypothesis structures guided by a search heuristic (often an iterative hill-climbing heuristic), while measuring how well each structure corresponds to correlations in the data via a structure scoring function. Common scores include MDL [13], BDe [10], conditional likelihood (CL) [8], etc. Some scores require a BN's parameters to be trained (e.g., MDL and CL), but others marginalize out the parameters (e.g., BDe).

We will use the following notation. Let $\boldsymbol{X}$ be a set of n RVs, $\{X_1, X_2, \ldots, X_n\}$, with arities $r_1, r_2, \ldots, r_n$. A data point is a *fully observable* assignment of values to $\boldsymbol{X}$. A BN, B, over $\boldsymbol{X}$ is described by the pair $\langle B_S, B_\Theta \rangle$. B_S is the DAG representing the BN's structural topology. $B_\theta = \{\theta_{X_i,j,k} : 1 \le i \le n, 1 \le j \le q_i, 1 \le k \le r_i\}$ is the set of parameters where $\theta_{X_i,j,k} = P(X_i = k \mid Pa(X_i) = j)$. X_i's parent set is denoted $Pa(X_i)$. q_i is the number of configurations for the RVs in $Pa(X_i)$. Depending on context, "X_i" will also refer to the family with child RV X_i.

2.2 Shrinkage

For any system of at least three parameters, Stein [16] demonstrated there exists an estimator with lower quadratic risk than the MLE, where risk is measured as the expected difference between the true parameters and the estimated parameters. This holds even when the parameters are independently distributed. James and Stein [11] introduced such an estimator, the acclaimed James Stein Estimator (JSE), for normally distributed RVs with identity covariance matrices. The JSE shrinks the MLE towards a value computed from all the parameters being estimated. The inclusion of this bias reduces the estimator's risk. Similar results have been extended to the multinomial distributions that are used in discrete BNs [9]. The JSE also played a central role in empirical Bayesian methods in general [5].

McCallum et al. [14] demonstrated that shrinkage could also be applied to text document classification given hierarchically related document classes. Instead of shrinking the MLE estimate toward a single value (as done by Stein), the parameter estimate is shrunk towards a combination of estimates across multiple classes of data,

$$\breve{\theta} = \lambda^0 \hat{\theta}^0 + \lambda^1 \hat{\theta}^1 + \ldots + \lambda^n \hat{\theta}^n \tag{1}$$

where $\breve{\theta}$ is the shrinkage estimate, $\hat{\theta}^i$ is the estimate for the ith class's MLE and λ^i is a linear mixing weight for the ith class. The weights were set via an expectation maximization (EM) algorithm. McCallum et al. demonstrated increased classification performance when using shrinkage estimates relative to MLEs. Anderson, Domingos and Weld demonstrated how this form of shrinkage could also be applied in Relational Markov models [1]. They used a different method to learn mixture weights, but still found significant increases in model performance.

Building on the previous success of this form of shrinkage, we demonstrate how shrinkage can be applied among RVs within the same class of data. This allows shrinkage to be applied even when there are not hierarchically related classes of data, but instead hierarchically related RVs within the same class.

2.3 Random Variable Aggregation Hierarchies

There are many domains that have a natural hierarchical decomposition of RVs. For example, image analyses, where pixel neighborhoods of varying size can be aggregated together; genetic regulatory network reconstruction, where genes can be decomposed into families and super-families; word types in grammar trees; medical diagnoses, where diseases and symptoms are grouped into sub-categories; Fourier and wavelet analyses, where coefficients are spatially and temporally related; etc.

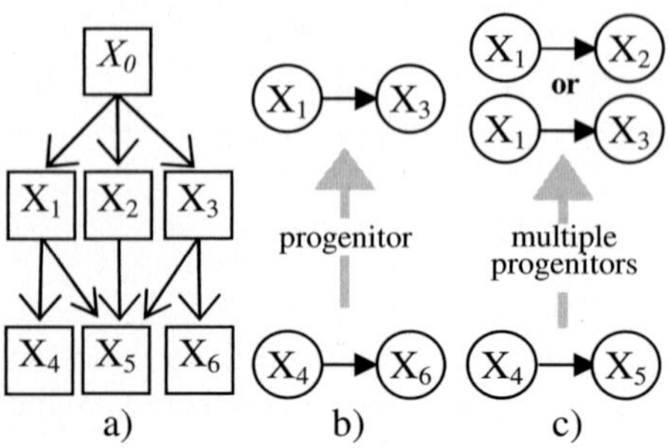

Fig. 1. a) Hypothetical trellis hierarchy. (this is not a BN). b) $X_4 \to X_6$ family and its progenitor. c) $X_4 \to X_5$ family and its multiple *valid* progenitors.

Start: Initialize coefficients

$$\lambda^p_{X_i,j} = 1/(V_i + 1)$$

'E' step: Gauge ability for CPTs to predict events in $\widetilde{D}'$

$$\beta^p_{X_i,j} = \sum_{d \in \widetilde{D}'} P\left(\hat{\theta}^p_{X_i,j} \; generated \; d\right) = \sum_{k=1}^{r_i} \frac{\lambda^p_{X_i,j}\hat{\theta}^p_{X_i,j,k}}{\sum_{m=1}^{V_i} \lambda^m_{X_i,j}\hat{\theta}^m_{X_i,j,k}} N^{\widetilde{D}'}_{X_i,j,k}$$

'M' step: Calculate guaranteed improved weights by normalizing β's.

$$\lambda^p_{X_i,j} = \beta^p_{X_i,j} / \sum_{m=1}^{V_i} \beta^m_{X_i,j}$$

Fig. 2. Coefficient learning algorithm

In the neuroimaging domain we demonstrate our methods on, there is a hierarchical relationship among neuroanatomical brain regions. Each brain region decomposes into a set of smaller brain regions and the activation associated with each brain region is calculated as the average weighted activation of the brain regions it comprises. From these hierarchical relationships, we build a hierarchy such that each node in the hierarchy corresponds to a brain region. The parents of a node in the hierarchy (referred to as an *h-parent* since *parent* describes relationships in BNs) correspond to brain regions the node is part of and children of a node in the hierarchy (*h-children*) are the regions the node is composed of.

A RV hierarchy is composed of *composite* and *atomic* RVs. The atomic RVs exist at the bottom level of the hierarchy and have no h-children. They correspond to the non-decomposable elements in the domain. In the neuroimaging domain, the smallest regions of the brain are represented as atomic RVs. Composite RVs have h-children and their values can be computed from their h-children via an *aggregation function*.

Let $\boldsymbol{X}$ contain both the atomic and composite RVs. Let $\hat{\boldsymbol{X}}$ be a subset of τ RVs in $\boldsymbol{X}$, $\{X_1, \ldots, X_\tau\}$. An *aggregation function* $Y = \xi(\hat{\boldsymbol{X}})$, is a scalar function of $\hat{\boldsymbol{X}}$ where Y is a composite RV whose distribution reflects an aspect of the joint distribution of the RVs in $\hat{\boldsymbol{X}}$. We use the weighed mean aggregation function in our experiments. Thus, a composite RV's value is the weighted mean of its h-children's values (this is a slight simplification as the weighted mean must be discretized).

A hierarchy over the RVs in $\boldsymbol{X}$, denoted as Λ, can be graphically represented as a *trellis* (Figure 1a). A trellis is a relaxation of a forest such that each node may have multiple parents. Let Λ_{X_i} denote the h-children of X_i, Λ^{X_i} denote the h-parents of X_i and $level_\Lambda(X_i)$ denote the integer-valued level X_i is located in. $\Lambda_{X_i} = \varnothing$ for leaves and $\Lambda^{X_i} = \varnothing$ for the root(s). If X_i is not a leaf node then $X_i = \xi(\Lambda_{X_i})$. An *h-level* corresponds to all RVs at one level in the hierarchy.

2.4 Calculating BN Parameters with Shrinkage

To demonstrate how to calculate a BN's parameters with shrinkage, assume we are computing the parameters for a BN family containing a RV X_4 as a parent and RV X_6 as a child and we need a distribution to smooth this family's MLE towards. To find this distribution, we can look to the hierarchy the RVs are in. Assume this is the hierarchy given in Figure 1a. X_4's and X_6's h-parents are X_1 and X_3, respectively.

Since X_1's value is partially determined by X_4's value, the probability distribution for X_1 is likely to be similar to the distribution for X_4. Likewise, X_3's distribution is likely to be similar to X_6's. Further, the CPT detailing the correlation between X_1 and X_3 may also be similar to the CPT detailing the correlation between X_4 and X_6. Thus, we propose using the CPT in the $X_1 \to X_3$ family as a distribution to smooth the MLE for the $X_4 \to X_6$ family's CPT towards. We refer to the $X_1 \to X_3$ family as a *progenitor* for the $X_4 \to X_6$ family, Figure 1b. Specifically, the *progenitor* for a family with *P* parents $\{X_{i_1},..., X_{i_P}\}$ and child X_j is a family with parents $\{X_{\hat{i}_1},..., X_{\hat{i}_P}\}$ and child $X_{\hat{j}}$ such that, $1 \le p \le P$, is the h-parent of X_{ip} and $X_{\hat{j}}$ is the h-parent of X_j The $X_4 \to X_6$ family is referred to as the $X_1 \to X_3$ family's *progeny*.

The progenitor and progeny for a family X_i are denoted $\vec{\Lambda}^{X_i}$ and $\vec{\Lambda}_{X_i}$, respectively. As family X_i's progenitor is also a family, it will also have a progenitor. This family is X_i's progenitor's progenitor, or more simply, X_i's second-order progenitor. We denote family X_i's p^{th}-order progenitor as $\vec{\Lambda}^{p,X_i}$ and the pth order progeny as $\vec{\Lambda}_{p,X_i}$. A family's 0th-order progenitor, $\vec{\Lambda}^{0,X_i}$ refers to the family itself.

For the moment, we assume the topology of the hierarchy is a forest and all of the nodes within a single BN family are in the same h-level (we return to the more complex case in the next subsection). In this case, determining a family's progenitor is straight-forward. The child in $\vec{\Lambda}^{X_i}$ is Λ^{X_i} and the parents in $\vec{\Lambda}^{X_i}$ are $\Lambda^{Pa(X_i)}$. Once a family's progenitor and higher-order progenitors have been determined, the MLE for the family can be smoothed towards their MLEs.

The MLE for a BN's parameters is $\hat{\theta}_{X_i,j,k} = N_{i,j,k} / N_{i,j}$, where $N_{i,j,k}$ is the number of times in the data that $X_i = k$ when $Pa(X_i) = j$ and $N_{i,j}$ is the number of times $Pa(X_i) = j$. The shrinkage estimate for family X_i's CPT is calculated as the linear combination of MLEs of the multiple orders of progenitors of X_i. This is done on a multinomial-by-multinomial basis resulting in the following estimate,

$$\breve{\theta}_{X_i,j} = \sum_{p=0}^{V_i} \lambda^p_{X_i,j} \hat{\theta}_{(\vec{\Lambda}^{p,X_i}),j} + \bar{\lambda}_{X_i,j} \bar{\theta}_{X_i,j}, \tag{2}$$

where $V_i = level_\Lambda(X_i)$ (i.e., the number of h-levels above X_i that exist in the hierarchy), $\bar{\theta}_{X_i,j}$ is the uniform multinomial s.t. $\bar{\theta}_{X_i,j,k} = 1/r_i$. $\bar{\lambda}_{X_i,j}$ is the uniform estimate's mixture weight, and $\sum_{p=1}^{V_i} \lambda^p_{X_i,j} + \bar{\lambda}_{X_i,j} = 1$. Inclusion of the uniform estimate prevents the need for any Laplace smoothing when calculating the MLE estimates. If the arity of hierarchically related RVs differs, a mapping function must be provided that maps elements in the domain for one RV into elements in the domain for the other RV (in essence, allowing the CPTs for RVs with different arities to have the same number of elements).

2.5 Progenitor Complications

In a BN family, one node can only be the family's child xor *one* of the family's parents. Progenitors do not necessarily conform to these constraints. For instance, take the hierarchy in Figure 1a. If the progenitor of family $X_4 \rightarrow X_5$ was needed (Figure 1c) three possible progenitors exist, $X_1 \rightarrow X_3$, $X_1 \rightarrow X_2$ and $X_1 \rightarrow X_1$. This is because X_5 has three h-parents, X_1, X_2 and X_3.

The $X_1 \rightarrow X_1$ family is invalid as it is a cyclic relationship. However, we are not proposing to add progenitors into a BN's topology. Progenitors are only used to generate distributions to be shrunk towards. The CPT for this (invalid) family would be the $P(X_1 \mid X_1)$ distribution, which is a valid, though uninteresting, identity matrix. We leave this distribution in the shrinkage process, though it could likely be omitted.

A similar event occurs when a family's progenitor contains two parents that are not unique. E.g., consider the family composed of the links $X_1 \rightarrow X_2$ and $X_1 \rightarrow X_2$ (two identical links). This does not represent a legal BN topology as only a single link is allowed to connect two unique nodes. The CPT for this (invalid) family is $P(X_2 \mid X_1, X_1)$, which contains two sets of multinomials: the $P(X_2 \mid X_1 = \alpha, X_1 = \alpha)$ multinomials, which are valid and equal $P(X_2 \mid X_1 = \alpha)$; and the $P(X_2 \mid X_1 = \alpha, X_1 = \beta)$, $\alpha \neq \beta$, multinomials, which contain untrainable parameters (as no data point could have $X_1 = \alpha$ and $X_1 = \beta$ simultaneously). Recall that we employ shrinkage at the multinomial level. Thus, the valid multinomials may be incorporated into the shrinkage process normally and the invalid multinomials are discarded.

When a node in the hierarchy has more than a single h-parent, i.e., when the topology is a trellis and not a forest, any BN family the node participates in will have multiple progenitors, Figure 1c. Each of those progenitors may in turn have multiple progenitors, resulting in a possibly exponential increase in the number of higher-order progenitors for a family. In our experiments, it was not uncommon to see thousands of progenitors for a single family.

Theoretically, the MLEs for each of these progenitors could be computed and used in a shrinkage process. This is not computationally tractable, particularly for dense trellis hierarchies. Thus, when a family has more than one p^{th}-order progenitor, we create a new *meta-progenitor* that represents a merging of all the pth-order progenitors. The meta-progenitor's child is a new RV representing the union of all the pth-order progenitors' children. Each of the meta-progenitor's parents are new RVs representing the union of the pth-order progenitors' corresponding parents.

The value for the new RVs given a data point is determined by a weighted voting procedure. E.g., if the RVs X_1, X_2 and X_3 are being merged into a new RV $\dot{X}$, if X_1 = 1 , X_2 = 1 and X_3 = 2 in a given data point, then $\dot{X} = 1$ for that data point since that was the most common value seen by the RVs merged into $\dot{X}$. Ties were broken arbitrarily, but occurred rarely due to weighted votes. The MLE for the multinomials in the meta-family's CPT can be computed and incorporated into the shrinkage estimate as a $\hat{\theta}_{(\bar{\Lambda}^{p,X_i}),j}$ term in Equation 2. In many domains, the hierarchy relating the RVs will be a forest (or even a tree) and this merging process will not be required.

Another slight complication occurs when a family contains nodes from different h-levels. E.g., assume the progenitor of family $X_1 \rightarrow X_6$ is needed. This family contains a node, X_0, at the highest level of the hierarchy given in Figure 1a, but also a node, X_3, at the second highest level. When constructing the progenitor of this family, the h-parent of any node at the highest level is set to be the node itself. Thus, the progenitor of family $X_0 \rightarrow X_3$ is $X_0 \rightarrow X_0$. This family does not have any progenitors as all nodes are at the highest level of the hierarchy.

2.6 Estimating Shrinkage Coefficients

Given the MLEs, $\hat{\theta} = \{\hat{\theta}_{(\bar{\Lambda}^{0,X_i}),j}, \hat{\theta}_{(\bar{\Lambda}^{1,X_i}),j}, \ldots, \hat{\theta}_{(\bar{\Lambda}^{V_i,X_i}),j}, \overline{\theta}_{X_i,j}\}$, the mixture weights, $\lambda = \{\lambda^0_{X_i,j}, \lambda^1_{X_i,j}, \ldots, \lambda^{V_i}_{X_i,j}, \overline{\lambda}_{X_i,j}\}$, are set to maximize the empirical likelihood of the learned BN. I.e., the estimates are set to those that result in the highest likelihood possible given a set of left out data, $\tilde{D}$ (the need for left-out data will be addressed shortly). When estimating the multinomial $\theta_{X_i,j}$, only the subset of data points in $\tilde{D}$ where $Pa(X_i) = j$ is needed. We refer to this subset as $\tilde{D}'$.

Maximizing the likelihood of the learned BN given $\tilde{D}$ can be done by selecting the parameters that match the MLE of the BN given $\tilde{D}$ as closely as possible. Thus, the shrinkage mixing coefficients are chosen by minimizing the following function: $\lambda = \arg\min_{\lambda'}(CPTLoss(\breve{\theta}, \tilde{\theta}))$, where $\breve{\theta}$ is the shrinkage estimate computed via Equation 2, $\tilde{\theta}$ is the MLE given the left-out data and $CPTLoss(\breve{\theta}, \tilde{\theta}) = \sum_{j=1}^{q_i} \sum_{k=1}^{r_i} | \breve{\theta}_{X_i,j,k} - \tilde{\theta}_{X_i,j,k} |$.

As the data likelihood of a mixture of multinomials is a convex function [14], a simple version of the EM algorithm can be used to find the optimum value for mixture coefficients. The algorithm is given in Figure 2.

This algorithm assumes that each data point, $d \in \tilde{D}'$, is drawn from a mixture of multinomials. I.e., a die roll determines which multinomial to use, and another roll determines what value X_i takes on given the multinomial. This algorithm selects mixture coefficients such that the linear combination of MLE estimates on the training data is as close to the MLE estimate for the left out data as is possible.

Two issues arise. First, requiring the algorithm to use left-out data inefficiently uses the available data and second, the set of left-out data may be biased (as it represents a relatively small amount of data). To address these issues, a form of cross validation is employed. During each stage of the cross validation, a different section of the training data is set aside as the left-out data. Mixing coefficients are learned that simultaneously maximize the fit of the shrinkage estimates to the left-out estimates across all folds. I.e., $\lambda = \arg\min_{\lambda'}(\sum_{v=1}^{\#\,folds} CPTLoss(\breve{\theta}_v, \tilde{\theta}_v)))$, where $\breve{\theta}_v$ and $\tilde{\theta}_v$ are the shrinkage estimates and left-out MLE for the vth fold, respectively. Thus, all the data is used both to draw MLE from and to train the coefficients.

The EM algorithm usually converged in hundreds of iterations. The convergence rate can be dramatically increased (usually to 10 or fewer iterations) by making significantly larger steps at each iteration than proposed by EM. See [4] for details.

3 Results

Experiments are performed on two domains. The first is a simulated domain where ground truth is known and controllable. Data with varying degrees of noise was

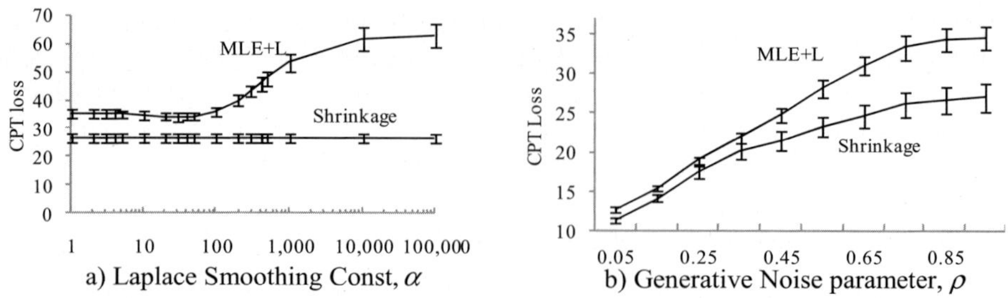

Fig. 3. Simulated data results

generated and the two estimators, MLE+L versus shrinkage, were tested to see how closely they could estimate the underlying generative parameters (comparisons to MLE without any smoothing are not possible as multinomials containing zero–valued probabilities will likely exist and yield invalid data log-likelihoods).

The second domain is a challenging real-world neuroimaging domain consisting of functional magnetic resonance imaging data (fMRI) datasets. Ten datasets were collected on patients that were either healthy, demented or suffered from schizophrenia [2, 6, 12]. For each group of patients, a BN was learned that modeled the correlations among approximately 150 regions in the brain. fMRI data is temporal and time was explicitly represented in the BN structures. Such BNs are referred to as dynamic Bayesian networks. See [4] for further modeling details.

3.1 Simulated Data

In all simulated experiments, a single hierarchy, Λ, over RVs $\boldsymbol{X} = \{X_1, \ldots, X_{57}\}$, is created with three h-levels containing 3, 9 and 45 nodes. A data-generating dynamic Bayesian network (DBN), G, is constructed with nodes $\{X_1^t, X_1^{t+1}, \ldots, X_{57}^t, X_{57}^{t+1}\}$. Each X_i^{t+1} node is given one, two or four random parents (depending on the experiment) from the $\boldsymbol{X}^t$ RVs. Each of these links correspond to a temporal correlation and the data points constructed are actually time series. The correlational strength for each random link can be quantified with a normalized mutual information score (NMIS) and CPTs consistent with NMIS are randomly generated. The method used to generate such CPTs is outside the scope of this paper, see [4] for more details. We refer to the distribution of generated CPTs as $P(\theta_i \mid \boldsymbol{M})$ where $\boldsymbol{M}$ is the set containing one NMIS for every parent in the X_i family. If X_i contains no parents, $\boldsymbol{M}$ is a value indicating the amount of information in $P(X_i)$.

The CPTs for families with no progenitors (X_1, X_2 and X_3) are generated from the $P(\theta_i^B \mid \{c\})$ distribution, yielding families that have increasingly strong correlations as c increases. The CPTs for families with progenitors are initially set as copies of their progenitor's CPTs. Then h random locations in the progeny's CPTs are chosen (with replacement) and a random amount of probability mass between 0 and 0.1 is moved into or out of the random location. The larger h is, the less similar the CPTs between hierarchically related families are, and the less helpful shrinkage should be.

Each simulated data point is not drawn directly from *G*. Instead, the ℓth data point is drawn from a new BN, G^{ℓ}, whose structure is identical to *G* but whose CPTs are noisy versions of *G*'s CPTs. The CPTs in G^{ℓ} are initially set as copies of the CPTs in *G*. For each CPT, $\theta_i^{G^{\ell}}$, a random tuple, $\langle j,k \rangle$, is chosen. The probability mass assigned to $\theta_{i,j,k}^{G^{\ell}}$ is increased by a value chosen between 0 and ρ, $0 < \rho < 1$, and the multinomial is renormalized. As ρ increases, the amount of noise introduced into G^{ℓ} increases and the more distinct each generated dataset is from *G*. The task is: given a set of *L* data points, $\{d_1, d_2, ..., d_L\}$, learn parameters that minimize the CPT loss between learned CPTs and the original CPTs in *G* (results were qualitatively similar across multiple noise models) .

3.1.1 Learning the Generative BN's Parameters

Laplace smoothing adds an additional hyper-parameter, α, into the learning process that controls how much the MLE+L is smoothed towards a uniform distribution. The first experiment compares MLE+L with varying Laplace smoothing constants to shrinkage estimates. Four simulated data points, each with 1000 time points, are generated from four generating BNs, $\{G^1, G^2, G^3, G^4\}$. Each family in the generative BNs contains a single random parent; *c* equals 0.05; ρ equals 0.1 and *h* equals 2. At these settings, families in the generating BNs have CPTs that are moderately correlated with their progenitors' CPTs, the parents and children in families are loosely correlated and the noise added to each dataset is significant, but not overwhelming. These settings are arbitrary and the qualitative features of the results are maintained with a wide ranges of values for *c*, ρ and *h*.

Figure 3a gives the results comparing the estimators' ability to reconstruct *G*'s CPTs across varying smoothing constants. The tests were repeated 20 times and confidence intervals representing one standard deviation above and below the mean are plotted. Shrinkage does not require a Laplace smoothing constant and is provided as a reference line. Even when the optimal Laplace smoothing constant is derived empirically, shrinkage results in CPTs with lower loss. I.e., shrinkage estimates result in parameters more similar to the generative BN's parameters before noise was added.

Figure 3b lists the results for varying degrees of noise. As the amount of probability mass randomly perturbed in G_1 through G_4's CPTs increases, MLE+Ls become more and more skewed. This is because they simply average the noisy observations into their estimates. Shrinkage estimates are less affected by the increasing noise and are capable of learning estimates with lower CPT loss.

The shrinkage estimates take advantage of the correlation between a family's CPT and the family's progenitor's CPT. The strength of this correlation will vary in real-world domains and may even be negligible. We've performed experiments with decreasing levels of correlation between progenitors' CPTs. As the correlation decreases (i.e., as *h* increases), the improvement gained by using shrinkage also decreases, but even when the progenitors' CPTs are drawn independently of their progenies' CPTs, shrinkage performs significantly ($p < 0.05$) better than MLE+L. This agrees with Stein's observations on shrinkage estimators [16].

3.2 Neuroimaging Data

We also estimated CPTs from the neuroimaging datasets with artificially introduced noise. Noise was added as random changes to the values of RVs in the training data.

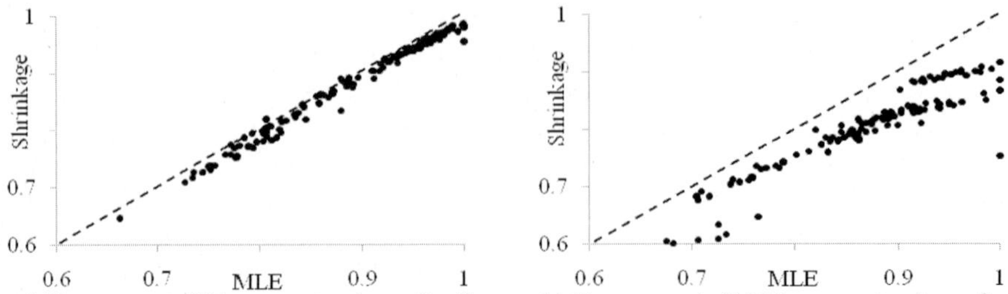

a) Two parents (64 parameters) per family b) Four parents (1024 parameters) per family

Fig. 4. Negative log likelihood of left-out data. The results from the ten fMRI datasets are plotted on each graph. The likelihood values have been normalized to range from zero to 1. Smaller values indicate higher data-likelihood, thus points under the line indicate left-out likelihood was higher for shrinkage estimates.

As in the simulated domain, shrinkage estimates were capable of estimating CPTs that were less affected by the noise and closer to the CPTs for the noiseless datasets (results were omitted due to space constraints, see [4] for additional details).

As shrinkage estimates result in lower risk than MLE+L estimates, the data likelihood of BNs given left-out data (of the same class) should also be higher with shrinkage estimates on average than with MLE estimates. We demonstrate that this is the case for the ten fMRI datasets via cross validation experiments.

For each cross-validation fold, the fMRI datasets are split into two portions. Approximately 80% of a data set is used for training and 20% is used as left-out data. BNs are then learned on the training data using either MLE+L or shrinkage estimates. The data-likelihood of the trained BNs given the left out data is then calculated.

Figure 4 lists the results for the ten datasets. The graphs plot the negative log likelihood (normalized across datasets) of BNs given the left-out datasets. Points under the line indicate that shrinkage resulted in higher log-likelihoods (lower negative log-likelihood) than MLE+L. As the number of parameters grow, the benefit of using shrinkage increases. When the average number of parents per node is two, shrinkage estimates result in higher left-out data likelihoods 92% of the time. That number jumps to 100% when the average number of parents per node is four. Further, the margin by which shrinkage beats MLE+L on individual left-out datasets also increases with the number of parameters.

Even though left-out generalization clearly improves with shrinkage estimates, it is not necessarily the case that classification accuracy will change. While classification is not a primary goal of this work, we have performed an array of classification experiments using the generative BDe score [10] (which does not require parameterization during the structure search) and the class-discriminative ACL-ML score [3] (which does require parameterization during the structure search).

Differences in classification accuracies due to shrinkage were not significantly changed from MLE+L. Of 590 classification experiments performed (with varying complexities of learned BNs), BNs trained with MLE+L correctly classified 382 datasets (64.7%) and BNs trained with shrinkage estimates correctly classified 372 datasets (63.1%); a statistically insignificant difference.

4 Conclusions

One component of learning Bayesian networks is the estimation of parameters. A widely employed estimator is the MLE with Laplace smoothing (MLE+L). Stein demonstrated that the MLE was inadmissible in certain cases [16]. Several machine learning modeling techniques were shown to benefit from shrinkage estimates [1, 14] by constructing a hierarchy of classes and shrinking a RV's MLE towards the MLE of RVs in the other classes.

We have proposed a similar means of shrinking a RV's MLE towards the MLEs of other hierarchically related RVs in the same class. Shrinkage estimates are calculated as weighted linear combinations of MLEs where the mixture coefficients are learned via an EM algorithm. To our knowledge, we are also the first to propose using a shrinkage estimator during BN structure search.

We performed experiments on a simulated domain where ground truth was known and controllable as well as on a challenging real-world neuroimaging domain. On the simulated data, we demonstrated that even when the ideal Laplace smoothing constant is known, shrinkage estimates allow for better parameter estimates in the presence of noisy data. As the amount of noise increased, shrinkage's benefit increased. This was true (though diminished) even if the RVs in the hierarchy were independent, which agrees with Stein's [16] original work with shrinkage.

On the fMRI data, we also found that shrinkage was capable of estimating fMRI parameters more effectively than MLE+L given noisy versions of the fMRI data. As the level of noise increased, the performance of shrinkage estimates also increased. We further showed that using shrinkage estimates increases the generalization of the learned BNs by increasing the likelihood of data points (of the same class) left out of training process. This increase was found not to be caused solely by shrinking towards a uniform distribution (a type of empirical Laplace smoothing), but that shrinkage towards other distributions found in the data was advantageous. This is in agreement with [1, 14]. Finally, we found that the application of shrinkage estimates did not diminish the classification performance of learned BNs.

Future work involves applying these shrinkage techniques to domains that do not have a preexisting hierarchy among their RVs. For such domains, a synthetic hierarchy could be constructed by aggregating sets of RVs together into new RVs. This raises yet unanswered questions such as which RVs should be aggregated together, how many levels the synthetic hierarchy should have, what aggregation should be used, etc. Given the results on the fMRI data—a domain in which hierarchically related brain regions often have significantly different functional behaviors—we believe our shrinkage estimates will perform well in general. Indeed, in preliminary experiments where the hierarchy used to guide shrinkage was randomized, shrinkage estimates still yielded better estimates than MLE+L.

Acknowledgments

We would like to thank the anonymous reviewers for their valuable feedback and Dr. Randy Buckner, Dr. Kent Kiehl, Dr. Vincent P. Clark and The MIND Institute for providing access to their neuroimaging datasets. This work was funded by grants DA012852, NIDA, NIH; 1R01MH076282-01, NIMH; DE-FG02-99ER62764, DOE.

References

1. Anderson, C., Domingos, P., Weld, D.: Relational Markov models and their application to adaptive web navigation. In: International Conference on Knowledge Discovery and Data Mining, pp. 143–152 (2002)
2. Buckner, R.L., Snyder, A., Sanders, A., Marcus, R., Morris, J.: Functional Brain Imaging of Young, Nondemented, and Demented Older Adults. Journal of Cognitive Neuroscience 12, 24–34 (2000)
3. Burge, J., Lane, T.: Class-Discriminative Dynamic Bayesian Networks. In: ICML, Bonn, Germany (2005)
4. Burge, J.: Learning Bayesian Networks from Hierarchically Related Data with a Neuroimaging Application. Ph.D. Dissertation. Computer Science. University of New Mexico, New Mexico (2007)
5. Carlin, B.P., Louis, T.A.: Bayes and Empirical Bayes Methods for Data Analysis. Chapman & Hall, London (1996)
6. Clark, V.P., Friedman, L., Manoach, D., Ho, B.C., Lim, K., Andreasen, N.: A collaborative fMRI study of the novelty oddball task in schizophrenia: Effects of illness duration. Society for Neuroscience Abstracts 474.474 (2005)
7. Friedman, N., Geiger, D., Goldszmidt, M.: Bayesian Network Classifiers. Mach. Learn. 29, 131–163 (1997)
8. Grossman, D., Domingos, P.: Learning Bayesian Network Classifiers by Maximizing Conditional Likelihood. In: International Conference on Machine Learning, pp. 361–368 (2004)
9. Gupta, A.K., Ehsanese Saleh, A.K.M.: Estimation of Multinomial Probabilities under a Model Constraint. Journal of Multinomial Estimation 58, 151–161 (1996)
10. Heckerman, D., Geiger, D., Chickering, D.M.: Learning Bayesian networks: The combination of knowledge and statistical data. Machine Learning 20, 197–243 (1995)
11. James, W., Stein, C.: Estimation with quadratic loss. In: Berkeley Symposium on Mathematical Statistics and Probability, vol. 1, pp. 361–379. University of California Press (1960)
12. Kiehl, K.: An event-related functional magnetic resonance imaging study of an auditory oddball task in schizophrenia. Schizophrenia Research 48, 159–171 (2001)
13. Lam, W., Bacchus, F.: Learning Bayesian Belief Networks. An Approach Based on the MDL Principle. Computational Intelligence 10, 269–293 (1992)
14. McCallum, A., Rosenfeld, R., Mitchell, T., Ng, A.Y.: Improving Text Classification by Shrinkage in a Hierarchy of Classes. In: International Conference on Machine Learning, pp. 359–367 (1998)
15. Pearl, J.: Fusion, Propagation, and Structuring in Belief Networks. AI 29, 241–288 (1986)
16. Stein, C.: Inadmissibility of the usual estimator for the mean of a multivariate normal distribution. In: Third Berkeley Symposium on Mathematical Statistics and Probability, vol. 1, pp. 197–206. University of California Press (1955)

Level Learning Set: A Novel Classifier Based on Active Contour Models

Xiongcai Cai[1,3] and Arcot Sowmya[1,2]

[1] School of Computer Science and Engineering, The University of New South Wales, Sydney, NSW 2052, Australia
[2] Division of Engineering, Science and Technology, UNSW Asia, Singapore
[3] National ICT Australia, Locked Bag 6016, NSW 1466, Australia
{xcai,sowmya}@cse.unsw.edu.au

Abstract. This paper presents a novel machine learning algorithm for pattern classification based on image segmentation and optimisation techniques employed in active contour models and level set methods. The proposed classifier, named *level learning set* (LLS), has the ability to classify general datasets including sparse and non sparse data. It moves developments in vision segmentation into general machine learning by utilising and extending level set-based active contour models from the field of computer vision to construct decision boundaries in any feature space. This model has advantages over traditional classifiers in its ability to directly construct complex decision boundaries, and in better knowledge representation. Various experimental results including comparisons to existing machine learning algorithms are presented, and the advantages of the proposed approach are discussed.

1 Introduction

Pattern recognition has been crucial for human survival, and development of reliable and accurate pattern recognition by machines is an important research area. Pattern classifier construction is central to pattern recognition. Although there are many techniques for pattern classification, it is well known in the field that each algorithm has its inherent drawbacks. The investigation and design of new efficient and accurate approaches are therefore vital for solving particular kinds of pattern recognition problems.

The research in learning object extraction indicates that machine learning techniques have great potential for automation and optimisation of object recognition from images. Based on existing research, there also remains the potential for generalising, testing and improving machine learning and computer vision techniques for general datasets.

In this paper, we propose a novel classification method that determines a decision boundary directly from any dataset based on active contour models and level set methods. We formulate the classifier learning problem as that of segmenting the feature space, and then apply an active contour (with a level set formulation) to perform the segmentation. The principal idea is that the

J.N. Kok et al. (Eds.): ECML 2007, LNAI 4701, pp. 79–90, 2007.

regularisation term included in the objective function that is minimised by the active contour provides some protection against over-fitting, because it penalises long boundaries. The approach is to utilise and extend level set based active contour models from the field of computer vision to create novel machine learning techniques, namely level learning set, for any general dataset. The optimisation mechanism of active contours is adapted to work in sparse feature spaces rather than in image space. In parallel, a decision boundary creation technique based on level set functions for classifier construction is proposed.

The approach explores a novel direction in pattern classifier construction and seeks to provide new insights into the application of active contours and the level set method. It moves developments in vision segmentation, based on optimisation, into general machine learning. In addition, it enables the level set method to handle sparse, non-spatial datasets rather than only spatial data. The paper shows how to embed a level set based active contour model in the framework of machine learning to achieve a very general pattern classifier. In experiments, our method is compared with standard machine learning and classification methods on the UCI repository dataset.

The rest of the paper is organised as follows. In Section 2 we review related work in classifier construction approaches and active contour models used in Level Learning Set Classifier. In Section 3, the proposed classifier is presented, where the algorithm is described in detail. In Section 4, the experimental results are shown where LLS is evaluated and compared to standard classifiers, and Section 5 concludes the paper.

2 Related Work

2.1 Pattern Classification

There are two general strategies for creating classifiers: namely generative learning and discriminative learning.

Generative learning [1,2] utilises an example data set to build a probability model by finding the best estimate of parameters for some known parametric form of distribution. One problem with these methods is that the best estimate of a parameter may not give the best classifier because the parametric model itself may not be correct. Another problem is that even a well trained classifier obtained using a parametric density model may not be an accurate description of the data due to limited number of parameters in the model.

Discriminative learning ignores probability and attempts to construct a good decision boundary directly, which is often extremely successful, especially when no reasonable prospect of modeling the data exists. It assumes that the decision boundary comes from one or another class of solutions and constructs a solution to choose the best element of that class. Techniques following the discriminative approach include nearest-neighbour methods [3], linear discriminative analysis [4], neural networks [5], support vector machines [6] and decision trees [7,8]. Recently, Yip et al. [9] proposed a data clustering method using level set methods to identify density peaks and valleys in the density landscape, which advances contours to form cluster cores.

2.2 Active Contours in Computer Vision

Machine vision provides interesting and challenging problems and rich techniques in advancing machine learning. Active contours are techniques in vision used to detect objects in a given image u_0 using methods of curve evolution. The basic idea is to deform a curve to the boundary of the object starting with an initial curve C, under some constraints from the image u_0. To address curve evolution, deformable contour models or snakes were first presented [10] for detection and localisation of boundaries. Cohen [11] uses the balloon model to reduce the initialisation requirement of the snake model. This has been improved [12] using a geodesic formulation in a Riemannian space for active contours derived from the image content. Cohen and Kimmel [13] describe a shape modeling method by interpretation of the snake as a path of minimal cost which is solved using numerical methods. The Level set method has been utilised for shape modeling [14] as it allows for detection of automatic topology changes, cusps and corners. Geman and Jedynak [15] present an active testing model to reduce uncertainty in tracking roads in satellite images using entropy and statistical inference. These approaches only work for low level segmentation and are not suitable for higher level object extraction or recognition due to their inability to learn and utilise prior object knowledge. Chan and Vese [16] extended the scalar Chan-Vese algorithm for active contours to the vector valued case. The model minimises a Mumford-Shah function over the length of the contour, as well as the sum of the fitting error over each component of the vector-valued image. We have recently developed a method [17] to introduce control parameters into the speed function of level set methods. It utilises a genetic algorithm to tune those parameters to adjust for the effects of intensity and gradient features and force the marching of the active contours to stop at the object boundaries. We have also presented a novel active contour model using information fusion techniques [18].

We now present a new classification algorithm for constructing a decision boundary in any feature space, based on level set methods.

3 Level Learning Set (LLS) Classifier

Given a set of observations and their labels, we define the decision boundary construction problem as an optimisation problem involving data set partition and using a geometric formulation, with respect to some constraints. In this paper, we first split the general classifier construction problem into many one-class classifier construction problems using the divide and conquer strategy. One-class classification [19] is a new branch in pattern recognition that tries to describe one class of objects, and distinguish it from all other possible outlier objects, in contrast to normal classification where one tries to distinguish between two or more classes of objects. For each class, we make the assumption that the space of measurements X is divided into two subsets: A belonging to the target class, and its complement outlier class $A^c = X \setminus A$. The classifier construction problem is then to seek a decision area in the feature space that maintains the characteristics of that class and represents the knowledge learned from the training data, which can be used to classify new data. The individual one-class classifiers may then be fused to construct the decision boundary for multi-class classification.

3.1 LLS in One-Class Classification

In one-class classification, often just the probability density of the training set is estimated. When new objects fall under some density threshold, they are considered to be outliers and are rejected. This approach has some shortcomings as discussed in 2.1. We propose a one-class LLS method which does not rely on density estimation. The method is inspired by the level set-based active contour model [12,14,16], which is an image segmentation method based on the minimisation of an energy function that models curve inflation, curve smoothness, and curve advection to image edges. It is designed to be geometric and robust and produces a one-class decision boundary that maximises a measure of within-class similarity, and minimises the length of the boundary and the area of the region inside the boundary, around a training set of objects.

Let Ω be a bounded open subset of $\Re^n$, with $\partial\Omega$ its boundary. Let $f(x)$ be a given function such that $f(x) : \overline{\Omega} \rightarrow \Re$, where $\overline{\Omega}$ is an order type of set Ω. Let $C(s) : [0, 1] \rightarrow \Re^n$ be a parameterised curve. The classifier decision boundary is defined as the zero level set of an implicit function $z = \phi(x, t)$ defined on the entire feature domain. The contour at time t must satisfy the function $\phi(x, t) = 0$. The area inside the boundary C then represents an open subset of Ω, in which data points have a strong likelihood of belonging to the class. An energy function modeling the constraint for constructing the decision boundary is defined by

$$F(c_1, c_2, C) = \mu.Length(C) + \nu.Area(inside(C)) + \lambda_1 \int_{inside(C)} |f(x) - c_1|^2 dx + \lambda_2 \int_{outside(C)} |f(x) - c_2|^2 dx \quad (1)$$

where $Length(C)$ is the length of the curve C and $Area(inside(C))$ is the area of the region inside C. x is an n-dimensional vector representing a location in the feature space, c_1 = average(f) inside C and c_2 = average(f) outside C. μ, ν, λ_1 and λ_2 are weighting parameters. $f(x)$, namely feature pixel intensity, is a function over the whole feature space defined by

$$f(x) = count(instance_x^i). \quad (2)$$

$f(x)$ is the number of instances of the class i having a feature vector value of x.

The transformation from non sparse image data to general sparse data is not straightforward. Traditionally, level sets perform two-class segmentation on images, where training instances cover the whole working space. For general datasets, multiple instances may map to a single point in feature space, and other areas in feature space may be left empty, which requires careful handling. We use definition (2) and divide the multi-class classification problem into several one-class ones to address this.

According to this configuration, the higher the feature pixel intensity that a data point in feature space has, the stronger the probability that it belongs to the class and resides inside the decision boundary C. We specifically use instances belonging to the target class to create the feature pixel intensity in (2), and ignore all other instances, as depicted in Figure 1. Information outside the boundary in definition (1) does not include instances from other classes.

Thus, the minimisation problem is defined as follows:

$$\inf_{c1,c2,C} F(c_1, c_2, C). \tag{3}$$

By calculus of variations [20], the Gateaux derivative of F in (1) is defined as

$$\frac{\partial \varepsilon}{\partial \phi} = -\delta_\epsilon(\phi)[\mu.div(\frac{\nabla\phi}{|\nabla\phi|}) - \nu - \lambda_1(f-c_1)^2 + \lambda_2(f-c_2)^2] \tag{4}$$

The function ϕ that minimises this functional also satisfies the Euler-Lagrange equation $\frac{\partial \varepsilon}{\partial \phi} = 0$, which is parameterised by an artificial time variable t as:

$$\frac{\partial \phi}{\partial t} = -\delta_\epsilon(\phi)[\mu.div(\frac{\nabla\phi}{|\nabla\phi|}) - \nu - \lambda_1(f-c_1)^2 + \lambda_2(f-c_2)^2] \tag{5}$$

We solve the level set problems by discretisation of the divergence operator as in [21] and iterative computing of the level set function value as in [22] using Equation (5). By iteratively computing the level set function value, we obtain a description in which the learned knowledge is represented by the level set function ϕ, inside average feature intensity c_1 and outside average feature intensity c_2.

Therefore, the one-class LLS classifier is built around construction of an indicator function that ties the location of the data to its class:

$$I_A(x) = \begin{cases} 1 \text{ if } x \in A \\ 0 \text{ if } x \in A^c. \end{cases} \tag{6}$$

To represent this indicator function, the implicit function $\phi(x)$ is used, which is in R^n. The implicit representation can be discretised, resolving an n-dimensional set D. This can even be avoided, in part, by placing all the points x very close to the boundary, leaving the rest of D unsolved. Since only the $\phi(x) = 0$ isocontour in dimension n-1 is important, only the points x near it are actually needed to accurately represent the boundary [23].

Instead of storing the complete training set, this knowledge representation is relatively simple. Moreover, due to the evolution of active contours, the learned contour can be directly used as the initial contour for learning from new training data, which makes it very suitable for incremental learning. Examples of decision boundaries created by one-class LLS classifiers are shown in Figure 1, where the two images in each row show the decision boundaries constructed for two different classes in each dataset separately, after 200 iterations, with bin size 30.

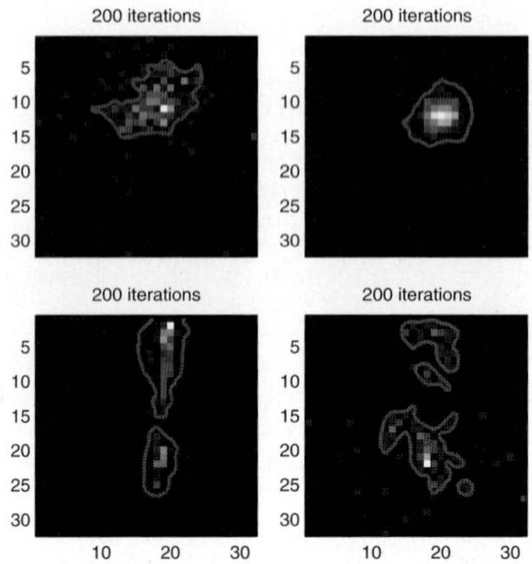

Fig. 1. Decision boundaries constructed by base one-class LLSs for dataset Wis-BC-Diag (top) and Ionosphere (bottom) from UCI dataset, are shown as closed curves

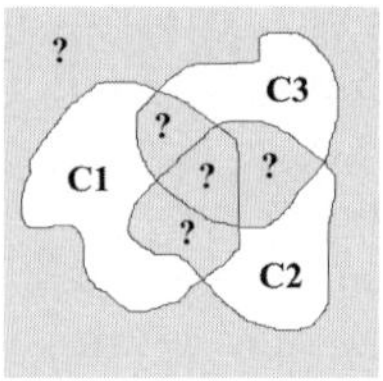

Fig. 2. The areas with question marks show areas where there is inconsistent output from one-class classifiers

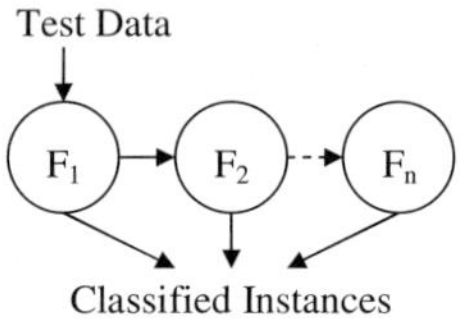

Fig. 3. LLS with cascade of classifiers where acceptance can occur at any stage

3.2 Extension to Multi-class Classification

When we have the one-class decision boundary in feature space for each class, the generalisation to multi-class classification is not straightforward for discriminants that are not based on density estimation. Simple combining methods use voting, but this has the drawback of inconsequent labellings and ties. Before proposing a method to construct the multi-class classifier from one-class classifiers, we first define the following decision areas in feature space:

$$Rejected\ Area_{i,j} = \sim Area(C_i) \cap \sim Area(C_j) \tag{7}$$

$$Competitive\ Area_{i,j} = Area(C_i) \cap Area(C_j) \tag{8}$$

$$Accepted\ Area_i = Area(C_i) \setminus_{j=1, j\neq i}^{n} Competitive\ Area_{i,j}. \tag{9}$$

where $Area(C_i)$ is a subspace of the feature space that remains within the decision boundary curve of class i.

According to the above definition, as shown in Figure 2, a one-class classifier is strongly confident in its decision when the test data point resides in its Accepted Area in feature space, since its decision does not conflict with that of other classifiers. However, dilemmas arise when decisions conflict with each other. Therefore, the decision function for multi-class classification is defined by

$$I_i(x) = \begin{cases} 1 & \text{if } x \in Accepted\ Area_i \\ unknown & \text{if } x \in Competitive\ Area_{i,j} \\ unknown & \text{if } x \in Rejected\ Area_{i,j}. \end{cases} \tag{10}$$

Algorithm 1. Learning(D) - left, Testing(k, T) - right.

Ensure: $k \leftarrow$learned model
  $Y \leftarrow$set of instances in training set D
  $R \leftarrow$set of reference class labels
  $B \leftarrow$subsets of downward projections on Y
  for all b in B **do**
    for all class i in R **do**
      $k_{b,i} \leftarrow$add one-class LLS function
    end for
  end for

Ensure: $d \leftarrow$class labels
  for all instance y in test set T **do**
    $B \leftarrow$create downward projections on y
    for all b in B **do**
      for all class i in k **do**
        $x_b \leftarrow$subset b in B
        $D_i(x_b) \leftarrow$decision area of $k_{b,i}(x_b)$
        if $D_i(x_b)$ is *Accepted Area* **then**
          $d(x) \leftarrow$class i
        else
          $p_i(x_b) \leftarrow$add class probability
        end if
      end for
    end for
    if d_y is not assigned **then**
      $d_y \leftarrow \arg\max_i \sum_{b \in B} p_i(x_b)$
    end if
  end for

To minimise the classification error, the algorithm assigns a class label i to a test instance x only when the location of the instance x remains in the class Accepted $Area_i$ in the feature space, that is the region is inside one decision boundary and not overlapped by others. Otherwise, it refuses to make any decision and defers it to the next step.

3.3 The Final Proposed LLS

As shown in the previous section, all classifiers might conclude that a certain sub feature space does not have their class characteristics and thus consider instances located in this sub space as not being in their class. In this case, the instance is rejected by all classifiers. In contrast, several classifiers might claim an instance and cause a conflict, and the instance has to be rejected in this case too. When rejection is not an option, these rejected instances should still be classified. To solve this problem, we build a classifier out of multiple multi-class LLS classifiers using a cascade fusion strategy based on a degenerate decision tree [24,25], as shown in Figure 3.

At each step, we train one multi-class LLS classifier for multiple classes using different subsets of the feature set of all instances in the training dataset using the following:

$$B = \{B_s | s = 1 \ldots n\},\ B_s = \{b_s\},$$
$$\text{where } b_s = \{s_{th} \text{ downward projection of } Y \text{ in a fixed order}\} \qquad (11)$$

where Y is the set of all instances in the training set D and s is the size of the feature subsets. This results in creating a sequence of multi-class LLS models.

Table 1. Datasets Used

DATA SET	♯FEATURES	♯CLASSES	♯CASES
PIMA	9	2	768
ECOLI	8	7	336
GLASS	19	6	214
ICONO'	35	2	351
IRIS	4	3	150
LIVER	7	2	345
SEGMENT'	20	7	1500
WINE	14	3	178
WIS-BC-D	31	2	569
WIS-BC-P	34	2	198
YEAST	9	10	1484

Table 2. Classifiers for Comparison

CLASSIFIER	DESCRIPTION
NAIVE BAYES	
BAYES NET	
KNN	INVERSE DISTANCE WEIGHTED
C4.5	DECISION TREE
C4.4	C4.5 NO PRUNING, LAPLACE SMOOTHING
NBTREE	
SVM	POLYNOMIAL KERNEL
RBF NET	RADIAL BASIS FUNCTION NETWORK

We treat the base classifiers as experts having subject-specific knowledge, whose contributions to the final decision are equally weighted. We employ the unanimity rule of decision making, except in the final step of cascade, where voting and ranking are used. Since different experts for the same target are trained by different feature subsets, the unanimity rule makes confident decisions at the beginning of the cascade, and defers more difficult decisions to later stages, when more training information is available.

The model in each step chooses its confident decision area to make a decision against classification and leaves instances in its dilemma area to be resolved by the models in subsequent steps. That is, b_ss are subsequently applied to each test instance until it gets accepted by one of them or until it misses them all. This is because each feature might strongly predict instances with certain characteristics and be weak for others. By creating a variety of models trained by different feature sets, each model works as an expert which only makes a decision in the area where it is confident. In the case of an instance missing all models, ranking and voting is employed to assign them a class, which is done by summing the class probabilities in each model and picking the class with highest total probability. The proposed algorithm is depicted in Algorithm 1.

In this way, most of the instances can be accepted at the beginning stages and therefore most of the classification time is spent on instances that are hard to classify. This means that the system is focusing on the hard-to-classify instances, which agrees with human decision making behaviours and can help to improve the overall performance of the classifier. Another advantage is that each of the stages need not be perfect; in fact, the stages are usually biased towards small false-alarm rate rather than towards high hit-rates.

4 Experiments

To test the performance of the proposed system on real world data, we implemented LLS in Matlab and tested it using datasets from the UCI Repository [26]. We utilised the Weka framework [27] for evaluation of the algorithms.

4.1 Setup

We chose 11 datasets with numerical attributes alone, shown in Table 1 from the UCI repository, since LLS currently handles only numerical attributes. We compared LLS with 8 standard classifiers, that covers most categories of state-of-the-art machine learning algorithms and listed in Table 2.

Due to the cascade strategy, LLS prefers to use the most discriminating features at the beginning of the cascade procedure. Therefore, we employ Principal Component Analysis (PCA) to preprocess the datasets and choose the principal component with large variance first. For visualisation purposes, the feature values are re-scaled to be in the range between 0 and 255 after PCA processing and we only use two features in each base LLS in the experiments by making an assumption that a class can be described well by a feature subset of size 2. We utilise binning to reduce noise and improve computational efficiency by empirically assigning 30 bins to each dimension of the feature space.

4.2 Results and Discussion

We evaluated the classifiers on the datasets by conducting 10-fold cross-validation, and the resulting prediction accuracy is depicted in Table 3, where the outputs of the paired t-test at 95% confidence level with LLS as the base classifier are also shown. The standard deviations are shown in brackets. Under LLS column, accuracies better than 80% appear in bold.

To compare the performance of algorithms under a variety of configurations, we calculated the values of AUC, the area under the ROC (Receiver Operating Characteristics) curve, shown in Table 4. We also show the Mean Square Error (MSE) which is another commonly used evaluation metric in Table 5. The classifiers are ordered left to right in decreasing order, based on their average measures. The bold entries in Tables 4 and 5 are LLS values better than average.

LLS are competitive with most of state-of-the-art machine learning algorithms besides exploiting a novel direction of classifier construction that is not based on any existing machine learning algorithm. From the AUC and MSE scores in Table 4 and 5, it is clear that LLS outperforms at least half of the other classifiers and is very competitive with the rest. The prediction accuracy measures in Table 3 shows that LLS outperforms all other classifiers on dataset Iris. It also outperforms about half of other classifiers on Liver, Wis-BC-D and Ecoli. Although it appears that some other classifiers produce a better prediction accuracy than LLS, the paired t-test shows that LLS is statistically competitive with most classifiers on most datasets except Segmentation and Yeast, where instances from different classes are mixed together, with very confusing boundaries. For these datasets, the use of binning with fixed size may have caused instances from different classes to be collected into the same bins and confused the boundary construction.

Table 3. Prediction Accuracy ('v' - better, '*' - worse than LLS)

DATA SET	NB TREE	RBF NET	C4.5	C4.4	SVM	BAYES NET	KNN	NAIVE BAYES	**LLS**	LLS RANK
IRIS	94.00	95.33	96.00	96.00	96.00	92.67	95.33	96.00	**96.67**	**1**
	(4.92)	(4.50)	(5.62)	(5.62)	(4.66)	(6.63)	(5.49)	(4.66)	(4.71)	
LIVER	66.13	64.35	68.71	68.99	58.28	56.25	58.25	55.39	62.61	**5**
	(8.31)	(6.86)	(8.74)	(6.80)	(1.48)	(3.65)	(6.39)	(8.86)	(9.60)	
WIS-D'	92.79	94.21	93.15	92.80	97.72	95.08	96.32	92.98	**93.50**	**5**
	(2.40)	(3.61)	(3.64)	(3.91)	(1.66)v	(2.58)	(2.92)	(4.30)	(3.10)	
ECOLI	80.94	83.63	81.55	80.07	84.82	79.14	84.80	85.40	**81.24**	**6**
	(5.12)	(4.88)	(7.61)	(8.36)	(5.52)v	(6.17)	(4.4)v	(5.87)	(3.22)	
GLASS	75.22	65.50	65.87	66.32	57.51	74.76	70.11	49.48	61.23	7
	(9.63)v	(9.33)	(8.91)	(8.37)	(8.22)	(6.26)v	(9.72)v	(9.02)	(7.88)	
IONO'	89.73	92.62	91.46	91.46	88.60	89.46	82.62	82.62	**86.89**	7
	(3.64)	(5.66)	(3.27)	(3.27)	(4.26)	(4.47)	(3.43)	(5.47)*	(2.86)	
WINE	96.63	98.30	93.86	93.86	98.33	98.89	95.00	96.63	**94.97**	7
	(2.90)	(2.74)	(5.52)	(5.52)	(2.68)v	(2.34)v	(4.86)	(5.38)	(4.11)	
WIS-P'	73.24	77.79	75.74	74.74	76.29	74.79	77.34	67.16	73.76	8
	(4.68)	(6.45)	(8.84)	(7.51)	(3.25)	(4.48)	(6.58)	(11.39)	(7.36)	
SEGM'	94.33	86.93	95.73	95.73	91.93	90.40	94.80	81.07	**85.60**	8
	(2.31)v	(3.03)	(0.72)v	(0.90)v	(2.40)v	(2.18)v	(1.66)v	(2.33)*	(2.74)	
PIMA	74.36	75.40	73.83	72.67	77.34	74.36	72.14	76.31	70.06	9
	(6.68)	(4.36)	(5.66)	(6.64)	(4.07)v	(4.71)	(4.36)	(5.52)v	(4.07)	
YEAST	56.80	59.16	55.99	54.78	57.08	56.74	55.19	57.61	50.95	9
	(3.55)v	(4.71)v	(4.77)v	(4.85)	(4.10)v	(3.79)v	(2.53)v	(3.01)v	(3.32)	

Table 4. Area under ROC curve ('v' - better, '*' - worse than LLS)

DATASET	NAIVE BAYES	BAYES NET	RBF NETWORK	**LLS**	KNN	C4.4	NB TREE	C4.5	SVM
ECOLI	0.99	0.99	0.98	**0.95**	0.98	0.97	0.97	0.95	0.97
GLASS	0.73*	0.91	0.82	0.82	0.88	0.82	0.89	0.79	0.77
IRIS	1.00	1.00	1.00	**1.00**	1.00	0.99	1.00	0.99	1.00
IONOSPHERE	0.94	0.95	0.96	**0.97**	0.90*	0.92*	0.91	0.89*	0.85*
LIVER	0.65	0.52*	0.67	0.62	0.65	0.69	0.66	0.67	0.5*
PIMA	0.82v	0.81v	0.79	0.72	0.75	0.77v	0.79	0.75	0.72
WIS-BC-D	0.98	0.99v	0.97	**0.96**	0.99v	0.97	0.95	0.93	0.97
WIS-BC-P	0.66	0.68	0.61	0.66	0.57	0.66	0.54	0.61	0.52
WINE	1.00	1.00	0.99	**0.99**	1.00	0.97	1.00	0.98	1.00
YEAST	0.75	0.76	0.78	0.73	0.72	0.74	0.76	0.70	0.72
SEGMENT	0.99	1.00	1.00	**0.99**	1.00	1.00	0.98	0.98	1.00
AVERAGE	0.87	0.87	0.87	**0.86**	0.86	0.86	0.86	0.84	0.82

All the above performances are achieved with a generic speed function. On a specific application, a more sophisticated speed function specially constructed with embedded domain knowledge may lead to even better performance.

Table 5. Mean Square Error ('v' - better, '*' - worse than LLS)

Dataset	Bayes Net	RBF Network	kNN	NB Tree	**LLS**	C4.4	C4.5	Naive Bayes	SVM
ECOLI	0.19	0.20	0.18v	0.20	**0.21**	0.21	0.21	0.17v	0.31*
GLASS	0.24v	0.27	0.24v	0.23v	0.29	0.28	0.29	0.33	0.32
IRIS	0.15	0.13	0.13	0.14	**0.06**	0.13	0.11	0.13	0.29*
IONOSPHERE	0.31	0.25	0.34*	0.30	**0.26**	0.27	0.28	0.39*	0.33*
LIVER	0.5	0.48	0.49	0.48	0.49	0.48	0.50	0.51	0.65*
PIMA	0.42	0.42	0.44	0.43	0.45	0.44	0.44	0.41	0.47
WIS-BC-D	0.21	0.21	0.16v	0.25	**0.24**	0.23	0.25	0.24	0.13v
WIS-BC-P	0.41	0.42	0.45	0.45	0.46	0.44	0.46	0.52	0.49
WINE	0.06v	0.06	0.14	0.11	**0.15**	0.18	0.17	0.09	0.28*
YEAST	0.24v	0.24v	0.25	0.24v	**0.26**	0.27*	0.27	0.24v	0.28*
SEGMENT	0.15v	0.16v	0.10v	0.12v	**0.20**	0.11v	0.11v	0.23*	0.30*
Average	0.26	0.26	0.27	0.27	**0.28**	0.28	0.28	0.30	0.35

5 Concluding Remarks

LLS has certain advantages over other classifiers. Firstly, it has an efficient knowledge representation where the knowledge learned is represented as the level learning set isocontours in the feature space. This makes the testing very efficient by requiring only a lookup of the class indicator value in the learned indicator function for each feature vector. Secondly, the proposed classifier constructs decision boundaries directly, thereby avoiding the difficulty of determining a correct parametric density model and its parameter values. In addition, the learned level set function can be directly used as the initialisation of an LLS training procedure for new instances, which makes it suitable for incremental learning.

Acknowledgement

National ICT Australia is funded through the Australian Government's *Backing Australia's Ability* initiative, in part through the Australian Research Council. The authors also thank Dr Mike Bain, School of Computer Science and Engineering, UNSW for asking the 'what if' question.

References

1. Braverman, D.: Learning filers for optimum pattern recognition. IRE Transactions on Information Theory IT-8, 280–285 (1962)
2. Baum, L.E., Petrie, T.: Statistical inference for probabilistic functions of finite state markov chains. Annals of Mathematical Statistics 37, 1554–1563 (1966)
3. Fix, E., Hodges, J.L.: Discriminatory analysis - nonparametric discrimination: Consistency properties. USAF School of Aviation medicine 4, 261–279 (1951)
4. Highleyman, W.H.: Linear decision functions with application ot pattern recognition. Processings of the IRE 50, 1501–1514 (1962)

5. McCulloch, W.S., Pitts, W.: A logical calculus of ideas imminent in nervous activity. Nulletin of Mathematical Biophysics 5(115-133) (1943)
6. Boser, B.E., Guyon, I., Vapnik, B.: A training algorithm for optimal margin classifers. In: Haussler, D. (ed.) Processings of the 4th Workshop on Computational Learning Theory, San Mateo, CA, pp. 144–152. ACM Press, New York (1992)
7. Breiman, L., Friedman, J.H., Olshen, R.A., Stone, C.J.: Classification and Regression Trees. Chapman and Hall, New York (1993)
8. Quinlan, J.R.: C4.5 Programs for machine Learning. Morgan Kaufmann, San Francisco, CA (1993)
9. Yip, A.M., Ding, C., Chan, T.F.: Dynamic cluster formation using level set methods. IEEE Transactions on Pattern Analysis and Machine Intelligence 28(6), 877–889 (2006)
10. Kass, M., Witkin, A., Terzopoulos, D.: Snakes: Active contour models. International Journal of Computer Vision, 321–331 (1988)
11. Cohen, L.: On active contour models and balloons. CVGIP Image Understanding 53 (1991)
12. Caselles, V., Kimmel, R., Sapiro, G.: Geodesic active contours. In: ICCV'95, Cambridge, USA, pp. 694–699 (1995)
13. Cohen, L.D., Kimmel, R.: Global minimum for active contour models: A minimal path approach. In: IEEE Computer Society Conference on Computer Vision and Pattern Recognition, pp. 666–673. IEEE Computer Society Press, Los Alamitos (1996)
14. Malladi, R., Sethian, J.A., Vemuri, B.C.: Shape modeling with front propagation: a level set approach. IEEE Transactions on Pattern Analysis and Machine Intelligence 17(2) (1995)
15. Geman, D., Jedynak, B.: An active testing model for tracking roads in satellite images. IEEE Trans. Pattern Anal. Machine Intell. 18(1) (1996)
16. Chan, T.F., Vese, L.A.: Active contours without edges. IEEE Transactions on Image Processing 10(2), 266–277 (2001)
17. Cai, X., Sowmya, A., Trinder, J.: Learning parameter tuning for object extraction. In: Narayanan, P.J., Nayar, S.K., Shum, H.-Y. (eds.) ACCV 2006. LNCS, vol. 3851, pp. 868–877. Springer, Heidelberg (2006)
18. Cai, X., Sowmya, A.: Active contour with neural networks-based information fusion kernel. In: King, I., Wang, J., Chan, L., Wang, D. (eds.) ICONIP 2006. LNCS, vol. 4233, pp. 324–333. Springer, Heidelberg (2006)
19. Tax, D.: One-class classification. PhD thesis, Delft University of Technology (2001)
20. Evans, L.: Partial Differential Equations. American Mathematical Society (2002)
21. Rudin, L.I., Osher, S., Fatemi, E.: Nonlinear total variation based noise removal algorithms. Physica D 60, 259–268 (1992)
22. Aubert, G., Vese, L.: A variational method in image recovery. SIAM Journal on Numerical Analysis 34(5), 1948–1979 (1997)
23. Osher, S.J., Fedkiw, R.P.: Level Set Methods and Dynamic Implicit Surfaces. Springer, Heidelberg (2003)
24. Amit, Y., Geman, D., Wilder, K.: Joint induction of shape features and tree classifiers. IEEE Transactions on Pattern Analysis and Machine Intelligence 19(11), 1300–1305 (1997)
25. Viola, P., Jones, M.J.: Rapid object detection using a boosted cascade of simple features. In: IEEE CVPR, pp. 511–518. IEEE Computer Society Press, Los Alamitos (2001)
26. Newman, D., Hettich, S., Blake, C., Merz, C.: Uci repository of machine learning databases (1998) http://www.ics.uci.edu/~mlearn/mlrepository.html
27. Witten, I.H., Frank, E.: Data Mining: Practical machine learning tools and techniques, 2nd edn. Morgan Kaufmann, San Francisco (2005)

Learning Partially Observable Markov Models from First Passage Times

Jérôme Callut[1,2] and Pierre Dupont[1,2]

[1] Department of Computing Science and Engineering, INGI
Université catholique de Louvain,
Place Sainte-Barbe 2,
B-1348 Louvain-la-Neuve, Belgium
{Jerome.Callut,Pierre.Dupont}@uclouvain.be
[2] UCL Machine Learning Group
http://www.ucl.ac.be/mlg/

Abstract. We propose a novel approach to learn the structure of Partially Observable Markov Models (POMMs) and to estimate jointly their parameters. POMMs are graphical models equivalent to Hidden Markov Models (HMMs). The model structure is built to support the First Passage Times (FPT) dynamics observed in the training sample. We argue that the FPT in POMMs are closely related to the model structure. Starting from a standard Markov chain, states are iteratively added to the model. A novel algorithm POMMPHit is proposed to estimate the POMM transition probabilities to fit the sample FPT dynamics. The transitions with the lowest expected passage times are trimmed off from the model. Practical evaluations on artificially generated data and on DNA sequence modeling show the benefits over Bayesian model induction or EM estimation of ergodic models with transition trimming.

1 Introduction

This paper is concerned with the induction of Hidden Markov Models (HMMs). These models are widely used in many pattern recognition areas, including speech recognition [9], biological sequence modeling [2], and information extraction [3], to name a few. The estimation of such models is twofolds: (i) the model structure, *i.e.* the number of states and the presence of transitions between these states, has to be defined and (ii) the probabilistic parameters of the model have to be estimated. The structural design is a discrete optimization problem while the parameter estimation is continuous by nature. In most cases, the model structure, also referred to as topology, is defined according to some prior knowledge of the application domain. However, automated techniques for designing the HMM topology are interesting as the structures are sometimes hard to define *a priori* or need to be tuned after some task adaptation. The work described here presents a new approach towards this objective.

Classical approaches to structural induction includes the Bayesian merging technique due to Stolcke [10] and the maximum likelihood state-splitting method of Ostendorf and Singer [8]. The former approach however has not been shown

J.N. Kok et al. (Eds.): ECML 2007, LNAI 4701, pp. 91–103, 2007.

to clearly outperform alternative approaches while the latter is specific to the subclass of left-to-right HMMs modeling speech signals. A more recent work [6] proposes a maximum *a priori* (MAP) technique using entropic model priors. This technique mainly focus on learning the correct number of states of the model but not its underlying transition graph. Another approach [11] attempts to design the model structure in order to fit the length distribution of the sequences. This problem can be considered as a particular case of the problem considered here since length distributions are the First Passage Times (FPT) between start and end sequence markers. Furthermore, in [11], sequence lengths are modeled with a mixture of negative binomial distributions which form a particular subclass of the general phase-type (PH) distributions considered here.

This paper presents a novel approach to the structural induction of Partially Observable Markov Models (POMMs). These models are equivalent to HMMs in the sense that they can generate the same class of distributions [1]. The model structure is built to support the First Passage Times (FPT) dynamics observed in the training sample. The FPT relative to a pair of symbols $(\mathtt{a}, \mathtt{b})$ is the number of steps taken to observe the next occurrence of $\mathtt{b}$ after having observed $\mathtt{a}$. The distribution of the FPT in POMMs are shown to be of phase type (PH). POMMStruct aims at fitting these PH distributions from the FPT observed in the sample. We motivate the use of the FPT in POMMStruct by showing that they are informative about the model structure to be learned. Starting from a standard Markov chain (MC), POMMStruct iteratively adds states to the model. The probabilistic parameters are estimated using a novel method based on the EM algorithm, called POMMPHit. The latter computes the POMM parameters that maximize the likelihood of the observed FPT. POMMPHit differs from the standard Baum-Welch procedure since the likelihood function to be maximized is concerned with times between events (*i.e.* emission of symbols) rather than with the complete generative process. Additionally, a procedure based on the FPT is proposed to trim unnecessary transitions in the model. In contrast with a previous work [1], POMMStruct does not only focus on the mean of the FPT but on the complete distribution of these dynamical features. Consequently, a new parameter estimation technique is proposed here. In addition, a transition trimming procedure as well as a feature selection method to select the most relevant pairs $(\mathtt{a}, \mathtt{b})$ are also proposed.

Section 2 reviews the FPT in sequences, POMMs, PH distributions and the Jensen-Shannon divergence used for feature selection. Section 3 focus on the FPT dynamics in POMMs. Section 4 presents the induction algorithm POMMStruct. Finally, section 5 shows experimental results obtained with the proposed technique applied on artificial data and DNA sequences.

2 Background

The induction algorithm POMMStruct presented in section 4 relies on the First Passage Times (FPT) between symbols in sequences. These features are reviewed in section 2.1. Section 2.2 presents Partially Observable Markov Models

(POMMs) which are the models considered in POMMSTRUCT. The use of POMMs is convenient in this work as the definition of the FPT distributions in these models readily matches the standard parametrization of phase-type (PH) distributions (see section 3). Discrete PH distributions are reviewed in section 2.3. Finally, the Jensen-Shannon (JS) divergence used to select the most relevant pairs of symbols is reviewed in subsection 2.4.

2.1 First Passage Times in Sequences

Definition 1. *Given a sequence s defined on an alphabet Σ and two symbols $\mathtt{a}, \mathtt{b} \in \Sigma$. For each occurrence of* a *in s, the first passage time to* b *is the finite number of steps taken before observing the next occurrence of* b*.* $\mathrm{FPT}_s(\mathtt{a}, \mathtt{b})$ *denotes the first passage times to* b *for all occurrences of* a *in s. It is represented by a set of pairs $\{(z_1, w_1), \ldots, (z_l, w_l)\}$ where z_i denotes a passage time and w_i is the frequency of z_i in s.*

For instance, let us consider the sequence $s = aababba$ defined over the alphabet $\Sigma = \{\mathtt{a}, \mathtt{b}\}$. The FPT from a to b in s are $\mathrm{FPT}_s(\mathtt{a}, \mathtt{b}) = \{(2, 1), (1, 2)\}$. The *empirical FPT distribution* relative to a pair $(\mathtt{a}, \mathtt{b})$ is obtained by computing the relative frequency of each distinct passage time from a to b. In contrast with N-gram features (*i.e.* contiguous substring of length N), the FPT does not only focus on the local dynamics in sequences as there is no *a priori* fixed maximum time (*i.e.* number of steps) between two events. For this reason, such features are well-suited to model long-term dependencies [1]. In section 3, we motivate the use of the FPT in the induction algorithm by showing that they are informative about the model topology to be learned.

2.2 Partially Observable Markov Models (POMMs)

Definition 2 (POMM). *A* Partially Observable Markov Model (POMM) *is a HMM $H = \langle \Sigma, Q, A, B, \iota \rangle$ where Σ is an alphabet, Q is a set of states, $A : Q \times Q \to [0, 1]$ is a mapping defining the probability of each transition, $B : Q \times \Sigma \to [0, 1]$ is a mapping defining the emission probability of each symbol on each state, and $\iota : Q \to [0, 1]$ is a mapping defining the initial probability of each state. Moreover, the emission probabilities satisfy: $\forall q \in Q, \exists a \in \Sigma$* such that $B(q, a) = 1$.

In other words, each state of a POMM only emits a single symbol. This model is called *partially* observable since, in general, several distinct states can emit the same symbol. As for a HMM, the observation of a sequence emitted by a POMM does not identify uniquely the states from which each symbol was emitted. However, the observations define *state subsets* or *blocks* from which each symbol may have been emitted. Consequently one can define a partition $\kappa = \{\kappa_\mathtt{a}, \kappa_\mathtt{b}, \ldots, \kappa_\mathtt{z}\}$ of the state set Q such that $\kappa_\mathtt{a} = \{q \in Q \,|\, B(q, \mathtt{a}) = 1\}$. Each block of the partition κ gathers the states emitting the same symbol. Whenever each block contains only a single state, the POMM is fully observable and equivalent to an order 1 MC. A POMM is depicted in the left part of Figure 1. The state label 1a indicates that it is the first state of the block $\kappa_{\mathtt{a}}$ and the emission distributions are defined according to state labels. There is a probability one to start in state 1d. Any probability distribution over Σ^* generated by a HMM with $|Q|$ states over an alphabet Σ can be represented by a POMM with $\mathcal{O}(|Q|.|\Sigma|)$ states [1].

2.3 Phase-Type Distributions

A discrete finite Markov chain (MC) is a stochastic process $\{X_t \mid t \in \mathbb{N}\}$ where the random variable X takes its value at any discrete time t in a finite set Q and such that: $P[X_t = q \mid X_{t-1}, X_{t-2}, \ldots, X_0] = P[X_t = q \mid X_{t-1}, \ldots, X_{t-p}]$. This condition states that the probability of the next outcome only depends on the last p values of the process (Markov property). A MC can be represented by a 3-tuple $T = \langle Q, A, \boldsymbol{\iota} \rangle$ where Q is a finite set of states, A is a $|Q| \times |Q|$ transition probability matrix and $\boldsymbol{\iota}$ is a $|Q|-$dimensional vector representing the initial probability distribution. A MC is *absorbing* if the process has a probability one to get trapped into a state q. Such a state is called *absorbing.* The state set can be partitioned into the *absorbing set* $Q_A = \{q \in Q \mid A_{qq} = 1\}$ and its complementary set, the *transient set* Q_T. The *time to absorption* is the number of steps the process takes to reach an absorbing state.

Definition 3 (Discrete Phase-type (PH) Distribution). *A probability distribution $\varphi(.)$ on $\mathbb{N}^0$ is a* distribution of phase-type *(PH) if and only if it is the distribution of the time to absorption in an absorbing MC.*

The probability distribution of $\varphi(.)$ is classically computed using matrix operations [5]. However, this computation is performed here via *forward* and *backward* variables, similar to those used in the Baum-Welch algorithm [9], which are useful in the POMMPhit algorithm (see section 4.2). Strictly speaking, computing $\varphi(.)$ only requires one of these two kinds of variables but both of them are needed in POMMPhit. Given a set $\mathcal{S} \subseteq Q_T$ of starting states, a state $q \in Q$ and a time $t \in \mathbb{N}$, the forward variable $\alpha^{\mathcal{S}}(q,t)$ computes the probability that the process started in $\mathcal{S}$ reaches state q after having moved over transient states during t steps: $\alpha^{\mathcal{S}}(q,t) = P[X_t = q, \{X_k\}_{k=1}^{t-1} \in Q_T \mid X_0 \in \mathcal{S}]$. Given a set $\mathcal{E} \subseteq Q_A$ of absorbing states, a state $q \in Q$ and a time $t \in \mathbb{N}$, the backward variable $\beta^{\mathcal{E}}(q,t)$ computes the probability that state q is reached by the process t steps before getting absorbed in $\mathcal{E}$: $\beta^{\mathcal{E}}(q,t) = P[X_0 = q, \{X_k\}_{k=1}^{t-1} \in Q_T \mid X_t \in \mathcal{E}]$. The forward variables can be computed using the following recurrence for $q \in Q$ and $t \in \mathbb{N}$:

$$\alpha^{\mathcal{S}}(q,0) = \begin{cases} \iota_q^{\mathcal{S}} & \text{if } q \in \mathcal{S} \\ 0 & \text{otherwise} \end{cases} \qquad \alpha^{\mathcal{S}}(q,t) = \sum_{q' \in Q_T} \alpha^{\mathcal{S}}(q',t-1) A_{q'q} \tag{1}$$

where $\boldsymbol{\iota}^{\mathcal{S}}$ denotes an initial distribution over $\mathcal{S}$. The following recurrence computes the backward variables for $q \in Q$ and $t \in \mathbb{N}$:

$$\beta^{\mathcal{E}}(q,0) = \begin{cases} 1 & \text{if } q \in \mathcal{E} \\ 0 & \text{otherwise} \end{cases} \qquad \beta^{\mathcal{E}}(q,t) = \begin{cases} 0 & \text{if } q \in \mathcal{E} \\ \sum_{q' \in Q} \beta^{\mathcal{E}}(q',t-1) A_{qq'} & \text{otherwise} \end{cases} \tag{2}$$

Using these variables, the probability distribution of φ is computed as follows for all $t \in \mathbb{N}^0$:

$$\varphi(t) = \sum_{q \in Q_A} \alpha^{Q_T}(q,t) = \sum_{q \in Q_T} \iota_q^{Q_T} \beta^{Q_A}(q,t) \tag{3}$$

where $\boldsymbol{\iota}^{Q_T}$ is the initial distribution of the MC for transient states. Each transient state of the absorbing MC is called a *phase.* This technique is powerful since it decomposes complex distributions such as the hyper-geometric or the Coxian distribution as a combination of phases. These distributions can be defined using specific absorbing MC structures. A distribution with an initial vector and a transition matrix with no structural constraints is called here a *general PH distribution.*

2.4 Jensen-Shannon Divergence

The Jensen-Shannon divergence is a function which measures the distance between two distributions [7]. Let $\mathcal{P}$ denote the space of all probability distributions defined over a discrete set of events Ω. The JS divergence is a function $\mathcal{P} \times \mathcal{P} \to \mathbb{R}$ defined by $D_{JS}(P_1, P_2) = H(M) - \frac{1}{2}H(P_1) - \frac{1}{2}H(P_2)$ where $P_1, P_2 \in \mathcal{P}$ are two distributions, $M = \frac{1}{2}(P_1 + P_2)$ and $H(P) = -\sum_{e \in \Omega} P[e] \log P[e]$ is the Shannon entropy. The JS divergence is non-negative and is bounded by 1 [7]. It can be thought of as a symmetrized and smoothed variant of the KL divergence as it is relative to the mean of the distributions.

3 First Passage Times in POMMs

In this section, the distributions of the FPT in POMMs are studied. We show that the FPT distributions between blocks are of phase-type by constructing their representing absorbing MC. POMMStruct aims at fitting these PH distributions from the FPT observed in a training sample. We motivate the use of these distributions by showing that they are informative about the model structure to be learned.

First, let us formally define the FPT for a pair of symbols (a, b) in a POMM.

Definition 4 (First Passage Times in POMMs). *Given a POMM* $H = \langle \Sigma, Q, A, B, \iota \rangle$, *the* first passage time *(FPT) is a function* $\mathrm{fpt} : \Sigma \times \Sigma \to \mathbb{N}^0$ *such that* $\mathrm{fpt}(\mathsf{a}, \mathsf{b})$ *is the number of steps before reaching the block* κ_{b} *for the first time, leaving initially from the block* κ_{a}*:* $\mathrm{fpt}(\mathsf{a}, \mathsf{b}) = \inf_t \{t \in \mathbb{N}^0 | X_t \in \kappa_{\mathsf{b}}$ *and* $X_0 \in \kappa_{\mathsf{a}}\}$.

The FPT from block κ_{a} to block κ_{b} are drawn from a phase-type distribution obtained by (i) defining an initial distribution[1] $\boldsymbol{\iota}^{\kappa_{\mathsf{a}}}$ over κ_{a} such that $\iota_q^{\kappa_{\mathsf{a}}}$ is the expected[2] proportion of time the process reaches state q relatively to the states in κ_a and (ii) transforming the states in κ_{b} to be absorbing. It is assumed here that

[1] $\boldsymbol{\iota}^{\kappa_{\mathsf{a}}}$ is not the initial distribution of the POMM but it is the initial distribution for the FPT starting in κ_{a}.

[2] This expectation can be computed using standard MC techniques (see [4]).

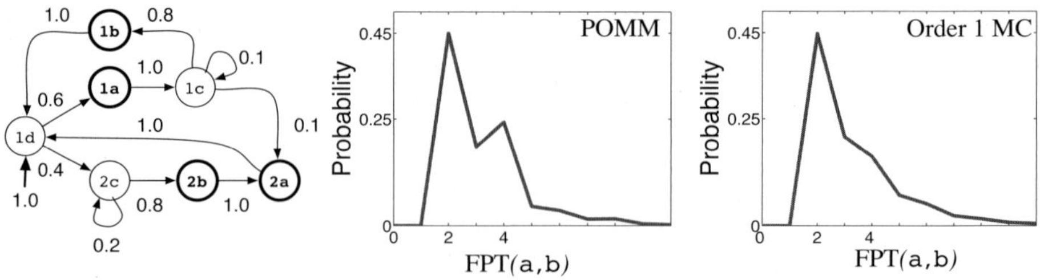

Fig. 1. Left: an irreducible POMM H. Center: the distribution of the FPT from block $\kappa_{\mathtt{a}}$ to block $\kappa_{\mathtt{b}}$ in H. Right: the FPT distribution from a to b in an order 1 MC estimated from 1000 sequences of length 100 generated from H.

$\mathtt{a} \neq \mathtt{b}$. Otherwise, a similar absorbing MC can be constructed but the states in $\kappa_{\mathtt{a}}$ have to be duplicated such that the original states are used as starting states and the duplicated ones are transformed to be absorbing. The probability distribution of fpt$(\mathtt{a}, \mathtt{b})$ is computed as follows for all $t \in \mathbb{N}^0$:

$$P[\text{fpt}(\mathtt{a}, \mathtt{b}) = t] \propto \sum_{q \in \kappa_{\mathtt{b}}} \alpha^{\kappa_{\mathtt{a}}}(q, t) = \sum_{q \in \kappa_{\mathtt{a}}} \iota_q^{\kappa_{\mathtt{a}}} \beta^{\kappa_{\mathtt{b}}}(q, t) \tag{4}$$

An irreducible POMM H and its associated PH distribution from block $\kappa_{\mathtt{a}}$ to block $\kappa_{\mathtt{b}}$ are depicted respectively in the left and center parts of Figure 1. The obtained PH distribution has several modes (*i.e.* maxima), the most noticeable being at times 2 and 4. These modes reveal the presence of paths of length[3] 2 and 4 from $\kappa_{\mathtt{a}}$ to $\kappa_{\mathtt{b}}$ having a large probability. For instance, the paths `1a,1c,1b` and `2a,1d,1a,1c,1b` have a respective probability equal to 0.45 and 0.21 (other paths of length 4 yield a total probability equal to 0.25 for this length). Other informations related to the model structure such as long-term dependencies can also be deduced from the FPT distributions [1]. These structural informations, available in the learning sequences, are exploited in the induction algorithm POMMStruct presented in section 4. It starts by estimating a standard MC from the training sequences. The right part of Figure 1 shows the FPT distribution from a to b in an order 1 MC estimated from sequences drawn from H. The FPT dynamics from a to b in the MC poorly approximates the FPT dynamics from $\kappa_{\mathtt{a}}$ to $\kappa_{\mathtt{b}}$ in H as there is only a single mode. POMMStruct iteratively adds states to the estimated model and reestimate its probabilistic parameters in order to best match the observed FPT dynamics.

4 The Induction Algorithm: POMMStruct

This section presents the POMMStruct algorithm which learns the structure and the parameters of a POMM from a set of training sequences S_{train}. The objective is to induce a model that best reproduces the FPT dynamics extracted

[3] The length of a path is defined here in terms of number of steps.

from S_{train}. Section 4.1 presents the general structure of the induction algorithm. Reestimation formulas for fitting FPT distributions are detailed in section 4.2.

4.1 POMM Induction

The pseudo-code of POMMSTRUCT is presented in Algorithm 1.

Algorithm POMMSTRUCT
Input:
- A training sample S_{train}
- The order r of the initial model
- The number p of pairs
- A precision parameter ϵ

Output: A collection of POMMs

$EP_0 \leftarrow$ `initialize`(S_{train}, r);
$FPT_{train} \leftarrow$ `extractFPT`(S_{train});
$\mathcal{F} \leftarrow$ `selectDivPairs`(EP_0, FPT_{train}, p);
$EP_0 \leftarrow$ POMMPHIT$(EP_0, FPT_{train}, \mathcal{F})$;
$Lik_{train} \leftarrow$ `FPTLikelihood`(EP_0, FPT_{train});
$i \leftarrow 0$
repeat
  $Lik_{last} \leftarrow Lik_{train}$;
  $\kappa_j \leftarrow$ `probeBlocks`(EP_i, FPT_{train});
  $EP_{i+1} \leftarrow$ `addStateInBlock`(EP_i, κ_j);
  $EP_{i+1} \leftarrow$ POMMPHIT$(EP_{i+1}, FPT_{train}, \mathcal{F})$
  $Lik_{train} \leftarrow$ `FPTLikelihood`(EP_{i+1}, FPT_{train});
  $i \leftarrow i + 1$
until $\frac{|Lik_{train} - Lik_{last}|}{|Lik_{last}|} < \epsilon$;
return $\{EP_0, \ldots, EP_i\}$

Algorithm 1. POMM Induction by fitting FPT dynamics

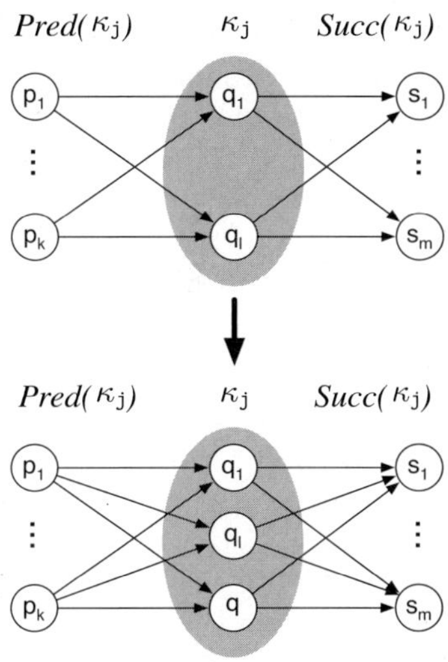

Fig. 2. Adding a new state q in the block κ_j

An initial order r MC is estimated first from S_{train} by the function `initialize`. Next, the function `extractFPT` extracts the FPT in the sample for each pair of symbols according to definition 1. Using the Jensen-Shannon (JS) divergence, `selectDivPairs` compares the FPT distributions of the initial MC with the empirical FPT distributions of the sample. The p most diverging pairs $\mathcal{F}$ are selected to be fit during induction process, where p is an input parameter. In addition, the selected pairs can be weighted according to their JS divergence in order to give more importance to the poorly fitted pairs. This is achieved by multiplying the parameters w_i in $FPT(\mathtt{a}, \mathtt{b})$ (see definition 1) by the JS divergence obtained for this pair. The JS divergence is particularly well-suited for this feature weighting as it is positive and upper bounded by one. The parameters of the initial model are reestimated using the POMMPHIT algorithm presented in section 4.2. This EM-based method computes the model parameters that maximize the likelihood of the selected FPT pairs.

States are iteratively added to the model in order to improve the fit to the observed dynamics. At the beginning of each iteration, the procedure `probeBlocks` determines the block κ_j of the model in which a new state is added. This block is selected as the one leading to the larger FPT likelihood improvement. To do so, `probeBlocks` tries successively to add a state in each block using the `addStateInBlock` procedure detailed hereafter. For each candidate block, a few iterations of POMMPHit is applied to reestimate the model parameters. The block κ_j offering the largest improvement is returned. The `addStateInBlock` function (illustrated in Figure 2) inserts a new state q in κ_j such that q is connected to all the predecessors (*i.e.* states having at least one outgoing transition to a state in κ_j) and successors (*i.e.* states having at least one incoming transition from a state in κ_j) of κ_j. These two sets need not to be disjoint and may include states in κ_j (if they are connected to some state(s) in κ_j).

The probabilistic parameters of the augmented model are estimated using POMMPHit until convergence. An interesting byproduct of POMMPHit are the expected transition passage times (see section 4.2). It provides the average number of times the transitions are triggered when observing the FPT in the sample. According to this criterion, the less frequently used transitions are successively trimmed off from the model. Whenever a transition is removed, the parameters of the model are reestimated using POMMPHit. In general, the convergence is attained after a few iterations as the parameters not affected by the trimming are already well estimated. Transitions are trimmed until the likelihood function no longer increases. This procedure has several benefits: (i) it can move POMMPHit away from a local minimum of the FPT likelihood function (ii) it makes the model sparser and therefore reduces the computational resources needed in the forward-backward computations (see section 4.2) and (iii) the obtained model is more interpretable. POMMStruct is iterated until convergence of the FPT likelihood up to a precision parameter ϵ. A validation procedure is used to select the best model from the collection of models $\{EP_0, \ldots, EP_i\}$ returned by POMMStruct. Each model is evaluated on an independent validation set of sequences and the model offering the highest FPT likelihood is chosen. At each iteration, the computational complexity is dominated by the complexity of POMMPHit (see section 4.2).

POMMStruct does not maximize the likelihood of the training sequences in the model but the likelihood of the FPT extracted from these sequences. We argued in section 3 that maximizing this criterion is relevant to learn an adequate model topology. If one wants to perform sequence prediction, *i.e.* predicting the next outcomes of a process given its past history, the parameters of the model may be adjusted towards this objective. This can be achieved by applying the standard Baum-Welch procedure initialized with the model resulting from POMMStruct.

4.2 Fitting the FPT: POMMPHit

In this section, we introduce the POMMPHit algorithm for fitting the FPT distributions between blocks in POMMs from the FPT observed in the sequences.

POMMPHIT is based on the Expectation-Maximization (EM) algorithm and extends the PHIT algorithm presented in [1] for fitting a single PH distribution. For each pair of symbol $(\mathtt{a}, \mathtt{b})$, the observations consist of the FPT $\{(z_1, w_1), \ldots, (z_l, w_l)\}$ extracted from the sequences according to definition 1. The observations for a given pair $(\mathtt{a}, \mathtt{b})$ are assumed to be independent from the observations for the other pairs. While this assumption is generally not satisfied, it drastically simplifies the reestimation formula and consequently offers an important computational speed-up. Moreover, good results are obtained in practice. A passage time z_i is considered here as an incomplete observation of the pair (z_i, h_i) where h_i is the sequence of states reached by the process to go from block $\kappa_{\mathtt{a}}$ to block $\kappa_{\mathtt{b}}$ in z_i steps. In the sequel, $\mathcal{H}^{\mathtt{a},\mathtt{b}}$ denotes the set of hidden paths from block $\kappa_{\mathtt{a}}$ to block $\kappa_{\mathtt{b}}$. Before presenting the expectation and maximization steps in POMMPHIT, let us introduce auxiliary hidden variables which provide sufficient statistics to compute the complete FPT likelihood function $P[Z, \mathcal{H} \mid \lambda]$ conditioned to the model parameters λ:

- $S^{\mathtt{a},\mathtt{b}}(q)$: the number of observations in $\mathcal{H}^{\mathtt{a},\mathtt{b}}$ starting in state $q \in \kappa_{\mathtt{a}}$,
- $N^{\mathtt{a},\mathtt{b}}(q, q')$: the number of times state q' immediately follows state q in $\mathcal{H}^{\mathtt{a},\mathtt{b}}$.

The complete FPT likelihood function is defined as follows:

$$P[Z, \mathcal{H} \mid \lambda] = \prod_{\mathtt{a},\mathtt{b} \in \mathcal{F}} \prod_{q \in \kappa_{\mathtt{a}}} (\iota_q^{\kappa_{\mathtt{a}}})^{S^{\mathtt{a},\mathtt{b}}(q)} \prod_{q,q' \in Q} A_{qq'}^{N^{\mathtt{a},\mathtt{b}}(q,q')} \tag{5}$$

where $\boldsymbol{\iota}^{\kappa_{\mathtt{a}}}$ is the initial distribution over $\kappa_{\mathtt{a}}$ for the FPT starting in $\kappa_{\mathtt{a}}$.

Expectation step

The expectation of the variables $S^{\mathtt{a},\mathtt{b}}(q)$ and $N^{\mathtt{a},\mathtt{b}}(q, q')$ are conveniently computed using the *forward* and *backward* variables respectively introduced in equations (1) and (2). These reccurences are efficiently computed using a $|Q| \times L^{\mathtt{a},\mathtt{b}}$ lattice structure where $L^{\mathtt{a},\mathtt{b}}$ is the longest observed FPT from $\mathtt{a}$ to $\mathtt{b}$. The conditional expectation of the auxiliary variables given the observations $\overline{S^{\mathtt{a},\mathtt{b}}}(q) = E[S^{\mathtt{a},\mathtt{b}}(q) \mid FPT(\mathtt{a}, \mathtt{b})]$ and $\overline{N^{\mathtt{a},\mathtt{b}}}(q, q') = E[N^{\mathtt{a},\mathtt{b}}(q, q') \mid FPT(\mathtt{a}, \mathtt{b})]$ are:

$$\overline{S^{\mathtt{a},\mathtt{b}}}(q) = \sum_{(z,w) \in FPT(\mathtt{a},\mathtt{b})} w \frac{\iota_q^{\kappa_{\mathtt{a}}} \beta^{\kappa_{\mathtt{b}}}(q, z)}{\sum_{q \in \kappa_{\mathtt{a}}} \iota_q^{\kappa_{\mathtt{a}}} \beta^{\kappa_{\mathtt{b}}}(q, z)} \tag{6}$$

$$\overline{N^{\mathtt{a},\mathtt{b}}}(q, q') = \sum_{(z,w) \in FPT(\mathtt{a},\mathtt{b})} w \sum_{t=0}^{z-1} \frac{\alpha^{\kappa_{\mathtt{a}}}(q, t) A_{qq'} \beta^{\kappa_{\mathtt{b}}}(q', z - t - 1)}{\sum_{q \in \kappa_{\mathtt{a}}} \iota_q^{\kappa_{\mathtt{a}}} \beta^{\kappa_{\mathtt{b}}}(q, z)} \tag{7}$$

The previous computations assume that $\mathtt{a} \neq \mathtt{b}$. In the other case, the states in $\kappa_{\mathtt{a}}$ have to be preliminary duplicated as described in section 3. The obtained conditional expectations are used in the maximization step of POMMPHIT but also in the trimming procedure of POMMSTRUCT. In particular, $\sum_{(\mathtt{a},\mathtt{b}) \in \mathcal{F}} \overline{N^{\mathtt{a},\mathtt{b}}}(q, q')$ provides the average number of times the transition $q \rightarrow q'$ is triggered while observing the sample FPT.

Maximization step
Given the conditional expectations, $\overline{S^{\mathtt{a},\mathtt{b}}}(q)$ and $\overline{N^{\mathtt{a},\mathtt{b}}}(q,q')$, the maximum likelihood estimates of the POMM parameters are the following for all $q, q' \in Q$:

$$\iota_q^{\kappa_{\mathtt{a}}} = \frac{\sum_{\mathtt{b}\in\{\mathtt{b}|(\mathtt{a},\mathtt{b})\in\mathcal{F}\}} \overline{S^{\mathtt{a},\mathtt{b}}}(q)}{\sum_{q\in\kappa_{\mathtt{a}}} \sum_{\mathtt{b}\in\{\mathtt{b}|(\mathtt{a},\mathtt{b})\in\mathcal{F}\}} \overline{S^{\mathtt{a},\mathtt{b}}}(q)} \text{ where } q \in \kappa_{\mathtt{a}}, \quad A_{qq'} = \frac{\sum_{\mathtt{a},\mathtt{b}\in\mathcal{F}} \overline{N^{\mathtt{a},\mathtt{b}}}(q,q')}{\sum_{q'\in Q} \sum_{\mathtt{a},\mathtt{b}\in\mathcal{F}} \overline{N^{\mathtt{a},\mathtt{b}}}(q,q')} \tag{8}$$

The computational complexity per iteration is $\Theta(pL^2m)$ where p is the number of selected pairs, L is the longest observed FPT and m is the number of transitions in the current model. An equivalent bound for this computation is $\mathcal{O}(pL^2|Q|^2)$, but this upper bound is tight only if the transition matrix A is dense.

5 Experiments

This section presents experiments conducted with POMMStruct on artificially generated data and on DNA sequences. In order to report comparative results, experiments were also performed with the Baum-Welch algorithm and the Bayesian state merging algorithm due to Stolcke [10]. The Baum-Welch algorithm is applied on fully connected graphs of increasing sizes. For each considered model size, three different random seeds are used and the model having the largest likelihood is kept. Additionally, a transition trimming procedure, based on the transition probabilities, has been used. The optimal model size is selected on a validation set obtained by holding out 25% of the training data. The Bayesian state merging technique of Stolcke has been reimplemented according to the setting described in the section 3.6.1.6 of [10]. The *effective sample size* parameter, defining the weight of the prior versus the likelihood, has been tuned[4] in the set $\{1, 2, 5, 10, 20\}$. The POMMStruct algorithm is initialized with an order $r \in \{1, 2\}$ MC. All observed FPT pairs are considered (*i.e.* $p = |\Sigma|^2$) without feature weighting. Whenever applied, the POMMPHit algorithm is initialized with three different random seeds and the parameters leading to the largest FPT likelihood are kept. The optimal model size is selected similarly as for the Baum-Welch algorithm.

Artificially generated sequences were drawn from target POMMs having a complex FPT dynamics and with a tendency to include long-term dependencies [1]. From each target model, 500 training sequences and 250 test sequences of length 100 were generated. The evaluation criterion considered here is the Jensen-Shannon (JS) divergence between the FPT distributions of the model and the empirical FPT distributions extracted from the test sequences. This is a good measure to assess whether the model structure represents well the dynamics in the test sample. The JS divergence is averaged over all pairs of symbols. The left part of Figure 3 shows learning curves for the 3 considered techniques on test sequences drawn from an artificial target model with 32 states and an

[4] The fixed value of 50 recommended in [10] performed poorly in our experiments.

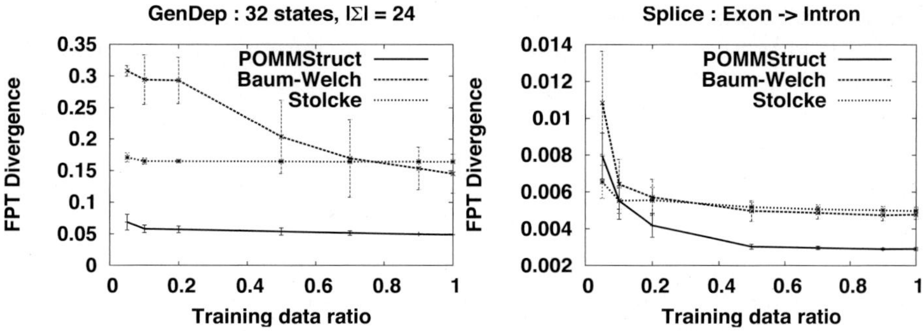

Fig. 3. Left: Results obtained on test sequences generated by an artificial target model with 32 states. Right: Results obtained on the `Splice` test sequences.

alphabet size equal to 24. For each training size, results are averaged over 10 samples of sequences[5]. POMMStruct outperforms its competitors for all training set sizes. Knowledge of the target machine size is not provided to our induction algorithm. However, if one would stop the iterative state adding using this target state number, the resulting number of transitions very often matches the target. The algorithm of Stolcke performed well for small amounts of data but the performance does not improve much when more training data are available. The Baum-Welch technique poorly fits the FPT dynamics when a small amount data is used. However, when more data are available ($\geq 70\%$), it provides slightly better results than the Stolcke's approach. Performances in sequence prediction (which is not the main objective of the proposed approach) can be assessed with test perplexity. The relative perplexity increases with respect to the target model, used to generate the sequences, for POMMStruct[6], the approach of Stolcke and the Baum-Welch algorithm are respectively 2%, 18% and 21%. When all the training data are used, the computational run-times are the following: about 3.45 hours for POMMStruct, 2 hours for Baum-Welch and 35 minutes for Stolcke's approach . Experiments were also conducted on DNA sequences containing exon-intron boundaries from the `Splice`[7] dataset. The training and the test sets contain respectively 500 and 235 sequences of length 60. The FPT dynamics in these sequences is less complex than in the generated sequences, leading to smaller absolute JS divergences for all techniques. The right part of Figure 3 shows learning curves for the 3 induction techniques. Again, POMMStruct, initialized here with an order 2 MC, exhibits the best overall performance. When more than 50% of the training data are used, the Baum-Welch algorithm performs slightly better than the technique of Stolcke. The perplexity obtained with POMMStruct and Baum-Welch are comparable while the approach of

[5] The errorbars in the plot represent standard deviations.

[6] Emissions and transitions probabilities of the model learned by POMMStruct have been reestimated here with the Baum-Welch algorithm without adapting the model structure.

[7] `Splice` is available from the UCI repository.

Stolcke performs slightly worse (4% of relative perplexity increase). When all the training data are used, the computational run-times are the following: 25 minutes for Baum-Welch and 17 minutes for Stolcke's approach and 6 minutes for POMMStruct.

6 Conclusion

We propose in this paper a novel approach to the induction of the structure of Partially Observable Markov models (POMMs) which are graphical models equivalent to Hidden Markov Models. A POMM is constructed to best fit the First Passage Times (FPT) dynamics between symbols observed in the learning sample. Unlike N-grams, these features are not local as there is no fixed maximum time (*i.e.* number of steps) between two events. Furthermore, the FPT distributions contain relevant informations, such as the presence of dominant path lengths or long-term dependencies, about the structure of the model to be learned. The proposed algorithm, POMMStruct, induces the structure and the parameters of a POMM that best fit the FPT observed in the training sample. Additionally, the less frequently used transitions in the FPT are trimmed off from the model. POMMStruct is iterated until the convergence of the FPT likelihood function. Experimental results illustrate that the proposed technique is better suited to fit a process with a complex FPT dynamics than the Baum-Welch algorithm applied with a fully connected graph with transition trimming or the Bayesian state merging approach of Stolcke.

Our future work includes extension of the proposed approach to model FPT between substrings rather than between individual symbols. An efficient way to take into account the dependencies between the FPT in the reestimation procedure of POMMPHit will also be investigated. Applications of the proposed approach to other datasets will also be considered, typically in the context of novelty detection where the FPT might be very relevant features.

References

1. Callut, J., Dupont, P.: Inducing hidden markov models to model long-term dependencies. In: Gama, J., Camacho, R., Brazdil, P.B., Jorge, A.M., Torgo, L. (eds.) ECML 2005. LNCS (LNAI), vol. 3720, pp. 513–521. Springer, Heidelberg (2005)
2. Durbin, R., Eddy, S., Krogh, A., Mitchison, G.: Biological sequence analysis. Cambridge University Press, Cambridge (1998)
3. Freitag, D., McCallum, A.: Information extraction with HMM structures learned by stochastic optimization. In: Proc. of the Seventeenth National Conference on Artificial Intelligence, AAAI, pp. 584–589 (2000)
4. Kemeny, J.G., Snell, J.L.: Finite Markov Chains. Springer, Heidelberg (1983)
5. Latouche, G., Ramaswami, V.: Introduction to Matrix Analytic Methods in Stochastic Modeling. Society for Industrial & Applied Mathematics, U.S. (1999)
6. Li, J., Wang, J., Zhao, Y., Yang, Z.: Self-adaptive design of hidden markov models. Pattern Recogn. Lett. 25(2), 197–210 (2004)

7. Lin, J.: Divergence measures based on the shannon entropy. IEEE Trans. Information Theory 37, 145–151 (1991)
8. Ostendorf, M., Singer, H.: HMM topology design using maximum likelihood successive state splitting. Computer Speech and Language 11, 17–41 (1997)
9. Rabiner, L., Juang, B.-H.: Fundamentals of Speech Recognition. Prentice-Hall, Englewood Cliffs (1993)
10. Stolcke, A.: Bayesian Learning of Probabilistic Language Models. Ph. D. dissertation, University of California (1994)
11. Zhu, H., Wang, J., Yang, Z., Song, Y.: A method to design standard hmms with desired length distribution for biological sequence analysis. In: Bücher, P., Moret, B.M.E. (eds.) WABI 2006. LNCS (LNBI), vol. 4175, pp. 24–31. Springer, Heidelberg (2006)

Context Sensitive Paraphrasing with a Global Unsupervised Classifier

Michael Connor and Dan Roth

Department of Computer Science
University of Illinois at Urbana-Champaign
connor2@uiuc.edu, danr@cs.uiuc.edu

Abstract. Lexical paraphrasing is an inherently context sensitive problem because a word's meaning depends on context. Most paraphrasing work finds patterns and templates that can replace other patterns or templates in **some** context, but we are attempting to make decisions for a **specific** context. In this paper we develop a global classifier that takes a word v and its context, along with a candidate word u, and determines whether u can replace v in the given context while maintaining the original meaning.

We develop an unsupervised, bootstrapped, learning approach to this problem. Key to our approach is the use of a very large amount of unlabeled data to derive a reliable supervision signal that is then used to train a supervised learning algorithm. We demonstrate that our approach performs significantly better than state-of-the-art paraphrasing approaches, and generalizes well to unseen pairs of words.

1 Introduction

The problem of determining whether a text snippet can be written somewhat differently while maintaining its meaning has attracted a lot of attention from NLP researchers in recent years. It has clear applications in generation and summarization [1], automatic evaluation of machine translation and other machine generated text [2], and has been brought to focus recently by the body of work on Textual Entailment [3,4]. Consider, for example sentence 1(a) in Tab. 1. Does it have the meaning of sentence 1(b)?

Table 1. Context Sensitive Paraphrasing

1(a)	The general *commanded* his troops	(b)	The general *spoke to* his troops	**Y**
2(a)	The soloist *commanded* attention	(b)	The soloist *spoke to* attention	**N**

There has been some work on generating rules or templates such as: 'X commanded Y' can be rewritten as 'X spoke to Y.' These rules do not specify when they should be applied or in what direction; they lack *context sensitivity.*

J.N. Kok et al. (Eds.): ECML 2007, LNAI 4701, pp. 104–115, 2007.

Consider sentence 2(a) in Tab.1. Is it still true that 'commanded' can be replaced with 'spoke to'? Alternatively one can ask: When can 'speak to' replace 'command' in the original sentence and not change the meaning of the sentence? This can be viewed as both a form of textual entailment and a weaker version of the common word sense disambiguation task [5]. If we knew the meaning of 'command' in the sentence and could compare it to the meaning of 'speak to,' we could decide if they are paraphrases here.

In this paper we develop a machine learning approach that learns *Context Sensitive Paraphrasing*: when one word can replace another in a given sentence without modifying its meaning. We address this task directly, without relying on any intermediate and possibly more difficult word sense assignment, and without attempting to compile a list of rules per word that say if and when another word or phrase can replace it. We will focus on verb paraphrasing; determining when one verb can replace another in a specific context. This limits our notion of context, but still provides a useful challenge because of the highly polysemous nature of verbs and their importance in encoding relations.

Our machine learning approach gives us a global classifier that is able to tackle this important and difficult task of context sensitive paraphrasing. The key difficulty from the machine learning perspective is how to derive a reliable supervision signal. By using domain knowledge and a large amount of data we are able to collect statistics over individual words to induce a reliable surrogate supervisory signal.

1.1 Related Work

One related line of inquiry is on *paraphrase generation*, namely given a sentence or phrase, generate paraphrases of that phrase that have the same or entailed meaning in *some* context. Often this would be represented as a fixed set of rules. Building these systems could require parallel or comparable corpora [6,7] which ties the systems to very specific topics. Other systems extract rules from dependency trees built over a large single corpora or the web [8,9,10]. These create more general rules, but they only say that a context *exists* where one phrase can replace another. They do not indicate *when* a rule can be applied, as we do.

A second line of work has approached the single word paraphrasing task as a sense disambiguation task. Kauchak and Barzilay [2] determine when one word can fit in a given context as part of a machine translation evaluation system by generating a separate simple classifier for every word. Dagan et al. [11] puts forward an implicit sense disambiguation task where two words are considered paraphrases if they share the specific sense for a given context. These approaches rely on a more standard word-sense word-expert approach with one classifier per word in the first case, or even one classifier per pair of words in the second. These approaches cannot classify unseen words; if they do encounter a new word they need to generate new training data and classifiers on the fly leading to scaling issues as the vocabulary increases.

Previous work employs either a single supervised rule (either through hand tuning or supervised signal present in parallel corpora) or a set of simple per-word classifiers. Our approach combines aspects of both so that we can train a supervised global classifier using a supervision signal induced from unsupervised per-word classifiers. We do not have to hand tune global classifier parameters, but are also able to apply our function to words outside of its original training set.

In Sec. 2 we present our learning problem and overall plan for context dependence. In Sec. 3 we define how we use context overlap to form rules for paraphrase decisions. A single global classifier encodes these rules for all words in Sec. 4, which is trained with bootstrapped examples from unsupervised local classifiers (sec. 4.2). Experimental results for both untrained context dependent rules and the single global classifier are presented in Sec. 5.

2 Formal Model

Formally, we are learning in an unsupervised way a binary function $f(S, v, u)$. f is given a sentence S, a word or phrase v in S, and a second word or phrase u. f returns 1 iff replacing v in S with u keeps the same or entailed meaning.

Looking at Tab. 1, if we set S to 1(a), v to 'command' and u to 'speak to', then $f(S, v, u)$ should return 1 indicating that the sentence in 1(b) is a correct paraphrase. However if u and v are kept the same but S changed to 2(a) then $f(S, v, u)$ should return a 0. 2(b) is not a correct paraphrase; 'command' does not replace 'speak to' *in this context* S.

2.1 Definition of Context

Much of our technique relies heavily on our notion of context. Context around a word can be defined as bag of words or collocations, or can be derived from parsing information. We view each of these as different aspects of the same context, with each aspect providing different amounts of information and different drawbacks (sparsity, distribution, etc) for the final decision. For most of this work we use dependency links from Minipar [12] dependency parser to define the local context of a word in a sentence, similar to what is used by DIRT and TEASE [10,9]. Throughout this paper each algorithm will make use of a specific aspect of context we'll call c which can be either subject and object of the verb, named entities that appear as subject or object, all dependency links connected to the target, all noun phrases in sentences containing the target, or all of the above. One of the goals of our system is to intelligently combine these sources of information about context in a single classifier framework.

2.2 Modeling Context Sensitive Paraphrasing

We consider the question of whether u can replace v in S as composed of two simpler questions: (1) can u replace v in *some* context and (2) can u fit in the context of S. In the first case, u must share some meaning with v. If the second condition also holds then we can theorize that u will get this meaning of v in S. We give the question 'can u replace v' context dependence by determining if u can belong in v's context in S.

We approach the first question using the same distributional similarity assumptions that others use, namely that we can determine whether u can replace v in some context by seeing what contexts they both appear in in a large corpus. To use this idea to answer the second question we restrict the context comparison to those similar to the given context S. If two words are seen in the same contexts then they may be paraphrases, but if they are seen in many of the same contexts that are also similar to the given context then they may be paraphrases in the local context.

3 Statistical Paraphrase Decisions

Most word paraphrasing systems work on similar principles: they find contexts that both words, u and v, appear in. Given enough such contexts then u and v are accepted as replacements. In the next two sections we define how we encode such rules and then add context sensitivity.

3.1 Context Insensitive Decisions

Given u and v the first goal is to find the sets of contexts that u and v have been seen with in a large corpora. S_v^c is the set of type c contextual features of contexts that v appears in and likewise for S_u^c. By looking at the overlap of these two sets we can see what sort of contexts both u and v appear in. Looking at the example in Tab. 2, and more specifically the $S_v \cap S_u$ row, we can see some features of contexts that 'suggest' and 'propose' appear in compared to those that 'suggest' and 'indicate' both appear in. With u = 'propose', the shared contexts are often related to political activity, with some politician suggesting or proposing an action or plan. On the other hand, in the contexts with u = 'indicate', the sense of both words is that the subject is a signal for the object.

To make a decision based on the amount of contextual overlap we set a threshold for the overlap coefficient score:

$$Score_c(u, v) = |S_v^c \cap S_u^c| / min(|S_v^c|, |S_u^c|)$$

This score represents what proportion of contexts the more specific (seen in fewer contexts) word shares with the other. The specific threshold that we select differs between notions of context, but is constant across words. Given this threshold value we now have a simple classifier that can determine if any u can replace any v in some context. To be able to apply this classifier to a u, v pair we only need to find their S_u^c and S_v^c sets by looking in a large body of text for occurrences of u and v.

Table 2. Similar Context Overlap Example. Given the above sentence the goal is to determine whether 'propose' and/or 'indicate' can replace 'suggest' and retain the original meaning. The aspect of context used is the subject and object of target verb and c notation has been left out. Note that each set only shows a subset of its members, unless otherwise noted.

Sentence		Marshall Formby of Plainview *suggested* a plan to fill by appointment future vacancies in the Legislature and Congress, eliminating the need for special elections.	
Query		v = suggest; u = propose	v = suggest; u = indicate
CIP	$S_v \cap S_u$	obj:alternative, subj:Clinton, obj:compromise, obj:solution	subj:presence, subj:history, obj:possibility, obj:need
CSP	Local Context	obj:plan, subj:NE:PER	
	V_S	foil, lay out, debate, consider, endorse, propose, discuss, change, disrupt, unveil, detail, disclose	
	S_S	obj:bid, obj:legislation, obj:approach, obj:initiative, subj:pronoun+obj:program, subj:George W. Bush, obj:project	
	$S_{S,v} \cap S_{S,u}$	subj:George W. Bush, obj:way, obj:policy, obj:legislation, obj:program, obj:idea	subj:George W. Bush (only one)

3.2 Adding Context Sensitive Decisions

The goal of this step of the algorithm is to restrict the set of contexts used to find overlap of u and v so that the overlap has some relation to the local context S. This process is described in more detail in Fig. 1(b). The system identifies contexts similar to S and sees if u and v overlap in these. By restricting the set of contexts that we use to find overlap of u and v as in Sec. 3.1 we are attempting to see if the usage of u and v overlap in a specific sense which relates to S.

We consider a context similar to the current one if they both appear with similar verbs. If two contexts can appear with the same set of verbs then the contexts convey the same set of possible meanings. We start by finding a set of verbs typical to the given context. Currently we use a very simple definition of the local context of v in S: the subject and object of v, if those exist. In many cases the subject and object restrict what verbs can be used and indicate a specific meaning for those verbs. For our example sentence in Tab. 2, the subject is a named entity which we indicate as NE:PER and the object is 'plan'. The V_S of this context are verbs that indicate actions someone does with a plan, including synonyms for creating, breaking or presenting. Verb $x \in V_S$ if x has been seen before with the subject and object of v, not necessarily all in the same sentence.

We now look for context features that these verbs appear in and are specific to the meaning of this set of verbs and context. S_S^c are those context features of type c that some percentage of the typical verbs are seen with (in experiments this percentage is empirically set to 25%). In Tab. 2 S_S shows a set of contextual features (subjects and objects) that are similar to the given: objects that are treated like plans and subjects that are people that do stuff with plans, which appears to be mostly politicians in our dataset.

So given a set of contextual features, S_S^c, from contexts similar to S, and contexts S_u^c for which u appear and S_v^c for which v appear, we want to restrict our attention to the set of contexts that both u and v appear in and that are similar to S: $S_S^c \cap S_v^c \cap S_u^c$. If we focus on the sets $S_{S,v}^c = S_S^c \cap S_v^c$ and $S_{S,u}^c = S_S^c \cap S_u^c$ then the intersection of these two sets is the same as the intersection of all three, and we can use the overlap score as we used above:

$$Score_c(S, v, u) = |S_{S,v}^c \cap S_{S,u}^c| / min(|S_{S,v}^c|, |S_{S,u}^c|)$$

This time we know the contexts of v and u are related to the given context, giving this overlap measure context sensitivity.

If we return to our example in Tab. 2 and look at the $S_{S,v} \cap S_{S,u}$ row we can see that 'propose' and 'indicate' have separated themselves for this specific context. The similar contexts of 'indicate' and 'suggest' have a very low intersection with the contexts similar to the given local context since they are used with a different sense of 'suggest'. On the other hand 'propose' can be used in the same sense as 'suggest' in this sentence, so it has a higher overlap with similar contexts. This higher overlap indicates that for this context, 'propose' can replace 'suggest', but 'indicate' cannot.

Algorithm UV-CIP
 INPUT: (S, v, u)
 OUTPUT: $f(S, v, u) \in \{0, 1\}$

 Generate S_u^c and S_v^c:
  Depends on notion of context
 Compute $\text{Score}_c(u, v)$
  Based on $S_u^c \cap S_v^c$
 Return $\text{Score}_c(u, v) > \text{Threshold}_c$

(a) Context Insensitive Paraphrase Rule

Algorithm SVU-CSP
 INPUT: (S, v, u)
 OUTPUT: $f(S, v, u) \in \{0, 1\}$

 Generate S_u^c and S_v^c
 Find contexts similar to S: S_S^c
  Find local context of v in S
  Determine V_S
  Determine S_S^c
 Find $S_{S,u}^c = S_S^c \cap S_u^c$
 Find $S_{S,v}^c = S_S^c \cap S_v^c$
 Determine $\text{Score}_c(S, v, u)$
  Based on $S_{S,u}^c \cap S_{S,v}^c$
 Return $\text{Score}_c(S, v, u) > \text{Threshold}_c$

(b) Context Sensitive Paraphrase Rule

Fig. 1. Statistics Based Context Sensitive Paraphrasing. Contextual overlap depends on a specific aspect of context c, be it the subject and object, bag of words, named entities, or all available.

4 Global Context Sensitive Paraphrase Classifier

Each paraphrasing rule above (context sensitive and insensitive for each contextual aspect) forms a simple classifier that can be applied to any pair of words and only has one parameter to tune, the threshold. We form our single global classifier as a linear combination of these different paraphrasing rules. We can use the overlap scores for each contextual aspect that the separate rules produce as features for the global classifier, and thus leverage the powers of multiple notions of context and both context sensitive and insensitive information at the same time. To create training data for this single global classifier we use large amounts of untagged text to train local per-word classifiers that are able to identify new contexts where a specific word can act as a paraphrase. These local classifiers are used to tag new data to be used to train the single global classifier.

4.1 Shared Context Features

The flexibility of a classifier architecture allows us to incorporate additional features other than just the raw $\text{Score}_c(u, v)$ and $\text{Score}_c(S, v, u)$. For each context type c we still compile the sets of similar contexts S^c_u, S^c_v, $S^c_{S,u}$, and $S^c_{S,v}$ but now we use the size of the overlaps as features. Fig. 2(a) describes this process further. We create three features for context insensitive overlap (UV features: only depend on u and v), and three for context sensitive (SUV features: depend on S, u and v). By including context insensitive features the classifier can still rely on a context independent decision when encountering a rare or malformed local context. For both UV and SUV feature types we create three features which show the direction of overlap: score, uIntersect, and vIntersect. The score feature is the same as the $\text{Score}_c(u, v)$ for UV and $\text{Score}_c(S, u, v)$ for SUV used in the statistics based rules above. The uIntersect and vIntersect actually give directionality to the feature representation. If uIntersect is close to 1 then we know that u primarily appears in contexts that v appears in, and thus u may be a specialization of v, and if this is an SUV feature then we know the directionality holds in contexts similar to S. The classifier can now learn that its possibly more important for v to specialize u, and can say yes for replacing A by B in a given context, but not B by A.

For any new word w, all we need to know about w to generate features are S^c_w for every c; contextual features of contexts that w is seen with. If we can find contexts that w appears in in our large corpora then we can create the S^c_w sets and use these to compute overlap with other words, the only features that our classifier relies on. A separate classifier does not need to be trained on contexts that w appears in, we can rely on our global classifier even if it never saw an example of w during training.

4.2 Unsupervised Training: Bootstrapping Local Classifiers

The single global classifier requires training to be able to determine the importance of each context type in the global paraphrasing decision. To generate tagged S, v, u examples for the single global classifier we employ a set of bootstrapping local classifiers similar to Kauchak and Barzilay[2] or Context-Sensitive Spelling Correction[13]. Each classifier learns what contexts one specific word can appear in. Once we have these classifiers we generate candidate examples to train the global classifier and use the local classifiers to filter and label confident examples. These examples are then tagged with global features and used to train our global binary classifier. This process is detailed in Fig. 2(b).

```
Algorithm GLOBAL FEATURE TAGGING
    INPUT: (S, v, u)
    OUTPUT: Feature vector

    For each context type c:
      Find S^c_u, S^c_v
      Generate S^c_{u,v} = S^c_u ∩ S^c_v
      Generate u, v features
        uIntersect.UV.c: |S^c_{u,v}|/|S^c_u|
        vIntersect.UV.c: |S^c_{u,v}|/|S^c_v|
        score.UV.c:
          |S^c_{u,v}|/min(|S^c_u|, |S^c_v|)
      Find V_S, S^c_S
      Generate S^c_{S,u} = S^c_S ∩ S^c_u
      Generate S^c_{S,v} = S^c_S ∩ S^c_v
      Generate S^c_{S,v,u} = S^c_{S,u} ∩ S^c_{S,v}
      Generate S, v, u features
        uIntersect.SVU.c: |S^c_{S,v,u}|/|S^c_{S,u}|
        vIntersect.SVU.c: |S^c_{S,v,u}|/|S^c_{S,v}|
        score.SVU.c:
          |S^c_{S,v,u}|/min(|S^c_{S,u}|, |S^c_{S,v}|)
    Place feature values into buckets
    Return feature vector
      contains all features
      of all context types
```

(a) Global Feature Tagging

```
Algorithm TRAINING GENERATION
    INPUT: Set of words U
    OUTPUT: Training data (S, v, u, {0, 1})

    For each u ∈ U:
      Generate f_u(S, v) classifier:
        Collect S, u → positive examples
          u can replace itself.
        Collect S, v → negative examples
          Random v, unrelated to u
        Train f_u using local features
      Label new examples:
        Collect S, v examples
          v similar to u
        Apply f_u to every similar example
        If confidence above threshold:
          Add S, v, u and predicted
          label to global training data.
    Return global training data
      from all U words
```

(b) Unsupervised Training Data Generation

Fig. 2. Procedures for training data generation and tagging. Although our final global classifier is a supervised learner, we use multiple unsupervised local classifiers to generate the set of training examples. The local classifiers work on local features while the global classifier looks at features related to the contextual overlap of its input.

The key fact that allows us to build classifiers this way and train a single global classifier is that we can extract large amounts of training examples for such local classifiers from free, untagged text.

To learn what contexts a specific word u can belong in, we use trivial positive and negative examples that can be collected from flat text. Trivial positive examples are of u replacing itself, and trivial negatives are of u replacing a random x that is unrelated to u (not connected in WordNet). The positive examples identify contexts that u is known to fit in, and the negative examples represent contexts that u likely does not, so we can eliminate irrelevant contextual features. We encode this knowledge of what contexts u does and does not belong in in local f_u binary classifiers.

For each word u in our training set of words, we create an $f_u(S, v)$ classifier: the input is the context of v in S and the output is 1 or 0, depending if u can replace v in S or not. Notice this is a local form of the global $f(S, v, u)$ function, if it were possible to train local classifiers for every possible u. The local f_u use their implicit knowledge about the given u to tag interesting examples such that the global classifier can extract patterns that hold for all words.

Our feature representation for the context of v in S that f_u uses includes bag of words, collocations, nearest noun and verb to the left and right of target, and named dependency links of length 1 and 2 from target from Minipar. These features are richer than the simple surrounding word and collocation features employed in [2], which allow us to get the same accuracy for local f_u classifiers using many fewer examples (their local classifiers used on average 200k training examples, ours at most 30k).

Once we have trained local bootstrapping classifiers we use them to tag examples of S, v, where v is similar to u (from Lin's similarity list [14]). If the local classifiers confidently label an example, that example is added with its label to the global training set. The confidence is tuned to less than 5% error on a development set for each f_u. We generated 230 local classifiers, where the seed U set was selected so that about half the words were seen in our test data, and half random verbs with at least 1000 occurrences in our text corpora. These local classifiers confidently tagged over 400k examples for our global classifier.

5 Experimental Results

5.1 Methodology

As a large source of text we used the 2000 New York Times section of the AQUAINT corpus. Each sentence was tagged with part of speech and named entities then parsed with Minipar. To implement both the f_u and the single global classifier we used the SNoW learning architecture[15] with perceptron update rule.

Our test set goal was to select one example sentence representing each sense (and thus a different word to replace) for each of a set of verbs so that we can highlight the context sensitivity of paraphrasing. We started with an initial random selection of polysemous verbs that occur in WordNet 2.1 sense tagged data (Semcor)[16]. For each verb we selected a possible synonym for each of a coarse sense mapping (Navigli's mappings of WordNet 2.1 to coincide with ODE entries [17]) since the coarse word senses provide clearer distinctions between meanings of words than regular WordNet. We then selected one representative sentence where each coarse synonym could replace the target verb. For every S, v sentence the possible u were exactly the coarse synonyms for v, the intent being that exactly one of them would be replaceable for each sense of v, although this was not always the case. Two humans (native English speaking graduate students) annotated each S, v, u example for whether u could replace v or not in S. The interannotator agreement was over 83% of instances, with a kappa of 0.62, corresponding to substantial agreement[18]. This kappa is comparable to our previous tagging efforts and others reported in similar efforts [19]. Overall our test set has 721 S, v, u examples with 57 unique v verbs and 162 unique u.

5.2 Results

The results of the global classifier on the test set is shown in Fig. 3. The varying precision/recall points were achieved by setting the SNoW confidence threshold for the global classifier and setting the score threshold for the statistical rules. As

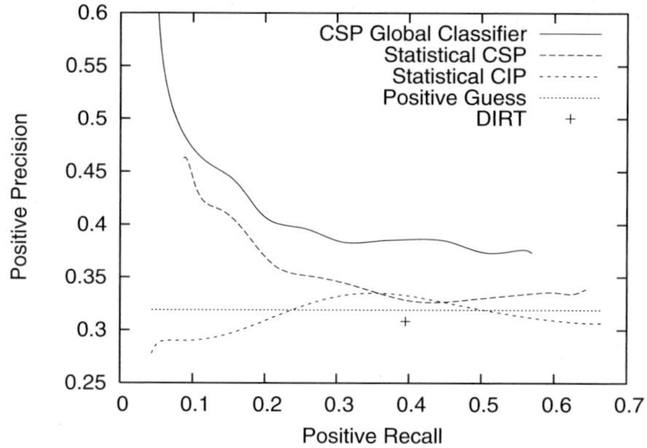

Fig. 3. Positive precision/recall curve for our global CSP classifier compared to statistical context sensitive and insensitive paraphrasing rules using all contextual features. Also shown is the single point of precision/recall given by current top of the line paraphrasing system DIRT on our test set. The positive guess line illustrates the precision of always guessing yes for every example: 32% of test cases are positive.

we can see the single global classifier is able to exploit both the u, v and S, v, u rules and different definitions of context to improve both recall and precision. As an additional comparison we include the results if we used slightly modified DIRT rules to make paraphrase judgments. Each DIRT rule specifies a dependency pattern that can be rewritten as another dependency pattern. For our verb paraphrase task we restricted the rules to those that could be interpreted as single verb rewrite rule where each pattern is a verb with two dependency links coming off of it. In a similar setup, recent experiments have shown that DIRT is the top of the line for verb paraphrasing [19].

Both classifier and statistical based rules performed better on this test set than DIRT probably because we do not rely on a fixed set of patterns (that are generated on a separate corpus). Instead we use classifiers that can be instantiated with any word encountered in the test set. During training our global classifier only saw examples generated for a subset of the words that appear in testing. The classifier can still apply to any S, v, u example as long as we can collect contexts that v and u have been seen in. Any per-word classifier approach such as Kauchak and Barzilay could not have handled unseen examples such as these, they would need to collect examples of u and generate a new classifier.

To test the ability of our classifier to learn a global hypothesis that applies across words we tested the performance of the classifier when it was trained with unsupervised data generated for a varying number of words while keeping the final number of training examples fixed. If the classifier can learn a hypothesis just as well by looking at statistics for 50 words vs. 250 then its hypothesis is not dependent on the specific words used in training, but on global statistics that exist for paraphrasing. Fig. 4(a) shows that the number of words used to

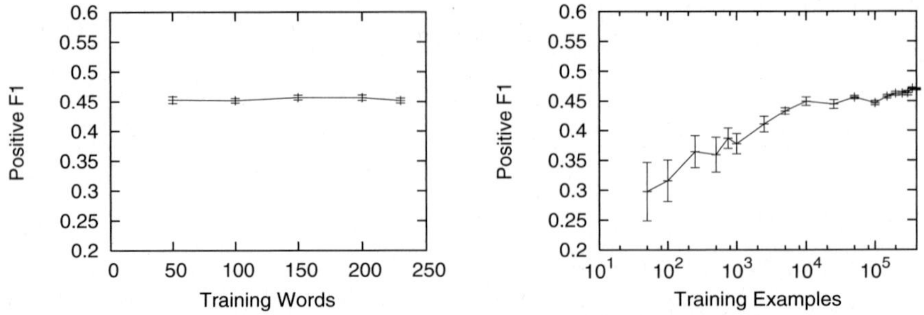

(a) Number of Words (b) Number of Examples

Fig. 4. Generalization to unseen words: Plot (a) shows that performance on the test data does not depend on the number of words seen in training (recall: training set is created w/o supervision). What does affect performance is the number of training examples generated (plot (b)). Each point represents the mean positive F1 over 20 different random resamplings of the training set. This plot represents one point selected from the precision/recall curve above.

generate training data has little effect on the positive F1 of the classifier, the same rules learned on 50 words is learned on 200 and beyond. On the other hand, if we look at the number of examples used to train the classifier we do see improvement. Fig 4(b) shows the results of varying the number of examples used to train the classifier, but keeping the number of words these examples are drawn from fixed. If we are only able to create accurate bootstrapping classifiers for a small set of words, this should still prove adequate to generate data to train the global classifier, as long as we can generate a lot of it.

6 Conclusion and Future Work

In this project we presented an approach to adding context sensitivity to a word paraphrasing system. By only looking for distributional similarity over contexts similar to the given sentence we are able to decide if one verb can replace another in the given context. Further we incorporate this approach into a classifier architecture that is able to successfully combine multiple definitions of context and context sensitive and insensitive information into a unified whole. Our machine learning approach allowed us to leverage a large amount of data regarding the local statistics of word occurrences to generate training data for a traditionally supervised global classifier in an unsupervised manner.

Our experiments indicate that it is important to have as much data per word as possible, both in terms of representation and training, so we plan to expand our knowledge sources. The eventual goal for the system is to incorporate it into a full textual entailment system and see if this context sensitive paraphrasing can benefit a larger NLP task.

Acknowledgments

We would like to thank those who have given us comments throughout this project, especially Idan Szpektor, Kevin Small, and anonymous reviewers. This research is supported by NSF grants BCS-0620257 and ITR-IIS-0428472.

References

1. Barzilay, R., Lee, L.: Catching the drift: Probabilistic content models, with applications to generation and summarization. In: Proceedings HLT-NAACL (2004)
2. Kauchak, D., Barzilay, R.: Paraphrasing for automatic evaluation. In: Proceedings of HLT-NAACL 2006 (2006)
3. Dagan, I., Glickman, O., Magnini, B.: The pascal recognizing textual entailment challenge. In: Proceedings of the PASCAL Challenges Workshop on Recognizing Textual Entailment (2005)
4. de Salvo Braz, R., Girju, R., Punyakanok, V., Roth, D., Sammons, M.: An inference model for semantic entailment in natural language. In: Proceedings of the National Conference on Artificial Intelligence (AAAI), pp. 1678–1679 (2005)
5. Ide, N., Veronis, J.: Word sense disambiguation: The state of the art. Computational Linguistics (1998)
6. Barzilay, R., Lee, L.: Learning to paraphrase: An unsupervised approach using multiple-sequence alignment. In: Proceedings HLT-NAACL, pp. 16–23 (2003)
7. Barzilay, R., McKeown, K.: Extracing paraphrases from a parallel corpus. In: Proceedings ACL-01 (2004)
8. Glickman, O., Dagan, I.: Identifying lexical paraphrases from a single corpus: A case study for verbs. In: Recent Advantages in Natural Language Processing (RANLP-03) (2003)
9. Szpektor, I., Tanev, H., Dagan, I., Coppola, B.: Scaling web-based acquisition of entailment relations. In: Proceedings of EMNLP 2004 (2004)
10. Lin, D., Pantel, P.: Discovery of inference rules for question answering. Natural Language Engineering 7(4), 343–360 (2001)
11. Dagan, I., Glickman, O., Gliozzo, A., Marmorshtein, E., Strapparava, C.: Direct word sense matching for lexical substitution. In: Proceedings ACL-06, pp. 449–456 (2007)
12. Lin, D.: Principal-based parsing without overgeneration. In: Proceedings of ACL-93, pp. 112–120 (1993)
13. Golding, A.R., Roth, D.: A Winnow based approach to context-sensitive spelling correction. Machine Learning 34(1-3), 107–130 (1999)
14. Lin, D.: Automatic retrieval and clustering of similar words. In: COLING-ACL-98 (1998)
15. Carlson, A., Cumby, C., Rosen, J., Roth, D.: The SNoW learning architecture. Technical Report UIUCDCS-R-99-2101, UIUC Computer Science Department (May 1999)
16. Fellbaum, C.: Wordnet: An Electronic Lexical Database. Bradford Books (1998)
17. Navigli, R.: Meaningful clustering of senses helps boost word sense disambiguation performance. In: Proceedings of COLING-ACL 2006 (2006)
18. Landis, J., Koch, G.: The measurement of observer agreement for categorical data. In: Biometrics (1977)
19. Szpektor, I., Shnarch, E., Dagan, I.: Instance-based evaluation of entailment rule acquisition. In: Proceedings of ACL 2007 (2007)

Dual Strategy Active Learning

Pinar Donmez[1], Jaime G. Carbonell[1], and Paul N. Bennett[2]

[1] School of Computer Science, Carnegie Mellon University, 5000 Forbes Ave, Pittsburgh PA, 15213 USA
{pinard,jgc}@cs.cmu.edu

[2] Microsoft Research, 1 Microsoft Way, Redmond, WA 98052 USA
Paul.N.Bennett@microsoft.com

Abstract. Active Learning methods rely on static strategies for sampling unlabeled point(s). These strategies range from uncertainty sampling and density estimation to multi-factor methods with learn-once-use-always model parameters. This paper proposes a dynamic approach, called DUAL, where the strategy selection parameters are adaptively updated based on estimated future residual error reduction after each actively sampled point. The objective of dual is to outperform static strategies over a large operating range: from very few to very many labeled points. Empirical results over six datasets demonstrate that DUAL outperforms several state-of-the-art methods on most datasets.

1 Introduction

Active learning has received significant attention in recent years, but most work focuses on presenting a new algorithm and showing how for some datasets and under some operating range it outperforms earlier methods [17,16,6]. Some active learning methods perform best when very few instances have been sampled, whereas others perform best only after substantial sampling. For instance, density estimation methods perform well with minimal labeled data since they sample from maximal-density unlabeled regions, and thus help establish the initial decision boundary where it affects the most remaining unlabeled data [8]. On the other hand, uncertainty sampling methods "fine tune" a decision boundary by sampling the regions where the classifier is least certain, regardless of the density of the unlabeled data [2,4]. Such methods work best when a larger number of unlabeled points may be sampled, as we show later in this paper. This paper takes a step towards a principled ensemble-based sampling approach for active learning that dominates either method individually, largely by selecting sampling methods based on estimated residual classification error reduction. Different active learning methods use different selection criteria. For example, *Query-by-Committee* [1,2] selects examples that cause maximum disagreement amongst an ensemble of hypotheses. Hence, it reduces the version space [5] and is similar to Tong and Koller's approach [4] which halves the version space in an SVM setting. *Uncertainty sampling* [3] selects the example on which the learner has lowest classification certainty. Version-space reduction methods eliminate

J.N. Kok et al. (Eds.): ECML 2007, LNAI 4701, pp. 116–127, 2007.

areas of the parameter space that have no direct effect on the error rate, but may have indirect effects. Uncertainty sampling is not immune to selecting outliers since they have high uncertainty [6], but the underlying data distribution is ignored. Several active learning strategies including [9,8,6] propose ways to trade-off uncertainty vs. data density. Xu et al. [8] propose a representative sampling method which uses the k-means algorithm to cluster the data within the margin of an SVM classifier and selects the cluster centroids for labeling. McCallum and Nigam [6] also suggest a clustering based approach using the EM algorithm. All these methods aim to balance the uncertainty of the sample with its representativeness, but do so in a fixed manner, rather than by dynamically selecting or reweighing, based on residual error estimation. In this paper, we introduce a **Du**al strategy for **A**ctive **L**earning, DUAL, which is a context-sensitive sampling method. DUAL significantly improves upon the work of [9] by incorporating a robust combination of density weighted uncertainty sampling and standard (uniform) uncertainty sampling. The primary focus of DUAL is to improve active learning for the later portion of the process, rather than traditional methods that concentrate primarily on the initial dataset labeling. Baram et al. [10] present an ensemble active learning method that is complementary to ours, but does not subsume our mid-course strategy-switching method. Baram et al. develop an online algorithm that selects among three alternative active sampling strategies using a variant of the multi-armed bandit algorithm [11] to decide the strategy to be used at each iteration. They focus primarily on selecting which sampling method is optimal for a given dataset; in contrast, we focus on selecting the operating range among the sampling methods. Empirical results demonstrate that DUAL generally leads to better performance. Furthermore, it is also empirically shown that 1) DUAL is reliably better than the best of the single strategies, and 2) it is better across various domains and for both minimal and copious labeled data volumes.

The paper is organized as follows: Section 2 presents further motivation. Section 3 summarizes the method of [9]. Section 4 describes our new DUAL algorithm and presents the results of our empirical studies. In Section 5, we offer our observations and concluding remarks as well as suggestions for potential future directions.

2 Motivation for DUAL

Nguyen and Smeulders [9] suggest a probabilistic framework where clustering information is incorporated into the active sampling scheme. They argue that data points lying on the classification boundary are informative, but using information about the underlying data distribution helps to select better examples. They assume higher density samples lying close to the decision boundary are more informative. We call their method density weighted uncertainty sampling, or DWUS for short. DWUS uses the following active selection criterion:

$$s = \arg\max_{i \in I_u} E[(\hat{y}_i - y_i)^2 \mid x_i] p(x_i) \tag{1}$$

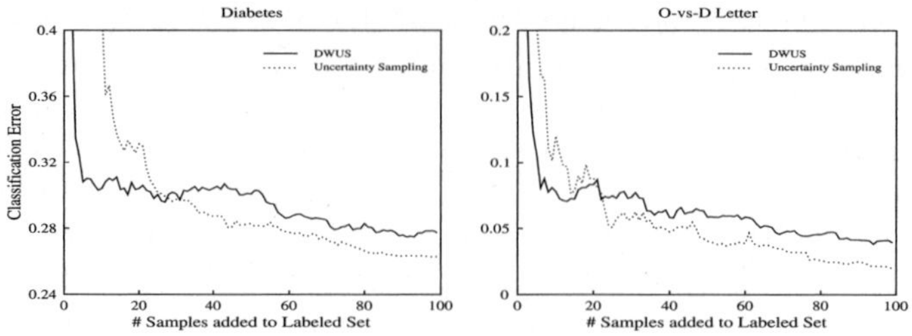

Fig. 1. Comparison of Density Weighted versus (standard) uniformly weighted Uncertainty Sampling on two UCI benchmark datasets

where $E[(\hat{y}_i - y_i)^2 \mid x_i]$ and $p(x_i)$ are the expected error and density of a given data point x_i, respectively. I_u is the index for the unlabeled data. This criterion favors points that have the largest contribution to the current classification error. In contrast, one can use an uncertainty-based selection criterion within the same probabilistic framework as illustrated by the following formula:

$$s = \arg\max_{i \in I_u} E[(\hat{y}_i - y_i)^2 \mid x_i] \quad (2)$$

We refer to the above principle as Uncertainty Sampling for the rest of this paper. Consider Fig. 1, which displays the performance of DWUS and Uncertainty Sampling on two of the datasets that we explore in more detail later. Combining uncertainty with the density of the underlying data is a good strategy to reduce the error quickly. However, after rapid initial gains, DWUS exhibits very slow additional learning while uncertainty sampling continues to exhibit more rapid improvement.[1] A similar behavior is also evident in [8] where their representative sampling method increases accuracy in the initial phase while uncertainty sampling has a slower learning rate, but gradually outperforms their method.

We investigated the Spearman's ranking correlation over candidates to be labeled by density and uncertainty in our scenario, and found that they seldom reinforce each other, but instead they tend to disagree on sample point selection. At early iterations, many points are highly uncertain. Thus, DWUS can pick high density points which are lower down in the uncertainty *ranking* but have a high absolute uncertainty score. Later, points with high absolute uncertainty are no longer in dense regions. As a result, DWUS picks points that have moderate density but low uncertainty because such points are scored highly according to the criterion in Equation 1. Hence, it wastes effort picking instances whose selection does not have a large effect on error rate reduction.

Fortunately, we can do better across the full spectrum of labeled instances by our algorithm DUAL which adopts a dynamically reweighed mixture of density and uncertainty components and achieves performance superior to its competitors over a variety of datasets. In the following section, we review essential parts of DWUS and then describe DUAL.

[1] Although a quick drop in classification error for DWUS is also observed in [9], they did not compare with uncertainty sampling.

3 Density Weighted Uncertainty Sampling (DWUS)

Nguyen and Smeulders [9] assume a clustering structure of the underlying data. $\mathbf{x}$ is the data and $y \in \{+1, 0\}$ is the class label. The cluster label $k \in \{1, 2, .., K\}$ indicates the hidden cluster information for every single data point where K is the number of total clusters. In order to calculate the posterior $P(y \mid x)$, they use the following marginalization:

$$P(y \mid x) = \sum_{k=1}^{K} P(y, k \mid x) = \sum_{k=1}^{K} P(y \mid k, x) P(k \mid x) \tag{3}$$

where $P(y \mid k, x)$ is the probability of the class label y given the cluster k and the data point x, and $P(k \mid x)$ is the probability of the cluster given the data point. But once k is known, y and x are independent since points in one cluster are assumed to share the same label as the cluster; hence knowing the cluster label k is enough to model the class label y. Thus:

$$P(y \mid x) = \sum_{k=1}^{K} P(y, k \mid x) = \sum_{k=1}^{K} P(y \mid k) P(k \mid x) \tag{4}$$

$P(k \mid x)$ is calculated only once unless the data is re-clustered, whereas $P(y \mid k)$ is updated each time a new data point is added to the training set. Before explaining how to estimate these two distributions, we illustrate below how the algorithm works:

1. Cluster the data.
2. Estimate $P(y \mid k)$.
3. Calculate $P(y \mid x)$ (Equation 4).
4. Choose an unlabeled sample based on (Equation 1) and label.
5. Re-cluster if necessary.
6. Repeat steps 2-5 until stop.

We first explain how to induce $P(k \mid x)$ according to [9]. A Gaussian mixture model is used to estimate the data density using the clustering structure such that $p(x)$ is a mixture of K Gaussians with weights $P(k)$. Hence, $p(x) = \sum_{k=1}^{K} p(x \mid k) P(k)$. where $p(x \mid k)$ is a multivariate Gaussian sharing the same variance σ^2 for all clusters k:

$$p(x \mid k) = (2\pi)^{-d/2} \sigma^{-d} \exp\{\frac{-\left\|x - c_k\right\|^2}{2\sigma^2}\} \tag{5}$$

where c_k is the centroid of the k-th cluster which is determined via the K-medoid algorithm [12]. It is similar to the K-means algorithm since they both try to minimize the squared error between the points assigned to a cluster and the cluster centroid. In K-means, the centroid is the average of all points in the cluster, whereas in K-medoid the most centrally located point in the cluster is the centroid. Moreover, K-medoid is more robust to noise or outliers.

Once the cluster representatives are identified, an EM procedure is applied to estimate the cluster prior $P(k)$ using the following two steps:

E-step: *M-step:*

$$P(k \mid x_i) = \frac{P(k)\exp\{\frac{-||x_i - c_k||^2}{2\sigma^2}\}}{\sum_{\acute{k}=1}^{K} P(\acute{k})\exp\{\frac{-||x_i - c_{\acute{k}}||^2}{2\sigma^2}\}} \qquad P(k) = \frac{1}{n}\sum_{i=1}^{n} P(k \mid x_i) \quad (6)$$

The cluster label distribution $P(y \mid k)$ is calculated using the following logistic regression model: $P(y \mid k) = \frac{1}{1+\exp(-y(c_k.\mathbf{a}+b))}$, $\mathbf{a} \in R^d$ and $b \in R$ are logistic regression parameters. c_k is the k-th cluster centroid, so $P(y \mid k)$ models the class distribution for a representative subset of the entire dataset. Points are assigned to a cluster with the probability $P(k \mid x)$ so that their labels will be affected by their cluster membership probabilities (See Equation 4). Hence, a distribution is learned at each cluster and no cluster purity requirement is forced.

The parameters of the logistic regression model are estimated via the following likelihood maximization:

$$L = \sum_{i \in I_l \cup I_u} \ln p(x_i; c_1, ..., c_K, P(1), ..., P(K)) + \sum_{i \in I_l} \ln P(y_i \mid x_i; \mathbf{a}, b) \quad (7)$$

where I_l and I_u are the indices for labeled and unlabeled data, respectively. The parameters of the first summand have already been determined by the K-medoid algorithm and the EM routine in Equation 6. The second summand is used to estimate the parameters $\mathbf{a}$ and b via Equation 4, as follows:

$$L(\mathbf{a}, b) = \frac{\lambda}{2}||\mathbf{a}||^2 - \sum_{i \in I_l} \ln\left\{\sum_{k=1}^{K} P(k \mid x_i) P(y_i \mid k; \mathbf{a}, b)\right\} \quad (8)$$

The regularization parameter λ is given initially independently of the data. Since the problem is convex, it has a unique solution which can be solved via Newton's algorithm. Then we can calculate the probability $P(y_i \mid k; \hat{\mathbf{a}}, \hat{b})$ using the logistic regression model and obtain the class posterior probability $P(y_i \mid x_i; \hat{\mathbf{a}}, \hat{b})$ using Equation 4. The label $\hat{y}_i$ is predicted for each unlabeled point x_i according to Bayes rule. Finally, active point selection is done by Equation 1. The error expectation for a given unlabeled point $E[(\hat{y}_i - y_i)^2 \mid x_i]$ in that equation is:

$$E[(\hat{y}_i - y_i)^2 \mid x_i] = (\hat{y}_i - 1)^2 P(y_i = 1 \mid x_i) + (\hat{y}_i)^2 P(y_i = 0 \mid x_i) \quad (9)$$

Since the probability $P(y_i \mid x_i)$ is unknown, its current approximation $P(y_i \mid x_i; \hat{\mathbf{a}}, \hat{b})$ is used instead. Additionally, data points are re-clustered into smaller clusters as the expected error reduces. The reason is that it is important to make significant changes in the decision boundary during the early iterations of active sampling. Later the classification boundary becomes more stable and thus needs to be finely tuned. Additional details can be found in [9].

4 DUAL Algorithm and Experimental Results

4.1 Description of the DUAL Algorithm

DUAL works as follows: It starts executing DWUS up until it estimates a cross-over point with uncertainty sampling by predicting a low derivative of the expected error, e.g. $\frac{\partial \epsilon(DWUS)}{\partial x_t} \leq \delta$. The derivative estimation need not be exact, requiring only the detection of diminishing returns which we explain soon. Then, it switches to execute a combined strategy of density-based and uncertainty-based sampling. In practice, we do not know the future classification error of DWUS, but we can approximate it by calculating the average expected error of DWUS on the unlabeled data. It will not give us the exact cross-over point, but it will provide a rough estimate of when we should consider switching between methods. The expected error of DWUS on the unlabeled data can be evaluated as follows:

$$\hat{\epsilon}_t(DWUS) = \frac{1}{n_t} \sum_{i \in I_u} E[(\hat{y}_i - y_i)^2 \mid x_i] \tag{10}$$

where $E[(\hat{y}_i - y_i)^2 \mid x_i]$ is calculated as in Equation 9. Moreover, it is re-calculated at each iteration of active sampling. t is the iteration number, and n_t is the number of unlabeled instances at the t-th iteration and I_u is the set of indices of the unlabeled points at time t. By monitoring the average expected error at every single iteration, we can estimate when DWUS' performance starts to saturate, i.e., $\frac{\partial \hat{\epsilon}(DWUS)}{\partial x_t} \leq \delta$. δ is assigned a fixed small value in our evaluations [See Section 4.2 for how it was estimated]. When it is near zero, this is equivalent to detecting when a method is stuck in local minima/plateau in gradient descent methods. In fact, this principle is flexible enough to work with any two active learning methods where one is superior for labeling the initial data and the other is favorable later in the process. It generalizes to N sampling methods by introducing additional estimated switchover points based on estimated derivative of expected error for each additional sampling strategy.

We know that the strength of DWUS comes from the fact that it incorporates the density information into the selection mechanism. However, as the number of iterations increases uncertainty sampling outperforms DWUS and DWUS exhibits diminishing returns. We propose to use a mixture model for active sampling after we estimate the cross-over:

$$x_s^* = \arg\max_{i \in I_u} \pi_1 * E[(\hat{y}_i - y_i)^2 \mid x_i] + (1 - \pi_1) * p(x_i) \tag{11}$$

It is desirable for the above model to minimize the expected future error. If we were to select based on only the uncertainty, then the chosen point would be $x_{US}^* = \arg\max_{i \in I_u} E[(\hat{y}_i - y_i)^2 \mid x_i]$. After labeling x_{US}^*, the expected loss is:

$$f_{US} = \frac{1}{n} \sum_j E_{L+\{x_{US}^*, y\}}[(\hat{y}_j - y_j)^2 \mid x_j] \tag{12}$$

The subscript $L+\{x^*_{US}, y\}$ indicates that the expectation is calculated from the model trained on the data $L+\{x^*_{US}, y\}$. Assume f_{US}=0, then we can achieve the minimum expected loss by forcing $\pi_1 = 1$; hence $x^*_s = x^*_{US}$. The appropriate weight in this scenario is inversely related with the expected error of uncertainty sampling. Thus, we can replace the weights by $\pi_1 = 1 - f_{US}$, and $1 - \pi_1 = f_{US}$, and obtain the following model:

$$x^*_s = \arg\max_{i \in I_u} (1 - f_{US}) * E[(\hat{y}_i - y_i)^2 \mid x_i] + f_{US} * p(x_i) \tag{13}$$

Achieving the minimum expected loss is guaranteed only for the extreme case where the expected error, f_{US}, of uncertainty sampling is equal to 0. However, correlating the weight of uncertainty sampling with its generalization performance increases the odds of selecting a better candidate after the cross-over.

In the real world, we do not know the true value of f_{US}. So we need to approximate it. After estimating the cross-over, we are interested in giving higher priority to uncertainty, reflecting how well uncertainty sampling would perform on the unlabeled set. Therefore, we approximate f_{US} as $\hat{\epsilon}(US)$, the average expected error of uncertainty sampling on the unlabeled portion of the data. This leads us to the following selection criterion for DUAL:

$$x^*_s = \arg\max_{i \in I_u} (1 - \hat{\epsilon}(US)) * E[(\hat{y}_i - y_i)^2 \mid x_i] + \hat{\epsilon}(US) * p(x_i) \tag{14}$$

$\hat{\epsilon}(US)$ is updated at every iteration t after the cross-over. Its calculation is exactly the same as in Equation 10. However, the data to sample from is restricted to the already labeled examples by active selection. We construct a set with the actively sampled examples by DWUS until the cross-over, and call it set A. Uncertainty sampling is allowed to choose the most uncertain data point from only among elements in set A by estimating the posterior $P(y_i \mid x_i; \hat{\mathbf{a}}, \hat{b})$ over the initially labeled data. The chosen point is added to to the initial labeled set for uncertainty sampling and removed from set A. The average expected error of uncertainty sampling is calculated on the remaining unlabeled data. Then, DUAL selects the next data point to label via the criterion in Equation 14. This labeled point is also added to set A. Hence, set A is dynamically updated at each iteration with the actively sampled points. Consequently, in order to calculate the expected error of uncertainty sampling the algorithm never requests the label of a point that has not already been sampled during the active learning process. Such a restriction will prevent an exact estimate of the expected error. But, it is a reasonable alternative, and introduces no additional cost of labeling. The pseudo-code for the DUAL algorithm is given as *The Dual Algorithm*.

The DUAL Algorithm

```
program DUAL(Labeled data L, Unlabeled data U, max number of
iterations T, and δ.)
begin
  Set the iteration counter t to 0.
  while(not switching point) do
```

```
    Run DWUS algorithm and compute ∂ε̂(DWUS)/∂x_t.
    if(∂ε̂(DWUS)/∂x_t > δ)
      Choose the point to label:
      x*_s = arg max_{i∈I_u} E[(ŷ_i − y_i)^2 | x_i]p(x_i)
      t=t+1 (Increment counter t)
    else Hit the switching point.
  while(t < T)
      Compute E[(ŷ − y)^2|x], p(x) via DWUS, and ε̂_t(US) via
      uncertainty sampling.
      Choose the point according to:
      x*_s = arg max_{i∈I_u} (1 − ε̂_t(US)) * E[(ŷ_i − y_i)^2 | x_i] + ε̂_t(US) * p(x_i)
      t=t+1
end.
```

4.2 Experimental Setup

To evaluate the performance of DUAL, we ran experiments on UCI benchmarks: diabetes, splice, image segment, and letter recognition [18]. Some of these problems are not binary tasks so we used the random partitioning into two classes as described by [13]. For the letter recognition problem, we picked three pairs of letters (M-vs-N, O-vs-D, V-vs-Y) that are most likely to be confused with each other. Thus, we examine six binary discrimination tasks. For each dataset, the initial labeled set is 0.4% of the entire data and contains an equal number of positive and negative instances. For clustering, we followed the same procedure used by [9] where the initial number of clusters is 20 and clusters are split until they reach a desired volume. The values of the parameters are given in Table 1 along with the basic characteristics of the datasets. These parameters and the δ parameter used for switching criteria were estimated on other data sets and held constant throughout our experiments, in order to avoid over-tuning. We compared the performance of DUAL with that of DWUS, uncertainty sampling, representative sampling[2] [8], density-based sampling and the COMB method of [10]. Density-based sampling adopts the same probabilistic framework as DWUS but uses only the density information for active data selection: $x_s^* = \arg\max_{i \in I_u} p(x_i)$. COMB uses an ensemble of uncertainty sampling, sampling method of [16], and a distance-based strategy choosing the unlabeled instance that is farthest from the current labeled set. COMB uses SVM with Gaussian kernel for all three strategies. For further implementation details on COMB, see [10].

The performance of each algorithm was averaged over 4 runs. At each run, a different initial training set was chosen randomly. At each iteration of each algorithm, the active learner selected a sample from the unlabeled pool to be labeled. After it has been added to the training set, the classifier is re-trained and tested on the remaining unlabeled data and the classification error is reported. We also

[2] We used k=10 for k-means clustering as it produced better performance in [8], and selected the centroid of the largest cluster in the linear SVM margin.

Table 1. Characteristics of the Datasets, Values of the Parameters and p-value for significance tests after 40 iterations

Dataset	Total Size	+/- Ratio	dims(d)	sigma(σ)	lambda(λ)	DUAL>DWUS
Diabetes	768	0.536	8	0.5	0.1	$p < 0.0001$
Splice	3175	0.926	60	3	5	$p < 0.0001$
Image	2310	1.33	18	0.5	0.1	$p < 0.0001$
M-vs-N	1575	1.011	16	0.1	0.1	$p < 0.0001$
O-vs-D	1558	0.935	16	0.1	0.1	$p < 0.0001$
V-vs-Y	1550	0.972	16	0.1	0.1	$p < 0.0001$

conducted significance tests between DUAL and DWUS to report whether they perform significantly different. In order to determine whether two active learning systems differ statistically significantly, it is common to compare the difference in their errors averaged over a range of iterations [14,20]. Comparing performance over all 100 iterations would suppress detection of statistical differences since DUAL executes DWUS until cross-over. We conducted the comparison when they start to differ, which is on average after 40 iterations; we compute the two-sided paired t-tests by averaging from the 40th to 100th iteration. Table 1 shows that DUAL statistically outperforms DWUS in that range. For the remaining comparisons, we compute 2-sided paired t-tests over the full operating range since we want to know if DUAL is superior to the other methods more generally and DUAL does not execute these other methods at any iteration.

5 Observations and Conclusion

Figure 2 presents the improvement in error reduction using DUAL over the other methods. We only display results on 4 datasets due to space limitations. For the results on all datasets see `www.cs.cmu.edu/~pinard/DualResults`. DUAL outperforms DWUS and representative sampling both with $p < 0.0001$ significance. DUAL outperforms COMB with $p < 0.0001$ significance on 4 out of 6 datasets, and with $p < 0.05$ on Image and M-vs-N data sets. We also calculate the error reduction of DUAL compared to the strong baseline DWUS. For instance, at the point in each graph after 3/4 of the sampling iterations after cross-over occurs, we observe 40% relative error reduction on O-vs-D data, 30% on Image, 50% on M-vs-N, 27% on V-vs-Y, 10% on Splice, and 6% on Diabetes dataset. These results are significant both statistically and also with respect to the magnitude reduction in relative residual error. DUAL is superior to Uncertainty sampling ($p < 0.001$) on 5 out of 6 datasets. We see on the V-vs-Y data that the cross-over between DWUS and uncertainty sampling occurs at a very early stage, but the current estimate of the expected error of DWUS to switch selection criteria is not accurate at the very early points in that dataset. Clearly, DUAL might have benefited from changing its selection criterion at an earlier iteration.

As part of a failure analysis and in order to test this hypothesis, we conducted another set of experiments where we simulated a better relative error estimator

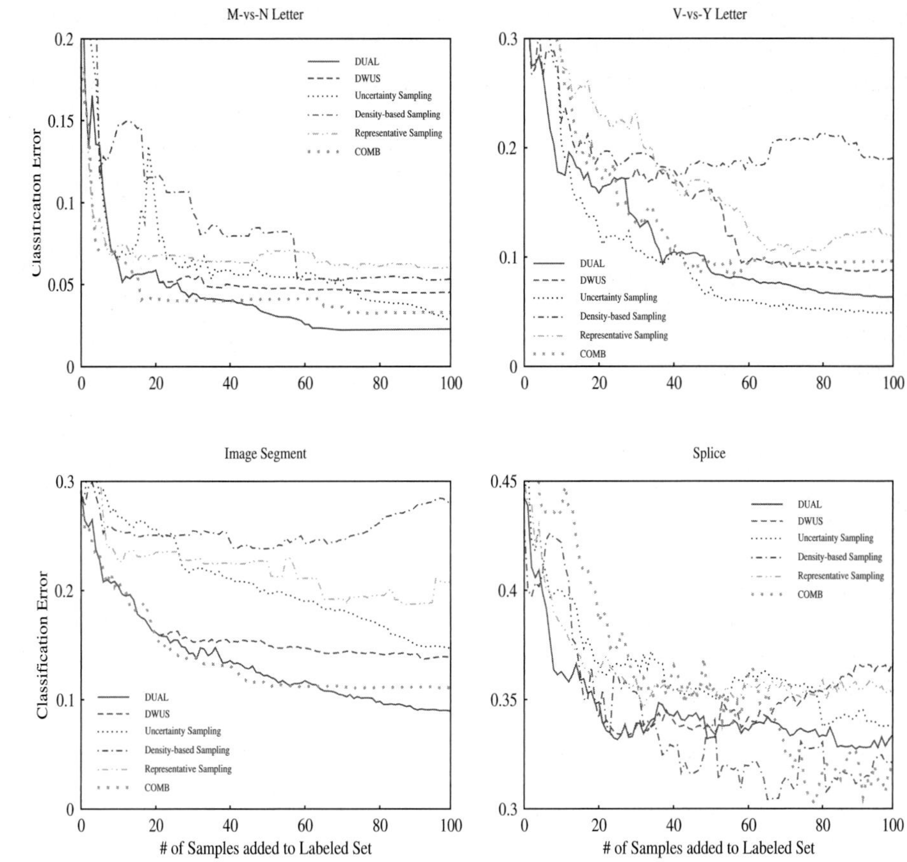

Fig. 2. Results on 4 different UCI benchmark datasets

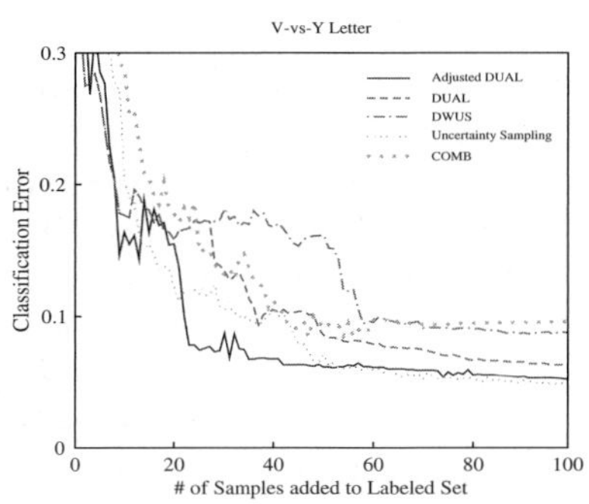

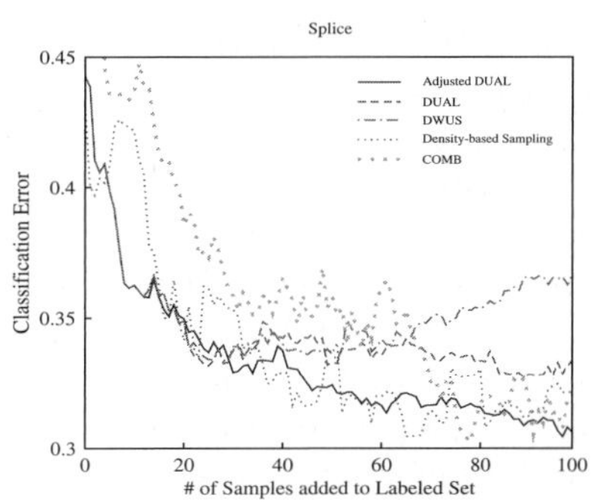

Fig. 3. Results after adjusting the switching point for DUAL on the V-vs-Y Letter data

Fig. 4. Results when DUAL is adjusted using Equation 15 on the splice data for strategy switching. Fig. 3 demonstrates that DUAL outperforms all other methods when the true cross-over point is identified, indicating that better error estimation is a profitable area of research. In fact, one hypothesized solution is to switch when $P(error(M_2) \mid X) < P(error(M_1) \mid X) + \epsilon$, which considers the probability that over future selected instances method 2, M_2, will have less error than method 1, M_1. We plan to study more robust switching criteria.

DUAL outperforms Density-based sampling ($p < 0.0001$) on all but splice data. Density-based sampling performs worst for almost 40 iterations but then beats all of the others thereafter, totally breaking the pattern observed in the other datasets. Currently, DUAL only estimates how likely the uncertainty score is to lead to improvement, but the density-based method may also be likely to improve. One strategy is to calculate the expected error $\hat{\epsilon}(DS)$ of density-based sampling and modify Equation 14 to obtain the following:

$$x_s^* = \arg\max_{i \in I_u} \{\hat{\epsilon}(DS) * E[(\hat{y}_i - y_i)^2 \mid x_i] + (1 - \hat{\epsilon}(DS)) * p(x_i)\} \tag{15}$$

Fig. 4 presents the result after the modification in Equation 15. The adjustment helps DUAL make a significant improvement on the error reduction. Moreover, it consistently decreases the error as more data is labeled, hence its error reduction curve is smooth as opposed to the higher variance of density-based sampling. This suggests that pure density-based sampling is inconsistent in reducing error since it only considers the underlying data distribution regardless of the current model. Thus, we argue that DUAL may be more reliable than individual scoring based on density due to its combination formula that adaptively establishes balance between two selection criteria. Even though a strategy such as uncertainty or density based sampling performs well individually, Figures 2, 3 and 4 illustrate that it is more advantageous to use their combination.

To conclude, we presented DUAL which robustly combines uncertainty and density information. Empirical evaluation shows that, in general, this approach leads to more effective sampling than the other strategies. Xu et al. [8] also propose a hybrid approach to combine representative sampling and uncertainty sampling. Their method, however, only applies to SVMs and only tracks the better performing strategy rather than outperforming both individual strategies. Baram et al. also reports comparable performance for COMB to the best individual sampling strategy, but it is sometimes marginally better, and sometimes marginally worse and hence is not consistently the best performer. Our performance, on the contrary, exceeds that of the individually best sampling strategy in most cases by statistically significant margins. Hence, DUAL clearly goes beyond COMB in terms of lower classification error and faster convergence. Furthermore, our framework is general enough to fuse active learning methods that exhibit differentiable performance on the whole operating range. It can also be easily generalized to multi-class problems: one can estimate the error reduction globally or per-class using class-weighted or instance-weighted average, and then use the same cross-over criterion. While we use logistic regression, any probabilistic classifier can be adapted for use in DUAL. Our main contributions are in estimating the error of one method using the labeled data selected by another, and robustly integrating their outputs when one method is dominant (Equation 14 vs. Equation 15). Our future plan is to generalize DUAL to using a relative success weight, and to extend this work to ensemble methods that involve more than two strategies, maximizing ensemble diversity [15,14,10]. Moreover, we plan to investigate better methods for estimating the cross-over, such as estimating a smoothed version of $\frac{\partial \hat{\epsilon}}{\partial x_t}$ rather than a local-only version.

References

1. Seung, H.S., Opper, M., Sompolinsky, H.: Query by committee. In: Proceedings of the Fifth Annual ACM Workshop on Computational Learning Theory, pp. 287–294. ACM Press, New York (1992)
2. Freund, Y., Seung, H., Shamir, E., Tishby, N.: Selective sampling using the Query By Committee algorithm. Machine Learning Journal 28, 133–168 (1997)
3. Lewis, D., Gale, W.: A sequential algorithm for training text classifiers. In: SIGIR '94, pp. 3–12 (1994)
4. Tong, S., Koller, D.: Support vector machine active learning with applications to text classification. In: ICML '00, pp. 999–1006 (2000)
5. Mitchell, T.M.: Generalization as search. Artificial Intelligence Journal 18 (1982)
6. McCallum, A., Nigam, K.: Employing EM and pool-based active learning for text classification. In: ICML '98, pp. 359–367 (1998)
7. Cohn, D.A., Ghahramani, Z., Jordan, M.I.: Active learning with statistical models. Journal of Artificial Intelligence Research 4, 129–145 (1996)
8. Xu, Z., Yu, K., Tresp, V., Xu, X., Wang, J.: Representative sampling for text classification using support vector machines. In: Sebastiani, F. (ed.) ECIR 2003. LNCS, vol. 2633, Springer, Heidelberg (2003)
9. Nguyen, H.T., Smeulders, A.: Active learning with pre-clustering. In: ICML '04, pp. 623–630 (2004)
10. Baram, Y., El-Yaniv, R., Luz, K.: Online choice of active learning algorithms. In: ICML '03, pp. 19–26 (2003)
11. Auer, P., Cesa-Bianchi, N., Freund, Y., Schapire, R.E.: The nonstochastic multiarmed bandit problem. SIAM Journal on Computing 32(1), 48–77 (2002)
12. Struyf, A., Hubert, M., Rousseeuw, P.: Integrating robust clustering techniques in s-plus. Computational Statistics and Data Analysis 26, 17–37 (1997)
13. Rätsch, G., Onoda, T., Muller, K.R.: Soft margins for AdaBoost. Machine Learning Journal 42(3), 287–320 (2001)
14. Melville, P., Mooney, R.J.: Diverse ensembles for active learning. In: ICML '04, pp. 584–591 (2004)
15. Melville, P., Mooney, R.J.: Constructing diverse classifier ensembles using artificial training examples. In: IJCAI '03, pp. 505–510 (2003)
16. Roy, N., McCallum, A.: Toward optimal active learning through sampling estimation of error reduction. In: ICML '01, pp. 441–448 (2001)
17. Schohn, G., Cohn, D.: Less is more: Active Learning with support vector machines. In: ICML '00, pp. 839–846 (2000)
18. Newman, D.J., Hettich, S., Blake, C.L., Merz, C.J.: UCI Repository of machine learning databases (1998)
19. Saar-Tsechansky, M., Provost, F.: Active learning for class probability estimation and ranking. In: IJCAI '01, pp. 911–920 (2001)
20. Guo, Y., Greiner, R.: Optimistic Active Learning using Mutual Information. In: IJCAI '07, pp. 823–829 (2007)

Decision Tree Instability and Active Learning

Kenneth Dwyer and Robert Holte

Department of Computing Science, University of Alberta,
Edmonton AB, Canada
{dwyer,holte}@cs.ualberta.ca

Abstract. Decision tree learning algorithms produce accurate models that can be interpreted by domain experts. However, these algorithms are known to be unstable – they can produce drastically different hypotheses from training sets that differ just slightly. This instability undermines the objective of extracting knowledge from the trees. In this paper, we study the instability of the C4.5 decision tree learner in the context of active learning. We introduce a new measure of decision tree stability, and define three aspects of active learning stability. Several existing active learning methods that use C4.5 as a component are compared empirically; it is determined that query-by-bagging yields trees that are more stable and accurate than those produced by competing methods. Also, an alternative splitting criterion, DKM, is found to improve the stability and accuracy of C4.5 in the active learning setting.

Keywords: Decision tree learning, evaluation of learning methods, active learning, ensemble methods.

1 Introduction

Decision tree learners constitute one of the most well studied classes of machine learning algorithms. The relative ease with which a decision tree classifier can be interpreted is one of its most attractive qualities. However, decision tree learners are known to be highly unstable procedures – they can produce dramatically different classifiers from training sets that differ just slightly [1,2]. This instability undermines the objective of extracting knowledge from decision trees. Turney [2] describes a situation in which decision trees were used by engineers to help them understand the sources of low yield in a manufacturing process: "The engineers frequently have good reasons for believing that the causes of low yield are relatively constant over time. Therefore the engineers are disturbed when different batches of data from the same process result in radically different decision trees. The engineers lose confidence in the decision trees, even when we can demonstrate that the trees have high predictive accuracy."

We have studied the instability of the C4.5 decision tree learner [3] in the context of both passive and active learning [4]. In this paper, we present the results of the active learning study. Instability is a concern in active learning because the decision tree may change substantially whenever new examples are labelled and added to the training set.

J.N. Kok et al. (Eds.): ECML 2007, LNAI 4701, pp. 128–139, 2007.

This paper asks an important new question: How stable are the decision trees produced by some well-known active learning methods? Experiments are conducted that compare the performance of several active learning methods, which use C4.5 as a component learner, on a collection of benchmark datasets. It is determined that the query-by-bagging method [5] is more stable *and* more accurate than its competitors. This is an interesting result because no previous active learning study has trained a single decision tree on examples selected by a committee of trees. Query-by-bagging tends to yield larger trees than do the other methods; yet, we provide evidence that these increases in size do not usually entail a loss of interpretability. Our second contribution is a set of new definitions of "stability," which fill an important gap between the extremities represented by existing measures. Finally, the DKM splitting criterion [6,7] is shown to improve the stability and accuracy of C4.5 in the active learning setting.

2 Decision Tree Instability

A learning algorithm is said to be *unstable* if it is sensitive to small changes in the training data. When presented with training sets that differ by some small amount, an unstable learner may produce substantially different classifiers. On the other hand, stable learning algorithms, such as nearest neighbour, are less sensitive in this regard [8]. As a concrete example of instability, consider the decision trees shown in Fig. 1. These two trees were grown and pruned by C4.5 using data from the lymphography dataset, which was obtained from the UCI repository [9]. For clarity, each attribute is denoted by a single letter,[1] and the class labels are 'malign lymph' (+) and 'metastases' (−). The data was converted to a two-class problem by deleting the examples belonging to the 'normal find' and 'fibrosis' classes, which account for 6 of the 148 instances. Figure 1(a) displays a tree, T_{106}, that was induced from a random sample consisting of 106 (roughly 75%) of the available examples. A single instance, randomly chosen from the unused examples, was appended to this training set, from which C4.5 produced the tree T_{107} that is shown in Fig. 1(b). The two trees differ considerably in size, as T_{107} contains nearly double the number of decision nodes appearing in T_{106}. Moreover, there is just one path from the root to a leaf node along which both trees perform the same set of tests when classifying an example; this is the path that consists of the tests {A≤3=T, B=B2, D=D4} and predicts the negative class. In all other cases, the trees apply different reasoning when making predictions. The fact that these changes were caused by the addition of one training example illustrates the instability of the C4.5 algorithm.

3 Quantifying Stability

In this paper, two types of stability are examined: *semantic* and *structural* stability. A learner that is semantically stable will, when presented with similar

[1] The values of each discrete attribute are enumerated, whereas the possible outcomes for a test on a continuous attribute are T (true) and F (false).

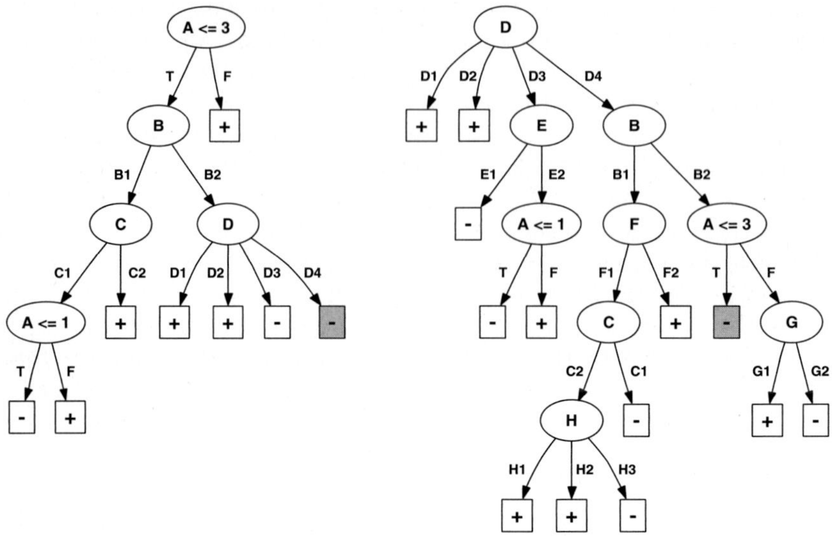

(a) Tree grown from 106 examples (b) Tree grown from 107 examples

Fig. 1. Decision trees grown from two subsets of the lymphography dataset that differ in a single training example. The shaded leaf in each tree highlights the only case in which both trees perform the same set of tests when predicting the class label.

data samples, tend to produce hypotheses that make similar predictions. For a learner to be structurally stable, a stronger condition must be satisfied, namely, the hypotheses that it creates from closely related data sets must be syntactically similar. Thus, structural stability is a sufficient condition for semantic stability, but the converse is not true. It is also possible to formulate a measure of stability that is not purely semantic or purely structural, but which considers some characteristics of a classifier's structure.

To measure semantic stability, we adopt a learner-independent measure called *agreement* [2]. Given two training sets, the learner induces a pair of hypotheses; the agreement is defined as the probability that a randomly chosen unlabelled example is assigned to the same class by both models. In practice, agreement is estimated by having the models classify a randomly selected set of examples.

There is no consensus on how to quantify the structural stability of decision trees. Two existing measures, called *Discrepant* [10] and *Common* [11], report minimal stability when two trees differ at the root node. However, it is possible for trees to differ at the root, and yet be quite similar or even identical elsewhere; neither of these metrics are sensitive to such an occurrence. We propose a novel measure, called *region stability*, that we argue is more appropriate for comparing the structure of decision trees.

Each leaf in a decision tree is a decision region whose boundaries are defined by the unordered set of nodes and branches that make up the path from the root to the leaf. The region stability measure compares the decision regions in one tree with those of another. Specifically, it estimates the probability that two trees classify a randomly selected example in "equivalent" decision regions. Two decision regions are considered to be equivalent if they perform the same set of tests and predict the same class label.

Region stability is estimated by having the two trees classify a randomly chosen set of unlabelled examples. As an illustration, suppose that the region stability score for the trees in Fig. 1 is computed using 100 examples, 5 of which are classified in the shaded leaf in each tree. Since this is the only decision region that the trees have in common (all other pairs of regions differ in at least one test), the region stability score is 0.05. The effect of using unlabelled examples in the calculation is that more weight is assigned to a region that classifies a larger portion of these examples in the event that their distribution is non-uniform.

When comparing two decision regions that test a particular continuous attribute, the thresholds (or cut-points) are checked for equality. However, C4.5 only places a threshold at a value that exists in the training data, and so it can be impossible for identical thresholds to appear in two trees that are induced from slightly different samples. In some learning tasks, small discrepancies of this sort may be considered superficial. For this reason, the region stability measure accepts a parameter $\epsilon \in [0, 100]\%$ that specifies a permitted margin of error between thresholds defined on a continuous attribute a. Let $\min(a)$ and $\max(a)$ be the minimum and maximum values for a in the entire dataset. Two thresholds defined on a are considered equal if they are within $\epsilon \cdot [\max(a) - \min(a)]/100$ units of one another. Note that the path from the root to a leaf may contain multiple tests on the same continuous attribute that specify distinct thresholds. The leftmost path in Fig. 1(a), for example, contains the tests A$\leq$3 and A$\leq$1. Since the first of these tests is redundant given the second, only the test A$\leq$1 is considered when comparing this decision region to another.

4 Instability in Active Learning

In active learning, the learner has the ability to choose points from the instance space on which to train a classifier. Although the ability of active learning methods to make more efficient use of unlabelled data has been well documented [5,12,13,14], little attention has been given to the stability of these techniques. This study focuses on pool-based active learning, or *selective sampling*, in which the learner draws a batch of m examples from a pool of unlabelled examples U on each iteration. The selective sampling methods tested in this study all make use of a base learning algorithm, which in this case is C4.5.

The stability of a sampling method is measured with respect to the decision trees that are induced by C4.5 from the training examples chosen by that method. We propose three different aspects of stability in active learning, which are named *PrevStab*, *FinalStab*, and *RunStab*. Each of these is quantified by applying a distance measure Φ (e.g. region stability or agreement) to specific pairs of trees. Let T_i denote the tree induced from the labelled data at iteration i of selective sampling. PrevStab quantifies the similarity of trees that are induced on consecutive iterations. For $i > 1$, trees from iterations i and $i-1$ are compared; that is, the score $\Phi(T_i, T_{i-1})$ is computed. Calculating this score for all consecutive pairs of trees induced during active learning reveals the amount of change that occurs as a result of adding each new batch of examples to the training set. FinalStab compares the tree induced at each iteration to the tree that is induced on the final iteration of selective sampling. At iteration i of n, for $i < n$, FinalStab computes $\Phi(T_i, T_n)$; thus, it evaluates the manner in which the sequence of trees progresses toward the final tree that is produced. Finally, RunStab quantifies stability across different selective sampling "runs," in which distinct initial training sets are used. This score may be interpreted as the degree to which an active learning method yields similar trees from different initial training data. Given r runs of selective sampling, the RunStab score at iteration i is obtained by computing $\Phi(T_i^j, T_i^k)$ for each pair of runs $\{j, k\} \leq r, j \neq k$, and then taking the average of these values. Here, T_i^p is the set of labelled examples at iteration i when using the pth initial training set.

When assessing the stability of a selective sampling procedure, some properties of the stability scores are desirable. For example, the FinalStab scores should increase as more examples are labelled and added to the training set, reaching reasonably high levels in the later stages of active learning. An increasing sequence of FinalStab scores implies that the learner produces decision trees that have progressively more structure in common with the final tree. PrevStab scores are expected to be low during the initial iterations, as the selective sampling method explores the instance space. Later, when the sampling method presumably begins refining the hypothesis, the PrevStab scores should increase and maintain a fairly high level. Last of all, high RunStab scores are desirable, especially in the late stages of selective sampling. If this is not the case, then the sampling method is sensitive to the particular examples that form the initial training set, and the trees it produces during different runs are dissimilar.

5 Experiments

5.1 Experimental Procedure

Experiments were carried out using four selective sampling methods: uncertainty sampling [13], query-by-bagging and query-by-boosting [5], and bootstrap-LV [14]. These are all uncertainty-based approaches, which heuristically select examples based on how confidently their true labels can be predicted. The latter three methods each form a committee of decision trees (a committee size of 10 was used here), and request the labels of the examples for which the committee "vote" is most evenly split. It is worth noting, however, that active learners exist which optimize other criteria, such as the expected future error [15]. Random sampling was also included in these experiments as a basis for comparison.

The sampling methods used C4.5 Release 8 [3] as a base learner. Experiments were duplicated using C4.5's default gain ratio splitting criterion (hereafter called entropy) and the DKM criterion [6,7] to grow trees. Each of these splitting criteria are defined by an impurity function $f(a, b)$, which is $a\log_2(a) + b\log_2(b)$

for entropy and $\sqrt{2ab}$ for DKM. Here, a and b represent the probabilities of each class within a given subset of examples formed by the split. Additionally, C4.5 Release 8 applies a penalty term to splits on continuous attributes that is specifically designed for entropy; our modification for DKM is described in [4].

Sixteen datasets were obtained from the UCI repository that each contained at least 500 training examples; this ensured that the unlabelled pool was reasonably large. Since DKM only handles two-class problems, multi-class datasets were converted to two-class ones by designating a single class as the target concept, and aggregating the remaining classes into the class "other." The target class used for each dataset is shown in Table 1. Furthermore, the region stability measure requires that each example be classified by exactly one leaf. Thus, attributes with an unknown value rate greater than 10 percent were removed, and any remaining instances that still contained missing values were deleted. The modified datasets are available online at `http://www.cs.ualberta.ca/~dwyer/ecml2007/`.

For each dataset, one third of the data from each class was randomly set aside for evaluation; these examples were used to measure the stability and error rate of the induced classifiers. Of the remaining instances, 15 percent were randomly chosen to form the initial training set, while the others constituted the pool of unlabelled examples. The batch size m was set to be 2 percent of the number of examples in a given dataset, to a minimum of 10 and a maximum of 50, and active learning ceased once two-thirds of the pool examples had been labelled. For a given dataset, 25 runs were performed, using different initial training sets. The same evaluation set was used during each run, in order to remove a source of variation when comparing stability and error rate across runs. Finally, the region stability scores were computed using ϵ values of 0, 5, and 10 percent.

5.2 Evaluation

In order to determine whether one selective sampling method was superior to another on a given dataset, a summary statistic was devised to convert each sequence of scores into a single value. Our summary statistic is a weighted average that assigns greater weight to later iterations. It was argued in Sect. 4 that structural stability is most desirable in the later stages of active learning; ideally, the learner will have a reasonable grasp of the target concept at this point, and new examples will serve mainly to refine the model, rather than to alter it significantly. A high level of stability during early iterations of active learning is of little value if stability deteriorates in later rounds.

After completing 25 runs of n iterations on a given dataset, the mean score for a statistic was calculated on each iteration. A weighted average was then computed as $\frac{1}{n}\sum_{i=1}^{n} w_i \cdot s_i$, where s_i is the mean score on iteration i; the weights w_i increased linearly as a function of i, according to the equation $w_i = \frac{2i}{n(n+1)}$. Semantic and structural stability were measured by calculating FinalStab, PrevStab, and RunStab using Turney's agreement and the region stability measure. The learning curve for error rate was summarized using the same weighted averaging scheme as for stability, under the assumption that a lower error rate is also most desirable in the later stages of active learning.

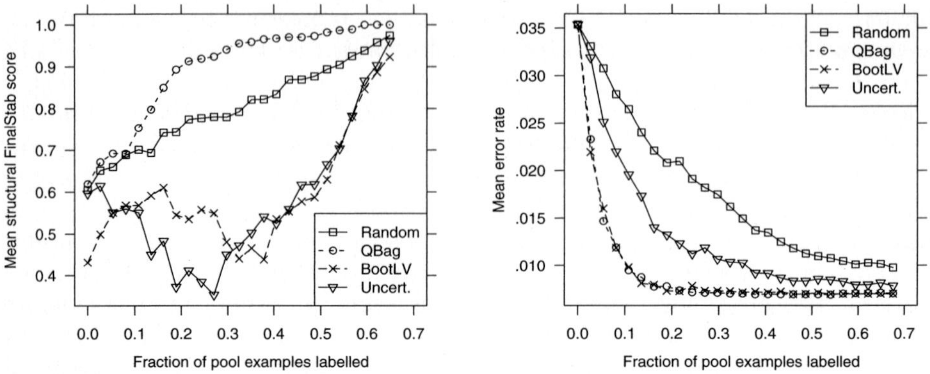

(a) Structural FinalStab ($\epsilon = 0$) (b) Error rate

Fig. 2. Plots of two statistics for the kr-vs-kp dataset when using DKM. QBag is the most stable and the most accurate sampling method in this case. In all experiments, learning ceased when 2/3 of the instances in the pool had been labelled.

To exemplify how the weighted averaging scheme characterizes the scores that are produced by the selective sampling procedures, consider Fig. 2(a). Here, the structural FinalStab scores for 4 of the 5 sampling methods on the kr-vs-kp dataset are plotted as a function of the training set size. Query-by-bagging (QBag) was clearly the most stable method on this dataset, with a weighted score of .953, while random sampling (Random) placed second, at .858. Bootstrap-LV (BootLV) and uncertainty sampling (Uncert), were more closely matched. Although Uncert was marginally more stable than BootLV during the final iterations, the former's instability between $x = .13$ and $x = .27$ dropped its weighted score (.638) below that of BootLV (.644).

In order to assess the statistical significance of the experimental results, the following methodology was applied [16]. The null hypothesis is that all the sampling methods are equivalent. For each dataset, ranks were assigned to the methods based on their weighted scores. Next, the Friedman test[2] was applied to each method's average rank, and the critical value was computed using the F_F statistic. If the null hypothesis could be rejected based on this value at a chosen significance level α, the Nemenyi test was used to determine whether significant differences existed between any given pair of sampling methods.

To illustrate this process, consider the weighted error rates displayed in Table 1. For each dataset, ranks (shown in parentheses) are assigned in order of increasing error rate, with averages used in the event of a tie. With an average rank of 4.375 over all datasets, Random is the worst-ranking method, while QBag ranks the best, on average (1.625). At $\alpha = .05$, the null hypothesis is rejected based on the Friedman test. The critical difference is 1.527, and so differences between average ranks of at least this amount are statistically significant. Thus, QBag, QBoost, and BootLV are each significantly more accurate than Random;

[2] The tests of statistical significance that were applied are described in [16].

Table 1. Weighted average error rates when using the DKM splitting criterion, (ranks in parentheses). For each dataset, the lowest observed error rate is bolded.

Dataset (target class)	Random (R)	QBag (G)	QBoost (T)	BootLV (L)	Uncert (U)
anneal (not-3)	.144 (4)	**.121** (1)	.135 (3)	.125 (2)	.150 (5)
australian (+)	**.129** (1.5)	**.129** (1.5)	.131 (5)	.130 (3.5)	.130 (3.5)
car (acceptable)	.090 (5)	**.077** (1)	.082 (4)	.078 (2)	.081 (3)
german (bad)	.293 (5)	**.274** (1)	.285 (2)	.290 (4)	.289 (3)
hypothyroid (+)	.006 (5)	**.002** (2)	**.002** (2)	**.002** (2)	.004 (4)
kr-vs-kp (no-win)	.014 (5)	**.007** (1.5)	.008 (3)	**.007** (1.5)	.010 (4)
letter (k)	.015 (5)	**.011** (2)	**.011** (2)	**.011** (2)	.013 (4)
nursery (priority)	.056 (5)	**.038** (1.5)	.039 (3)	**.038** (1.5)	.044 (4)
pendigits (9)	.016 (5)	**.010** (1.5)	**.010** (1.5)	.012 (4)	.011 (3)
pima-indians (+)	.286 (5)	.283 (2)	**.280** (1)	.284 (3)	.285 (4)
segment (cement)	.020 (5)	**.011** (1)	.012 (2.5)	.012 (2.5)	.019 (4)
tic-tac-toe (−)	.217 (5)	**.197** (1)	.201 (2)	.207 (3)	.211 (4)
vehicle (opel)	**.227** (1)	.231 (5)	.229 (3.5)	.228 (2)	.229 (3.5)
vowel (hud)	.056 (5)	**.033** (1)	.036 (2)	.037 (3)	.049 (4)
wdbc (malignant)	.073 (4)	.068 (2)	**.067** (1)	.069 (3)	.076 (5)
yeast (nuclear)	.256 (4.5)	**.250** (1)	.253 (2.5)	.256 (4.5)	.253 (2.5)
Avg. rank	(4.375)	(1.625) **R,U**	(2.500) **R**	(2.719) **R**	(3.781)

also, QBag is superior to Uncert. A letter beside the average rank of a sampling method S indicates that S is significantly better than the method corresponding to that letter. For example, the R and U in the QBag column of Table 1 imply that QBag is significantly more accurate than Random and Uncert, respectively.

5.3 Experimental Results

Due to space limitations, only the average ranks are presented for each statistic; these are displayed in Table 2. Although the average ranks are sufficient for demonstrating our findings, detailed results may be viewed at `http://www.cs.ualberta.ca/~dwyer/ecml2007/`. In Table 2, the level of significance that was tested for each statistic is shown in the "α" column.

Error Rate. The committee-based methods achieved significantly lower error rates than did Random, independent of the splitting criterion employed. Uncert was also significantly less accurate than QBag.

Overall, the results support the findings of previous active learning studies that involved these sampling methods, in that Random was certainly the inferior approach, and committee-based methods usually produced lower error rates than Uncert [5,14]. However, there is a subtle, yet important factor distinguishing our experiments from existing research involving active learning with decision trees. The committee-based results reported in our experiments represent the performance of a single C4.5 decision tree that is trained on examples selected by a committee of trees. By contrast, in the original experiments involving QBag,

Table 2. Average ranks for the sampling methods on each statistic. The top half of the table diplays the results for the entropy criterion; bottom half: DKM criterion.

	Statistic	ϵ	α	**Random (R)**	**QBag (G)**	**QBoost (T)**	**BootLV (L)**	**Uncert (U)**
Entropy criterion	Error Rate	–	.05	4.406	2.000 **R,U**	2.188 **R**	2.719 **R**	3.688
	Tree Size	–	.01	1.062 **G,T,U**	4.062	3.938	2.500	3.250
	Seman. FinalStab	–	.05	4.281	1.969 **R**	3.000	3.094	2.656 **R**
	Seman. PrevStab	–	.05	4.000	2.062 **R**	3.531	3.094	2.312 **R**
	Seman. RunStab	–	.01	4.625	1.344 **R,U**	2.625 **R**	2.656 **R**	3.750
	Struct. FinalStab	0		3.562	2.875	2.875	3.000	2.688
	Struct. FinalStab	5	.10	3.375	3.031	2.875	2.812	2.906
	Struct. FinalStab	10		3.344	3.000	2.938	2.750	2.969
	Struct. PrevStab	0		3.312	2.719	3.406	3.062	2.500
	Struct. PrevStab	5	.10	3.188	2.812	3.469	2.969	2.562
	Struct. PrevStab	10		3.062	2.812	3.594	2.969	2.562
	Struct. RunStab	0		4.469	1.750 **R,U**	2.000 **R,U**	2.656	4.125
	Struct. RunStab	5	.01	4.188	1.656 **R,U**	2.188 **R,U**	2.594	4.375
	Struct. RunStab	10		4.156	1.656 **R,U**	2.250 **R,U**	2.562	4.375
DKM criterion	Error Rate	–	.05	4.375	1.625 **R,U**	2.500 **R**	2.719 **R**	3.781
	Tree Size	–	.01	1.125 **G,T,U**	4.125	3.938	2.625	3.125
	Seman. FinalStab	–	.05	4.000	2.188 **R**	3.250	2.750	2.812
	Seman. PrevStab	–	.05	3.594	2.312 **T**	3.844	2.812	2.438
	Seman. RunStab	–	.01	4.531	1.562 **R,U**	2.750 **R**	2.469 **R**	3.688
	Struct. FinalStab	0		3.281	2.562	3.188	3.094	2.875
	Struct. FinalStab	5	.10	3.156	2.594	3.125	3.031	3.094
	Struct. FinalStab	10		3.281	2.562	3.125	3.125	2.906
	Struct. PrevStab	0		2.875	2.812	3.844	2.906	2.562
	Struct. PrevStab	5	.10	2.844	2.875	3.688	2.938	2.656
	Struct. PrevStab	10		2.812	2.938	3.688	2.844	2.719
	Struct. RunStab	0		4.031	1.875 **R,U**	2.125 **R,U**	2.625	4.344
	Struct. RunStab	5	.01	3.719	2.031 **U**	2.188 **U**	2.750	4.312
	Struct. RunStab	10		3.875	1.938 **R,U**	2.344 **U**	2.562	4.281

for instance, a committee of C4.5 trees selected unlabelled examples that were subsequently used to train a bagged committee of trees [5]. Note that although a single decision tree trained from labelled data L is likely to be less accurate than a bagged committee trained from L, the committee is no longer intelligible [1].

Other methods have been proposed for training one type of classifier on examples selected by another type. Lewis and Catlett [13] employed a probabilistic classifier to select training examples for C4.5, and Domingos [17] used a committee to generate labelled data, from which a single classifier was trained. However, we are not aware of any previous study in which a committee of decision trees was used to train a single tree within the active learning framework.

Tree Size. In terms of the number of leaf nodes, the selective sampling methods consistently yielded larger trees than did Random (see "Tree Size" in Table 2). The trees grown by QBag tended to be the largest, containing 38 percent more leaves, on average, than those of Random. Does this imply that trees grown using QBag, for example, are more difficult to interpret than trees produced by Random? While no agreed-upon criterion exists for distinguishing between a tree that is interpretable and a tree that is not, one simple criterion is that there might exist a threshold t, such that any tree containing more than t leaves is uninterpretable. The datasets on which the weighted average leaf count for Random is at most t and the count for QBag is greater than t would then represent cases where QBag sacrifices intelligibility. Testing all integer values of t ranging from 1 to 25, we find that this occurs on at most 5 datasets ($t = 13$) when using DKM, and at most 3 datasets ($t = 11, 12$) with entropy. Thus, QBag's gains in accuracy are not typically made at the expense of intelligibility.

Stability. With regard to semantic stability, QBag achieved the best average rank on FinalStab, PrevStab, and RunStab, for both splitting criteria. Random was the least stable method in all but one case (PrevStab with DKM). Although Uncert also performed well on FinalStab and PrevStab, it was significantly less stable than QBag on the RunStab measure, as was Random. No strong conclusions could be drawn regarding the semantic stability of QBoost or BootLV.

As for structural stability, the RunStab results were highly significant. QBag and QBoost were the two best-ranked methods for all three values of ϵ that were used, while Random and Uncert were the worst. By definition, QBag and QBoost always choose the m highest scoring examples from the pool – the ones for which the committee vote is most divided. Therefore, a given example will be added to the training set if it receives a sufficiently high score at some iteration. BootLV, on the other hand, does not necessarily choose the highest scoring examples; it samples m times from a probability distribution in which the weight of an example is proportional to its score. Random is completely stochastic, which accounts for its instability across runs. As for Uncert, its low RunStab scores are a consequence of assigning scores to unlabelled examples based on the hypothesis of a single decision tree. Since this tree is generally unstable, the score assigned to a given example is likely to change considerably when the tree is induced from different training data. This problem is mitigated by the committee-based methods, as a committee of trees tends to be more stable than a single tree [1].

The results for structural FinalStab and PrevStab did not reveal any statistically significant differences between the sampling methods, even at $\alpha = .10$.

Table 3. Pairwise comparisons involving the QBag sampling method. The significance level α is indicated in parentheses where applicable.

(a) Structural FinalStab win-loss counts for QBag vs. Random

ϵ	**Entropy**	**DKM**
0	10-6 (.05)	11-4 (.05)
5	9-7 (.10)	10-6
10	9-6 (.10)	10-6

(b) Structural stability win-loss counts for DKM vs. entropy when using QBag

ϵ	**FinalStab**	**PrevStab**	**RunStab**
0	10-6 (.10)	11-5 (.05)	9-7
5	11-5 (.05)	12-4 (.05)	11-5 (.05)
10	12-4 (.05)	12-4 (.05)	10-6 (.10)

The ranges of the average ranks were smaller for these statistics; yet, Random had the worst average rank on FinalStab, for example, for all values of ϵ that were tested. A direct comparison between Random and QBag – the best method on most of the statistics – does in fact reveal significant differences. Table 3(a) compares QBag and Random on the structural FinalStab measure. Here, a win is recorded for the sampling method that achieves the higher weighted score on a given dataset. QBag obtains the most wins under all 6 conditions, and the Wilcoxon signed-ranks test, which is recommended when comparing two methods [16], finds that the QBag scores are significantly better in 4 of these cases. With regard to the PrevStab scores, there were no significant differences detected between QBag and Random by this test.

Comparison of Splitting Criteria. The weighted scores obtained when using the entropy splitting criterion were compared to those obtained with DKM, and the Wilcoxon signed-ranks tests was used to assess statistical significance. With respect to error rates, DKM was significantly more accurate than entropy when QBag or BootLV were used ($\alpha = .10$), and DKM never recorded less than 9 wins with any of the other methods. DKM frequently grew smaller trees, but the difference was significant only with BootLV ($\alpha = .10$). Remarkably, DKM yielded higher scores on the majority of datasets for every sampling method and every measure of structural stability, at all values of ϵ. We highlight the comparison between DKM and entropy when using QBag, as it has been shown in previous sections to be the superior sampling method. As the data in Table 3(b) reveals, the FinalStab and PrevStab scores for QBag improved significantly when DKM was used to grow trees. Similarly, QBag's RunStab scores improved for all values of ϵ when using DKM instead of entropy. Here, permitting a small margin of error between continuous thresholds revealed that DKM produced decision regions that were more similar than those formed with entropy. Finally, the semantic stability of C4.5 was less influenced by the choice of splitting criterion, as significant differences were detected only for PrevStab when using BootLV ($\alpha = .05$) or Random ($\alpha = .10$). In both instances, DKM was superior.

6 Conclusions

We have presented a methodology for evaluating the stability of decision tree learners in the context of active learning, which includes a novel measure of decision tree stability. The main conclusions drawn from our experiments are, first of all, that query-by-bagging (QBag) is the method of choice for training a single, interpretable decision tree, when using the C4.5 algorithm. QBag was found to be superior based on many of the stability measures, and was never significantly less stable than any other sampling method. Moreover, QBag produced the most accurate decision trees, and so the increased stability did not correspond with higher error rates. Although QBag yielded trees that were larger, on average, than those of the competing methods, we provided evidence that this would not usually be detrimental to intelligibility. The second important finding is that the

DKM splitting criterion improves the stability and accuracy of C4.5 in the active learning setting. In particular, since QBag performed better with DKM, this combination is recommended for training a single tree. It is important to emphasize that these conclusions are based on average performance across datasets, as no sampling method was superior on all the datasets that were tested.

Acknowledgments. This research was funded by NSERC, the Informatics Circle of Research Excellence (iCORE), and the Alberta Ingenuity Fund.

References

1. Breiman, L.: Bagging predictors. Machine Learning 24(2), 123–140 (1996)
2. Turney, P.D.: Bias and the quantification of stability. Machine Learning 20(1-2), 23–33 (1995)
3. Quinlan, J.R.: Improved use of continuous attributes in C4.5. JAIR 4, 77–90 (1996)
4. Dwyer, K.D.: Decision tree instability and active learning. Master's thesis, University of Alberta (2007)
5. Abe, N., Mamitsuka, H.: Query learning strategies using boosting and bagging. In: Proc. ICML '98, pp. 1–9 (1998)
6. Dietterich, T.G., Kearns, M., Mansour, Y.: Applying the weak learning framework to understand and improve C4.5. In: Proc. ICML '96, pp. 96–104 (1996)
7. Drummond, C., Holte, R.C.: Exploiting the cost (in)sensitivity of decision tree splitting criteria. In: Proc. ICML '00, pp. 239–246 (2000)
8. Alpaydin, E.: Introduction to Machine Learning. MIT Press, Cambridge (2004)
9. Newman, D.J., Hettich, S., Blake, C.L., Merz, C.J.: UCI ML Repository (1998)
10. Shannon, W.D., Banks, D.L.: Combining classification trees using MLE. Statistics in Medicine 18(6), 727–740 (1999)
11. Pérez, J.M., Muguerza, J., Arbelaitz, O., Gurrutxaga, I., Martín, J.I.: Consolidated trees: Classifiers with stable explanation. In: Singh, S., Singh, M., Apte, C., Perner, P. (eds.) ICAPR 2005. LNCS, vol. 3686, pp. 99–107. Springer, Heidelberg (2005)
12. Cohn, D.A., Atlas, L.E., Ladner, R.E.: Improving generalization with active learning. Machine Learning 15(2), 201–221 (1992)
13. Lewis, D.D., Catlett, J.: Heterogeneous uncertainty sampling for supervised learning. In: Proc. ICML '94, pp. 148–156 (1994)
14. Saar-Tsechansky, M., Provost, F.: Active sampling for class probability estimation and ranking. Machine Learning 54(2), 153–178 (2004)
15. Roy, N., McCallum, A.: Toward optimal active learning through sampling estimation of error reduction. In: Proc. ICML '01, pp. 441–448 (2001)
16. Demšar, J.: Statistical comparisons of classifiers over multiple data sets. JMLR 7, 1–30 (2006)
17. Domingos, P.M.: Knowledge acquisition from examples via multiple models. In: Proc. ICML '97, pp. 98–106 (1997)

Constraint Selection by Committee: An Ensemble Approach to Identifying Informative Constraints for Semi-supervised Clustering

Derek Greene and Pádraig Cunningham

University College Dublin, Ireland
{derek.greene,padraig.cunningham}@ucd.ie

Abstract. A number of clustering algorithms have been proposed for use in tasks where a limited degree of supervision is available. This prior knowledge is frequently provided in the form of pairwise must-link and cannot-link constraints. While the incorporation of pairwise supervision has the potential to improve clustering accuracy, the composition and cardinality of the constraint sets can significantly impact upon the level of improvement. We demonstrate that it is often possible to correctly "guess" a large number of constraints without supervision from the co-associations between pairs of objects in an ensemble of clusterings. Along the same lines, we establish that constraints based on pairs with uncertain co-associations are particularly informative, if known. An evaluation on text data shows that this provides an effective criterion for identifying constraints, leading to a reduction in the level of supervision required to direct a clustering algorithm to an accurate solution.

1 Introduction

Recently, a considerable amount of attention has been paid to the application of machine learning algorithms in problems that do not perfectly correspond to the standard distinction between supervised and unsupervised learning [1]. In many domains, a limited degree of background knowledge will be available when performing exploratory data analysis. While this may take the form of labelled training data, in other situations a simpler type of supervision will be available that describes the relations between pairs of data objects. The latter is commonly represented as a set of pairwise constraints, where each constraint indicates that two objects should either always be assigned to the same cluster (*must-link*) or never be assigned together (*cannot-link*). A number of popular clustering algorithms, such as standard k-means, have been adapted to incorporate this type of information. While the addition of pairwise supervision has the potential to improve clustering accuracy, the choice of constraints will often dictate the level of improvement attained [2]. Many semi-supervised clustering tasks will be active in nature, where the constraint oracle takes the form of a human expert. In such applications, the number of queries for constraints that can be made will be strictly limited.

J.N. Kok et al. (Eds.): ECML 2007, LNAI 4701, pp. 140–151, 2007.

In this paper, we tackle the problem of identifying constraints that are "informative" in the context of semi-supervised clustering. That is, we seek constraints that will be most effective in guiding a clustering algorithm to produce more accurate solutions. We differentiate these from constraints whose presence does not lead to any noticeable improvement in clustering accuracy. To make this distinction, we firstly establish a connection between hard pairwise constraints and the frequency of co-assignment, or *co-association*, between pairs of objects in an ensemble of clusterings. Specifically, Section 3.1 describes a process by which it is often possible to "guess" or impute a large number of constraints without supervision by examining these co-association values. Following from this, in Section 3.2 we propose a new approach for selecting informative constraints by identifying objects whose cluster assignments are ambiguous. In Section 4 we evaluate this approach on text data, where it is shown to lead to a reduction in the number of actual oracle queries required to produce a significant improvement in clustering accuracy.

2 Related Work

2.1 Semi-supervised Clustering

Given a set of n data objects $\mathcal{X} = \{x_1, \ldots, x_n\}$, a common representation for background information pertaining to $\mathcal{X}$ is in the form of pairwise constraint sets: must-link constraints $\mathcal{M}$ and cannot-link constraints $\mathcal{C}$. This information can be incorporated into traditional partitional clustering algorithms by adapting the objective function to include penalties for violated constraints. For instance, the Pairwise Constrained k-means (PCKM) algorithm [2] modifies the standard sum of squared errors function to take into account both object-centroid distortions in a clustering $\mathcal{P} = \{\pi_1, \ldots, \pi_k\}$ and any associated constraint violations

$$J_{pckm}(\mathcal{P}) = \sum_{c=1}^{k} \sum_{x_i \in \pi_c} ||x_i - \mu_c||^2 + \sum_{(x_i,x_j)\in\mathcal{M}, li \neq lj} w_{ij} + \sum_{(x_i,x_j)\in\mathcal{C}, li = lj} \bar{w}_{ij} \quad (1)$$

where μ_c is the centroid of the cluster π_c, and l_i denotes the cluster label of the object x_i in $\mathcal{P}$. The weight w_{ij} signifies the size of the penalty incurred when a must-link constraint between a pair (x_i, x_j) is violated, while $\bar{w}_{ij}$ is the penalty for violating a cannot-link constraint between the pair. These weights control the influence given to external information during the assignment phase of the algorithm. The objective (1) has been shown to have a probabilistic basis related to the assignment of labels in Hidden Markov Random Fields (HMRFs).

As with standard partitional algorithms, the choice of initialisation strategy for semi-supervised methods such as PCKM can greatly affect clustering accuracy. An effective strategy in this context involves computing the transitive closure of the graph formed by the constraints in $\mathcal{M}$, and using the centroids of the resulting λ neighbourhoods. If $\lambda > k$, where k is the desired number of clusters, then a weighted variant of farthest-first initialisation may be employed to select a subset of k well-separated centroids [3].

While research in the area of semi-supervised clustering has largely focused on the development of new clustering algorithms, relatively little emphasis has been placed on the important issue of selecting useful constraints. An initial foray into this area was made with the two-stage *Explore and Consolidate* (E&C) approach proposed by Basu *et al.* [2]. In the exploration stage, a set of k initial well-separated neighbourhoods is identified, each of which belongs to be a different natural class. Once the neighbourhoods have been formed, the consolidation stage proceeds by randomly selecting unlabelled objects and assigning them to correct neighbourhoods in a manner that requires as few constraints as possible. The resulting centroids and constraint sets were used to provide supervision for the PCKM algorithm.

2.2 Ensemble Clustering

It has been shown that combining the strengths of a diverse set of clusterings can often yield more accurate and robust solutions [4]. Unsupervised ensemble approaches typically involves two phases: a *generation* phase where a collection of base clusterings is produced, and an *integration* phase where an aggregation function is applied to the ensemble members to produce a consensus solution. The most frequently employed integration strategy has been to use the information provided by an ensemble to determine the level of association between pairs of objects in a dataset [4,5]. The fundamental assumption underlying this strategy is that pairs belonging to the same natural class will frequently be co-assigned during repeated executions of a clustering algorithm. In practice, these pairwise co-associations are represented using a symmetric co-association matrix. A consensus solution is recovered by applying a similarity-based algorithm to the matrix, such as single-linkage agglomerative clustering.

Pairwise co-association values have also been used to gather information from unlabelled data in order to improve the performance of kernel-based classification algorithms. The *bagged cluster kernel* technique proposed by Weston *et al.* [6] involves modifying a base kernel to include co-association information aggregated from multiple k-means clusterings, which are generated on bootstrap samples.

2.3 Uncertainty Sampling

For many learning problems, large numbers of training examples will not be available due to the expense of providing class labels. In these cases, active learning techniques can be employed to identify and label informative data objects that will serve to maximise classification accuracy. One approach to active learning that has widely been used is *uncertainty sampling* [7], where unlabelled objects are prioritised based upon the level of uncertainty regarding their class membership. An intuitive basis for measuring uncertainty is to consider the disagreement between the predictions made by a committee of classifiers [8]. For instance, Melville & Mooney [9] suggested measuring the uncertainty for an unlabelled object based on the margin between its maximum class probability and the probability of the next best competing class.

3 Constraint Identification

The composition and cardinality of the sets $\mathcal{M}$ and $\mathcal{C}$ can significantly impact upon the improvements achieved by semi-supervised algorithms. In addition, as the number of data objects n increases, the number of possible constraints also significantly increases. If constraints are selected at random, many oracle queries may be required before any noticeable improvement in clustering accuracy is achieved. To illustrate this, Figure 1 shows the effect of adding constraints for randomly chosen pairs on the normalised mutual information (NMI) [4] scores produced when the PCKM algorithm is applied to the *3-news-similar* dataset. Even after the addition of 1000 constraints, little significant increase in accuracy is evident. For many semi-supervised tasks, it will be the case that the oracle is a human expert. Since it is unrealistic to expect a human to respond to so many queries, an intelligent strategy for choosing constraints is desirable.

3.1 Imputing Constraints from Pairwise Co-associations

When seeking to choose a small set of highly informative constraints, it may be helpful to eliminate those "easy" constraints that can be found without the aid of a supervisor. In this section, we show that it is possible to identify such constraints by examining the relationship between pairs of objects over a large collection of base clusterings, denoted $\mathbb{P} = \{\mathcal{P}_1, \ldots, \mathcal{P}_\tau\}$.

Like their supervised counterparts, it has been demonstrated that unsupervised ensembles are most effective when constructed from solutions that are both accurate and diverse [4]. To encourage diversity, a commonly employed strategy has been to apply a partitional clustering algorithm, such as standard k-means, to different subsamples of the same dataset. In practice, typically 60-80% of the data is included when generating each base clustering. After each sample is clustered, membership assignments for the out-of-sample objects are determined by applying a suitable classification scheme, such as a nearest centroid classifier.

Once an ensemble $\mathbb{P}$ has been generated, it is customary to represent the co-assignments between objects across all clusterings in the form of a symmetric

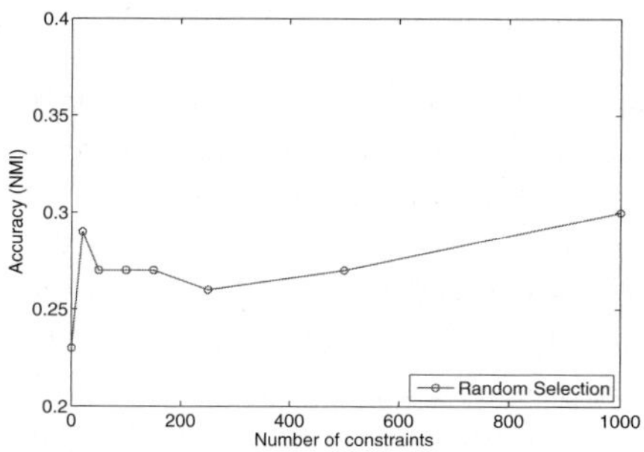

Fig. 1. Effect of randomly selected constraints on *3-news-similar* dataset

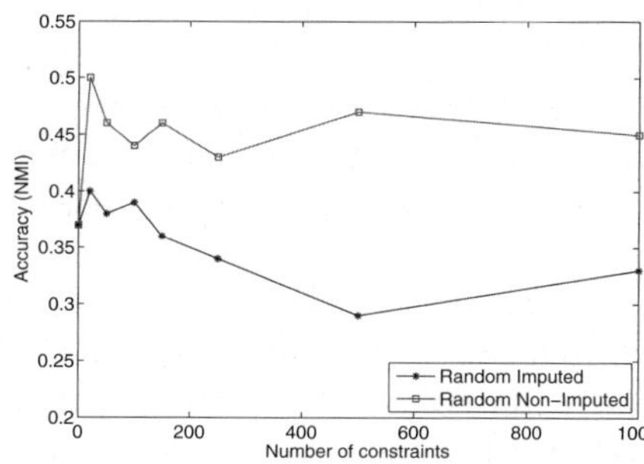

Fig. 2. Effect of randomly selected imputed constraints on *3-news-related* dataset

1. Initialise **A** as the $n \times n$ empty co-association matrix for the dataset **X**.
2. For $t = 1$ to τ:
   1. Draw a sample of objects $\mathcal{X}_t$ by random sampling without replacement.
   2. Generate a base clustering $\mathcal{P}_t$ by clustering the sample $\mathcal{X}_t$.
   3. Classify each out-of-sample object based on the clusters in $\mathcal{P}_t$.
   4. For each pair (x_i, x_j) assigned to the same cluster in $\mathcal{P}_t$, update **A**:

$$A_{ij} = A_{ij} + 1/\tau$$

3. Construct imputed constraint sets $(\mathcal{M}', \mathcal{C}')$ based on the co-association of each unique pair (x_i, x_j), according to the rule given in Eqn. 2.

Fig. 3. Pairwise constraint imputation procedure

$n \times n$ co-association matrix **A**. In this matrix, an entry $A_{ij} \in [0, 1]$ denotes the fraction of clusterings in $\mathbb{P}$ in which the objects x_i and x_j were assigned to the same cluster. Both the ensemble and cluster kernel techniques discussed in Section 2.2 are motivated by the assumption that the matrix **A** encodes information describing the probability or confidence with which a pair of objects will be grouped together in the natural classes of the data. For a sufficient number of base clusterings, a value $A_{ij} \approx 1$ is a strong indicator that the pair (x_i, x_j) belong to the same class, while $A_{ij} \approx 0$ indicates that they belong to different classes. On the other hand, a value $A_{ij} \approx 0.5$ implies that we are highly unsure about whether the objects are actually conceptually related to one another.

When performing ensemble clustering, we are typically interested in producing a complete disjoint partition of the data. This can result in "uncertain" pairs being grouped together in the consensus clustering. For instance, the integration approach described in [5] only requires a value $A_{ij} > 0.5$ for a pair to be placed in the same consensus cluster. However, given the goal of accurately deducing constraints, we focus on pairs with unambiguous associations. By thresholding the values in **A**, we can eliminate uncertain pairs from consideration. Specifically, we choose a threshold value κ_m for must-link constraints, which represents the minimum level of confidence required for the co-assignment of two objects, and a threshold κ_c for cannot-link constraints, which represents the maximum level of uncertainty allowed when concluding that two objects are unrelated. Both values lie in the range $[0, 1]$, with the natural requirement that $\kappa_m >> \kappa_c$. Formally, we construct imputed constraint sets $(\mathcal{M}', \mathcal{C}')$ by using the rule:

$$\begin{array}{ll} A_{ij} \geq \kappa_m & \text{add } (x_i, x_j) \text{ to } \mathcal{M}' \\ A_{ij} \leq \kappa_c & \text{add } (x_i, x_j) \text{ to } \mathcal{C}' \\ \kappa_c < A_{ij} < \kappa_m & \text{ignore.} \end{array} \tag{2}$$

The application of the method outlined in Figure 3 frequently produces constrained pairs that correspond to those generated from natural class labels.

While ensemble clustering can often provide a more comprehensive picture of the natural structures present in a dataset, it is interesting to note that constraints imputed in this way, even if correct, will rarely prove directly useful in semi-supervised clustering. Surprisingly, in some situations these constraints can actually prove harmful. We suggest that this phenomenon is due to the fact that these easily imputed constraints leave regions in certain underlying classes under-represented, so that initial clusters resulting from the imputed must-link constraints are skewed. As an example, Figure 2 shows the effect of randomly adding constraints from the set of pairs that were correctly imputed on the *3-news-related* dataset. Here, the addition of a large number of imputed constraints actually results in less accurate solutions. In contrast, when randomly choosing from among non-imputed pairs, the quality of the resulting clusterings increases.

3.2 Selecting Informative Constraints

Motivated by the observations made in the previous section, we now describe a new ensemble-based selection procedure that makes use of pairwise co-associations to focus on informative constraints. This procedure consists of two phases: firstly we use the imputed set $\mathcal{M}'$ to identify a set of representative objects $\{r_1, \ldots, r_k\}$ which correspond to distinct classes in the data; subsequently we construct clusters around these representatives by adding constraints relating to objects whose cluster assignments are difficult to determine.

While imputed constraints may not be directly useful for semi-supervised clustering, they do provide a starting point for finding representative objects. This can be achieved by examining the set of neighbourhoods produced by computing transitive closure of the imputed must-link constraints in $\mathcal{M}'$. We frequently observe that the largest neighbourhoods produced in this way will correspond to distinct natural classes in the data. This provides a basis for selecting representatives for k different classes using only a small number of oracle queries. Firstly, the neighbourhoods are arranged in descending order by size, and the median object of each neighbourhood is identified (*i.e.* the object nearest the neighbourhood centroid). The median of the largest neighbourhood is elected to be the first

---

1. Identify imputed constraint sets $(\mathcal{M}', \mathcal{C}')$ from a co-association matrix $\mathbf{A}$.
2. Compute the transitive closure of $\mathcal{M}'$, and identify the median objects of each neighbourhood based on the values in $\mathbf{A}$.
3. Choose the first representative r_1 to be the median of the largest neighbourhood.
4. For $c = 2$ to k:
   - Select r_c as the median of the next largest neighbourhood, such that a cannot-link constraint exists between r_c and each of $\{r_1, \ldots, r_{c-1}\}$.
5. Output a clustering $\mathcal{P} = \{\pi_1, \ldots, \pi_k\}$, where $r_c \in \pi_c$, together with any other object with a must-link constraint to r_c.

Fig. 4. Constraint set initialisation phase

representative r_1. Each of the $(k-1)$ other representatives is chosen to be the median object of the largest remaining neighbourhood, such that a cannot-link constraint exists between that median and all previously selected representatives (*i.e.* it belongs to a new class). The application of this initialisation scheme leads to an initial clustering $\mathcal{P} = \{\pi_1, \ldots, \pi_k\}$, where $r_c \in \pi_c$. Any objects involved in must-link constraints are also assigned to the appropriate cluster in $\mathcal{P}$. The complete initialisation procedure is outlined in Figure 4. A particular advantage of this approach is that, even if constraints are only available for a subset of objects, good representatives can be identified using imputed neighbourhoods derived from clusterings of the entire dataset.

In the second phase of the proposed constraint selection procedure, we expand the clustering $\mathcal{P}$ by incrementally assigning objects using pairwise supervision. Objects are processed using an ordering based upon the level of uncertainty regarding their association to the existing clusters, thereby prioritising those objects for which queries to an external oracle are particularly necessary. Formally, let $\mathbf{S} \in \mathbb{R}^{n \times k}$ denote the object-cluster association matrix, such that S_{ic} is the mean co-association between the object x_i and the members of the cluster π_c:

$$S_{ic} = \frac{1}{|\pi_c|} \sum_{x_j \in \pi_c} A_{ij} \tag{3}$$

To evaluate the degree of uncertainty in assigning an object to a cluster in $\mathcal{P}$, we use a criterion based on the well-known *silhouette index* [10], which is often employed in internal cluster validation. Rather than using distance values computed on the raw data, we consider the margin between competing clusters based on object-cluster associations. Specifically, for a candidate query object x_i, let π_a denote the cluster with which it has the highest level of association, and let π_b denote the next best alternative cluster. The certainty of the assignment of x_i can be measured using the expression:

$$u(x_i) = \frac{2 \cdot S_{ia}}{S_{ia} + S_{ib}} - 1 \tag{4}$$

Since it is always the case that $S_{ia} \geq S_{ib}$, Eqn. 4 produces an evaluation in the range $[0, 1]$, where a smaller value is indicative of a greater degree of uncertainty.

Unfortunately, if objects are chosen based on an ordering of the uncertainty scores $u(x_i)$, this can potentially result in the generation of a large succession of constraints for a single natural class. The use of such unbalanced constraint sets can reduce the performance gain achieved by semi-supervised algorithms when using small constraint sets. To address this problem, we introduce a bias in favour of under-represented classes. This is accomplished by weighting object-cluster association values with respect to cluster size, leading to an adjusted certainty criterion

$$w(x_i) = \frac{2 \cdot T_{ia}}{T_{ia} + T_{ib}} - 1 \quad \text{such that} \quad T_{ic} = \frac{|\pi_c|}{\sum_j |\pi_j|} \cdot S_{ic} \tag{5}$$

where T_{ia} denotes the maximum weighted object-cluster association value, and T_{ib} is the next highest value. This weighting has the effect of producing higher

1. Update the object-cluster association matrix $\mathbf{S}$.
2. Select the next most uncertain object x_i with the minimum value for $w(x_i)$, as calculated using Eqn. 5.
3. Arrange the clusters in descending order using the values in the i-th row of $\mathbf{S}$.
4. For each cluster π_c:
   - Query the oracle for the pair (x_i, r_c) until a must-link constraint is found.
5. Assign x_i to the cluster containing the correct representative.
6. Repeat from Step 1 until no further oracle queries are possible.

Fig. 5. Constraint set expansion phase

scores for objects that have strong associations with large clusters. Since objects with lower scores are prioritised, this encourages the selection of constraints for objects that are likely to be assigned to smaller clusters.

Once an unassigned object x_i has been selected based on the minimal value for Eqn. 5, its correct cluster in $\mathcal{P}$ is found by querying the oracle for constraints between x_i and each of the k representatives. Following the observations made in [2], it is apparent that the correct cluster can be located using at most $(k-1)$ queries. We can potentially further reduce the number of queries required by sorting the values in the i-th row of $\mathbf{S}$ in descending order. Candidate clusters are processed in this order until a must-link pair (x_i, r_c) is generated. If such a constraint is not found after $(k-1)$ queries, it can be assumed that the object belongs to the final cluster without the requirement for an additional query. After assigning x_i to the correct cluster, uncertainty scores for the remaining objects are recalculated. An outline of the expansion phase is provided in Figure 5.

4 Evaluation

In this section, we describe the results of two sets of experimental evaluations conducted on text data. Firstly, we assess the veracity of constraints imputed using the approach discussed in Section 3.1. In the second set of experiments, we evaluate the performance of semi-supervised clustering when constraints are selected using the ensemble-based procedure proposed in Section 3.2.

Both sets of experiments were performed on six text corpora, which present different degrees of difficulty when performing document clustering. The *bbc* corpus contains news articles pertaining to five topical areas: business, entertainment, politics, sport and technology. The *bbcsport* corpus consists of a smaller set of sports news articles from the same source[1]. The *cstr* dataset[2] represents a small collection of technical abstracts. The *3-news-related* dataset (also referred to as *ng17-19*) is a commonly used subset of the *20-newsgroups* collection[3],

[1] Both available from `http://mlg.ucd.ie/datasets/`
[2] Original abstracts available from `http://www.cs.rochester.edu/trs`
[3] Available from `http://people.csail.mit.edu/jrennie/20Newsgroups/`

consisting of three groups pertaining to politics that exhibit some overlap. Another benchmark subset, the *3-news-similar* dataset, consists of three IT-related newsgroups that overlap significantly. The *reuters5* dataset is a subset of the widely-used *Reuters-21578* corpus of news articles, containing documents from the five largest categories. To pre-process the datasets, we applied standard stop-word removal and stemming techniques. We subsequently removed terms occurring in less than three documents and applied log-based *tf-idf* normalisation.

4.1 Validation of Imputed Constraints

To investigate the effectiveness of the constraint imputation technique, we generated an ensemble consisting of 2000 members for each dataset. These clusterings were formed by applying standard k-means with cosine similarity and random initialisation to samples of documents, using a subsampling rate of 80%. We subsequently constructed a co-association matrix and a corresponding set of imputed constraints for each corpus by following the procedure outlined in Figure 3. In practice, we found that conservative thresholds of $\kappa_m = 0.98$ and $\kappa_c = 0$ were suitable for use with a variety of text datasets.

Table 1 presents details of the imputed must-link and cannot-link constraint sets generated for each dataset. Note that the numbers reported do not take into account any additional cannot-link constraints that can be inferred from the imputed must-link constraints. We compare the imputed sets to the correct pairwise relations defined by the natural classification of the datasets, using measures of *pairwise precision* (PP) and *pairwise recall* (PR). Given an imputed set $\mathcal{Y}'$, the former refers to the fraction of imputed pairs that are correctly constrained, while the latter represents the fraction of the complete set $\mathcal{Y}$ recovered:

$$PP(\mathcal{Y}', \mathcal{Y}) = \frac{|\mathcal{Y}' \cap \mathcal{Y}|}{|\mathcal{Y}'|} \qquad PR(\mathcal{Y}', \mathcal{Y}) = \frac{|\mathcal{Y}' \cap \mathcal{Y}|}{|\mathcal{Y}|} \tag{6}$$

On each of the datasets considered, a large number of must-link and cannot-link constraints are correctly imputed. In all but one case, pairwise precision scores of 0.9 or higher were achieved for both constraint types. Table 1 also lists the mean NMI scores of the base clusterings in each ensemble. It is interesting to observe that, even when the quality of the base clusterings used to construct

Table 1. Details of imputed constraint sets for text datasets

Dataset	n	Base NMI	Must-Link Selected	Must-Link PP	Must-Link PR	Cannot-Link Selected	Cannot-Link PP	Cannot-Link PR
bbc	2225	0.80	191619	0.98	0.38	1021257	1.00	0.52
bbcsport	737	0.71	4842	1.00	0.08	19516	1.00	0.09
cstr	505	0.64	4389	0.99	0.12	40874	0.99	0.44
reuters5	2317	0.46	145336	0.94	0.15	1202021	0.91	0.61
3-news-related	2625	0.41	245886	0.90	0.19	12620	1.00	0.01
3-news-similar	2938	0.22	17761	0.67	0.01	3025	0.95	0.01

a co-association matrix is poor, it is still possible to produce an accurate set of imputed constraints. Due to the use of conservative threshold values in the imputation process, the level of recall is significantly lower than the level of precision. However, for all the datasets under consideration, the number of correctly imputed pairs is significantly higher than the number of constraints we could expect to be provided by a human resource.

4.2 Constraint Selection Evaluation

We now compare the performance of the constraint selection approach proposed in Section 3.2 with that of two alternative strategies. The first is the *Explore and Consolidate* (E&C) approach described in [2]. As a baseline, we also consider the random selection of constraints from all the available pairs in the data. As our choice of semi-supervised clustering algorithm, we employ PCKM with cosine similarity, and set the value of k to correspond to the number of natural classes in the data. When evaluating the case where no constraints are present, initial centroids are selected for the clustering algorithm using farthest-first initialisation. The constraint selection approaches were evaluated over 50 two-fold cross validation trials. As an oracle, we use the natural classification supplied for each dataset. Each oracle query results in either a must-link or a cannot-link constraint. In each trial, constraints are available for 90% of the data, while the remaining 10% of the data constitutes the test set. In the assignment phase of PCKM, all constraints are given an equal weighting of 0.001.

Figure 6 shows a comparison of the mean NMI scores achieved by the three constraint selection strategies when applied to the six datasets under consideration. Note that the reported scores are calculated solely based on the assignment of objects in the test set. We focus on the performance of the three selection strategies for the first 150 queries, since the selection of a larger number of constraints by a human oracle in this context is unrealistic. For all three methods, the points on the validation plots indicate the mean NMI score achieved using the first p selected constraints. This ensures that each method has the same level of supervision.

Firstly, it is clear that both the E&C and ensemble strategies represent significantly better options than simply choosing constrained pairs at random. For data with poorly separated clusters, such as the *3-news-related* and *3-news-similar* datasets, little improvement in clustering accuracy is evident after 150 random queries. In contrast, the ensemble strategy leads to a significant increase in accuracy, even after the addition of only 10 constraints. In general, we observed that ensemble-based selection led to greater increases in accuracy after the first 10–30 constraints than afforded by the E&C technique. This may be attributed to the selection of good representatives based on imputed must-link constraints, and, in particular, the use of the weighted uncertainty criterion (5) to encourage the selection of constraints from under-represented classes. For the *bbc* and *bbcsport* datasets, both intelligent selection methods did result in an initial drop in accuracy when using a very small number of constraints. However, the subsequent increases in accuracy were substantial. It is interesting to note

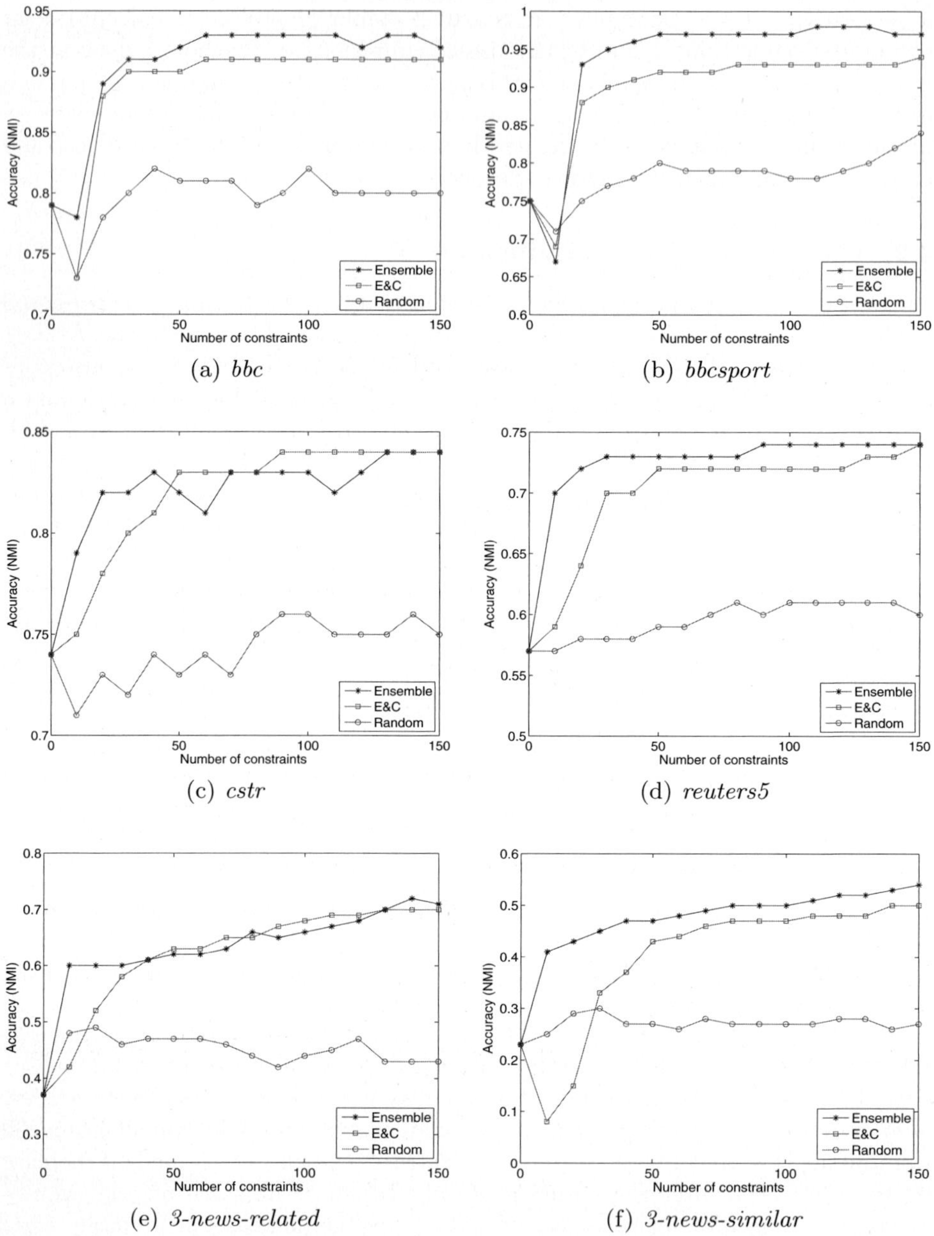

Fig. 6. Comparison of mean accuracy (NMI) scores for constraint selection strategies when applied to text datasets

that the recall of the imputed constraints did not have a direct impact on the choice of suitable representatives for the first phase of ensemble-based selection. Also, in the case of the *3-news-similar* dataset, which achieved a relatively low level of pairwise precision as shown in Table 1, both the imputed constraints and the related co-association values still proved useful when selecting real constraints. While initialising the proposed ensemble approach does require more time than the E&C strategy, the running times were not prohibitive in practice. We suggest that, for many applications, the cost of additional machine cycles will be less than the expense of making additional queries to a human oracle.

5 Conclusion

In this paper, we demonstrated that it is often possible to correctly impute sets of pairwise constraints for data by examining the co-associations in an ensemble of clusterings. Furthermore, we proposed a new approach for selecting informative constraints for use in semi-supervised clustering tasks, based upon the uncertainty of object-cluster associations. Evaluations on text data have shown this approach to be effective in improving clustering accuracy, particularly when working with a small number of constraints. We suggest that the notion of imputed constraints may also be relevant in other contexts, such as when integrating information from different feature spaces, or where prior knowledge is available in the form of one or more existing clusterings of the data.

References

1. Chapelle, O., Schölkopf, B., Zien, A. (eds.): Semi-Supervised Learning. MIT Press, Cambridge (2006)
2. Basu, S., Banerjee, A., Mooney, R.: Active semi-supervision for pairwise constrained clustering. In: Proc. 4th SIAM Int. Conf. Data Mining, pp. 333–344 (2004)
3. Basu, S., Bilenko, M., Mooney, R.J.: A probabilistic framework for semi-supervised clustering. In: Proc. 10th ACM SIGKDD Int. Conf. Knowledge Discovery and Data Mining, pp. 59–68. ACM Press, New York (2004)
4. Strehl, A., Ghosh, J.: Cluster ensembles - a knowledge reuse framework for combining multiple partitions. J. Machine Learning Research 3, 583–617 (2002)
5. Fred, A.: Finding consistent clusters in data partitions. In: Kittler, J., Roli, F. (eds.) MCS 2001. LNCS, vol. 2096, pp. 309–318. Springer, Heidelberg (2001)
6. Weston, J., Leslie, C., Ie, E., Zhou, D., Elisseeff, A., Noble, W.: Semi-supervised protein classification using cluster kernels. Bioinformatics 21(15), 3241–3247 (2005)
7. Lewis, D.D., Catlett, J.: Heterogeneous uncertainty sampling for supervised learning. In: Proc. 11th Int. Conf. Machine Learning, pp. 148–156 (1994)
8. Seung, H.S., Opper, M., Sompolinsky, H.: Query by committee. In: Proc. 5th Workshop on Computational Learning Theory, pp. 287–294. Morgan Kaufmann, San Francisco (1992)
9. Melville, P., Mooney, R.: Diverse ensembles for active learning. In: Proc. 21st Int. Conf. Machine Learning, pp. 584–591 (2004)
10. Rousseeuw, P.: Silhouettes: a graphical aid to the interpretation and validation of cluster analysis. J. Computational and Applied Mathematics 20(1), 53–65 (1987)

The Cost of Learning Directed Cuts

Thomas Gärtner[1] and Gemma C. Garriga[2]

[1] Fraunhofer IAIS, Schloß Birlinghoven, 53754 Sankt Augustin, Germany
[2] HIIT Basic Research Unit, Helsinki University of Technology, Finland
thomas.gaertner@iais.fraunhofer.de, gemma.garriga@hut.fi

Abstract. In this paper we investigate the problem of classifying vertices of a directed graph according to an unknown directed cut. We first consider the usual setting in which the directed cut is fixed. However, even in this setting learning is not possible without in the worst case needing the labels for the whole vertex set. By considering the size of the minimum path cover as a fixed parameter, we derive positive learnability results with tight performance guarantees for active, online, as well as PAC learning. The advantage of this parameter over possible alternatives is that it allows for an a priori estimation of the total cost of labelling all vertices. The main result of this paper is the analysis of learning directed cuts that depend on a hidden and changing context.

1 Introduction

Classifying vertices in directed graphs is an important machine learning setting with many applications. In this paper we consider learning problems on directed graphs with three characteristic properties: (*i*) The target concept defines a directed cut; (*ii*) the total cost of finding the cut has to be bounded before any labels are observed to asses whether it will exceed some given budget; and (*iii*) the target concept may change due to a hidden context.

For one example consider the problem of finding the source of contamination in waste water systems where the pipes are the edges of the digraph and the direction is given by the direction of the water flow. Often uncontaminated waste water can be used to fertilise fields and it is important to find the cause of contamination as quickly as possible. As each test costs time and money, we aim at a strategy that needs the least number of tests. The pipes connecting uncontaminated water with contaminated water form a directed cut.

For another example consider classifying intermediate products in some process, e.g., for manufacturing cars, as faulty or correct. The process can be represented by a directed graph and the concept defines a directed cut as typically faults that appear in an intermediate product will also be present in later stages of the product. The directed cut we are interested in consists of all edges connecting correct to faulty intermediate products. Furthermore, the concept may depend on a hidden variable as some pre-assembled parts may vary and the fault may occur only for some charges and not for others. In order to be able to trade off between the cost of having a faulty product and the costs for finding the cause of the fault, tight performance guarantees are needed.

J.N. Kok et al. (Eds.): ECML 2007, LNAI 4701, pp. 152–163, 2007.

Performance guarantees proposed in machine learning literature can be distinguished into concept-dependent and concept-independent. *Concept-dependent guarantees* state that the performance of the learning algorithm depends on the *unknown* target concept's complexity. *Concept-independent guarantees* state that the performance of the learning algorithm depends on the instance space's complexity, or in a transductive setting on the given training and test sets. For real-world applications, one often faces the question whether the costs of labelling a whole dataset exceeds a given budget or not. In this case, concept-independent, transductive, bounds are to be preferred over concept-dependent guarantees.

Our first result is that for learning directed cuts we can achieve tight, concept-independent guarantees. Based on a fixed size of the minimum path cover, we establish logarithmic performance guarantees for online learning, active learning, and PAC learning. We furthermore show which algorithms and results carry over to learning intersections of monotone with anti-monotone concepts.

We then turn to the more complex setting of learning with a hidden context, i.e., the unknown concept depends on an unobservable variable that can change any time. In order to enable query learning algorithms to identify one of the true concepts, the usual query model is not sufficient. We hence propose a novel type of queries and give learning algorithms able to cope with concept drift due to hidden changes in the context. In particular, it is necessary (and sufficient) that the learning algorithm can query three different vertices at a time where it is ensured that the answers will be provided on the basis of the same concept. Worst case guarantees in this setting are related to adverserial learning.

The main purpose of this paper is to summarise our findings on the application of the size of the minimum pathcover as a concept-independent, transductive learning parameter for learning directed cuts with and without changing context. Due to space limitations we only sketch proofs.

2 Preliminaries

2.1 Directed Graphs

For any $k \in \mathbb{N}$ we denote $\{1, \ldots, k\}$ by $[\![k]\!]$ and the Boolean values '*true*', '*false*' by $\top, \bot$, respectively with $\Omega = \{\top, \bot\}$.

A *directed graph* (*digraph*) is a pair (V, E) where V is the set of *vertices* and $E \subseteq V^2$ is the set of *edges*. For a digraph G we will sometimes denote its vertices by $V(G)$ and its edges by $E(G)$. The *induced subgraph* of $G = (V, E)$ by a subset of vertices $U \subseteq V$ is the digraph $G[U] = (U, E[U])$ where $E[U] = E \cap U^2$. A *subgraph* of G is any digraph $G' = (V', E')$ with $V' \subseteq V(G)$ and $E' \subseteq E[V']$.

For a digraph (V, E) and two sets $U, U' \subseteq V$ we define $E(U, U') = \{(u, u') \in E \mid u \in U \setminus U' \wedge u' \in U' \setminus U\}$. The *children* of U in a digraph (V, E) are then expressed as $\delta^+(U) = \{v \in V \mid (u, v) \in E(U, V \setminus U)\}$ and its *parents* as $\delta^-(U) = \{v \in V \mid (v, u) \in E(V \setminus U, U)$. The *contraction* of a set of vertices $U \subseteq V$ on a digraph $G = (V, E)$ is the digraph $(\{u\} \cup V \setminus U, E[V \setminus U] \cup (\{u\} \times E(U, V \setminus U)) \cup (E(V \setminus U, U) \times \{u\}))$, i.e., a new digraph which has U replaced by a single vertex $u \notin V$.

A *walk* in a directed graph G is a sequence $p_1 \dots p_i \dots p_n$ of vertices of G such that $\forall i \in [\![n-1]\!] : (p_i, p_{i+1}) \in E$ and $|p| = n$ is the *length* of the walk p. We denote the (possibly infinite) set of walks in G by $\mathcal{P}(G)$ and define the binary relations $\leq_G, \geq_G$ such that $u \geq_G v \Leftrightarrow v \leq_G u \Leftrightarrow \exists p \in \mathcal{P}(G) : p_1 = u \wedge p_{|p|} = v$. Whenever G is clear from the context it will be omitted. For any directed graph, these relations form a preorder on the vertex set. For any preorder $\leq$ and vertex set $U \subseteq V(G)$ we will use $\min U = \{u \in U \mid \nexists v \in U \setminus \{u\} : v \leq u\}$ and similarly $\max U = \{u \in U \mid \nexists v \in U \setminus \{u\} : u \leq v\}$. A digraph G is *strongly connected* iff $\forall u, v \in V(G) : u \geq v \wedge v \geq u$. A *strongly connected component* of a graph is a maximal strongly connected induced subgraph. A directed graph G is *acyclic* or a *DAG* iff it does not have a strongly connected component. On a directed acyclic graph the relations $\leq_G, \geq_G$ form a partial order on the vertex set. A walk on a directed acyclic graph is called a *path* or a *chain*. A set of vertices $U \subseteq V(G)$ is an *antichain* if $\forall u, v \in U : u \geq v \vee v \geq u \Rightarrow u = v$.

2.2 Learning Directed Cuts

Classification on graphs involves identifying a subset of the vertices, say $C \subseteq V$. We investigate identifying directed cuts. Formally, a set C defines a *directed cut* $E(C, V \setminus C)$ in a digraph if and only if $E(V \setminus C, C) = \emptyset$ (see, e.g., [1]). Due to the bijection between sets C defining directed cuts and the set of *cut edges* $E(C, V \setminus C)$ we will us the term *directed cut* to refer to C as well as to $E(C, V \setminus C)$. In the partially contaminated water system example, the uncontaminated water defines a directed cut corresponding to the set of pipes connecting contaminated to uncontaminated water.

In terms of the partial order $\geq$ induced by the digraph (V, E), a directed cut can then be seen as a set of vertices $U \subset V$ such that $\nexists u \in U, v \in V \setminus U : v \geq u$. Furthermore, identifying a directed cut can be seen as learning a labelling function $y : V \to \Omega$ where $\forall (u, v) \in E : y(v) \Rightarrow y(u)$. We call such a labelling a *monotone concept on a digraph* or *consistent with the directed graph* in the sense that the preorder of the vertices is respected by the labelling. A monotone concept y corresponds to the directed cut $C_y = \{v \in V \mid y(v)\}$ which we will sometimes call the *extension* of y and $E \cap (C_y \times V \setminus C_y)$ will be called the *concept cut*. The elements of the concept cut will be referred to as *cut edges*.

Without loss of generality it is sufficient to consider learning on DAGs. Any result for DAGs (defining a partial order) directly carries over to general digraphs (defining a preorder). This holds as directed cuts can never "cut" a strongly connected component. Learning on a general digraph is hence equivalent to learning on a digraph that has all strongly connected components contracted. Also, without loss of generality we can always add a 'super-source' and a 'super-sink' such that the new graph has a unique minimum and maximum.

2.3 The Cost of Learning

We consider the following question: Given an oracle that can provide us with hints about the fixed but unknown concept to be learned and some cost for each hint, what is the worst case total cost needed to induce a satisfactory hypothesis? This question is important, for instance, when only a given budget is available for the task of finding a satisfactory hypothesis. Different concrete learning settings considered in literature are distinguished by the type of the hints given by the oracle, the cost function, and the definition of satisfactory hypotheses.

For *active learning* the oracle supplies the learning algorithm with the true label of any instance selected by the learning algorithm. Each hint, i.e., answer to a query, has a fixed cost and the hypothesis is satisfactory iff it is equal to the concept. Calls to the labelling oracle are called *membership queries.* For *online learning* the oracle selects an instance, makes the learning algorithm guess its label and then supplies the learning algorithm with the true label. Each wrong guess has a fixed cost and the hypothesis is satisfactory iff it is equal to the concept. The maximum total cost is the *worst case missclassification bound.* For *PAC learning* the oracle supplies the learning algorithm with a labelled instance drawn according to a fixed but unknown distribution. Each example has a fixed cost and a hypothesis is satisfactory iff it can be guaranteed that its error for examples drawn from the same distribution is smaller than some ϵ with probability larger than $1-\delta$ for some δ. The total cost is the *sample complexity.*

As we are considering a transductive setting, i.e., the whole vertex set (without any labels) is input to the learning algorithm, we are interested in achieving costs logarithmic in the size of the graph. Hence, we consider a concept not learnable on a digraph in one of the above settings if we can not achieve polylogarithmic cost bounds. It can be seen that the general problem of identifying a directed cut is not learnable in any of the above settings. Consider the DAG $(\llbracket n+2\rrbracket, (\{n+1\} \times \llbracket n\rrbracket) \cup (\llbracket n\rrbracket \times \{n+2\}))$. Given $y(n+1) \wedge \neg y(n+2)$, and any information about the vertices $\llbracket n\rrbracket \setminus \{u\}$ for some $u \in \llbracket n\rrbracket$, we can not infer the label of u. This implies that—in the worst case—it is impossible to identify the correct directed cut without costs in the order of the size of the graph.

2.4 Fixed Parameter Learnability

As directed cuts are in general not learnable, it is important to identify tractable subclasses. Performance parameters proposed in machine learning literature can be distinguished into concept-dependent and concept-independent parameters. Concept-dependent parameters define subclasses of the concept class. Concept-independent parameters define subclasses of the instance space. An example of the first case is the VC dimension of k-term monotone DNF formulae; an example of the latter case is the VC dimension of monotone Boolean formulae over n variables. Concept-independent parameters may be further distinguished into transductive ones and inductive ones.

The related setting of identifying a cut in an undirected graph (see e.g. [2] for a derivation of the VC dimension of small cuts) has been found to be fixed parameter learnable where the parameter is the size of the concept cut, i.e., the number of edges between differently labelled vertices. Although we can show that directed cuts are also fixed parameter learnable if the size of the directed concept cut is considered as the parameter, the dependency of the total cost on

Table 1. Total cost of learning monotone concepts as well as intersections of monotone and anti-monotone concepts in a DAG (V, E) for various cost models and fixed size of the minimum path cover Q^*. A '=' indicates an exact result for all directed graphs, '$\leq$' ('$\geq$') indicate tight upper (lower) bounds.

	Monotone Concepts	Intersections
Active query bound	$\leq \lvert Q^*\rvert \log \lvert V\rvert$	$= \lvert V\rvert$
Online mistake bound	$\leq \lvert Q^*\rvert \log \lvert V\rvert$	$\leq \lvert Q^*\rvert + 2\lvert Q^*\rvert \log \lvert V\rvert$
VC dimension	$= \lvert Q^*\rvert$	$\leq 2\lvert Q^*\rvert; \geq \lvert Q^*\rvert$
PAC sample complexity	$\leq \left\lceil \frac{\lvert Q^*\rvert}{\epsilon} \ln \frac{\lvert Q^*\rvert}{\delta} \right\rceil$	$\leq \left\lceil \frac{2\lvert Q^*\rvert}{\epsilon} \ln \frac{2\lvert Q^*\rvert}{\delta} \right\rceil$

a parameter of the concept is often not desireable. In particular in cases where we want or need to estimate the total cost of learning the cut a priori, concept-dependent parameters such as the size of the concept cut are not sufficient.

In this paper we concentrate on learning monotone concepts on DAGs for which the size of the minimum path cover of the vertices is bounded. This parameter is concept-independent and transductive. Hence, opposed to the size of the concept cut, it can be used to a priori estimate the total cost of classification.

3 Learning with Fixed Minimum Path Cover Size

Table 1 summarises the results that can be obtained when the size of the minimum path cover Q^* of the DAG is fixed. In all but one of the considered learning settings, monotone concepts (directed cuts) as well as the intersection of monotone and anti-monotone concepts are fixed-parameter learnable, i.e., the total cost of learning is $O(|Q^*| \log |V|)$. The remainder of this section first introduces path covers and then describes the performance guarantees in more details.

3.1 Path Covers of DAGs

A *path cover* of $U \subseteq V$ in a DAG $G = (V, E)$ is a set $Q \subseteq \mathcal{P}(G)$ of paths such that $U = \bigcup_{p \in Q} V(p)$. The algorithms we present later and/or their analysis rely on a minimum path cover of $V(G)$. We refer to an arbitrary minimum path cover as Q^* and assume wlog that Q^* contains only maximal paths and hence that each path starts at the source (labelled $\top$) and ends at the sink (labelled $\perp$).

The size of the minimum path cover is upper bounded by the maximum dicut which is hard to find. In contrast to the concept cut it is not lower bounded by the minimum dicut and can be computed in polynomial time (see, e.g., [3] for algorithms) from the graph without knowing the concept. It can indeed be much smaller than the concept cut.In fact, while the concept cut size is lower bounded by the minimum dicut, the minimum path cover can even be smaller than the minimum dicut. Last but not least, the minimum path cover has the intuitive property that learning gets the easier the more edges we observe. Note that this is not the case when using the size of the concept cut.

3.2 Learning Monotone Concepts

To see that the results of Table 1 are tight when learning directed cuts (i.e. monotone concepts), consider the digraph $([\![n{+}2]\!], (\{n{+}1\}\times[\![n]\!])\cup([\![n]\!]\times\{n{+}2\}))$. Given $y(n+1)\wedge\neg y(n+2)$, and any information about the labels of the vertices $[\![n]\!]\setminus\{u\}$ for some $u\in[\![n]\!]$, we can not infer the label of u.

The algorithms for active and online learning perform binary search on each path in the path cover independently. For active learning this means always querying the vertex furthest from the nearest vertex with known or inferred label in the path, i.e., the vertex half way between the smallest known positive and the largest known negative of the path. With each query we can then learn the label of at least half of the remaining vertices. For online learning binary search means always predicting according to the closest vertex in the path. With each mistake we can deduce the label of at least half of the remaining vertices.

That the VC dimension is smaller than the size of the minimum path cover follows by induction over the path cover size and two observations: Firstly, on each path, monotone concepts can only shatter one vertex. Secondly, introducing more edges can not allow us to shatter more vertices. That the VC dimension is equal to the size of the minimum path cover follows then by Dilworth's theorem [4]. This theorem relates the size of the minimum path cover to the size of the largest antichain. Observing that each antichain can be shattered by monotone concepts gives the desired result. As efficiently finding a consistent hypothesis is trivial, directed cuts can be efficiently PAC learned. A direct proof of the sample complexity is very similar to the proof for axis-aligned rectangles and will be included in an extended version of the paper.

Notice that learning directed cuts generalises learning of monotone Boolean formulae by considering each Boolean instance as a vertex of a directed hypercube, i.e., the digraph $(2^{[\![n]\!]}, \{(U, U\cup\{v\})\mid U\subseteq[\![n]\!]\wedge v\notin U\})$. An antichain of size $\binom{n}{\lceil n/2\rceil}$ in this graph is found as $\{U\subseteq V\mid |U|=\lceil n/2\rceil\}$ and that this is indeed the largest anti-chain follows from Sperner's theorem [5]. This VC dimension is exactly the one obtained (without path covers) in [6]. However, for data that is only a subset of the hypercube, our transductive guarantee can be (much) better. For instance, it can be seen that the size of the minimum path cover of a set of Boolean instances does not change when redundant attributes are introduced. Most other results on learning of monotone Boolean formulae consider particular sets of functions with restricted complexity, e.g. the size of the smallest decision tree representing the concept [7]. As complexity is a concept dependent parameter, we can not use it to estimate classification costs a priori. Our results are complementary to these bounds, as depending on the concept class and the training and test instances, one or the other bound is tighter.

3.3 Learning Intersections of (Anti-) Monotone Concepts

Given some functions $y_i : V \to \Omega$ monotone on a digraph (V, E) and constants $b_i \in \Omega$ we call the concept $y_\cap(v) = \bigwedge_i b_i \operatorname{xor} y_i(v)$ an *intersection of monotone and anti-monotone concepts* on G. The total cost of learning such concepts is summarised in the second column of Table 1.

To see that active learning is not possible in this setting, consider any ordering $i_1, \ldots i_{|V|}$ in which an algorithms queries the vertices of any digraph. As the intersection concept class contains the empty set as well as any singleton vertex, given $y(i_1), \ldots y(i_{|V|-1}) = \bot$ we can not conclude the label of $i_{|V|}$.

For online learning, on the other hand, a small modification of the above described algorithm for learning directed cuts suffices to obtain a mistake bound logarithmic in the number of vertices: As long as we have not observed any label on a path, we predict $\bot$. As soon as we make the first mistake on a path, we split the problem in two subproblems, each equivalent to learning a directed cut.

The proof of the VC dimension being upper bounded by twice the size of the minimum path cover follows along the lines of the proof of the monotone case. However, we now only have a bound, not an exact result. To see that there are graphs for which the VC dimension of intersections of monotone and anti-monotone concepts is smaller than twice the size of the minimum path cover, consider the graph $([4], \{(1, 2), (2, 4), (1, 3), (3, 4)\})$. This graph has an antichain of size two and hence no smaller path cover. However, we can not shatter all four vertices as we can never achieve that $y(1) = y(4) = \top = \neg y(2) = \neg y(3)$. The precise VC dimension depends in this case on the maximum $\mathcal{U} \subseteq [V]^2$ with $\forall U, U' \in \mathcal{U}, u \in U, u' \in U' : u \leq u' \vee u' \leq u \Rightarrow U = U'$.

4 Learning Despite Changing Concepts

In many real world learning problems the target concept may change depending on a hidden context such as unobservable variations in the environment. For instance, consider again the directed graph representing the assembly of a product from subparts. Learning a directed cut corresponds in this example to finding those stages of the process that introduced faults. Indeed, whether a fault is introduced at some stage or not, may depend on an unknown property, like variations in basic parts. Hence, the fault may occur only sometimes, depending on this hidden context. In order to be able to trade off between the cost of having a faulty product and the costs needed to find the cause of the fault, tight performance guarantees for learning with hidden contexts are needed.

For that, we consider a variant of active learning where the target concept $y_b : V \to \Omega$ also depends on a *hidden context* b that may change at any time. We can view this as having different monotone concepts C_b for each value of b and the oracle chooses a b for each query. For simplicity we restrict ourselves to Boolean contexts $b \in \Omega$. The aim of the learning algorithm is to discover either of the true concepts, $C_\top$ or $C_\bot$, despite the changing concepts.

To obtain worst case bounds for this setting, we consider the oracle as an adversarial 'evil' oracle that chooses the hidden context to maximise the cost of learning either of the directed cuts. Although the context does not need to be (and often will not be) a function of the query, to prove negative results it will be useful to sometimes view it in this way. Key roles in the analysis of the learning algorithms will be played by the edges connecting vertices with different labels in one of the concepts, the *cut edges*, as well as by the elements of the symmetric difference of the two true concepts, the *distinction points* $C_\top \triangle C_\perp$ (the elements in either of the concepts but not in both).

Similar to the settings without a hidden context, a setting will be called learnable if there is a learning algorithm that can be guaranteed to identify one of the true concepts while asking only a number of queries (poly-) logarithmic in the number of vertices. However, we will now also encounter settings in which we can not find a true concept even by querying all vertices.

In the remainder we will show that traditional membership queries are not sufficient to learn directed cuts when a hidden context is present. One way to enable learning is to allow the algorithm to ask for the label of multiple vertices at the same time, which the oracle is then forced to answer according to the same concept. We will call these "m-ary" queries, where $m \in \mathbb{N}$ is the number of vertices that can be queried at once and will be answered from the same concept, i.e., during one m-ary query the context does not to change. We use the notation $\langle\cdot\rangle_m : V^m \to \Omega^m$ for m-ary queries. We will show that 2-ary queries are only slightly more powerful than 1-ary queries and that in general directed cuts with a hidden context are not learnable with 2-ary queries. However, we will also describe an algorithm that is able to correctly identify one of the true concepts with logarithmically (in the size of the graph) many 3-ary queries.

4.1 1-Ary Membership Queries

With traditional membership queries, directed cuts with hidden context are not learnable even if the size of the minimum path cover is fixed. We distinguish two cases depending on the size of the symmetric difference $C_\perp \triangle C_\top$ of the concepts.

Consider first the case $|C_\perp \triangle C_\top| \geq 2$. Here, we can find an adversarial context such that any learning algorithm can discover neither of the two true concepts. Let $v \in \max C_\perp \triangle C_\top$ where the maximum is taken with respect to the partial order induced by the DAG and assume without loss of generality that $v \in C_\top$. Then, any vertex before v in the partial order (an ancestor) belongs to both $C_\top$ and $C_\perp$. Hence, the set $S = C_\perp \cup \{v\}$ is monotone. The oracle can pretend to answer from S by choosing $C_\perp$ for all queries u with $u \neq v$ and choosing $C_\top$ only if $u = v$. Observing these answers from the oracle, the learning algorithm can not guess either of the true concepts.

In fact, even in the extreme case with the symmetric difference $|C_\perp \triangle C_\top| \leq 1$, directed cuts are not learnable: The answers of the oracle can not be distinguished from the above case without knowing $|C_\perp \triangle C_\top| \leq 1$.

For an illustrative example consider the path $(\llbracket 4 \rrbracket, \{(1,2),(2,3),(3,4)\})$ with the concepts $C_\perp = \llbracket 1 \rrbracket$ and $C_\top = \llbracket 3 \rrbracket$. If the query $u \in \llbracket 2 \rrbracket$, the oracle answers according to $C_\top$, otherwise according to $C_\perp$. Then, no matter the queries, the learning algorithm will only observe the 'fake' concept $\llbracket 2 \rrbracket$. Now, consider the concepts $C_\bot = [\![1]\!]$ and $C_\top = [\![2]\!]$. Even if the oracle answers consistently according to $C_\top$, the learning algorithm has no means of distinguishing this case from the previous one. Even more surprisingly, also in the seemingly trivial case $C_\top = C_\bot = [\![2]\!]$, we have no means to distinguish the answers of the oracle from the answers in the previous case.

4.2 2-Ary Membership Queries

We consider now 2-ary membership queries, i.e., the learning algorithm can ask for the label of two vertices simultaneously and the answers will be given from the same concept. After each 2-ary query, the context may change. We denote 2-ary queries of vertices v and v' by $\langle v, v'\rangle_2$.

As one would expect, 2-ary queries are more powerful than traditional (1-ary) queries. For an example where this holds, consider a single path $([\![n]\!], \{(i, i+1) \mid i \in [\![n-1]\!]\})$ and coinciding concepts $C_\top = C_\bot = [\![c]\!]$ for some $1 < c < n$. In this case we can find out whether $[\![i]\!]$ is a true concept or not by simply querying the vertices $\langle i, i+1\rangle_2$ in one 2-ary query. If the answer is $\langle i, i+1\rangle_2 = (\top, \bot)$ we have found a true concept ($i = c$) otherwise not. As we assumed $C_\top = C_\bot$ we can find this cut edge with logarithmically many queries.

However, already the simple setting of a single path with symmetric difference $|C_\top \triangle C_\bot| \geq 1$ is not learnable with 2-ary queries. In this case, no matter which queries the learning algorithm asks, the oracle can always answer such that it only reveals a distinction point (an element of the symmetric difference) and 'hides' the concept cut. In fact, a naive learning algorithm that queries all pairs of vertices connected by an edge suffices to find at least one distinction point. If the oracle would try not to reveal a distinction point, it would need to answer one 2-ary query of adjacent vertices by $\top, \bot$ and it would hence reveal us one true concept, which it will—of course—avoid.

If we find a distinction point we can query the pair of vertices adjacent to the distinction point, say u, v. Through the answer we can either identify another distinction point or we can be sure that one of the two concepts has a cut bettween u and v. We can repeat this procedure, now querying the vertices adjacent to the distinction area, until we find no further distinction point. Then, we can be sure that the distinction area is adjacent to a cut edge, however, we cannot be sure which side of the distinction area is adjacent to the cut.

Consider the illustrative example $([\![3]\!], \{(1,2), (2,3)\})$. We will show that even when asking the full set of possible query combinations, the corresponding answers can be such that deducing one of the true concepts is not possible. Suppose now, all possible 2-ary queries are answered as follows: $\langle 1, 2\rangle_2 = (\top, \top)$; $\langle 2, 3\rangle_2 = (\bot, \bot)$; $\langle 1, 3\rangle_2 = (\top, \bot)$. The learning algorithm knows from these answers that: First, vertex 2 belongs to the symmetric difference of the two true concepts, i.e. $2 \in C_\top \triangle C_\bot$; second, there is one of the true concepts that contains vertices 1, 2; and third, there is one of the true concepts that does not contain vertices 2, 3. Yet this information does not allow the learning algorithm to certainly identify a true concept. It might be that: (*i*) $C_\top = [\![1]\!], C_\bot = [\![2]\!]$; (*ii*) $C_\top = [\![1]\!], C_\bot = [\![3]\!]$; and (*iii*) $C_\top = \emptyset, C_\bot = [\![2]\!]$. For each possibility, there is a context such that the oracle will produce the above mentioned set of answers. Hence, the learning algorithm has no means to distinguish these possibilities. Notice that in this case knowing $|C_\top \triangle C_\bot| = 1$ would help us identify both true concepts while even knowing $|C_\top \triangle C_\bot| = 2$ would not be sufficient to surely identify one concept.

4.3 3-Ary Membership Queries

In this section, we consider 3-ary membership queries. We give an algorithm that is guaranteed to find one of the true concepts for any DAG and any pair of concepts with at most $|Q^*|^2 + 2|Q^*| \log |V|$ many 3-ary membership queries. The learning algorithm can be summarised in three steps:

1. Find an edge that corresponds to a cut edge in one of the true concepts on each path in the path cover or find a distinction point ($\leq |Q^*| \log |V|$).
2. Check that the cut edges (from step 1) on each path belong to the same true concept or find a distinction point ($\leq |Q^*|^2$).
3. Given a distinction point, find any of the two concepts ($\leq 2|Q^*| \log |V|$).

Note that the main difference between 3-ary queries and 2-ary ones is that as soon as we have a distinction point, we can use it to perform a coordinated binary search in both true concepts at the same time.

Step one (*finding a cut edge or a distinction point*) could in principle proceed as described above for 2-ary membership queries, however, with 3-ary queries we can find the cut or a distinction point on each path p in $\log |V|$ many queries: We repeatedly perform binary search by querying the smallest known positive on p, the largest known negative on p as well as the vertex half way between them. As long as we do not get a distinction point on a path, we assume all answers of the oracle correspond to the same concept. Notice that even if the oracle changed the concept but the answers stay consistent with those received so far, the strategy of the learning algorithm needs no change. Unless we get a distinction point, we can reduce the number of vertices on this path for which we do not know any label by half. Hence, after $\log |V|$ many queries we will either get a distinction point or a cut edge. If we do not have a distinction point yet, we proceed with the same procedure on the next path.

Step two (*finding a distinction point*) needs to check wether the individual cut edges that we found in step one for each path, correspond all to the same concept. If this is the case then we are done, otherwise we find a distinction point. This can be achieved with $|Q^*|^2$ many queries as follows: For a pair of paths $p, q \in Q^*$ denote the corresponding cut edges found in step one by (u_p, v_p) and (u_q, v_q), respectively. The learning algorithm can find out if there is one true concept which both edges correspond to, by asking only two 3-ary queries $\langle u_p, v_p, u_q \rangle_3$ and $\langle u_p, v_p, v_q \rangle_3$. If the oracle answers consistently with its previous answers then such a true concept exists. If the oracle deviates from its previous answers, we have found a distinction point. We proceed with the next pair of paths until we get a distinction point or have checked that there is a concept in which all edges found in step one are correct cut edges.

Step three (*finding a concept given a distinction point*) is the simplest of the three steps and will be performed after in step one or two the learning algorithm found a distinction point. It proceeds simply by performing a binary search on each path in the path cover for both concepts at the same time. The 3-ary query will always include the distinction point as one of the queries, and the two remaining ones will be used for the binary search. After at most $2|Q^*|\log|V|$ many queries (in fact we may subtract the number of queries made in step one) we can be sure to have found one of the two concepts.

5 Related Work

Recently, the use of cuts in learning on graphs is becoming more and more popular. Usually motivated by the 'cluster assumption' [8] one tries to find a small cut separating positive labeled vertices from negative labeled ones. for instance, work in [9] extends an earlier approach based on finding the minimum cuts in a graph by adding randomness to the graph structure. In [2] it is shown that the VC dimension of small cuts is bounded by the size of the cut. The disadvantage of these approaches is that the performance depends on a property of the concept and not on an efficiently computable property of the graph like the minimum path cover. Furthermore, in the kind of applications we mentioned in the introduction, it is questionable whether the concept cut is indeed small.

It is also possible to derive concept-dependent results for learning directed cuts. We show this here for active learning: As long as there is a walk from source to sink, choose the shortest such walk and perform binary search on this path. As soon as a concept cut edge is found, remove it and iterate. At least every $\log|V|$ iterations a concept cut edge is removed and the algorithm terminates with the corret cut after as many iterations as there are edges in the cut.

Learning directed cuts is also closely related to learning monotone Boolean formulae as these can be modelled by directed cuts on the directed hypercube. Most performance guarantees for learning monotone Boolean formulae are concept-dependent. We showed that our results imply concept-independent and transductive performance guarantees for learning monotone Boolean formulae.

Learning with concept drift due to hidden context has for instance been investigated in [10,11]. The setting is different from ours in that once a concept is learned, it can become invalid only after a certain interval of time. To the best of our knowledge, learning monotone concepts with hidden context that can change at arbitrary points in time has not been investigated.

6 Conclusions

The question whether a learning task is feasible with a given budget is an important problem in real world machine learning applications. Recent learning theoretical work has concentrated on performance guarantees that depend on the complexity of the target function or at least on strong assumptions about the target function. In this paper we proposed performance guarantees that only make natural assumptions about the target concept and that otherwise depend just on properties of the unlabelled training and test data. This is in contrast to related work on learning small cuts in undirected graphs where usually the size of the concept cut is taken as a (concept-dependent) learning parameter.

Concepts on digraphs, which are a natural model, e.g., for technical processes, are typically monotonic. In this paper we proposed the size of the minimum path cover as a performance parameter for learning directed cuts (i.e., monotone concepts on digraphs). On the one hand, this parameter can efficiently be computed from unlabelled training and test data only; and is, on the other hand, sufficiently powerful to make directed cuts fixed parameter learnable in the active, online, as well as PAC learning frameworks.

In many real world learning problems, an additional challenge is often that the concept that a learning algorithm tries to identify changes depending on some hidden context. We hence extended the usual query learning model to include a hidden context that can change at any time and explored learnability with a more powerful query model. In particular, we show that to enable learnability despite a changing concept, it is necessary (and sufficient) that the learning algorithm can query three different vertices at a time where it is ensured that the answers will be provided on the basis of the same concept. While, in this paper, we concentrated on learning on directed graphs, we believe that this setting can also have significant impact in other domains where some relevant variables are unobservable. We will study such domains as part of our future work.

References

1. Korte, B., Vygen, J.: Combinatorial Optimization: Theory and Algorithms. Springer, Heidelberg (2002)
2. Kleinberg, J.: Detecting a network failure. In: FOCS, IEEE, Los Alamitos (2000)
3. Ntafos, S., Hakimi, S.: On path cover problems in digraphs and applications to program testing. IEEE Transactions on Software Engineering (1979)
4. Dilworth, R.: A decomposition theorem for partially ordered sets. Annals of Mathematics (1948)
5. Sperner, E.: Ein satz über untermengen einer endlichen menge. Mathematische Zeitschrift (1928)
6. Procaccia, A.D., Rosenschein, J.S.: Exact vc-dimension of monotone formulas. Neural Information Processing — Letters and Reviews (2006)
7. O'Donnell, R., Servedio, R.A.: Learning monotone decision trees in polynomial time. In: IEEE Conference on Computational Complexity, IEEE, Los Alamitos (2006)
8. Chapelle, O., Zien, A.: Semi-supervised classification by low density separation. In: AISTATS (2005)
9. Blum, A., Lafferty, J., Rwebangira, M.R., Reddy, R.: Semi-supervised learning using randomized mincuts. In: ICML'04, vol. 13 (2004)
10. Harries, M.B., Sammut, C., Horn, K.: Extracting hidden context. Machine Learning 32(2), 101–126 (1998)
11. Widmer, G., Kubat, M.: Effective learning in dynamic environments by explicit context tracking. In: ECML '93, pp. 227–243 (1993)

Spectral Clustering and Embedding with Hidden Markov Models

Tony Jebara, Yingbo Song, and Kapil Thadani

Department of Computer Science, Columbia University, New York NY 10027, USA
{jebara,yingbo,kapil}@cs.columbia.edu

Abstract. Clustering has recently enjoyed progress via spectral methods which group data using only pairwise affinities and avoid parametric assumptions. While spectral clustering of vector inputs is straightforward, extensions to structured data or time-series data remain less explored. This paper proposes a clustering method for time-series data that couples non-parametric spectral clustering with parametric hidden Markov models (HMMs). HMMs add some beneficial structural and parametric assumptions such as Markov properties and hidden state variables which are useful for clustering. This article shows that using probabilistic pairwise kernel estimates between parametric models provides improved experimental results for unsupervised clustering and visualization of real and synthetic datasets. Results are compared with a fully parametric baseline method (a mixture of hidden Markov models) and a non-parametric baseline method (spectral clustering with non-parametric time-series kernels).

1 Introduction

This paper explores unsupervised learning in the time-series domain using a combination of parametric and non-parametric methods. Some parametric assumptions, such as Markov assumptions and hidden state assumptions, are quite useful for time-series data. However, it is also advantageous to remain non-parametric and agnostic about the overall shape that a collection of time-series data forms. This paper provides surprising empirical evidence that a semi-parametric [1,2] method can outperform both fully parametric methods of describing multiple time-series observations and fully non-parametric methods. These improvements include better clustering performance as well as better embedding and visualization over existing state-of-the-art time-series techniques.

There are a variety of parametric and non-parametric algorithms for discovering clusters within a dataset; however, the application of these techniques for clustering sequential data such as time-series data poses a number of additional challenges. Time-series data has inherent structure which may be disregarded by a fully non-parametric method. Additionally, a clustering approach for time-series data must be capable of detecting similar hidden properties or behavior between sequences of different lengths with no obvious alignment principle across temporal observations.

J.N. Kok et al. (Eds.): ECML 2007, LNAI 4701, pp. 164–175, 2007.

Alternatively, standard parametric clustering methods are popular but can make excessively strict assumptions about the overall distribution of a dataset of time-series samples. Expectation Maximization (EM), for example, estimates a fully parametric mixture model by iteratively adjusting the parameters to maximize likelihood [3,4,5]. In the time-series domain, a mixture of hidden Markov models (HMMs) can be used for clustering [5]. This is sensible since the underlying Markov process assumption is useful for a time series. However, the parametric *mixture* of HMMs may make invalid assumptions about the shape of the overall distribution of the collection of time-series exemplars. Just as a mixture of Gaussians assumes a radial shape for each cluster, many fully parametric time series models make assumptions about the shape of the variation across the many time series in a dataset. This is only sensible if data is organized into radial or symmetric clusters. In practice, though, clusters (of points or of time series) might actually be smoothly varying in a non-radially distributed manner.

Recent graph-theoretic approaches to clustering [6,7,8], on the other hand, do not make assumptions about the underlying distribution of the data. Data samples are treated as nodes in a weighted graph, where the edge weight between any two nodes is given by a similarity metric or kernel function. A k-way clustering is represented as a series of cuts which remove edges from the graph, dividing the graph into a set of k disjoint subgraphs. This approach clusters data even when the underlying parametric form is unknown (as long as there are enough samples) and far from radial or spherical. Unfortunately, recovering the optimal cuts is an NP-complete problem as was shown by Shi and Malik [8] who proposed the Normalized Cut (NCut) criterion. Spectral clustering is a relaxation of NCut into an linear system which uses eigenvectors of the graph Laplacian to cluster the data [7].

This article takes a semi-parametric approach to combine the complementary advantages of both methods. It applies recent work in spectral clustering [7] to the task of clustering time-series data. However, each time series is individually modeled using HMMs. This assumes HMM structure for each time-series datum on its own yet assumes no underlying structure in the overall distribution of the time-series data. The sequences are clustered only according to their individual pairwise proximity in HMM parameter space. It should be noted that though HMMs are used in this paper, the approach is applicable to clustering other time-series datasets under different parametric assumptions such as linear dynamical systems.

2 HMMs and Kernels

2.1 Hidden Markov Models

Assume a dataset of $n = 1 \ldots N$ time-series sequences where each datum $\mathbf{x}_n$ is an ordered sequence of $t = 1, \ldots, T_n$ vectors $x_{n,t}$ in some Euclidean space. A natural parametric model for representing a single time series or sequence $\mathbf{x}_n$ is the hidden Markov model (HMM), whose likelihood is denoted $p(\mathbf{x}_n|\theta_n)$. Note that the model θ_n is different for each sequence. This replaces the common *iid* (independent identically distributed) assumption on the dataset with a weaker *id* (independently distributed) assumption. More specifically, for $p(\mathbf{x}_n|\theta_n)$, consider a first-order stationary HMM with Gaussian emissions. The probability model of a sequence is $p(\mathbf{x}|\theta)$ where $\mathbf{x} = \{x_1, \ldots, x_T\}$ is a sequence of length T where each observation vector is $x_t \in \Re^d$. In addition, an HMM has a hidden state at each time point $\mathbf{q} = \{q_1, \ldots, q_T\}$ where each state takes on a discrete value $q_t = \{1, \ldots, M\}$. The likelihood of the HMM factorizes as follows:

$$p(\mathbf{x}|\theta) = \sum_{q_0,\ldots,q_T} p(x_0|q_0)p(q_0)\prod_{t=1}^{T} p(x_t|q_t)p(q_t|q_{t-1}) \tag{1}$$

The HMM is specified by the parameters: $\theta = (\pi, \alpha, \mu, \Sigma)$

1. The initial state probability distribution $\pi_i = p(q_0 = i)$, $i = 1 \ldots M$.
2. The state transition probability distribution given by a matrix $\alpha \in \Re^{M\times M}$ where $\alpha_{ij} = p(q_t = j|q_{t-1} = i)$.
3. The emission density $p(x_t|q_t = i) = \mathcal{N}(x_t|\mu_i, \Sigma_i)$, for $i = 1 \ldots M$, where $\mu_i \in \Re^d$ and $\Sigma_i \in \Re^{d\times d}$ are the mean and covariance of the Gaussian in state i. Take $\mu = \{\mu_1, \ldots, \mu_M\}$ and $\Sigma = \{\Sigma_1, \ldots, \Sigma_M\}$ for short.

Estimating the parameters of an HMM for a single sequence is typically done via EM. The E-step uses a forward-backward pass or junction tree algorithm (JTA) to obtain posterior marginals over the hidden states given the observations: $\gamma_t(i) = p(q_t = S_i|\mathbf{x}_n, \hat{\theta}_n)$ and $\xi_t(i,j) = p(q_t = S_i, q_{t+1} = S_j|\mathbf{x}_n, \hat{\theta}_n)$. The M-step updates the parameters θ using these E-step marginals as follows: $\hat{\pi}_i = \gamma_1(i)$

$$\hat{\alpha}_{ij} = \frac{\sum_{t=1}^{T-1}\xi_t(i,j)}{\sum_{t=1}^{T-1}\sum_{j=1}^{M}\xi_t(i,j)} \quad \hat{\mu}_i = \frac{\sum_{t=1}^{T}\gamma_t(i)x_t}{\sum_{t=1}^{T}\gamma_t(i)} \quad \hat{\Sigma}_i = \frac{\sum_{t=1}^{T}\gamma_t(i)(x_t-\mu_i)(x_t-\mu_i)^T}{\sum_{t=1}^{T}\gamma_t(i)}.$$

2.2 Probability Product Kernels

A natural choice of kernel between HMMs is the probability product kernel (PPK) described in [9] since it computes an affinity between distributions. The generalized inner product is found by integrating a product of the distributions of pairs of data sequences over the space of all potential observable sequences $\mathcal{X}$: $\mathcal{K}(p(\mathbf{x}|\theta), p(\mathbf{x}|\theta')) = \int p^{\beta}(\mathbf{x}|\theta)p^{\beta}(\mathbf{x}|\theta')d\mathbf{x}$. When $\beta = 1/2$, the PPK becomes the classic Bhattacharyya affinity metric between two probability distributions. The Bhattacharyya affinity is favored over other probabilistic divergences and affinities such as Kullback-Leibler (KL) divergence because it is symmetric and positive semi-definite (it is a Mercer kernel). In addition, it is computable in closed form for a variety of distributions including HMMs while the KL between two HMMs cannot be exactly recovered efficiently.

This section discusses the computation of the PPK between two HMMs $p(\mathbf{x}|\theta)$ and $p(\mathbf{x}|\theta')$. For brevity, we denote $p(\mathbf{x}|\theta)$ as p and $p'(\mathbf{x}|\theta')$ as p' where $\mathbf{x}$ represents a sequence of emissions x_t for $t = 1...T$. While the brute force evaluation

Table 1. The probability product kernel

Probability product kernel $\mathcal{K}(\theta, \theta')$:
$\mathcal{K}(\theta, \theta') = \sum_{q_T} \sum_{q'_T} \Psi(q_T, q'_T)$
$\prod_{t=1}^{T} \sum_{q_{t-1}} \sum_{q'_{t-1}} p(q_t|q_{t-1})^\beta p'(q'_t|q'_{t-1})^\beta \Psi(q_{t-1}, q'_{t-1}) p(q_0)^\beta p'(q'_0)^\beta$
Elementary kernel $\Psi(\cdot)$:
$\Psi(q_t = i, q'_t = j) = \int_{x_t} p(x_t|q_t = i)^\beta p'(x_t|q'_t = j)^\beta dx_t$

An efficient iterative method to calculate the PPK $\tilde{\mathcal{K}}(\theta, \theta')$:
$\Phi(q_0, q'_0) = p(q_0)^\beta p'(q'_0)^\beta$
for $t = 1 \dots T$
$\Phi(q_t, q'_t) = \sum_{q_{t-1}} \sum_{q'_{t-1}} p(q_t|q_{t-1})^\beta p(q'_t|q'_{t-1})^\beta \Psi(q_{t-1}, q'_{t-1}) \Phi(q_{t-1}, q'_{t-1})$
end
$\tilde{\mathcal{K}}(\theta, \theta') = \sum_{q_T} \sum_{q'_T} \Phi(q_T, q'_T) \Psi(q_T, q'_T)$

of the integral over **x** is expensive, an exact efficient formula is possible. Effectively, the kernel takes advantage of the factorization of the HMMs to set up an efficient iterative formula.

Initially, an elementary kernel $\Psi(\theta, \theta') = \int_{x_t} p^\beta(x_t|\theta) p^\beta(x_t|\theta') dx_t$ is computed; this is the Bhattacharyya affinity between the emissions models for p and p' integrated over the space of all emissions. For the exponential family of distributions this integral can be calculated in closed form. For HMMs with Gaussian emissions, this integral is proportional to:

$$\Psi(i, j) = \frac{|\Sigma^\dagger|^{1/2}}{|\Sigma_i|^{\beta/2} |\Sigma_j|^{\beta/2} \exp(-\frac{\beta}{2}(\mu_i^T \Sigma_i^{-1} \mu_i + \mu_j{}^T \Sigma_j{}^{-1} \mu_j - \mu^{\dagger T} \Sigma^\dagger \mu^\dagger)}$$

where $\Sigma^\dagger = (\Sigma_i^{-1} + \Sigma_j{}^{-1})^{-1}$ and $\mu^\dagger = \Sigma_i^{-1} \mu_i + \Sigma_j{}^{-1} \mu_j$. Given the elementary kernel, the kernel between two HMMs is solved in $\mathcal{O}(TM^2)$ operations using the formula in Table 1 (further details can be found in [9]). Given a kernel affinity between two HMMs, a non-parametric relationship between time series sequences emerges. It is now straightforward to apply non-parametric clustering and embedding methods which will be described in section 4. The next section, however, first describes a more typical fully parametric clustering setup using a mixture of HMM models to couple the sequences and parameters θ_n. This has the undesirable effect of coupling pairs of sequences by making global parametric assumptions on the whole dataset instead of only on pairs of sequences.

3 Clustering as a Mixture of HMMs

Parametric approaches to clustering of time-series data using HMMs assume that each observation sequence $\mathbf{x}_n$ is generated from a mixture of K components and use different clustering formulations in order to estimate this mixture. Two such techniques for estimating a mixture of K HMMs are the hard-clustering k-means approach and the soft-clustering EM approach.

A k-means approach is used in [3,4] to assign sequences to clusters in each iteration and use only the sequences assigned to a cluster for re-estimation of its HMM parameters. Each sequence can only be assigned to *one* cluster per iteration and it can run into problems when there is no good separation between the processes that generated the data approximated by the HMM parameters. A soft-clustering approach that overcomes these problems is described in [5]; here each sequence has a prior probability $p(z = k)$ of being generated by the k'th HMM. This reduces to a search for the set of parameters $\{\theta_1, \ldots, \theta_K, p(z)\}$ where $z \in \{1, \ldots K\}$ that maximize the likelihood function $\prod_{n=1}^{N} \sum_{k=1}^{K} p(z = k) p(\mathbf{x}_n | \theta_k)$. The E-step is similar to the E-step in the HMM-training algorithm run separately for each of the K HMMs. The posterior likelihood $\tau_n^k = \frac{p(z=k)p(\mathbf{x}_n|\theta_k)}{\sum_{k=1}^{K} p(z=k)p(\mathbf{x}_n|\theta_k)}$ is estimated as the probability that sequence $\mathbf{x}_n$ was generated by HMM k. The M-step incorporates the posterior τ_n^k of each sequence n into its contribution to the updated parameters for the kth HMM.

$$\hat{\alpha}_{ij} = \frac{\sum_{n=1}^{N} \tau_n^k \sum_{t=1}^{T_n - 1} \xi_{n,t}^k(i,j)}{\sum_{n=1}^{N} \tau_n^k \sum_{t=1}^{T_n - 1} \sum_{j=1}^{M} \xi_{n,t}^k(i,j)} \qquad \hat{\mu}_i = \frac{\sum_{n=1}^{N} \tau_n^k \sum_{t=1}^{T_n} \gamma_{n,t}^k(i) x_{n,t}}{\sum_{n=1}^{N} \tau_n^k \sum_{t=1}^{T_n} \gamma_{n,t}^k(i)}$$

$$\hat{\pi}_i = \frac{\sum_{n=1}^{N} \tau_n^k \gamma_{n,1}^k(i)}{N} \qquad \hat{\Sigma}_i = \frac{\sum_{n=1}^{N} \tau_n^k \sum_{t=1}^{T_n} \gamma_{n,t}^k(i)(x_{n,t} - \mu_i)(x_{n,t} - \mu_i)^T}{\sum_{n=1}^{N} \tau_n^k \sum_{t=1}^{T_n} \gamma_{n,t}^k(i)}.$$

The responsibility terms τ_n^k also provide the priors $p(z = k)$ for the next iteration and determine the final clustering assignment at convergence.

In summary, this method makes strict parametric assumptions about the underlying distribution of all the sequences in the dataset and attempts to find a parameter setting that maximizes the posterior probabilities given such models for the underlying distributions. However, these parametric assumptions aren't always intuitive and, as our experiments show, often negatively affect clustering performance as opposed to the non-parametric methods that are being investigated in this article.

4 Spectral Clustering of HMMs

The spectral approach to HMM clustering involves estimating an HMM model for each sequence using the approach outlined in section 2.1. The PPK is then computed between all pairs of HMMs to generate a Gram matrix which is used for spectral clustering. This approach leverages both parametric and non-parametric techniques in the clustering process; parametric HMMs make some assumptions about the structure of the individual sequences (such as Markov assumptions) but the spectral clustering approach makes no assumptions about the overall distribution of the sequences (for instance, *i.i.d* assumptions). Empirically, this approach (Spectral Clustering of Probability Product Kernels or SC-PPK) achieves a noticeable improvement in clustering accuracy over fully parametric models such as mixtures of HMMs or naive pairwise likelihood comparisons.

Listed below are the steps of our proposed algorithm. It is a time-series analogue of the Ng-Weiss algorithm presented in [7].

The SC-PPK algorithm

1. Fit an HMM to each of the $n = 1 \ldots N$ time-series sequences to retrieve models $\theta_1 \ldots \theta_N$.
2. Calculate the Gram matrix $A \in \mathbb{R}^{N \times N}$ where $A_{m,n} = \mathcal{K}(\theta_m, \theta_n)$ for all pairs of models using the probability product kernel (default setting: $\beta = 1/2$, T=10).
3. Define $D \in \mathbb{R}^{N \times N}$ to be the diagonal matrix where $D_{m,m} = \sum_n A_{m,n}$ and construct the Laplacian matrix: $L = D^{-1/2} A D^{-1/2}$.
4. Find the K largest eigenvectors of L and form matrix $X \in \mathbb{R}^{N \times K}$ by stacking the eigenvectors in columns. Renormalize the rows of matrix X to have unit length.
5. Cluster the N rows of X into K clusters via k-means or any other algorithm that attempts to minimize distortion.
6. The cluster labels for the N rows are used to label the corresponding N HMM models.

Another well-known approach to clustering time-series data is Dynamic-Time-Warping, introduced in [3]. This method was surpassed in performance by the spectral clustering method proposed by Yin and Yang [10] which uses a direct comparison of HMM likelihoods as the kernel affinity. The SC-PPK method outperforms Yin and Yang's method due to the fact that it doesn't calculate the affinities based on a pair of time-series samples but integrates over the entire space of all possible samples given the HMM models. Thus, the SC-PPK approach recovers a stronger and more representative affinity score between HMM models. Furthermore, since the PPK computes the integration by solving a closed form kernel using an efficient iterative method, it achieves a significant gain in speed over the kernel used in [10].

5 Experiments

This section details the experiments that were conducted to compare semi-parametric spectral approaches and fully parametric approaches to clustering of time-series data. k-Means and EM versions of a mixture of HMMs approach were used to represent the parametric setting. The two spectral clustering algorithms investigated were Yin and Yang's algorithm[10], which computes a likelihood-based kernel between pairs of sequences, and the SC-PPK algorithm which computes a kernel over the HMM model parameters. Note that there are parameters which can be adjusted for both of the spectral clustering methods: the σ fall-off ratio for the Yin-Yang kernel and the mixing proportion T for the SC-PPK method. In the following experiments, the default settings were used for both methods, i.e. $\sigma = 1$ and $T = 10$. Stability results for these kernels are shown in Fig 1.

5.1 Datasets

The evaluations were run over a variety of real-world and synthesized datasets which are described below.

MOCAP: The Motion Capture dataset (available from Carnegie Mellon University[1]) consists of time-series data representing human locomotion and actions. The sequences consist of 123-dimensional vectors representing 41 body markers tracked spatially through time for various physical activities. For these experiments, simple activities that were likely to be hard to cluster were considere; tests compared either similar activities or the same activity for different subjects. Table 2 contains the results of the evaluation over these real-world datasets.
Rotated MOCAP: A synthesized dataset was generated by rotating two MOCAP sequences 5° at a time through 360 degrees. The seed sequences used were a walking sequence from WALK(#7) and a running sequence from RUN(#9). This dataset, which provides us with clusters of sequences that lie on a regular manifold, is used for comparing clustering in Table 3, comparing running times in Table 6 and embedding in Fig 2. An additional dataset SWERVING was generated by rotating the walking and running sequence left and right periodically to make their movements seem zig-zagged.
Arabic handwriting: This dataset consists of 2-dimensional time-series sequences which represent written word-parts of Arabic characters extracted from the dataset used in [11]. Table 4 shows the results of clustering pairs of similar word-parts (identified by their Unicode characters) and Fig 3(a) shows an MDS embedding of three symbols.
Australian sign language: This dataset (from the University of California-Irvine[2]) consists of multiple sign-language gestures, each represented by 27 instances of 22-dimensional time-series sequences. Semantically-related expressions such as *write* and *draw* or antonyms such as *give* and *take* were assumed to have similar real-world symbols and formed the basis of all experiments with this dataset. Table 5 shows the average accuracy over the clustering of 18 such pairs of sequences while varying the number of HMM states used and Fig 3(b) shows an embedding of three gestures.

5.2 Results

The tables in this section show the results of experiments over these various datasets. Experiments were restricted to pairwise clustering over datasets of similar size. The standard accuracy metric is used for comparison of results. The results reported were averaged over multiple folds - five folds for the spectral clustering algorithms and ten folds for the fully parametric techniques since these algorithms converge to local maxima and have highly variable performance).

In general, the kernel-based methods outperformed the parametric methods and the PPK performed favorably compared to Yin and Yang's kernel.

[1] http://mocap.cs.cmu.edu/

[2] http://www.cse.unsw.edu.au/w̃aleed/tml/data

Table 2. Clustering accuracy with 2-state HMMs on MOCAP data. The numbers in the parentheses identify the index of the subject performing that particular specified action.

Dataset	k-Means	EM	Yin-Yang	SC-PPK
simple walk vs run set	**100%**	**100%**	**100%**	**100%**
run(#9) vs run/jog(#35)	57%	52%	76%	**100%**
walk(#7) vs walk(#8)	59%	60%	**68%**	**68%**
walk(#7) vs run/jog(#35)	71%	69%	71%	**95%**
jump(#13) vs jump forward(#13)	50%	50%	75%	**87%**
jump(#13,#16) vs jump forward(#13,#16)	50%	50%	60%	**66%**

Table 3. Clustering accuracy with 2-state HMMs on synthesized MOCAP dataset. A single pair of walking and running time-series samples were used, subsequent samples were generated by rotating the seed pair 5° at a time to generate 72 unique pairs.

rotation limit	step size	k-Means	EM	Yin-Yang	SC-PPK
30°	5°	**100%**	**100%**	92%	**100%**
60°	5°	54%	71%	63%	**100%**
90°	5°	50%	50%	75%	**100%**
180°	5°	51%	51%	71%	**100%**
360°	5°	50%	50%	60%	**100%**
360°	10°	50%	50%	50%	**100%**
360°	15°	50%	50%	50%	**100%**
360°	30°	54%	50%	50%	**100%**
Swerving	–	50%	50%	85%	**100%**

Table 4. Clustering accuracy with 2-state HMMs on Arabic handwriting dataset

Dataset	k-Means	EM	YY	SC-PPK
U0641 vs U0643	68%	64%	86%	**97%**
U0645 vs U0647	70%	66%	86%	**100%**
U062D vs U062F	78%	80%	93%	**95%**
U0621 vs U062D	66%	65%	86%	**93%**
U0628 vs U0631	71%	70%	94%	**100%**
U0635 vs U0644	74%	76%	95%	**100%**
U0621 vs U0647	71%	66%	96%	**98%**

Improvements in accuracy well as better runtime performance were seen in both quantitative clustering accuracy and qualitative embedding performance. In addition, experiments were conducted to investigate the stability of the SC-PPK method over the T parameter. Fig 1 shows stability comparisons for both spectral clustering kernels over the respective parameters. The accuracies were averaged over five-fold testing. It was noted that a useful setting for T usually lay within the interval of 5 to 25. In practice, cross validation would be useful for recovering the optimal setting.

Table 5. Clustering accuracy on Australian sign language dataset; 18 semantically related pairs of signs compared. Top: 5 representative pairs are shown for a range of SC-PPK clustering accuracies. Bottom: averages for the 18 pairs over different number of states.

Sample pairs (2-state)	k-Means	EM	Yin-Yang	SC-PPK
'hot' vs 'cold'	64%	98%	96%	**100%**
'eat' vs 'drink'	52%	50%	52%	**93%**
'happy' vs 'sad'	73%	54%	50%	**87%**
'spend' vs 'cost'	58%	53%	52%	**80%**
'yes' vs 'no'	51%	51%	52%	**59%**
# of hidden states	k-Means	EM	Yin-Yang	SC-PPK
2	64.5%	72.1%	69.3%	**76.1%**
3	64.4%	73.3%	**75.5%**	**75.5%**
4	65.4%	**74.9%**	74.7%	74.3%

Table 6. Average runtimes in seconds on a 3-Ghz machine with emissions $x_t \in \mathbb{R}^{123\times 1}$, includes HMM training time

# of time-series samples	k-Means	EM	Yin-Yang	SC-PPK
5	20.6s	23.5s	4.1s	**3.6s**
10	47.1s	59.7s	11.1s	**6.1s**
25	68.29s	185.0s	49.9s	**15.4s**
50	111.6s	212.9s	171.8s	**30.1s**
75	178.3s	455.6s	382.8s	**48.6s**
100	295.9s	723.1s	650.2s	**64.5s**

5.3 Runtime Advantages

Unlike EM-HMM, which needs to calculate posteriors over $N \times k$ HMM-sequence pairs and maximize over k HMMs at *every* iteration until convergence, SC-PPK requires a single HMM to be trained once for each sequence in the dataset. The SC-PPK method calculates the integration between two HMM parameters in closed form directly without needing to evaluate the likelihood of the individual time-series samples, resulting in a dramatic reduction of in total runtime. In practice, we noticed around two orders of magnitude improvement in clustering speed over EM, as shown in Table 6. These runtimes include HMM training times as well as clustering times.

6 Visualization of HMM Parameters

Visualization and manifold learning is another important component of unsupervised learning. Starting from a set of high dimensional data points $\mathcal{X}$ with $x_i \in \mathbb{R}^N$, embedding and visualization methods recover a set of corresponding low dimensional datapoints $\mathcal{Y}$ (typically with typically $y_i \in \mathbb{R}^2$) such that the

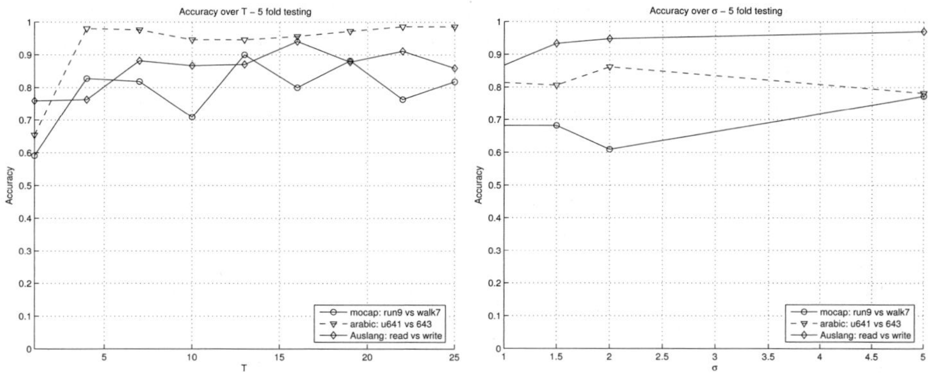

(a) (b)

Fig. 1. Kernel stability over their respective parameters (a) SC-PPK - T (b) YY kernel - σ. Accuracies averaged over five runs.

distance between y_i and y_j is similar to the distance between x_i and x_j for all $i, j = 1...N$. These techniques permit visualization of high dimensional datasets and can help confirm clustering patterns. Classic visualization and embedding techniques include multi-dimensional scaling (MDS) [12] as well as recent contenders such as semi-definite embedding (SDE) [13].

To further analyze the usefulness of the PPK at capturing an accurate representation of the kernel affinity between two sequences, embedding using MDS was applied to the datasets. This corresponds to training an HMM over each of the time-series sequences and recovering the $\mathbb{R}^{N \times N}$ Gram matrix where $A_{m,n} = \mathcal{K}(\theta_m, \theta_n)$ – identical to steps 1 and 2 of the SC-PPK algorithm. From the Gram matrix, the dissimilarity matrix $D \in \mathbb{R}^{N \times N}$ is given by $D_{i,j} = 1/A_{i,j}$. This matrix is then used as the input for the standard MDS algorithm as in [12]. MDS is chosen because of its simplicity although more sophisticated methods such as SDE are equally viable. Fig 2 shows the embedding for the rotated data using a rotation step size of 10° under the Yin and Yang kernel (a) and the PPK (b). From the figure, we can see that the Yin and Yang kernel captures some of the periodic structure of the dataset in the embedding but it is only locally useful and does not adequately capture the expected global circular structure in the rotation. Conversely, the result from the PPK method is much clearer. The PPK integrates over the sample space providing a less brittle description of each time series. Thus the kernel affinity captures an accurate representation of the the distance between HMM parameters with respect to all of the data samples, forming a perfectly circular global embedding of the 360° rotated MOCAP dataset. Fig 3(a) shows PPK-based embeddings for three classes from the Arabic handwriting dataset. The method recovered an accurated embedding as the three classes are separated from one-another. Similarly, Fig 3(b) shows the embeddings for three classes from the Australian sign language dataset.

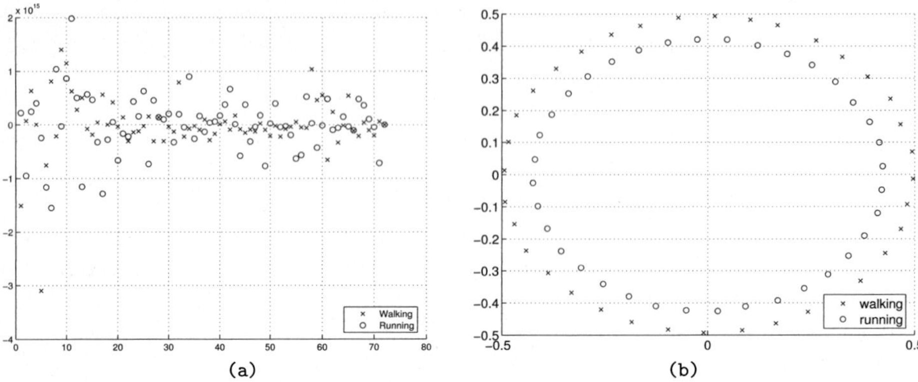

Fig. 2. MDS embedding of HMM parameters using the synthesized 360° rotated MOCAP dataset with (a) the Yin-Yang kernel and (b) the probability product kernel

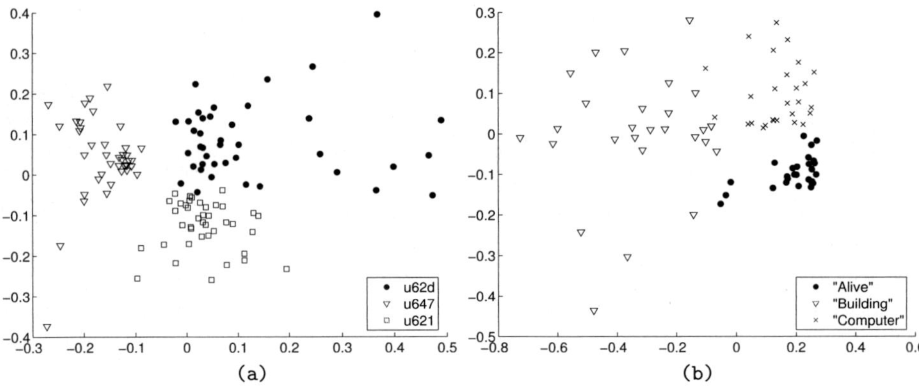

Fig. 3. MDS embedding of HMM parameters (a) Arabic handwriting dataset and (b) Australian sign Language dataset

7 Conclusions

This paper presented a semi-parametric approach for clustering time-series data that exploits some parametric knowledge about the data including its Markov properties and the presence of latent states, and at the same time utilizes non-parametric principles and remains agnostic about the shape of the clusters a multitude of time series can form. This works surprisingly well for time-series data in experiments on real-world data. By avoiding parametric assumptions about the underlying distributions or the variations across the time series, improved clustering accuracy is possible.

The method combines both a non-parametric spectral clustering approach using the probability product kernel with a fully parametric maximum likelihood estimation approach for each singleton time series. We showed that spectral clustering with a probability product kernel method provides improvements in clustering accuracy over fully parametric mixture modeling as well as spectral clustering with non-probabilistic and non-parametric affinity measures. Furthermore, embedding and visualization of time series data is also improved. Finally, the proposed method has computational efficiency benefits over prior approaches.

For future work, we are investigating spectral clustering with the probability product kernel for other generalized graphical models and parametric distributions. In addition, we are investigating a general formalism and generalized cost functions for semi-parametric estimation that unify both parametric and non-parametric criteria and leverage the complementary advantages of both approaches.

References

1. Dey, D.: Practical Nonparametric & Semiparametric Bayesian Statistics, vol. 133. Springer, Heidelberg (1998)
2. Hoti, F., Holstrom, L.: A semiparametric density estimation approach to pattern classification. Pattern Recognition (2004)
3. Tim Oates, L.F., Cohen, P.R.: Clustering time series with hidden Markov models and dynamic time warping. In: IJCAI-99 Workshop on Neural, Symbolic and Reinforcement Learning Methods for Sequence Learning (1998)
4. Smyth, P.: Clustering sequences with hidden Markov models. In: Advances in Neural Information Processing Systems, pp. 648–654 (1997)
5. Alon, J., Sclaroff, S., Kollios, G., Pavlovic, V.: Discovering clusters in motion time-series data. IEEE Computer Vision and Pattern Recognition (2003)
6. Shental, N., Zomet, A., Hertz, T., Weiss, Y.: Pairwise clustering and graphical models. In: Advances in Neural Information Processing Systems (2003)
7. Ng, A., Jordan, M., Weiss, Y.: On Spectral Clustering: Analysis and an algorithm. In: Advances in Neural Information Processing Systems (2001)
8. Shi, J., Malik, J.: Normalized cuts and image segmentation. IEEE Transactions on Pattern Analysis and Machine Intelligence 22, 888–905 (2000)
9. Jebara, T., Kondor, R., Howard, A.: Probability product kernels. Journal of Machine Learning Research 5, 819–844 (2004)
10. Yin, J., Yang, Q.: Integrating hidden Markov models and spectral analysis for sensory timeseries clustering. In: Proceedings of the Fifth IEEE International Conference on Data Mining (ICDM'05), IEEE Computer Society Press, Los Alamitos (2005)
11. Biadsy, F., El-Sana, J., Habash, N.: Online arabic handwriting recognition using hidden Markov models. In: The 10th International Workshop on Frontiers of Handwriting Recognition (2006)
12. Kruskal, J.B., Wish, M.: Multidimensional Scaling. In: Quantitative Application in the Social Sciences, Sage University Paper (1978)
13. Weinberger, K.Q., Saul, L.K.: Unsupervised learning of image manifolds by semidefinite programming. International Journal of Computer Vision 70(1), 77–90 (2006)

Probabilistic Explanation Based Learning

Angelika Kimmig[1], Luc De Raedt[1], and Hannu Toivonen[2]

[1] Department of Computer Science, Katholieke Universiteit Leuven
[2] Department of Computer Science, University of Helsinki

Abstract. Explanation based learning produces generalized explanations from examples. These explanations are typically built in a deductive manner and they aim to capture the essential characteristics of the examples.

Probabilistic explanation based learning extends this idea to probabilistic logic representations, which have recently become popular within the field of statistical relational learning. The task is now to find the most likely explanation why one (or more) example(s) satisfy a given concept. These probabilistic and generalized explanations can then be used to discover *similar* examples and to reason by *analogy*. So, whereas traditional explanation based learning is typically used for speed-up learning, probabilistic explanation based learning is used for discovering new knowledge.

Probabilistic explanation based learning has been implemented in a recently proposed probabilistic logic called ProbLog, and it has been applied to a challenging application in discovering relationships of interest in large biological networks.

1 Introduction

During the 80s, explanation based learning (EBL) was a popular research theme within the field of machine learning. It aimed at finding plausible and generalized explanations for particular examples using a logical domain theory, cf. [2] for an overview and introduction. These generalized explanations were then typically turned into rules that would be added to the theory, often with the aim of speeding up further inference or extending an imperfect domain theory. Traditional explanation based learning was largely studied within first order logic representations and explanations were built using deduction [8,16], though there was sometimes also an abductive component [1]. In the past few years, the machine learning and artificial intelligence communities have become interested in statistical relational learning [7] and probabilistic logic learning [4]; these are techniques that lie at the intersection of machine learning, logical representations and probabilistic modelling. These fields have contributed many different probabilistic logics, and have used them for various applications.

A natural question that arises in this context is whether explanation based learning can be applied to these probabilistic logics. A first step in this direction is done in [3], where logical and empirical evidence are combined in explanation based learning to get explanations with a certain confidence. The question is investigated and positively answered within this paper. More specifically, we introduce probabilistic explanation based learning within a recently introduced

J.N. Kok et al. (Eds.): ECML 2007, LNAI 4701, pp. 176–187, 2007.

simple extension of Prolog, called ProbLog [5], and demonstrate its use on a challenging application within biological link mining. Probabilistic explanation based learning computes the most likely generalized explanation from one or more positive examples and then uses these generalized explanations to identify other examples that possess this explanation (with high probability). In this way, probabilistic explanation based learning realizes a kind of probabilistic similarity or analogical reasoning. This type of reasoning is required within scientific link mining tasks in large biological networks. These are networks that consist of a large set of entities (such as proteins, tissues, diseases, genes, ...) as well as the relationships that hold amongst them. The task faced by the biologist is to investigate these networks in order to understand particular phenomenae and to discover new knowledge and relationships, cf. [15,11]. Using probabilistic explanation based learning with ProbLog allows the life scientist, for instance, to discover probable explanations for specific phenomenae (such as a gene being related to a particular disease – say Alzheimer disease), and then to apply the discovered generalized explanation to identify other genes that are related to this disease with a similar explanation. Furthermore, it allows to rank these genes according to the likelihood of the explanation.

Probabilistic explanation based learning as introduced here is also related to probabilistic abduction, as studied by Poole [12], and to abductive explanation based learning. The difference with Poole's work however is that we compute *generalized* explanations and also apply them for analogical reasoning. In contrast to abductive explanation based learning, probabilistic reasoning is employed here.

This paper is organized as follows: we briefly review ProbLog in Section 2 and explanation based learning in Section 3. Section 4 introduces probabilistic EBL, which is evaluated using experiments in biological link mining in Section 5. Finally, Section 6 concludes and touches upon related work.

2 ProbLog: Probabilistic Prolog

ProbLog is a simple probabilistic extension of Prolog introduced in [5]. A ProbLog program consists – as Prolog – of a set of definite clauses. However, in ProbLog every clause c_i is labeled with the probability p_i that it is true, and those probabilities are assumed to be mutually independent.

Example 1. Within bibliographic data analysis, the similarity structure among items can improve information retrieval results. Consider a collection of papers $\{\mathbf{a}, \mathbf{b}, \mathbf{c}, \mathbf{d}\}$ and some pairwise similarities $\mathtt{similar(a, c)}$, e.g., based on key word analysis. Two items X and Y are related(X, Y) if they are similar (such as a and c) or if X is similar to some item Z which is related to Y. Uncertainty can elegantly be represented by the attached probabilities:

$$
\begin{array}{ll}
1.0 : \mathtt{related(X,Y)} :- \mathtt{similar(X,Y)}. & \\
0.8 : \mathtt{related(X,Y)} :- \mathtt{similar(X,Z)}, \mathtt{related(Z,Y)}. & \\
0.8 : \mathtt{similar(a,c)}. & 0.7 : \mathtt{similar(c,b)}. \\
0.6 : \mathtt{similar(d,c)}. & 0.9 : \mathtt{similar(d,b)}. \\
0.7 : \mathtt{similar(e,c)}. & 0.5 : \mathtt{similar(f,a)}.
\end{array}
$$

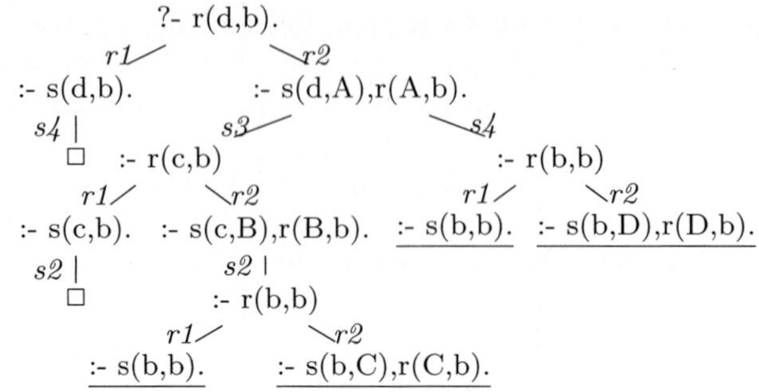

Fig. 1. SLD tree for `related(d,b)`

A ProbLog program $T = \{p_1 : c_1, \cdots, p_n : c_n\}$ defines a probability distribution over logic programs $L \subseteq L_T = \{c_1, \cdots, c_n\}$ in the following way:

$$P(L|T) = \prod_{c_i \in L} p_i \prod_{c_i \in L_T \setminus L} (1 - p_i). \tag{1}$$

Unlike in Prolog, where one is typically interested in determining whether a query succeeds or fails, ProbLog specifies the probability that a query succeeds. The *success probability* $P(q|T)$ of a query q in a ProbLog program T is defined by

$$P(q|T) = \sum_{L \subseteq L_T} P(q, L|T) = \sum_{L \subseteq L_T} P(q|L) \cdot P(L|T), \tag{2}$$

where $P(q|L) = 1$ if there exists a θ such that $L \models q\theta$, and $P(q|L) = 0$ otherwise. In other words, the success probability of query q corresponds to the probability that the query q has *a* proof in a logic program randomly sampled from T.

The evaluation of the success probability of ProbLog queries is computationally hard. In [5], this problem is tackled by employing a reduction to the computation of the probability of a monotone DNF formula, an NP-complete problem.

Example 2. Figure 1 shows the SLD-tree for proving `related(d,b)` in our example program (see Section 3 for details). This tree contains two successful proofs, and therefore the success probability of `related(d,b)` corresponds to $P((r_1 \wedge s_4) \vee (r_2 \wedge s_3 \wedge r_1 \wedge s_2))$. This probability cannot be computed as $P((r_1 \wedge s_4)) + P((r_2 \wedge s_3 \wedge r_1 \wedge s_2))$ because the two expressions are not mutually disjoint.

The key contribution of our previous work on ProbLog was the implementation of an efficient approximative inference procedure for computing the success probabilities in large ProbLog programs for the biological network mining domain (cf. also Section 5). The inference procedure employs Binary Decision Diagrams in combination with an approximation algorithm based on iterative deepening, cf. [5] for more details.

However, in probabilistic explanation based learning as introduced here, cf. Section 4, the probability of interest will not be the total probability of a query but rather the probability of a single derivation d for a given example. This probability corresponds to

$$P(d|T) = \prod_{c_i \in d} p_i \quad (3)$$

and can thus be computed exactly in an efficient way. Intuitively, it corresponds to the probability that a randomly sampled subprogram of T contains all clauses employed in the derivation d.

Example 3. There are two proofs for `related(d,b)`. The first one uses the base case of `related/2` and the fact `similar(d,b)` and thus has a probability of $1.0 \cdot 0.9 = 0.9$, the second one uses the recursive case and two facts, thus getting a probability of $0.8 \cdot 0.6 \cdot 1.0 \cdot 0.7 = 0.336$.

3 Explanation Based Learning

The central idea of explanation-based learning (EBL) as conveniently formalized for Prolog [8,16] is to compute a generalized explanation from a concrete proof of an example. Explanations use only so-called *operational* predicates, i.e. predicates that capture essential characteristics of the domain of interest and should be easy to prove. Operational predicates are to be declared by the user as such.

Following the work by [8,16], explanation based learning starts from a definite clause theory T, that is a pure Prolog program, and an example in the form of a ground atom $p(t_1, ..., t_n)$. It then constructs a refutation proof of the example using SLD-resolution. SLD-resolution takes a goal of the form $? - g, g_1, ..., g_n$, a clause $h \leftarrow b_1, ..., b_m$ such that g and h unify with most general unifier θ, and then produces the resolvent $? - b_1\theta, ..., b_m\theta, g_1\theta, ..., g_n\theta$. This process then continues until the empty goal is reached. SLD-resolution is illustrated in Figure 1, where each path from the root of the tree to the empty clause $\Box$ corresponds to a refutation proof of `related(d,b)`. Given the resolution proof for the example $p(t_1, ..., t_n)$, explanation based learning will generalize the proof and produce a generalized explanation. To realize this, it starts from the variabelized goal, i.e. $p(X_1, ..., X_n)$ where the X_i are different variables, and then performs the same SLD-resolution steps as in the proof for the example. The only difference is that in the general proof constructed in explanation based learning atoms $q(s_1, ..., s_r)$ for operational predicates q in a goal $? - g_1, ..., g_i, q(s_1, ..., s_r), g_{i+1}, ..., g_n$ are not resolved away. Also, the proof procedure stops when the goal contains only atoms for operational predicates. The resulting goal provides a *generalized explanation* for the example. In terms of the SLD-resolution proof tree, explanation based learning cuts off branches below operational predicates. It is easy to implement the explanation based proof procedure as a meta-interpreter for Prolog [16,8].

Example 4. Reconsider the logic program of Example 1, ignoring the probability labels for now. We define `similar/2` to be the only operational predicate, and use `related(a,b)` as training example. EBL proves this goal using two instances of the operational predicate, namely `similar(a,c)` and `similar(c,b)`,

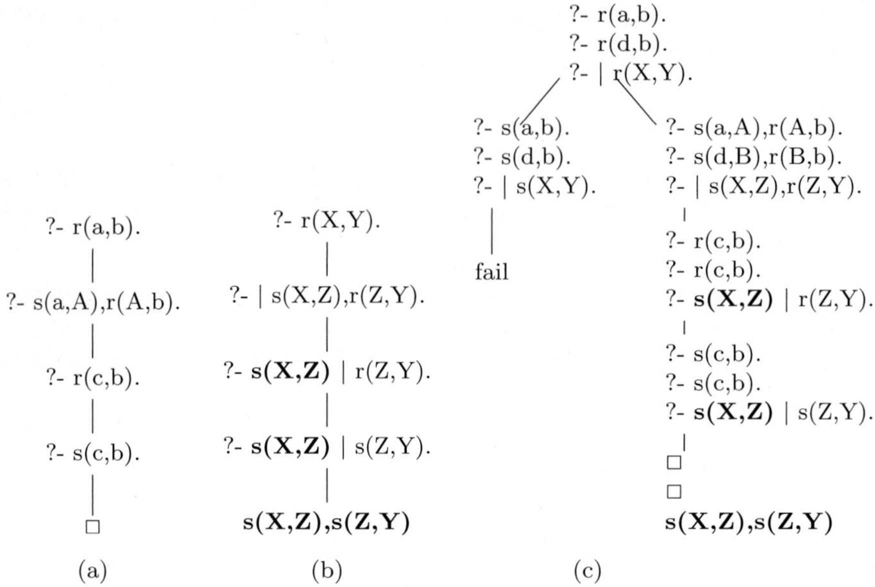

Fig. 2. (a) The successful branch of the SLD tree for `related(a,b)`. (b) The corresponding branch for general goal `related(X,Y)`, where bold atoms are part of the explanation and the bar marks the position to continue the proof. (c) A partial SLD tree for Example 6, where each node contains the current status for the two training examples as well as the general version.

and then produces the explanation `similar(X,Z), similar(Z,Y)` for the generalized example `related(X,Y)`. The result can be represented as the clause `exp_related(X,Y)`← `similar(X,Z), similar(Z,Y)`. We will call such clauses *explanation clauses*. To be able to identify the examples covered by this clause, we rename the predicate in the head of explanation clauses. The successful branches of the SLD trees for `related(a,b)` and the generalized example `related(X,Y)` are depicted in Figure 2.

4 Probabilistic Explanation Based Learning

Probabilistic explanation based learning (PEBL) extends EBL to probabilistic logic representations. In this paper, we use ProbLog as the underlying language for PEBL, but the general idea can easily be transferred to other probabilistic logics, such as Poole's ICL [12] or Sato's PRISM [14].

Within ProbLog, as already discussed in Section 2, a probability is associated to each proof of a query. Therefore, the adaptation of explanation based learning to ProbLog is direct. The key difference now is that for each example, we compute the most likely proof and then compute the generalized explanation as sketched in the previous section.

The probability of a given single proof is calculated simply as the product $\prod_i p_i$ of probability labels of all clauses c_i used (at least once) in that proof, as defined in Equation 3 and illustrated in Example 3. This corresponds to the probability of randomly sampling a subprogram of the ProbLog program that contains all clauses used in the proof and thus admits the proof. The set of clauses C used in the proof of the example that is to be generalized can be partitioned into two sets. Indeed, define $G = \{c|c \in C$ such that c is used in the generalized proof$\}$, and $E = C - G$, i.e. E contains the example-specific clauses used to prove operational predicates. We then have that

$$\prod_{c_i \in C} p_i = \prod_{c_j \in G} p_j \prod_{c_k \in E} p_k.$$

Thus, the probability of the orginal proof is equal to the product of the probability of the generalized proof and the probability of the operational predicates for the example.

Example 5. In Example 4, $C = \{r_2, s_1, r_1, s_2\}$, $G = \{r_1, r_2\}$ and $E = \{s_1, s_2\}$. The probability $\prod_{c_j \in G} p_j = 0.8 \cdot 1.0$ also denotes the probability that the explanation clause `related(X,Y)`$\leftarrow$ `similar(X,Z), similar(Z,Y)` is logically entailed by the original ProbLog program.

Computing the most likely proof for a given goal in ProbLog is straightforward: instead of traversing the SLD-tree in a left-to-right depth-first manner as in Prolog, nodes are expanded in order of the probability of the derivation leading to that node. This realizes a best-first search with the probability of the current proof as an evaluation function. In the application sketched in Section 5, we need to deal however with goals having very many candidate proofs (each corresponding to a particular path in a large biological network). Implementing best-first search in a naive manner rapidly results in memory problems. We therefore employ the traditional solution of iterative deepening [13] to avoid these problems in our implementation. Using iterative deepening depth first search, we cut off the search at proofs with probability below a threshold. We start with a minimum probability of 0.5. If at least one explanation was found in the last completed iteration, the algorithm outputs the most probable one and stops, otherwise the next iteration uses half the probability threshold of the last one. The algorithm can also be used to return the k most probable structurally distinct explanations.

Probabilistic explanation based learning as incorporated in ProbLog offers natural solutions to two issues traditionally discussed in the context of explanation based learning [10,9]. The first one is the *multiple explanation* problem, which is concerned with choosing the explanation to be generalized for examples having multiple proofs. This problem arises in many applications such as the one sketched in Section 5 on mining biological networks, where there are various possible explanations as to why a particular query succeeds, for instance, a gene being linked to a particular disease. The use of a sound probabilistic framework naturally deals with this issue by selecting the *most likely* proof. The second problem is that of *generalizing from multiple examples*, another issue that received quite some attention in traditional explanation based learning. To realize this in our setting, we modify the best-first search algorithm so that it searches for the most likely generalized explanation shared by the n examples $e_1, ..., e_n$. Starting from the variabelized atom e, we compute $n+1$ SLD-resolution derivations in parallel. A resolution step resolving an atom for a non-operational predicate in the generalized proof for e is allowed only when the same resolution step can also be applied to each of the n parallel derivations. Atoms corresponding to operational predicates are – as sketched above – not resolved in the generalized proof, but it is nevertheless required that for each occurrence of these atoms in the n parallel derivations, there exists a resolution derivation.

Example 6. Consider again our running example, and assume that we now want to construct a common explanation for `related(a,b)` and `related(d,b)`. We thus have to simultaneously prove both examples and the variabelized goal `related(X,Y)`. This is illustrated in Figure 2(c). After resolving all three goals with the first clause for `related/2`, we reach the first instance of the operational predicate `similar/2` and thus have to prove both `similar(a,b)` and `similar(d,b)`. As proving `similar(a,b)` fails, the last resolution step is rejected and the second clause for `related/2` used instead. As both `similar(a,A)` and `similar(d,B)` can be proven, `similar(X,Z)` is added to the explanation, and the procedure continues with the goals `related(c,b)`, `related(c,b)` and `related(Z,Y)`. This succeeds using the base case and adds `similar(Z,Y)` to the explanation, which thus is `similar(X,Z),similar(Z,Y)`.

Because PEBL generates a generalized explanation, which can be turned into an explanation clause, the technique can be employed to identify similar instances and to reason by analogy. Indeed, by asserting such an explanation clause and posing queries to the resulting predicate one obtains similar examples. Furthermore, the success probabilities of the examples can be used to rank them according to likelihood, and hence, similarity.

Example 7. Using the explanation clause `exp_related(X,Y)`$\leftarrow$ `similar(X,Z)`, `similar(Z,Y)` to query for covered instances would return the following answer: `exp_related(a,b)` $(0.8 \cdot 0.7 = 0.56)$, `exp_related(e,b)` $(0.7 \cdot 0.7 = 0.49)$, `exp_related(d,b)` $(0.6 \cdot 0.7 = 0.42)$, `exp_related(f,c)` $(0.5 \cdot 0.8 = 0.40)$.

5 Experiments

Research on ProbLog and PEBL is meant to support the life scientist analysing large biological networks that can be automatically constructed from the enormous amounts of molecular biological data that are available from public sources, such as Ensembl[1], NCBI Entrez[2], OMIM[3], and many others. They contain knowledge about various types of objects, such as genes, proteins, tissues, organisms, biological processes, and molecular functions. Information about their

[1] `www.ensembl.org`

[2] `www.ncbi.nlm.nih.gov/Entrez/`

[3] www.ncbi.nlm.nih.gov/Omim

```
e_path(A,B) ← node(A,gene), edge(A,C,belongs_to), node(C,homologgroup),
      edge(B,C,refers_to), node(B,phenotype), nodes_distinct([B,C,A]).
e_path(A,B) ← node(A,gene), edge(A,C,codes_for), node(C,protein),
      edge(D,C,subsumes), node(D,protein), edge(D,E,interacts_with),
      node(E,protein), edge(B,E,refers_to), node(B,phenotype),
      nodes_distinct([B,E,D,C,A])
e_path(A,B) ← node(A,gene), edge(A,C,participates_in), node(C,pathway),
      edge(D,C,participates_in), node(D,gene), edge(D,E,codes_for),
      node(E,protein), edge(B,E,refers_to), node(B,phenotype),
      nodes_distinct([B,E,D,C,A])
e_path(A,B) ← node(A,gene), edge(A,C,is_found_in),
      node(C,cellularcomponent), edge(D,C,is_found_in), node(D,protein),
      edge(B,D,refers_to), node(B,phenotype), nodes_distinct([B,D,C,A])
```

Fig. 3. Some explanation clauses for `path(A,B)`, connecting gene `A` to phenotype `B`

known or predicted relationships is also available, e.g., that gene A of organism B codes for protein C, which is expressed in tissue D, or that genes E and F are likely to be related since they co-occur often in scientific articles. Analysing such networks and data has been identified as an important and challenging task (see, e.g., [11]) and only few tools exist that support life scientists in this task.

Such a collection of interlinked heterogeneous biological data can be seen as a weighted network, where nodes are entities and the weight of an edge corresponds to the probability that the corresponding nodes are related [15]. It can thus be represented as a ProbLog database, which in the most simple case consists of probabilistic `edge/2` facts. Probabilities of the edges can be obtained from methods that predict their existence based on, e.g., co-occurrence frequencies or sequence similarities [15]. Within ProbLog, it is straightforward to add more information such as the type of relation encoded by an edge or explicit information on nodes, see Figure 3 for some examples.

Using ProbLog, one can pose queries that ask for the probability that a particular relationship holds. Typically, this will involve background knowledge of biological concepts as well as types of relations that form strong chains between two given nodes. In ProbLog this can be modeled by using a `path` predicate that computes the probability of a path as the product of the probabilities of the used edges, thus assuming that they are mutually independent [15,5].

We implemented PEBL in Yap-5.1.2 and performed experiments in the context of the weighted biological database of [15]. As an example problem to be studied, we looked at connections between disease genes and the corresponding phenotype for Alzheimer disease (resp. asthma). Since the key motivation for employing probabilistic explanation based learning is to be able to reason by analogy or to find similar examples, we set up experiments to answer the following questions:

Q1 Does PEBL produce meaningful examples when reasoning by analogy?
Q2 Can we find common explanations?

Q3 Can PEBL's explanations induced on one domain (say Alzheimer disease) be transferred to another one (say Asthma)?

To answer those questions, we extracted graphs around both diseases from the database. The genes were obtained by searching Entrez for human genes with the relevant annotation (AD or asthma); phenotypes are from OMIM. Most of the other information comes from EntrezGene, String, UniProt, HomoloGene, Gene Ontology, and OMIM databases. We did not include articles since they would dominate the graphs otherwise. Weights were assigned to edges as described in [15]. In the experiments below, we used a fixed number of randomly chosen (Alzheimer disease or asthma) genes for graph extraction. Subgraphs were extracted by taking all acyclic paths of length at most 4 or 5, and of probability at least 0.01, between any given gene and the corresponding phenotype. Some of the genes did not have any such paths to the phenotype and are thus disconnected from the rest of the graph. Table 1 gives a summary of the properties of the resulting graphs, obtained using two diseases, a varying number of annotated example genes, and a search depth of 4 or 5. (Remaining columns are explained below). Graphs Alz1 and Alz2 were obtained using the same 17 Alzheimer disease genes, but three of them were not connected to the Alzheimer disease phenotype with a path of length at most 4 (Alz1). Alz3 and Alz4 were extracted starting with all 142 annotated Alzheimer disease genes, and Ast1 and Ast2 with 17 asthma genes. As a basic representation, a modified path-predicate was employed that takes into account the node and edge types. We defined predicates related to node and edge types as operational. To answer question **Q1**, we start by studying example explanations for `path(A,B)` obtained from the graphs, where `A` is a gene and `B` a phenotype (Figure 3). These explanations are all semantically meaningful. For instance, the first one indicates that gene A is related to phenotype B if A belongs to a group of homologous (i.e., evolutionarily related) genes that relate to B. The three other explanations are based on interaction of proteins: either an explicit one, by participation in the same pathway, or by being found in the same cellular component. This last discovery suggests that a clause to describe different kinds of possible interactions would be a useful feature in the logical theory. It thus seems that PEBL can produce useful explanations and can help the user discover and synthesize new information, which answers **Q1** positively.

To further study the questions more objectively, we consider a slightly artifical setting. We define a target predicate `connect/3` as `connect(X,Y,Z) :- path(X,Z),path(Y,Z),path(X,Y).` This predicate succeeds if three nodes are connected to each other. We use examples where genes `X` and `Y` and phenotype `Z` are connected, and construct explanations on graphs Alz1 and Ast1.

We consider ordered triplets `(G1,G2,P)` of nodes, where `G1` and `G2` are different genes and `P` is a phenotype. We call such a triplet positive with respect to the given network if both genes are annotated with the graph's disease and `P` is the corresponding phenotype, and negative otherwise. Thus for Alz1, there are $14 \cdot 13 \cdot 1 = 182$ positive and $29 \cdot 28 \cdot 3 - 182 = 2254$ negative triplets. Those numbers are also given in Table 1.

Table 1. Graph characteristics: search depth used during graph extraction, numbers of nodes and edges, number of genes annotated resp. not annotated with the corresponding disease and number of phenotypes, number of positive and negative examples for connecting two genes and a phenotype.

	depth	nodes	edges	ag	ng	pt	pos	neg
Alz1	4	122	259	14	15	3	182	2254
Alz2	5	658	3544	17	20	4	272	5056
Alz3	4	351	774	72	33	3	5112	27648
Alz4	5	3364	17666	130	55	6	16770	187470
Ast1	4	127	241	7	12	2	42	642
Ast2	5	381	787	11	12	2	110	902

Table 2. Averaged results over all examples learned on Alz1 (left column) resp. Ast1 (right column) and evaluated on 6 different graphs (lines Alz1–4, Ast1–2): number of positives among the first k answers (pos(k)), number of positives returned before the first negative (pos_n), absolute number of positives among examples with non-zero probability (pos_a), and precision w.r.t. all examples with non-zero probability (prec).

	Alz1						Ast1					
	pos(1)	pos(3)	pos(5)	pos_n	pos_a	prec	pos(1)	pos(3)	pos(5)	pos_n	pos_a	prec
Alz1	0.95	2.53	3.95	6.91	16.82	0.46	1.00	3.00	4.86	6.86	10.57	0.23
Alz2	0.84	2.24	3.60	7.37	18.65	0.42	0.86	2.86	4.71	6.86	14.56	0.22
Alz3	0.99	2.64	4.09	23.20	126.09	0.48	1.00	2.71	4.14	6.86	28.00	0.24
Alz4	0.84	2.23	3.58	7.37	18.80	0.42	0.86	2.29	3.43	5.14	28.00	0.15
Ast1	0.09	0.26	0.44	2.07	2.07	0.02	1.00	3.00	4.86	17.14	17.14	0.34
Ast2	0.08	0.23	0.38	2.00	2.00	0.01	0.86	2.57	4.29	16.57	16.57	0.20

We use `connect(G1,G2,P)` for positive triplets as training examples. As `connect` is symmetric in the first two arguments, we only consider one ordering per pair of genes, which yields in total $14 \cdot 13/2 = 91$ training examples for Alz1 (resp. 21 for Ast1). The aim is to construct explanations for connections between the nodes of positive triplets, and use those to obtain for each test graph a ranked list of triplets covered by the explanation. To do so, we first compute the most likely explanation for each individual training example e, and then rank all instances covered by the resulting explanation clause according to their maximal probability. Table 2 summarizes classification accuracies obtained using those rankings and the classification criterion on triplets as described above. Values are averaged over all training examples. On graphs describing the same disease as the training graph, the top k instances for $k = 1, 3, 5$ are mostly positive, which again gives a positive answer to **Q1**. We obtained 26 different explanations from Alz1 and 3 different explanations from Ast1. Most explanations have been learned on at least two examples, and the biggest set of examples which shared most likely explanation contains 12 examples. Figure 4 shows an example explanation found both on Alz1 and on Ast1. This indicates a positive answer to question **Q2**, discovery of common explanations. The answer to **Q3**,

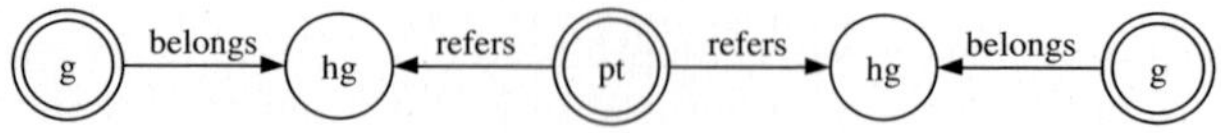

Fig. 4. One explanation for `connect(G1,G2,P)`, where double circles mark answer variables, and node types used are gene (g), phenotype (pt) and homologgroup (hg)

if explanations can be transferred, is less conclusive: while transfer from Asthma to Alzheimer disease achieves good results, the other direction is a lot worse. However, one has to take into account that 23 of the 26 explanations learned on Alzheimer disease do not return any example at all on Asthma graphs, one only returns negative instances and the remaining 2 carry over very well, returning 30 resp 16 positive instances before returning negative ones. At the same time, two of the three explanations learned on Asthma were also learned on Alzheimer disease, which might explain their good performance there.

6 Conclusions and Related Work

We have introduced probabilistic explanation based learning, which applies principles of explanation based learning to probabilistic logic representations. Within this paper this was realized using a simple probablistic extension of Prolog, called ProbLog [5], even though the technique can easily be adapted towards other logics such as ICL [12] or PRISM [14]. Whereas the original version of ProbLog was intended as an inference engine for answering queries to a kind of probabilistic database efficiently, the present work is meant to support reasoning by analogy, similarity, or cases. The idea is that the most likely explanation for a particular example is employed to compute similar instances. Experiments on mining biological networks have shown promising results.

Probabilistic explanation based learning builds upon the existing work in both explanation based learning and probabilistic logics. From an explanation based learning point of view it is a simple extension of the formalisations within Prolog due to [8,16] with probabilistic inference. From a probabilistic logic point of view, it extends the work of Poole [12] in that it finds *generalized* explanations. We have argued that using probabilities in the explanations provides a natural solution to the multiple explanation problem whereas the use of a resolution based proof procedure allows one to naturally deal with multiple examples and identify common explanations. Finally, the work is related to that on analogical, similarity and case based reasoning. In this regard, it provides a notion of similarity that is based on background knowledge (as in the definition of the `connect` predicate) as well as likelihood.

ProbLog and PEBL have been motivated by and applied to challenging and realistic biological network mining tasks [15]. Within the framework of ProbLog we have also studied the problem of compressing a large network from positive as well as negative examples [6]. Our future work will be aimed at making this set of tools available to the life scientist and to evaluate their utility there.

Acknowledgements. This research has been partially supported by IQ (European Union Project IST-FET FP6-516169), Research Foundation-Flanders (FWO-Vlaanderen), Tekes and Humboldt foundation.

References

1. Cohen., W.: Abductive Explanation-Based Learning: A Solution to the Multiple Inconsistent Explanation Problem. Machine Learning 8(2) (1992)
2. DeJong, G.: Explanation-based learning. In: Tucker, A. (ed.) Computer Science Handbook, 2nd edn., CRC (2004)
3. DeJong, G.: Toward Robust Real-World Inference: A New Perspective on Explanation-Based Learning. In: Fürnkranz, J., Scheffer, T., Spiliopoulou, M. (eds.) ECML 2006. LNCS (LNAI), vol. 4212, Springer, Heidelberg (2006)
4. De Raedt, L., Kersting, K.: Probabilistic Logic Learning. SIGKDD Explorations 5(2) (2003)
5. De Raedt, L., Kimmig, A., Toivonen, H.: ProbLog: A probabilistic Prolog and its application in link discovery. In: Proceedings of 20th International Joint Conference on Artificial Intelligence, pp. 2468–2473 (2007)
6. De Raedt, L., Kersting, K., Kimmig, A., Revoredo, K., Toivonen, H.: Compressing Probabilistic Prolog Programs. Machine Learning Journal (to appear, 2007)
7. Getoor, L., Taskar, B. (eds.): Statistical Relational Learning. MIT Press, Cambridge (to appear, 2007)
8. Hirsh, H.: Explanation-based Generalization in a Logic-Programming Environment. In: Proceedings of 15th International Joint Conference on Artificial Intelligence, pp. 221–227 (1987)
9. Langley, P.: Unifying themes in empirical and explanation-based learning. In: Proceedings of the sixth international workshop on Machine learning, pp. 2–4 (1989)
10. Mitchell, T.M., Keller, R.M., Kedar-Cabelli, S.T.: Explanation-based generalization: A unifying view. Machine Learning 1(1), 47–80 (1986)
11. Perez-Iratxeta, C., Bork, P., Andrade, M.A.: Association of genes to genetically inherited diseases using data mining. Nature Genetics 31, 316–319 (2002)
12. Poole, D.: Probabilistic Horn abduction and Bayesian networks. Artificial Intelligence 64(1) (2003)
13. Russel, S., Norvig, P.: Artificial Intelligence: A Modern Approach, 2nd edn. Prentice-Hall, Englewood Cliffs (2002)
14. Sato, T., Kameya, Y.: Parameter learning of logic programs for symbolic-statistical modeling. Journal of AI Research 15, 391–454 (2001)
15. Sevon, P., Eronen, L., Hintsanen, P., Kulovesi, K., Toivonen, H.: Link discovery in graphs derived from biological databases. In: Leser, U., Naumann, F., Eckman, B. (eds.) DILS 2006. LNCS (LNBI), vol. 4075, Springer, Heidelberg (2006)
16. Van Harmelen, F., Bundy, A.: Explanation-Based Generalisation = Partial Evaluation. Artificial Intelligence 36(3), 401–412 (1988)

Graph-Based Domain Mapping for Transfer Learning in General Games

Gregory Kuhlmann and Peter Stone

Department of Computer Sciences, The University of Texas at Austin
1 University Station C0500, Austin, Texas 78712-1188
{kuhlmann,pstone}@cs.utexas.edu

Abstract. A general game player is an agent capable of taking as input a description of a game's rules in a formal language and proceeding to play without any subsequent human input. To do well, an agent should learn from experience with past games and transfer the learned knowledge to new problems. We introduce a graph-based method for identifying previously encountered games and prove its robustness formally. We then describe how the same basic approach can be used to identify similar but non-identical games. We apply this technique to automate domain mapping for value function transfer and speed up reinforcement learning on variants of previously played games. Our approach is fully implemented with empirical results in the general game playing system.

1 Introduction

We consider the problem of General Game Playing (or Meta-Game Playing as it was introduced by [10]). In this paradigm, the challenge is to design an agent that can receive descriptions of previously unseen games and play them without subsequent human input. In its lifetime, a GGP agent will encounter a variety of different games. To leverage this experience, the agent must transfer knowledge from past games in a way that is beneficial to a new task that it is given.

In the transfer learning paradigm, an agent trains on a *source* task and leverages that experience to speed up learning on a *target* task. In particular, we are interested in transferring a value function found through temporal difference learning. The intention is to provide a reasonable starting place for learning, while allowing refinement for the specifics of the target task.

Because the source task and target task may have different state and action spaces, and different goals, a prerequisite for value function transfer is a domain mapping between the two. We present a set of general mapping functions to automatically translate a value function between certain classes of game variants, a process that is typically carried out manually. Also, unlike typical transfer scenarios, an agent in our paradigm is responsible for selecting the appropriate source task from its database, rather than being given a specific source task to use. We contribute a graph-based method for recognizing similar games and prove that it is robust even when game descriptions are intentionally obfuscated.

J.N. Kok et al. (Eds.): ECML 2007, LNAI 4701, pp. 188–200, 2007.

```
1.  (role white) (role black)
2.  (init (cell a 1 b)) (init (cell a 2 b)) (init (cell a 3 b))
3.  (init (cell a 4 bk))  ...  (init (cell d 1 wr))  ...  (init (cell d 4 b))
4.  (init (control white)) (init (step 1))
5.  (<= (legal white (move wk ?u ?v ?x ?y))
6.      (true (control white)) (true (cell ?u ?v wk)) (kingmove ?u ?v ?x ?y)
7.      (true (cell ?x ?y b)) (not (restricted ?x ?y)))
8.  (<= (legal white noop) (true (control black)))
9.  (<= (next (cell ?x ?y ?p)) (does ?player (move ?p ?u ?v ?x ?y)))
10. (<= (next (step ?y)) (true (step ?x)) (succ ?x ?y))
11. (succ 1 2) (succ 2 3) (succ 3 4) (succ 4 5) ... (succ 7 8) (succ 8 9) (succ 9 10)
12. (nextcol a b) (nextcol b c) (nextcol c d)
13. (<= (goal white 100) checkmate)
14. (<= (goal black 100) (not checkmate))
15. (<= terminal (true (step 10)))
16. (<= terminal stuck)
```

Fig. 1. Partial game description for "Minichess". GDL keywords shown in **bold**.

The following section provides background on GGP and discusses the key elements of the game description language as well as our method for analyzing such descriptions. Section 3 introduces our graph-based game recognition algorithm, sketches a proof of its robustness, and outlines the recognized game variant classes. In Section 4, we discuss how to map learned value functions between game variants. Our complete approach is evaluated in the GGP framework in Section 5. Section 6 surveys related work and Section 7 concludes.

2 General Game Playing

The general game playing scenario adopted for this work is taken from the AAAI General Game Playing competition [8]. In the competition setup, the *Game Manager* connects to each player process and sends the game description along with time limits called the *start clock* and *play clock*. Players have the duration of the start clock to analyze the game description before the game begins and the duration of the play clock to choose their moves each turn. The game continues until a terminal state is reached. No human intervention is permitted at any point: the general game player must be a complete and fully autonomous agent.

2.1 Game Description Language

For an agent to interpret a game, it must be described in a well-defined language. In the Game Description Language (GDL), used in the competition, games are modeled as state machines. An agent can derive its legal moves, the next state given the moves of all players, and whether or not it has won by applying resolution theorem proving. Part of the description for a game called "Minichess" is shown in Figure 1. A GGP agent must be able to play any game, given such a description. We illustrate the features of GDL through this example.

First, GDL declares the game's roles (line 1). "Minichess" has two roles, `white` and `black`. Next, the initial state of the game is defined (2–4). Each functional term inside an `init` relation is true in the initial state. Besides `init`, none of the tokens in these lines are GDL keywords. The predicates `cell`, `control` and `step` are all game-specific. With the exception of goal values, even the numbers do not have any external meaning. If any of these tokens were to be replaced by a different token throughout, the meaning would not change.

GDL also defines the set of legal moves available to each role through `legal` rules (5–8). The `<=` symbol is the reverse implication operator. Tokens beginning with a question mark are variables. The `true` relation is affirmative if its argument can be satisfied in the current state. The state transition function is defined using the `next` keyword (9–10). The `does` predicate is true if the given player selected the given action in the current state. Finally, GDL defines rules to determine when the game state is `terminal` (15–16). When the game ends, each player receives the reward defined by the game's `goal` rules.

A game description may define additional relations to simplify the conditions of other rules and support numerical relationships. For instance, the `succ` relation (11) defines how the game's step counter is incremented, and the `nextcol` relation (12) orders the columns of the chess board. Identifying such relationships is valuable because they bridge logical and numerical representations.

2.2 Automated Domain Analysis

An approach common to most computer game playing systems is heuristic search, in which game states are evaluated based on the contribution of various features. Although these features are typically supplied by the system designer [3,11], the general game playing setting prohibits such human involvement, motivating the development of automated methods.

In prior work on automated domain analysis [9], we developed techniques for generating features automatically from GDL game descriptions. The structures identified during domain analysis are also valuable in domain mapping. One of the most basic structures to look for is a *successor* relation. This type of relation induces an ordering over a set of objects. We have already seen two examples in lines 11–12 of Figure 1. A major challenge for automated domain analysis in GGP is that, during the competition, the description's non-keyword tokens are scrambled to prevent the use of lexical clues. In a competition setting, the same successor relations may look something like: `(tcsh pico cpio) (tcsh cpio grep) ... (tcsh echo ping)`.

Our system can still identify these relations as successors because order is a structural, rather than lexical, property. Based on these relations, the agent identifies additional structures such as a step counter, which is a functional term in the game's state that increments each time step. Our system identifies it by looking for a rule such as the one on line 10 of Figure 1.

Another example of a structure that our agent attempts to identify is a *board*. A board is a two dimensional grid of cells that change state, such as a chess or checkers board. Once a board is identified, the system looks for *markers*, which are objects that occupy the cells of the board and *pieces*, special markers that

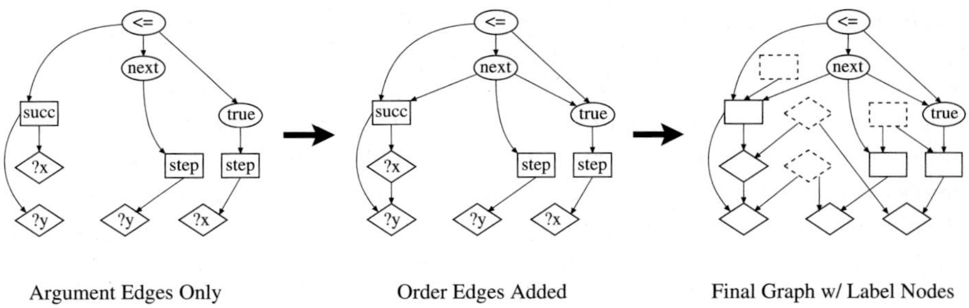

Fig. 2. Rule graph construction for step counter rule on line 10 of Figure 1

occupy only one cell at a time. In "Minichess", the white rook, `wr`, and the black king `bk` are examples of pieces. Games like Othello have only markers.

3 Graph-Based Domain Mapping

An important step in transferring knowledge from a known game to a new, unknown game is recognizing the extent to which the games are similar. Because their rules are reordered and tokens scrambled during a competition, it is not clear from the GDL descriptions even if two games are identical. To address this problem, we introduce the concept of rule graphs, canonical form graph structures that capture the important aspects of the game description while ignoring inconsequential elements such as token names and rule order.

3.1 Rule Graphs

Rule graphs are colored, directed graph representations of game rules. To describe rule graph construction, we use the example of the step counter rule in line 10 of Figure 1. Conceptually, a rule graph is constructed in three stages. These stages for the step counter graph are show from left to right in Figure 2.

First, the graph contains a node for each logical sentence, relational sentence, constant and variable in the rule. For each of these terms, an *argument edge* is added from the term's node to all of the term's arguments. Variable nodes are shown as diamonds. Logical sentence nodes are labeled by the sentence's operator. Relational sentences and constants are labeled with their functor's name and shown as circles, if they are keywords, and shown as squares, otherwise. The resulting graph is shown on the far left in Figure 2. For the purpose of matching, each circular node with a different label is considered a different color.

As shown in the center graph in the figure, we add additional edges to force ordering constraints on arguments. For each relational sentence with arity greater than one, we add an *order edge* from each argument to the argument that follows it. The edge between the two arguments of the `succ` relation in the figure is an example of such an edge. Also, we constrain the consequent of an implication to precede the antecedents without enforcing an order on the antecedents themselves. We achieve this constraint by adding edges from the consequent to each of the antecedents, as in the edge from `next` to `succ` and from `next` to `true`.

Finally, we must identify which variables and constants are the same without keeping the specific labels. For each unique variable in a rule and for each unique non-keyword constant in the game description, we create a new *label node* and add edges to each of their instances. Variable label nodes are shown as dashed diamonds and non-keyword constant label nodes as dashed squares. The final graph for the step counter rule is shown on the far right in Figure 2.

To determine if two rules graphs are isomorphic, one must simply use any off-the-shelf graph isomorphism algorithm. Through informal experimentation we found VF [4] to be relatively efficient for the structure of rule graphs.

3.2 Correctness Proof

In this section, we sketch a proof for the correctness of rule graph isomorphism as a means to determine if two games are the same, modulo scrambling. We begin with a few definitions, followed by the formal statement of the theorem.

In GDL, an *atomic sentence* is a relation constant of arity k applied to k terms: $p(x_1, \ldots, x_k)$ or equivalently $p(x_1^k)$. An example of an atomic sentence is father(bob, X). If k is 0 then the sentence is called an *object constant.* A *term* is either a *variable* (e.g. X) or an atomic sentence. A more complex example of an atomic sentence is the following: f(X, g(Y, h(p)), q). The constants may be user-defined, such as `cell`, or GDL keywords such as `not`, `terminal`, or `distinct`.

A *rule* is an implication of the form: $h \Leftarrow b_1 \wedge \cdots \wedge b_n$, where h, the head, and each b_i in the body are atomic sentences. Although GDL supports disjunction in the body, it is always possible to remove this disjunction and write rules in this form. Because conjunction is associative and commutative, we can represent the body of a rule as a set, B. Therefore, we represent such a rule as a pair $h \Leftarrow B$ where $B = \{b_1, b_2, \ldots, b_n\}$. If the set B is empty, then the head of the rule is an unconditionally true fact.

A *game description* is a set of rules. A *variable scrambling* is a one-to-one function over the variable labels present in a rule. A *constant scrambling* is a one-to-one function over the constant labels present in a game description. A *game scrambling* of a game description γ is a constant scrambling of γ and a set of variable scramblings, one for each rule in γ. Two game descriptions γ and γ' are *scramble-equivalent* if there exists a scrambling η such that $\gamma' = \eta(\gamma)$.

Theorem 1. *Two game descriptions γ and γ' are scramble-equivalent if and only if the rule graph G created from γ and rule graph G' created from γ' are isomorphic.*

Proof Sketch

The forward implication of the theorem is fairly straightforward to prove. If two game descriptions are scramble-equivalent, then their corresponding rule graphs will be isomorphic. A simple argument for this statement is that the graph construction algorithm is deterministic and does not depend on the exact names of the non-keyword tokens.

The reverse direction is a bit more subtle. We will prove that isomorphic rule graphs imply scramble-equivalent game descriptions by induction on the size of the game description. Beginning with the base case of $\gamma = \emptyset$, we can construct any game description by composing the following operations:

1. Add new rule with object constant head and empty body:
   $\gamma \longrightarrow \gamma \cup \{c \Leftarrow \emptyset\}$
2. Add object constant as antecedent of existing rule:
   $\gamma \cup \{h \Leftarrow B\} \longrightarrow \gamma \cup \{h \Leftarrow B \cup \{c\}\}$
3. Append object constant to some atomic sentence in head of existing rule:
   $\gamma \cup \{p(\ldots r(x_1^k)\ldots) \Leftarrow B\} \longrightarrow \gamma \cup \{p(\ldots r(x_1^k, c)\ldots) \Leftarrow B\}$
4. Append variable to some atomic sentence in head of existing rule:
   $\gamma \cup \{p(\ldots r(x_1^k)\ldots) \Leftarrow B\} \longrightarrow \gamma \cup \{p(\ldots r(x_1^k, X)\ldots) \Leftarrow B\}$
5. Append object constant to some atomic sentence in body of existing rule:
   $\gamma \cup \{h \Leftarrow B \cup \{p(\ldots r(x_1^k)\ldots)\}\} \longrightarrow \gamma \cup \{h \Leftarrow B \cup \{p(\ldots r(x_1^k, c)\ldots)\}\}$
6. Append variable to some atomic sentence in body of existing rule:
   $\gamma \cup \{h \Leftarrow B \cup \{p(\ldots r(x_1^k)\ldots)\}\} \longrightarrow \gamma \cup \{h \Leftarrow B \cup \{p(\ldots r(x_1^k, X)\ldots)\}\}$

For each of the above operations, we construct a corresponding abstract rule graph, G. This graph can be divided into two partitions: the nodes and edges present prior to applying the operation, and those added by the operation. By the definition of isomorphism, the isomorphic rule graph, G', can then be partitioned in the same way. By applying the graph building algorithm in reverse, we get a partitioned game description γ'. By the induction hypothesis, the original subgraph isomorphism implies scramble-equivalent subgames. What remains is to show that there exists a scrambling compatible with the subgame scrambling that makes the induction step rule equivalent to its partner in the isomorphic game. The same procedure proves the induction step for each operation.

3.3 Identifying Similar Games

While it is undoubtedly useful to recognize identical games, the applicability of our algorithm is much greater if we extend it to similar, but non-identical games. Our approach is to continue using identical rule graph isomorphism, but to test against generated variants of previously played games. We begin by identifying the classes of variants that we have determined to produce small, local changes to rule graph structure. Each variant defines a transformation procedure, which modifies the original rule graph by adding and/or deleting nodes and edges.

The first class of variants are those that change only the initial state of the game. By comparing all of the rules other than the initial state declarations, the standard graph isomorphism algorithm can identify these variants: **Num Markers**, in which the number of markers on the board differs and **Piece Configuration**, in which the location of pieces is different.

A more challenging class of variants to identify are those that change one or more of the game's successor relations. For example, the `nextcol` relation defined on line (12) of Figure 1 could be made longer by adding another rule: `(nextcol d e)` or shorter by removing the rule `(nextcol c d)`. Alternatively, we could make the sequence cyclic by adding the rule: `(nextcol d a)`. Each of these game description changes correspond to rule graph transformations. By applying these candidate transformations prior to matching, we can identify the **Board Size** variant, in which the length successor relation ordering the coordinates of one or more of the board dimensions has been changed. The **Cylindrical/Toroidal Board** variant makes cyclic the successor relation that orders one or more of the coordinates of the board. Finally, **Step Limit** alters the maximum number of steps before forced termination by changing the step number in the termination condition and expanding the counter's successor relation as necessary.

Step Limit is a composite variant in that it modifies both a successor relation and a goal condition. Another goal variant is **Inverted Goal**, in which the constants "100" and "0" are swapped in the second argument of all instances of `goal`. In **Switched Role**, the rule graph is unchanged but the player's assigned role is different (e.g. playing as O instead of X in tictactoe). Lastly, in the **Missing Feature** variants, a state feature present in the source task state is absent in the target task state. The transformation procedure removes all instances of the feature and the rules that include it, (e.g. removal of a step counter).

Offline, the agent generates a rule graph for each applicable transformation of each previously played game. When faced with a new game, the agent generates its rule graph and attempts to match it against every graph in the database. Non-matching graphs are typically rejected very quickly; only correct matches require any significant amount of computation. With a database of roughly 100 games, the entire process never requires more than 27 secs on a 2.80GHz machine.

Although this approach can detect quite complicated transformations of games, there are limits to its power. Game variants that affect many rules at once are particularly difficult to handle. For example, the board topologies in 3 and 4 player Chinese checkers games differ by too many rules to describe their difference as a concise, generally-applicable transformation procedure.

To this point, we have described our procedure for identifying game variants. In the next section, we describe our approach to transferring knowledge between these games for the purpose of speeding up learning.

4 Value Function Transfer

The approach detailed in this work transfers a learned value function from a source task to initialize the value function of a target task, identified to be similar through the graph-based method described in the previous section. Before introducing our approach to value function transfer, we provide some background on the reinforcement learning paradigm and detail the assumptions and design choices of our learning algorithm.

4.1 Reinforcement Learning in Games

In a Reinforcement Learning (RL) problem [13], an environment is modeled as a Markov Decision Process (MDP), defined by a transition function, T, and a reward function, R. Many common algorithms for solving RL problems are based on learning a value function, Q, which approximates the expected long-term reward for executing action a in state s.

Mapping	Initial $V_T[s]$	Applicable Variants
Direct	$V_S[s]$	Step Limit Num Markers Piece Configuration
Inverse	$100 - V_S[s]$	Inverted Goal Switched Role
Average	$1\frac{1}{B}(s)\vert\sum_{s' \in B(s)} V_S[s']$	Board Size Missing Feature

Fig. 3. Value function initialization formulas for three mappings, along with applicable game variants. V_S and V_T are the value functions for the source and target tasks, respectively. $B(s)$ is the set of source task afterstates mapped to target afterstate s.

In GGP, R is known, but for multiplayer games, T is only partially known, because the transition function depends on the opponent's unknown policy. If we consider only turn-taking games, in which the next state is uniquely determined by the agent's action on its turn, then we need only learn a function V over what are commonly called *afterstates*. Although it is still possible to learn Q, V has fewer values, increasing generalization. Also, this representation simplifies transfer mapping by requiring only a mapping between the states of the two tasks and not the actions.

A popular algorithm for learning value functions is an incarnation of temporal difference learning called Sarsa [13]. Taking into account the assumptions discussed thus far and that R is defined only for terminal states, our learning algorithm can be described by the following update rule:

$$V[s_{t-1}] \leftarrow V[s_{t-1}] + \alpha \cdot \begin{cases} (R(s_t) - V[s_{t-1}]) & \text{if } s_t \text{ is terminal,} \\ (V[T(s_t, a_t)] - V[s_{t-1}]) & \text{otherwise.} \end{cases}$$

where α is the learning rate (0.3 in our experiments), s_t is the current state, a_t is the agent's chosen action, and s_{t-1} is the afterstate following the agent's previous action. This algorithm and the rest of the transfer learning approach described in this work make no assumptions about the representation of V. In our experiments, each $V[s]$ is stored as a single real value in a table. However, there is nothing in principle that would prevent our method from working with a function approximator, such as a neural network.

4.2 Value Function Mapping

To translate afterstate values in the source into afterstate values in the target we must construct a mapping between their state spaces. The appropriate mapping depends on the identified relationship of the tasks. In Figure 3 we propose three possible mapping functions and, for each, identify applicable game variants.

The *direct* mapping simply copies the value of an afterstate in the source task directly to afterstate value in the target task. This mapping assumes that the two tasks have the same state space and roughly the same goal condition.

Because the Step Limit variant effects only the duration of the game and Num Markers and Piece Configuration effect only the game initial state, the direct mapping seems to be appropriate.

The *inverse* mapping also assumes that the state space is the same between tasks, but that the goal has changed. In particular, it assumes that the goal of the target task is the exact opposite of the source task. This mapping is clearly applicable in the case of Inverted Goal. Assuming that the game is zero sum, then the mapping is also appropriate for Switched Role.

The final mapping, *average*, assumes only that there is a function, B, that for a given target afterstate, returns the set of relevant source afterstates. In the case of Missing Feature, $B(s)$ would return all source task afterstates with feature values matching those of s for the features remaining in the target afterstate. The Board Size variant uses a particular B, detailed in the next section.

4.3 Case Studies

In this section, we discuss the application of the complete mapping procedure to three concrete examples, one from each mapping category. Our first transfer scenario involves a miniature checkers game played on a 5×5 board. The rules are identical to normal checkers, except that an available jump must be taken.

This source-target pair is an example of the Num Markers variant. In the target task, each player begins with only 4 pieces instead of 5. The goal in both tasks is the same: to capture your opponent's markers before they capture yours. It is reasonable to assume that there will be some overlap in the states visited in the source task and those in the target task, so the Direct mapping appears to be the logical choice. At the same time, the degree to which the transfer may help (or hurt) must be answered empirically.

In the class of games appropriate for the Inverse mapping, we looked at the game of tictactoe and a variant in which the goal is inverted. Because the goal of the game is the opposite of the original goal, highly valued states of the source task should have low values in the target task and vice-versa.

Finally, "Minichess", the chess variant introduced in Section 2.1 is used as an example of a Board Size variant. For a target task with board size $N \times N$, we assume that the source task has a board size of $N-1 \times N-1$. In particular, we use the 3×3 game as the source task and the 4×4 game as the target task. The afterstate mapping function B, is constructed as follows. An afterstate represented by the 4×4 board in the target task is mapped to four candidate afterstates in the source task, each represented by a 3×3 board, which we call a *subboard*. The first subboard consists of the top-left 3×3 cells of the board. The next subboard consists of the

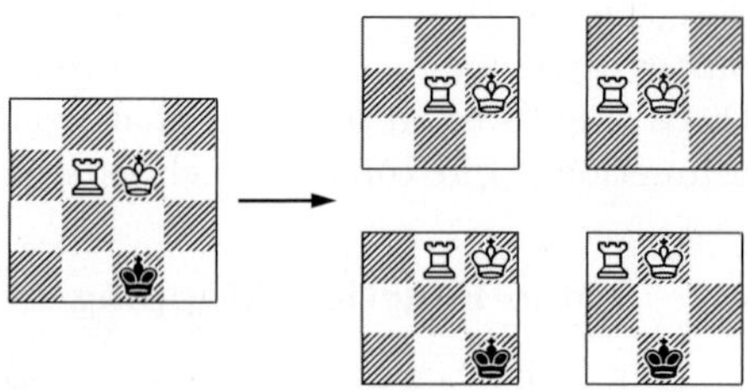

Fig. 4. Full 4×4 "Minichess" state and all four candidate subboards

top-right cells, continuing clockwise. Figure 4 shows a source task afterstate and its four candidate subboards. Each of these candidates is not necessarily a valid afterstate in the source task. If no subboards are valid, the afterstate value is initialized to the default value.

5 Experiments

We conducted experiments to determine the impact of value function transfer in each of the described scenarios, using different amounts of training on the source task. Each learning trial consists of an independent source task learning phase followed by a target task learning phase. The target task agent's value function is initialized by the source task value function, according to the domain's generated mapping function. Each trial was repeated 30 times, with a sliding window average of 100 matches used to generate learning curves. To determine statistical significance, we evaluated the curves at several points using a one-tailed T-test with 95% confidence. All figures show averaged learning curves.

The results of our "Checkers" experiments are shown on the left in Figure 5. Value function transfer produces an initial performance improvement that persists until convergence. The other two curves eventually catch up, beyond the scale of the graph. The visible differences are statistically significant for all data points shown. The average number of state values transferred for the most experience player was 1,113, which is roughly a third of all unique afterstates encountered during target task learning. To make learning more valuable in these experiments, we used an opponent agent trained for an extensive period of time with temporal different learning rather than a random player.

The "TicTacToe" results, shown on the right in Figure 5, again demonstrate the positive impact of transfer. In this case, the average hit rate was 68% for the learner with 10,000 matches of source task experience. This substantial reuse of source task values helps to explain the significance of the transfer benefit.

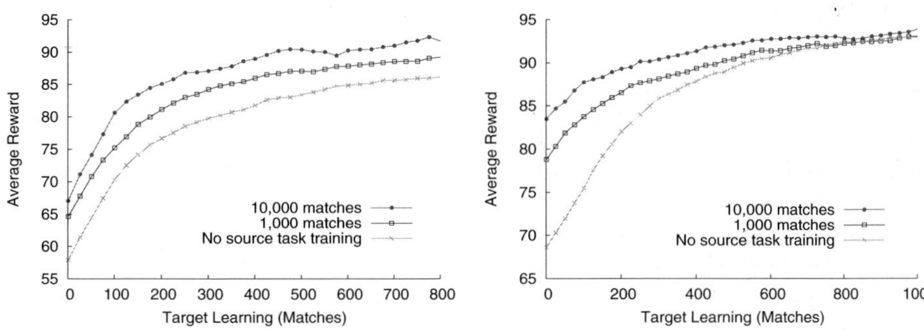

Fig. 5. Transfer learning results with varying source experience. *Left:* "Checkers" game with Num Markers variant. *Right:* "TicTacToe" game with Inverted Goal variant.

The performance improvement of the player with 10,000 matches of source task experience is significantly better than the from-scratch learner until 700 matches.

To make the problem more interesting for learning, at the start of each match, for both source and target learning, the state is initialized to a random configuration of the pieces. In only about half of the initial states can the white player force a win. However, in our experiments, the black player is controlled by a one-move lookahead player, and thus, by exploiting the suboptimality of the opponent, a learner is able to earn an average score above 50.

The transfer results for "Minichess" are shown in Figure 6. Transfer clearly improves the learner's initial performance. The experienced learners do significantly better than the agent learning from scratch up until 1,200 target matches. The agent learning from scratch then performs better than the experienced players between 2,500 and 4,000 matches. The fact that the slowdown is more pronounced for the 1,000 match learner than for the 100 match learner indicates that the agent may be overfitting to the source task. The negative effect is short-lived, however, and by 4,000 target task matches, all three learners converge.

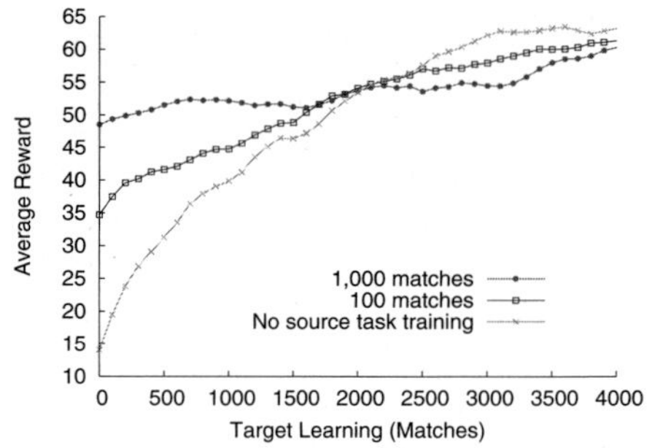

Fig. 6. Transfer from 3 × 3 board to 4 × 4 board in "Minichess"

6 Related Work

Graph theoretic structures have long been recognized for their value to logic programming. Scheffer et al. [12] define an *occurrence graph* and demonstrate its utility in efficiently solving the θ-subsumption problem for ILP. This graph relates the shared variables between a pair of clauses, but does not relate symbol names across clauses like our rule graphs.

In other work [6,5], *dependency graphs*, used to check for consistency in logic programs with negation, have been extended to apply under the stable model semantics. Dependency graphs are defined over the predicate symbols of a knowledge base and capture a different abstraction than that in our work.

The most similar graph structure to our own is that defined by Xu and Tao [15]. With this structure, they demonstrate that the isomorphism problem for definite logic programs (those with only Horn clauses) is equivalent to the graph isomorphism problem. Our proof in Section 3.2 extends this result to general Datalog programs with negation.

In their recent work, Taylor et al. [14] demonstrate that value function transfer is able to speed up learning between tasks when the domain mapping is given. Their work also makes progress towards automating mapping by employing a classification algorithm to map actions between tasks. This method requires that the states are defined in terms of objects and each state feature is associated with one of those objects.

Other work on Relational Reinforcement Learning (RRL) has shown that by maintaining the relational structure of the domain in the representation of the value function, it is possible to learn to solve differently parametrized tasks simultaneously [7]. As our work makes no assumptions about value function representation, future work may reveal RRL to be complementary to our approach. RRL has even been applied in GGP. Asgharbeygi et al. [1] learn the values of handcrafted relational predicates to speed up learning considerably.

Another successful example of transfer learning in GGP is the work of Banerjee and Stone [2], in which features of the game tree alone are leveraged for transfer. Although the features are somewhat expensive to compute because they require search, the learner is able to transfer learned knowledge across games with significantly different state and action spaces.

7 Conclusion

This work makes progress toward the complete automation of domain mapping for value function-based transfer learning. The first main contribution is the introduction of the *rule graph* structure, which is useful for representing games in canonical form. Beyond its use in this paper, the rule graph is likely to be of general interest within the GGP community, as a way to leverage past experience. The second main contribution of this paper is that rule graphs, along with a set of identified variant classes, can be be used as part of a practical method for recognizing variants of previously played games and speeding up learning in the General Game Playing framework.

References

1. Asgharbeygi, N., Stracuzzi, D., Langley, P.: Relational temporal difference learning. In: ICML (2006)
2. Banerjee, B., Stone, P.: General game learning using knowledge transfer. In: The 20th International Joint Conference on Artificial Intelligence, January 2007, pp. 672–677 (2007)
3. Campbell, M., Hoane Jr., A.J., Hsu, F.H.: Deep blue. Artificial Intelligence 134(1–2), 57–83 (2002)
4. Cordella, L.P., Foggia, P., Sansone, C., Vento, M.: An improved algorithm for matching large graphs. In: Proc. of the 3rd IAPR-TC-15 Internation Workshop on Graph-based Representations, Italy, pp. 149–159 (2001)
5. Costantini, S.: Comparing different graph representations of logic programs under the answer set semantics. In: Proceedings of the AAAI Spring Symposium on Answer Set Programming (2001)
6. Dimopoulos, Y., Torres, A.: Graph theoretical structures in logic programs and default theories. Theoretical Computer Science 170(1), 209–244 (1996)
7. Dzeroski, S., De Raedt, L., Driessens, K.: Relational reinforcement learning. Machine Learning 43, 7–52 (2001)

8. Genesereth, M., Love, N.: General game playing: Overview of the AAAI competition. AI Magazine 26(2) (2005)
9. Kuhlmann, G., Dresner, K., Stone, P.: Automatic heuristic contruction in a complete general game player. In: Proceedings of the Twenty-First National Conference on Artificial Intelligence (July 2006)
10. Pell, B.: Strategy generation and evaluation for meta-game playing. PhD thesis, University of Cambridge (1993)
11. Schaeffer, J., Culberson, J.C., Treloar, N., Knight, B., Lu, P., Szafron, D.: A world championship caliber checkers program. Artificial Intelligence 53(2-3), 273–289 (1992)
12. Scheffer, T., Herbrich, R., Wysotzki, F.: Efficient theta-subsumption based on graph algorithms. In: Inductive Logic Programming Workshop (1996)
13. Sutton, R.S., Barto, A.G.: Reinforcement Learning: An Introduction. MIT Press, Cambridge, MA (1998)
14. Taylor, M.E., Whiteson, S., Stone, P.: Transfer via inter-task mappings in policy search reinforcement learning. In: The Sixth International Joint Conference on Autonomous Agents and Multiagent Systems (May 2007)
15. Xu, D.-Y., Tao, Z.-H.: Complexities of homomorphism and isomorphism for definite logic programs. Journal of Computer Science and Technology 20(6), 758–762 (2005)

Learning to Classify Documents with Only a Small Positive Training Set

Xiao-Li Li[1], Bing Liu[2], and See-Kiong Ng[1]

[1] Institute for Infocomm Research, Heng Mui Keng Terrace, 119613, Singapore
[2] Department of Computer Science, University of Illinois at Chicago, IL 60607-7053
xlli@i2r.a-star.edu.sg, liub@cs.uic.edu, skng@i2r.a-star.edu.sg

Abstract. Many real-world classification applications fall into the class of positive and unlabeled (PU) learning problems. In many such applications, not only could the negative training examples be missing, the number of positive examples available for learning may also be fairly limited due to the impracticality of hand-labeling a large number of training examples. Current PU learning techniques have focused mostly on identifying reliable negative instances from the unlabeled set *U*. In this paper, we address the oft-overlooked PU learning problem when the number of training examples in the positive set *P* is small. We propose a novel technique LPLP (Learning from Probabilistically Labeled Positive examples) and apply the approach to classify product pages from commercial websites. The experimental results demonstrate that our approach outperforms existing methods significantly, even in the challenging cases where the positive examples in *P* and the hidden positive examples in *U* were not drawn from the same distribution.

1 Introduction

Traditional supervised learning techniques typically require a large number of labeled examples to learn an accurate classifier. However, in practice, it can be an expensive and tedious process to obtain the class labels for large sets of training examples. One way to reduce the amount of labeled training data needed is to develop classification algorithms that can learn from a set of labeled positive examples augmented with a set of unlabeled examples. That is, given a set *P* of positive examples of a particular class and a set *U* of unlabeled examples (which contains both hidden positive and hidden negative examples), we build a classifier using *P* and *U* to classify the data in *U* as well as future test data. We call this the PU learning problem.

Several innovative techniques (e.g. [1], [2], [3]) have been proposed to solve the PU learning problem recently. All of these techniques have focused on addressing the lack of labeled negative examples in the training data. It was assumed that there was a sufficiently large set of positive training examples, and also that the positive examples in *P* and the hidden positive examples in *U* were drawn from the same distribution. However, in practice, obtaining a large number of positive examples can be rather difficult in many real applications. Oftentimes, we have to do with a fairly small set of positive training data. In fact, the small positive set may not even adequately represent

J.N. Kok et al. (Eds.): ECML 2007, LNAI 4701, pp. 201–213, 2007.

the whole positive class, as it is highly likely that there could be hidden positives in *U* that may not be similar to those few examples in the small positive set *P*. Moreover, the examples in the positive set *P* and the hidden positive examples in the unlabeled set *U* may not even be generated or drawn from the same distribution. A classifier trained merely on the few available examples in *P* would thus be incompetent in recognizing all the hidden positives in *U* as well as those in the test sets.

In this work, we consider the problem of learning to classify documents with only a small positive training set. Our work was motivated by a real-life business intelligence application of classifying web pages of product information. The richness of information easily available on the World Wide Web has made it routine for companies to conduct business intelligence by searching the Internet for information on related products. For example, a company that sells computer printers may want to do a product comparison among the various printers currently available in the market. One can first collect sample printer pages by crawling through all product pages from a consolidated e-commerce web site (e.g., amazon.com) and then hand-label those pages containing printer product information to construct the set *P* of positive examples. Next, to get more product information, one can then crawl through all the product pages from other web sites (e.g., cnet.com) as *U*. Ideally, PU learning techniques can then be applied to classify all pages in *U* into printer pages and non-printer pages. However, we found that while the printer product pages from two websites (say, amazon.com and cnet.com) do indeed share many similarities, they can also be quite distinct as the different web sites invariably present their products (even similar ones) in different styles and have different focuses. As such, directly applying existing methods would give very poor results because 1) the small positive set *P* obtained from one site contained only tens of web pages (usually less than 30) and therefore do not adequately represent the whole positive class, and 2) the features from the positive examples in *P* and the hidden positive examples in *U* are not generated from the same distribution because they were from different web sites.

In this paper, we tackle the challenge of constructing a reliable document (web page) classifier based on only a few labeled positive pages from a single web site and then use it to automatically extract the hidden positive pages from different web sites (i.e. the unlabeled sets). We propose an effective technique called LPLP (Learning from Probabilistically Labeling Positive examples) to perform this task. Our proposed technique LPLP is based on probabilistically labeling training examples from *U* and the EM algorithm [4]. The experimental results showed that LPLP significantly outperformed existing PU learning methods.

2 Related Works

A theoretical study of PAC learning from positive and unlabeled examples under the statistical query model was first reported in [5]. Muggleton [6] followed by studying the problem in a Bayesian framework where the distribution of functions and examples are assumed known. [1] reported sample complexity results and provided theoretical elaborations on how the problem could be solved. Subsequently, a number of practical PU learning algorithms were proposed [1], [3] and [2]. These PU learning algorithms all conformed to the theoretical results presented in [1] by following a common two-step strategy, namely: (1) identifying a set of reliable negative documents from the unlabeled set; and then (2) building a classifier using EM or SVM iteratively. The specific differences between the various algorithms in these two steps are as follows. The S-EM method proposed in [1] was based on naïve Bayesian classification and the EM algorithm [4]. The main idea was to first use a spying technique to identify some reliable negative documents from the unlabeled set, and then to run EM to build the final classifier. The PEBL method [3] uses a different method (1-DNF) for identifying reliable negative examples and then runs SVM iteratively for classifier building. More recently, [2] reported a technique called Roc-SVM. In this technique, reliable negative documents were extracted by using the information retrieval technique Rocchio [7]. Again, SVM is used in the second step. A classifier selection criterion is also proposed to catch a good classifier from iterations of SVM. Despite the differences in algorithmic details, the above methods all focused on extracting reliable negative instances from the unlabeled set.

More related to our current work was the recent work by Yu [8], which proposed to estimate the boundary for the positive class. However, the amount of positive examples they required was around 30% of the whole data, which was still too large for many practical applications. In [9], a method called PN-SVM was proposed to deal with the case when the positive set is small. However, it (like all the other existing algorithms of PU learning) relied on the assumption that the positive examples in *P* and the hidden positives in *U* were all generated from the same distribution. For the first time, our LPLP method proposed in this paper will address such common weaknesses of current PU learning methods, including handling challenging cases where the positive examples in *P* and the hidden positive examples in *U* were not drawn from the same distribution.

Note that the problem could potentially be modeled as a one-class classification problem. For example, in [10], a one-class SVM that uses only positive data to build a SVM classifier was proposed. Such approaches are different from our method in that they do not use unlabeled data for training. However, as previous results reported in [2] have already showed that they were inferior for text classification, we do not consider them in this work.

3 The Proposed Technique

Figure 1 depicts the general scenario of PU learning with a small positive training set *P*. Let us denote a space ψ that represents the whole positive class, which is located above the hyperplane H_2. The small positive set *P* only occupies a relatively small subspace *SP* in ψ ($SP \subseteq \psi$), shown as the oval region in the figure. The examples in the unlabelled set *U* consists of both hidden positive examples (represented by circled "+") and hidden negative examples (represented by "-"). Since *P* is small, and ψ contains positive examples from different web sites that present similar products in different styles and focuses, we may not expect the distributions of the positive examples in *P* and those of the hidden positive examples in *U* to be the same. In other words, the set of hidden positive examples that we are trying to detect may have a very small intersection or is even disjoint with *SP*. If we naively use the small set *P* as the positive training set and the entire unlabelled set *U* as the negative set, the resulting classifier (corresponds to hyperplane H_1) will obviously perform badly in identifying the hidden positive examples in *U*.

On the other hand, we can attempt to use the more sophisticated PU learning methods to address this problem. Instead of merely using the entire unlabelled set *U* as the negative training data, the first step of PU learning extracts some reliable negatives from *U*. However, this step is actually rather difficult in our application scenario as depicted in Figure 1. Since the hidden positive examples in *U* are likely to have different distributions from those captured in the small positive set *P*, not all the training examples in *U* that are dissimilar to examples in *P* are negative examples. As a result, the so-called reliable negative set that the first step of PU learning extracts based on dissimilarity from *P* would be a very noisy negative set, and therefore not very useful for building a reliable classifier.

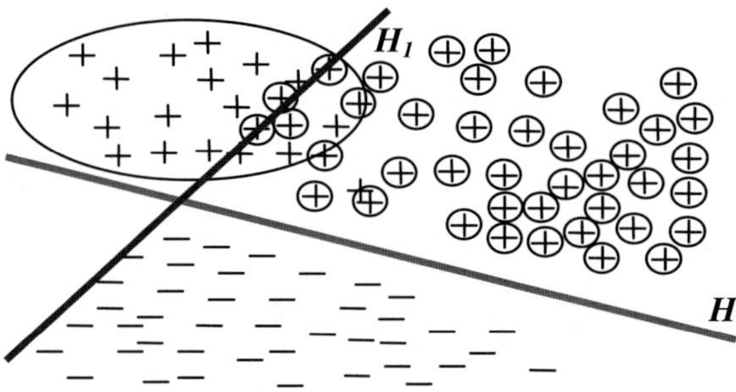

Fig. 1. PU learning with a small positive training set

Let us consider the possibility of extracting a set of likely positive examples (*LP*) from the unlabeled set *U* to address the problem of *P*'s being not sufficiently representative of the hidden positive documents in *U*. Unlike *P*, the distribution of *LP* will be similar with the other hidden positive examples in *U*. As such, we could expect that a more accurate classifier can be built with the help of set *LP* (together with *P*). Pictorially, the resulting classifier would correspond to the optimal hyperplane H_2 shown in Figure 1. Instead of trying to identify a set of noisy negative documents from the unlabeled set *U* as existing PU learning techniques do, our proposed technique LPLP therefore focuses on extracting a set of likely positive documents from *U*.

While the positive documents in *P* and the hidden positive documents in *U* were not drawn from the same distribution, they should still be similar in some underlying feature dimensions (or subspaces) as they belong to the same class. For example, the printer pages from two different sites, say amazon.com and cnet.com, would share the representative word features such as "printer", "inkjet", "laser", "ppm" etc, though their respective distributions may be quite different. Particularly, the pages from cnet.com whose target readers are more technically-savvy may contain more frequent mentioning of keyword terms that correspond to the technical specifications of printers than those pages from amazon.com whose primary focus is to reach out to the less technically-inclined customers. However, we can safely expect that the basic keywords (representative word features) that describe computer printers should be presented in both cases. In this work, we therefore assume that the representative word features for the documents in *P* should be similar to those for the hidden positive documents in *U*. If we can find such a set of representative word features (*RW*) from the positive set *P*, then we can use them to extract other hidden positive documents from *U*.

We are now ready to present the details of our proposed technique LPLP. In Section 3.1, we first introduce a method to select the set of representative word features *RW* from the given positive set *P*. Then, in Section 3.2, we extract the likely positive documents from *U* and probabilistically label them based on the set *RW*. With the help of the resulting set *LP*, we employ the EM algorithm with a good initialization to build an accurate classifier to identify the hidden positive examples from *U* in Section 3.3.

3.1 Selecting a Set of Representative Word Features from P

As mentioned above, we expect the positive examples in *P* and the hidden positive examples in *U* share the same representative word features as they belong to the same class. We extract a set *RW* of representative word features from the positive set *P* containing the top *k* words with the highest $s(w_i)$ scores. The scoring function *s*() is based on TFIDF method [11] which gives high scores to those words that occur frequently in the positive set *P* and not in the whole corpus $P \cup U$ since *U* contains many other unrelated documents. Figure 2 shows the detailed algorithm to select the keyword set *RW*.

1. $RW = \Phi$, $F = \Phi$;
2. **For** each word feature $w_i \in P$
3.   **If** (stopwords (w_i)!=true)
4. $F = F \cup$ {stemming(w_i)};
5. *total*=0;
6. **For** each word feature $w_i \in F$
7. $N(w_i, P) = \sum_{j=1}^{|P|} \frac{N(w_i, d_j)}{\max_{w_i} (N(w_i, d_j))}$;
8. $total \mathrel{+}= N(w_i, P)$;
9. **For** each word feature $w_i \in F$
10. $s(w_i) = \frac{N(w_i,P)}{total} * \log \frac{|P|+|U|}{df(w_i,P)+df(w_i,U)}$;
11. Rank the word feature's $s(w_i)$ from big to small into a list *L*;
12. Pr_{TOP}= the *k*-th $s(w_i)$ in the list *L*, $w_i \in F$;
13. **For** $\forall w_i \in F$
14.   **If** ($s(w_i)$ >= Pr_{TOP})
15. $RW = RW \cup \{ w_i \}$;

Fig. 2. Selecting a set of representative word features from *P*

In step 1, we initialize the representative word set *RW* and unique feature set *F* as empty sets. After removing the stop words (step 3) and performing stemming (step 4) [11], all the word features are stored into the feature set *F*. For each word feature w_i in the positive set *P*, steps 6 to 8 compute the accumulated word frequency (in each document d_j, the word w_i's frequency $N(w_i, d_j)$ is normalized by the maximal word frequency of d_j in step 7). Steps 9 to 10 then compute the scores of each word feature, which consider both w_i's probabilities of belonging to a positive class and its inverted document frequency, where $df(w_i, P)$ and $df(w_i, U)$ are w_i's document frequencies in *P* and *U* respectively. After ranking the scores into the rank list *L* in step 11, we store into *RW* those word features from *P* with top *k* scores in *L*.

3.2 Identifying *LP* from *U* and Probabilistically Labeling the Documents in *LP*

Once the set *RW* of representative keywords is determined, we can regard them together as a representative document (*rd*) of the positive class. We then compare the similarity of each document d_i in *U* with *rd* using the cosine similarity metric [11], which automatically produces a set *LP* of probabilistically labeled documents with $\Pr(d_i|+) > 0$. The algorithm for this step is given in Figure 3. In step 1, the likely positive set *LP* and the remaining unlabelled set *RU* are both initialized as empty sets. In steps 2 to 3, each unlabeled document d_i in *U* is compared with *rd* using the cosine similarity. Step 4 stores the largest similarity value as *m*. For each document d_i in *U*, if its cosine similarity $sim(rd, d_i)>0$, we assign a probability $Pr(+|d_i)$ that is based on the ratio of its similarity and *m* (step 7) and we store it into the set *LP* in step 8. Otherwise, d_i is included in *RU* instead (step 10). The documents in *RU* have zero similarity with *rd* and can be considered as a purer negative set than *U*.

1. $LP = \Phi$; $RU = \Phi$;
2. **For** each $d_i \in U$
3. $sim(rd, d_i) = \dfrac{\sum_j w_{rd,j} * w_{d_i,j}}{\sqrt{\sum_j w_{rd,j}^2}\sqrt{\sum_j w_{d_i,j}^2}}$;
4. Let $m = \max_{d_i}(sim(rd, d_i))$, $d_i \in U$;
5. **For** each $d_i \in U$
6.   **If** ($sim(rd, d_i) > 0$)
7. $Pr(+|d_i) = sim(rd, d_i)/m$;
8. $LP = LP \cup \{d_i\}$;
9.   **Else**
10. $RU = RU \cup \{d_i\}$;

Fig. 3. Probabilistically labeling a set of documents

Note that in step 7, the hidden positive examples in *LP* will be assigned high probabilities while the negative examples in *LP* will be assigned very low probabilities. This is because the representative features in *RW* were chosen based on those words that occurred frequently in *P* but not in the whole corpus $P \cup U$. As such, the hidden positive examples in *LP* should also contain many of the features in *RW* while the negative examples in *LP* would contain few (if any) of the features in *RW*.

3.3 The Classification Algorithm

Next, we employ the naïve Bayesian framework to identify the hidden positives in *U*. Given a set of training documents *D*, each document is considered an list of words and each word in a document is from the vocabulary $V = < w_1, w_2, \ldots, w_{|v|} >$. We also have a set of predefined classes, $C=\{c_1, c_2, \ldots, c_{|C|}\}$ For simplicity, we will consider two class classification in this discussion, i.e. $C=\{c_1, c_2\}$, c_1="+" and c_2="-". To perform classification for a document d_i, we need to compute the posterior probability, $Pr(c_j|d_i)$, $c_j \in \{+,-\}$. Based on the Bayesian probability and the multinomial model [12], we have

$$\Pr(c_j) = \frac{\sum_{i=1}^{|D|} \Pr(c_j \mid d_i)}{|D|} . \tag{1}$$

and with Laplacian smoothing,

$$\Pr(w_t \mid c_j) = \frac{1 + \sum_{i=1}^{|D|} N(w_t, d_i)\Pr(c_j \mid d_i)}{|V| + \sum_{s=1}^{|V|}\sum_{i=1}^{|D|} N(w_s, d_i)\Pr(c_j \mid d_i)}. \tag{2}$$

Here, $Pr(c_j|d_i) \in \{0,1\}$ depending on the class label of the document.

Assuming that the probabilities of words are independent given the class, we obtain the naïve Bayesian classifier:

$$\Pr(c_j \mid d_i) = \frac{\Pr(c_j)\prod_{k=1}^{|d_i|}\Pr(w_{d_i,k} \mid c_j)}{\sum_{r=1}^{|C|}\Pr(c_r)\prod_{k=1}^{|d_i|}\Pr(w_{d_i,k} \mid c_r)}. \tag{3}$$

In the naive Bayesian classifier, the class with the highest $Pr(c_j|d_i)$ is assigned as the class of the document. The NB method is known to be an effective technique for text classification even with the violation of some of its basic assumptions (e.g class conditional independence) [13] [14] [1].

The Expectation-Maximization (EM) algorithm is a popular class of iterative algorithms for problems with incomplete data. It iterates over two basic steps, the Expectation step, and the Maximization step. The Expectation step basically fills in the missing data, while the Maximization step then estimates the parameters. When applying EM, equations (1) and (2) above comprise the Expectation step, while equation (3) is used for the Maximization step. Note that the probability of the class given the document now takes the value in [0, 1] instead of {0, 1}.

The ability of EM to work with missing data is exactly what we need here. Let us regard all the positive documents to have the positive class value "+". We want to know the class value of each document in the unlabeled set U. EM can help to properly assign a probabilistic class label to each document d_i in the unlabeled set, i.e., $Pr(+|d_i)$ or $Pr(-|d_i)$. Theoretically, in EM algorithm, the probabilities of documents in U will converge after a number of iterations [4]. However, a good initialization is important in order to find a good maximum of the likelihood function. For example, if we directly use P as positive class and U as negative class (initially), then EM algorithm will not build an accurate classifier as the negative class would be too noisy (as explained previously). Thus, in our algorithm, after extracting likely positive set LP, we re-initialize the EM algorithm by treating the probabilistically labeled LP (with/without P) as positive documents. The resulting classifier is more accurate

1. **For** each $d_i \in RU$,
2. $\quad Pr(+ \mid d_i) = 0$;
3. $\quad Pr(- \mid d_i) = 1$;
4. $PS = LP \cup P$ (or LP);
5. **For** each $d_j \in PS$
6. $\quad$ **If** $d_j \in P$
7. $\qquad Pr(+ \mid d_j) = 1$;
8. $\qquad Pr(- \mid d_j) = 0$;
9. $\quad$ **Else**
10. $\qquad Pr(+ \mid d_j) = sim(rd, d_j) / m$;
11. $\qquad Pr(- \mid d_j) = 0$;
12. Build an *NB*-C classifier *C* using *PS* and *RU* based on equations (1), (2);
13. **While** classifier parameters change
14. $\quad$ **For** each $d_i \in PS \cup RU$
15. $\qquad$ Compute $Pr(+|d_i)$ and $Pr(-|d_i)$ using *NB-C*, i.e., equation (3);
16. $\qquad$ Update $Pr(c_j)$ and $Pr(w_t|c_j)$ by replacing equations (1) and (2) with the new probabilities produced in step 15 (a new *NB-C* is being built in the process)

Fig. 4. The detailed LPLP algorithm

because 1) *LP* has the similar distributions with other hidden positive documents in *U*, and 2) the remaining unlabeled set *RU* is also much purer than *U* as a negative set.

The detailed LPLP algorithm is given in Figure 4. The inputs to the algorithm are *LP*, *RU* and *P*. Steps 1 to 3 initialize the probabilities for each document d_i in *RU*, which are all treated as negative documents initially. Step 4 sets the positive set *PS*; there are two possible ways to achieve this: we either (1) combine *LP* and *P* as *PS*, or (2) use only *LP* as *PS*. We will evaluate the effect of the inclusion of *P* in *PS* in the next section. Steps 5 to 11 will assign the initial probabilities to the documents in *P* (if *P* is used) and *LP*. Each document in *P* is assigned to the positive class while each document in *LP* is probabilistically labeled using the algorithm in Figure 3. Using *PS* and *RU*, a NB classifier can be built (step 12). This classifier is then applied to the documents in ($LP \cup RU$) to obtain the posterior probabilities ($Pr(+|d_i)$ and $Pr(-|d_i)$) for each document (step 15). We can then iteratively employ the revised posterior probabilities to build a new (and better) NB classifier (step 16). The EM process continues until the parameters of the NB classifier converge.

4 Evaluation Experiments

In this section, we evaluate the proposed LPLP technique under different settings and compare it with existing methods, namely, Roc-SVM [2] and PEBL [3]. Roc-SVM is available on the Web as a part of the LPU system[1]. We implemented PEBL ourselves as it is not publicly available. The results of S-EM [1] were not included here because the performance was generally very poor due to its reliance on similarity of positive documents in *P* and in *U*, as expected.

4.1 Datasets

Our evaluation experiments were done using product Web pages from 5 commercial Web sites: Amazon, CNet, PCMag, J&R and ZDnet. These sites contained many introduction/description pages of different types of products. The pages were cleaned using the web page cleaning technique in [15], i.e., navigation links and advertisements have been detected and eliminated. The data contained web pages of the following product categories: Notebook, Digital Camera, Mobile Phone, Printer and TV. Table 1 lists the number of pages from each site, and the corresponding product categories (or classes). In this work, we treat each page as a text document and we do not use hyperlinks and images for classification.

Table 1. Number of Web pages and their classes.

	Amazon	CNet	J&R	PCMag	ZDnet
Notebook	434	480	51	144	143
Camera	402	219	80	137	151
Mobile	45	109	9	43	97
Printer	767	500	104	107	80
TV	719	449	199	0	0

[1] http://www.cs.uic.edu/~liub/LPU/LPU-download.html

Note that we did not use standard text collections such as Reuters[2] and 20 Newsgroup data[3] in our experiments as we want to highlight the performance of our approach on data sets that have different positive distributions in *P* and in *U*.

4.2 Experiment Settings

As mentioned, the number of available positively labeled documents in practice can be quite small either because there were few documents to start with, or it was tedious and expensive to hand-label the training examples on a large scale. To reflect this constraint, we experimented with different number of (randomly selected) positive documents in *P*, i.e. $|P|$ = 5, 15, or 25 and allpos. Here "allpos" means that all documents of a particular product from a Web site were used. The purpose of these experiments is to investigate the relative effectiveness of our proposed method for both small and large positive sets.

We conducted a comprehensive set of experiments using all the possible *P* and *U* combinations. That is, we selected every entry (one type of product from each Web site) in Table 1 as the positive set *P* and use each of the other 4 Web sites as the unlabeled set *U*. Three products were omitted in our experiments because their $|P|<10$, namely, Mobile phone in J&R (9 pages), TV in PCMag (no page), and TV in ZDnet (no page). A grand total of 88 experiments were conducted using all the possible *P* and *U* combinations of the 5 sites. Due to the large number of combinations, the results reported below are the average values for the results from all the combinations.

To study the sensitivity of the number of representative word features used in identifying likely positive examples, we also performed a series of experiments using different numbers of representative features, i.e. k = 5, 10, 15 and 20 in our algorithm.

4.3 Experimental Results

Since our task is to identify or retrieve positive documents from the unlabeled set *U*, it is appropriate to use *F* value to evaluate the performance of the final classifier. *F* value is the harmonic mean of precision (p) and recall (r), i.e. $F=2*p*r/(p+r)$. When either of p or r is small, the *F* value will be small. Only when both of them are large, *F* value will be large. This is suitable for our purpose as we do not want to identify positive documents with either too small a precision or too small a recall. Note that in our experiment results, the reported *F* values give the classification (retrieval) results of the positive documents in *U* as *U* is also the test set.

Let us first show the results of our proposed technique LPLP under different experimental settings. We will then compare it with two existing techniques.

The bar chart in Figure 5 shows the *F* values (Y-axis) of LPLP using different numbers of positive documents (X-axis) and different numbers of representative words (4 data series). Recall that we had presented two options to construct the positive set *PS* in step 4 of the LPLP algorithm (Figure 4). The first option is to add the extracted likely positive documents (*LP*) to the original set of positive documents *P*, represented in Figure 5 by "with *P*". The second option is to use only the extracted likely positive documents as the positive data in learning, i.e., dropping the original

[2] http://www.research.att.com/~lewis/reuters21578.html

[3] http://www.cs.cmu.edu/afs/cs/project/theo-11/www/naive-bayes/20_newsgroups.tar.gz

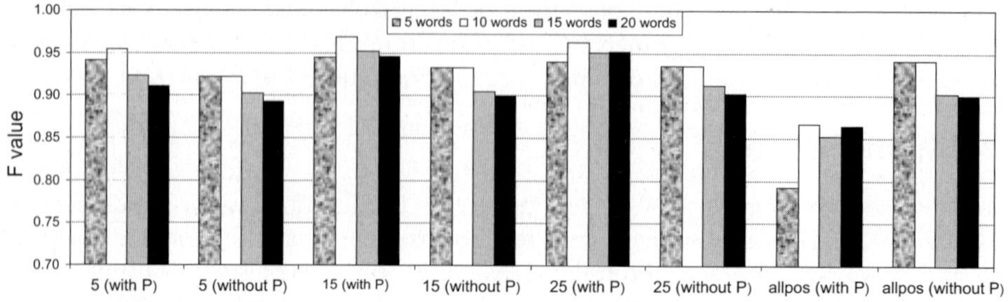

Fig. 5. F values of LPLP with different numbers of positive documents

positive set *P* (since it is not representative of the hidden positive documents in *U*). This option is denoted by "without P" in Figure 5.

Inclusion of *P* for constructing *PS*: If there were only a small number of positive documents (|*P*| = 5, 15 and 25) available, we found that using option 1 (with *P*) to construct the positive set for the classifier is better than using option 2 (without *P*), as expected. However, interestingly, if there is a large number of positive documents (allpos in Figure 5), then option 1 is actually inferior to option 2. The reason is that the use of a big positive set *P*, which is not representative of the positive documents in *U*, would have introduced too much negative influence on the final classifier (many hidden positive examples in *U* will be classified as negative class). However, when the given positive set *P* is small, its potential negative influence is much less, and it will therefore help to strengthen the likely positive documents by providing more positive data. This is a subtle and rather unexpected trade-off here.

Number of positive documents in *P*: From Figure 5, we also observe that the number of the given positive documents in *P* does not influence the final results a great deal. The reason for this is that the computed likely positive documents from *U* are actually more effective positive documents for learning than the original positive documents in *P*. This is a very compelling advantage of our proposed technique as this means that the user does not need to label or to find a large number of positive examples for effective learning. In fact, as discussed above, we also notice that even without using any original positive document in *P*, the results were very good as well.

Number of representative word features: The results in Figure 5 also showed that there is no need to use many representative words for detecting positive documents. In general, 5-15 representative words would suffice. Including the less representative word features beyond the top *k* most representative ones would introduce unnecessary noise in identifying the likely positive documents in *U*.

Next, we compare the results of our LPLP technique with those of the two best existing techniques mentioned earlier, namely, Roc-SVM [2] and PEBL [3]. Figure 6 shows two series of results. The first series, marked "*P*", showed the classification results of all three methods using all positive documents ("allpos"), without the use of the likely positive documents *LP* as suggested in this paper. In other words, learning was done using only *P* and *U*. Note that for the strictest comparison what we have shown here are the best possible results for Roc-SVM and PEBL, which may not be obtainable in practice because it is hardly possible to determine which SVM iteration would give the best results in these algorithms (both Roc-SVM and PEBL algorithms run SVM many times). In fact, their results at convergence were actually much worse.

We can see that PEBL performed better than both LPLP and Roc-SVM. However, the absolute *F* value of PEBL is still very low (0.54). Note also that because of the use of "allpos" for training, the LPLP's result for this was obtained without using the likely positive set *LP* (it is now the EM standard algorithm), hence it was unable to perform as well as it should have.

The second series in Figure 6 shows the comparative results of using the extracted likely positive documents instead of *P* for learning. Here, our LPLP algorithm performs dramatically better (*F*=0.94) even against the best possible results of PEBL (*F*=0.84) and Roc-SVM (*F*=0.81). Note that here PEBL and Roc-SVM also use the likely positive documents *LP* extracted from *U* by our method (we boosted the PEBL and Roc-SVM for the purpose of comparison). The likely positives were identified from *U* using 10 representative words selected from *P*. Unlike our LPLP algorithm, both Roc-SVM and PEBL do not take probabilistically labels, but only binary labels. As such, for these two algorithms, we chose the likely positive documents from *U* by requiring each document (*d*) to contain at least 5 (out of 10) selected representative words. All the likely positive documents identified were then treated as positive documents, i.e., $Pr(+|d)$ = 1. We also tried using other numbers of representative words in *RW* and found that 5 words performed well for these two algorithms with our datasets. We can see that with the use of the likely positives (set *LP*) identified by our method (instead of *P*), the classification results of these two existing algorithms have also improved dramatically as well. In fact, by using *LP* instead of *P*, the previously weaker Roc-SVM has caught up so substantially that the best possible result of PEBL is only slightly better than that of Roc-SVM now.

Finally, in Figure 7, we show the comparative results when the number of the positive documents is small, which is more often than not the case in practice. Again, we see that our new method LPLP performed much better than the best possible

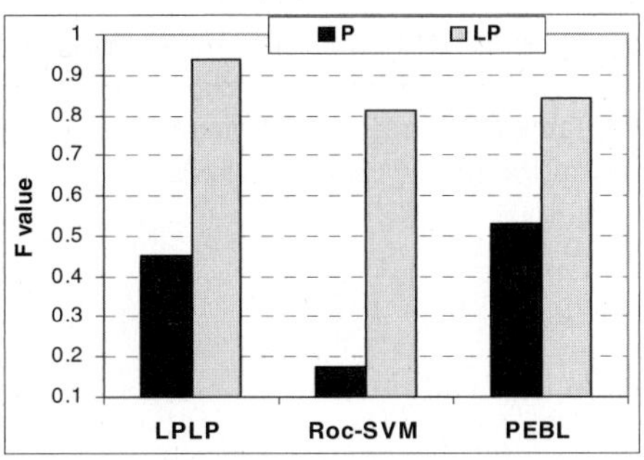

Fig. 6. F values of LPLP, the best results of Roc-SVM and PEBL using all positive documents

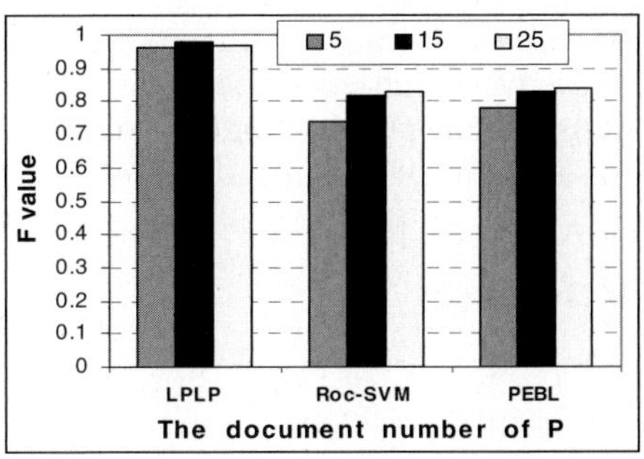

Fig. 7. F values of LPLP, the best results of Roc-SVM and PEBL using *P* together with *LP*

results of the two existing methods Roc-SVM and PEBL (which may not be obtainable in practice, as explained earlier) when there were only 5, 15, or 25 positive documents in *P*. As explained earlier, including *P* together with *LP* (for all the three techniques) gave better results when *P* is small.

In summary, the results in Figures 6 and 7 showed that the likely positive documents *LP* extracted from *U* can be used to help boost the performance of classification techniques for PU learning problems. In particular, LPLP algorithm benefited the most and performed the best. This is probably because of its ability to handle probabilistic labels and is thus better equipped to take advantage of the probabilistic (and hence potentially noisy) *LP* set than the SVM-based approaches.

5 Conclusions

In many real-world classification applications, it is often the case that not only the negative training examples are hard to come by, but the number of positive examples available for learning can also be fairly limited as it is often tedious and expensive to hand-label large amounts of training data. To address the lack of negative examples, many PU learning methods have been proposed to learn from a pool of positive data (*P*) without any negative data but with the help of unlabeled data (*U*). However, PU learning methods still do not work well when the size of positive examples is small.

In this paper, we address this oft-overlooked issue for PU learning when the number of positive examples is quite small. In addition, we consider the challenging case where the positive examples in *P* and the hidden positive examples in *U* may not even be drawn from the same distribution. Existing techniques have been found to perform poorly in this setting. We proposed an effective technique LPLP that can learn effectively from positive and unlabeled examples with a small positive set for document classification. Instead of identifying a set of reliable negative documents from the unlabeled set *U* as existing PU techniques do, our new method focuses on extracting a set of likely positive documents from *U*. In this way, the learning can rely less on the limitations associated with the original positive set *P*, such as its limited size and potential distribution differences. Augmented by the extracted probabilistic *LP* set, our LPLP algorithm can build a much more robust classifier. We reported experimental results with product page classification that confirmed that our new technique is indeed much more effective than existing methods in this challenging classification problem. In our future work, we plan to generalize our current approach to solve similar classification problems other than document classification.

References

1. Liu, B., Lee, W., Yu, P., Li, X.: Partially Supervised Classification of Text Documents. In: ICML, pp. 387–394 (2002)
2. Li, X., Liu, B.: Learning to Classify Texts Using Positive and Unlabeled Data. In: IJCAI, pp. 587–594 (2003)
3. Yu, H., Han, J., Chang, K.C.-C.: PEBL: Positive Example Based Learning for Web Page Classification Using SVM. In: KDD, pp. 239–248 (2002)

4. Dempster, A.P., Laird, N.M., Rubin, D.B.: Maximum Likelihood from Incomplete Data via the EM Algorithm. Journal of the Royal Statistical Society (1977)
5. Denis, F.: PAC Learning from Positive Statistical Queries. In: ALT, pp. 112–126 (1998)
6. Muggleton, S.: Learning from Positive Data. In: Proceedings of the sixth International Workshop on Inductive Logic Programming, pp. 358–376. Springer, Heidelberg (1997)
7. Rocchio, J.: Relevance feedback in information retrieval. In: Salton, G. (ed.) The SMART Retrieval System: Experiments in Automatic Document Processing (1971)
8. Yu, H.: General MC: Estimating boundary of positive class from small positive data. In: ICDM, pp. 693–696 (2003)
9. Fung, G.P.C., et al.: Text Classification without Negative Examples Revisit. IEEE Transactions on Knowledge and Data Engineering 18(1), 6–20 (2006)
10. Schölkopf, B., et al.: Estimating the Support of a High-Dimensional Distribution. Neural Comput 13(7), 1443–1471 (2001)
11. Salton, G., McGill, M.J.: Introduction to Modern Information Retrieval (1986)
12. McCallum, A., Nigam, K.: A comparison of event models for naïve Bayes text classification. In: AAAI Workshop on Learning for Text Categorization (1998)
13. Lewis, D.D.: A sequential algorithm for training text classifiers: corrigendum and additional data. In: SIGIR Forum, 13–19 (1995)
14. Nigam, K., et al.: Text Classification from Labeled and Unlabeled Documents using EM. Machine Learning 39(2-3), 103–134 (2000)
15. Yi, L., Liu, B., Li, X.: Eliminating noisy information in Web pages for data mining. In: KDD, pp. 296–305 (2003)

Structure Learning of Probabilistic Relational Models from Incomplete Relational Data

Xiao-Lin Li and Zhi-Hua Zhou

National Key Laboratory for Novel Software Technology
Nanjing University, Nanjing 210093, China
{lixl,zhouzh}@lamda.nju.edu.cn

Abstract. Existing relational learning approaches usually work on complete relational data, but real-world data are often incomplete. This paper proposes the MGDA approach to learn structures of probabilistic relational model (PRM) from incomplete relational data. The missing values are filled in randomly at first, and a maximum likelihood tree (MLT) is generated from the complete data sample. Then, Gibbs sampling is combined with MLT to modify the data and regulate MLT iteratively for obtaining a well-completed data set. Finally, probabilistic structure is learned through dependency analysis from the completed data set. Experiments show that the MGDA approach can learn good structures from incomplete relational data.

1 Introduction

Most machine learning algorithms work with the attribute-value setting which only allows the analysis of fairly simple objects described by a single table. To deal with complex and structured objects, one choice is to employ a relational structure which involves multiple tables. Thus, each complex object can be described by multiple records in multiple tables. To be able to analyze relational databases containing multiple relations properly, learning algorithms have to be designed for coping with the structural information in relational databases [8].

Relational learning has a precursor going back over a decade in the field of inductive logic programming (ILP) [18]. One of the most significant developments in recent years is the convergence of ILP and probabilistic reasoning and learning). ILP endows the ability of handling multiple relations; probabilistic methods endow the ability of handling uncertainty. Many approaches containing those ingredients have been proposed [19,11,1,15,16,9,21,5].

It is noteworthy that most relational learning algorithms operate on complete data, while real-world data are often incomplete, i.e., with missing attribute values. Although learning with incomplete data has been studied in attribute-value setting [6,12], few techniques can be directly applied to relational setting since the case of incomplete relational data is substantially more complex. An attribute-value learning algorithm can be seen as a relational learning algorithm which only deals with a database containing a single table. It will be computationally more expensive and the result will be much worse if such algorithms

J.N. Kok et al. (Eds.): ECML 2007, LNAI 4701, pp. 214–225, 2007.

are applied to incomplete relational data directly since there exist more poor local maxima. Actually, learning from incomplete relational data is a challenging problem in relational learning.

This paper proposes the MGDA (Maximum likelihood tree and Gibbs sampling-based Dependency Analysis) approach to learn structures of probabilistic relational models from incomplete relational data. Firstly, we fill in the incomplete relational data randomly. Then, we generate a maximum likelihood tree (MLT) [4] from the completed data sample. After that, Gibbs sampling is combined with MLT to modify the data and regulate MLT iteratively for obtaining a well-completed data set. Finally, probabilistic structure is learned through dependency analysis from the completed data set.

The rest of this paper is organized as follows. Section 2 briefly introduces the research background. Section 3 describes the proposed method. Section 4 reports on the experiments. Finally, section 5 concludes.

2 Background

Probabilistic relational model (PRM) [11] is one of the fundamental models in relational learning, which extends the standard attribute-value-based Bayesian network representation to incorporate a richer relational structure. Briefly, given a relational database of a specific schema (or a set of instances and relations between them), a PRM defines a probability distribution which specifies probabilistic dependencies between related objects (or the attributes of the instances).

Definition. [11] A PRM for a relational schema σ is defined as follows. For each entity type X and each propositional attribute $X.A$,

- A set of parents $Pa(X.A) = \{Pa_1, Pa_2, \cdots, Pa_n\}$, where each Pa_i has the form $X.B$ or $\gamma(X.\tau.B)$. τ is a chain of relations and $\gamma(\cdot)$ is an aggregation function.
- A conditional probability model for $P\left(X.A|Pa\left(X.A\right)\right)$.

The probability distribution over complete instantiation $\mathcal{L}$ of σ represented by the PRM is given by:

$$P\left(\mathcal{L}|\sigma, \mathcal{S}, \theta_{\mathcal{S}}\right) = \prod\nolimits_{X_i} \prod\nolimits_{A \in \mathcal{A}(X_i)} \prod\nolimits_{x \in \mathcal{O}^{\sigma}(X_i)} P(\mathcal{L}_{x_i.a}|\mathcal{L}_{Pa(x_i.a)})$$

As indicated by [11], the task of learning a PRM from complete data has two aspects, i.e., parameter estimation and structure learning. In parameter estimation, the input consists of the schema and training database, as well as a qualitative dependency structure. In structure learning, there is only the training database as input, while the goal is to extract an entire PRM schema from the training database automatically.

Obviously, structure learning is the key of learning a PRM. There are two general approaches to graphical probabilistic model learning, i.e., the *search & scoring* approaches and the *dependency analysis* approaches. The main difficulty in the first kind of approaches is how to find out a good dependency structure from the many possible ones, which are potentially infinite. For Bayesian networks, the task of finding the highest scoring network is NP-hard [3]. PRM learning is at least as hard as Bayesian network learning. The second kind of approaches, i.e. dependency analysis approaches, try to discover the dependency relationship from the data, and then use these dependencies to infer the structure. The approach proposed in this paper belongs to this category.

Many applications and extensions of PRM have been described. Getoor and Sahami [13] applied PRM to collaborative filtering. Getoor *et al.* [14] applied PRM to hypertext classification. Taskers *et al.* [23] proposed a general class of models for classification and clustering based on PRM. They have considered incomplete data for parameter estimation, but have not touched structure learning. Sanghai *et al.* [22] extended dynamic Bayesian networks where each time slice is represented by a PRM. To the best of our knowledge, structure learning of PRM from incomplete relational data has only been studied recently [17], where an evolutionary algorithm is used and the PRM structure is learned by filling in the missing data with the best evolved structure in each generation.

In traditional attribute-value setting, learning from incomplete data has been studied by many researchers. In particular, approaches for learning Bayesian networks from incomplete data require an approximation for incomplete data. One kind of approaches is based on Monte-Carlo or sampling [12]. These approximations can be very accurate, but these approaches are often intractable when the sample size is very large. Another kind of approaches is based on the expectation-maximization (EM) algorithm [6]. EM algorithm can be powerful for parameter estimation in relational learning with missing data, but for structure learning, since the number of possible structures to be explored is too huge, in the E step of EM it would be difficult to efficiently determine how to modify the current structure. It has been noted [10] that such algorithms often get stuck in local maxima when the search landscape is large and multi-modal.

3 The MGDA Approach

The MGDA approach is summarized in Table 1, which will be introduced step-by-step in this section.

3.1 Initialization

Incomplete data make the dependency relationship between attributes more disordered and it is difficult to learn an creditable PRM structure directly. If the incomplete data can be filled in accurately, then the fittest structure can be learned. Standard Gibbs sampling conducts sampling from full conditional distribution. As the conditional set is with high dimensionality, the complexity is exponential in the number of attributes. It will be computationally expensive if standard Gibbs sampling is extended to relational learning directly. So, an improved approach needs to be proposed.

Table 1. The MGDA approach

1. Fill in the incomplete relational data randomly and generate an MLT from the obtained complete data set (details in Section 3.1);
2. Repeat until the stop criterion is satisfied:
   a) Modify the incomplete relational data (details in Section 3.2.1);
   b) Modify the corresponding parameter according to the latest modified data set (details in Section 3.2.2);
   c) Regulate the MLT structure according to the completed relational data and test the stop criterion (details in Section 3.2.3);
3. Regulate the PRM structure learned from the well-completed data set by using the proposed dependency analysis approach (details in Section 3.3).

Here we combine Gibbs sampling with MLT to modify the incomplete data and regulate MLT iteratively for obtaining a well-completed data set. The incomplete relational data are filled in randomly at first. Then, an MLT is generated from the completed data set. MLT is the fittest tree-like structure of Bayesian network, which has a simple structure. Chow and Liu [4] proposed a well-known method for learning tree-like Bayesian networks, which reduces the problem of constructing an MLT to the finding of a maximal weighted spanning tree. We extend this procedure on relational conditions as follows:

1. Compute $I(X_i.A; X_j.B)$ between each pair of attributes ($A \neq B$), where

$$I(X_i.A; X_j.B) = \sum_{\substack{X_i,\\ X_j}} \sum_{\substack{A\in A(X_i),\\ B\in B(X_j)}} \sum_{\substack{x_i.a,\\ x_j.b}} P(x_i.a, x_j.b) \log \frac{P(x_i.a, x_j.b)}{P(x_i.a)P(x_j.b)};$$

2. Build a complete undirected graph where the weight of the edge connecting $X_i.A$ to $X_j.B$ is $I(X_i.A; X_j.B)$;
3. Choose a root attribute for the tree and set the direction of all edges to be outward from it.

Then, we use the learned MLT structure to decompose the joint probability. This process can convert the sampling from n-order full conditional probability to second-order conditional probability since each attribute of an MLT has only one parent at most. So, it can not only meet the requirement of full conditional distribution in standard Gibbs sampling but also reduce the computational cost. After modifying the incomplete data, a new MLT can be generated.

3.2 Modification and Regulation

There are three tasks in each iteration, i.e., modifying the incomplete relational data, modifying the parameters, and regulating the MLT structure. The order of sampling attributes with incomplete data is based on the order of nodes (attributes) of the learned MLT structure and the order of records of the data set. Assume that $X_i.A$ has a missing entry in the mth record, which is denoted by $x_{im}.a$ and the modified value is denoted by $\hat{x}_{im}.a$. The possible values of $X_i.A$ are $x_i^1.a, \cdots, x_i^r.a$. MGDA uses the latest modified data set to modify the next missing attribute value.

Modifying the Incomplete Relational Data. If $P(L|\sigma, S, \theta_s)$ contains non-zero probabilities, MGDA modifies the missing data by Gibbs sampling. For a random λ, the value of $X_i.A$ is:

$$\hat{x}_{im}.a = \begin{cases} x_i^1.a, \ 0 < \lambda \leq \hat{p}\left(L_{x_{i.a}^1} | L_{P_a(x_{im}.a)}\right) \\ \cdots \quad \cdots \\ x_i^h.a, \sum_{j=1}^{h-1} \hat{p}\left(L_{x_{i.a}^j} | L_{P_a(x_{im}.a)}\right) < \lambda \leq \sum_{j=1}^{h} \hat{p}\left(L_{x_{i.a}^j} | L_{P_a(x_{im}.a)}\right) \\ \cdots \quad \cdots \\ x_i^r.a, \ \lambda > \sum_{j=1}^{r-1} \hat{p}\left(L_{x_{i.a}^j} | L_{P_a(x_{im}.a)}\right) \end{cases}$$

Modifying the Parameters. If $P(L|\sigma, S, \theta_s)$ contains zero probabilities, i.e. $\hat{p}\left(L_{x_{i.a}^u} | L_{P_a(x_{im}.a)}\right) = 0$, MGDA modifies the probabilities by using Laplacian-correction [7]:

$$\hat{p}\left(L_{x_{i.a}^u} | L_{P_a(x_{im}.a)}\right) = \frac{1}{N\|P_a(x_{im}.a)\| + \|x_i^u.a\|}$$

where N is the number of records, $\|x_i^u.a\|$ is the number of the values of attribute $X_i.A$, and $\|P_a(x_{im}.a)\|$ is the number of the parent combination of $Pa(X_i.A)$.

If $x_{im}.a \neq \hat{x}_{im}.a$, the corresponding parameters are modified as follows:

$$\hat{p}\left(L_{\hat{x}_{im}.a} | L_{P_a(x_{im}.a)}, \hat{D}_m\right) = \hat{p}\left(L_{\hat{x}_{im}.a} | L_{P_a(x_{im}.a)}, D_m\right) + 1/N$$

$$\hat{p}\left(L_{x_{im}.a} | L_{P_a(x_{im}.a)}, \hat{D}_m\right) = \hat{p}\left(L_{x_{im}.a} | L_{P_a(x_{im}.a)}, D_m\right) - 1/N$$

where D_m and $\hat{D}_m$ are respectively the database before and after modifying $x_{im}.a$.

Regulating the MLT Structure. After modifying the incomplete relational data, MGDA generates a new MLT structure from the completed data set. The MGDA modifies the incomplete relational data and regulates MLT iteratively for obtaining a well-completed data set. The iteration will stop when the stop criterion is satisfied. For the modification on the incomplete relational data and parameters, we test the coherence of two consecutive iterations. $x_1^t, x_2^t, \cdots, x_k^t, \ldots, x_n^t$ and $x_1^{t+1}, x_2^{t+1}, \cdots, x_k^{t+1}, \ldots, x_n^{t+1}$ $(k \in \{1, \cdots, n\})$ are two sequences of the incomplete relational data in two consecutive iterations, respectively, then

$$sig(x_k^t, x_k^{t+1}) = \begin{cases} 0, \ x_k^t = x_k^{t+1} \\ 1, \ x_k^t \neq x_k^{t+1} \end{cases}$$

For a given threshold $\eta > 0$, if $\frac{1}{n}\sum_{k=1}^{n} sig(x_k^t, x_k^{t+1}) < \eta$ then stop the modification and generate an MLT structure from the latest modified data set. Thus, when the above process terminates, a well-completed data set and a well-regulated MLT are obtained.

3.3 Structure Learning of PRM

MGDA uses class dependency graph [11] structures as the candidate PRMs. The MLTs here are also class dependency graphs. In those graphs, an attribute can depend on any attributes of all the classes except itself. If parents of the attribute are attributes of other class, they relate with the attribute by chains of relations. In this way, we can get the class dependency graph which contains latent relations and also get PRM structure with relations.

There are three basic dependencies [20] between attributes, i.e., transitive dependencies, non-transitive dependencies and induced dependencies, which can be described by the Bayesian network framework of information channels and pipelines [2]: (1) Transitive dependencies indicate that information flow can directly pass two nodes in Bayesian networks and not be blocked by any other nodes. In other words, the two nodes are conditional dependent. (2) Non-transitive dependencies indicate that information flow can not directly pass two nodes in Bayesian networks, but can pass through the open path which connects the two nodes and be blocked by the nodes in cut-set. Namely, the two nodes are conditional independent given the nodes in cut-set. (3) Induced dependencies are induced by V-structure. Information flow can not directly pass two nodes and be induced by the collider in V-structure [20]. [1] Learning Bayesain network is to keep transitive dependencies and get rid of other dependencies. As an extension of Bayesian network, PRM can be learned through the new dependency analysis approach from the well-completed data set.

To measure the conditional independence, we use mutual information and conditional mutual information. Conditional mutual information is defined as:

$$I(X_i.A; X_j.B|C) = \sum_{\substack{X_i,\\X_j}} \sum_{\substack{A,\\B}} \sum_{\substack{x_i.a,\\x_j.b}} P(x_i.a, x_j.b|c) \log \frac{P(x_i.a, x_j.b|c)}{P(x_i.a|c)P(x_j.b|c)}$$

where C is a set of nodes. When $I(X_i.A, X_j.B|C)$ is smaller than a certain small value ε, we say that $X_i.A$ and $X_j.B$ are conditionally independent given C. Then, we use dependency analysis to regulate the PRM structure from the well-completed data set.

Transitive Dependencies Regulation. We use the latest regulated MLT as the initial PRM structure. For each pair of nodes $(X_i.A, X_j.B)$ ($X_i.A$ is in front of $X_j.B$ in node ordering) without edge connection, compute conditional mutual information $I(X_i.A, X_j.B|Pa)$, where Pa are the nodes in all the parents of $X_j.B$ that are on the path linking $X_i.A$ and $X_j.B$. If $I(X_i.A, X_j.B|Pa) > \varepsilon$, add an edge $X_i.A \rightarrow X_j.B$. This process requires at most $\frac{(n-1)(n-2)}{2}$ number of conditional independence (CI) tests. The regulated structure is denoted by G_1.

Non-transitive Dependencies Regulation. For G_1, compute $I(X_i.A, X_j.B|Pa)$ for each pair of nodes $(X_i.A, X_j.B)$ with edge connection, where Pa are the

[1] For three nodes X, Y and Z, there are only three possible types of V-structures, i.e. (1) $X \rightarrow Y \rightarrow Z$, (2) $X \leftarrow Y \rightarrow Z$, and (3) $X \rightarrow Y \leftarrow Z$. Among them only the third type makes X and Z depend conditionally on $\{Y\}$.

nodes in all the parents of $X_j.B$ that are on the path linking $X_i.A$ and $X_j.B$. If $I(X_i.A, X_j.B|Pa) < \varepsilon$, delete the edge between them. This process requires at most $n(n-1)$ number of CI tests. The regulated structure is denoted by G_2.

Inductive Dependencies Regulation and Edges Orienting. For each pair of nodes, compute $I(X_i.A, X_j.B)$ according to the node ordering. If $I(X_i.A, X_j.B) < \varepsilon$, test the pairs of nodes by collider identification. Any nodes which can form a V-structure with $X_i.A$ and $X_j.B$ are denoted as $X_{m1}, \cdots, X_{mt}$ ($X_{mh} \neq X_i.A, X_j.B$, $h \in \{1, \cdots, t\}$). For a given threshold $\delta > 0$, if $\frac{I(X_i.A, X_j.B|X_{mh})}{I(X_i.A, X_j.B)} > 1+\delta$, then $X_i.A$, $X_j.B$ and X_{mh} form a V-structure and orient edges $X_i.A \rightarrow X_{mh}$ and $X_j.B \rightarrow X_{mh}$. If there is an edge between $X_i.A$ and $X_j.B$, then delete the edge. This process requires at most $\frac{n(n-1)(n-2)}{2}$ number of CI tests.

Using collider identification, we can identify all the V-structures of the third type in a probabilistic model and orient the edges in such structures using tests on conditional independence. The number of edges which can be oriented by collider identification is constrained by the network structure. In an extreme case, when the network does not contain any V-structure of the third type, these methods could not orient any edges at all. However, this method is popular in Bayesian network learning owing to its efficiency and reliability.

For edges that could not be oriented by collider identification, we orient them by computing the joint cross-entropy. For two discrete attributes $X_i.A = \{x_{i1}.a, x_{i2}.a, \cdots, x_{iM}.a\}$ and $X_j.B = \{x_{j1}.b, x_{j2}.b, \cdots, x_{jN}.b\}$, suppose the joint probabilistic distribution of $X_i.A$ and $X_j.B$ is $p_1(x_{im}.a, x_{jn}.b)$ under assumption H_1; the joint probabilistic distribution of $X_i.A$ and $X_j.B$ is $p_2(x_{im}.a, x_{jn}.b)$ under assumption H_2, where $m = 1, 2, \cdots, M$, $n = 1, 2, \cdots, N$. Then the joint cross-entropy of $X_i.A$ and $X_j.B$ can be defined as:

$$I(p_2, p_1; X_i.A, X_j.B) = \sum\nolimits_{m=1}^{M} \sum\nolimits_{n=1}^{N} p_2(x_{im}.a, x_{jn}.b) \cdot \log \frac{p_2(x_{im}.a, x_{jn}.b)}{p_1(x_{im}.a, x_{jn}.b)}$$

Let the assumptions H_1 and H_2 be $X_i.A \rightarrow X_j.B$ and $X_i.A \leftarrow X_j.B$, respectively. Compute $I(p_1, p_2; X_i.A, X_j.B)$ and $I(p_2, p_1; X_i.A, X_j.B)$:

if $I(p_1, p_2; X_i.A, X_j.B) > I(p_2, p_1; X_i.A, X_j.B)$,
then orient edges $X_i.A \rightarrow X_j.B$; **otherwise**, orient edges $X_i.A \leftarrow X_j.B$.

4 Experiments

We begin by evaluating the proposed MGDA approach on a synthetic data set generated by a school domain whose structure is shown in Fig. 2(a). The learning approach takes only the data set as input. We generate 4 data sets with the same size 5,000. Here the size of a data set corresponds to the number of students involved. These data sets are with 10%, 20%, 30%, and 40% missing data, respectively. These missing data are generated by randomly removing 10%, 20%, 30%, and 40% attribute-values from the original data sets, respectively.

We compare MGDA with FR, FM and MLTEC. FR and FM are two straightforward approaches. FR fills in the incomplete relational data randomly and then

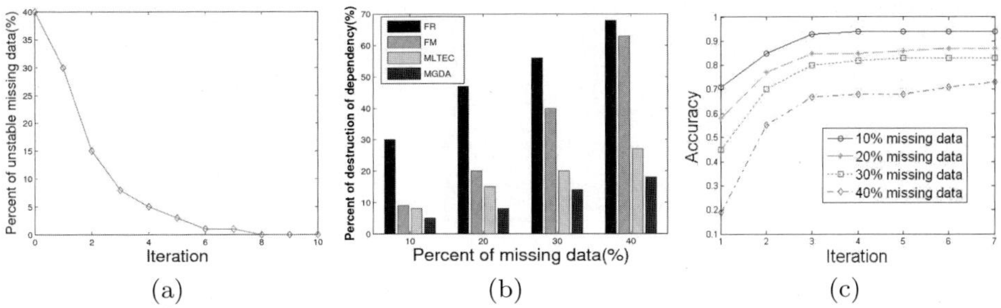

Fig. 1. Results on the school domain. (a) Percentage of unstable missing data on the database with 40% missing data when MGDA is used; (b) Comparison of the destruction of dependency relations in structures learned from data sets; (c) Average accuracy of the structures learned by MGDA.

learns the structures of PRMs from the obtained complete data. FM fills in the incomplete relational data with the mean values of attributes and then learns the structures of PRMs from the obtained complete data. To the best of our knowledge, MLTEC [17] is the only approach for learning PRM structure from incomplete relational data, where an evolutionary algorithm is used and the PRM structure is learned by filling in the missing data with the best evolved structure in each generation. We run MLTEC for ten times on each data set and regard the median PRM structure of the ten runs as the result. This is because that MLTEC is an approach based on evolutionary computation, whose result could be very different in different runs. We wish that the median PRM structure of the ten runs could reflect the median performance of MLTEC.

Fig. 1(a) shows the percentage of unstable missing data, i.e., the portion of missing data being modified in each iteration of MGDA, on the data set with 40% missing data. It can be found that the missing data to be modified become fewer and fewer as the iteration proceeds. Moreover, by comparing the filled values and real values, we found that among the values filled in by MGDA, 93% are correct; for MLTEC, 90% are correct; while for FR and FM the correctness is only 61% and 66%, respectively.

Fig. 1(b) presents the comparison between FR, FM, MLTEC and MGDA on the destruction of dependency relations in the learned structures. It can be found that the performance of MGDA is apparently better than that of FR. This is not difficult to understand. When the missing data are filled in randomly, noises are introduced and thereby the dependency relations between attributes are corrupted to a great extent. By taking advantage of the information in the observed data, the noises will be smoothed through refining the missing data iteratively. Thus the corrupted dependency relations are recovered. The performance of MGDA is also apparently better than FM, especially when the level of missing data is high. This is not difficult to understand either. When the level of missing data is low, the mean values of attributes filled in the missing data can represent the distribution of the real data to some degree. With the increasing of the level of missing data, the mean values of attributes could not represent

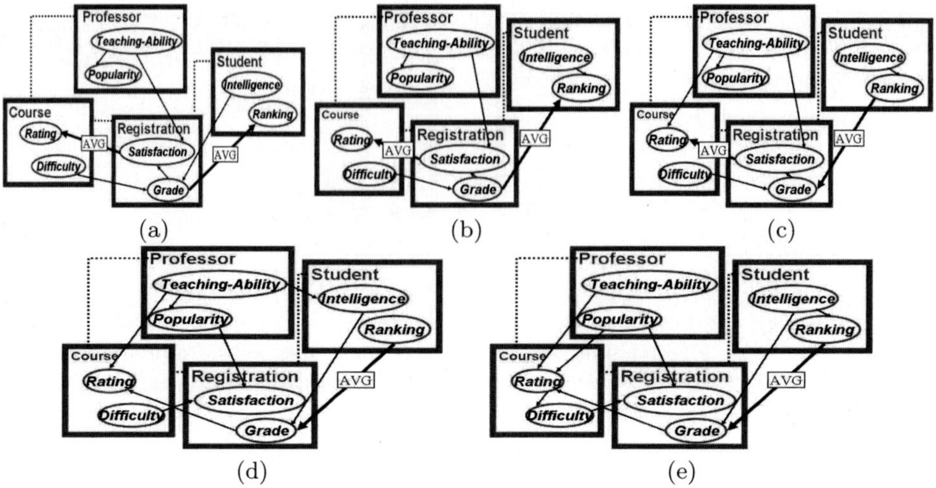

Fig. 2. The PRM structures on the school domain. (a) True structure. Dotted lines indicate relations between classes while solid arrows indicate probabilistic dependencies; (b) Result of MGDA; (c) Result of MLTEC; (d) Result of FM; (e) Result of FR.

the distribution of the real data well any more. Therefore, the performance of FM degenerates seriously. It can also be found that although the performance of MLTEC is better than FR and FM, it is worse than MGDA.

Fig. 1(c) compares the accuracies of the structures learned by MGDA on different data sets. Here we define *accuracy* in the following way. Suppose the ground-truth structure has a edges, the learned structure added b redundant edges but missed c edges, then the accuracy of the learned structure is $1-(b+c)/a$. It is obvious that the accuracy of a perfect model is 1, while the accuracy of some very poor models could be negative. Since very poor models are useless, it is not meaningful to distinguish them. Thus, we assign zero accuracy to them.

It can be found from Fig. 1(c) that as the iteration proceeds, the accuracy of MGDA increases. The accuracies of FR, FM and MLTEC are respectively 57%, 80% and 86% on 10% missing data, 14%, 57% and 80% on 20% missing data, 0, 14% and 71% on 30% missing data, and 0, 0 and 57% on 40% missing data. It is evident that the accuracy of MGDA is better than them. By inspecting the structures, we find that MGDA did not produce many redundant edges even in a high level of missing data. This might owe to the combination of Gibbs sampling with MLT, which has simple structure to modify the incomplete data and thus suffers less from overfitting.

The PRM structure learned by MGDA on the data set with 40% missing data is shown in Fig. 2(b). Comparing it with Fig. 2(a) we can find that it missed a dependency between the *Intelligence* of a student and the *Grade* of the registration and added a dependency between the *Intelligence* of a student and its *Ranking*. Fig. 2(c) shows the structure learned by MLTEC, which also missed the dependency between the *Intelligence* of a student and the *Grade* of

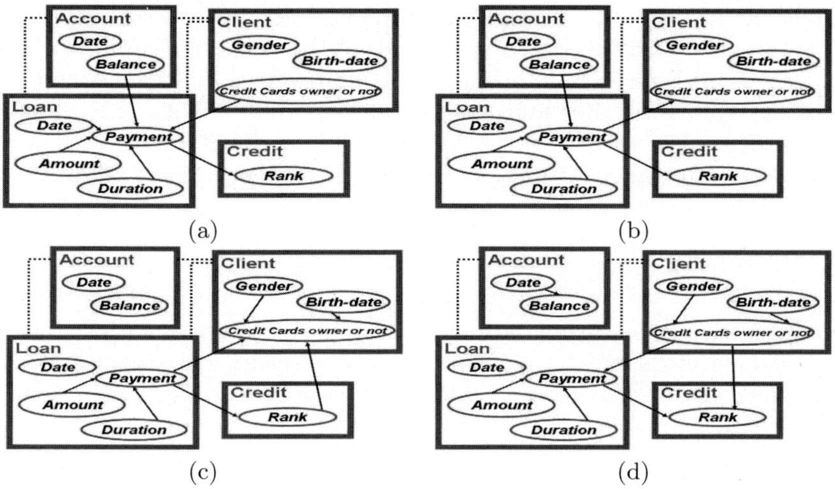

Fig. 3. The PRM structures learned on the financial domain. (a) By MGDA; (b) By MLTEC; (c) By FM; (d) By FR.

the registration. Moreover, it reversed the dependency between the *Grade* of the registration and the *Ranking* of a student, and added two redundant dependencies. Figs. 2(d) and (e) show the structures learned by FM and FR, respectively. Comparing them with Fig. 2(a) we can find that they have many redundant dependencies and missed many dependencies. In short, the structure learned by MGDA is more credible than those learned by the compared approaches.

We also evaluate the proposed MGDA approach on a real-world domain. This domain is a financial database taken from the PKDD2000 Discovery Challenge. The database contains data from a Czech bank, which describes the operation of 5,369 clients holding 4,500 accounts. The bank wants to improve their services by finding interesting groups of clients. The eight tables in the database are: *account*, *client*, *disposition*, *permanent*, *order*, *transaction*, *loan*, *credit card*, and *demographic data*. We focus on the question of clients' credit and choose a subset from the database, which consists of 4 relations, i.e. *account*, *client*, *loan* and *credit*. The extraction results in an incomplete data set. Since the data are from real-world and the ground-truth model is not known, it is not feasible to compare the proposed approach with other approaches quantitatively. Thus, we adopt the experimental methodology used by previous research [11,22], i.e., qualitatively comparing the learned structures.

The PRM structures learned by MGDA, MLTEC, FM and FR are shown in Figs. 3(a) to (d), respectively. MGDA learned that the *Payment* of a loan depends on its *Date*, *Amount* and *Duration*, the *Balance* of the account, and *the Credit cards owner or not* of the client. It also learned a dependency which can relate the tables: the *Rank* of Credit depends on the *Payment* of the loan. By comparing the structure learned by MLTEC with that learned by MGDA, we can find that MLTEC missed a dependency relation between the *Date* and the *Payment* of the loan and reversed the dependency between the *Payment* of a loan and the *Credit cards owner or not* of the client. However, the missed dependency seems not very important and the reversed dependency looks still reasonable. From Figs. 3(c) and (d) we can find that FM and FR missed an important dependency between the *Balance* of the account and the *Payment* of the loan and both generated more redundant dependency relationships.

5 Conclusion

Relational learning algorithms are capable of dealing with multiple tables or relations which could not be tackled by attribute-value-based methods. However, although real-world data are often incomplete, learning with incomplete relational data is largely understudied. In this paper, we propose the MGDA approach and experiments show that it can learn reasonable structures from incomplete relational data.

We observed that MGDA did not produce many redundant edges even when the missing rate was quite high. So, its performance may be improved by incorporating some mechanism for dealing with missing edges. This will be studied in the future. When several values for an attribute are almost equally likely, the current stopping criterion might encounter some problem. A possible solution may be to compute the Euclidean distance between the parameters for two consecutive steps and stop when this distance goes below a threshold. This is another future issue. Moreover, combining MGDA with collective classification is also worth studying in the future.

Acknowledgments

We wish to thank the anonymous reviewers for their helpful comments and suggestions. This work was supported by NSFC (60635030), the China Postdoctoral Science Foundation (20060390921) and the Jiangsu Planned Projects for Postdoctoral Research Funds (0601017B).

References

1. Anderson, C., Domingos, P., Weld, D.: Relational Markov models and their application to adaptive web navigation. In: KDD'02, Edmonton, Canada, pp. 143–152 (2002)
2. Cheng, J., Greiner, R., Kelly, J.: Learning Bayesian networks from data: An efficient algorithm based on information theory. Artificial Intelligence 137, 43–90 (2002)
3. Chickering, D.M.: Learning Bayesian networks is NP-complete. In: Fisher, D., Lenz, H.J. (eds.) Learning from Data: Artificial Intelligence and Statistics V, pp. 121–130. Springer, Berlin (1996)
4. Chow, C.K., Liu, C.N.: Approximating discrete probability distributions with dependence trees. IEEE Trans. Information Theory 14, 462–467 (1968)

5. De Raedt, L., Kimmig, A., Toivonen, H.: ProbLog: A probabilistic prolog and its application in link discovery. In: IJCAI'07, Hyderabad, India, pp. 2462–2467 (2007)
6. Dempster, A., Laird, N., Rubin, D.: Maximum likelihood from incomplete data via the EM algorithm. Journal of the Royal Statistical Society - B 39, 1–39 (1977)
7. Domingos, P., Pazzani, M.: On the optimality of the simple Bayesian classifier under zero-one loss. Machine Learning 29, 103–130 (1997)
8. Dzeroski, S., Lavrac, N. (eds.): Relational Data Mining. Springer, Berlin (2001)
9. Flach, P., Lachiche, N.: Naive Bayesian classification of structured data. Machine Learning 57, 233–269 (2004)
10. Friedman, N.: The Bayesian structural EM algorithm. In: UAI'98, Madison, WI (1998)
11. Friedman, N., Getoor, L., Koller, D., Pfeffer, A.: Learning probabilistic relational models. In: IJCAI'99, Stockholm, Sweden, pp. 1300–1307 (1999)
12. Geman, S., Geman, D.: Stochastic relaxation: Gibbs distributions and the Bayesian restoration of images. IEEE Trans. Pattern Analysis and Machine Intelligence 6, 721–742 (1984)
13. Getoor, L., Sahami, M.: Using probabilistic relational models for collaborative filtering. In: Masand, B., Spiliopoulou, M. (eds.) WebKDD'99. LNCS (LNAI), vol. 1836, Springer, Heidelberg (2000)
14. Getoor, L., Segal, E., Taskar, B., Koller, D.: Probabilistic models of text and link structure for hypertext classification. In: IJCAI'01 Workshop on Text Learning, Seattle, WA, pp. 24–29 (2001)
15. Getoor, L., Friedman, N., Koller, D., Taskar, B.: Learning probabilistic models of link structure. Journal of Machine Learning Research 3, 679–707 (2002)
16. Kersting, K., De Raedt, L.: Basic principles of learning Bayesian logic programs. Technical report, Institute for Computer Science, University of Freiburg, Freiburg, Germany (2002)
17. Li, X.L., Zhou, Z.H.: An approach to learning of PRM from incomplete relational data (in chinese). Chinese Journal of Software (2007) (in press)
18. Muggleton, S. (ed.): Inductive Logic Programming. Academic Press, London (1992)
19. Muggleton, S.: Stochastic logic programs. In: De Raedt, L. (ed.) Advances in Inductive Logic Programming, pp. 254–264. IOS, Amsterdam, The Netherland (1996)
20. Pearl, J.: Probabilistic Reasoning in Intelligent Systems: Networks of Plausible Inference. Morgan Kaufmann, San Mateo, CA (1988)
21. Richardson, M., Domingos, P.: Markov logic networks. Technical report, Department of Computer Science and Engineering, University of Washington, Seattle, WA (2005)
22. Sanghai, S., Domingos, P., Weld, D.: Relational dynamic Bayesian networks. Journal of Artificial Intelligence Research 24, 1–39 (2005)
23. Taskar, B., Segal, E., Koller, D.: Probabilistic classification and clustering in relational data. In: IJCAI'01, Seattle, WA, pp. 870–876 (2001)

Stability Based Sparse LSI/PCA: Incorporating Feature Selection in LSI and PCA*

Dimitrios Mavroeidis[1] and Michalis Vazirgiannis[1,2]

[1] Department of Informatics, Athens University of Economics and Business, Greece
[2] GEMO Team, INRIA/FUTURS, France

Abstract. The stability of sample based algorithms is a concept commonly used for parameter tuning and validity assessment. In this paper we focus on two well studied algorithms, LSI and PCA, and propose a feature selection process that provably guarantees the stability of their outputs. The feature selection process is performed such that the level of (statistical) accuracy of the LSI/PCA input matrices is adequate for computing meaningful (stable) eigenvectors. The feature selection process "sparsifies" LSI/PCA, resulting in the projection of the instances on the eigenvectors of a principal submatrix of the original input matrix, thus producing sparse factor loadings that are linear combinations solely of the selected features. We utilize bootstrapping confidence intervals for assessing the statistical accuracy of the input sample matrices, and matrix perturbation theory in order to relate the statistical accuracy to the stability of eigenvectors. Experiments on several UCI-datasets verify empirically our approach.

1 Introduction

The intuitiveness of requiring that small changes in the input do not significantly affect the output of sample-based algorithms has made stability a very popular tool in machine learning. Many researchers have proposed the use of stability for assessing the validity (such as [14]) and for tuning the parameters of clustering algorithms (such as [17,13]). In this context an issue that presents several interesting challenges, is the analysis of the contribution that individual features have to the instability of the output and the derivation of necessary conditions that would guarantee stability, when a subset of the features is used. This analysis would allow for the introduction of feature selection algorithms that guarantee the stability of the output.

In this paper we focus on the stability of two well studied data preprocessing algorithms, Latent Semantic Indexing (LSI) [9], and Principal Components Analysis (PCA) [11]. These algorithms have been extensively used/studied in several machine learning papers (such as in [6,15]). Although they are not learning algorithms themselves, when they are used as a preprocessing step of a deterministic learning algorithm, their stability guarantees the stability of the output of the learning algorithm. Apart from

* This research project was co-financed by E.U.-European Social Fund (75%) and the Greek Ministry of Development-GSRT (25%). In particular, Dr. Vazirgiannis was supported by the Marie Curie Intra-European Fellowship NGWeMiS: Next Generation Web Mining and Searching (MEIF-CT-2005-011549).

J.N. Kok et al. (Eds.): ECML 2007, LNAI 4701, pp. 226–237, 2007.

the stability requirement, a motivation for performing feature selection stems from the fact that the factor loadings that are derived by LSI and PCA are linear combinations of all the input features, thus incorporating noise and making results difficult to interpret. The introduction of a feature selection process would resolve this issue, as it would result in sparse factor loadings that are linear combinations only of the selected features. Using analogous motivations, researchers have introduced "sparse" versions for various factor analysis techniques (an account of the related work can be found in section 3).

In general, the concept of stability is concerned with sample-based algorithms. In this setting, it is assumed that there exists a fixed (unknown) probability distribution that generates the data, and that the training set presents an i.i.d. sample drawn from this distribution. In the case of PCA and LSI, the input i.i.d. training set is used to construct the sample input matrices (the sample Covariance matrix in the case of PCA), that are essentially statistical estimates of the "true" input matrices that would be derived if we had complete knowledge of the data generating distribution. In this paper we focus on the instability that is related to the sampling variability (statistical accuracy) of the LSI/PCA input matrices, that can be naturally quantified using confidence intervals. In the context of our work, we assume that we do not have access to the data distribution and we utilize bootstrapping confidence intervals [10], which present a standard approach for measuring statistical accuracy (sampling variability) without making distributional assumptions.

In standard LSI/PCA the eigenvectors rely on the correlations/covariances between all the input features. However, some feature-correlations could be inaccurate in the statistical sense, thus degrading the quality of the resulting eigenvectors. In the proposed Stability based Sparse LSI/PCA (*SbS-LSI*, *SbS-PCA*) approach, we select the subset of features such that the level of accuracy of the term-term similarities/covariances is adequate for computing meaningful (stable) eigenvectors. Naturally this raises the need for determining the level of statistical accuracy that is needed for producing reliable (stable) eigenvectors. In order to address this issue we utilize matrix perturbation theory [20], which relates the eigenvalues and eigenvectors of matrices A and $A + E$. In order to employ matrix perturbation theory we consider A to be our input term-term similarity/covariance matrix and E to express the statistical inaccuracy of the term-term similarities/covariances, as quantified by the length of the respective bootstrap confidence intervals. *SbS-LSI* and *SbS-PCA* select a subset of the original features such that the eigenvectors of A' (the term-similarity/covariance matrix that is defined by the selected features, which is a principal submatrix of the original feature-similarity/covariance matrix) are stable with respect to perturbation E' (the respective principal submatrix of E).

The main innovation of *SbS-LSI* and *SbS-PCA* and the main differentiation from the related Sparse factor analysis approaches, is the fact that we utilize the stability criterion for "sparsifying" LSI/PCA (as we require the eigenvectors to be stable with respect to resampling variability). Concerning the practical impact of our work, experimental results on several real world UCI-datasets verify that the *SbS-LSI* and *SbS-PCA* algorithms can retrieve stable principal submatrices for various termination criteria.

2 Preliminaries

2.1 Latent Semantic Indexing and Principal Component Analysis

The Vector Space Model, used traditionally for representing documents, assumes that the terms are orthogonal, thus ignoring possible term-correlations. LSI aims at addressing this issue by projecting the documents to the k left singular vectors that corresponds to the k largest singular values of the term-document (feature-instance) Singular Value Decomposition (SVD). The SVD of a matrix A is defined as $A = U\Sigma V^T$ where U contains the left-singular vectors, V contains the right singular vectors and Σ contains the singular values. The left-singular matrix U can be considered as the eigenvector matrix of AA^T (the term-term similarity matrix). LSI projects the data using the equation: $A_k^T = V_k\Sigma_k$, or equivalently $A_k = U_k^T A$, where A_k is the new term-document matrix, containing only k dimensions (rows). There exist several variations of LSI, that have small differences with the generic approach described above. In this paper we adopt the variation where AA^T, the term similarity matrix, is derived by the cosine similarity measure rather than the inner-product.

Principal Components Analysis (PCA) is a dimensionality reduction technique that aims in retaining the maximal amount of variance in the projected space. PCA works by projecting the data in the first k eigenvectors (also called principal components) that correspond to the largest eigenvalues of the feature Covariance matrix. Thus, it can be observed that the low dimensionality transformations are derived by the same formula, as in LSI $A_k = U_k^T A$, with the difference being that the eigenvectors contained in U_k are derived by the feature Covariance matrix, instead of the feature-feature similarity (inner-product or cosine) matrix. This observation allows us to treat LSI and PCA in a uniform manner and define a feature selection framework that applies to both.

2.2 Bootstrapping

Bootstrapping [10] is a statistical method that can be used for measuring the accuracy of statistical estimates. In order to employ bootstrapping in estimating confidence intervals for the feature-feature similarities/covariances, we consider that the features are random variables with an unknown probability distribution. Thus, our input data can be considered as a random i.i.d. sample, where the observed feature values are derived by the unknown probability distribution. Taking the above into account, the cosine similarity/covariance abides to the definition of a statistic and as such its accuracy can be measured in the statistical sense.

Percentile Intervals present the most natural approach for constructing bootstrap confidence intervals. The Bias Corrected and Accelerated (BCa) bootstrap intervals present an improvement over the simple percentile intervals, in the sense that they account for the bias and the acceleration of the estimated parameter. The BCa intervals have several theoretical advantages over standard percentile intervals [10] that make them more appropriate in the context of our work.

A natural question that arises when employing the bootstrapping approach, for estimating confidence intervals, concerns the number of bootstrap samples needed to achieve accurate intervals. Based mainly on empirical evidence several researchers [10] have reported that 1000 bootstrap samples are enough for accurately estimating bootstrap confidence intervals.

A more principled approach is presented in [1], where the authors introduce a three-step method, that allows for computing the number of bootstrap samples needed, in order to achieve a guaranteed accuracy with high probability. The level of approximation is user-defined and involves two parameters, the percentage deviation pdb, which measures the deviation of the computed interval from the ideal interval (i.e. the interval that is computed using infinite bootstrap samples) and the confidence τ. Using these parameters, their method computes the number of bootstrap samples that are sufficient for achieving the desired level of accuracy with probability $1 - \tau$.

2.3 Matrix Perturbation Theory

Matrix perturbation theory and more precisely Stewart's theorem on the perturbation of Invariant Subspaces [20] provides the means for assessing whether there exists a space that is spanned by k eigenvectors of the input term-term similarities/covariances that is not severely affected by the resampling variability (that quantifies the level of statistical inaccuracy) of the term-term similarities/covariances.

Although it would be more intuitive to consider the stability of the eigenvectors and not the spaces spanned by the eigenvectors, this would result in a not well-defined problem, since the eigenvectors that correspond to a tight cluster of eigenvalues are ill conditioned [20]. The inappropriateness of using eigenvectors can be also observed if we consider a matrix with two eigenvectors that have equal eigenvalues. In this case, it can be easily verified that any two orthogonal vectors in the subspace spanned by these two eigenvectors can be used to represent the eigenvectors of the original matrix. Theorem 1 presents a slightly modified version of the original Stewart's theorem, as presented by Papadimitriou et al. in [18]:

Theorem 1 (Stewart's theorem [20]). *Let A and $A + E$ be $n \times n$ symmetric matrices and let $V = [V_1\ V_2]$ be an orthogonal matrix, with $V_1 \in \mathbb{R}^{d \times n}$ and $V_2 \in \mathbb{R}^{(n-d) \times n}$, where $range(V_1)$ is an invariant subspace for A. Partition the matrices $V^T AV$ and $V^T EV$ as follows:*

$$V^T AV = \begin{bmatrix} Q_1 & 0 \\ 0 & Q_2 \end{bmatrix}$$

$$V^T EV = \begin{bmatrix} E_{11} & E_{12} \\ E_{21} & E_{22} \end{bmatrix}$$

if

$$\delta = \lambda_{min} - \mu_{max} - ||E_{11}||_2 - ||E_{22}||_2 > 0$$

where λ_{min} is the smallest eigenvalue of Q_1 and μ_{max} is the largest eigenvalue of Q_2 and $||E_{12}||_2 \leq \delta/2$, then there exists a matrix $P \in \mathbb{R}^{(n-d) \times d}$ with $||P||_2 \leq \frac{2}{\delta}||E_{21}||_2$, such that the columns of $V_1' = (V_1 + V_2 P)(I + P^T P)^{\frac{1}{2}}$ form an orthonormal space that is invariant for $A + E$. Moreover, then

$$dist(range(V_1), range(V_1')) \leq \frac{2}{\delta}||E_{21}||_2$$

Using some elementary linear algebra we can simplify the above theorem and state that the space spanned by k eigenvectors that correspond to the largest k eigenvalues of matrix A will have small distance with the space spanned by k eigenvectors of matrix $A + E$, if the difference between the k-th and the $(k + 1)$-th eigenvalue of matrix A is at least 4 times larger than the Euclidean norm of the perturbation E.

2.4 Cauchy's Interlacing Theorem

Stewart's theorem, presented in the previous section, derives the stability of a matrix's eigenvector spaces by examining its eigenvalues. Thus, the naive approach for examining the stability of the matrix's principal submatrices, would be to compute all the respective eigenvalue decompositions. In order to avoid the prohibitive cost of computing all decompositions, we need to relate the eigenvalues of a matrix with the eigenvalues of its principal submatrices.

A well known theorem in the field of Linear Algebra that relates the eigenvalues of a matrix with the eigenvalues of its principal submatrices is Cauchy's Interlacing Theorem [20]. Cauchy's interlacing theorem is stated formally as follows:

Theorem 2 (Cauchy's Interlacing Theorem). *Let A be a matrix of order n with eigenvalues $\lambda_1 \geq \lambda_2 \geq ... \geq \lambda_n$ and let B be a principal submatrix of A of order $n - 1$ with eigenvalues $\mu_1 \geq \mu_2 \geq ... \geq \mu_{n-1}$. Then $\lambda_1 \geq \mu_1 \geq \lambda_2 \geq \mu_2 \geq ... \geq \mu_{n-1} \geq \lambda_n$.*

Cauchy's Interlacing can be extended easily to rank $n - k$ principal submatrices.

Corollary 1. *Let A be a matrix of order n with eigenvalues $\lambda_1 \geq \lambda_2 \geq ... \geq \lambda_n$ and let B be a principal submatrix of order $n-k$ of A with eigenvalues $\mu_1 \geq \mu_2 \geq ... \geq \mu_{n-k}$. Then $\lambda_i \geq \mu_i \geq \lambda_{i+k}$, $i = 1, 2, ..., n - k$.*

3 Related Work

In the context of supervised learning, the connection between the stability and the generalization performance has been studied (i.e in [4]). These studies derive generalization bounds for the performance of learning algorithms, based on their stability. In unsupervised learning the stability criterion has been used widely for choosing the parameters of clustering algorithms (i.e. selecting the number of clusters [17,13]), and for assessing the validity of clustering results [14].

Albeit the popularity of using stability for choosing the appropriate number of clusters, recent theoretical results have suggested that the stability criterion may not be appropriate for this task. More precisely, in [2] the authors prove for centroid based and spectral clustering that stability is determined by the symmetries of the data, which are not necessarily related to the parameters of the clustering algorithm. In [2] the authors focus on the stability concerning the structure of the clustering space and do not study the instability related to the sampling variability (which is related to the statistical accuracy). Our approach for "sparsifying" LSI/PCA is based on the analysis of the sampling variability affect, thus the result in [2] do not affect our approach.

The notion of stability has been studied within the contents of Principal Components Analysis (PCA). [3,8] present some early attempts to study stability of PCA by means of resampling (bootstrapping and jackknife). Potential applications of the stability criterion for PCA are presented in [3] where the stability is used for determining the appropriate dimension in PCA. Using different methodological approaches, the stability of the PCA has been also studied in [19].

Researchers working on PCA, have also identified the possible drawbacks of producing factor loadings that are a linear combination of all the input variables. This observation has led to attempts for "sparsifying" PCA [16,5,7,21]. Most of these approaches define the PCA problem as a cardinality constrained optimization problem and propose approximate algorithms for solving it. There are also a some research effort that use several heuristics for "sparsifying" LSI (such as [12]). Although we share the same motivation with Sparse PCA/LSI approaches, we utilize the stability criterion for "sparsifying" LSI/PCA. This differentiates significantly our approach from the Sparse PCA/LSI approaches.

4 Stability Based Sparse LSI/PCA

After introducing all the necessary notions and having presented the related work, we can move on to describe our proposed approach for "sparsifying" LSI/PCA. Recall that the main intuition in the proposed approach for Sparse LSI/PCA, is to select a feature subset such that the level of accuracy of the term-term similarities/covariances is adequate for computing stable PCA/LSI solutions.

4.1 Measuring Resampling Variability of Term-Term Similarities/Covariances

For quantifying the resampling variability of the estimated term-term similarities/ covariance, we utilize a principled statistical approach, bootstrapping BCa confidence intervals, that enable the non-parametric calculation of the statistical accuracy of the sample term-term similarities/covariances. We illustrate the method adopted, with the following example:

Example 1. Consider that we have the terms *"graduation"* and *"unemployment"* that are contained in a sample of 5 documents. The sample can be represented as a set of 2-tuples, where each 2-tuple contains the frequency of occurrence of the two terms in each document $\{d_1, d_2, d_3, d_4, d_5\} = \{(0,1),(2,3),(4,3),(3,0),(1,0)\}$. The cosine similarity of the two terms is 0.75. Taking only the cosine into account one could derive that the two terms are semantically similar, however if we take 5 bootstrap samples we may have:

bootstrap sample	cosine
{(0,1),(0,1),(4,3),(3,0),(1,0)}	0.70
{(0,1),(2,3),(3,0),(3,0),(1,0)}	0.40
{(0,1),(2,3),(4,3),(2,3),(1,0)}	0.96
{(0,1),(3,0),(1,0),(3,0),(1,0)}	0.0
{(2,3),(2,3),(4,3),(2,3),(4,3)}	1.0

The percentile confidence interval at 0.6 coverage is [0.0,0.96], which quantifies the variability of the values of the cosine similarity with respect to resampling of the input data. This implies that more data are needed in order to conclude on the two terms semantic similarity.

In the case we want to compute the confidence interval for the covariance, we can work in an analogous manner, using the covariance instead of the cosine formula. From the example it can be observed that the calculated interval may have variability itself (different runs could result in different intervals). In order to address this issue, we use 1000 bootstrap samples for calculating the confidence intervals. As it has been mentioned in the preliminaries section, 1000 bootstrap samples are considered to be adequate for computing accurate confidence intervals [10].

4.2 Relating Variability to Stable Sub-spaces

Since we aim at selecting stable sub-spaces with respect to the resampling variability of the term-term similarities/covariances, we need the means for relating the variability expressed by the BCa intervals (which quantify the statistical accuracy of the term-similarities/covariances) to the stability of the eigenvectors of the term-term similarity/covriance matrix. For this purpose we utilize Matrix Perturbation Theory and more precisely Stewart's Theorem that essentially relates the eigenvector spaces of matrices A and $A+E$, with respect to the eigenvalues of A and the norm of E. In the context of our work A contains the term-term similarities/covariances, while $A+E$ contains the perturbed version of A.

For determining the elements of matrix E we adopt the conservative approach of computing the elements of matrix E as the maximum difference between the term-term similarities/covariances and the endpoints of the corresponding confidence intervals. The intuition behind selecting the matrix E to contain the largest differences stems from a property of the Euclidean norm stating that $||E||_2$ lies in the interval $[\frac{1}{\sqrt{n}}||E||_1, \sqrt{n}||E||_1]$ where n is the number of columns (or rows) of E and $||E||_1 = max_{1\leq j\leq n}\sum_i^n |a_{ij}|$ (a_{ij} are the elements of the matrix). Thus by defining the elements of matrix E to include the maximum differences, we force the $||E||_2$ to lie within an interval of larger values (worst case scenario). Moreover this property of the Euclidean norm justifies the heuristic of removing the rows and columns with highest norm (later introduced in Algorithm 1). Since $||E||_1$ is defined using the absolute values of the matrix elements, it makes no difference (in the estimated interval) if we include negative values in the definition of E. In order to illustrate our approach, we provide the following example (continuation of example in section 4.1):

Example 2. Consider the case where we have terms i: *"graduation"* and j: *"unemployment"*, then taking after the example in section 4.1 we will have the $(i, j)^{th}$ and $(j, i)^{th}$ element of matrix A to be $A(i, j) = 0.75$. Since the confidence interval produced by bootstrap samples is [0.0,0.96], the $(i, j)^{th}$ and $(j, i)^{th}$ element of matrix E will be determined by $E(i, j) = max\{|0.75 - 0.0|, |0.75 - 0.96|\} = 0.75$.

Having determined the elements of matrix E we can apply Stewart's theorem in a straight forward manner. This will allow for assessing whether there exists some k for which the space spanned by the k eigenvectors is stable. If no such k exists, we should investigate sparser representations, removing the terms that exhibit high variance in their similarity estimations. The problem of searching for stable principal submatrices presents several challenges which we investigate in the subsequent section.

4.3 Stable Principal Submatrices

As we have argued in the introductory section, the problem of identifying stable principal submatrices is related to the problem of feature selection for LSI/PCA. In our approach we formulate two requirements for selecting the feature subset.

1. The feature-feature similarity/covariance matrix induced by the subset of features (which is a principal submatrix of the original similarity/covariance matrix), should contain stable eigenvector spaces for some k.
2. The E matrix induced by the subset of features (which is a principal submatrix of the original E matrix) should contain the most accurate similarity/covariance estimations.

The main difficulty for identifying stable principal submatrices is that the stability of the eigenvector spaces is assessed using the eigenvalues of the matrix. Thus, the naive approach would require that the eigenvalue decomposition is performed on every candidate matrix, making the cost of searching stable submatrices prohibitive.

In order to reduce the computational cost, we make use of Proposition 1, that is derived from the Cauchy's interlacing theorem. Proposition 1 allows for evaluating, whether it is possible for stable eigenvector spaces to exist in a principal submatrix, prior to computing its eigenvalue decomposition. Consequently the number of eigendecompositions that are performed can be significantly reduced. In Proposition 1, we do not check directly the requirements of Stewart's theorem but the requirements stated in Lemma 1. The proofs for Lemma 1 and Proposition 1 can be found in the Appendix.

Lemma 1. *Let A and $A + E$ be $n \times n$ symmetric matrices and let the eigenvalues of A and E be $\lambda_1^{(A)} \geq ... \geq \lambda_n^{(A)}$ and $\lambda_1^{(E)} \geq ... \geq \lambda_n^{(E)}$ respectively. If $\lambda_1^{(E)} > 0$ and $\lambda_i^{(A)} - \lambda_{i+1}^{(A)} > 4 \cdot \lambda_1^{(E)}$ for some i, then the prerequisites of Stewart's theorem will hold, and the space spanned by the first i eigenvectors of A will be stable.*

Proposition 1. *Let A and E be matrices of order n with eigenvalues $\lambda_1^{(A)} \geq \lambda_2^{(A)} \geq ... \geq \lambda_n^{(A)}$ and $\lambda_1^{(E)} \geq \lambda_2^{(E)} \geq ... \geq \lambda_n^{(E)}$ respectively. Moreover let A' and E' be principal submatrices of A and E of order $n - k$. If $\lambda_i^{(A)} - \lambda_{i+k+1}^{(A)} \leq 4 \cdot \lambda_{1+k}^{(E)}$, for all $i = 1, 2, ..., n - k - 1$, then the prerequisites of lemma 1 do not hold for matrices A' and $A' + E'$.*

In order to retrieve stable principal submatrices, we adopt the approach of incrementally reducing the order of the input term-term similarity/covariance A_n matrix at each step by 1. The choice of the principal submatrix of order $n - 1$ is done with respect to retaining the most accurate term-term similarities/covariances. This is done by removing the term that corresponds to the row (and column) of E_n that has the highest norm. Subsequently, using Proposition 1 we check whether it is possible for A_{n-1} to satisfy the prerequisites of Lemma 1 (and thus to contain stable eigenvector spaces). Until this condition is satisfied, we continue to reduce the order of the similarity matrix by 1. When proposition 1 cannot guarantee that the prerequisites of Lemma 1 will fail, we compute the eigenvalue decomposition and verify analytically whether the prerequisites of Lemma 1 hold. If we derive (using Lemma 1) that there exist stable eigenvector spaces, then we can check the standard LSI/PCA termination criteria (i.e. in PCA we can require that the stable eigenvector spaces retain a required amount of the initial variance). If the standard termination criteria are met, then we terminate the algorithm and output the stable principal submatrix. Otherwise we continue to iterate until such such stable submatrix is found. Our algorithm for detecting stable principal submatrices is illustrated as Algorithm 1.

Algorithm 1. SbS-LSI/PCA(S,A,E,TerminationCriteria)

```
Compute the eigenvalues of A
Compute the eigenvalues of E
if (The prerequisites of Lemma 1 are satisfied) AND (TerminationCriteria are met) then
    return A and the k for which the TerminationCriteria are met.
else
    repeat
        Find row r (feature t) of E with the highest norm
        S' ←Remove from S feature t
        A' ←Remove from A row and column r
        E' ←Remove from E row and column r
    until Proposition 1 cannot guarantee that the preconditions of Lemma 1 will not be satis-
    fied
    call SbS-LSI/PCA(S',A',E',TerminationCriteria)
end if
```

In order to illustrate the use of the traditional termination criteria, consider that we are provided with a dataset that contains m objects with n features. This input dataset induces an initial $n \times n$ covariance matrix C. Moreover, consider that we aim in projecting the data in a stable sub-space such that $a\%$ of the variance of the original input data is retained. Each time we find a principal submatrix of C that has stable eigenvectors, it will contain stable eigenspaces for a certain number k of eigenvectors (i.e. $k = k_1$,$k = k_2$ and $k = k_3$, recall that stability for a certain number of eigenvectors k depends on the difference of eigenvalues λ_k and λ_{k+1}, thus it can be achieved for various values of k). Then we should check whether retaining k (for all possible "stable values" of k) eigenvectors of the principal submatrix is adequate for satisfying the termination criterion set (i.e. expressing $a\%$ of the original data variance).

5 Experiments

In the experimental section we empirically demonstrate the behavior of *SbS-LSI* in three real world UCI-datasets. The datasets are the Ionosphere dataset that contains radar data (with 351 objects, 35 dimensions and 2 class labels), the Segmentation dataset that contains outdoor image segmentations (with 2000 objects, 19 dimensions and 7 class labels) and the Spambase dataset that contains emails classified as spam/non spam (with 4601 objects, 58 attributes and 2 class labels). In the experimental setup, we have set the confidence level to 0.9 for the BCa intervals. Moreover, we consider that the termination criteria for *SbS-LSI* is set to be a certain proportion of the Frobenius norm of the original data (i.e. we require that the projected space expresses $a\%$ of the Frobenius norm of the original space). Usually, in the context of LSI, the termination criterion is set to be a number k that represents the number of eigenvectors used to project the data (and thus the dimensionality of the reduced space), however this is not appropriate in *SbS-LSI* as the k values have different semantics with respect to different principal submatrices (the first k eigenvectors of a 500×500 matrix are not comparable to the first k eigenvectors of a 5000×5000 matrix).

In the Ionosphere dataset, we can easily evaluate using Proposition 1 that the input data (using all the features), do not contain stable eigenvectors. If we set the proportion $a \geq 33\%$, then the algorithm removes 2 features that contribute maximally to the instability of LSI and finds a principal submatrix that has stable eigenvector spaces for $k = 1$. Using the values of the respective eigenvectors, the algorithm verifies that the termination criteria (concerning the proportion a) is satisfied and the algorithm terminates. A similar behavior is exhibited by the Spambase dataset, that does not contain stable eigenvectors in the original space. If we set the proportion $a \geq 25\%$, then the algorithm removes 43 features and finds a principal submatrix that has stable eigenvector spaces for $k = 13$. Then the algorithm verifies that the termination criteria (concerning the proportion a) is satisfied and thus the algorithm terminates.

A more interesting behavior is exhibited by the Segmentation datasets. If we set the proportion $a \geq 45\%$, then the algorithm, verifies that the first eigenvector of the original input matrix (using all the features) is stable and satisfies the termination criteria. However, if we set $a \geq 55\%$, then the input matrix is not adequate and *SbS-LSI* has to examine the stability of principal submatrices. For $a \geq 55\%$ the algorithm removes 3 features and finds a principal submatrix that has stable eigenvector spaces for $k = 1$ and $k = 3$. For $k = 3$ the termination criteria are met, and the algorithm terminates. If we set $a \geq 65\%$, then the algorithm removes another two features and retrieves a principal submatrix that has stable eigenvectors for $k = 1, 2, 3, 4$. For $k = 4$, the termination criteria are met and the algorithm terminates.

The experiments demonstrate the practical applications of *SbS-LSI* and *SbS-PCA*. If we take into account the intuitiveness of the stability criterion, then it is natural to consider preferable to choose the stable sub-spaces that are derived by *SbS-LSI* and *SbS-PCA* over the standard LSI and PCA results. For example in the Segmentation dataset if we set as a termination criteria $a \geq 65\%$, standard LSI will return a certain number of k eigenvectors from the original input data, that are not stable with respect to sampling variability. On the contrary *SbS-LSI* performs feature selection, removes 5 features that contribute maximally to the instability of LSI, and returns $k = 4$ eigenvector of the resulting principal submatrix that are guaranteed to be stable. In the cases where the termination criteria are not met (i.e. no stable principal submatrix is found) , then it would be a sound practice to avoid using LSI or PCA as a preprocessing step to machine learning algorithms.

6 Conclusions and Further Work

Motivated by the intuitiveness of the stability criterion, we have introduced a feature selection process for "sparsifying" LSI and PCA. The proposed *SbS-LSI* and *SbS-PCA* algorithms select a feature subset such that the level of the statistical accuracy of the term-term similarities/covariances is adequate for computing stable eigenvectors (and thus stable sub-spaces). The main theoretical innovation of *SbS-LSI* and *SbS-PCA* is the fact that they present the first approach that utilizes the concept of stability for "sparsifying" LSI/PCA.

Concerning further work, we aim at investigate possible solutions for reducing the computational cost of retrieving stable submatrices. We also intend to investigate the theoretical properties of using the stability criterion for sparsifying LSI/PCA and its potential applications in Spectral Clustering.

References

1. Andrews, D.W., Buchinsky, M.: On the number of bootstrap repetitions for BCa confidence intervals. Econometric Theory (2002)
2. Ben-David, S., von Luxburg, U., Pal, D.: A sober look at clustering stability. In: Lugosi, G., Simon, H.U. (eds.) COLT 2006. LNCS (LNAI), vol. 4005, Springer, Heidelberg (2006)
3. Besse, P.: PCA stability and choice of dimensionality. Statistic & Probability Letters (1992)
4. Bousquet, O., Elisseeff, A.: Stability and generalization. Journal of Machine Learning Research (2002)
5. Cadima, J., Jolliffe, I.T.: Loadings and correlations in the interpretation of principal components. Journal of Applied Statistics (1995)
6. Cristianini, N., Shawe-Taylor, J., Lodhi, H.: Latent Semantic Kernels. Journal of Intelligent Information Systems (2002)
7. d'Aspremont, A., Ghaoui, L.E., Jordan, M.I., Lanckriet, G.R.G.: A direct formulation for sparse PCA using semidefinite programming. In: NIPS (2004)
8. Daudin, J., Duby, C., Trecourt, P.: Stability of principal component analysis studied by the bootstrap method. Statistics (1988)
9. Deerwester, S., Dumais, S., Furnas, G., Landauer, T., Harshman, R.: Indexing by latent semantic analysis. Journal of the American Society For Information Science (1990)
10. Efron, B., Tibshirani, R.: An introduction to the bootstrap. Chapman Hall (1993)
11. Jolliffe, I.T.: Principal Components Analysis. Springer, Heidelberg (2002)
12. Kontostathis, A., Pottenger, W.M., Davison, B.D.: Identification of critical values in Latent Semantic Indexing (LSI). In: Lin, T.Y., Ohsuga, S., Liau, C.J., Tsumoto, S. (eds.) Foundations of Data Mining and Knowledge Discovery, Springer, Heidelberg (2005)
13. Lange, T., Roth, V., Braun, M.L., Buhmann, J.M.: Stability-based validation of clustering solutions. Neural Computation (2004)
14. Levine, E., Domany, E.: Resampling method for unsupervised estimation of cluster validity. Neural Computation (2001)
15. Mika, S., Schölkopf, B., Smola, A.J., Müller, K.-R., Scholz, M., Rätsch, G.: Kernel PCA and De-Noising in Feature Spaces. In: NIPS 1998 (1998)
16. Moghaddam, B., Weiss, Y., Avidan, S.: Spectral bounds for sparse PCA: Exact and greedy algorithms. In: NIPS 2005 (2005)
17. Monti, S., Tamayo, P., Mesirov, J., Golub, T.: Consensus clustering: A resampling-based method for class discovery and visualization of gene expression microarray data. Machine Learning (2003)

18. Papadimitriou, C.H., Raghavan, P., Tamaki, H., Vempala, S.: Latent semantic indexing: A probabilistic analysis. In: PODS 1998 (1998)
19. Shawe-Taylor, J., Williams, C.K.I.: The stability of kernel principal components analysis and its relation to the process eigenspectrum. In: NIPS 2002 (2002)
20. Stewart, G., Sun, J.-G.: Matrix perturbation theory. Academic Press, London (1990)
21. Zou, H., Hastie, T., Tibshirani, R.: Sparse principal component analysis. Journal of Computational and Graphical Statistics (2006)

Appendix

Proof (Lemma 1). We have:

$\lambda_i^{(A)} - \lambda_{i+1}^{(A)} > 4 \cdot \lambda_1^{(E)} \Rightarrow$
$\lambda_i^{(A)} - \lambda_{i+1}^{(A)} > 4 \cdot ||E||_2 \Rightarrow$
$\lambda_i^{(A)} - \lambda_{i+1}^{(A)} - 2 \cdot ||E||_2 > 2 \cdot ||E||_2 \Rightarrow$
$\lambda_i^{(A)} - \lambda_{i+1}^{(A)} - ||E_{11}||_2 - ||E_{22}||_2 \geq \lambda_i^{(A)} - \lambda_{i+1}^{(A)} - 2 \cdot ||E||_2 > 2 \cdot ||E||_2 \geq 2 \cdot ||E_{12}||_2$
(eq. 1)

From equation 1 we can derive $\delta \geq 2 \cdot ||E_{12}||_2$
Moreover we have:

$\lambda_1^{(E)} > 0 \Rightarrow ||E||_2 > 0 \Rightarrow$(using equation 1) $\delta > 0$

Thus the prerequisites set by Stewart's theorem are met and the space spanned by the first i eigenvectors of matrix A sill be stable under perturbation E.

Note that for deriving the result we have used the fact that $||E||_2 \geq ||E_{ij}||_2$ and the definition for δ from Stewart's theorem.

Proof (Proposition 1). Let the eigenvalues of A' and E' be $\mu_1^{(A')} \geq ... \geq \mu_{n-k}^{(A')}$ and $\mu_1^{(E')} \geq ... \geq \mu_{n-k}^{(E')}$ respectively.

Concerning the eigenvalues of A and A' we can derive from corollary 1 that:

$$\begin{matrix} \mu_i^{(A')} \leq \lambda_i^{(A)} \\ \mu_{i+1}^{(A')} \geq \lambda_{i+1+k}^{(A)} \end{matrix} \Rightarrow \mu_i^{(A')} - \mu_{i+1}^{(A')} \leq \lambda_i^{(A)} - \lambda_{i+1+k}^{(A)}$$

Concerning the eigenvalues of E and E' we can derive from corollary 1 that $\lambda_{1+k}^{(E)} \leq \mu_1^{(E')}$

Thus if we have:

$\lambda_i^{(A)} - \lambda_{i+k+1}^{(A)} \leq 4 \cdot \lambda_{1+k}^{(E)}$ for all $i = 1, 2, ..., n-k-1 \Rightarrow$
$\mu_i^{(A')} - \mu_{i+1}^{(A')} \leq 4 \cdot \mu_1^{(E')}$ for all $i = 1, 2, ..., n-k-1$

Thus the prerequisites of Lemma 1 do not hold for matrices A' and $A' + E'$.

Bayesian Substructure Learning - Approximate Learning of Very Large Network Structures

Andreas Nägele[1,2], Mathäus Dejori[1], and Martin Stetter[1]

[1] Siemens AG, Corporate Technology, CT IC 4, D-81730 Munich, Germany
[2] Dept. of Computer Science, Technical University of Munich, D-85747 Garching, Germany

Abstract. In recent years, Bayesian networks became a popular framework to estimate the dependency structure of a set of variables. However, due to the NP-hardness of structure learning, this is a challenging task and typical state-of-the art algorithms fail to learn in domains with several thousands of variables. In this paper we introduce a novel algorithm, called substructure learning, that reduces the complexity of learning large networks by splitting this task into several small subtasks. Instead of learning one complete network, we estimate the network structure iteratively by learning small subnetworks. Results from several benchmark cases show that substructure learning efficiently reconstructs the network structure in large domains with high accuracy.

Keywords: Graphical Models, Bayesian Networks, Structure Learning.

1 Introduction

Bayesian networks (BNs) are popular graphical models to describe the dependencies between a set of random variables in a probabilistic as well as graph theoretic way. They provide a consistent and intuitive graphical representation of higher-order statistics between these variables. One important task for BNs that became important in recent years is the learning of the qualitative dependency structure from data. Due to the NP-completeness of structure learning [6], many interesting domains for Bayesian network learning face the problem of high dimensionality. The computational time of learning Bayesian networks can be reduced by applying heuristic assumptions about possible network structures combined with heuristic search strategies. For example, the "Sparse Candidate" algorithm with polynomial computational complexity was introduced [11]. This algorithm restricts the number of possible parents for each variable to a small number and allows only edges between a variable and its "candidate" parents. The basic idea behind this algorithm is following heuristic argument: If variables X_1 and X_2 are almost independent in the data, they are unlikely to be connected in a Bayesian network and, thus, the search space of possible network structures can be restricted on those that have no edge between X_1 and X_2. Recently, a very competitive algorithm was introduced [16]. This so called *MMHC* algorithm uses a constraint based method to detect possible parent-child relationships and

J.N. Kok et al. (Eds.): ECML 2007, LNAI 4701, pp. 238–249, 2007.

combines all these relationships to an undirected skeleton of the network structure. Afterwards, a score-based greedy search procedure is used to learn the edge orientation based on the skeleton.

However, structure learning in domains with tens of thousands of variables is intractable for current learning methods given the available computational power except for very restricting cases with boolean variables paired with very sparsely linked graphs [12]. Areas of applications for large networks are, besides others, social networks, warehousing or biological processes. For learning in such large domains, one typically restricts the feature dimensions on a feasible subset of relevant variables that are of high interest, as it was done in [10] for the estimation of biological processes.

Here we introduce the *substructure learning* algorithm which combines the approach of restricting possible network structures with dimensionality reduction. This approach is shown to be efficient in terms of accuracy and scalability for structure learning in large domains. In a first step, we learn the skeleton of the network structure. In a second step, for each variable, we learn one small subnetwork to estimate the local structure "around" this variable. Thereby, the possible network structures are restricted, based on the undirected skeleton. By learning one subnetwork for each variable in the complete network, we systematically estimate the complete directed network structure step by step, without learning one single Bayesian network for the whole domain. Based on all subnetworks, we provide a graphical representation of the directed dependency structure using the framework of a fPDAG (feature partial directed graph) to enable a unifying representation of all small and local subnetworks.

2 Methods

2.1 Background

At first, we provide a brief summary of learning multinomial Bayesian networks (BNs) and instead direct the interested reader to [14,16] for further information. Bayesian networks can be used to describe the joint probability distribution of n random variables $\mathbf{X} = \{X_1, X_2, X_3, ..., X_n\}$. A Bayesian network $B = (\mathcal{G}, \Theta)$ consists of two parts. The first part is the network structure which is a directed acyclic graph (DAG) $\mathcal{G}$ with each variable X_i represented as a node. The edges in the DAG represent statistical dependencies between the variables. The second part is a set of parameters describing the probability density. With the independence statements encoded in the DAG the joint probability function over $\mathbf{X}$ can be decomposed into the product form

$$p(X_1, X_2, ..., X_n) = \prod_{i=1}^{n} p(X_i|\mathbf{Pa}_i, \Theta, \mathcal{G}), \tag{1}$$

where $\mathbf{Pa}_i$ are the parents of variable X_i in the DAG $\mathcal{G}$.

Learning the structure and the parameters of a Bayesian network from a data set $\mathbf{D}$ can be formulated as the following problem: Given a finite data set $\mathbf{D} = (\mathbf{d}^1, ..., \mathbf{d}^N)$ with N different independent observations, where each data point $\mathbf{d}^l = (d_1^l, ..., d_n^l)$ is an observation of all n variables, find the graph structure $\mathcal{G}$ and the parameters Θ that best match data set $\mathbf{D}$. In the Bayesian approach this implies maximizing the function

$$p(\mathcal{G}|\mathbf{D}) = \frac{p(\mathbf{D}|\mathcal{G})p(\mathcal{G})}{p(\mathbf{D})}, \tag{2}$$

where $p(\mathcal{G})$ is the prior for the structure, $p(\mathbf{D})$ a normalization constant and $p(\mathbf{D}|\mathcal{G})$ the marginal likelihood of $\mathbf{D}$ given the model graph $\mathcal{G}$.

By using an uniform prior over all possible network structures, the learning problem can be reduced by searching solely the structure with best marginal likelihood

$$p(\mathbf{D}|\mathcal{G}) = \int p(\mathbf{D}|\mathcal{G}, \Theta)p(\Theta|\mathcal{G})d\Theta, \tag{3}$$

where $p(\mathbf{D}|\Theta, \mathcal{G})$ is the likelihood of the data set $\mathbf{D}$ given the Bayesian network $(\mathcal{G}, \Theta)$ and $p(\Theta|\mathcal{G})$ denotes the prior for the local probability distributions Θ of the Bayesian network with structure $\mathcal{G}$.

The approach described so far is commonly referred to as "score-based" approach since the DAGs are rated by their score. Constraint-based methods form the second class of structure learning algorithms. Instead of searching the optimal scoring DAG, they reconstruct the network by applying conditional independence tests on the data. Recently, a new and quite competitive algorithm that combines both approaches was developed [16]. The so called MMHC (max-min hill-climbing) algorithm performs Bayesian network learning in two steps: firstly, an undirected network skeleton is estimated with MMPC (max-min parents and children) that employs constraint-based techniques. Afterwards, a score-based greedy search is performed to orient the edges in order to obtain a high-scoring DAG.

Our substructure algorithm utilizes the same approach to estimate the skeleton, thus we shortly summarize the MMPC algorithm. For more details we direct the interested reader to [16]. MMPC is a local discovery algorithm to assess the set of parents and children $\mathbf{PC}_i$ of a variable X_i. This is done in two phases. In the first phase, conditionally dependent variables can enter the set of candidate parents and children according to a heuristic function which is called Max-Min heuristic: This variable enters next the candidate set that maximizes the minimum association to X_i given the current candidate set. Thereby, the minimum association is defined as the minimal conditional dependency of a variable and X_i, tested for all possible subsets of the current candidate set. This means that this variable enters the candidate set which is most unlikely to be conditionally independent from X_i. The growing phase stops after all dependent variables have entered the candidate set. In the second phase, the false positive variables are removed which possibly entered the candidate set in the first phase. False positives are such variables that are independent of X_i given some subset of all variables. Thus, all variables that are conditionally independent given a subset of the candidates are removed from the candidate set. The authors of MMPC have shown that under the assumption of faithfulness this algorithm will return no false negatives. It also returns no false positives if the **PC** relation is made symmetric, i.e. for all $X_j \in \mathbf{PC}_i$ it is tested whether $X_i \in \mathbf{PC}_j$; if this condition is not fulfilled, X_j is removed from $\mathbf{PC}_i$. To construct the skeleton of the Bayesian network, the MMPC algorithm is performed for all variables, and each variable is connected to all members of its set of parents and children.

It has been shown that the MMHC algorithm has a good performance in terms of quality as well as runtime and outperforms many state-of-the-art BN learning algorithms such as the Sparse-Candidate algorithm [16,11]. However, MMHC faces the problem of its computational complexity if applied in a domain with more than several thousand variables. While the skeleton reconstruction phase is quite efficient, the edge orientation phase is the limiting part in the MMHC algorithm. The authors have reported from a benchmark with 5000 variables where the first phase took 19 hours on a Pentium Xeon with 2.4 GHz, while the edge orientation took almost two weeks [16].

2.2 Substructure Learning

In this section we introduce substructure learning as an efficient and scalable method for estimating the structural dependencies in large and sparse domains. The general idea behind this algorithm is that subparts of very large networks can be learned by omitting unimportant variables, as it is done e.g. for the estimation of the genetic regulatory network where the large amount of about 30,000 genes (variables) is reduced to a small set of relevant genes [10]. How the selection of important network nodes for one subnetwork can influence the learned structure is exemplarily shown in Fig. 1, that is taken from [4]. The removal of one important node (X_7 in this example) can disrupt the structure of the BN. The direct relationships that pass originally over X_7 in left hand network must be represented by indirect relationships between the remaining nodes in the subnetwork on the right hand side, which leads to a massive appearance of false positive and false negative edges, thus leading to an entirely wrong set of relationships.

Based on the idea of dimensionality reduction and instead of learning the whole network, we learn a set of small subnetworks that together resemble the original global structure with high accuracy. The algorithm itself is a two-step process (see Table 1): Firstly, the skeleton $\mathcal{S}$ of the complete network structure is reconstructed. Secondly, small subnetworks are learned independently of each other for an estimation of the complete network structure. The new approach of substructure learning is to estimate the complete network structure by learning several subnetworks, one for each variable in the complete network.

In the first step, our algorithm (lines 2 – 5) is identical to the first phase of MMHC and determines the set of parents and children $\mathbf{PC}_i$ of each variable X_i to reconstruct the skeleton $\mathcal{S}$ of the complete network. In the second step (lines 6 – 12), we introduce a variable selection component by leaving, for each variable X_i, a subnetwork that is centered "around" the variable. This estimation starts with

Table 1. Substructure learning algorithm

1: **procedure** SUBSTRUCTURE($\mathbf{D}$)
  Input: data $\mathbf{D}$
  Output: set of Bayesian subnetworks $\mathbf{B}$
  // skeleton reconstruction
2: **for each** variable $X_i \in \mathbf{X}$ do
3:   $\mathbf{PC}_i$:= MMPC(X_i,$\mathbf{D}$);
4: **end for**
5: create skeleton $\mathcal{S}$ by all $\mathbf{PC}_i$
  // structure learning
6: **for each** variable $X_i \in \mathbf{X}$ do
7:   $\mathbf{M}_i$:= NEIGHBOURHOOD(X_i,$\mathcal{S}$);
8:   $\mathbf{D}_{\mathbf{M}_i}$:= restrict data $\mathbf{D}$ on variables in $\mathbf{M}_i$
9:   B_i := LEARN_BN($\mathbf{M}_i, \mathbf{D}_{\mathbf{M}_i}, \mathcal{S}$);
10:   B_i := restrict B_i on the Markov blanket of X_i and X_i;
11:   $\mathbf{B} := \mathbf{B} \cup B_i$
12: **end for**
13: **return** $\mathbf{B}$;
14: **end procedure**

the selection of variables $\mathbf{M}_i$ for learning one BN (line 7). For that purpose we utilize the skeleton $\mathcal{S}$ to determine the set $\mathbf{M}_i$ of structurally important variables which is calculated by NEIGHBOURHOOD(X_i,$\mathcal{S}$). This procedure returns a set of variables which includes X_i, the neighbours of X_i in $\mathcal{S}$ and their neighbours. Thus, the central variable X_i of the local structure, the parents and children of X_i and their parents and children are all put together for learning one single BN. This variable selection is the first crucial step since a suboptimal selection with missing variables which are structurally important can lead to false positives as well as false negatives, as it was shown before examplarily.

The second crucial step is the learning of the local Bayesian subnetworks (line 9). As done for MMHC, we restrict edges in the subnetwork to edges that also appear (as undirected edges) in the skeleton, this means an edge between two variables can only be added during structure search if the variables are also connected in the

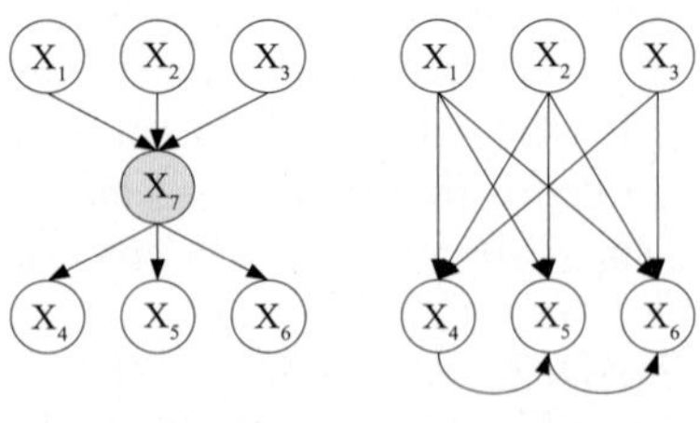

Fig. 1. The left Bayesian network is an example for a complete Bayesian network, the network on the right-hand side is the simplest Bayesian network that encodes the same probability distribution, but without node X_7. Note that the nodes X_4, X_5 and X_6 are no longer independent given their parents.

skeleton. To increase the quality of the network estimation we afterwards restrict the learned subnetwork to the Markov blanket of X_i by removing all variables and edges that do not belong to the Markov blanket or X_i itself. The Markov blanket of a variable is a subset of variables that render this variable independent from all others. In a BN, the Markov blanket of a variable consists of its parents, its children and the parents of its children. The result of the substructure algorithm is the set $\mathbf{B}$, containing all local Bayesian subnetworks B_i, one for each variable. All the local subnetworks allow a structural estimation of the complete DAG and, as well, build a quantitative model for each single variable given its Markov blanket, encoded as a BN.

2.3 Structure Representation

The set of partially overlapping subnetworks $\mathbf{B}$ lacks of a unifying representation of the network structure. While the structure of a single subnetwork forms a DAG, the edges of all subnetworks together need neither to be acyclic nor to have all edges with conforming orientations in all subnetworks. For example, it is likely that there exists an edge between two variables in one subnetwork that has the opposite direction in another subnetwork, or it does not occur in the other subnetwork at all. For a unifying representation of such structural uncertainties we use the framework of feature partial directed graphs (fPDAG) [8,9], which assigns confidences to edge features. The features of an edge between two variables X_i and X_j can be described by a probability distribution with four states, that is

$$p_{i \leftrightarrow j} = \{p_{i \rightarrow j}, p_{i - j}, p_{i \leftarrow j}, p_{i \perp j}\} \ . \tag{4}$$

$p_{i \rightarrow j}$ denotes the probability of a directed edge from X_i to X_j, $p_{i \leftarrow j}$ the probability of a directed edge from X_j to X_i, p_{i-j} the probability of an undirected edge and $p_{i \perp j}$ the probability that there is no edge between the two variables. We estimate the confidence of a feature as the empirical mean of the confidences in the subnetworks:

$$p_{i \leftrightarrow j}(k) = \frac{1}{\alpha} \sum_{g=1}^{n} f_{i \leftrightarrow j}(B_g)(k), \tag{5}$$

where $f(B_g)$ is the truth-value of the feature in network B_g: it is one if the feature appears in the network, otherwise it is zero. The normalization constant α denotes the number of networks that can make a statement about the feature. In more detail, the normalization constant of an edge feature with X_i and X_j as endpoints is the number of networks that contain both variables X_i and X_j. If there is no network that contains both variables, the probability of the edge is set to zero. As the direction of edges that do not belong to a collider structure can be ambiguous [18], the features are not calculated directly from the structure of a Bayesian network but from the PDAG (partial directed acyclic graph) representation of its network structure [7].

The fPDAG of Bayesian networks is a graph which contains all variables that are present in the Bayesian networks. Each edge between two variables X_i and

X_j is weighted with its feature $p_{i \leftrightarrow j}$. Thus, unlike Bayesian networks or PDAGs, the structure of a fPDAG is neither an acyclic directed nor a partially directed acyclic graph. Instead, it is a weighted graph that has edges between related variables, and these edges are labeled with $p_{i \leftrightarrow j}$.

2.4 Time Complexity of Substructure Learning

In the first phase of the substructure algorithm, the skeleton of the underlying dependency structure is reconstructed using MMPC. Each single call on MMPC has a computational complexity of $O(|\mathbf{X}||\mathbf{PC}|^{l+1})$ with l as the maximum size of all conditioning subsets. Thus, the overall cost for reconstructing the whole skeleton is $O(|\mathbf{X}|^2|\mathbf{PC}|^{l+1})$, where $|\mathbf{PC}|$ is the largest set of parents and children over all variables in $\mathbf{X}$ (we refer to [16] for more details). So far, the substructure algorithm does not differ from MMHC. However, in the edge orientation phase substructure learning splits the structure search problem into several small problems.

We now estimate the influence of this splitting on the number of possible network structures. Given a skeleton where each variable has at least two neighbours (or parents in the case of the sparse candidate algorithm), finding the best DAG is NP-hard in the number of variables [11,6]. Thus, learning one subnetwork is NP-hard in $|\mathbf{PC}|^2$, since $|\mathbf{PC}|^2$ is an upper bound for the number of variables in one subnetwork. This means, if $|\mathbf{PC}|$ is much smaller than the number of all variables, the substructure approach dramatically reduces the number of possible network structures. This affects the performance of heuristic search strategies like hill climbing, as well. For an estimation of the impact, we define the cost of a search strategy, depending on the maximum number of parents and children and the size of the domain, as $F(|\mathbf{PC}|, |\mathbf{X}|)$. For one subnetwork, the cost becomes $f(|\mathbf{PC}|, |\mathbf{PC}|^2)$. Thus, the overall cost for the second phase of substructure learning is $|\mathbf{X}|f(|\mathbf{PC}|, |\mathbf{PC}|^2)$. For large networks with small $|\mathbf{PC}|$ we expect the substructure algorithm to perform faster than approaches that learn the complete DAG. If we restrict $|\mathbf{PC}|$ on a fixed value, the second phase performs even linearly in the number of variables.

3 Results

In this section, we empirically benchmark the substructure algorithm by a comparison to MMHC. We use only MMHC for comparison as it has been shown in [16] to outperform many other structure learning algorithms in terms of accuracy and time efficiency. For the benchmark, we sample training data from known benchmark networks and request both algorithms to reconstruct the original network structures. These reconstructed networks are then compared to the original network to assess the quality of the learned structures. As benchmark networks we have chosen the Alarm [3] and the Insurance network [4]. Both networks are relatively small and have only a few variables (Alarm: 37; Insurance: 27). However, we are particularly interested in the performance in large domains.

Thus, we used the tiling method described in [17], which uses one network as tile and puts several tiles together, to enlarge both networks in size. We generated several large networks with the 10-fold, 20-fold and 30-fold size of the original network using the Causal Explorer software package [2]. The resulting networks are denoted as Alarm_10, Alarm_20, Alarm_30, Insurance_10, Insurance_20 and Insurance_30 (or abbreviated: A._10, ..., I._30). From each of the benchmark networks we sampled data sets of different sizes (100, 200, 500, 1000 and 5000 samples).

For the structure learning part of the substructure algorithm we use random hill climbing as heuristic search method. This means we select randomly two variables, calculate the scores for arc addition, arc removal and arc reversal and apply the highest scoring local change until no action can improve the total score. As scoring function that solves (3), we use the Bayesian Dirichlet equivalent (BDeu) score [14] with an equivalent sample size of ten. For the MMHC algorithm we used the implementation of the original authors from the Causal Explorer software package [2]. For the DAG search, they implemented Greedy Hill Climbing and used the BDeu score with an equivalent sample size of ten, as well. The here presented approach is focused on optimally reconstructing the original structure. Thus, we assess the accuracy by using evaluation measures that are based on structural features only. Other quality measures that take the density distribution into account are not considered here. As first evaluation measure we use the structural hamming distance (SHD) which is defined as the number of the following operations to make two PDAGs match [16]: (1) insert or remove an undirected edge or (2) insert, reverse or remove a directed edge. For feature graphs (fPDAGs), we extend the definition in such a way that each operation counts not as one but as the confidence of the corresponding feature. Additionally, we report the number of false positives (FP) and false negatives (FN) defined as the number of operations to remove all false positive or false negative edges. For runtime comparisons we use the real-time of both algorithms in seconds on a computer with an Intel Pentium M processor, 2 GHz, and two GB working memory.

Table 2. Performance results for different networks and sample sizes

	500		1000		5000	
	Runtime	SHD	Runtime	SHD	Runtime	SHD
A.	1.22 (5.43)	1.25 (26.2)	1.23 (7.31)	1.03 (16.4)	1.30 (26.4)	1.85 (18.5)
A._10	**0.64** (162.8)	1.01 (382.4)	**0.73** (228.3)	**0.99** (314.5)	**0.85** (862.1)	1.10 (253.9)
A._20	**0.40** (582.9)	**0.91** (742.8)	**0.45** (802.4)	**0.89** (620.9)	–	–
A._30	**0.24** (1265)	**0.88** (1066)	**0.33** (1741)	**0.85** (867.0)	–	–
I.	1.18 (5.1)	1.00 (42.1)	1.09 (7.66)	**0.90** (36.1)	1.11 (57.2)	**0.92** (34.1)
I._10	**0.78** (129.3)	1.11 (405.0)	**0.88** (199.6)	1.04 (327.1)	**0.98** (1348)	1.08 (201.6)
I._20	**0.54** (398.5)	1.03 (757.0)	**0.65** (598.0)	1.01 (592.3)	–	–
I._30	**0.39** (815.7)	1.02 (1137)	**0.45** (1202)	**0.97** (885.2)	–	–

Table 3. Average performance results

Network	Size	Edges	Runtime	SHD	FP	FN
Alarm	37	46	1.32	1.37	**0.98**	1.31
Alarm_10	370	570	**0.74**	1.21	**0.81**	1.06
Alarm_20*	740	1101	**0.43**	**0.90**	**0.32**	1.09
Alarm_30*	1110	1580	**0.29**	**0.86**	**0.31**	1.08
Insurance	27	52	1.31	1.00	1.04	1.09
Insurance_10	270	556	1.27	1.15	1.40	1.04
Insurance_20*	540	1074	**0.59**	1.02	**0.86**	1.03
Insurance_30*	810	1619	**0.42**	**0.99**	**0.87**	1.01

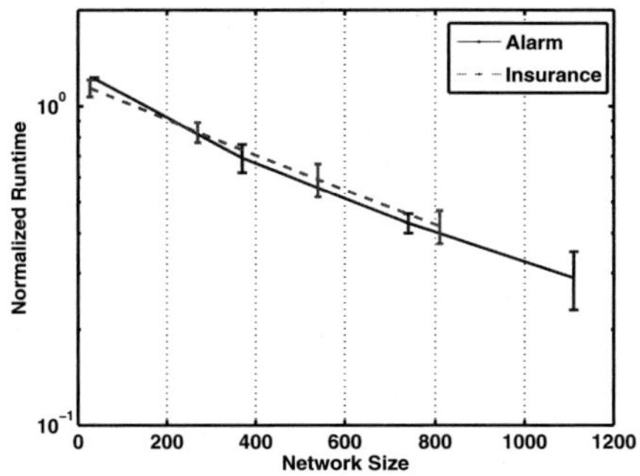

Fig. 2. Speed-up of substructure learning increases with the size of the network

Table 2 shows the relative performance of substructure learning compared to MMHC for different sample sizes (500, 1000 and 5000 samples) and networks by means of runtime (in seconds) and SHD. The numbers denote the normalized performance of substructure learning. This means that we divided each measure for substructure learning by the corresponding measure for MMHC. Thus, a value smaller than one denotes that substructure learning performs better than MMHC. The number in brackets denote the original, unnormalized measures for substructure learning. Additionally, in table 3 we report the network-wise averaged values over all sample sizes (100, 200, 500, 1000 and 5000 samples). Some of the networks (denoted by an asterisk in the table) are only learned with 500 and 1000 samples due to the large amount of time needed for one network reconstruction. As we can see, the substructure algorithm generally shows a good performance in terms of runtime and network quality compared to MMHC, especially for large networks. There is only one prominent outlier: the relatively small Alarm network is reconstructed poorly for 5000 samples with a normalized hamming distance of 1.85. For all other cases, however, the structural hamming distances are comparable for both approaches, in some cases substructure learning even outperforms MMHC. Besides, the number of false positives are even less in most substructure networks, while there are slightly more false negatives (see table 3).

In Fig. 2, the normalized and averaged runtimes for 500 and 1000 samples are plotted against the size of the network. As MMHC shows better runtime results for small networks, the reduced complexity of substructure learning shows its advantage for larger networks: For the Insurance_30 benchmark case, substructure learning needs only about 40 % of MMHCs runtime, while for the largest Alarm network only about 30 % of the runtime is needed. We also tried to learn larger networks, thus we created a tiled Alarm network with 1850 variables and 2853 egdes. However, MMHC failed to learn the complete network within one day (we interrupted the algorithm because of time issues). In contrast, substructure learning reconstructed the whole network within 255 minutes with a hamming distance of 1378, 88 false positives, 661 false negatives and 1564 correctly identified edges. Thereby, the network learning phase of substructure learning took only 10 minutes, while the skeleton reconstruction phase took the rest.

4 Discussion

Many other approaches for efficient network learning optimize the search procedure to find a good DAG by utilizing the sparseness of the structure. Recently, an algorithm that deals with domains up to hundreds of thousands of variables was introduced [12]. However, it restricts on binary variables paired with very sparsely linked graphs. Another approach that is closely related to MMHC was introduced in [5]. While, in the worst case, the skeleton reconstruction phase using MMPC can have an exponential cost, they developed an polynomial algorithm (called PMMS) for learning the skeleton. Empirically results on benchmark cases have shown that this algorithm significantly improves the runtime with a comparable quality of the reconstructed skeleton. In future we plan to include this algorithm in our substructure learning.

Since substructure learning detects the Markov blanket for each variable and thus renders this variable independent from all other variables given the Markov blanket, it can also be seen as a feature selection algorithm. In [15] a variation of MMPC is developed that estimates the Markov blanket using conditional independency tests. A comparison of different other approaches can be found in [1]. However, these methods return only the set of variables that belong to the Markov blanket, without discovering the probability distribution and its underlying network structure.

Another approach that is somehow related to our work is the framework of dependency networks [13]. There, the joint distribution is defined by a set of conditional probabilities. Unlike BNs where the conditional probability of a variable is defined given its parents, the conditional probability for each variable is determined by the complete Markov blanket. Subnetworks, resulting from substructure learning, can be easily transformed into a dependency network: The conditional probability of variable X_i is given by the joint distribution of subnetwork B_i, conditioned on the Markov blanket of X_i. For inference in a dependency network, the original authors have introduced a Gibbs-sampling method. Since subnetworks can be transformed into dependency networks, this inference method can also be applied to subnetworks.

5 Conclusion

The problem of learning the best scoring Bayesian network from data is NP-hard. In this paper, we have introduced the substructure algorithm that efficiently estimates the features of the underlying network structure by independently learning small subnetworks. Results from benchmark cases show that structural features of large networks can be learned with high accuracy, comparable to the results of MMHC. However, substructure learning scales much better for large domains, if the network is only sparsely linked. We have also shown that the framework of dependency networks can be utilized to perform inference on subnetworks.

References

1. Aliferis, C.F., Tsamardinos, I., Statnikov, A.: HITON: a novel Markov Blanket algorithm for optimal variable selection. In: AMIA: Annual Symposium proceedings, American Medical Informatics Association (2003)
2. Aliferis, C.F., Tsamardinos, I., Statnikov, A., Brown, L.E.: Causal Explorer: A Causal Probabilistic Network Learning Toolkit for Biomedical Discovery. In: Valafar, F., Valafar, H. (eds.) Proceedings of the International Conference on Mathematics and Engineering Techniques in Medicine and Biological Scienes, METMBS '03, June 2003, pp. 371–376. CSREA Press (2003)
3. Beinlich, I.A., Suermondt, H.J., Chavez, R.M., Cooper, G.F.: The ALARM Monitoring System: A Case Study with Two Probabilistic Inference Techniques for Belief Networks. In: Second European Conference on Artificial Intelligence in Medicine, London, Great Britain, vol. 38, pp. 247–256. Springer, Berlin (1989)
4. Binder, J., Koller, D., Russell, S., Kanazawa, K.: Adaptive Probabilistic Networks with Hidden Variables. Machine Learning 29(2-3), 213–244 (1997)
5. Brown, L.E., Tsamardinos, I., Aliferis, C.F.: A Comparison of Novel and State-of-the-Art Polynomial Bayesian Network Learning Algorithms. In: AAAI, pp. 739–745 (2005)
6. Chickering, D.M., Geiger, D., Heckerman, D.: Learning Bayesian Networks is NP-Hard. Technical Report MSR-TR-94-17, Microsoft Research, Redmond, WA, USA (November 1994)
7. Chickering, D.M.: A Transformational Characterization of Equivalent Bayesian Network Structures. In: Proceedings of the Eleventh Conference on Uncertainty in Artificial Intelligence, pp. 87–98 (1995)
8. Dejori, M.: Inference Modeling of Gene Regulatory Networks. PhD thesis, TU München, Garching, Germany (2005)
9. Friedman, N., Goldszmidt, M., Wyner, A.J.: On the Application of The Bootstrap for Computing Confidence Measures on Features of Induced Bayesian Networks. In: Seventh International Workshop on Artificial Intelligence and Statistics (January 1999)

10. Friedman, N., Linial, M., Nachman, I., Pe'er, D.: Using Bayesian networks to analyze expression data. In: RECOMB, pp. 127–135 (2000)
11. Friedman, N., Nachman, I., Pe'er, D.: Learning Bayesian Network Structure from Massive Datasets: The "Sparse Candidate" Algorithm. In: UAI 99, pp. 206–215 (1999)
12. Goldenberg, A., Moore, A.: Tractable Learning of Large Bayes Net Structures from Sparse Data. In: ICML '04: Proceedings of the twenty-first international conference on Machine Learning, p. 44. ACM Press, New York (2004)
13. Heckerman, D., Chickering, D.M., Meek, C., Rounthwaite, R., Kadie, C.: Dependency networks for inference, collaborative filtering, and data visualization. Journal of Machine Learning Research 1, 49–75 (2001)
14. Heckerman, D., Geiger, D., Chickering, D.M.: Learning Bayesian Networks: The Combination of Knowledge and Statistical Data. Machine Learning 20(3), 197–243 (1995)
15. Tsamardinos, I., Aliferis, C.F., Statnikov, A.: Time and Sample Efficient Discovery of Markov Blankets and Direct Causal Relations. In: KDD '03: Proceedings of the ninth ACM SIGKDD international conference on Knowledge discovery and data mining, pp. 673–678. ACM Press, New York (2003)
16. Tsamardinos, I., Brown, L.E., Aliferis, C.F.: The max-min hill-climbing Bayesian network structure learning algorithm. Machine Learning 65(1), 31–78 (2006)
17. Tsamardinos, I., Statnikov, A., Brown, L.E., Aliferis, C.F.: Generating Realistic Large Bayesian Networks by Tiling. In: 19th International Florida Artificial Intelligence Research Society (FLAIRS) Conference (May 2006)
18. Verma, T.S., Pearl, J.: Equivalence and synthesis of causal models. In: Bonissone, P.P., Henrion, M., Kanal, L.N., Lemmer, J.F. (eds.) Uncertainty in Artificial Intelligence, pp. 255–268. North Holland, Elsevier Science Publishers B.V, Amsterdam (1991)

Efficient Continuous-Time Reinforcement Learning with Adaptive State Graphs

Gerhard Neumann, Michael Pfeiffer, and Wolfgang Maass

Institute for Theoretical Computer Science, Graz University of Technology
A-8010 Graz, Austria
{neumann,pfeiffer,maass}@igi.tugraz.at

Abstract. We present a new reinforcement learning approach for deterministic continuous control problems in environments with unknown, arbitrary reward functions. The difficulty of finding solution trajectories for such problems can be reduced by incorporating limited prior knowledge of the approximative local system dynamics. The presented algorithm builds an adaptive state graph of sample points within the continuous state space. The nodes of the graph are generated by an efficient principled exploration scheme that directs the agent towards promising regions, while maintaining good online performance. Global solution trajectories are formed as combinations of local controllers that connect nodes of the graph, thereby naturally allowing continuous actions and continuous time steps. We demonstrate our approach on various movement planning tasks in continuous domains.

1 Introduction

Finding near-optimal solutions for continuous control problems is of great importance for many research fields. In the weighted region path-planning problem, for example, one needs to find the shortest path to a goal state through regions of varying movement costs. In robotics specific reward functions can be used to enforce obstacle avoidance or stable and energy-efficient movements. Most existing approaches to these problems require either complete knowledge of the underlying system, or are restricted to simple reward functions. In this paper we address the problem of learning high quality continuous-time policies for tasks with arbitrary reward functions and environments that are initially unknown, except for minimal prior knowledge of the local system dynamics.

Reinforcement learning (RL) [1] is an attractive framework for the addressed problems, because it can learn optimal policies through interaction with an unknown environment. For continuous tasks, typical approaches that use parametric value-function approximation suffer from various problems concerning the learning speed, quality, and robustness of the solutions [2]. Several authors have therefore advocated non-parametric techniques [3,4], where the value function for the continuous problem is only computed on a finite set of sample states. In this case stronger theoretical convergence and performance guarantees apply [3]. Still, few RL algorithms can cope with continuous actions and time steps.

J.N. Kok et al. (Eds.): ECML 2007, LNAI 4701, pp. 250–261, 2007.

Sampling-based planning methods [5,6], on the other hand, can efficiently construct continuous policies as combinations of simple *local controllers*, which navigate between sampled points. Local controllers for small regions of the state space are often easily available, and can be seen as minimal prior information about the task's underlying system dynamics. Local controllers do not assume complete knowledge of the environment (e.g. location of obstacles), and are therefore not sufficient to find globally optimal solutions. Instead, a graph is built, consisting of random sample points that are connected by local controllers. A global solution path to the goal is constructed by combining the paths of several local controllers.

Planning techniques are very efficient, but their application is limited to completely known environments. Guestrin and Ormoneit [6], e.g., have used combinations of local controllers for path planning tasks in stochastic environments. Their graph is built from uniform samples over the whole state space, rejecting those that result in collisions. They also assume that a detailed simulation of the environment is available to obtain the costs and success probabilities of every transition. In this paper we address problems in which the exact reward function is unknown, and the agent has no knowledge of the position of obstacles.

We propose an algorithm for efficiently exploring such unknown continuous environments in order to construct sample-based models. The algorithm builds an *adaptive state graph* of sample points that are connected by given local controllers. Feedback from the environment, like reward signals or unexpected transitions, is incorporated online. Efficiently creating adaptive state graphs can be seen as an optimal exploration problem [7]. The objective is to quickly find good paths from the start to the goal region, not necessarily optimizing the online performance. Initial goal-directed exploration creates a sparse set of nodes, which yields solution trajectories that are later improved by refining the sampling in critical regions. Planning with adaptive models combines the advantages of reinforcement learning and planning. We regard our algorithm more as a RL method, in the spirit of model-based RL [1,8], since the agent learns both its policy and its world model from actual experience.

The adaptive state graph transforms the continuous control problem into a discrete MDP, which can be exactly solved e.g. by dynamic programming [1]. This results in more accurate policies and reduced running time in comparison to parametric function approximation. The obtained policy still uses continuous actions and continuous time steps, leading to smoother and more natural trajectories than in discretized state spaces. In this paper we address primarily deterministic and episodic tasks with known goal regions, but with small modifications these restrictions can be relaxed. Prior knowledge of the goal position, for example, speeds up the learning process, otherwise the agent will uniformly explore the state space. We demonstrate in comparisons of our algorithm to standard RL and planning techniques that fast convergence and accurate solution trajectories can be achieved at the same time.

In the next section we introduce the basic setup of the problem. We show the structure of the algorithm in Section 3 and present the details of the adaptive state graph construction in Section 4. In Section 5 we evaluate our algorithm on a continuous path finding task and a planar 3-link arm reaching task, before concluding in Section 6.

2 Graph Based Reinforcement Learning

We consider episodic, deterministic control tasks in continuous space and time. The agent's goal is to move from an arbitrary starting state to a fixed goal region, maximizing a reward function, which evaluates the goodness of every action. In the beginning, the agent only knows the locations of the start state and the goal region, and can use local controllers to navigate to a desired target state in its neighborhood.

Let $\mathcal{X}$ define the state space of all possible inputs $x \in \mathcal{X}$ to a controller. We require $\mathcal{X}$ to be a metric space with given metric $d : \mathcal{X} \times \mathcal{X} \to \mathbb{R}_0^+$. Control outputs $u \in \mathcal{U}$ change the current state x according to the system dynamics $\dot{x} = f(x, u)$. In this paper we assume that only an approximative local model $\hat{f}(x, u)$ is known, which does not capture possible nonlinearities due to obstacles. The objective is to find a control policy $\mu : \mathcal{X} \to \mathcal{U}$ for the actual system dynamics $f(x, u)$ that returns for every state x a control output $u = \mu(x)$ such that the agent moves from a starting state $x^S \in \mathcal{X}$ to a goal region $X^G \subset \mathcal{X}$ with maximum reward.

Our algorithm builds an adaptive state graph $\mathcal{G} = \langle \mathcal{V}, E \rangle$, where the nodes in $\mathcal{V} = \{x_1, \ldots, x_N\} \subset \mathcal{X}$ form a finite subset of sample points from $\mathcal{X}$. We start with $\mathcal{V}_0 = \{x^S\}, E_0 = \emptyset$ and let the graph grow in subsequent exploration phases. The edges in $E \subseteq \mathcal{V} \times \mathcal{V}$ correspond to connections between points in $\mathcal{V}$ that can be achieved by a given *local controller*. The local controller $a(e)$ for an edge $e = (x_i, x_j)$ tries to steer the system from x_i to x_j, assuming that the system dynamics along the path corresponds to $\hat{f}(x, u)$. If an edge can be traversed with a local controller, it is inserted into E, and $r(e)$, the total reward obtained on the edge is stored. The combination of multiple edges yields globally valid trajectories.

For a given graph $\mathcal{G}$ the actual task is to find an optimal *task policy* π from the starting state x^S to the goal region X^G. We therefore have to find the optimal sequence of edges $\langle e_i \rangle$ in the graph from x^S to X^G such that the sum of rewards $R^\pi := \sum_{i=0}^{n} r(e_i)$ is maximized. The problem is solved by calculating the optimal value function V^π through dynamic programming. This method is guaranteed to converge to an optimal policy [1], based on the knowledge contained in the adaptive state graph.

The quality of the resulting policy depends on the available edges and nodes of the graph, but also on the quality of the local controllers. We assume here that local controllers can compute near-optimal solutions to connect two states in the absence of unforeseen events. Feedback controllers can compensate small stochastic effects, but the presented algorithm in general assumes deterministic dynamics. We restrict ourselves here to rather simple system dynamics, for which controllers are easily available, e.g. straight-line connections in Euclidean spaces.

While the agent is constructing the graph it is following an *exploration policy* π^{exp}, which can be different from the task policy π. π^{exp} does not always take the best known path to the goal, but also traverses to nodes where the creation of additional nodes and edges may lead to better solutions for the actual task. Virtual *exploration edges* to unvisited regions with heuristic *exploration rewards* are therefore inserted into the graph. This creates incentives for the algorithm to explore new regions. Whenever such virtual edges are chosen by the exploration policy, the graph is expanded to include new nodes and edges.

3 Structure of the Algorithm

The adaptive state graph $\mathcal{G}$ is grown from the start state towards the goal region. We use the approximative model $\hat{f}(x, u)$ to generate new potential successor states from existing nodes, and rank them by a heuristic exploration score. An exploration queue $\mathcal{Q}$ stores the most promising candidates for exploration, and the exploration policy, defined via the value function V^{exp} directs the agent towards one of these targets. Since our goal is finding a good policy from the start, not necessarily maximizing the online performance, the selection of the exploration target involves an exploration-exploitation trade-off inherent to all RL methods. Our method uses the information in the graph to efficiently concentrate on relevant regions of the state space. Whenever a new state is visited, it is added as a node into the graph. We also add all possible edges to and from neighboring nodes that can be achieved by local controllers. Initial optimistic estimates for the reward come from the local controller, but are updated when actual experience becomes available.

Algorithm 1 shows a pseudo-code implementation of the basic algorithm. Details of the subroutines are explained in Section 4. Roughly the algorithm can be structured into 3 parts: the first part in lines 5-11 deals with the generation of new exploration nodes and is described in Sections 4.1-4.3. The second part in lines 12-15 first updates the value functions, and then executes the local controller to move to a different node (see Sections 4.4-4.5). In the remaining part (lines 16-26) we incorporate the feedback received from the environment to update the graph (see Section 4.6).

4 Building the Adaptive State Graph

A key for efficient exploration of the state space is the generation of sample states. Previous approaches for sampling-based planning, e.g. [6,5], have used uniform random sampling of nodes over the whole state space. This requires a large number of nodes, of which many will lie in irrelevant or even unreachable regions of the state space. On the other hand, a high density of nodes in critical regions is needed for fine-tuning of trajectories. The presented algorithm iteratively builds a graph by adding states that are visited during online exploration. It thereby fulfills two objectives: Firstly, the exploration is directed to search towards a goal

Algorithm 1. Graph-based RL

Input: Start x^S, goal region X^G, local controller a

```
Initialize 𝒱 = {x^S}, E = ∅, 𝒢 = ⟨𝒱, E⟩, 𝒬 = ∅
repeat (for each episode):
  Initialize x = x^S
  repeat (for each step of the episode):
    for i = 1 to N_t do
      x̃_i = sample_new_node()
      [σ(x̃_i), var_σ(x̃_i)] = exploration_score(x̃_i, V)
      if var_σ(x̃_i) > θ^exp_min then
        insert_exploration_node(x̃_i)
      end if
    end for
    [V, V^exp, 𝒬] =replan(𝒢)
    Select next edge e = (x, x') stochastically (e.g. ε-greedy) from V^exp
    Execute local controller a(x, x')
    Receive actual state x̂' and reward r of transition
    if d(x', x̂') > δ then {different state than predicted was reached}
      Delete edge (x, x') from 𝒢 and insert edge (x, x̂')
      Set x' = x̂'
    end if
    if x' was previously unvisited then
      insert_new_node(x')
      update_edge(x, x', r)
      [V, V^exp, 𝒬] =replan(𝒢)
    else
      update_edge(x, x', r)
    end if
  until x is terminal
```

Output: Task policy π, derived from $\mathcal{G}$ and V

state, and secondly, it optimizes the current policy in regions where the number of nodes is insufficient.

4.1 Generating Samples: `sample_new_node`

Whenever a node x in the graph is visited the algorithm stochastically creates a number of potential *exploration nodes* for that state. New exploration nodes are created uniformly in the neighborhood of the current node. We therefore first uniformly sample an execution time $t_i \in [t_{\min}, t_{\max}]$, and a constant control action u_i in U. Then we simulate the local dynamics $\hat{f}(x, u)$ from x with action u_i for time t_i, and reach a new node $\tilde{x}_i$. For efficiency reasons the number of generated samples N_t should be reduced over time. Similarly the minimum and maximum execution time is reduced over time to create finer sampling and achieve fine-tuning of the policy.

4.2 Evaluating Exploration Nodes: `exploration_score`

Efficient exploration preferentially visits regions where an improvement of the task policy is possible, but avoids creating unnecessary nodes in already densely sampled regions. We estimate the utility of every potential exploration target $\tilde{x}$ by an *exploration score* $\sigma(\tilde{x})$, and direct the agent towards the most promising such nodes. Informed search methods like A* [9] estimate the utility of $\tilde{x}$ as the expected return of a path from the start x^S to the goal region X^G via $\tilde{x}$. This can be decomposed into the path costs $c(x^S, \tilde{x})$ from x^S to $\tilde{x}$ plus the estimated value $\hat{V}(\tilde{x})$, i.e. the estimated rewards-to-goal. Therefore $\sigma(\tilde{x}) = c(x^S, \tilde{x}) + \hat{V}(\tilde{x})$.

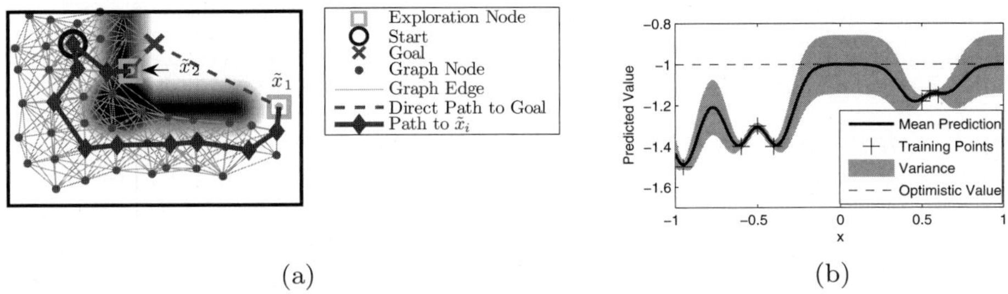

Fig. 1. (a) Illustration of the exploration process. Exploration node $\tilde{x}_1$ is preferred over $\tilde{x}_2$, because the reward to reach $\tilde{x}_2$ is strongly negative. (b) Illustration of value prediction with Gaussian processes on an artificial 1-D dataset. The prediction approaches the optimistic value and has larger variance for points that are farther away from training points.

For calculating the path costs $c(x^S, \tilde{x})$ we use only visited edges of the state graph. Otherwise the optimistic initialization of edge rewards will almost always lead to an underestimation of the path costs, and therefore all exploration nodes will appear similarly attractive. $\hat{V}(\tilde{x})$ must be an optimistic estimate of the value, e.g. the estimated costs of the direct path to the goal in the absence of obstacles. If the goal is not known, a constant value must be used. This prior estimate for the value of a new node $\tilde{x}$ can be improved by considering also the task-policy values $V(x')$ of nearby existing nodes x'. Gaussian process regression [10] is a suitable method to update predictions of a prior function by taking information from a finite set of training examples into account, thereby creating a more-exact posterior. The contributions of individual training examples are weighted by a kernel $k(x, x')$, which measures the similarity between a training point x' and test point x. Typical kernels monotonically decrease with growing distance to a training point. Therefore the prediction for a new node that is far away from existing points approaches the optimistic prior estimation, whereas a point close to existing nodes will receive a prediction similar to the weighted mean of values from neighboring nodes. The range in which training points contribute to predictions can be controlled by a *bandwith* parameter β of the kernel, which is task dependent and needs to be chosen in advance. In our experiments we use a standard squared exponential kernel $k(x, x') = \exp\left(-\frac{d(x,x')^2}{2\beta^2}\right)$.

Since the prior estimate is an optimistic estimation of the true value, the predictions for an exploration node will usually increase the further the new node is away from existing nodes (see Figure 1(b)). Therefore this approach enforces exploration into unvisited areas. Additionally to the value estimate $\hat{V}(\tilde{x})$ the Gaussian process returns the variance $\text{var}_\sigma(\tilde{x})$ of the prediction. Since the variance increases with distance to training points, we can use $\text{var}_\sigma(\tilde{x})$ as a measure for the sampling density around $\tilde{x}$. To control the number of nodes we reject exploration nodes with variance lower than $\theta_{\text{min}}^{\text{exp}}$. This threshold may be lowered over time, to ensure refinement of the adaptive state graph in later episodes.

4.3 Integrating New Exploration Nodes: `insert_exploration_node`

Newly generated exploration nodes $\tilde{x}_i$ are placed on the *exploration queue* $\mathcal{Q}$, which is a priority queue ranked by the exploration scores $\sigma(\tilde{x}_i)$. The highest scored exploration targets in $\mathcal{Q}$ are the most promising candidates for exploration. If σ_{max} is the best score of a node on the queue, we consider all exploration nodes with a score not worse than $\sigma_{\text{max}} - \theta_\sigma$, with $\theta_\sigma \geq 0$ as targets for the exploration policy π^{exp}. Virtual and terminal *exploration edges* are added to the graph for each such node $\tilde{x}$, originating from the node from which $\tilde{x}$ was created. The rewards of these edges are the estimated rewards-to-goal, given by $\hat{V}$. The exploration policy may then either choose an exploration edge, thereby adding a new node to the adaptive state graph, or move to an already visited node. The latter indicates that exploring from other nodes seems more promising than continuing the exploration at the current node.

The threshold parameter θ_σ has an interesting interpretation in the context of the exploration-exploitation dilemma. If $\theta_\sigma = 0$ then the agent will always choose the most promising exploration target, similar to A* search [9] on a partially unknown graph. This will however yield a bad online performance, because the agent may have to travel all the way through the state space if it discovers that another node promises better solutions. $\theta_\sigma = \infty$ will lead to greedy search, and ultimately to inefficient uniform sampling of the whole state space. By adjusting $\theta_\sigma > 0$ one can balance the trade-off between online performance and finding near-optimal start-to-goal paths as soon as possible.

4.4 Re-planning Within the Graph: `replan`

The adaptive state graph yields a complete model of the reduced MDP, which can be solved by dynamic programming methods. In practice we use efficient re-planning techniques like Prioritized Sweeping [8] to minimize the number of updates in every iteration. In most steps this requires only a very small number of iterations on a small set of nodes. Only when important connections are found, and the value of many states changes, we need to compute more iterations.

Re-planning is run twice: once on the graph that includes only exploration targets in $\mathcal{Q}$ with score larger than $\sigma_{\max} - \theta_\sigma$ as terminal states. This yields the value function $V^{\exp}$ for the *exploration policy* $\pi^{\exp}$. We also compute the value function V for the task policy π, using all available targets from $\mathcal{Q}$ as terminal nodes. This policy attempts to reach the goal optimally, without performing exploratory actions. It is therefore used in the computation of exploration scores, because there we are only interested in the optimistic rewards-to-goal.

4.5 Action Selection and Incorporation of Actual Experience

At the current node x the agent selects an outgoing edge $e = (x, x')$ through its exploration policy $\pi^{\exp}$, which is derived stochastically (e.g. ε-greedy) from $V^{\exp}$. The local controller $a(x, x')$ then moves towards x'. If the agent reaches a small neighborhood around x' the controller is deactivated, and the reward of the traversed edge in $\mathcal{G}$ is updated. If the local controller does not reach the vicinity of x' within a given maximum time, the controller stops at a state $\hat{x}'$. We then delete the edge $e = (x, x')$ from the graph $\mathcal{G}$, since it cannot be completed by a local controller, and insert an edge from x to $\hat{x}'$ instead.

4.6 Inserting New Nodes: `insert_new_node`

When a node x' is visited for the first time, it is inserted as a new node into the graph. Local controllers to and from all nodes in a certain neighborhood around x' are simulated to create incoming and outgoing edges. If a connection seems possible we insert the edge into $\mathcal{G}$ and store an optimistic estimate of the reward, e.g. the negative estimated transition time of the local controller in absence of obstacles. Inserting a new node x' also invalidates existing exploration nodes in the neighborhood, if their exploration score variance would fall below the threshold $\theta^{\exp}_{\min}$ (see Section 4.2).

If a newly inserted edge $e = (x', x'')$ with estimated reward $\hat{r}(e)$ reduces the path costs from x^S to x'', the edge becomes an attractive target for exploration. We then insert e as an exploration edge into the queue $\mathcal{Q}$. The exploration score is $\sigma(e) = c(x^S, x') + \hat{r}(e) + V(x'')$, which is the estimated return of a path from x^S to X^G that uses e. For the exploration policy the agent may then equally select exploration nodes or edges as its best exploration targets.

4.7 Practical Implementation Issues

Efficient data structures like *kd*-trees reduce the search time for neighbors during the training phase. The CPU time is still higher than for model-based RL methods with fixed discretizations, e.g. Prioritized Sweeping [8]. The construction of an adaptive state graph is an overhead, but on the other hand, it permits better solutions and faster learning.

5 Experiments

In this section we show that our algorithm can solve several continuous control problems that are challenging for standard reinforcement learning techniques. We show that the algorithm requires less actual experience than existing methods and finds more accurate trajectories.

5.1 Static Puddle World

The puddle world task is a well-known benchmark for reinforcement learning algorithms in continuous domains. The objective is to navigate from a given starting state to a goal state in a 2-dimensional environment which contains *puddles*, representing regions of negative reward. Every transition inflicts a reward equal to the negative required time, plus additional penalties for entering a puddle area. The puddles are oval shapes, and the negative reward for entering a puddle is proportional to the distance inside the puddle. The 2-dimensional control action $u = (v_x, v_y)$ corresponds to setting velocities in x and y directions, leading to the simple linear system dynamics $(\dot{x}, \dot{y}) = (v_x, v_y)$. We can safely assume to know this dynamics, but planning a path to the goal state and avoiding the unknown puddles remains a difficult task.

Figure 2 shows various stages of the exploration process in a maze-like puddle world with multiple puddles. As optimistic value estimate $\hat{V}(\tilde{x})$ we use the negative time needed for the direct path to the goal (ignoring any puddles). In Figure 2(a) it can be observed that the agent directs its initial exploration towards the goal, while avoiding paths through regions of negative reward. Less promising regions like the upper left part are avoided. When the agent has reached the goal the first time (Figure 2(b)) the agent knows a coarse path to the goal. With continuing learning time, the agent refines the graph and adds more nodes in relevant regions, which is illustrated in Figure 2(c). The path is almost optimal and avoids all puddles on the way to the goal.

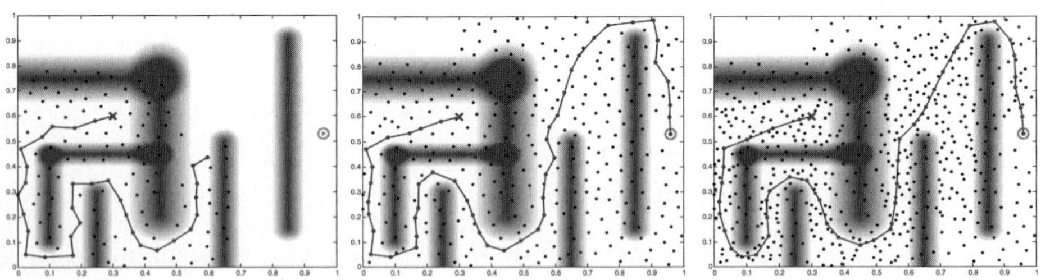

(a) (b) (c)

Fig. 2. Static Puddle World: (a) and (b) shows the graph at the beginning of learning and when the agent has found the goal for the first time. (c) results from further optimization of the graph. The red line indicates the best known policy to the target.

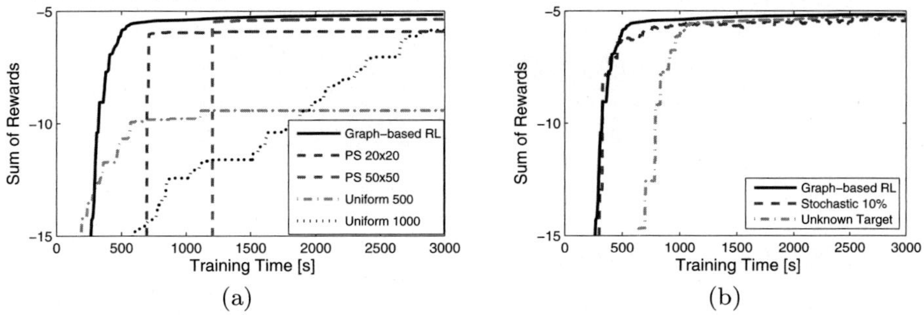

Fig. 3. Learning performance on static puddle world from Figure 2. (a) Comparison of RL with adaptive state graphs to prioritized sweeping (PS), and greedy search on uniformly sampled nodes (Uniform) with different discretization densities. (b) Influence of stochasticity (10% movement noise) and unknown target states on performance of graph-based RL. (Average over 10 trials).

Standard TD-learning [1] with CMAC or RBF function approximation needs several thousands of episodes to converge on this task, because a rather fine discretization is required. It is therefore not considered for comparison. Better results were achieved by Prioritized Sweeping [8], a model-based RL algorithm which discretizes the environment and learns the transition and reward model from experience. In Figure 3 we compare the performance of RL with adaptive state graphs to prioritized sweeping with different discretization densities. We also compare the performance of a greedy search method on a graph with 500 and 1000 uniformly sampled nodes, which updates its reward estimates after every step. We evaluate the performance of the agent by measuring the sum of rewards obtained by its greedy policy at different training times. The training time is the total amount of time spent by the agent for actually moving within the state space during the training process. Figure 3(a) shows that the graph-based RL algorithm achieves reasonable performance faster than prioritized sweeping (even with coarse discretization), and the best found policy slightly outperforms all other methods. Our refined graph in the end contains about 730 nodes, which is approximately a fourth of the number of states used by prioritized sweeping on the fine grid. Greedy search on estimated edges initially finds the goal faster, but it either converges to a suboptimal policy, which is due to the uniform sampling, or needs longer to optimize its policy.

In Figure 3(b) we added small Gaussian movement noise (variance is 10% of movement velocity), and used local feedback-controllers. Our algorithm still converges quickly, but due to the stochasticity it cannot reach the same performance as in the deterministic case. We also investigated the (deterministic) problem in which the goal state is unknown. Since the agent has to explore uniformly in the beginning, it needs longer to converge, but ultimately reaches the same performance level.

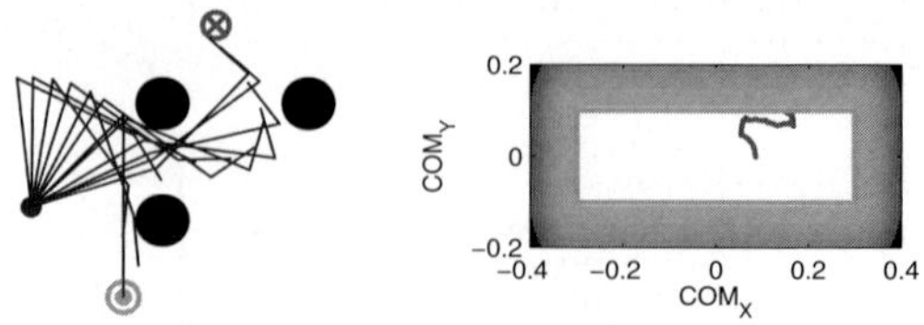

Fig. 4. Arm reaching task with stability constraints. Left: Solution trajectory found by our algorithm. The agent must reach the goal region (red) from the starting position (green), avoiding the obstacles. Right: Trajectory of the CoM of the robot (red) inside the neutral zone (green).

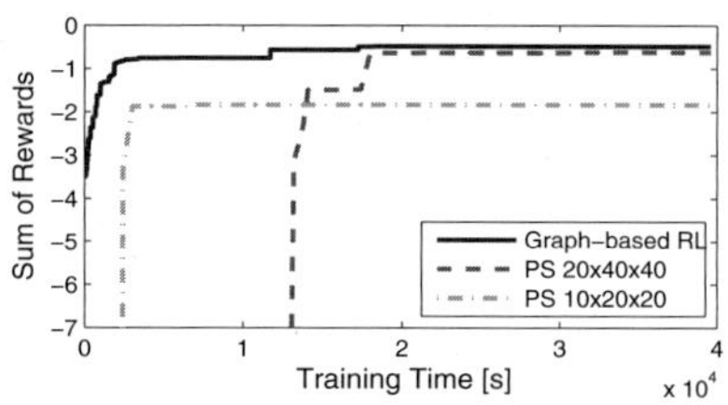

Fig. 5. Learning performance on the 3-link arm reaching task for RL with adaptive state graphs and prioritized sweeping (PS) with different discretization densities. (Average over 10 trials).

5.2 3-Link Arm Reaching Task

The joints of a simulated planar 3-link robot arm are steered under static stability constraints in an environment with several obstacles (see Figure 4). The objective is to reach a goal area with the tip. The robot consist of a body (point mass with 1 kg), around which the arm - modeled as upper arm (length 0.5 m / weight 0.2 kg), fore arm (0.5 m / 0.1 kg) and hand (0.2 m / 0.05 kg) - can rotate. The center of mass (CoM) of the robot needs to be kept inside a finite support polygon. If the CoM leaves a neutral zone of guaranteed stability ($[-0.2, 0.2]$ in x and $[-0.1, 0.1]$ in y), the agent receives negative reward that grows quadratically as the CoM approaches the boundary of the support polygon. Under these constraints the trivial solution of rotating the arm around the top left obstacle achieves lower reward than the trajectory that maneuvers the arm through the narrow passage between the obstacles.

The 3-dimensional state space consists of the three joint angles, and the control actions correspond to setting the angular velocities. The approximative model $\hat{f}$ is a simple linear model, but the true system dynamics f contains nonlinearities due to obstacles, which are not captured by $\hat{f}$. The optimistic value estimate $\hat{V}(x)$ is the negative time needed by a local controller to reach a target configuration, calculated by simple inverse kinematics. Figure 5 shows that graph-based RL converges much faster to more accurate trajectories than prioritized sweeping with different levels of discretization.

6 Conclusion and Future Work

In this paper we introduced a new efficient combination of reinforcement learning and sampling-based planning for continuous control problems in unknown environments. We use minimal prior knowledge in the form of approximative models and local controllers to increase the learning speed. Our algorithm builds an adaptive state graph through goal-directed exploration. We demonstrated on various movement planning tasks with difficult reward functions that RL with adaptive state graphs requires less actual experience than existing methods to obtain high quality solutions. The approach is particularly promising for complicated tasks that can be projected to low dimensional representations, such as balancing humanoid robots using motion primitives [11]. In the future we will extend the approach to non-deterministic and non-episodic, discounted tasks. Extending the approach to non-linear dynamics or even learning the local controllers for more complex dynamical systems is also part of future work.

Acknowledgments. This work was supported in part by the Austrian Science Fund FWF under project number P17229 and PASCAL Network of Excellence, IST-2002-506778. This publication only reflects the authors' views.

References

1. Sutton, R., Barto, A.: Reinforcement Learning: An Introduction. MIT Press, Cambridge (1998)
2. Boyan, J.A., Moore, A.W.: Generalization in reinforcement learning: Safely approximating the value function. In: NIPS 7, pp. 369–376 (1995)
3. Ormoneit, D., Sen, S.: Kernel-based reinforcement learning. Machine Learning 49(2-3), 161–178 (2002)
4. Jong, N., Stone, P.: Kernel-based models for reinforcement learning. In: ICML Workshop on Kernel Machines and Reinforcement Learning (2006)
5. Kavraki, L., Svestka, P., Latombe, J., Overmars, M.: Probabilistic roadmaps for path planning in high-dimensional configuration spaces. IEEE T-RA 12(4) (1996)
6. Guestrin, C.E., Ormoneit, D.: Robust combination of local controllers. In: Proc. UAI, pp. 178–185 (2001)
7. Simsek, Ö., Barto, A.: An intrinsic reward mechanism for efficient exploration. In: ICML, pp. 833–840 (2006)
8. Moore, A.W., Atkeson, C.G.: Prioritized sweeping: Reinforcement learning with less data and less real time. Machine Learning 13, 103–130 (1993)
9. Hart, P., Nilsson, N., Raphael, B.: A formal basis for the heuristic determination of minimum cost paths. IEEE Trans. SSC 4, 100–107 (1968)
10. Rasmussen, C., Williams, C.: Gaussian Processes for Machine Learning. MIT Press, Cambridge (2006)
11. Hauser, H., Ijspeert, A., Maass, W.: Kinematic motion primitives to facilitate control in humanoid robots (2007) (submitted for publication)

Source Separation with Gaussian Process Models

Sunho Park and Seungjin Choi

Department of Computer Science
Pohang University of Science and Technology
San 31 Hyoja-dong, Nam-gu, Pohang 790-784, Korea
{titan,seungjin}@postech.ac.kr

Abstract. In this paper we address a method of source separation in the case where sources have certain temporal structures. The key contribution in this paper is to incorporate Gaussian process (GP) model into source separation, representing the latent function which characterizes the temporal structure of a source by a random process with Gaussian prior. Marginalizing out the latent function leads to the Gaussian marginal likelihood of source that is plugged in the mutual information-based loss function for source separation. In addition, we also consider the leave-one-out predictive distribution of source, instead of the marginal likelihood, in the same framework. Gradient-based optimization is applied to estimate the demixing matrix through the mutual information minimization, where the marginal distribution of source is replaced by the marginal likelihood of the source or its leave-one-out predictive distribution. Numerical experiments confirm the useful behavior of our method, compared to existing source separation methods.

1 Introduction

Source separation assumes that multivariate observation data $\boldsymbol{x}_t = [x_{1,t} \cdots x_{n,t}]^\top$ ($x_{i,t}$ represents the ith element of $\boldsymbol{x}_t \in \mathbb{R}^n$) are generated by

$$\boldsymbol{x}_t = \boldsymbol{A}\boldsymbol{s}_t, \tag{1}$$

where $\boldsymbol{A} \in \mathbb{R}^{n \times n}$ is the mixing matrix and $\boldsymbol{s}_t = [s_{1,t}, \ldots, s_{n,t}]^\top$ is the source vector whose elements are assumed to statistically independent. Source separation is an unsupervised learning task, the goal of which is to restore unknown independent sources $\boldsymbol{s}_t$ up to scaling and permutation ambiguities, without the knowledge of the invertible mixing matrix $\boldsymbol{A}$, given a set of data points, $\{\boldsymbol{x}_t\}_{t=1}^N$. In other words, source separation aims to estimate a demixing matrix $\boldsymbol{W}$ such that $\boldsymbol{W}\boldsymbol{A} = \boldsymbol{P}\boldsymbol{\Lambda}$ is a *transparent transform*, where $\boldsymbol{P}$ is the permutation matrix and $\boldsymbol{\Lambda}$ is an arbitrary invertible diagonal matrix.

Various methods for source separation have been developed (for example, see [1] and references therein). Two exemplary independent component analysis (ICA) methods might be Infomax [2] and FastICA [3] where only spatial independence is exploited, assuming that sources follow non-Gaussian distributions.

J.N. Kok et al. (Eds.): ECML 2007, LNAI 4701, pp. 262–273, 2007.

Infomax is indeed maximum likelihood source separation where sources are latent variables that are treated as nuisance parameters [4]. In cases where individual source is temporally correlated, it is well known that second-order statistics (e.g., time-delayed correlations) is sufficient to achieve separation. SOBI [5] is a widely-used algebraic method where a set of several time-delayed correlation matrices of whitened data is jointly diagonalized by a unitary transform in order to estimate a demixing matrix. Alternatively, a linear latent function of parametric form (e.g., auto-regressive (AR) model) was often used as a source generative model in order to characterize the temporal structure of sources [6,7,8]. In such cases, parameters involving AR source generative models should be estimated in learning a mixing matrix or a demixing matrix.

Gaussian process (GP) model is a nonparametric method, which recently attracts extensive interests in machine learning. For a recent tutorial, see [9,10] with references therein. In this paper we use a GP model to characterize the temporal structure of a source, representing the latent function (which relates the current sample of source to past samples) by a random process with Gaussian prior. The marginal likelihood of source is Gaussian, which is computed by integrating out the latent function. We incorporate the GP source model into source separation based on the mutual information minimization, modeling the probability distribution of source by the marginal likelihood of source in the mutual information-based loss function. Alternatively, we also consider the leave-one-out (LOO) predictive distribution, instead of the marginal likelihood of source, in the same framework. We use a gradient-based optimization to estimate the demixing matrix, through the mutual information minimization, where the marginal likelihood of source or LOO predictive distribution of source is used to model the marginal entropy of source.

2 GP Models for Sources

The latent function $f_i(\cdot)$ relates the current sample of source $s_{i,t}$ to past p samples, leading to

$$s_{i,t} = f_i\left(\boldsymbol{s}_{i,t-1:t-p}^{\top}\right) + \varepsilon_{i,t}, \tag{2}$$

where $\boldsymbol{s}_{i,t-1:t-p} = \left[s_{i,t-1}, s_{i,t-2}, \ldots, s_{i,t-p}\right]$ is a collection of past p samples and $\epsilon_{i,t}$ is the white Gaussian noise with zero mean and unit variance, i.e., $\epsilon_{i,t} \sim \mathcal{G}(\epsilon_{i,t}; 0, 1)$. In the case of linear AR model, the latent function is parameterized by

$$f_i\left(\boldsymbol{s}_{i,t-1:t-p}^{\top}\right) = \sum_{\tau=1}^{p} h_{i,\tau} s_{i,t-\tau}, \tag{3}$$

where $h_{i,\tau}$ are AR coefficients.

GP model represents the latent function $f_i(\cdot)$ by a random process with Gaussian prior, unlike AR model employs the parametric form (3). We place a GP prior over the function $f_i(\cdot)$, i.e.,

$$f_i \sim \mathcal{GP}\left(0, k\left(\boldsymbol{s}_{i,t:t-p+1}^{\top}, \boldsymbol{s}_{i,\tau:\tau-p+1}^{\top}\right)\right), \tag{4}$$

where $k\left(\boldsymbol{s}_{i,t:t-p+1}^\top, \boldsymbol{s}_{i,\tau:\tau-p+1}^\top\right)$ is a *covariance function*. We use the squared exponential covariance function, i.e.,

$$k\left(\boldsymbol{s}_{i,t:t-p+1}^\top, \boldsymbol{s}_{i,\tau:\tau-p+1}^\top\right) = \exp\left\{-\lambda_i \|\boldsymbol{s}_{i,t:t-p+1}^\top - \boldsymbol{s}_{i,\tau:\tau-p+1}^\top\|^2\right\}, \tag{5}$$

where λ_i is a length-scale hyperparameter.

We refer to the source generative model (2) with GP prior (4) as *GP source model.* The GP source model follows the standard GP regression in which $\boldsymbol{s}_{i,1:N}^\top = [s_{i,1}, \ldots, s_{i,N}]^\top$ is a collection of responses and $\mathcal{S}_i = \left\{\boldsymbol{s}_{i,t-1:t-p}^\top\right\}_{t=1}^N$ is a set of regressors.

We define the vector $\boldsymbol{f}_i \in \mathbb{R}^N$ as

$$\boldsymbol{f}_i = [f_{i,0}, f_{i,1}, \ldots, f_{i,N-1}]^\top,$$

where $f_{i,t} = f_i\left(\boldsymbol{s}_{i,t:t-p+1}^\top\right)$. Then the likelihood of source i is given by

$$p\left(\boldsymbol{s}_{i,1:N}^\top | \boldsymbol{f}_i, \mathcal{S}_i\right) = \mathcal{G}(\boldsymbol{s}_{i,1:N}^\top; \boldsymbol{f}_i, \boldsymbol{I}_N), \tag{6}$$

where $\boldsymbol{I}_N$ is the $N \times N$ identity matrix. Then the marginal likelihood of source i is obtained by integrating the likelihood times the prior

$$p_i\left(\boldsymbol{s}_{i,1:N}^\top | \mathcal{S}_i\right) = \int p\left(\boldsymbol{s}_{i,1:N}^\top | \boldsymbol{f}_i, \mathcal{S}_i\right) p\left(\boldsymbol{f}_i | \mathcal{S}_i\right) d\boldsymbol{f}_i, \tag{7}$$

where the prior is given by (4),

$$p\left(\boldsymbol{f}_i | \mathcal{S}_i\right) = \mathcal{G}(\boldsymbol{f}_i; 0, \boldsymbol{K}_i),$$

where $\boldsymbol{K}_i$ is a $N \times N$ matrix whose (u, v)-element is given by

$$[\boldsymbol{K}_i]_{u,v} = k(\boldsymbol{s}_{i,u-1:u-p}, \boldsymbol{s}_{i,v-1:v-p}).$$

The log of the marginal likelihood, denoted by $\log p_i^{ML}$, is of the form

$$\begin{aligned} \log p_i^{ML}\left(\boldsymbol{s}_{i,1:N}^\top\right) &= \log p\left(\boldsymbol{s}_{i,1:N}^\top | \mathcal{S}_i\right) \\ &= -\frac{1}{2}\boldsymbol{s}_{i,1:N} \boldsymbol{\Sigma}_i^{-1} \boldsymbol{s}_{i,1:N}^\top - \frac{1}{2}\log|\boldsymbol{\Sigma}_i| - \frac{N}{2}\log 2\pi, \end{aligned} \tag{8}$$

where $\boldsymbol{\Sigma}_i = \boldsymbol{K}_i + \boldsymbol{I}_N$.

We also consider the LOO predictive distribution which is Gaussian:

$$p_i^{LOO}\left(\boldsymbol{s}_{i,1:N}^\top\right) = \prod_{t=1}^N p\left(s_{i,t} | \mathcal{S}_i, \boldsymbol{s}_{i,1:N}^{-t}\right) = \prod_{t=1}^N \mathcal{G}(s_{i,t}; \mu_{i,t}, \sigma_{i,t}^2), \tag{9}$$

where $\boldsymbol{s}_{i,1:N}^{-t} = [s_{i,1}, \ldots, s_{i,t-1}, s_{i,t+1}, \ldots, s_{i,N}]$ denotes all samples of source i but $s_{i,t}$. The LOO predictive mean $\mu_{i,t}$ and variance $\sigma_{i,t}^2$ are given by

$$\begin{aligned} \mu_{i,t} &= s_{i,t} - \left[\boldsymbol{\Sigma}_i^{-1}\boldsymbol{s}_{i,1:N}^\top\right]_t / \left[\boldsymbol{\Sigma}_i^{-1}\right]_{t,t}, \\ \sigma_{i,t}^2 &= 1/\left[\boldsymbol{\Sigma}_i^{-1}\right]_{t,t}. \end{aligned}$$

Thus the log of LOO predictive distribution is of the form

$$\log p_i^{LOO}(\boldsymbol{s}_{i,1:N}^\top) = -\frac{1}{2}\sum_{t=1}^{N}\left\{-\log\left[\boldsymbol{\Sigma}_i^{-1}\right]_{t,t} + \frac{\left(\left[\boldsymbol{\Sigma}_i^{-1}\boldsymbol{s}_{i,1:N}^\top\right]_t\right)^2}{\left[\boldsymbol{\Sigma}_i^{-1}\right]_{t,t}} + \log 2\pi\right\} \quad (10)$$

The log LOO predictive distribution (10) is often referred to as *log pseudo-likelihood* that is an approximation of the log marginal likelihood (8)[11]. The marginal likelihood or LOO predictive distribution is used to learn hyperparameters in GP regression. We use the marginal likelihood or the LOO predictive distribution as an estimate of the source distribution which is required in the source separation based on the mutual information minimization. It is known that the LOO predictive distribution is more robust to model mis-specification, compared to [12,10]. The model mis-specification occurs when the model assumption is not suitable to describe the observation data. In the case of source separation using GP models, the model mis-specification might arise when inappropriate model order p is chosen or the selected kernel function is not suitable. The marginal likelihood represents the probability distribution of source given a certain model assumption, so it might be affected by the model mis-specification. Fortunately the aim in this paper is to estimate a demixing matrix for source separation rather than to estimate hyperparameters for source model fitting. Thus, the mis-specification problem is not critical in source separation. This issue is investigated through experiments (see Sec. 5.3).

3 Source Separation with GP Models

In this section we present the main contribution of this paper, developing methods which incorporate the GP source model (illustrated in Sec 2) into source separation based on the mutual information minimization.

Let us consider the demixing model:

$$\boldsymbol{y}_t = \boldsymbol{W}\boldsymbol{x}_t, \quad (11)$$

where $\boldsymbol{W} \in \mathbb{R}^{n\times n}$ is the demixing matrix. The goal of source separation is to learn the demixing matrix $\boldsymbol{W}$ such that $\boldsymbol{y}_t = \boldsymbol{P}\boldsymbol{\Lambda}\boldsymbol{s}_t$, i.e., $\boldsymbol{W}\boldsymbol{A}$ is a transparent transform.

Sources are assumed to be mutually independent, which satisfies

$$p\left(\boldsymbol{s}_{1,1:N}^\top, ..., \boldsymbol{s}_{n,1:N}^\top\right) = \prod_{i=1}^{n} p_i\left(\boldsymbol{s}_{i,1:N}^\top\right). \quad (12)$$

The factorial model (12) leads to the mutual information-based risk $R(\boldsymbol{W})$ that is of the form

$$\boldsymbol{R}(\boldsymbol{W}) = \mathbb{E}\{L(\boldsymbol{W})\} = \frac{1}{N}\mathbb{E}\left\{\log\frac{p\left(\boldsymbol{y}_{1,1:N}^\top, ..., \boldsymbol{y}_{n,1:N}^\top\right)}{\prod_{i=1}^n p_i\left(\boldsymbol{y}_{i,1:N}^\top\right)}\right\}, \quad (13)$$

where $L(\boldsymbol{W})$ is the loss function. The risk (13) is nothing but the normalized Kullback-Leibler divergence between the joint distribution $p\left(\boldsymbol{y}_{1,1:N}^\top, ..., \boldsymbol{y}_{n,1:N}^\top\right)$ and the product of marginal distributions $\prod_{i=1}^n p_i\left(\boldsymbol{y}_{i,1:N}^\top\right)$. Since $\boldsymbol{y}_t$ is a linear transform of $\boldsymbol{x}_t$, joint distributions satisfies

$$p\left(\boldsymbol{y}_{1,1:N}^\top, ..., \boldsymbol{y}_{n,1:N}^\top\right) = \frac{p\left(\boldsymbol{x}_{1,1:N}^\top, ..., \boldsymbol{x}_{n,1:N}^\top\right)}{|\det \boldsymbol{W}|^N}. \tag{14}$$

Taking this into account, the loss function $L(\boldsymbol{W})$ is given by

$$L(\boldsymbol{W}) = -\log|\det \boldsymbol{W}| - \frac{1}{N}\sum_{i=1}^n \log p_i\left(\boldsymbol{y}_{i,1:N}^\top\right), \tag{15}$$

where $\frac{1}{N}\log p\left(\boldsymbol{x}_{1,1:N}^\top, ..., \boldsymbol{x}_{n,1:N}^\top\right)$ is omitted since it does not depend on $\boldsymbol{W}$.

Now we use the log of the marginal likelihood (8) or the log of LOO predictive distribution (10) as an substitute to $\log p_i\left(\boldsymbol{y}_{i,1:N}^\top\right)$ in the loss function (15). In the case of the marginal likelihood, the loss function becomes

$$\begin{aligned} L_{ML}(\boldsymbol{W}) &= -\log|\det \boldsymbol{W}| - \frac{1}{N}\sum_{i=1}^n \log p_i^{ML}\left(\boldsymbol{y}_{i,1:N}^\top\right) \\ &= -\log|\det \boldsymbol{W}| + \frac{1}{2N}\sum_{i=1}^n \left\{\boldsymbol{y}_{i,1:N}\boldsymbol{\Sigma}_i^{-1}\boldsymbol{y}_{i,1:N}^\top + \log|\boldsymbol{\Sigma}_i|\right\}, \end{aligned} \tag{16}$$

where $\frac{1}{2N}\log 2\pi$ (which does not depend on $\boldsymbol{W}$) is left out. In (16), $\boldsymbol{\Sigma}_i = \boldsymbol{K}_i + \boldsymbol{I}_N$ is computed using $y_{i,t}$ which is the estimate of $s_{i,t}$, i.e.,

$$[\boldsymbol{K}_i]_{u,v} = k\left(\boldsymbol{y}_{i,u-1:u-p}^\top, \boldsymbol{y}_{i,v-1:v-p}^\top\right).$$

We use a gradient-based optimization to find a solution which minimizes (16). In order to compute the gradient, we first define

$$\boldsymbol{\alpha}_i = \boldsymbol{\Sigma}_i^{-1}\boldsymbol{y}_{i,1:N}^\top, \tag{17}$$

$$\boldsymbol{Z}_i^{kl} = \boldsymbol{\Sigma}_i^{-1}\frac{\partial \boldsymbol{K}_i}{\partial w_{k,l}}, \tag{18}$$

where the derivative of the covariance matrix $\boldsymbol{K}_i$ w.r.t $w_{k,l}$ (which is the (k,l)-element of the demixing matrix $\boldsymbol{W}$) is computed as

$$\left[\frac{\partial \boldsymbol{K}_i}{\partial w_{k,l}}\right]_{u,v} = -2\lambda_i k\left(\boldsymbol{y}_{i,u-1:u-p}^\top, \boldsymbol{y}_{i,v-1:v-p}^\top\right)\left[\boldsymbol{\Delta}\boldsymbol{\Delta}^\top \boldsymbol{w}_{i,:}^\top\right]_l \delta_{i,k},$$

where $\delta_{i,k}$ is the Kronecker delta, $\boldsymbol{w}_{i,:}$ represents the ith row vector of $\boldsymbol{W}$, and

$$\boldsymbol{\Delta} = \left[(\boldsymbol{x}_{u-1} - \boldsymbol{x}_{v-1}), \ldots, (\boldsymbol{x}_{u-p} - \boldsymbol{x}_{v-p})\right].$$

With this definition, the gradient of (16) w.r.t $w_{k,l}$ is determined by

$$
\begin{aligned}
\frac{\partial L_{ML}}{\partial w_{k,l}} &= -\mathrm{tr}\left\{\boldsymbol{W}^{-1}\frac{\partial \boldsymbol{W}}{\partial w_{k,l}}\right\} + \frac{1}{2N}\sum_{i=1}^{n}\mathrm{tr}\left\{\boldsymbol{y}_{i,1:N}\frac{\partial \boldsymbol{\Sigma}_i^{-1}}{\partial w_{k,l}}\boldsymbol{y}_{i,1:N}^{\top}\right. \\
&\quad \left. + 2\frac{\partial \boldsymbol{y}_{i,1:N}}{\partial w_{k,l}}\boldsymbol{\Sigma}_i^{-1}\boldsymbol{y}_{i,1:N}^{\top} + \boldsymbol{\Sigma}_i^{-1}\frac{\partial \boldsymbol{K}_i}{\partial w_{k,l}}\right\} \\
&= -\mathrm{tr}\left\{\boldsymbol{W}^{-1}\frac{\partial \boldsymbol{W}}{\partial w_{k,l}}\right\} \\
&\quad - \frac{1}{2N}\sum_{i=1}^{n}\delta_{i,k}\mathrm{tr}\left\{\boldsymbol{\alpha}_i\boldsymbol{\alpha}_i^{\top}\frac{\partial \boldsymbol{K}_i}{\partial w_{k,l}} - 2\boldsymbol{x}_{l,1:N}\boldsymbol{\alpha}_i - \boldsymbol{Z}_i^{kl}\right\}.
\end{aligned}
\tag{19}
$$

The hyperparameters λ_i can also be learned through minimizing the loss function and the gradient w.r.t them can be easily computed. However, here we fix them as constant values and learn only demixing matrix. Empirical results show that the performance does not much depend on the values of hyperparameters (see Fig. 1 (a)).

In a similar manner, we also consider the log of LOO predictive distribution (10), leading to the following loss function

$$
\begin{aligned}
&L_{LOO}(\boldsymbol{W}) \\
&= -\log|\det\boldsymbol{W}| - \frac{1}{N}\sum_{i=1}^{n}\log p_i^{LOO}\left(\boldsymbol{y}_{i,1:N}^{\top}\right) \\
&= -\log|\det\boldsymbol{W}| + \frac{1}{2N}\sum_{i=1}^{n}\sum_{t=1}^{N}\left\{-\log\left[\boldsymbol{\Sigma}_i^{-1}\right]_{t,t} + \frac{\left(\left[\boldsymbol{\Sigma}_i^{-1}\boldsymbol{y}_{i,1:N}^{\top}\right]_t\right)^2}{\left[\boldsymbol{\Sigma}_i^{-1}\right]_{t,t}}\right\}.
\end{aligned}
\tag{20}
$$

The gradient of (20) w.r.t $w_{k,l}$ is calculated by

$$
\begin{aligned}
\frac{\partial \mathcal{L}_{LOO}}{\partial w_{k,l}} &= -\mathrm{tr}\left\{\boldsymbol{W}^{-1}\frac{\partial \boldsymbol{W}}{\partial w_{k,l}}\right\} \\
&\quad + \frac{1}{2N}\sum_{i=1}^{n}\sum_{t=1}^{N}\frac{\delta_{i,k}}{\left[\boldsymbol{\Sigma}_i^{-1}\right]_{t,t}}\left\{[\boldsymbol{\alpha}_i]_t\left(2\left[\boldsymbol{\Sigma}_i^{-1}\boldsymbol{x}_{l,1:N}^{\top} - \boldsymbol{Z}_i^{kl}\boldsymbol{\alpha}_i\right]_t\right)\right. \\
&\quad \left. + \left(1 + \frac{[\boldsymbol{\alpha}_i]_t^2}{\left[\boldsymbol{\Sigma}_i^{-1}\right]_{t,t}}\right)\left[\boldsymbol{Z}_i^{kl}\boldsymbol{\Sigma}_i^{-1}\right]_{t,t}\right\}.
\end{aligned}
\tag{21}
$$

The derivative (21) is easily derived based on the derivative of the log of LOO predictive distribution for single regression problem (see Chap. 5 in [10]). Throughout this paper, we refer to source separation methods based on the minimization of (16) and (20) as GPSS-ML and GPSS-LOO, respectively.

4 Implementation Issues

Our loss function (16) or (20) involves the matrix inversion ($\boldsymbol{\Sigma}_i^{-1}$), which requires high computational complexity and is often numerically unstable. As in kernel methods, we use Cholesky decomposition instead of the direct inversion of $\boldsymbol{\Sigma}_i$. For example, in (17), $\boldsymbol{\alpha}_i$ is calculated by solving the following linear systems

$$\left(\boldsymbol{L}_i \boldsymbol{L}_i^\top\right) \boldsymbol{\alpha}_i = \boldsymbol{y}_{i,1:N}^\top,$$

where $\boldsymbol{L}_i$ be the lower-triangular matrix in the Cholesky decomposition of $\boldsymbol{\Sigma}_i$. Furthermore, the log of the determinant of $\boldsymbol{\Sigma}_i$ is easily calculated through

$$\log|\det \boldsymbol{\Sigma}_i| = 2\sum_{t=1}^{N} \log\left[\boldsymbol{L}_i\right]_{t,t}.$$

A widely-used method to approximate the kernel matrix$\boldsymbol{K}_i$ is the *Nyström* method where we choose $M < N$ landmark points and use only the information in $M \times M$ submatrix $\boldsymbol{K}^{M,M}$ and $N \times M$ submatrix $\boldsymbol{K}^{N,M}$ to extrapolate elements in $\boldsymbol{K}^{N-M,N-M}$. The Nyström approximation of $\boldsymbol{K}_i$ [13], denoted by $\widetilde{\boldsymbol{K}}_i$, takes the form

$$\widetilde{\boldsymbol{K}}_i = \boldsymbol{K}_i^{N,M}(\boldsymbol{K}_i^{M,M})^{-1}\boldsymbol{K}_i^{M,N}. \tag{22}$$

In addition, other approximation methods include subset of regressor (SoR) [14], projected process (PP) [15,10], and sparse Gaussian process (SGP) using pseudo-input [16]. A unifying view of such approximation methods is given in [17]. In this paper we only consider the marginal likelihood of $\boldsymbol{y}_{i,1:N}^\top$ (the LOO predictive distribution is not considered in approximation methods). In our case, all those approximation methods (SoR, PP, SGP, Nyström) lead to the same approximation of the marginal likelihood that is of the form

$$\begin{aligned}\log \widetilde{p}(\boldsymbol{y}_{i,1:N}|\mathcal{Y}_i) = &-\frac{1}{2}\log|\det(\widetilde{\boldsymbol{K}}_i + \boldsymbol{\Lambda}_i)| \\ &-\frac{1}{2}\boldsymbol{y}_{i,1:N}(\widetilde{\boldsymbol{K}}_i + \boldsymbol{\Lambda}_i)^{-1}\boldsymbol{y}_{i,1:N}^\top - \frac{N}{2}\log 2\pi,\end{aligned} \tag{23}$$

where $\widetilde{\boldsymbol{K}}_i$ is the approximation of $\boldsymbol{K}_i$, given in (22). Depending on approximation methods, only $\boldsymbol{\Lambda}_i$ is different. In the case of SoR, PP and Nyström, we use $\boldsymbol{\Lambda}_i = \boldsymbol{I}_N$. For SGP, $\boldsymbol{\Lambda}_i = \mathrm{diag}(\boldsymbol{K}_i - \widetilde{\boldsymbol{K}}_i) + \boldsymbol{I}_N$ for SGP. Plugging (23) into the loss function (16) leads to two different approximations: (1) GPSS-ML-Nyström (where SoR, PP, or Nyström is used for approximation); (2) GPSS-ML-SGP.

With a low-rank approximation where $\boldsymbol{K}_i \approx \widetilde{\boldsymbol{K}}_i = \boldsymbol{Q}\boldsymbol{Q}^\top$ (for instance, in Nyström method, $\boldsymbol{Q} = \boldsymbol{K}_i^{N,M}(\boldsymbol{K}_i^{M,M})^{-\frac{1}{2}}$ where $\boldsymbol{Q} \in \mathbb{R}^{N\times M}$ and $M \ll N$), the following relations are useful in saving computational load:

$$(\widetilde{\boldsymbol{K}}_i + \boldsymbol{I}_N)^{-1} = \boldsymbol{I}_N - \boldsymbol{Q}\left(\boldsymbol{I}_M + \boldsymbol{Q}^\top\boldsymbol{Q}\right)^{-1}\boldsymbol{Q}^\top, \tag{24}$$

$$\det\left(\widetilde{\boldsymbol{K}}_i + \boldsymbol{I}_N\right) = \det\left(\boldsymbol{I}_M + \boldsymbol{Q}^\top\boldsymbol{Q}\right), \tag{25}$$

where calculations are done with lower dimension M.

5 Numerical Experiments

We present three empirical results with comparison to FastICA, Infomax, and SOBI, in cases where: (1) sources are nonlinear time series; (2) sources have similar spectra; (3) sources do not match the model assumptions. In all experiments, we evaluate the performance of algorithms considered here using the following performance index (PI)

$$\mathrm{PI} = \frac{1}{n}\sum_{i=1}^{n}\left\{\left(\sum_{k=1}^{n}\frac{|g_{i,k}|^2}{\max_j |g_{i,j}|^2}-1\right)+\left(\sum_{k=1}^{n}\frac{|g_{k,i}|^2}{\max_j |g_{j,i}|^2}-1\right)\right\}, \quad (26)$$

where $g_{i,j}$ is the (i,j)-element of the global transformation $\boldsymbol{G} = \boldsymbol{W}\boldsymbol{A}$. When perfect separation is achieved, PI=0. In practice, PI < 0.005 gives good performance. We conduct 20 independent runs for each algorithm with different initial conditions and report the statistical quantity of PI, i.e., box-plot of PI of each method and the average of value of PI. For SOBI, we use 10 different time-delayed correlation matrices to estimate the demixing matrix.

5.1 Experiment 1

We use two nonlinear time series as sources to generate $\boldsymbol{x}_t$. One source is *Santa Fe* competition laser and the other source is *Mackey-Glass* MG_{30}. In this case, our method and SOBI successfully achieve separation, while FastICA and Infomax have difficulty in separating out those two nonlinear time series (see Fig. 1).

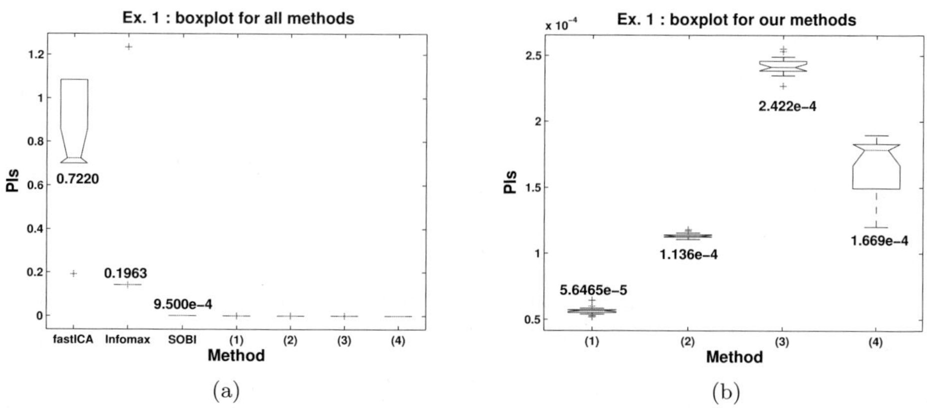

Fig. 1. Box plots of PIs (over 20 independent runs) are shown in (a), for methods which include FastICA, Infomax, SOBI, GPSS-ML (1), GPSS-LOO (2), GPSS-ML-Nyström (3), and GPSS-ML-SPR (4). PIs of only our methods, (1)-(4), are shown in (b), over a smaller dynamic range. In the case of GPSS-ML-Nyström and GPSS-ML-SPR, $M = N/10$.

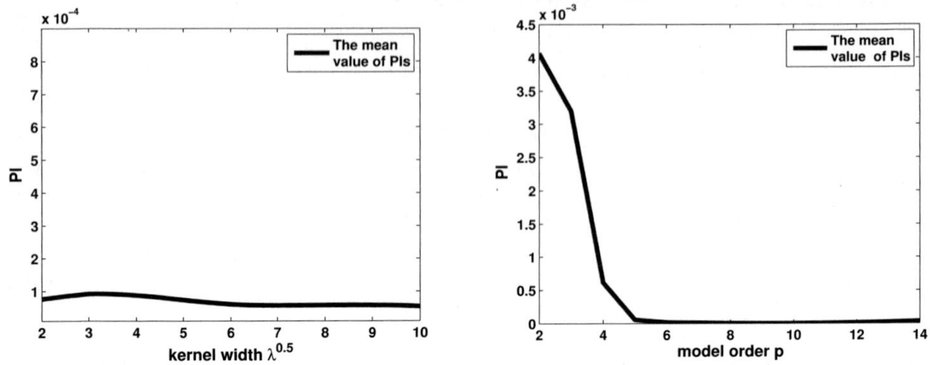

Fig. 2. The performance (in terms of PI) behavior of GPSS-ML in Experiment 1 is shown, with respect to: (a) square root of the length scale hyperparameter λ (with $p = 5$ fixed); (b) model order p (with $\lambda = 50$ fixed)

In principle, length-scale hyperparameters $\{\lambda_i\}$ can also be learned. However, pre-specified values of hyperparameters provide satisfactory results as well. Exemplary empirical result is shown in Fig. 2 (a) where PI of our method is evaluated with respect to $\lambda = \lambda_1 = \cdots = \lambda_n$ varying over$[4, 100]$. The model order p determines how many past samples of source are used to calculate the covariance function. Fig. 2 (b) shows the PI of our method with respect to different values of p, where $p \geq 5$ gives quite a good performance. In the rest of experiments, we use $\lambda = 50$ and $p = 5$.

5.2 Experiment 2

We use two independent colored Gaussian sources and one music signal whose distribution is close to Gaussian to generate the observation data. Two colored Gaussian sources are generated by AR models, the coefficients of which, $\boldsymbol{h}_i \triangleq \{h_{i,\tau}\}$, are given by

$$\boldsymbol{h}_1 = \{1.3117, -0.8664, 0.5166, -0.2534\},$$
$$\boldsymbol{h}_2 = \{0.7838, 0.3988, -0.4334, -0.1792\}.$$

Certainly FastICA and Infomax do not work in this case, since sources are Gaussian. With randomly generated Gaussian innovation sequences, we chose the case where power spectra of two colored Gaussian sources are similar each other (see Fig. 3). In such a case, the performance of SOBI degrades, while our method still retains satisfactory performance (see Fig. 4-(a)). In this experiment we set $M = N/6$.

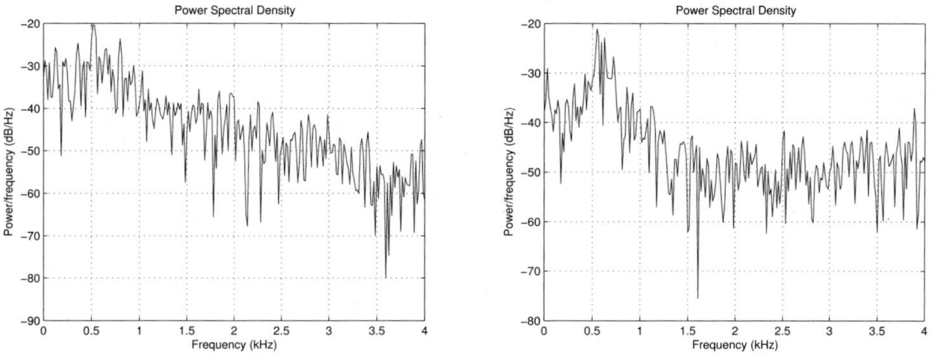

Fig. 3. Power spectrum of two synthetic colore Gaussian sources used in Experiment 2

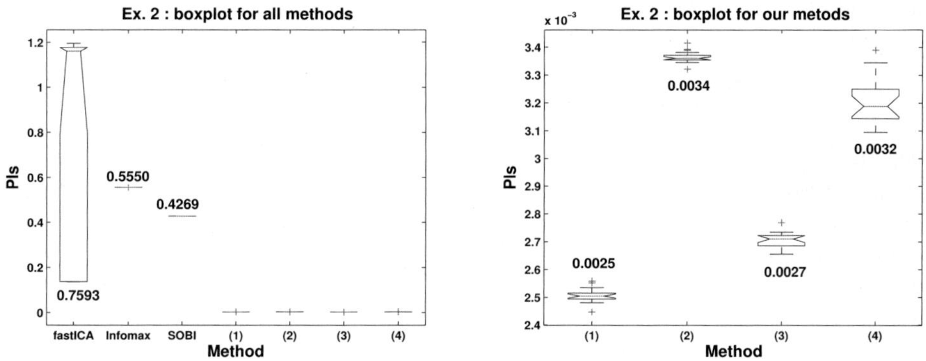

(a) (b)

Fig. 4. The box-plots of PIs are shown in the case of Experiment 2, where (1) GPSS-ML, (2) GPSS-LOO, (3) GPSS-ML-Nyström, (4) GPSS-ML-SPR

5.3 Experiment 3

Fig. 2 (b) shows that the performance of our methods (GPSS-ML and GPSS-LOO) does not vary much in the case for overestimating p. In Experiment 3, we consider the case where we underestimate the model order p which determines how many past samples are taken into account in calculating the covariance matrix. We generate two synthetic colored Gaussian sources using linear AR models of order 20 (see Fig. 5 (a)). The case for underestimating p can be viewed as a model mis-specification. GPSS-ML and GPSS-LOO are compared in this case where $p = 5$ is used in computing $\boldsymbol{K}_i$. The marginal likelihood represents the probability of a source given the assumption of the model. In contrast, the LOO value given an estimate for the predictive distribution whether or not the assumptions of the model may be fulfilled. In this sense Wahba has

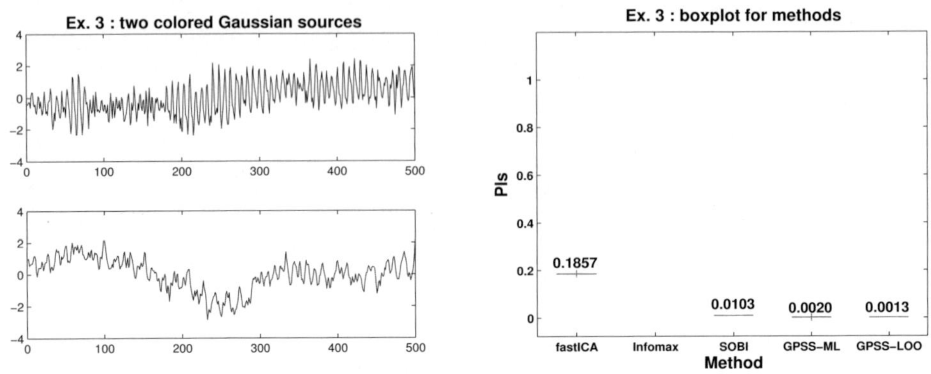

(a) (b)

Fig. 5. Two colored Gaussian sources generated by AR models of order 20, are shown in (a). Performance comparison is shown in (b) in the case where we underestimate the model order p in our GPSS-ML and GPSS-LOO ($p = 5$ is used). In (b), the result of Infomax is omitted since its mean value of PIs is greater than 1.

argued that the LOO-based method should be more robust against the model mis-specification [12]. In our experiment, GPSS-LOO gives slightly better performance than GPSS-ML (see Fig. 5 (b)), although the performance difference is negligible.

6 Conclusions

We have presented methods of source separation where we use GPs to model the temporal structure of sources and learn the demixing matrix through the mutual information minimization. The marginal likelihood of source or the LOO predictive distribution was used to model the probability distribution of source, leading to two different source separation algorithms (GPSS-ML and GPSS-LOO). Approximation methods (such as Nyström and SGP) were also used, leading to GPSS-ML-Nyström and GPSS-ML-SGP. Compared to source separation methods where a parametric method (e.g., AR model) was used to model the temporal structure of sources, our method is more flexible in the sense that: (1) sources are allowed to be nonlinear time series; (2) it is not sensitive to the model order mismatch. Compared to SOBI, our method successfully worked even in the case where sources have similar power spectra. The computational scalability in our current method is not as good as existing methods. Although we have applied several approximation methods for marginal likelihood, our method is limited to large scale data yet. This is the main drawback to be further studied, possibly adopting sparse approximations [18] that have exploited for kernel machines.

Acknowledgments. This work was supported by Korea MCIE under Brain Neuroinformatics Program and by KOSEF Basic Research Program (grant R01-2006-000-11142-0).

References

1. Cichocki, A., Amari, S.: Adaptive Blind Signal and Image Processing: Learning Algorithms and Applications. John Wiley & Sons, Inc., Chichester (2002)
2. Bell, A., Sejnowski, T.: An information maximisation approach to blind separation and blind deconvolution. Neural Computation 7, 1129–1159 (1995)
3. Hyvärinen, A., Oja, E.: A fast fixed-point algorithm for independent component analysis. Neural Computation 9, 1483–1492 (1997)
4. Amari, S., Cardoso, J.F.: Blind source separation: Semiparametric statistical approach. IEEE Trans. Signal Processing 45, 2692–2700 (1997)
5. Belouchrani, A., Abed-Merain, K., Cardoso, J.F., Moulines, E.: A blind source separation technique using second order statistics. IEEE Trans. Signal Processing 45, 434–444 (1997)
6. Pearlmutter, B., Parra, L.: A context-sensitve generalization of ICA. In: Proceedings of International Conference on Neural Information Processing, pp. 151–157 (1996)
7. Attias, H., Schreiner, C.E.: Blind source separation and deconvolution: The dynamic component analysis algorithms. Neural Computation 10, 1373–1424 (1998)
8. Cheung, Y.M.: Dual auto-regressive modelling approach to Gaussian process identification. In: Proceedings of IEEE International Conference on Multimedia and Expo., pp. 1256–1259. IEEE Computer Society Press, Los Alamitos (2001)
9. Seeger, M.: Gaussian processes for machine learning. International Journal of Neural Systems 14, 69–106 (2004)
10. Rasmussen, C.E., Williams, C.K.I.: Gaussian Processes for Machine Learning. MIT Press, Cambridge (2006)
11. Besag, J.: Statistical analysis of non-lattice data. The Statistician 24(3), 179–195 (1975)
12. Wahba, G.: Spline Models for Observational Data. SIAM [Society for Industrial and Applied Mathematics] (1990)
13. Williams, C.K.I., Seeger, M.: Using the Nyström method to speed up kernel machines. In: Advances in Neural Information Processing Systems, vol. 13, MIT Press, Cambridge (2001)
14. Silverman, B.W.: Some aspects of the spline smoothing approach to non-parametric regression curve fitting. Journal of the Royal Statistical Society 47, 1–52 (1985)
15. Seeger, M., Williams, C.K.I., Lawrence, N.D.: Fast forward selection to speed up sparse Gaussian process regression. In: Proceedings of International Workshop on Artificial Intelligence and Statistics (2003)
16. Snelson, E., Ghahramani, Z.: Sparse Gaussian processes using pseudo-inputs. In: Advances in Neural Information Processing Systems, vol. 18, MIT Press, Cambridge (2006)
17. Quiñonero-Candela, J., Rasmussen, C.E.: A unifying view of sparse approximate Gaussian process regression. Journal of Machine Learning Research 6, 1939–1959 (2005)
18. Csató, L., Opper, M.: Sparse on-line Gaussian processes. Neural Computation 14, 641–668 (2002)

Discriminative Sequence Labeling by Z-Score Optimization

Elisa Ricci[1], Tijl de Bie[2], and Nello Cristianini[2,3]

[1] Dept. of Electronic and Information Engineering, University of Perugia, 06125, Perugia, Italy
elisa.ricci@diei.unipg.it
[2] Dept. of Engineering Mathematics, University of Bristol, Bristol, BS8 1TR, UK
tijl.debie@gmail.com
[3] Dept. of Computer Science, University of Bristol, Bristol, BS8 1TR, UK
nello@support-vector.net

Abstract. We consider a new discriminative learning approach to sequence labeling based on the statistical concept of the Z-score. Given a training set of pairs of hidden-observed sequences, the task is to determine some parameter values such that the hidden labels can be correctly reconstructed from observations. Maximizing the Z-score appears to be a very good criterion to solve this problem both theoretically and empirically. We show that the Z-score is a convex function of the parameters and it can be efficiently computed with dynamic programming methods. In addition to that, the maximization step turns out to be solvable by a simple linear system of equations. Experiments on artificial and real data demonstrate that our approach is very competitive both in terms of speed and accuracy with respect to previous algorithms.

1 Introduction

Sequence labeling is one of the most important tasks in many applications, such as in part-of-speech tagging or named entity recognition (NER) in the Natural Language Processing (NLP) field, and gene finding or protein homology detection in bioinformatics. This task represents a generalization of the standard classification problem since prediction is made not only to a single hidden variable, but to a sequence of mutually dependent hidden variables (the labels). Traditionally, Hidden Markov Models (HMMs) have been used for sequence labeling. The HMM conditional probabilities are trained using the maximum likelihood criterium, after which the HMM can be used for prediction by means of the Viterbi algorithm. However, the HMM approach is arguably suboptimal for this task, as it is designed for modeling, rather than for discrimination.

In the last few years, a number of discriminative methods have been proposed to improve the performance achieved by generative HMM based sequence labeling. Recently studied methods include Maximum Entropy Markov Models [6], Conditional Random Fields (CRFs) [5], Hidden Markov Perceptron (HMP) [3], boosting-based algorithms [1] and Maximal Margin (MM) methods [2,7].

J.N. Kok et al. (Eds.): ECML 2007, LNAI 4701, pp. 274–285, 2007.

In particular MM algorithms have been shown to provide accurate labeling (see [2] for a comparison between different methods). These methods rely on the definition of a linear score function for observed-hidden sequence pairs. Parameter estimation is performed by imposing that for each observed sequence in the training set, the score of the pair with the correct given hidden sequence should be bigger than the score of all other possible hidden sequences. These conditions can be simply specified by a set of linear constraints. Subject to these constraints, the squared norm of the parameters is minimized, which guarantees that the minimal difference between the score of the correct pair and the closest runner-up is maximal. Clearly, a direct implementation of this strategy would be totally infeasible, as the number of possible hidden sequences associated to an observed one (and hence the number of constraints) is exponential in the length of the sequences. Altun *et al.* [2] have attacked this problem by adding constraints incrementally. With this approach, for each constraint to be added a Viterbi decoding needs to be performed, so it quickly becomes expensive for long sequences and large training sets. In [8] the number of added constraints is demonstrated to increase polynomially with the length of the sequences. An exponential number of constraints is required also by the algorithm proposed by Collins [4]. In [7] a different strategy is applied where the optimization problem is reparameterized in terms of marginal variables but a certain number of constraints (scaling linearly with the length of the sequences) is still required.

Since in practical applications data are often nonseparable, in MM methods slack variables (one for each training pair) are introduced to allow some constraints to be violated. With this approach the number of incorrectly reconstructed sequences is minimized. However in these cases, choosing other optimization criteria could be desirable. To this aim, in this paper, we approach the problem from a different perspective. We consider the full distribution of the scores for all possible observed-hidden sequence pairs and we compute the mean and the variance of this distribution as a function of the parameters. Then, we maximize the Z-score of the correct observed-hidden sequence pairs subject to the parameters, where the Z-score is defined as the number of standard deviations the score is away from its mean. In this way, the number of incorrect pairs which scores higher than the optimal ones is minimized. Moreover the score of the correct pair is optimally separated from the bulk of all possible scores without considering each of these separately. A crucial observation enabling this strategy is that the Z-score of any fixed pair can be computed exactly and efficiently as a function of the parameters. This is done by means of a dynamic program analogous to the classical forward algorithm for HMMs. Additionally, we show that the Z-score is a convex function of the scoring parameters, and consequently it can be maximized exactly by simply solving a linear system.

2 Hidden Markov Models

We define a state alphabet set $\Sigma_y = \{Y_1 \ \dots \ Y_{n_s}\}$ and an observation alphabet set $\Sigma_x = \{X_1 \ \dots \ X_{n_o}\}$ and we consider an observed sequence

$\mathbf{x} = (x_1, x_2, ..., x_m)$, $\mathbf{x} \in \mathcal{X} = \Sigma_x{}^m$ and the corresponding hidden sequence $\mathbf{y} = (y_1, y_2, ..., y_m)$, $\mathbf{y} \in \mathcal{Y} = \Sigma_y{}^m$. Formally an HMM is an object (E, T). The emission matrix E stores the probability of observation i being produced from the state j, i.e. it is an $n_o \times n_s$ matrix with elements $e_{ij} = \log P(X_i|Y_j)$, $1 \leq i \leq n_o$, $1 \leq j \leq n_s$. The transition matrix T is the matrix with elements $t_{ij} = \log P(Y_i|Y_j)$, $1 \leq i, j \leq n_s$. The probability of a given observed-hidden sequence pair can be computed as:

$$s(\mathbf{x}, \mathbf{y}) = \sum_{k=1}^{m} (\log P(y_k|y_{k-1}) + \log P(x_k|y_k))$$

Defining $\psi_{kk-1}^{ij} = \log P(y_k = Y_i|y_{k-1} = Y_j)$ and $\psi_k^{ij} = \log P(x_k = X_i|y_k = Y_j)$, the scoring function can be rewritten as:

$$s(\mathbf{x}, \mathbf{y}) = \sum_{k=1}^{m} (\sum_{i,j=1}^{n_s} \psi_{kk-1}^{ij} I_{kk-1}^{ij} + \sum_{i=1}^{n_o} \sum_{j=1}^{n_s} \psi_k^{ij} I_k^{ij}) = \sum_{i,j=1}^{n_s} t_{ij} C_t^{ij} + \sum_{i=1}^{n_o} \sum_{j=1}^{n_s} e_{ij} C_e^{ij}$$

where I_{kk-1}^{ij} is equal to 1 if the k-th hidden label is Y_i and the $(k-1)$-th label is Y_j and analogously $I_k^{ij} = 1$ means that the k-th observation is X_i and the associated label is Y_j. Therefore $C_t^{ij} = \#(y_k = Y_i|y_{k-1} = Y_j)$ and $C_e^{ij} = \#(x_k = X_i|y_k = Y_j)$ count the number of each of the possible transitions and emissions.

For notational convenience, define the vector of parameters $\boldsymbol{\theta} \in R^d$, $\boldsymbol{\theta} = [e_{11} \cdots e_{n_o n_s} t_{11} \cdots t_{n_s n_s}]^T$, with $d = n_s n_o + n_s n_s$. Correspondingly, for a given pair of observed and hidden sequences $(\mathbf{x},\mathbf{y})$ define a vector $\boldsymbol{\phi}(\mathbf{x}, \mathbf{y}) = [C_e^{11} \cdots C_e^{n_o n_s} C_t^{11} \cdots C_t^{n_s n_s}]^T \in R^d$ containing the sufficient statistics associated to each parameter. Then we can express the scoring function $s(\mathbf{x}, \mathbf{y})$ as a linear function of the parameters $\boldsymbol{\theta}$:

$$s(\mathbf{x}, \mathbf{y}) = \boldsymbol{\theta}^T \boldsymbol{\phi}(\mathbf{x}, \mathbf{y})$$

We call $s(\mathbf{x}, \mathbf{y})$ the *score* associated to the observed-hidden sequence pair $(\mathbf{x},\mathbf{y})$.

Once the parameters are fixed, the actual labeling task predicts the hidden state sequence $\bar{\mathbf{y}}$ that is most likely in conjunction with the given observation sequence $\mathbf{x}$. Hence, labeling is done by solving $h(\mathbf{x}) = \arg\max_{\mathbf{y}} s(\mathbf{x}, \mathbf{y})$. A brute force calculation of $h(\mathbf{x})$ is intractable for realistic problems, as the number N of possible assignments in $\mathcal{Y}$ is exponential in the length of the sequences m. However such prediction can be done efficiently by the Viterbi algorithm. In the following the score of the optimal pair will be denoted by $s(\mathbf{x}, \bar{\mathbf{y}})$.

3 The Z-Score

Given $\mathbf{x}$, we can consider the mean values $\mu(\mathbf{x})$ of the scores of all possible N hidden sequences $\mathbf{y}_j$ and show that it is also a linear function:

$$\mu(\mathbf{x}) = \frac{1}{N} \sum_{j=1}^{N} \boldsymbol{\theta}^T \boldsymbol{\phi}(\mathbf{x}, \mathbf{y}_j) = \boldsymbol{\theta}^T \boldsymbol{\mu}_{\phi}$$

where $\boldsymbol{\mu}_{\boldsymbol{\phi}} = [\mu_1 \dots \mu_d]^T$ is the vector with components given by the average values of the components of $\boldsymbol{\phi}(\mathbf{x}, \mathbf{y}_j)$. Similarly, for the variance $\sigma^2(\mathbf{x})$ we have:

$$\sigma^2(\mathbf{x}) = \frac{1}{N}\sum_{j=1}^{N}(\boldsymbol{\theta}^T\boldsymbol{\phi}(\mathbf{x}, \mathbf{y}_j) - \mu(\mathbf{x}))^2 = \boldsymbol{\theta}^T\boldsymbol{C}\boldsymbol{\theta}$$

The matrix $\boldsymbol{C}$ is a covariance matrix with elements:

$$c_{pq} = \frac{1}{N}\sum_{j=1}^{N}\phi_p(\mathbf{x}, \mathbf{y}_j)\phi_q(\mathbf{x}, \mathbf{y}_j) - \mu_p\mu_q = v_{pq} - \mu_p\mu_q \tag{1}$$

where $1 \leq p, q \leq d$. Based on this mean and variance, expressed in terms of the parameters $\boldsymbol{\theta}$, we can now define the Z-score parameterized by $\boldsymbol{\theta}$:

Definition 1. *Let $\mu(\boldsymbol{x})$ and $\sigma^2(\boldsymbol{x})$ be the mean and the variance of the scores for all possible hidden sequences generating $\boldsymbol{x}$. We define the Z-score $Z(\boldsymbol{x})$:*

$$Z(\boldsymbol{x}) = \frac{s(\boldsymbol{x}, \bar{\boldsymbol{y}}) - \mu(\boldsymbol{x})}{\sigma(\boldsymbol{x})} = \frac{\boldsymbol{\theta}^T\boldsymbol{b}}{\sqrt{\boldsymbol{\theta}^T\boldsymbol{C}\boldsymbol{\theta}}} \tag{2}$$

where the right expression is obtained with $\boldsymbol{b} = \boldsymbol{\phi}(\boldsymbol{x}, \bar{\boldsymbol{y}}) - \boldsymbol{\mu}_{\boldsymbol{\phi}}$.

In general, we are interested in computing the Z-score for a set of ℓ pairs of sequences $S = \{(\mathbf{x}_1, \bar{\mathbf{y}}_1)(\mathbf{x}_2, \bar{\mathbf{y}}_2) \dots (\mathbf{x}_\ell, \bar{\mathbf{y}}_\ell)\}$. In such cases, we can define the global score as the sum of the scores for each sequence pair in the set. Its mean is the sum of the means for all sequence pairs $(\mathbf{x}_i, \mathbf{y}_i)$ separately, and can be summarized by $\boldsymbol{b}^* = \sum_i \boldsymbol{b}_i$. Similarly, the covariance of the sum of (independent) scores is the sum of the covariances: $\boldsymbol{C}^* = \sum_i \boldsymbol{C}_i$. Hence, the Z-score can be extended to the case where there is more than one given sequence pair by using for $\boldsymbol{b}^*$ and $\boldsymbol{C}^*$ instead of $\boldsymbol{b}$ and $\boldsymbol{C}$ in Eqn. 2 above.

We will now proceed to show that $\boldsymbol{C}^*$ and $\boldsymbol{b}^*$ can be computed efficiently. Then we will show that based on these the Z-score can be maximized efficiently, and that it represents a theoretically and empirically interesting criterium for discriminative sequence labeling.

4 Computing the Z-Score as a Function of the Parameters

In this section we show how the elements of $\boldsymbol{b}$ and $\boldsymbol{C}$ can be computed exactly and efficiently by dynamic programming (DP) routines. Therefore the Z-score can be fully determined, as a function of the parameter vector $\boldsymbol{\theta}$.

Proposition 1. *Each element of the vector $\boldsymbol{b}$ and of the matrix $\boldsymbol{C}$ can be computed in a time $O(mn_s^2)$.*

Algorithm 1. Dynamic programming algorithm to compute $\mu_k,\ 1 \le k \le n_s n_o$

Input: $\mathbf{x} = (x_1, x_2, ..., x_m)$, p, q.

$\pi(i,1) := 1 \quad \forall i$
if $q = x_1 \wedge p = i$, $\mu^e_{pq}(i,1) := 1$
for $j = 2$ **to** m
  for $i = 1$ **to** n_s
    $M := 0$
    $\pi(i,j) := \sum_i \pi(i, j-1)$
    if $q = x_j \wedge p = i$, $M := 1$
    $\mu^e_{pq}(i,j) := \frac{\sum_i (\mu^e_{pq}(i,j-1)+M)\pi(i,j-1)}{\pi(i,j)}$
  end
end

Output: $\frac{\sum_i \mu^e_{pq}(i,m)}{\sum_i \pi(i,m)}$

Outline of proof. We consider a pair of observed-hidden sequences $(\mathbf{x}, \bar{\mathbf{y}})$. The vector $\boldsymbol{b}$ is given by $\boldsymbol{b} = \boldsymbol{\phi}(\mathbf{x}, \bar{\mathbf{y}}) - \boldsymbol{\mu}_{\boldsymbol{\phi}}$. The first term can be calculated computing the statistics associated to each parameter.

The elements of the vector $\boldsymbol{\mu}_{\boldsymbol{\phi}}$ can be obtained with DP routines. We construct the vector $\boldsymbol{\mu}_{\boldsymbol{\phi}}$ such that its first $n_s n_o$ elements contain the mean values associated with the emission probabilities. Each value can be determined by Algorithm 1. Here a $n_s \times m$ DP table μ^e_{pq} is considered and initialized to zero values. The index p denotes the hidden state $(1 \le p \le n_s)$ and q refers to the observation $(1 \le q \le n_o)$. For example the first component of $\boldsymbol{\mu}_{\boldsymbol{\phi}}$ corresponds to the DP matrix μ^e_{11}. First a $n_s \times m$ matrix $\boldsymbol{\pi}$ is progressively filled. Each cell $\pi(i,j)$ contains the number of all possible paths from the origin of the trellis to position (i,j). Then a recursive relation is considered to compute each element of the matrix μ^e_{pq}. Further details are shown in Algorithm 1.

A similar algorithm is adopted to compute the mean values for the transition probabilities. A DP matrix μ^t_{pz} is filled, where $1 \le p, z \le n_s$. The only difference is the recursive formula that can be found in Algorithm 2.

Analogously the elements of the covariance matrix $\boldsymbol{C}$ can be computed. We have five sets of values: variances of emission probabilities $(c^e_{pq},\ 1 \le p \le n_s, 1 \le q \le n_o)$, variances of transition probabilities $(c^t_{pz},\ 1 \le p, z \le n_s)$, covariances of emission probabilities $(c^e_{pqp'q'},\ 1 \le p, p' \le n_s, 1 \le q, q' \le n_o)$, covariances of transition probabilities $(c^t_{pzp'z'},\ 1 \le p, p', z, z' \le n_s)$ and mixed covariances $(c^{et}_{pqp'z},\ 1 \le p, p', z \le n_s, 1 \le q \le n_o)$. To determine each of them we consider Eqn. 1. It suffices to calculate the values v_{pq} since the mean values are already known. The computation of v_{pq} is again performed following Algorithm 1 but with recursive relations given in Algorithm 2.

Computational Cost Analysis. In general the calculation of the matrices $\boldsymbol{b}$ and $\boldsymbol{C}$ requires running a DP algorithm like Algorithm 1 respectively d times for mean values and d^2 times for the covariance matrix. Hence the overall

Algorithm 2. Extra formulas for computing mean and variance values

9: **if** $z = i,\ M := 1$

10: $\mu^t_{pz}(i,j) := \frac{\sum_i \mu^t_{pz}(i,j-1)\pi(i,j-1)+M\pi(p,j-1)}{\pi(i,j)}$

4: **if** $q = x_1\ \wedge\ p = i,\ v^e_{pq}(i,1) := 1$

9: **if** $q = x_j\ \wedge\ p = i,\ M := 1$

10: $v^e_{pq}(i,j) := \frac{\sum_i (v^e_{pq}(i,j-1)+2M\mu^e_{pq}(i,j-1)+M)\pi(i,j-1)}{\pi(i,j)}$

9: **if** $q' = x_j\ \wedge\ p' = i,\ M_1 := 1$

if $q = x_j\ \wedge\ p = i,\ M_2 := 1$

10: $v^e_{pqp'q'}(i,j) := \frac{\sum_i (v^e_{pqp'q'}(i,j-1)+M_1\mu^e_{pq}(i,j-1)+M_2\mu^e_{p'q'}(i,j-1))\pi(i,j-1)}{\pi(i,j)}$

4: **if** $p = i,\ v^t_{pz}(i,2) = 1$

9: **if** $p = i,\ M := 1$

10: $v^t_{pz}(i,j) := \frac{\sum_i v^t_{pz}(i,j-1)\pi(i,j-1)+(2M\mu^t_{pz}(p,j-1)+M)\pi(p,j-1)}{\pi(i,j)}$

9: **if** $p' = j,\ M_1 := 1$

if $p = j,\ M_2 := 1$

10: $v^t_{pzp'z'}(i,j) := \frac{\sum_i v^t_{pzp'z'}(i,j-1)\pi(i,j-1)+M_1\mu^t_{pz}(p',j-1)\pi(p',j-1)+M_2\mu^t_{p'z'}(p,j-1)\pi(p,j-1)}{\pi(i,j)}$

9: **if** $z' = i,\ M_1 := 1$

if $q = x_j\ \wedge\ p = i,\ M_2 := 1$

10: $v^{et}_{pqp'z}(i,j) := \frac{\sum_i v^{et}_{pqp'z}(i,j-1)\pi(i,j-1)+M_1\mu^e_{pq}(p',j-1)\pi(p',j-1)+M_2\mu^t_{p'z'}(p,j)\pi(p,j)}{\pi(i,j)}$

computational cost considerably increases for large d. However, most of the DP routines are redundant since many cells of $\boldsymbol{b}$ and $\boldsymbol{C}$ have the same values. In particular:

Proposition 2. *The number of dynamic programming routines required to calculate* $\boldsymbol{b}$ *and* $\boldsymbol{C}$ *increases linearly with the size* n_o *of the observation alphabet.*

Outline of proof. In the mean vector $\boldsymbol{\mu}_\phi$ there are $n_o + 1$ different values. All the elements associated to transition probabilities assume the same values while for emission probability $\mu^e_{pq} = \mu^e_{ef}$, $\forall q = f$.

The covariance matrix $\boldsymbol{C}$ is a symmetric block matrix made basically by three components: the block associated to emission probabilities, that of transition probabilities and that relative to mixed terms. To compute it $6n_o+5$ DP routines are required. In the emission part there are $2n_o$ possible different values since $c^e_{pq} = c^e_{ef}$, $\forall q = f$, $c^e_{pqp'q'} = 0$, $\forall q \neq q'$ and $c^e_{pqp'q'} = c^e_{efe'f'}$ $\forall q = q' = f = f'$. In the transition block there are only 5 possible different values. In particular for the variances, it is $c^t_{pz} = c^t_{eg}$, $\forall p = z = e = g$ and $c^t_{pz} = c^t_{eg}$, $\forall p = e$, $z = g$ and $p \neq z$. The other three values are associated to covariances since $c^t_{pzp'z'} = 0$, $\forall p \neq p'$, $z \neq z'$, $c^t_{pzp'z'} = c^t_{ege'g'}$, $\forall p = p'$, $z \neq z'$, $e = e'$, $g \neq g'$ and $c^t_{pzp'z'} = c^t_{ege'g'}$, $\forall p \neq p'$, $z = z'$, $e \neq e'$, $g = g'$. The block relative to mixed terms is made of $4n_o$ possible different value. In fact there are n_o values $c^{et}_{pqp'z}$ with $p = p' = z'$, n_o values $c^{et}_{pqp'z}$, with $p = p'$, $p' \neq z'$, n_o values $c^{et}_{pqp'z}$, with $p = z'$, $p' \neq z'$ and n_o values $c^{et}_{pqp'z}$, with $p \neq p'$, $z \neq z'$.

4.1 Dealing with Arbitrary Features

A nice property of our method is that it can be easily extended to the case of arbitrary features. In general the vector $\phi(\mathbf{x}, \mathbf{y})$ contains not only statistics associated to transition and emission probabilities but also any feature that reflects the properties of the objects represented by the nodes of the HMM. For example in most of the NLP tasks, observations are words and the problem is to assign opportune labels to them. In this case, feature vectors can contain information about the occurrence of a certain word in a sentence as well as about its spelling properties (e.g. if the word is capitalized, if it contains numerical symbols). Sometimes also overlapping features [5] are needed, i.e. features that indicate relations between observations and some previous and future labels. It means that at instant k all the indicator functions I^{ij}_s are considered, with $k - w \leq s \leq k + w$ where w is the size of a window around the k-th observation. In this way it is possible to deal with high order dependencies between labels.

To compute the Z-score in these situations the derivation of appropriate formulas similar to those of μ^e_{pq}, c^e_{pq} and $c^{et}_{pqp'z}$ is straightforward. It suffices to set the values M, M_1 and M_2 equal to 1 when the considered features are active. For example, if $\mathbf{x}$ represents a sequence of words and we want to compute the mean for the feature "*The word is capitalized*", we use Algorithm 1 with the parameter M equal to 1 in correspondence to observation x_i if the first letter of x_i is an upper case latter. Unfortunately the computational cost increases with the number of features since the number of different parameters in the matrix $\boldsymbol{C}^*$ scales quadratically with the observations alphabet size n_o. However we show that in this case approximate algorithms can be used to obtain close estimates of the mean and the variance values with a significantly reduced computational cost. The experiments reported in the last section support this claim.

5 *Z*-Score Optimization

Suppose we have a training set of pairs of observed and hidden sequences $S = \{(\mathbf{x}_1, \bar{\mathbf{y}}_1)(\mathbf{x}_2, \bar{\mathbf{y}}_2) \dots (\mathbf{x}_\ell, \bar{\mathbf{y}}_\ell)\}$. One often considers the task to find the parameter values $\boldsymbol{\theta}$ such that the optimal sequence of hidden states $\bar{\mathbf{y}}_i$ can be reconstructed from $\mathbf{x}_i$, $\forall \;\; 1 \leq i \leq \ell$. In formulas this condition can be expressed as:

$$\boldsymbol{\theta}^T \phi(\mathbf{x}_i, \bar{\mathbf{y}}_i) \geq \boldsymbol{\theta}^T \phi(\mathbf{x}_i, \mathbf{y}_i) \;\; \forall \mathbf{y}_i \neq \bar{\mathbf{y}}_i, \; \forall \, 1 \leq i \leq \ell \tag{3}$$

This set of constraints defines a convex set in the parameter space and its number is exponential in the length of the sequences. To obtain an optimal vector $\boldsymbol{\theta}$ that successfully fulfills (3) an optimization problem can be considered, i.e. a suitable objective function must be chosen. Several choices are possible. For example in

[1,7] a maximal margin solution is considered: between all possible values of $\boldsymbol{\theta}$ such that (3) is verified, they pick the values such that the highest scoring sequence is maximally separated from the others. Interestingly, with this approach, an upper bound on the zero-one error (i.e. on the number of incorrectly reconstructed sequences) is minimized. Similarly CRFs [5] use a conditional likelihood criterion to minimize a different upper bound on this loss.

Here a different philosophy is investigated, which we believe to be more appropriate in the cases where there exists no parameter setting for which the given pairs are optimal. Our purpose is to minimize the number of incorrect pairs that are ranked higher than the correct one. To this aim we choose as objective function the Z-score since we are motivated by statistical reasoning. The Z-score can be regarded as a measure of ranking quality. To give an intuition, a pair of sequences $(\mathbf{x}, \mathbf{y})$ corresponds to a high Z-score if few other pairs have probability of having a higher score. On the other hand, a small Z-score means a low position of the given $(\mathbf{x}, \mathbf{y})$ in the ranking associated with that scoring model. Interestingly, under normality assumptions, this Z-score is directly equivalent to a p-value. Hence, maximizing the Z-score can be interpreted as maximizing the significance of the correct pair score: the larger the Z-score, the more significant it is, or the more different it is from the majority of others pairs. Intriguingly, we can interpret the Z-score maximization as a special case of Fisher's discriminant analysis (FDA), where one class reduces to a single data point: we consider the distribution of all possible scores and contrast this with the 'distribution' of the score for the given training example (which is obviously non-zero only for one value). Therefore learning theory applicable to FDA would be directly translated to our algorithm. (We will not go into this aspect in the present paper).

Following the definition of Z-score given at the end of Section 3, the optimization problem we are interested in is:

$$\max_{\boldsymbol{\theta}} \frac{\boldsymbol{\theta}^T \boldsymbol{b}^*}{\sqrt{\boldsymbol{\theta}^T \boldsymbol{C}^* \boldsymbol{\theta}}} \tag{4}$$

We note that, $\boldsymbol{C}^*$ being a positive semidefinite matrix, the objective function is convex and the problem admits a global solution. We can find the optimal $\boldsymbol{\theta}$ simply by inverting the covariance matrix ($\boldsymbol{\theta} = {\boldsymbol{C}^*}^{-1} \boldsymbol{b}^*$). Alternatively, considering the invariance of the problem to positive rescaling and the monotonicity of the square root, (4) becomes:

$$\begin{aligned} \min_{\boldsymbol{\theta}} \ & \frac{1}{2} \boldsymbol{\theta}^T \boldsymbol{C}^* \boldsymbol{\theta} \\ \text{s.t.} \ & \boldsymbol{\theta}^T \boldsymbol{b}^* \geq 1 \end{aligned} \tag{5}$$

Classical Lagrangian duality enables the primal problem (5) to be transformed into the associated dual, which can be easier to solve for large values of d. It is simple to verify that the dual problem is:

$$\max_{\boldsymbol{\alpha} \geq 0} \ -\frac{1}{2} \boldsymbol{\alpha}^T \boldsymbol{J} \boldsymbol{\alpha} + \boldsymbol{h} \boldsymbol{\alpha} \tag{6}$$

where we have defined $\boldsymbol{J} = \boldsymbol{b}^{*T}\boldsymbol{C}^{*-1}\boldsymbol{b}^*$ and $\boldsymbol{h} = 1$. The solution of the primal is given by $\boldsymbol{\theta} = \boldsymbol{C}^{*-1}\boldsymbol{b}^*\boldsymbol{\alpha}$. The computational cost in the optimization phase is dominated by the inversion of the matrix $\boldsymbol{C}^*$. General matrix inversions usually take $O(d^3)$ time. However since $\boldsymbol{C}^*$ is a symmetric positive definite matrix the use of iterative methods as conjugate gradient greatly speed up the computation.

5.1 Incorporating Hamming Loss Function

Imposing constraints (3) a zero-one loss $\ell_{0/1}(\mathbf{y}, \mathbf{y}') = I(\mathbf{y} \neq \mathbf{y}')$ is implicitly considered: unfortunately $\ell_{0/1}(\mathbf{y}, \mathbf{y}')$ is 1 if the complete sequence is not labeled correctly, both when the entire sequence is wrong and when only one label is predicted incorrectly. A better loss function that discriminates between similar pairs of sequences and very different ones, is the Hamming loss $\ell_H(\mathbf{y}, \mathbf{y}') = \sum_i I(y_i \neq y_i')$. Originally proposed in [7] for MM algorithms it can be also used in our method. For each pair of sequences $(\mathbf{x}, \mathbf{y})$ we consider the score:

$$s(\mathbf{x}, \mathbf{y}) = \boldsymbol{\theta}^T \boldsymbol{\phi}(\mathbf{x}, \mathbf{y}) + \ell_H(\mathbf{y}, \bar{\mathbf{y}}) = \boldsymbol{\theta}'^T \boldsymbol{\phi}'(\mathbf{x}, \mathbf{y})$$

where we define the vectors $\boldsymbol{\theta}'^T = [\boldsymbol{\theta} \;\; 1]^T$ and $\boldsymbol{\phi}'(\mathbf{x}, \mathbf{y})^T = [\boldsymbol{\phi}(\mathbf{x}, \mathbf{y}) \;\; \ell_H(\mathbf{y}, \bar{\mathbf{y}})]^T$. It is easy to verify that the associate Z-score turns out into a dual convex optimization problem with the same form of (6), with $\boldsymbol{h} = 1 - \mu_\ell - \boldsymbol{b}^{*T}\boldsymbol{C}^{*-1}\boldsymbol{c}_\ell$. The optimal vector of parameters in the primal is $\boldsymbol{\theta} = \boldsymbol{C}^{*-1}(\boldsymbol{b}^*\boldsymbol{\alpha} - \boldsymbol{c}_\ell)$, which is used to perform decoding with Viterbi algorithm. Here μ_ℓ represents the mean value of the terms $\ell_H(\mathbf{y}, \bar{\mathbf{y}})$ computed along all possible paths while $\boldsymbol{c}_\ell$ is the vector containing the covariance values between the loss term and all the other parameters. The computation of μ_ℓ and $\boldsymbol{c}_\ell$ is realized with Algorithm 1 and recursive relations similar to those in Algorithm 2. For example the value μ_ℓ is computed with Algorithm 1 with the only difference that at line 11 $M = 1$ if $y_j \neq \bar{y}_j$. It is worth noting that in general every loss function that can be computed by DP can be used in our method.

6 Experimental Results

Artificial Data. In the first series of experiments our method has been tested with artificial data. An HMM with $n_s = 3$, $n_o = 4$ has been considered. The parameters to be determined are the transition and emission probabilities. Sequences with length $m = 10$ have been generated randomly, so that the optimal parameter vector may not exist. In the experiments the size of training set varies while the number of pairs in the test set is fixed to 100. We compared the performance of our approach with CRFs, and the HMP and the MM method in [2] with linear kernel. For the latter and for the Z-score a formulation with a Hamming loss is also considered. For MM algorithms the soft margin parameter C has been set to 0.1 and 1 for the standard and the rescaled margin version respectively, a constant $\epsilon = 10^{-12}$ specifies the accuracy for constraints to be satisfied. The maximum number of iterations of the HMP is $T = 100$. The CRFs have been optimized using a conjugate gradient method. Parameter values have been determined by cross-validation. The performance are evaluated in terms of labeling error on test set (average number of misclassified labels) (Fig 1.a). Results are averaged over 100 runs. The simple Z-score maximization is only slightly outperformed by Z-score and MM methods with Hamming loss which have comparable performance. For the two latter algorithms we also examine the computational cost. Figure 1.b shows, for the same experiment, the training time as function of the training set size: our approach is definitely faster, especially for larger datasets.

We performed similar experiments for different datasets and HMMs and we observed that maximizing the Z-score the performance is comparable or better than MM method for nonseparable data (which is the more common situation with real-life data). In the separable case, we can also impose the constraints (3) with an iterative algorithm similar to that proposed in [2]. In this way labeling accuracy is comparable to MM method but much less constraints are used. We do not report associated simulation results due to lack of space. In terms of computation time our approach is generally much faster.

For very large numbers of parameters, however, the time required to compute $\boldsymbol{b}^*$ and $\boldsymbol{C}^*$ may exceed the computation time of competing MM approaches. However, in this case, good approximations for $\boldsymbol{b}$ and $\boldsymbol{C}$ can be used by considering a randomly sampled subset of paths in the trellis, rather than using DP. Results in Table 6 demonstrate this is a valid approach. Here, sequences of length 100 have been considered, the training and test set sizes are 50 and 100. Various HMM models have been used: the hidden alphabet size is fixed to $n_s = 2$, while n_o varies. The average test error and the computation time are reported for the Z-score method with exact $\boldsymbol{b}$ and $\boldsymbol{C}$, when they are computed on a set of 100 random paths, and for the MM method with Hamming loss.

Named Entity Recognition. NER is a subtask of information extraction which deals with finding phrases containing person, organization and locations

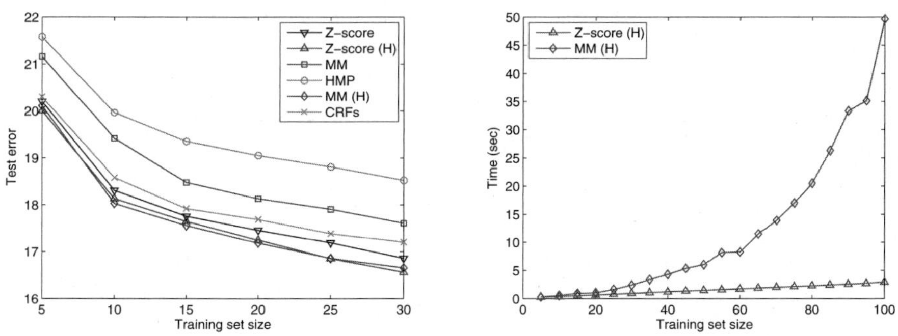

Fig. 1. (a) Average number of uncorrect labels and (b) computational time as function of the training set size for an HMM with $n_s = 3$ and $n_o = 4$

Table 1. Test error. Time (sec) in parenthesis.

n_o	Z-SCORE	Z-SCORE (100)	MM (H)
3	15.82 (0.88)	15.91 (0.43)	15.81 (5.63)
5	10.10 (1.28)	10.13 (0.63)	10.02 (8.29)
7	7.49 (1.80)	7.58 (0.68)	7.22 (10.68)
9	4.99 (2.48)	4.99 (0.69)	4.94 (14.24)
11	4.74 (3.29)	4.78 (0.72)	4.58 (16.03)

names or temporal and numerical expressions. The experimental setup is similar to [2]. We considered 300 sentences extracted from the Spanish news wire article corpus used for the Special Session of CoNLL-2002 on NER. Our subset contains more than 7000 tokens (about 2000 unique) and each sentence has an average length of 30 words. The hidden alphabet is limited to $n_s = 9$ different labels, since the expression types are only persons, organizations, locations and miscellaneous names. We use only a small subset of CoNLL-2002 since our aim here is simply to compare Z-score with previous methods and not to compete with large scale NER systems. We performed experiments with 5-fold crossvalidation and two different sets of binary features: $\mathcal{S}_1$ (HMM features) and $\mathcal{S}_2$ ($\mathcal{S}_1$ and HMM features for the previous and the next word). We compared the performance of our approach with CRFs and with the HMP and the MM method with linear kernel. As for artificial datasets, we also report results for our method and MM with Hamming loss. For MM algorithms the soft margin parameter C has been set to 1, while the required accuracy for constraints to be satisfied is given by $\epsilon = 0.01$. The number of iterations of the HMP is $T = 200$.

The results shown in Table 6 demonstrate the competitiveness of the proposed method. Here the test error is reported. Optimizing the Z-score, we obtain performance very close to MM-methods. Admittedly, since the length of feature vectors is large, our approach results generally slower than the other methods. However experiments have been performed with a naive implementation of our algorithm based on a conjugate gradient method for inverting $\boldsymbol{C}^*$. Perhaps more sophisticated iterative methods exploiting the sparseness of $\boldsymbol{C}^*$ and the use of approximate matrices can speed up the computation. For example the average running times with features $\mathcal{S}_1$ is about 9465.34 sec for Z-score, while the MM approach (SVM-struct implementation [8], $\epsilon = 0.01$) takes 1043.16 sec. However computing $\boldsymbol{b}^*$ and $\boldsymbol{C}^*$ with sampling (150 paths) the time required by Z-score optimization decreases to 607.45 sec.

Table 2. Classification error on test set on NER

	Z-SCORE	Z-SCORE (H)	MM	MM (H)	HMP	CRFs
$\mathcal{S}_1$	11.66	11.07	13.94	10.97	20.99	12.01
$\mathcal{S}_2$	8.01	7.89	9.04	8.11	13.78	8.29

7 Conclusions

In this paper a new discriminative algorithm for sequence labeling has been proposed. The algorithm is fast and easy to implement. It relies on DP to compute the Z-score as a function of the parameters, and a simple linear system to maximize it. Similar to recent discriminative methods, the learning problem is a convex optimization with an objective function that takes into account arbitrary dependencies between input and output labels and penalizes incorrect decoded sequences based on the Hamming distance from the given output. Our approach avoids the need to explicitly consider the exponential number of constraints that arise in this kind of problems and, unlike previous works, naturally and adequately deals with the infeasible case where there exists no parameter setting for which the correct given pairs are optimal. Moreover the proposed algorithm does not rely on any parameter that needs to be tuned with time-consuming procedures as cross-validation. We are currently developing a kernelized version of our algorithm which will enable us to circumvent the computational problems when the size of the features vectors becomes large. A further investigation includes the analysis of approximate algorithms to obtain mean and covariance matrices in order to reduce the computational cost.

Acknowledgments

This work was partially supported by NIH grant R33HG003070-01, and the EU Project SMART.

References

1. Altun, Y., Hofmann, T., Johnson, M.: Discriminative learning for label sequences via boosting. In: Advances in Neural Information Processing Systems (NIPS) (2003)
2. Altun, Y., Tsochantaridis, I., Hofmann, T.: Hidden markov support vector machines. In: 20th International Conference on Machine Learning (ICML) (2003)
3. Collins, M.: Discriminative training methods for hidden markov models: Theory and experiments with perceptron algorithms. In: Proc. Conference on Empirical Methods in Natural Language Processing (EMNLP) (2002)
4. Collins, M.: Parameter estimation for statistical parsing models: Theory and practice of distribution-free methods. In: IWPT (2001)
5. Lafferty, J., Pereira, F., McCallum, A.: Conditional random fields: Probabilistic models for segmenting and labeling sequence data. In: International Conference on Machine Learning (ICML) (2001)
6. McCallum, A., Freitag, D., Pereira, F.: Maximum entropy Markov models for information extraction and segmentation. In: Proceedings of the International Conference on Machine Learning (ICML) (2000)
7. Taskar, B., Guestrin, C., Koller, D.: Max-margin markov networks. In: Neural Information Processing Systems (NIPS) (2003)
8. Tsochantaridis, I., Hofmann, T., Joachims, T., Altun, Y.: Support vector machine learning for interdependent and structured output spaces. In: Proceedings of the International Conference on Machine Learning (ICML) (2004)

Fast Optimization Methods for L1 Regularization: A Comparative Study and Two New Approaches

Mark Schmidt[1], Glenn Fung[2], and Rómer Rosales[2]

[1] Department of Computer Science University of British Columbia
[2] IKM CKS, Siemens Medical Solutions, USA

Abstract. L1 regularization is effective for feature selection, but the resulting optimization is challenging due to the non-differentiability of the 1-norm. In this paper we compare state-of-the-art optimization techniques to solve this problem across several loss functions. Furthermore, we propose two new techniques. The first is based on a smooth (differentiable) convex approximation for the L1 regularizer that does not depend on any assumptions about the loss function used. The other technique is a new strategy that addresses the non-differentiability of the L1-regularizer by casting the problem as a constrained optimization problem that is then solved using a specialized gradient projection method. Extensive comparisons show that our newly proposed approaches consistently rank among the best in terms of convergence speed and efficiency by measuring the number of function evaluations required.

1 Introduction

Parsimonious models are normally preferred over more complex ones. Sparsity, a concept commonly employed to describe model complexity, can be defined in terms of the training examples that are used to define the model (as in Support Vector Machines), or in terms of the covariates (feature selection). In addition to parsimony, feature selection can help prevent overfitting in problems with many input features relative to the amount/variability of the data; see [9,18] for an overview.

The problem of obtaining an optimal subset of features for a linear classifier is known to be NP-hard [18], and is computationally unsolvable in most large applications. A popular strategy is to use a continuous, convex relaxation of the non-convex feature selection problem, through the use of a prior or a regularizer that encourages sparsity in the model[1].

In recent years, there has been an increasing interest in the L1 regularizer, since it has the beneficial effects of regularizing model coefficients (as in L2 regularization), but yields sparse models that are more easily interpreted [17].

[1] *E.g.,* the number of nonzero components of the normal to a hyperplane classifier is equivalent to the number of features it needs to employ.

J.N. Kok et al. (Eds.): ECML 2007, LNAI 4701, pp. 286–297, 2007.

Logarithmic sample complexity bounds[2] allow L1-regularized models to learn effectively even under an exponential number of irrelevant features (relative to training samples) [13], giving better performance than ridge (L2) penalties in these scenarios. Furthermore, L1-regularization has appealing asymptotic sample-consistency in terms of variable selection [19].

For this paper, we will consider problems with the general form:

$$\min_x f(x) \equiv L(x) + \lambda||x||_1. \tag{1}$$

Here, $L(x)$ is a loss function, and the goal is to minimize this loss function with the L1-penalty, yielding a regularized sparse solution. Efficient algorithms have been proposed for the special cases where $L(x)$ has a specific functional form, such as a Gaussian [3] or Logistic [11] negative log-likelihood. In this paper, we focus on the more general case where $L(x)$ is simply a twice-differentiable continuous function, no specific form is assumed.

Since the objective function is non-differentiable when x contains values of 0, this precludes the use of standard unconstrained methods. This has lead to a wide variety of approaches proposed in the literature to solve problems of this form. In this paper we evaluate twelve classical and state-of-the-art L1 regularization methods over several loss functions in this general scenario (in most cases these are generalized versions of algorithms for specific loss functions proposed in the literature). In addition, we propose two new methods:

(i) The first proposed method, *SmoothL1*, uses a smooth approximation to the L1-regularizer that is continuous and differentiable, allowing us to formulate Newton (or Quasi-Newton) methods to solve the resulting optimization problems independently of the loss function used.
(ii) The second method proposed, *ProjectionL1*, addresses the differentiability by reformulating the problem as a non-negatively constrained optimization problem. We further describe the use of the *Two-Metric Projection* method put forward by [7] to solve the resulting optimization problem efficiently.

Our numerical results indicate that some strategies for addressing the non-differentiable loss are much more efficient than others, while our two simple proposed strategies are competitive with the best strategies (including more complex algorithms). We end with a discussion of the choice of algorithms in different scenarios.

2 Fast Optimization Methods for L1 Regularization

In this section, we review various previously proposed approaches and propose two new optimization techniques that can be used for L1-regularized optimization (Table 1 at the end gives a high level overview of these approaches). Although most methods proposed in the literature have been for individual loss

[2] Number of training examples required to learn a function.

functions, we focus on methods that can be extended to handle a general unconstrained differentiable loss. We concentrate on a single scalar λ value, although all techniques below are easily generalized to include a λ for each element (that may be equal to zero to avoid penalizing some elements). Except where otherwise noted, the algorithms are stabilized (to ensure global convergence) by using a back-tracking line search that finds a step length t satisfying the Armijo condition (we generate trial points using cubic interpolation of function and directional derivative values, and use a sufficient decrease parameter of 0.0001). In this section we will assume analytic second derivatives, and defer discussion of methods that avoid explicit Hessian calculation until the end.

2.1 SubGradient Strategies

We first examine optimization strategies that use sub-gradients to extricate the task of dealing with the non-differentiable gradient. At a local minimizer $\bar{x}$ of $f(x)$, we observe the following first-order optimality conditions:

$$\begin{cases} \nabla_i L(\bar{x}) + \lambda sign(\bar{x_i}) = 0, & |\bar{x_i}| > 0 \\ |\nabla_i L(\bar{x})| \leq \lambda, & \bar{x_i} = 0 \end{cases}$$

These conditions can be used to define a sub-gradient for each x_i whose negation represents the coordinate-wise direction of maximum descent:

$$\nabla_i f(x) = \begin{cases} \nabla_i L(x) + \lambda sign(x_i), & |x_i| > 0 \\ \nabla_i L(x) + \lambda, & x_i = 0, \nabla_i L(x) > -\lambda \\ \nabla_i L(x) - \lambda, & x_i = 0, \nabla_i L(x) > \lambda \\ 0, & x_i = 0, -\lambda \leq \nabla_i L(x) \leq \lambda \end{cases}$$

Using this sub-gradient, the *Gauss-Seidel* algorithm of [16] uses a working set of variables, and does an exact line search to optimize the working set variable whose sub-gradient is largest. Variables begin at $x_i = 0$ with an empty working set, and the variable with the largest sub-gradient magnitude is introduced whenever the working set satisfies the optimality conditions. This continues until no variable can be introduced. The *Grafting* procedure uses a variation that jointly solves the working set variable optimization with standard unconstrained techniques [15]. In contrast, rather than separating variables into active and working sets, and introducing the working set variable with the largest sub-gradient magnitude, the *Shooting* algorithm simply cycles through all variables, optimizing each in turn [6]. Analogously, we can also define a *Sub-Gradient Descent* strategy that attempts to minimize $f(x)$ in terms of x jointly using the above sub-gradient, and defines the working set at each iteration to be those variables not satisfying the optimality conditions[3].

[3] In our experiments, we used the line search of [16] for both the Gauss-Seidel and Shooting algorithm. For Grafting and Sub-Gradient Descent, we use Newton steps of the form $x := x - t\nabla^2 f(x)^{-1}\nabla f(x)$ for a step length t to optimize the working set.

2.2 Unconstrained Approximations

An alternative to working directly with $f(x)$ and using sub-gradients to address non-differentiability, is to replace $f(x)$ with an (often continuous and twice-differentiable) approximation $g(x)$. The problem of minimizing $g(x)$ can then be solved with unconstrained optimization techniques, such as performing Newton iterations of the form $x := x - t\nabla^2 g(x)^{-1}\nabla g(x)$ for a suitable step length t. A simple example is the *epsL1* approximation [11]:

$$g(x) = L(x) + \lambda\sqrt{x^T x + \epsilon}$$

This function is differentiable and approximates $f(x)$ for small ϵ. An alternative approximation is the class of log-barrier functions:

$$g(x) = L(x) + \lambda||x||_1 - \mu \log c(x)$$

In the *Log-Barrier* method, the constraint function $c(x)$ forces feasibility of iterates in a constrained formulation (see Section 2.3). In the *Log(norm(x))* method, $c(x)$ is set to $||x||_2^2$, preventing any variable from becoming exactly 0. For these methods, the unconstrained optimizer must implement truncation of the step lengths in order to maintain positivity of $c(x)$. Although the optimization can be performed for a fixed small value of μ, in the Log-Barrier method it is standard to solve (or approximately solve) the unconstrained problem with a decreasing sequence of μ values, which avoids ill-conditioning of the Hessian preventing convergence (see [14] for additional details).

SmoothL1 Approximation Method. We propose another type of smooth approximation, that takes advantage of the non-negative projection operator $(x)_+ = \max(x, 0)$. This projection function can be smoothly approximated, by the integral of a sigmoid function:[1]:

$$(x)_+ \approx p(x, \alpha) = x + \frac{1}{\alpha}\log(1 + \exp(-\alpha x)) \tag{2}$$

$p(x, \alpha)$ is a member of the class of smoothing functions presented in [1] proposed to solve complementarity problems. This smooth approximation of the projection has been used to transform the standard L2-penalized SVM formulation into an efficiently-solved unconstrained problem [12]. We also make use of the nice properties of $p(x, \alpha)$, but aiming for the different goal of achieving sparsity in the covariates.

By combining $p(x, \alpha)$ with the identity $|x| = (x)_+ + (-x)_+$ we arrive at the following smooth approximation for the absolute value function that consists of the sum of the integral of two sigmoid functions:

$$\begin{aligned} |x| &= (x)_+ + (-x)_+ \approx p(x, \alpha) + p(-x, \alpha) \\ &= \tfrac{1}{\alpha}\left[\log(1 + \exp(-\alpha x)) + \log(1 + \exp(\alpha x))\right] \\ &\stackrel{\text{def}}{=} |x|_\alpha \end{aligned} \tag{3}$$

The corresponding loss function is: $g(x) = L(x) + \lambda \sum_i |x_i|_\alpha$; we called it the *SmoothL1* approximation. It can be shown that $|x|_\alpha$ converges to $|x|$ as α approaches ∞ (the proof is similar to [12]), while $|x|_\alpha$ is twice differentiable:

$$\nabla(|x|_\alpha) = (1 + \exp(-\alpha x))^{-1} - (1 + \exp(\alpha x))^{-1} \tag{4}$$

$$\nabla^2(|x|_\alpha) = 2\alpha \exp(\alpha x)/(1 + \exp(\alpha x))^2 \tag{5}$$

With a smooth approximation, an unconstrained optimization method can be applied to $g(x)$ for a large value of α as a proxy for minimizing $f(x)$. However, for large α the SmoothL1 approximation is not appropriately modeled by a quadratic for variables near 0. To account for this, we use a continuation strategy analogous to Log-Barrier methods, where we take Newton steps between increasing the parameter α (beginning from a small α where the quadratic approximation is appropriate, and terminating at a sufficiently large value of α). The advantage of this new approach over Log-Barrier approximations is that a specialized line search that truncates the step to maintain constraint feasibility is not required (allowing the potential use of more sophisticated line search criteria), and that it does not involve solving a problem with double the number of variables (associated with using a constrained formulation).

An approach related to unconstrained approximations are Expectation Maximization (EM) approaches (see [4]). These approaches use a scale mixture of normals prior on the variables ($x_i|\tau_i \sim N(0, \tau_i)$), where the variances of the individual Gaussians have an exponential prior: $p(\tau_i|\sqrt{\lambda}) = \frac{\sqrt{\lambda}}{2} \exp(\frac{-\tau_i\sqrt{\lambda}}{2})$. Under this representation, integrating over τ_i yields a Laplacian density (and thus an L1-regularizer after taking logarithms) for $p(x_i|\lambda)$. In the *EM* approach the individual τ_i are treated as missing variables, and the 'E-step' computes the expectation of τ_i. Subsequently, the 'M-Step' uses this expectation to (exactly or approximately) compute the MAP parameters with the scale mixture (L2) prior. Algorithmically, this is equivalent to using the following approximation (where x^{old} is the value from the previous iteration)[4]:

$$g(x) = L(x) + \lambda \sum_i \frac{||x_i||_2^2}{|x_i^{old}|_1}$$

Although this approach has previously been presented as a fixed-point Iteratively Reweighted Least Squares (IRLS) update, it is straightforward to modify it in order to compute the Newton descent direction under this approximation (allowing the method to be applied to loss functions that do not yield an IRLS approximation).

2.3 Constrained Formulations

A third general approach to address the non-differentiability of the L1-regularizer is to cast the problem as a constrained optimization problem. One approach

[4] Numerical instability of this approach arises as x_i approaches 0. Strategies to avoid this include using a pseudo-inverse [17], reformulation [4], or by defining the working set as those variables whose magnitude is above a threshold.

to do this is to replace λ with a variable $t \propto 1/\lambda$ and solve the constrained problem:

$$\min_x L(x) \quad s.t. ||x||_1 \leq t \tag{6}$$

Recently, [11] presented an algorithm for L1-regularized Logistic Regression, where the Logistic Regression IRLS update is computed subject to the constraint $||x||_1 \leq t$. The solution to the constrained Weighted Least Squares problem can be efficiently calculated using the LARS algorithm [3]. This 'IRLS-LARS' algorithm (with an Armijo backtracking linesearch) proved more efficient than other approaches examined in [11] for L1-regularized Logistic Regression. This specific strategy can clearly be more generally applied to any loss function that yields an IRLS update, but it is not a general strategy since many loss functions do not yield an IRLS approximation[5].

We can extend the IRLS-LARS algorithm to a general algorithm by observing that the algorithm is an IRLS reformulation of a Sequential Quadratic Programming (SQP) update (where a unit step length is assumed). That is, IRLS-LARS minimize a Quadratic approximation to the function, subject to a linearization of the constraints (the linearization is redundant in this case). To handle the L1 constraint in a more general setting, we split x into non-negative variables representing positive and negative components, by defining new variables $x^+ = max(0, x)$ and $x^- = -min(0, w)$ (thus, $x = x^+ - x^-$). This gives the following constrained problem (a general form of a formulation used in [17]):

$$\min_{x^+, x^-} L(x^+ - x^-) \quad s.t. \sum_i [x_i^+ + x_i^-] \leq t, \forall_i x_i^+ \geq 0, x_i^- \geq 0 \tag{7}$$

From a probabilistic perspective, a difficulty with this formulation is that the constraints become degenerate as t approaches the L1-norm of the Maximum Likelihood Estimate (an analogous problem is present for non-probabilistic losses), a value that may not be known or desirable to compute. We use the following alternative formulation that avoids this problem, makes clear the strength of the Laplacian regularizer, and yields simple bound constraints on the variables:

$$\min_{x^+, x^-} L(x^+ - x^-) + \lambda \sum_i [x_i^+ + x_i^-] \quad s.t. \forall_i x_i^+ \geq 0, x_i^- \geq 0 \tag{8}$$

A general *SQP* algorithm takes descent steps of the form $x := x - td$ for a step length t, where the descent direction d is calculated by solving the following Quadratic Program [8]:

$$\min_d \nabla(L(x^+ - x^-)^T + \lambda 1)^T d + \frac{1}{2} d^T \nabla^2 L(x^+ - x^-) d \tag{9}$$

$$s.t. \forall_i x_i^+ + d_i^+ \geq 0, x_i^- + d_i^- \geq 0 \tag{10}$$

[5] IRLS updates are typically applicable in cases where the loss is an affine function of the covariates.

The linear constraints allow the objective function $f(x)$ to be used directly as a measure of progress (assuming the variables are initially non-negative and the step length is never greater than one), avoiding the need to use special techniques to avoid a scenario known as the Maratos effect [14]. For strictly convex problems, the SQP iterates converge super-linearly to the optimal solution [8], explaining the low number of iterates reported by [11] for IRLS-LARS. This general SQP algorithm can be considerably less efficient than the IRLS-LARS algorithm, since a general Quadratic Program must be solved at each iteration (although warm-starting is possible), and the algorithm does not take advantage of the form of the constraints.

ProjectionL1 Method. We propose to take advantage of the non-negative bound constraints by using a *Two-Metric Projection* method [7], which we now outline. Using the notation $x^* = [x^+ \; x^-]^T$, the active set of constraints for non-negative bounds $x_i^* \geq 0$ at an iterate x_* is defined as $\{i | x_i^* = 0, \nabla L(x^+ - x^-) + \lambda > 0\}$. To avoid very small steps, we replace the test $x_i^* = 0$ with $0 \leq x_i^* \leq \epsilon$, for a small ϵ. At each iteration, we optimize the variables whose bound constraint is not active (the working set) using a projected-gradient strategy. A standard projected-gradient algorithm would take descent steps on the working set of the form: $x^* := [x^* - t\nabla f(x^+ - x^-)]^+$, where t represents the step length[6] and the element-wise 'plus' function projects onto the non-negative orthant.

The gradient projection strategy is appealing since it allows rapid changes in the active set, and is especially suited to handle this type of problem due to the simplicity of the constraint projection operator. However, its convergence may be slow due to the use of the steepest decent direction. Hence, the 'Two-Metric Projection' strategy scales the descent direction by the inverse of the working set's Hessian matrix, yielding the following simple update: $x^* := [x^* - t\nabla^2 f(x^*)^{-1}\nabla f(x^*)]^+$. As in SQP, this algorithm achieves a superlinear rate of convergence [7]. However, it has a substantially reduced iteration cost compared to SQP (or IRLS-LARS).

To complete our discussion of the L1-regularized optimization methods proposed in the literature, we note that in the Basis Pursuit Denoising literature, Interior Point (primal-dual log-barrier) methods have been used (for example, [2]). These methods, closely related to Log-Barrier methods, simultaneously optimize both the primal variables x^* and a set of dual variables ν corresponding to the Lagrange multipliers. It is straightforward to adapt these methods to the general case using the bound-constrained formulation above. Assuming x^* is feasible and ν is non-negative, for a barrier parameter μ the remaining (modified) first-order optimality (KKT) conditions for the bound-constrained problem can be written as follows (where $\circ$ denotes the element-wise Hadamard product):

$$0 = r(x^*, \nu) \equiv \begin{bmatrix} \nabla L(x^+ - x^-) - \nu \\ -\nu \circ x^* - \mu 1 \end{bmatrix}.$$

[6] The line search along the projection arc requires a modified Armijo condition [7].

This equation corresponds to the gradient of the Lagrangian, and the (modified) complementary condition. We seek to solve the equation $r(x^*, \nu) = 0$ by taking Newton-Raphson steps of the form $[x^* \ \nu]^T := [x^* \ \nu]^T - t\nabla r(x^*, \nu)^{-1} r(x^*, \nu)$, where the step length t is truncated to ensure that x^* and ν are non-negative (computing $\nabla r(x^*, \nu)^{-1} r(x^*, \nu)$ requires some algebraic manipulation). Between iterates, the barrier parameter μ is updated based on an update rate (we use 10), the number of constraints m, and the duality gap $\nu^T x^*$:$\mu = 10m(\nu^T x^*)^{-1}$ (see [5] for a review of Interior Point methods).

3 Experiments

We have applied the above strategies to a variety of loss functions and data sets. Specifically, we looked at a generalized version of the **Gauss-Seidel**, **Shooting**, **Grafting**, **Sub-Gradient**, **epsL1**, **Log-Barrier**, **EM**, **Log(norm(w))**, **SmoothL1**, **SQP**, **ProjectionL1**, and **Interior Point** methods. Although the general-L1 framework make no assumptions about convexity, we have restricted our experiments to convex functions.

All methods were run until the same convergence criteria was met (*i.e.*, where appropriate, that the step length between iterates, change in function value between iterates, negative directional derivative, or optimality condition was less than 10^{-6}). We assessed the ability of the methods to optimize a loss function known only through a 'black box' function that returns the objective value and derivatives for a given parameter setting. Convergence was measured based on function evaluations; this is, the number of times the algorithm invoked the 'black box' (to make the comparisons fair, all of the implementations were designed and tuned with this in mind). The iterates were truncated to 250 such evaluations, and methods whose final loss was greater than 10^{-3} times the minimum found across the methods were assigned the maximum value of 250 evaluations to punish for low accuracy. This was only needed in a small minority of cases, since all methods typically either found a high accuracy solution, or reached the maximum number of iterations. We used a second-order (Hessian-based Newton) strategy across all methods examined.

3.1 Binary Classification

Our first experiment focused on the problem of optimizing the negative log-likelihood associated with binary Probit Regression (using y as class labels, z as the features, ϕ as the error function, and x as the paramters): $L(x) = \log(\phi(\frac{y_i x^T z_i}{\sqrt(2)}))$. We applied all 12 optimization strategies to 12 publicly available data sets[7] from the UCI repository[8]. All methods were initialized with $x = 0$

[7] 1: Wisconsin Breast Cancer, 2: Australian Heart, 3: Pima Diabetes, 4: Australian Credit, 5: Sonar, 6: Ionosphere, 7: German, 8: Bright, 9: Dim, 10: Adult, 11: Census, 12: 2Norm.

[8] http://www.ics.uci.edu/~mlearn/MLRepository.html

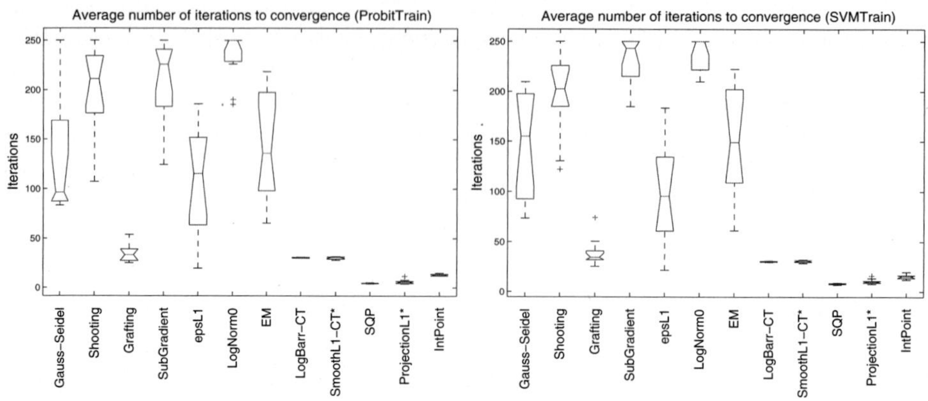

Fig. 1. Distribution of function evaluations (averaged over λ) across 12 data sets to train: (left) a Probit Regression classifier with L1-regularization and (right) a Smooth Support Vector Machine classifier with L1-regularization (*=new method)

(those that do not allow this used $x = 0.01$). Using $\lambda_{max} \stackrel{\text{def}}{=} \max_i |\nabla L(0)|$ as the maximum value of λ for each data set[9], we evaluated each data set at λ_{max} multiplied by each of $[.1, .3, .5, .7, .9]$.

Since the methods discussed in this report apply to general differentiable loss functions, we can easily replace the binary Probit Regression loss function with other loss functions. We tested the optimizers using a differentiable loss function closely related to the hinge loss used in Support Vector Machines: $l(x) = (1 - y_i x^T z_i)^+$. In 'Smooth' Support Vector Machines, the projection ('plus') function in the hinge loss is replaced with the smooth approximation in Section 2.2, yielding a differentiable objective [12]. We repeated the Probit Regression experiment with the Smooth Support Vector Machine loss function (we set the parameter α controlling the accuracy of the loss approximation to 5). Fig. 1 plots the distribution of the mean number of iterations to convergence across the data sets for both binary classification loss functions. We also examined the binary Logistic Regression loss (not shown due to space limit), finding results similar to the Probit Regression experiment (these results are consistent with the findings reported in [11]).

3.2 Multinomial and Structured Classification

We examined optimizing two more complicated objectives than those described above: Multinomial Logistic Regression (using the Softmax function) and (2-dimensional) Conditional Random Fields (CRFs). These represent more challenging scenarios since the Hessians of these models are often indefinite. We

[9] This and higher values produce $x = 0$ as their solution, following from the first-order optimality conditions of the unconstrained problem.

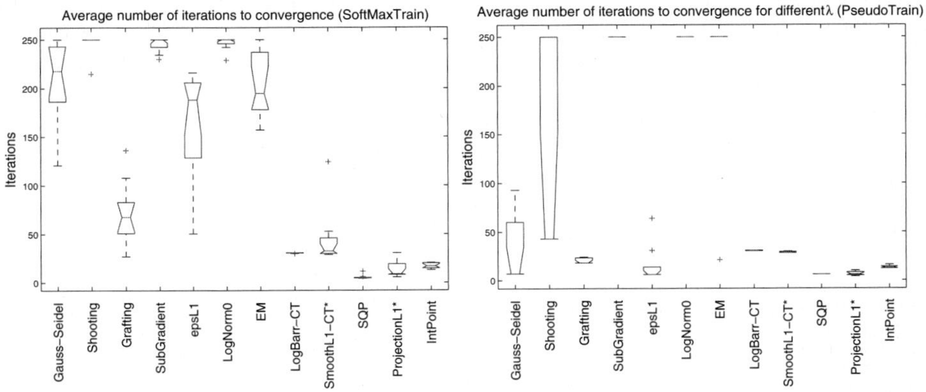

Fig. 2. Left: Distribution of function evaluations (averaged over λ) across 11 data sets to train a Multinomial Logistic Regression classifier with L1-regularization. Right: evaluations on the image patch classification data set to train an L1-regularized 2D Conditional Random Field evaluated for various λ values (*=new method).

trained Multinomial Logistic Regression classifiers on 11 data sets[10] from the UCI repository and the Statlog project[11]. We trained the 2D Conditional Random Field on an image patch classification task [10], using the following Pseudo-likelihood (v represents edge weights that are also penalized).

$$l(x, v) = \log(1 + \exp(y_i x^T z_i + \sum_{j \in nei(i)} y_i y_j v^T z_{ij})) \tag{11}$$

A clear advantage of our approach of treating the loss as a generic function, is that it is trivial to apply the methods to these more complicated objectives (once the loss function and its partial derivatives are defined). We used the 'CRF2D' software to provide the CRF loss that we augmented with L1-regularization[12]. The summarized results of these experiments are shown in Fig. 2.

4 Discussion

Table 1 summarizes the different methods we have examined, including an aggregate convergence ranking across the experiments (ie. number of times the loss is evaluated over all training examples), and a ranking of the iteration speed of the different methods (which typically only depends on the number of variables). If we were to completely ignore iteration cost, SQP would be the fastest

[10] 1:Iris, 2:Glass, 3:Wine, 4:Vowel, 5:Vehicle, 6:LED, 7:Satellite, 8:Waveform21, 9:DNA, 10:Waveform40, 11:Shuttle.

[11] `http://www.liacc.up.pt/ML/old/statlog/`

[12] http://www.cs.ubc.ca/~murphyk/Software/CRF/crf.html

Table 1. Convergence ranking is determined by the average number of iterations to convergence across the 405 experiments (methods whose average values are within 5 are grouped, the methods that required the fewest iterations are ranked 1, methods requiring the most iterations ranked 8). Iteration speed is based on the cost of computing the descent direction if all variables are non-zero (the fastest methods are ranked 1, the slowest ranked 4). Notes: *: method improves the approximation between iterations. **: method uses a constrained objective that is improved between iterations. ***: methods use the correct gradient, but only for the working set (other sub-gradient methods also restrict to the working set).

Optimization Method	Approx Objective	Sub-Gradient	Explicit Constraints	Convergence Ranking	Iteration Speed Ranking
Gauss-Seidel [16]	N	Y	N	6	1
Shooting [15]	N	Y	N	8	1
Grafting [6]	N	Y	N	4	2
Sub-Gradient	N	Y	N	9	2
epsL1 [11]	Y	N	N	5	2
Log(norm(x))	Y	N	N	10	2
EM [4]	Y*	Y***	N	7	2
Log-Barrier [14]	Y*	N	Y	3	3
SmoothL1 [ThisPaper]	Y*	N	N	3	2
SQP [11]	N	N	Y	1	4
ProjectionL1 [ThisPaper]	Y	Y***	Y	1	3
Interior Point [5]	Y**	N	Y	2	3

method. However, in terms of runtime, ProjectionL1 was typically the fastest method across the experiments, since its iteration cost (solving a symmetric linear system) is substantially smaller than the cost of solving a quadratic program (even if LARS is used). Although the approaches that explicitly enforced constraints were generally superior to the unconstrained approaches, the SmoothL1 approach was the most effective approach that did not use a constrained approach (the constrained approaches have a higher iteration cost since they solve a linear system with double the number of variables). The 250 iteration limit may have favorably skewed the convergence of methods that reached this limit (making it difficult to draw definite conclusions on these). However, overall our experiments indicated that the proposed ProjectionL1 strategy was the most efficient in terms of runtime on the test problems, although the proposed SmoothL1 algorithm may be efficient on problems with many variables, while SQP may be more efficient on problems with very expensive function evaluations.

In some scenarios, it might not be practical to compute (or store) analytic Hessians. If we replace the analytic Hessian with a suitable (limited-memory) Hessian approximation (ie. L-BFGS), all of the above methods can be applied without modification (with the exception of the InteriorPoint method). This substantially reduces the iteration cost and memory requirements (for all but the coordinate descent strategies), at the cost of an increase in function evaluations.

In this work, we have reviewed 12 methods for solving general L1-regularized optimization problems, and provided a numerical comparison on several standard machine learning problems. Two of these methods are novel (introduced in this paper) and prove to be among the most efficient overall. Due to space constraints, we have omitted some information that we would have liked to include. Online[13], we have made available additional details/proofs on some of the methods, code (to enable reproducible research), and additional experimental results.

References

1. Chen, C., Mangasarian, O.L.: A class of smoothing functions for nonlinear and mixed complementarity problems. Comput. Optim. Appl 5(2), 97–138 (1996)
2. Chen, S., Donoho, D., Saunders, M.: Atomic decomposition by basis pursuit. SIAM J. Sci. Comput. 20(1), 33–61 (1999)
3. Efron, B., Johnstone, I., Hastie, T., Tibshirani, R.: Least angle regression. Ann. Stat. 32(2), 407–499 (2004)
4. Figueiredo, M.: Adapative sparseness for supervised learning. IEEE. Trans. Pattern. Anal. Mach. Intell. 25(9), 1150–1159 (2003)
5. Freund, R.M., Mizuno, S.: Interior point methods: Current status and future directions. Optima 51, 1–9 (1996)
6. Fu, W.: Penalized regressions: The bridge versus the LASSO. J. Comput. Graph. Stat. 7(3), 397–416 (1998)
7. Gafni, E., Bertsekas, D.: Two-metric projection methods for constrained optimization. SIAM J. Contr. Optim. 22(6), 936–964 (1984)
8. Garcia Palomares, U.M., Mangasarian, O.L.: Superlinearly convergent Quasi–Newton algorithms for nonlinearly constrained optimization problems. Math. Program. 11, 1–13 (1976)
9. Guyon, I., Elisseeff, A.: An introduction to variable and feature selection. J. Mach. Learn. Res. 3, 1157–1182 (2003)
10. Kumar, S., Hebert, M.: Discriminative random fields: A discriminative framework for contextual interaction in classification. In: ICCV (2003)
11. Lee, S.-I., Lee, H., Abbeel, P., Ng, A.Y.: Efficient L1 regularized logistic regression. In: AAAI (2006)
12. Lee, Y.-J., Mangasarian, O.L.: SSVM: A smooth support vector machine. Comput. Optim. Appl. 20, 5–22 (2001)
13. Ng, A.: Feature selection, L1 vs. L2 regularization, and rotational invariance. In: ICML, pp. 78–85. ACM Press, New York (2004)
14. Nocedal, J., Wright, S.J.: Numerical Optimization. Springer, New York (1999)
15. Perkins, S., Lacker, K., Theiler, J.: Grafting: Fast, incremental feature selection by gradient descent in function space. J. Mach. Learn. Res. 3, 1333–1356 (2003)
16. Shevade, S., Keerthi, S.: A simple and efficient algorithm for gene selection using sparse logistic regression. Bioinformatics 19(17), 2246–2253 (2003)
17. Tibshirani, R.: Regression shrinkage and selection via the lasso. J. Roy. Stat. Soc. B 58(1), 267–288
18. Weston, J., Elisseeff, A., Scholkopf, B., Tipping, M.: Use of the zero norm with linear models and kernel methods. J. Mach. Learn. Res. 3, 1439–1461 (2003)
19. Zhao, P., Yu, B.: On model selection consistency of LASSO. J. Mach. Learn. Res. 7, 2541–2567 (2007)

[13] http://www.cs.wisc.edu/~gfung/GeneralL1

Bayesian Inference for Sparse Generalized Linear Models

Matthias Seeger, Sebastian Gerwinn, and Matthias Bethge

Max Planck Institute for Biological Cybernetics
Spemannstr. 38, Tübingen, Germany

Abstract. We present a framework for efficient, accurate approximate Bayesian inference in generalized linear models (GLMs), based on the expectation propagation (EP) technique. The parameters can be endowed with a factorizing prior distribution, encoding properties such as sparsity or non-negativity. The central role of posterior log-concavity in Bayesian GLMs is emphasized and related to stability issues in EP. In particular, we use our technique to infer the parameters of a point process model for neuronal spiking data from multiple electrodes, demonstrating significantly superior predictive performance when a sparsity assumption is enforced via a Laplace prior distribution.

1 Introduction

The framework of *generalized linear models* (GLM) [5] is a cornerstone of modern Statistics, offering unified estimation and prediction methods for a large number of models frequently used in Machine Learning. In a *Bayesian* generalized linear model (B-GLM), assumptions about the model parameters (sparsity, non-negativity, *etc*) are encoded in a prior distribution. For example, it is common to use an overparameterized model with many features together with a sparsity prior. Only such features relevant for describing the data will end up having significant weight under the Bayesian posterior. Importantly, for the models of interest in this paper, inference does not require combinatorial computational efforts, but can be done even with a large number of parameters.

Exact Bayesian inference is not analytically tractable in most B-GLMs. In this paper, we show how to employ the expectation propagation (EP) technique for approximate inference in GLMs with factorizing prior distributions. We focus on models with log-concave (therefore unimodal) posterior, for which a careful EP implementation is numerically robust and tends to convergence rapidly to an accurate posterior approximation. The code used in our experiments will be made publicly available.

We apply our technique to a point process model for neuronal spiking data from multiple electrodes. Here, each neuron is assumed to receive causal input from an external stimulus and the spike history, represented by features in a GLM. In the presence of high-dimensional stimuli (such as images), with many neurons recorded at a reasonable time resolution, we end up with a lot of features, but we can assume that the system can be described by a much smaller number

J.N. Kok et al. (Eds.): ECML 2007, LNAI 4701, pp. 298–309, 2007.

of parameters. This calls for a sparsity prior, and we are able to confirm the importance of this prior assumption through our experiments, where our model achieves much better predictive performance with a Laplace sparsity prior than with a (traditionally favoured) Gaussian prior, especially for small to moderate sample sizes. Our model is inspired by [10], who identify commonly used spiking models as log-concave GLMs, but the Bayesian treatment as well as the usage of sparsity in this context is novel.

The structure of the paper is as follows. In Section 2, we introduce and motivate the model class of B-GLMs. In Section 3, we show how the expectation propagation method can be applied to B-GLMs, motivating the central role of log-concavity in this context. Our multi-neuron spiking model is presented in Section 4, and experimental results are presented in Section 5. We close with a discussion in Section 6.

2 Bayesian Generalized Linear Models

The models we are interested in here are specified in terms of primary parameters $\boldsymbol{w}$ (or weights) and hyperparameters $\boldsymbol{\theta}$. If D denotes the set of observations, the likelihood is $P(D|\boldsymbol{w})$, and the (Bayesian) prior distribution is $P(\boldsymbol{w})$. We require that

$$P(\boldsymbol{w}|D) \propto \prod_j \phi_j(u_j), \quad u_j = \boldsymbol{w}^T \boldsymbol{\psi}_j, \tag{1}$$

where $P(\boldsymbol{w}|D) \propto P(D|\boldsymbol{w})P(\boldsymbol{w})$ is the (Bayesian) posterior. u_j is a scalar-valued[1] linear function of $\boldsymbol{w}$, and the *sites* $\phi_j(\cdot)$ are non-negative scalar functions. We require that all ϕ_j are *log-concave*, *i.e.* each $-\log\phi_j$ is convex[2]. The role of log-concavity is clarified shortly, see also Section 3. Note that our framework can be extended with no additional difficulties to models with an additional joint Gaussian factor $N(\boldsymbol{w}|\boldsymbol{\mu}_0, \boldsymbol{\Sigma}_0)$ in (1). Here, $\boldsymbol{\Sigma}_0$ need not be diagonal. Most Gaussian process models fall in our class, for example [9].

Perhaps the simplest B-GLM is the *linear* one, where the likelihood is Gaussian and given by factors $\phi_j(u_j) = N(y_j|u_j, \sigma^2)$, describing data $D = \{(\boldsymbol{\psi}_j, y_j)\}$, $y_j \in \mathbb{R}$. Equivalently, $y_j = \boldsymbol{\psi}_j^T\boldsymbol{w} + \varepsilon_j$, where $\varepsilon_j \sim N(0, \sigma^2)$ is noise. If the linear model is used with a Gaussian prior on $\boldsymbol{w}$, Bayesian inference can be done analytically, essentially by solving the normal equations. However, this convenient conjugate choice does not encode any strong assumptions about $\boldsymbol{w}$ and can severely underperform in situations where such assumptions are reasonable. What non-Gaussian priors can we use within our model class? We restrict ourselves to factorizing priors: $P(\boldsymbol{w}) = \prod_k P(w_k)$. Log-concave choices include the *Laplace* (or double exponential) $P(w_k) \propto e^{-\rho_k|w_k|}$ (sparsity); *positive Gaussian* $P(w_k) \propto N(w_k|0, \sigma_k^2)\mathrm{I}_{\{w_k>0\}}$ (non-negativity); or *exponential* distribution $P(w_k) \propto e^{-\rho_k w_k}\mathrm{I}_{\{w_k>0\}}$ (sparsity and non-negativity). Furthermore, any product of log-concave functions is log-concave again.

[1] Our framework applies just as well if the u_j are low-dimensional vectors, but this is not in the scope of this paper.

[2] We allow for generalized convex functions, which may take the value $+\infty$.

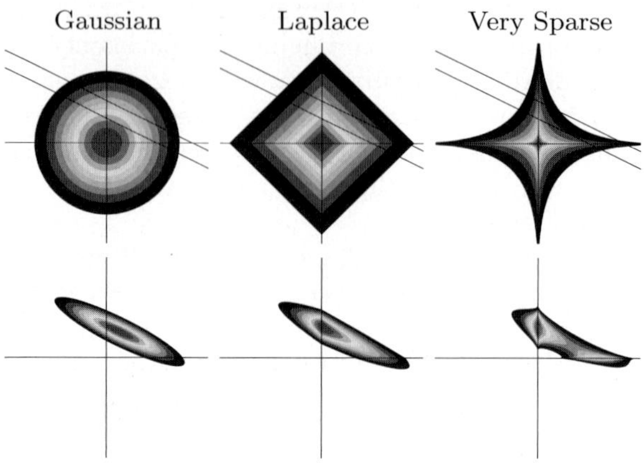

Fig. 1. Different prior distributions over coefficients of $\boldsymbol{w}$

In this paper, we are principally interested in the *Laplace* distribution as a sparsity prior. The linear model with this prior is the basis of the *Lasso* [19], extensively used in Machine Learning (under names such as L_1 regularization, basis pursuit, and others). In the Lasso, we compute point estimates for the parameters, by maximizing the sum of the log likelihood and the log of the Laplace sparsity prior. The latter L_1 regularizer tends to force coefficient estimates to zero exactly if they are not required. L_1 penalization can be applied to nonlinear GLMs as well, resulting in a convex estimation problem, for which several algorithms have been proposed in Machine Learning.

The Bayesian inference approach is quite different. Rather than just estimating a single parameter value, a posterior distribution over parameters is computed. More than a point estimate, we obtain credibility regions and information about parameter correlations from the posterior. Parameters are never forced exactly to zero under the posterior, since such a conclusion could not be justified from finite observations. The function of the Laplace sparsity prior in Bayesian inference is motivated in Figure 1. It leads to shrinkage of posterior mass towards coordinate axes (vertical in the figure), something a Gaussian prior does not do. On the other hand, the posterior remains log-concave, so that all contours enclose convex sets. The stronger sparsity prior $\propto e^{-|a_{ij}|^{0.4}}$ is not log-concave and induces a multimodal posterior, which can be very hard to approximate. Note that the role of the Laplace prior in our work here is not to provide feature selection or sparse estimation, but rather to improve our inference for an over-parameterized model from limited data. Note that the method proposed here has been applied to Bayesian inference for the sparse *linear* model underlying the Lasso in [16]. However, our application here requires a nonlinear model, since the data are event times rather than real-valued responses.

Generalized linear models [5] extend the linear model to a range of different tasks beyond real-valued regression estimation, while maintaining desirable properties such as identifiability, efficient estimation, and simple asymptotics. All log-concave GLMs are of the form (1). The likelihood has exponential family form, in that $P(D|\boldsymbol{w}) = \exp(\boldsymbol{\phi}(D)^T\boldsymbol{g} - l(\boldsymbol{g}) - a(D))$, where $\boldsymbol{g} = \boldsymbol{g}(\boldsymbol{w})$ are the natural parameters, and $l(\boldsymbol{g})$ is the log partition function, which is convex in $\boldsymbol{g}$. If $\boldsymbol{g}$ is linear in $\boldsymbol{w}$, then $P(D|\boldsymbol{w})$ is log-concave in $\boldsymbol{w}$, since $-\log P(D|\boldsymbol{w}) = -\boldsymbol{\phi}(D)^T\boldsymbol{w} + l(\boldsymbol{g})$ up to a constant. Therefore, any log-concave factorizing prior on $\boldsymbol{w}$ induces a B-GLM. If $\boldsymbol{g}(\boldsymbol{w})$ is composed of a linear map and a nonlinear link function, log-concavity must be established separately. A concrete example of a B-GLM of this kind is given in Section 4.

Importantly, the posteriors of B-GLMs are log-concave in $\boldsymbol{w}$, therefore unimodal. This property is quite crucial to ensure that our approximate inference[3] method is accurate and can be implemented in a numerically stable manner. Note that many models of general interest are not B-GLMs, such as mixture models, models with Student-t likelihoods. Many of the commonly used sparsity priors, such as "spike-and-slab" (mixture of narrow and wide Gaussian), Student-t, or $\propto \exp(-\rho|w_k|^\alpha)$, $\alpha < 1$ (see Figure 1 for $\alpha = 0.4$), are not log-concave, and accurate approximate inference is in general a very hard problem. Furthermore, most approximate inference methods known today are numerically unstable when applied to such models.

Several approximate inference methods for B-GLMs have been proposed. The MCMC technique of [11] could be applied, together with adaptive rejection sampling [3] for the likelihood factors. Our approach is significantly faster and more robust than MCMC (where convergence is very hard to assess). Sparse Bayesian Learning (SBL) [20] is the most well-known method for the sparse *linear* model. SBL is related to our EP variant in [16]. It has been combined with EP and applied to B-GLMs in [12]. The main technical difference to our proposal is that they use separate techniques to deal with likelihood sites (EP, moment matching) and prior sites (scale mixture decomposition of Student-t), while we employ EP for all sites. The EP update for Laplace prior sites is numerically challenging, and an equivalent direct EP variant for a non-log-concave Student-t prior (used in SBL) is likely to behave non-robustly (Malte Kuss, pers. comm.). The scale mixture treatment circumvents these numerical difficulties, and stronger sparsity Student-t priors can be used. On the other hand, our direct approach runs significantly faster on models of interest here, where there are many more likelihood than prior factors. The method of [12] is a double-loop algorithm, where EP is run to convergence on the likelihood sites after each update of the (prior) scale mixture parameters. Our method is also more transparent, not mixing two different approximate inference principles[4]. Finally, their method approximates a multimodal posterior with a single Gaussian in a variational lower-bound fashion (SBL can be interpreted

[3] Faced with non-log-concave models with multimodal posteriors, most approximate inference techniques somewhat break down, with the exception of MCMC techniques, which however typically become very inefficient in such situations.

[4] These principles may in fact be based on qualitatively different divergence measures, noting that SBL has variational mean-field character [22], which uses a different divergence than EP [6]. Since these divergences focus on different aspects of approximation [6], mixing them is non-transparent and may lead to algorithmic problems such as slow convergence.

in a variational way, see [22]), which is often quite loose. Typical robustness and "symmetry-breaking" problems in such methods are hidden in the optimization over the scale mixture (prior) parameters, which may be hard to solve properly. Even if their SBL approach is applied to a model with Laplace priors (by using the scale mixture decomposition of the Laplace, see [11]), the implications of posterior log-concavity for their method are less clear.

Note that the Laplace approximation frequently used for approximate Bayesian inference cannot be applied directly to the sparse GLM, since the Hessian does not exist at the posterior mode. A double-loop method can be derived by applying the Laplace approximation to the likelihood only, this has been proposed in [20].

3 Expectation Propagation

Exact Bayesian inference is not analytically tractable for the application considered here, or for most B-GLMs in general. However, it can be approximated, and our approach is based on the *expectation propagation* (EP) method [7,9]. EP results in a Gaussian approximation $Q(\boldsymbol{w})$ to a posterior $P(\boldsymbol{w}|D)$ of the form (1). While the latter is not Gaussian, its log-concavity (and unimodality) motivates such an approximation. EP is used for a linear model (Gaussian likelihood) with Laplace prior in [16], and has been used for a range of models with Gaussian prior and log-concave likelihood [9], albeit not for point process data (as is done here; an application to discrete-state continuous-time Markov processes was given in [8]). In general, there has not been much work on approximate inference for nonlinear models with sparsity priors (an exception is [12]).

The posterior $P(\boldsymbol{w}|D)$ in (1) is formally a product of J sites ϕ_j, normalized to integrate to one. Each site ϕ_j is either part of the likelihood $P(D|\boldsymbol{w})$ or of the prior $P(\boldsymbol{w})$. Let K be the number of variables: $\boldsymbol{w} \in \mathbb{R}^K$. We use a factorizing Laplace prior on $\boldsymbol{w}$,

$$P(\boldsymbol{w}) = \prod_{k=1}^{K} \phi_k(w_k), \quad \phi_k(w_k) \propto e^{-\rho|w_k|}, \quad \rho > 0, \tag{2}$$

whose sparsity-enducing role has been motivated above. The likelihood sites ϕ_j, $j = K+1, \dots, J$ in (1) are log-concave and will be specified further below for the model of interest.

The EP posterior approximation of (1) has the form $Q(\boldsymbol{w}) \propto \prod_j \tilde{\phi}_j(u_j)$, where $\tilde{\phi}_j(u_j) = \exp(b_j u_j - \frac{1}{2}\pi_j u_j^2)$ are *site approximations* of Gaussian form, the b_j, π_j are called *site parameters*. The log-concavity of the model implies that all $\pi_j \geq 0$. Some of them may be 0, as long as $Q(\boldsymbol{w})$ is a (normalizable) Gaussian throughout. An EP update at j consists of computing the Gaussian *cavity distribution* $Q^{\setminus j} \propto Q\tilde{\phi}_j^{-1}$ and the non-Gaussian *tilted distribution* $\hat{P} \propto Q^{\setminus j}\phi_j$, then updating b_j, π_j such that the new Q' has the same mean and covariance as $\hat{P}$ (moment matching). This is iterated in some random ordering over the sites until convergence.

Let $Q(\boldsymbol{w}) = N(\boldsymbol{w}|\boldsymbol{h}, \boldsymbol{\Sigma})$. An EP update at site j leads to a rank-one update of $\boldsymbol{\Sigma}$, featuring $\boldsymbol{v}_j = \boldsymbol{\Sigma}\boldsymbol{\psi}_j$, and costs $O(K^2)$. Details are given in the appendix. It is shown in [15] that for log-concave sites this update can always be done, and results in $\pi_j \geq 0$. In this case, EP updates can typically be done in a stable way, and empirically the method converges reliably and quickly. In contrast to this, EP tends to be very problematic to run on non-log-concave models. Full updates may not always be possible (for example resulting in negative variances), and damping techniques are typically required to attain convergence at all. Cases of EP divergence for multimodal posteriors have been reported [7]. EP updates often become inherently unstable operations in these cases[5].

A good initialization of $\boldsymbol{b}$, $\boldsymbol{\pi}$ depends on the concrete B-GLM. For our sparse spiking model (see Section 4), we start with $\boldsymbol{b} = \boldsymbol{0}$, and $\pi_j = 0$ for all likelihood sites, but $\pi_k = \rho^2/2$ for prior sites, ensuring that ϕ_k (2) and $\tilde{\phi}_k$ have the same first and second moments initially, $k = 1, \ldots, K$.

It is reported in [16] that in the presence of a factorizing Laplace prior, EP can behave extremely unstably if $\boldsymbol{w}$ is only weakly constrained by the likelihood. This happens in strongly underdetermined linear models (more variables than observations), but will typically not be the case in parametric B-GLMs. For example, in our spiking model application, we have many more likelihood sites than $\boldsymbol{w}$ components. In such cases, an initial EP update sweep over all likelihood sites is recommended, before any Laplace prior sites are updated. In an underdetermined case, the measures developed in [16] may have to be applied.

The marginal likelihood $P(D|\boldsymbol{\theta})$ is the probability of the data, given model and hyperparameters $\boldsymbol{\theta}$, where primary parameters $\boldsymbol{w}$ have been integrated out. It is the normalization constant in (1). This quantity, also known as partition function or evidence, can be used to conduct Bayesian tests (via Bayes factors), or to adjust $\boldsymbol{\theta}$ in a way robust to overfitting. EP comes with a marginal likelihood approximation, which in our case can be derived from [16,15], together with its gradient w.r.t. $\boldsymbol{\theta}$. Details will be described in a longer version of this paper.

4 Sparse Feature Neuronal Spiking Model

An important approach to understanding neural systems is to build models in order to predict spike responses to natural stimuli [2]. Traditionally, single cell responses are characterized using spike-triggered averaging techniques[6], allowing for efficient estimation of the *linear receptive field*, a concise description of what the cell is most sensitive to. For example, a neuron in the early visual cortex may

[5] In this case, a multimodal posterior is approximated by a unimodal Gaussian, so that spontaneous "symmetry breaking" does occur. The outcome may then depend significantly on artificial choices such as site ordering for the updates, or numerical roundoff errors during the updates.

[6] Statistics are obtained by averaging over a window $[t_i - \Delta, t_i)$, t_i a spike, characterizing effects which precede a spike emission [14].

act as a detector of certain features such as edges or lighting/texture gradients of particular orientation in a small area of the visual field: its receptive field can be thought of as a localized, oriented filter, and only the appearance of the specific event will elicit a strong response. This notion can be grounded in a specific GLM: the linear-nonlinear cascade model [10]. Recent developments apply this formalism to multi-neuron responses [4,10]. We present another important conceptual extension: rather than computing point estimates of model parameters only, we employ a full Bayesian inference scheme, allowing us to encode desirable properties via the prior. The resulting posterior gives quantitative answers about localization and dispersion of inferred model parameters, together with credibility intervals ("error bars") describing the range of uncertainty in the parameters. Assessing uncertainty is essential in this application, since neural response models come with many parameters, and only a limited amount of data is available.

We adopt *linear-nonlinear-Poisson* (LNP) cascade models [17], where spikes $D_i = \{t_{j,i}\}$ of neuron i come from an inhomogeneous Poisson process, whose instantaneous firing rate $\lambda_i(t)$ is a nonlinear function of the output of a linear filter. The filter coefficients are the primary parameters $\boldsymbol{w}_i$. $\lambda_i(t)$ depends on both stimulus events as well as the spiking history of all neurons. There are *stimulus-neuron* dependencies (normally described by the *linear receptive field*) as well as *neuron-neuron* dependencies: $\lambda_i(t)$ may depend on spikes from $D = \cup_i D_i$, lying in $[0, t)$. In summary, LNP models are obtained as $\lambda_i(t) = \lambda_i(\boldsymbol{w}_i^T \boldsymbol{\psi}(t))$, where $\boldsymbol{\psi}(t)$ does not depend on primary parameters: a linear filter is followed by a nonlinear transfer function λ_i, which feeds into an inhomogeneous Poisson process. According to general point process theory [18], the negative log likelihood for spike data D is

$$\sum_i \left(-\sum_j \log \lambda_i(\boldsymbol{w}_i^T \boldsymbol{\psi}(t_{j,i})) + \int \lambda_i(\boldsymbol{w}_i^T \boldsymbol{\psi}(t))\, dt \right).$$

It has been shown in [10] that the likelihood is log-concave in $\boldsymbol{w}_i$ if $\lambda_i(\cdot)$ is convex and log-concave.

The model we consider here is a generalization of a Poisson Network [13], and a special LNP model. For a sequence of *changepoints* $0 = \tilde{t}_0 < \tilde{t}_1 < \dots < \tilde{t}_j < \dots$, we assume that $\boldsymbol{\psi}(t)$ is constant in each $[\tilde{t}_{j-1}, \tilde{t}_j)$, attaining the value $\boldsymbol{\psi}_j$ there. The semantics of changepoints are given below, here we note that all spikes (from all neurons) are changepoints, with $\xi_{j,i} = 1$ iff $\tilde{t}_j \in D_i$ and $\xi_{j,i} = 0$ otherwise. Under this assumption, the likelihood is $P(D|\{\boldsymbol{w}_i\}) = \prod_i L_i(\boldsymbol{w}_i)$, where each $L_i(\boldsymbol{w}_i)$ has the form (1), with $\phi_{j,i}(u_{j,i}) = \lambda_i(u_{j,i})^{\xi_{j,i}} \exp(-\tau_j \lambda_i(u_{j,i}))$, $\tau_j = \tilde{t}_j - \tilde{t}_{j-1}$. Importantly, while we require that all rates $\lambda_i(t)$ are piecewise constant, we do not restrict ourselves to a uniform quantization of the time axis. The changepoint spacing is far from uniform, but rather tracks current spiking activity and stimulus quantization.

A simple transfer function is $\lambda_i(u) = e^u$, giving rise to a log-linear point process model. Another option is $\lambda_i(u) = e^u \mathrm{I}_{\{u<0\}} + (1+u)\mathrm{I}_{\{u\geq 0\}}$, which grows linearly only [4]. The class of admissable λ_i is characterized in [10].

The piecewise constant features $\psi(t)$ encode spike history and input stimulus (with some history as well) by using windows back in time. In order to infer the precise timing of relationships, we need a narrow spacing, and thus end up with many features, only a small part of which will be necessary to describe the data. This notion is embodied in the Laplace sparsity prior. We use $P(\{\boldsymbol{w}_i\}) = \prod_i P(\boldsymbol{w}_i)$, each factor having the form (2). The posterior for our sparse multi-neuron spiking model factorizes w.r.t. $\boldsymbol{w}_i$, each factor constituting a B-GLM of the form (1). The prior sites have the form $\phi_{k,i}(u_{k,i}) = \frac{\rho_i}{2}\exp(-\rho_i|u_{k,i}|)$ with $\psi_k = \boldsymbol{\delta}_k = (\mathrm{I}_{\{l=k\}})_l$. EP is used for approximate inference, as detailed in Section 3. It can be run in parallel across neurons, although the feature vectors ψ_j are shared among them.

We describe the composition of $\psi(t)$ informally only. A more formal description will be given in a longer version of this paper. The spike-history part of $\psi(t)$ depends on windows $I_l(t) = (t - \Delta_l^H, t - \Delta_{l-1}^H]$, $0 = \Delta_0^H < \Delta_1^H < \dots$, components are $n_{i,l}(t) = |\{j|\, t_{j,i} \in I_l(t)\}|$. These give rise to changepoints $t_{j,i} + \Delta_l$ for all j, i, and $l \geq 0$. The input stimulus $\boldsymbol{x}(t)$ is a step function, changing at t_j^I, $j \geq 1$. This adds components $\boldsymbol{x}(t - \Delta_l^I)$ to $\psi(t)$ for another system of lags $0 \leq \Delta_0^I < \Delta_1^I < \dots$. The corresponding changepoints are $t_j^I + \Delta_l^I$ for all j, l. The list of changepoints can be computed from the dataset, it does not depend on parameter settings. We also use a constant feature in $\psi(t)$, whose parameter controls the mean firing rate.

For fixed parameters $\boldsymbol{w}_i$, we can easily compute the log likelihood for some data by an accumulation of $\log \phi_{j,i}$. Here, the list of changepoints can be grown sequentially. The posterior expected log likelihood can be approximated by averaging over a sample drawn from $Q(\{\boldsymbol{w}_i\})$, or by just plugging in the posterior means. We can also sample data exactly from the model for fixed parameters $\boldsymbol{w}_i$, using a simple variant of the Gillespie algorithm (*e.g.*, [21]). This is possible only because we restrict ourselves to piecewise constant features $\psi(t)$. Sampling from the model is useful to approximate predictive probabilities for essentially arbitrary queries.

5 Experimental Results

In this section we present results for the multi-neuron spiking model of Section 4, applied to data recorded from retinal ganglion cells stimulated with white noise in a whole-mount preparation. More precisely, the stimulus has been generated from an m-sequence, yielding 16x16 bitmaps of spatially and temporally decorrelated light intensity patterns presented at about 50 Hz (20 ms between stimulus onset and offset). We selected four out of 27 neurons for our analysis, with average mean firing rate of 9 Hz for a recording time of 658 s . Details about the recording technique and the spike-sorting method can be found in [23].

The goal of our first analysis is to investigate how the Gaussian and the Laplace priors differentially affect the inference in our neuronal spiking model, depending on the amount of data used. This study is carried out for one out of the four neurons, with a substantially reduced set of parameters, in that we use a single time

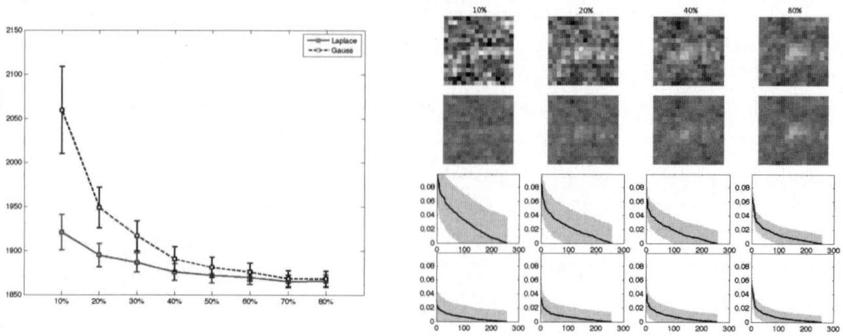

Fig. 2. Left: Comparison between Gaussian and Laplace prior for the reduced model. Hyperparameters are chosen by crossvalidation (see text). The negative log-likelihood value on the test dataset is plotted as a function of dataset size of the training set. Errorbars are obtained by sampling from the approximative posterior distribution and correspond to 2 standard deviations. **Right**: Receptive fields (shown are posterior means) under model with Gaussian (upper) and with Laplace prior (lower), for different training set sizes. Curves below show marginal posteriors (absolute value of mean, one std. dev. error bars, cut off at zero), decreasing order.

lag $\Delta_0^I = 120\,\text{ms}$ for stimulus dependence, six windows $\Delta_l^H = 0, 1, 10, 20, 40, 80, 160\,\text{ms}$ for spike history, and a constant offset feature. The complete data set was partitioned into test set, validation set (10% each), and a training pool (80%). The training sets are selected as increasing portions of the latter, in steps of 10%. Our B-GLM at present comes with a single hyperparameter ρ, the scale of the prior. This parameter is determined, independently for the Gaussian and the Laplace variant, by maximizing the log likelihood of the validation set under the posterior mean parameters for a training set of size 10%.

The log likelihood scores on the test set (Figure 2, left) show that the Laplace prior configuration of our model clearly outperforms the Gaussian prior variant. As expected, the difference is most pronounced for small training set sizes, and does eventually vanish for large data sets, when the prior has less and less influence on the inference. This confirms the *statistical* validity of the sparseness assumption for this task. As discussed in Section 2 and Figure 1, the Gaussian has a strong tendency to push large values towards zero, while the Laplace prior concentrates more on shrinking smaller values strongly to zero (see Figure 2, right; 80%, lower panel). The intolerance of even a small number of large coefficients means that the prior variance of the Gaussian has to be chosen larger than for the Laplace, leading to very diffuse receptive field estimates (see Figure 2, right).

The goal of our second study is to demonstrate that the sparse Bayesian estimation framework allows us to obtain reliable results also for more complex models with a large number of parameters. We did the same experiments as above with a full setup consisting of $n = 4$ neurons, five time lags for stimulus dependency (20, 40, 80, 120, 160 ms), the same six windows for spike history

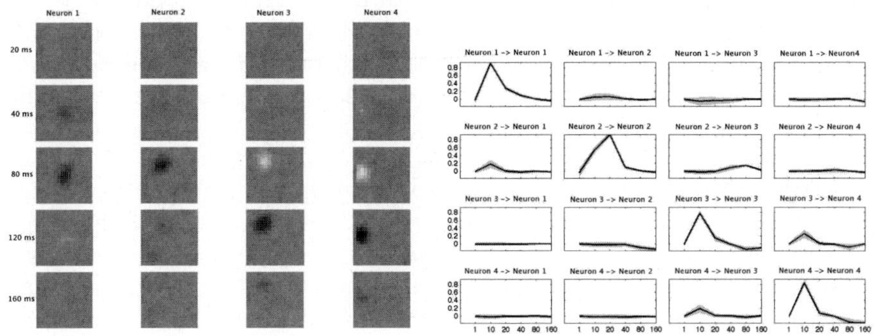

Fig. 3. Left: Stimulus dependence for the four neurons (columns) at different time lags (rows). Shown are posterior means. Gray scale from dark (minimum) to light (maximum). **Right**: Causal dependencies between the four neurons. Each plot shows the parameter value as function of increasing time lag. Shown are posterior mean and three std. dev. Note that all inter-dependency parameter estimates are positive, while the offset parameters for each of the neurons is significantly negative. Self-excitation can be clearly seen, explaining the bursting behaviour seen in the data.

and constant offset feature as above, resulting in a total number of parameters $K = 1305$ (versus $K = 263$ for the restricted setup). We use training set size 10%, and score Gaussian and Laplace variant by the negative test set log likelihood for the one neuron used in the restricted setup. We have $\text{nlh}_{1,\text{Gauss}} = 1953.14$, $\text{nlh}_{1,\text{Laplace}} = 1920.35$, $\text{diff}_{1,\text{Gauss}-\text{Laplace}} = 32.79$ for the restricted, and $\text{nlh}_{4,\text{Gauss}} = 2984.5$, $\text{nlh}_{4,\text{Laplace}} = 1992.59$, $\text{diff}_{4,\text{Gauss}-\text{Laplace}} = 991.91$ for the full setup. Both Gaussian and Laplace variant become worse on the full setup, owing to the fact that there is a much larger number of parameters and interdependence features, explaining the same number of spikes (although the data from the other neurons can be used as well in the full setup). In summary the Laplace prior becomes more import the more parameters the model has.

Using the full training pool (80%, 178326 changepoints), we obtain reliable posterior mean estimates for both the *stimulus-neuron* and the *neuron-neuron* dependencies (we used the ρ value determined for the restricted setup). The receptive fields (Figure 3, left) are localized in space and time, as is typical for retinal ganglion cells. Self-feedback dominates the spike history parameters (Figure 3, right), allowing the model to explain short burst behaviour of retinal cells [1].

6 Conclusion

We have presented a method for approximate Bayesian inference in generalized linear models with factorizing priors, which is accurate, efficient, and numerically robust. In particular, we applied this method to a multi-neuron spiking model and showed that the usage of a Laplace sparsity prior leads to superior prediction performance at no extra cost, compared to the standard Gaussian choice.

Our method is versatile and flexible, catering to various applications as the family of B-GLMs is large, containing the sparse linear model, the generalized linear and Gaussian process models for classification, robust regression, ordinal regression, survival analysis and many more. While these models are often fitted to data by point estimation techniques, our framework can be used to obtain a good approximation to the full posterior distribution efficiently.

In future work, we will explore ideas to speed up our method drastically, for example by exploiting the fact that $\boldsymbol{\psi}_{j+1} - \boldsymbol{\psi}_j$ is sparse. We will also consider factor representations of the parameters $\boldsymbol{w}_i$, for example to learn wide-horizon, fine-grained spatio-temporal receptive fields, and extensions of our basic model by latent variables. Both will render the complete model non-log-concave, but our method here will still be useful as subroutine in a surrounding belief propagation architecture.

Acknowledgments

We thank G. Zeck for providing us with data, and J. Macke for helpful discussions. Supported in part by the IST Programme of the European Community, under the PASCAL Network of Excellence, IST-2002-506778.

References

1. Berry, M., Warland, D., Meister, M.: The structure and precision of retinal spike trains (1997)
2. Carandini, M., Demb, J., Mante, V., Tolhurst, D., Dan, Y., Olshausen, B., Gallant, J., Rust, N.: Do we know what the early visual system does? J Neurosci 25(46), 10577–10597 (2005)
3. Gilks, W.R., Wild, P.: Adaptive rejection sampling for Gibbs sampling. Applied Statistics 41(2), 337–348 (1992)
4. Harris, K., Csicsvari, J., Hirase, H., Dragoi, G., Buzsaki, G.: Organization of cell assemblies in the hippocampus. Nature 424(6948), 552–556 (2003)
5. McCullach, P., Nelder, J.A.: Generalized Linear Models. In: Monographs on Statistics and Applied Probability, 1st edn. no. 37, Chapman & Hall (1983)
6. Minka, T.: Divergence measures and message passing. Technical Report MSR-TR-2005-173, Microsoft Research, Cambridge (2005)
7. Minka, T.: Expectation propagation for approximate Bayesian inference. Uncertainty in AI 17 (2001)
8. Nodelman, U., Koller, D., Shelton, C.: Expectation propagation for continuous time Bayesian networks. Uncertainty in AI 21, 431–440 (2005)
9. Opper, M., Winther, O.: Gaussian processes for classification: Mean field algorithms. N. Comp. 12(11), 2655–2684 (2000)
10. Paninski, L.: Maximum likelihood estimation of cascade point-process neural encoding models. Network: Computation in Neural Systems 15, 243–262 (2004)
11. Park, T., Casella, G.: The Bayesian Lasso. Technical report, University of Florida (2005)
12. Qi, Y., Minka, T., Picard, R., Ghahramani, Z.: Predictive automatic relevance determination by expectation propagation. In: Proceedings of ICML 21 (2004)

13. Rajaram, S., Graepel, T., Herbrich, R.: Poisson networks: A model for structured point processes. AI and Statistics 10 (2005)
14. Rieke, F., Warland, D., van Steveninck, R.R., Bialek, W.: Spikes: Exploring the Neural Code, 1st edn. MIT Press, Cambridge (1999)
15. Seeger, M.: Expectation propagation for exponential families. Technical report, University of California at Berkeley (2005) See `http://www.kyb.tuebingen.mpg.de/bs/people/seeger`
16. Seeger, M., Steinke, F., Tsuda, K.: Bayesian inference and optimal design in the sparse linear model. AI and Statistics 11 (2007)
17. Simoncelli, E., Paninski, L., Pillow, J., Schwartz, O.: Characterization of neural responses with stochastic stimuli. In: Gazzaniga, M. (ed.) The Cognitive Neurosciences, 3rd edn., MIT Press, Cambridge (2004)
18. Snyder, D., Miller, M.: Random point processes in time and space. Springer Texts in Electrical Engineering (1991)
19. Tibshirani, R.: Regression shrinkage and selection via the Lasso. J. Roy. Stat. Soc. B 58, 267–288 (1996)
20. Tipping, M.: Sparse Bayesian learning and the relevance vector machine. J. M. Learn. Res. 1, 211–244 (2001)
21. Wilkinson, D.: Stochastic Modelling for Systems Biology. Chapman & Hall (2006)
22. Wipf, D., Palmer, J., Rao, B.: Perspectives on sparse Bayesian learning. In: Advances in NIPS 16 (2004)
23. Zeck, G., Xiao, Q., Masland, R.: The spatial filtering properties of local edge detectors and brisk-sustained retinal ganglion cells. Eur J Neurosci 22(8), 2016–2026 (2005)

Appendix

EP update: Match moments of $\hat{P}(u_j) \propto \phi_j(u_j)\tilde{\phi}_j(u_j)^{-1}Q(u_j)$ and $Q'(u_j)$, so $b_j \to b'_j = b_j + \Delta b_j$, $\pi_j \to \pi'_j = \pi_j + \Delta\pi_j$. If $Q(\boldsymbol{w}) = N(\boldsymbol{h}, \boldsymbol{\Sigma})$, then $Q'(\boldsymbol{w}) \propto \exp((\Delta b_j)u_j - \frac{1}{2}(\Delta\pi_j)u_j^2)Q(\boldsymbol{w})$ with $u_j = \boldsymbol{\psi}_j^T\boldsymbol{w}$. If $\boldsymbol{v}_j = \boldsymbol{\Sigma}\boldsymbol{\psi}_j$, $a_j = \boldsymbol{\psi}_j^T\boldsymbol{v}_j$, $\mu_j = \boldsymbol{\psi}_j^T\boldsymbol{h}$:

$$\boldsymbol{\Sigma}' = \boldsymbol{\Sigma} - \frac{\Delta\pi_j}{1 + \Delta\pi_j a_j}\boldsymbol{v}_j\boldsymbol{v}_j^T, \quad \boldsymbol{h}' = \boldsymbol{h} + \frac{\Delta b_j - \Delta\pi_j\mu_j}{1 + \Delta\pi_j a_j}\boldsymbol{v}_j.$$

The computation of b'_j, π'_j depends on the exact form of $\phi_j(u_j)$. For Laplace sites, the computation is analytic, but numerically challenging [16]. For the likelihood sites of our spiking model, the required one-dimensional integrals are numerically harmless and can be approximated with Gauss-Hermite quadrature.

Classifier Loss Under Metric Uncertainty

David B. Skalak[1], Alexandru Niculescu-Mizil[2], and Rich Caruana[2]

[1] Highgate Predictions, LLC, Ithaca, NY 14850 USA
[2] Cornell University, Ithaca, NY 14853 USA
{skalak,alexn,caruana}@cs.cornell.edu
http://www.cs.cornell.edu/

Abstract. Classifiers that are deployed in the field can be used and evaluated in ways that were not anticipated when the model was trained. The final evaluation metric may not have been known at training time, additional performance criteria may have been added, the evaluation metric may have changed over time, or the real-world evaluation procedure may have been impossible to simulate. Unforeseen ways of measuring model utility can degrade performance. Our objective is to provide experimental support for modelers who face potential "cross-metric" performance deterioration. First, to identify model-selection metrics that lead to stronger cross-metric performance, we characterize the expected loss where the selection metric is held fixed and the evaluation metric is varied. Second, we show that the number of data points evaluated by a selection metric has substantial impact on the optimal evaluation. While addressing these issues, we consider the effect of calibrating the classifiers to output probabilities influences. Our experiments show that if models are well calibrated, cross-entropy is the highest-performing selection metric if little data is available for model selection. With these experiments, modelers may be in a better position to choose selection metrics that are robust where it is uncertain what evaluation metric will be applied.

Keywords: performance metric, evaluation, calibration, cross-metric.

1 Introduction

Most machine learning research on classification has assumed that it is best to train and select a classifier according to the metric upon which it ultimately will be evaluated. However, this characterization makes several assumptions that we question here. What if we don't know the metric upon which the classifier will be judged? What if the classification objective is not optimal performance, but simply robust performance across several metrics? Does it make any difference how much data is available on which to base model performance estimates? What if we want at least to avoid the worst-performing selection metrics?

In this paper we give experimental results to begin to answer questions like the ones we have just posed. The results show that the choice of selection metric depends to a large degree on how much data is available to measure performance and depends also on whether the underlying models produce accurate probabilities.

J.N. Kok et al. (Eds.): ECML 2007, LNAI 4701, pp. 310–322, 2007.

It is not so far-fetched that we may not have as much knowledge of — and access to — the ultimate evaluation metric as is usually assumed. In some situations a modeler may have the discretion to build models that optimize one of several metrics but not have access to a classification algorithm that directly optimizes the evaluation metric. For example, the modeler may decide between optimizing cross-entropy or root-mean-squared error through the choice of model class and training algorithm. But if these models are evaluated with respect to the F-score metric, it would be important to compare expected performance losses in going from cross-entropy to F-score and from root-mean-squared error to F-score. These considerations arise in natural language processing (NLP) tasks, such as noun phrase coreference resolution, where classification models may be built to maximize accuracy, but where F-score or average precision provides the ultimate measure of success [1]. In fact, NLP tasks are often evaluated on multiple reporting metrics, compounding the cross-metric problem.

The complex data processing required for NLP systems often places NLP classifiers in a pipeline where they are judged according to the performance they enable in downstream modules that receive the class predictions. Embedded classifiers may be subjected to evaluation(s) that cannot easily be tested and that may change according to evolving criteria of the entire system.

A marketing group in a large organization may request a model that maximizes response lift at 10% of the universe of customers. After the model has been built, the marketing budget for the campaign is cut, but the marketing group has the campaign ready to roll out and so not have the time to commission another model. In that case the database marketing group may decide to contact only 5% of the customers. The model that optimized response at the 10% level will now be judged in the field according to a different criterion: response from 5% of the customers. (Alternatively, the marketing group may not even specify its performance criterion, but may request a model that "simply" yields optimal profits, accuracy, and lift.) What model should be selected to be robust to changes such as these?

The availability of multiple performance metrics also poses questions for machine learning research. For example, an author may want to use a test metric that would be most acceptable to a wide readership. An author might also want to apply a second test metric under which performance is most likely to vary meaningfully from the first, and therefore provide complementary guidance.

Thus real-world considerations make evaluation more complicated than might be generally assumed. Performance metrics may change over time, may not be known, may be difficult to simulate, or may be numerous. In this paper we examine uncertain evaluation by providing experimental answers to two questions:

1. What selection metrics yield the highest performance across commonly applied evaluation metrics?
2. What is the effect of the number of data points available for making model selection judgments where the ultimate evaluation metric may be unknown?

In our experiments, we show one important factor is whether a classifier has been calibrated to output accurate probabilities. Context for all these results is provided by a brief survey of closely related research (Section 2) and a discussion of the characteristic shape of distributions gleaned from plotting selection metric performance against evaluation metric performance (Section 6).

2 Related Research

As part of an extensive set of experiments, Huang and Ling defined a model selection ability measure called MSA to reflect the relative abilities of eight metrics to optimize one of three target metrics: accuracy, area under the ROC curve ("AUC") and lift [2]. Given one of these three "goal" metrics, MSA measures the probability that one of the eight metrics correctly identifies which member of all pairs of models will be better on the goal metric. While this is an attractive summary approach, our experiments hew more closely to how we see model selection done in practice. Our experiments measure how one metric's *best* performing models perform when measured by a second metric. Since practitioners tend to focus on superior models only, our methodology also reflects that bias. Our empirical study below also evaluates all our metrics as reporting methods rather than limiting the study to a proper subset of three goal metrics. The roles of probability calibration and classifier combination in reducing performance loss are also studied additionally here.

Several related efforts to develop algorithms to handle multiple performance criteria have also been made [3,4,5]. Additionally, Ting and Zheng [6] have provided an approach to deal with changes in costs over time.

In 2004 as part of a statistical study of AUC, Rosset showed empirically that, even where the goal is to maximize accuracy, optimizing AUC can be a superior strategy for Naive Bayes and k-nearest neighbor classifiers [7]. Joachims has extended support vector methodology to optimize directly non-linear performance measures that cannot be decomposed into measures over individual examples, and any measure derived from a contingency table [8]. Cortes and Mohri give a statistical analysis of accuracy and AUC and show that classifiers with the same accuracy can yield different AUC values when accuracy is low [9].

3 Experimental Design

3.1 Performance Metrics

The performance metrics we study are accuracy (ACC), lift at the 25th percentile (LFT), F-score (FSC), area under the ROC curve (ROC), average precision (APR), precision-recall break-even point (BEP), root-mean squared error (RMS), and mean cross-entropy (MXE). We also synthesize a hybrid metric that is defined as the equally-weighted mean performance under RMS, ROC and ACC (called "ALL"). We follow the definitions of these performance metrics found in Caruana and Niculescu [10], since they are implemented in the PERF code that was made available by Caruana in connection with the KDD Cup 2004.

We have also adopted the same conventions as to the normalization of classifier performance with respect to various metrics. Unfortunately, normalization is necessary in order to compare directly metrics with different measurement scales. Metrics have been normalized to values in $[0, 1]$ where 0 represents the baseline performance of classifying all instances with the most frequent class in the data, and 1 corresponds to the best performance of any model developed in our lab on that data [1].

3.2 Problems

Eleven binary classification problems were used in these experiments. ADULT, COV_TYPE and LETTER are from the UCI Repository [11]. COV_TYPE has been converted to a binary problem by treating the largest class as the positive and the rest as negative. We converted LETTER to boolean in two ways. LETTER.p1 treats "O" as positive and the remaining 25 letters as negative, yielding a an unbalanced problem. LETTER.p2 uses letters A-M as positives and the rest as negatives, yielding a well-balanced problem. HS is the IndianPine92 data set [12] where the difficult class Soybean-mintill is the positive class. SLAC is a problem from the Stanford Linear Accelerator. MEDIS and MG are medical data sets. COD, BACT, and CALHOUS are three of the datasets used in [13]. ADULT, COD, and BACT contain nominal attributes. For neural networks, SVMs, KNNs, and logistic regression we transform nominal attributes to boolean (one boolean per value). Each decision tree, bagged decision tree, boosted tree, boosted stump, random forest and naive Bayes model is trained twice, once with transformed attributes and once with the original ones.

3.3 Model Types

The 10 model types that we used in this experiment were: back-propagation neural networks, bagging of decision trees, boosting of decision trees, k-nearest neighbor, logistic regression, Naive Bayes, random forests, decision trees, boosting decision stumps and support vector machines. We create a library of approximately 2,000 models trained on training sets of size 4,000. We train each of these models on each of the 11 problems to yield approximately 22,000 models. The models are all as described in [14].

The output of such learning methods as boosted decision trees, boosted decision stumps, SVMs and Naive Bayes cannot be interpreted as well-calibrated posterior probabilities [15]. This has a negative impact on the metrics that interpret predictions as probabilities: RMS, MXE and ALL (which invokes RMS). To address this problem, we use post-training calibration to transform the predictions of all the methods into well-calibrated probabilities. In this paper calibration is done via Platt scaling [16].

---

[1] The performance upper bounds are available to interested researchers.

To fit the calibrated model we use a set of 1000 points reserved solely for calibration (i.e. they are not part of the training, validation or final test set).[2] While in practice one would use the same set of points both for calibration and for model selection, here we use separate sets in order to separate the effects of calibration from the effects of model selection on performance. The effect of calibration is further discussed in Section 5.

4 The Effect of Sample Size on Selection Metric Choice

In this section we discuss the effect of small data sample size on the decision of which selection metrics to use. Our primary objective in this section is to quantify the loss in selecting on one metric but reporting on another. To obtain the results in this section, we use the following methodology. For each problem, we train each of the approximately 2000 models on a 4000 points training set, and calibrate it using the extra 1000 points calibration set. All the trained models are then evaluated on a validation (selection) set, and the model with the best performance on the selection metric is found. Finally, we report the evaluation (reporting) metric performance of the best model on a final independent test set. To ensure that the results are not dependent on the particular train/validation/test set split, we repeat the experiment five times and report the average performance over the five trials.

To investigate how the size of the selection set affects the performance of model selection for different selection metrics, we consider selection sets of 100, 200, 500 and 1000 points. For comparison we also show results for "optimal" selection, where the final test set is used as the selection set.

We use the following experimental procedure. We are given a problem, a selection metric, s, and a reporting metric, r. We choose from our library the classifier C_s that has the highest normalized score under the selection metric s. We then measure the score of that classifier C_s under the reporting metric r. Call that score $r(C_s)$.

Next we identify the classifier C^* that has the highest performance on the reporting metric. Call that score $r(C^*)$. The difference $r(C^*) - r(C_s)$ is the loss we report. The selection of C_s is done on a validation set and the reporting metric performance of both classifiers is computed on an independent test set.

Figure 1 shows the loss in performance due to model selection for nine selection metrics averaged across the nine reporting metrics. The tenth line, ORM (Optimize to the Right Metric), shows the loss of always selecting using the evaluation metric (i.e. select using ACC when the evaluation metric is ACC, ROC when the evaluation metric is ROC, etc.). On the X axis we vary the size of the selection set on a log scale. The right-most point on the graph, labeled

[2] This approach could give metrics affected by calibration (*e.g.,* RMS and MXE) an advantage for model selection over metrics not affected by calibration (*e.g.,* ACC, ROC, and LFT). To verify that this is not a problem we repeated the experiments with well-calibrated models that do not require post-training calibration (and thus do not use extra calibration data) and obtained similar results.

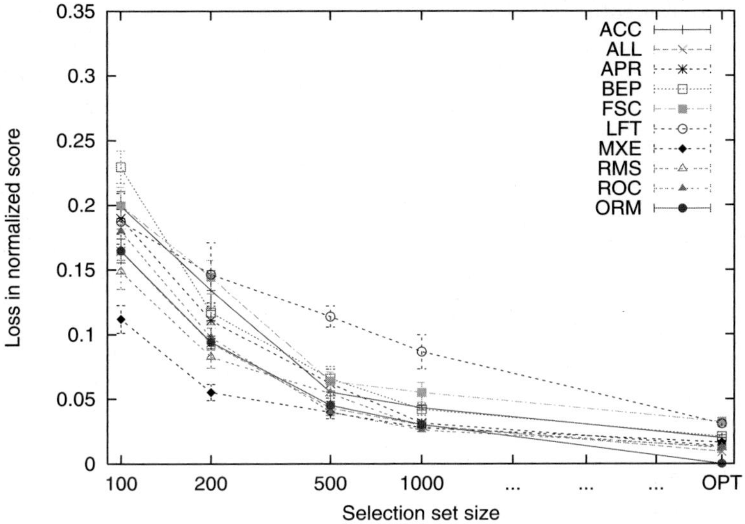

Fig. 1. Average across all nine reporting metrics

OPT, shows the loss when selection is done "optimally" (by cheating) using the final test set. This represents the best achievable performance for any selection metric, and can be viewed as a bias, or mismatch between the selection metric and the evaluation metric.[3]

The most striking result is the good performance of selecting on mean cross-entropy (MXE) for small sizes of the selection set. When the selection set has only 100 or 200 points, using cross-entropy as the selection metric incurs the lowest loss. In fact, at 100 and 200 points, selecting on MXE has the lowest loss for every individual reporting metric, not only on average! This may be a surprising result in that it undermines the common belief that it is always better to optimize to the metric on which the classifier will be evaluated.

We propose two hypotheses that would account for the superior performance of MXE for small data sets, but we do not yet have support for these possible explanations. MXE provides the maximum likelihood probability estimation of the binary targets. Under this hypothesis, MXE reflects the "correct" prior for target values as a binomial distribution [17]. Priors are particularly important where data are scarce. The second hypothesis recognizes that (of the metrics we consider) MXE assesses the largest penalty for large errors, which may be desirable where not much data is available.

For larger selection sets, MXE continues to be competitive, but ROC and ALL catch up when the selection set has 500 points. At 1000 points all metrics except BEP, ACC, FSC, and LFT have similar performance (on average across reporting metrics). This result suggests that, when the evaluation metric is uncertain, cross

[3] Of course, this bias/mismatch depends on the underlying set of classifiers to select among.

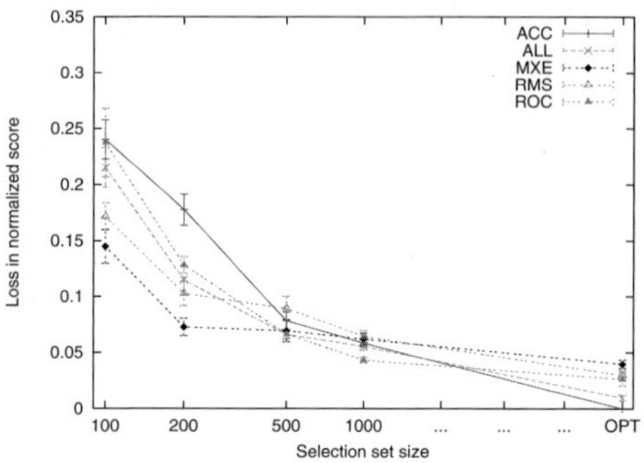

Fig. 2. Loss when reporting on ACC

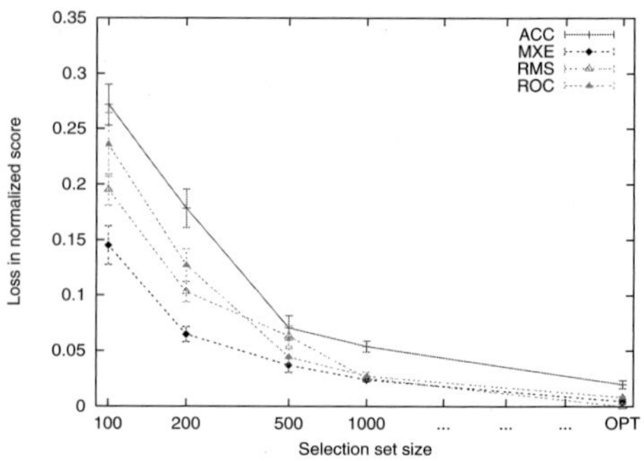

Fig. 3. Loss when reporting on RMS

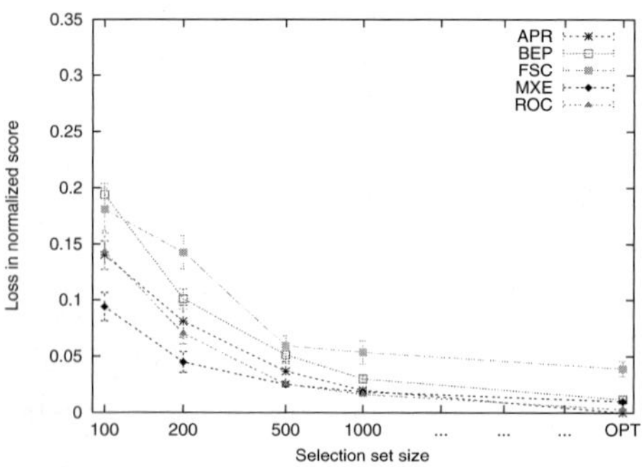

Fig. 4. Loss when reporting on APR

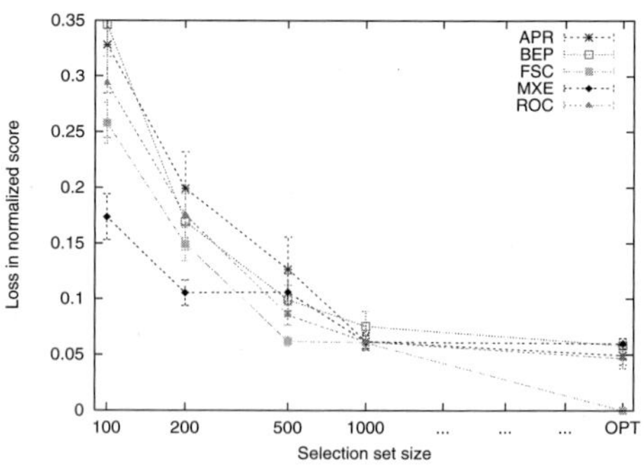

Fig. 5. Loss when reporting on FSC

entropy should be used as a selection metric, especially when validation data is scarce. When the validation set is larger, ROC, RMS and ALL also are robust selection metrics. LFT and FSC seem to be the least robust metrics, followed by BEP and ACC. Contrary to common belief, directly optimizing the evaluation metric (the ORM line) actually yields worse performance than both using MXE and RMS as a selection metric. Even for larger validation set sizes optimizing to the right metric does not yield a benefit on average.

Figure 2 shows the performance for a few selection metrics when ACC is the evaluation metric. The figure shows ROC is superior as a selection metric to ACC even when the evaluation metric is ACC. ROC-based selection yields lower loss across all selection set sizes (except of course OPT, where ACC has zero loss by definition). This confirms the observation made by Rosset [7], which was discussed in Section 2. Although at low selection set sizes MXE has the best performance (followed by RMS), looking at the OPT point, we see that MXE has the largest bias (followed by RMS). Of all metrics ALL has the smallest bias.

In the Information Retrieval (IR) community, APR is often preferred to ROC as a ranking evaluation metric because it is more sensitive to the high end of the ranking and less sensitive to the low end. Figure 4 shows the loss in normalized

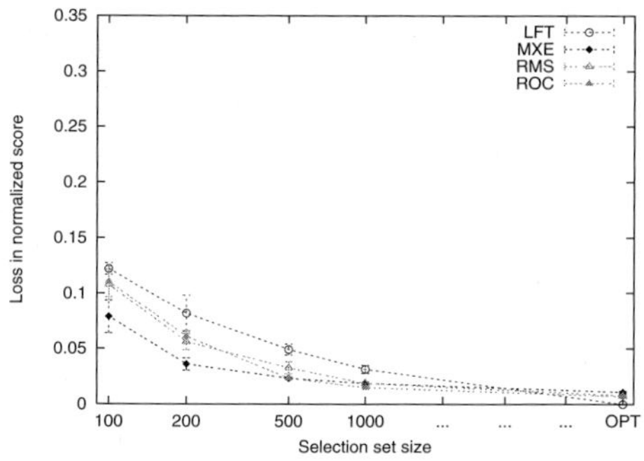

Fig. 6. Loss when reporting on LFT

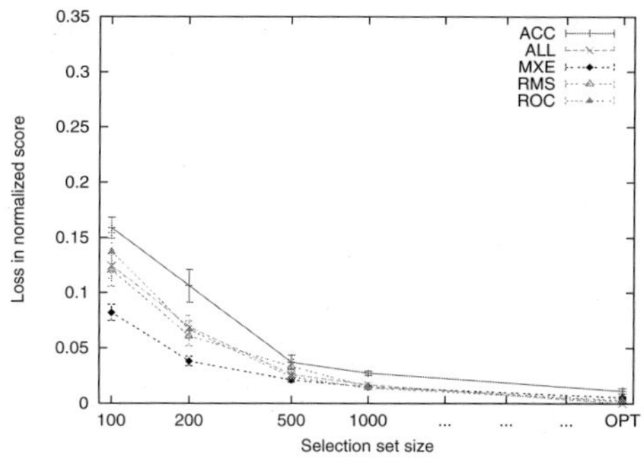

Fig. 7. Loss when reporting on ALL

score when the evaluation metric is APR. Besides APR and ROC, we also show the selection performance of MXE and two other IR metrics: BEP and FSC. The results suggest that selection based on ROC performs the same, or slightly better than selecting on APR directly. In fact ROC has a very low bias relative to APR, as shown by the OPT point in the graph. The other two IR metrics have lower performance, with FSC incurring a significantly higher loss.

Figure 5 depicts the loss in normalized score when using FSC as an evaluation metric. This figure may also be of interest to IR practitioners, since FSC is often relied upon in that field. The figure shows that, except for small validation set sizes, if FSC is the metric of interest, then FSC should also be used as a selection metric. For small validation sets, MXE again provides significantly lower loss. One other interesting observation is the large mismatch between FSC and the other metrics (the OPT point in the graph). This mismatch is one reason why, given enough validation data, FSC is the preferred selection metric when one is interested in optimizing FSC.

One other interesting case is shown in Figure 6 for LFT as the evaluation metric. The figure shows that even if one is interested in lift, one should not select based on it. MXE, RMS and ROC all lead to selecting better models.

Figure 7 shows the case when the performance is evaluated using a combination of multiple metrics. For the figure, the reporting metric is ALL which is an equally weighed average of ACC, RMS and ROC. Selecting on the more robust RMS or ROC metrics performs as well as selecting on the evaluation metric ALL. This is not the case for ACC, which is a less robust metric. For small validation sets, cross-entropy is again the best selection metric.

5 The Effect of Model Probability Calibration on Selection Metric Choice

In this section we investigate how cross-metric optimization performance is affected by models with poor calibration such as boosted trees, boosted stumps,

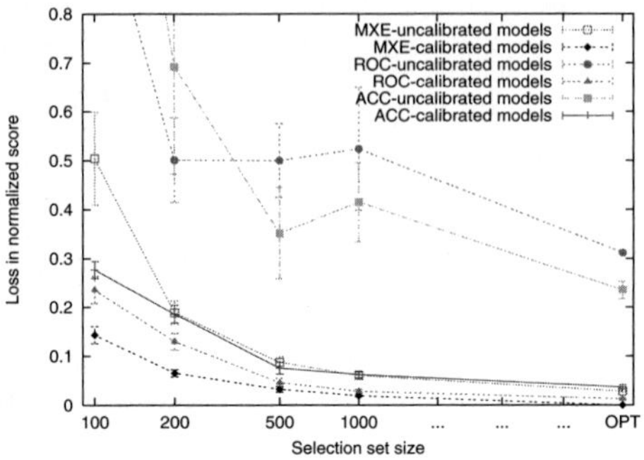

Fig. 8. Evaluation metric MXE

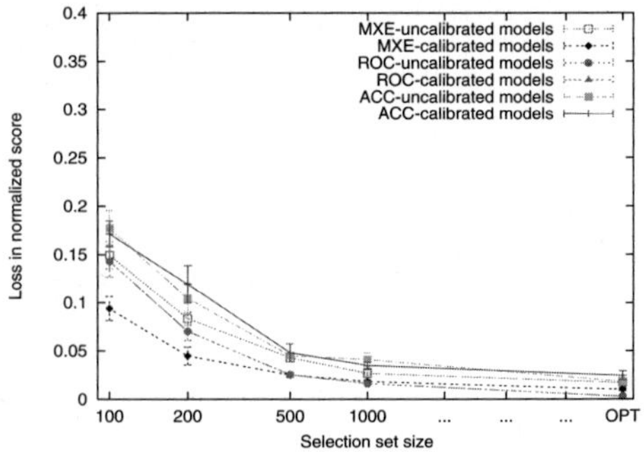

Fig. 9. Evaluation metric APR

SVMs and Naive Bayes. To this end, we repeat the experiments in Section 4, but use the original uncalibrated models instead of the Platt-calibrated ones.

As expected, having a mix of well calibrated and poorly calibrated models hurts cross-metric optimization. The effect of poorly calibrated models is two-fold. On one hand, when selecting on a metric such as ROC, APR or ACC that does not interpret predictions as probabilities, and evaluating on a metric such as RMS, MXE or ALL that is sensitive to probability calibration, the selected model, while performing well on the "non-probability" measures, may be poorly calibrated, thus incurring a high loss on the "probability" measures.

This effect can be clearly seen in Figure 8. The figure shows the loss in normalized score when the reporting metric is MXE, and the selection metric is MXE, ROC or ACC. For each selection metric, two lines are shown: one for selecting from uncalibrated models, and the other for selecting from Platt-calibrated models. When selecting from uncalibrated models, using either ROC or ACC as selection metrics (the top two lines) incurs a very large loss in performance (note the scale). In fact, quite often, the MXE performance of the selected models is worse than that of the baseline model (the model that predicts, for each instance, the ratio of the positive examples in the training set). Using calibrated models eliminates this problem driving down the loss.

On the other hand, when selecting on one of the "probability" measures (RMS, MXE or ALL), the poorly calibrated models will not be selected because of their low performance on such metrics. Some of these models, however, do perform very well on "non-probability" measures such as ROC, APR or ACC. This leads to increased loss when selecting on probability measures and evaluating on non-probability ones because, in a sense, selection is denied access to some of the best models.

Figure 9 shows the loss in normalized score when the reporting metric is APR, and the selection metric is MXE, ROC or ACC. Looking at MXE as a selection metric we see that, as expected, the loss from model selection is higher when using uncalibrated models than when using calibrated ones. Since calibration does not affect ROC or APR, selecting on ROC and evaluating on APR yields

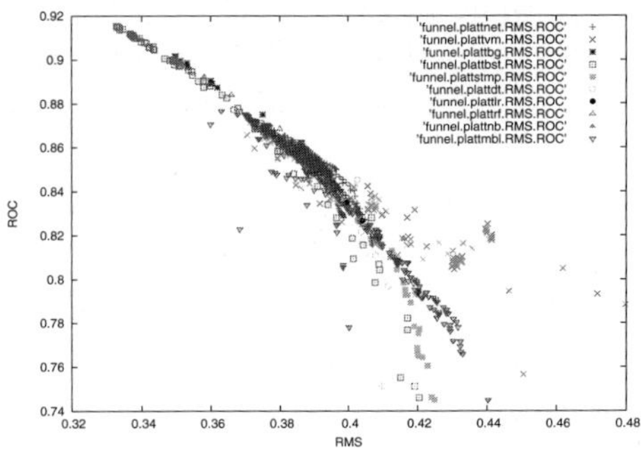

Fig. 10. Covertype data funnel

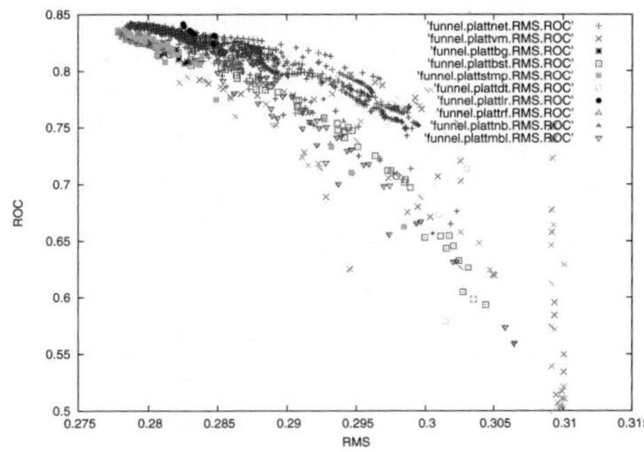

Fig. 11. Medis data funnel

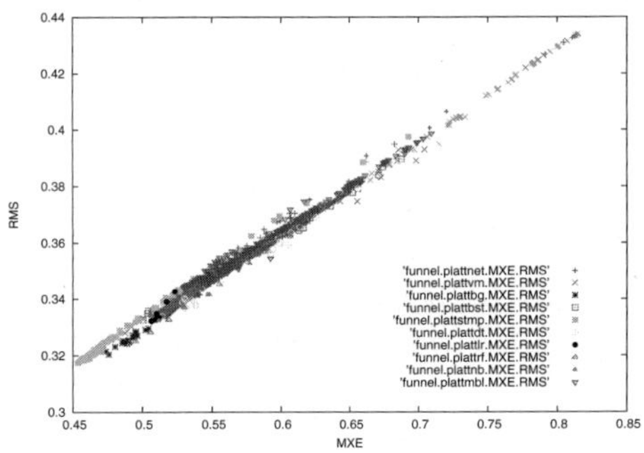

Fig. 12. Adult data funnel

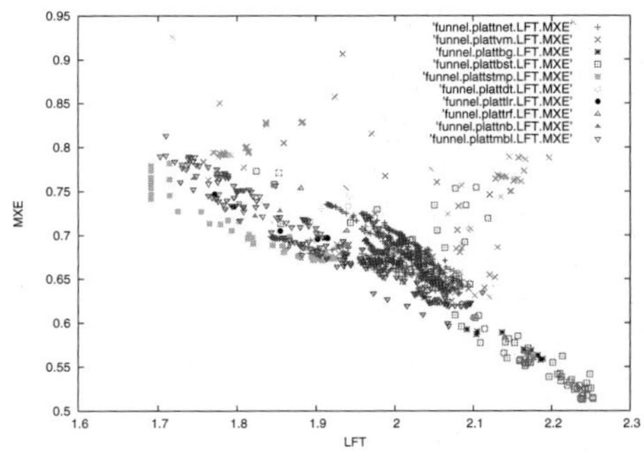

Fig. 13. Covertype data funnel

the same results no matter if the models were calibrated or not. The same is not true when selecting using ACC because calibration can affect threshold metrics by effectively changing the threshold.

6 Visualizing the Joint Distribution of Selection and Evaluation Metric Performance

One way to gain further insight is to graph for each pair of metrics the distribution of performances for a large set of classifiers. For this experiment we rely on the pool of classifiers trained for the previous experiments. Recall that these classifiers came from 10 model classes. A variety of parameter settings for each model class yielded 8,910 classifiers, each of which may be evaluated according to its test-set performance for pairs of metrics. With 9 performance metrics, there are 36 plots of pairs of metrics to examine for each problem. Figures 10, 11, 12 and 13 show four of these that illustrate a variety of behaviors.

Figure 10 is a scatterplot of the ROC vs. RMS performance of the models on the Covertype problem. In this figure boosted decision trees (purple boxes) clearly dominate all other model types on both ROC and MXE. Bagged decision trees (blue stars) are the second best model. At the better-performing end of the spectrum (upper left of the plot) there is a strong correlation between performance on the two metrics. This correlation is reduced as performance worsens, leading to the broadening of the "funnel".

Figure 11 shows a scatterplot for the same two metrics (ROC vs. RMS) but on the Medis problem. The shape of the funnel differs somewhat from that of Figure 10. On this problem, there is no one model type that dominates the other model types on both metrics. Calibrated boosted stumps have the best RMS, but neural nets and logistic regression yield somewhat better ROC. Also, there is less correlation between the two performance measures for different families of algorithms – the thread for each family is more distinguishable in this plot.

Figure 12 shows RMS vs. MXE performance for the Adult data set. As one might expect for two measures such as RMS and MXE that are so similar, this scatterplot shows a remarkably strong linear correlation between the two measures, with the best-performing models being neural nets and SVMs. Figure 13 shows MXE vs. LFT for Covertype. In this scatterplot there is a reasonably strong correlation between the two measures for most algorithms, but SVMs (green Xs) form a cloud of outliers with overall worse MXE.

One general feature of these "funnel" plots is that there is a narrowing at the high-performing end of the graph because it is difficult with most metrics to achieve near-optimal performance on one metric while achieving poorer performance on the other metric. When performance is poorer, however, often the funnel widens because when performance is poor on one metric it is possible to achieve a wide range of performances on other metrics. When performance is not optimal, it makes a larger difference what metric is used for selection.

The shape of the distribution of scores is seen many times for pairs of metrics. Often a wedge-shaped distribution can be seen reflecting the relatively wide variance in performance for classifiers that do not perform well along one or both of the two metrics. But we see a much tighter distribution at the vertex of the wedge for classifiers that do perform well under both metrics.

These distinctive distributions may provide a clue as to why calibrated classifiers suffer less cross-metric loss. Ensemble classifiers and calibrated classifiers both tend to yield higher-performing classifiers for a variety of metrics. In many graphs, they fall towards the narrow, extreme vertex of the wedge. At this thin edge of the plot, little variance in performance from metric to metric is seen. Consequently, cross-metric loss is lower in that region of the plot, which is inhabited by superior classifiers.

7 Conclusion

Our experiments have shown that when only a small amount of data is available, cross-entropy yields the strongest cross-metric performance. The experiments have also shown that calibration can affect the performance of selection metrics in general, and of cross-entropy in particular. In general, MXE and ROC performed strongly as selection metrics and FSC, LFT, ACC, and BEP performed poorly. The next step in our research is to go beyond the empirical results presented in this paper and try to create a formal decomposition of cross-metric loss.

Acknowledgments. This work was supported by NSF Award 0412930.

References

1. Munson, A., Cardie, C., Caruana, R.: Optimizing to arbitrary NLP metrics using ensemble selection. In: Proc. of Human Language Technology Conference and Conference on Empirical Methods in Natural Language Processing (HLT/EMNLP), pp. 539–546 (2005)
2. Huang, J., Ling, C.X.: Evaluating model selection abilities of performance measures. In: Evaluation Methods for Machine Learning, Papers from the AAAI workshop, Technical Report WS-06-06, AAAI, pp. 12–17 (2006)
3. Soares, C., Costa, J., Brazdil, P.: A simple and intuitive measure for multicriteria evaluation of classification algorithms. In: ECML 2000. Proceedings of the Workshop on Meta-Learning: Building Automatic Advice Strategies for Model Selection and Method Combination, Barcelona, Spain (2000)
4. Nakhaeizadeh, C., Schnabl, A.: Development of multi-criteria metrics for evaluation of data mining algorithms. In: Heckerman, D., Manilla, H., Pregibon, D. (eds.) Proceedings of the 3rd International Conference on Knowledge Discovery in Databases, Newport Beach, CA, AAAI Press, Menlo Park, CA (1997)
5. Spiliopoulou, M., Kalousis, A., Faulstich, L.C., Theoharis, T.: NOEMON: An intelligent assistant for classifier selection. In: FGML98. Number 11 in 98, Dept. of Computer Science, TU Berlin, pp. 90–97 (1998)
6. Ting, K.M., Zheng, Z.: Boosting trees for cost-sensitive classifications. In: Nédellec, C., Rouveirol, C. (eds.) ECML 1998. LNCS, vol. 1398, pp. 190–195. Springer, Heidelberg (1998)
7. Rosset, S.: Model selection via the auc. In: ICML '04: Proceedings of the Twenty-first International Conference on Machine Learning, p. 89. ACM Press, New York (2004)
8. Joachims, T.: A support vector method for multivariate performance measures
9. Cortes, C., Mohri, M.: Auc optimization vs. error rate minimization. In: Thrun, S., Saul, L., Scholkopf, B. (eds.) Advances in Neural Information Processing Systems 16, MIT Press, Cambridge (2004)
10. Caruana, R., Niculescu-Mizil, A.: Data mining in metric space: an empirical analysis of supervised learning performance criteria. In: KDD '04: Proceedings of the tenth ACM SIGKDD international conference on Knowledge discovery and data mining, pp. 69–78. ACM Press, New York (2004)
11. Blake, C., Merz, C.: UCI repository of machine learning databases (1998)
12. Gualtieri, A., Chettri, S.R., Cromp, R., Johnson, L.: Support vector machine classifiers as applied to aviris data. In: Proc. Eighth JPL Airborne Geoscience Workshop (1999)
13. Perlich, C., Provost, F., Simonoff, J.S.: Tree induction vs. logistic regression: a learning-curve analysis. J. Mach. Learn. Res. 4, 211–255 (2003)
14. Caruana, R., Niculescu-Mizil, A.: An empirical comparison of supervised learning algorithms. In: ICML '06: Proceedings of the 23rd International Conference On Machine Learning, pp. 161–168. ACM Press, New York (2006)

15. Niculescu-Mizil, A., Caruana, R.: Predicting good probabilities with supervised learning. In: Proc. 22nd International Conference on Machine Learning (ICML'05) (2005)
16. Platt, J.C.: Probabilistic outputs for support vector machines and comparisons to regularized likelihood methods. In: Smola, A., Bartlett, P., Schlkopf, B., Schuurmans, D. (eds.) Advances in Large Margin Classifiers, pp. 61–74. MIT Press, Cambridge (1999)
17. Mitchell, T.M.: Machine Learning. McGraw-Hill, New York (1997)

Additive Groves of Regression Trees

Daria Sorokina, Rich Caruana, and Mirek Riedewald

Department of Computer Science, Cornell University, Ithaca, NY, USA
{daria,caruana,mirek}@cs.cornell.edu

Abstract. We present a new regression algorithm called Groves of trees and show empirically that it is superior in performance to a number of other established regression methods. A Grove is an additive model usually containing a small number of large trees. Trees added to the Grove are trained on the residual error of other trees already in the Grove. We begin the training process with a single small tree in the Grove and gradually increase both the number of trees in the Grove and their size. This procedure ensures that the resulting model captures the additive structure of the response. A single Grove may still overfit to the training set, so we further decrease the variance of the final predictions with bagging. We show that in addition to exhibiting superior performance on a suite of regression test problems, bagged Groves of trees are very resistant to overfitting.

1 Introduction

We present a new regression algorithm called Grove, an ensemble of additive regression trees. We initialize a Grove with a single small tree. The Grove is then gradually expanded: on every iteration either a new tree is added, or the trees that already are in the Grove are made larger. This process is designed to try to find the simplest model (a Grove with the fewest number of small trees) that captures the underlying additive structure of the target function. As training progesses, this algorithm yields a sequence of Groves of slowly increasing complexity. Eventually, the largest Groves may begin to overfit the training set even as they continue to learn important additive structure. This overfitting is reduced by applying bagging on top of the Grove learning process.

In Section 2 we describe the Grove algorithm step by step, beginning with the classical way of training additive models and incrementally making this process more complicated – and better performing – at each step. In Section 3 we compare bagged Groves with two other regression ensembles: bagged regression trees and stochastic gradient boosting. The results show that bagged Groves outperform these other methods and work especially well on highly non-linear data sets. In Section 4 we show that bagged Groves are resistant to overfitting. We conclude and discuss future work in Section 5.

J.N. Kok et al. (Eds.): ECML 2007, LNAI 4701, pp. 323–334, 2007.

2 Algorithm

Bagged Groves of Trees, or bagged Groves for short, is an ensemble of regression trees. Specifically, it is a bagged additive model of regression trees where each individual additive model is trained in an adaptive way by gradually increasing both number of trees and their complexity.

Regression Trees. The unit model in a Grove is a regression tree. Algorithms for training regression trees differ in two major aspects: (1) the criterion for choosing the best split in a node and (2) the way in which tree complexity is controlled. We use trees that optimize RMSE (root mean squared error) and we control tree complexity (size) by imposing a limit on the size (number of cases) at an internal node. If the fraction of the data points that reach a node is less than a specified threshold α, then the node is declared a leaf and is not split further. Hence the smaller α, $0 \leq \alpha \leq 1$, the larger the tree. (See Table 7.)

Note that because we will later bag the tree models, the specific choice of regression tree is not particularly important. The main requirement is that the complexity of the tree should be controllable.

2.1 Additive Models — Classical Algorithm

A Grove of trees is an additive model where each additive term is represented by a regression tree. The prediction of a Grove is computed as the sum of the predictions of these trees: $F(\mathbf{x}) = T_1(\mathbf{x}) + T_2(\mathbf{x}) + \cdots + T_N(\mathbf{x})$. Here each $T_i(\mathbf{x})$, $1 \leq i \leq N$, is the prediction made by the i-th tree in the Grove. The Grove model has two main parameters: N, the number of trees in the Grove, and α, which controls the size of each individual tree. We use the same value of α for all trees in a Grove.

In statistics, the basic mechanism for training an additive model with a fixed number of components is the *backfitting algorithm* [1]. We will refer to this as the Classical algorithm for training a Grove of regression trees (Algorithm 1).

The algorithm cycles through the trees until the trees converge. The first tree in the Grove is trained on the original data set, a set of training points $\{(\mathbf{x}, y)\}$. Let $\hat{T}_1$ denote the function encoded by this tree. Then we train the second tree, which encodes $\hat{T}_2$, on the residuals, i.e., on the set $\{(\mathbf{x}, y-\hat{T}_1(\mathbf{x}))\}$. The third tree then is trained on the residuals of the first two, i.e., on $\{(\mathbf{x}, y-\hat{T}_1(\mathbf{x})-\hat{T}_2(\mathbf{x}))\}$, and so on.

After we have trained N trees this way, we *discard* the first tree and retrain it on the residuals of the other $N-1$ trees, i.e. on the set $\{(\mathbf{x}, y-\hat{T}_2(\mathbf{x})-\hat{T}_3(\mathbf{x})-\cdots-\hat{T}_N(\mathbf{x}))\}$. Then we similarly discard and retrain the second tree, and so on. We keep cycling through the trees in this way until there is no significant improvement in the RMSE on the training set.

Bagging. As with single decision trees, a single Grove tends to overfit to the training set when the trees are large. Such models show a large variance with respect to specific subsamples of the training data and benefit significantly from

Algorithm 1. Classical additive model training

function Classical(α,N,{**x**,y})
  for $i = 1$ **to** N **do**
    $\text{Tree}_i^{(\alpha,N)} = 0$
  Converge(α,N,{**x**,y}, $\text{Tree}_1^{(\alpha,N)}, \ldots, \text{Tree}_N^{(\alpha,N)}$)

function Converge(α,N,{**x**,y},$\text{Tree}_1^{(\alpha,N)}, \ldots, \text{Tree}_N^{(\alpha,N)}$)
  repeat
    for $i = 1$ **to** N **do**
      newTrainSet = $\{\mathbf{x}, y - \sum_{k \neq i} \text{Tree}_k^{(\alpha,N)}(\mathbf{x})\}$
      $\text{Tree}_i^{(\alpha,N)}$ = TrainTree(α, newTrainSet)
  until (change from the last iteration is small)

bagging, a well-known procedure for improving model performance by reducing variance [2]. On each iteration of bagging, we draw a bootstrap sample (bag) from the training set, and train the full model (in our case a Grove of additive trees) from that sample. After repeating this procedure a number of times, we end up with an ensemble of models. The final prediction of the ensemble on each test data point is an average of the predictions of all models.

Example. In this section we illustrate the effects of different methods of training bagged Groves on synthetic data. The synthetic data set was generated by a function of 10 variables that was previously used by Hooker [3].

$$F(x) = \pi^{x_1 x_2}\sqrt{2x_3} - sin^{-1}(x_4) + log(x_3 + x_5) - \frac{x_9}{x_{10}}\sqrt{\frac{x_7}{x_8}} - x_2 x_7 \qquad (1)$$

Variables x_1, x_2, x_3, x_6, x_7, x_9 are uniformly distributed between 0.0 and 1.0 and variables x_4, x_5, x_8 and x_{10} are uniformly distributed between 0.6 and 1.0.[1]

Figure 1 shows a contour plot of how model performance depends on both α, the size of tree, and N, the number of trees in a Grove, for 100 bagged Groves trained with the classical method on 1000 training points from the above data set. The performance is measured as RMSE on an independent test set consisting of 25,000 points. Notice that lower RMSE implies better performance. The bottom-most horizontal line for $N = 1$ corresponds to bagging single trees. The plot clearly indicates that by introducing additive model structure, with $N > 1$, performance improves significantly. We can also see that the best performance is achieved by Groves containing 5-10 relatively small trees (large α), while for larger trees performance deteriorates.

2.2 Layered Training

When individual trees in a Grove are large and complex, the Classical additive model training algorithm (Section 2.1) can overfit even if bagging is applied.

[1] Ranges are selected to avoid extremely large or small function values.

Algorithm 2. Layered training

function Layered(α,N,train)
  $\alpha_0 = 0.5, \alpha_1 = 0.2, \alpha_2 = 0.1, \ldots, \alpha_{\max} = \alpha$
  for $j = 0$ **to** max **do**
    if $j = 0$ **then**
      for $i = 1$ **to** N **do**
        $\text{Tree}_i^{(\alpha_0,N)} = 0$
    else
      for $i = 1$ **to** N **do**
        $\text{Tree}_i^{(\alpha_j,N)} = \text{Tree}_i^{(\alpha_{j-1},N)}$
    Converge(α_j,N,train,$\text{Tree}_1^{(\alpha_j,N)}, \ldots, \text{Tree}_N^{(\alpha_j,N)}$)

Consider the extreme case $\alpha = 0$, i.e., a Grove of full trees. The first tree will perfectly model the training data, leaving residuals with value 0 for the other trees in the Grove. Hence the intended Grove of several large trees will degenerate to a single tree.

One could address this issue by limiting trees to very small size. However, we still would like to be able to use large trees in a Grove so that we can capture complex and non-linear functions. To prevent the degeneration of the Grove as the trees become larger, we developed a "layered" training approach. In the first round we grow N small trees. Then in later cycles of discarding and re-training the trees in the Grove we gradually increase tree size.

More precisely, no matter what the value of α, we *always* start the training process with small trees, typically using a start value $\alpha_0 = 0.5$. Let α_j denote the value of the size parameter after j iterations of the Layered algorithm (Algorithm 2). After reaching convergence for α_{j-1}, we increase tree complexity by setting α_j to approximately half the value of α_{j-1}. We continue to cycle through the trees, re-training all trees in the Grove in the usual way, but now allow them to reach the size correspondent to the new larger α_j, and as before, we proceed until the Grove converges on this layer. We keep gradually increasing tree size until $\alpha_j \approx \alpha$.

For a training set with 1000 data points and $\alpha = 0$, we use the following sequence of values of α_j: $(0.5, 0.2, 0.1, 0.05, 0.02, 0.01, 0.005, 0.002, 0.001)$. It is worth noting that while training a Grove of large trees, we automatically obtain all Groves with the same N for all smaller tree sizes in the sequence. Figure 2 shows how 100 bagged Groves trained by the layered approach perform on the synthetic data set. Overall performance is much better than for the classical algorithm and bagged Groves of N large trees now perform at least as well as bagged Groves of N smaller trees.

2.3 Dynamic Programming Training

There is no reason to believe that the best (α, N) Grove should always be constructed from a $(\approx 2\alpha, N)$ Grove. In fact, a large number of small trees might overfit the training data and hence limit the benefit of increasing tree size in later iterations. To avoid this problem, we need to give the Grove training algorithm additional flexibility in choosing the right balance between increasing tree size and the number of trees. This is the motivation behind the *Dynamic Programming* Grove training algorithm.

This algorithm can choose to construct a new Grove from an existing one by either adding a new tree (while keeping tree size constant) or by increasing tree size (while keeping the number of trees constant). Considering the parameter grid, the Grove for a grid point (α_j, n) could be constructed either from its left neighbor (α_{j-1}, n) or from its lower neighbor $(\alpha_j, n-1)$. Pseudo-code for this approach is shown in Algorithm 3. We make a choice between the two options for computing each Grove (adding another tree or making the trees larger) in a greedy manner, i.e., the one that results in better performance of the Grove on the validation set. We use the out-of-bag data points [4] as the validation set for choosing which of the two Groves to use at each step.

Figure 3 shows how the Dynamic Programming approach improves bagged Groves over the layered training. Figure 4 shows the choices that are made during the process: it plots the average difference between RMSE of the Grove created from the lower neighbor (increase n) and performance of the Grove created from the left neighbor (decrease α_j). That is, a negative value means that the former is preferred, while a positive value means that the latter is preferred at that grid point. We can see that for this data set increasing the tree size is the preferred direction, except for cases with many small trees.

This dynamic programming version of the algorithm does not explore all possible sequences of steps to build a Grove of trees, because we require that every grove built in the process should contain trees of equal size. We have tested several other possible approaches that don't have this restriction, but they failed to produce any improvements and were noticeably worse from the running time point of view. For these reasons we prefer the dynamic programming version over other, less restricted options.

2.4 Randomized Dynamic Programming Training

Our bagged Grove training algorithms so far performed bagging in the usual way, i.e., create a bag of data, train all Groves for different vallues of (α, N) on that bag, then create the next bag, generate all models on this bag; and so on for 100 different bags. When the Dynamic Programming algorithm generates a Grove using the same bag, i.e., the same train set that was used to generate its left and lower neighbors, complex models might not be very different from their neighbors because those neighbors already might have overfitted and there is not enough training data to learn anything new. We can address this problem by using a different bag of data on every step of the Dynamic Programming algorithm, so that every Grove has some new data to learn from. While performance of a single Grove might become worse, performance of bagged Groves improves due to increased variability in the models. Figure 5 shows the improved performance of this final version of our Grove training approach. The most complex Groves are

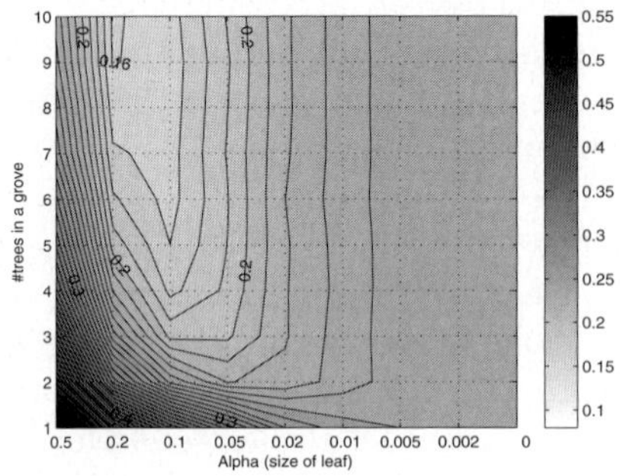

Fig. 1. RMSE of bagged Grove, Classical algorithm

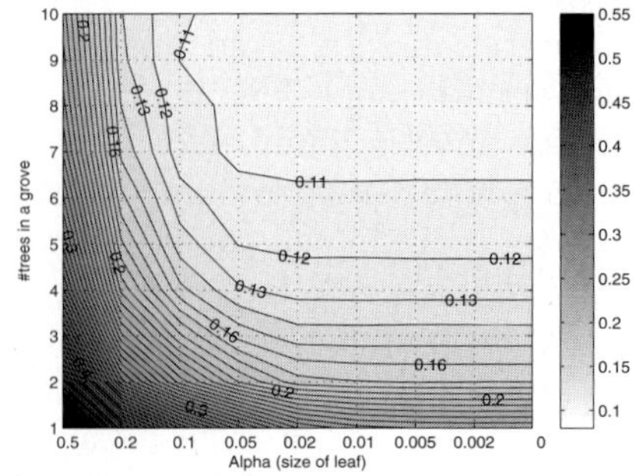

Fig. 2. RMSE of bagged Grove, Layered algorithm

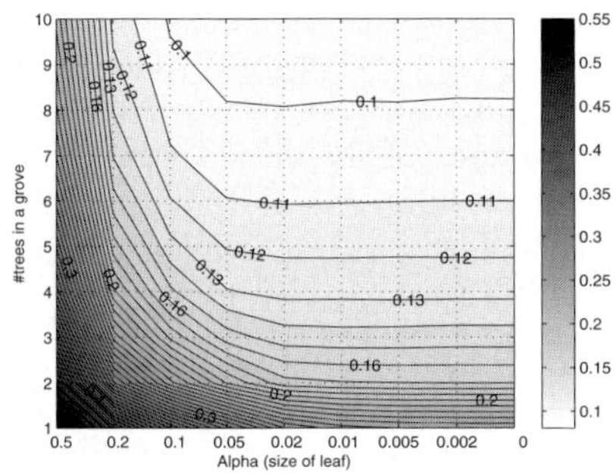

Fig. 3. RMSE of bagged Grove, Dynamic Programming algorithm

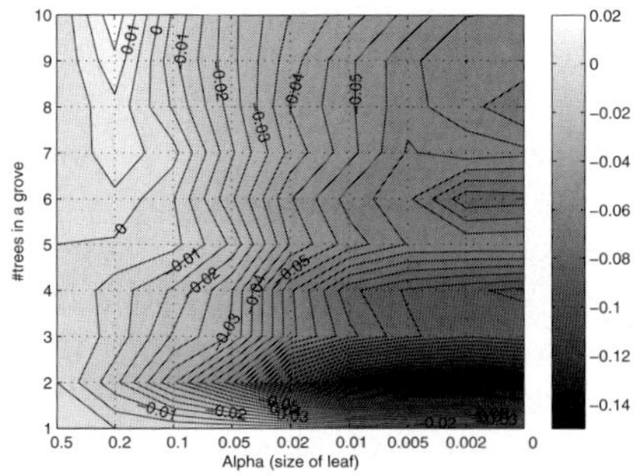

Fig. 4. Difference in performance between "horizontal" and "vertical" steps

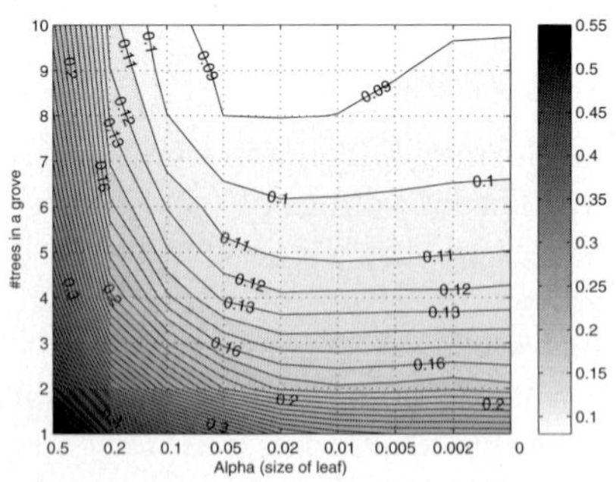

Fig. 5. RMSE of bagged Grove (100 bags), Randomized Dynamic Programming algorithm

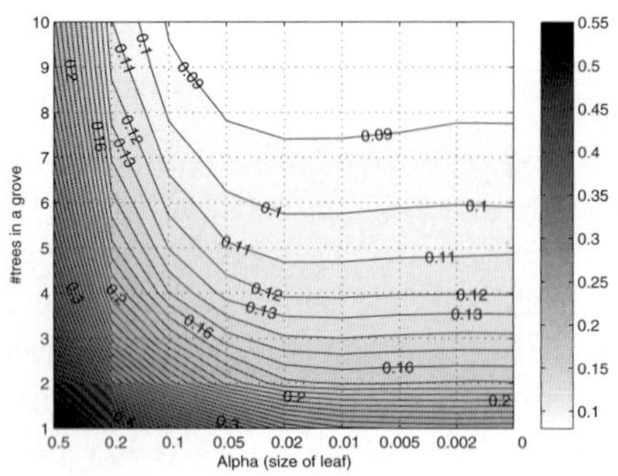

Fig. 6. RMSE of bagged Grove (**500 bags**), Randomized Dynamic Programming algorithm

Algorithm 3. Dynamic Programming Training

```
function DP(α,N,trainSet)
  α_0 = 0.5, α_1 = 0.2, α_2 = 0.1, ..., α_max = α
  for j = 0 to max do
    for n = 1 to N do

      for i = 1 to n − 1 do
        Tree_{attempt1,i} = Tree_i^{(α_j,n−1)}
      Tree_{attempt1,n} = 0
      Converge(α_j,n,train,Tree_{attempt1,1}, ..., Tree_{attempt1,n})

      if j > 0 then
        for i = 1 to n do
          Tree_{attempt2,i} = Tree_i^{(α_{j−1},n)}
        Converge(α_j,n,train,Tree_{attempt2,1}, ..., Tree_{attempt2,n})

      winner = Compare Σ_i Tree_{attempt1,i} and Σ_i Tree_{attempt2,i} on validation set
      for i = 1 to n do
        Tree_i^{(α_j,n)} = Tree_{winner,i}
```

now performing worse than their left neighbors with smaller trees. This happens because those models need more bagging steps to converge to their best quality. Figure 6 shows the same plot for bagging with 500 iterations where the property "more complex models are at least as good as their less complex counterparts" is restored.

3 Experiments

We evaluated bagged Groves of trees on 2 synthetic and 5 real-world data sets and compared the performance to two other regression tree ensemble methods that are known to perform well: stochastic gradient boosting and bagged regression trees. Bagged Groves consistently outperform both of them. For real data sets we performed 10 fold cross validation: for each run 8 folds were used as a training set, 1 fold as a validation set for choosing the best set of parameters and the last fold was used as the test set for measuring performance. For the two synthetic data sets we generated 30 blocks of data containing 1000 points each and performed 10 runs using different blocks for training, validation and test sets. We report mean and standard deviation of the RMSE on the test set. Table 1 shows the results; for comparability across data sets all numbers are scaled by the standard deviation of the response in the dataset itself.

3.1 Parameter Settings

Groves. We trained 100 bagged Groves using the Randomized Dynamic Programming technique for all combinations of parameters N and α with $1 \leq N \leq$

Table 1. Performance of bagged Groves (Randomized Dynamic Programming training) compared to boosting and bagging. RMSE on the test set averaged over 10 runs.

	California Housing	Elevators	Kinematics	Computer Activity	Stock	Synthetic No Noise	Synthetic Noise
Bagged Groves							
RMSE	0.38	0.309	0.364	0.117	0.097	0.087	0.483
StdDev	0.015	0.028	0.013	0.0093	0.029	0.0065	0.012
Boosting							
RMSE	0.403	0.327	0.457	0.121	0.118	0.148	0.495
StdDev	0.014	0.035	0.012	0.01	0.05	0.0072	0.01
Bagged trees							
RMSE	0.422	0.44	0.533	0.136	0.123	0.276	0.514
StdDev	0.013	0.066	0.016	0.012	0.064	0.0059	0.011

15 and $\alpha \in \{0.5, 0.2, 0.1, 0.05, 0.02, 0.01, 0.005\}$. Notice that with these settings the resulting ensemble can consist of at most 1500 trees. From these models we selected the one that gave the best results on the validation set. The performance of the selected Grove on the test set is reported.

Stochastic Gradient Boosting. The obvious main competitor to bagged Groves is gradient boosting [5] [6], a different ensemble of trees also based on additive models. There are two major differences between boosting and Groves. First, boosting never discards trees, i.e., every generated tree stays in the model. Grove iteratively retrains its trees. Second, all trees in a boosting ensemble are always built to a fixed size, while groves of large trees are trained first using groves of smaller trees. We believe that these differences allow Groves to better capture the natural additive structure of the response function.

The general gradient boosting framework supports optimizing for a variety of loss functions. We selected squared-error loss because this is the loss function that our current version of the Groves algorithm optimizes for. However, like gradient boosting, Groves can be modified to optimize for other loss functions.

Friedman [6] recommends boosting small trees with at most 4–10 leaf nodes for best results. However, we discovered for one of our datasets that using larger trees with gradient boosting did significantly better. This is not surprising since some real datasets contain complex interactions, which cannot be accurately modeled by small trees. For fairness we therefore also include larger boosted trees in the comparison than Friedman suggested. More precisely, we tried all $\alpha \in \{1, 0.5, 0.2, 0.1, 0.05\}$. Table 7 shows the typical correspondence between α and number of leaf nodes in a tree, which was very similar across the data sets. Preliminary results did not show any improvement for tree size beyond $\alpha = 0.05$.

Stochastic gradient boosting deals with overfitting by means of two techniques: regularization and subsampling. Both techniques depend on user-set parameters. Based on recommendations in the literature and on our own evaluation we used the following values for the final evaluation: 0.1 and 0.05 for the regularization

α	# leaf nodes
1	2 (stump)
0.5	3
0.2	8
0.1	17
0.05	38
0.02	100
0.01	225
0.005	500
0	full tree

Fig. 7. Typical number of leaf nodes for different values of α

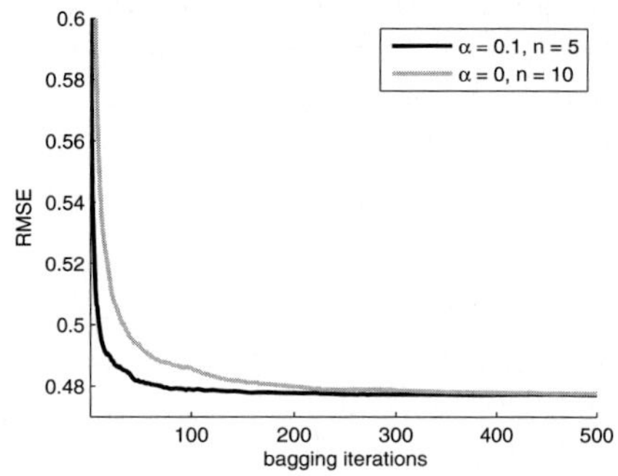

Fig. 8. Performance of bagged Grove for simpler and more complex models

coefficient and 0.4, 0.6, and 0.8 as the fraction of the subsampling set size from the whole training set.

Boosting can also overfit if it is run for too many iterations. We tried up to 1500 iterations to make the maximum number of trees in the ensemble equal for all methods in comparison. The actual number of iterations that performs best was determined based on the validation set, and therefore can be lower than 1500 for the best boosted model.

In summary, to evaluate stochastic gradient boosting, we tried all combinations of the values described above for the 4 parameters: size of trees, number of iterations, regularization coefficient, and subsampling size. As for Groves, we determine the best combination of values for these parameters based on a separate validation set.

Bagging. Bagging single trees is known to provide good performance by significantly decreasing variance of the individual tree models. However, compared with Groves and boosting, which are both based on additive models, bagged trees do not explicitly model the additive structure of the response function. Increasing the number of iterations in bagging does not result in overfitting and bagging of larger trees usually produces better models than bagging smaller trees. Hence we omitted parameter tuning for bagging. Instead we simply report results for a model consisting of 1500 bagged full trees.

3.2 Datasets

Synthetic Data without Noise. This is the same data set that we used as a running example in the earlier sections. The response function is generated by Equation 1. The performance of bagged Groves on this dataset is much better than the performance of other methods.

Synthetic Data with Noise. This is the same synthetic dataset, only this time Gaussian noise is added to the response function. The standard deviation σ of the noise distribution is chosen as 1/2 of the standard deviation of the response in the original data set. As expected, the performance of all methods drops. Bagged Groves still perform clearly better, but the difference is smaller.

We have used 5 regression data sets from the collection of Luís Torgo [7] for the next set of experiments.

Kinematics. The Kinematics family of datasets originates from the Delve repository [8] and describes a simulation of robot arm movement. We used a *kin8nm* version of the dataset: 8192 cases, 8 continuous attributes, high level of non-linearity, low level of noise. Groves show 20% improvement over gradient boosting on this dataset. It is worth noticing that boosting preferred large trees on this dataset; trees with $\alpha = 0.05$ showed clear advantage over smaller trees. However, there was no further improvement for boosting even larger trees. We attribute these effects to high non-linearity of the data.

Computer Activity. Another dataset from the Delve repository, describes the state of multiuser computer systems. 8192 cases, 22 continuous attributes. The variance of performance for all algorithms is low. Groves show small (3%) improvement compared to boosting.

California Housing. This is a dataset from the StatLib repository [9] and it describes housing prices in California from the 1990 Census: 20,640 observations, 9 continuous attributes. Groves show 6% improvement compared to boosting.

Stock. This is a relatively small (960 data points) regression dataset from the StatLib repository. It describes daily stock prices for 10 aerospace companies: the task is to predict the first one from the other 9. Prediction quality from all methods is very high, so we can assume that the level of noise is small. This is another case when Groves give significant improvement (18%) over gradient boosting.

Elevators. This data set is obtained from the task of controlling an aircraft [10]. It seems to be noisy, because the variance of performance is high although the data set is rather large: 16,559 cases with 18 continuous attributes. Here we see a 6% improvement.

3.3 Discussion

Based on the empirical results we conjecture that Bagged Groves outperform the other algorithms most when the datasets are highly non-linear and not very noisy. (Noise can obscure some of the non-linearity in the response function, making the best models that can be learned from the data more linear than they would have been for models trained on the response without noise.) This can be explained as follows. Groves can capture additive structure yet at the same time use large trees. Large trees capture non-linearity and complex interactions well, and this gives Groves an advantage over gradient boosting which relies mostly on additivity. Gradient boosting usually works best with small trees, and fails to make effective use of large trees. At the same time most data sets, even non-linear ones, still have significant additive structure. The ability to detect and model this additivity gives Groves an advantage over bagging, which is effective with large trees, but does not explicitly model additive structure.

Gradient boosting is a state of the art ensemble tree method for regression. Chipman et al [11] recently performed an extensive comparison of several algorithms on 42 data sets. In their experiments gradient boosting showed performance similar to or better than Random Forests and a number of other types of models. Our algorithm shows performance consistently better than gradient boosting and for this reason we do not expect that Random Forests or other methods that are not superior to gradient boosting would outperform our bagged Groves.

In terms of computational cost, bagged Groves and boosting are comparable. In both cases a large number of tree models has to be trained (more for Groves) and there is a variety of parameter combinations that need to be examined (more for boosting).

4 Bagging Iterations and Overfitting Resistance

In our experiments we used a fixed number of bagging iterations and did not consider this a tuning parameter because bagging rarely overfits. In bagging the number of iterations is not as crucial as it is for boosting: if we bag as long as we can afford, we will get the best value that we can achieve. In that sense the experimental results we report are conservative and Bagged Groves could potentially be improved by additional bagging iterations.

We observed a similar trend for parameters α and N as well: more complex models (larger trees, more trees) are at least as good as their less complex counterparts, but only if they are bagged sufficiently many times. Figure 8 shows how the performance on the synthetic data set with noise depends on the number of bagging iterations for two bagged Groves. The simpler one is trained with $N = 5$ and $\alpha = 0.1$ and the more complex one is trained with $N = 10$ and $\alpha = 0$. We can see that eventually they converge to the same performance and that the simpler model only does better than the complex model when the number of bagging iterations is small. [2]

We observed similar behavior for the other datasets. This suggests that one way to get good performance with bagged Groves might be to build the most complex Groves (large trees, many trees) that can be afforded and bag them many, many times until performance tops out. In this case we might not need a validation set to select the best parameter settings. However, in practice the most complex models can require many more iterations of bagging than simpler models that achieve almost the same level of performance much faster. Hence the approach that used in our experiments can be more useful in practice: select

[2] Note that this is only true because of the layered approach to training Groves which trains Groves of trees of smaller size before moving on to Groves with larger trees. If one initialized a Grove with a single large tree, performance of bagged Groves might still decrease with increasing tree size because the ability of the Grove to learn the additive structure of the problem would be injured.

a computationally acceptable number of bagging iterations (100 seems to work fine, but one could also use 200 or 500 to be more confident) and search for the best N and α for this number of bagging iterations on the validation set.

5 Conclusion

We presented a new regression algorithm, bagged Groves of trees, which is an additive ensemble of regression trees. It combines the benefits of large trees that model complex interactions with benefits of capturing additive structure by means of additive models. Because of this, bagged Groves perform especially well on complex non-linear datasets where the structure of the response function contains both additive structure (which is best modeled by additive trees) and variable interactions (which is best modeled within a tree). We have shown that on such datasets bagged Groves outperform state-of-the-art techniques such as stochastic gradient boosting and bagging. Thanks to bagging, and the layered way in which Groves are trained, bagged Groves resist overfitting—more complex Groves tend to achieve the same or better performance as simpler Groves.

Groves are good at capturing the additive structure of the response function. A future direction of our work is to develop techniques for determining properties inherent in the data using this algorithm. In particular, we believe we can use Groves to learn useful information about statistical interactions between variables in the data set.

References

1. Hastie, T., Tibshirani, R., Friedman, J.H.: The Elements of Statistical Learning. Springer, Heidelberg (2001)
2. Breiman, L.: Bagging Predictors. Machine Learning 24, 123–140 (1996)
3. Hooker, G.: Discovering ANOVA Structure in Black Box Functions. In: Proc. ACM SIGKDD, ACM Press, New York (2004)
4. Bylander, T.: Estimating Generalization Error on Two-Class Datasets Using Out-of-Bag Estimates. Machine Learning 48(1–3), 287–297 (2002)
5. Friedman, J.: Greedy Function Approximation: a Gradient Boosting Machine. Annals of Statistics 29, 1189–1232 (2001)
6. Friedman, J.: Stochastic Gradient Boosting. Computational Statistics and Data Analysis 38, 367–378 (2002)
7. Torgo, L.: Regression DataSets, `http://www.liacc.up.pt/~ltorgo/Regression/DataSets.html`
8. Rasmussen, C.E., Neal, R.M., Hinton, G., van Camp, D., Revow, M., Ghahramani, Z., Kustra, R., Tibshirani, R.: Delve. University of Toronto, `http://www.cs.toronto.edu/~delve`
9. Meyer, M., Vlachos, P.: StatLib. Department of Statistics at Carnegie Mellon University, `http://lib.stat.cmu.edu`
10. Camacho, R.: Inducing Models of Human Control Skills. In: Nédellec, C., Rouveirol, C. (eds.) Machine Learning: ECML-98. LNCS, vol. 1398, Springer, Heidelberg (1998)
11. Chipman, H., George, E., McCulloch, R.: Bayesian Ensemble Learning. In: Advances in Neural Information Processing Systems 19, pp. 265–272 (2007)

Efficient Computation of Recursive Principal Component Analysis for Structured Input

Alessandro Sperduti

Department of Pure and Applied Mathematics, University of Padova, Italy
sperduti@math.unipd.it

Abstract. Recently, a successful extension of Principal Component Analysis for structured input, such as sequences, trees, and graphs, has been proposed. This allows the embedding of discrete structures into vectorial spaces, where all the classical pattern recognition and machine learning methods can be applied. The proposed approach is based on eigenanalysis of extended vectorial representations of the input structures and substructures. One problem with the approach is that eigenanalysis can be computationally quite demanding when considering large datasets of structured objects. In this paper we propose a general approach for reducing the computational burden. Experimental results show a significant speed-up of the computation.

1 Introduction

In many real-world applications it is natural to represent data in a structured form. Just to name a few, in Chemistry chemical compounds can be represented as undirected annotated graphs; in Natural Language Processing, the semantics of a sentence is described in terms of a parse tree. In addition, many problems in these application domains are characterized by the presence of noise and/or uncertainty in the data. Moreover, these problems can naturally be formulated as clustering, or classification, or regression tasks, which are well suited to be treated by machine learning approaches. Many standard machine learning approaches, however, can deal only with numerical vectors. Thus, a first necessary step to their application to structured objects is the apriori selection of a set of structural features of interest which will constitute the dimensions of a vectorial space where each structure can be represented according to its own degree of matching.

Recently, different an more direct approaches have been proposed and successfully applied to structured domains, such as Recursive Neural Networks (e.g. see [11,2,4,1,9]), and Kernel Methods for structured patterns (see [3] for a survey). Both these approaches, however, have their problems, such has local minima for Neural Networks, and the a priori definition of the kernel for Kernel Methods.

More recently, an alternative approach has been proposed. The idea is to devise vectorial representations of structures, belonging to a data set, which preserve all the information needed to discriminate among each other. This approach hinges on the calculation of Principal Component Analysis (PCA) for structured objects, such as sequences, trees, and graphs [10,8]. The aim is to provide a method to generate informative representations which are amenable to be used into already well known unsupervised and supervised techniques for clustering, classification, and regression.

J.N. Kok et al. (Eds.): ECML 2007, LNAI 4701, pp. 335–346, 2007.

A problem with this approach, however, is that it is computationally quite demanding. In this paper, we address this problem by proposing some techniques to reduce the computational burden. After presenting in Section 2 the basic concepts about PCA for vectors and structures, we discuss in Section 3 three different approaches that, if applied simultaneously, can significantly reduce the computational burden in the case of structures. This is experimentally demonstrated in two datasets of relevant size and complexity (Section 4).

2 Principal Components Analysis for Vectors and Structures

In the following we present the main ideas underpinning the computation of PCA for vectors and structured inputs. We briefly recall the standard PCA with a perspective that will allow us to readily introduce its extension to the case of sequences. The suggested approach is then further extended to cover the direct treatment of trees, and finally we discuss our proposal to deal with directed or undirected graphs.

2.1 Vectors

The aim of standard PCA [6] is to reduce the dimensionality of a data set, while preserving as much as possible the information present in it. This is achieved by looking for orthogonal directions of maximum variance within the data set. The principal components are sorted according to the amount of variance they explain, so that the first few retain most of the variation present in all of the original variables. It turns out that the qth principal component is given by the projection of the data onto the eigenvector of the (sample) covariance matrix $\mathbf{C}$ of the data corresponding to the qth largest eigenvalue.

From a mathematical point of view, PCA can be understood as given by an orthogonal linear transformation of the given set of variables (i.e., the coordinates of the vectorial space in which data is embedded):

$$\mathbf{y}_i = \mathbf{W}_\mathbf{x}\mathbf{x}_i \tag{1}$$

where $\mathbf{x}_i \in \mathbb{R}^k$ are the vectors belonging to the data set, and $\mathbf{W}_\mathbf{x}$ is the orthogonal matrix whose qth row is the qth eigenvector of the covariance matrix. Typically, larger variances are associated with the first $p < k$ principal components. Thus one can conclude that most relevant information occur only in the first p dimensions. The process of retaining only the first p principal components is known as *dimensional reduction*. Given a fixed value for p, principal components allow also to minimize the reconstruction error, i.e. the square error of the difference between the original vector $\mathbf{x}_i$ and the vector obtained by projecting its principal components $\mathbf{y}_i$ back into the original space by the linear transformation $\mathbf{W}_\mathbf{x}^\mathsf{T}\mathbf{y}_i$:

$$\mathbf{W}_\mathbf{x} = \arg\min_{\mathbf{M}\in\mathbb{R}^{p\times k}} \sum_i \|\mathbf{x}_i - \mathbf{M}^\mathsf{T}\mathbf{M}\mathbf{x}_i\|^2$$

where the rows of $\mathbf{W}_\mathbf{x}$ corresponds to the first p eigenvectors of $\mathbf{C}$.

2.2 Sequences

In [10] it is shown how PCA can be extended to the direct treatment of sequences. More specifically, given a temporal sequence $\mathbf{x}_1, \mathbf{x}_2, \ldots, \mathbf{x}_t, \ldots$ of input vectors, where t is a discrete time index, we are interested in modeling the sequence through the following linear dynamical system:

$$\mathbf{y}_t = \mathbf{W}_\mathbf{x}\mathbf{x}_t + \mathbf{W}_\mathbf{y}\mathbf{y}_{t-1} \tag{2}$$

which extends the linear transformation defined in eq. (1) by introducing a *memory term* involving the matrix $\mathbf{W}_\mathbf{y}$ and the principal components $\mathbf{y}_{t-1}$ computed up to time step $t-1$, i.e. the principal components describing the input sequence up to time step $t-1$. The aim is to define proper matrices $\mathbf{W}_\mathbf{x}$ and $\mathbf{W}_\mathbf{y}$ such that $\mathbf{y}_t$ can be considered a good "encoding" of the input sequence read till time step t, i.e., the sequence is first encoded using eq. (2), and then, starting from the obtained encoding $\mathbf{y}_t$, it should be possible to reconstruct backwards the original sequence using the transposes of $\mathbf{W}_\mathbf{x}$ and $\mathbf{W}_\mathbf{y}$. This requirement implies that the following equations

$$\mathbf{x}_t = \mathbf{W}_\mathbf{x}^\mathsf{T}\mathbf{y}_t \tag{3}$$

$$\mathbf{y}_{t-1} = \mathbf{W}_\mathbf{x}\mathbf{x}_{t-1} + \mathbf{W}_\mathbf{y}\mathbf{y}_{t-2} = \mathbf{W}_\mathbf{y}^\mathsf{T}\mathbf{y}_t \tag{4}$$

should hold. In fact, the perspective of this proposal for recursive principal component analysis is to find a low-dimensional representation of the input sequence such that the expected reconstruction error, i.e. the sum of the (squared) differences between the vectors generated by equation (3) and the original input vectors for different values of t

$$error(t) = \sum_{i=1}^{t} \|\mathbf{x}_i - \mathbf{W}_\mathbf{x}^\mathsf{T}(\mathbf{W}_\mathbf{y}^\mathsf{T})^{t-i}\underbrace{\sum_{j=1}^{t}(\mathbf{W}_\mathbf{y})^{t-j}\mathbf{W}_\mathbf{x}\mathbf{x}_i}_{\mathbf{y}_t}\|^2 \tag{5}$$

is as small as possible, i.e. given a fixed value of p, where $\mathbf{y}_t \in \mathbb{R}^p$, we look for

$$(\mathbf{W}_\mathbf{x}, \mathbf{W}_\mathbf{y}) = \underset{\substack{\mathbf{M} \in \mathbb{R}^{p\times k}\\ \mathbf{N} \in \mathbb{R}^{p\times p}}}{\arg\min} \sum_{i=1}^{t} \|\mathbf{x}_i - \mathbf{M}^\mathsf{T}(\mathbf{N}^\mathsf{T})^{t-i}\sum_{j=1}^{t}\mathbf{N}^{t-j}\mathbf{M}\mathbf{x}_i\|^2.$$

In [10] it has been shown that, when considering several sequences for the same linear system, it is possible to find a value of p where the reconstruction error is zero by performing eigenanalysis of extended vectorial representations (belonging to the so called state space) of the input sequences, where a sequence at time t is represented by the vector

$$[\mathbf{x}_t^\mathsf{T}, \ldots, \mathbf{x}_1^\mathsf{T}, \underbrace{\mathbf{0}^\mathsf{T}, \ldots, \mathbf{0}^\mathsf{T}}_{(T-t)}] \tag{6}$$

being T the maximum length for any input sequence. This representation can be understood as an explicit representation of a stack where a new input vector, e.g. $\mathbf{x}_{t+1}$, is pushed into the stack by shifting to the right the current content by k positions, and inserting (adding) $\mathbf{x}_{t+1}$ into the freed positions:

$$[\mathbf{0}^\mathsf{T}, \mathbf{x}_t^\mathsf{T}, \ldots, \mathbf{x}_1^\mathsf{T}, \underbrace{\mathbf{0}^\mathsf{T}, \ldots, \mathbf{0}^\mathsf{T}}_{(T-t-1)}] + [\mathbf{x}_{t+1}^\mathsf{T}, \underbrace{\mathbf{0}^\mathsf{T}, \ldots, \mathbf{0}^\mathsf{T}}_{(T-1)}] = [\mathbf{x}_{t+1}^\mathsf{T}, \mathbf{x}_t^\mathsf{T}, \ldots, \mathbf{x}_1^\mathsf{T}, \underbrace{\mathbf{0}^\mathsf{T}, \ldots, \mathbf{0}^\mathsf{T}}_{(T-t-1)}]$$

More precisely, let $\mathbf{X}$ be the matrix which collects all the vectors of the above form by columns (for all sequences at any time step), if the input vectors $\mathbf{x}_i \in \mathbb{R}^k$ have zero mean, $s = T \cdot k$, $\mathbf{U}\mathbf{\Lambda}\mathbf{U}^\mathsf{T}$ is the eigenvalue decomposition of $\mathbf{X}\mathbf{X}^\mathsf{T}$ and $\widetilde{\mathbf{U}} \in \mathbb{R}^{s \times p}$ is the matrix obtained by $\mathbf{U}$ removing all the eigenvectors corresponding to null eigenvalues λ_i, the "optimal" matrices for an encoding space of dimension p can be defined as:

$$\widetilde{\mathbf{W}}_\mathbf{x} \equiv \widetilde{\mathbf{U}}^\mathsf{T} \underbrace{\begin{bmatrix} \mathbf{I}_{k\times k} \\ \mathbf{0}_{(s-k)\times k} \end{bmatrix}}_{\text{adding to the first } k \text{ positions}} \quad \text{and} \quad \widetilde{\mathbf{W}}_\mathbf{y} \equiv \widetilde{\mathbf{U}}^\mathsf{T} \underbrace{\begin{bmatrix} \mathbf{0}_{k\times(s-k)} & \mathbf{0}_{k\times k} \\ \mathbf{I}_{(s-k)\times(s-k)} & \mathbf{0}_{(s-k)\times k} \end{bmatrix}}_{\text{shifting to the right of } k \text{ positions}} \widetilde{\mathbf{U}}.$$

2.3 Trees

In [10] a similar, but a bit more elaborated result than the one presented for sequences, has been obtained for trees (with maximum outdegree b). Specifically, for trees the linear dynamical system to be considered is

$$\mathbf{y}_u = \mathbf{W}_\mathbf{x}\mathbf{x}_u + \sum_{c=0}^{b-1} \mathbf{W}_\mathbf{c}\mathbf{y}_{ch_c[u]} \tag{7}$$

where u is a node of the tree, $ch_c[u]$ is the $c+1$-th child of u, and a different matrix $\mathbf{W}_\mathbf{c}$ is defined for each child.

Let us illustrate what happens for binary complete trees. For $b = 2$, we have the following linear model

$$\mathbf{y}_u = \mathbf{W}_\mathbf{x}\mathbf{x}_u + \mathbf{W}_\mathbf{l}\mathbf{y}_{ch_l[u]} + \mathbf{W}_\mathbf{r}\mathbf{y}_{ch_r[u]} \tag{8}$$

where u is a vertex of the tree, $ch_l[u]$ is the left child of u, $ch_r[u]$ is the right child of u, $\mathbf{W}_\mathbf{l}, \mathbf{W}_\mathbf{r} \in \mathbb{R}^{s\times s}$, where s is the dimension of the state space. In this case, the basic idea is to partition the state space $\mathbb{S}$ according to a perfectly balanced binary tree. More precisely, each vertex u of the binary tree is associated to a binary string $id(u)$ obtained as follows: the binary string "1" is associated to the root of the tree. Any other vertex has associated the string obtained by concatenating the string of its parent with the string "0" if it is a left child, "1" otherwise. Then, all the dimensions of $\mathbb{S}$ are partitioned in s/k groups of k dimensions. The label associated to vertex v is stored into the j-th group, where j is the integer represented by the binary string $id(u)$. E.g. the label of the root is stored into group 1, since $id(root)$ ="1", the label of the vertex which can be reached by the path ll starting from the root is stored into group 4, since $id(u)$ ="100", while the label of the vertex reachable through the path rlr is stored into group 13, since $id(u)$ ="1101". Notice that, if the input tree is not complete, the components corresponding to missing vertexes are set to be equal to 0. Using this convention, extended state space vectors maintain the definition of eq. (6), where the first k components are used to store the current input label, i.e. the label associated to the root of the (sub)tree presented up to now as input, while the remaining components are defined according to the scheme described above.

Matrices $\mathbf{W_l}$ and $\mathbf{W_r}$ are defined as follows. Both matrices are composed of two types of blocks, i.e. $\mathbf{I}_{k\times k}$ and $\mathbf{0}_{k\times k}$. Matrix $\mathbf{W_l}$ has to implement a push-left operation, i.e. the tree $\mathcal{T}$ encoded by a vector $\mathbf{y}_{root(\mathcal{T})}$ has to become the left child of a new node u whose label is the current input $\mathbf{x}_u$. Thus $root(\mathcal{T})$ has to become the left child of u and also all the other vertexes in $\mathcal{T}$ have their position redefined accordingly. From a mathematical point of view, the new position of any vertex a in $\mathcal{T}$ is obtained by redefining $id(a)$ as follows: *i)* the most significative bit of $id(a)$ is set to "0", obtaining the string $id_0(a)$; *ii)* the new string $id_{new}(a)$ ="1"+$id_0(a)$ is defined, where + is the string concatenation operator. If $id_{new}(a)$ represents a number greater than s/k then this means that the vertex has been pushed outside the available memory, i.e. the vertex a is *lost*. Consequently, groups which correspond to *lost* vertexes have to be annilated. Thus, $\mathbf{W_l}$ is composed of $(q+1)\times(q+1)$ blocks, all of type $\mathbf{0}_{k\times k}$, except for the blocks in row $id_{new}(a)$ and column $id(a)$, with $id_{new}(a) \leq s/k$, where a block $\mathbf{I}_{k\times k}$ is placed. Matrix $\mathbf{W_r}$ is defined similarly: it has to implement a push-right operation, i.e.: *i)* the most significative bit of $id(a)$ is set to "1", obtaining the string $id_1(a)$; *ii)* the new string $id_{new}(a)$ ="1"+$id_1(a)$ is defined. Matrix $\mathbf{W_x}$ is defined as in the case of sequences. Performing the eigenspace analysis, we obtain the solution matrices $\widetilde{\mathbf{W}}_\mathbf{x} \equiv \widetilde{\mathbf{U}}^\mathsf{T}\mathbf{W_x}$, $\widetilde{\mathbf{W}}_\mathbf{l} \equiv \widetilde{\mathbf{U}}^\mathsf{T}\mathbf{W_l}\widetilde{\mathbf{U}}$, and $\widetilde{\mathbf{W}}_\mathbf{r} \equiv \widetilde{\mathbf{U}}^\mathsf{T}\mathbf{W_r}\widetilde{\mathbf{U}}$. A description of the construction for the general case, i.e. when $b > 2$, can be found in [10].

A problem in dealing with complete trees is that very soon there is a combinatorial explosion of the number of paths to consider, i.e. in order for the machine to deal with moderately deep trees, a huge value for s needs to be used. In practical applications, however, the observed trees tend to follow a specific generative model, and thus there may be many topologies which are never, or very seldomly, generated. Thus, in practice, instead of considering each possible path in the complete tree, only paths that are present into the dataset are considered.

2.4 Graphs

When considering the possibility to extend Recursive PCA to graphs either with directed or undirected edges we have to face two problems: *i)* how to deal with cycles during the encoding; *ii)* how to identify the origin and destination of an edge during decoding.

In [8], these two problems are solved through a coding trick. The basic idea is to enumerate the set of vertexes following a given convention and representing a (directed or undirected) graph as an (inverted) ordered list of vertex's labels associated with a list of edges for which the vertex is origin and where the position in the associated list is referring to the destination vertex. The idea is that the list is used by the linear dynamical system during encoding to read one by one the information about each vertex and associated edges, pushing the read information into the internal stack. Decoding is obtained by popping from the internal stack, one by one, the information about vertexes and associated edges.

The proposed linear dynamical system supporting the above idea is defined as

$$\mathbf{y}_i = \mathbf{W_v}[\mathbf{v}_{label}^\mathsf{T}, \mathbf{v}_{edges}^\mathsf{T}]^\mathsf{T} + \mathbf{W_y}\mathbf{y}_{i-1} \tag{9}$$

where i ranges over the enumeration of the vertexes, i.e. positions in the list representing the graph, $\mathbf{v}_{label} \in \mathbb{R}^k$ is the numerical encoding of the current label, $\mathbf{v}_{edges} \in \mathbb{R}^N$ is the vector representing the information about the edges entering the current vertex where N is the maximum number of vertexes that the system can manage for a single input graph, and $\mathbf{y}_0$ is the null vector. Thus $[\mathbf{v}_{label}^\mathsf{T}, \mathbf{v}_{edges}^\mathsf{T}]^\mathsf{T} \in \mathbb{R}^{k+N}$ and the space embedding the explicit representation of the stack is $N(k+N)$ since no more than N vertexes can be inserted. It should be noted that this size of the stack is needed only if the input graphs are directed, and the above system is basically equivalent to system (2) for sequences.

However, if undirected graphs are considered, a specific state space optimization can be performed. In fact, when inserting the first vertex into the internal stack only the first entry of the vector $\mathbf{v}_{edges}$ may be non null (the one encoding the self-connection), since no other vertex has already been presented to the system. In general, if vertex i is being inserted, only the first i components of $\mathbf{v}_{edges}$ may be non null. Because of that, the shift operator embedded into matrix $\mathbf{W_y}$ may "forget" the last component of each field into which the internal stack is organized. Formally, the shift operator described above can be implemented by the following matrix

$$\mathbf{S} \equiv \begin{bmatrix} \mathbf{0}_{d\times s} & & \\ \mathbf{I}_{(d-1)\times(d-1)} & \mathbf{0}_{(d-1)\times(s-d+1)} & \\ \mathbf{0}_{(d-2)\times d} & \mathbf{I}_{(d-2)\times(d-2)} & \mathbf{0}_{(d-2)\times(s-2(d-1))} \\ \mathbf{0}_{(d-3)\times(2d-1)} & \mathbf{I}_{(d-3)\times(d-3)} & \mathbf{0}_{(d-3)\times(s-3(d-1))} \\ & \cdots & \\ & \mathbf{0}_{(k+1)\times(s-k-1)} & \mathbf{I}_{(k+1)\times(k+1)} \end{bmatrix}$$

and the solution matrices defined as $\widetilde{\mathbf{W}}_\mathbf{v} \equiv \widetilde{\mathbf{U}}^\mathsf{T}\begin{bmatrix}\mathbf{I}_{d\times d} \\ \mathbf{0}_{(s-d)\times d}\end{bmatrix}$ and $\widetilde{\mathbf{W}}_\mathbf{y} \equiv \widetilde{\mathbf{U}}^\mathsf{T}\mathbf{S}\widetilde{\mathbf{U}}$.

3 Improving the Computation

In the previous section we have presented the theoretical basis for the definition of PCA for structured inputs. In this section we discuss some practical problems which are encountered when trying to apply the theory "as is". Then we make some observations about some specific features of structured domains. Finally, on the basis of these observations we suggest some techniques that help in reducing the computational burden, thus allowing the application of PCA for structures to larger and more complex datasets.

3.1 Practical Problems

The definition of PCA for structures, as outlined above, hinges on the explicit definition of the state space in order to get the "compressed" solution of the problem, i.e. the weights matrices. From a practical point of view this implies that when considering datasets of significant size and complexity (in terms of number of components for single structure) a quite large matrix $\mathbf{X}$ describing the state space should be explicitly defined. Specifically, $\mathbf{X}$ will have a column for each single component of the dataset and a given number[1] of rows for each element of the encoding scheme. More precisely, in the case of sequences, k rows for each time step; in the case of trees, k rows for each path explicitly defined in the training data; finally, in the case of graphs, $k + N - i$ rows for each item in the internal stack at distance i from the top. It is not difficult to understand that when considering a large number of components and sufficiently deep structures, the global size of $\mathbf{X}$ can soon become unmanageable because of storage requirements. In addition to that, computing the eigenvalues and eigenvectors of $\mathbf{X}$ can become problematic even for small dimensions since additional storage is required for the internal data structures used for the computation. Least, but not last, even if storage requirements are satisfied, the time needed to perform the eigenanalysis is more than quadratic with respect to the size of $\mathbf{X}$. Thus, it is clear that strategies which try to keep $\mathbf{X}$ as small as possible and to reduce the computational time for its eigenanalysis should be defined in order to allow the treatment of datasets of significative size and complexity.

In the next subsection we observe that, even before resorting to more or less sophisticated numerical analysis techniques and algorithms, the structured nature of the data can be exploited to get a significative reduction of the size of $\mathbf{X}$, as well as a (fractional) reduction of the time needed to perform its eigenanalysis.

3.2 Some Basic Observations and Their Exploitation

Let make some observations about the structure of $\mathbf{X}$: *i)* the number of rows is determined by both the size of the representation of each possible component and the adopted structural encoding scheme; *ii)* if the components are finite and discrete, then it is quite probable that different structures will have one or more components in common. This implies that columns in $\mathbf{X}$ that correspond to these common components will be identical; this can be exploited by redefining a more compact version of $\mathbf{X}$ where each distinct component is represented only once, but considering its multiplicity; *iii)* a quicker eigenanalysis of $\mathbf{X}$ can be computed by precomputing a QR decomposition of either $\mathbf{X}$ or $\mathbf{X}^\mathsf{T}$.

Observation *i)* leads to a general scheme for defining a "minimal" state space. Observation *ii)* may lead to a significative reduction in size of $\mathbf{X}$ when considering structures compounded of discrete components, while observation *iii)* can be exploited in general.

In the following three subsections we discuss the above points, according to the order of presentation given above.

3.3 Defining a "Minimal" State Space

The state space defined in Section 2 is designed to be able to potentially represent all possible structures up to a given predefined limit. For example, when considering sequences, all the possible sequences up to length T can be represented in the state

[1] We previously assumed that each component could be described by a vector of dimension k.

space. The same is true for graphs. Only for trees, a strategy which tries not to represent all possible paths has been suggested: only paths defined in the dataset are represented in the state space. However, any input vector can be associated to any position within the defined paths. In conclusion, it is clear that, since PCA is computed on a specific dataset, there is no point in having such a general encoding scheme for the state space. It is better to devise from the beginning an encoding scheme for the state space which takes into account the dataset.

Here we suggest to define a state space where for each structural component only items which occur associated to it in the dataset are explicitly represented. For example, if we consider the set of sequences $Tr = \{\mathbf{x}^{(1)}, \ldots, \mathbf{x}^{(N)}\}$ up to length T, then given position i, the state space is designed to be able to represent only those input vectors $\mathbf{x}_i^{(s_1)}, \ldots, \mathbf{x}_i^{(s_i)}$ (more precisely, the subspace $Subs(Tr, i) = spanned(\mathbf{x}_i^{(s_1)}, \ldots, \mathbf{x}_i^{(s_i)})$ spanned by the input vectors) which occur at position i when they are processed. Please, note that: *i)* an input vector $\mathbf{x}_p^{(j)} \in \mathbb{R}^k$ that occurs at position p into the sequence j of length l_j, occurs into the state space as a sub-vector from position $k \cdot p$ to position $k(l_j - p)$, i.e. into the state space vectors

$$[\mathbf{x}_p^{(j)^\mathsf{T}}, \ldots, \mathbf{x}_1^{(j)^\mathsf{T}}, \underbrace{\mathbf{0}^\mathsf{T}, \ldots, \mathbf{0}^\mathsf{T}}_{(T-i)}], \quad \cdots \quad , [\mathbf{x}_{l_j}^{(j)^\mathsf{T}}, \ldots, \mathbf{x}_p^{(j)^\mathsf{T}}, \ldots, \mathbf{x}_1^{(j)^\mathsf{T}}, \underbrace{\mathbf{0}^\mathsf{T}, \ldots, \mathbf{0}^\mathsf{T}}_{(T-l_j)}];$$

ii) the matrix obtained by using the input vectors $\mathbf{x}_i^{(s_1)}, \ldots, \mathbf{x}_i^{(s_i)}$ as columns may have rank $r < k$ (full rank is k), which implies that if with B_i we refer to a basis of $Subs(Tr, i)$, then a "minimal" state space can be obtained by using as basis of the space the union of these bases, i.e. $B_{ss} = \bigcup_{i=1}^{T} B_i$. A suitable shift operator performing a change of basis at each position should correspondingly be defined, which is always possible.

If we consider the special case of structures where each component may be one among k different labels represented by vectors of the canonical basis, B_i will correspond to the subset of canonical vectors associated to the labels occurring at position i into the "state space stack". In this case the shift operator will just "forget" the components that are not present from that point up to the last components of the state space.

3.4 Representing Unique Substructures in the Case of Discrete Components

When each component is described by a discrete entity, e.g. a symbol or label, the likelihood that different input structures share a common substructure is often not marginal. This is particularly true if the structures are created by a generative source, such as a generative model, e.g. a grammar. Repeated components correspond to repeated identical columns in $\mathbf{X}$. Without loss of generality, let assume that the columns of $\mathbf{X}$ are sorted so to have identical columns in contiguous positions. Let $\mathbf{r}_1, \ldots, \mathbf{r}_z$ be the all different columns occurring in $\mathbf{X}$, and $\mu_1, \ldots, \mu_z$ their multiplicity in $\mathbf{X}$. Then it is not difficult to verify that the matrix $\mathbf{X}^{\mathbf{red}} \equiv [\sqrt{\mu_1}\mathbf{r}_1, \ldots, \sqrt{\mu_z}\mathbf{r}_z]$ has the same covariance matrix as $\mathbf{X}$, and thus it shares the same column eigenvectors with $\mathbf{X}$. However, $\mathbf{X}^{\mathbf{red}}$ has only z columns versus $\sum_{i=1}^{z} \mu_i \geq z$ columns of $\mathbf{X}$. The problem, then, is to discover these repeated components, and their multiplicity, even before generating

```
MinimalDAG

Input: A tree forest F = {T_1, ..., T_N}
  /* l ≡ label, f ≡ frequency, tree ≡ tree_rooted_at */
  Initialize: μD ← void DAG;
   for j ← 1 to N do
   vertex_list ← InvTopologOrder(T_j);
   while vertex_list ≠ ∅ do
       v = pop(vertex_list);
       if ∃u ∈ μD s.t. tree(u) ≡ tree(v) then f(u) ← f(u) + 1
            else add to μD a node w where l(w) = l(v) and f(w) = 1
             forall children ch_i[v] of v
               add arc (w, c_i) to μD where c_i ∈ Nodes(μD) and tree(c_i) ≡ tree(ch_i[v])
   return μD
```

Fig. 1. The algorithm to transform a tree-forest into a minimal DAG, where all the subtrees are represented only once

columns representing them. Since graphs are basically treated as a special type of lists, here we focus on trees, which constitute the most general case since a list can be considered as a tree with outdegree 1. The problem is how to efficiently remove from the dataset repeated occurrences of (sub)trees. A dataset consisting of trees can be represented as a tree forest F. We define a procedure that merges all the trees in F into a single *minimal* DAG, i.e., a DAG with a *minimal* number of vertices. We will refer to this DAG as $\mu D = \mu DAG(F)$.

In Figure 1, we give an algorithm to efficiently compute shared subtrees, and to efficiently represent a forest as an annotated DAG (ADAG). More formally, with annotated DAG, we refer to a DAG where each node is annotated with a pair (*label,frequency*). The *label* field represents information associated with the node, while the *frequency* field is used to count how many repetitions of the same subtree rooted in that node are present in the tree forest. The frequency can then be used to define $\mathbf{X}^{\mathbf{red}}$ The procedure `InvTopologOrder`(T_j) used in the algorithm returns a total order of vertexes of T_j which is compatible with the (inverted) partial order defined by the arcs of T_j. Thus, the first vertexes of the list will be vertexes with zero outdegree, followed by vertexes which have only children with zero outdegree, and so on. Using this order guarantees the (unique) existence of vertexes $c_i \in \mu D$ s.t. $tree\_rooted\_at(c_i) \equiv tree\_rooted\_at(ch_i[v])$. In fact, for each i, the vertex $ch_i[v]$ is processed before vertex v and is either inserted in μD or recognized as a duplicated of a vertex already present in μD.

It should be noted that the function $tree\_rooted\_at(\cdot)$ can be implemented quite efficiently by an indexing mechanism, where a unique code is defined for a void child, and a unique code for the root of each different (sub)tree is generated by recursively considering the label of the root and the (unique) codes computed for its children.

Exploiting the indexing mechanism described above, the overall time complexity of the algorithm is $O(n \log(n))$, where n is the total number of vertexes of the forest F.

Please, notice that both the encoding scheme (i.e. the different paths defined by the forest) and the columns of $\mathbf{X}^{\mathbf{red}}$ can be generated by a visit of $\mu DAG(F)$.

3.5 Exploiting QR Decomposition

Eigenanalysis of the correlation matrix $\mathbf{XX}^{\mathsf{T}}$ can be performed in a robust and "economic" way by performing an SVD decomposition of either $\mathbf{X}$, in the case the number of rows is higher than the number of columns, or $\mathbf{X}^{\mathsf{T}}$ in the case the number of columns is higher than the number of rows. In fact, if we consider the SVD decomposition of $\mathbf{X} = \mathbf{USV}^{\mathsf{T}}$, where $\mathbf{U}$ and $\mathbf{V}$ are orthogonal matrices, and $\mathbf{S}$ is a diagonal matrix containing the singular values, the eigenvectors of $\mathbf{XX}^{\mathsf{T}}$ are the columns of matrix $\mathbf{U}$ and the corresponding eigenvalues are the square of the singular values stored in $\mathbf{S}$.

The SVD of $\mathbf{X}$ can be performed by first performing a QR decomposition of $\mathbf{X} = \mathbf{QR}$, where $\mathbf{Q}$ is an orthogonal matrix, and $\mathbf{R}$ is an upper triangular matrix, and then performing an SVD decomposition of $\mathbf{R} = \mathbf{USV}^{\mathsf{T}}$. In this way the eigenvectors are obtained by computing $\mathbf{QU}$. The decomposition described above is quicker than the direct SVD decomposition of $\mathbf{X}$ or $\mathbf{X}^{\mathsf{T}}$ if we choose to start from the matrix that produces a smaller $\mathbf{R}$, so that the successive SVD decomposition is quicker. Moreover, we do not need to compute the full product between $\mathbf{Q}$ and $\mathbf{U}$, since, already knowing the singular values returned in $\mathbf{S}$, only the relevant columns of the product need to be computed, savings additional computations.

4 Experimental Evaluation

Two datasets were used to test our approach. The first one is derived from the data set of the PTC (Predictive Toxicology Challenge, [5]) originally provided by the U.S. National Institute for Environmental Health Sciences - US National Toxicology Program (NTP) in the context of carcinogenicity studies. The publicly available dataset (see http://www.predictive-toxicology.org/data/ntp/) is a collection of about four hundred chemical compounds. The dataset includes a range of molecular classes and molecular dimension spanning from small and simple cases to medium size with multi-cycles. In order to represent these chemical structures and their components, we used undirected graphs with labels associated to vertexes and edges. The vertexes of these graphs correspond to the various atoms and the vertexes labels correspond to the type of atoms. The edges correspond to the bonds between the atoms and the edges labels correspond to the type of bonds. This explicit graph modeling can be obtained through the information directly extracted by standard formats based on connection table representation, limited, in our case, to the information on atoms type (including C and H), bond type (single, double or triple) and their 2D-topology, as implicit in the set of vertexes connections. Here, we do not assume any specific canonical ordering of such information, assuming directly the form provided in the original PTC data set.

For testing our approach, we have considered molecules with atoms occurring at least more than 3 times in the original data set and with a maximum dimension (number of vertexes) of 70. In all, 394 distinct chemical compounds are considered, with the smallest having 4 atoms. 10 distinct atoms occur in the used data set, corresponding to

Table 1. Occurrences of atoms symbols in the chemical dataset and some of its statistical properties

Chemical Symbol	C	N	O	P	S	F	Cl	Br	H	Na
Frequency	3608	417	766	25	76	11	326	46	4103	22

# examples	Max. number atoms	Max. number bonds	Avg. number atoms (bonds)	Tot. number items (atoms+bonds)
394	70	73	23.86 (24.20)	18,936

Sentence	*Noun Phrase*	*Verb Phrase*	*Prepositional Phrase*	*Adjectival Phrase*
s → np vp	np → D ap	vp → V np		ap → A ap
s → np V	np → D N	vp → V pp	pp → P np	ap → A N
	np → np pp			

Fig. 2. Context-Free Grammar used in the experiments

Table 2. Experimental results

Dataset	# components for "minimal" state space (size full space)	Time in sec. direct SVD full matrix	Time in sec. QR+SVD full matrix	# col. in μDAG matrix	Time in sec. direct SVD μDAG matrix	Time in sec. QR+SVD μDAG matrix
Graphs	1587 (3115)	313.25	222.87	2020	182.36	138.91
Trees	2795 (7158)	1556.95	1063.41	1217	77.3	63.08

the following chemical symbols: C, N, O, P, S, F, Cl, Br, H, Na. In Table 1 we report the frequencies of such atoms through the compounds as well as some general statistics.

Symbols are represented by 10-dimensional vectors (i.e. $k = 10$) following a "one-hot" coding scheme. Bond's type is coded by integers in the set $\{0, 1, 2, 3\}$, where 0 represents the absence of a bond and the other numbers are for single, double and triple bonds, respectively. Triple bonds occur only 5 times in the dataset. Double bonds occur 1509 times in the dataset. The remaining bonds are single. Since the graphs do not have self-connections for vertexes, we can avoid to represent the information about self-connections. Since the maximum number of vertexes in the dataset is $N = 70$, a standard full representation of the state space (stack size) would require $s = \sum_{i=0}^{N-1}(d-i) = 3115$ different components, since the graphs are undirected. We used the dummy state $\mathbf{y}_{dummy}$ described in [10] to get zero-mean vectors.

The second dataset is given by parse trees derived by the context-free grammar shown in Figure 2, and already used by Pollack [7]. In all 421 distinct parse trees have been randomly generated for a total of $14,815$ nodes. Terminal and nonterminal symbols are represented by 6-dimensional vectors (i.e. $k = 6$), where the first component is 0 for terminal symbols and 3 for nonterminal symbols, while the remaining 5 components follow a "one-hot" coding scheme. Since in the dataset there were 1193 distinct paths when processing the trees, a standard full representation of the state space (stack size) would require $s = 1193 \times 6 = 7158$ components.

In Table 2 we have reported the results obtained by using an Intel Xeon E5345 based computer using Scilab.

5 Conclusion

We have suggested a way to speed-up the computation of principal components for structured input. The validity of the proposed approach has been experimentally evaluated with quite good results. Additional improvements, not explored in this paper, can be obtained by considering the sparsity of the $\mathbf{X}$ matrix, and the adoption of more sophisticated numerical algorithms for its eigenanalysis.

References

1. Baldi, P., Pollastri, G.: The principled design of large-scale recursive neural network architectures-DAG-RNNs and the protein structure prediction problem. Journal of Machine Learning Research 4, 575–602 (2003)
2. Frasconi, P., Gori, M., Sperduti, A.: A general framework for adaptive processing of data structures. IEEE Trans. Neural Networks 9(5), 768–786 (1998)
3. Gärtner, T.: A survey of kernels for structured data. SIGKDD Explor. Newsl. 5(1), 49–58 (2003)
4. Hammer, B.: Learning with Recurrent Neural Networks. Springer Lecture Notes in Control and Information Sciences. Springer, Heidelberg (2000)
5. Helma, C., King, R.D., Kramer, S., Srinivasan, A.: The predictive toxicology challenge 2000-2001. Bioinformatics 17(1), 107–108 (2001)
6. Jolliffe, I.: Principal Component Analysis. Springer, Heidelberg (2002)
7. Pollack, J.B.: Recursive distributed representations. Artificial Intelligence 46, 77–105 (1990)
8. Micheli, A., Sperduti, A.: Recursive Principal Component Analysis of Graphs. In: Marques de Sá, J., Alexandre, L.A., Duch, W., Mandic, D. (eds.) ICANN 2007. LNCS, vol. 4669, pp. 826–835. Springer, Heidelberg (2007)
9. Micheli, A., Sperduti, A., Starita, A., Bianucci, A.M.: Analysis of the internal representations developed by neural networks for structures applied to quantitative structure-activity relationship studies of benzodiazepines. Journal of Chem. Inf. and Comp. Sci. 41(1), 202–218 (2001)
10. Sperduti, A.: Exact Solutions for Recursive Principal Components Analysis of Sequences and Trees. In: Kollias, S., Stafylopatis, A., Duch, W., Oja, E. (eds.) ICANN 2006. LNCS, vol. 4131, pp. 349–356. Springer, Heidelberg (2006)
11. Sperduti, A., Starita, A.: Supervised neural networks for the classification of structures. IEEE Transactions on Neural Networks 8, 714–735 (1997)

Hinge Rank Loss and the Area Under the ROC Curve

Harald Steck

Siemens Medical Solutions, IKM CAD & Knowledge Solutions,
51 Valley Stream Parkway E51, Malvern, PA 19355, USA
harald.steck@siemens.com

Abstract. In ranking as well as in classification problems, the Area under the ROC Curve (AUC), or the equivalent Wilcoxon-Mann-Whitney statistic, has recently attracted a lot of attention. We show that the AUC can be lower bounded based on the hinge-rank-loss, which simply is the rank-version of the standard (parametric) hinge loss. This bound is asymptotically tight. Our experiments indicate that optimizing the (standard) hinge loss typically is an accurate approximation to optimizing the hinge rank loss, especially when using affine transformations of the data, like e.g. in ellipsoidal machines. This explains for the first time why standard training of support vector machines approximately maximizes the AUC, which has indeed been observed in many experiments in the literature.

1 Introduction

The equivalence of the Area under the Receiver Operating Characteristics Curve (AUC) and the Wilcoxon-Mann-Whitney statistic has in recent years sparked a lot of interesting work toward a better understanding of classification and ranking problems. While the AUC is a valuable measure for *assessing* the quality of a given classifier or ranking method, it was typically not used as an objective function when *training / optimizing* a classifier, mainly due to its high computational cost or different preferences concerning performance measures in the past (e.g., 0/1-loss). Only recently, computationally tractable optimization methods were developed for the use of AUC during training. These approaches are reviewed in Section 8.

This paper aims to better understand the interrelationship among the performance measures AUC (cf. Section 3), 0/1-loss, and our new hinge rank loss (cf. Section 4). It is not concerned with algorithms for optimizing these measures. In Section 5, we first show that the AUC is determined by the difference between the hinge rank loss and the 0/1-loss; and secondly, that the hinge rank loss provides an asymptotically-tight lower-bound on the AUC. Thirdly, Section 6 argues that the AUC is approximately maximized by the standard training of support vector machines; this can be improved by using affine transformations of the data, e.g., employing (kernel) PCA [1] or ellipsoidal machines [2]. This is supported by our experiments in Section 7 as well as by many experimental findings in the literature [3,4,5,6], as discussed in Section 8.

J.N. Kok et al. (Eds.): ECML 2007, LNAI 4701, pp. 347–358, 2007.

2 Notation

This section introduces relevant notation concerning classifiers and their parametric (real-valued) vs. rank outputs. Like in much of the machine learning literature, we consider *binary* classification in this paper. Assume we are given data $D = \{(x_i, y_i)\}_{i=1,...,N}$ with N examples, class labels $y_i \in \{-1, +1\}$, and input vectors x_i; the number of positive examples (i.e., where $y_i = +1$) is N^+, and the number of negative examples is $N^- = N - N^+$.

Given a classifier C with real-valued output c_i, we have $c_i = C(x_i)$ for each input x_i, $i = 1, ..., N$. For simplicity, we assume that there are no ties, i.e., $c_i \neq c_j$ for all $i \neq j$.[1] Given the real-valued threshold θ, the classification rule is $\text{sign}(c_i - \theta)$. The rank-version of this classifier is denoted as follows: let the values c_i be ordered in *ascending* order, i.e., the smallest output-value gets assigned the lowest rank. Let $r_i \in \{1, ..., N\}$ be the rank of example $i = 1, ..., N$. Moreover, let r_j^+ denote the ranks of the positive examples, $j = 1, ..., N^+$; and r_k^- be the ranks of the negative ones, $k = 1, ..., N^-$. As the counterpart of the real-valued threshold θ, a natural definition of the rank-threshold is $\tilde{\theta} = \max\{r_i : c_i \leq \theta\} + 1/2 = \min\{r_i : c_i > \theta\} - 1/2$, as it is located half way between the two neighboring ranks at the (real-valued) threshold.[2] The classification rule is $\text{sign}(r_i - \tilde{\theta})$, so that the real-valued version and the rank-version of the classifier yield identical classification results.

3 Area Under the Curve

This section briefly reviews the Area under the Receiver Operating Characteristics (ROC) Curve (AUC). While the AUC, denoted by A, had been used as a measure for assessing *classifier performance* in machine learning (e.g., see [7] for an overview), in recent years it has also become popular as a quality measure in *ranking problems*. This is because of its well-known equivalence to the Wilcoxon-Mann-Whitney (WMW) statistic [9,10]; it can be written in terms of pairwise comparisons of ranks:

$$A = \frac{1}{N^+ N^-} \sum_{j=1}^{N^+} \sum_{k=1}^{N^-} \mathbf{1}_{r_j^+ > r_k^-}, \tag{1}$$

where $\mathbf{1}$ is the indicator function: $\mathbf{1}_a = 1$ if a is true and 0 otherwise. Essentially, it counts the number of pairs of examples that are ranked correctly, i.e., positive examples are supposed to have a higher rank than negative ones. The AUC takes values $A \in [0, 1]$; $A = 1$ indicates perfect classification/ranking, and a random classification/ranking results in $A = 0.5$. The AUC is independent of the threshold value θ used in classification.

---

[1] Given continuous inputs, and assuming that the classifier does not discretize or use a step-function internally, there are no ties in the outputs to be expected in general.

[2] Again, no ties concerning the c_i's are assumed.

Even though the computational cost of evaluating Eq. 1 for all pairs of positive and negative examples (of which there are N^+N^-) seems to grow quadratically with N at first glance, it is easy to see that the WMW statistic can be evaluated in linear time in N given the ranks (if the continuous outputs c_i are given, the ranks can be determined by sorting them in time $N \log N$) [7,8]:

$$A = \frac{1}{N^+N^-} \sum_{j=1}^{N^+} (r_j^+ - j) = \frac{1}{N^+N^-} \left[\left(\sum_{j=1}^{N^+} r_j^+ \right) - \binom{N^+ + 1}{2} \right] . \tag{2}$$

4 Hinge Rank Loss

In this section, we define the *hinge rank loss* as a rank-version of the standard (parametric) hinge loss, which is commonly used for learning support vector machines (SVM). We show that it can be calculated by summing over the ranks of the positive examples (or equivalently of the negative ones), similar to Eq. 2.

While classification accuracy is often *assessed* in terms of the 0/1-loss, the 0/1-loss is computationally expensive to optimize when *training* the classifier. For the optimization task, researchers thus typically resort to approximations or bounds of the 0/1-loss. Among other loss functions, the (linear) *hinge loss* [11] (plus a penalty for regularization) is commonly used as objective function when learning SVMs. The hinge loss has several favorable properties, including: (1) it is an upper bound on the 0/1-loss, (2) it is differentiable everywhere except for one point, and (3) leads to a convex optimization problem. The hinge loss [11] of the real-valued classifier-outputs c_i, given the threshold θ and the data D, is typically defined as $L_\theta^{\mathrm{H}} = \sum_{i=1}^{N} [1 - y_i(c_i - \theta)]_+$, where $[\cdot]_+$ denotes the positive part, i.e., $[a]_+ = a$ if $a > 0$, and 0 otherwise. In analogy, we propose the following rank-version of the standard hinge loss:

Definition 1 (Hinge Rank Loss). *We define as the* hinge rank loss, *based on the ranks r_i w.r.t. the rank-threshold $\tilde{\theta}$:*

$$L_{\tilde{\theta}}^{\mathrm{HR}} = \sum_{i=1}^{N} \left[\frac{1}{2} - y_i(r_i - \tilde{\theta}) \right]_+ . \tag{3}$$

Note that $r_i - \tilde{\theta} \in \{\pm 1/2, \pm 3/2, ...\}$, cf. Section 2, so that $[1/2 - y_i(r_i - \tilde{\theta})]_+ \in \{0, 1, 2, ...\}$. Both L^{H} and L^{HR} share the same relevant properties: the loss incurred due to each misclassified example i is at least 1 (hence both are an upper bound on the 0/1-loss), and it increases linearly in r_i.[3] Conversely, no loss L^{HR} is incurred for any correctly classified example, as desirable (in contrast to hinge loss). Note that the 'hinge ranking loss' defined in [12] is different from our definition, as discussed in Section 8.

Next, we re-write the hinge rank loss in terms of the sum over the ranks of the positive examples. For notational convenience, we will use the definition

[3] If we had defined the hinge rank loss with 1 in place of 1/2, the results in this paper would hold with only minor changes.

$\bar{\theta} = \tilde{\theta} - 1/2 \in \mathbb{N}$ for the rank-threshold in place of the (equivalent) definition in Section 2. Hence, the examples with ranks $r_i \leq \bar{\theta}$ get classified as negatives, and the examples with ranks $r_i \geq \bar{\theta} + 1$ as positives. Now we can present

Proposition 1. *For the hinge rank loss from Definition 1 holds*

$$L_{\bar{\theta}}^{\mathrm{HR}} = N_{\bar{\theta}}^{\mathrm{fn}} + N^{+}\bar{\theta} + \binom{N - \bar{\theta} + 1}{2} - \sum_{j=1}^{N^{+}} r_j^{+} , \tag{4}$$

with the number of false negatives $N_{\bar{\theta}}^{\mathrm{fn}} = \sum_{j=1}^{N^{+}} \mathbf{1}_{r_j^{+} \leq \bar{\theta}}$.

Proof: Decomposing the sum in the definition in Eq. 3 into one for either class, and summing only over the non-zero arguments, one obtains $L_{\bar{\theta}}^{\mathrm{HR}} = \sum_{j=1:r_j^{+} \leq \bar{\theta}}^{N^{+}} (1 - r_j^{+} + \bar{\theta}) + \sum_{k=1:r_k^{-} > \bar{\theta}}^{N^{-}} (r_k^{-} - \bar{\theta})$. Concerning the right-most sum, we use the following identity regarding all the ranks greater than $\bar{\theta}$, $\sum_{j=1:r_j^{+} > \bar{\theta}}^{N^{+}} (r_j^{+} - \bar{\theta}) + \sum_{k=1:r_k^{-} > \bar{\theta}}^{N^{-}} (r_k^{-} - \bar{\theta}) = \binom{N - \bar{\theta} + 1}{2}$. Now the former equation can be rewritten in terms of sums over the positive examples only (or equivalently over the negative ones only). Merging the two sums over the positive examples into one, it follows $L_{\bar{\theta}}^{\mathrm{HR}} = \sum_{j=1:r_j^{+} \leq \bar{\theta}}^{N^{+}} 1 - \sum_{j=1}^{N^{+}} (r_j^{+} - \bar{\theta}) + \binom{N - \bar{\theta} + 1}{2}$, which yields Eq. 4. □

5 Hinge Rank Loss and AUC

In this section, we decompose the AUC or Wilcoxon-Mann-Whitney-statistic used in ranking problems in terms of the hinge rank loss and the 0/1-loss used in classification tasks. From Eqs. 2 and 4, it follows immediately:

Proposition 2. *The AUC is related to the hinge rank loss and the number of false negatives as follows:*

$$A = 1 - \frac{L_{\bar{\theta}}^{\mathrm{HR}} - \mathrm{const}_{D,\bar{\theta}} - N_{\bar{\theta}}^{\mathrm{fn}}}{N^{+}N^{-}} \quad \text{and} \quad A \geq 1 - \frac{L_{\bar{\theta}}^{\mathrm{HR}} - \mathrm{const}_{D,\bar{\theta}}}{N^{+}N^{-}}, \tag{5}$$

where $\mathrm{const}_{D,\bar{\theta}} = \binom{N^{-} - \bar{\theta} + 1}{2}$ *if* $N^{-} \geq \bar{\theta}$ *and* $\mathrm{const}_{D,\bar{\theta}} = \binom{\bar{\theta} - N^{-}}{2}$ *otherwise;* $\mathrm{const}_{D,\bar{\theta}}$ *is a constant given the data* D *(and thus* N^{+} *and* N^{-}*) and the rank-threshold* $\bar{\theta}$*, i.e., it is independent of the classifier* C.

Not only is the hinge rank loss $L_{\bar{\theta}}^{\mathrm{HR}}$ an upper bound on the 0/1-loss (as discussed earlier), but also it is the decisive term in the lower bound on the AUC, as apparent from the non-negativity of $N_{\bar{\theta}}^{\mathrm{fn}}$ in Eq. 5.

Proposition 3. *The lower bound in Eq. 5 is tight in the asymptotic limit* $N \to \infty$ *under the mild assumption that* $N^{+}/N \to \mathrm{const}_D^{+}$*, where* $0 < \mathrm{const}_D^{+} < 1$ *is a constant.*

Proof: It has to be shown that $N_{\bar{\theta}}^{\mathrm{fn}}/(N^{+}N^{-}) \to 0$ as $N \to \infty$, as this is the only term omitted from Eq. 5 as to obtain the bound in Eq. 5. This is trivial because

$0 \leq N_{\bar{\theta}}^{\text{fn}} \leq N$, and $N/(N^+N^-) \to 0$ as $N \to \infty$ under the assumption $N^+/N \to \text{const}_D^+ > 0$. Hence, in the non-separable case, we have $1 - A > \text{const} > 0$, while $N_{\bar{\theta}}^{\text{fn}}/(N^+N^-) \to 0$, which hence becomes negligible for large N. In the separable case, we have $A = 1$ and from Eq. 5 thus $L_{\bar{\theta}}^{\text{HR}} - \text{const}_{D,\bar{\theta}} = N_{\bar{\theta}}^{\text{fn}}$, so that the bound indeed approaches 1 in the asymptotic limit and thus becomes tight. □

The asymptotic tightness of this bound implies that the minimum of the hinge rank loss indeed coincides with the maximum of the AUC in the asymptotic limit (our experiments in Section 7 indicate that this holds already for rather small data sets in excellent approximation). This desirable property is not guaranteed for the loose bounds on the AUC used in the literature, cf. Section 8.

Apart from that, Eq. 5 relates the AUC, which is independent of threshold $\bar{\theta}$, with the terms $L_{\bar{\theta}}^{\text{HR}}$, $\text{const}_{D,\bar{\theta}}$ and $N_{\bar{\theta}}^{\text{fn}}$, which all depend on $\bar{\theta}$. The validity of Eq. 5 implies that the effect of different values $\bar{\theta}$ cancels out among those terms.

An interesting special case of Eq. 5 is obtained for the natural choice of the threshold $\bar{\theta} = N^-$, so that the *predicted number* of positive (negative) examples equals the *true number* of positives (negatives); or equivalently, the number of false positives equals the number of false negatives. This choice has two effects: (1) it minimizes the constant $\text{const}_{D,\bar{\theta}}$, namely it vanishes; (2) it holds that $N_{N^-}^{\text{fn}} = L_{N^-}^{0/1}/2$, where the latter is the 0/1-loss. We thus obtain the

Corollary: *For the choice $\bar{\theta} = N^-$, the relation among AUC, hinge rank loss and 0/1-loss reads:*

$$A = 1 - \frac{L_{N^-}^{\text{HR}} - \frac{1}{2} L_{N^-}^{0/1}}{N^+N^-} \quad \text{and} \quad A \geq 1 - \frac{L_{N^-}^{\text{HR}}}{N^+N^-}. \tag{6}$$

6 Hinge Loss as a Parametric Approximation

In this section, we argue that minimizing the (standard) hinge loss—as it is the parametric counterpart of the hinge rank loss—can be expected to be a good approximation to maximizing the AUC, especially after pre-processing the data by an affine transformation, like (kernel-) PCA (principal component analysis) [1] with subsequent rescaling along each principal component, or the ellipsoidal machine [2].

While minimizing the hinge rank loss during training would provide an asymptotically tight bound on the AUC (as shown in the previous section), this is computationally expensive due to its discrete nature. For computational reasons, a standard approach is to approximate a discrete function by a continuous (and possibly differentiable or convex) one, which then can be optimized more efficiently. For instance, the Wilcoxon-Mann-Whitney-statistic has been approximated by various differentiable functions in [14,15] for efficient optimization by means of gradient descent (but then suffered from quadratic computational complexity due to the gradient).

Our propositions suggest an alternative approximation for efficient optimization: as the asymptotically-tight lower bound on the AUC is maximized by minimizing the hinge rank loss, the latter may simply be approximated by its parametric counterpart: the standard hinge loss, which is computationally less costly to minimize (as done e.g. in standard SVM training). The rank-threshold $\bar{\theta}$ is accordingly replaced by (real-valued) threshold θ, cf. Sections 2 and 4.

Note that there exist rank and parametric versions of many commonly-used statistics, like the Pearson correlation coefficient and the Spearman rank correlation; or the paired Student's t-test and the Wilcoxon signed-rank test. In general, the ranked and the parametric versions of a statistic were found to yield similar results in experiments, even though no theoretical proofs exist in general. Further experimental insights include that there can also be some differences; in particular, rank statistics are independent of an (assumed) distribution of the examples, and are typically less affected by outliers in the data.

Even though the validity of the approximation of the hinge rank loss by the (standard) hinge loss cannot be proven theoretically, it is strongly supported not only by our experiments in Section 7 but also by many experimental findings in the literature, where standard SVM training yielded surprisingly high AUC values [3,4,5,6], cf. also Section 8.

Given a linear classifier (in feature space), consider an arbitrary orientation of its hyperplane: regarding the hinge rank loss, the contribution of an individual misclassified example grows monotonically with its distance from the hyperplane for both the parametric hinge loss and the hinge rank loss, however at possibly different rates. Note that the maximum possible contribution of a misclassified example to the hinge rank loss is a constant (determined by the number of examples) for *any* orientation of the hyperplane; this does not hold for the standard hinge loss, especially if the examples are squished along some dimensions. This suggests a necessary condition for the hinge loss to be a good approximation to the hinge rank loss: rescaling the (feature) space such that the examples have the *same spread in every direction*. This can be achieved by the ellipsoidal machine [2], which determines the bounding ellipsoid of the examples (possibly allowing for outliers for robustness) and transforms the examples such that they lie within a *sphere*. Alternatively, a similar affine transformation can be obtained by using principal component analysis and rescaling / normalizing along every principal component j by a factor N/std_j (where std_j is the standard deviation along principal component j, cf. Section 7 for an example), or using its kernelized version [1]. The resulting improvement is illustrated in Section 7, which also shows that such an affine transformation can make the hinge loss more robust against outliers. Moreover, note that such an affine transformation is independent of and has a different effect than the (standard) penalty term for regularization; for instance, the latter would not solve the issue in the third example in Fig. 1.

7 Experiments

In this section, we experimentally evaluated how the hinge rank loss, the (standard) hinge loss and the 0/1-loss are related to the AUC. We assessed this in two different ways, as outlined in the following, using artificial data as well as 8

Table 1. This table shows the AUC values obtained after optimizing the following measures: AUC, hinge rank loss (L^{HR}), (standard) hinge loss (L^{H}),(standard) hinge loss after affine transformation of data (aff. L^{H}), and 0/1-loss ($L^{0/1}$) on artificial data (cf. Fig. 1) and 8 data sets from the UCI repository

data set	dim.	examples	AUC	L^{HR}	L^{H}	aff. L^{H}	$L^{0/1}$
artificial data 1	2	1000	0.998	0.998	0.998	0.998	0.998
artificial data 2	2	1000	0.848	0.848	0.848	0.848	0.848
artif. with outliers	2	1000	0.796	0.796	0.574	0.796	0.796
Sonar	60	208	0.996	0.996	0.973	0.996	0.950
Glass	10	214	0.992	0.992	0.987	0.988	0.957
Ionosphere	33	351	0.983	0.983	0.976	0.981	0.958
SPECTF	44	267	0.956	0.952	0.930	0.937	0.910
Pima	8	768	0.841	0.841	0.819	0.837	0.835
Hayes-Roth	4	129	0.730	0.730	0.704	0.710	0.703
Hepatitis	19	80	1.000	1.000	1.000	1.000	0.972
Echocardiogram	7	107	0.826	0.826	0.724	0.798	0.793

data sets from the UCI machine learning repository.[4] In a pre-processing step, we discarded the examples with missing values for simplicity, as the remaining examples still provide a 'real-world distribution' for comparing the measures.

As a linear classifier, we used a hyperplane. When learning this classifier w.r.t. the various measures, only the hinge loss is not invariant under re-scaling of the data. We thus re-scaled the data in two different ways, as to illustrate the improvements due to the affine transformation discussed in Section 6. In the first version, we re-scaled each dimension k by the factor N/std_k, where std_k is the standard deviation of the examples regarding dimension k. In the second version, we applied PCA and re-scaled along each principal component analogously (called the affine transformation in the remainder).

Tab. 1 summarizes the AUC-values achieved after optimizing the various performance measures.[5,6] As expected, direct maximization of the AUC resulted in the highest AUC-values, but the difference to minimizing the hinge rank loss appeared negligible, as expected due to the asymptotic tightness of our bounds in Eqs. 5 and 6. Moreover, minimizing the standard hinge loss also yielded quite good AUC-scores. As expected, the affine transformation leads to a notable improvement. In comparison, optimizing the 0/1-loss was clearly inferior to minimizing the hinge rank loss, as expected. Moreover, the 0/1-loss was also slightly worse than the (standard) hinge loss applied to the data after the affine transformation. This suggests that the latter can indeed serve as a useful parametric

---

4 `http://www.ics.uci.edu/~mlearn/MLRepository.html`

5 We omitted the standard penalty term here, as regularization is an important but different problem. It can simply be included when classifying *unseen* examples, after the preprocessing step regarding the affine transformation.

6 For ease of implementation, we used a simulated annealing scheme with random distortions of the hyperplane as to optimize the 'discrete' measures directly.

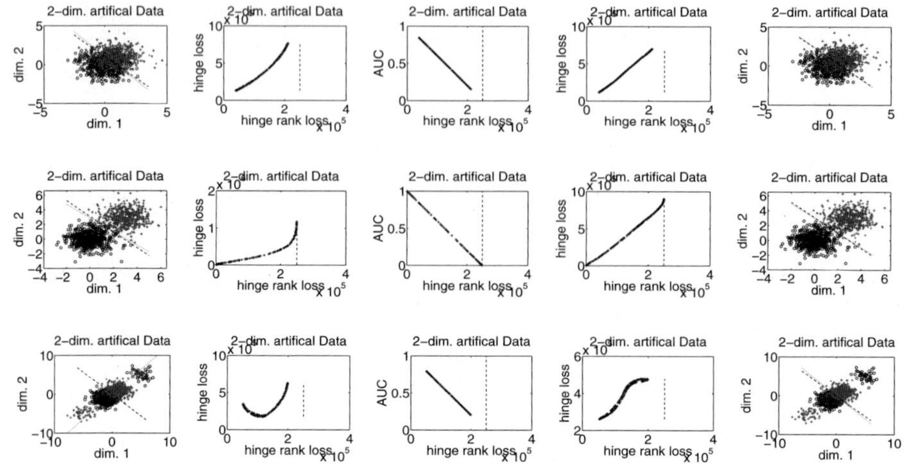

Fig. 1. Two-dimensional artificial data: either class (+, ∘) is represented by 500 examples, sampled from a standard normal distribution. The first two experiments differ in the distance between the centroids of the two classes. In the third experiment, both classes contain 10% of outliers. The two leftmost columns show the results for the hinge loss without the affine transformation, and the two rightmost columns show the results (in the original space) when using the affine transformation. The column in the center applies to both cases. The dashed line is the optimal hyperplane based on the hinge rank loss, while the dotted line is optimal w.r.t. the (standard) hinge loss.

approximation to the hinge rank loss, as it is computationally less expensive to optimize.

While the previous evaluation is only concerned with the *optimum* AUC-value, in our second assessment we evaluated the relationship between the hinge loss and the AUC for *all possible* AUC-values. For each data set, we randomly sampled various orientations of the hyperplane. We chose the rank-threshold $\bar{\theta} = N^-$, as in the Corollary, and determined the corresponding (parametric) threshold as the average parametric classifier-output for the two examples with ranks N^- and $N^- + 1$.[7] Then we calculated—for each orientation of the hyperplane—the parametric hinge loss, the hinge rank loss and the AUC; the scatter-plots in Figs. 1 and 2 illustrate the relationship between these measures (each point corresponds to a different random orientation of the hyperplane). The vertical dashed line indicates the largest possible value of the hinge rank loss given N^+ positive and N^- negative examples: it equals $N^+N^- + \min\{N^+, N^-\}$, but its value may not be attained for a given data set due to the configuration of the examples.

Concerning the first two artificial data sets in Fig. 1, the scatter-plots indicate a clear monotonic relationship between the parametric hinge loss (with and

[7] As long as the parametric and rank thresholds correspond to each other, any other choice may have been used as well.

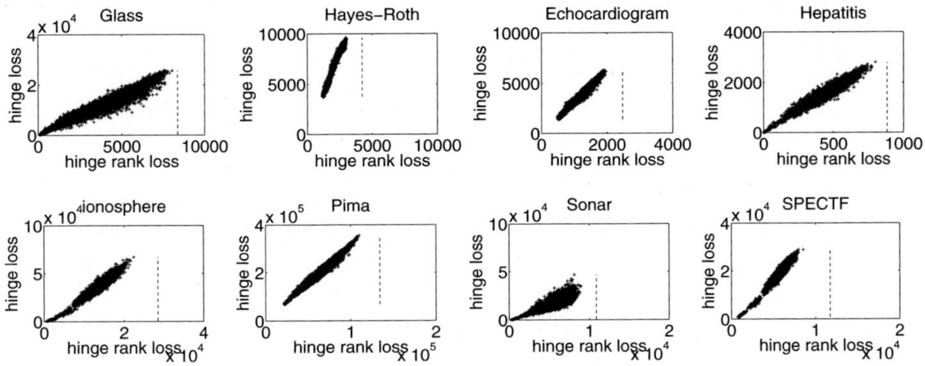

Fig. 2. The scatter-plots show the relationship of our hinge rank loss with the hinge loss on 8 data sets from the UCI machine learning repository

without the affine transformation) and the hinge rank loss, and between the hinge rank loss and the AUC. Hence, minimizing the hinge loss is an excellent approximation to minimizing the hinge rank loss, and to maximizing the AUC. Only in the third experiment, where many outliers are present, the optimal hyperplane w.r.t. the hinge loss (without affine transformation) differs significantly from the result based on the hinge rank loss, as expected (cf. Section 6); the corresponding scatter-plot shows a non-monotonic relationship, illustrating that the minima of the two loss functions are vastly different. The graphs on the lower right in Fig. 1 show the benefit of the affine transformation: when the (standard) hinge loss is applied to the data after the affine transformation, the scatter-plot shows a monotonic relationship, as desired, and the optimal hyperplanes w.r.t. either loss function are very similar. Apart from that, note that the relationship of the hinge rank loss and the AUC is well approximated by a linear function, as expected from the asymptotic tightness of the lower bounds in Eqs. 5 and 6.

Fig. 2 shows the relationship of the hinge rank loss and the (standard) hinge loss applied to 8 data sets from the UCI repository after the affine transformation: also here, it is notably monotonic. The fact that this relationship is different for each data set is irrelevant for minimization as long as it is monotonic. Apart from that, this relationship is much more 'noisy' for these real-world data sets than for our artificial data sets. Interestingly, the 'noise level' typically decreases as the hinge loss decreases, so that minimizing the hinge loss appears to be a good approximation to optimizing the hinge rank loss, and hence the AUC. Only for the data set 'Echocardiogram', the noise level is large for small values of the hinge loss, and thus the optimal hyperplanes with respect to the two loss functions are notably different, possibly due to dominating outliers.

Like in Fig. 1, we also found for these real-world data sets that the relationship between the hinge rank loss and the AUC is linear in excellent approximation (the plots have to be omitted due to lack of space), as expected.

8 Related Work

This section describes related work concerning boosting and SVMs in the context of ranking, and points out differences to our approach. A 'hinge ranking loss' was first defined in [12]. Its main difference to our Definition 1 is that they measure the difference in the ranks among all incorrectly ordered *pairs* of examples, so their measure is essentially quadratic in the rank-differences, while our measure is linear. As our hinge rank loss provides an asymptotically tight bound on the AUC, it is clear that the 'hinge ranking loss' does not.

Boosting can be understood as gradient descent, and the various flavors of boosting essentially differ in the objective function or in the (heuristic) minimization method, e.g., [16]. The objective function minimized by RankBoost [17], L^{RBoost}, provides a lower bound on the AUC [13], namely $1-L^{\text{RBoost}}/(N^+N^-) \leq A$. It has essentially the same form as our bounds in Eqs. 5 or 6 involving the hinge rank loss. While our bounds are asymptotically tight, RankBoost optimizes a loose bound, as $L^{\text{RBoost}} = \sum_{j=1}^{N^+}\sum_{k=1}^{N^-} \mathrm{e}^{c_k^- - c_j^+} \geq \sum_{j=1}^{N^+}\sum_{k=1}^{N^-} \mathbf{1}_{c_j^+ < c_k^-} = N^+N^-(1-A)$, cf. [13], where each c_j^+ (or c_k^-) denotes the weighted sum over the weak learners' outputs for the positive (or negative) example j (or k). In [13], it was also shown that AdaBoost's loss function equals the one of RankBoost in the case where the positive and negative examples contribute equally to the loss.

The average and the variance of the AUC statistic were derived in [18], revealing interesting relations to the misclassification rate, among other properties. In [19], confidence intervals for the AUC were obtained from these results by applying Chebyshev's inequality. The average and variance of the AUC was calculated with respect to all possible rankings with fixed misclassification rate, where each ranking got implicitly assigned the same probability/weight. This average-case analysis of a combinatorial problem may only be of limited use in practice: given fixed data, it is unlikely that all possible rankings occur with the same probability; in fact, many rankings may not occur at all in a given data set (e.g., cf. the scatter-plots in Section 7, where the extreme (small and large) values are actually not reached in many data sets). A different kind of generalization bounds were derived in [20].

It was mentioned in [3] that optimizing standard SVMs leads to maximizing the AUC in the special (trivial) case when the given data is separable. As a perfect separation implies an AUC of 1 (which is maximal), the more interesting case is non-separable data. Our results are derived without any assumptions on the kind of classifier used or the (non-)separability of the given data.

Apart from that, it was experimentally observed in [3] that there was no significant difference in AUC-scores between SVMs trained in the standard way and other approaches tailored to directly maximize the AUC, like RankBoost [17], AUCsplit (local optimization of AUC) [21], or ROC-SVM [3]. This provides additional support for the point made in this paper, namely that the hinge rank loss can indeed be accurately approximated by its parametric counterpart, the standard hinge loss.

In [4], the objective was to directly maximize the AUC when learning SVMs, which led to slight experimental improvements over the standard SVM training. This approach may be considered a special case of the SVM-approach to ordinal regression [22]. Both gradient-descent methods suffered from quadratic computational complexity, which made additional approximations necessary for computational reasons.

In [5], a generalized SVM approach was developed that is able to optimize multivariate non-linear performance measures in polynomial time, including AUC among others. The experiments focused on 4 data sets with unbalanced class distributions: in this scenario, their new approach was superior to standard SVMs when assessed with respect to the F_1-score or the precision/recall breakeven area. However, when assessed with respect to the AUC, the superiority of their new approach over standard SVMs appeared less convincing on the 4 data sets presented.

Among the many performance measures compared experimentally in [6], it was found that '... maximum margin methods such as boosting and SVMs ... surprisingly ... also yield excellent performance on the ordering metrics.'

In summary, the experimental observations in the literature, e.g., [3,4,5,6], suggest that—despite the various sophisticated methods tailored to directly maximize the AUC—standard SVMs could not be consistently outperformed when assessed with respect to the AUC. This paper provides a simple explanation: minimizing the (standard) hinge loss typically is an accurate approximation to maximizing the AUC.

9 Conclusions

We have derived a simple equation that relates the Area under the ROC Curve (AUC) with the hinge-rank-loss and the number of false negatives. This immediately yields an asymptotically-tight lower bound on the AUC, based on the hinge rank loss. While the surprisingly high AUC-scores after standard SVM training in the literature provide indirect evidence, our experiments corroborate directly that minimization of the (standard) hinge loss typically is an accurate approximation to minimizing the hinge rank loss, especially after applying affine transformations like in ellipsoidal machines. In summary, this suggests that standard SVM training typically is a simple, yet effective and computationally efficient way of approximately maximizing the AUC.

Acknowledgments. I am grateful to R. Bharat Rao for encouragement and support of this work, and to the anonymous reviewers for excellent comments.

References

1. Schölkopf, B., Smola, A., Müller, K.: Nonlinear component analysis as a kernel eigenvalue problem. Neural Computation 10, 1299–1319 (1998)
2. Shivaswamy, P., Jebara, T.: Ellipsoidal machines. In: Proc. Int. Conf. on Artificial Intelligence and Statistics, pp. 481–488 (2007)

3. Rakotomamonjy, A.: Optimizing area ROC curve with SVMs. In: workshop "ROC Analysis in AI" at the European Conference on Artificial Intelligence (2004)
4. Brefeld, U., Scheffer, T.: AUC maximizing support vector learning. In: workshop "ROC Analysis in Machine Learning" at Int. Conf. on Machine Learning (2005)
5. Joachims, T.: A support vector method for multivariate performance measures. In: Proc. Int. Conf. on Machine Learning, pp. 377–384 (2005)
6. Caruana, R., Niculescu-Mizil, A.: Data mining in metric space: an empirical analysis of supervised learning performance criteria. In: Proc. Int. Conf. on Knowledge Discovery and Data Mining, pp. 69–78 (2004)
7. Hand, D.J., Till, R.J.: A simple generalization of the area under the ROC curve for multiple class classification problems. Machine Learning 45, 171–186 (2001)
8. Wu, S., Flach, P.: A scored AUC metric for classifier evaluation and selection. In: workshop "ROC Analysis in Machine Learning" at Int. Conf. on Machine Learning (2005)
9. Wilcoxon, F.: Individual comparisons by ranking methods. Biometrics 1, 80–83 (1945)
10. Mann, H.B., Whitney, D.R.: On a test whether one of two random variables is stochastically larger than the other. Ann. Math. Stat. 18, 50–60 (1947)
11. Cortes, C., Vapnik, V.: Support-vector networks. Machine Learning 20, 273–297 (1995)
12. Agarwal, S., Niyogi, P.: Stability and generalization of bipartite ranking algorithms. In: Proc. Conf. on Learning Theory, pp. 32–47 (2005)
13. Rudin, C., Cortes, C., Mohri, M., Schapire, R.: Margin-based ranking meets boosting in the middle. In: Proc. Conf. on Learning Theory, pp. 63–78 (2005)
14. Yan, L., Dodier, R., Mozer, M.C., Wolniewicz, R.: Optimizing classifier performance via the Wilcoxon-Mann-Whitney statistics. In: Proc. Int. Conf. on Machine Learning, pp. 848–855 (2003)
15. Herschtal, A., Raskutti, B.: Optimising the area under the ROC curve using gradient descent. In: Proc. Int. Conf. on Machine Learning, pp. 49–56 (2004)
16. Friedman, J., Hastie, T., Tibshirani, R.: Additive logistic regression: A statistical view of boosting. The Annals of Statistics 38, 337–374 (2000)
17. Freund, Y., Iyer, R., Schapire, R., Singer, Y.: An efficient boosting algorithm for combining preferences. Journal of Machine Learning Research 4, 933–969 (2003)
18. Cortes, C., Mohri, M.: AUC optimization vs. error rate minimization. Advances in Neural Information Processing Systems 16, 313–320 (2003)
19. Cortes, C., Mohri, M.: Confidence intervals for the area under the ROC curve. Advances in Neural Information Processing Systems 17, 305–312 (2004)
20. Agarwal, S., Graepel, T., Herbrich, R., Har-Peled, S., Roth, D.: Generalization bounds for the area under the ROC curve. Journal of Machine Learning Research 6, 393–425 (2005)
21. Ferri, C., Flach, P., Hernandez-Orallo, J.: Learning decision trees using the area under the ROC curve. In: Proc. Int. Conf. on Machine Learning, pp. 139–146 (2002)
22. Herbrich, R., Graepel, T., Obermayer, K.: Support vector learning for ordinal regression. In: Proc. Int. Conf. on Neural Networks, pp. 97–102 (1999)

Clustering Trees with Instance Level Constraints

Jan Struyf[1] and Sašo Džeroski[2]

[1] Dept. of Computer Science, Katholieke Universiteit Leuven
Celestijnenlaan 200A, 3001 Leuven, Belgium
Jan.Struyf@cs.kuleuven.be

[2] Dept. of Knowledge Technologies, Jožef Stefan Institute
Jamova 39, 1000 Ljubljana, Slovenia
Saso.Dzeroski@ijs.si

Abstract. Constrained clustering investigates how to incorporate domain knowledge in the clustering process. The domain knowledge takes the form of constraints that must hold on the set of clusters. We consider instance level constraints, such as must-link and cannot-link. This type of constraints has been successfully used in popular clustering algorithms, such as k-means and hierarchical agglomerative clustering. This paper shows how clustering trees can support instance level constraints. Clustering trees are decision trees that partition the instances into homogeneous clusters. Clustering trees provide a symbolic description for each cluster. To handle non-trivial constraint sets, we extend clustering trees to support disjunctive descriptions. The paper's main contribution is ClusILC, an efficient algorithm for building such trees. We present experiments comparing ClusILC to COP-k-means.

1 Introduction

Clustering methods partition a given set of instances into subsets (clusters) such that the instances in a given cluster are similar [1]. Traditional clustering algorithms, such as k-means and hierarchical agglomerative clustering (HAC), are unsupervised, that is, they only have access to the attributes describing each instance; no direct information about the actual assignment of instances to clusters is available. This distinguishes clustering from supervised classification, where the class of each instance is given.

Constrained clustering investigates how domain knowledge can improve clustering performance. Domain knowledge is given as a set of constraints that must hold on the clusters. We consider two common types of instance level (IL) constraints: must-link and cannot-link [2]. A must-link constraint ML(a,b) specifies that instances a and b must belong to the same cluster, and a cannot-link constraint CL(a,b) specifies that a and b must not be placed in the same cluster. IL constraints provide additional information about the assignment of instances to clusters. Clustering with IL constraints is therefore considered to be a form of semi-supervised learning.

IL constraints have been successfully incorporated in popular clustering algorithms, such as k-means [3,4,5,6] and HAC [7,8]. This paper shows how clustering

J.N. Kok et al. (Eds.): ECML 2007, LNAI 4701, pp. 359–370, 2007.

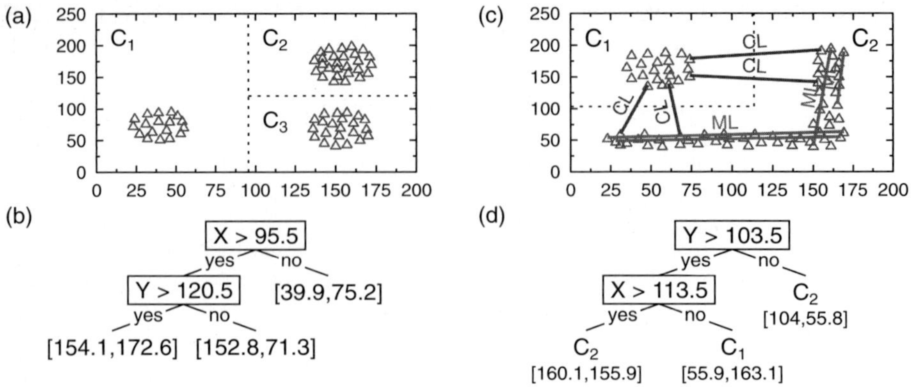

Fig. 1. (a) A simple data set with three clusters. (b) A clustering tree for (a). Each leaf is labeled with the cluster's centroid (the attribute-wise mean of the instances). (c) Data with must-link (ML) and cannot-link (CL) constraints. (d) A disjunctive clustering tree for (c), which takes the IL constraints into account.

trees can support IL constraints. Clustering trees are decision trees that are used for clustering [9] (Fig. 1.b). Each leaf of a clustering tree corresponds to a cluster and is labeled with the cluster's centroid. Similar to regular decision trees, the internal nodes of a clustering tree contain attribute-value tests. The main advantage of clustering trees is that they provide a symbolic description for each cluster (i.e., they perform conceptual clustering [10]). For example, cluster C_2 in Fig. 1.a is the set of instances for which $X > 95.5$ and $Y > 120.5$.

A disadvantage of clustering trees is that they only allow conjunctive cluster descriptions. This corresponds to rectangular clusters in the two-dimensional case (Fig. 1.a). One of the main goals of constrained clustering is dealing with non-trivial cluster shapes. In this paper, we therefore adapt clustering trees to support disjunctive cluster descriptions. To this end, we introduce cluster labels in the leaves of the clustering tree. All leaves that share the same label make up one cluster. We call a clustering tree with such labels a *disjunctive clustering tree*. For example, the L-shaped cluster C_2 in Fig. 1.c is represented by two leaves in Fig. 1.d and its disjunctive description is $Y \leq 103.5 \vee (Y > 103.5 \wedge X > 113.5)$. Note that this is similar to how classification trees represent disjunctive concepts, but here the labels are not given in the data.

2 Top-Down Induction of Clustering Trees

Clustering tree learning algorithms, such as Tilde [9] or Clus [11], are similar to top-down induction (TDI) algorithms for regular decision trees, such as C4.5 [12]. A TDI algorithm builds a tree starting from the root node in a depth-first manner. Given a set of instances, it considers all possible attribute-value tests, and selects the test t^* that maximizes a certain heuristic function. Next, it creates a new internal node, labels it t^*, and calls itself recursively to create a subtree for each subset in the partition induced by t^* on the instances. If, at a given point, no suitable test can be found, then it creates a leaf.

To induce a clustering tree, the TDI algorithm computes the heuristic value of a test t given instances I as $H(t, I) = \text{Var}(I) - \sum_{I_k \in \mathcal{P}(t,I)} \frac{|I_k|}{|I|} \text{Var}(I_k)$, with $\text{Var}(I)$ the variance of I, and $\mathcal{P}(t, I)$ the partition induced by t on I. $H(t, I)$ takes all attributes into account, that is, $\text{Var}(I)$ is the variance summed over all attributes. $H(t, I)$ guides the algorithm to a tree with homogeneous (low variance) leaves. If no test yields a significant reduction in variance, then the algorithm creates a leaf and labels it with the attribute-wise mean of the instances.

3 ClusILC

This section presents ClusILC, the main contribution of this paper. ClusILC is an algorithm that constructs a disjunctive clustering tree given a set of instances and a set of IL constraints. ClusILC performs soft constrained clustering [4,5,6], that is, the output is not guaranteed to satisfy all the given constraints.

3.1 ClusILC's Heuristic

Decision tree learners that follow the TDI approach (Section 2) employ a local heuristic: $H(t, I)$ only depends on the instances local to the node that is being constructed. ClusILC uses a global heuristic. Such a heuristic measures the quality of the entire tree and takes all instances into account. The heuristic that we propose for ClusILC is

$$H(T, I, IL) = (1 - \gamma) \cdot \frac{1}{\text{Var}(I)} \sum_{l \in T} \frac{|I_l|}{|I|} \text{Var}(I_l) + \gamma \cdot \frac{|\{c \in IL | \text{violated}(T, I, c)\}|}{|IL|},$$

with T the disjunctive clustering tree for which the heuristic is to be computed, I the set of instances, IL the set of IL constraints, and I_l the instances in leaf l of T. The first term of $H(T, I, IL)$ measures the average variance in the leaves of the tree, normalized by the data's total variance. The second term is the proportion of IL constraints that is violated by the tree. The heuristic trades off both terms by means of a parameter γ. Note that it is not possible to convert this heuristic into an equivalent local one because of the second term. This term cannot be split into a term for each leaf that only depends on local instances because IL constraints may link these instances to instances in other leaves.

3.2 ClusILC's Search Strategy

ClusILC (Fig. 2) searches greedily for a tree that minimizes $H(T, I, IL)$. It starts with a tree that consists of only a single leaf covering all instances. In each main loop iteration, it refines the current tree by replacing one of its leaves with a subtree consisting of a new test node and two new leaves. The candidate refined

```
procedure ClusILC(I,IL)
T = leaf(I,C1,mean(I))
h = H(T,I,IL)
while true do
    (T*,h*) = (null,h)
    for each Tr ∈ Refine(T) do
        hr = H(Tr,I,IL)
        if hr < h* then
            (T*,h*) = (Tr,hr)
    if h* < h then
        (T,h) = (T*,h*)
    else
        return T
```

```
procedure Refine(T)
R = ∅
for each leaf l ∈ T do
    Il = instances(l)
    for each attribute a do
        for each split point v do
            t = "a > v"
            (I1,I2) = apply(Il,t)
            for each label pair (c1,c2) do
                l1 = leaf(I1,c1,mean(I1))
                l2 = leaf(I2,c2,mean(I2))
                n = node(t,l1,l2)
                Tr = replace l by n in T
                R = R ∪ {Tr}
return R
```

Fig. 2. The ClusILC algorithm

trees are constructed by the procedure Refine. ClusILC computes for each such tree its heuristic value and selects the one with the smallest heuristic value (T^*). If T^* is better than the current tree, then T^* becomes the current tree and the search continues. If, on the other hand, no refined tree is able to improve on the heuristic value of the current tree, then the search ends and the current tree is returned.

Refine computes the set of candidate refined trees R. It consists of four nested loops. The first loop iterates over all leaves of the current tree. For each such leaf, Refine considers all attributes that can be used to construct an attribute-value test. For each attribute, it considers all possible split points and constructs a test of the form $a > x$. This test introduces two new leaves in the tree, where each should be assigned a cluster label (Fig. 1.d). The label can be either a label that already appears in the tree, or it can be a new label. For each pair of such labels (one for each leaf), Refine creates an internal node with the test and the two leaves, and then uses this node to create a new refined tree.

Note that ClusILC does not follow the depth-first approach of most TDI algorithms. The reason is that such a search strategy is not suitable for optimizing a global heuristic. (For a local heuristic, both methods produce the same tree and TDI algorithms use depth-first construction because it is more efficient and easier to implement.)

The efficiency of the algorithm in Fig. 2 can be improved in several ways. The most obvious optimization is that the candidate generation and the evaluation part of the algorithm can be integrated. Instead of storing all candidate refined trees, ClusILC only stores the current best refinement. Each time a new refinement is generated, ClusILC immediately computes its heuristic value and updates the current best refinement if the new refinement is better. The next two sections discuss how to efficiently assign cluster labels and how to find the best split point for a numerical attribute.

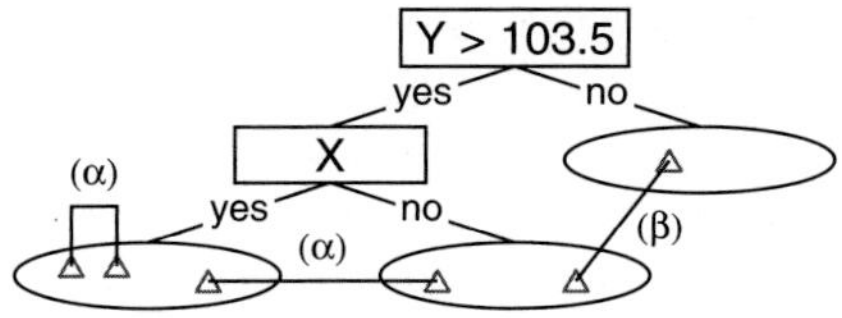

Fig. 3. We distinguish two constraint groups when refining the leaf marked "X": (α) constraints either local to one of the new leaves, or connecting the two new leaves, and (β) constraints connecting one of the two new leaves to another leaf already in the tree

3.3 Assigning Cluster Labels

The second optimization is that ClusILC does not consider all pairs of cluster labels when generating refined trees. The reason is that the choices (select a label for each leaf) are mostly independent. We distinguish two groups of constraints when refining a leaf: α and β (defined in Fig. 3). The number of violated constraints in group α does not depend on the actual labels (c_1, c_2) of the new leaves (ClusILC only considers splits with $c_1 \neq c_2$). The heuristic value therefore only changes if $v_1^\beta(c_1) + v_2^\beta(c_2)$ changes, with $v_k^\beta(c)$ the number of violated group β constraints when labeling leaf k with c. Because the two leaves have disjoint sets of constraints in group β, the two terms in the sum can be optimized separately, that is, the optimal labels can be assigned sequentially to the leaves. The optimal label c_k^* for leaf l_k is the label that minimizes $v_k^\beta(c)$. There is, however, one problem with this approach: the constraint $c_1 \neq c_2$ introduces a dependency between the two labels. Therefore, two cases must be considered. The first case is to first select the optimal label c_1^* for leaf l_1, then select the label $c_2 \neq c_1^*$ for leaf l_2 that minimizes $v_2^\beta(c_2)$. The second case is symmetrical, but starts with labeling l_2. ClusILC picks the case that minimizes $v_1^\beta(c_1) + v_2^\beta(c_2)$. The resulting labeling is the same as when the labeling would be obtained by considering all pairs (c_1,c_2). This optimization makes the labeling step linear in the number of possible cluster labels (instead of quadratic).

3.4 Selecting a Split Point

When refining a given leaf, ClusILC considers for each attribute all possible split points in one pass over the leaf's instances. This is similar to how TDI algorithms such as C4.5 select the best split point for a numerical attribute. The main difference is that ClusILC computes a number of additional statistics to be able to efficiently compute, for each candidate split, the number of violated constraints. We first discuss the basic algorithm and then the required modifications.

BestSplit (Fig. 4) considers all possible tests $a > x$ in one iteration over the instances. It first sorts the instances by their value for a from large to small. Each value x in the middle of two subsequent values in this sorted list is a candidate split point (line 7). To compute the corresponding heuristic value, the algorithm needs to compute the variance in the two subsets induced by

procedure BestSplit(l,a,h_0)

1: initialize S_1, S_2, h^*, r^*

2: initialize v^α, $\mathrm{ML}_1^\beta, \mathrm{ML}_2^\beta, \mathrm{CL}_1^\beta$, and CL_2^β

3: $a_{\mathrm{prev}} = \infty$

4: **for each** $i \in$ instances(l) sorted by a from large to small **do**

5:     **if** $i[a] \neq a_{\mathrm{prev}} \wedge a_{\mathrm{prev}} \neq \infty$ **then**

6:         $x = (i[a] + a_{\mathrm{prev}})/2$

7:         $t =$ "$a > x$"

8:         $v^\beta =$ AssignLabels($\mathrm{ML}_1^\beta, \mathrm{ML}_2^\beta, \mathrm{CL}_1^\beta$, CL_2^β)

9:         $h =$ Heuristic(h_0,S_1,S_2,$v^\alpha + v^\beta$)

10:         **if** $h < h^*$ **then**

11:             $h^* = h$; $r^* =$ "refine l using t"

12:         $a_{\mathrm{prev}} = i[a]$

13:     Update(S_1, i, +1); Update(S_2, i, -1)

14:     **for each** $il \in IL^\alpha(i)$ **do**

15:         Update(v^α, il)

16:     **for each** $il \in IL^\beta(i)$ **do**

17:         Update(ML_1^β, CL_1^β, il, +1); Update(ML_2^β, CL_2^β, il, -1)

Fig. 4. Selecting the split point for an attribute

the split on the instances. This can be done in constant time if appropriate statistics for the two subsets are available (S_1 and S_2 in the algorithm). Subset 1 contains the instances for which the test succeeds; subset 2 the instances for which it fails. S_k summarizes the instances in subset k; it counts the number of instances, and for each attribute, the sum of its values and the sum of its squared values. Based on these numbers, the variances of the attributes can be computed ($\mathrm{Var}(a) = \overline{a^2} - (\overline{a})^2$). The algorithm starts with all instances in subset 2 (test $a > \infty$). S_2 is therefore initialized to represent all instances and S_1 is initialized to all zeros. Each iteration of the loop decreases the value of the split point x (assuming no identical attribute values) and correspondingly moves one instance from subset 2 to subset 1. This is reflected in line 13, which adds the instance to S_1 and removes it from S_2. These updates simply correspond to adding (subtracting) the (squared) attribute values of the given instance to (from) the corresponding components of S_1 (S_2).

The first modification is required to be able to assign cluster labels for the two new leaves in $O(|C|)$ time with C the set of cluster labels already in the tree. To this end, the algorithm uses the arrays ML_k^β and CL_k^β. Similar to the S_k statistics, there is one array of a given type for each of the two subsets. The arrays are used to count, for each cluster label, the number of ML and CL constraints in group β (Fig. 3). For example, $\mathrm{ML}_k^\beta[c]$ counts the number of ML constraints that connect the instances in subset k to one of the label c leaves already in the tree. The number of group β constraints $v_k^\beta(c)$ that are violated by assigning label c to subset k can now be computed as $v_k^\beta(c) = \mathrm{CL}_k^\beta[c] + \sum_{c_j \neq c} \mathrm{ML}_k^\beta[c_j]$; the number of constraints violated by assigning a new label is $v_k^\beta(new) = \sum_{c_j \in C} \mathrm{ML}_k^\beta[c_j]$

(all ML constraints violated). The former can be rewritten as $v_k^\beta(c) = \mathrm{CL}_k^\beta[c] + (v_k^\beta(new) - \mathrm{ML}_k^\beta[c])$. By first computing $v_k^\beta(new)$ and then computing for each $c \in C$, $v_k^\beta(c)$ using the second formula, all v_k^β values can be computed in $O(|C|)$ time. The v_k^β values are used to assign optimal labels (Section 3.3). Line 17 updates the CL_k^β arrays based on the group β constraints in which instance i participates. Such an update consists of retrieving the cluster label of the other instance participating in the constraint and updating the corresponding component of the ML or CL array (depending on the constraint's type). To make this step efficient, each instance stores its current cluster label and associated set of group β constraints $IL^\beta(i)$.

To be able to compute the heuristic value BestSplit needs, in addition to the optimal labeling and its corresponding number of violated group β constraints (v^β, line 8), also the number of violated group α constraints. It counts this number in the variable v^α. Initially, all instances are in subset 2. As a result, all ML constraints of group α are satisfied and all CL constraints are violated. v^α is initialized to the latter. Each time an instance moves from subset 2 to subset 1, v^α is updated to take into account the group α constraints in which it participates. v^α is increased by one for each such constraint that becomes violated by moving the instance; it is decreased by one for each constraint that was violated before and becomes satisfied by moving the instance. Note that group α constraints change state (from violated to satisfied and the other way around) if one of their associated instances changes subset.

Based on the above statistics, BestSplit computes the heuristic value of a split $a > x$ and the optimal labeling of the corresponding new leaves (line 9). It uses S_1 and S_2 to compute the first term of the heuristic (the variance part) and the number of violated constraints $v^\alpha + v^\beta$ for the second term. Note that these statistics only account for the variance in the new leaves and the constraints associated to their instances. To compute the heuristic of the entire tree (T with l replaced by node(t,l_1,l_2)), the algorithm adds the offset h_0. h_0 is computed as $H(T - \{l\}, I, IL - IL_l)$; h_0 takes the variance in the other leaves of T and the violated constraints that do not have a participating instance in l into account.

3.5 Algorithm Complexity

BestSplit(l,a,h_0) sorts the instances, which takes $O(|I_l| \log |I_l|)$ time, with I_l leaf l's instances. Its main loop iterates over I_l. The main loop's most expensive steps are the call to AssignLabels, which takes $O(|C|)$ time (C is the set of cluster labels), and updating the S_k, which takes $O(|A|)$ time (A is the attribute set). BestSplit also processes the constraints in which the instances participate. Each such constraint is processed at most once (β) or twice (α). As a result, the total cost of BestSplit is $O(|I_l| \log |I_l| + |I_l| \cdot (|C| + |A|) + |IL_l|)$, with IL_l the constraints in which l participates.

To iterate over all refinements of T, ClusILC calls BestSplit for each of T's leaves and for each attribute in the data set. For a given attribute, the cost of calling BestSplit for all leaves is $O(|I| \log |I| + |I| \cdot (|C| + |A|) + |IL|)$ because each instance occurs in at most one leaf and each constraint is included for at most two leaves. Each such iteration yields two additional nodes. As a result, the cost of building a tree with N nodes is $O(N \cdot |A| \cdot (|I| \log |I| + |I| \cdot (|C| + |A|) + |IL|))$. This is more expensive than the TDI algorithm. The complexity of the latter is $O(D \cdot |A| \cdot (|I| \log |I| + |I| \cdot |A|))$, with D the depth of the tree ($D < N$).

4 Experimental Evaluation

4.1 Setup

We present preliminary experiments with ClusILC, which has been implemented in the Clus system[1]. ClusILC has two parameters. The parameter γ trades off the relative variance and the proportion of violated constraints in the heuristic. The parameter m lower bounds the number of instances in each leaf. We set both parameters (ad-hoc) to their default values $\gamma = 0.5$ and $m = 2$.

We compare ClusILC to COP-k-means [3]. COP-k-means is a version of k-means that takes IL constraints into account. During each iteration, k-means assigns each instance in turn to its closest cluster. COP-k-means instead assigns each instance to the closest cluster center such that none of the constraints in which it participates are violated. If a given instance can't be assigned to one of the clusters without violating constraints, then COP-k-means fails (it performs hard constrained clustering).

The experimental setup is similar to that of Wagstaff et al. [3]. We use classification data sets from the UCI [13] repository as input (Table 1). The clustering algorithms only use the descriptive attributes. The class attribute is used to generate constraints. To generate a constraint, two instances are picked at random. If they belong to the same class, then the constraint becomes a ML constraint; if they belong to different classes then it becomes a CL constraint. We augment the IL constraints by adding all entailed constraints (during the initialization of the learners) [3]. The ML constraints represent an equivalence relation over the instances. We therefore add all constraints in the transitive closure of the original ML constraints. Assuming consistency, a CL constraint between two instances can be extended to their ML equivalence classes. That is, for each pair of ML equivalence classes A and B that are linked by at least one CL constraint, we add a CL constraint between every pair of instances $(a, b), a \in A, b \in B$.

The number of classes k is given in each classification task. We use this number to set the parameter k (number of clusters) of COP-k-means. We also introduce an upper bound on the number of cluster labels in ClusILC. This can be accomplished by changing the AssignLabels procedure so that it does not introduce a new cluster label if there are already k labels in the tree.

We compare the result of the clustering algorithms to the correct labels in terms of the Rand index. Given two clusterings C_1 and C_2, $\text{Rand}(C_1, C_2) = \frac{a+b}{|I| \cdot (|I|-1)/2}$, with a the number of instance pairs (i_1, i_2) where i_1 and i_2 are in

[1] Available at `http://www.cs.kuleuven.be/~dtai/clus`.

Table 1. Data set properties: number of instances $|I|$, attributes $|A|$, and classes k

	Name	$\|I\|$	$\|A\|$	k		Name	$\|I\|$	$\|A\|$	k
1	iris	150	4	3	7	liver-disorders	345	6	2
2	hayes-roth	160	4	4	8	ionosphere	351	34	2
3	wine	178	13	3	9	balance	625	4	3
4	glass	214	9	6	10	yeast	1484	8	10
5	heart-statlog	270	13	2	11	image	2310	19	7
6	ecoli	336	7	8	12	pendig	7494	16	10

the same cluster in both C_1 and C_2, and b the number of pairs where i_1 and i_2 are assigned to different clusters by both C_1 and C_2.

We report, besides the Rand index for all instances (i.e., cluster all instances and compute the Rand index for that clustering), also the cross-validated Rand index. The latter indicates how the algorithms perform on unconstrained instances. We use 10 fold cross-validation. In each iteration, constraints are generated for nine folds. The tenth fold is used to compute the Rand index. (The algorithms cluster the data in all folds.) The cross-validated Rand index is the average of the values computed for each of the folds. The results (both all data and cross-validated) are averages over 60 random sets of constraints[2].

4.2 Results

Fig. 5 presents the results. Consider first the curves for the clustering of all instances (labeled "All"). The Rand index of COP-k-means increases with the number of constraints and, in 8 out of 12 data sets, clearly surpasses that of ClusILC for a sufficiently large number of generated constraints. This was to be expected because COP-k-means only returns a clustering if it can satisfy all constraints: given enough constraints, the Rand index will become 1.0. (For the large data sets image and pendig COP-k-means requires many constraints.) ClusILC, on the other hand, may also return a solution that does not satisfy all constraints. This can happen either because, even if a solution exists, the greedy search fails to find it, or because the target concept cannot be expressed as a clustering tree with the given set of features. The result in both cases is a lower Rand index.

Next consider the cross-validation results (labeled "CV"). For these results, ClusILC does better for wine, ecoli, ionosphere, balance, image, and pendig (6 out of 12 data sets). It only does clearly worse for one data set (yeast). For the other 5 data sets it performs comparable to COP-k-means. One reason for the good generalization performance of ClusILC is that it can represent

[2] For wine, heart-statlog, liver-disorders, and ionosphere, COP-k-means was, for large constraints sets, unable to find a consistent clustering. To obtain results for these data sets, we generated in each trial different random constraint sets until it found a solution (up to 10^5). The probability of finding a consistent solution strongly depends on the number of constraints. E.g., for wine, the peak was at 300 constraints and required on average 1087 sets before a consistent solution was found.

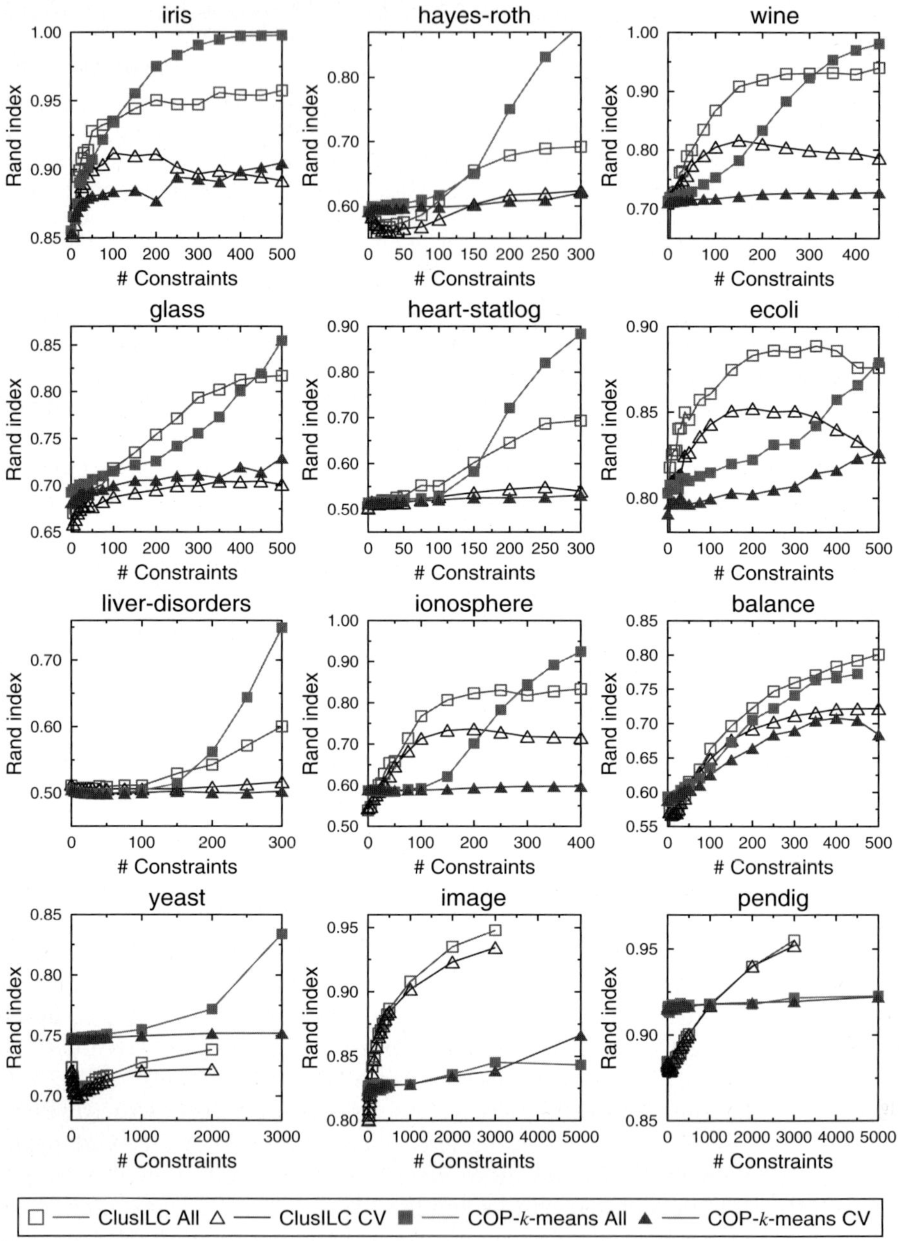

Fig. 5. Results for ClusILC and COP-k-means

more complex clusters than COP-k-means, which essentially assumes spherical clusters (i.e., a strong bias). Note also that not all constraints are useful and the possibility to ignore constraints can be beneficial [14].

We also measure the execution times and clustering tree sizes of ClusILC. The maximum execution time (over all sets of constraints) for one run ranges from 1.4 seconds (on balance) to 9 minutes (on heart-statlog). The maximum tree size ranges from 23 nodes (iris) to 773 nodes (yeast). Typically, the more constraints, the larger the tree. Note that this may yield to overfitting as can be seen, for example, from the graphs for iris and ecoli. The experiments were run on a cluster of AMD Opteron processors (1.8 - 2.4GHz, >2GB RAM) running Linux.

5 Conclusion and Further Work

Clustering trees are decision trees used for clustering tasks. The main advantage of such trees over other clustering methods is that they provide a symbolic description for each cluster. This paper shows how clustering trees can support instance level (IL) constraints. We extend clustering trees to be able to represent disjunctive descriptions by assigning cluster labels to the leaves. This modification is required to handle non-trivial constraint sets.

The main contribution is ClusILC, an algorithm that builds a disjunctive clustering tree given a set of instances and a set of IL constraints. ClusILC is a greedy algorithm guided by a global heuristic that takes the constraints into account. We discuss two important optimizations that are implemented in ClusILC: an algorithm for efficiently assigning cluster labels, and an algorithm for efficiently finding the optimal split point for a numeric attribute.

The experimental evaluation compares ClusILC to COP-k-means. While COP-k-means performs better on all data (its solution satisfies all constraints if it finds one), ClusILC has a better or comparable generalization performance.

We consider data sets with numeric attributes only. In future work, we plan to extend ClusILC to support data with mixed numeric and nominal attributes. The main modification that is required to this end is to redefine the variance metric used in the heuristic (e.g., to use the Gini index for nominal attributes [15]). ClusILC uses greedy hill-climbing search. We plan to investigate alternative search strategies, such as beam search, for which we have shown that it improves the performance of predictive clustering trees [16]. We also consider experiments comparing ClusILC to other constrained clustering algorithms, such as k-means algorithms that implement soft constrained clustering [4,5,6], metric learning approaches (e.g., [4,5]), and HAC [7,8]. Finally, we plan to investigate how other constraint types, such as constraints on the size of the tree [11], can be integrated in ClusILC.

Acknowledgments. Jan Struyf is a postdoctoral fellow of the Research Foundation - Flanders (FWO-Vlaanderen). The authors thank Siegfried Nijssen and Elisa Fromont for the fruitful discussion on clustering trees and IL constraints, and the anonymous reviewers for their constructive comments.

References

1. Jain, A., Murty, M., Flynn, P.: Data clustering: A review. ACM Computing Surveys 31(3), 264–323 (1999)
2. Wagstaff, K., Cardie, C.: Clustering with instance-level constraints. In: 17th Int'l Conf. on Machine Learning, pp. 1103–1110 (2000)
3. Wagstaff, K., Cardie, C., Rogers, S., Schroedl, S.: Constrained K-means clustering with background knowledge. In: 18th Int'l Conf. on Machine Learning, pp. 577–584 (2001)
4. Bilenko, M., Basu, S., Mooney, R.: Integrating constraints and metric learning in semi-supervised clustering. In: 21st Int'l Conf. on Machine Learning, pp. 81–88 (2004)
5. Basu, S., Bilenko, M., Mooney, R.: A probabilistic framework for semi-supervised clustering. In: 10th ACM SIGKDD Int'l Conf. on Knowledge Discovery and Data Mining, pp. 59–68. ACM Press, New York (2004)
6. Davidson, I., Ravi, S.: Clustering with constraints: Feasibility issues and the K-means algorithm. In: SIAM Int'l Data Mining Conf. (2005)
7. Davidson, I., Ravi, S.: Agglomerative hierarchical clustering with constraints: Theoretical and empirical results. In: 9th European Conf. on Principles and Practice of Knowledge Discovery in Databases, pp. 59–70 (2005)
8. Klein, D., Kamvar, S., Manning, C.: From instance-level constraints to space-level constraints: Making the most of prior knowledge in data clustering. In: 19th Int'l Conf. on Machine Learning, pp. 307–314 (2002)
9. Blockeel, H., De Raedt, L., Ramon, J.: Top-down induction of clustering trees. In: 15th Int'l Conf. on Machine Learning, pp. 55–63 (1998)
10. Michalski, R., Stepp, R.: Learning from observation: Conceptual clustering. In: Machine Learning: An Artificial Intelligence Approach, vol. 1, Tioga Publishing Company (1983)
11. Struyf, J., Džeroski, S.: Constraint based induction of multi-objective regression trees. In: 4th Int'l Workshop on Knowledge Discovery in Inductive Databases: Revised Selected and Invited Papers, pp. 222–233 (2006)
12. Quinlan, J.: C4.5: Programs for Machine Learning. Morgan Kaufmann Series in Machine Learning. Morgan Kaufmann, San Francisco (1993)
13. Merz, C., Murphy, P.: UCI repository of machine learning databases, University of California, Department of Information and Computer Science, Irvine, CA (1996), http://www.ics.uci.edu/~mlearn/MLRepository.html
14. Davidson, I., Wagstaff, K., Basu, S.: Measuring constraint-set utility for partitional clustering algorithms. In: 10th European Conf. on Principles and Practice of Knowledge Discovery in Databases, pp. 115–126 (2006)
15. Raileanu, L., Stoffel, K.: Theoretical comparison between the Gini index and information gain criteria. Annals of Mathematics and Artificial Intelligence 41(1), 77–93 (2004)
16. Kocev, D., Struyf, J., Džeroski, S.: Beam search induction and similarity constraints for predictive clustering trees. In: 5th Int'l Workshop on Knowledge Discovery in Inductive Databases: Revised Selected and Invited Papers (to appear, 2007)

On Pairwise Naive Bayes Classifiers

Jan-Nikolas Sulzmann[1], Johannes Fürnkranz[1], and Eyke Hüllermeier[2]

[1] Department of Computer Science, TU Darmstadt
Hochschulstr. 10, D-64289 Darmstadt, Germany
{sulzmann,juffi}@ke.informatik.tu-darmstadt.de
[2] Informatics Institute, Marburg University
Hans-Meerwein-Str., Lahnberge, D-35032 Marburg, Germany
eyke@mathematik.uni-marburg.de

Abstract. Class binarizations are effective methods for improving weak learners by decomposing multi-class problems into several two-class problems. This paper analyzes how these methods can be applied to a Naive Bayes learner. The key result is that the pairwise variant of Naive Bayes is equivalent to a regular Naive Bayes. This result holds for several aggregation techniques for combining the predictions of the individual classifiers, including the commonly used voting and weighted voting techniques. On the other hand, Naive Bayes with one-against-all binarization is not equivalent to a regular Naive Bayes. Apart from the theoretical results themselves, the paper offers a discussion of their implications.

1 Introduction

The Naive Bayes classifier is a Bayesian learner that often outperforms more sophisticated learning methods such as neural networks, nearest neighbor estimation, or decision tree learning in many application areas. It is widely esteemed because of its simplicity, versatility, efficiency, and comprehensibility to domain experts (Kononenko, 1993). Even though the Naive Bayes classifier is directly amenable to multi-class problems, we consider the question whether its performance can be improved by combining it with class binarization methods. This question is motivated by the fact that class binarization has yielded good results for other multi-class learners as well (Fürnkranz, 2003).

The paper starts with a brief recapitulation of the Naive Bayes classifier (Section 2) and class binarization methods (Section 3). The main results are then presented in Section 4. We first derive a general method for combining pairwise Bayesian classifiers (Section 4.1), and then show that this method and the commonly used weighted and unweighted voting techniques are equivalent to the regular classifier (Sections 4.2 and 4.3). In Section 5, we address the same question for the alternative one-against-all class binarization technique and show that, in this case, equivalence to the regular Naive Bayes learner is lost. Finally, in Section 6, we briefly recapitulate the results and discuss some implications thereof.

J.N. Kok et al. (Eds.): ECML 2007, LNAI 4701, pp. 371–381, 2007.

2 Naive Bayes Classifier

Consider a simple setting of classification learning, in which the goal is to predict the class $c \in C = \{c_1, \ldots, c_m\}$ of an query input $x = (a_1, \ldots, a_n)$, given a training set of pre-classified examples; instances are characterized in terms of an attribute-value representation, and a_i is the value of the ith attribute.

In general, the classification error can be minimized by selecting

$$\arg\max_{c_i \in C} \Pr(c_i|x), \tag{1}$$

i.e., the class with maximum posterior probability. To identify this class, estimates of the conditional probabilities $\Pr(c_i|x)$, $i = 1, \ldots, m$, are needed. Bayes theorem states that

$$p_i = \Pr(c_i|x) = \frac{\Pr(x|c_i) \cdot \Pr(c_i)}{\Pr(x)}, \tag{2}$$

and therefore allows one to reverse the original (direct) estimation problem into a more tractable (indirect) one: instead of estimating the probability of a class given the input, it suffices to estimate the probability of an input given a class.

The denominator in (2), $\Pr(x) = \sum_j \Pr(x|c_j) \cdot \Pr(c_j)$, is a normalizing constant that does not influence the solution of the maximization problem (1). Thus, the following basic version of a Bayesian learner is obtained:

$$\begin{aligned} c_B &= \arg\max_{c_i \in C} \Pr(x|c_i) \cdot \Pr(c_i) \\ &= \arg\max_{c_i \in C} \Pr(a_1, a_2, ..., a_n|c_i) \cdot \Pr(c_i) \end{aligned}$$

Under the so-called *Naive Bayes assumption*, which assumes the probabilities of attributes to be conditionally independent given the class, the difficult estimation of the (high-dimensional) probability $\Pr(x|c_i)$ can be reduced to the estimation of (one-dimensional) class-conditional attribute probabilities $\Pr(a_j|c_i)$:

$$\Pr(x|c_i) = \Pr(a_1, a_2, ..., a_n|c_i) \stackrel{!}{=} \prod_{j=1}^{n} \Pr(a_j|c_i)$$

The probabilities $\Pr(c_i)$ and $\Pr(a_j|c_i)$ can now be estimated from the training data, which is typically done by referring to corresponding relative frequencies. Even though the Naive Bayes assumption is usually violated in practice, and the probability estimates for $\Pr(c_i|x)$ are often not very accurate, the Naive Bayes prediction

$$c_{NB} = \arg\max_{c_i \in C} \left(\Pr(c_i) \cdot \prod_{j=1}^{n} \Pr(a_j|c_i) \right)$$

achieves surprisingly high classification rates. This is because, for a correct classification, it is only important that the true class receives the highest (estimated) probability. In other words, only the *order* of the probability estimates $\Pr(c_i|x)$ is relevant, and this order is, to some extent, robust toward deviations of the estimated from the real probabilities (Domingos and Pazzani, 1997).

3 Class Binarization

Class binarization techniques turn multi-class problems into a set of binary problems. Prominent examples include one-against-all binarization (Clark and Boswell, 1991; Anand et al., 1995; Cortes and Vapnik, 1995; Rifkin and Klautau, 2004), pairwise classification (Friedman, 1996; Hastie and Tibshirani, 1998; Fürnkranz, 2002), and error-correcting output codes (Dietterich and Bakiri, 1995). A general framework for such techniques is presented in (Allwein et al., 2000).

The main goal of these methods is to enable machine learning methods which are inherently designed for binary problems (e.g., perceptrons, support vector machines, etc.) to solve multi-class problems. However, there is also evidence that ensembles of binary classifiers may improve the performance of multi-class learners (Dietterich and Bakiri, 1995; Fürnkranz, 2003).

There are several reasons why such approaches can work. First, the binary problems are typically less complex and will often have a simpler decision boundary that is easier to model. For example, Knerr et al. (1992) observed that the classes of a digit recognition task were pairwise linearly separable, while it was not possible to discriminate each class from all other classes with linear perceptrons. It is well-known that Naive Bayes is essentially a linear classifier (Duda and Hart, 1972), and thus it can be expected to profit from such a pairwise decomposition of the task. Furthermore, a large number of binary classifiers introduces an ensemble effect in the sense that mistakes of a single classifier have a smaller impact on the final predictions, thus increasing the robustness of the classifier. For Naive Bayes classifiers in particular, which is known for giving good predictions but uncalibrated probabilities, class binarization is of importance because most calibration techniques operate on two-class problems (Zadrozny and Elkan, 2002). Finally, regarding computational efficiency, training a large number of classifiers from subsets of the training examples may be cheaper than training an entire classifier, in particular when the base classifier has a super-linear time or space complexity.

4 Pairwise Bayesian Classification

We are primarily interested in *pairwise classification*, which transforms an m-class problem into $m(m-1)/2$ two-class problems $\langle i,j\rangle$, one for each pair of classes $\{i,j\}$, $1 \le i < j \le m$. The binary classifier for problem $\langle i,j\rangle$ is trained with examples of classes c_i and c_j, whereas examples of classes $k \neq i,j$ are ignored for this problem. At classification time, a query x is submitted to all binary models, and the predictions of the binary classifiers are combined to yield a final overall prediction.

A pairwise probabilistic classifier, R_{ij}, is therefore trained to estimate *pairwise probabilities* of the form

$$p_{ij} = \Pr(c_i|x, c_{ij}),$$

that is, the probability of class c_i given that the example x either belongs to class c_i or c_j (abbreviated as c_{ij}). These probabilities can, for example, be estimated by training a Bayes classifier on training sets D_{ij} which only contain the examples of classes c_i and c_j. More specifically, such a Bayes classifier estimates the pairwise probabilities $\Pr(c_i|x, c_{ij})$ and $\Pr(c_j|x, c_{ij})$ of class pair c_{ij} as follows:

$$\Pr(c_i|x, c_{ij}) = \frac{\Pr(x|c_i, c_{ij}) \cdot \Pr(c_i|c_{ij})}{\Pr(x|c_i, c_{ij}) \cdot \Pr(c_i|c_{ij}) + \Pr(x|c_j, c_{ij}) \cdot \Pr(c_i|c_{ij})}$$

$$\Pr(c_j|x, c_{ij}) = 1 - \Pr(c_i|x, c_{ij})$$

Again, a naive implementation of a Bayes classifier expands $\Pr(x|c_i, c_{ij})$ into $\Pr(a_1|c_i, c_{ij}) \cdot \Pr(a_2|c_i, c_{ij}) \cdots \Pr(a_m|c_i, c_{ij})$.

4.1 Bayesian Combination of Votes

The probabilities $p_{ij} = \Pr(c_i|x, c_{ij})$ need to be combined into probabilities (scores) $s_i = \Pr(c_i|x)$, a process that is known as *pairwise coupling* (Hastie and Tibshirani, 1998; Wu et al., 2004). In particular, we will consider simple *linear combiners* of the form

$$s_i = \sum_{j \neq i} w_{ij} \cdot \Pr(c_i|x, c_{ij}) \tag{3}$$

Interestingly, linear combination of that kind is sufficient to imitate regular Bayes classification:

Theorem 1. *Weighting the pairwise probabilities with*

$$w_{ij} = \frac{\Pr(c_{ij}|x)}{m-1} = \frac{\Pr(c_i|x) + \Pr(c_j|x)}{m-1} \tag{4}$$

reduces a pairwise Bayes classifier to a regular Bayes classifier.

Proof. Noting that

$$\begin{aligned}(m-1)\Pr(c_i|x) &= \sum_{j \neq i} \Pr(c_i|x) \\ &= \sum_{j \neq i} \Pr(c_i|x, c_{ij}) \cdot \Pr(c_{ij}|x),\end{aligned}$$

replacing w_{ij} in (3) by (4) yields

$$\begin{aligned} s_i &= \sum_{j \neq i} w_{ij} \cdot \Pr(c_i|x, c_{ij}) \\ &= \frac{1}{m-1} \sum_{j \neq i} \Pr(c_i|x, c_{ij}) \cdot \Pr(c_{ij}|x) \\ &= \frac{1}{m-1} \sum_{j \neq i} \Pr(c_i|x) \\ &= \Pr(c_i|x) = p_i \end{aligned}$$

□

This result is interesting, as it shows that an optimal Bayes decision can in principle be derived from an ensemble of pairwise learners. Or, stated differently, the binary decomposition of the original multi-class problem does not cause a loss of information. Moreover, the result shows how the weights w_{ij} should ideally be defined. As will be seen later on, the voting methods commonly used in practice refer to more simple weighting schemes, which can hence be considered as approximations of the ideal weights w_{ij}.

Anyway, as mentioned previously, the main interest in classification does not concern the probability estimates $\Pr(c_i|x, c_{ij})$ themselves, but only the resulting predictions. In the following, we will show that the use of voting or weighted voting will yield the same predictions as the Naive Bayes classifier.

4.2 Weighted Voting

Weighted Voting simply sums up the pairwise probability estimates of each class, i.e., it uses $w_{ij} \equiv 1$ in (3):

$$c_{WV} = \arg\max_{c_i} \sum_{j \neq i} \Pr(c_i|x, c_{ij})$$

Weighted voting has been frequently used in empirical studies and maintained a good performance. More importantly, Hüllermeier and Fürnkranz (2004) have shown that pairwise classification with weighted voting optimizes the Spearman rank correlation between the predicted ranking of all class labels and the true ranking, given that the predicted pairwise probabilities are unbiased estimates of their true values.

Theorem 2. *A pairwise Naive Bayes classifier with* weighted voting *predicts the same class ranking as a regular Naive Bayes classifier, i.e.,*

$$\Pr(c_i|x) \leq \Pr(c_j|x) \Leftrightarrow \sum_{k \neq i} \Pr(c_i|x, c_{ik}) \leq \sum_{k \neq j} \Pr(c_j|x, c_{jk})$$

$$\Pr(c_i|x) < \Pr(c_j|x) \Leftrightarrow \sum_{k \neq i} \Pr(c_i|x, c_{ik}) < \sum_{k \neq j} \Pr(c_j|x, c_{jk})$$

Proof. Let $p_i = \Pr(c_i|x)$ and $s_i = \sum_{k \neq i} \Pr(c_i|x, c_{ik})$. Then

$$s_i - s_j = (p_{ij} - p_{ji}) + \sum_{k \neq i,j} p_{ik} - p_{jk}$$

$$= \frac{p_i - p_j}{p_i + p_j} + \sum_{k \neq i,j} \frac{p_k(p_i - p_j)}{(p_i + p_k)(p_j + p_k)}$$

From this, it immediately follows that $(p_i < p_j) \Rightarrow (s_i < s_j)$, and that $(p_i \leq p_j) \Rightarrow (s_i \leq s_j)$. The other directions can thus be obtained by contraposition: $(s_i < s_j) \Rightarrow (p_i < p_j)$ and $(s_i \leq s_j) \Rightarrow (p_i \leq p_j)$. □

Obviously, due to their construction, the pairwise probabilities p_{ij} are in full agreement with the total order induced by the regular Bayes probabilities p_i. In particular, it is interesting to note that these probabilities satisfy a certain type of *transitivity property*, namely

$$(p_{ij} < 1/2) \wedge (p_{jk} < 1/2) \;\Rightarrow\; (p_{ik} < 1/2). \tag{5}$$

This obviously holds, since $p_{ij} < 1/2$ means that $p_i < p_j$, $p_{jk} < 1/2$ means that $p_j < p_k$, and therefore $p_i < p_k$, which in turn implies $p_{ik} < 1/2$. It deserves mentioning, however, that, for many other pairwise base classifiers, this type of transitivity is not guaranteed. In fact, it is well possible that classifier R_{ik} predicts class c_k, classifier R_{kj} predicts class c_j, but classifier R_{ij}, predicts class c_i, resulting in a tie between the three classes. In fact, for rule learning algorithms not even symmetry will hold, i.e., $R_{ij} \neq R_{ji}$ (Fürnkranz, 2002).

On the other hand, one should also note that transitivity of a pairwise classifier is not enough to imply equivalence to the original (m-class) classifier. For example, suppose that $p_1 = 0.6$, $p_2 = 0.3$, $p_3 = 0.1$. The pairwise classifier with $p_{12} = p_{13} = 0.6$ and $p_{23} = 0.9$ is clearly transitive in the sense of (5) and also in agreement with the ranking $c_1 \succ c_2 \succ c_3$. Still, weighted voting gives $s_1 = 1.2$, $s_2 = 1.3$, $s_3 = 0.5$, and therefore the ranking $c_2 \succ c_1 \succ c_3$.

4.3 Unweighted Voting

An even simpler combination scheme for the predictions of pairwise classifiers is *unweighted voting*. To classify a new example, each of the learned base classifiers determines which of its two classes is the more likely one. The winning class receives a vote, and the algorithm eventually predicts the class that accumulates the highest number of votes. Essentially, it adds up the number of cases where class c_i has a higher pairwise probability than some other class c_j, i.e., the number of indexes j such that $\Pr(c_i|x, c_{ij}) \geq 0.5$ holds:

$$c_V = \arg\max_{c_i} \sum_{j \neq i} [\Pr(c_i|x, c_{ij})] = \sum_{j \neq i} \frac{[\Pr(c_i|x, c_{ij})]}{\Pr(c_i|x, c_{ij})} \cdot \Pr(c_i|x, c_{ij})$$

where $[x]$ is the rounding operator that returns $\lceil x \rceil$ if $x \geq \lfloor x \rfloor + 1/2$ and $\lfloor x \rfloor$ otherwise; thus, $w_{ij} = \frac{[\Pr(c_i|x, c_{ij})]}{\Pr(c_i|x, c_{ij})}$ in (3).

Again, we can show that this algorithm is equivalent to a regular Naive Bayes learner.

Theorem 3. *A pairwise Naive Bayes classifier with* unweighted voting *predicts the same class ranking as a regular Naive Bayes classifier.*

Proof. Let $p_i = \Pr(c_i|x)$ and $p_{ij} = \Pr(c_i|x, c_{ij}) = p_i/(p_i + p_j)$. Ignoring the issue of ties (i.e., $p_i \neq p_j$ for all $i \neq j$), one obviously has $(p_i < p_j) \Leftrightarrow (p_{ij} < p_{ji})$. Therefore, the number of votes received by class c_i is

$$s_i = \sum_{k \neq i} [p_{ik}]$$

and just corresponds to the number of classes c_k such that $p_i > p_k$. Therefore, the class with the k-th highest probability receives $m - k$ votes, which in turn means that the two rankings are identical. □

Remark 1. The above result can easily be generalized to the case of ties: If one splits up a vote in the case $p_{ij} = 1/2$, i.e., both classes receive one half of the vote, then $s_i = s_j$ iff $p_i = p_j$.

From the above proof it becomes immediately clear that the result in principle holds for all probabilistic or scoring classifiers that are "class-order-invariant" in the following sense: A class c_i receives a higher score than class c_j in the original m-class problem if and only if it is also favored in the direct (pairwise) comparison with c_j. In other words, the pairwise order between c_i and c_j is not reversed due to the consideration of additional classes, i.e., it is not influenced by the complementary set of classes $C \setminus \{c_i, c_j\}$. This property, which is quite interesting by itself, is obviously satisfied by a Bayes classifier but does not necessarily hold for other classifiers. Note that a class-order-invariant classifier also satisfies the transitivity property (5).

The above result is also interesting in light of the well-known robustness of Naive Bayes classification. As it shows in a rather explicit way, the main prerequisite for correct classification or, more generally, ranking of class labels, is not a very accurate estimation of probabilities. In fact, these probabilities are used by the pairwise classifier only in a very crude way, namely in the form of binary votes. Therefore, the only important thing is to correctly decide which among two given classes is the more probable one.

5 One-Against-All Class Binarization

In the previous section, we have seen that three versions of pairwise Naive Bayes classification are equivalent to a regular Naive Bayes classifier. At first sight, this is somewhat surprising, because what the Naive Bayes classifier does is modeling separate probability distributions for each individual class c_i first, and predicting the class with the maximum probability afterward. Thus, it seems to have much more in common with one-against-all classifiers than with pairwise decomposition. However, it is not difficult to see that just the opposite is true, at least for the naive implementation of Bayes classification.

In one-against-all classification, an m-class problem is split into m binary problems that discriminate one class c_i, $i = 1 \dots m$, from all other classes. These classifiers are trained using all examples of class c_i as positive examples and the examples of the union of all other classes $\bar{c}_i = \bigcup_{j \neq i} c_j$ as negative examples. If we compare the two probabilities

$$\Pr(c_i|x)_{OA} = \frac{\Pr(x|c_i) \cdot \Pr(c_i)}{\Pr(x|c_i) \cdot \Pr(c_i) + \Pr(x|\bigcup_{j \neq i} c_j) \cdot \Pr(\bigcup_{j \neq i} c_j)}$$

$$\Pr(c_i|x)_{NB} = \frac{\Pr(x|c_i) \cdot \Pr(c_i)}{\Pr(x|c_i) \cdot \Pr(c_i) + \sum_{j \neq i} \Pr(x|c_j) \cdot \Pr(c_j)}$$

we can see that the difference lies in the normalizing constant, which in the case of the one-against-all Naive Bayes classifier estimates the probabilities from the sum of all counts over all classes $c_j, j \neq i$, whereas the regular Naive Bayes classifier sums the probabilities over these classes.

Since the equality relation

$$\Pr\left(x|\bigcup_{j \neq i} c_j\right) \cdot \Pr\left(\bigcup_{j \neq i} c_j\right) = \sum_{j \neq i} \Pr(x|c_j) \cdot \Pr(c_j)$$

generally holds, there is indeed no difference for a true Bayesian classifier. However, this equality is not valid for the probability estimates that are derived by Naive Bayes. If we use

$$f(c) = \Pr(c) \prod_{k=1}^{n} \Pr(a_k|c)$$

to denote the score that Naive Bayes computes for each class c, then

$$f(\bigcup_{j \neq i} c_j) \neq \sum_{j \neq i} f(c_j)$$

and, consequently, $\Pr(c_i|x)_{OA} \neq \Pr(c_i|x)_{NB}$. In particular, the probabilities $\Pr(c_i|x)_{OA}$ will in general not sum up to 1 ($\sum_i \Pr(c_i|x)_{OA} \neq 1$, but instead $\Pr(c_i|x)_{OA} + \Pr(\bar{c}_i|x)_{OA} = 1$ for all $i = 1, \dots, m$).

To see that this may also lead to different classifications (rankings of class labels), let us consider a sample problem with three classes A, B, and C, and 10 examples for each of them. We have two binary attributes X and Y. For $X = 1$ we have observed 15 examples distributed as $(1, 10, 4)$. Likewise, for $Y = 1$, we have 12 examples distributed as $(8, 1, 3)$. This gives

$$f(A) = \Pr(A) \cdot \Pr(X = 1|A) \cdot \Pr(Y = 1|A) = \frac{1}{3} \cdot \frac{1}{10} \cdot \frac{8}{10} = \frac{2}{75}$$

$$f(\overline{A}) = \Pr(\overline{A}) \cdot \Pr(X = 1|\overline{A}) \cdot \Pr(Y = 1|\overline{A}) = \frac{2}{3} \cdot \frac{14}{20} \cdot \frac{4}{20} = \frac{7}{75}$$

Analogously, we get

$$f(B) = \frac{1}{30}, \quad f(\overline{B}) = \frac{11}{120}; \qquad f(C) = \frac{1}{25}, \quad f(\overline{C}) = \frac{33}{200}$$

For a regular Naive Bayes, normalization yields

$$\Pr(A|X=1,Y=1)_{NB} = \frac{f(A)}{f(A)+f(B)+f(C)} = \frac{4}{15},$$

$$\Pr(B|X=1,Y=1)_{NB} = \frac{5}{15}; \quad \Pr(C|X=1,Y=1)_{NB} = \frac{6}{15},$$

and therefore the prediction C, whereas

$$\Pr(A|X=1,Y=1)_{OA} = \frac{f(A)}{f(A)+f(\overline{A})} = \frac{8}{36},$$

$$\Pr(B|X=1,Y=1)_{OA} = \frac{8}{30}; \quad \Pr(C|X=1,Y=1)_{OA} = \frac{8}{41},$$

and class B is predicted.

6 Discussion

The results obtained in this work, showing that various pairwise versions of a Naive Bayes classifier are equivalent to a regular Naive Bayes classifier, are interesting for several reasons. As a first consequence, decomposing a multi-class problem into a pairwise ensemble of binary classifiers does not work for Naive Bayes classifiers, that is, it is not possible no improve classification performance in this way.

The weights derived in Theorem 1 are not specific to Naive Bayes, but apply to probabilistic algorithms in general. It remains to be seen whether this technique can be applied to other base classifiers as well. The main practical impediment is the estimation of $\Pr(c_{ij}|x)$. For example, one could try to estimate them using a pairwise variant of Naive Bayes that predicts a *pair* of classes instead of a single class. First experiments with a few related variants, presented in (Sulzmann, 2006), were not very encouraging, however.

Hüllermeier and Fürnkranz (2004) have shown that weighted voting optimizes the Spearman rank correlation, provided the pairwise probabilities are estimated correctly. In this work, we have shown the equivalence of Naive Bayes to pairwise Naive Bayes using weighted voting. Combining these two results lets us conclude that the regular Naive Bayes also optimizes the Spearman rank correlation. The main problem, of course, is that its probability estimation is biased because of the independence assumption, which will in general not hold. However, just as the bias in the probability estimation does not necessarily affect the prediction of the top rank (Domingos and Pazzani, 1997), it might well turn out that its effect on the entire ranking of the classes is not very strong; the equivalence result for pairwise Naive Bayes with unweighted voting in Section 4.3 is clearly indicative in this regard, as is the generally good performance of Naive Bayes on ranking tasks (Zhang and Su, 2004). We plan to elaborate on this issue in future work.

Another interesting issue concerns the generalization of the results obtained in this paper. For example, we already mentioned that the equivalence between regular Bayes and pairwise Bayes with unweighted voting in principle holds for all "class-order-invariant" classifiers. Finding a characterizing property of a similar kind appears to be more difficult in the case of weighted voting. For Bayes classification, there is a very simple relationship between the multi-class probabilities p_i and the pairwise probabilities p_{ij}: the latter are directly proportional to the former. As we have seen, this relationship assures that the order of the classes remains unchanged, that is, this property is sufficient to guarantee equivalence. However, it is presumably not a necessary condition.

Acknowledgments

This research was supported by the *German Science Foundation (DFG).*

References

Allwein, E.L., Schapire, R.E., Singer, Y.: Reducing multiclass to binary: A unifying approach for margin classifiers. Journal of Machine Learning Research 1, 113–141 (2000)

Anand, R., Mehrotra, K.G., Mohan, C.K., Ranka, S.: Efficient classification for multiclass problems using modular networks. IEEE Transactions on Neural Networks 6, 117–124 (1995)

Clark, P., Boswell, R.: Rule induction with CN2: Some recent improvements. In: Kodratoff, Y. (ed.) EWSL 1991. LNCS, vol. 482, pp. 151–163. Springer, Heidelberg (1991)

Cortes, C., Vapnik, V.: Support-vector networks. Machine Learning 20(3), 273–297 (1995)

Dietterich, T.G., Bakiri, G.: Solving multiclass learning problems via error-correcting output codes. Journal of Artificial Intelligence Research 2, 263–286 (1995)

Domingos, P., Pazzani, M.J.: On the optimality of the simple bayesian classifier under zero-one loss. Machine Learning 29(2-3), 103–130 (1997)

Duda, R.O., Hart, P.E.: Pattern Classification and Scene Analysis. John Wiley, New York (1972)

Friedman, J.H.: Another approach to polychotomous classification. Technical report, Department of Statistics, Stanford University, Stanford, CA (1996)

Fürnkranz, J.: Round robin classification. Journal of Machine Learning Research (JMLR) 2, 721–747 (2002)

Fürnkranz, J.: Round robin ensembles. Intelligent Data Analysis 7(5), 385–403 (2003)

Hastie, T., Tibshirani, R.: Classification by pairwise coupling. In: Jordan, M.I., Kearns, M.J., Solla, S.A. (eds.) Advances in Neural Information Processing Systems 10 (NIPS-97), pp. 507–513. MIT Press, Cambridge (1998)

Hüllermeier, E., Fürnkranz, J.: Ranking by pairwise comparison: A note on risk minimization. In: Proceedings of the IEEE International Conference on Fuzzy Systems (FUZZ-IEEE-04), Budapest, Hungary (2004)

Kononenko, I.: Inductive and bayesian learning in medical diagonsis. Applied Artificial Intelligence 7(4), 331–337 (1993)

Knerr, S., Personnaz, L., Dreyfus, G.: Handwritten digit recognition by neural networks with single-layer training. IEEE Transactions on Neural Networks 3(6), 962–968 (1992)

Rifkin, R., Klautau, A.: In defense of one-vs-all classification. Journal of Machine Learning Research 5, 101–141 (2004)

Sulzmann, J.-N.: Pairwise Naive Bayes classifier. In: Althoff, K.-D., Schaaf, M. (eds.) Proceedings of the LWA 2006, Lernen Wissensentdeckung Adaptivität, Hildesheim, Germany, pp. 356–363. Gesellschaft für Informatik e. V (GI) (2006)

Wu, T.-F., Lin, C.-J., Weng, R.: Probability estimates for multi-class classification by pairwise coupling. Journal of Machine Learning Research (JMLR) 5, 975–1005 (2004)

Zadrozny, B., Elkan, C.: Transforming classifier scores into accurate multiclass probability estimates. In: Proceedings of the 8th International Conference on Knowledge Discovery and Data Mining (KDD-02), pp. 694–699 (2002)

Zhang, H., Su, J.: Naive Bayesian Classifiers for Ranking. In: Boulicaut, J.-F., Esposito, F., Giannotti, F., Pedreschi, D. (eds.) ECML 2004. LNCS (LNAI), vol. 3201, pp. 501–512. Springer, Heidelberg (2004)

Separating Precision and Mean in Dirichlet-Enhanced High-Order Markov Models

Rikiya Takahashi

IBM Tokyo Research Laboratory,
1623-14 Shimo-tsuruma, Yamato-shi, Kanagawa 242-8502, Japan
rikiya@jp.ibm.com

Abstract. Robustly estimating the state-transition probabilities of high-order Markov processes is an essential task in many applications such as natural language modeling or protein sequence modeling. We propose a novel estimation algorithm called Hierarchical Separated Dirichlet Smoothing (HSDS), where Dirichlet distributions are hierarchically assumed to be the prior distributions of the state-transition probabilities. The key idea in HSDS is to *separate* the parameters of a Dirichlet distribution into the precision and mean, so that the precision depends on the context while the mean is given by the lower-order distribution. HSDS is designed to outperform Kneser-Ney smoothing especially when the number of states is small, where Kneser-Ney smoothing is currently known as the state-of-the-art technique for N-gram natural language models. Our experiments in protein sequence modeling showed the superiority of HSDS both in perplexity evaluation and classification tasks.

1 Introduction

To precisely predict or detect time-series sequences of discrete symbols, we desire robust inference techniques to estimate the state-transition probabilities in high-order Markov processes. Using state-transition probabilities for N-grams, a high-order Markov process is often used to model natural language [1], protein sequences [2], or the dynamics of consumers [3], where one state is assigned to each word, amino acid, or customer type, respectively. In these applications, the statistical robustness of the estimated state-transition probabilities often becomes a crucial issue for the predictive accuracy of the model, because the training data of the state-transition frequencies are limited. For example, word error rates in automatic speech recognition become high if we use N-gram language models trained with limited corpora.

In prior work, the state-of-the-art estimation techniques are not effective for cases when the number of states is small, such as a protein sequence, unless we use Markov Chain Monte Carlo (MCMC) methods. Generally, a standard strategy to robustly estimate the state-transition probabilities is to properly interpolate the probabilities of the N-grams, $(N-1)$-grams, and lower order distributions. In natural language modeling, the most advanced smoothing techniques currently used are Kneser-Ney smoothing [4] and its derivative versions [1]. The essence of Kneser-Ney smoothing and its derivatives is a modification of the state-transition

J.N. Kok et al. (Eds.): ECML 2007, LNAI 4701, pp. 382–393, 2007.

frequencies in calculating the lower order distributions, so that any frequency of a state-transition larger than one is reduced to one while the zero-frequency remains at zero. Such modifications of the frequencies are derived as a fast approximated inference of a hierarchical Poisson-Dirichlet (Pitman-Yor) process [5,6,7,8]. If we do not use that approximation, precisely estimating the parameters of hierarchical Pitman-Yor processes requires Gibbs sampling, which is a computationally intensive MCMC method. In addition, since the approximation is adequate only when the number of states is unbounded or sufficiently large, we are seeking another advanced estimation technique for when the number of states is bounded and small.

In this paper, we propose a novel technique to smooth the state-transition probabilities more effectively than Kneser-Ney smoothing when the number of states is small, and which does not require MCMC algorithms. We call our method Hierarchical Separated Dirichlet Smoothing (HSDS), because Dirichlet distributions are hierarchically assumed to be prior distributions of the state-transition probabilities. Our main idea is to *separate* the parameters of a Dirichlet distribution into a context-dependent precision and a mean given by the lower order distribution, and to estimate them alternately. Using the Dirichlet precision, we can quantify the effective frequency. Since the modified frequency adopted in Kneser-Ney smoothing is a special case of our effective frequency when the number of states is sufficiently large, HSDS can work flexibly when the number of states is small or large. In addition, since optimizing the parameters of a Dirichlet distribution does not require MCMC methods, HSDS runs relatively fast.

The rest of the paper is organized as follows. Section 2 introduces the hierarchical Dirichlet distributions that we use. Section 3 describes procedures to estimate the parameters of Dirichlet distributions and discusses when HSDS outperforms Kneser-Ney smoothing. Section 4 shows experimental results in the tasks of perplexity evaluation and classification, using natural language and protein sequence data. Section 5 concludes the paper.

2 Hierarchical Dirichlet Distributions for Prior

In this section, we introduce our custom Dirichlet distributions as the prior distributions of the state-transition probabilities, where our key idea is to impose different constraints on the precision and mean of the Dirichlet distribution. We hierarchically calculate the expectation of the state-transition probability on the posterior distribution, which is determined by the training data and the prior distribution. The mean of the Dirichlet distribution is given by lower-order distributions such as the $(N-1)$-gram models, which are more robust than the higher-order distributions. The precision of the Dirichlet distribution is a specific parameter for each context, to incorporate the numbers of unique states depending on that context. Our model is an extension of the hierarchical Dirichlet language model [9].

For a given discrete-state space $\mathcal{S}$ whose size is $|\mathcal{S}|$, assume we want to predict a prospective state s_N that will follow a state sequence $s_1, s_2, \cdots, s_{N-1}$ with bounded length $N \geq 1$. Since s_N is a random variable, we need a model of $\Pr(s|h)$, the probability with which a state $s \in \mathcal{S}$ follows a $(N-1)$-length context $h \in \mathcal{S}^{N-1} \equiv \mathcal{S} \times \mathcal{S} \times \cdots \times \mathcal{S}$. We aim to estimate precise values of $p_{hs} \equiv \Pr(s|h)$ for each s and h from limited training data $\mathcal{D} = \{n_{hs}; s \in \mathcal{S}, h \in \mathcal{S}^{N-1}\}$, where n_{hs} is the frequency of state s that follows context h. A vector of estimated probabilities $\boldsymbol{p}_h$, whose i-th element p_{hi} is the probability with which the i-th state follows h, is defined as a random variable, because the estimated probability fluctuates around the true probability. For simplicity, hereinafter when a vector is defined with a bold face, such as $\boldsymbol{x}$, it is assumed that we simultaneously define its elements with a normal typeface of the same letter, such as x_s, where the element with the subscript s is a variable related to the state s.

Our aim is to estimate the expectation of $\boldsymbol{p}_h$ on the posterior distribution $P(\boldsymbol{p}_h|\mathcal{D})$. To compute a relevant posterior distribution, we need to specify a proper prior distribution $P(\boldsymbol{p}_h)$ for applying Bayes theorem. The expectation of the state-transition probability and the posterior distribution is given as

$$\langle p_{hs}|\mathcal{D}\rangle = \int_{\boldsymbol{p}_h} p_{hs} P(\boldsymbol{p}_h|\mathcal{D}) d\boldsymbol{p}_h \tag{1}$$

$$P(\boldsymbol{p}_h|\mathcal{D}) = \frac{P(\mathcal{D}|\boldsymbol{p}_h)P(\boldsymbol{p}_h)}{\int_{\boldsymbol{p}_h} P(\mathcal{D}|\boldsymbol{p}_h)P(\boldsymbol{p}_h) d\boldsymbol{p}_h}, \tag{2}$$

where $\langle \cdot|\mathcal{D}\rangle$ is the expectation on the posterior distribution.

We assume a Dirichlet distribution in $P(\boldsymbol{p}_h)$ because its probability density function and its likelihood function are analytically tractable, and in order to avoid MCMC methods. This is contrast to adopting hierarchical Pitman-Yor processes that are more general stochastic processes but which require MCMC methods. With the parameters of the Dirichlet distribution $\boldsymbol{\phi}_h$ and the observed frequencies $\boldsymbol{n}_h$, the prior and posterior distributions are given as follows:

$$P(\boldsymbol{p}_h) = Dir\left(\boldsymbol{p}_h; \boldsymbol{\phi}_h\right) \equiv \frac{\Gamma\left(\sum_{s\in\mathcal{S}} \phi_{hs}\right)}{\prod_{s\in\mathcal{S}} \Gamma\left(\phi_{hs}\right)} \cdot \prod_{s\in\mathcal{S}} p_{hs}^{\phi_{hs}-1} \tag{3}$$

$$P(\boldsymbol{p}_h|\mathcal{D}) = Dir\left(\boldsymbol{p}_h; \boldsymbol{n}_h + \boldsymbol{\phi}_h\right) \equiv \frac{\Gamma\left(\sum_{s\in\mathcal{S}} n_{hs} + \phi_{hs}\right)}{\prod_{s\in\mathcal{S}} \Gamma\left(n_{hs} + \phi_{hs}\right)} \cdot \prod_{s\in\mathcal{S}} p_{hs}^{n_{hs}+\phi_{hs}-1} \tag{4}$$

Here we introduce the main idea of *separating* the parameters of the Dirichlet distribution into a precision and a mean that have different constraints from each other. We denote a truncated context, which is generated by removing the earliest state from h, by $\pi(h)$. We parameterize $\boldsymbol{\phi}_h$ as a product of the coefficient $\alpha_h = \sum_{s\in\mathcal{S}} \phi_{hs}$ and the normalized vector $\boldsymbol{\theta}_{\pi(h)}$. The expectation of the state transition probability p_{hs} on the posterior distribution is given as

$$\langle p_{hs}|\mathcal{D}\rangle = \frac{n_{hs} + \alpha_h \theta_{\pi(h)s}}{n_h + \alpha_h}. \tag{5}$$

Following Minka in [10], we call α_h the “Dirichlet precision” and $\boldsymbol{\theta}_{\pi(h)}$ the “Dirichlet mean”.

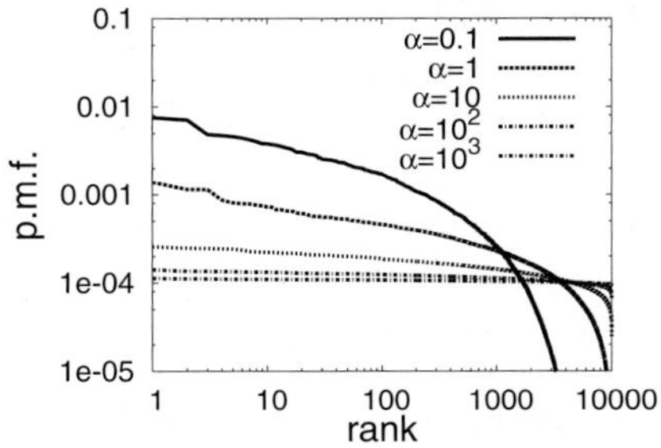

Fig. 1. Distributions of the states controlled by the Dirichlet precision α

The Dirichlet mean is hierarchically given by the expectation of the lower-order distribution, making use of the robustness of the lower-order distributions. We give $\boldsymbol{\theta}_{\pi(h)} = \langle \boldsymbol{p}_{\pi(h)} | \mathcal{D} \rangle$, assuming the prior $P(\boldsymbol{p}_{\pi(h)})$ by a Dirichlet distribution which has a precision $\alpha_{\pi(h)}$ and a mean $\boldsymbol{\theta}_{\pi(\pi(h))}$. Analogously, for each lower-order distribution from the $(N-2)$-gram to the 1-gram, the Dirichlet distribution is hierarchically assumed as its prior distribution. For the 1-gram, where h is empty, we define its Dirichlet mean by the 0-gram distribution $\boldsymbol{\theta}_0 = (1/|\mathcal{S}|, \cdots, 1/|\mathcal{S}|)^T$.

The Dirichlet precision depends on the context after which the different numbers of unique states will appear. Fig. 1 shows the multinomial distributions sorted in rank of probability with a log-log scale, where their parameters obey the 10,000-dimension symmetric Dirichlet distribution $Dir(\alpha/10000, \cdots, \alpha/10000)$. In Fig. 1, we see power-law distributions except when the states are extremely sporadic and that the higher Dirichlet precision α will yield larger numbers of unique states. Since a different number of unique states can follow from a different context h, we define the Dirichlet precision α_h for each context h. For example, in the 2-gram natural language model, α_h will be high if h is an article which does not strongly limit the following word, and α_h will be low if h is some specific verb such as "quantify", which tends to limit the following word.

HSDS can be regarded as an extension of the smoothing used in the hierarchical Dirichlet language model [9]. We believe MacKay and Peto were the first to use a Dirichlet distribution to smooth the probabilities of the 2-grams, where the prior distribution is given by $P(\boldsymbol{p}_h) = Dir(\boldsymbol{p}_h; \alpha \boldsymbol{\theta}_{\pi(h)h})$. Yet the original MacKay and Peto hierarchical Dirichlet language model was shown to be non-competitive with other smoothing techniques [8]. Since they discuss extensions to have the Dirichlet precision be context-dependent with classifying the contexts, HSDS is the first competitive method to extend the hierarchical Dirichlet language model.

3 Variational Inference by Effective Frequency

In this section, we present an algorithm to estimate the optimal Dirichlet precision and mean, and discuss when HSDS will outperform Kneser-Ney smoothing.

Our inference scheme is based on a variational approximation, where the infimum of the likelihood in a Dirichlet-multinomial distribution is maximized. The Dirichlet precision is optimized by a kind of Newton-Raphson method and the Dirichlet mean is calculated with the effective frequency, which is a frequency controlled by the Dirichlet precision. We explain when HSDS outperforms Kneser-Ney smoothing based on the meaning of the effective frequency.

First, we introduce the concept of the effective frequency by deriving the infimum of the likelihood of the training data. Since the observed frequencies $\boldsymbol{n}_h$ obey a Dirichlet-multinomial (Polya) distribution, Eq. (6) gives the likelihood of $\mathcal{D}$ under the set of hyperparameters $\Phi = \{\alpha_h, \boldsymbol{\theta}_{\pi(h)}; h \in \mathcal{S}^{N-1}\}$. We referred to [10] in deriving Inequality (7).

$$P(\mathcal{D}|\Phi) \propto \prod_h \frac{\Gamma(\alpha_h)}{\Gamma(n_h + \alpha_h)} \prod_{s:n_{hs}>0} \frac{\Gamma\left(n_{hs} + \alpha_h \theta_{\pi(h)s}\right)}{\Gamma\left(\alpha_h \theta_{\pi(h)s}\right)} \tag{6}$$

$$\geq \prod_h \frac{\Gamma(\bar{\alpha}_h)}{\Gamma(n_h + \bar{\alpha}_h)} \exp\left[\left(\Psi(n_h + \bar{\alpha}_h) - \Psi(\bar{\alpha}_h)\right)(\bar{\alpha}_h - \alpha_h)\right]$$

$$\prod_{s:n_{hs}>0} \left[\frac{\Gamma\left(n_{hs} + \bar{\alpha}_h \bar{\theta}_{\pi(h)s}\right)}{\Gamma\left(\bar{\alpha}_h \bar{\theta}_{\pi(h)s}\right)} \left(\bar{\alpha}_h \bar{\theta}_{\pi(h)s}\right)^{-\widetilde{n}_{hs}}\right] \left(\alpha_h \theta_{\pi(h)s}\right)^{\widetilde{n}_{hs}}, \tag{7}$$

where $\Psi(\cdot)$ denotes a *digamma* function such that $\Psi(x) \equiv \frac{\partial}{\partial x} \log \Gamma(x)$, and

$$\widetilde{n}_{hs} = \bar{\alpha}_h \bar{\theta}_{\pi(h)s} \left(\Psi\left(n_{hs} + \bar{\alpha}_h \bar{\theta}_{\pi(h)s}\right) - \Psi\left(\bar{\alpha}_h \bar{\theta}_{\pi(h)s}\right)\right). \tag{8}$$

We call $\widetilde{n}_{hs}$ the "effective frequency", because the infimum of the likelihood has the same formulation as a multinomial distribution for context h where the observed frequency of state s is $\widetilde{n}_{hs}$. Minka also discusses the effective frequency in [10], by differentiating the likelihood of the Polya distribution with respect to the Dirichlet mean. We explain the meaning of the effective frequency in Section 3.2. For convenience, we also define $\widetilde{n}_h \equiv \sum_{s \in \mathcal{S}} \widetilde{n}_{hs}$, $\widetilde{n}_{\pi(h)s} \equiv \sum_u \widetilde{n}_{hs}$ where u is the earliest state in context h and thus $h \equiv u\pi(h)$, and $\widetilde{n}_{\pi(h)} \equiv \sum_{s \in \mathcal{S}} \widetilde{n}_{\pi(h)s}$.

3.1 Estimating the Dirichlet Precision

Next, we estimate the Dirichlet precision as the expectation of α_h on an approximated posterior distribution. The procedure for estimation is divided into the following two cases. First, when $n_{hs} = 1$ for all s such that $n_{hs} > 0$, we initially set $\alpha_h = \infty$, which is equivalent to using only the state-transition probability of the $(N-1)$-gram[1]. Second, in all other cases, α_h is given by the expectation of a gamma distribution that approximates the posterior distribution of α_h. We assume the prior for α_h is a non-informative uniform distribution. Since the part of the likelihood related to α_h can be expressed as

$$P(\mathcal{D}|\alpha_h) \propto \exp\left[-\left(\Psi(n_h + \bar{\alpha}_h) - \Psi(\bar{\alpha}_h)\right)\alpha_h\right] \alpha_h^{\widetilde{n}_h}, \tag{9}$$

[1] If $\forall s, n_{hs} = 1$, then the exact likelihood expressed by Eq. (6) becomes a function of the Dirichlet mean alone. Therefore, the posterior distribution of α_h becomes the non-informative uniform distribution $U[0, \infty]$, whose expectation is infinity.

we can derive the approximated posterior $Q(\alpha_h|\mathcal{D})$ as

$$\begin{aligned} Q(\alpha_h|\mathcal{D}) &\propto P(\mathcal{D}|\alpha_h)P(\alpha_h) \\ &\propto Ga\left(\alpha_h; \widetilde{n}_h + 1, \Psi\left(n_h + \bar{\alpha}_h\right) - \Psi\left(\bar{\alpha}_h\right)\right), \end{aligned} \tag{10}$$

where we denote a gamma distribution by $Ga(\cdot,\cdot)$. The expectation of α_h on the approximated posterior $Q(\alpha_h|\mathcal{D})$ is given as

$$\langle \alpha_h|\mathcal{D}\rangle = \frac{\widetilde{n}_h + 1}{\Psi\left(n_h + \bar{\alpha}_h\right) - \Psi\left(\bar{\alpha}_h\right)}. \tag{11}$$

To calculate the optimal Dirichlet precision α_h^*, we assume $\langle \alpha_h|\mathcal{D}\rangle = \bar{\alpha}_h$, which means that the likelihood of the Polya distribution is approximated by the gamma distribution that has the same expectation. We can immediately derive the following equation, which we can solve quickly with the modified Newton-Raphson method proposed in [11].

$$\Psi\left(n_h + \alpha_h^*\right) - \Psi\left(\alpha_h^*\right) = \frac{1}{\alpha_h^*} + \sum_{s:n_{hs}>0} \theta_{\pi(h)s}\left[\Psi\left(n_{hs} + \alpha_h^*\theta_{\pi(h)s}\right) - \Psi\left(\alpha_h^*\theta_{\pi(h)s}\right)\right] \tag{12}$$

Note that the estimated α_h^* values tend to be underestimated when n_h is small, because the true posterior distribution of α_h has a heavier-tail than the gamma distribution. Based on several earlier experiments, we decided to multiply α_h^* by 2 if $\alpha_h^* > 10$. This is a simple heuristic rule, but it works for many datasets. A better estimation technique should be developed.

3.2 Estimating the Dirichlet Mean

The optimal Dirichlet mean $\theta_{\pi(h)s}^*$ is calculated from the effective frequency and the Dirichlet precision of the lower-order distributions. The terms related to $\theta_{\pi(h)s}$ in the infimum of the represented likelihood are also given by multinomial distributions that have effective frequencies as

$$Q(\mathcal{D}|\Phi) \propto \prod_{\pi(h)} \prod_{s:n_{hs}>0} \theta_{\pi(h)s}^{\widetilde{n}_{\pi(h)s}}. \tag{13}$$

Since we also assume a Dirichlet distribution in $P(\boldsymbol{p}_{\pi(h)})$, the optimal Dirichlet mean $\theta_{\pi(h)s}^*$ is given as

$$\theta_{\pi(h)s}^* = \frac{\widetilde{n}_{\pi(h)s} + \alpha_{\pi(h)}\theta_{\pi(\pi(h))s}}{\widetilde{n}_{\pi(h)} + \alpha_{\pi(h)}}. \tag{14}$$

Because the optimal Dirichlet precision and Dirichlet mean must be estimated iteratively, we summarized the computational procedure in Algorithm 1, except for the last heuristic multiplication for the Dirichlet precision.

Algorithm 1. Estimating the Dirichlet precision and Dirichlet mean

Initialize all the parameters $\{\alpha_h, \boldsymbol{\theta}_{\pi(h)}\}$.
repeat
  for $n = N$ downto 1 **do**
    for all $h \in \mathcal{S}^{n-1}$ **do**
      if $\exists s, n_{hs} > 1$ **then**
        $\alpha_h \Leftarrow \alpha_h^*$ by solving Eq. (12).
      end if
      for all $s \in \mathcal{S}$ **do**
        Calculate $\widetilde{n}_{hs}$ by Eq. (8).
      end for
    end for
    if $n \geq 2$ **then**
      for all $h \in \mathcal{S}^{n-1}$ **do**
        Update $\boldsymbol{\theta}_{\pi(h)}$ by Eq. (14).
      end for
    end if
  end for
until all the parameters have converged.

3.3 Effects of the Effective Frequency

Finally, we discuss the cases when HSDS outperforms Kneser-Ney smoothing, by clarifying the meaning of the effective frequency. Fig. 2 shows the relationships between the effective frequency $\widetilde{n}$ and the raw frequency n, as functions of the Dirichlet precision α where $\widetilde{n} = \alpha\left(\Psi(\alpha + n) - \Psi(\alpha)\right)$. When $\alpha \to 0$, the effective frequency converges to an indicator function of the raw frequency: $\widetilde{n} = 1$ if $n > 0$ and $\widetilde{n} = 0$ if $n = 0$ and it is the same as the modified frequency adopted in Kneser-Ney smoothing.

Fig. 2 and the actual effective frequency defined by Eq. (8) suggest that approximating the effective frequency by the modified frequency of Kneser-Ney smoothing is adequate only for s and h such that $\alpha_h \theta_{\pi(h)s}$ is low. When the

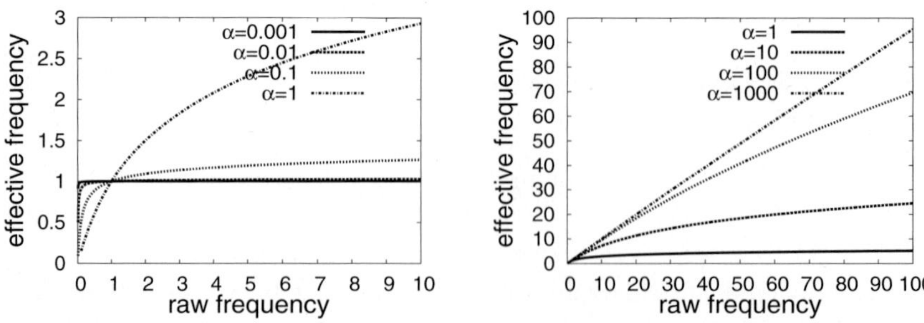

(a) In case α is low (b) In case α is high

Fig. 2. Effective frequencies with various values of the Dirichlet precision α

number of states is large, which is true for natural language modeling, the approximation is adequate because most of the values of $\theta_{\pi(h)s}$ are very low.

HSDS will outperform Kneser-Ney smoothing in two cases: when the number of states is small, or when the order of the Markov processes is high, in that $\alpha_h \theta_{\pi(h)s}$ is not too low in either case. First, if the number of states is small, some of the $\{\theta_{\pi(h)s}\}$ are not low. Second, if N is high and n_h is too small, α_h becomes a high value in estimating the Dirichlet precision. At such times, the effective frequency approaches the raw frequency. Intuitively, if the observed frequency of N-grams is too low, we should ignore the frequency of that N-grams and should just use the raw frequency of the $(N-1)$-grams.

4 Experiments

In this section, we experimentally show that HSDS outperforms Kneser-Ney smoothing when the number of states is small, by comparing the results for two different types of datasets: a natural language corpus and some protein sequence data. A natural language is chosen as a sequence with large number of states, because natural languages have large and potentially infinite vocabularies. Protein sequences are chosen as sequences with small number of states, because any protein sequence consists of only 20 types of amino acids, which means the number of states in a protein sequence N-gram is also limited to 20.

To evaluate the performance of each model, we focused on calculating the test-set perplexity, where its low values usually mean better predictive accuracies. In addition, we checked the results of classification tests for protein sequence modeling. For a K-length sequence $s_1^K \equiv s_1 s_2 \cdots s_K$, its perplexity evaluated by the N-gram model $\Theta = \{Pr(s|h), s \in \mathcal{S}, h \in \mathcal{S}^0, \mathcal{S}^1 \cup \cdots \cup \mathcal{S}^{N-1}\}$ is given as

$$PP\left(s_1^K|\Theta\right) = \exp\left[-\frac{1}{K}\sum_{k=1}^{K} \log Pr\left(s_k|s_{\max\{1,k-N+1\}}, \cdots, s_{k-1}\right)\right]. \quad (15)$$

The other experimental conditions, which are common in natural language modeling and protein sequence modeling, are given below. After studying the numbers of unique N-grams in the training data, we decided to train the 2-, 3-, 4-, and 5-gram models. The 6-gram models were also trained for the protein sequence data. To compare the smoothing methods, we tested Hierarchical Separated Dirichlet Smoothing (HSDS), Interpolated Kneser-Ney Smoothing (IKNS), Modified Kneser-Ney Smoothing (MKNS), Absolute Discounting (ABSD) [12], and Witten-Bell smoothing (WBS) [13]. The smoothing methods except for IKNS and MKNS were selected to compare the performances broadly. The formulas used in IKNS and MKNS are described in [1], where we adopted the versions without cross-validation in estimating the discounting factors.

4.1 Natural Language Modeling

As natural language data, we used the `Reuters-21578` text categorization test collection [14], which is a popular English corpus mainly used for text

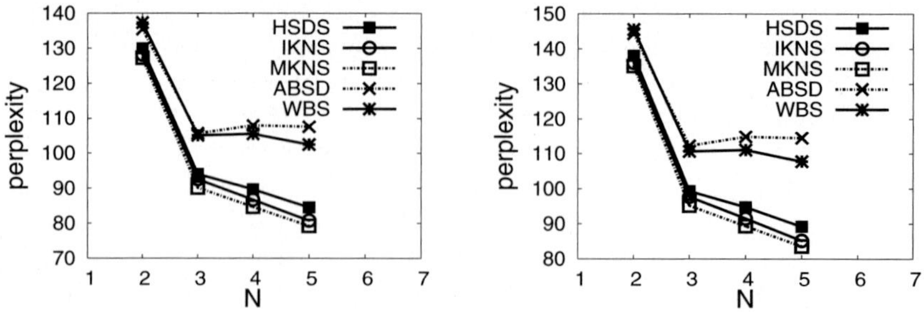

(a) When OOV words were included. (b) When OOV words were excluded.

Fig. 3. Test-set perplexity in `Reuters-21578` dataset

categorization research. By extracting all of the text, we prepared 172,900 sentences that consisted of a total of 2,804,960 words, and divided them into 162,900 training sentences and 10,000 test sentences. The training data had 118,602 unique words that appeared at least once, and we chose the most frequent 20,000 words as the vocabulary set. We calculated test-set perplexity both when out-of-vocabulary (OOV) words were included and excluded. When the OOV words were included, we replaced all of the OOV words with the same special token.

Fig. 3 shows each model's test-set perplexity and HSDS is inferior to both IKNS and MKNS. We think that the relatively weak performance of HSDS is because the Dirichlet distribution cannot precisely capture the power-law in the frequencies of the words. As shown in Fig. 1, the Dirichlet distribution cannot represent the heavy-tail of the frequencies of the words, while the Pitman-Yor process and Kneser-Ney smoothing can control the exponent of the power-law [8], which is important for the distribution within a potentially infinite vocabulary.

Still, HSDS outperformed the other smoothing techniques except for IKNS and MKNS. We think that the effective frequency in HSDS worked more effectively than the raw-frequencies, in calculating the lower-order distributions.

4.2 Protein Sequence Modeling

For protein sequence data, we performed classification tests as well as a perplexity evaluation, using the `DBsubloc` dataset [15]. Though `DBsubloc` is a protein database mainly used for protein subcellular localization, because of the amount of available data, we only classified the unlabeled data into one of 4 types of organisms: viruses, archaea, bacteria, and eukaryotes. After dividing the non-redundant dataset into training data and test data, we independently trained 4 types of N-gram models. In the training data, the numbers of unique sequences were 1,082 for the viruses, 1,131 for the archaea, 9,701 for the bacteria, and 18,043 for the eukaryotes. The test data consisted of 100 unique sequences for each organism, where their numbers of amino acids were 43,990 for the viruses, 26,455 for the archaea, 29,075 for the bacteria, and 62,286 for the eukaryotes.

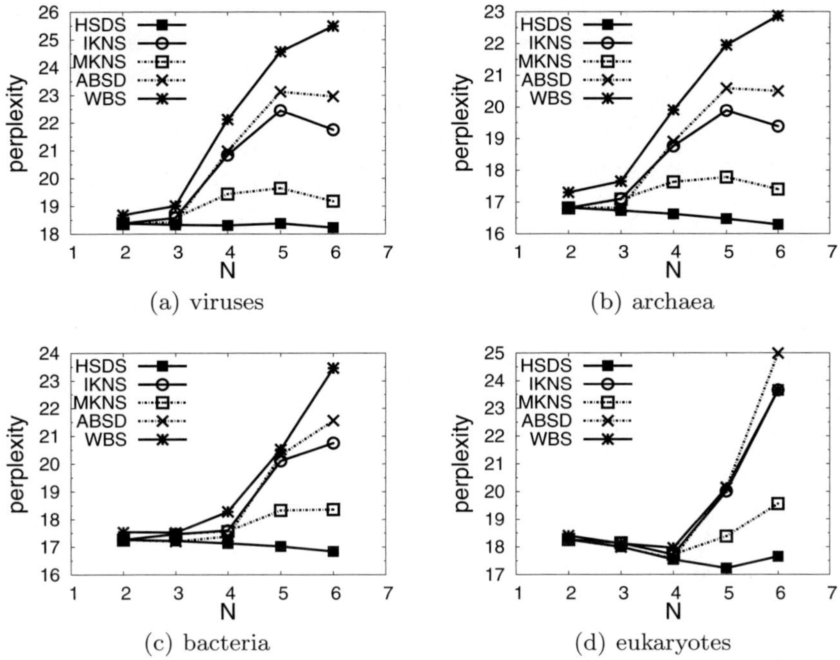

(a) viruses (b) archaea

(c) bacteria (d) eukaryotes

Fig. 4. Test-set perplexity in `DBsubloc` dataset

Perplexity Evaluation. In the perplexity evaluation task, each test-set was evaluated by a model of the same organism. i.e. The viruses test data was evaluated with viruses model. Fig. 4 shows the test-set perplexity for each organism.

HSDS achieved the lowest test-set perplexity, and its performance was slightly improved even when N became larger, while the other smoothing techniques had worse performances. As mentioned in Section 3.3, in protein sequence modeling, the effective frequency seemed to work more effectively than the modified frequency adopted in Kneser-Ney smoothing.

Classification. In the classification task, we made unlabeled data by removing the labels from all of the test data, and classified the unlabeled data into one of the 4 organism types using a naive Bayes classifier. Let c_i be one of the 4 organism types. For a sequence s_1^K, the organism type of the sequence $c(s_1^K)$ was determined as

$$c(s_1^K) = \arg\max_{c_i} P(s_1^N|c_i)P(c_i), \tag{16}$$

where $P(s_1^N|c_i)$ was calculated by the trained N-gram model of the organism type c_i, and $\forall c_i, P(c_i) = 0.25$. For each organism, we calculated the recall, precision, and F_1-measure. We used the arithmetic average of the 4 organism types as a performance metric of our multi-class classification.

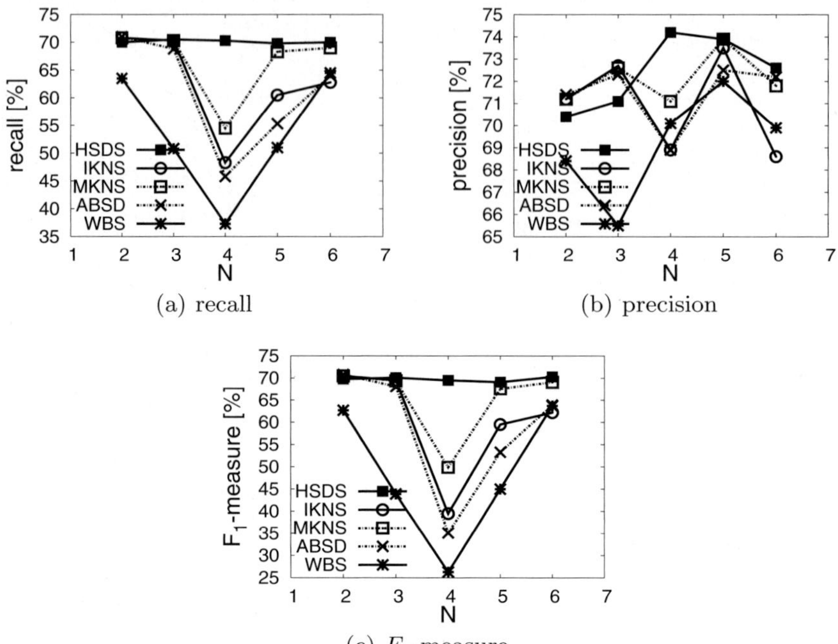

(a) recall (b) precision (c) F_1-measure

Fig. 5. Performances in classifying 4 organism-types

The results also show that HSDS is stable as N increases. Fig. 5 shows the averages of the recall, precision, and F_1-measure for the 4 organism types when the order of the N-gram changes. As in the perplexity evaluation, the performance of HSDS was stable even as N increased, while the performances of the other methods peaked for the 2-gram models. If we only look at the absolute performance, the 2-gram model with ABSD recorded the highest F_1-measure, but the other methods also recorded almost the same performances in 2-gram models.

5 Conclusion

We proposed a smoothing method for probabilistic N-gram models, which we named Hierarchical Separated Dirichlet Smoothing (HSDS). We hierarchically assumed a Dirichlet distribution to be a prior distribution of the state-transition probabilities, and separated the parameters of a Dirichlet distribution into precision and mean. The context-specific Dirichlet precision can reflect the context-dependent number of unique states, and the Dirichlet mean based on the effective frequencies gives appropriate lower-order distributions. Theoretically and experimentally, HSDS was shown to outperform Kneser-Ney smoothing when the number of states is small and N increases.

In the future, we will extend our context-specific formulation for more general stochastic process models such as the hierarchical Pitman-Yor processes, to more precisely incorporate the effects of the power-law in the observed frequencies.

Acknowledgment

The author wishes to thank Gakuto Kurata and Hisashi Kashima for many fruitful discussions about Kneser-Ney smoothing and other related topics.

References

1. Chen, S., Goodman, J.: An empirical study of smoothing techniques for language modeling. Technical Report TR-10-98, Harvard Computer Science (1998)
2. Ganapathiraju, M., Manoharan, V., Klein-Seetharaman, J.: BLMT: Statistical sequence analysis using n-grams. Applied Bioinformatics 3 (November 2004)
3. Netzer, O., Lattin, J.M., Srinivasan, V.: A Hidden Markov Model of Customer Relationship Dynamics. Stanford GSB Research Paper (July 2005)
4. Kneser, R., Ney, H.: Improved backing-off for m-gram language modeling. In: Proceedings of the IEEE International Conference on Acoustics, Speech and Signal Processing, vol. 1, pp. 181–184 (May 1995)
5. Pitman, J., Yor, M.: The two-parameter Poisson-Dirichlet distribution derived from a stable subordinator. The Annals of Probability 25(2), 855–900 (1997)
6. Goldwater, S., Griffiths, T., Johnson, M.: Interpolating between types and tokens by estimating power-law generators. In: Advances in Neural Information Processing Systems (NIPS), vol. 18 (2006)
7. Teh, Y.W.: A Bayesian interpretation of interpolated Kneser-Ney. Technical Report TRA2/06, School of Computing, National University of Singapore (2006)
8. Teh, Y.W.: A hierarchical Bayesian language model based on Pitman-Yor processes. In: Proceedings of the Annual Meeting of the Association for Computational Linguistics, vol. 44 (2006)
9. MacKay, D.J.C., Peto, L.: A hierarchical Dirichlet language model. Natural Language Engineering 1(3), 1–19 (1994)
10. Minka, T.: Estimating a Dirichlet distribution. Technical report, Microsoft Research (2003)
11. Minka, T.: Beyond Newton's method. Technical report, Microsoft Research (2000)
12. Ney, H., Essen, U., Kneser, R.: On structuring probabilistic dependences in stochastic language modeling. Computer, Speech, and Language 8, 1–38 (1994)
13. Witten, I.H., Bell, T.C.: The zero-frequency problem: Estimating the probabilities of novel events in adaptive text compression. IEEE Transactions on Information Theory 37(4), 1085–1094 (1991)
14. Lewis, D.D.: Reuters-21578 text categorization test collection distribution 1.0 (1997) Available at `http://www.daviddlewis.com/resources/testcollections/reuters21578/`
15. Guo, T., Sun, Z.: Dbsubloc: Database of protein subcellular localization (2005) Available at `http://www.bioinfo.tsinghua.edu.cn/~guotao/`

Safe Q-Learning on Complete History Spaces

Stephan Timmer and Martin Riedmiller

Neuroinformatics Group, University of Osnabrueck, Germany

Abstract. In this article, we present an idea for solving deterministic partially observable markov decision processes (POMDPs) based on a history space containing sequences of past observations and actions. A novel and sound technique for learning a Q-function on history spaces is developed and discussed. We analyze certain conditions under which a history based approach is able to learn policies comparable to the optimal solution on belief states. The algorithm presented is model-free and can be combined with any method learning history spaces. We also present a procedure able to learn history spaces especially suited for our Q-learning algorithm.

1 Introduction

In a POMDP setting, the learning agent does not have full information about the current state of the system. The common approach for solving POMDPs is therefore to replace the original state space S by the belief space of probability distributions over S. The belief space is huge and computing the optimal value function over beliefs can be very costly even for small state spaces. A still bigger problem is solving POMDPs without a model. In general, estimating the model (stochastic transitions and stochastic observations) is hard, since the current state $s_t \in S$ is unknown at any time step.

In this article, we investigate the technique of including short-time memory into the representation of the POMDP. By using short-time memory, we can maintain an estimate of the current state $s_t \in S$ of the system, which is adaptable with respect to size and precision. A reasonable way of establishing such an estimate is to consider a sequence of past observations and actions. Such a sequence is called a history list. In contrast to the history list approach, the belief space formulation of the POMDP is a perfect solution to the problem of estimating the current state, since all information about past events is merged into a probability distribution over states. However, due to the enormous complexity of learning policies on belief states, we restrict ourselves to suboptimal, but good policies that can be found with an algorithm based on history lists.

The overall problem of solving POMDPs without a model using history lists can be divided into two subproblems:

1. Building a set of history lists constituting a history space
2. Learning a policy on history lists after substituting the state space by the history space

J.N. Kok et al. (Eds.): ECML 2007, LNAI 4701, pp. 394–405, 2007.

First, we will concentrate on the second problem mentioned above, assuming that a history space is already available. We want to analyze certain conditions under which a history space can be used to learn near optimal policies by a variant of Q-learning. We will then present a procedure for learning history spaces, which is especially suited for our Q-learning algorithm. Unfortunately, it does not suffice to compute a Q-function on history lists and then extract a greedy policy. Before the Q-function can be exploited it is necessary to establish a sequence of observations and actions providing reliable information about the current state. We will discuss how such an approach relates to the optimal solution on belief states and present empirical evidence for a benchmark with more than one hundred states.

Although we will consider only deterministic systems, we choose to stay within the POMDP framework. Our work aims at solving reinforcement learning problems. The task of learning policies for deterministic POMDPs can be naturally formulated as such a problem.

2 Basic Facts About History Lists

Throughout the paper, we will assume a deterministic POMDP $(T, S, U, O, r, f, \Omega)$ such that T is a discrete set of time steps, S is a discrete state space, U is a discrete action space, O is a discrete observation space, $r : S \times U \to \mathbb{R}$ is the reward function, $f : S \times U \to S$ is a deterministic transition function and $\Omega : S \times U \to O$ is a deterministic observation model. To illustrate the use of history lists, consider the maze given in Figure 1. The agent, which is denoted by an arrow in a circle, is expected to find a certain goal cell in the maze. To determine the current position of the agent, only *bump-sensors* are available. These sensors, denoted by black dots, can tell the agent if there are walls at the four surrounding cells. The observation space therefore consists of sixteen combinations of walls plus an additional goal observation. The action space contains four distinct actions for moving left, right, up or down. If the agent tries to break through a wall or tries to leave the maze, the position of the agent remains the same.

How can the agent make use of history lists in this situation? The basic idea is to determine the current position of the agent by comparing history lists at

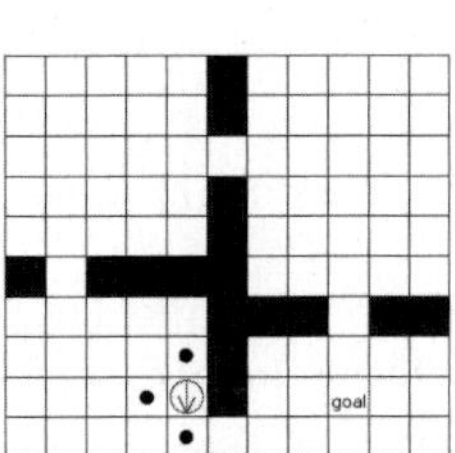

Fig. 1. Maze with partial observability

different time steps. If the same sequence of past wall observations and actions is given at two time steps $t \neq t'$, it is likely that also the position of the agent is the same at these time steps ($s_t = s_{t'}$). We do not expect a history list to contain the complete sequence of past observations and actions. In general, history lists can be of arbitrary length.

Definition 1. *History Lists*
A history list $h \in (U \times O)^*$ is a possibly empty sequence of action-observation pairs. The length $|h|$ of a history list is defined as the number of observations it contains. The space of possible history lists $H^* \subseteq (U \times O)^*$ contains all history lists which can be generated by the transition function f and the observation model Ω.[1]

Every time the agent notices a sequence of observations and actions that matches a history list $h \in H$ of a given history space $H \subseteq H^*$, an action u_h with respect to history h is executed. Assume that the sequence of observations and actions until time step $t \in T$ is given by $[u_0, o_1, u_1, o_2 ..., u_{t-1}, o_t]$. We call a history list $h \in H$ the current history list at time step $t \in T$ if h is a maximal suffix of this sequence with respect to the history space H. The current history list at time step t is denoted by h_t similar to the current state $s_t \in S$. To be compatible with the literature [1], we decided not to include reward signals into the definition of a history list. However, our algorithm will make use of reward signals.

A history list $h \in H$ is especially useful if it helps us to determine the current state $s_t \in S$ of the system. We will now give a more general definition of such sequences.

Definition 2. *Identifying History Lists*
A history list $h \in H^*$ is called identifying for a set of states $S' \subseteq S$, if $|h| > 0$ and the following proposition holds: If $[u_0, o_1, ..., u_{t-1}, o_t]$ is a sequence of observations and actions that can be generated by the transition function f and the observation model Ω, and h is a suffix of this sequence, then it holds that $s_t \in S'$.

In the following, we will use the term "identifying history list" only in the context of single states ($|S'| = 1$), unless the set S' is explicitly specified. What makes identifying history lists interesting is the fact that these lists are closed under some typical list operations.

Lemma 1. *Extension of History Lists (at the front)*
Let h be an identifying history list for a set of states $S' \subseteq S$. If h' is an extension of h such that h is a suffix of h', then h' is identifying for the set of states S'.

Proof. Let h' be a suffix of a possible sequence $[u_0, o_1, ..., u_{t-1}, o_t]$. Since h is a suffix of h', h is also a suffix of this sequence. Thus, it holds that $s_t \in S'$ because h is identifying for S'.

[1] If the observation model solely depends on the state ($\Omega : S \to O$) we allow history lists to have an additional observation at the front, representing the observation of the initial state of the history sequence.

Lemma 2. *Extension of History Lists (at the end)*
Let h be an identifying history list for a single state $s \in S$. Let h' be an extension of h such that an action $u \in U$ and an observation $o \in O$ is added at the end of h. If $h' \in H^*$, then h' is identifying for the single state $s' = f(s, u)$

3 Solving POMDPs with History Lists

Our algorithm consists of two separate modules.

1. At time step $t = 0$, a preferably short sequence of actions is executed, such that the current history list at time step $t' \geq 0$ becomes identifying for a single state. This corresponds to establishing a belief state in which a single state $s \in S$ has probability $p(s) = 1$, while all other states have probability zero. This module is called the efficient exploration strategy
2. From time step t' on, follow a greedy policy extracted from a Q-function defined on identifying history lists. This is reasonable, since every identifying history list corresponds to a single state $s \in S$. If at some time step later than t', the current history list becomes non-identifying, jump back to the first step of this enumeration (to reestablish an identifying history list)

To implement a procedure as described above, it is necessary to have a criterion able to decide whether a history list $h \in H$ is identifying or not. Furthermore, we need an efficient exploration strategy leading to an identifying history list as quickly as possible. We will now develop two criterions for detecting identifying history lists, as well as an efficient exploration strategy.

Definition 3. *Sufficient History Length*
Given a deterministic POMDP $M := (T, S, U, O, r, f, \Omega)$, the sufficient history length l_{su} is defined as
$l_{su} := max_{s \in S}\ min_{\ h \in H^*}\ \{|h|, h \text{ identifies state } s\}$

It is possible to find an identifying history list no longer than l_{su} for an arbitrary state $s \in S$. Thus, every history space $H \subseteq H^*$ should contain identifying history lists having a size at least equal to l_{su}. Otherwise, it would be impossible to identify every state in S.

Definition 4. *k-Complete History Space*
Let H_k denote the set of identifying history lists (for single states) which have a length less or equal to k. Let the set of minimal suffixes $H_k^{min} \subseteq H_k$ contain all identifying history lists $h \in H_k$ such that $\nexists h' \in H_k : h' \neq h$ and h' is a suffix of h. A history space $H \subseteq H^*$ is k-complete if $H_k^{min} \subseteq H$ and there are no identifying history lists $h, h' \in H, h \neq h'$ with $h \in H_{k-l_{su}}^{min}$ such that h is a suffix of h'.

A k-complete history space must contain an identifying history list h of length $|h| \leq k$, if h is a minimal suffix of an identifying history list. If h is such a suffix with length no longer than $k - l_{su}$, a k-complete history space must not contain extensions at the front of h.

Theorem 1. *Detection of Identifying History Lists*
Let $H \subseteq H^*$ be a history space and $h \in H$ a history list of length $\hat{k} := |h|$. If $k - \hat{k} \geq l_{su}$ for a fixed $k \in \mathbb{N}$, then the following two propositions hold:
H is k-complete : h is identifying $\Rightarrow \nexists h' \in H : h' \neq h$ and h is a suffix of h'
$H_k^{min} \subseteq H$: h is identifying $\Leftarrow \nexists h' \in H : h' \neq h$ and h is a suffix of h'

Proof. ($\Rightarrow$):
Let $h \in H$ be an identifying history list and let h^{min} be the minimal identifying suffix of h. Since $|h^{min}| \leq |h| = \hat{k} \leq k - l_{su} < k$ and H is k-complete, it must hold that $h^{min} \in H$. We assume that there exists a history list $h' \in H$ such that h is a suffix of h'. From Lemma 1, it follows that h' is an identifying history list. In this situation, H would not be k-complete since both h^{min} and h' are identifying history lists in H, $h^{min} \in H^{min}_{k-l_{su}}$ and h^{min} is a suffix of h'.
($\Leftarrow$):
Let $[u_0^*, o_1^*, ..., u_{t-1}^*, o_t^*]$ be a possible sequence of observations and actions and $[s_0, ..., s_{t-\hat{k}}, ..., s_t]$ be a corresponding sequence of system states.

Let $h := [u_0, o_1, ..., u_{\hat{k}-1}, o_{\hat{k}}]$ be a suffix of the above sequence. By definition of the sufficient history length l_{su}, there exists an identifying history list $h' \in H^*$, $h' := [u_0', o_1', ..., u_{r-1}', o_r']$ for state $s_{t-\hat{k}}$ with $r \leq l_{su}$. Consider the history list $h'' := [u_0', o_1', ..., u_{r-1}', o_r', u_0, o_1, ..., u_{\hat{k}-1}, o_{\hat{k}}]$ which is built by extending h' with history list h (at the end). It is easy to see that $h'' \in H^*$. By applying Lemma 2 several times, it follows that h'' is an identifying history list for state s_t. Furthermore, h'' has a length of at most k, since $|h| = \hat{k}$ and $|h'| \leq l_{su}$. Since $H_k^{min} \subseteq H$, there must exist an identifying history list $h''' \in H$ such that h''' is a minimal suffix of h'' and an identifying history list for state s_t . Since also h is a suffix of h'', it must hold that either h is a suffix of h''' or h''' is a suffix of h. Since we assume that there is no history list in H containing h as a suffix, h''' must be a suffix of h. Thus by Lemma 1, h is an identifying history list for s_t.

Note that it is not necessary to know the exact value of l_{su}. An overestimation of l_{su} will not affect the proof of the above theorem. It is easy to show that if the observation model only depends on the current state ($\Omega : S \rightarrow O$), the above theorem also holds for an extended history list $h = [o_0, u_0, .., u_{t-1}, o_t]$ including the observation of the initial state of the history sequence.

Since the criterion above can be checked solely by inspecting the history space H, it is possible to compute an efficient exploration strategy on the basis of H and a set of transitions $\mathcal{F}$ sampled from the underlying POMDP. These sample transitions can also be used to establish an alternative criterion: For a deterministic system, the sequence of observations and rewards is uniquely determined given a starting state and a sequence of actions. A history list h contains a link to all sampled episodes in which h became the current history list at some time t. By examining these episodes, it can be checked whether for an action sequence occurring after time t, the corresponding sequence of observations and rewards is uniquely determined. If this is the case for all action sequences (occurred after time t), the history list h is considered to be identifying. The idea for this

Safe Q-Learning on History Lists
Initialization
1. $N := 0, \mathcal{F} = \emptyset, \forall h \in H, u \in U : \hat{Q}_0(h, u) := 0$

Main Loop
1. Sample a set $\mathcal{F}_{new}$ of transition instances by applying an ϵ-greedy exploration
2. $\mathcal{F} = \mathcal{F} \cup \mathcal{F}_{new}$
3. $\mathcal{F}^{vl} := \{(h_t, u_t, r_t, h_{t+1}) \in \mathcal{F} \mid u_t \in U^{vl}_{h_t}$ and h_{t+1} is identifying $\}$

Q-Learning Update Loop
1. $\forall (h_t, u_t, r_t, h_{t+1}) \in \mathcal{F}^{vl}$
   $\hat{Q}_{N+1}(h_t, u_t) = r_t + \gamma \max_{u \in U^{vl}_{h_t}} \hat{Q}_N(h_{t+1}, u)$
2. $N = N + 1$

Until $\hat{Q}_N$ converges
End of Main Loop

Fig. 2. Q-Learning on Identifying History Lists

criterion was already introduced in [1] for building a prediction suffix tree, but without considering reward signals.

- To apply Q-learning on history spaces, two alternative criterions are available to detect identifying history lists.
  Criterion A A history list $h \in H$ is considered to be identifying if this can be proved by Theorem 1, assuming a k-complete history space or at least $H^{min}_k \subseteq H$. Additionally, h is considered to be identifying if it is an extension of another history list $h' \in H$ which can be proved to be identifying. Otherwise, h is considered to be non-identifying.
  Criterion B If the sequence of observations and rewards following a history list h is uniquely determined for action sequences occurred on sampled episodes, h is considered to be identifying. Otherwise, h has been proven to be non-identifying.
- Transition instances are represented by four tuples $(h_t, u_t, r_t, h_{t+1}) \in \mathcal{F}$, where r_t denotes the reward
- The set of valid actions $U^{vl}_h \subseteq U$ for history list h is empty if h is not identifying. Otherwise, the set U^{vl}_h contains action $u \in U$ if there exists a transition instance $(h_t = h, u_t = u, r_t, h_{t+1}) \in \mathcal{F}$ such that h_{t+1} is identifying
- The greedy action of $h \in H$ is computed with respect to the set of valid actions U^{vl}_h. If $U^{vl}_h = \emptyset$, a random action is taken

We implemented an efficient exploration strategy (Figure 3) trying to minimize the expected length of a path to an identifying history list. It would also be possible to develop a reward-based exploration which maximizes the rewards on a path to an identifying history list.

Theorem 2. *Safe Q-Learning on History Lists*
Let H be a history space. If criterion A is used to detect identifying history lists and it holds $H^{min}_k \subseteq H$, then the Q-function will converge to a unique fix point. If criterion B is used, then the Q-function will converge without any assumptions with respect to H.

Efficient Exploration Strategy
Input Set of sampled transitions $\mathcal{F}$, Q-function Q_N, current history list h_t
Algorithm

1. Estimate transition probabilities $p((h,u) \rightarrow h')$ for the history space H based on transition instances from $\mathcal{F}$.
2. If h_t is identifying, return the greedy action according to the function Q_N. If h_t is not identifying, compute an action sequence probably leading to an identifying history list. This can be implemented by considering action sequences of length $1 < l \leq l_{max}$ starting from the current history list $h_t \in H$. By inspecting the estimated transition model, every possible current history list $h_{t+l} \in H$ after l time steps can be discovered and added to a candidate set. Then, it can be checked by criterion A or criterion B, how many candidates are identifying history lists.

Fig. 3. Efficient Exploration Strategy

Proof. A detailed proof is omitted due to space constraints. If criterion A is used, convergence immediately follows from Theorem 1, since updates of the Q-function are made only on sequences consisting of identifying history lists. Since every identifying history list corresponds to a single state $s \in S$, the subset of the history space used to update the Q-function is markovian. If criterion B is used, then a similar argument holds: For an updated history list h, it holds that all stored sequences of observations and rewards (occurred on a sampled episode) are deterministic after history list h becomes the current history list. Thus, it is possible to create a new deterministic POMDP with a new state space S' and observation model Ω' such that all sampled episodes are compatible with the new POMDP and h is an identifying history list for a state in S'.

Now we want to discuss which criterion is better suited to detect identifying history lists. If a k-complete history space is available, it is preferable to choose criterion A, because it has been proven to work correctly and can be checked efficiently. Note that if the history space used is not k-complete, but at least it holds that $H_k^{min} \subseteq H$, then Q-learning will still converge, but the criterion will detect only a subset of all identifying history lists. If the history space used is of very poor quality, it seems to be better to choose criterion B. Criterion B gives only empirical evidence that a history list identifying, but at least guarantees convergence of the Q-learning algorithm. The problem with criterion B is that even if the Q-function converges, the extracted policy is not necessarily successful if applied to the problem. This comes from the fact that a history list classified as identifying by criterion B can actually be non-identifying. In such a situation, the efficient exploration strategy might lead to non-identifying history lists. Thus, we propose to consider a history list as identifying only if this is confirmed by both criterions. By this procedure we achieve guaranteed convergence and the performance of the exploration strategy will gradually improve with the quality of the history space used. The reason for this is that criterion B will never classify a history list as non-identifying if this is not truly the case but it will revise wrong classifications made by criterion A. In other words, if the criterions are combined, the resulting classification will always be better than a classification solely based on criterion A.

The question arises whether the learned Q-function gives a policy of high performance. It is easy to see that if H (or rather k) is sufficiently large, then the safe Q-learning algorithm will converge to a near optimal policy. This is due to the fact that every extension (at the end) of an identifying history list is again identifying (Lemma 2). If H contains identifying history lists corresponding to an optimal path from a starting state to the goal, Q-learning will investigate this path.

4 Empirical Results

We applied our algorithm to the partially observable maze shown in Figure 1. The size of the state space is $|S| = 104$, which is rather large compared to typical POMDP benchmarks from the literature. The reward is -1 at all non-goal cells. Note that for the maze considered it holds that $l_{su} = 5$. Since there are many cells in the maze having no walls surrounding them, it is necessary to take a couple of well advised steps to identify the current state. Since the observations only depend on the state, we used history lists with an additional (initial) observation at the front.

We compared our algorithm against the optimal solution on belief states computed by the Witness algorithm [2] and a random exploration strategy. The initial probability distribution over states (belief state) is chosen according to the initial observation of the sampled episode. By this procedure, we incorporate knowledge about the observation of the initial state of an episode into the belief state. Unfortunately, we were not able to compute the optimal policy on belief states for the whole maze. Since the state space contains more than one hundred states, the computational effort for establishing the optimal value function becomes intractable. We therefore conducted an additional experiment in which only the lower right part of the maze is considered. This reduced maze only has twenty states. For both mazes, we computed the optimal solution of the corresponding MDP (fully observable maze). This solution always bounds the optimal solution of the POMDP mazes.

The random exploration samples an action at random if it is not possible to prove that the current history list is identifying. Otherwise, it takes the greedy action according to the learned Q-function. The efficient exploration (Figure 3) tries to identify the current state as quickly as possible and then takes a greedy policy to the goal. Thus, the resulting policy is not optimal, but reasonably close to the optimum.

We conducted experiments with three k-complete history spaces such that each experiment corresponds to a different choice of the parameter $k \in \{6, 7, 8\}$. Only criterion A was used to detect identifying history lists, because for k-complete history spaces this criterion works perfectly (Theorem 1). All values presented are mean values from ten runs of the algorithm. Every run of an

Table 1. Performance of learned policies. The fourth/fifth column gives the number of steps to the goal averaged over every possible starting state. The values given in braces are the performance of the policy learned after the third iteration of the main loop.

Algorithm	History Space	Size ($\|H\|$)	Efficient	Random	Maze
MDP Opt.	-	-	2.2	-	small
POMDP Opt.	-	-	2.7	-	small
Safe Q	7-complete	3200	3.48	4.40	small
MDP Opt.	-	-	7.77	-	large
Safe Q	8-complete	119082	12.40 (13.83)	32.15 (34.75)	large
Safe Q	7-complete	30712	13.46 (19.37)	39.39 (40.36)	large
Safe Q	6-complete	14850	14.00 (22.78)	61.59 (55.17)	large

Table 2. Results of the second experiment. The setup of the experiment is equal to the first experiment (large maze, 8-complete) but with a reduced history space. The third (fifth) column of the last row shows an experiment in which all extensions of history lists of size six (seven) are deleted.

Deletion Method	# Deleted Lists	# Steps	# Deleted Lists	# Steps
Random	10000	12.52 (13.54)	20000	13.57 (14.59)
Random	30000	13.52 (22.76)	-	-
No Extensions	77432	13.08 (14.33)	96428	13.62 (14.19)

experiment (large maze) consists of fifteen iterations of the main loop of the safe Q-learning algorithm. In every iteration, 10^5 transition instances are collected by applying an ϵ-greedy policy. For the small maze, only a single iteration of the main loop is carried out, sampling a total number of 50000 transition instances. An episode sampled to collect transition instances ends if the goal state is reached or the number of collected transition instances exceeds the threshold max_step $= 200$. Sampling 10^5 transition instances approximately corresponds to 660 sampled episodes. The exploration rate is set to $\epsilon = 0.1$.

Table 1 shows that it is possible to learn good policies based on a Q-function defined on history lists. The performance of the algorithm develops with the size of the history space and with the length of the history lists, respectively. Moreover, the efficient exploration strategy achieves significantly better results than the random exploration strategy. The optimal solution on belief states for the large maze is presumably close to ten steps. To show the robustness of the algorithm against non k-complete spaces, we conducted an additional experiment with the efficient exploration strategy in which a number of identifying history lists are randomly selected from all lists having size eight (8-complete history space) and then deleted from the history space. To detect identifying history lists, we used a combination of criterions as discussed in the previous section. Table 2 shows that even if it holds that $H_k^{min} \not\subseteq H$, the algorithm still performs well.

5 Discussion

In this section, we want to discuss the applicability of history based approaches to real world problems. From our perspective, two questions are especially important in this context.

1. Is it possible to learn a k-complete history space?
2. Is it possible to scale the approach to stochastic POMDPs?

We performed preliminary experiments in which it was possible to learn k-complete history spaces by the following procedure based on sampling a number of episodes at random.

- Initially, the history space H consists of all possible history lists of length one (e.g. $h = uo$), $l := 0$
- Loop (until the history space H does no longer changes)
  - $l = l + 1$
  - Delete old data and collect new data by sampling a number of episodes. An episode is a sequence consisting of actions, observations and rewards.
  - Build all one step extensions (at the end and at the front) of all history lists in H having a size equal to l. One step means a single action-observation pair. If the size of an extended list does not exceed the threshold $k - l_{su}$, add the list to H.
  - If a history list in H is a (possibly multi step) front extension of another history list in H, which is classified as identifying by criterion B, then shorten the extended list by deleting the first (at the front) action-observation pair of the list
- End of loop
- Add all possible history lists to H having size $k - l_{su} < |h| \leq k$ except for front extensions of those identifying history lists, which were previously included during the loop (detected with criterion B)

The above procedure can be proven not to include front extensions of an identifying history list $h \in H$ with $|h| \leq k - l_{su}$. This is a critical aspect of learning a k-complete history space. We were able to learn a 8-complete history space for the large maze.

In the past, it has already been demonstrated that history list approaches are practical and can be scaled to complex problems, e.g. continuous, multidimensional state spaces ([3], [4]). In fact, even in cases in which it is not possible to learn k-complete history spaces, e.g. for infinite state spaces, the convergence proof for our algorithm still applies (criterion B). A certain benefit of k-complete history spaces is that the size of the history space learned can be adjusted by the parameter k. Even for small values of k, it will be possible to learn good policies on a k-complete space because of the efficient exploration strategy. While applying a policy, the efficient exploration strategy establishes exactly those identifying history lists for which stored Q-values are available.

We think that the basic idea of this approach can be carried over to the general case of stochastic POMDPs. It may always be advantageous to explicitly search for belief states in which the probability mass concentrates on few states. This is the reason why our definition of identifying history lists also covers sets of states. We think that a search procedure as mentioned above is much more efficient than computing Q-values for every single belief as it is done in classical POMDP algorithms. Following this idea, we currently work on an extension of our algorithm to sparse stochastic systems (systems with less stochasticity).

6 Related Work

This section contains a summary of existing work concerning the issue of learning POMDP representations with short-time memory as well as learning policies on those representations.

For a deterministic transition function and a deterministic observation model, a POMDP can be represented by a Finite State Automaton (FSA). To learn a model of an FSA, the concept of tests is introduced in [5]. A test itself consists of a sequence of actions, while the outcome of a test is defined as the observation made after executing the action sequence. A randomized algorithm is presented which is able to learn a sufficient number of tests such that future observations can be perfectly predicted. In [6], this idea is generalized to the stochastic case yielding Predictive State Representations (PSRs). In the context of PSRs, tests are considered to be sequences of observations and actions such that probabilities can be assigned to these sequences. Precisely, the expression $p(t|h) = p(o_1, .., o_k|hu_1, ..., u_k)$ for a test $t = u_1 o_1 ... u_k o_k$ denotes the probability of observing a certain sequence of observations, given that a certain sequence of actions is executed and a certain history h (past events) occurred. Similar to the work in [5], it can be shown that the model of an arbitrary POMDP of finite size can be expressed by a sufficiently large set of tests $\{t_1, ..., t_n\}$ which is then called a PSR. The prediction vector $p(h) = [p(t_1|h), ..., p(t_n|h)]$ constitutes a sufficient statistic of the system. In [1], it is shown that for the deterministic case, it is possible to derive a PSR from a prediction suffix tree, which can be decomposed into a set of history lists. Existing literature about PSRs focuses only on predicting the state, but not on learning policies.

In [1], predictions of future observations of an FSA are made by building a prediction suffix tree with loops. A path through this tree starts at the root node and corresponds to a certain, possibly cyclic sequence of past observations and actions. The leaf nodes of the tree contain predictions about future observations. By allowing the tree to have loops, it is possible to deal with long subsequences of useless information which can be sandwiched into an enclosing sequence. This procedure can substantially reduce the number of history lists (branches of the tree) needed to be stored in memory. In our approach, we did not include loops, because loop detection is a potential source of error. An incorrectly detected loop (by inspecting sampled episodes) could damage the performance of the efficient exploration strategy. However, it would be easily possible to include the looping mechanism by inserting links from longer (identifying) history lists to shorter (identifying) history lists. In contrast to our algorithm, the suffix tree is only designed for prediction purposes. Neither an efficient exploration is used to identify the current state in minimal time nor is a policy learned. Moreover, the concept of k-complete history spaces makes it possible to bound the size of the history space by the parameter k. A suffix tree always provides perfect prediction, but is possibly of great depth.

In [3], a Q-learning variant is used to learn policies for POMDPs based on a tree structure called UTree. The tree is used to estimate the current state by distinguishing future rewards of sequences of observations and actions. Unfortunately, there is no guarantee that Q-learning will eventually converge in such a setting. Thus, UTree can only heuristically be applied to POMDPs.

7 Conclusion

We developed a variant of Q-learning able to learn near optimal policies for deterministic POMDPs without a model. This is accomplished by substituting the state space by a history space consisting of sequences of past observations and actions. The algorithm is sound in the sense that convergence can by achieved without any assumptions with respect to the history space used. By introducing the concept of k-complete history spaces, we showed that the performance of the algorithm gradually improves with the quality of the history space available. We empirically showed that the algorithm is robust against "incomplete" history spaces and a relatively simple algorithm is able to learn k-complete history spaces.

References

1. Holmes, M.P., Isbell, C.L.: Looping suffix tree-based inference of partially observable hidden state. In: Proceedings of the 23th International Conference on Machine Learning (ICML), Pittsburgh, Pennsylvania, USA, pp. 409–416 (2006)
2. Littman, M.L., Cassandra, A.R., Kaelbling, L.P.: Efficient dynamic-programming updates in partially observable markov decision processes. Technical Report CS-95-19, Brown University (1995)
3. McCallum, A.: Learning to use selective attention and short-term memory in sequential tasks. In: From Animals to Animats 4: Proceedings of the Fourth International Conference on Simulation of Adaptive Behavior, pp. 315–324. The MIT Press, Cambridge (1996)
4. Timmer, S., Riedmiller, M.: Abstract state spaces with history. In: Proceedings of the 25th International Conference of NAFIPS, the North American Fuzzy Information Processing Society (2006)
5. Rivest, R.L., Schapire, R.E.: Diversity-based inference of finite automata. Journal of the Association for Computing Machinery 43, 555–589 (1994)
6. Littman, M., Sutton, R., Singh, S.: Predictive representations of state. In: Proceedings of the 14th International Conference on Neural Information Processing Systems (NIPS), pp. 1555–1561 (2002)

Random k-Labelsets: An Ensemble Method for Multilabel Classification

Grigorios Tsoumakas and Ioannis Vlahavas

Department of Informatics,
Aristotle University of Thessaloniki
54124 Thessaloniki, Greece
{greg,vlahavas}@csd.auth.gr

Abstract. This paper proposes an ensemble method for multilabel classification. The RAndom k-labELsets (RAKEL) algorithm constructs each member of the ensemble by considering a small random subset of labels and learning a single-label classifier for the prediction of each element in the powerset of this subset. In this way, the proposed algorithm aims to take into account label correlations using single-label classifiers that are applied on subtasks with manageable number of labels and adequate number of examples per label. Experimental results on common multilabel domains involving protein, document and scene classification show that better performance can be achieved compared to popular multilabel classification approaches.

1 Introduction

Traditional *single-label* classification is concerned with learning from a set of examples that are associated with a single label λ from a set of disjoint labels L, $|L| > 1$. If $|L| = 2$, then the learning task is called *binary* classification (or *filtering* in the case of textual and web data), while if $|L| > 2$, then it is called *multi-class* classification. In *multilabel* classification, the examples are associated with a set of labels $Y \subseteq L$.

Multilabel classification is a challenging research problem that emerges in several modern applications such as music categorization [1], protein function classification [2,3,4,5] and semantic classification of images [6,7]. In the past, multilabel classification has mainly engaged the attention of researchers working on text categorization [8,9,10], as each member of a document collection usually belongs to more than one semantic category.

Multilabel classification methods can be categorized into two different groups [11]: i) *problem transformation* methods, and ii) *algorithm adaptation* methods. The first group of methods are algorithm independent. They transform the multilabel classification task into one or more single-label classification, regression or label ranking [12] tasks. The second group of methods extend specific learning algorithms in order to handle multilabel data directly. There exist multilabel extensions of decision tree [2], support vector machine [13,14], neural network

J.N. Kok et al. (Eds.): ECML 2007, LNAI 4701, pp. 406–417, 2007.

[15,5], Bayesian [9], lazy learning [16] and boosting [10] learning algorithms. This paper focuses on the former group of methods.

The most widely-used problem transformation method considers the prediction of each label as an independent binary classification task. It learns one binary classifier $h_\lambda : X \rightarrow \{\neg\lambda, \lambda\}$ for each different label $\lambda \in L$. It transforms the original data set into $|L|$ data sets D_λ that contain all examples of the original data set, labeled as λ if the labels of the original example contained λ and as $\neg\lambda$ otherwise. It is the same solution used in order to deal with a multi-class problem using a binary classifier, commonly referred to as one-against-all or one-versus-rest. Following [12], we will refer to this method as Binary Relevance (BR) learning, a name popular within the Information Retrieval community. BR is criticized for not considering correlations among the labels.

A less common problem transformation method considers each different subset of L as a single label. It so learns one single-label classifier $h : X \rightarrow P(L)$, where $P(L)$ is the powerset of L, containing all possible label subsets. We will refer to this method as Label Powerset (LP) learning. LP has the advantage of taking label correlations into account, but suffers from the large number of label subsets, the majority of which are associated with very few examples.

This paper proposes an approach that constructs an ensemble of LP classifiers. Each LP classifier is trained using a different small random subset of the set of labels. The proposed approach, dubbed RAKEL (RAndom k-labELsets), aims at taking into account label correlations and at the same time avoiding the aforementioned problems of LP. Ensemble combination is accomplished by thresholding the average zero-one decisions of each model per considered label. The paper investigates the issue of selecting appropriate parameters (subset size, number of models, threshold) for RAKEL through an experimental study on three domains concerning protein, image and document classification. Results of performance comparison against the BR and LP methods are in favor of the proposed approach.

A secondary contribution of this paper is a unified presentation of existing evaluation measures for multilabel classification, including their categorization into example-based and label-based measures. The categorization goes further discussing micro and macro averaging operations for any label-based measure.

The remainder of this paper is organized as follows: Section 2 introduces the proposed approach and Section 3 presents the categorization of evaluation measures. Section 4 gives the setup of the experimental study and Section 5 discusses the results. Finally, Section 6 concludes and points to future work.

2 The RAKEL Algorithm

We first define the concept of *k-labelsets* and introduce notation that is subsequently used. Let $L = \{\lambda_i\}$, $i = 1..|L|$ be the set of labels in a multilabel classification domain. A set $Y \subseteq L$ with $k = |Y|$ is called k-labelset. We will use the term L^k to denote the set of all distinct k-labelsets on L. The size of L^k is given by the binomial coefficient: $|L^k| = \binom{|L|}{k}$.

The RAKEL (RAndom k-LabELsets) algorithm iteratively constructs an ensemble of m Label Powerset (LP) classifiers. At each iteration, $i = 1..m$, it randomly selects a k-labelset, Y_i, from L^k without replacement. It then learns an LP classifier $h_i : X \rightarrow P(Y_i)$. The pseudocode of the ensemble production phase is given in Figure 1.

```
Input: Number of models m, size of labelset k, set of labels L, training set D
Output: An ensemble of LP classifiers h_i and corresponding k-labelsets Y_i
R ← L^k;
for i ← 1 to min(m, |L^k|) do
    Y_i ← a k-labelset randomly selected from R;
    train an LP classifier h_i : X → P(Y_i) on D;
    R ← R \ {Y_i};
```

Fig. 1. The ensemble production phase of RAKEL

The number of iterations (m) is a user-specified parameter with acceptable values ranging from 1 to $|L^k|$. The size of the labelsets (k) is another user-specified parameter with meaningful values ranging from 2 to $|L| - 1$. For $k = 1$ and $m = |L|$ we get the binary classifier ensemble of the Binary Relevance (BR) method, while for $k = |L|$ (and consequently $m = 1$) we get the single-label classifier of the LP method. We hypothesize that using labelsets of small size and an adequate number of iterations, RAKEL will manage to model label correlations effectively. The experimental study in Section 5 provides evidence in support of this hypothesis and guidelines on selecting appropriate values for k and m.

For the multilabel classification of a new instance x, each model h_i provides binary decisions $h_i(x, \lambda_j)$ for each label λ_j in the corresponding k-labelset Y_i. Subsequently, RAKEL calculates the average decision for each label λ_j in L and outputs a final positive decision if the average is greater than a user-specified threshold t. An intuitive value for t is 0.5, but RAKEL performs well across a wide range of t values as it shown by the experimental results. The pseudocode of the ensemble production phase is given in Figure 2.

2.1 Computational Complexity

If the complexity of the single-label base classifier is $O(g(|C|, |D|, |A|))$ for a dataset with $|C|$ class values, $|D|$ examples and $|A|$ predictive attributes, then the computational complexity of RAKEL is $O(mg(2^k, |D|, |A|))$. The complexity is linear with respect to the number of models m, as in most ensemble methods, and it further depends on the complexity of the base classifier.

One important thing to note is the high number of class values (2^k) that each LP classifier of RAKEL must learn. This may become an important hindrance of the proposed algorithm, especially if the base classifier has quadratic or greater

```
Input: new instance x, ensemble of LP classifiers h_i, corresponding set of
       k-labelsets Y_i, set of labels L
Output: multilabel classification vector Result
for j ← 1 to |L| do
    Sum_j ← 0;
    Votes_j ← 0;
for i ← 1 to m do
    forall labels λ_j ∈ Y_i do
        Sum_j ← Sum_j + h_i(x, λ_j);
        Votes_j ← Votes_j + 1;
for j ← 1 to |L| do
    Avg_j ← Sum_j/Votes_j;
    if Avg_j > t then
        Result_j ← 1 ;
    else Result_j ← 0 ;
```

Fig. 2. The ensemble combination phase of RAKEL

complexity with respect to the number of class values, as in the case of support vector machine classifiers. In practice however, the actual number of class values is never 2^k, because LP can simply consider the label subsets that appear in the training data. The number of these subsets is typically significantly smaller than 2^k. See for example the number of label subsets for the multilabel datasets considered in the experimental study of this paper (Section 4, Table 1).

3 Evaluation Measures

Multilabel classification requires different evaluation measures than those used in traditional single-label classification. Several measures have been proposed in the past for the evaluation of multilabel classifiers. Some of them are calculated based on the average differences of the actual and the predicted sets of labels over all test examples. Others decompose the evaluation process into separate evaluations for each label, which they subsequently average over all labels. We call the former *example-based* and the latter *label-based* evaluation measures.

3.1 Example-Based

Let D be a multilabel evaluation data set, consisting of $|D|$ multilabel examples (x_i, Y_i), $i = 1..|D|, Y_i \subseteq L$. Let h be a multilabel classifier and $Z_i = h(x_i)$ be the set of labels predicted by h for example x_i.

Schapire and Singer [10] consider the Hamming Loss, which is defined as:

$$HammingLoss(h, D) = \frac{1}{|D|} \sum_{i=1}^{|D|} \frac{|Y_i \triangle Z_i|}{|L|}$$

where $\triangle$ stands for the symmetric difference of two sets, which is the set-theoretic equivalent of the exclusive disjunction (XOR operation) in Boolean logic.

Classification Accuracy [17] or Subset Accuracy [18] is defined as follows:

$$ClassificationAccuracy(h, D) = \frac{1}{|D|}\sum_{i=1}^{|D|} I(Z_i = Y_i)$$

where I(true)=1 and I(false)=0. This is a very strict evaluation measure as it requires the predicted set of labels to be an exact match of the true set of labels.

The following measures are used in [14]:

$$Precision(h, D) = \frac{1}{|D|}\sum_{i=1}^{|D|} \frac{|Y_i \cap Z_i|}{|Z_i|} \qquad Recall(h, D) = \frac{1}{|D|}\sum_{i=1}^{|D|} \frac{|Y_i \cap Z_i|}{|Y_i|}$$

$$F(h, D) = \frac{1}{|D|}\sum_{i=1}^{|D|} \frac{2|Y_i \cap Z_i|}{|Z_i| + |Y_i|} \qquad Accuracy(h, D) = \frac{1}{|D|}\sum_{i=1}^{|D|} \frac{|Y_i \cap Z_i|}{|Y_i \cup Z_i|}$$

3.2 Label-Based

Any known measure for binary evaluation can be used here, such as accuracy, area under the ROC curve, precision and recall. The calculation of these measures for all labels can be achieved using two averaging operations, called *macro-averaging* and *micro-averaging* [8]. These operations are usually considered for averaging precision, recall and their harmonic mean (F-measure) in Information Retrieval tasks.

Consider a binary evaluation measure $M(tp, tn, fp, fn)$ that is calculated based on the number of true positives (tp), true negatives (tn), false positives (fp) and false negatives (fn). Let tp_λ, fp_λ, tn_λ and fn_λ be the number of true positives, false positives, true negatives and false negatives after binary evaluation for a label λ. The macro-averaged and micro-averaged versions of M, are calculated as follows:

$$M_{macro} = \frac{1}{|L|}\sum_{\lambda=1}^{|L|} M\left(tp_\lambda, fp_\lambda, tn_\lambda, fn_\lambda\right)$$

$$M_{micro} = M\left(\sum_{\lambda=1}^{|L|} tp_\lambda, \sum_{\lambda=1}^{|L|} fp_\lambda, \sum_{\lambda=1}^{|L|} tn_\lambda, \sum_{\lambda=1}^{|L|} fn_\lambda\right)$$

Note that micro-averaging has the same result as macro-averaging for some measures, such as accuracy, while it differs for other measures, such as precision, recall and area under the ROC curve. Note also that the average (macro/micro) accuracy and Hamming loss sum up to 1, as Hamming loss is actually the average binary classification error.

4 Experimental Setup

4.1 Datasets

We experiment with 3 datasets from 3 different application domains: bioinformatics, semantic scene analysis and document categorization. The biological dataset *yeast* [13] is concerned with protein function classification. The image dataset *scene* [6] is concerned with semantic indexing of still scenes. The textual dataset *tmc2007* [19] concerns aviation safety reports. These and other multilabel datasets are available for download in Weka's ARFF format at: http://mlkd.csd.auth.gr/multilabel.html

Table 1 shows certain standard statistics of these datasets, such as the number of examples in the train and test sets, the number of numeric and discrete attributes and the number of labels, along with multilabel data statistics, such as the number of distinct label subsets, the label cardinality and the label density [11]. Label cardinality is the average number of labels per example, while label density is the same number divided by $|L|$.

Table 1. Standard and multilabel statistics for the data sets used in the experiments

	Examples		Attributes			Distinct	Label	Label
Dataset	Train	Test	Numeric	Discrete	Labels	Subsets	Cardinality	Density
scene	1211	1196	294	0	6	15	1.074	0.179
tmc2007	21519	7077	0	48981	22	1341	2.158	0.098
yeast	1500	917	103	0	14	198	4.327	0.302

Feature selection was applied on *tmc2007*, in order to reduce the computational cost of training. We used the χ^2 feature ranking method separately for each label in order to obtain a ranking of all features for that label. We then selected the top 500 features based on the their maximum rank over all labels. A similar approach was found to have high performance in previous experimental work on textual datasets [20].

4.2 Multilabel Methods

We compare RAKEL against the BR and LP methods. In all datasets we experiment with 9 different threshold values for RAKEL, ranging from 0.1 to 0.9 with a 0.1 step. We also experiment with a range of subset sizes and number of models, that differ depending on the dataset. We evaluate the performance of methods using a hold-out set. In particular, we use the original train and test set splits that come with the distributions of the datasets. Although we calculate most of the evaluation measures of Section 3, we only present results for Hamming loss and the micro-averaged F-measure, due to limited space. These two metrics are widely-used in the literature and indicative of the performance of multilabel classification methods.

The BR, LP and RAKEL methods can utilize any learning algorithm for classifier training. Evaluating the performance of different algorithms was out of the scope of this paper. We selected the support vector machine (SVM) [21] for the experiments, based on its strong performance in a past study [11]. The SVM was trained with a linear kernel and the complexity constant C equal to 1. The one-against-one strategy is used for dealing with multi-class tasks.

We have implemented a package of Java classes for multilabel classification based on Weka [22]. The package includes implementations of BR, LP, RAKEL and other methods, an evaluation framework that supports the measures presented in Section 3 and code for the calculation of multilabel statistics. It has a command line interface similar to Weka but the full feature set is available only as an API. The package contains source code and a compiled library. Java v1.5 or better and Weka v3.5.5 is required to run the software, which is available for download at http://mlkd.csd.auth.gr/multilabel.html.

5 Results and Discussion

5.1 *Scene* Dataset

For the *scene* dataset we experiment with all meaningful values for k (2 to 5). We also build incrementally the ensemble with values for m ranging from 1 to $|L^k|$. Figures 3(a) and 3(b) show the Hamming loss and F-measure respectively (y-axis) of BR, LP and RAKEL for t = 0.5, with respect to the number of iterations m (x-axis).

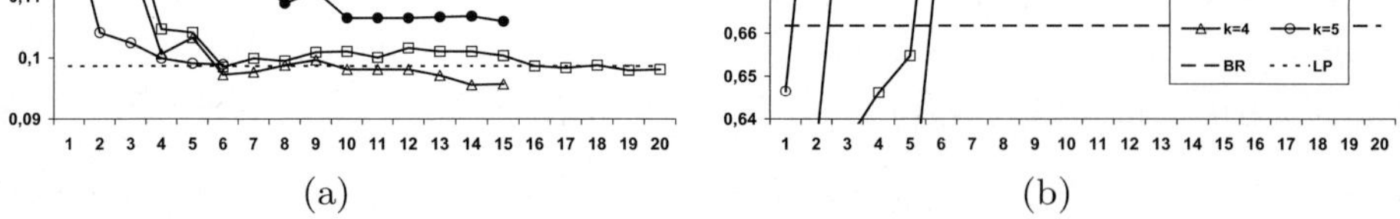

Fig. 3. Hamming loss (a) and F-measure (b) of BR, LP and RAKEL for t=0.5

We first notice that LP is better than the more popular BR in this dataset. The small number of labels (6) and label subsets (15) are factors that may contribute to this result. We also notice that for all values of k RAKEL has better performance than BR after the construction of a few models. For k = 3, RAKEL achieves the best results, which are better than LP for m >= 10. Better

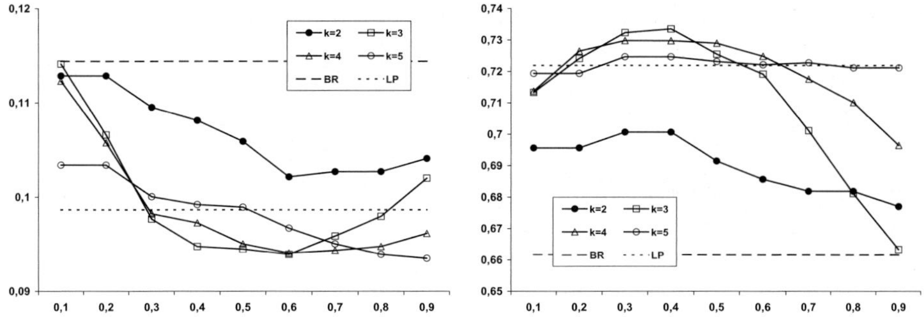

Fig. 4. Hamming loss (a) and F-measure (b) of BR, LP and RAKEL for optimal m

results than LP are also achieved for certain values of m in the cases where $k = 4$ and $k = 5$. These results show that for the default threshold value (0.5) the performance of RAKEL exceeds that of BR and LP for a range of subset sizes and iterations.

Figures 4(a) and 4(b) show the minimum Hamming loss and maximum F-Measure respectively (y-axis) for RAKEL across all iterations m, with respect to all values of t. The performance of BR and LP is given too. These figures show the best performance that can be achieved by RAKEL irrespectively of the number of models for the different threshold values.

We notice that low Hamming loss can be achieved for a range of t values for $k = 3$ and $k = 4$, with the best results being achieved for $t = 0.6$. The F-measure on the other hand seems to be favored by threshold values around 0.4. RAKEL can achieve higher F-measure than LP for $k = 3$ or $k = 4$ for threshold values ranging from 0.2 to 0.5.

5.2 *Yeast* Dataset

For the *yeast* dataset we experimented with k values from 2 to 7 (half of all labels). The number of iterations (m) were ranging from 1 to $min(|L^k|, 300)$. Similarly to the *scene* dataset, Figures 5(a) and 5(b) show the Hamming loss and F-measure respectively (y-axis) of BR, LP and RAKEL for $t = 0.5$, with respect to the number of iterations m (x-axis). For clarity of presentation, we grouped the values in batches of 5 models and calculated the average.

In Figure 5(a) we notice that the Hamming loss of BR and LP is not displayed, as their values (BR=0.1997 and LP=0.2022) are beyond the focus of the plot. RAKEL achieves better Hamming loss than BR and LP for all values of k after the first 20 models. Hamming loss has a decreasing trend up to around 150 models, while from then on it seems to have a slightly increasing trend. In Figure 5(b) we notice similar results for F-measure, but this time for $k > 3$. As a conclusion we can argue that RAKEL using the default threshold value (0.5) attains better performance than BR and LP for a wide range of k and m values.

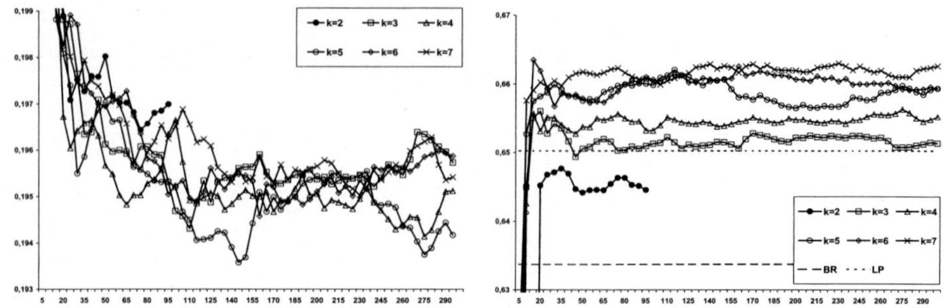

(a) (b)

Fig. 5. Hamming loss (a) and F-measure (b) of BR, LP and RAKEL for t=0.5

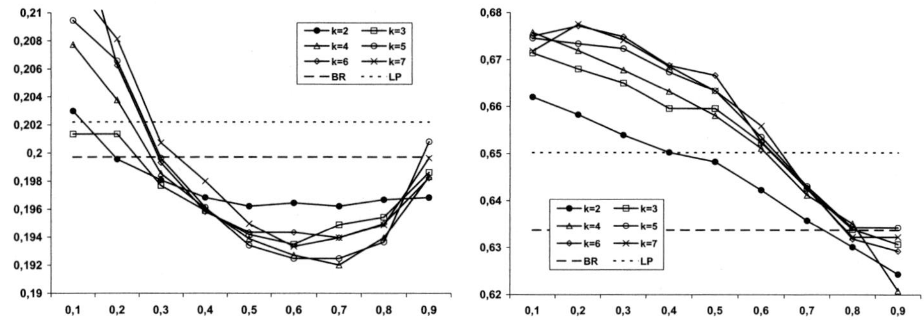

(a) (b)

Fig. 6. Hamming loss (a) and F-measure (b) of BR, LP and RAKEL for optimal m

In Figure 6(a), we notice that irrespectively of the subset size, RAKEL has lower Hamming loss than BR and LP for a range of t values (0.4 to 0.8). Regarding the different subset sizes, we notice high performance for $k = 4$ and $k = 5$ consistently for a range of t values (0.5 to 0.8). The lowest Hamming loss is achieved for k=4 and t=0.7. In Figure 6(b), we notice that similarly to the Hamming loss results, RAKEL has higher F-measure than BR and LP for a range of t values (0.1 to 0.6), but this time for $k > 2$. We also notice that compared to Hamming loss, the F-measure is favored by low threshold values. In fact, it seems that F-measure is linearly decreasing with t. The highest F-measure is achieved for $k = 7$ and $t = 0.2$. For $k > 4$ we notice consistently higher performance than for $k \leq 4$ for a range of t values (0.2 to 0.5).

5.3 *Tmc2007* Dataset

For the *tmc2007* dataset we present preliminary experiments for $k = 5$, $k = 7$ and m ranging from 1 to 50. Similarly to the previous datasets, Figures 7(a) and 7(b) show the Hamming loss and F-measure respectively (y-axis) of BR and

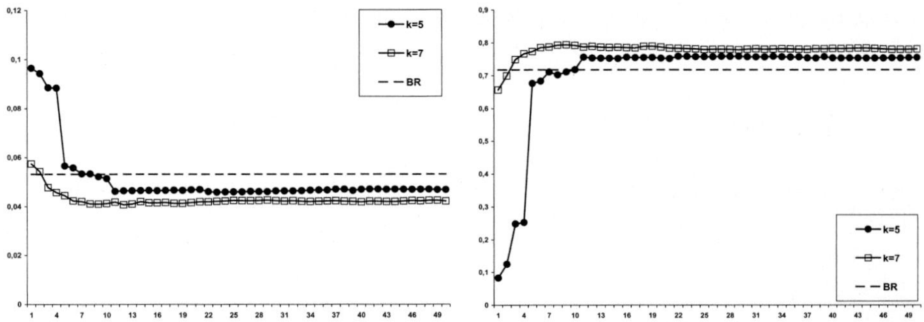

(a) (b)

Fig. 7. Hamming loss (a) and F-measure (b) of BR, LP and RAKEL for t=0.5

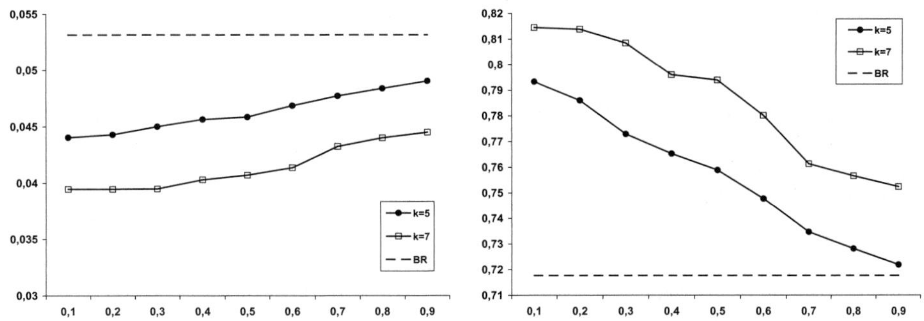

(a) (b)

Fig. 8. Hamming loss (a) and F-measure (b) of BR, LP and RAKEL for optimal m

RAKEL for $t = 0.5$, with respect to the number of iterations m (x-axis). The performance of the full LP classifier was not computed, due to the high memory requirements and computational complexity that comes from the high number of distinct subsets and the quadratic complexity of SVM with respect to the classes.

In Figure 7, we notice that RAKEL achieves better Hamming loss and F-measure than BR for both values of k after the first 10 models. For $k = 7$ the results are better than for $k = 5$. Once more, we conclude that RAKEL using the default $t = 0.5$ value has better performance than BR for a wide range of m values and for both the two k values of the preliminary experiments.

In Figures 8, we notice that irrespectively of the subset size and the threshold value, RAKEL has better Hamming loss and F-measure than BR. Similarly to the *yeast* dataset, we notice that the F-measure is linearly decreasing with t. This behavior of the F-measure with respect to the threshold is consistent in all three datasets, so we can conclude that low t values lead to higher F measure. Similar behavior is noticed for Hamming loss in this dataset, which is linearly increasing with respect to t. This result is different from the previous datasets where large t values seemed to favor Hamming loss.

6 Conclusions and Future Work

This paper has presented a new ensemble method for multilabel classification that is based on random projections of the label space. We train an ensemble of Label Powerset (LP) classifiers in this work and show that higher performance can be achieved than the popular Binary Relevance (BR) method and the LP classifier on the full set of labels. We consider the novel idea of label space projection an important contribution, as it offers a framework for the development of new multilabel ensemble methods, using different multilabel classifiers than LP at the base level and heuristic projection approaches, instead of random.

The latter issue definitely deserves further investigation, as the random nature of RAKEL may be leading to the inclusion of models that affect the ensemble's performance in a negative way. To alleviate this problem, we plan as future work to couple RAKEL with an ensemble selection method [23] in order to select those models that will lead to increased performance.

Acknowledgements

The authors would like to thank Robert Friberg for his valuable contribution in the development of the Java software for multilabel classification. This work is partly funded by the Greek General Secretariat for Research and Technology, project Regional Innovation Pole of Central Macedonia.

References

1. Li, T., Ogihara, M.: Detecting emotion in music. In: Proceedings of the International Symposium on Music Information Retrieval, Washington D.C., USA, pp. 239–240 (2003)
2. Clare, A., King, R.: Knowledge discovery in multi-label phenotype data. In: Siebes, A., De Raedt, L. (eds.) PKDD 2001. LNCS (LNAI), vol. 2168, pp. 42–53. Springer, Heidelberg (2001)
3. Diplaris, S., Tsoumakas, G., Mitkas, P., Vlahavas, I.: Protein classification with multiple algorithms. In: Bozanis, P., Houstis, E.N. (eds.) PCI 2005. LNCS, vol. 3746, pp. 448–456. Springer, Heidelberg (2005)
4. Roth, V., Fischer, B.: Improved functional prediction of proteins by learning kernel combinations in multilabel settings. In: Proceeding of 2006 Workshop on Probabilistic Modeling and Machine Learning in Structural and Systems Biology (PMSB 2006), Tuusula, Finland (2006)
5. Zhang, M.L., Zhou, Z.H.: Multi-label neural networks with applications to functional genomics and text categorization. IEEE Transactions on Knowledge and Data Engineering 18, 1338–1351 (2006)
6. Boutell, M., Luo, J., Shen, X., Brown, C.: Learning multi-label scene classification. Pattern Recognition 37, 1757–1771 (2004)

7. Kang, F., Jin, R., Sukthankar, R.: Correlated label propagation with application to multi-label learning. In: CVPR '06: Proceedings of the 2006 IEEE Computer Society Conference on Computer Vision and Pattern Recognition, New York City, NY, USA, pp. 1719–1726. IEEE Computer Society Press, Los Alamitos (2006)
8. Yang, Y.: An evaluation of statistical approaches to text categorization. Journal of Information Retrieval 1, 78–88 (1999)
9. McCallum, A.: Multi-label text classification with a mixture model trained by em. In: Proceedings of the AAAI' 99 Workshop on Text Learning (1999)
10. Schapire, R.E., Singer, Y.: Boostexter: a boosting-based system for text categorization. Machine Learning 39, 135–168 (2000)
11. Tsoumakas, G., Katakis, I.: Multi-label classification: An overview. International Journal of Data Warehousing and Mining 3, 1–13 (2007)
12. Brinker, K., Furnkranz, J., Hullermeier, E.: A unified model for multilabel classification and ranking. In: Proceedings of the 17th European Conference on Artificial Intelligence (ECAI '06), Riva del Garda, Italy, pp. 489–493 (2006)
13. Elisseeff, A., Weston, J.: A kernel method for multi-labelled classification. Advances in Neural Information Processing Systems 14 (2002)
14. Godbole, S., Sarawagi, S.: Discriminative methods for multi-labeled classification. In: Dai, H., Srikant, R., Zhang, C. (eds.) PAKDD 2004. LNCS (LNAI), vol. 3056, pp. 22–30. Springer, Heidelberg (2004)
15. Crammer, K., Singer, Y.: A family of additive online algorithms for category ranking. Journal of Machine Learning Research 3, 1025–1058 (2003)
16. Zhang, M.L., Zhou, Z.H.: A k-nearest neighbor based algorithm for multi-label classification. In: Proceedings of the 1st IEEE International Conference on Granular Computing, pp. 718–721. IEEE Computer Society Press, Los Alamitos (2005)
17. Zhu, S., Ji, X., Xu, W., Gong, Y.: Multi-labelled classification using maximum entropy method. In: Proceedings of the 28th annual international ACM SIGIR conference on Research and development in Information Retrieval, pp. 274–281. ACM Press, New York (2005)
18. Ghamrawi, N., McCallum, A.: Collective multi-label classification. In: Proceedings of the 3005 ACM Conference on Information and Knowledge Management (CIKM '05), Bremen, Germany, pp. 195–200. ACM Press, New York (2005)
19. Srivastava, A., Zane-Ulman, B.: Discovering recurring anomalies in text reports regarding complex space systems. In: 2005 IEEE Aerospace Conference, IEEE Computer Society Press, Los Alamitos (2005)
20. Rogati, M., Yang, Y.: High-performing feature selection for text classification. In: CIKM '02: Proceedings of the eleventh international conference on Information and knowledge management, pp. 659–661 (2002)
21. Cristianini, N., Shawe-Taylor, J.: An Introduction to Support Vector Machines and other kernel-based learning methods. Cambridge University Press, Cambridge (2000)
22. Witten, I.H., Frank, E.: Data Mining: Practical machine learning tools and techniques. Morgan Kaufmann, San Francisco (2005)
23. Tsoumakas, G., Angelis, L., Vlahavas, I.: Selective fusion of heterogeneous classifiers. Intelligent Data Analysis 9, 511–525 (2005)

Seeing the Forest Through the Trees: Learning a Comprehensible Model from an Ensemble

Anneleen Van Assche and Hendrik Blockeel

Computer Science Department, Katholieke Universiteit Leuven, Belgium
{anneleen.vanassche,hendrik.blockeel}@cs.kuleuven.be

Abstract. Ensemble methods are popular learning methods that usually increase the predictive accuracy of a classifier though at the cost of interpretability and insight in the decision process. In this paper we aim to overcome this issue of comprehensibility by learning a single decision tree that approximates an ensemble of decision trees. The new model is obtained by exploiting the class distributions predicted by the ensemble. These are employed to compute heuristics for deciding which tests are to be used in the new tree. As such we acquire a model that is able to give insight in the decision process, while being more accurate than the single model directly learned on the data. The proposed method is experimentally evaluated on a large number of UCI data sets, and compared to an existing approach that makes use of artificially generated data.

Keywords: ensembles, decision trees, comprehensibility.

1 Introduction

In the process of knowledge discovery, one seeks to extract useful knowledge from data bases. But for knowledge to be useful, predictive accuracy is not sufficient: the extracted models also need to be understood by human users in order to trust them and accept them. Moreover users often construct models to gain insight in the problem domain rather than to obtain an accurate classifier only. For this reason, researchers have advocated machine learning methods which yield comprehensible models, such as decision tree learners and rule learners. Another issue in knowledge discovery is the stability of the classifier. A classifier may be very accurate and also comprehensible, but as long as the model is very instable, meaning that small changes in the data might have a large influence on the predictions of the model, users may have a hard time accepting it.

For quite some years now, a lot of interest has been shown to a class of learning methods called ensembles. The main goal in the design of ensemble methods is to increase the predictive accuracy of the classifier. And indeed, studies have shown the discrimination power of ensemble methods both theoretically and empirically [1,2,6], and in propositional as well as relational learning [12,11,5,17]. Ensemble methods are learning algorithms that first construct a set of (diverse) classification models and then classify new data points by combining the predictions of each of these models. Exactly by doing so, they are often able to increase

J.N. Kok et al. (Eds.): ECML 2007, LNAI 4701, pp. 418–429, 2007.

the stability and predictive accuracy significantly over the single models. On the other hand the comprehensibility of the learned hypothesis drops significantly, since the result of an ensemble method is a large set of models with (weighted) votes connected to each of them, which obviously becomes harder to interpret.

Some authors have pointed out that striving for comprehensibility is one of the important issues in ensemble learning requiring future investigations [1,14]. Quite some successful research has been carried out already in this area. More in particular researchers have tried to obtain comprehensibility by means of extracting a new interpretable model from an existing (ensemble) model without sacrificing too much accuracy. Craven and Shavlik [4] presented an algorithm TREPAN for extracting comprehensible, symbolic representations from trained neural networks. TREPAN extracts a decision tree using the network as an oracle to answer queries during the extraction process. Domingos [7] proposed Combined Multiple Models (CMM). CMM first builds an ensemble of multiple models and then reapplies the base learner to recover the partitioning implicit in the multiple model ensemble. This is achieved by giving the base learner a new training set, composed of a large number of examples generated and classified according to the ensemble. Zhou et al. [19] utilize neural network ensembles to generate new instances and then extract symbolic rules from those instances. Ferri et al. [8] describe a method to learn a comprehensible model from an ensemble by selecting the single hypothesis from a multi-tree that is most similar to the combined hypothesis according to a similarity measure.

The approaches described above all rely on artificially generated data to tackle the problem of finding an interpretable model that approximates the ensemble: either by classifying this new data by the ensemble and constructing a new interpretable model on it, or by using this new data to measure similarity between the ensemble model and candidate interpretable models. However in some domains, generating artificial data is not straightforward: for instance when dealing with relational data, data distributions are far more complex and examples no longer have a fixed set of attributes.

For this reason, we propose a method to learn a single interpretable model from an ensemble without the need of generating artificial data. Instead of first generating artificial data and computing class distributions for different possible tests on this data, class distributions are estimated directly from the information available from the different decision trees in the ensemble in order to decide which tests are to be used in the new tree. In this paper we investigate how well this method performs in a propositional context, though most of its benefit might lie in a relational context, where other methods, based on artificial data, become hard to apply. We describe the proposed approach in detail in the next section. Afterwards it is evaluated on a large number of benchmark data sets comparing accuracy, complexity and stability to the original single tree and the ensemble classifier as well as to the single tree obtained by using the CMM method [7] that makes use of artificially generated data. In the last section we formulate conclusions and some ideas for future research.

2 Algorithm

In the remainder of the paper we will propose a method to learn a single decision tree from an ensemble that is constructed via bagging but the method applies to other ensemble learners such as boosting [9] or random forests [3] as well.

2.1 Motivation

Dietterich [6] describes three fundamental reasons why an ensemble may work better than a single classifier. The first reason is statistical: without sufficient data, a learner may find several different hypotheses that correctly classify all training data. Constructing an ensemble consisting of these different hypotheses and then averaging over them may reduce the risk of choosing a wrong hypothesis. The second reason is computational. By performing some form of local search, learning algorithms may end up in different local optima and an ensemble consisting of these classifiers may give a better approximation to the true unknown function than the individual classifiers. The last reason is representational. Often the true function cannot be represented by any of the hypotheses in the hypotheses space of the learner. By applying weighted voting among these hypotheses the hypotheses space may be expanded. However, in the particular case of ensembles of decision trees, the reason of representability does not hold: actually a single decision tree in itself is able to represent any function described over the instance space as it can separate the instance space completely if necessary. The improvement obtained by ensembles of decision trees thus follows from the statistical and computational reasons. We aim to retain at least part of this improvement by constructing a tree that approximates the ensemble.

2.2 Constructing a Single Tree Exactly Representing an Ensemble

Assume E is an ensemble of N decision trees, which we would like to represent by one single decision tree. The ensemble E gives predictions to new examples x according to a combination of the predictions of each of its base trees, in this case the average:

$$L_E(x) = argmax_{C_i}(\frac{1}{N}\sum_{k}^{N} P_k(C_i|x)) \qquad (1)$$

As a decision tree is able to represent any function described over the instance space, there also exists a decision tree that exactly represents the function described by the ensemble. Depending on the order of the tests in the nodes, the tree that represents the same concept as the ensemble, can consist of up to 2^d leaves, with d the number of different tests in the ensemble. So although it represents the same concept as the ensemble, such a tree would not satisfy our needs, namely be interpretable and give insight in the ensemble's decisions, simply because it is too big. Very often even the smallest tree exactly representing the concept in the ensemble might be far too large to be considered interpretable and an approximation to the ensemble will be preferred over the exact representation of the ensemble.

2.3 Computing Heuristics from the Ensemble

In order to give insight into the ensemble, the tests placed in the nodes of the new tree should be the '*most informative*' nodes at that point according to the ensemble. Usually tests with a higher information gain or gain ratio are considered more informative than tests with a lower value for these heuristics. So we need a way of computing these heuristics from the ensemble. The aim is to approximate the concept in the ensemble, therefore the class distributions predicted by the ensemble are used and not those directly available in the training data. Let's say we want to compute which test has the highest information gain according to the ensemble in a certain node n of the new tree. Suppose B is the conjunction of tests that occurred along the path from the root until node n, then the regular formula of information gain IG for a certain test T in n is

$$\begin{aligned} IG(T|B) = entropy(B) \quad & -P(T|B)entropy(T \wedge B) \\ & -P(\neg T|B)entropy(\neg T \wedge B) \end{aligned} \tag{2}$$

where

$$entropy(A) = \sum_{i=1}^{c} -P(C_i|A) \log_2 P(C_i|A) \tag{3}$$

with c the total number of classes, C_i the ith class and A any set of conditions.

A decision tree is constructed to model class distributions in the data and thus can be used to estimate these $P(C_i|A)$. Suppose we have a decision tree DT_k, now for any A we can estimate $P(C_i|A)$ by propagating it through the tree, applying the law of total probability in each node, until we end up in the leaves. Then we get:

$$P_k(C_i|A) = \sum_{\text{leaves } l_{kj} \text{ in } DT_k} P(C_i|Y_{kj} \wedge A)P(Y_{kj}|A) \tag{4}$$

where Y_{kj} is the conjunction of tests from the root of tree DT_k until leaf l_{kj} and $P_k()$ is the estimate of $P()$ by tree DT_k. The class probability estimate $P_E(C_i|A)$ of the ensemble E is then the average over the class probability estimates $P_k(C_i|A)$ of the N trees in E.

Now the probability $P(C_i|Y_{kj} \wedge A)$ corresponds to the probability estimate $P_k(C_i|Y_{kj})$ given by leaf l_{kj} (by using example frequencies in that leaf). Indeed, either $A \subseteq Y_{kj}$ and $P(C_i|Y_{kj}) = P(C_i|Y_{kj} \wedge A)$ or , $A \nsubseteq Y_{kj}$ and then we can assume that the class C_i is conditionally independent from the tests in A given the tests in Y_{kj}, because if not, the leaf l_{kj} would have been split at least once more on a test $T \in A \setminus Y_{kj}$.

For the other probability $P(Y_{kj}|A)$, we can distinguish 3 possible cases:

- $Y_{kj} \subseteq A$: then $P(Y_{kj}|A) = 1$ and for other leaves $Y_{kl} : P(Y_{kl}|A) = 0$ hence $P_k(C_i|A) = P_k(C_i|Y_{kj})$
- $\exists T : T \in Y_{kj}, \neg T \in A$: then $P(Y_{kj}|A) = 0$ and leaf l_{kj} of tree DT_k will not contribute in the probability $P_k(C_i|A)$

– else: $0 < P(Y_{kj}|A) < 1$ and leaf l_{kj} of tree DT_k partly contributes to the probability $P_k(C_i|A)$

To be able to estimate these probabilities $P(Y_{kj}|A)$ from the trees, we need to make the assumption that Y_{kj} is conditionally independent from $A \setminus \{Te \in A | Te \in Y_{kj} \vee \neg Te \in Y_{kj}\}$. Then $P(Y_{kj}|A) = P(Y_{kj}|\{Te \in A | Te \in Y_{kj} \vee \neg Te \in Y_{kj}\})$, which can be estimated from the tree by looking at the proportion of examples in the tree fulfilling these constraints. This assumption is exactly the same as made by Quinlan [13], when classifying instances with missing values by a tree. But since decision trees are not specifically constructed to model distributions among the tests, another, maybe better way to estimate the probabilities $P(Y_{kj}|A)$ is by computing them on the training set (if the test set is already available, using both training and test set might provide an even better estimate). The same holds for the $P(T|B)$, as requested in equation 2.

Using the method described above to compute the information gain for tests according to an ensemble E, a decision tree is built representing the ensemble E, each time replacing a leaf n in the tree by an internal node as long as we can find a test T where $IG_E(T|n) \geq IG_E(T_i|n)$ and $IG_E(T|n) > 0$ for all possible tests T_i. On the other hand, if $IG_E(T_i|n) = 0$ for all tests T_i, all examples ending up in n will be labeled the same by the ensemble, and no further splitting is required to represent the ensemble.

2.4 Stop Criteria

The tree obtained using the method described above (where all probabilities are estimated from the ensemble), represents the ensemble but is often very large and also constructing it will be very time consuming. For that reason, it will be necessary to impose some stop criteria to avoid the tree from becoming too big. First we describe a way to do safe prepruning in order to avoid splits to be added that will not have an influence on the predicted class. This will not change the eventual predictions of the tree. Next, we will impose a none equivalence preserving stop criterion, to make the tree even more interpretable.

Safe Prepruning. At the end of the tree construction, some redundant splits will still be present in the tree, as they might change the class distributions in the leaves but not the eventual classes predicted by the leaves. Usually in decision tree algorithms, these nodes are removed by postpruning. The same can be applied here, but since the tree deduced from an ensemble usually becomes rather large, quite some time might be spent in adding all these redundant splits and it would be desirable to preprune the tree if possible.

We will check whether indeed all possible examples that end up in a node n of the new tree will be predicted the same class by the ensemble as follows. Examples that end up in n are examples that succeed for D_n, where D_n is the conjunction of tests along the path from the root until node n of the new tree. For each tree DT_k of the ensemble we keep track of the possible leaves l_{kj} in that tree where these examples fulfilling D_n might end up. Each of these leaves l_{kj}

gives a prediction of the probability of a class $P(C_i|Y_{kj})$, with Y_{kj} the tests along the path from the root of tree k to leaf l_{kj}. Then we can define a lower bound on the class probability prediction of the ensemble E for examples fulfilling D_n as follows:

$$P_{Emin}(C_i|D_n) = \frac{1}{N}\sum_k \min_{l_{kj}^{D_n}} P(C_i|Y_{kj})$$

and equivalently an upper bound:

$$P_{Emax}(C_i|D_n) = \frac{1}{N}\sum_k \max_{l_{kj}^{D_n}} P(C_i|Y_{kj})$$

where $l_{kj}^{D_n}$ are all the leaves in DT_k where examples satisfying D_n can possibly end up. Then if

$$\exists C \in \mathcal{C}, \forall C_i \in \mathcal{C} \setminus \{C\} : P_{Emin}(C|D_n) > P_{Emax}(C_i|D_n)$$

(where $\mathcal{C}$ contains all possible class values), all examples in n will be predicted as C by the ensemble, and the tree should not be split any further in that node.

None Equivalence Preserving Stop Criterion. As mentioned before, the tree constructed using safe prepruning might still be very large. Because of this, we will introduce another stop criterion, such that a more comprehensible approximation to the ensemble is obtained. If all training examples ending up in a node are classified the same by the ensemble, no further splitting will be performed and the node will become a leaf. As a consequence, the training examples will be labeled the same by the new tree as by the ensemble, but for other new examples this is not necessarily the case.

3 Implementation

The method described above was implemented in the WEKA data mining system [18]. Bagging with J48 (WEKA's C4.5) as base learner was used as the ensemble to start from. Theoretically it is sufficient to use the tests that were used in the ensemble in order to represent the hypothesis of the ensemble by a single tree. And also intuitively, it makes sense only to use these tests to construct a new tree as these were probably the most important amongst all possible tests. Moreover in practice, tests not appearing in the ensemble will always have a lower information gain than the tests appearing in the ensemble and would never be chosen. As detailed in Section 2.3, to find the best test in a certain node of the new tree, each of the possible candidate tests are assigned a heuristic value by propagating them through the ensemble trees, and using the class probability estimates of the leaves they end up in. To estimate the probability that examples satisfying a set of tests A end up in a certain leaf Y_{kj} (so $P(Y_{kj}|A)$) or to find the probability of a certain test T given the tests B appearing already in the new tree along the path from the root until the current node, we can either use the ensemble or the data as indicated before. We distinguish the following three cases in the implementation:

1. both $P(Y_{kj}|A)$ from equation 4 and $P(T|B)$ from equation 2 are estimated from the trees in the ensemble. Then the assumption is made that Y_{kj} is independent from $A \setminus \{Te \in A | Te \in Y_{kj} \vee \neg Te \in Y_{kj}\}$, the same for $P(T|B)$. This means we assume tests are independent from each other unless the tree indicates they're not. [**Ism_t**]
2. $P(Y_{kj}|A)$ from equation 4 is estimated from the ensemble assuming independencies as above, but $P(T|B)$ is estimated from the available data. [**Ism_td**]
3. both $P(Y_{kj}|A)$ and $P(T|B)$ are estimated from the available data, and only the conditional class probabilities are estimated from the ensemble. [**Ism_d**]

Without using the stop criterion based on the data, applying Ism_t will result in a (often very large) tree that exactly represents the decisions of the ensemble. This is no longer necessarily the case when applying Ism_td or Ism_d as probabilities on the data are used and they might be 0 if no data is available for certain conditions. As 'available data' we usually have the training data to estimate certain probabilities. Sometimes the test set is also available on beforehand, or in a transductive learning setting, unlabeled examples might be at our disposal. When data is used to compute probabilities, the predictions of the new tree will be equivalent to those of the ensemble at least for all provided (unlabeled) instances. For other unseen examples there is no guarantee as the (shorter) tree is now only an approximation to the ensemble.

We also implemented Cmm as described by Domingos [7]. But while the original version describes it for rule sets, for comparison with our method, we applied the general framework to decision trees. N artificial examples are generated as follows: suppose we have m trees obtained via bagging, then Cmm generates N/m examples from each tree. For each leaf in the tree, if it classified r of the s examples in the bootstrap sample it was induced from, $(r/s)(N/m)$ examples covered by it will be generated. For each example this is done by ensuring that it satisfies all the tests from the root of the tree until that leaf, and beyond that by setting the values of its attributes according to a uniform distribution. The label of the new example is the prediction given by the ensemble. After having constructed a new training set, J48 is again applied to learn a new tree.

4 Empirical Evaluation

We will investigate empirically whether the proposed method can indeed retain some of the accuracy and stability gains of bagging while providing a more interpretable model. Experiments were carried out using a representative sample of 34 data sets from the UCI repository [10]. We omitted a few data sets where bagging performed worse than a single model, as these are cases where it actually makes no sense to apply the method described above. We used 25 iterations of bagging. This was also described by Domingos [7] to be a sufficiently large number: 50 models did not perform significantly better, while 10 models led to poor

Table 1. Win-draw-loss table using a 90% two-tailed significance test comparing the different algorithms on 34 benchmark data sets from the UCI repository

(w/d/l)	Bagging	Ism_t	Ism_td	Ism_d	Cmm(up)	Cmm(p)	Ism_tu	Ism_tdu	Ism_du
J48	(19/15/0)	(9/25/0)	(9/25/0)	(6/23/5)	(5/25/4)	(5/29/0)	(17/17/0)	(19/15/0)	(18/16/0)
Bagging	/	(0/13/21)	(0/13/21)	(0/12/22)	(0/12/22)	(0/9/25)	(0/31/3)	(0/31/3)	(0/31/3)
Ism_t	/	/	(5/26/3)	(1/22/11)	(1/22/11)	(2/23/9)	(19/15/0)	(19/15/0)	(19/14/1)
Ism_td	/	/	/	(1/19/14)	(0/24/10)	(1/25/8)	(18/16/0)	(18/16/0)	(18/16/0)
Ism_d	/	/	/	/	(4/23/6)	(8/23/3)	(19/15/0)	(20/14/0)	(19/15/0)
Cmm(up)	/	/	/	/	/	(8/25/1)	(21/13/0)	(21/13/0)	(21/13/0)
Cmm(p)	/	/	/	/	/	/	(24/10/0)	(24/10/0)	(24/10/0)
Ism_tu	/	/	/	/	/	/	/	(2/32/0)	(2/32/0)
Ism_tdu	/	/	/	/	/	/	/	/	(0/34/0)

results. The number of artificial examples generated by Cmm to learn a new tree was set to 1000, augmented with the training examples[1]. As Cmm applies J48 after generating new data, C4.5's pruning procedure could be used as well: we both build a pruned (Cmm(p)) and an unpruned tree (Cmm(up)) on the data. We compare the different versions of the Ism method (Ism_t, Ism_td, Ism_d as detailed in Section 3) all using the stop criteria described in Section 2.4. For deciding on stopping and (if necessary) estimating probabilities, these versions are only provided with the training data. Moreover we also evaluate the same algorithms in a transductive learning setting where also the unlabeled test instances are provided (Ism_tu, Ism_tdu, Ism_du). All results were obtained averaging over five 10-fold cross-validations. Binary decision trees were used in all methods.

4.1 Predictive Accuracy

Table 1 describes the significant wins and losses on the 34 data sets comparing the different algorithms to each other, to J48, Bagging and Cmm.

Comparing the different versions of Ism we find that Ism_d is clearly inferior to the other two versions that make more use of information available in the ensemble instead of the data. It is significantly outperformed on 11 data sets by Ism_t and on 14 by Ism_td while it outperforms those only on one data set. Moreover Ism_d was also significantly outperformed by J48 on some data sets, while this is not the case for the other versions of Ism. For space limitations and as it is clearly inferior we will not consider Ism_d in further results. Table 2 shows more detailed accuracy results for all data sets. As can be seen, the other versions were able to do at least as good as J48, but in almost all cases accuracies were higher (9 significantly).

Surprisingly the unpruned version of Cmm did not improve the results of J48. This might support the claim of Domingos [7] that a good match is needed between the learner's bias and that of the probability estimation procedure and that estimating probabilities from the frequencies in the leaves of the trees in

[1] Note that the results for Cmm and bagging here do not easily compare to the results obtained by Domingos [7]. This is because both the base learner of bagging as the learner for Cmm differ from [7], moreover a different set of data sets was used.

Table 2. Test accuracy of the different algorithms on some benchmark data sets from the UCI repository

Data Set	J48	Bagging	ISM_t	ISM_td	CMM(up)	CMM(p)	ISM_tu	ISM_tdu
anneal.ORIG	92.65	94.07 ∘	93.52	93.94	94.63 ∘	94.28 ∘	93.76	94.12 ∘
audiology	78.26	80.50 ∘	81.47 ∘	80.94 ∘	80.86 ∘	80.13	80.50 ∘	80.50 ∘
autos	76.21	79.59	79.88 ∘	80.58 ∘	78.49	77.32	79.10	79.59
balance-scale	77.59	81.30 ∘	79.15 ∘	79.05 ∘	79.09 ∘	79.98 ∘	81.20 ∘	81.20 ∘
breast-cancer	69.95	71.67	70.49	70.20	67.48	69.65	71.67	71.67
breast-w	94.99	96.02 ∘	95.19	95.16	95.22	95.22	96.02 ∘	96.05 ∘
car	97.16	97.35	97.50	97.42	97.15	97.05	97.35	97.35
cmc	52.96	52.74	52.23	51.62	49.69	52.34	52.73	52.74
colic	85.57	85.25	85.35	85.46	82.70 •	85.52	85.41	85.41
credit-a	83.91	85.10	83.97	83.77	81.86 •	83.91	85.13	85.10
credit-g	69.70	74.30 ∘	72.38 ∘	71.88 ∘	67.38 •	71.04	74.30 ∘	74.30 ∘
cylinder-bands	73.52	78.78 ∘	75.81	76.93	72.48	72.85	78.89 ∘	78.78 ∘
dermatology	95.35	96.11	95.41	95.52	95.18	95.73	96.11	96.11
glass	70.97	73.65	68.02	69.44	68.70	67.36	73.65	73.65
heart-c	76.88	80.28 ∘	79.55	79.15	79.02	79.09	80.41 ∘	80.28 ∘
ionosphere	90.59	92.70	91.92	92.04	91.51	91.16	92.70	92.70
iris	94.67	95.33	95.33	95.20	95.07	95.47	95.33	95.33
kropt	77.95	80.88 ∘	80.94 ∘	80.75 ∘	77.39 •	78.16 ∘	80.81 ∘	80.82 ∘
letter	88.31	93.50 ∘	89.67 ∘	89.69 ∘	88.23	88.16	93.50 ∘	93.50 ∘
liver-disorders	65.16	70.50 ∘	66.36	67.86	66.94	67.46	70.50 ∘	70.50 ∘
lymph	73.05	81.27 ∘	77.20	76.64	76.62	75.32	81.27 ∘	81.27 ∘
mfeat-pixel	88.30	93.00 ∘	89.17	89.55 ∘	87.36	87.53	93.00 ∘	93.00 ∘
nursery	99.31	99.59 ∘	99.56 ∘	99.56 ∘	99.43 ∘	99.36 ∘	99.56 ∘	99.56 ∘
optdigits	90.94	95.59 ∘	90.40	90.83	90.99	90.88	95.59 ∘	95.59 ∘
page-blocks	96.89	97.33 ∘	97.01	97.05	96.86	97.05	97.33 ∘	97.33 ∘
primary-tumor	43.07	45.96 ∘	43.83	43.18	43.07	44.07	45.78	45.95 ∘
segment	96.93	97.52 ∘	96.61	97.01	96.85	96.87	97.52 ∘	97.52 ∘
sonar	74.05	80.05	70.32	71.63	70.00	71.55	80.05	80.05
soybean	91.81	92.39	91.25	91.42	91.16	91.63	91.22	91.48
tae	58.25	60.81	60.97	60.97	61.07	60.43	60.81	60.81
tic-tac-toe	94.26	97.60 ∘	96.79 ∘	96.89 ∘	96.30 ∘	96.43 ∘	97.60 ∘	97.60 ∘
vehicle	73.87	75.32	74.47	74.82	72.67	72.60	75.32	75.32
yeast	55.46	61.07 ∘	57.18 ∘	56.35	55.72	56.52	61.07 ∘	61.07 ∘
zoo	91.09	91.67	91.89	91.89	91.47	91.87	91.67	91.67
average accuracy	80.58	83.2	81.49	81.6	80.54	81	83.14	83.17
(∘/ / •)		(19/15/0)	(9/25/0)	(9/25/0)	(5/25/4)	(5/29/0)	(17/17/0)	(19/15/0)

∘, • statistically significant improvement/degradation over J48

the ensemble is not the best way to go. Pruning of these CMM trees on the other hand increased overall performance.

Although ISM also estimates class probabilities from the frequencies in the leaves, it is less disturbed by it. ISM seems to retain more of the accuracy gains of bagging than CMM(p) did: it outperforms J48 in more cases, its average accuracy is slightly higher, and moreover it is in less cases significantly different from bagging than CMM(p). Also comparing ISM and CMM(p) directly to each other we find that while ISM_t and ISM_td win 9 and 8 times significantly of CMM(p), CMM(p) wins respectively only 2 and 1 time.

If we take a look at the results for the transductive learning setting (rightmost two columns in Table 2), where the unlabeled test set is also provided to ISM, we see that ISM is able to retain usually all of bagging's accuracy gain on the test set. This means that, for the provided examples, ISM can give exactly the decisions needed to label these examples as the bagging ensemble does. Note that these decisions might not necessarily be sufficient to classify unseen examples exactly as the ensemble does.

Table 3. Average relative model size compared to J48 and CMM(p) of the different models

	CMM(p)	CMM(up)	Bagging	ISM_t	ISM_td	ISM_tu	ISM_tdu
J48	1.82	3.08	25.73	3.28	2.4	3.36	2.5

4.2 Comprehensibility

To compare the comprehensibility of different models usually the complexity of the model is considered. As all the models we are dealing with consist of decision trees, we can here define the complexity of a model to be the number of nodes occurring in the tree[2]. Assuming a single tree learned with J48 provides a comprehensible model, we compare the complexity of the new models to that of J48. Table 3 reports the average relative model size of a model X to J48 ($nb\_nodes(X)/nb\_nodes(\mathrm{J48})$).

As could be expected, the model size of a bagged ensemble (of 25 iterations) is about 25 times larger than that of a single model. ISM_td is able to reduce this to 2.4 times. Provided we are dealing with binary trees, this means that in a tree built with ISM_td on average only 1.2 extra tests are occurring on a path from the root to a leaf compared to a tree built by J48. In general, models induced by ISM_t are slightly larger than those of ISM_td. Since the information gain is completely estimated from the ensembles, in ISM_t splits might occur where all training examples go in one branch. In ISM_td, tests that give rise to such splits will get an information gain of zero as the probability that examples end up in one of the branches is computed on the training set. Additionally, the more (labeled or unlabeled) data is provided, the larger the models induced by ISM can become. The complexity of CMM with pruning is still smaller than that of ISM_td. Overall we assume that, provided an end-user is able to interpret a tree induced by J48, he should be able to interpret a tree induced by ISM as well.

4.3 Stability

Semantic stability is often measured by estimating the probability that models generated by the same learner on different training sets will give the same prediction to a randomly selected instance. Following the method described by Turney [15], for each data set 1000 unlabeled examples were generated from a uniform distribution and predictions of models obtained on the different folds of the data in cross-validations were compared to each other. The exact formula of the stability S of a certain learner X is then given below:

$$S(X) = \frac{1}{1000}\sum_{i=0}^{1000}[\frac{2}{(n-1)n}\sum_{k=1}^{n}\sum_{l=0}^{k-1}\delta(X_k(i), X_l(i))] \tag{5}$$

[2] Note that in case of an ensemble this is still an overly optimistic measure for comprehensibility because to understand the decisions it is not sufficient to look at all tests used in the trees but also how the trees are combined.

Table 4. Average stability of the different models

J48	Bagging	ISM_t	ISM_td	CMM(up)	CMM(p)	ISM_tu	ISM_tdu
73.74%	80.73%	74.89%	74.51%	76.08%	76.63%	75.64%	75.26%

where n is the number of folds, $X_k(i)$ is the prediction for example i from the model learned by learner X on fold k and $\delta(L, M)$ is 1 if L equals M else 0.

Table 4 presents the average stability of the different algorithms over all data sets. As can be seen, ISM is able to increase the stability only with about 1% over J48. Providing ISM with more information about the complete data distribution (by offering extra unlabeled data[3]) results in a further small increase of the stability. Bagging on the other hand, led to an improvement of 7% and CMM 2.8%. While ISM retains more of the accuracy gain of bagging than CMM, CMM seems to preserve more of the stability gain.

5 Conclusions and Future Work

In this paper we presented a method to learn a decision tree that approximates the decisions made by an ensemble of decision trees. The tree is constructed without the need of generating artificial data. Instead, heuristics are computed for each of the possible tests by predicting class distributions for these tests using the ensemble. We show that we indeed obtain a tree that is able to retain some of the accuracy (and less of the stability) gains of bagging, while providing a model that keeps most of the comprehensibility of a single model directly learned on the data. Moreover the method can easily benefit from a transductive learning setting, where unlabeled instances are already available in the training phase. The supplied examples will be predicted the same as the ensemble by the new tree. Our method is also clearly competitive with an existing approach CMM, which makes use of artificially generated data. In general, our method outperforms CMM with respect to accuracy, while CMM has a higher stability. Since for CMM postpruning was very beneficial, both in terms of accuracy and complexity, this should be considered as future work for our method as well. To ensure comprehensibility of the obtained model one might even want to impose user defined size constraints on the model. The effect on the accuracy of constraining the size of the models further should be investigated. We would also like to assess our method using other ensemble learners, such as random forests and boosting. Furthermore this method should be extensively evaluated in the relational case. First experiments, reported in Van Assche et al. [16], already show promising results. Last, we would also like to extend the method for regression. This means a heuristic based on variance should be estimated from the ensemble instead of entropy. As variance is an additive measure, the variance for a certain test can be estimated based on the variances in the ensemble leaves that are consistent with the test.

[3] This is the unlabeled test data from the train-test folds, not the unlabeled data generated to compute the stability, if so, the stability would be the same as bagging.

Acknowledgements

Anneleen Van Assche is supported by the Institute for the Promotion of Innovation by Science and Technology in Flanders (I.W.T.-Vlaanderen). Hendrik Blockeel is Postdoctoral Fellow of the Fund for Scientific Research - Flanders (Belgium) (F.W.O.-Vlaanderen).

References

1. Bauer, E., Kohavi, R.: An empirical comparison of voting classification algorithms: Bagging, boosting, and variants. Machine Learning 36, 105 (1999)
2. Breiman, L.: Bagging predictors. Machine Learning 24(2), 123–140 (1996)
3. Breiman, L.: Random forests. Machine Learning 45(1), 5–32 (2001)
4. Craven, M.W.: Extracting Comprehensible Models from Trained Neural Networks. PhD thesis, University of Wisconsin, Madison (2003)
5. de Castro Dutra, I., Page, D., Costa, V., Shavlik, J.: An empirical evaluation of bagging in inductive logic programming. In: Proc. of the 12th International Conference on Inductive Logic Programming, pp. 48–65 (2002)
6. Dietterich, T.: Ensemble methods in machine learning. In: Proc. of the 1th International Workshop on Multiple Classifier Systems, pp. 1–15 (2000)
7. Domingos, P.: Knowledge discovery via multiple models. Intelligent Data Analysis 2, 187–202 (1998)
8. Ferri, C., Hernández-Orallo, J., Ramírez-Quintana, M.: From Ensemble Methods to Comprehensible Models. In: Lange, S., Satoh, K., Smith, C.H. (eds.) DS 2002. LNCS, vol. 2534, pp. 165–177. Springer, Heidelberg (2002)
9. Freund, Y., Schapire, R.E.: Experiments with a new boosting algorithm. In: Saitta, L. (ed.) Proc. of the 13th International Conference on Machine Learning, pp. 148–156. Morgan Kaufmann, San Francisco (1996)
10. Hettich, S., Blake, C.L., Merz, C.J.: UCI repository of machine learning databases (1998)
11. Hoche, S., Wrobel, S.: Relational learning using constrained confidence-rated boosting. In: Rouveirol, C., Sebag, M. (eds.) Proc. of the 11th International Conference on Inductive Logic Programming, pp. 51–64. Springer, Heidelberg (2001)
12. Quinlan, J.: Boosting first-order learning. In: Arikawa, S., Sharma, A.K. (eds.) ALT 1996. LNCS, vol. 1160, Springer, Heidelberg (1996)
13. Quinlan, J.R.: Induction of decision trees. Machine Learning 1, 81–106 (1986)
14. Ridgeway, G., Madigan, D., Richardson, J., adn O'Kane, T.: Interpretable boosted naive bayes classification. In: Proc. of the 4th International Conference on Knowledge Discovery in Databases, pp. 101–104. AAAI Press (1998)
15. Turney, P.: Bias and quantification of stability. Machine Learning 20, 23–33 (1995)
16. Van Assche, A., Blockeel, H.: Seeing the forest through the trees: Learning a comprehensible model from a first order ensemble. In: Proc. of the 17th International Conference on Inductive Logic Programming (to appear, 2007)
17. Van Assche, A., Vens, C., Blockeel, H., Džeroski, S.: First order random forests: Learning relational classifiers with complex aggregates. Machine Learning 64(1-3), 149–182 (2006)
18. Witten, I., Frank, E.: Data Mining: Practical Machine Learning Tools and Techniques, 2nd edn. Morgan Kaufmann, San Francisco (2005)
19. Zhou, Z., Jiang, Y., Chen, S.: Extracting symbolic rules from trained neural network ensembles. AI Communications 16(1), 3–15 (2003)

Avoiding Boosting Overfitting by Removing Confusing Samples

Alexander Vezhnevets and Olga Barinova

Moscow State University, dept. of Computational Mathematics and Cybernetics,
Graphics and Media Lab
119992 Moscow, Russia
{avezhnevets,obarinova}@graphics.cs.msu.ru

Abstract. Boosting methods are known to exhibit noticeable overfitting on some datasets, while being immune to overfitting on other ones. In this paper we show that standard boosting algorithms are not appropriate in case of overlapping classes. This inadequateness is likely to be the major source of boosting overfitting while working with real world data. To verify our conclusion we use the fact that any overlapping classes' task can be reduced to a deterministic task with the same Bayesian separating surface. This can be done by removing "confusing samples" – samples that are misclassified by a "perfect" Bayesian classifier. We propose an algorithm for removing confusing samples and experimentally study behavior of AdaBoost trained on the resulting data sets. Experiments confirm that removing confusing samples helps boosting to reduce the generalization error and to avoid overfitting on both synthetic and real world. Process of removing confusing samples also provides an accurate error prediction based on the work with the training sets.

1 Introduction

Problem of overfitting is one of the key problems in machine learning. Boosting was first believed to be immune to overfitting. It was even reported to eventually lower its test error while training after the training error reaches zero. Later, Dietterich [4] found that boosting is very sensitive to noise and overfits it greatly. Grove [11] and Friedman et al [9] noted that boosting actually overfits on some real-world datasets, although much less then one should expect from such general model after considerable amount of iterations.

The best explanation of boosting generalization capabilities so far is margin theory [26]. It was put under serious doubt by Briemans experiments, but was rehabilitated recently [22]. Margin theory provides an upper generalization bound independent of number of iterations made by boosting. This bound suggests that boosting may not overfit even if ran for many rounds. But as stated by authors: "unfortunately, however, in their current form, our upper bounds are too pessimistic to be used as actual numerical estimates of the error". Although margin theory explains why boosting may not overfit it does not provide any explanation why boosting actually does overfit in practice on real world data even with constant complexity base learner (stump). Domingos [5] showed the relation between margin theory explanation of boosting and

J.N. Kok et al. (Eds.): ECML 2007, LNAI 4701, pp. 430–441, 2007.

bias-variance explanation. He also made an interesting statement that reducing variance (increasing margins) is beneficial only for unbiased samples, while for biased samples it is preferable to have high variance (lower margin). Biased sample is a sample, for which the optimal prediction, for a given loss and the family of classifiers, differs from its current label. Freund & Schapire [7] in their discussion on Friedmans paper suggest that for overlapping classes (when Bayesian error is not zero) "AdaBoost is not the optimal method in this case". It should be noted that in real world applications it is a rare case if Bayesian error is zero and classes are perfectly separable due to imperfect feature vector representation of objects, limitations of measuring equipment and noise.

2 Related Work

After the discovery of the fact that boosting does overfit many works were devoted to explaining and avoiding this phenomenon. Several authors reported that boosting tends to increase the weights of few hard-to-learn samples, which leads to overfitting. Several modifications of the reweighting scheme were proposed that make weights change more smoothly. Domingo et al. [6] propose a modification of AdaBoost in which the weights of the examples are kept bounded by its initial value, however the authors admit no significant difference between AdaBoost and its modification in experiments on noisy data. Friedman [10] suggests that shrinking the weights of base hypothesis would increase boosting generalization capability.

The property of concentrating on few hard-to-learn patterns can be interpreted in terms of margin maximization; this view leads to regularized modifications. Ratsch et al. [21] view boosting as minimization of cost functional through an approximate gradient descent with respect to a margin. The authors propose regularization methods to achieve "soft margins" for AdaBoost which should avoid boosting from concentrating on misclassified samples with large negative margins. Friedman [10] also considers regularization methods through introducing proportional shrinkage into gradient boosting.

In contrast to regularization methods and weight shrinking methods, we do not penalize algorithm's behavior that can lead to overfitting and concentrate on removing samples that we prove to be harmful for boosting (Section 3.). We consider such approach more appropriate because it explicitly and strictly defines samples to be ignored, rather then penalize behavior that seems to lead to overfitting, but also may be the fitting of hard data.

Other authors see unboundness of loss function as the major source of overfitting. Viewing boosting as a gradient descent search for a good fit in function space allows modifying loss functions. Mason et al. [15] views boosting as gradient descent on an appropriate cost functional in a suitable inner product space. Proposed modification of boosting algorithm with normalized sigmoid cost function was reported to outperform AdaBoost when boosting decision stumps, particularly in the presence of label noise. Friedman [10] considers Huber loss function.

Rosset [23] proposes an approach of weight decay for observation weights which is equivalent to "robustifying" the underlying loss function. However the author admits that in experiments on real-world data there is no consistent winner between the non-decayed and the decayed versions of boosting algorithm.

In contrast to referenced methods, we see the main source of boosting overfitting not in an inappropriateness of particular loss function, but in general concept of average loss minimization (Section 3.). We show that this procedure is not adequate for tasks with overlapping classes'.

A large body of research addresses learning in the presence of noise. Robust statistics emerged in the 1960s in the statistical community [12]. However in classification tasks we cannot use the usual definition of robustness from statistics. In random classification noise model, the binary label of each example which the learner receives is independently inverted from the true label with fixed probability, which is referred to as the noise rate.

Krause & Singer [14] suggest employing EM algorithm and changing loss function to make boosting tolerant to known level of noise. Takenouchi & Eguchi [27] develop a modification of AdaBoost for classification noise case. The authors modify loss function and show that proposed method moderates the overweighting for outliers using a uniform weight distribution.

In contrast to the works described above we do not assume presence of classification noise and do not request any prior knowledge about data such as noise level. It should be noted that our method provides performance gain on real world data without adding artificial noise, while most methods show performance gain only if noise is present, and several even note degraded performance if no artificial noise added.

Previous research demonstrates that removing hard examples is worthwhile [17][16][1]. The main goal of these approaches is to enhance the classification accuracy by improving the quality of training data. These methods have various mechanisms to identify examples "suspicious, surprising or close to the boundary" [1]. In most works the decision as to which of the examples should be excluded is based on observations of algorithm behavior. In [17] analysis of dynamical evolution of AdaBoost weights is performed for estimating 'hardness' of every training example. Then the points with hardness above certain threshold, which is a parameter of the algorithm, are removed from the training set. In contrast to referenced works we explicitly and strictly define samples to be removed and propose non-parametric algorithm for removing these samples.

Our underlying concept resembles comments provided by Domingos [5] who states that increasing margin (lowering variance) for some samples can actually be harmful for the learner.

In this paper we study the reasons of overfitting of boosting in case of noiseless data with overlapping classes. In this case both samples $(x,+1)$ and $(x,-1)$ (considering binary classification task) can occur with positive probabilities. We show that minimization of average loss over the training set, which is used by all boosting-like algorithms, is not adequate in case of overlapping classes. We call training samples that have conditional probability of their own label lower than of the opposite "confusing samples". Forcing classifier to fit confusing samples by minimizing average loss over the training set can lead to non-optimal solutions. We view this as one of the main reasons of boosting overfitting on real-world data.

Removing confusing samples from the dataset leads to a deterministic task with the same Bayesian separating surface. This finding suggests that by removing these samples from training set we can enhance boosting capabilities and avoid overfitting.

Described below is the algorithm for removing confusing samples, which requires no prior information about data. We also show how generalization error can be predicted from the training set only, by estimating the amount of confusing samples. In order to support our conclusions we perform experiments on both synthetic and real world data from UCI-repository. Experiments confirm that removing confusing samples helps avoiding overfitting and increasing the accuracy of classification. The error prediction is also experimentally confirmed to be quite accurate.

Other sections of this paper are organized as follows. In section 3. we present reasoning explaining boosting inadequateness in case of overlapping classes. In section 4. we describe an algorithm for removing confusing samples from training set. Section 5 describes our experiments and section 6. is left for conclusion.

3 Average Loss and Confusing Samples

Let $T = (x_i, y_i), i = 1,...,n$ be the training set, where $x_i \in X$ is the vector of attributes and $y_i \in \{-1,+1\}$ is the class label (for simplicity we consider binary classification task). We take the assumption, that the pairs *(x,y)* are random variables distributed according to an unknown distribution $P(x, y)$.

We consider the general case of overlapping classes, which means that for some instances x the probability of both labels is positive.

$$\exists x : p(x,+1) > 0, p(x,-1) > 0$$

Definintion 1. Let us call $\{(x_i, y_i) \in T : P(-y_i \mid x_i) > 0.5 > P(y_i \mid x_i)\}$ "confusing samples". Samples $\{(x_i, y_i) \in T : P(-y_i \mid x_i) < 0.5 < P(y_i \mid x_i)\}$ will be called "regular samples".

Lemma 1. The fraction of confusing samples in the training set converges (in probability) to Bayesian rate with training set size increasing indefinitely.

Proof. Let us denote Bayesian rule by $B(x)$. The exposition immediately follows from classical Bernoulli theorem and the fact that confusing samples are those samples, which are misclassified by the perfect Bayesian classifier:

$$P(-y_i \mid x_i) > 0.5 > P(y_i \mid x_i) \Leftrightarrow B(x_i) = -y_i .$$

Lemma 1 says that in case of overlapping classes training set $T = (x_i, y_i), i = 1,...,n$ contains a mixture of regular and confusing samples; the fraction of confusing samples in the training set is governed by the value of Bayesian rate. This lemma provides us with error prediction algorithm, which will be described in section 4.1 .

Lemma 2. Removing all confusing samples from the training set reduces overlapping classes' task to a deterministic classification task with the same Bayesian separating surface.

Proof. Removing confusing samples leads to a deterministic classification task with conditional class distribution

$$\tilde{P}(y \mid x) = \begin{cases} 1, & P(-y \mid x) < 0.5 < P(y \mid x) \\ 0, & P(-y \mid x) \geq 0.5 \geq P(y \mid x) \end{cases} .$$

One can see that Bayesian rule for this derived task and original task are the same, which proves the lemma.

In standard boosting algorithms, training set is sequentially reweighed and fitted by weak learner in order to minimize average loss $C:\mathbb{R}\times\mathbb{R}\rightarrow\mathbb{R}$ on the training set:

$$\frac{1}{n}\sum_{i=1}^{n}C(y_i,F(x_i))\rightarrow\min_F,$$

where $F(x)$ is the current classifiers ensemble. In case of probabilistic setup, one seeks to minimize the conditional expectation of loss for all instances x [9]

$$E\big(C\big(y,F(x)\big)\,|\,x\big)=C\big(1,F(x)\big)P(1\,|\,x)+C\big(-1,F(x)\big)P(-1\,|\,x)$$

Consider overlapping classes' task. Let n stand for a number of samples with feature vector x in a given training set

$$\frac{1}{n}\sum_{i=1}^{n}C(y_i,F(x_i))=\sum_{x\in T}\left(\frac{n_x}{n}\times\frac{1}{n_x}\sum_{x_i=x}C\big(y_i,F(x)\big)\right)=$$

$$=\sum_{x\in T}\frac{n_x}{n}\times\left(\frac{1}{n_x}\cdot\sum_{x_i=x,y_i=+1}C\big(+1,F(x)\big)+\frac{1}{n_x}\cdot\sum_{x_i=x,y_i=-1}C\big(-1,F(x)\big)\right)=$$

$$=\sum_{x\in T}\frac{n_x}{n}\times\left(\frac{n_{x,+1}}{n_x}\cdot C\big(+1,F(x)\big)+\frac{n_{x,-1}}{n_x}\cdot C\big(-1,F(x)\big)\right),$$

where $n_{x,+1},n_{x,-1}$ respectively denote amount of samples $(x,+1)$ and $(x,-1)$.

Consider the score of a fixed instance x from T in average loss:

$$Score(x)=\frac{n_{x,+1}}{n_x}\cdot C\big(+1,F(x)\big)+\frac{n_{x,-1}}{n_x}\cdot C\big(-1,F(x)\big).$$

One can see that the score of every instance x from T in average loss converges to the conditional loss expectation with indefinitely increasing number of copies of instance x in training set. Training set can contain several copies of an instance only in case of very large and dense training set, that almost never holds in practice.

Usually $n_x=1$, and $Score(x)=C\big(y_i,F(x)\big)$. In this case minimizing the score of a confusing sample actually increases the true expectation of loss for the fixed instance. Broadly speaking, minimizing average loss means forcing classifier to fit all training samples, including the confusing samples, while correct classification of confusing samples is undesirable. Removing confusing samples reduces classification task with overlapping classes to deterministic, which makes PAC learning framework (in which boosting is formulated) directly applicable.

In this paper we rely on Lemma 2 and reduce task with overlapping classes' to a deterministic one with the same Bayesian separating surface. We propose an algorithm that removes confusing samples and experimentally study the performance of boosted stumps being trained on reduces training set.

4 Algorithm

Our goal is to roughly estimate the conditional probabilities of training set samples labels and to exclude those samples, for which

$$P(-y_i \mid x_i) > 0.5 > P(y_i \mid x_i).$$

A. Niculescu-Mizil and R. Caruana [19] suggested using Platt scaling or Isotonic regression to obtain calibrated probabilities from boosting. Platt's scaling method fits the sigmoid into raw classifier output, thus approximating posterior as:

$$P(y \mid x) \approx \frac{1}{1+\exp\left(A \cdot F(x)+B\right)}$$

We build an iterative process. During iterations we randomly divide data into 3 parts. We train a boosted committee on the first part, calibrate probabilities on the second and estimate posterior for samples labels in the third part (using the built classifier and estimated calibration parameters). We repeat this procedure several times. At each step we acquire an estimate of class probabilities for training instances. Posterior estimates for every sample are averaged.

Algorithm. Removing "confusing samples"

Input: A training set $T = \{(x_i, y_i)\}_{i=1}^{n}$; number of epochs K;

1. **for** k=1 to K
2. Divide a training set into three subsets $\bigcup_{i=1}^{3} T_k^i = T$ and $\bigcap_{i=1}^{3} T_k^i = \varnothing$
3. Train boosted weak learners on T_k^1 and obtain classifier $F^k(x)$
4. Estimate calibration parameters A and B for posterior output on T_k^2 using Platt scaling
5. Estimate posterior probability of labels for samples in T_k^3,

   $$p^k(y \mid x_i) \approx \frac{1}{1+\exp\left(A \cdot F^k(x_i)+B\right)}$$

6. **end for**
7. Calculate the average of posterior probability:

   $$p(y \mid x_i) = \underset{k:x_i \in T_k^3}{mean}\left(p^k(y \mid x_i)\right)$$

8. Construct reduced training set T' from those samples, for which

   $$\arg\max_y \left\{p(y \mid x_i)\right\} = y_i$$

9. return T'

Those samples that have average posterior probability estimate of their label lower than of its opposite are considered to be "confusing samples". After removing "confusing samples" the reduced training set can be learned by boosted committee.

Averaging of estimates was extensively studied in context of regression tasks [28]. Perrone [20] proved that averaging estimates always generates improved estimate in the sense of any convex optimization measure even without independence assumption on the estimates. Brieman [3] experimented with averaging class probability estimates obtained by learning decision trees on bootstrap replicates of the training set. He showed that averaging decreases error of class probability estimation.

Proposed algorithm is in relation with data editing approach [13] [24] [17]. Data editing methods are developed for improving the Nearest Neighbor classification accuracy by removing (or relabelling) outliers from the training set. In [13] [24] ensembles of neural networks, built by bagging, are employed to identify outliers. In contrast, we use calibrated boosted trees, which provide better posterior estimation [19].

4.1 Error Estimation

Since we are reducing classification task with overlapping classes to deterministic task, then the percent of detected confusing samples should, according to Lemma 1, be the prediction of error. Our experiments, described below, confirm this.

5 Experiments

In order to study the behavior of Boosting incorporated with removing of confusing samples we have conducted a set of experiments on both synthetic and real world data. We compare the performance of boosted stumps trained on full training set with boosted stumps trained on reduced dataset. We use Boosting algorithm described by Schapire, R., & Singer, Y. [25]. Stumps were chosen as base learners to avoid possible issues with base learner complexity [22].

5.1 Synthetic Data

We used two overlapping Gaussians to check our conclusions. Each Gaussian has standard deviation σ=1 and centers at *(1,0)* and *(-1,0)*. A perfect, Bayesian classifier would be a straight line coinciding with the second coordinate axis (a stump). We take 10000 random samples drawn from these Gaussians as a test set and randomly construct a training set of 200, 500 and 1000 samples. In each experiment the test set was fixed and the training set was randomly drawn from distribution. This was repeated for 100 times and the results were averaged. We measured the quality of pruning as the precision of detecting confusing and regular samples in the training set. We could do it explicitly since the Bayesian classifier is known. Precision is defined as

$$Pn = \frac{Tp}{Tp + Fp},$$

where *Tp* is the number of correct detections (of confusing or regular samples) and the *Fp* is the number of false positive detections. It is the ratio of correctly detected confusing or regular samples in the full set.

Figure 1 illustrates performance on our toy example. AdaBoost applied to full set overfitts greatly and produces cluttered separating surface. Removing confusing samples allows AdaBoost to produce smooth boundary, very close to Bayesian.

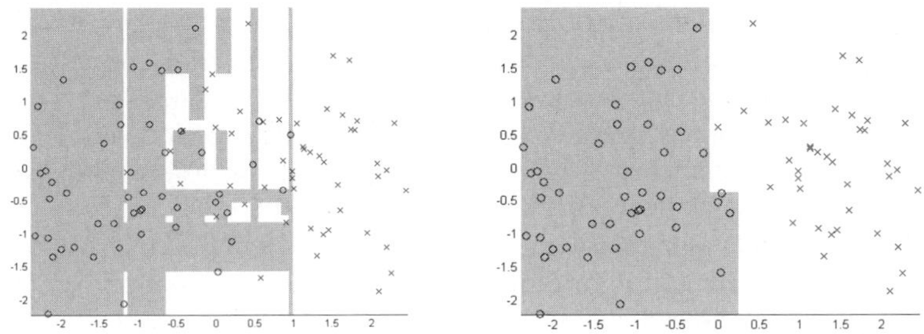

Fig. 1. Artificial data points and separating surfaces. From left to right: full dataset; dataset reduced by proposed algorithm.

Table 1 lists the results. It is clear that AdaBoost does overfit on confusing samples, especially in case of modest training set size. The estimated error comes to be quite consistent with actual error on the test set while is somewhat higher then error of the Bayesian classifier. Accuracy of error prediction is also confirmed by experiments on real world data presented in the next section. Looking at precision of pruning we can see that confusing samples precision is significantly lower then the precision of regular samples detection. This means that some percentage (10-15%) of removed samples is actually regular, while most (~98%) of samples marked as regular are marked correctly. It seems that losing some regular samples does not really degrade the performance of boosting, while removing the majority of confusing ones helps noticeably.

The more data we have, the closer is average loss to its expectation. Also, the less iterations boosting does, the smaller is the effect of overfitting. Thus, with a lot of data and after only few iterations AdaBoost should not noticeably overfit, while

Table 1. Test error (%) of AdaBoost trained on raw and reduced data, error estimation and pruning precision on synthetic data

Set Size	Estimated error	10 iterations		100 iterations		Bayesian classifier error		Regular samples precision	Confusing samples precision
		Full	Reduced	Full	Reduced	Train	Test		
200	16.48	17.38	**16.45**	19.72	**16.55**	15.49	16.07	97.93	89.26
500	16.39	16.13	**15.98**	17.38	**16.01**	15.70	15.66	98.05	86.04
1000	16.39	**16.14**	16.33	16.89	**16.37**	15.89	15.95	97.67	85.34

AdaBoost trained on reduced data may start suffering form underfitting, because of smaller training set. This happened in an experiment with training set containing 1000 samples and 10 iterations of boosting.

5.2 Measuring the Quality of Pruning on Real World Data

In case of synthetic data one can explicitly measure the error of confusing samples detection, but in case of real world data this is impossible. The important issue here is how to devise an appropriate metric for the quality of pruning algorithm for real world data. Consider dividing dataset into two parts and separately pruning both of them. If pruning is done correctly, a classifier trained on first reduced part is expected to misclassify samples marked as confusing in the other part and vice-versa. Thus, we propose to measure the precision of detecting regular and confusing samples by the classifier trained on the separate, reduced part of the same set.

The precision of regular samples detection is the ratio of samples that were marked as regular samples by pruning algorithm that were correctly classified by classifier trained on the separate, reduced subset. Analogously, precision of confusing samples detection is the ratio of samples marked as confusing in the set of samples that were misclassified by classifier trained on another separate, reduced subset.

Table 2. Test error (%) of AdaBoost trained on raw and reduced data; test error of MadaBoost and error estimation and pruning precision on various data sets

Dataset	Esti-mated	100 iterations Full	100 iterations Reduced	100 iterations Mada	1000 iterations Full	1000 iterations Reduced	1000 iterations Mada	Regular samples precision	Conf. samples precision
BREAST	3.73	4.6±0.08	**3.65±0.09**	4.01±0.09	4.77±0.1	**3.67±0.09**	4.15±0.22	98.83	72.91
AUSTRALIAN	13.06	15.2±0.17	**13.8±0.17**	14.93±0.23	17.68±0.17	**13.88±0.16**	16.23±0.64	96.78	74.43
GERMAN	24.66	25.72±0.16	25.35±0.14	**23.4±0.38**	28.4±0.18	25.05±0.16	**24.9±0.03**	91.22	71.54
HABERMAN	25.96	29.67±0.29	**26.33±0.31**	27.78±0.31	34.50±0.36	**26.37±0.32**	34.97±0.1	92.14	77.14
HEART	18.34	21.41±0.36	18.36±0.30	**16.66±0.58**	23.13±0.36	**18.07±0.30**	20.37±0.35	92.60	68.26
PIMA	24.03	25.58±0.20	**23.99±0.16**	25.26±0.17	28.07±0.20	**24.10±0.17**	28.26±0.12	93.38	79.29
SPAM	5.79	6.19±0.04	6.02±0.04	**5.59±0.03**	6.35±0.04	**5.97±0.04**	6.26±0.03	98.83	78.01
TIC-TAC-TOE	6.49	**8.47±0.20**	13.59±0.29	12.84±0.03	2.04±0.05	2.12±0.08	**1.67±0.07**	97.83	35.70
VOTE	4.51	4.75±0.13	**4.61±0.1**	5.51±0.43	5.90±0.14	**4.63±0.10**	7.35±0.29	99.51	88.84

5.3 UCI-Repository Data

In order to measure the performance of our algorithm on real world data we have selected 9 datasets from UCI-repository [2]. In our experiments we split the dataset in two subsets of equal size and use one subset for training and the other for testing and vice-versa. We measured the test error, pruning precision (as described above) and the error prediction from the training set (as described in section 2.3). This procedure was repeated 50 times for a total of 100 runs (50x2 cross-validation). We had to use equally sized training and test set to be able to measure the quality of pruning. We also compared our approuch with one of the regularized boosting methods, namely MadaBoost [6].

Table 2 presents the results of our experiments, the lowest error is shown in bold. AdaBoost trained on reduced dataset has lowest test error on 5 of 9 datasets if ran for 100 iterations and is best on 7 of 9 if ran for 1000 iterations. It performs better than AdaBoost trained on full set on all, but Tic-Tac-Toe dataset. The failure on Tic-tac-toe dataset is actually anticipated, because the data is perfectly separable and the Bayesian error is zero. As the number of learning iteration increases, AdaBoost trained on full dataset tends to overfit on most datasets, while AdaBoost trained on reduced data has almost non-increasing error very close to the predicted estimate. Moreover, MadaBoost is also prone to overfitting when ran for 1000 iterations despite regularization. This confirms our conclusions that the source of boosting overfitting are the confusing samples, and that for most real world data class overlapping is present.

Figure 2 provides test curves for two datasets. On Breast dataset AdaBoost does not have any significant gain in error with the increase of training iterations, what was also noted before [22], but it still benefits from pruning.

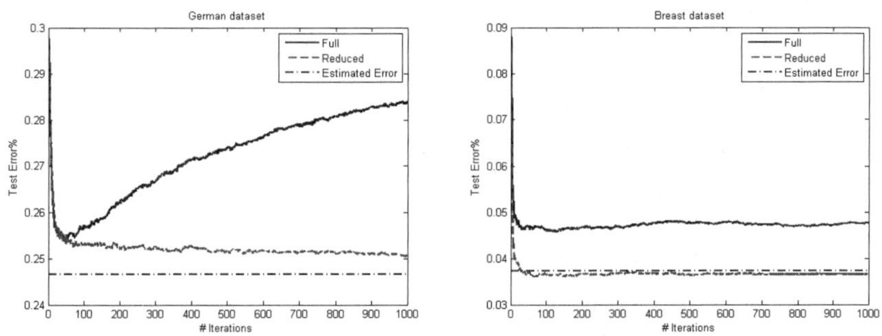

Fig. 2. Test and training error curves. From top left to bottom right: test error on German dataset; test error on Breast dataset.

5.4 Margins

It is common to interpret the performance of Boosting in terms of margins maximization. Figure 3 shows the cumulative margin for AdaBoost trained on full and reduced Breast and Tic-Tac-Toe datasets after 100 rounds of training. On Breast dataset AdaBoost trained on reduced dataset has lower minimal margin but has uniformly higher margin for the margins higher than a small threshold (0.03). Low minimal margin is a direct consequence of pruning – it is natural to expect negative margins for the removed samples. Pruning makes the data simpler and allows AdaBoost to maximize the margins of regular samples more efficiently. The behavior of margins on Tic-Tac-Toe is the same, but in case of Tic-Tac-Toe, gain in margins on lower cumulative frequencies is insignificant. Thus sacrificing minimal margin does not actually give any benefit and only worsens the performance.

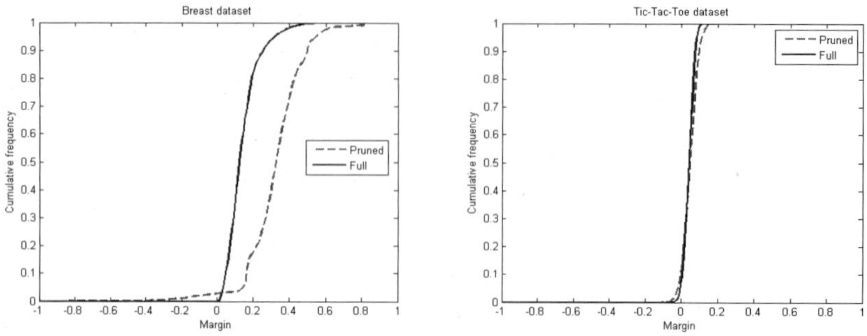

Fig. 3. Cumulative margins for AdaBoost trained on full and reduced dataset after 100 rounds. From left to right: Breast dataset; Tic-Tac-Toe dataset.

As pointed out by Reyzin & Schapire [22], margin theory would suggest sacrificing minimal margin for the higher margin at low cumulative frequencies. Removing confusing samples seems to make AdaBoost perform in such manner.

6 Conclusion

We described the problem of overfitting in boosting in case of overlapping classes. In this case, it is likely that overfitting is induced by fitting so called "confusing samples", that are samples misclassified by "perfect" Bayesian classifier. Overfitting in boosting seems to occur only when target distributions overlap or the noise is present, thus boosting could show no overfitting on some datasets and overfit greatly on others. An algorithm for removing the confusing samples is described, which is experimentally confirmed to help boosting get lower test error and avoid overfitting. We also show that by pruning confusing samples one can effectively predict the generalization error of the classifier by analyzing only the training set. We prove our conclusion by the experiments on both synthetic data and nine UCI-repository datasets.

Acknowledgments. Authors would like to thank Dr. D. Vetrov, D. Kropotov and Dr. V. Vezhnevets for inspiring discussions; and E. Vezhnevets for proof reading.

References

1. Angelova, A., Abu-Mostafa, Y., Perona, P.: Pruning Training Sets for Learning of Object Categories. In: Proc. IEEE Conf. on Computer Vision and Pattern Recognition (2005)
2. Blake, C.L., Merz, C.J.: UCI repository of machine learning databases (1998)
3. Breiman, L.: Bagging Predictors. Machine Learning 24, 2, 123–140 (1996)
4. Dietterich, T.G.: An experimental comparison of three methods for constructing ensembles of decision trees: Bagging, boosting, and randomization. Machine Learning 40(2) (1999)
5. Domingos, P.: A Unified Bias-Variance Decomposition for Zero-One and Squared Loss. In: Proc. of the 17th National Conference on Artificial Intelligence (2000)
6. Domingo, C., Watanabe, O.: Madaboost: A modication of adaboost. In: 13th Annual Conference on Comp. Learning Theory (2000)

7. Freund, Y., Schapire, R.: Discussion of the paper Additive logistic regression: a statistical view of boosting. Friedman, J., Hastie, T., Tibshirani, R., The Annals of Statistics 38, 2, 391–393 (2000)
8. Freund, Y.: An Adaptive Version of the Boost by Majority Algorithm. Machine Learning 43(3), 293–318 (2001)
9. Friedman, J., Hastie, T., Tibshirani, R.: Additive Logistic Regression: a Statistical View of Boosting. The Annals of Statistics 28, 2, 337–407 (2000)
10. Friedman, J.: Greedy function approximation: A gradient boosting machine. Annals of Statistics 29, 5 (2001)
11. Grove, A.J., Schuurmans, D.: Boosting in the limit: Maximizing the margin of learned ensembles. In: Proceedings of the Fifteenth National Conference on Artifical Intelligence (1998)
12. Hampel, F.R., Rousseeuw, P.J., Ronchetti, E.M., Stahel, W.A.: Robust Statistics: the Approach Based on Influence Functions. Wiley, New York (1986)
13. Jiang, Zhou: Editing training data for kNN classifiers with neural network ensemble. LNCS (2004)
14. Krause, N., Singer, Y.: Leveraging the Margin More Carefully. In: ACM International Conference Proceeding Series, vol. 69 (2004)
15. Mason, L., Baxter, J., Bartlett, P., Frean, M.: Boosting algorithms as gradient descent. In: Neural Information Processing Systems 12, pp. 512–518. MIT Press, Cambridge (2000)
16. Merler, S., Caprile, B., Furlanello, C.: Bias-variance control via hard points shaving. International Journal of PatternRecognition and Artificial Intelligence (2004)
17. Muhlenbach, F., Lallich, S., Zighed, D.A.: Identifying and handling mislabelled instances. Intelligent Information Systems 22, 1, 89–109 (2004)
18. Nicholson, A.: Generalization Error Estimates and Training Data Valuation, Ph.D. Thesis, California Institute of Technology (2002)
19. Niculescu-Mizil, A., Caruana, R.: Obtaining Calibrated Probabilities from Boosting. In: Proc. 21st Conference on Uncertainty in Artificial Intelligence (2005)
20. Perrone, M.: Improving regression estimation: Averaging methods for Variance reduction with extension to General Convex Measure Optimization, Ph.D. Thesis, Brown University (1993)
21. Ratsch, G.: Robust Boosting and Convex Optimization. Doctoral dissertation, University of Potsdam (2001)
22. Reyzin, L., Schapire, R.: How boosting the margin can also boost classifier complexity. In: Proceedings of the 23rd International Conference on Machine Learning (2006)
23. Rosset, S.: Robust Boosting and Its Relation to Bagging. In: KDD-05 (2005)
24. Sanchez, et al.: Analysis of new techniques to obtain quality training sets. Pattern Recognition Letters (2003)
25. Schapire, R., Singer, Y.: Improved Boosting Algorithms Using Confidence-rated Predictions. Machine Learning 37, 3, 297–336 (1999)
26. Schapire, R., Freund, Y., Bartlett, P., Lee, W.S.: Boosting the margin: A new explanation for the effectiveness of voting methods. In: Machine Learning: Proceedings of the Fourteenth International Conference (1997)
27. Takenouchi, T., Eguchi, S.: Robustifying AdaBoost by adding the naive error rate. Neural Computation 16 (2004)
28. Taniguchi, M., Tresp, V.: Averaging Regularized Estimators. Neural Computation (1997)

Planning and Learning in Environments with Delayed Feedback

Thomas J. Walsh, Ali Nouri, Lihong Li, and Michael L. Littman

Rutgers, The State University of New Jersey
Department of Computing Science
110 Frelinghuysen Rd., Piscataway, NJ 08854
{thomaswa,nouri,lihong,mlittman}@cs.rutgers.edu

Abstract. This work considers the problems of planning and learning in environments with constant observation and reward delays. We provide a hardness result for the general planning problem and positive results for several special cases with deterministic or otherwise constrained dynamics. We present an algorithm, Model Based Simulation, for planning in such environments and use model-based reinforcement learning to extend this approach to the learning setting in both finite and continuous environments. Empirical comparisons show this algorithm holds significant advantages over others for decision making in delayed environments.

1 Introduction

In traditional reinforcement learning [1], or RL, an agent's observations of its environment are almost universally assumed to be immediately available. However, as tasks and environments grow more complex, this assumption falters. For example, the Mars Rover program has tremendously broadened the theater of engagement available to roboticists, but direct control of these agents from Earth is limited by the vast communication latency. Delayed observations are also a challenge for agents that receive observations through terrestrial networks [2], such as the Internet or a multi-agent sensor network. Even solo agents that do advanced processing of observations (such as image processing) will experience delay between *observing* the environment, and *acting* based on this information. Such delay is not limited to a single timestep, especially when processing may occur in a pipeline of parallel processors. These scenarios involving delayed feedback have generated interest within the academic community, leading to the inclusion of a delayed version of the "Mountain Car" environment in the First Annual Reinforcement Learning Competition[1]. This paper considers *practical* solutions for dealing with constant observation and reward delays.

Prior work in the area of delayed environments dates back over thirty years [3] and several important theoretical results have been developed, including the insight that action and observation delays are two sides of the same coin [4] and that planning can be performed for both finite- and infinite-horizon delayed

[1] http://rlai.cs.ualberta.ca/RLAI/rlc.html.

J.N. Kok et al. (Eds.): ECML 2007, LNAI 4701, pp. 442–453, 2007.

MDPs or POMDPs using algorithms for their undelayed counterparts in much larger state spaces constructed using the last observation and the actions afterward [5,6]. We cover this and several other approaches for planning and learning in delayed environments in Section 3. We then show that such augmented approaches can lead to an exponential state space expansion and provide a hardness result for the planning problem in general delayed MDPs. In light of these results, we develop algorithms for planning and learning in four special cases of Markovian (if not for the delay) environments: finite and continuous worlds with deterministic transitions, "mildly stochastic" finite environments, and continuous environments with bounded noise and smooth value functions. In Section 5, we provide the *first* empirical studies of learning agents in such delayed environments. We assume throughout this work that the delay value is constant and provided to the planner or learner at initialization.

2 Definitions

A *finite* Markov Decision Process [7] is defined as a 5-tuple $\langle S, A, P, R, \gamma \rangle$, where S is a set of states, A is a set of actions, and P is a mapping: $S \times A \times S \mapsto [0, 1]$ indicating the probability of an action taking the agent from state $s \in S$ to state $s' \in S$. R is a mapping: $S \mapsto \Re$, which governs the reward an agent receives in state s (similar results to those in this paper hold for $R : S \times A \mapsto \Re$), and γ is the discount factor. A deterministic Markov policy, $\pi : S \mapsto A$, maps states to actions. We refer to such policies as *memoryless*, as they depend only on the current state. The value function $V^{\pi}(s)$ represents the expected cumulative sum of discounted reward, and satisfies the Bellman equation: $V^{\pi}(s) = R(s) + \gamma \sum_{s'} P(s, \pi(s), s')V^{\pi}(s')$. Every finite MDP has an optimal policy $\pi^* = \mathrm{argmax}_{\pi} V^{\pi}(s)$ and a unique optimal value function $V^*(s)$. Given an MDP, techniques exist for determining $V^*(s)$ and $\pi^*(s)$ in time polynomial in the size of the MDP [7].

In this work, we will also consider *continuous* MDP's where $S \subseteq \Re^n$ and A may also be continuous ($A \subseteq \Re^m$). Computing value functions in this case often requires approximation methods, an issue we treat in Sections 3.3 and 4.2.

We define a *constant delayed MDP* (CDMDP) as a 6-tuple $\langle S, A, P, R, \gamma, k \rangle$, where k is a non-negative integer indicating the number of timesteps between an agent occupying a state and actually receiving its feedback (the state observation and reward). We assume that k is bounded by a polynomial function of the size of the underlying MDP and the agent observes its initial state in response to each of its first k actions.

One may think of a CDMDP *policy* as a mapping from previous state observations and actions (that is, histories) to actions, since the current state is not revealed at the time an action is taken if $k > 0$. It is known that an optimal CDMDP policy can be determined using $I_k \in S \times A^k$, the last observation and previous k actions, following [5]. In light of this fact, we formally define a CDMDP policy as $\pi : (S \times A^k) \mapsto A$. The *CDMDP planning problem* is defined as: given a CDMDP, initial state I_k^0, and a reward threshold θ, determine whether a policy exists that achieves an expected discounted reward (from the initial state) of at least θ. In the *CDMDP learning problem*, an agent deployed in a delayed-feedback environment knowing only S, A, γ, and k is tasked with finding an optimal policy for the environment online.

The positive results of this paper pertain to the following special cases for the underlying (undelayed) Markovian dynamics:

I **Deterministic finite:** The undelayed MDP is finite and $\forall s \exists s' P(s,a,s') = 1$.
II **Deterministic continuous:** Same as Case I except S and A are continuous.
III **Mildly stochastic finite:** The undelayed MDP is finite and there is some $\delta \geq 0$ s.t. $\forall s \exists s' P(s,a,s') \geq 1 - \delta$. Case I is a degenerate case where $\delta = 0$.
IV **Bounded-noise continuous:** The underlying MDP is continuous, and transitions are governed by $s_{t+1} = T(s_t, a_t) + w_t$, where T is a deterministic transition function: $S \times A \mapsto S$, and w_t is bounded noise: $\|w_t\|_\infty \leq \Delta$ for some $\Delta \geq 0$. We further assume that the CDMDP's optimal value function is Lipschitz continuous when the action sequences for two I_k's coincide. That is, $|V^*(s, a_1, \cdots, a_k) - V^*(s', a_1, \cdots, a_k)| \leq C_V \|s - s'\|$ for some constant $C_V > 0$. This assumption is a consequence of smoothness of the underlying MDP's dynamics. We note that this case covers a wide class of dynamical systems, including those with linear transitions and bounded white noise.

3 Strategies for Dealing with Delay

We now cover several known methods for acting in delayed environments and introduce a new method for planning in the special cases covered above.

3.1 General Approaches

The first solution we consider is the **wait agent**, which "waits" for k steps, and acts using the optimal action in the undelayed MDP. More formally, this approach corresponds to a CDMDP policy of $\pi(I_k) = \pi^*(s)$ if $I_k = (s, \emptyset^k)$, and $\emptyset$ otherwise. Here, $\emptyset$ is the "wait" action. Some environments, such as Mountain Car, where the agent is rarely at a standstill, will not permit waiting, and even in those that do, the resultant policies will usually be suboptimal.

Another intuitive planning approach is to just treat the CDMDP as an MDP and use the **memoryless** policy $\pi(I_k) = \{\pi^*(s) \mid I_k = (s, a_1, \cdots, a_k)\}$. In some environments, this simple solution can produce reasonable policies, especially if the delay is relatively small compared to the magnitude of the state transitions. For the CDMDP learning problem, searching for the best policy that ignores delay is intimately connected to the search for good memoryless policies in POMDPs. One known technique that has shown empirical success in the latter theater is the use of eligibility traces [8], particularly in the online value-function-learning algorithm Sarsa(λ). Using $\lambda > 0$, the values of states in the same trajectory become "blurred" together, mitigating the effect of partial observability (in our case, delayed observations). As such, we include Sarsa(λ) in our empirical study (see Section 5) of the CDMDP Learning Problem.

The traditional method for modeling MDPs with constant delay is the **augmented** approach [5], which involves explicitly constructing an MDP equivalent to the original CDMDP in the much larger state space $S \times A^k$. The formal construction of such an MDP is covered in previous work [4]. One can then use any of the standard MDP planning algorithms to determine $V^*(I_k)$ for $I_k \in S \times A^k$. The corresponding optimal policy is known to be an optimal policy for the CDMDP [6]. Unfortunately, this expansion renders traditional MDP planning algorithms intractable for all but the smallest values of k. In Section 4.1, we show that the exponential state space growth is unavoidable in general, but in Section 3.2, we describe an approach that averts this computational burden and provides optimal or near-optimal policies in the special cases from Section 2. In Section 4.3, we outline a practical way to learn the augmented model with a polynomial number of samples. We note here that several RL modeling techniques that have an intuitive relationship to the CDMDP paradigm reduce, in the worst case, to the augmented approach and are therefore equally infeasible. These include modeling CDMDPs via factored MDPs, POMDPs, or POMDPs with variable length wait actions. The focus of this paper is on *practical* solutions for CDMDPs, and so we do not further discuss these generally intractable solutions, comparing simply against the augmented approach.

3.2 A New Approach: Model Based Simulation (MBS)

We now introduce a planning algorithm, Model Based Simulation (MBS), designed for the restricted CDMDP cases from Section 2. The intuition behind MBS is that, in a deterministic or benignly stochastic environment, given I_k, one can use P to "simulate" the most likely single-step outcomes of the last k actions, starting from the last observed state, thus determining, or at least closely approximating, the current state of the agent. In the deterministic cases, this prediction is straightforward. In the other two cases, (mildly stochastic and bounded noise) the algorithm will use the most likely or expected outcome, respectively. The MBS algorithm appears in Algorithm 1.[2]

Extending MBS to the learning setting is fairly straightforward in the context of finite CDMDPs (Cases I and III). One needs only to employ a model-based RL algorithm such as R-max [9] to learn the parameters (P and R) of the underlying zero-delay MDP. However, to extend MBS to *continuous* CDMDPs, simply discretizing the environment is not sufficient because this approach can easily turn deterministic (Case II) or slightly perturbed (Case IV) state transitions into far less benign dynamics, making the action simulations unsuitable. Instead, we require a method that trains a model of the transitions in the continuous space itself, but still plans in the discretized space (in order to make valid comparisons against the policies of the other finite-space algorithms). The next section defines such an algorithm.

[2] Note: for continuous MDPs, some steps may require approximation, see Section 4.2.

Algorithm 1. Model Based Simulation

Input: A CDMDP $M = \langle S, A, P, R, \gamma, k \rangle$, and $I_k = (s, a_1, a_2, \cdots, a_k) \in S \times A^k$.
Output: The optimal action $a^* = \pi^*(I_k)$
Construct a regular MDP $\bar{M} = \langle S, A, \bar{P}, R, \gamma \rangle$ where $\bar{P}(s, a, s') = 1$ for the most likely (finite) or expected (continuous) outcome of a in s.
Find the optimal value function $\bar{V}^*$ and an optimal policy $\bar{\pi}^*$ for $\bar{M}$.
Compute the current (but unobserved) state $\bar{s}$ by applying action sequence $(a_1, \cdots, a_k)$ to s according to $\bar{P}$.
Return $\bar{\pi}^*(\bar{s})$.

Algorithm 2. Model Parameter Approximation

Input:
    A collection of N sample instances $X = \{(s_i, a_i, r_i, s_i') \mid i = 1, 2, \cdots, N\}$
    S, A, γ and $R_{\max}$ from a continuous MDP
    Function approximators T_A and R_A
    The current continuous observation s
Output: The action to be taken from s.
Train T_A and R_A using X.
Construct discrete MDP $\hat{M} = \langle \hat{S}, A, \hat{P}, \hat{R}, \gamma \rangle$; for any $\bar{s} \in \hat{S}$ and $a \in A$:
if we have enough samples in X **then**
    use maximum-likelihood estimates
else if T_A and R_A have high confidence **then**
    generate an artificial sample set X' using T_A and R_A, build model using $X \cup X'$
else
    $\hat{P}(\bar{s}, a, \bar{s}) = 1$ and $\hat{R}(\bar{s}, a) = R_{\max}$.
end if
Find the optimal value function $\hat{V}^*$ and an optimal policy $\hat{\pi}^*$ for $\hat{M}$.
$\hat{s} = \text{Discretize}(s)$
Return $\hat{\pi}^*(\hat{s})$.

3.3 Model Parameter Approximation

Model Parameter Approximation, or MPA, (Algorithm 2) is a model-based RL algorithm designed for MDPs with bounded, continuous state and action spaces. MPA is closely related to Lazy Learning [10], which uses locally weighted regression to build approximations of the MDP dynamics and then plans in a discretized version of the MDP, using the trained regressor as a generative model. MPA performs a similar construction, but it can use any function approximator and borrows from the R-max algorithm by tagging state/action pairs as "known" or "unknown" and encouraging exploration of the unknown areas.

MPA is a model-based reinforcement-learning algorithm for zero-delay MDPs whose planning component is very similar to MBS without simulation. Therefore, to use MPA in the continuous CDMDP learning setting, we perform MBS's simulation *before* the discretization of the current state using MPA's transition function approximator, T_A, to apply the action sequence (using the expected one-step outcomes). We then discretize the outcome of that simulation and use the appropriate action. This CDMDP learning algorithm, MBS+MPA, produces a "discretized" policy, valid for comparison against the other algorithms we will investigate in Section 5.

4 Theoretical Analysis of Delayed Problems

In this section, we develop several theoretical properties of the CDMDP planning and learning problems for CDMDPs as described in Section 2. Our treatment includes a hardness result in the general case, positive results for the four special cases, and an efficient way to learn augmented models.

4.1 Planning Results I: The General Case

The augmented approach represents a sound and complete method for finding an optimal policy. Although in certain cases it is unnecessary to fully expand the state space to $S \times A^k$, Theorem 1 below shows that converting the CDMDP representation to an equivalent augmented MDP representation can require an exponential expansion over the size of the compact CDMDP model.

Theorem 1. *The smallest regular MDP $\bar{M} = \langle \bar{S}, A, \bar{P}, \bar{R}, \gamma \rangle$ induced by a finite CDMDP $M = \langle S, A, P, R, \gamma, k \rangle$ can have a lower bound of $|\bar{S}| = \Omega(|A|^k)$.*

Proof (sketch). In an MDP, applying action a from state s produces a probability distribution over next states. It follows from the Markov assumption that in an MDP with $|S|$ states, there can be at most $|S|$ distinct probability distributions over next states for any possible action. Thus, the compact CDMDP representation, which has only $|S|$ states, requires $|S| \cdot |A|$ probability distributions. In the worst case, however, we're able to construct an MDP such that each action can result in $\Theta(|A|^k)$ probability distributions based on different k-step histories $(s, a_1, ..., a_k)$. Thus, the representation of the induced augmented MDP provably has $|S| \cdot |A|^k$ states and $|S| \cdot |A|^{k+1}$ distributions. □

The exponential increase in the number of states suggests that this approach is intractable in general, and the next theorem establishes that it is unlikely the CDMDP planning problem can be solved in polynomial time.

Theorem 2. *The general CDMDP planning problem is NP-Hard.*

Proof (sketch). The proof is by reduction from the problem of planning in a finite-horizon unobservable MDP (UMDP). The construction takes a UMDP with $|S|$ states and horizon k and turns it into an infinite-horizon CDMDP with delay k and $k + k|S| + 1$ states. The first k states are merely "dummy" states needed to define I_k^0. Each of the next $k|S|$ states represents one of the UMDP states at a timestep t, the new rewards are $r(s)/\gamma^t$, and extra transitions are added from the old "final" states to a new final trap state with 0 reward. A solution to this problem would provide an answer to whether any policy from a given start state in a finite horizon UMDP can have a value of at least θ, which is known to be NP-Complete [11]. □

A more complicated reduction from 3-SAT shows this problem is indeed *strongly* NP-Hard. We note that if P $\neq$ NP, then Theorem 1 would be a direct consequence of Theorem 2 since an MDP can be solved in time polynomial in the size of its representation. However, Theorem 1 gives a stronger result, showing an exponential blowup in representation is unavoidable when converting a CDMDP to an MDP, even if P=NP. The NP-Hardness result for CDMDP planning motivates the search for constrained cases where one can take advantage of special structure within the problem to avoid the worst case. We now provide theoretical results concerning the four special cases previously defined.

4.2 Planning Results II: Special Cases

The following results provide bounds on $\left\|\bar{V}^* - V^*\right\|_\infty$, where $\bar{V}^*$ is the value function for $\bar{\pi}^*$ computed by MBS in its deterministic approximation $\bar{M}$ (*c.f.* Algorithm 1), and V^* is the true CDMDP value function. These bounds are also accuracy bounds for answering the CDMDP planning problem using $\bar{M}$ instead of M and can be used to derive the *actual* online performance bounds when using greedy policies w.r.t. $\bar{V}^*$ compared to the optimal CDMDP policy [12].

We begin with the finite-state cases, starting with the more general "mildly stochastic" setting (Case III) where MBS will assume that the last k transitions have each had the most likely one-step outcome.

Theorem 3. *In Case III,* $\left\|\bar{V}^* - V^*\right\|_\infty \leq \frac{\gamma\delta R_{\max}}{(1-\gamma)^2}$. *Hence, MBS solves the CDMDP planning problem for such CDMDPs with this accuracy in polynomial time.*

Proof (sketch). We first bound the error on the one-step backup of the deterministic approximation, and then extend this result over the value function. Answering the CDMDP planning problem within this accuracy can then be done by approximating the current state s through simulation and comparing $\bar{V}^*(s)$ to the reward bound θ. The major operation for MBS is the computation of $\bar{V}^*$ for a deterministic MDP $\bar{M}$, which can be done in $O(SA + S^3)$ [13]. □

We note that, by definition, $\bar{V}^*$ has taken the k-step prediction error into account; therefore, Theorem 3 provides a bound (indirectly) for the performance of MBS when it has to predict forward k steps using an inaccurate model. The bound above is only practically useful for small values of δ, because larger values could cause $\bar{M}$ to be a very poor approximation of M. At the opposite extreme, setting $\delta = 0$, we arrive at the following result for Case I:

Corollary 1. *In Case I, MBS solves the CDMDP planning problem exactly in polynomial time.*

In the continuous cases (II and IV), computing $\bar{V}^*$ and its maximum, even in the undelayed case, requires approximation (e.g. discretization [14]) that will introduce an additional error, denoted ϵ, to $\bar{V}^*$ as compared to V^*. Computing $\bar{V}^*$ will also require some (possibly not polynomially bounded) time, T. In Case IV, we assume the magnitude of the noise is bounded by Δ and the optimal CDMDP value function is Lipschitz continuous with constant C_V, leading to the following result.

Theorem 4. *In Case IV, assuming an approximation algorithm for computing $\bar{V}^*$ within ϵ accuracy, MBS solves the CDMDP planning problem with accuracy $\frac{2\gamma C_V \Delta}{1-\gamma} + \epsilon$ in time polynomial in the size of the input and T.*

Proof (sketch). We establish an error bound on the one-step backup of the deterministic approximation using the Lipschitz condition given in Section 2. The major step in this proof is showing $\left|\max_a \int_S P(s, a_1, s')V^*(s', a_2, \cdots, a_k, a)ds' - \max_a V^*(s_0, a_2, \cdots, a_k, a)\right| \leq 2C_V\Delta$, where s_0 is the expected next state by taking a in s. From there, the proof is similar to Theorem 3, using the approximation algorithm when appropriate. □

Similarly to Case III, this bound is only of interest if Δ and ϵ are small. By setting $\Delta = 0$, we arrive at the following result that says planning in deterministic continuous CDMDPs is the same as in their equivalent undelayed ones:

Corollary 2. *In Case II, the MBS algorithm, using an approximation algorithm to compute $\bar{V}^*$, can answer the CDMDP planning problem with accuracy ϵ in time polynomial in the size of the input and T.*

4.3 A Remark on Learning

A *naive* approach to the general CDMDP learning problem would be to apply standard RL algorithms in the augmented state space. While theoretically sound, this tack requires gathering experience for every possible I_k (an exponential sampling requirement). A preferable alternative is to instead learn the one-step model from experience, then build the augmented model and use it to plan, in conjunction with an algorithm, like R-max [9], that facilitates exploration. While this *compact learning approach* still suffers in the worst case from the unavoidable exponential burden of planning (Theorems 1 and 2), its sampling requirement is polynomially bounded, making it somewhat more practical.

5 Empirical Algorithm Comparisons

We now evaluate several of the methods discussed in Section 3 in the learning setting for each of the four cases. Agents were evaluated in episodic domains based on average cumulative reward for 200 episodes with a cap of 300 steps per episode. All data points represent an average over 10 runs. We implemented the "wait agent" using R-max in the finite-state setting and with MPA for continuous environments. Several variants of the memoryless-policy strategy were appraised, including model-based RL algorithms, R-max and MPA, as well as Sarsa(0)[3], Sarsa(.9), and "Batch" versions of Sarsa (B-Sarsa) that used experience replay [15] every 1000 steps. The Sarsa learning rate was set to .3 (empirically tuned) and exploration in these cases was guided by optimistic initialization of the value function along with an ϵ-greedy [1] approach for picking actions, with ϵ initialized to .1 and decaying by a factor of .95 per episode. Due to the large

[3] Variants of Q(λ)-learning were also tried, yielding similar results to Sarsa(λ).

number of variations, only the best and worst of these "memoryless" approaches are plotted for each environment. For the "augmented" MDP approaches, we investigated both the *naive* and *compact* learners described in Section 4.3, with planning taking place in the augmented space using R-max. We also evaluated a *naive* Sarsa(λ) learner in the augmented space. Unfortunately, the computational burden of planning made these augmented approaches infeasible beyond delays of 5. Finally, for MBS, we again used R-max or MPA, as appropriate.

5.1 Delayed W-Maze I: A Deterministic Finite Environment

We begin with a deterministic finite (Case I) world, the "W-maze", as depicted in Figure 1 (left). The agent starts in a random cell and its goal is to escape the maze through the top center square by executing the "up" action. All steps within the maze garner a reward of -1. The environment is designed to thwart memoryless approaches, which have trouble finding the right situation to begin going "up" and instead alternate between the extreme branches.

Figure 1 (right) shows the results of this experiment. The "wait" agent performs well in this environment, but sub-optimally for $k > 0$. In contrast, MBS+R-max quickly achieves optimality for all delay values. The best memoryless performer was B-Sarsa(.9), but its performance drops well below the random agent at higher delays. The worst memoryless learner was R-max, which fails to learn the transition function for $k > 0$. The *compact* version of the augmented learner performs comparably to MBS+R-max, but the planning for this method becomes intractable beyond a delay of 5. As expected, the *naive* augmented learners see a significant performance drop-off as delay increases. Unlike the memoryless approaches, which learn fast but can't represent the optimal policy, these learners are too slow to learn from the finite samples available to them.

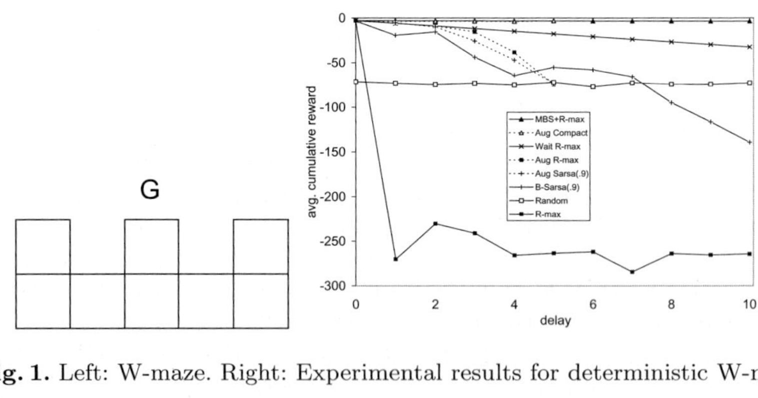

Fig. 1. Left: W-maze. Right: Experimental results for deterministic W-maze.

5.2 Delayed Mountain Car: A Case II Environment

We further investigated these algorithms in a domain with deterministic *continuous* dynamics (Case II), a delayed version of "Mountain Car" [1], which was an event in the First Annual Reinforcement Learning Competition. The environment is made up of two continuous variables, representing the car's location and speed. The car has 3 actions (forward, neutral, reverse) and rewards of −1 for all steps and 0 at the top of the hill. For the "memoryless", and "augmented" approaches, we continued to use the algorithms described in the previous section and overlaid a 10 × 10 (empirically tuned) grid for discretization. The "wait" agent strategy was not applicable because this domain has momentum. For MPA, we used Locally Weighted Progression Regression (LWPR) [16] to approximate the transition function, and an averager to approximate the reward function. The results are illustrated in Figure 2 (left). Again, the best performer was MBS+MPA, which has the advantage of modeling continuous actions and efficiently compensating for delay. However, for many delay values, Batch Sarsa(.9) performed almost as well, because action effects in Mountain Car are quite small. By focusing on the results of the memoryless learners (Figure 2 (right)), we see the clear benefit of eligibility traces as both B-Sarsa(.9) and Sarsa(.9) outperform B-Sarsa(0), Sarsa(0) and MPA (without MBS) when $k > 0$.

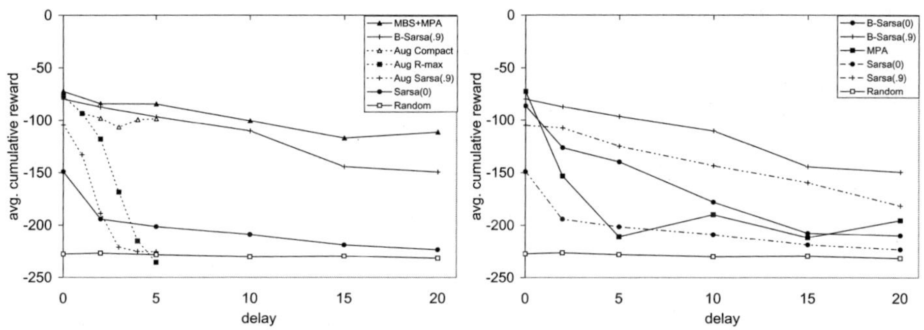

Fig. 2. Mountain Car Results. Left: various strategies. Right: memoryless learners.

5.3 Delayed W-Maze II: A Stochastic Finite Environment

We also considered a mildly stochastic (Case III) version of W-maze, where actions succeed with a probability of .7 and "slip" in one of the other three directions with probability .1 each. The results of this experiment are illustrated in Figure 3 (left). Despite the non-determinism in the domain, MBS+R-max performed comparably to the *compact* augmented learner and outperformed all of the other approaches. The memoryless approaches all flounder with increasing delay, being outdone even by the *naive* augmented R-max and "wait" learners.

5.4 Delayed Puddle World: A Case IV Environment

Finally, we investigated a Case IV environment, Stochastic Puddle World [17] where action outcomes were perturbed by bounded Gaussian noise. The 2-D environment contains two puddles and a goal. Steps within the puddles garner large

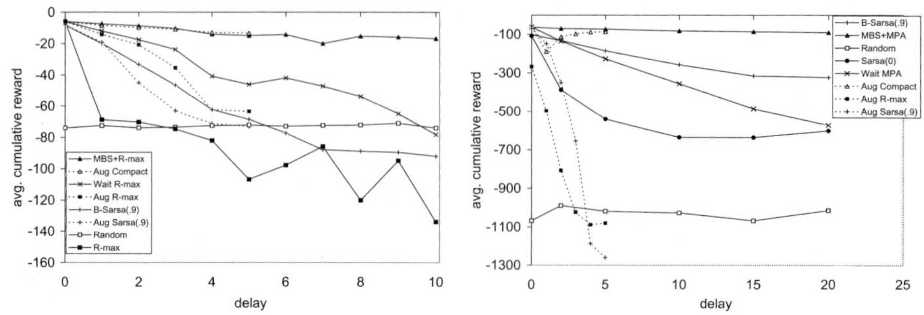

Fig. 3. Experimental results for stochastic W-maze (left) and Puddle World (right)

negative rewards while all other steps yield -1. A 10×10 tiling was used for discretization. The batch learners used experience replay every 2500 steps because of noise effects. The results are reported in Figure 3 (right). MBS+MPA clearly outperforms its memoryless counterparts, though eligibility traces help maintain performance with increasing delay. As with Mountain Car, MBS+MPA outperforms some augmented learners at $k = 0$ because MPA's function approximators quickly and accurately learn the domain dynamics. The "wait" agent, which loiters in the puddles, performs poorly for large delays. This domain dramatically exhibits the benefits of the *compact* augmented approach over the *naive* ones.

6 Conclusions and Future Work

In this paper, we evaluated algorithms for environments with constant observation and reward delay. We showed the general CDMDP planning problem is NP-Hard, but planning can be done in polynomial time in the deterministic finite setting, and we provided loss bounds in three other settings. We introduced Model Based Simulation (MBS) for planning in CDMDPs, and Model Parameter Approximation (MPA) to extend MBS for learning in continuous environments. Our experiments show this approach outperforms various natural alternatives in several benchmark delayed MDPs.

Several open research topics in this area remain. In the learning setting, one could relax the assumption that the delay is known, perhaps learning the delay values using clustering. A related problem is variable delay, or *jitter*, which is common when dealing with network latency and has been studied in prior work on augmented models [4]. Also, though we covered two important *stochastic* special cases, there may be more conditions that facilitate efficient planning. A related open question is whether an algorithm that exploits structure within the belief space (for instance, if the number of reachable belief states from any start state within k steps is small) could plan in time not influenced by the potential exponential expansion. We note that MBS is an extreme case of such an algorithm, which considers only $|S|$ reachable belief states, all of them pure.

Acknowledgments. This work was supported in part by NSF IIS award 0329153. We thank the First Annual Reinforcement Learning Competition, Adam White, and the anonymous reviewers for their contributions.

References

1. Sutton, R.S., Barto, A.G.: Reinforcement Learning: An Introduction. MIT Press, Cambridge, MA (1998)
2. Altman, E., Nain, P.: Closed-loop control with delayed information. In: Proc. 1992 ACM SIGMETRICS and PERFORMANCE, 1-5 1992, pp. 193–204. ACM Press, New York (1992)
3. Brooks, D.M., Leondes, C.T.: Markov decision processes with state-information lag. Operations Research 20(4), 904–907 (1972)
4. Katsikopoulos, K.V., Engelbrecht, S.E.: Markov decision processes with delays and asynchronous cost collection. IEEE Transactions on Automatic Control 48, 568–574 (2003)
5. Bertsekas, D.P.: Dynamic Programming and Optimal Control, 2nd edn., vol. 1/2. Athena Scientific (2001)
6. Bander, J.L., White III, C.C.: Markov decision processes with noise-corrupted and delayed state observations. The Journal of the Operational Research Society 50, 660–668 (1999)
7. Puterman, M.L.: Markov Decision Processes: Discrete Stochastic Dynamic Programming. Wiley, New York (1994)
8. Loch, J., Singh, S.: Using eligibility traces to find the best memoryless policy in partially observable Markov decision processes. In: ICML, pp. 323–331 (1998)
9. Brafman, R.I., Tennenholtz, M.: R-max–a general polynomial time algorithm for near-optimal reinforcement learning. Journal of Machine Learning Research 3, 213–231 (2002)
10. Atkeson, C.G., Moore, A.W., Schaal, S.: Locally weighted learning for control. Artificial Intelligence Review 11(1–5), 75–113 (1997)
11. Papadimitriou, C.H., Tsitsiklis, J.N.: The complexity of Markov decision processes. Mathematics of Operations Research 12(3), 441–450 (1987)
12. Singh, S.P., Yee, R.C.: An upper bound on the loss from approximate optimal-value functions. Machine Learning 16(3), 227–233 (1994)
13. Littman, M.L.: Algorithms for Sequential Decision Making. PhD thesis, Brown University, Providence, RI (1996)
14. Munos, R., Moore, A.W.: Rates of convergence for variable resolution schemes in optimal control. In: ICML, pp. 647–654 (2000)
15. Lin, L.J.: Reinforcement Learning for Robots using Neural Networks. PhD thesis, Carnegie Mellon University, Pittsburgh, PA (1993)
16. Vijayakumar, S., Schaal, S.: Locally weighted projection regression: An o(n) algorithm for incremental real time learning in high dimensional space. In: ICML, pp. 1079–1086 (2000)
17. Boyan, J.A., Moore, A.W.: Generalization in reinforcement learning: Safely approximating the value function. In: NIPS, pp. 369–376 (1995)

Analyzing Co-training Style Algorithms

Wei Wang and Zhi-Hua Zhou

National Key Laboratory for Novel Software Technology,
Nanjing University, Nanjing 210093, China
{wangw,zhouzh}@lamda.nju.edu.cn

Abstract. Co-training is a semi-supervised learning paradigm which trains two learners respectively from two different views and lets the learners label some unlabeled examples for each other. In this paper, we present a new PAC analysis on co-training style algorithms. We show that the co-training process can succeed even without two views, given that the two learners have large difference, which explains the success of some co-training style algorithms that do not require two views. Moreover, we theoretically explain that why the co-training process could not improve the performance further after a number of rounds, and present a rough estimation on the appropriate round to terminate co-training to avoid some wasteful learning rounds.

1 Introduction

Unlabeled training data are usually much easier than labeled training data to be obtained in many practical machine learning applications, so semi-supervised learning which attempts to exploit unlabeled data to help improve the performance of learning with limited labeled training data has attracted much attention during the past few years [5,9,13,6,12,10,17,3]. *Co-training* is a well-known semi-supervised learning paradigm. In its initial form [5], co-training trains two classifiers separately on two *sufficient and redundant views*, i.e., two attribute sets each of which is sufficient for learning and conditionally independent to the other given the class label, and lets the two classifiers label some unlabeled instances for each other. Since in most real-world scenarios sufficient and redundant views do not exist, variants of co-training that do not require two views have been developed. For example, rather than using two views, Goldman and Zhou [8] used two different supervised learning algorithms, Zhou and Li [16] used two different parameter configurations of the same base learner, etc.

There are several theoretical studies on co-training. Dasgupta et al. [7] proved that when the requirement of sufficient and redundant views is met, the co-trained classifiers could make fewer generalization errors by maximizing their agreement over the unlabeled data. Balcan et al. [2] showed that given appropriately strong PAC-learners on each view, an assumption of *expansion* on the underlying data distribution, which is weaker than the assumption of sufficient and redundant views, is sufficient for *iterative co-training* to succeed. This tells that the *conditional independence* [5] or even the *weak dependence* [1] between

J.N. Kok et al. (Eds.): ECML 2007, LNAI 4701, pp. 454–465, 2007.

the two views is not needed, at least, for iterative co-training which is the popular routine taken by many variants of co-training.

Previous theoretical studies mainly investigate co-training with two views. Although the applicability of co-training style algorithms that do not require two views is better in practice and empirical studies have shown the effectiveness of those algorithms, there is no theoretical analysis that can explain that why co-training without two views can succeed. On the other hand, in experiments we have observed that the co-training process could not improve the learning performance further after a number of rounds, which has not been analyzed by previous theoretical studies.

In this paper, we present a new PAC analysis which addresses the above issues. In detail, we derive a theorem on why co-training can work without two views, and a theorem on why co-training could not improve the performance after a number of learning rounds. The second theorem provides a rough estimation on the appropriate round to terminate the co-training process to avoid some wasteful learning rounds, which is validated by an empirical study in this paper.

The rest of this paper is organized as follows. After stating some preliminaries in Section 2, we present our theoretical results in Section 3, then report on our empirical study on determining the appropriate round to terminate co-training in Section 4, and finally conclude the paper in Section 5.

2 Preliminaries

Given data set $\mathcal{S} = \mathcal{L} \cup \mathcal{U}$, where $\mathcal{L} = \{(x_1, y_1), \cdots, (x_l, y_l)\} \subset \mathcal{X} \times \mathcal{Y}$ is the labeled data set and $\mathcal{U} = \{(x_{l+1}, x_{l+2}, \cdots, x_n)\} \subset \mathcal{X}$ is the unlabeled data set. $\mathcal{Y} = \{-1, +1\}$; $\mathcal{X}$ is with distribution $\mathcal{D}$. Let $\mathcal{H} : \mathcal{X} \to \mathcal{Y}$ denote the hypothesis space. Assume that $|\mathcal{H}|$ is finite, and $\mathcal{D}$ is generated by the ground truth $h^* \in \mathcal{H}$. It is obvious that the generalization error of h^* is zero. Since we have only finite sample, it is hard to achieve h^* over $\mathcal{S}$. Suppose we obtain a classifier $h^i \in \mathcal{H}$ from $\mathcal{S}$, which is somewhat different from h^*. Let $d(h^i, h^*)$ denote the difference between the two classifiers h^i and h^*, then

$$d(h^i, h^*) = Pr_{x \in \mathcal{D}}[h^i(x) \neq h^*(x)]. \tag{1}$$

Let ϵ bound the generalization error of the classifiers what we wish to achieve finally. That is, if $d(h^i, h^*) = Pr_{x \in \mathcal{D}}[h^i(x) \neq h^*(x)] < \epsilon$, we say that we have obtained a desired classifier since the difference between this classifier and the ground truth h^* is very small; otherwise we say that the classifier h^i is 'bad'. Of course we wish to have a high probability to achieve a good classifier. The confidence parameter δ can play this role. The learning process is said to do probably approximately correct learning of h^* if and only if $Pr[d(h^i, h^*) \geq \epsilon] \leq \delta$, where the probability is taken over all possible training data. Formally, the requirement is that the difference between the ground truth h^* and the hypothesis h^i be small (less than ϵ) with high probability (more than $1 - \delta$).

3 Main Results

Given the initial labeled data $\mathcal{L}$ and unlabeled data $\mathcal{U}$, consider the following co-training learning process:

Co-Training Process: *At first, two initial classifiers h_1^0 and h_2^0 are trained using $\mathcal{L}$ which contains l labeled examples. Then, h_1^0 selects u number of unlabeled instances from $\mathcal{U}$ to label, and puts these newly labeled examples into the data set σ_2 which contains all the examples in $\mathcal{L}$; at the same time, h_2^0 selects u number of unlabeled instances from $\mathcal{U}$ to label, and puts these newly labeled examples into the data set σ_1 which contains all the examples in $\mathcal{L}$. h_1^1 and h_2^1 are trained from σ_1 and σ_2, respectively. After that, h_1^1 selects u number of unlabeled instances to label, and uses these newly labeled examples to update σ_2; while h_2^1 also selects u number of unlabeled instances to label, and uses these newly labeled examples to update σ_1. Such a process is repeated for a pre-set number of learning rounds.*

Different learners have different biases, which is an intuitive explanation to that why co-training style algorithms can succeed. The two classifiers that have different biases will label some instances with different labels. The difference $d(h^i, h^j)$ between the two classifiers h^i and h^j implies the different biases between them. If the examples labeled by the classifier h^i is useful for the classifier h^j, h^i should know some information that h^j does not know. In other words, h^i and h^j should have large difference. As the Co-Training Process proceeds, the two classifiers will become more and more similar and the difference between them will become smaller and smaller since the two classifiers label more and more unlabeled instances for each other. The difference can be helpful for analyzing the co-training style algorithms.

In the i-th learning round, let a_i and b_i denote the upper bound of the generalization error of h_1^i and h_2^i, respectively; let $d(h_1^{i-1}, h_2^i)$ denote the difference between h_1^{i-1} and h_2^i, and let $d(h_1^i, h_2^{i-1})$ denote the difference between h_1^i and h_2^{i-1}. It is feasible to estimate the difference when there are a large mount of unlabeled instances. Now we present our main result.

Theorem 1. *Given the initial labeled data set $\mathcal{L}$, assuming that the size of $\mathcal{L}$ is sufficient to learn two classifiers h_1^0 and h_2^0 whose upper bound of the generalization error is $a_0 < 0.5$ and $b_0 < 0.5$ respectively with high probability (more than $1-\delta$) in the PAC model, i.e., $l \geq max\{\frac{1}{a_0}ln\frac{|\mathcal{H}|}{\delta}, \frac{1}{b_0}ln\frac{|\mathcal{H}|}{\delta}\}$. Then h_1^0 selects u number of unlabeled instances from $\mathcal{U}$ to label and puts them into σ_2 which contains all the examples in $\mathcal{L}$, and then h_2^1 is trained from σ_2 by minimizing the empirical risk. If $lb_0 \leq e\sqrt[M]{M!} - M$, then*

$$Pr[d(h_2^1, h_*) \geq b_1] \leq \delta. \tag{2}$$

where $M = ua_0$ and $b_1 = \max\{\frac{lb_0 + ua_0 - ud(h_1^0, h_2^1)}{l}, 0\}$.

Proof. Firstly, we analyze the expected rate of disagreement between the classifier h^i and the sample sequence σ_2 which consists of u number of newly labeled examples and $\mathcal{L}$. By minimizing the empirical risk, the classifier which has the lowest observed rate of disagreement with the sample sequence σ_2 will be generated. Let $d(h^i, \sigma_2)$ denote the expected rate of disagreement between h^i and σ_2. Then

$$d(h^*, \sigma_2) = \frac{u \times d(h_1^0, h^*)}{l+u} \tag{3}$$

$$d(h_2^1, \sigma_2) = \frac{l \times d(h_2^1, h^*) + u \times d(h_1^0, h_2^1)}{l+u} \tag{4}$$

In order to achieve 'good' classifiers whose generalization errors are less than b_1 by minimizing the empirical risk, the sample sequence σ_2 must be sufficient to guarantee that no classifier whose generalization error is no smaller than b_1 has a lower observed rate of disagreement with σ_2 than h^* with a probability bigger than $1-\delta$.

Since the upper bound of the generalization error of the classifier h_1^0 is a_0, $d(h^*, \sigma_2)$ is no more than $\frac{ua_0}{l+u}$. Let $M = ua_0$, the probability that the classifier h_2^1 has a lower observed rate of disagreement with σ_2 than h^* is less than

$$C_{l+u}^M d(h_2^1, \sigma_2)^M [1 - d(h_2^1, \sigma_2)]^{l+u-M}. \tag{5}$$

Let $b_1 = \max\{\frac{lb_0 + ua_0 - ud(h_1^0, h_2^1)}{l}, 0\}$, if $d(h_2^1, h^*) \geq b_1$,

$$\begin{aligned} d(h_2^1, \sigma_2) &= \frac{l \times d(h_2^1, h^*) + u \times d(h_1^0, h_2^1)}{l+u} \\ &\geq \frac{lb_1 + u \times d(h_1^0, h_2^1)}{l+u} \\ &\geq \frac{lb_0 + ua_0}{l+u} \\ &> \frac{M}{l+u}. \end{aligned}$$

The function $C_m^s x^s (1-x)^{m-s}$ is monotonically decreasing as x increases when $s/m < x < 1$. So, if $d(h_2^1, h^*) \geq b_1$, the value of Eq.5 is smaller than

$$C_{l+u}^M (\frac{lb_0 + ua_0}{l+u})^M (1 - \frac{lb_0 + ua_0}{l+u})^{l+u-M}. \tag{6}$$

In other words, the probability for that the classifier with generalization error no less than b_1 has a lower observed rate of disagreement with σ_2 than h^* is smaller than the value of Eq.6.

The calculation of the real value of Eq.6 is quite complex, so we approximate it by using the Poisson Theorem:

$$C_{l+u}^M (\frac{lb_0 + ua_0}{l+u})^M (1 - \frac{lb_0 + ua_0}{l+u})^{l+u-M} \approx \frac{(lb_0 + ua_0)^M}{M!} e^{-(lb_0 + ua_0)} \tag{7}$$

When $lb_0 \leq e\sqrt[M]{M!} - M$, the right-hand term of Eq.7 is no more than e^{-lb_0}. Since the classifier h_2^0 is PAC-learnable and the sample size of $\mathcal{L}$ is at least $\frac{1}{b_0} ln \frac{|\mathcal{H}|}{\delta}$,

$e^{-lb_0} \leq \delta/|\mathcal{H}|$. Therefore, the value of Eq.6 is no more than $\delta/|\mathcal{H}|$. Considering that there are at most $|\mathcal{H}| - 1$ classifiers with generalization error no less than b_1 having a lower observed rate of disagreement with σ_2 than h^* in $\mathcal{H}$, the probability that $Pr[d(h_2^1, h^*) \geq b_1]$ is at most δ. □

Theorem 1 shows that given the initial labeled data, if we can train two learners which have large difference, the learners can be improved by exploiting the unlabeled data through the Co-Training Process. It is easy to see that the Co-Training Process reassembles the main process of existing co-training style algorithms [5,8,16]. It can be recognized that the two views used in the standard co-training algorithm [5], the two different supervised learning algorithms used in Goldman and Zhou's algorithm [8], and the different configurations of the base learner used in Zhou and Li's algorithm [16] are actually exploited to make the classifiers to have large difference. This explains why co-training without two views [8,16] can succeed.

When co-training style algorithms are executed, the number of labeled examples is usually small while the initial classifiers are usually not very bad, thus the condition that $lb_0 \leq e\sqrt[M]{M!} - M$ in Theorem 1 can be satisfied. Note that using a bigger u will increase the upper bound of lb_0. This is because that a bigger u will result in a bigger M since $M = ua_0$, while Fig. 1 shows that the value of the function $f(M) = e\sqrt[M]{M!} - M$ increases as M increases.

In Theorem 1 we know that when the difference $d(h_1^0, h_2^1)$ is bigger than a_0, the upper bound $b_1 = \max\{\frac{lb_0 + ua_0 - ud(h_1^0, h_2^1)}{l}, 0\}$ is smaller than b_0. The bigger the difference $d(h_1^0, h_2^1)$, the smaller the upper bound of the generalization error of the classifiers h_2^1. In the Co-Training Process, the difference between the two learners decreases as the value of u increases. When u increases to a certain degree, the difference between the two learners becomes very small. This is easy to understand since the learner h_2^1 is trained by minimizing the empirical risk with a large number of examples provided by h_1^0.

From the above we know that when $d(h_1^0, h_2^1)$ is larger than a_0, we can generate 'good' classifiers according to Theorem 1. But when $d(h_1^0, h_2^1)$ is smaller than a_0,

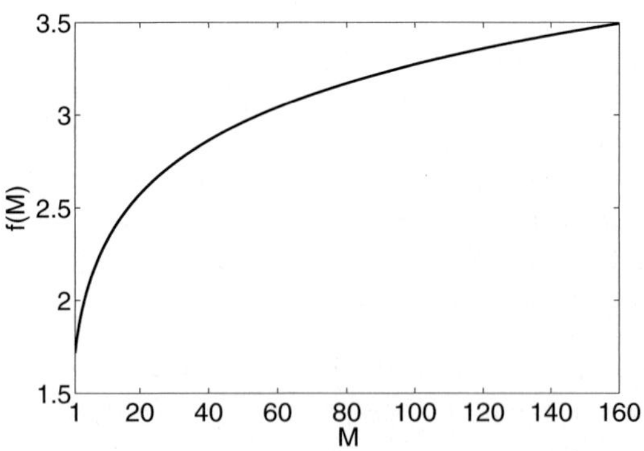

Fig. 1. The value of $f(M) = e\sqrt[M]{M!} - M$

what is the performance of the Co-Training Process? In this case, if $d(h_2^1, \sigma_2)$ is bigger than $d(h^*, \sigma_2)$ (for any $d(h_2^1, h^*) \geq b_1$), we can still obtain 'good' classifiers ($d(h_2^1, h^*) < b_1$) by minimizing the empirical risk because the expected rate of disagreement between the 'bad' classifiers and sample sequence is bigger than that between the ground truth h^* and sample sequence. So, with the Co-Training Process we can obtain classifiers which satisfy $d(h_2^1, h^*) < b_1$ with big probability. It is requested that u should be smaller than $lb_1/[a_0 - d(h_1^0, h_2^1)]$ for searching the 'good' classifiers. Thus, if $d(h_1^0, h_2^1)$ is smaller than a_0, the Co-Training Process will work well when $u < lb_1/[a_0 - d(h_1^0, h_2^1)]$. For $u \gg l$, we have Theorem 2:

Theorem 2. *In the Co-Training Process, if $u \gg l$, then for any $0 < \epsilon < 1$,*

$$Pr[d(h_1^0, h_2^1) \geq \epsilon] \leq \delta, \tag{8}$$

and

$$Pr[|d(h_1^0, h^*) - d(h_2^1, h^*)| \geq \epsilon] \leq \delta. \tag{9}$$

Proof. In the Co-Training Process, the training data of the classifier h_2^1 contain the l number of initial labeled examples and the u number of newly labeled examples given by the classifier h_1^0 . When $u \gg l$, it could be considered that the training data of the classifier h_2^1 comes from another distribution $\mathcal{D}'$ generated by the classifier h_1^0 which is different from h^*. In distribution $\mathcal{D}'$, the ground truth is h_1^0. According to the PAC learning theory, for any $0 < \epsilon < 1$, in distribution $\mathcal{D}'$ if u is large enough,

$$Pr[d(h_1^0, h_2^1) \geq \epsilon] \leq \delta.$$

Eq.9 is true considering

$$\begin{aligned}
&Pr_{x \in \mathcal{D}}[h_1^0(x) \neq h^*(x))] - Pr_{x \in \mathcal{D}}[h_2^1(x) \neq h_1^0(x))] \\
&\leq Pr_{x \in \mathcal{D}}[h_2^1(x) \neq h^*(x))] \\
&\leq Pr_{x \in \mathcal{D}}[h_1^0(x) \neq h^*(x))] + Pr_{x \in \mathcal{D}}[h_2^1(x) \neq h_1^0(x))]
\end{aligned}$$

□

From Theorem 2 we can find that when $u \gg l$, the difference between the two learners is very small (less than ϵ). The two learners become very similar and could not improve each other any more. In Section 4, we will report on an empirical study to show that whether the appropriate learning round of co-training could be estimated based on Theorem 2.

In the above we have discussed the situation when we should proceed with the Co-Training Process to improve the two learners, and when we should terminate the Co-Training Process. As a short summary, our theoretical study shows that

- If the two initial learners have large difference, they can be improved through the Co-Training Process;
- If the two initial learners have small difference, they can be improved if u/l is small;

– As the Co-Training Process proceeds, more and more unlabeled data are labeled for the learners each other, which makes the difference between the two learners become smaller and smaller. Thus, after a number of learning rounds the Co-Training Process could not improve the performance further.

4 Empirical Study

In order to study that whether the appropriate number of learning rounds of co-training could be estimated based on Theorem 2, we perform an empirical study.

4.1 Configurations

In the experiments we use the *course* data set [5], *ads* data set [11] and three UCI data sets , i.e. *kr-vs-kp*, *mushroom* and *tic-tac-toe* [4]. The *course* and *ads* data sets have multiple views but the UCI data sets have only one view.

The *course* data set has two views (*pages* view and *links* view) and contains 1,051 examples each corresponds to a web page, and the task is to predict whether an unseen web page is a *course page* or not. There are 230 positive examples (roughly 22%). Sixty-six attributes are used in *pages* view and five attributes in *links* view. The *ads* data set has five views. We use the 1st and 3rd views since the standard co-training algorithm only uses two views. This data set contains 983 examples, among which there are 138 positive examples (roughly 14%). As for the UCI data sets, *kr-vs-kp* contains 3,196 examples, among which there are 1,527 positive examples (roughly 48%); *mushroom* contains 8,124 examples, among which there are 3,916 positive examples (roughly 48%); *tic-tac-toe* contains 958 examples, among which there are 332 positive examples (roughly 35%). For each of these data sets, we randomly use 25% data as the test set while using the remaining 75% data to generate a labeled data set $\mathcal{L}$ whose concrete size will be mentioned later, and using the rest of the 75% data to generate the unlabeled data set $\mathcal{U}$.

In each learning round, each classifier labels the positive and negative examples on which it is with the most confidence for the other classifier, and the number of newly labeled positive and negative examples is in proportion to that of the positive and negative examples in $\mathcal{L}$. Since the size of $\mathcal{L}$ plays an important role in the Co-Training Process, we run experiments with different sizes of $\mathcal{L}$ on each data set. Moreover, each experiment is repeated for 20 runs and the average performance is recorded.

We study whether we can estimate the appropriate number of learning rounds to terminate the co-training process for avoiding wasteful further training. Here we estimate the value of $d(h_1^i, h_2^i)$ using $\mathcal{L} \cup \mathcal{U}$. Note that this is a simplification since as described in Section 3, the difference between h_1^{i-1} and h_2^i and that between h_1^i and h_2^{i-1} should be estimated. When the difference between the two classifiers is smaller than $min[a_i, b_i]$ and $u > max\{Lb_i/[a_{i-1} - d(h_1^{i-1}, h_2^i)], La_i/[b_{i-1} - d(h_1^i, h_2^{i-1})]\}$, we terminate the Co-Training Process.

Since in real-world tasks we do not have the test data to estimate the error of the two classifiers, we could not estimate the value of a_i and b_i directly. In Theorem 2 we know that the difference between the two classifiers will be stable when u is large, so we could utilize the stability of the difference to roughly estimate the appropriate round for termination. Note that this is an approximation which may cause the estimated round inaccurate. In our experiments we set to terminate the Co-Training Process when the change of the difference in consecutive three rounds is smaller than 0.001. We run the Co-Training Process with various classifiers including SMO, NaiveBayes and MultilayerPerceptron in WEKA [15].

4.2 Results on Data with Two Views

Firstly, we run experiments with the same classifier (SMO) on data sets with two views (i.e., the *course* and *ads* data sets) using the standard co-training algorithm [5]. The results are shown in Table 1.

Table 1. Experimental results on data sets with two views. *SMO* is used to train the classifiers. *data-a-b-c-d* means that on the data set *data*, the initial labeled training set contains a positive examples and b negative examples, and in each round each classifier labels c positive and d negative examples for the other classifier. e_{C_1} and e_{C_2} denote the error rates of the two classifiers trained in the two views, respectively. *dis* denotes the disagreement of the two classifiers. r denotes the number of learning rounds.

	Initial round				Estimated round				Last round			
Data set	e_{C_1}	e_{C_2}	*dis*	r	e_{C_1}	e_{C_2}	*dis*	r	e_{C_1}	e_{C_2}	*dis*	r
course-3-9-1-3	.151	.179	.157	0	.119	.127	.145	60	.119	.127	.145	60
course-6-18-1-3	.127	.155	.177	0	.124	.121	.166	20	.113	.122	.143	60
course-9-27-1-3	.125	.136	.171	0	.118	.116	.154	49	.114	.118	.148	60
ads-4-24-1-6	.114	.100	.046	0	.086	.075	.038	15	.079	.068	.032	25
ads-8-48-1-6	.104	.081	.055	0	.079	.067	.034	21	.078	.062	.031	25
ads-12-72-1-6	.093	.072	.058	0	.082	.065	.041	11	.076	.059	.034	25

We can find from Table 1 that the performances of the classifiers at the estimated round can be quite close to the performances of the classifiers at the last learning round, e.g. on *course*-9-27-1-3. This suggests that estimating the appropriate terminating round based on Theorem 2 is feasible for the standard co-training algorithm.

4.3 Results on Data Without Two Views

Then, we run experiments on data sets without two views, by using two different classifiers on the same view. Here we use SMO and NaiveBayes as the two different base learners on the *kr-vs-kp*, *mushroom* and *tic-tac-toe* data set. The results are shown in Table 2.

Table 2. Experimental results on data sets without two views. *SMO* and *NaiveBayes* are used to train the two classifiers, respectively. *data-a-b-c-d* means that on the data set *data*, the initial labeled training set contains a positive examples and b negative examples, and in each round each classifier labels c positive and d negative examples for the other classifier. e_{C_1} and e_{C_2} denote the error rates of the classifiers *SMO* and *NaiveBayes*, respectively. *dis* denotes the disagreement of the two classifiers. r denotes the number of learning rounds.

	Initial round				Estimated round				Last round			
Data set	e_{C_1}	e_{C_2}	*dis*	r	e_{C_1}	e_{C_2}	*dis*	r	e_{C_1}	e_{C_2}	*dis*	r
kr-vs-kp-35-35-1-1	.137	.220	.175	0	.134	.164	.096	50	.134	.164	.096	50
kr-vs-kp-50-50-1-1	.096	.186	.178	0	.097	.136	.079	50	.097	.136	.079	50
kr-vs-kp-65-65-1-1	.087	.182	.172	0	.090	.128	.079	50	.090	.128	.079	50
mushroom-3-3-1-1	.173	.168	.060	0	.130	.129	.026	32	.130	.134	.027	50
mushroom-6-6-1-1	.096	.100	.059	0	.089	.093	.044	26	.082	.088	.028	50
mushroom-12-12-1-1	.077	.097	.064	0	.069	.085	.043	19	.066	.080	.030	50
tic-tac-toe-10-10-1-1	.432	.433	.197	0	.423	.419	.099	39	.424	.424	.084	50
tic-tac-toe-15-15-1-1	.378	.410	.191	0	.370	.403	.104	31	.373	.399	.102	50
tic-tac-toe-20-20-1-1	.355	.392	.181	0	.353	.403	.102	39	.359	.396	.093	50

We can find that the performances of the classifiers at the estimated round can be quite close to the performances of the classifiers at the last learning round, e.g. on *mushroom*-3-3-1-1. This suggests that estimating the appropriate terminating round based on Theorem 2 is also feasible for co-training style algorithms which do not require two views, e.g. [8,16].

The estimated round is sometimes relatively loose, but the results shown in Tables 1 and 2 verify that after a number of learning rounds, continuing the co-training process could not improve the performance further. It is expected that by developing better methods for estimating the difference between the learners, tighter estimation on the appropriate terminating round could be obtained, which is a future issue.

4.4 Further Experiments and Discussion

In order to study the influence of the difference between the two learners further, more experiments are conducted. We run the Co-Training Process with two different groups of base learners on the *pages* view of the *course* data set. The first group is SMO and MultilayerPerceptron and the second group is SMO and NaiveBayes. With this experiment, it could be more clear that whether the learners with larger difference could be improved more than the learners with smaller difference. The results are shown in Table 3.

It can be found from Table 3 that the difference between the second group of classifiers is larger than that between the first group of classifiers. Note that the SMO classifier appears in both groups, while its improvement is larger in the second group than in the first group. This confirms that the larger the

Table 3. Comparing the performance of co-training using two different groups of base learners on the *pages* view of the *course* data set. *SMO* and *MultilayerPerceptron* (or *SMO* and *NaiveBayes*) denote the two classifiers, respectively. *data-a-b-c-d* means that on the data set *data*, the initial labeled training set contains a positive examples and b negative examples, and in each round each classifier labels c positive and d negative examples for the other classifier. e_{C_1} and e_{C_2} denote the error rates of the classifiers *SMO* and *MultilayerPerceptron*(or *SMO* and *NaiveBayes*), respectively. *dis* denotes the disagreement of the two classifiers. r denotes the number of learning rounds.

	Initial round				Estimated round				Last round			
Data set	e_{C_1}	e_{C_2}	*dis*	r	e_{C_1}	e_{C_2}	*dis*	r	e_{C_1}	e_{C_2}	*dis*	r
	C_1 = SMO & C_2 = MultilayerPerceptron											
pagesview-3-9-1-3	.137	.139	.018	0	.127	.126	.043	11	.123	.118	.026	50
pagesview-9-27-1-3	.113	.118	.036	0	.107	.108	.041	13	.099	.105	.028	50
pagesview-15-45-1-3	.100	.101	.038	0	.089	.090	.033	35	.087	.087	.029	50
	C_1 = SMO & C_2 = NaiveBayes											
pagesview-3-9-1-3	.137	.133	.069	0	.106	.095	.040	15	.097	.087	.031	50
pagesview-9-27-1-3	.113	.097	.075	0	.096	.085	.045	23	.087	.078	.036	50
pagesview-15-45-1-3	.100	.081	.076	0	.089	.075	.048	20	.078	.074	.032	50

difference between the two learners, the more the improvement from the Co-Training Process.

5 Conclusion

In this paper, we present a new PAC analysis on co-training style algorithms. We theoretically explain that why co-training without two views can succeed, and that why co-training could not improve the performance further after a number of learning rounds. Our theoretical result on the second issue provides a feasible approach for estimating the appropriate learning rounds to terminate the co-training process to avoid wasteful learning rounds. We study the effectiveness of the approach in empirical study.

The current estimation of the appropriate learning rounds requires information on the generalization ability of the learners. Since such information is not available in real-world tasks, we use an approximation to realize the approach. So, although the approach has a theoretical foundation and empirical study shows that it works not bad, the approximation makes the estimation not as accurate as we have expected. To improve the estimation in real-world tasks is a future issue.

Note that in some empirical study of the natural language processing community, it has been found that sometimes the performances of the two learners can degrade if the co-training process is run to convergence [14]. Our theoretical study in this paper gives an explanation to this phenomenon. That is, after a number of learning rounds the co-training process could not improve the performance further since the difference between the learners becomes very small. In other words, the two learners becomes very similar. Thus, if the co-training process is continued to convergence, these two learners will have very high chance to make similar errors. Since the co-trained learners are usually combined to use, the similar errors will be reinforced. Thus, overfitting is aggravated and therefore the degradation of performance is observed.

Acknowledgment

We want to thank the anonymous reviewers for their helpful comments and suggestions. This work was supported by the National Science Foundation of China (60635030, 60505013) and the Foundation for the Author of National Excellent Doctoral Dissertation of China (200343).

References

1. Abney, S.: Bootstrapping. In: Proceedings of the 40th Annual Meeting of the Association for Computational Linguistics, Philadelphia, PA, pp. 360–367 (2002)
2. Balcan, M.F., Blum, A., Yang, K.: Co-training and expansion: Towards bridging theory and practice. In: Saul, L.K., Weiss, Y., Bottou, L. (eds.) Advances in Neural Information Processing Systems 17, pp. 89–96. MIT Press, Cambridge, MA (2005)
3. Belkin, M., Niyogi, P.: Semi-supervised learning on Riemannian manifolds. Machine Learning 56, 209–239 (2004)
4. Blake, C., Keogh, E., Merz, C.J.: UCI repository of machine learning databases. Department of Information and Computer Science, University of California, Irvine, CA (1998), http://www.ics.uci.edu/~mlearn/MLRepository.html
5. Blum, A., Mitchell, T.: Combining labeled and unlabeled data with co-training. In: Proceedings of the 11th Annual Conference on Computational Learning Theory, Madison, WI, pp. 92–100 (1998)
6. Chapelle, O., Weston, J., Schölkopf, B.: Cluster kernels for semi-supervised learning. In: Becker, S., Thrun, S., Obermayer, K. (eds.) Advances in Neural Information Processing Systems 15, pp. 585–592. MIT Press, Cambridge, MA (2003)
7. Dasgupta, S., Littman, M., McAllester, D.: PAC generalization bounds for co-training. In: Dietterich, T.G., Becker, S., Ghahramani, Z. (eds.) Advances in Neural Information Processing Systems 14, pp. 375–382. MIT Press, Cambridge, MA (2002)
8. Goldman, S., Zhou, Y.: Enhancing supervised learning with unlabeled data. In: Proceedings of the 17th International Conference on Machine Learning, San Francisco, CA, pp. 327–334 (2000)
9. Joachims, T.: Transductive inference for text classification using support vector machines. In: Proceedings of the 16th International Conference on Machine Learning, Bled, Slovenia, pp. 200–209 (1999)
10. Krogel, M.A., Scheffer, T.: Effectiveness of information extraction, multi-relational, and semi-supervised learning for predicting functional properties of genes. In: Proceedings of the 3rd IEEE International Conference on Data Mining, Melbourne, FL, pp. 569–572. IEEE Computer Society Press, Los Alamitos (2003)
11. Kushmerick, N.: Learning to remove internet advertisements. In: Proceedings of the 3rd Annual Conference on Autonomous Agents, Seattle, WA, pp. 175–181 (1999)

12. Mladenic, D.: Modeling information in textual data combining labeled and unlabeled data. In: Proceedings of the ESF Exploratory Workshop on Pattern Detection and Discovery, pp. 170–179
13. Nigam, K., McCallum, A.K., Thrun, S., Mitchell, T.: Text classification from labeled and unlabeled documents using EM. Machine Learning 39, 103–134 (2000)
14. Pierce, D., Cardie, C.: Limitations of co-training for natural language learning from large data sets. In: Proceedings of the 2001 Conference on Empirical Methods in Natural Language Processing, Pittsburgh, PA, pp. 1–9 (2001)
15. Witten, I.H., Frank, E.: Data Mining: Practical Machine Learning Tools and Techniques, 2nd edn. Morgan Kaufmann, San Francisco, CA (2005)
16. Zhou, Z.H., Li, M.: Semi-supervised regression with co-training. In: Proceedings of the 19th International Joint Conference on Artificial Intelligence, Edinburgh, Scotland, pp. 908–913 (2005)
17. Zhu, X., Ghahramani, Z., Lafferty, J.: Semi-supervised learning using Gaussian fields and harmonic functions. In: Proceedings of the 20th International Conference on Machine Learning, Washington, DC, pp. 912–919 (2003)

Policy Gradient Critics

Daan Wierstra[1] and Jürgen Schmidhuber[1,2]

[1] Istituto Dalle Molle di Studi sull'Intelligenza Artificiale (IDSIA),
CH-6928 Manno-Lugano, Switzerland
daan@idsia.ch

[2] Department of Embedded Systems and Robotics, Technical University Munich,
D-85748 Garching, Germany
schmidhu@in.tum.de

Abstract. We present Policy Gradient Actor-Critic (PGAC), a new model-free Reinforcement Learning (RL) method for creating *limited-memory stochastic policies* for Partially Observable Markov Decision Processes (POMDPs) that require long-term memories of past observations and actions. The approach involves estimating a policy gradient for an Actor through a Policy Gradient Critic which evaluates probability distributions on actions. Gradient-based updates of history-conditional action probability distributions enable the algorithm to learn a mapping from memory states (or event histories) to probability distributions on actions, solving POMDPs through a combination of memory and stochasticity. This goes beyond previous approaches to learning purely reactive POMDP policies, without giving up their advantages. Preliminary results on important benchmark tasks show that our approach can in principle be used as a general purpose POMDP algorithm that solves RL problems in both continuous and discrete action domains.

1 Introduction

Reinforcement Learning [1] algorithms often need to deal with partial observability problems naturally arising in real-world tasks. A naive approach would be to learn *reactive stochastic policies* [2] which simply map observations to probabilities for actions. The underlying philosophy here is that utilizing random actions, as opposed to deterministic actions, will prevent the agent from getting stuck. In general this is clearly suboptimal, and the employment of some form of memory seems essential for many realistic RL settings. However, for cases where our memory system's capacity is *limited* – that is, imperfect, like for example all Recurrent Neural Network architectures – reactive stochasticity may still facilitate learning good policies for realistic environments. Hence the need to stress the importance of learning what we define as *limited-memory stochastic policies*, that is, policies that map limited memory states to probability distributions on actions.

In spite of their apparent advantages, work on limited-memory stochastic policies has been scarce so far, notable exceptions being finite state-based policy gradients [3,4] and evolutionary search (e.g. [5]). We propose a novel approach to learning limited-memory stochastic policies in partially observable environments. Conventional policy gradient approaches update policy parameters using a sampling-based Monte Carlo estimate of

J.N. Kok et al. (Eds.): ECML 2007, LNAI 4701, pp. 466–477, 2007.

the gradient in policy space – they constitute a framework of Actor-only methods – but this tends to lead to high variance estimates. Our new approach Policy Gradient Actor-Critic (PGAC), however, is a dual Actor-Critic [1] architecture and updates a policy's parameters – the Actor – using a *model-based* estimated gradient on action probabilities, the model being the Policy Gradient Critic. Since PGAC uses a gradient that is provided directly by a Policy Gradient Critic, representing an action distribution evaluation function over pairs of history / action distribution parameters, we can avoid brute force Monte Carlo sampling, which provides numerous advantages including the power of function approximator generalization. Computing the gradient from the Policy Gradient Critic has the potential to yield a substantially improved estimate of beneficial policy updates for the Actor. Moreover, by representing a Q-function over action probability distributions rather than over concrete actions, we can explicitly represent the value of stochasticity.

We use Long Short-Term Memory (LSTM) [6] as our memory-capable differentiable recurrent function approximator (DRFA) for both Actor and Policy Gradient Critic. DRFA-based RL algorithms are a perfect example of limited-memory algorithms. The recurrency or *memory* of DRFAs can capture hidden state effects, which enables the algorithm to deal with the partial observability that plagues many real-world tasks. Like other DRFAs, they are limited in their learning capacity, however, and prone to local minima. These limitations can be partly compensated for by using PGAC's explicitly learned value of stochasticity in action probabilities. We show that the resulting PGAC method using LSTM is able to solve three fundamentally different benchmark tasks: continuous control in a non-Markovian pole balancing task, discrete control on the *deep memory* T-maze task, and discrete control on the extremely stochastic 89-state Maze.

2 The Algorithm

In this section we explain our basic algorithm for learning limited-memory stochastic policies. First, we summarily review the Reinforcement Learning framework as used in this paper. The particular differentiable recurrent function approximator applied, LSTM, is briefly described. Then we outline how PGAC operates within the RL framework using LSTM as DRFA for both Actor and Policy Gradient Critic.

2.1 Reinforcement Learning – Generalized Problem Statement

First let us introduce the notation used in this paper and the corresponding RL framework (see Figure 1 for a schematic depiction of the framework used). The environment, which is assumed to be Markovian, produces a state g_t at every time step. Transitions from state to state are governed by probabilities $T(g_{t+1}|a_t, g_t)$ dependent upon action a_t executed by the agent. Let r_t be the reward assigned to the agent at time t, and let o_t be the corresponding observation produced by the environment. Both quantities, governed by fixed distributions $p(o|g)$ and $p(r|g)$, are solely dependent on the state g_t. Let $R_t = \sum_{k=t+1}^{\tau} r_k \gamma^{t-k-1}$ be the *return* at time t, where $0 < \gamma < 1$ denotes a discount factor and τ denotes the length of the episode. The agent operates in episodes on the stochastic environment, executing action a_t at every time step t, after observing observation o_t and special 'observation' r_t (the reward) which both depend only on g_t. The

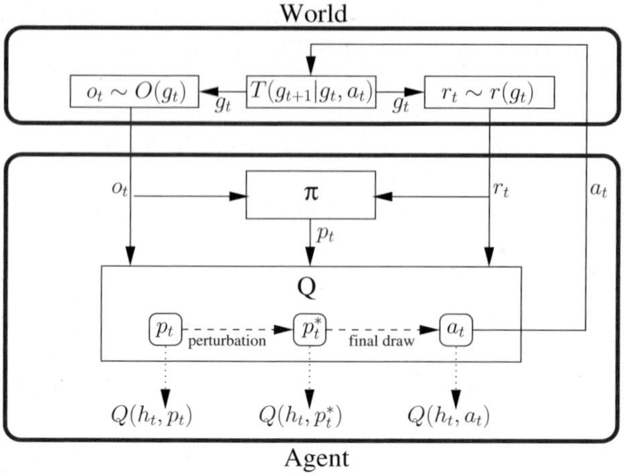

Fig. 1. PGAC in the reinforcement learning framework. Shown is the interaction between the Agent and the World. The Agent consists of two components, the Actor π_θ parameterized by weights θ and the Policy Gradient Critic Q_w parameterized by weights w. Q evaluates Actor-provided action probability distribution parameters $\mathbf{p}$, its perturbation $\mathbf{p}^*$ and the actually executed action a. Using the Jacobian of the Policy Gradient Critic, the parameters/weights of the DRFA defining the Actor are updated using regular gradient ascent.

environment-generated experience consists of finite episodes. A *history* h_t is the string of observations, rewards and actions up to moment t since the beginning of the episode: $h_t = \langle o_0, r_0, a_0, o_1, r_1, a_1, \ldots, o_t, r_t \rangle$. Policy $\pi(s_t; \theta)$ produces a vector $\mathbf{p}_t$ of probability distribution parameters (describing $\mathcal{D}_{\mathbf{p_t}}$) over actions given a memory state, from which actions a_t are drawn $a_t \sim \mathcal{D}_{\mathbf{p}_t}$. Here, internal state variable s is some DRFA-trained representation of the agent's entire history of actions, rewards and observations $s_t = f^*(\langle o_0, r_0, a_0, o_1, r_1, a_1, \ldots, o_t, r_t \rangle; \theta) = f^*(h_t; \theta) = f(s_{t-1}, (o_t, r_t); \theta)$. Now the objective of our algorithm is to optimize expected future discounted reward $\mathbf{E}[R_1] = \mathbf{E}\left[\sum_{t=1}^{T} \gamma^t r_t\right]$ by adjusting action probabilities $\mathcal{D}_{\mathbf{p}_t}$ appropriately. The estimate on the quality of action probabilities described by some parameter vector $\mathbf{p}$ can be expressed by a Q-function-like quantity: $Q(h_t, \mathbf{p}) = Q(f(h_t), \mathbf{p}) = Q(s_t, \mathbf{p})$ is a function that indicates the estimated expected future discounted reward of choosing actions following distribution $\mathcal{D}_\mathbf{p}$ at time step t after history h_t, *and following policy* π *thereafter*: $Q(h_t, \mathbf{p}) \approx \mathbf{E}\left[R_t | h_t, a_t \sim \mathcal{D}_{\mathbf{p}_t}, a_{k>t} \sim \mathcal{D}_\pi\right]$.

2.2 LSTM Recurrent Function Approximators

Differentiable recurrent function approximators constitute a class of architectures designed to deal with issues of time, such as approximating time series. A crucial feature of this class of architectures is that they are capable of relating events in a sequence, in principle even if placed arbitrarily far apart. A typical DRFA π maintains an *internal state* s_t (its memory so to say) which it uses to pass on (compressed) history information to the next moment by using recurrent connections. At every time step, the DRFA takes an input vector o_t and produces an output vector $\pi(s_t; \theta)$ from its internal state, and since the internal state s_t of any step is a function f of the previous state and the current input signal $s_t = f(o_t, s_{t-1}; \theta)$, it can take into account the entire history of past observations by using its recurrent connections for recalling events. Like conventional neural networks, DRFAs can be trained using backpropagation and related techniques based on gradient information. However, backpropagation is modified such that it works through time (BackPropagation Through Time (BPTT) [7,8]).

Recurrent Neural Networks (RNNs), a subset of this class of algorithms, have attracted some attention in the past decade because of their simplicity and potential power. However, though powerful in theory, they turn out to be quite limited in practice due to their inability to capture long-term time dependencies – they suffer from the problem of *vanishing gradient* [9], the fact that the gradient vanishes as the error signal is propagated back through time. Because of this, events more than 10 time steps apart can typically not be related.

One method purposely designed to circumvent this problem is Long Short-Term Memory (LSTM), a special RNN architecture capable of capturing long term time dependencies. The defining feature of this architecture is that it consists of a number of *memory cells*, which can be used to store activations arbitrarily long. Access to the memory cell is *gated* by units that learn to open or close depending on the context – context being present observations o_t and the previous internal state s_{t-1}.

LSTM has been shown to outperform other RNNs on time series requiring the use of deep memory [10]. Therefore, they seem well-suited for usage in RL algorithms for complex, deep memory requiring tasks. Whereas DRFAs are typically used for next step prediction, we use them as a function approximator to both estimate *value change* (the Policy Gradient Critic) and to *control* (the Actor) given histories of observations, actions and rewards.

2.3 Policy Gradient Actor-Critic

PGAC Reinforcement Learning for stochastic policies relies on the following observation: actions can be represented as special cases of *probability distribution parameters*. For example, any discrete action a can be represented as a special vector $\mathbf{p}$ where one element of $\mathbf{p}$ is 1 and the other 0. Action a_2 in a three-dimensional discrete action space can be expressed $\mathbf{p} = [0, 1, 0]$. We can apply this representation to conventional value functions, but now we can express more. Representing actions as probability distribution parameters enables us to construct Q-value functions over *action probabilities*. For example, $Q(s, [0.5, 0.5])$ would denote the value of executing a_1 with probability 0.5 and executing a_2 with probability 0.5 in state s. For a one-dimensional Gaussian case, a single action could be represented as $\mathbf{p} = [\mu, \sigma] = [3.0, 0.0]$ with $\mu = 3.0$ and $\sigma = 0.0$, but now this vector is more expressive: $Q(s, [\mu, \sigma])$ represents the estimated expected value of executing a continuous action a drawn from normal distribution $a \sim \mathcal{N}(\mu, \sigma^2)$.

Like many conventional temporal difference learning algorithms for POMDPs, the PGAC algorithm uses two differentiable recurrent function approximators: one Actor π_θ parameterized by θ, and one Critic Q_w parameterized by w. The crucial difference

Algorithm 1. Policy Gradient Actor-Critic

for each episode e **do**
  for each time step t **do**
    Actor produces parameter vector $\mathbf{p}_t$ from $\pi(h_t;\theta)$
    Perturb vector $\mathbf{p}_t$ to $\mathbf{p}_t^*$: $\mathbf{p}_t^* \sim \mathcal{P}(\mathbf{p}_t)$
    Finally draw an action a_t according to $\mathbf{p}_t^*$: $a_t \sim \mathcal{D}_{\mathbf{p}_t^*}$
    Execute action a_t, observe effects o_{t+1} and r_{t+1}
    Update (SARSA-fashion) the Policy Gradient Critic's Q_w-value function for $\langle h_t, \{\mathbf{a}_t, \mathbf{p}_t, \mathbf{p}_t^*\}\rangle$ pairs using the following TD-errors for updating w:

$$E^{TD}\langle h_{t-1}, \mathbf{p}_{t-1}\rangle = r_t + \gamma Q(h_t, \mathbf{p}_t) - Q(h_{t-1}, \mathbf{p}_{t-1})$$
$$E^{TD}\langle h_{t-1}, \mathbf{p}_{t-1}^*\rangle = r_t + \gamma Q(h_t, \mathbf{p}_t) - Q(h_{t-1}, \mathbf{p}_{t-1}^*)$$
$$E^{TD}\langle h_{t-1}, \mathbf{a}_{t-1}\rangle = r_t + \gamma Q(h_t, \mathbf{p}_t) - Q(h_{t-1}, \mathbf{a}_{t-1})$$

    Update Actor's parameters θ defining policy π as

$$\Delta\theta = \sum_i \alpha \overbrace{\frac{\partial Q(h_t, \mathbf{p}_t; w)}{\partial \mathbf{p}_t^{(i)}}}^{Critic} \underbrace{\frac{\partial \mathbf{p}_t^{(i)}}{\partial \theta}}_{Actor}$$

  end for
end for

between PGAC and other methods is the fact that its Policy Gradient Critic's Q-function evaluates probability distributions over actions rather than single actions. The Policy Gradient Critic is forced to operate on incomplete information, i.e. it has to be able to provide estimates on the quality of the policy given that the agent intends to let the actual action be drawn from a probability distribution governed by $\mathbf{p}$. This way, the agent explicitly includes the value of stochasticity in action selection in its Q-function. The fact that this extended Policy Gradient Critic evaluates action probability distributions, combined with the fact that the Actor provides the parameters for such a distribution, eliminates the need for a prewired exploration policy, since exploration is adjusted online while executing the policy. Another important reason for explicitly representing the value of stochasticity is that, because of limited memory, a stochastic policy might be the optimal one for some real-world tasks. It has been shown [2] that for some domains deterministic policies can produce arbitrarily worse performance than stochastic policies.

The Actor π_θ outputs, at every time step t, deterministically given history h_t, probability distribution parameters $\mathbf{p_t} = \pi(h_t;\theta)$ from which the agent's actions are drawn $a_t \sim \mathcal{D}_{p_t}$. Additionally, the Policy Gradient Critic $Q(h_t, \mathbf{p}; w)$ estimates the value $\mathbf{E}\Big[R_t | h_t, a_t \sim \mathcal{D}_{\mathbf{p}}, a_{k>t} \sim \mathcal{D}_\pi\Big]$ for Actor-produced $\mathbf{p_t}$. After every episode, the Actor's policy can be updated by using the Policy Gradient Critic as a teacher which provides a derivative for the direction in which to adjust Actor-provided policy $\mathbf{p}_t = \pi(h_t;\theta)$. The Policy Gradient Critic can be taught using on-policy Temporal Difference Learning techniques.

Actor Learning. The Actor is updated by updating Actor-defining parameters θ in the direction of higher expected future discounted reward *as predicted by the Policy Gradient Critic*:

$$\Delta\theta = \alpha \sum_i \frac{\partial Q(h_t, \mathbf{p}_t)}{\partial \mathbf{p}_t^{(i)}} \frac{\partial \mathbf{p}_t^{(i)}}{\partial \theta}$$

where $\mathbf{p}_t^{(i)}$ denotes parameter i of distribution parameter vector $\mathbf{p}_t = \pi(h_t)$ produced by the Actor at time t, and α denotes the learning rate. In order to compute this, using a fixed Policy Gradient Critic, we backpropagate a gradient signal towards higher Q-values from the Policy Gradient Critic's inputs $\mathbf{p}$, yielding the Jacobian of the Policy Gradient Critic, the quantities $\frac{\partial Q(h_t, \mathbf{p}_t^{(i)})}{\partial \mathbf{p}_t^{(i)}}$ for all i action probability distribution parameters. These values are then further backpropagated from the Policy Gradient Critic into the Actor architecture, now updating parameters θ along the way. In essence, the Policy Gradient Critic provides an estimate of the expected steepest gradient ascent for future discounted reward on the current incoming action distribution parameters. These estimated derivatives are then used by the Actor to update its policy, exactly in the direction of better value suggested by the Policy Gradient Critic. The algorithm pseudocode is provided in Algorithm 1.

Policy Gradient Critic Learning. The Actor can only be updated if the Policy Gradient Critic provides sufficiently accurate estimations on future discounted reward. To train the Policy Gradient Critic, on-policy Temporal Difference Learning is used. Unlike most reinforcement learning algorithms, PGAC does not learn a Q-value for actions performed $Q(h, a; w)$, it rather learns a Q-value for distributions on actions: the Q-value $Q(h_t, \mathbf{p}; w)$, represented by the Policy Gradient Critic, learns the expected value of executing one action randomly drawn from probability distribution $\mathcal{D}_{\mathbf{p}}$, and following stochastic policy π_θ thereafter.

The Q-function estimates the value of a stochastic action under the policy provided by the Actor. The Temporal Difference (TD) Errors E^{TD} that can be easily extracted from the experience are (history, action probability distribution) pairs $\langle h_{t-1}, \mathbf{p}_{t-1} \rangle$ and $\langle h_{t-1}, \mathbf{a}_{t-1} \rangle$:

$$E^{TD}\langle h_{t-1}, \mathbf{p}_{t-1} \rangle = r_t + \gamma Q(h_t, \mathbf{p}_t) - Q(h_{t-1}, \mathbf{p}_{t-1})$$
$$E^{TD}\langle h_{t-1}, \mathbf{a}_{t-1} \rangle = r_t + \gamma Q(h_t, \mathbf{p}_t) - Q(h_{t-1}, \mathbf{a}_{t-1})$$

where $\mathbf{p}$ is the Actor-produced vector of action probability distribution parameters, and $\mathbf{a}$ denotes the actually executed action. The algorithm uses the Policy Gradient Critic's Jacobian to update the Actor, that is, it has to be able to represent how a *difference* in action probabilities relates to a *difference* in value. The above two TD-errors might not provide enough data points to reliably estimate such derivatives, though, since the region *around* $\mathbf{p}_t$ is not sampled by the Actor, although that is the region where the most useful training information is localized. Therefore, we want to add perturbed samples around $\mathbf{p}_t$ in order to be able to estimate how the Q-value changes with respect to $\mathbf{p}_t$.

Providing such samples *without biasing learning* can be done using what we call a 'perturbation / final draw' operation. A 'perturbation' operation $\mathcal{P}$ perturbs probability distribution parameters $\mathbf{p}$ – provided by the Actor – onto a new parameter vector $\mathbf{p}^* \sim \mathcal{P}(\mathbf{p})$, such that the expected distribution of actions a drawn from $a \sim \mathcal{D}_{\mathbf{p}^*}$ follow the same distribution as actions drawn from the original $a \sim \mathcal{D}_{\mathbf{p}}$.

Example distributions that can be perturbed are finite discrete distributions, where all elements of vector $\mathbf{p}$ sum up to 1 (which, in our experiments, is implemented as a softmax layer), or a Gaussian distribution, e.g. $\mathbf{p} = [\mu.\sigma]$. For finite discrete distributions, one way to construct a perturbation operation is to use a random number generator u_i where each u_i represents a uniformly distributed random number between 0 and 1. Good approximate values for $\mathbf{p}^*$ can then be generated by $p_i^* = \frac{p_i + \beta p_i u_i}{\sum_j p_j + \beta p_j u_j}$ where β is a constant, taken to be 1 in this paper. For the simple Gaussian case $\mathbf{p} = [\mu_p, \sigma_p]$, we could construct perturbation $\mathbf{p}^* = [\mu_{p^*} \sim \mathcal{N}(\mu_p, \sigma_p/2), 0.866\sigma_p]$.

Thus constructing $\mathbf{p}^*$ values around $\mathbf{p}$ provides us with informative extra samples – we could see them as hypothetical stochastic actions – that enable the function approximator to estimate the value of other action probabilities than just those provided by the Actor. This yields the following SARSA-like TD-errors for $\mathbf{p}$, $\mathbf{p}^*$ and $\mathbf{a}$:

$$E^{TD}\langle h_{t-1}, \mathbf{p}_{t-1}\rangle = r_t + \gamma Q(h_t, \mathbf{p}_t) - Q(h_{t-1}, \mathbf{p}_{t-1})$$
$$E^{TD}\langle h_{t-1}, \mathbf{p}^*_{t-1}\rangle = r_t + \gamma Q(h_t, \mathbf{p}_t) - Q(h_{t-1}, \mathbf{p}^*_{t-1})$$
$$E^{TD}\langle h_{t-1}, \mathbf{a}_{t-1}\rangle = r_t + \gamma Q(h_t, \mathbf{p}_t) - Q(h_{t-1}, \mathbf{a}_{t-1})$$

It seems prudent to choose $\mathcal{P}$ such that $\mathbf{p}^*$ are generated reasonably close to $\mathbf{p}$.

Because of *limited memory*'s inheritantly imperfect state-from-history extraction capabilities, there will always be a measure of hidden state present. If the amount of state uncertainty reaches undesirable levels, it may be appropriate *not* to use TD-learning techniques to train the Policy Gradient Critic, since conventional TD-updates are essentially flawed in hidden state situations with discounted payoff [2]. Instead, one would use direct history-to-return mappings. In essence, this can already be accomplished by simply using eligibility traces, which achieves a similar effect as λ approaches 1.

3 Experiments

We carried out experiments on three fundamentally different problem domains. The first task, pole balancing with incomplete state information, is a *continuous* control task that has been a benchmark in the RL community for many years. The second task, the T-maze, is a difficult discrete control task that requires the agent to learn to remember its initial observation until the end of the episode. The third task, the 89-state Maze [11], is an extremely stochastic discrete control task.

All experiments were carried out with 15-cell LSTMs with direct input-output connections for both Actor and Policy Gradient Critic, and learning took place in batches of 100 sequences (251 in the case of the 89-state Maze). Plain gradient descent and ascent were used for Policy Gradient Critic and Actor, respectively. All experiments used an eligibility trace with $\lambda = 0.8$.

3.1 Continuous Control: Non-markovian Pole Balancing

This task involves trying to balance a pole hinged to a cart that moves on a finite track (see Figure 2). The single control consists of the force F applied to the cart (in Newtons), and observations usually include the cart's position x and the pole's angle β and velocities $\dot{x}$ and $\dot{\beta}$. It provides a perfect testbed for algorithms focussing on learning fine control in continuous state and action spaces. However, recent successes in the RL field have made the standard pole balancing setup too easy and therefore obsolete. To make the task more challenging, an extension is made: remove velocity information $\dot{x}$ and $\dot{\beta}$ such that the problem becomes non-Markov. This yields non-Markovian pole balancing [12], a more challenging task.

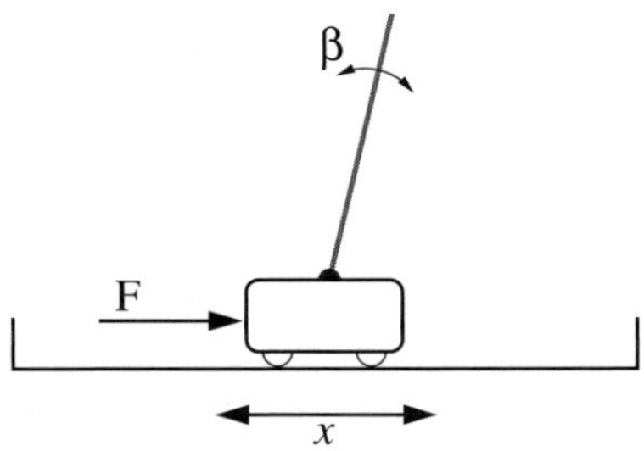

Fig. 2. The non-Markov pole balancing task. The task consists of a moving cart on a track, with a pole hinged on top. The controller applies a (continuous) force F to the cart at every time step, after observing the pole angle β (but not the angular velocity, making this a non-Markovian problem). The objective is to indefinitely keep the pole from falling.

We applied PGAC to the pole balancing task, using a Gaussian output structure, consisting of a μ output neuron (which was interpreted linearly) and a σ output neuron (which was scaled with the logistic function in order to prevent σ from being negative). Using $\gamma = 0.99$, reward was set to 0.0 at all time steps, except for the last time step when one of the poles falls over, where the reward is -1.0.

A run was considered a *success* when the pole did not fall over for $5,000$ time steps. Averaged over 20 runs, it took $34,823$ evaluations until the success criterion was reached. Interesting is that during learning, often the full stochastic policy had a higher value than the greedy policy (setting σ to 0), showing the usefulness of learning stochastic policies. The results for non-Markovian control clearly outperform most other single-agent memory-based continuous RL methods as far as we are aware (e.g. compare [4]'s finite state controller which cannot hold up the pole for more than 1000 time steps even after half a million evaluations), but some methods that are not single-agent, like evolutionary methods (e.g. [5]), still hold a competitive edge over PGAC.

3.2 Discrete Control: The Long Term Dependency T-Maze

The second experiment was carried out on the T-maze [13] (see Figure 3), a discrete control task with output neurons that code for a softmax layer from which an action is

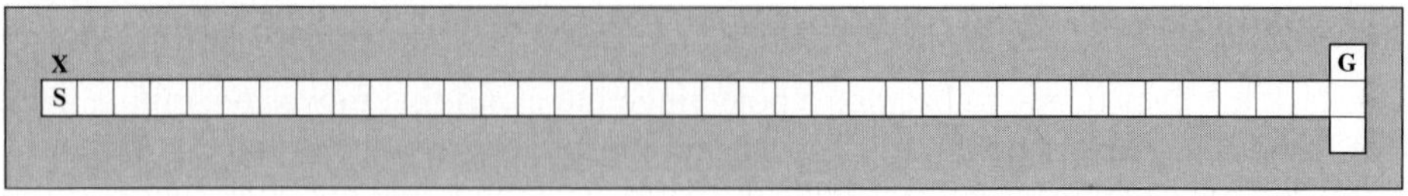

Fig. 3. The T-maze task. The agent observes its immediate surroundings and is capable of the actions north, east, south, and west. It starts in the position labeled 'S', there and only there observing either the signal 'up' or 'down', indicating whether it should go up or down at the T-junction. It receives a reward if it goes in the right direction, and a punishment if not. In this example, the direction is 'up' and N, the length of the alley, is 35.

drawn probabilistically. Designed to test an RL algorithm's ability to correlate events far apart in history, it involves having to *learn* to remember the observation from the first time step until the episode ends. At the first time step, it starts at position **S** and perceives the **X** either north or south – meaning that the goal state **G** is in the north or south part of the T-junction, respectively. Additionally to the first state's **X**-flag, the agent perceives only its immediate surroundings – whether there is a wall north, east, south or west of it. The agent has four possible actions: North, East, South and West. While in the corridor, if the agent bumps into the wall, it receives a punishment of -0.1, while if it goes east or west, it receives a reward of 0.0. When the agent makes the correct decision at the T-junction, i.e. go south if the **X** was south and north otherwise, it receives a reward of 4.0, otherwise a reward of -0.1. In both cases, this ends the episode. Note that the corridor length N can be increased to make the problem more difficult, since the agent has to learn to remember the initial 'road sign' for $N + 1$ time steps. In Figure 3 we see an example T-maze with corridor length 35.

Corridor length N was systematically varied from 10 to 60, and for each length 10 runs were performed. Discount factor $\gamma = 0.98$ was used. In Figure 4 the results are displayed. Using LSTM, PGAC is able to capture the relevant long term dependencies (up to 40 time steps) necessary for solving this task. This is only slightly worse than the best performing algorithm known to solve this task [13] which learns the task up to corridor length 70.

3.3 Discrete Control: The 89-State Maze

In this extremely noisy benchmark task (see Figure 5; see [11] for a complete description) the aim is to get to the goal as fast as possible (where the reward is 1), but within 251 time steps. Discount factor $\gamma = 0.98$ is used.

Good results were achieved for 10 runs of the algorithm. Each run was executed for $30,000,000$ iterations. After that, the resulting policy was evaluated. The median number of steps to achieve the goal (in case the goal is achieved) was 70, and the goal was reached in 85% of cases. This compares favorably with memory-less SARSA(λ) [14], one of the best (and similar) model-free approaches on this task, with numbers 73 steps and 77%, respectively. However, Bakker's RL-LSTM method [15] still clearly outperforms the PGAC algorithm with 61 steps and 93.9%, respectively.

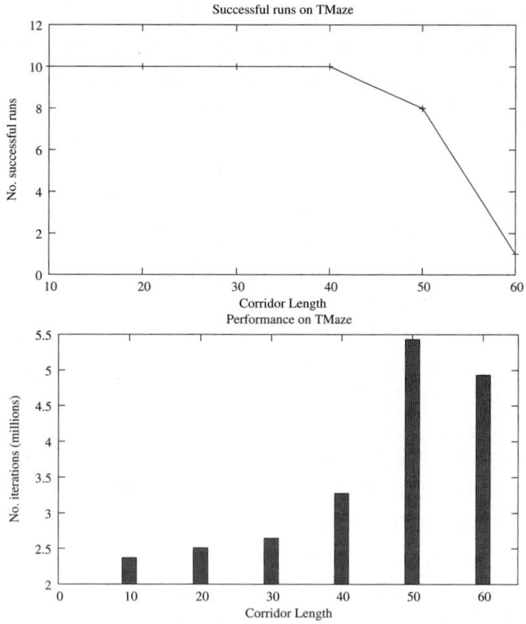

Fig. 4. T-maze results. The upper chart shows the number of successful runs for $N = 10, \ldots, 60$. PGAC Reinforcement Learning's performance starts to degrade at length $N = 50$. The lower plot shows the number of average iterations required to solve the task, averaged over the successful runs.

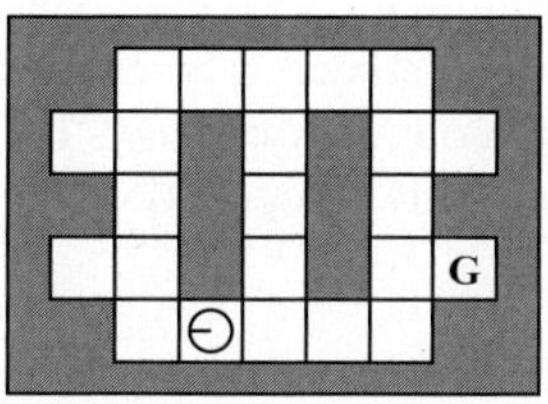

Fig. 5. The 89-state maze. In this extremely stochastic maze, the agent has a position, an orientation, and can execute five different actions: forward, turnleft, turnright, turnabout, and doNothing. The agent starts every trial in a random position. Its goal is to move to the square labeled 'G'. Observations comprise the local walls but are noisy (there is a high probability of observing walls where there are none and vice versa). Action outcomes are noisy and cannot be relied on. See [11] for a complete description of this problem domain. It is interesting to note that, to the authors' knowledge, this domain has as of yet not been satisfactorily solved, that is, solved up to human-comparable performance. That is what makes this a very interesting task.

4 Discussion

Initial results with PGAC Reinforcement Learning show that it is competitive with some of the best approaches on very different benchmark tasks. It does not yet outperform the best available approaches, though. This might be due to two reasons. First, the selection of the perturbation operator has a large influence on estimation variance. Further research into adjusting the choice of this operator might include investigating the appropriate finetuning of perturbations given the entropy in action distributions. Second, since the algorithm uses a limited-memory algorithm, some measure of hidden state remains present. This means that using on-policy temporal difference value updates as discussed above is essentially flawed, although this problem is largely overcome by the use of eligibility traces. A more correct but likely slower approach would involve estimating returns directly from histories.

Since the algorithm addresses learning limited-memory stochastic policies – an under-researched general class of problems which is essential to numerous real-world reinforcement learning tasks – in a simple, natural framework, we hope its performance will be boosted in future research by further analysis and the use of more advanced techniques in, for example, gradient-based learning methods, temporal difference algorithms and DRFA architectures. One area for improvement could include the development of a more principled method for creating action distribution perturbations, or, alternatively, the use of noise in the executed actions while weighting the obtained data points proportionally to their respective probability densities.

Although policy gradient methods can also learn stochastic policies, PGAC is specifically designed to both learn memory and to assign explicit value to stochasticity, making it ideally suited to learning limited-memory stochastic policies. A key feature of the algorithm is that the resulting stochastic policies are not learnt from brute force sampling, but by using an actual Policy Gradient Critic model, with the advantage of generalization and possibly lower estimation variance.

PGAC can be seen as an instance of generalized policy iteration, where value and policy iteratively improve, reinforcing each other. Since a gradient is used to update the action probabilities, it is not guaranteed to converge to a global optimum. However, the use of stochasticity in continuous action spaces holds the promise of overcoming at least part of the sensitivity normally associated with gradient-based continuous reinforcement learning.

5 Conclusion

We have introduced PGAC Reinforcement Learning, a new RL method for learning limited-memory stochastic policies which updates continuous and stochastic policies. A Policy Gradient Critic explicitly attributes value to stochasticity, yielding a flexible algorithm that does not need a prewired exploration strategy since it *learns* to adapt its stochastic action probabilities through experience. Using an appropriate recurrent function approximator, Long Short-Term Memory, the algorithm is capable of solving difficult tasks in environments with long time dependencies and continuous action spaces. Showing competitive results on three benchmark tasks, this algorithm seems promising for extensions to real-world RL tasks.

Acknowledgments

This research was funded by SNF grant 200021-111968/1.

References

1. Sutton, R., Barto, A.: Reinforcement learning: An introduction. MIT Press, Cambridge, MA (1998)
2. Singh, S., Jaakkola, T., Jordan, M.: Learning without state-estimation in partially observable markovian decision processes. In: International Conference on Machine Learning, pp. 284–292 (1994)
3. Aberdeen, D.: Policy-Gradient Algorithms for Partially Observable Markov Decision Processes. PhD thesis, Australian National University (2003)
4. Meuleau, N.L., Kim, K., Kaelbling, L.P.: Learning finite-state controllers for partially observable environments. In: Proc. Fifteenth Conference on Uncertainty in Artificial Intelligence (UAI '99), pp. 427–436. Morgan Kaufmann, San Francisco (1999)
5. Gomez, F.J., Schmidhuber, J.: Co-evolving recurrent neurons learn deep memory POMDPs. In: Proc. of the 2005 conference on genetic and evolutionary computation (GECCO), Washington, D. C., ACM Press, New York (2005)
6. Hochreiter, S., Schmidhuber, J.: Long short-term memory. Neural Computation 9(8), 1735–1780 (1997)
7. Werbos, P.: Back propagation through time: What it does and how to do it. Proceedings of the IEEE 78, 1550–1560 (1990)
8. Williams, R.J., Zipser, D.: A learning algorithm for continually running fully recurrent networks. Neural Computation 1(2), 270–280 (1989)
9. Hochreiter, S., Bengio, Y., Frasconi, P., Schmidhuber, J.: Gradient flow in recurrent nets: the difficulty of learning long-term dependencies. In: Kremer, S.C., Kolen, J.F. (eds.) A Field Guide to Dynamical Recurrent Neural Networks, IEEE Press, Los Alamitos (2001)
10. Schmidhuber, J.: RNN overview, with links to a dozen journal publications (2004) `http://www.idsia.ch/~juergen/rnn.html`
11. Littman, M., Cassandra, A., Kaelbling, L.: Learning policies for partially observable environments: Scaling up. In: Prieditis, A., Russell, S. (eds.) Machine Learning: Proceedings of the Twelfth International Conference, pp. 362–370. Morgan Kaufmann Publishers, San Francisco, CA (1995)
12. Wieland, A.: Evolving neural network controllers for unstable systems. In: Proceedings of the International Joint Conference on Neural Networks, Seattle, WA, pp. 667–673. IEEE, Piscataway, NJ (1991)
13. Bakker, B.: Reinforcement learning with long short-term memory. Advances in Neural Information Processing Syst. 14 (2002)
14. Loch, J., Singh, S.: Using eligibility traces to find the best memoryless policy in partially observable Markov decision processes. In: Proc. 15th International Conf. on Machine Learning, pp. 323–331. Morgan Kaufmann, San Francisco, CA (1998)
15. Bakker, B.: The State of Mind: Reinforcement Learning with Recurrent Neural Networks. PhD thesis, Leiden University (2004)

An Improved Model Selection Heuristic for AUC

Shaomin Wu[1], Peter Flach[2], and Cèsar Ferri[3]

[1] Cranfield University, United Kingdom
Shaomin.Wu@cranfield.ac.uk
[2] University of Bristol, United Kingdom
Peter.Flach@bristol.ac.uk
[3] Universitat Politècnica de València, Spain
cferri@dsic.upv.es

Abstract. The area under the ROC curve (AUC) has been widely used to measure ranking performance for binary classification tasks. AUC only employs the classifier's scores to rank the test instances; thus, it ignores other valuable information conveyed by the scores, such as sensitivity to small differences in the score values. However, as such differences are inevitable across samples, ignoring them may lead to overfitting the validation set when selecting models with high AUC. This problem is tackled in this paper. On the basis of ranks as well as scores, we introduce a new metric called *scored AUC* (sAUC), which is the area under the *sROC curve*. The latter measures how quickly AUC deteriorates if positive scores are decreased. We study the interpretation and statistical properties of sAUC. Experimental results on UCI data sets convincingly demonstrate the effectiveness of the new metric for classifier evaluation and selection in the case of limited validation data.

1 Introduction

In the data mining and machine learning literature, there are many learning algorithms that can be applied to build candidate models for a binary classification task. Such models can be decision trees, neural networks, naive Bayes, or ensembles of these models. As the performance of the candidate models may vary over learning algorithms, effectively selecting an optimal model is vitally important. Hence, there is a need for metrics to evaluate the performance of classification models.

The predicted outcome of a classification model can be either a class decision such as positive and negative on each instance, or a score that indicates the extent to which an instance is predicted to be positive or negative. Most models can produce scores; and those that only produce class decisions can easily be converted to models that produce scores [3,11]. In this paper we assume that the scores represent likelihoods or posterior probabilities of the positive class.

The performance of a classification model can be evaluated by many metrics such as recall, accuracy and precision. A common weakness of these metrics is that they are not robust to the change of the class distribution. When the ratio of positive to negative instances changes in a test set, a model may no longer perform optimally, or even acceptably. The ROC (Receiver Operating Characteristics) curve, however, is invariant to changes in class distribution. If the class distribution changes in a test set,

J.N. Kok et al. (Eds.): ECML 2007, LNAI 4701, pp. 478–489, 2007.

but the underlying class-conditional distributions from which the data are drawn stay the same, the ROC curve will not change. It is defined as a plot of a model's true positive rate on the y-axis against its false positive rate on the x-axis, and offers an overall measure of model performance, regardless of the different thresholds used. The ROC curve has been used as a tool for model selection in the medical area since the late 1970s, and was more recently introduced to evaluate machine learning algorithms [9,10].

The area under the ROC curve, or simply AUC, aggregates the model's behaviour for all possible decision thresholds. It can be estimated under parametric [13], semi-parametric [6] and nonparametric [5] assumptions. The nonparametric estimate of the AUC is widely used in the machine learning and data mining research communities. It is the summation of the areas of the trapezoids formed by connecting the points on the ROC curve, and represents the probability that a randomly selected positive instance will score higher than a randomly selected negative instance. It is equivalent to the Wilcoxon-Mann-Whitney (WMW) U statistic test of ranks [5]. Huang and Ling [8] argue that AUC is preferable as a measure for model evaluation over accuracy.

The nonparametric estimate of the AUC is calculated on the basis of the ranks of the scores. Its advantage is that it does not depend on any distribution assumption that is commonly required in parametric statistics. Its weakness is that the scores are only used to rank instances, and otherwise ignored. The AUC, estimated simply from the ranks of the scores, can remain unchanged even when the scores change. This can lead to a loss of useful information, and may therefore produce sub-optimal results.

In this paper we argue that, in order to evaluate the performance of binary classification models, both ranks and scores should be combined. A scored AUC metric is introduced for estimating the performance of models based on their original scores. The paper is structured as follows. Section 2 reviews ways to evaluate scoring classifiers, including AUC and Brier score, and gives a simple and elegant algorithm to calculate AUC. Section 3 introduces the *scored ROC curve* and the new *scored AUC* metric, and investigates its properties. In Section 4 we present experimental results on 17 data sets from the UCI repository, which unequivocally demonstrate that validation sAUC is superior to validation AUC and validation Brier score for selecting models with high test AUC when limited validation data is available. Section 5 presents the main conclusions and suggests further work. An early version of this paper appeared as [12].

2 Evaluating Classifiers

There are a number of ways of evaluating the performance of scoring classifiers over a test set. Broadly, the choices are to evaluate its *classification* performance, its *ranking performance*, or its *probability estimation* performance. Classification performance is evaluated by a measure such as accuracy, which is the proportion of test instances that is correctly classified. Probability estimation performance is evaluated by a measure such as mean squared error, also called the *Brier score*, which can be expressed as $\sum_x(\hat{p}(x) - p(x))^2$, where $\hat{p}(x)$ is the estimated probability for instance x, and $p(x)$ is 1 if x is positive and 0 if x is negative. The calculation of both accuracy and Brier score is an $O(n)$ operation, where n is the size of the test set.

Ranking performance is evaluated by sorting the test instances on their score, which is an $O(n\log n)$ operation. It thus incorporates performance information that neither accuracy nor Brier score can access. There are a number of reasons why it is desirable to have a good ranker, rather than a good classifier or a good probability estimator. One of the main reasons is that accuracy requires a fixed score threshold, whereas it may be desirable to change the threshold in response to changing class or cost distributions. Good accuracy obtained with one threshold does not imply good accuracy with another. Furthermore, good performance in both classification and probability estimation is easily obtained if one class is much more prevalent than the other. For these reasons we prefer to evaluate ranking performance. This can be done by constructing an ROC curve.

An ROC curve is generally defined as a piecewise linear curve, plotting a model's true positive rate on the y-axis against its false positive rate on the x-axis, evaluated under all possible thresholds on the score. For a test set with t test instances, the ROC curve will have (up to) t linear segments and $t+1$ points. We are interested in the area under this curve, which is well-known to be equivalent to the Wilcoxon-Mann-Whitney sum of ranks test, and estimates the probability that a randomly chosen positive is ranked before a randomly chosen negative. AUC can be calculated directly from the sorted test instances, without the need for drawing an ROC curve or calculating ranks, as we now show.

Denote the total number of positive instances and negative instances by m and n, respectively. Let $\{y_1,\dots,y_m\}$ be the scores predicted by a model for the m positives, and $\{x_1,\dots,x_n\}$ be the scores predicted by a model for the n negatives. Assume both y_i and x_j are within the interval $[0,1]$ for all $i = 1,2,...,m$ and $j = 1,2,...,n$; high scores are interpreted as evidence for the positive class. By a slight abuse of language, we will sometimes use positive (negative) score to mean 'score of a positive (negative) instance'.

AUC simply counts the number of pairs of positives and negatives such that the former has higher score than the latter, and can therefore be defined as follows:

$$\hat{\theta} = \frac{1}{mn}\sum_{i=1}^{m}\sum_{j=1}^{n}\psi_{ij} \tag{1}$$

where ψ_{ij} is 1 if $y_i - x_j > 0$, and 0 otherwise. Let Z_a be the sequence produced by merging $\{y_1,\dots,y_m\}$ and $\{x_1,\dots,x_n\}$ and sorting the merged set in ascending order (so a good ranker would put the positives after the negatives in Z_a), and let r_i be the rank of y_i in Z_a. Then AUC can be expressed in terms of ranks as follows:

$$\hat{\theta} = \frac{1}{mn}\left(\sum_{i=1}^{m} r_i - \frac{m(m+1)}{2}\right) = \frac{1}{mn}\sum_{i=1}^{m}(r_i - i) = \frac{1}{mn}\sum_{i=1}^{m}\sum_{t=1}^{r_i-i} 1 \tag{2}$$

Here, $r_i - i$ is the number of negatives before the ith positive in Z_a, and thus AUC is the (normalised) sum of the number of negatives before each of the m positives in Z_a.

Dually, let Z_d be the sequence produced by sorting $\{y_1,\dots,y_m\}\cup\{x_1,\dots,x_n\}$ in descending order (so a good ranker would put the positives before the negatives in Z_d). We then obtain

$$\hat{\theta} = \frac{1}{mn}\sum_{j=1}^{n}(s_j - j) = \frac{1}{mn}\sum_{j=1}^{n}\sum_{t=1}^{s_j-j} 1 \tag{3}$$

Table 1. Column-wise algorithm for calculating AUC

Inputs: m positive and n negative test instances, sorted by decreasing score;
Outputs: $\hat{\theta}$: AUC value of the model;
Algorithm:

1: Initialise: $AUC \leftarrow 0$, $c \leftarrow 0$
2: **for** each consecutive instance in the ranking **do**
3:     **if** the instance is positive **then**
4:         $c \leftarrow c + 1$
5:     **else**
6:         $AUC \leftarrow AUC + c$
7:     **end if**
8: **end for**
9: $\hat{\theta} \leftarrow \frac{AUC}{mn}$

where s_j is the rank of x_j in Z_d, and $s_j - j$ is the number of positives before the jth negative in Z_d. From this perspective, AUC represents the normalised sum of the number of positives before each of the n negatives in Z_d.

From Eq. (3) we obtain the algorithm shown in Table 1 to calculate the value of the AUC. The algorithm is different from other algorithms to calculate AUC (e.g., [4]) because it doesn't explicitly manipulate ranks. The algorithm works by calculating AUC column-wise in ROC space, where c represents the (un-normalised) height of the current column. For simplicity, we assume there are no ties (this can be easily incorporated by reducing the increment of AUC in line 6). A dual, row-wise algorithm using the ascending ordering Z_a can be derived from Eq. (2). Alternatively, we can calculate the *Area Over the Curve (AOC)* row-wise using the descending ordering, and set $\hat{\theta} \leftarrow \frac{mn-AOC}{mn}$ at the end.

3 sROC Curves and Scored AUC

Our main interest in this paper is to select models that perform well as rankers. To that end, we could simply evaluate AUC on a validation set and select those models with highest AUC. However, this method may suffer from overfitting the validation set whenever small difference in the score values lead to considerable differences in AUC.

Example 1. Two models, M_1 and M_2, are evaluated on a small test set containing 3 positives and 3 negatives. We obtain the following scores:

$$M_1 : 1.0+\ 0.7+\ 0.6+\ 0.5-\ 0.4-\ 0.0-$$
$$M_2 : 1.0+\ 0.9+\ 0.6-\ 0.5+\ 0.2-\ 0.0-$$

Here, for example, $0.7+$ means that a positive instance receives a score of 0.7, and $0.6-$ means that a negative instance receives a score of 0.6. In terms of AUC, M_1 achieves the perfect ranking, while M_2 has $AUC = 8/9$. In terms of Brier score, both models perform equally, as the sum of squared errors is 0.66 in both cases, and the mean squared error is 0.11. However, one could argue that M_2 is preferable as its ranking is much less sensitive

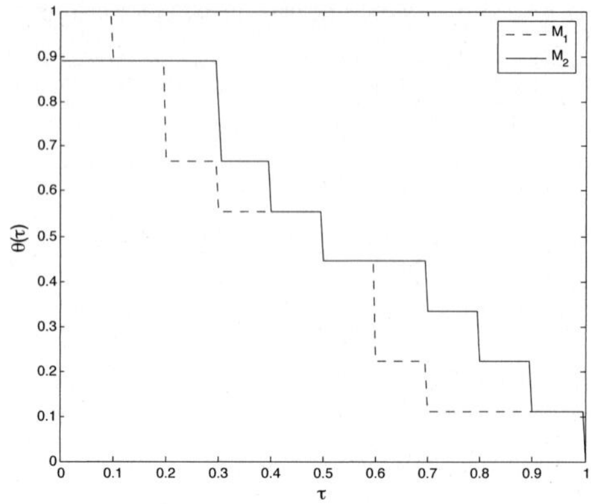

Fig. 1. sROC curves for example models M_1 and M_2 from Example 1

to drift of the scores. For instance, if we subtract 0.25 from the positive scores, the AUC of M_1 decreases to $6/9$, but the AUC of M_2 stays the same.

In order to study this more closely, we introduce the following parameterised version of AUC.

Definition 1. *Given a* margin τ *with* $0 \leq \tau \leq 1$, *the* margin-based AUC *is defined as*

$$\hat{\theta}(\tau) = \frac{1}{mn} \sum_{i=1}^{m} \sum_{j=1}^{n} \psi_{ij}(\tau) \tag{4}$$

where $\psi_{ij}(\tau)$ *is 1 if* $y_i - x_j > \tau$, *and 0 otherwise.*

Clearly, $\hat{\theta}(0) = \hat{\theta}$, and $\hat{\theta}(1) = 0$. More generally, $\hat{\theta}(\tau)$ is a non-increasing step function in τ. It has (up to) mn horizontal segments. For a given τ, $\hat{\theta}(\tau)$ can be interpreted as the AUC resulting from decreasing all positive scores with τ (or increasing all negative scores with τ). Figure 1 plots $\hat{\theta}(\tau)$ of models M_1 and M_2 from Example 1. It is clear that the margin-based AUC of M_1 deteriorates more rapidly with τ than that of M_2, even though its initial AUC is higher. We call such a plot of $\hat{\theta}(\tau)$ against τ an *sROC curve*.

Consider the area under the sROC curve, denoted by $\hat{\theta}_s$. This is a measure of how rapidly the AUC deteriorates with increasing margin. It can be calculated without explicitly constructing the sROC curve, as follows.

Theorem 1. $\hat{\theta}_s = \frac{1}{mn} \sum_{i=1}^{m} \sum_{j=1}^{n} (y_i - x_j)\psi_{ij}$.

Proof

$$\begin{aligned}\hat{\theta}_s &= \int_0^1 \hat{\theta}(\tau) d\tau = \int_0^1 \frac{1}{mn} \sum_{i=1}^{m} \sum_{j=1}^{n} \psi_{ij}(\tau) d\tau \\ &= \frac{1}{mn} \sum_{i=1}^{m} \sum_{j=1}^{n} \int_0^1 \psi_{ij}(\tau) d\tau = \frac{1}{mn} \sum_{i=1}^{m} \sum_{j=1}^{n} (y_i - x_j)\psi_{ij}\end{aligned} \tag{5}$$

Thus, just as $\hat{\theta}$ is the area under the ROC curve, $\hat{\theta}_s$ is the area under the sROC curve; we call it *scored AUC (sAUC)*. An equivalent definition of sAUC was introduced in [12], and independently by Huang and Ling, who refer to it as *soft AUC* [7]. Its interpretation as the area under the sROC curve is, to the best of our knowledge, novel. The sROC curve depicts the stability of AUC with increasing margins, and sAUC aggregates this over all margins into a single statistic.

Whereas in Eq. (1) the term ψ_{ij} is an indicator that only reflects the ordinal comparison between the scores, $(y_i - x_j)\psi_{ij}$ in Eq. (5) measures how much y_i is larger than x_j. Notice that, by including the ordinal term, we combine information from both ranks and scores. Indeed, if we omit ψ_{ij} from Eq. (5) the expression reduces to $\frac{1}{m}\sum_{i=1}^{m} y_i - \frac{1}{n}\sum_{i=1}^{n} x_i = M^+ - M^-$; i.e., the difference between the mean positive and negative scores. This measure (a quantity that takes scores into account but ignores the ranking) is investigated in [2].

We continue to analyse the properties of sAUC. Let $R^+ = \frac{1}{m}\sum_{i=1}^{m} \frac{r_i - i}{n} y_i$ be the weighted average of the positive scores, weighted by the proportion of negatives that are correctly ranked relative to each positive. Similarly, let $R^- = \frac{1}{n}\sum_{j=1}^{n} \frac{s_j - j}{m} x_j$ be the weighted average of the negative scores, weighted by the proportion of positives that are correctly ranked relative to each negative (i.e., the height of the column under the ROC curve). We then have the following useful reformulation of sAUC.

Theorem 2. $\hat{\theta}_s = R^+ - R^-$.

Proof

$$\hat{\theta}_s = \frac{1}{mn}\sum_{i=1}^{m}\sum_{j=1}^{n}(y_i - x_j)\psi_{ij} = \frac{1}{mn}\sum_{i=1}^{m}\sum_{j=1}^{n} y_i\psi_{ij} - \frac{1}{mn}\sum_{i=1}^{m}\sum_{j=1}^{n} x_j\psi_{ij} =$$

$$= \frac{1}{mn}\sum_{i=1}^{m}\sum_{j=1}^{r_i - i} y_i - \frac{1}{mn}\sum_{j=1}^{n}\sum_{i=1}^{s_j - j} x_j = \frac{1}{m}\sum_{i=1}^{m}\frac{r_i - i}{n} y_i - \frac{1}{n}\sum_{j=1}^{n}\frac{s_j - j}{m} x_j = R^+ - R^-$$

This immediately leads to the algorithm for calculating $\hat{\theta}_s$ in Table 2. The algorithm calculates R^+ column-wise as in the AUC algorithm (Table 1), and the complement of R^- row-wise (so that the descending ordering can be used in both cases).

Example 2. Continuing Example 1, we have

M_1: $R^+ = 0.77$, $R^- = 0.3$ and $\hat{\theta}_s = 0.47$;
M_2: $R^+ = 0.74$, $R^- = 0.2$ and $\hat{\theta}_s = 0.54$.

We thus have that M_2 is somewhat better in terms of sAUC than M_1 because, even though its AUC is lower, it is robust over a larger range of margins.

The following theorems relate $\hat{\theta}_s$, $\hat{\theta}$ and $M^+ - M^-$.

Theorem 3. *(1) $R^+ \leq M^+$ and $R^- \leq M^-$.*
(2) $M^+ - M^- \leq \hat{\theta}_s \leq \hat{\theta}$.

Table 2. Algorithm for calculating sAUC

Inputs: m positive and n negative test instances, sorted by decreasing score;
Outputs: $\hat{\theta}_s$: scored AUC;
Algorithm:

```
Initialise: AOC ← 0, AUC ← 0, r ← 0, c ← 0
for each consecutive instance with score s do
    if the instance is positive then
        c ← c + s
        AOC ← AOC + r
    else
        r ← r + s
        AUC ← AUC + c
    end if
end for
R⁻ ← (mr − AOC)/(mn)
R⁺ ← AUC/(mn)
θ̂_s ← R⁺ − R⁻
```

Proof. (1)

$$R^+ = \frac{1}{mn}\sum_{i=1}^{m}\sum_{j=1}^{r_i-i} y_i \le \frac{1}{mn}\sum_{i=1}^{m}\sum_{j=1}^{n} y_i = M^+$$

$$R^- = \frac{1}{mn}\sum_{j=1}^{n}\sum_{i=1}^{s_j-j} x_j \le \frac{1}{mn}\sum_{j=1}^{n}\sum_{i=1}^{m} x_j = M^-$$

(2)

$$\begin{aligned} M^+ - M^- &= \frac{1}{mn}\sum_{i=1}^{m}\sum_{j=1}^{n}(y_i - x_j) \le \frac{1}{mn}\sum_{i=1}^{m}\sum_{j=1}^{n}(y_i - x_j)\psi_{ij} \\ &= \hat{\theta}_s \le \frac{1}{mn}\sum_{i=1}^{m}\sum_{j=1}^{n}\psi_{ij} = \hat{\theta} \end{aligned}$$

The last step follows because $y_i \le 1$ and $0 \le x_j \le 1$, hence $y_i - x_j \le 1$, for any i and j.

Theorem 4. *(1) For separated scores (i.e., $y_i > x_j$ for any i and j), $M^+ - M^- = \hat{\theta}_s \le \hat{\theta} = 1$.*
(2) For perfect scores (i.e., $y_i = 1$ and $x_j = 0$ for any i and j), $M^+ - M^- = \hat{\theta}_s = \hat{\theta} = 1$.

Proof. (1) For separated scores we have $\psi_{ij} = 1$ for any i and j, hence $M^+ - M^- = \hat{\theta}_s$ and $\hat{\theta} = 1$.
(2) For perfect scores we additionally have $y_i - x_j = 1$ for any i and j, hence $\hat{\theta}_s = 1$.

Finally, we investigate the statistical properties of sAUC. We note that $\hat{\theta}_s$ is an unbiased estimate of $\theta_s = \int_0^1 P(y > x + \tau)d\tau$, which is proved in the following theorem.

Theorem 5. *$\hat{\theta}_s$ is an unbiased estimate of θ_s.*

Proof. From Eq. (5), we have

$$E(\hat{\theta}_s) = \mathrm{E}\left[\frac{1}{mn}\sum_{i=1}^{m}\sum_{j=1}^{n}\int_0^1 \psi_{ij}(\tau)d\tau\right] = \int_0^1 \left(\mathrm{E}\left[\frac{1}{mn}\sum_{i=1}^{m}\sum_{j=1}^{n}\psi_{ij}(\tau)\right]\right)d\tau$$
$$= \int_0^1 P(y > x+\tau)d\tau$$

The variance of the estimate $\hat{\theta}_s$ can be obtained using the method of DeLong et al. [1] (we omit the proof due to lack of space).

Theorem 6. *The variance of* $\hat{\theta}_s$ *is estimated by*

$$\mathrm{var}(\hat{\theta}_s) = \frac{n-1}{mn(m-1)}\sum_{i=1}^{m}\left(\frac{1}{n}\sum_{j=1}^{n}(y_i - x_i)\psi_{ij} - \hat{\theta}_s\right)^2 + \frac{m-1}{mn(n-1)}\sum_{j=1}^{n}\left(\frac{1}{m}\sum_{i=1}^{m}(y_i - x_i)\psi_{ij} - \hat{\theta}_s\right)^2.$$

4 Experimental Evaluation

Our experiments to evaluate the usefulness of sAUC for model selection are described in this section. Our main conclusion is that sAUC outperforms AUC and BS (Brier score) for selecting models, particularly when validation data is limited. We attribute this to sAUC having a lower variance than AUC and BS. Consequently, validation set values generalise better to test set values.

In the first experiment, we generated two artificial data sets (A and B) of 100 examples, each labelled with a 'true' probability p which is uniformly sampled from $[0,1]$. Then, we label the instances (+ if $p \geq 0.5$, $-$ otherwise). Finally, we swap the classes of 10 examples of data set A, and of 11 examples of data set B. We then construct 'models' M_A and M_B by giving them access to the 'true' probabilities p, and record which one is better (either M_A on data set A or M_B on data set B). For example, by thresholding p at 0.5, M_A has accuracy 90% on data set A, and M_B has accuracy 89% on data set B. We then add noise to obtain 'estimated' probabilities in the following way: $p' = p + k * U(-0.5, 0.5)$, where k is a noise parameter, and $U(-0.5, 0.5)$ obtains a pseudo-random number between -0.5 and 0.5 using a uniform distribution (if the corrupted values are > 1 or < 0, we set them to 1 and 0 respectively).

After adding noise, we again determine which model is better according to the four measures. In Figure 2, we show the proportion of cases where noise has provoked a change in the selection of the better model, using different values of the noise parameter k (averaged over 10,000 runs for each value of k). As expected, the percentage of changes increases with respect to noise for all four measures, but sAUC presents the most robust behaviour among all these four measures. This simple experiment shows that AUC, BS and accuracy are more vulnerable to the existence of noise in the predicted probabilities, and therefore, in this situation, the model selected by sAUC is more reliable than the models selected by the other three measures.

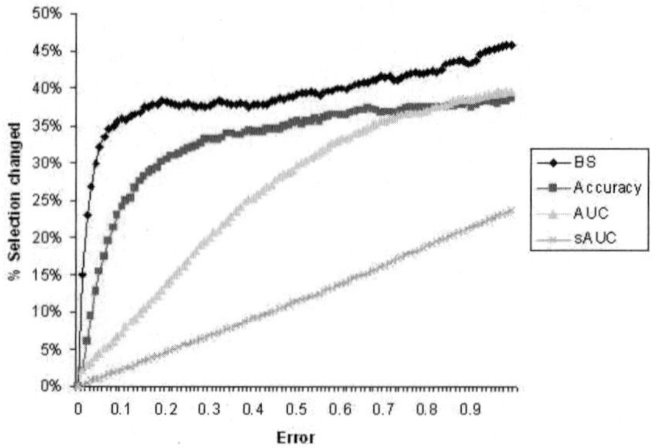

Fig. 2. The effect of noise in the probability estimates on four model selection measures

We continue reporting our experiments with real data. We use the three metrics (AUC, sAUC and BS) to select models on the validation set, and compare them using the AUC values on the test set. 17 two-class data sets are selected from the UCI repository for this purpose. Table 3 lists their numbers of attributes, numbers of instances, and relative size of the majority class.

Table 3. UCI data sets used in the experiments (larger data sets used in separate experiment in **bold face**)

# Data set	#Attrs	#Exs	%Maj.Class
1 Monk1	6	556	50.00
2 Monk2	6	601	65.72
3 Monk3	6	554	55.41
4 **Kr-vs-kp**	36	3,196	52.22
5 Tic-tac-toe	9	958	64.20
6 Credit-a	15	690	55.51
7 German	20	1,000	69.40
8 **Spam**	57	4,601	60.59
9 House-vote	16	435	54.25
10 Breast Cancer	9	286	70.28
11 Breast-w	9	699	65.52
12 Colic	22	368	63.04
13 Heart-statlog	13	270	59.50
14 **Sick**	29	3,772	93.87
15 **Caravan**	85	5,822	94.02
16 **Hypothyroid**	25	3,163	95.22
17 **Mushroom**	22	8,124	51.80

The configuration of the experiments is as follows. We distinguish between small data sets (with up to 1,000 examples) and larger data sets. For the 11 small data sets, we randomly split the whole data set into two equal-sized parts. One half is used as training set; the second half is again split into 20% validation set and 80% test set. In order to obtain models with sufficiently different performance, we train 10 different classifiers with the same learning technique (J48 unpruned with Laplace correction, Naive Bayes, and Logistic Regression, all from Weka) over the same training data, by randomly removing three attributes before training. We select the best model according to three measures: AUC, sAUC and BS using the validation set. The performance of each selected model is assessed by AUC on the test set. Results are averaged over 2000 repetitions of this

Table 4. Experimental results (AUC) on small data sets. Figures in **bold face** indicate a win of sAUC over AUC/BS. The last line indicates the total number of wins, which is never smaller than the critical value (9 out of 11).

	J48			Naive Bayes			Logistic Regression		
#	sAUC	AUC	BS	sAUC	AUC	BS	sAUC	AUC	BS
1	86.34	**83.76**	**85.81**	70.80	**67.98**	**69.96**	70.07	**67.28**	**69.23**
2	51.79	**51.32**	**51.05**	51.19	51.81	51.78	51.19	51.76	51.80
3	95.92	**93.20**	**95.47**	95.47	**92.21**	**94.96**	95.98	**92.65**	**95.58**
5	79.48	**77.72**	**78.16**	72.13	**70.88**	**71.05**	74.62	**72.11**	**72.68**
6	90.16	**89.25**	**89.56**	89.70	**89.06**	**89.61**	91.12	**90.62**	**90.55**
7	68.95	**68.75**	**68.85**	77.69	**77.24**	**77.25**	77.60	**77.29**	**77.20**
9	98.11	**97.81**	**97.98**	96.90	**96.74**	**96.81**	98.36	**98.24**	**98.28**
10	61.75	62.10	62.09	69.62	**69.09**	**68.98**	65.19	**64.94**	65.33
11	97.68	**97.64**	**97.67**	98.01	**97.94**	**98.00**	99.24	**99.18**	**99.22**
12	87.13	**85.65**	**86.13**	83.85	**83.60**	**83.82**	84.18	**83.74**	**83.76**
13	83.42	83.56	83.45	88.69	**88.68**	**88.49**	89.24	**89.12**	**89.13**
wins		9	9		10	10		10	9

experiment to reduce the effect of the random selection of attributes. These results are reported in Table 4. We performed a sign test over these results to compare the overall performance. The critical value for a two-tailed sign test over 11 data sets at $\alpha = 0.05$ is 9 wins. We conclude that sAUC significantly outperforms AUC/BS in all experiments. Given that the sign test is relatively weak, we consider this to be strong experimental evidence that sAUC is a good model selector for AUC in cases where we have limited validation data.

For the 6 larger data sets we employed a slightly different experimental configuration. In this case we employ 50% of the data for training the models, 25% for validation, and 25% for test. Here we only run 100 iterations. Our intuition is that when we have enough validation data, sAUC demonstrates less of an advantage for selecting models with higher test AUC because the variance of validation AUC is drastically reduced. The results included in Table 5 confirm this intuition, as the critical number of wins or losses (6 at $\alpha = 0.10$) is never achieved, and thus no significant differences in performance are observed.

Table 5. Experimental results (AUC) on larger data sets. Figures in **bold face** indicate a win of sAUC over AUC/BS. According to the sign test, the numbers of wins and losses are not significant.

	J48			Naive Bayes			Logistic Regression		
#	sAUC	AUC	BS	sAUC	AUC	BS	sAUC	AUC	BS
4	99.92	**99.91**	**99.91**	95.88	96.45	96.45	99.59	**99.55**	**99.57**
8	96.69	96.78	**96.67**	95.88	96.50	96.45	96.95	**96.93**	**96.91**
14	98.70	**98.67**	**98.65**	91.85	92.00	**91.62**	93.68	93.78	**93.59**
15	69.55	69.67	69.90	70.47	70.59	70.75	94.83	96.55	94.90
16	96.73	97.28	**96.59**	98.00	**97.99**	**97.90**	96.91	97.01	96.98
17	100	100	100	99.80	99.88	**99.79**	100	100	100
wins		2	3		1	3		2	3

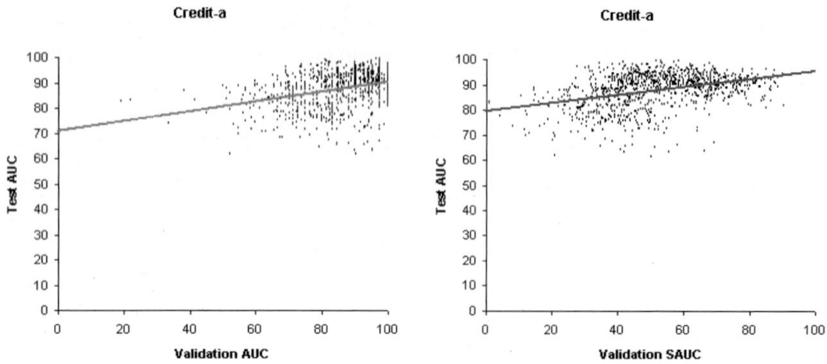

Fig. 3. Scatter plots of test AUC vs. validation AUC (left) and test AUC vs. validation sAUC (right) on the Credit-a data set.

Finally, Figure 3 shows two scatter plots of the models obtained for the Credit-a data set, the first one plotting test AUC against validation AUC, and the second one plotting test AUC against validation sAUC. Both plots include a straight line obtained by linear regression. Since validation sAUC is an underestimate of validation AUC (Theorem 3), it is not surprising that validation sAUC is also an underestimate of test AUC. Validation AUC appears to be an underestimate of test AUC on this data set, but this may be caused by the outliers on the left. But what really matters in these plots is the proportion of variance in test AUC not accounted for by the linear regression (which is $1-g^2$, where g is the linear correlation coefficient). We can see that this is larger for validation AUC, particularly because of the vertical lines observed in Figure 3 (left). These lines indicate how validation AUC fails to distinguish between models with different test AUC. This phenomenon particularly occurs for a number of models with perfect ranking on the validation set. Since sAUC takes the scores into account, and since these models do not have perfect scores on the validation set, the same phenomenon is not observed in Figure 3 (right).

5 Conclusions

The ROC curve is useful for visualising the performance of scoring classification models. ROC curves contain a wealth of information about the performance of one or more classifiers, which can be utilised to improve their performance and for model selection. For example, Provost and Fawcett [10] studied the application of model selection in ROC space when target misclassification costs and class distributions are uncertain.

In this paper we introduced the scored AUC (sAUC) metric to measure the performance of a model. The difference between AUC and scored AUC is that the AUC only uses the ranks obtained from scores, whereas the scored AUC uses both ranks and scores. We defined sAUC as the area under the sROC curve, which shows how quickly AUC deteriorates if the positive scores are decreased. Empirically, sAUC was found to select models with larger AUC values then AUC itself (which uses only ranks) or the Brier score (which uses only scores).

Evaluating learning algorithms can be regarded as a process of testing the diversity of two samples, that is, a sample of the scores for positive instances and that for negative instances. As the scored AUC takes advantage of both the ranks and the original values of samples, it is potentially a good statistic for testing the diversity of two samples, in a similar vein as the Wilcoxon-Man-Whitney U statistic. Preliminary experiments suggest that sAUC has indeed higher power than WMW. Furthermore, while this paper only investigates sAUC from the non-parametric perspective, it is worthwhile to study its parametric properties. We plan to investigate these further in future work.

Acknowledgments

We thank José Hernández-Orallo and Thomas Gärtner for useful discussions. We would also like to thank the anonymous reviewers for their helpful comments.

References

1. DeLong, E.R., DeLong, D.M., Clarke-Pearson, D.L.: Comparing the areas under two or more correlated receiver operating characteristic curves: a nonparametric approach. Biometrics 44, 837–845 (1988)
2. Ferri, C., Flach, P., Hernández-Orallo, J., Senad, A.: Modifying ROC curves to incorporate predicted probabilities. In: Proceedings of the Second Workshop on ROC Analysis in Machine Learning (ROCML'05) (2005)
3. Fawcett, T.: Using Rule Sets to Maximize ROC Performance. In: Proc. IEEE Int'l Conf. Data Mining, pp. 131–138 (2001)
4. Fawcett, T.: An introduction to ROC analysis. Pattern Recognition Let. 27-8, 861–874 (2006)
5. Hanley, J.A., McNeil, B.J.: The Meaning and Use of the AUC Under a Receiver Operating Characteristic (ROC) Curve. Radiology 143, 29–36 (1982)
6. Hsieh, F., Turnbull, B.W.: Nonparametric and Semiparametric Estimation of the Receiver Operating Characteristic Curve. Annals of Statistics 24, 25–40 (1996)
7. Huang, J., Ling, C.X.: Dynamic Ensemble Re-Construction for Better Ranking. In: Proc. 9th Eur. Conf. Principles and Practice of Knowledge Discovery in Databases, pp. 511–518 (2005)
8. Huang, J., Ling, C.X.: Using AUC and Accuray in Evaluating Learing Algorithms. IEEE Transactions on Knowledge and Data Engineering 17, 299–310 (2005)
9. Provost, F., Fawcett, T., Kohavi, R.: Analysis and Visualization of Classifier Performance: Comparison Under Imprecise Class and Cost Distribution. In: Proc. 3rd Int'l Conf. Knowledge Discovery and Data Mining, pp. 43–48 (1997)
10. Provost, F., Fawcett, T.: Robust Classification for Imprecise Environments. Machine Learning 42, 203–231 (2001)
11. Provost, F., Domingos, P.: Tree Induction for Probability-Based Ranking. Machine Learning 52, 199–215 (2003)
12. Wu, S.M., Flach, P.: Scored Metric for Classifier Evaluation and Selection. In: Proceedings of the Second Workshop on ROC Analysis in Machine Learning (ROCML'05) (2005)
13. Zhou, X.H., Obuchowski, N.A., McClish, D.K.: Statistical Methods in Diagnostic Medicine. John Wiley and Sons, Chichester (2002)

Finding the Right Family: Parent and Child Selection for Averaged One-Dependence Estimators

Fei Zheng and Geoffrey I. Webb

Faculty of Information Technology, Monash University, VIC 3800, Australia
{feizheng,Geoff.Webb}@infotech.monash.edu.au

Abstract. Averaged One-Dependence Estimators (AODE) classifies by uniformly aggregating all qualified one-dependence estimators (ODEs). Its capacity to significantly improve naive Bayes' accuracy without undue time complexity has attracted substantial interest. Forward Sequential Selection and Backwards Sequential Elimination are effective wrapper techniques to identify and repair harmful interdependencies which have been profitably applied to naive Bayes. However, their straightforward application to AODE has previously proved ineffective. We investigate novel variants of these strategies. Our extensive experiments show that elimination of child attributes from within the constituent ODEs results in a significant improvement in probability estimate and reductions in bias and error relative to unmodified AODE. In contrast, elimination of complete constituent ODEs and the four types of attribute addition are found to be less effective and do not demonstrate any strong advantage over AODE. These surprising results lead to effective techniques for improving AODE's prediction accuracy.

1 Introduction

Semi-naive Bayesian techniques further improve naive Bayes' accuracy by relaxing its assumption that the attributes are conditionally independent [1, 2, 3, 4, 5, 6, 7, 8, 9, 10, 11, 12, 13, 14, 15, 16]. One approach to weakening this assumption is to use an *x-dependence classifier* [7], in which each attribute depends upon the class and at most x other attributes. Examples include Tree Augmented Naive Bayes (TAN) [9], Super Parent TAN (SP-TAN) [11], NBTree [5], Lazy Bayesian rules (LBR) [12] and Averaged One-Dependence Estimators (AODE) [13]. Among these techniques, TAN, SP-TAN and AODE restrict themselves to one-dependence classifiers, which readily admit to efficient computation. Another approach to remedying violations of the attribute independence assumption is to apply naive Bayes with a new attribute set by deleting or merging highly related attributes. Key such approaches include Backwards Sequential Elimination (BSE) [1], Forward Sequential Selection (FSS) [4], Backward Sequential Elimination and Joining (BSEJ) [6] and Hierarchical Naive Bayes (HNB) [16]. An extensive comparative study of semi-naive Bayes techniques [17] shows that

J.N. Kok et al. (Eds.): ECML 2007, LNAI 4701, pp. 490–501, 2007.

AODE has a significant advantage in error over many other semi-naive Bayesian algorithms, with the exceptions of LBR and SP-TAN. It shares similar levels of error with these two algorithms, while having considerably lower training time complexity relative to SP-TAN and test time complexity relative to LBR. AODE is a powerful alternative to naive Bayes, significantly reducing its error, while retaining much of its attractive simplicity and efficiency. Consequently it has received substantial attention. Indeed, at the time of writing, the paper introducing AODE [13] is the most cited paper from 2005 in the Machine Learning journal [18].

FSS and BSE use a simple heuristic wrapper approach that seeks to minimize error on the training set. Starting from the empty attribute set, FSS operates by iteratively adding attributes, each time adding the attribute whose addition best reduces training set error. BSE uses the opposite search direction and operates by iteratively removing attributes, each time removing the attribute whose elimination most improves training set accuracy. When applied to naive Bayes, FSS and BSE have proved to be beneficial in domains with highly correlated attributes. It is therefore surprising that two attempts to apply these approaches to AODE have proved ineffective [15, 19]. Where the training time overheads of attribute selection are not a major concern, attribute selection has the potential of two beneficial effects, both of improving accuracy and also of reducing test time due to the need to process fewer attributes. This paper investigates why previous approaches to attribute selection for AODE have proved ineffective, and develops novel attribute selection algorithms that do prove effective when applied to AODE and which have potential for wider application.

2 Averaged One-Dependence Estimators (AODE)

The Bayesian classifier [20] predicts a class for an unseen example $\mathbf{x}=\langle x_1,\ldots,x_n\rangle$ by selecting

$$\underset{y}{\operatorname{argmax}}\left(\hat{P}(y \mid x_1,\ldots,x_n)\right), \tag{1}$$

where $\hat{P}(\cdot)$ is an estimate of the probability $P(\cdot)$, x_i is a value of the ith attribute X_i, and $y \in \{c_1,\ldots,c_k\}$ is a value of the class variable Y. Naive Bayes estimates $\hat{P}(y \mid x_1,\ldots,x_n)$ by assuming that the attributes are independent given the class, and hence classifies $\mathbf{x}$ by selecting

$$\underset{y}{\operatorname{argmax}}\left(\hat{P}(y)\prod_{i=1}^{n}\hat{P}(x_i \mid y)\right). \tag{2}$$

Domingos and Pazzani (1996) point out that interdependencies between attributes will not affect naive Bayes' accuracy, so long as it can generate the correct ranks of conditional probabilities for the classes. However, the success of semi-naive Bayesian methods show that appropriate relaxation of the conditional independence assumption is effective.

One natural extension to naive Bayes is to relax the independence assumption by utilizing a one-dependence classifier (ODE) [7], such as TAN [9], in which each attribute depends upon the class and at most one other attribute. To avoid model selection, AODE [13] selects a limited class of ODEs and aggregates the probability estimates of all qualified classifiers within this class. A single attribute, called the *parent* attribute, is selected as the parent of all the other attributes in each ODE. In order to avoid unreliable base probability estimates, when classifying an object $\langle x_1, \ldots, x_n \rangle$ the original AODE excludes ODEs with parent x_i where the frequency of the value x_i is lower than limit m=30, a widely used minimum on sample size for statistical inference purposes. However, subsequent research [14] shows that this constraint actually increases error and hence the current research uses m=1.

From the definition of conditional probability we have

$$P(y \mid \mathbf{x}) = P(y, \mathbf{x})/P(\mathbf{x}) \propto P(y, \mathbf{x}), \tag{3}$$

and for any attribute value x_i,

$$P(y, \mathbf{x}) = P(y, x_i)P(\mathbf{x} \mid y, x_i). \tag{4}$$

This equality holds for every x_i. Therefore,

$$P(y, \mathbf{x}) = \frac{\sum_{i:1 \leq i \leq n \wedge F(x_i) \geq m} P(y, x_i)P(\mathbf{x} \mid y, x_i)}{|\{i : 1 \leq i \leq n \wedge F(x_i) \geq m\}|}, \tag{5}$$

where $F(x_i)$ is the frequency of attribute-value x_i in the training sample.

To this end, AODE classifies by selecting:

$$\operatorname*{argmax}_y \left(\sum_{i:1 \leq i \leq n \wedge F(x_i) \geq m} \hat{P}(y, x_i) \prod_{j=1}^{n} \hat{P}(x_j \mid y, x_i) \right). \tag{6}$$

At training time AODE generates a three-dimensional table of probability estimates for each attribute-value, conditioned by each other attribute-value and each class. The resulting space complexity is $O(k(nv)^2)$, where v is the mean number of values per attribute. The time complexity of forming this table is $O(tn^2)$, where t is the number of training examples, as an entry must be updated for every training case and every combination of two attribute-values for that case. Classification requires the tables of probability estimates formed at training time of space complexity $O(k(nv)^2)$. The time complexity of classifying a single example is $O(kn^2)$ as we need to consider each pair of qualified parent and child attribute within each class.

AODE maintains the robustness and much of the efficiency of naive Bayes, and at the same time exhibits significantly higher classification accuracy for many data sets. Therefore, it has the potential to be a valuable substitute for naive Bayes over a considerable range of classification tasks.

3 Attribute Selection

In naive Bayes, all attributes are used during prediction, and hence all influence classification. When two attributes are strongly related, the influence from these two attributes may be given too much weight, and the influence of the other attributes may be reduced, which can result in prediction bias. Selecting an appropriate attribute subset, which excludes highly correlated attributes, might alleviate this problem.

Since there are 2^n candidate subsets of n attributes, an exhaustive search of the space is prohibitive. This necessitates the use of heuristic search. Greedy hill climbing is a simple and widely used technique, which adds or removes an attribute irrevocably at each step. That is, once an attribute is added or removed, it cannot be respectively removed from or added to the set. To measure the goodness of alternative attribute subsets, we need an evaluation function, which commonly measures the discriminating ability of an attribute or an attribute set among classes. The *Wrapper* [22] approach uses accuracy estimates on the target induction algorithm as the evaluation function. Leave-one-out cross validation is an attractive technique for estimating accuracy from the training set in Bayesian classifier, as it can be efficiently performed by simply modifying the frequency tables.

Another two issues in hill climbing search are the direction of search and stopping criteria. Forward Sequential Selection (FSS) [4] begins with the empty attribute set and successively adds attributes, while Backwards Sequential Elimination (BSE) [1] starts with the complete attribute set and successively removes attributes. There are three commonly used options for halting the search. We call the first strategy Stop on First Nonimprovement (SFN), as it terminates the search when there is no classification accuracy improvement [1, 6]. The second option, called Stop on First Reduction (SFR), considers performing selection continually so long as the accuracy is not reduced [4]. The third, called Continue Search and Select Best (CSSB), continues the search until all attributes have been added or removed and then selects the attribute subset with the highest accuracy evaluation [19].

In the context of naive Bayes, FSS and BSE select a subset of attributes using leave-one-out cross validation error as a selection criterion and apply naive Bayes to the new attribute set. The subset of selected attributes is denoted as S. Independence is assumed among the resulting attributes given the class. Hence, FSS and BSE classify $\mathbf{x}$ by selecting

$$\underset{y}{\operatorname{argmax}} \left(\hat{P}(y) \prod_{x \in S} \hat{P}(x|y) \right). \tag{7}$$

4 Attribute Selection for AODE

In theory, AODE would appear to be a promising candidate for attribute selection. While an individual ODE can factor out harmful attribute inter-dependencies in which the parent is involved, it will not help when the parent is not. When there are many more attributes than those that participate in a particular inter-dependency, the majority of ODEs will not factor out the inter-dependency, and hence it is credible that deleting one of the attributes should be beneficial. Why then have previous attempts [15,19] to apply attribute-selection to AODE proved unfruitful?

One difference between applying attribute selection in NB compared to AODE may be the greater complexity of an AODE model, resulting in greater variance in estimates of performance as the model is manipulated through attribute elimination and hence reduced reliability in these estimates. Another difference may be that attributes play multiple roles in an AODE model (either a parent or a child) whereas they play only a single role of child in an NB model.

To explore the first issue, we evaluate the use of a statistical test to assess whether an observed difference in holdout evaluation scores should be accepted as meaningful during the attribute selection process.

To explore the second issue, we investigate the separate selection of attributes in each of the parent and child roles, as well as in both roles together.

In the context of AODE, FSS and BSE use leave-one-out cross validation error on AODE as a selection criterion. Each available selection is attempted and the one that results in the lowest error is implemented. The process is repeated for successive attributes until the decrease in error fails a one-tailed binomial sign test at a significance level of 0.05.

To formalize the various attribute selection strategies we introduce into AODE the use of a *parent* (p) and a *child* (c) set, each of which contains the set of indices of attributes that can be employed in respectively a parent or child role in the AODE. The number of indices in each set is denoted respectively as $\|p\|$ and $\|c\|$. We define $\text{AODE}_{p,c}$ as

$$\underset{y}{\text{argmax}} \left(\sum_{i \in p : F(x_i) \geq m} \hat{P}(y, x_i) \prod_{j \in c} \hat{P}(x_j \mid y, x_i) \right). \tag{8}$$

Assume that attribute x_i is related to other attributes, and that these harmful interdependencies can be detected and repaired by FSS or BSE. The exclusion of x_i from c may have influence on $\|p\|$ - 1 ODEs, while the exclusion of x_i from p may only factor out the effect of the single ODE in which x_i is the parent. In $\text{AODE}_{p,c}$, a linear function is used to combine constituent ODEs, and a multiplicative function is used to combine attributes within each ODE. Large improvements are possible because of the multiplicative influence, and hence exclusion of a child may have greater effect than exclusion of a parent.

4.1 FSS for AODE

There are four different types of attribute addition. The first type of attribute addition, called *parent addition* (PA), starts with p and c initialized to the empty and full sets of $\{1 \dots n\}$ respectively. It adds attribute indexes to p, effectively adding a single ODE at each step. The second type of attribute addition, called

Table 1. Data sets

No.	Domain	Case	Att	Class	No.	Domain	Case	Att	Class
1	Abalone	4177	9	3	29	Liver Disorders (bupa)	345	7	2
2	Adult	48842	15	2	30	Lung Cancer	32	57	3
3	Annealing	898	39	6	31	Lymphography	148	19	4
4	Audiology	226	70	24	32	Mfeat-mor	2000	7	10
5	Autos Imports-85	205	26	7	33	Mushrooms	8124	23	2
6	Balance Scale	625	5	3	34	Nettalk(Phoneme)	5438	8	50
7	Breast Cancer (Wisconsin)	699	10	2	35	New-Thyroid	215	6	3
8	Car Evaluation	1728	7	4	36	Optical Digits	5620	49	10
9	Chess	551	40	2	37	Page Blocks	5473	11	5
10	Contact Lenses	24	5	3	38	Pen Digits	10992	17	10
11	Credit Approval	690	16	2	39	Pima Indians Diabetes	768	9	2
12	Dmplexer	1000	15	2	40	Postoperative Patient	90	9	3
13	Echocardiogram	131	7	2	41	Primary Tumor	339	18	22
14	German	1000	21	2	42	Promoter Gene Sequences	106	58	2
15	Glass Identification	214	10	3	43	Satellite	6435	37	6
16	Heart	270	14	2	44	Segment	2310	20	7
17	Heart Disease (cleveland)	303	14	2	45	Sign	12546	9	3
18	Hepatitis	155	20	2	46	Sonar Classification	208	61	2
19	Horse Colic	368	23	2	47	Splice-junction Gene Sequences	3190	62	3
20	House Votes 84	435	17	2	48	Syncon	600	61	6
21	Hungarian	294	14	2	49	Sick-euthyroid	3772	30	2
22	Hypothyroid(Garavan Institute)	3772	30	4	50	Tic-Tac-Toe Endgame	958	10	2
23	Ionosphere	351	35	2	51	Vehicle	846	19	4
24	Iris Classification	150	5	3	52	Volcanoes	1520	4	4
25	King-rook-vs-king-pawn	3196	37	2	53	Vowel	990	14	11
26	Labor negotiations	57	17	2	54	Waveform-5000	5000	41	3
27	LED	1000	8	10	55	Wine Recognition	178	14	3
28	Letter Recognition	20000	17	26	56	Zoo	101	18	7

child addition (CA), begins with p and c initialized to the full and empty sets respectively. It adds attribute indexes to c, effectively adding an attribute to within every ODE at each step. Starting with the empty set for both p and c, *Parent and child addition* (P∧CA) at each step adds the same value to both p and c , hence selecting it for use in any role in the classifier. *Parent or child addition* (P∨CA) performs any one of the other types of attribute additions in each iteration, selecting the option that most improves the accuracy.

4.2 BSE for AODE

All four types of attribute elimination start with p and c initialized to the full set. The first approach, called *parent elimination* (PE), deletes attribute indexes from p, effectively deleting a single ODE at each step. The second approach, called *child elimination* (CE), deletes attribute indexes from c, effectively deleting an attribute from within every ODE at each step. *Parent and child elimination* (P∧CE) [15] at each step deletes the same value from both p and c, thus eliminating it from use in any role in the classifier. *Parent or child elimination* (P∨CE) performs any one of the other types of attribute eliminations in each iteration, selecting the option that best reduces error.

4.3 Complexity

As child selection requires modifying the probability estimates for $\|p\|$ ODEs at each step, it has higher training time complexity than that of parent selection, which only considers one ODE at each step. At training time PA and PE generate a three-dimensional table of probability estimates, as AODE does. They must also store the training data, with additional space complexity $O(tn)$, to perform leave-one-out cross validation on AODE. A three-dimensional table, indexed by instance, class and attribute, is introduced to speed up the process of evaluating the classifiers, with space complexity $O(tkn)$. Therefore, the resulting space complexity is $O(tkn + k(nv)^2)$. Deleting attributes has time complexity of $O(tkn^2)$, as a single leave-one-out cross validation is order $O(tk)$ and it is performed at most $O(n^2)$ times. They have identical time and space complexity with AODE at classification time. For the strategies involving child selection, they have identical space complexity and classification time complexity with PA and PE, but higher training time complexity of $O(tkn^3)$, as a single leave-one-out cross validation is order $O(tkn)$.

4.4 Statistical Test

It is quite likely that small improvements in leave-one-out error may be attributable to chance. In consequence it may be beneficial to use a statistical test to assess whether an improvement is significant. We employ a standard binomial sign test. Treating the examples for which an attribute addition or deletion corrects a misclassification as a *win* and one for which it misclassifies a previously correct example as a *loss*, a change is accepted if the number of wins exceeds the number of losses and the probability of obtaining the observed number of wins and losses if they were equiprobable was no more than 0.05.

5 Empirical Comparison

The main goal in this comparison is to assess the efficacy of the statistical test and study the influence of the use of different types of attribute selection in AODE. The fifty-six natural domains from the UCI Repository of machine learning [23] used in our experiments are shown in Table 1. Continuous attributes were discretized using MDL discretization [24] and missing values were replaced with the modes and means from the training data. The base probabilities were estimated using Laplace estimation [25]. Algorithms are implemented in the Weka workbench [26], and the experiments were performed on a dual-processor 1.7 GHz Pentium 4 Linux computer with 2 Gb RAM.

We compare the classification error of AODE with different attribute selection techniques on AODE using the repeated cross-validation bias-variance estimation method proposed by Webb (2000). This is preferred to the default method in Weka, which uses 25% of the full data set as training sets, because it results in the use of substantially larger training sets. In order to maximize the variation in the training data from trial to trial we use two-fold cross validation. The training data are randomly divided into two folds. Each fold is used as a test set for a classifier generated from the other fold. Hence, each available example is classified once for each two-fold cross-validation. Bias and variance are estimated by fifty runs of two-fold cross-validation in order to give a more accurate estimation of the average performance of an algorithm. The advantage of this technique is that it uses the full training data as the training set and test set, and every case in the training data is used the same number of times in each of the roles of training and test data. In addition to the classification error, we use the information loss function to evaluate the probabilistic prediction of each technique.

Two variants of attribute selection were evaluated, one employing a binomial sign test and the other not. Algorithms using a binomial sign test are superscripted by ^{S} and those without by ^{NS}. We use Stop on First Reduction with attribution addition algorithms and Stop on First Nonimprovement with attribute elimination algorithms as these produce the best performance (results not presented due to lack of space). The number of times that an algorithm performs better, worse or equally to the others is summarized into pairwise win/loss/draw records which are presented in Table 2. Algorithms are sorted in descending order on the value of wins minus losses against AODE on each metric. Each entry compares the algorithm with which the row is labelled (L) against the algorithm with which the column is labelled (C). We assess a difference as significant if the outcome of a one-tailed binomial sign test is less than 0.05. For space reason, we only present bias, variance and information loss results for the attribute elimination algorithms.

5.1 Error

CE^S, $\text{P}\vee\text{CE}^S$ and $\text{P}\wedge\text{CE}^S$, enjoy a significant advantage in error over AODE ($p = 0.011$, $p = 0.011$ and $p = 0.048$ respectively), while attribute addition (both with and without statistical test) always has a significant disadvantage to AODE. The rest of the algorithms share a similar level of error with AODE.

The algorithms using attribute elimination share a similar level of error with the exception that CE^S and $\text{P}\vee\text{CE}^S$ outperform PE^S, PE^{NS} outperforms CS^{NS} and $\text{P}\wedge\text{CE}^{NS}$ outperforms CE^{NS}. The advantage of all the attribute elimination algorithms is significant compared with all the attribute addition algorithms but PA^{NS}. PA^{NS} has a significant advantage over CA, P$\wedge$CA and P$\vee$CA (with and without statistical test). The reason the performances of CA, P$\wedge$CA and P$\vee$CA are disappointing might be that they are susceptible to getting trapped into poor selections by local minima during the first several child additions.

5.2 Bias and Variance

All the attribute elimination algorithms, except PE^S, have a significant advantage in bias over AODE and PE^S. $\text{P}\wedge\text{CE}^{NS}$, CE^{NS} and $\text{P}\vee\text{CE}^{NS}$ outperform PE^{NS} and the remaining four algorithms with statistical tests. The advantage of $\text{P}\wedge\text{CE}^{NS}$ is significant compared with CE^{NS}. AODE enjoys a significant advantage over all the algorithms with respect to variance. The algorithms with statistical tests have a significant advantage over the algorithms without a statistical test. PE^S has a significant advantage over $\text{P}\wedge\text{CE}^S$.

5.3 Information Loss

Two algorithms, P$\wedge$CE^S and CE^S, significantly improve AODE's probability estimate. PE^{NS} is the only algorithm that has a significant disadvantage over AODE. It also has a significant disadvantage over P$\wedge$CE^S, CE^S, P$\vee$CE^S and PE^S. The advantage of P$\vee$CE^S is marginal compared with AODE and is significant compared with CE^S and PE^{NS}.

5.4 Continue Search and Select Best (CSSB)

To observe the behaviors of parent and child selection, we also examine the attribute selection techniques with CSSB. Due to the significantly increasing variance, all of these selection approaches have proved ineffective. Figure 1 shows the error ratio of PA [19], PE, CA and CE against AODE as a function of the number of attributes on 3 data sets with more than 3000 instances, in which both selection of parent and child have lower error compared with AODE (for the space reason, the other 6 data sets are not presented). The values on the x-axis are the number of attributes in the p set for PA and PE, and the number of attributes in the c set for CA and CE. The values on the y-axis are the classification error of each selection algorithm divided by that for AODE. The smaller the ratio, the more accuracy improvement will be.

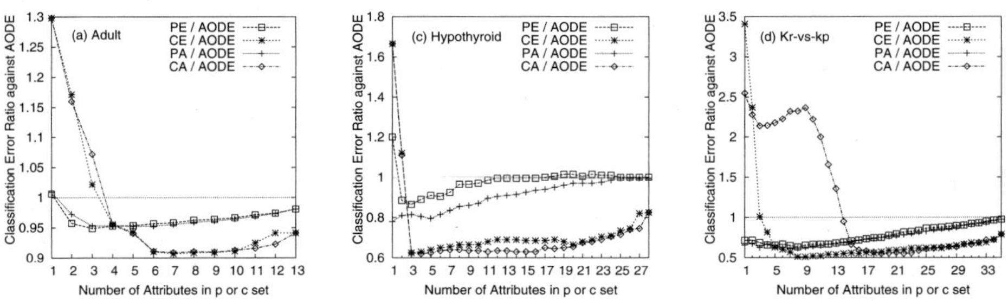

Fig. 1. Error ratio of parent and child selection using CSSB against AODE, as function of the number of attributes

Slight error differences between PA and PE are observed as shown in the graph (win/draw/loss being 25/8/23). Notice that PA tends to achieve the minima at an early stage, while PE appears to reach it at a late stage. CE has greater error reduction compared with PE until there are a small number of children left, after which it increases error sharply. The error ratios for PE and CE for the first attribute elimination are 0.98 and 0.94, 0.99 and 0.96, 1 and 0.83, and 0.98 and 0.79 for Adult, Nettalk, Hypothyroid and King-rook-vs-king-pawn respectively. The performance of CA fluctuates over the first several attribute additions for King-rook-vs-king-pawn. Similar behavior is observed for many other data sets in our collection.

Table 2. Win/Loss/Draw records on 56 data sets with binomial sign test

Error

W/L/D	CE^{S}	P∨CE^{S}	P∧CE^{S}	PE^{NS}	PE^{S}	CE^{NS}	P∨CE^{NS}	P∧CE^{NS}	PA^{NS}	P∧CA^{NS}	PA^{S}	CA^{NS}	P∨CA^{NS}	P∨CA^{S}	P∧CA^{S}	CA^{S}
CE^{S}																
P∨CE^{S}	6//5/45															
P∧CE^{S}	8/6/42	3/8/45														
PE^{NS}	24/23/9	24/23/9	24/23/9													
PE^{S}	**4/13/39**	**4/14/38**	6/12/38	20/25/11												
CE^{NS}	24/27/5	24/27/5	24/27/5	**19/34/3**	25/26/5											
P∨CE^{NS}	24/29/3	24/29/3	24/29/3	23/28/5	24/28/4	32/18/6										
P∧CE^{NS}	25/28/3	24/29/3	24/29/3	21/31/4	23/29/4	**33/17/6**	19/31/6									
PA^{NS}	22/32/2	22/31/3	22/31/3	21/33/2	23/31/2	29/23/4	21/32/3	26/26/4								
P∧CA^{NS}	**17/37/2**	**17/37/2**	**17/37/2**	**13/41/2**	**17/37/2**	**15/38/3**	**10/44/2**	**12/40/4**	**13/41/2**							
PA^{S}	**13/41/2**	**12/42/2**	**12/42/2**	**10/43/3**	**14/40/2**	**13/41/2**	**10/44/2**	**11/43/2**	**4/49/3**	24/29/3						
CA^{NS}	**14/40/2**	**14/40/2**	**14/40/2**	**10/44/2**	**13/41/2**	**8/44/4**	**7/47/2**	**7/46/3**	**10/44/2**	**15/35/6**	**18/36/2**					
P∨CA^{NS}	**12/42/2**	**12/42/2**	**12/42/2**	**12/42/2**	**12/42/2**	**17/37/2**	**16/38/2**	**16/38/2**	**15/39/2**	21/32/3	23/31/2	29/25/2				
P∨CA^{S}	**11/43/2**	**11/43/2**	**11/43/2**	**10/44/2**	**10/44/2**	**15/39/2**	**14/40/2**	**14/40/2**	**13/41/2**	**19/35/2**	**19/35/2**	28/26/2	**4/20/32**			
P∧CA^{S}	**9/46/1**	**9/46/1**	**9/46/1**	**9/46/1**	**10/45/1**	**7/48/1**	**6/49/1**	**6/49/1**	**7/48/1**	**4/50/2**	**10/44/2**	**14/41/1**	**18/37/1**	**20/34/2**		
CA^{S}	**6/49/1**	**6/49/1**	**6/49/1**	**6/49/1**	**7/48/1**	**5/50/1**	**6/49/1**	**6/49/1**	**6/49/1**	**3/51/2**	**7/47/2**	**6/47/3**	**13/42/1**	**16/39/1**	**19/34/3**	
AODE	**3/13/40**	**3/13/40**	**5/13/38**	20/25/11	4/3/49	26/24/6	28/24/4	29/23/4	31/23/2	**37/17/2**	**40/14/2**	**41/13/2**	**42/12/2**	**44/10/2**	**45/10/1**	**48/7/1**

Bias

W/L/D	P∧CE^{NS}	CE^{NS}	P∨CE^{NS}	PE^{NS}	P∨CE^{S}	CE^{S}	P∧CE^{S}	PE^{S}
P∧CE^{NS}								
CE^{NS}	**14/36/6**							
P∨CE^{NS}	28/26/2	32/23/1						
PE^{NS}	**12/40/4**	**12/40/4**	**12/42/2**					
P∨CE^{S}	**6/47/3**	**7/45/4**	**8/47/1**	19/28/9				
CE^{S}	**6/47/3**	**7/45/4**	**9/46/1**	19/28/9	3/8/45			
P∧CE^{S}	**6/47/3**	**7/45/4**	**8/47/1**	19/28/9	2/7/47	7/5/44		
PE^{S}	**6/47/3**	**7/45/4**	**9/46/1**	**14/30/12**	**1/16/39**	**2/16/38**	**2/15/39**	
AODE	**6/47/3**	**7/45/4**	**9/46/1**	**14/30/12**	**1/16/39**	**2/16/38**	**2/15/39**	2/5/49

Variance

W/L/D	PE^{S}	CE^{S}	P∧CE^{S}	P∨CE^{S}	PE^{NS}	CE^{NS}	P∧CE^{NS}	P∨CE^{NS}
PE^{S}								
CE^{S}	6/13/37							
P∧CE^{S}	**5/14/37**	4/8/44						
P∨CE^{S}	6/11/39	4/9/43	6/4/46					
PE^{NS}	**14/32/10**	**16/32/8**	**16/31/9**	**17/31/8**				
CE^{NS}	**10/42/4**	**11/42/3**	**11/42/3**	**10/43/3**	**14/39/3**			
P∧CE^{NS}	**11/42/3**	**11/42/3**	**11/41/4**	**11/41/4**	**12/41/3**	20/27/9		
P∨CE^{NS}	**11/40/5**	**11/40/5**	**11/40/5**	**11/40/5**	**16/37/3**	**31/16/9**	**37/14/5**	
AODE	**6/0/50**	**14/5/37**	**15/5/36**	**13/5/38**	**33/14/9**	**43/10/3**	**42/11/3**	**40/11/5**

Info Loss

W/L/D	CE^{NS}	P∧CE^{NS}	P∧CE^{S}	CE^{S}	P∨CE^{NS}	P∨CE^{S}	PE^{S}	PE^{NS}
CE^{NS}								
P∧CE^{NS}	26/27/3							
P∧CE^{S}	21/33/2	22/32/2						
CE^{S}	21/33/2	21/33/2	7/8/41					
P∨CE^{NS}	28/27/1	27/28/1	33/23/0	32/24/0				
P∨CE^{S}	21/33/2	21/32/3	9/5/42	**11/2/43**	23/33/0			
PE^{S}	22/32/2	22/32/2	7/14/35	6/13/37	24/32/0	7/13/36		
PE^{NS}	26/28/2	25/29/2	**16/36/4**	**16/36/4**	25/31/0	**16/36/4**	**16/35/5**	
AODE	22/32/2	22/32/2	**6/15/35**	**5/13/38**	24/32/0	7/14/35	2/6/48	**35/16/5**

6 Conclusion

AODE efficiently induces classifiers that have competitive classification performance with other state-of-the-art semi-naive Bayes algorithms. Its accuracy and classification time complexity might be further improved if harmful ODEs are excluded. In view of their effectiveness with naive Bayes, it is surprising that previous applications of FSS and BSE to AODE have proved ineffective. In this paper we explore two explanations of this phenomenon. One is that AODE has higher variance compared with naive Bayes, and hence appropriate variance management is required. Another is that child selection appears to have greater effect than parent selection, as ODEs are combined using a linear function but attributes within an ODE are combined using a multiplicative function.

Our extensive experiments suggest that the types of attribute elimination that remove child attributes from within the constituent ODEs can significantly reduce bias and error, but only if a statistical test is employed to provide variance management. In contrast, elimination of complete constituent ODEs does not consistently provide error reduction. CE and P$\wedge$CE also significantly improve probability estimates when used with a statistical test. The types of attribute addition that add child attributes to within the constituent ODEs do not provide any positive benefits, possibly due to being mislead early in the search by local minima. These results suggest that the elimination of a child is more effective than the elimination of a parent, leading to effective approaches to further enhance AODE's accuracy.

References

1. Kittler, J.: Feature selection and extraction. In: Young, T.Y., Fu, K.-S. (eds.) Handbook of Pattern Recognition and Image Processing, pp. 60–81. Academic Press, New York (1986)
2. Kononenko, I.: Semi-naive Bayesian classifier. In: Proc. 6th European Working Session on Machine learning, pp. 206–219. Springer, Berlin (1991)
3. Langley, P.: Induction of recursive Bayesian classifiers. In: Proc. 1993 European Conf. Machine Learning, pp. 153–164. Springer, Berlin (1993)
4. Langley, P., Sage, S.: Induction of selective Bayesian classifiers. In: Proc. 10th Conf. Uncertainty in Artificial Intelligence, pp. 399–406. Morgan Kaufmann, San Francisco (1994)
5. Kohavi, R.: Scaling up the accuracy of naive-Bayes classifiers: a decision-tree hybrid. In: Proc. 2nd ACM SIGKDD Int. Conf. Knowledge Discovery and Data Mining, pp. 202–207. ACM Press, New York (1996)
6. Pazzani, M.J.: Constructive induction of Cartesian product attributes. In: ISIS: Information, Statistics and Induction in Science, pp. 66–77 (1996)
7. Sahami, M.: Learning limited dependence Bayesian classifiers. In: Proc. 2nd Int. Conf. Knowledge Discovery in Databases, pp. 334–338. AAAI Press, Menlo Park, CA (1996)
8. Singh, M., Provan, G.M.: Efficient learning of selective Bayesian network classifiers. In: Proc. 13th Int. Conf. Machine Learning, pp. 453–461. Morgan Kaufmann, San Francisco (1996)

9. Friedman, N., Geiger, D., Goldszmidt, M.: Bayesian network classifiers. Machine Learning 29(2), 131–163 (1997)
10. Webb, G.I., Pazzani, M.J.: Adjusted probability naive Bayesian induction. In: Proc. 11th Australian Joint Conf. Artificial Intelligence, pp. 285–295. Springer, Berlin (1998)
11. Keogh, E.J., Pazzani, M.J.: Learning augmented Bayesian classifers: A comparison of distribution-based and classification-based approaches. In: Proc. Int. Workshop on Artificial Intelligence and Statistics, pp. 225–230 (1999)
12. Zheng, Z., Webb, G.I.: Lazy learning of Bayesian rules. Machine Learning 41(1), 53–84 (2000)
13. Webb, G.I., Boughton, J., Wang, Z.: Not so naive Bayes: Aggregating one-dependence estimators. Machine Learning 58(1), 5–24 (2005)
14. Cerquides, J., Mántaras, R.L.D.: Robust Bayesian linear classifier ensembles. In: Gama, J., Camacho, R., Brazdil, P.B., Jorge, A.M., Torgo, L. (eds.) ECML 2005. LNCS (LNAI), vol. 3720, pp. 70–81. Springer, Heidelberg (2005)
15. Zheng, F., Webb, G.I.: Efficient lazy elimination for averaged-one dependence estimators. In: Proc. 23th Int. Conf. Machine Learning (ICML 2006), pp. 1113–1120. ACM Press, New York (2006)
16. Langseth, H., Nielsen, T.D.: Classification using hierarchical naive Bayes models. Machine Learning 63(2), 135–159 (2006)
17. Zheng, F., Webb, G.I.: A comparative study of semi-naive Bayes methods in classification learning. In: Proc. 4th Australasian Data Mining Conference (AusDM05), pp. 141–156 (2005)
18. Thomson ISI: Web of science (2007), `http://scientific.thomson.com/products/wos/`
19. Yang, Y., Webb, G., Cerquides, J., Korb, K., Boughton, J., Ting, K.M.: To select or to weigh: A comparative study of model selection and model weighing for SPODE ensembles. In: Proc. 18th European Conf. Machine Learning (ECML2006), pp. 533–544. Springer, Berlin (2006).
20. Duda, R.O., Hart, P.E.: Pattern Classification and Scene Analysis. John Wiley and Sons, New York (1973)
21. Domingos, P., Pazzani, M.J.: Beyond independence: Conditions for the optimality of the simple Bayesian classifier. In: Proc. 13th Int. Conf. Machine Learning, pp. 105–112. Morgan Kaufmann, San Francisco (1996)
22. John, G.H., Kohavi, R., Pfleger, K.: Irrelevant features and the subset selection problem. In: Proc. 11th Int. Conf. Machine Learning, pp. 121–129. Morgan Kaufmann, San Francisco, CA (1994)
23. Newman, D.J., Hettich, S., Blake, C.L., Merz, C.J.: UCI repository of machine learning databases. University of California, Department of Information and Computer Science, Irvine, CA (1998)
24. Fayyad, U.M., Irani, K.B.: Multi-interval discretization of continuous-valued attributes for classification learning. In: Proc. 13th Int. Joint Conf. Artificial Intelligence (IJCAI-93), pp. 1022–1029. Morgan Kaufmann, San Francisco (1993)
25. Cestnik, B.: Estimating probabilities: A crucial task in machine learning. In: Proc. 9th European Conf. Artificial Intelligence, pp. 147–149. Pitman, London (1990)
26. Witten, I.H., Frank, E.: Data Mining: Practical Machine Learning Tools and Techniques. Morgan Kaufmann, San Francisco (2005)
27. Webb, G.I.: Multiboosting: A technique for combining boosting and wagging. Machine Learning 40(2), 159–196 (2000)

Stepwise Induction of Multi-target Model Trees

Annalisa Appice[1] and Saso Džeroski[2]

[1] Dipartimento di Informatica, Università degli Studi di Bari
via Orabona, 4 - 70126 Bari - Italy
[2] Department of Knowledge Technologies, Jožef Stefan Institute
Jamova 39 - Ljubljana, Slovenia 1000
appice@di.uniba.it, Saso.Dzeroski@ijs.si

Abstract. Multi-target model trees are trees which predict the values of several target continuous variables simultaneously. Each leaf of such a tree contains several linear models, each predicting the value of a different target variable. We propose an algorithm for inducing such trees in a stepwise fashion. Experiments show that multi-target model trees are much smaller than the corresponding sets of single-target model trees and are induced much faster, while achieving comparable accuracies.

1 Introduction

Many problems encountered in ecological applications involve the prediction of several targets associated with a case. More formally, given a set of observed data $(\mathbf{x}, \mathbf{y}) \in \mathbf{X} \times \mathbf{Y}$, where $\mathbf{X}$ consists of m explanatory (or independent) variables X_i, the goal is to predict several target (or dependent) variables $Y_1, \ldots, Y_n$. The range of each Y_j can be either a finite set of unordered category labels for classification or a subset of real number $\Re$ for regression.

The problem of predicting several target variables simultaneously has been approached in the *predictive clustering* framework [1], where now methods exist to construct clusters of examples which are similar to each other and simultaneously associate a predictive model (classification or regression) with each constructed cluster. Several systems have been developed to induce decision and regression trees [1,9,5] or rules [8] within the predictive clustering framework, but to the best of our knowledge there is no attempt of inducing a *model tree* to predict the values of several continuous target variables simultaneously.

Model trees [3,10,6,7,4] are decision trees whose leaves contain linear regression models that predict the value of a single continuous target variable. In this paper, we address the task of inducing *multi-target* model trees that predict the values of several target continuous variables simultaneously. We propose an algorithm named MTSMOTI (*M*ulti *T*arget *S*tepwise *Mo*del *T*ree *I*nduction) that induces the multi-target trees in a stepwise fashion [2]. The tree is induced top-down by choosing at each step to either partition the training space (split nodes) or introduce a regression variable in the set of linear models to be associated with leaves (regression nodes).

J.N. Kok et al. (Eds.): ECML 2007, LNAI 4701, pp. 502–509, 2007.

The paper is organized as follows. The stepwise induction of multi-target model trees is presented in Section 2. Experimental results are reported in Section 3 and some conclusions are drawn in Section 4.

2 The Algorithm

Our system for the induction of multi-target model trees employs the basic stepwise construction of a regression model as it is implemented in SMOTI [4].

To explain the stepwise procedure, let us consider an example: suppose we are interested in analyzing a target variable Y in a region R described by two continuous explanatory variables X_1 and X_2 when R can be partitioned into two regions R_1 and R_2 and two linear regression models involving both X_1 and X_2 can be built independently for each region R_i. It may be found that the Y value is proportional to X_1 and this behavior is independent of any partitioning of R. In this case, the effect of X_1 on Y is *global*, since it can be reliably predicted for the whole region R. The initial regression model is approximated by regressing on X_1 for the whole region $R : \hat{Y} = \hat{a}_0 + \hat{b}_0 X_1$. The effect of another variable in the partially constructed regression model is introduced by eliminating the effect of X_1: we have to compute the regression model for the whole region R, that is, $\hat{X_2} = \hat{a}_{20} + \hat{b}_{21} X_1$, as well as the residuals $X'_2 = X_2 - \hat{X_2}$ and $Y' = Y - \hat{Y} = Y - (\hat{a}_0 + \hat{b}_0 X_1)$. The partitioning of R into R_1 and R_2 leads to building two independent regression models to capture the effect of the variable X_2 *locally* in the subregions R_1 and R_2, respectively. Obviously, a straight-line regression now involves the residual variables Y' and X'_2, but can be automatically translated into a multiple linear function involving Y, X_1 and X_2.

This stepwise procedure corresponds to a tree structure with split nodes that produce binary partitions of the training data and regression nodes that perform straight-line regressions. Similarly to SMOTI, MTSMOTI induce such trees. However, MTSMOTI differs from SMOTI in several ways. First, MTSMOTI predicts several target variables simultaneously, assuming there is some (linear) dependence among target variables. Second, it resorts to a MAUVE [7]-based heuristic function to reduce the SMOTI time complexity of evaluating a node, yielding trees with better accuracy. Finally, it adopts some different stopping criteria and a post-pruning method. We discuss these topics below.

2.1 Model Tree Construction

The top-level description of the model tree construction performed by MTSMOTI is sketched in Algorithm 1.

A split node t on a variable X_i performs a binary test. If X_i is continuous, the split test is in the form $X_i \leq \alpha$ vs $X_i > \alpha$. Possible values of α are found by sorting the distinct values of X_i in the training sample falling in t, then identifying one threshold for each distinct value. If X_i is discrete, a discrete split partitions attribute values into two complementary sets, so that a binary tree is always built. To determine discrete split thresholds, we use the same criterion applied in CART. If $S_{X_i} = \{x_{i_1}, \ldots, x_{i_k}\}$ is the set of distinct values of X_i in t, S_{X_i} is sorted according to the sample mean of the target variable Y (or residual of Y) over all training cases falling in t, that is, $\bar{Y}_1, \ldots, \bar{Y}_k$. In the multi-target case, the set of distinct values of X_i is sorted according to the "average" of the sample means for each target variable Y_j from $\mathbf{Y}$. Since the range of different target variables may differ by several orders of magnitude, the sample means are scaled within the range $[0, 1]$. The scaled value of $\bar{Y}_{j_s}$ is $\bar{Y}_{j_{s \to [0,1]}} = \frac{|\bar{Y}_{j_s} - min_j|}{(max_j - min_j)}$, where $min_j = \min_{s=1,\ldots,k} \{\bar{Y}_{j_s}\}$ and $max_j = \max_{s=1,\ldots,k} \{\bar{Y}_{j_s}\}$.

Algorithm 1. MTSMOTI top-level description.

```
function build-MTSMOTI-tree(X, Y, R, E) return T
X → set of m continuous (X_C) and discrete (X_D) explanatory variables
Y → set of n continuous target variables
R → set of residuals of continuous variables; initially R = X_C ∪ Y
E → {(x_j, y_j)|j = 1...N} a training sample
T → a multi-target model tree with regression and split nodes
begin
RegList=regressionCandidates(X, Y, R, E);
if stopping criteria then
    t is the best regression node on RegList; T =leaf(best_t);
else
    SplitList=splitCandidates(X, Y, R, E); t is the best node on RegList∪SplitList;
    if t is a regression node on variable X_i then
        R' is a copy of R; R_{X_i} is residual of X_i in R';
        for each R_i ∈ R' do
            if R_i represents either a target variable or a continuous explanatory variable
            not yet included in the current model then
                replace R_i in R' with its new residual by removing effect of R_{X_i};
            end if
        end for
        T' =build-MTSMOTI-tree(X, Y, R', E); T = tree with root in t and child T';
    end if
    if t is a split node on variable X_i then
        T_L =build-MTSMOTI-tree(X, Y, R, {(x_j, y_j) ∈ E| test in t is true});
        T_R =build-MTSMOTI-tree(X, Y, R, {(x_j, y_j) ∈ E| test in t is false});
        T is the tree with root in t, left branch T_L, right branch T_R;
    end if
end if
end
```

A regression node performs a set of straight-line regressions on a continuous variable X_i, one for each target variable Y_j. Straight-line regressions in the subtree rooted in a regression node will involve residuals of both the target variables and the continuous explanatory variables not yet included in the model.

2.2 Split and Regression Node Evaluation

The choice of either a split test or a regression step at a node t is based on the evaluation measures $s(t, \boldsymbol{Y})$ and $r(t, \boldsymbol{Y})$, respectively.

Let t be a split on X_i then $s_j(t, Y_j)$ is computed as $s_j(t; Y_j) = \frac{N(t_L)}{N(t)} RE(t_L; Y_j) + \frac{N(t_R)}{N(t))} RE(t_R; Y_j)$, where $N(t)$ is the number of cases reaching t, $N(t_L)$ $(N(t_R))$ is the number of cases passed down to the left (right) child, and $RE(t_L)$ $(RE(t_R))$ is the resubstitution error of the left (right) child. The resubstitution error is computed as $RE(t; Y_j) = \sqrt{\frac{1}{N(t)} \sum_{i=1}^{N(t)} (y_{j_i} - \hat{y}_{j_i})^2}$. For the left(right) child of a split t, the estimate $\hat{y}_j$ combines the straight-line regressions associated with regression nodes along the path from the root to t_L (t_R) with the straight-line regression on X_i computed on t_L (t_R). In case X_i is a discrete variable, straight-line regression on t_L (t_R) is replaced with the sample mean of Y_j (or residual of Y_j) values falling in t_L (t_R). This evaluation function is derived by MAUVE [7] as an alternative to consider no regression (M5')[10], simple regression on all continuous variables (SMOTI) or multiple regression on all continuous variables together (RETIS) [3]. The motivation in favor of the MAUVE measure is in its lower computational complexity. In fact, similarly to M5', MAUVE is linear in the number of variables, but the MAUVE split evaluation avoids some pathological behaviors of M5' [7]. The evaluation of a regression step $Y_j = \alpha_j + \beta_j X_i$ at node t is based on the resubstitution error $RE(t; Y_j)$. In this way, the selection of the best regression step requires the computation of a straight-line regression with complexity linear by number of examples falling in t, for each of the m target variables. Measures obtained at t for separate target variables are scaled to the interval $[0, 1]$ and combined as $s(t, \boldsymbol{Y}) = \frac{1}{n} \sum_{j=1}^{n} s_{\rightarrow[0,1]}(t; Y_j)$ $\left(r(t, \boldsymbol{Y}) = \frac{1}{n} \sum_{j=1}^{n} RE_{\rightarrow[0,1]}(t; Y_j)\right)$. The most promising split (regression) minimizes the evaluation measure s (r) on the set of split (regression) candidates.

As pointed in [4], a regression step on X_i would result in values of $r(t; Y_j)$ less than or equal to values of $s(t; Y)$ for some split test involving X_i. Hence, the split selection criterion in MTSMOTI is improved to consider the special case of identical regression models associated with both children (left and right): a useless split is replaced with a regression candidate. To check for this case, MTSMOTI compares pairs of lines associated with the children according to a statistical test for coincident regression lines [11] with linear time complexity.

2.3 Stopping Criteria

Three different stopping criteria are implemented. The first uses the partial F-test to evaluate the actual contribution provided by a new explanatory variable to the model [2]. The F-test is performed separately for each target variable. Hence, stopping can operate at different tree depth for different target variables. The second requires the number of examples in each node to be greater than a minimum value. The third stops the induction process when all continuous explanatory variables along the path from the root to the current node are used in regression steps and there are no discrete variables in the training set.

2.4 Pruning

MTSMOTI adopts a pruning procedure to determine which nodes of the tree should be taken as leaves and compute the set of linear models for each interior node of the un-pruned tree. Linear models built in a stepwise fashion at each node are expanded by sequentially adding variables, one at a time, on the basis of the strength of the average resubstitution error. The models are built by using only the continuous variables tested or regressed in the subtree below this node. For each target variable, the contribution of an added term is immediately evaluated according to the F-test and eventually dropped whenever it is not statistically significant. Once a linear model is in place for an interior node, the tree is pruned back from the leaves so long as the expected estimated error decreases. The estimate of the expected error is the average of the resubstitution errors (scaled in the range [0,1]) on the training cases reaching that node for each target variable. To avoid the underestimation of the expected error on unseen cases, the average resubstitution error is multiplied by the factor $(N(t)-\nu(t))/(N(t)+\nu(t))$, where $N(t)$ is the number of training cases that reach t an $\nu(t)$ is the number of variables in the linear model associated with the node.

3 Experimental Results

The performance of MTSMOTI is evaluated on both single-target and multi-target datasets by 10-fold cross-validation. For each target variable Y_j, we estimate the basis of the average relative mean square error ($RRMSE(D, Y_j) = \frac{1}{10}\sum_{i=1}^{10}(\sqrt{\sum_{h=1}^{N(D_i)}(y_{j_h} - \widehat{y}_{j_h}(D/D_i))^2}/\sqrt{\sum_{h=1}^{N(D_i)}(y_{j_h} - \bar{y}_j(D_i))^2})$), where $\widehat{y}_{j_h}(D/D_i)$ is the value predicted for the j-th target variable of the h-th testing case by the model tree induced on D/D_i and $\bar{y}_j$ is the mean value of y_j on D_i. RRMSE is averaged on separate target variables. The complexity of trees is evaluated on the basis of the number of leaves. All the multi-target datasets as well as the results for PC-Tree reported in this Section are provided by Bernard Ženko [8].

3.1 Single-Target Datasets

MTSMOTI is tested on single-target datasets taken from the UCI Machine Learning Repository (http://www.ics.uci.). MTSMOTI is run in two settings. In the former setting (SR), model trees are built in a stepwise fashion, while in the latter setting (S), model trees are built by partitioning the training sample and then associating leaves with multiple linear models by post-pruning the tree. MTSMOTI is compared with REGTREE, i.e., our implementation of a regression tree learner, SMOTI, M5', predictive clustering trees (PCT) and rules (PCR). SMOTI and M5' are run with default stopping thresholds. The pruning of M5' is enabled, but no smoothing is used. Results are reported in Table 1.

Several conclusions are drawn from these experimental results. First, model trees outperform regression trees in accuracy and size. Second, our implementation of the stepwise tree construction generally improves performance of SMOTI

Table 1. Single-target regression: comparison of the average RRMSE and average size

	RRMSE						Size					
Dataset	MT (SR)	MT (S)	REG TR.	SMO TI	M5	PCT	MT (SR)	MT (S)	REG TR.	SMO TI	M5	PCT
AutoHorse	0.38	0.43	0.47	0.49	0.35	0.41	3.8	4.2	6.8	6.6	2.4	23
AutoMpg	0.40	0.44	0.44	0.46	0.37	0.45	12.7	10.5	16.5	10	4.8	16
AutoPrice	0.48	0.46	0.60	0.53	0.40	0.49	7.2	4.5	10.2	6.6	7.4	9
Tumor	1.00	1.16	1.16	1.34	0.99	0.96	4.7	17	16.6	8	1.1	3
Cloud	0.53	0.68	0.82	0.70	0.52	0.58	3.2	4.2	6.9	5	2.4	9
CPU	0.17	0.34	0.65	0.80	0.20	0.33	8.3	3.9	13	7	3.1	12
Housing	0.45	0.47	0.49	0.45	0.44	0.43	4.5	18.5	21.1	11	13.5	32
Quake	0.99	1.12	1.03	2.38	1.01	0.99	2.3	29	28.8	23	3.3	3
Sensory	0.93	0.93	0.93	1.00	0.96	0.94	16.5	16.5	16.5	12	4.7	7
Servo	0.60	0.60	0.60	0.45	0.43	0.42	7	7	7	7	5.6	11
Strike	0.94	0.91	0.96	1.88	1.24	0.98	3.9	18.7	18.7	12	6.5	12
Veteran	1.20	1.15	1.34	2.40	1.22	0.99	3.2	6.1	7.8	6	1	2

in accuracy. Third, the comparison between trees built in a stepwise fashion (SR) and trees in classical mode (S) show that trees with split and regression nodes achieve better (or at worst comparable) accuracy than trees with only split nodes. No general conclusion can be drawn on the tree size. Fourth, the comparison with M5' accuracy shows that MTSMOTI is sometime better, at worst comparable, to M5', but M5' typically builds smaller trees. In any case, MTSMOTI is able to detect the presence of global effects without significantly affecting accuracy. Finally, the comparison with predictive clustering trees shows that MTSMOTI does not exhibit an irrefutable superiority with respect to PC-TREE, although results are still good.

3.2 Multi-target Datasets

The multi-target datasets in this study are not public available. Only solar-flare (SOLARF) is available in the UCI Machine Learning Repository. A brief description of these datasets is reported in Table 2.

Table 2. Properties of multi-target datasets used in our study

Dataset	#Cases	#Explan. Var.	#Target Var.	Dataset	#Cases	#Explan. Var.	#Target Var.
EDM	154	16	3	SOLARF	323	10	3
MICROA	1944	142	3	WATERQ	1060	16	14
SIGMEAR	817	6	2	LANDSAT	60607	160	11
SIGMEAS	10368	11	2				

Table 3. Multi-target regression: comparison of the average RRMSE and average size

	RRMSE				Size			
Dataset	MTSMOTI	STSMOTI	MTREG TREE	PC T	MTSMOTI	STSMOTI	MTREG TREE	PC T
EDM	0.86	0.86	0.83	0.72	4	5	7	11
MICROA	0.78	0.60	0.87	1.01	18	47	17	50
SIGMEAR	0.71	0.91	1.15	0.85	3	8	11	7
SIGMEAS	0.03	0.03	0.03	0.03	23	27	49	166
SOLARF	1.02	1.06	1.02	1	13	30	13	2
WATERQ	0.96	0.97	0.98	0.96	12	92	13	5
LANDSAT	0.67	0.64	0.69	0.62	21	238	31.9	518

For each dataset, multi-target model trees (MTSMOTI) are first compared with the set of single-target model trees (STSMOTI), induced one for each target variable. The RRMSE is averaged over the target variables. The tree size for STSMOTI is the sum of size for all separate trees. Secondly, multi-target model trees are compared with multi-target regression trees (MTREGTREE) as well as predictive clustering trees. Results are reported in Table 3.

Results show that multi-target model trees are much smaller than the set of single-target model trees, while achieving comparable (sometime better) accuracy. MICROA is the only dataset where the multi-target model tree performs significantly worse than the set of single-target trees (0.78 vs. 0.60). A deeper analysis reveals that the worst performance involves only the prediction of one target variable (Shannon biodiversity: 0.7 vs. 0.28), while the accuracy estimates are comparable for the remaining two target variables (mites: 0.85 vs 0.82 and springehrtails: 0.78 vs 0.72). This negative result suggests the absence of a "linear" dependence between the Shannon biodiversity and the variables mites and springertails. In any case, multi-target trees are always induced much faster than the set of single-target ones (18 vs 25 (EDM), 202 vs 412 (MICROA), 5 vs 9 (SIGMEAR), 69 vs 84 (SIGMEAS), <1 vs 2 (SOLARF), 718 vs 1272 (WATERQ) and 9214 vs 25372 (LANDSAT): running times are in secs.

The comparison between multi-target model trees and regression trees reveals that although model trees are typically smaller than regression trees, they achieve comparable (or sometime better) accuracy than corresponding the regression trees. MTSMOTI is capable of detecting the presence of a global effect of some explanatory variable on "all" of the target variables that no previous study on these datasets have revealed. In this way, regression nodes implicitly reveal the existence of some linear dependences among the target variables at different depth of the tree hierarchy. Finally, the comparison with predictive clustering trees confirms are sometime more accurate than model trees (EDM and SIGMEA-REAL), but clustering trees can be significantly more complex. Finally, clustering trees predict the same constant values (for each example covered by the same leaf), and they are not be able of capturing any linear pattern in the data.

4 Conclusions

In this work, we present MTSMOTI, a system that induces multi-target model trees and predict the values of several target variables simultaneously. Leaves of such a tree contain several linear models, each predicting the value of a different target variable. Multi-target model trees are built with two types of nodes: split nodes and regression nodes. Experiments on single-target datasets shows that MTSMOTI is competitive with respect to regression tree learners, SMOTI and M5', as well as predictive clustering trees. Experiments on multi-target datasets confirm that multi-target model trees are much smaller than the set of single-target model trees, while achieving comparable accuracies. In addition, they are induced much faster. As future work, we plan to combine decision trees and model trees to predict continuous and discrete target variables, simultaneously. A comparison to predictive clustering rules should be interesting. Finally, adding linear regression models to predictive clustering rules is worth to be explored.

References

1. Blockeel, H., Raedt, L.D., Ramon, J.: Top-down induction of clustering trees. In: Shavlik, J. (ed.) Proceedings of the 15th International Conference on Machine Learning, pp. 55–63. Morgan Kaufmann, San Francisco (1998)
2. Draper, N.R., Smith, H.: Applied regression analysis. John Wiley & Sons, Chichester (1982)
3. Karalic, A.: Linear regression in regression tree leaves. In: Proceedings of International School for Synthesis of Expert Knowledge, Slovenia, pp. 151–163 (1992)
4. Malerba, D., Esposito, F., Ceci, M., Appice, A.: Top down induction of model trees with regression and splitting nodes. IEEE Transactions on Pattern Analysis and Machine Intelligence 26(5), 612–625 (2004)
5. Struyf, J., Dzeroski, S.: Constraint based induction of multi-objective regression trees. In: Bonchi, F., Boulicaut, J.-F. (eds.) Workshop on Knowledge Discovery in Inductive Databases, pp. 222–233 (2005)
6. Torgo, L.: Functional models for regression tree leaves. In: Fisher, D. (ed.) Proceedings of the 14th International Conference on Machine Learning, pp. 385–393. Morgan Kaufmann, San Francisco (1997)
7. Vens, C., Blockeel, H.: A simple regression based heuristic for learning model trees. Intelligent Data Analysis 10(3), 215–236 (2006)
8. Ženko, B.: Learning Predictive Clustering Rules. PhD thesis, Faculty of Computer and Information Science, University of Ljubljana, Slovenia (2007)
9. Suzuki, M.G.W., Choki, Y.: k-nearest neighbour classification of symbolic objects. In: De Raedt, L., Siebes, A. (eds.) PKDD 2001. LNCS (LNAI), vol. 2168, pp. 436–446. Springer, Heidelberg (2001)
10. Wang, Y., Witten, I.: Inducing model trees for continuous classes. In: van Someren, M., Widmer, G. (eds.) ECML 1997. LNCS, vol. 1224, pp. 128–137. Springer, Heidelberg (1997)
11. Weisberg, S.: Applied regression analysis, 2nd edn. Wiley, Chichester (1985)

Comparing Rule Measures for Predictive Association Rules*

Paulo J. Azevedo[1] and Alípio M. Jorge[2,3]

[1] CCTC, Departamento de Informática, Universidade do Minho
pja@di.uminho.pt
[2] Faculdade de Economia, Universidade do Porto
amjorge@fep.up.pt
[3] LIAAD, INESC PORTO L.A.

Abstract. We study the predictive ability of some association rule measures typically used to assess descriptive interest. Such measures, namely conviction, lift and χ^2 are compared with confidence, Laplace, mutual information, cosine, Jaccard and ϕ-coefficient. As prediction models, we use sets of association rules. Classification is done by selecting the best rule, or by weighted voting. We performed an evaluation on 17 datasets with different characteristics and conclude that conviction is on average the best predictive measure to use in this setting. We also provide some meta-analysis insights for explaining the results.

1 Introduction

Association rule mining is primarily used for exploratory data mining. In that setting it is useful to discover relations between sets of variables, which may represent products in an on-line store, disease symptoms, keywords, demographic characteristics, to name a few. To guide the data analyst identifying interesting rules, many objective interestingness rule measures have been proposed in the literature [10]. Although these measures have descriptive aims, we will evaluate their use in predictive tasks. One of these measures, conviction, will be shown as particularly successful in classification.

The general idea of classification based on association rules [7] is to generate a set of association rules with a fixed class attribute in the consequent and then use subsets of these rules to classify new examples. This approach has the advantage of searching a larger portion of the rule version space, since no search heuristics are employed, in contrast to decision tree and traditional classification rule induction. The extra search is done in a controlled manner enabled by the good computational behavior of association rule discovery algorithms. Another advantage is that the produced rich rule set can be used in a variety of ways without relearning, which can be used to improve the classification accuracy [5].

* Supported by Fundação Ciência e Tecnologia, Project Site-o-matic, FEDER e Programa de Financiamento Plurianual de Unidades de I & D.

J.N. Kok et al. (Eds.): ECML 2007, LNAI 4701, pp. 510–517, 2007.

2 The Measures

We now describe the measures used in this work (Table 1), after introducing some notation. Let r be a rule of the form $A \rightarrow C$ where A and C are sets of items. In a classification setting, each item in A is a pair $< attribute = value >$, and C has one single pair $< class\_attribute = class\_value >$. The rules are obtained from a dataset D of size N.

Table 1. Measures

Measure	Definition	Range
confidence	$conf(A \rightarrow C) = \frac{sup(A \cup C)}{sup(A)}$	[0, 1]
Laplace	$lapl(A \rightarrow C) = \frac{sup(A \cup C)+1}{sup(A)+2}$	[0, 1[
lift	$lift(A \rightarrow C) = \frac{conf(A \rightarrow C)}{sup(C)}$	[0, +∞[
conviction	$conv(A \rightarrow C) = \frac{1-sup(C)}{1-conf(A \rightarrow C)}$	[0.5, +∞[
leverage	$leve(A \rightarrow C) = sup(A \cup C) - sup(A) \times sup(C)$	[−0.25, 0.25]
χ^2	$\chi^2(A \rightarrow C) = N \times \sum_{X \in \{A,\neg A\}, Y \in \{C, \neg C\}} \frac{(sup(X \cup Y) - sup(X).sup(Y))^2}{sup(X) \times sup(Y)}$	[0, +∞[
Jaccard	$jacc(A \rightarrow C) = \frac{sup(A \cup C)}{sup(A)+sup(C)-sup(A \cup C)}$	[0, 1]
cosine	$cos(A \rightarrow C) = \frac{sup(A \cup C)}{\sqrt{sup(A) \times sup(C)}}$	[0, 1]
ϕ-coeff	$\phi(A \rightarrow C) = \frac{leve(A \rightarrow C)}{\sqrt{(sup(A) \times sup(C)) \times (1-sup(A)) \times (1-sup(C))}}$	[−1, 1]
mutual inf.	$MI(A \rightarrow C) = \frac{\sum_i \sum_j sup(A_i \cup C_j) \times log(\frac{sup(A_i \cup C_j)}{sup(A_i) \times sup(C_j)})}{min(\sum_i -sup(A_i) \times log(sup(A_i)), \sum_j -sup(C_j) \times log(sup(C_j)))}$	[0, 1]

In association rule discovery, *Confidence* (of $A \rightarrow C$) is a standard measure. It is an estimate of $\Pr(C \mid A)$, the probability of observing C given A. After obtaining a rule set, one can immediatly use confidence as a basis for classifying one new case x. Of all the rules that apply to x (i.e., the rules whose antecedent is true in x), we choose the one with highest confidence. *Laplace* is a measure mostly used in classification. It is a confidence estimator that takes support into account, becoming more pessimistic as the support of A decreases.

Confidence alone (or Laplace) is not be enough to assess the descriptive interest of a rule. Rules with high confidence may occur by chance. Such spurious rules can be detected by determining whether the antecedent and the consequent are statistically independent. This inspired a number of measures for association rule interest. One of them is *Lift* which measures how far from independence are A and C. Values close to 1 imply that A and C are independent and the rule is not interesting. Lift measures co-occurrence only (not implication) and is symmetric with respect to antecedent and consequent.

Conviction [3] measures the degree of implication of a rule, but also assesses the independence between A and C. Its value is 1 in case of independence and is infinite for logical implications (confidence 1). Unlike lift, it is sensitive to rule direction ($conv(A \rightarrow C) \neq conv(C \rightarrow A)$). Unlike confidence, the support of both antecedent and consequent are considered in conviction. *Leverage* was recovered by Webb for the Magnus Opus system [11], but previously proposed by Piatetsky-Schapiro [9]. The idea is to measure, through a difference, how much

A and C deviate from independence (from zero). The definite way for measuring the statistical independence between antecedent and consequent is the χ^2 test. As stated in [2], χ^2 does not assess the strength of correlation between antecedent and consequent. It only assists in deciding about the independence of these items which suggests that the measure is not feasible for ranking purposes. Our results will corroborate these claims.

The following measures evaluate the degree of overlap between the cases covered by A and C. The *Jaccard* coefficient is the binary similarity between the sets of cases covered by both sides of the rule, whereas *Cosine* views A and C as two binary vectors. In both cases, higher values mean similarity The ϕ-coefficient is analogous to the discrete case of the Pearson correlation coeficient. In [10], it is shown that $\phi^2 = \frac{\chi^2}{N}$. The last measure, *Mutual Information*, measures the amount of reduction in uncertainty of the consequent when the antecedent is known [10]. In the definition (table 1), $A_i \in \{A, \neg A\}$ and $C_j \in \{C, \neg C\}$. Notice that measures lift, leverage, χ^2, Jaccard, cosine, ϕ and MI are symmetric, whereas confidence, Laplace and conviction are asymmetric. We will see that this makes all the difference in terms of prediction. Other measures could have been considered, but we focused mainly on the ones used in association rules.

2.1 Prediction

The simplest approach for prediction with association rules is *Best Rule*, where we choose, among the rules that apply to a new case, the one with the highest value of the chosen predictive measure. Ties can be broken by support [7]. A kind of best rule strategy, combined with a coverage rule generation method, provided encouraging empirical results when compared with state of the art classifiers on some datasets from UCI [8]. Our implementation of Best Rule follows closely the rules ordering described in CMAR [6]:

$$R_1 \prec R_2 \;\; if \;\; meas(R_1) > meas(R_2) \;\; or \;\; meas(R_1) == meas(R_2) \wedge sup(R1) > sup(R2)$$
$$or \;\; meas(R_1) == meas(R_2) \wedge sup(R1) == sup(R2) \wedge ant(R1) < ant(R2).$$

where *meas* is the used interest measure and *ant* is the length of the antecedent.

For prediction, we have also tried *Weighted Voting*. This strategy combines the rules $F(x)$ that fire upon a case x. The answer of each rule is a *vote*, and the final decision is obtained by assigning a specific weight to each vote.

$$pred_{wv} = arg \max_{g \in G} \sum_{x' \in antec(F(x))} vote(x', g). \max meas(x' \to g).$$

3 Experiments

We have tested the effects of each measure on benchmark datasets. For that, we ran CAREN [1] using "Best Rule" and "Weighted Voting". For reference we show the results of the *rpart* and the *c4.5* TDIDT algorithms (see [5] for more details). Stratified 10 fold cross-validation was used to estimate error rates(Table 3) and to derive algorithm ranking (Table 4). The datasets used for evaluation (table 2) have varied sizes, number of attributes and classes and were obtained

Table 2. Datasets used for the empirical evaluation

Dataset	nick	#examples	#classes	#attr	#numerics	norm. Gini	norm. entropy
australian	aus	690	2	14	6	0.99	0.99
breast	bre	699	2	9	8	0.90	0.93
pima	pim	768	2	8	8	0.91	0.93
yeast	yea	1484	10	8	8	0.86	0.75
flare	fla	1066	2	10	0	0.61	0.70
cleveland	cle	303	5	13	5	0.81	0.80
heart	hea	270	2	13	13	0.99	0.99
hepatitis	hep	155	2	19	4	0.66	0.73
german	ger	1000	2	20	7	0.84	0.88
house-votes	hou	435	2	16	0	0.95	0.96
segment	seg	2310	7	19	19	1.00	1.00
vehicle	veh	846	4	18	18	1.00	1.00
adult	adu	32561	2	14	6	0.73	0.80
lymphography	lym	148	4	18	0	0.71	0.61
sat	sat	6435	6	36	36	0.97	0.96
shuttle	shu	58000	7	9	9	0.41	0.34
waveform	wav	5000	3	21	21	1.00	1.00

Table 3. Error rates (in percent) for rpart, c4.5 and the different CAREN variants

	aus	bre	pim	yea	fla	cle	hea	hep	ger	hou	seg	veh	adu	lym	sat	shu	wav
rpart	16.23	6.15	24.72	43.27	17.73	46.16	20.00	26.00	25.20	4.87	8.31	31.76	15.55	25.27	19.04	0.53	26.64
c4.5	13.92	5.00	24.36	44.27	17.44	50.04	21.09	21.32	30.20	3.25	3.21	25.96	13.61	23.07	13.97	0.05	22.73
BR.conf	14.21	4.57	22.78	41.27	19.14	45.70	18.52	19.99	28.50	8.11	9.91	38.74	14.81	17.29	19.75	0.47	17.40
BR.lift	36.09	18.88	41.66	44.57	21.66	44.09	31.48	47.51	63.80	46.67	9.91	43.92	36.49	47.75	34.51	21.74	29.82
BR.conv	14.35	4.28	22.38	42.07	19.78	44.09	18.89	16.78	26.70	8.11	9.91	38.63	14.27	18.00	19.39	0.45	17.42
BR.chi	32.89	14.02	33.71	45.10	21.66	44.09	27.04	47.51	63.30	40.95	31.77	46.21	36.49	47.08	32.43	20.59	21.04
BR.lapl	14.22	5.86	25.25	44.29	18.86	45.70	17.04	20.58	28.90	6.48	10.61	39.22	15.70	18.00	19.86	0.47	17.34
BR.lev	14.51	11.58	30.71	48.13	18.85	44.09	21.85	21.68	29.30	5.55	36.58	48.82	20.10	27.40	47.64	1.64	26.82
BR.jacc	14.51	19.45	34.89	44.81	18.86	45.70	38.15	20.58	30.00	5.55	34.03	48.81	24.08	34.32	42.14	15.58	26.74
BR.cos	14.51	23.17	34.89	55.80	18.86	45.70	44.44	20.58	30.00	5.55	33.94	49.75	24.08	43.62	42.75	15.58	32.16
BR.phi	14.51	6.85	27.85	44.55	19.22	44.09	18.89	30.27	30.70	5.55	33.12	49.06	17.91	28.69	36.25	6.45	26.46
BR.MI	25.81	5.85	24.20	46.14	17.90	44.09	27.04	19.99	29.90	15.88	14.50	37.90	17.41	45.76	35.29	6.04	28.52
Voting.conf	16.24	3.57	22.64	42.61	18.47	45.70	17.41	16.27	24.10	13.35	15.11	35.43	16.35	27.37	35.17	2.85	17.28
Voting.lift	15.37	3.29	25.63	42.01	19.50	45.70	16.67	17.14	27.50	14.73	15.11	35.55	20.02	32.19	33.43	9.20	17.24
Voting.conv	18.40	4.72	22.77	41.87	18.56	45.70	19.63	17.45	26.50	13.80	20.22	36.04	15.07	22.50	23.17	0.60	28.42
Voting.chi	16.10	3.43	25.63	42.88	18.94	45.70	17.04	15.22	25.70	13.81	15.89	36.03	18.42	32.19	35.79	3.60	17.12
Voting.lapl	16.39	3.57	22.77	42.41	18.38	45.70	17.41	16.27	23.90	13.35	15.15	35.55	16.41	27.37	35.17	2.84	17.22
Voting.Lev	15.82	4.58	24.72	46.04	18.56	45.70	17.78	14.12	24.40	14.50	22.34	39.00	17.04	32.72	36.60	2.69	19.72
Voting.Jacc	17.41	4.87	24.07	43.34	18.19	45.70	17.78	15.53	24.40	14.26	21.52	38.89	18.14	32.10	35.04	2.55	19.96
Voting.Cos	16.98	4.29	23.29	43.41	17.91	45.70	17.04	14.86	24.40	13.57	18.40	38.30	16.50	30.72	35.21	2.14	18.30
Voting.Phi	15.52	3.43	24.59	42.68	18.93	45.70	17.41	15.88	26.00	14.50	18.31	38.17	18.03	30.72	34.50	5.54	17.98
Voting.MI	77.84	49.08	34.36	45.03	18.66	45.70	73.33	80.09	66.00	80.63	97.71	74.69	34.88	93.25	84.38	40.84	90.90

Table 4. Ranks

	mean	aus	bre	pim	yea	fla	cle	hea	hep	ger	hou	seg	veh	adu	lym	sat	shu	wav
BR.conv	6.35	4	6	1	4	20	3.5	11.5	8	10	8.5	4	11	2	2.5	3	2	7
BR.conf	7.18	2	8	5	1	17	13.5	10	11.5	12	8.5	4	12	3	1	4	3.5	6
Voting.conf	7.44	14	4.5	2	6	7	13.5	6	6.5	2	10.5	8.5	3	7	7.5	12.5	12	4
Voting.lapl	7.47	15	4.5	3.5	5	6	13.5	6	6.5	1	10.5	10	4.5	8	7.5	12.5	11	2
c4.5	7.65	1	12	9	12	1	22	15	16	18	1	1	1	1	5	1	1	13
rpart	8.74	13	15	11.5	9	2	21	14	18	6	2	2	2	5	6	2	5	15
BR.lapl	8.79	3	14	13	13	13	13.5	3	14	13	7	6	15	6	2.5	5	3.5	5
Voting.Cos	9	16	7	6	11	4	13.5	3	2	4	12	13	10	9	11.5	14	8	9
Voting.conv	9.38	18	10	3.5	2	8.5	13.5	13	10	9	13	14	7	4	4	6	6	18
Voting.chi	10	12	2.5	14.5	8	16	13.5	3	3	7	14	11	6	15	14.5	16	13	1
Voting.Phi	10	10	2.5	10	7	15	13.5	6	5	8	16.5	12	9	13	11.5	9	14	8
Voting.lift	10.03	9	1	14.5	3	19	13.5	1	9	11	18	8.5	4.5	16	14.5	8	17	3
Voting.Jacc	10.65	17	11	7	10	5	13.5	8.5	4	4	15	15	13	14	13	11	9	11
Voting.Lev	11.56	11	9	11.5	19	8.5	13.5	8.5	1	4	16.5	16	14	10	16	18	10	10
BR.MI	13.15	19	13	8	20	3	3.5	17.5	11.5	15	19	7	8	11	19	15	15	19
BR.phi	13.82	6.5	16	16	14	18	3.5	11.5	19	19	4.5	18	20	12	10	17	16	14
BR.lev	14.03	6.5	17	17	21	11	3.5	16	17	14	4.5	21	19	17	9	21	7	17
BR.jacc	15.97	6.5	20	20.5	16	13	13.5	20	14	16.5	4.5	20	18	18.5	17	19	18.5	16
BR.cos	16.97	6.5	21	20.5	22	13	13.5	21	14	16.5	4.5	19	21	18.5	18	20	18.5	21
BR.chi	17.15	20	18	18	18	21.5	3.5	17.5	20.5	20	20	17	17	21.5	20	7	20	12
BR.lift	17.47	21	19	22	15	21.5	3.5	19	20.5	21	21	4	16	21.5	21	10	21	20
Voting.MI	20.21	22	22	19	17	10	13.5	22	22	22	22	22	22	20	22	22	22	22

from [8]. Since the existence of minority classes may be important to explain the results, we have also measured class balancing. For that, we use normalized Gini, defined as $\sum_i {p_i}^2/(1 - nclasses^{-1})$, where p_i is the proportion of class i, and normalized entropy, $-\sum_i p_i log_2(p_i)/log_2(nclasses)$. Both measures equal 1 when the classes are balanced and tend to 0 otherwise. The two measures are not very different in value for these 17 datasets.

We have preprocessed numerical attributes using Fayyad and Irani's supervised discretization method [4]. Minimal support was set to 0.01 or 10 training cases. The only exception was the *sat* dataset, where we used 0.02 for computational reasons. Minimal improvement was 0.01 and minimal confidence 0.5. We have also used the χ^2 filter to eliminate potentially trivial rules. C4.5 and rpart were ran using the original raw data.

4 Discussion

The first observation is that conviction gets the best mean rank. This confirms the experiments in [5] which motivated the present study of this measure. We observe that, using a t-test with 5% significance, conviction has 2 out of 17 significant wins over confidence and 3 over Laplace (and loses none). This seems to be a marginal but consistent advantage, which is not observed for the Voting strategy. The second observation is that the other 7 measures do not produce competitive classifiers. Notice that these are the symmetric rule interest measures. Using the error rate arrays, we can group the pairs strategy-measure using hierarchical clustering. The distance between strategies was measured using plain Euclidean distance and the clusters were aggregated using complete linkage. The obtained clustering (Fig. 1) indicates the predictive proximity of confidence, conviction and Laplace (the three symmetric measures employed), when used with best rule. Almost all Voting strategies are clustered together, except for Voting.conv (which is clustered with the top performing best rule approaches) and Voting.MI which performs particularly poorly. Other expected pairs of measures also cluster together. These are Jaccard and cosine (for best rule), lift and χ^2, leverage and ϕ and also rpart and C4.5.

We now try to study if some features of the data set (meta features) may indicate whether to use either conviction, confidence or laplace. As meta features

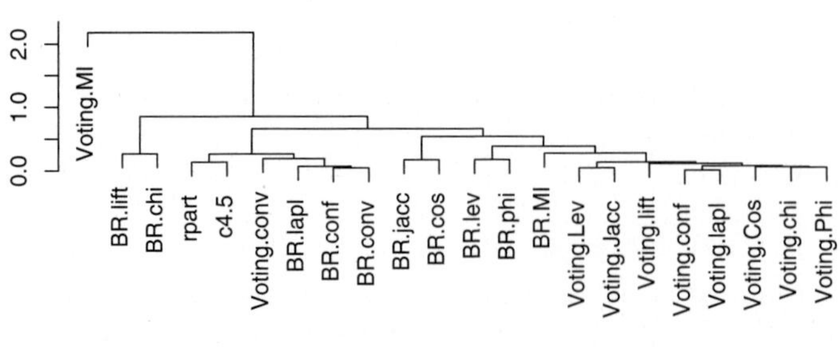

Fig. 1. Clustering measures and strategies using complete linkage and Euclidean distance

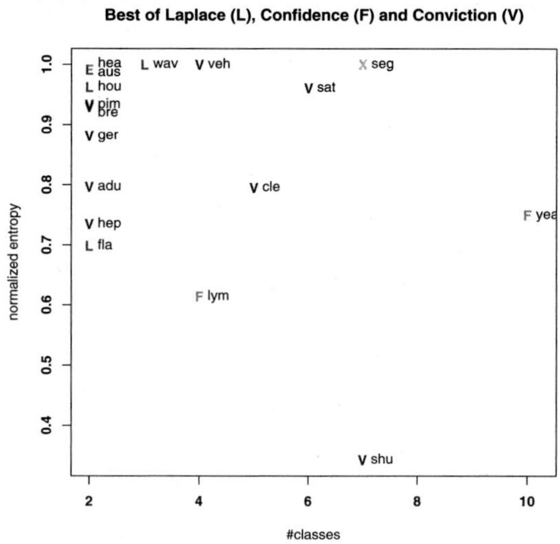

Fig. 2. Meta exploration of the results. The chart plots the datasets in a two dimensional space. Each dataset is represented by the symbol corresponding to the best performing measure. Ties are represented by "X".

we have selected *nclasses*, the number of classes and *n.entropy*, normalized class entropy, which measures the balance of class distribution. Given the relatively small number of datasets, we performed visual exploration using 2-dimensional xy-plots. In Fig. 2 we can see which of the three measures performed better with a best rule approach. The chart represents the datasets in the "number of classes" × "class distribution" space. Each dataset is represented by the measure that performed better within the considered pool. Conviction is represented by "V", confidence by "F" and Laplace by "L". When there is a tie between the two best ones the dataset point is signaled by an "X".

As we observe, there is no clear pattern explaining the success of each measure. Conviction dominates in general. Confidence is successful with the yeast dataset (10 classes, relatively unbalanced), and with two other. Laplace has a visible but not dominating presence in datasets with 2 or 3 classes. Regarding class balancing, there is no visible tendency. We observe, however, that the most unbalanced dataset is won by conviction.

Confidence and conviction differ in the rule ranking they produce when rules of different classes are involved. For rules of the same class, or of classes with the same support, conviction preserves the ordering given by confidence. This is because conviction (table 1) has the same numerator for rules with classes with the same support. The denominator increases when confidence of the rule decreases and vice-versa. The datasets considered are never exactly balanced (The values of normalized entropy and Gini shown in table 2 are 1.00 only because of rounding). In Fig. 3 we can compare the rule rankings provided by confidence and conviction for some datasets. These charts were built by generating a rule set

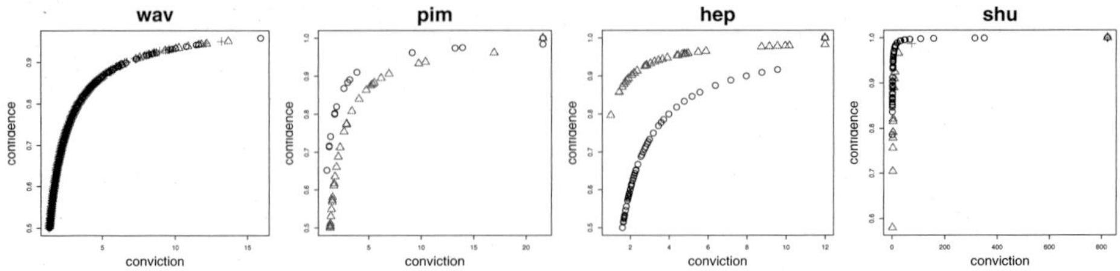

Fig. 3. Visualization of the comparison of the rule rankings produced by conviction and confidence. Each point represents one rule generated for the respective dataset. Different rule classes are represented with different characters.

for each dataset, and plotting each rule on a 2 dimensional space defined by confidence and conviction. For the almost balanced datasets (segment, vehicle and waveform), the ranking is practically preserved. This explains the almost equal error values of BR.conf and BR.conv (Table 3). For datasets with normalized entropy above 0.9 and two classes (australian, pima, heart and house-votes) we can observe two different curves, one for each class (each class is represented with a different marker). Despite the small difference between class supports, the different effects of conviction and confidence are quite visible. However, in these cases, the difference in error is still very small. The two significant wins of BR.conv over BR.conf are in datasets adult and hepatitis. These are datasets with mid-range entropy and 2 classes. In the case of hepatitis we can see that confidence tends to rank first the rules of one of the classes, whereas conviction tends to interleave rules of the two classes. The dataset with lowest entropy (highly unbalanced) is shuttle. It has 7 classes, but only rules for 3 of the classes were derived. For this dataset, conviction has advantage over confidence. In summary, what we observe is that conviction favours rules with less frequent classes, and ranks the rules differently from confidence. This is relatively innocuous for most of the datasets, although more frequently advantageous to conviction. When there is a significant difference it is in favour of BR.conv.

5 Conclusion

We have compared conviction with a few different measures and concluded that it shows a systematic advantage with best rule classifier. Compared to confidence, conviction favours low frequency classes and produces different rule orderings. This is mainly visible with unbalanced datasets. Besides conviction, confidence and Laplace, all the other yielded uninteresting results for best rule. In the case of Voting confidence and Laplace ranked relatively high, whereas conviction ranked amid the other measures. However Voting.conviction clustered close to the top performing best rule approaches. The negative results of conviction with the voting strategy may be due to the fact that rule ordering is diluted by the combined effect of voting rules. Another difficulty in using conviction with a voting strategy may be related with its overly stretched value range. Asymmetric measures obtained superior results with respect to symmetric ones. For future work it would be worthwhile to combine different measures to produce ensembles of classifiers.

References

1. Azevedo, P.J.: A data structure to represent association rules based classifiers. Technical report, Universidade do Minho, Departamento de Informática (2005)
2. Brin, S., Motwani, R., Silverstein, C.: Beyond market baskets: Generalizing association rules to correlations. In: Peckham, J. (ed.) SIGMOD Conference, pp. 265–276. ACM Press, New York (1997)
3. Brin, S., Motwani, R., Ullman, J.D., Tsur, S.: Dynamic itemset counting and implication rules for market basket data. In: Peckham, J. (ed.) Proceedings of the 1997 ACM SIGMOD International Conference on Management of Data, Tucson, Arizona, 13–15 June 1997, pp. 255–264. ACM Press, New York (1997)
4. Fayyad, U.M., Irani, K.B.: Multi-interval discretization of continuous-valued attributes for classification learning. In: IJCAI, pp. 1022–1029 (1993)
5. Jorge, A., Azevedo, P.J.: An experiment with association rules and classification: Post-bagging and conviction. In: Hoffmann, A., Motoda, H., Scheffer, T. (eds.) DS 2005. LNCS (LNAI), vol. 3735, pp. 137–149. Springer, Heidelberg (2005)
6. Li, W., Han, J., Pei, J.: Cmar: Accurate and efficient classification based on multiple class-association rules. In: Cercone, N., Lin, T.Y., Wu, X. (eds.) ICDM, pp. 369–376. IEEE Computer Society Press, Los Alamitos (2001)
7. Liu, B., Hsu, W., Ma, Y.: Integrating classification and association rule mining. In: KDD '98: Proceedings of the fourth ACM SIGKDD International Conference on Knowledge Discovery and Data Mining, pp. 80–86. ACM Press, New York (1998)
8. Merz, C.J., Murphy, P.: UCI repository of machine learning database (1996) `http://www.cs.uci.edu/~mlearn`
9. Piatetsky-Shapiro, G.: Discovery, analysis, and presentation of strong rules. In: Knowledge Discovery in Databases, pp. 229–248. AAAI/MIT Press (1991)
10. Tan, P.-N., Kumar, V., Srivastava, J.: Selecting the right objective measure for association analysis. Inf. Syst. 29(4), 293–313 (2004)
11. Webb, G.I.: Efficient search for association rules. In: KDD '00: Proceedings of the sixth ACM SIGKDD international conference on Knowledge discovery and data mining, pp. 99–107. ACM Press, New York (2000)

User Oriented Hierarchical Information Organization and Retrieval

Korinna Bade, Marcel Hermkes, and Andreas Nürnberger

Otto-von-Guericke-University, D-39106 Magdeburg, Germany
{kbade,nuernb}@iws.cs.uni-magdeburg.de, marcel.hermkes@googlemail.com

Abstract. In order to organize huge document collections, labeled hierarchical structures are used frequently. Users are most efficient in navigating such hierarchies, if they reflect their personal interests. Thus, we propose in this article an approach that is able to derive a personalized hierarchical structure from a document collection. The approach is based on a semi-supervised hierarchical clustering approach, which is combined with a biased cluster extraction process. Furthermore, we label the clusters for efficient navigation. Besides the algorithms itself, we describe an evaluation of our approach using benchmark datasets.

1 Introduction

With the increasing number of data publicly available also the personal collections of documents have become larger. A useful personal organization of these files is necessary to allow efficient re-finding of information. Hierarchical folder structures have proven to be useful in the past, e.g. in personal file folders or library catalogs. These structures have the advantage that they provide at the same time a (categorized) overview of the collection and direct access to all documents therein. However, users are most efficient in navigating such hierarchies if they reflect their personal interests instead some generally applicable criteria.

The goal of the work presented in the following is to provide the user a tool for building and maintaining such a personal hierarchy. We consider the following scenario. A starting point for the user can be a completely unstructured collection. At this point, the system can provide the user with an initial although unpersonalized structure purely based on standard document similarities. Once the user starts with explicitly filing documents in his own personal structure, either by himself or assisted by the system, this information is used to adapt the structuring of the still unstructured part of the collection towards user specific structuring preferences. Furthermore, these preferences can be applied to other, external collections, which the user is viewing. This allows the user faster access to interesting information therein.

In this paper, we present and evaluate an approach that is capable of extracting such a personal structure, while having different amounts of previously structured data available. The approach consists of three main steps: hierarchical clustering, extraction of clusters from the obtained dendrogram, and labeling. Each step is presented in an own section, also including important related work.

J.N. Kok et al. (Eds.): ECML 2007, LNAI 4701, pp. 518–526, 2007.

2 Personalized Hierarchical Clustering

Our considered task is a two-fold semi-supervised hierarchical learning problem with having unlabeled documents as well as unknown classes. The predominant classes C in the collection are split into the set of known classes C_k and a set of unknown classes C_u. As a consequence, the given labeled documents D_k are only mapped to classes in C_k. The task of the algorithm is to map the unlabeled documents D_u to classes in $C = C_k \bigcup C_u$. This means that the algorithm either derives a mapping to a known class or extracts new classes by grouping similar documents and assigning a class label to this group. Furthermore, we assume hierarchical relations R_H between the classes in form of a tree structure. When structuring a collection into classes, the algorithm should preserve the existing structure R_{Hk} and extract the relations of discovered classes in C_U to each other and to the classes in C_k. Considering our user scenario, C_k and R_{Hk} are defined by the hierarchical filing system of the user. D_k are the documents, which were filed in the past. D_u consists of the documents, which are still unstructured.

Considering related work, semi-supervised clustering is often performed by constraint based clustering. Here, the supervised information is used to generate Must-Link and Cannot-Link constraint sets [9], which influence the clustering. Several approaches exist that either change the underlying similarity space or directly modify the clustering process itself, e.g. [9,6,10,2]. All these approaches search for a flat partitioning of the data, while we want to find a hierarchical structure. In principle, these algorithms could be applied recursively to create a hierarchy. However, partitioning algorithms require the number of clusters as input parameter, which is not known in our scenario and hard to determine automatically. Additionally, it needs to be determined on each hierarchy level. Therefore, we decided to use Hierarchical Agglomerative Clustering (HAC) that directly produces a hierarchical representation of the data by a dendrogram. Furthermore, hierarchical approaches produce more stable and more accurate results, especially if the data of the used collection is naturally hierarchical.

In our approach, labeled data is used to change the underlying similarity space of a HAC algorithm to express personal structuring preferences. We assume that the extracted features are sufficient to describe these preferences. In our current work, we restricted ourselves to content features, i.e. occurring terms in text documents. For each feature f_i, a weight w_i is computed that expresses its influence in the clustering. These weights are integrated in the cosine similarity measure: $sim(fv_1, fv_2, w) = \sum_i w_i \cdot fv_{1,i} \cdot fv_{2,i}$. In [1], we present a method to learn and apply these weights in detail. Its evaluation showed that feature weighting improves the initial clustering towards a user specific structure.

3 Cluster Extraction

The goal of cluster extraction is to compress the dendrogram representation to the most "meaningful" nested clusters, i.e. to the clusters describing classes in $C = C_k \bigcup C_u$. In our setting, "meaningful" is partially defined by the given labeled data. However, it is usually rare, does not cover all classes and might be erroneous. Therefore, we first develop an unsupervised algorithm, which is then enhanced with labeled data.

An Unsupervised Approach. In published research, there is a common understanding that clusters could be extracted by two basic approaches. The dendrogram is either recursively cut with similarity thresholds or clusters are extracted on a node to node basis (e.g. by looking for significant changes in the merging similarity between a node (i.e. the similarity of its two child clusters) and its parent node). Both algorithm need a threshold as parameter. While the second approach can better handle different densities of sibling clusters, the first approach allows the use of a "global" criterion that helps in the extraction of less obvious clusters by using more obvious sibling clusters. Furthermore, it can also be used to always reduce the dendrogram, even without obvious sub-clusters. Nevertheless, cluster extraction is not widely discussed in the literature. To our knowledge, no work was published that dealt with this problem more thoroughly. Some work was done on extracting clusters from reachability plots produced by density based clustering (see [7,3]). The authors of [7] also show the similarities between reachability plots and dendrograms making it possible to apply their algorithms to dendrograms. However, these algorithms require specific assumptions that do not necessarily hold in our setting. The work in [7] works best with sharp cluster distinctions usually obtained, when data points are only assigned to leaf-clusters, which violates our problem definition. The work in [3] focused on extraction of narrowing sub-clusters. However, their approach requires a very smooth reachability plot, which is not produced in our application.

In this paper, we used a threshold approach. A recursive procedure is applied that starts at the root of the dendrogram and is repeated for each top node of an extracted cluster. A threshold t is computed in each iteration depending on the standard deviation σ of merging similarities in the considered sub-tree. The idea is to skip a top fraction of nodes with merging similarities that are "outstanding" from the others. As reference value the merging similarity of the current top node is used, which is also the minimum merging similarity of the whole sub-tree sim_{min}. t is computed by $sim_{min} + p \cdot \sigma$. While sim_{min} and σ are computed from the dendrogram, p is a parameter to determine the size of the fraction of minimal merging similarities to skip. Further parameters can restrict the cluster extraction, which are useful from the application point of view, i.e. the minimum number of items per cluster (preventing the extraction of too small clusters), the minimum difference in item size between a cluster and its parent cluster (preventing narrowing sub-clusters of being too similar to their parents), a minimum standard deviation (underneath it, merging similarities are supposed to be indistinguishable). Appropriate values for these are highly dependent on personal preference. Their values are not very crucial for the extraction process and adaptations to them can be made during interaction with the collection.

Using Supervision. The labeled data is used locally to make known class extraction more robust, i.e. avoiding the split of such a class. However, one has to be cautious in doing so, as this "robustness" should not overextend onto unknown classes. Due to this, we use the labeled data in a post-processing step after the unsupervised extraction rather than integrating it directly. First, the extracted clusters are labeled with known classes, if possible, as described in Sec. 4. We then merge sibling clusters labeled equally. As simple merge, we create intermediary clusters for groups of at least two equally labeled siblings. More interesting is what we call a deep merge based on the original dendrogram. Here, the sibling nodes are merged by extracting the common ancestor node from the dendrogram. The idea is that other items that also belong to the common ancestor node, but were not extracted or labeled as such, also belong to the same class. This combines more items of one class. However, it only works correctly, if the initial clustering represents the desired cluster structure appropriately. This can be detected, if integrated clusters are labeled differently, in which case the merge is not performed. However, this can especially not be detected for unknown classes, making it vulnerable for mislabeling.

Additionally and maybe more important is the use of the labeled data for estimating initial parameter values. Especially if the user starts interacting with the collection, he might not know how to set the parameters appropriately. Once he has a first result, it is easier to adapt parameters according to preference. For estimation, we label the clusters in the dendrogram. For each labeled cluster, we use the distance in merging similarity between this cluster and the cluster labeled with the parent class to estimate p. The mean value of all estimates is the final estimate. Minimum cluster size and standard deviation could be set to the maximum value that still allows the extraction of all labeled clusters.

4 Cluster Labeling

Labeling extracted clusters is crucial for the effectiveness of the hierarchy as it guides the user in browsing it. A good label must be capable of summarizing the content of a cluster. At the same time, it must be very short. In a hierarchy, the label must also be able to distinguish a cluster from its sibling clusters. Furthermore, it must show the differences between the cluster and its parent cluster. Although there are different approaches to automatically extract good cluster labels, a label given by the user himself is most descriptive. Therefore, we try to reuse known labels, if possible, before computing user independent labels.

Labeling Clusters as Known Classes. Known classes can be identified with the labeled data. As it is rare and possibly erroneous, we cannot trust every single instance but can also not assume high support or confidence of a labeling decision. In our work, we use two parameters to deal with this problem and constrain the labeling. We require to have a minimum precision for one class in all labeled items of the cluster and a minimum number of items labeled as such. The higher we set the thresholds of these parameters the less errors we make. However, this also means labeling less data. Good parameter values depend on the available amount of labeled data and on the clustering quality.

The clusters are labeled in a recursive procedure starting from the root of the cluster tree. If a label following the defined criteria is found, it is assigned to the cluster. All sub-clusters of it are then restricted to be labeled with sub-labels. This ensures the consistency of the hierarchy of known classes. Furthermore, labels are propagated upwards during cluster merges.

Labeling Clusters of Unknown Classes. The basis for most existing approaches are term statistics. Unfortunately, most related work only considers a flat cluster environment, which makes them not necessarily applicable to a hierarchical structure. [5] dealt with hierarchies by distinguishing three different concepts: terms describing the cluster itself, terms that are more general and thus better describe the parent cluster, and terms that are more specific, describing a child cluster. The distinction between these three concepts is made by predefined thresholds on term frequencies. However, these thresholds are hard to determine. Furthermore, it is questionable, whether one threshold works for different hierarchy levels as the distribution of term frequencies might vary. [4] uses a linear function that combines different statistical features that include hierarchical labeling criteria. In contrast to our work, they try to learn weights for different features by using linear regression on the basis of a set of labeled data. Our approach also uses statistical measures. As [5] and [4], we integrate parent and child clusters to avoid several occurrences of the same label along pathes in the hierarchy. A score of descriptiveness $Des_{t,C}$ is computed for each term t and each cluster C mainly based on the (absolute) document frequencies $df_{t,C}$, i.e. the number of documents that contain t (see (1), (2)). Here, each cluster is handled as containing all documents assigned to it and its child clusters.

$$Des_{t,C} = \log\left(\frac{rank_P(df_{t,P})}{rank_C(df_{t,C})}\right) \cdot (1 - SI_{t,P} + SI_{t,C})/2 \tag{1}$$

$$SI_{t,C} = \begin{cases} 1 & \text{if } Child(C) = \emptyset \\ \left(\sum_{c_i \in Child(C)} -\frac{df_{t,c_i}}{df_{t,C}} \log_2 \frac{df_{t,c_i}}{df_{t,C}}\right) / \log_2 |Child(C)| & \text{else} \end{cases} \tag{2}$$

The first factor measures the boost in document frequency ranking of t in comparison to the parent cluster P (as $rank_C(df_{t,C})$ is the rank of t in an descending order according to the document frequency of t in C, as in [4]). This assures that terms get higher scores that were not already good descriptors for the parent cluster and are therefore too general for the current cluster. The second factor considers information on how the term is distributed in sibling and child nodes, expressed by SI, which is bound to $[0;1]$. Terms occurring in several child clusters are favored by $SI_{t,C}$, while terms that are also descriptors of sibling clusters are penalized by $1 - SI_{t,P}$. For each cluster, n terms with highest descriptiveness are used as label. Unfortunately, our score cannot completely avoid that a term occurs several times along pathes through the cluster hierarchy (i.e. pathes from the root cluster to all leaf nodes). Therefore, we go through all such pathes in a post-processing step. If we encounter a term in the selected n descriptive labels occurring several times in a path, we remove it from the set of descriptive labels in all clusters except the one with highest $Des_{t,C}$. All clusters now having less than n terms as label get added new terms by taking the next best descriptive terms from the initially computed list.

5 Evaluation

In this evaluation, the general performance of the algorithms is evaluated using two different datasets of web pages that simulate the problem. The first is the banksearch dataset [8] (see Fig. 1). The second was created by us by downloading parts of the open directory (www.dmoz.org). The properties can be summarized as: hierarchy depth 4, 3 to 16 direct child nodes per inner node, about 50 documents directly in each node, 2119 documents in total. All documents were represented with standard tfidf document vectors.

We evaluated different settings to simulate different user data. For both datasets, we evaluated a setting with 10 labeled documents per class, i.e. a classification scenario (settings (1), (5)). For the banksearch data, we also evaluated settings with unknown classes: (2) *Motor Sport*, (3) *Science*, (4) *Science* and *Sport*. As measure, we used the f-score gained in accordance to the given dataset, which is supposed to be the true user defined class structure that shall be recovered. For its computation in an unlabeled cluster tree, we followed a common approach that selects for each class in the dataset the cluster gaining the highest f-score on it. When evaluating cluster labeling, the f-score of known classes is determined based on all documents labeled as such. The unknown classes are again extracted as best f-score clusters, however only in hierarchy consistent unlabeled parts of the cluster tree.

As we already evaluated the baseline performance of the clustering algorithm in [1], we focus here on evaluating cluster extraction and labeling. The competitiveness of our approach for classification can briefly be shown by comparison with SVM. For the banksearch data, the SVM reaches a mean F-score of 0.6892, while our approach reaches 0.7570 on the dendrogram. For the open directory data, the SVM reaches 0.6198, while our approach reaches 0.6100. Hence, our algorithm has a good baseline performance.

In Tables 1 and 2, we evaluate our cluster extraction methods (CE - unsupervised extraction, SM - simple merge, DM - deep merge) in comparison to the baseline given by the dendrogram (DG). As we consider here only a single cluster per class, this evaluation shows how good the algorithms are in preserving the best cluster. We only varied p for cluster extraction as the other parameters only do pruning of the cluster tree. We set the minimum cluster size and the minimum

• **Finance** (0)	• **Programming** (0)	• **Science** (0)	• **Sport** (100)
∘ Commercial Banks (100)	∘ C/C++ (100)	∘ Astronomy (100)	∘ Soccer (100)
∘ Building Societies (100)	∘ Java (100)	∘ Biology (100)	∘ Motor Sport (100)
∘ Insurance Agencies (100)	∘ Visual Basic (100)		

Fig. 1. Class structure of the banksearch dataset

Table 1. F-Score for different cluster extraction methods using the banksearch data

Setting	DG	$p = 0.1$ CE	SM	DM	$p = 0.05$ CE	SM	DM	$p = 0.03$ CE	SM	DM	$p = 0.01$ CE	SM	DM
(1)	0.757	0.693	0.733	0.723	0.735	0.737	0.735	0.718	0.760	0.745	0.754	0.754	0.754
(2)	0.771	0.699	0.727	0.752	0.713	0.724	0.724	0.762	0.762	0.762	0.767	0.767	0.767
(3)	0.734	0.582	0.654	0.667	0.676	0.705	0.709	0.717	0.729	0.731	0.732	0.732	0.732
(4)	0.697	0.542	0.585	0.583	0.575	0.622	0.617	0.641	0.653	0.643	0.694	0.694	0.694

Table 2. F-Score open directory data for CE/SM/DM

Setting	(5)
DG	0.610
$p = 0.2$	0.551/0.581/0.568
$p = 0.1$	0.577/0.587/0.585
$p = 0.01$	0.586/0.590/0.587

Table 3. Estimation p

Setting	p
(1)	0.196
(2)	0.072
(3)	0.047
(4)	0.030
(5)	0.212

Table 4. F-Score after labeling

Setting	SM	DM	SM-l	DM-l
(1)	0.760	0.745	0.696	0.696
(2)	0.762	0.762	0.728	0.728
(3)	0.729	0.731	0.692	0.694
(4)	0.653	0.643	0.624	0.519
(5)	0.587	0.585	0.525	0.521

Table 5. Example labeling for the banksearch data

Class	Five selected terms
Banking	mortgage, savings, payments, debit, income
Commercial Banks	bank, depositor, internet, abbey, advert
Building Societies	society, interest, building, telegraphic, superseeded
Insurance Agencies	insurance, cover, claims, wording, policy

difference in cluster size between parent and child cluster to 10. The minimum standard deviation was set to 0. Increasing p leads in general to broader cluster trees and a fewer number of extracted clusters. A too high value for p therefore will split a "class cluster" into several clusters, causing a decrease in the f-score. There is always a value for p that can (almost) recover the best f-score clusters from the dendrogram, while highly condensing the dendrogram representation, shrinking the number of clusters from over 2000 to about 100 or less for the banksearch data and from over 4000 to 200 or less. Furthermore, it seems that good values for p are quite stable for different data. Its order of magnitude, which is quite low, is in our opinion given by the fact that we cluster high dimensional text data. Both merging methods are useful for getting back lost performance due to splits in the cluster tree with similar results. Although hypothesized differently by us, the deep merge seems not to be better. This suggest that a simple merge, which also requires less computation time, is a sufficient and therefore better choice. Table 3 shows the estimations for p as computed based on the labeled data. Although these values are not perfect, they provide a good initial starting point for the exploration of the cluster tree.

Table 4 evaluates the identification of given classes using a minimum precision of 0.6 and a minimum number of labeled items of 2. We used a fixed p of 0.03 for the banksearch settings and 0.1 for the open directory setting. Both merges are considered. Labeling f-score is always less than the best cluster f-score as the given labeled data is not sufficient to always identify the best clusters. In setting (4), the deep merge performs a lot worse than the simple merge as it overextends the label of the known class *Programming* onto the unknown *Science* class. This suggests that the deep merge might be problematic in the case of unknown classes. Nevertheless, the identification of existing classes works well in general.

Table 5 gives an inside on how the labeling of unknown classes works with a small example. The labeling algorithm was directly applied to the dataset hierarchies to compute class labels. In general, the manually chosen labels are in about 70% of the classes among the five selected terms. The computed terms seem quite descriptive for the classes. Nevertheless, a more thorough evaluation of the labeling method is still necessary.

6 Conclusion

In this paper, we presented an integrated approach that provides a personalized hierarchical cluster structure for a certain collection. The algorithm comprises of several steps, i.e. (1) do personalized HAC, (2) extract clusters unsupervised, (3) label clusters according to known classes, (4) merge clusters, and (5) label still unlabeled clusters. We evaluated each step and showed the validity of our approach. The algorithms presented as solutions to certain steps can also be applied in different settings and are not necessarily restricted to our application.

References

1. Bade, K., Nürnberger, A.: Personalized hierarchical clustering. In: Proceedings of the 2006 IEEE/WIC/ACM Int. Conference on Web Intelligence, pp. 181–187 (2006)
2. Basu, S., Banerjee, A., Mooney, R.: Active semi-supervision for pairwise constrained clustering. In: Proc. of SIAM Int. Conf. on Data Mining, pp. 333–344 (2004)
3. Brecheisen, S., Kriegel, H.P., Kröger, P., Pfeifle, M.: Visually mining through cluster hierarchies. In: Proc. of SIAM Int. Conf. on Data Mining, pp. 400–412 (2004)
4. Callan, J., Treeratpituk, P.: Automatically labeling hierarchical clusters. In: Proceedings of the 2006 International Conference on Digital Government Research. ACM International Conference Proceeding Series, vol. 151, pp. 167–176. ACM Press, New York (2006)
5. Glover, E., Pennock, D., Lawrence, S., Krovetz, R.: Inferring hierarchical descriptions. In: Proceedings of 11th International Conference on Information and Knowledge Management, pp. 507–514 (2002)
6. Kim, H., Lee, S.: An effective document clustering method using user-adaptable distance metrics. In: Proceedings of the 2002 ACM symposium on Applied computing, pp. 16–20. ACM Press, New York (2002)

7. Sander, J., Qin, X., Lu, Z., Niu, N., Kovarsky, A.: Automatic extraction of clusters from hierarchical clustering representations. In: Advances in Knowledge Discovery and Data Mining: 7 th Pacific-Asia Conference (Proc.), pp. 75–87 (2003)
8. Sinka, M., Corne, D.: A large benchmark dataset for web document clustering. In: Soft Computing Systems: Design, Management and Applications, Frontiers in Artificial Intelligence and Applications, vol. 87, pp. 881–890 (2002)
9. Wagstaff, K., Cardie, C., Rogers, S., Schroedl, S.: Constrained k-means clustering with background knowledge. In: Proceedings of 18 th International Conference on Machine Learning, pp. 577–584 (2001)
10. Xing, E., Ng, A., Jordan, M., Russell, S.: Distance metric learning, with application to clustering with side-information. Advances in Neural Information Processing Systems 15, 505–512 (2003)

Learning a Classifier with Very Few Examples: Analogy Based and Knowledge Based Generation of New Examples for Character Recognition

S. Bayoudh[1], H. Mouchère[2], L. Miclet[1], and E. Anquetil[2]

[1] IRISA-ENSSAT
{bayoudh,miclet}@enssat.fr
[2] IRISA-INSA
{mouchere,anquetil}@irisa.fr

Abstract. This paper is basically concerned with a practical problem: the on-the-fly quick learning of handwritten character recognition systems. More generally, it explores the problem of *generating new learning examples*, especially from very scarce (2 to 5 per class) original learning data. It presents two different methods. The first one is based on applying distortions on original characters using *knowledge* on handwriting properties like speed, curvature etc. The second one consists in generation based on the notion of *analogical dissimilarity* which quantifies the analogical relation "A is to B almost as C is to D". We give an algorithm to compute the k-least dissimilar objects D, hence generating k new objects from three examples A, B and C. Finally, we experimentally prove the efficiency of both methods, especially when used in conjunction.

Keywords: instance generation, sequence generation by analogy, knowledge-based generation, handwritten character recognition.

1 Introduction

In a number of Pattern Recognition systems, the acquisition of labeled data is user unfriendly. Still, the classification system has to be retrained with as many examples as possible. A way to overcome this difficulty is to generate artificial new examples. It can be done either in the feature space or on the raw representation of the data.

The first technique has already been studied and experimented. [1] combines feature selection and generation of "corrupted" examples to avoid overfitting when boosting on small samples. [2] analyzes the regularization performed by adding noise on the learning data. In the framework of neural networks, the effect of generating more examples is known as a good way to avoid overfitting.

For on-line character recognition systems, several image distortions have been used [3]: slanting, shrinking, ink erosion and ink dilatation; [4] extends the learning data base by elastic distortions before training a neural network. Text lines can also be distorted as in [5] before training a Hidden Markov Model.

J.N. Kok et al. (Eds.): ECML 2007, LNAI 4701, pp. 527–534, 2007.

Bishop [6] gives no theoretical coverage about example generation, but draws a pragmatic conclusion: " (...) the addition of random noise to the inputs (...) has been shown to improve generalization in appropriate circumstances".

In this paper, we deal with the quick tuning of a handwritten character recognition to a new user, when only a very small set of examples is available. We describe in section 2 our system and the representation used to generate new examples. This operation is realized along two different axes, before transforming the data into the feature space. Firstly, we consider the inputs as sequences of a combination of Freeman chain-codes and of special symbols (*anchorage points*) describing pen up and downs, extrema, etc. Then, in section 3, we use an original method of generating: from any three examples, we produce as many examples as required, provided that they are in weak *analogical dissimilarity* from the three basic patterns. Secondly, as described in section 4, we extract high-level information from the characters : slant, writing speed, etc. and we randomly vary these parameters to generate new examples. To finish, we combine the two methods and we describe in section 5 our experimental protocol. We show in particular in this section that generating hundreds of fake examples from a very small number of real samples per class is a better learning strategy than using 10 real samples per class and comparable to use 30 real samples per class.

2 On-Line Handwriting Signal Description

The on-line characters used in this paper have been gathered on a PDA using a specialized pen-based human-computer interface. The characters are isolated. They are acquired without any context, in a random order, and on-line.

When acquired on-line, a character is considered as a function $p(t)$ describing the pen positions. Each point $p(t)$ is defined by its x and y geometric position.

Contrary to the knowledge-based generation, the generation based on Analogical Proportion (AP) requires a slightly more elaborated representation of the signal. Hence, before the AP generation, the signal is re-sampled in space and basically transformed into a Freeman chain-code. In this paper we use the extended 16-Freeman code $\Sigma = \{0, 1, .., 16\}$, where the direction 0 corresponds to an isolated point in the original signal. The AP generation produces characters in Freeman chain-code. Then they are decoded into an on-line signal by following the direction sequence using the same inter-point distance.

For the needs of the AP generation we have extended the Freeman code with a set of 8 capital letters $\{C, D, E, H, K, L, M, N\}$ each one corresponding to a special point in a handwritten character. They are called *anchorage points* and they lead to a better AP generation. These anchorage points come from an analysis of the stable handwriting properties, as defined in [7]: pen-up/down, y-extrema, angular points and in-loop y-extrema.

Figure 1 shows a global overview of the complete generation process of new examples using knowledge-based distortions and AD generation on Freeman encoding. After generation, the characters are transformed in a vector of 21 features. These features are the input of our handwriting recognition system. They

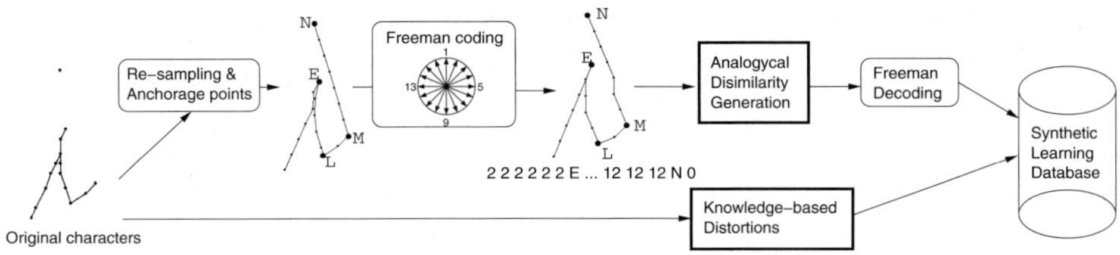

Fig. 1. Overview of the generation process of synthetic learning data base using knowledge-based distortions and AD generation on Freeman encoding.

are based on stable properties of handwriting like downstrokes [7]. The classification and test processes of the section 5 are done in this 21-dimension feature space.

3 Analogy Based Generation

In this section, we give general notions on analogy and explain how it can be used to generate new examples. Generally speaking, an *analogy*, or to be more specific, an *analogical proportion*, involves four objects (or terms) such that "*the second term is to the first as the fourth is to the third*" according to the seminal definition by Aristotle. Analogy has been widely used as a model of reasoning, in philosophy [8], Artificial Intelligence [9], computational linguistics [10].

3.1 Analogical Proportion

An *analogical proportion* (AP) between four objects A, B, C and D, in the same universe, is expressed by : "A `is to` B `as` C `is to` D". If an element x of the analogical equation is unknown, finding it is called resolving an *analogical equation*. For example, in "*fins is to fish as wings is to* x", the solution x would be *bird* in the semantic domain.

Definition 1. *An AP on a set* $\mathbf{X}$ *is a relation between four elements of* $\mathbf{X}$ *(i.e. a subset of* $\mathbf{X}^4$*). An element of this relation writes "*$a : b :: c : d$*" and reads "*a *is to* b *as* c *is to* d*", or "*a, b, c *and* d *are in AP". According to [10], an AP must fulfill the three properties:*

Symmetry of the "as" relation:	$(a : b :: c : d) \Leftrightarrow (c : d :: a : b)$
Exchange of the means:	$(a : b :: c : d) \Leftrightarrow (a : c :: b : d)$
Determinism:	$(a : a :: b : x) \Rightarrow (x = b)$

How can we use this definition in pattern generation ? Suppose that the handwritten character "a" is encoded as a sequence and that we have 3 examples a_1, a_2 and a_3 of this character. We can generate more "a" characters by solving analogical equations on sequences like: "$a_1 : a_2 :: a_3 : x$" or "$a_3 : a_2 :: a_1 : x$". If we have n examples, the number of new "a" that we can generate is $n^2 \times (n-1)/2$. We can even go further, as we show in the following paragraph, by relaxing the definition of the solution to an analogical equation.

3.2 Analogical Dissimilarity Between Objects

We give in this section a precise definition of the approximate *analogical proportion* "a `is to` b `almost as` c `is to` d". For this purpose, we have introduced a quantity that reflects how far are four objects from being in AP. This measure is called *Analogical Dissimilarity* (AD) [11]. To coherently extend the AP, it has to verify the following properties:

1. $\forall u, v, w, x, AD(u, v, w, x) = 0 \Leftrightarrow u : v :: w : x$
2. $\forall u, v, w, x, AD(u, v, w, x) = AD(w, x, u, v) = AD(v, u, x, w)$
3. $\forall u, v, w, x, z, t, AD(u, v, z, t) \leq AD(u, v, w, x) + AD(w, x, z, t)$
4. In general, $\forall u, v, w, x, AD(u, v, w, x) \neq AD(v, u, w, x)$.

3.3 Analogical Dissimilarity Between Sequences

Let $\Sigma = \{1, 2, \ldots, 16, 0, C, \ldots, N\}$ be the alphabet of the Freeman symbols code and of the anchorage points. A handwritten character is represented by a sequence of letters of Σ. We introduce a new letter $\backsim$ to Σ, to be added anywhere in a sequence without changing its semantics ("$35C4$" means the same as "$3 \backsim 5C \backsim\backsim 4$"). With this augmented alphabet, we can define an alignment between four sequences and the notion of analogical dissimilarity.

Alignment. An alignment of four sequences of different lengths is realized by inserting letters $\backsim$ so that all the four sequences have the same length. Once this is done, we consider in each column of the alignment the analogical dissimilarity in the augmented alphabet. For example $AD(1, 5, 2, 6) = 0$ because they are in exact AP, $AD(3, A, 4, A) = 1$ (because shifting 4 to 3, which are at distance 1, would give an exact AP).

The principle of our generation process is to align three sequences of characters "`h`" for example, and resolving column after column to generate the fourth sequence (see Figure 2). We define the cost of an alignment as the sum of the AD on columns, and an *optimal alignment* as one of minimal cost. The Analogical Dissimilarity between four Sequences (ADS) is the cost of an optimal alignment. It has all the properties given above, except the third point (the triangular inequality).

To generate the k best sequences regarding to ADS, we use the general search algorithm $A^\star$ [12] used to find the k shortest paths in a graph [13], with a heuristic value set to 0.

$$
\begin{aligned}
h_1 &= 9 \backsim 9 \backsim 9\,9\,9\,9\,9 \backsim H\;1\;2 \backsim 4\;K\;6\;9\;9\;9 \\
h_2 &= 1\;K \backsim 8\;9\,9\,9\,9\,9\;10\;H \backsim 2\;2\;4\;K \backsim 8\;8\;9 \\
h_3 &= \backsim \backsim 9\;8\;9\,9\,9\,9\,9\;10\;H\;2\;2\;3\;3\;K\;8\;9\;9 \backsim \\
x &= 1\;K \backsim 8\;9\,9\,9\,9\,9\;10\;H\;2\;2\;3\;3\;K\;8\;8\;8 \backsim
\end{aligned}
$$

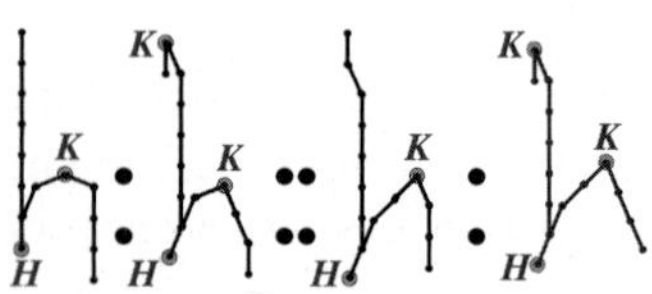

Fig. 2. Example of a resolution on Freeman direction sequences by AP and the corresponding characters representation

4 Knowledge Based Generation

In this section we present two classical image distortions and two new on-line distortions based on specificities of the on-line handwriting. Each distortion depends on one or more random parameters. To generate a synthetic character from an original one using a distortion, we first randomly choose a value for each corresponding parameter and then we apply it.

4.1 Generation by Image Distortions: Scaling and Slanting

To generate new learning examples, one has to choose distortions according to the data acquisition process. Indeed images captured with a camera or in a video can be perturbed by perspective, rotation, noise... while scanned handwriting is disturbed by ink thick variation only. In this paper we limit us to scaling and slanting deformations because of the nature of our data. Two random parameters correspond to the scale transformations, α_x and α_y which are the ratio of the corresponding scales. The slant allows to generate inclined handwriting. It depends of one random parameter α_s which represents the tangent of the slant.

4.2 Generation by On-Line Distortions

There are few works about using handwriting generation in order to increase on-line learning data. In [14] authors use works about handwriting generation [15] to increase the size of a learning database to train an off-line sentence writer-independent recognizer. The authors use a unique on-line handwriting model. This approach is unusable in our context because we need writer-dependent models. That is why we propose two simple distortions of on-line handwriting: *Speed Variation* and *Curvature Modification.*

Speed Variation. The aim of *Speed Variation* distortion is to modify the size of vertical and horizontal parts of the stroke, as shown in Figure 3, depending of a random parameter α_v. Indeed this straight parts of the writing can vary without changing the handwriting style. For this we modify the speed $\boldsymbol{V}(t) = (x(t+1) - x(t), y(t+1) - y(t))$ depending of its direction. If this vector is near one of the axes then it is increased or decreased by the ratio α_v. The new synthetic handwriting is defined by $p'(t)$:

$$p'(t) = p'(t-1) + \beta * \boldsymbol{V}(t-1), \text{ with } \beta = \begin{cases} 1 & \text{if } \arg(\boldsymbol{V}(t-1)) \left[\frac{\pi}{2}\right] \in \left[\frac{\pi}{8}, \frac{3\pi}{8}\right], \\ \alpha_v & \text{else.} \end{cases}$$

Curvature Modification. The *Curvature Modification* distortion modify the curvature of the writing as shown in Figure 3. It allows to close or open the loops of handwriting. The curvature modification uses a random parameter α_c. The curvature at the point $p(t-1)$ is defined by the angle $\hat{\theta}(t-1) = (p(t-2), \widehat{p(t-1)}, p(t))$ in $]-\pi, \pi]$. In order to keep the structure of the character, we do not modify the straight lines and cusps. The following equation gives the position of the point $p'(t)$ depending of the two previous points and of the original curvature $\hat{\theta}(t-1)$ modified by α_c:

$$(p'(t-2), \widehat{p'(t-1)}, p'(t)) = \hat{\theta}(t-1) - \alpha_c * 4 * \frac{|\hat{\theta}(t-1)|}{\pi} * (1 - \frac{|\hat{\theta}(t-1)|}{\pi}).$$

5 Experimentations

5.1 Experiment Protocol

Twelve different writers have written 40 times the 26 lowercase letters (1040 characters) on a PDA. Each writer database is randomly split in four parts with 10 characters per class. We use them in a 4-fold stratified cross validation: one fourth for $D10$ database (260 data) and three fourth for $D30$ database (780 data). Thus the experiment is done four times by switching these parts. The experimentations are composed of two phases in which three writer-dependent recognition systems are learned: a Radial Basis Function Network (RBFN) and a one-against-all Support Vector Machine (SVM).

Firstly, we compute two Reference recognition Rates without data generation : $RR10$ and $RR30$. For $RR10$, writer-dependent classifiers are learned for each writer on his $D10$ and evaluated on his $D30$ database for the four splits. For $RR30$, the classifiers are learned on $D30$ and tested on $D10$. Hence, $RR10$ is the recognition rate achievable with 10 original characters without character generation and $RR30$ gives an idea of achievable recognition rates with more original data. Practically speaking, in the context of on the fly learning phase we should not ask the user to input more than 10 characters per class.

Secondly the handwriting generation strategies are tested. For a given writer, one to ten characters per class are randomly chosen in his $D10$. Then 300 synthetic characters per class are generated to make a synthetic learning database. A classifier is learned with this base and tested on the database $D30$ of the writer. This experiment is done 3 times per cross validation split and per writer (12 times per user). Finally the means of the writer dependent mean recognition rate and the mean standard deviation are computed.

We study three different strategies for the generation of synthetic learning databases. The strategy *"Image Distortions"* chooses randomly for each generation one among the three image distortions. In the same way the strategy *"On-line and Image Distortions"* chooses randomly one distortion among the image distortions and on-line distortions. The *"Analogy and Distortions"* strategy generates two-thirds of the base with the previous strategy and the remaining third with AP generation.

5.2 Results

Figure 4 compares the recognition rates achieved by the three generation strategies for the three classifiers. Firstly we can note that the global behavior is the same for the two classifiers. Thus the following conclusions do not depend on the

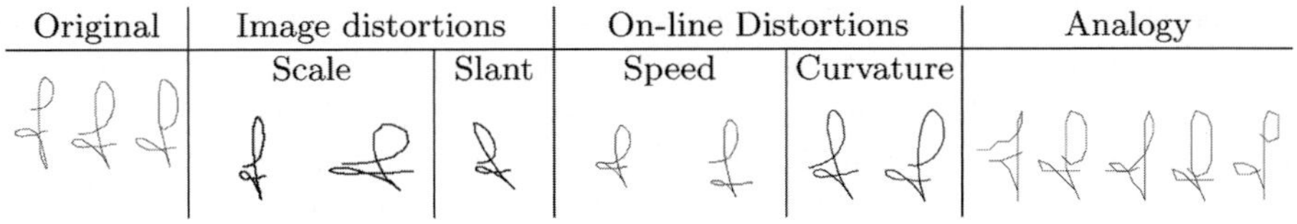

Fig. 3. Examples of synthetic characters generated by the three approaches

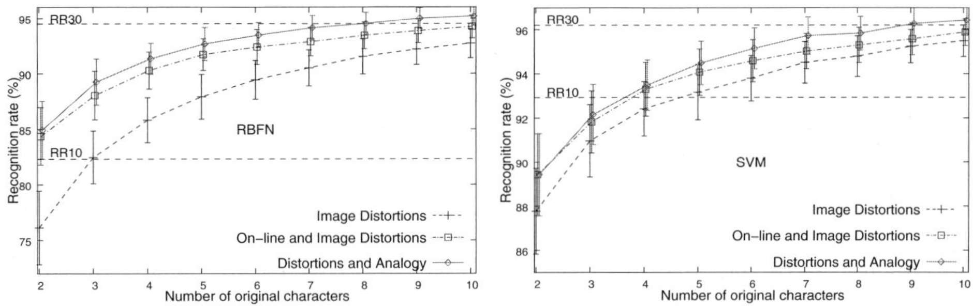

Fig. 4. Writer-dependent recognition rates and their standard deviation depending on the number of used original characters compared to reference rates using 10 or 30 characters per class for RBFN and SVM classifiers

classifier type. Secondly the three generation strategies are complementary because using *"On-line and Image Distortions"* is better than *"Image Distortions"* alone and *"Analogy and Distortions"* is better than using distortions. We proved statistically the signigicance of the improvement between the three generation strategies using the *t*-test and the *sign* test [16]. Thus, for each classifier and each number of original characters the difference between the strategies is due to chance has a probability less than 10^{-3} using the *t*-test and less than 10^{-30} using the *sign*-test.

Therefore, using only four original character with the complete generation strategy is better than the $RR10$. The $RR30$ is achieved by using 9 or 10 original characters. Thus we can conclude that using our generation strategies allows to learn classifier with very few original data as efficiently as using original data from a long input phase: we need about three times fewer original data to achieve the same recognition rate.

6 Conclusion

In this paper, we have shown how to generate synthetic examples for a quick tuning of a handwritten character classifier to a new writer. We have presented two complementary ways of generation, the first being based on the prior knowledge and the second on analogy on sequences. Both methods in conjunction have led to efficient results on writer-dependent recognition.

Although empirical, these experiments lead to the conclusion that it may be efficient to generate new samples, provided that the variation on few learning samples is not made in the feature decision space, but rather in a representation space close to the raw data. Knowledge-based and analogy-based generation, although of very different nature, have proved in this case to be both efficient.

References

1. Wolf, L., Martin, I.: Robust boosting for learning from few examples. In: IEEE Conf. on Computer Vision and Pattern Recognition (CVPR), IEEE Computer Society Press, Los Alamitos (2005)
2. Bishop, C.: Training with noise is equivalent to Tikhonov regularization. Neural Computation 7(1), 108–116 (1995)
3. Cano, J., Pérez-Cortes, J.C., Arlandis, J., Llobet, R.: Training set expansion in handwritten character recognition. In: Proc. of the 9th Int. Workshop on Structural and Syntactic Pattern Recognition, pp. 548–556 (2002)
4. Simard, P., Steinkraus, D., Platt, J.C.: Best practice for convolutional neural network applied to visual analysis. In: Proc. of the 7th Int. Conf. on Document Analysis and Recognition (2003)
5. Varga, T., Bunke, H.: Generation of synthetic data for an HMM-based handwriting recognition system. In: Proc. of 7th Int. Conf. on Document Analysis and Recognition, pp. 618–622 (2003)
6. Bishop, C.: Pattern Recognition and Machine Learning. Springer, Heidelberg (2007)
7. Anquetil, E., Lorette, G.: Perceptual model of handwriting drawing application to the handwriting segmentation problem. In: Proc. of the 4th Int. Conf. on Document Analysis and Recognition, pp. 112–117 (1997)
8. Hesse, M.: Aristotle's logic of analogy. The Philosophical Quarterly 15(61), 328–340 (1965)
9. Gentner, D., Holyoak, K.J., Kokinov, B.: The analogical mind: Perspectives from cognitive science. MIT Press, Cambridge (2001)
10. Lepage, Y.: Solving analogies on words: an algorithm. In: Proc. of COLING-ACL'98, vol. 1, pp. 728–735 (1998)
11. Bayoudh, S., Miclet, L., Delhay, A.: Learning by analogy: a classification rule for binary and nominal data. In: Proc. of the Int. Joint Conf. on Artificial Intelligence, vol. 20, pp. 678–683 (2007)
12. Nilsson, N.: Principles of Artificial Intelligence. Tioga Publishing Company (1980)
13. Eppstein, D.: Finding the k shortest paths. SIAM J. Computing 28(2), 652–673 (1998)
14. Varga, T., Kilchhofer, D., Bunke, H.: Template-based synthetic handwriting generation for the training of recognition systems. In: Proc. of 12th Conf. of the International Graphonomics Society, pp. 206–211 (2005)
15. Plamondon, R., Guerfali, W.: The generation of handwriting with delta-lognormal synergies. Biological Cybernetics 78, 119–132 (1998)
16. Gillick, L., Cox, S.J.: Some statistical issues in the comparison of speech recognition algorithms. In: IEEE (ed.) Proceedings of IEEE International Conference on Acoustics, Speech, and Signal Processing, Glasgow, Scotland, pp. 532–535. IEEE Computer Society Press, Los Alamitos (1989)

Weighted Kernel Regression for Predicting Changing Dependencies

Steven Busuttil and Yuri Kalnishkan

Computer Learning Research Centre and Department of Computer Science,
Royal Holloway, University of London,
Egham, Surrey, TW20 0EX, United Kingdom
{steven,yura}@cs.rhul.ac.uk

Abstract. Consider the online regression problem where the dependence of the outcome y_t on the signal $\mathbf{x}_t$ changes with time. Standard regression techniques, like Ridge Regression, do not perform well in tasks of this type. We propose two methods to handle this problem: WeCKAAR, a simple modification of an existing regression technique, and KAARCh, an application of the Aggregating Algorithm. Empirical results on artificial data show that in this setting, KAARCh is superior to WeCKAAR and standard regression techniques. On options implied volatility data, the performance of both KAARCh and WeCKAAR is comparable to that of the proprietary technique currently being used at the Russian Trading System Stock Exchange (RTSSE).

1 Introduction

Consider the online regression problem where the dependence of the outcome y_t on the signal $\mathbf{x}_t$ changes with time. An example of this is the prediction of financial options implied volatility described in Sect. 4.2. Standard regression techniques, like Ridge Regression, treat all training examples equally. In time series theory there is a method called GARCH (see, for example, [1, Chap. 19]), which assigns exponentially decreasing weights to old examples. This method is used to estimate historical volatility in finance. We would like to extend this idea to the more general problem of online regression.

In Sect. 3 we present two methods as a solution to this problem: WeCKAAR and KAARCh. WeCKAAR is a simple method that adds decaying weights to an existing regression technique. KAARCh is a new method based on the Aggregating Algorithm (AA). The AA (see [2]) allows us to merge experts from large pools to obtain optimal strategies. To get KAARCh, the AA is used to merge all predictors that can change with time.

We report the empirical performance of these methods in Sect. 4; first on an artificial dataset, and then on options implied volatility data. These results show that when dealing with changing dependencies, KAARCh is an improvement on standard and weighted regression techniques. In addition, the performance of WeCKAAR and KAARCh on options implied volatility data provided by the Russian Trading System Stock Exchange (RTSSE) is comparable to that of the specially designed proprietary technique currently being used.

J.N. Kok et al. (Eds.): ECML 2007, LNAI 4701, pp. 535–542, 2007.

2 Background

In the online regression framework at every moment in time $t = 1, 2, \ldots,$ the value of a signal $\mathbf{x}_t \in X$ arrives[1]. Statistician (or Learner) S observes $\mathbf{x}_t$ and then outputs a prediction $\gamma_t \in \mathbb{R}$, before the outcome $y_t \in \mathbb{R}$ arrives. The set X is a signal space which is assumed to be known to Statistician in advance. We will be referring to a signal-outcome pair as an example. The performance of S is measured by the sum of squared discrepancies between the predictions and the outcomes, known as square loss. Therefore, on trial t Statistician S suffers loss $(y_t - \gamma_t)^2$. The losses incurred after T trials sum up to the cumulative square loss at time T,

$$\mathrm{L}_T(S) = \sum_{t=1}^{T} (y_t - \gamma_t)^2 \ .$$

Clearly, a smaller value of $\mathrm{L}_T(S)$ means a better predictive performance.

2.1 Linear and Kernel Regression

If $X \subseteq \mathbb{R}^n$ we can consider simple linear regressors of the form $\mathbf{w} \in \mathbb{R}^n$. Given a signal $\mathbf{x} \in X$, such a regressor makes a prediction $\mathbf{w}'\mathbf{x}$. Linear methods are easy to manipulate mathematically but their use in the real world is limited since they can only model simple dependencies. The kernel trick (first used in this context in [3]) is now a widely used technique which can make a linear algorithm operate in feature space without the inherent complexities. For a function $k : X \times X \to \mathbb{R}$ to be a kernel it has to be symmetric, and for all ℓ and all $\mathbf{x}_1, \ldots, \mathbf{x}_\ell \in X$, the kernel matrix $\mathbf{K} = (k(\mathbf{x}_i, \mathbf{x}_j))_{i,j}$, $i, j = 1, \ldots, \ell$ must be positive semi-definite (have nonnegative eigenvalues). For every kernel there exists a unique reproducing kernel Hilbert space (RKHS) F such that k is the reproducing kernel of F. In fact, there is a mapping $\phi : X \to F$ such that kernels can be defined as $k(\mathbf{x}, \mathbf{z}) = \langle \phi(\mathbf{x}), \phi(\mathbf{z}) \rangle$. We will be referring to any function in the RKHS F as D. Intuitively $D(\mathbf{x})$ is a decision rule in F that produces a prediction for the object $\mathbf{x}$. We will be measuring the complexity of D by its norm $\|D\|$ in F. For more information on kernels and RKHS see, for example, [4] and [5].

2.2 Ridge Regression (RR)

Ridge Regression (RR), introduced to statistics in [6], is a popular regression technique that at time T aims to find a $\mathbf{w}_{\mathrm{R}}$ that minimises

$$\mathcal{L}_T(\mathrm{RR}) = a\|\mathbf{w}_{\mathrm{R}}\|^2 + \sum_{t=1}^{T-1} (y_t - \langle \mathbf{w}_{\mathrm{R}}, \mathbf{x}_t \rangle)^2 \ ,$$

[1] As usual, all vectors are identified with one-column matrices and $\mathbf{A}'$ stands for the transpose of matrix $\mathbf{A}$. We will not be specifying the size of simple matrices like the identity matrix $\mathbf{I}$ when this is clear from the context.

where a is a fixed positive real number. RR's solution is $\mathbf{w}_{\text{R}} = (a\mathbf{I}+\mathbf{X}'\mathbf{X})^{-1}\mathbf{X}'\mathbf{y}$, where $\mathbf{I}$ is the identity matrix, $\mathbf{X} = (\mathbf{x}_1, \ldots, \mathbf{x}_{T-1})'$ and $\mathbf{y} = (y_1, \ldots, y_{T-1})'$. The kernel version of RR, called Kernel Ridge Regression (KRR) (see [7]) calculates the prediction for a new example $\mathbf{x}_T$ by

$$\gamma_{\text{KRR}} = \mathbf{y}'(a\mathbf{I} + \mathbf{K})^{-1}\mathbf{k} \ , \tag{1}$$

where $\mathbf{k} = (k(\mathbf{x}_i, \mathbf{x}_T))$ and $\mathbf{K} = (k(\mathbf{x}_i, \mathbf{x}_j))_{i,j}$, $i, j = 1, \ldots, T-1$.

2.3 The Aggregating Algorithm for Regression (AAR)

The Aggregating Algorithm (AA) (see [2]), allows us to merge strategies (or experts) from large pools to obtain optimal strategies. Typically, such an optimal strategy performs nearly as good as the best expert in the pool in terms of the cumulative loss. The AA was applied to the problem of linear regression resulting in the AA for Regression (AAR) [2, Sect. 3] (also known as the Vovk-Azoury-Warmuth forecaster, see [8, Sect. 11.8]). Using a Gaussian prior, AAR merges all the static linear predictors that map signals to outcomes. AAR's solution to the regression problem is $\mathbf{w}_{\text{A}} = (a\mathbf{I}+\widetilde{\mathbf{X}}'\widetilde{\mathbf{X}})^{-1}\widetilde{\mathbf{X}}'\widetilde{\mathbf{y}}$, where $\widetilde{\mathbf{X}} = (\mathbf{x}_1, \ldots, \mathbf{x}_T)'$ and $\widetilde{\mathbf{y}} = (y_1, \ldots, y_{T-1}, 0)'$. It can be shown (see [9]) that this solution minimises

$$\mathcal{L}_T(\text{AAR}) = a\|\mathbf{w}_{\text{A}}\|^2 + \langle \mathbf{w}_{\text{A}}, \mathbf{x}_T\rangle^2 + \sum_{t=1}^{T-1}(y_t - \langle \mathbf{w}_{\text{A}}, \mathbf{x}_t\rangle)^2 \ .$$

The main property of AAR is that it is optimal in the sense that the total loss it suffers is only a little worse than that of any linear predictor. In [10] AAR was kernelised to get Kernel AAR (KAAR) which makes a prediction at time T by

$$\gamma_{\text{KAAR}} = \widetilde{\mathbf{y}}'(a\mathbf{I} + \widetilde{\mathbf{K}})^{-1}\widetilde{\mathbf{k}} \ ,$$

where $\widetilde{\mathbf{K}} = (k(\mathbf{x}_i, \mathbf{x}_j))_{i,j}$, $i, j = 1, \ldots, T$, and $\widetilde{\mathbf{k}} = \left(\mathbf{k}', k(\mathbf{x}_T, \mathbf{x}_T)\right)'$.

2.4 Controlled KAAR (CKAAR)

Controlled KAAR (CKAAR) [9] is a generalisation of both KRR and KAAR. At time T the linear version of CKAAR aims to find a solution $\mathbf{w}_{\text{C}}$ that minimises

$$\mathcal{L}_T(\text{CKAAR}) = a\|\mathbf{w}_{\text{C}}\|^2 + b\langle \mathbf{w}_{\text{C}}, \mathbf{x}_T\rangle^2 + \sum_{t=1}^{T-1}(y_t - \langle \mathbf{w}_{\text{C}}, \mathbf{x}_t\rangle)^2 \ ,$$

where $b \geq 0$. It is clear that when $b = 0$, CKAAR is equivalent to RR and equivalent to AAR when $b = 1$. Empirical results in [9] suggest that in general, the performance of CKAAR is as good as or better than that of both KAAR and KRR. The linear CKAAR solution is $\mathbf{w}_{\text{C}} = (a\mathbf{I} + \widehat{\mathbf{X}}'\widehat{\mathbf{X}})^{-1}\widehat{\mathbf{X}}'\widetilde{\mathbf{y}}$, where $\widehat{\mathbf{X}} = (\mathbf{X}', \sqrt{b}\,\mathbf{x}_T)'$. The kernel version of CKAAR makes a prediction at time T by

$$\gamma_{\text{CKAAR}} = \widetilde{\mathbf{y}}'(a\mathbf{I} + \widehat{\mathbf{K}})^{-1}\widehat{\mathbf{k}} \ ,$$

where $\widehat{\mathbf{K}} = \begin{bmatrix} \mathbf{K} & \sqrt{b}\,\mathbf{k} \\ \sqrt{b}\,\mathbf{k}' & b\,k(\mathbf{x}_T, \mathbf{x}_T) \end{bmatrix}$ and $\widehat{\mathbf{k}} = \left(\mathbf{k}', \sqrt{b}\,k(\mathbf{x}_T, \mathbf{x}_T)\right)'$.

3 Methods

We are interested in making predictions in online regression where the dependency of y_t on $\mathbf{x}_t$ changes with time. We present two solutions to this problem: a simple method named WeCKAAR and our new method KAARCh. It is interesting that the prediction formulae of these two methods are very similar.

3.1 WeCKAAR

Weighted CKAAR (WeCKAAR) is a simple modification of CKAAR that employs a decaying factor such that old examples are given less importance. The objective of WeCKAAR is to find a $\mathbf{w}$ that minimises

$$\mathcal{L}_T(\text{WeCKAAR}) = a\|\mathbf{w}\|^2 + b\langle \mathbf{w}, \mathbf{x}_T\rangle^2 + \sum_{t=1}^{T-1} d_t(y_t - \langle \mathbf{w}, \mathbf{x}_t\rangle)^2 \ , \tag{2}$$

where $d_t \in \mathbb{R}$ are nonnegative weights that increase with t. Let $d_T = b$ and $\mathbf{D} = \text{diag}(d_1, \ldots, d_T)$ be the diagonal matrix with elements $d_1 \ldots d_T$. It can be shown by differentiation that the minimum of (2) is achieved when $\mathbf{w} = \left(\widetilde{\mathbf{X}}'\mathbf{D}\widetilde{\mathbf{X}} + a\mathbf{I}\right)^{-1}\widetilde{\mathbf{X}}'\mathbf{D}\widetilde{\mathbf{y}}$. If we use the identity $(\mathbf{A}\mathbf{A}' + a\mathbf{I})^{-1}\mathbf{A} = \mathbf{A}(\mathbf{A}'\mathbf{A} + a\mathbf{I})^{-1}$ (see, for example, [10, Sect. 3.1]) to obtain the dual form of this and introduce kernels, WeCKAAR's prediction for the signal $\mathbf{x}_T$ becomes

$$\gamma_T = \widetilde{\mathbf{y}}'\sqrt{\mathbf{D}}\left(\sqrt{\mathbf{D}}\widetilde{\mathbf{K}}\sqrt{\mathbf{D}} + a\mathbf{I}\right)^{-1}\sqrt{\mathbf{D}}\widetilde{\mathbf{k}} \ , \tag{3}$$

where $\sqrt{\mathbf{D}} = \text{diag}(\sqrt{d_1}, \ldots, \sqrt{d_T})$, and

$$\sqrt{\mathbf{D}}\widetilde{\mathbf{K}}\sqrt{\mathbf{D}} = \begin{bmatrix} d_1 k(\mathbf{x}_1, \mathbf{x}_1) & \sqrt{d_1 d_2} k(\mathbf{x}_1, \mathbf{x}_2) & \cdots & \sqrt{d_1 d_T} k(\mathbf{x}_1, \mathbf{x}_T) \\ \sqrt{d_2 d_1} k(\mathbf{x}_2, \mathbf{x}_1) & d_2 k(\mathbf{x}_2, \mathbf{x}_2) & \cdots & \sqrt{d_2 d_T} k(\mathbf{x}_2, \mathbf{x}_T) \\ \vdots & \vdots & \ddots & \vdots \\ \sqrt{d_T d_1} k(\mathbf{x}_T, \mathbf{x}_1) & \sqrt{d_T d_2} k(\mathbf{x}_T, \mathbf{x}_2) & \cdots & d_T k(\mathbf{x}_T, \mathbf{x}_T) \end{bmatrix} .$$

3.2 KAARCh

The main idea behind our new method, the Kernel Aggregating Algorithm for Regression with Changing dependencies (KAARCh), is to apply the Aggregating Algorithm (AA) to the case where the pool of experts is made up of all linear predictors that can change with time. More formally, an expert in this case is a sequence $\theta_1, \theta_2, \ldots$, that at time T predicts $\mathbf{x}_T'(\theta_1 + \theta_2 + \ldots + \theta_T)$, where $\mathbf{x}_T \in \mathbb{R}^n$ and for every t, $\theta_t \in \mathbb{R}^n$.

Due to space limitations we are only going to give an overview of the main theoretical results achieved (for details see [11]). Let $a_1, \ldots, a_T$ be positive constants. Applying the AA to the pool of experts described above with a Gaussian prior and introducing kernels, we get KAARCh which makes a prediction by

$$\gamma_T = \widetilde{\mathbf{y}}'\left(\bar{\mathbf{K}} + \mathbf{I}\right)^{-1}\bar{\mathbf{k}} \ , \tag{4}$$

where $\bar{\mathbf{K}} = \left(\left(\sum_{t=1}^{\min(i,j)} \frac{1}{a_t}\right) k(\mathbf{x}_i, \mathbf{x}_j)\right)_{i,j}$, and $\bar{\mathbf{k}} = \left(\left(\sum_{t=1}^{i} \frac{1}{a_t}\right) k(\mathbf{x}_i, \mathbf{x}_T)\right)_i$, for $i, j = 1, \ldots, T$.

The main property of KAARCh is that its cumulative loss is less or equal to that of a wide class of experts plus a term of the order $o(T)$. Informally, this class is comprised of all the predictors that do not change very rapidly with time. We assume that outcomes are bounded by Y, therefore, for any t, $y_t \in [-Y, Y]$ (however, we do not require our algorithm to know Y).

Theorem 1. *Let k be a kernel on a space X, let D_t be decision rules in the RKHS induced by k and let $D = (D_1, D_2, \ldots, D_T)'$. Then for any point in time T and any $a_t > 0$, $t = 1, \ldots, T$,*

$$\mathrm{L}_T(\text{KAARCh}) \leq \inf_D \left(\mathrm{L}_T(D) + \sum_{t=1}^{T} a_t \|D_t\|^2 \right) + Y^2 \ln \det \left(\bar{\mathbf{K}} + \mathbf{I}\right) .$$

Let us bound the norm of D_1 by d and assume that T is known in advance. If each $\|D_t\|$, for $t = 2, \ldots, T$, is small, we can find $a_1, \ldots, a_T$ such that the extra terms become of the order $o(T)$.

Corollary 1. *Under the conditions of Theorem 1, let T be known in advance. For every positive d and ε, if $\|D_1\| \leq d$ and, for $t = 2, \ldots, T$, $\|D_t\| \leq \frac{d}{T^{0.5+\varepsilon}}$, we can choose $a_1, \ldots, a_T$ such that*

$$\mathrm{L}_T(\text{KAARCh}) \leq \mathrm{L}_T(D) + O\left(T^{\max(0.5, (1-\varepsilon))}\right) = \mathrm{L}_T(D) + o(T) .$$

This result can also be achieved if we assume that there are only a few nonzero D_t, for $t = 2, \ldots, T$. In this case, the nonzero D_t can have greater flexibility.

Implementation Notes. For simplicity, we may take all equal $a_1, a_2, \ldots, a_T = a$. In this case, (4) becomes

$$\gamma_T = \widetilde{\mathbf{y}}' \left(\breve{\mathbf{K}} + a\mathbf{I}\right)^{-1} \breve{\mathbf{k}} , \tag{5}$$

where

$$\breve{\mathbf{K}} = \begin{bmatrix} 1k(\mathbf{x}_1, \mathbf{x}_1) & 1k(\mathbf{x}_1, \mathbf{x}_2) & 1k(\mathbf{x}_1, \mathbf{x}_3) & \cdots & 1k(\mathbf{x}_1, \mathbf{x}_T) \\ 1k(\mathbf{x}_2, \mathbf{x}_1) & 2k(\mathbf{x}_2, \mathbf{x}_2) & 2k(\mathbf{x}_2, \mathbf{x}_3) & \cdots & 2k(\mathbf{x}_2, \mathbf{x}_T) \\ 1k(\mathbf{x}_3, \mathbf{x}_1) & 2k(\mathbf{x}_3, \mathbf{x}_2) & 3k(\mathbf{x}_3, \mathbf{x}_3) & \cdots & 3k(\mathbf{x}_3, \mathbf{x}_T) \\ \vdots & \vdots & \vdots & \ddots & \vdots \\ 1k(\mathbf{x}_T, \mathbf{x}_1) & 2k(\mathbf{x}_T, \mathbf{x}_2) & 3k(\mathbf{x}_T, \mathbf{x}_3) & \cdots & Tk(\mathbf{x}_T, \mathbf{x}_T) \end{bmatrix}, \breve{\mathbf{k}} = \begin{bmatrix} 1k(\mathbf{x}_1, \mathbf{x}_T) \\ 2k(\mathbf{x}_2, \mathbf{x}_T) \\ 3k(\mathbf{x}_3, \mathbf{x}_T) \\ \vdots \\ Tk(\mathbf{x}_T, \mathbf{x}_T) \end{bmatrix} .$$

Recalling that a scalar multiplied by a kernel is still a kernel, and making allowances such that steps in time can be skipped (for instance there is no data available for some steps), the coefficients $1, \ldots, T$ in $\breve{\mathbf{K}}$ and $\breve{\mathbf{k}}$ can be replaced with any increasing, positive real numbers $t_1, \ldots, t_T$, representing the real-world time at which examples arrive.

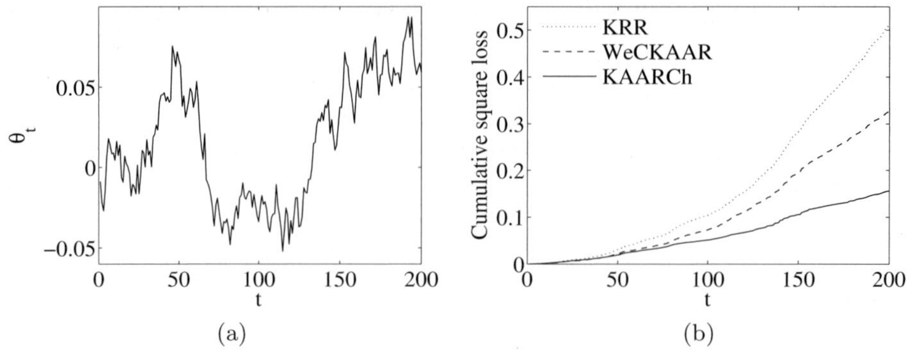

Fig. 1. The behaviour of θ_t with time (a), approximating Brownian motion, and the cumulative loss suffered by KRR, WeCKAAR and KAARCh on the artificial dataset (b)

4 Empirical Results

In this section we measure the empirical performance of our methods on an artificial dataset and on a real-world dataset on options implied volatility.

4.1 Artificial Dataset

Let $w_1, \ldots, w_T \in \mathbb{R}$ be T normally distributed random variables with mean 0 and variance σ^2, and $\theta_t = \sum_{i=1}^{t} w_i$. Drawing $\mathbf{x}_t \in \mathbb{R}$ from the interval $[0, 1]$ using a uniform distribution, we generate a dataset by the equation $y_t = \theta_t' \mathbf{x}_t$. In our experiments, we set $T = 200$ and $\sigma = 0.01$, and repeated the procedure 20 times on such randomly generated datasets. The typical behaviour of a resulting θ_t with time can be seen in Fig. 1 (a). In the normal regression setting (where the dependency does not change with time) this graph would simply be a flat line. In Fig. 1 (b) we show the mean over all runs of the cumulative square loss suffered by KRR, WeCKAAR and KAARCh using a linear kernel on these datasets.

4.2 Options Implied Volatility Data

The Russian Trading System Stock Exchange (RTSSE) have provided us with data containing the details of option transactions on several underlying assets. Options are types of derivative securities that give the right to buy or sell assets for a particular strike price in the future (see [1] for more details). The accurate pricing of these options is an important problem. The most popular approach to pricing options is based on the Black-Scholes (B-S) theory. This assumes that the asset price follows an exponential Wiener process with constant volatility σ which cannot be directly observed but can be estimated from historical data. In practice this model is often violated. Given the current prices of options and the underlying asset we can find σ that satisfies the B-S equations. This σ is known as the implied volatility and exhibits a dependence on the strike price

Table 1. Results on options implied volatility data. All mean square losses reported are $\times 10^{-3}$, apart from the ones for EERU1206 which are $\times 10^{-2}$.

RTSI1206 (10126 transactions) RTSSE: 2.91				RTSI0307 (8410 transactions) RTSSE: 2.78			
	KRR	WeCKAAR	KAARCh		KRR	WeCKAAR	KAARCh
Poly	36.56	2.19	(**2.16**)	Poly	8.29	2.40	**2.38**
Spline	2.63	(**2.23**)	(2.24)	Spline	3.49	2.29	**2.29**
RBF	3.31	2.33	**2.31**	RBF	3.87	2.33	**2.32**
GAZP1206 (9382 transactions) RTSSE: 1.29				GAZP0307 (10985 transactions) RTSSE: 2.13			
	KRR	WeCKAAR	KAARCh		KRR	WeCKAAR	KAARCh
Poly	1.59	1.54	**1.53**	Poly	3.16	2.45	**2.45**
Spline	5.21	**1.49**	1.49	Spline	2.85	2.47	**2.47**
RBF	1.59	**1.47**	1.48	RBF	3.53	**2.49**	2.49
EERU1206 (13152 transactions) RTSSE: 1.47				EERU0307 (14776 transactions) RTSSE: 4.74			
	KRR	WeCKAAR	KAARCh		KRR	WeCKAAR	KAARCh
Poly	162.43	**1.71**	1.72	Poly	5.49	4.58	**4.52**
Spline	1.92	**1.65**	1.66	Spline	5.07	**4.49**	4.50
RBF	6.36	**1.65**	1.65	RBF	5.83	(**4.46**)	4.49

and time. There is no generally recognised theory explaining the phenomenon of implied volatility; however, it remains a useful parameter and traders often use it to quote option prices. We are interested in using learning theory methods to predict implied volatility without assuming any model for its behaviour. In our experiments we treat the implied volatility of a transaction as the outcome and the parameters of the transaction and other market information as the signal.

For WeCKAAR's $d_1, \ldots, d_T$ and KAARCh's $t_1, \ldots, t_T$, we used a real number representing the time at which the transactions occurred. The kernels used were the spline, polynomial degree 2, and RBF with $\sigma = 1$ (see, for example, [5]). We employed a sliding window (of size 50) approach. The parameter a (see (1), (3), and (5)) was updated every 50 steps by finding a value that works well on previous examples. Due to computational limitations, we ran experiments on 100 randomly selected segments containing 200 transactions from every dataset.

In Table 1 we give the results obtained on different options data. EERU and GAZP are options on futures of liquid stocks and RTSI is related to options on futures of a popular RTSSE index (the appended numbers specify different transaction periods). The results show the mean square loss suffered by WeCKAAR, KAARCh and KRR, and also that of the proprietary method used at the RTSSE for comparison. To measure the statistical significance of the difference between the results of our methods and that of the RTSSE we used the Wilcoxon signed rank test. When there is no statistical significance in the difference (we use the conventional 5% threshold) the corresponding loss is enclosed in parentheses.

5 Discussion

KAARCh's performance on the artificial dataset is much better than that of WeCKAAR and KRR. We attribute this to KAARCh's superior theoretical properties. Six real-world datasets on options implied volatility were also considered. The results achieved by KAARCh and WeCKAAR on these datasets are always better than those of KRR and very close to those of the RTSSE (and slightly better in half of them). The proprietary method used at the RTSSE was specifically designed for this application and is constantly monitored and tuned by experts to predict better. Therefore, it is remarkable that our methods perform comparably. These results show that our new methods KAARCh and (to a lesser extent) WeCKAAR are capable of handling changing dependencies and, in this context, are an improvement on standard regression techniques.

Acknowledgements. We are grateful to Dr Michael Vyugin at the RTSSE for providing the data and sharing his expertise with us. We also thank Prof Volodya Vovk and Prof Alex Gammerman for useful discussions and comments.

References

1. Hull, J.C.: Options, Futures and Other Derivatives, 6th edn. Prentice-Hall, Englewood Cliffs (2005)
2. Vovk, V.: Competitive on-line statistics. International Statistical Review 69(2), 213–248 (2001)
3. Aizerman, M., Braverman, E., Rozonoer, L.: Theoretical foundations of the potential function method in pattern recognition learning. Automation and Remote Control 25, 821–837 (1964)
4. Aronszajn, N.: Theory of reproducing kernels. Transactions of the American Mathematical Society 68, 337–404 (1950)
5. Schölkopf, B., Smola, A.J.: Learning with Kernels — Support Vector Machines, Regularization, Optimization and Beyond. The MIT Press, USA (2002)
6. Hoerl, A.E.: Application of ridge analysis to regression problems. Chemical Engineering Progress 58, 54–59 (1962)
7. Saunders, C., Gammerman, A., Vovk, V.: Ridge regression learning algorithm in dual variables. In: Proceedings of the 15th International Conference on Machine Learning, pp. 515–521. Morgan Kaufmann, San Francisco (1998)
8. Cesa-Bianchi, N., Lugosi, G.: Prediction, Learning, and Games. Cambridge University Press, Cambridge (2006)
9. Busuttil, S., Kalnishkan, Y., Gammerman, A.: Improving the aggregating algorithm for regression. In: Proceedings of the 25th IASTED International Conference on Artificial Intelligence and Applications (AIA 2007), pp. 347–352. ACTA Press (2007)
10. Gammerman, A., Kalnishkan, Y., Vovk, V.: On-line prediction with kernels and the complexity approximation principle. In: Proceedings of the 20th Conference on Uncertainty in Artificial Intelligence, pp. 170–176. AUAI Press (2004)
11. Busuttil, S., Kalnishkan, Y.: Online regression competitive with changing predictors. In: Proceedings of the 18th International Conference on Algorithmic Learning Theory (ALT 2007). LNCS, Springer, Heidelberg (to appear, 2007)

Counter-Example Generation-Based One-Class Classification

András Bánhalmi, András Kocsor, and Róbert Busa-Fekete

Research Group on Artificial Intelligence of the Hungarian Academy of Sciences and of the University of Szeged,
H-6720 Szeged, Aradi vértanúk tere 1., Hungary
{banhalmi,kocsor,busarobi}@inf.u-szeged.hu

Abstract. For One-Class Classification problems several methods have been proposed in the literature. These methods all have the common feature that the decision boundary is learnt by just using a set of the positive examples. Here we propose a method that extends the training set with a counter-example set, which is generated directly using the set of positive examples. Using the extended training set, a binary classifier (here ν-SVM) is applied to separate the positive and the negative points. The results of this novel technique are compared with those of One-Class SVM and the Gaussian Mixture Model on several One-Class Classification tasks.

1 Introduction

In the field of machine learning there are several problems to which usual multi-class classification methods cannot be applied or do not perform that well. Among these problems an important one is the so-called "One-Class Classification" problem [1], where only positive examples are available for a particular class, or the negative examples are highly under-represented. These problems are also referred to as Data Description, Outlier Detection, and Novelty Detection in different fields. What the methods proposed for this task have in common is that since only positive examples are available from a particular class during the training phase, the decision boundary is learnt not between two or more classes, but it is a set of closed surfaces which surround the majority of the positive training instances. The area of one-class training includes several algorithms like generative probability density estimation methods (Gaussian Mixture Model (GMM), Parzen estimator), reconstruction methods (k-means, Autoencoder Neural Networks), and boundary estimators (k-centers, SVDD [2] [3] [4], NNDD [1]).

We propose here a new method for multidimensional real-valued one-class classification tasks. Firstly, our method selects the boundary points of the positive data. Next, these boundary points are used to generate counter-examples that surround the positives; and finally, a binary classifier (here ν-Support Vector Machine (SVM) [5]) is used to separate the positive and negative data samples. Overall, the goal of the proposed method is to force the binary classifier to learn a "multidimensional contour" at a distance from the positive examples.

J.N. Kok et al. (Eds.): ECML 2007, LNAI 4701, pp. 543–550, 2007.

2 Generation of Counter-Examples

In order to train the ν-SVM binary classifier by taking just the positive examples of a class, we propose a method for generating negative examples using the positive ones. Essentially, this method first finds the local boundary points of the input data. Then all the positive examples are transformed using the closest boundary point for each. The points obtained after these transformations will form the set of negative examples. This method is described below in more detail.

After, when we have negative examples surrounding the positives, a ν-SVM is trained to separate these two classes. During the testing phase the position of the decision boundary between the positive and negative sets can be controlled by setting a threshold for the acceptance.

2.1 Finding Boundary Points

Our goal is to find those points of the n-dimensional positive examples for which a hyperplane exists that separates this point from the other positive examples in its neighborhood. Here we suggest a method for solving this problem (see the pseudo-code in the Table 1).

Table 1. The Boundary Point Search Method

Input:	A set of N positive examples (X)
Output:	A set of K boundary points (B), and inner points (I)
0	$B = \emptyset$
1	For each x in X do
2	Take x_i, the k closest points (but with a positive distance) to x.
3	Compute the unit vectors: $e_i = \frac{x_i - x}{\\|x_i - x\\|}$
4	Try to separate e_i points from the origin using a hard margin linear SVM
5	If the optimization of SVM fails
	$I = I \cup \{x\}$
	else
	$B = B \cup \{x\}$, and form the vector: $x_{center} = \sum_{i=1}^{k} \alpha_i e_i$
	(this vector is needed for counter-example generation)

The explanation of this algorithm is the following. In the 2nd and 3rd rows the k closest points to x are determined (x_i), and unit vectors are computed from $x_i - x$ vectors. Then in the 4th row a linear SVM is applied to separate these normalized vectors from the origin. Next, if the separation process fails, then x is added to the set of inner points. If the points are separable, then x is added to the set of boundary points and an x_{center} vector is computed, which will be needed later for counter-example generation.

Here the center vector will be defined as follows. Let x_b a boundary point, and let x_i the k nearest neighbors of x_b ($i = 1 \ldots k$). Let e_i be defined by:

$e_i = \frac{x_i - x_b}{\|x_i - x_b\|}$. Then the *center vector* corresponding to x_b will be defined as the normal vector of the hyperplane separating the origin from the points e_i with maximal margin.

A hard-margin linear SVM is used to find the hyperplane separation with maximal margin, and the normal vector of this hyperplane is computed using the support vectors and the corresponding α_i values computed by the SVM. For more information and for a proof see [6].

2.2 Generating Counter-Examples

The method suggested here is based on the transformation of the positive examples using the boundary points chosen earlier and the corresponding center vectors. For more details about the algorithm, see Table 2 with the following explanation.

Table 2. The base method used to generate counter-examples

Input:	A set of N positive examples (X)
Output:	A set of M negative examples (Y)
0	$Y = \emptyset$, $B = boundaryPoints(X)$
1	For each x in X do
2	Find x_b, the closest boundary point (but with a positive distance) to x
3	Transform x to x_b using the following formula: $y = v(1 + T(x, x_b, X)/\|v\|) + x$, where $v = x_b - x$, T is a function of the X dataset, x, x_b
4	Check y to see if it is an inner point with the algorithm described in Table 1
5	If y is not an inner point, then $Y = Y \cup \{y\}$ else $B = B \backslash \{x_b\}$, and with the next closest boundary point repeat the procedure.

In the 2nd row the closest boundary point x_b to x is selected. The transformation of the point x will be a translation along the $v = x_b - x$ direction, and the distance of the transformed point y from the boundary point x_b depends on the $T(x, x_b, X)$ function. In the 4th and 5th rows the algorithm checks to see if y is an inner point, and if it is, then we do not take it as a negative example, and the boundary point will be deleted from the set. For the T function we suggest the following formula:

$$T(x, x_b, X) = \frac{dist}{dist \cdot curv + CosAngle(x, x_b, X)}, \tag{1}$$

where

$$CosAngle(x, x_b, X) = \frac{x_{b,center}^T \cdot (x - x_b)}{\left\|x_{b,center}^T\right\| \|x - x_b\|}, \tag{2}$$

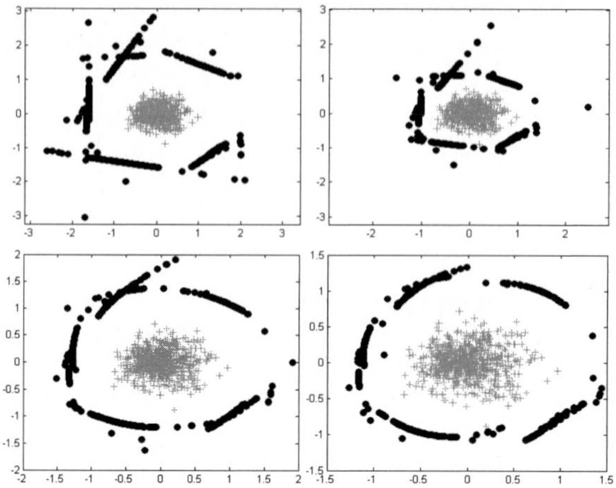

Fig. 1. These figures show the generated boundary points with different settings. Left to right: 1st: $(dist, curv) = (1, 0)$, 2nd: $(dist, curv) = (0.4, 0)$, 3rd: $(dist, curv) = (1, 0.5)$, 4th: $(dist, curv) = (1, 1)$. One can see that $curv = 0$ will generate points of a hyperplane, while $curv > 0$ will generate points of a better fitting boundary hyper-surface. With the *dist* parameter the distance between the boundary points and the generated counter-examples can be controlled.

and $x_{b,center}$ is the center vector for the x_b obtained and stored by the boundary point selection method (see Table 1). The constant parameter *dist* controls the distance between the transformed point and the boundary point, and the *curv* parameter controls the curvature of the hyper-surface of the counter-examples obtained by the transformation for the same boundary point. Figure 1 provides some examples with different *dist* and *curv* parameter values. The method generates N counter examples for a positive dataset of N data samples.

3 Refinements and Variants

The previously described boundary point selection algorithm is based on a local convexity condition. This method can also work on distinct or concave sets, but the condition may exclude many points from the boundary point set. To increase the number of the boundary points, we suggest some refinements.

The first modification we propose to apply can be used to increase the number of boundary points and also to filter extreme distal points. The idea is that we could also add some inner points to the set of the boundary points that are close to the local surface. The modified method iteratively separates new boundary points from the $X \backslash B$ dataset, where B is the set of the boundary points found in the previous iterations. The effect of this method on the dataset is shown in Figure 2.

The second modification of the base method is proposed for the counter-example generation algorithm. The boundary points do not necessarily have the same "popularity". In some cases there are a lot of boundary points which are

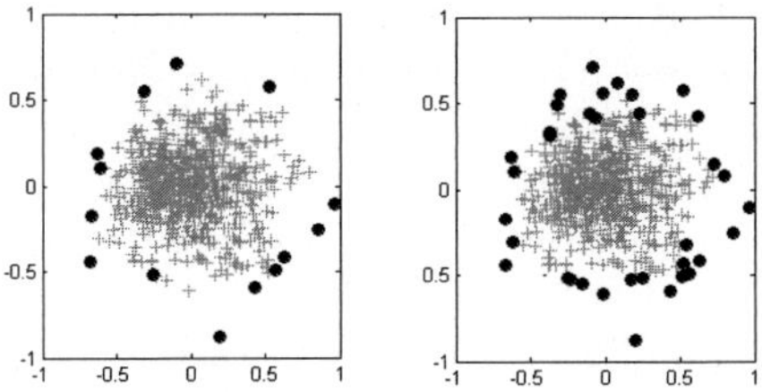

Fig. 2. The first picture shows the result of using the base method. The second picture is obtained with the proposed modification after 3 iterations.

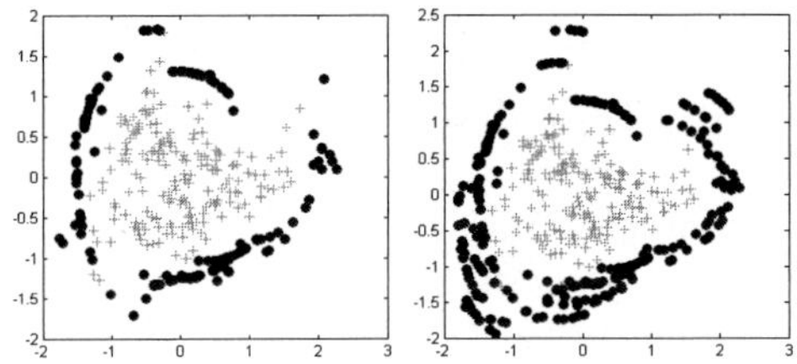

Fig. 3. The left picture shows the generated negative examples without applying the proposed modification, while the right picture shows the result when it is applied

rarely chosen for the point-transformation, and this can cause an imbalance in the density of the counter-examples. This problem can be handled by adding extra counter-examples to the original ones in the following way. First, the number of transformations have to be counted for all the boundary points. Then extra boundary points should be added using the following rule: *for each rarely used boundary point, select their k closest points, and after applying the transformation method add the new points to the set of counter-examples.* To define which boundary points the rule can be applied to, a frequency threshold has to be used. The effect of this modification can be seen in Figure 3 above.

4 Time Complexity and Applicability

The time complexity of counter-example generation depends on k and N, where k is the number of nearest neighbors used in the boundary point test, and N is the total number of positive training examples. The boundary point test method uses a linear SVM, so the time complexity is $o(k^3)$. To choose the k-nearest neighbors, $o(N \cdot log(N))$ time is needed, so altogether for N points the total time complexity is $o(k^3 \cdot N^2 \cdot logN)$. When generating counter-example for a specified point, we need the closest boundary point, and a test has to be done to see if the transformed point is an inner point. The combined time complexity of this part after summing for each training example is $o(|B| \cdot n \cdot k^3)$, where $|B|$ is the number of boundary points.

The time complexity of the training method depends on which method is chosen for this purpose. Here ν-SVM was applied, which has a time complexity of $o(N^3)$. However, some other methods which have a slightly lower time complexity could be applied for the classification task like the Core Vector Machine [7].

We suggest applying the method proposed here on those problems where the attributes are continuous real-valued variables. Some preprocessing should also be made to eliminate redundant or useless attributes. Since a hyperplane in an n-dimensional space is determined by at least n points (this is important when determining center vectors), we suggest that it also should be guaranteed that the size of the training data is higher than the dimension of the problem. However among our test cases there is an example which does not satisfy this condition, but the proposed method still works well.

5 Experiments and Results

In order to separate the examples from the artifically generated counter-examples ν-SVM with an RBF kernel function was applied using the WEKA system [8] [9]. For the boundary point tests the Matlab SVM Toolbox by Steve Gunn was applied [1]. For a comparison we used GMM (from the GMMBayes Matlab Toolbox [10]) and One-Class SVM (from WEKA) as baselines. All the models were trained using different free parameter settings, and the results with the best scores were taken. The free parameters are the number of clusters and confidence value for the GMM, the ν and γ values for the one-class SVM and the ν-SVM, the number of clusters, the $(curv, dist)$ parameters, the number of nearest neighbors that need to be considered (k) and the acceptance threshold for the counter-example generation-based method. The ν-SVM with n clusters is a construction where the positive training examples are grouped into n clusters using k-means. After that, the counter examples are generated, and a separate ν-SVM is trained for each cluster (the free parameters were set to the same value). In the decision phase the score of an example is the maximum value of the scores given by the SVM models corresponding to the clusters.

For testing purposes 10 one-class datasets were employed [2]. The "unvoiced DB", and "silence DB" were constructed by us and contain feature vectors of 25 Mel Filter Bank coefficients created from human speech samples. In the "Unvoiced" one-class problem the task was to train the examples of unvoiced phonemes. The "Silence" one-class database contained feature vectors of silent parts (and also contained the short silences in a plosive). The "Ball-Bearing", "Water Pump" train and test datasets (used in fault detection) were downloaded from [11]. That is, from the Ball-Bearing datasets the "rectangular window" version (containing 26-dimensional vectors), and from the "Water Pump" datasets the "autocorrelation function" version (containing 26-dimensional vectors) were utilized. In [12] these datasets are described in detail, and were used to find

[1] http://www.isis.ecs.soton.ac.uk/resources/svminfo/

[2] All the datasets can be downloaded from: http://www.inf.u-szeged.hu/oasis/oneclass/

Table 3. Best test results using different models in one-class tasks: classification accuracies, and rates of true positives and false positives

Accuracy/TP/ FP rates (%)	train DB size and dimension	one-class SVM	GMM	ν-SVM & counter examples
Silence DB [(1)]	301/12	82.4/89.7/24.8	**85.8**/82.5/36.8	85.6/ 83.8/12.4
Unvoiced DB [(2)]	405/12	78.6/86.3/29.0	78.1/82.9/26.6	**82.9**/ 80.0/14.4
Ball B. DB [(3)]	56/26	99.3/96.9/ 0.0	96.3/81.3/ 0.0	**100.0**/100.0/0.0
Water P. DB [(4)]	224/26	94.0/88.5/ 4.4	94.9/87.5/ 4.4	**95.7**/ 94.8/ 4.1
OC 507 DB [(5)]	163/13	67.2/78.8/44.4	60.3/26.9/ 6.3	**67.5**/ 77.5/42.5
OC 511 DB [(6)]	126/5	85.2/88.8/18.4	78.8/80.0/22.4	**86.8**/ 92.8/19.2
OC 514 DB [(7)]	236/278	70.9/82.6/40.9	67.7/53.2/17.9	**71.9**/ 68.3/34.4
OC 589 DB [(8)]	125/34	52.4/ 4.8/ 0.0	52.4/ 4.8/ 0.0	**71.6**/ 62.4/19.2
OC 598 DB [(9)]	300/21	**77.8**/76.0/20.3	50.5/ 1.0/ 0.0	77.7/ 86.3/31.0
OC 620 DB [(10)]	4490/10	**86.3**/89.6/17.0	84.9/93.1/23.2	84.6/ 91.1/22.1

the optimal parameter settings for the One-class SVM, and to choose the best preprocessing method. The other 6 datasets (OC xxx) were downloaded from the webpage given in [13]. More information about these datasets can be found there. These datasets did not contain separate train and test sets, so train sets and test sets were generated using a 5-fold cross-validation technique. In the experiments each test dataset contained an equal number of positive and negative examples. Moreover, when preprocessing the positive datasets a normalization and a PCA transformation was applied.

Table 3 below lists the best results of the different classification algorithms applied to one-class tasks[3].

6 Conclusions and Future Work

Based on the results of our experiments we can say that the proposed method seems superior to the statistical GMM, and the One-Class SVM in most cases.

[3] The settings of the free parameters of the models are the following. Here cn denotes the number of clusters (the default value is 1), $conf$ represents the confidence threshold for GMM (the default value is 1), ν and γ are the parameters of ν-SVM and One-Class SVM, $(dist, curv, k)$ are the parameters for counter-example generation – see Equation 1 – and the default values are $(1, 0.5, 2 \cdot dim)$. The acceptance threshold is represented by ath, whose default value is 0.5. Here G means that the second modification (see Section 3) was applied.
(1) $(\nu,\gamma) = (0.1, 0.01)$, $(conf, cn) = (1, 2)$, $(\nu, \gamma, cn, ath) = (0.1, 0.01, 2, 0.9)$; (2) $(\nu,\gamma) = (0.3, 0.01)$, $(conf, cn) = (1, 2)$, $(\nu, \gamma, cn, ath) = (0.1, 0.3, 2, 0.9)$ G; (3) $(\nu,\gamma) = (0.01, 0.01)$, $(conf, cn) = (0.95, 1)$, $(\nu, \gamma, ath, k) = (0.3, 0.01, 0.3, 56)$; (4) $(\nu,\gamma) = (0.05, 0.1)$, $(conf, cn) = (0.95, 1)$, $(\nu, \gamma, dist, curv, ath) = (0.3, 1, 1.5, 0.1, 0.9)$; (5) $(\nu,\gamma) = (0.1, 0.05)$, $(\nu, \gamma, ath) = (0.3, 0.3, 0.1)$ G; (6) $(\nu,\gamma) = (0.1, 0.5)$, $(\nu,\gamma) = (0.3, 0.3)$; (7) $(\nu,\gamma) = (0.1, 0.005)$, $(\nu, \gamma, ath) = (0.3, 0.01, 0.3)$; (8) $(\nu,\gamma) = (0.001, 0.5)$, $(\nu,\gamma) = (0.3, 0.3)$; (9) $(\nu,\gamma) = (0.1, 0.3)$, $(\nu, \gamma, ath) = (0.3, 0.3, 0.6)$; (10) $(\nu,\gamma) = (0.1, 0.3)$, $(\nu, \gamma, ath) = (0.3, 0.3, 0.8)$.

However, to make it work better in practice some improvements should be made to reduce the time complexity of our algorithm. Currently we are working on a faster iterative boundary-searching method that begins with a small subset of the whole, then modifies the boundary points by iteratively adding only suitable points to them from the database. In the near future we will implement a faster boundary point search method, and other distance-based classifiers will be tested to separate the positive and the negative examples.

Acknowledgement

We would like to thank György Szarvas, Richárd Farkas and László Tóth for their helpful advice and constructive comments, and also thank David Curley for checking this paper from a linguistic point of view.

References

1. Tax, D.: One-class classification; Concept-learning in the absence of counter-examples. PhD thesis, Delft University of Technology (2001)
2. Schölkopf, B., Platt, J.C., Shawe-Taylor, J., Smola, A.J., Williamson, R.C.: Estimating the support of a high-dimensional distribution. Neural Computation 13, 1443–1471 (2001)
3. Tax, D.M.J., Duin, R.P.W.: Support vector domain description. Pattern Recogn. Lett. 20, 1191–1199 (1999)
4. Tax, D.M.J., Duin, R.P.W.: Support vector data description. Mach. Learn. 54, 45–66 (2004)
5. Chen, P.H., Lin, C.J., Schölkopf, B.: A tutorial on ν-support vector machines: Research articles. Appl. Stoch. Model. Bus. Ind. 21, 111–136 (2005)
6. Vapnik, V.N.: Statistical Learning Theory. John Wiley and Son, Chichester (1998)
7. Tsang, I.W., Kwok, J.T., Cheung, P.M.: Core vector machines: Fast svm training on very large data sets. J. Mach. Learn. Res. 6, 363–392 (2005)
8. EL-Manzalawy, Y., Honavar, V.: WLSVM: Integrating LibSVM into Weka Environment (2005), Software available at `http://www.cs.iastate.edu/~yasser/wlsvm`
9. Witten, I.H., Frank, E.: Data Mining: Practical Machine Learning Tools and Techniques, 2nd edn. Morgan Kaufmann Series in Data Management Systems. Morgan Kaufmann Publishers Inc., San Francisco (2005)
10. Paalanen, P.: Bayesian classification using Gaussian mixture model and EM estimation: Implementations and comparisons. Technical report, Department of Information Technology, Lappeenranta University of Technology, Lappeenranta (2004)
11. Unnthorsson, R.: Datasets for model selection in one-class ν-svms using rbf kernels, `http://www.hi.is/~runson/svm/`
12. Unnthorsson, R., Runarsson, T.P., Jonsson, M.T.: Model selection in one-class ν-svms using rbf kernels. In: COMADEM – Proceedings of the 16th international congress (2003)
13. Tax, D.M.: Occ benchmark, `http://www-it.et.tudelft.nl/~davidt/occ/`

Test-Cost Sensitive Classification Based on Conditioned Loss Functions

Mumin Cebe and Cigdem Gunduz-Demir

Department of Computer Engineering
Bilkent University
Bilkent, Ankara 06800, Turkey
{mumin,gunduz}@cs.bilkent.edu.tr

Abstract. We report a novel approach for designing test-cost sensitive classifiers that consider the misclassification cost together with the cost of feature extraction utilizing the consistency behavior for the first time. In this approach, we propose to use a new Bayesian decision theoretical framework in which the loss is conditioned with the current decision and the expected decisions after additional features are extracted as well as the consistency among the current and expected decisions. This approach allows us to force the feature extraction for samples for which the current and expected decisions are inconsistent. On the other hand, it forces not to extract any features in the case of consistency, leading to less costly but equally accurate decisions. In this work, we apply this approach to a medical diagnosis problem and demonstrate that it reduces the overall feature extraction cost up to 47.61 percent without decreasing the accuracy.

1 Introduction

In classification, different types of cost have been investigated till date [1]. Among these costs, the most commonly investigated one is the *cost of misclassification errors* [2]. Compared to the misclassification cost, the other types are much less studied. The *cost of computation* includes both static complexity, which arises from the size of a computer program [3], and dynamic complexity, which is incurred during training and testing a classifier [4]. The *cost of feature extraction* arises from the effort of acquiring a feature. This type of cost is especially important in some real-world applications such as medical diagnosis in which one would like to balance the diagnosis accuracy with the cost of medical tests used for acquiring features.

In machine learning literature, a number of studies have investigated the cost of feature extraction [5,6,7,8,9,10,11,12,13,14,15]. The majority of these studies focus on the construction of decision trees in a least costly manner by selecting features based on both their information gain and their extraction cost [5,6,7,8,9]. While the earlier studies [5,6,7] consider only the feature extraction cost, more recent ones [8,9] consider the misclassification cost as well. Another group of studies focuses on the sequential feature selection also based on the information gain of features and their extraction cost [10,11,12]. In these studies, the

J.N. Kok et al. (Eds.): ECML 2007, LNAI 4701, pp. 551–558, 2007.

gain is measured as the difference in the amount of information before and after extracting the features. As the information after feature extraction cannot be known in advance, these studies estimate this information making use of maximum likelihood estimation [10], dynamic Bayesian networks [11], and neural networks [12]. The theoretical aspects of such feature selection are also studied in [13]. The other group of studies considers the feature selection as optimal policy learning and solves it formulating the classification problem as a Markov decision process [14] and a partially observable Markov decision process [15]. All of these studies select features based on the current decision and those obtained after features are extracted. None of them considers the consistency between these decisions.

In this paper, we report a novel cost-sensitive learning approach that takes into consideration the misclassification cost together with the cost of feature extraction utilizing the consistency behavior for the first time. In this approach, we make use of a Bayesian decision theoretical framework in which the loss function is conditioned with the current decision and the estimated decisions after the additional features are extracted in conjunction with the *consistency* among the current and estimated decisions. Using this proposed approach, the system tends to extract features that are expected to change the current decision (i.e., yield inconsistent decisions). It also tends to stop the extraction if all possible features are expected to confirm the current decision (i.e., yield consistent decisions), leading to less costly but equally accurate decisions. In this paper, working with a medical diagnosis problem, we demonstrate that the overall feature extraction cost is reduced up to 47.61% without decreasing the classification accuracy. To the best of our knowledge, this is the first demonstration of the use of conditioned loss functions for the purpose of test-cost sensitive classification.

2 Methodology

In our approach, we propose to use a Bayesian decision theoretical framework in which the loss function is conditioned with the current and estimated decisions as well as their consistency. For a given instance, the proposed approach decides whether or not to extract a feature, and in the case of deciding in favor of extraction, which feature to be extracted by using conditional risks computed with the new loss function definition.

In Bayesian decision theory, decision has to be made in favor of the action for which the conditional risk is minimum. For instance x, the conditional risk of taking action α_i is defined as

$$R(\alpha_i|x) = \sum_{j=1}^{N} P(C_j|x)\ \lambda(\alpha_i|C_j) \tag{1}$$

where $\{C_1, C_2, ..., C_N\}$ is the set of N possible states of nature and $\lambda(\alpha_i|C_j)$ is the loss incurred for taking action α_i when the actual state of nature is C_j. In

Table 1. Definition of the conditioned loss function for feature extraction, classification, and reject actions

	$\texttt{extract}_k$	$\texttt{classify}$	$\texttt{reject}$
Case 1: $C_{\texttt{actual}} = C_{\texttt{curr}} = C_{\texttt{est}_k}$	$\texttt{cost}_k$	$-\texttt{REWARD}$	$\texttt{PENALTY}$
Case 2: $C_{\texttt{actual}} \neq C_{\texttt{curr}} \neq C_{\texttt{est}_k}$	$\texttt{cost}_k + \texttt{PENALTY}$	$\texttt{PENALTY}$	$-\texttt{REWARD}$
Case 3: $C_{\texttt{curr}} = C_{\texttt{est}_k} \neq C_{\texttt{actual}}$	$\texttt{cost}_k + \texttt{PENALTY}$	$\texttt{PENALTY}$	$-\texttt{REWARD}$
Case 4: $C_{\texttt{actual}} = C_{\texttt{curr}} \neq C_{\texttt{est}_k}$	$\texttt{cost}_k + \texttt{PENALTY}$	$-\texttt{REWARD}$	$\texttt{PENALTY}$
Case 5: $C_{\texttt{actual}} = C_{\texttt{est}_k} \neq C_{\texttt{curr}}$	$\texttt{cost}_k - \texttt{REWARD}$	$\texttt{PENALTY}$	$\texttt{PENALTY}$

our approach, we consider C_j as the class that an instance can belong to and α_i as one of the following actions:

(a) $\texttt{extract}_k$: extract feature F_k,
(b) `classify`: stop the extraction and classify the instance using the current information, and
(c) `reject`: stop the extraction and reject the classification of the instance.

In the proposed framework, we use a new loss function definition in which the loss is conditioned with the current and estimated decisions along with their consistency. The loss function for each of the aforementioned actions is given in Table 1. In this table, $C_{\texttt{actual}}$ is the actual class, $C_{\texttt{curr}}$ is the class estimated by the current classifier, and $C_{\texttt{est}_k}$ is the estimated class when feature F_k is extracted. Here, $C_{\texttt{actual}}$ and $C_{\texttt{est}_k}$ should be estimated using the current information as it is not possible to know these values in advance.

As shown in Table 1, for a particular action, the loss function takes different values based on the consistency among the actual ($C_{\texttt{actual}}$), current ($C_{\texttt{curr}}$), and estimated ($C_{\texttt{est}_k}$) classes. In this definition, the actions that lead to correct classifications and the action that rejects the classification when the correct classification is not possible are rewarded with an amount of REWARD value by adding $-$REWARD to the loss function. When there are more than one feature that could be extracted, `reject` action is rewarded only if none of the classifiers using each of these features could yield the correct classification. On the contrary, the actions that lead to misclassifications and the action that rejects the classification when the correct classification is possible are penalized with an amount of PENALTY value. Additionally, the extraction cost ($\texttt{cost}_k$) is included in the loss function when feature F_k is to be extracted. In this definition of loss function, the only exception that does not follow these rules is the case of $\texttt{extract}_k$ action in Case 1. In this case, although it yields the correct classification, this action is not rewarded since it does not provide any additional information but brings about an extra feature extraction cost. By doing so, for Case 1, we force the algorithm not to extract an additional feature.

For a particular instance x, we express the conditional risk of each action using the definition of loss function above. With $\mathcal{C} = \{C_{\texttt{curr}}, C_{\texttt{est}_1}, C_{\texttt{est}_2}, ..., C_{\texttt{est}_M}\}$

being the set of the current class and the classes estimated after extracting each feature, the conditional risk of the $\texttt{extract}_k$ action is defined as follows.

$$R\,(\,\texttt{extract}_k|x,\mathcal{C}) = \sum_{j=1}^{N} P(C_{\texttt{actual}} = j|x) \times \tag{2}$$

$$\begin{bmatrix} P(C_{\texttt{curr}}=j|x)\ P(C_{\texttt{est}_k} = j|x)\ \texttt{cost}_k\ + \\ P(C_{\texttt{curr}}\neq j|x)\ P(C_{\texttt{est}_k}\neq j|x)\ P(C_{\texttt{curr}}=C_{\texttt{est}_k}|x)\ [\texttt{cost}_k + \texttt{PENALTY}]\ + \\ P(C_{\texttt{curr}}\neq j|x)\ P(C_{\texttt{est}_k}\neq j|x)\ P(C_{\texttt{curr}}\neq C_{\texttt{est}_k}|x)\ [\texttt{cost}_k + \texttt{PENALTY}]\ + \\ P(C_{\texttt{curr}}=j|x)\ P(C_{\texttt{est}_k}\neq j|x)\ [\texttt{cost}_k + \texttt{PENALTY}]\ + \\ P(C_{\texttt{curr}}\neq j|x)\ P(C_{\texttt{est}_k}=j|x)\ [\texttt{cost}_k - \texttt{REWARD}] \end{bmatrix}$$

$$R\,(\,\texttt{extract}_k|x,\mathcal{C}) = \sum_{j=1}^{N} P(C_{\texttt{actual}} = j|x) \times \tag{3}$$

$$\begin{bmatrix} P(C_{\texttt{curr}}=j|x) & P(C_{\texttt{est}_k}=j|x) & \texttt{cost}_k\ + \\ [1-P(C_{\texttt{curr}}=j|x)] & [1-P(C_{\texttt{est}_k}=j|x)] & [\texttt{cost}_k + \texttt{PENALTY}]+ \\ P(C_{\texttt{curr}}=j|x) & [1-P(C_{\texttt{est}_k}=j|x)] & [\texttt{cost}_k + \texttt{PENALTY}]+ \\ [1-P(C_{\texttt{curr}}=j|x)] & P(C_{\texttt{est}_k}=j|x) & [\texttt{cost}_k - \texttt{REWARD}] \end{bmatrix}$$

$$R\,(\,\texttt{extract}_k|x,\mathcal{C}) = \sum_{j=1}^{N} P(C_{\texttt{actual}} = j|x) \times \tag{4}$$

$$\begin{bmatrix} \texttt{cost}_k\ + \\ [1-P(C_{\texttt{est}_k} = j|x)]\ \texttt{PENALTY}\ + \\ P(C_{\texttt{est}_k} = j|x)\ [1-P(C_{\texttt{curr}} = j)|x]\ [-\texttt{REWARD}] \end{bmatrix}$$

Equation 4 implies that the extraction of feature F_k requires paying for its cost. It also implies that the $\texttt{extract}_k$ action is penalized with PENALTY if the class estimated after feature extraction is incorrect and is rewarded with REWARD if this estimated class is correct but it is different than the currently estimated class. Similarly, for a particular instance x, we derive the conditional risk of the classify and the reject actions in Equations 5 and 6, respectively.

$$R\,(\,\texttt{classify}|x,\mathcal{C}) = \sum_{j=1}^{N} P(C_{\texttt{actual}} = j|x) \times \tag{5}$$

$$\big[P(C_{\texttt{curr}} = j|x)\ [-\texttt{REWARD}] + [1-P(C_{\texttt{curr}} = j|x)]\ \texttt{PENALTY}\big]$$

$$R\,(\,\texttt{reject}|x,\mathcal{C}) = \sum_{j=1}^{N} P(C_{\texttt{actual}} = j|x) \times \tag{6}$$

$$\begin{bmatrix} \left[[1-P(C_{\texttt{curr}} = j|x)]\ \prod_{m=1}^{M} [1-P(C_{\texttt{est}_m} = j|x)]\right]\ [-\texttt{REWARD}]\ + \\ \left[1-[1-P(C_{\texttt{curr}} = j|x)]\ \prod_{m=1}^{M} [1-P(C_{\texttt{est}_m} = j|x)]\right]\ \texttt{PENALTY}\ + \end{bmatrix}$$

Equation 5 means that classifying the instance with the current classifier (classify action) is rewarded with REWARD if this is a correct classification and is penalized with PENALTY otherwise. Equation 6 means that rejecting the classification is only rewarded with REWARD if neither the estimated classes nor the current class is correct; otherwise, it is penalized with PENALTY.

As given in Equations 4, 5, and 6, the conditional risks are computed using the posterior probabilities. Posterior probabilities $P(C_{\texttt{curr}} = j|x)$ can be calculated by the current classifier before any possible feature extraction, since all of its features are already extracted. On the other hand, posterior probabilities $P(C_{\texttt{est}_k} = j|x)$ could not be known prior to extracting feature F_k. Thus, these posteriors should be estimated making use of the currently available information. For that, we use estimators which are trained as follows: First, we learn the parameters of the classifier Y_k that use both the previously extracted features and feature F_k on training samples. Then, for each of these samples, we compute the posterior probabilities using the classifier Y_k. Subsequently, we train the estimators to learn these posteriors by using only the previously extracted features. Note that similar posterior probability estimations have been achieved by using linear perceptrons [4] and dynamic Bayesian networks [11].

In the computation of posterior probabilities $P(C_{\texttt{actual}} = j|x)$ in Equation 4, we employ the posteriors computed for the current classifier as well as those estimated for the classifiers whose features are to be extracted. To do so, for each class, we multiply the corresponding posteriors, and then normalize them such that $\sum_{j=1}^{N} P(C_{\texttt{actual}} = j|x) = 1$. For Equations 5 and 6, we only use the posterior probabilities of the current classifier, since the corresponding actions (`classify` and `reject`) require stopping feature extraction, and thus, no additional features are extracted after taking these actions.

In order to dynamically select a subset of features for the classification of a given instance x, our algorithm first computes the conditional risk of the `classify` action, the $\texttt{extract}_k$ action for each feature F_k that is not extracted yet, and the `reject` action as given in Equations 4, 5, and 6, and then selects the action for which the conditional risk is minimum. This selection is sequentially conducted until either the `classify` or the `reject` action is selected.

3 Experiments

We conduct our experiments on the Thyroid Dataset[1] in which there are three classes (hypothyroid, hyperthyroid, and normal) and 21 features. The first 16 features are based on the answers of the questions that are asked to a patient; thus, we assign no cost to them. The next four features are obtained from the blood tests and the assigned cost of these blood tests is {\$22.78, \$11.41, \$14.51, \$11.41}. The last feature is calculated from the nineteenth and twentieth features; we use the last feature in classification only if these two features are already extracted.

In our experiments, we use decision tree classifiers and Parzen window estimators whose window function defines hypercubes. We train both classifiers and estimators on the training set. For Parzen window estimators, the test set

[1] This dataset is available at the UCI repository [16].

Table 2. Confusion matrix for the test set when our test-cost sensitive classification algorithm is used. Here, the reduction in the overall feature extraction cost is 47.61%.

		Selected class			Reject
		Hypothyroid	Hyperthyroid	Normal	cases
Actual class	Hypothyroid	70	0	0	3
	Hyperthyroid	0	173	0	4
	Normal	13	23	3140	2

Table 3. Confusion matrix for the test set when all features are used in classification

		Selected class		
		Hypothyroid	Hyperthyroid	Normal
Actual class	Hypothyroid	70	0	3
	Hyperthyroid	0	173	4
	Normal	13	29	3136

includes some samples for which there is no training sample falling in the specified hypercubes. For these samples, we do not penalize any feature extraction since the estimators provide no information and we consider only the posteriors obtained on the current classifier to compute the conditional risks.

In Table 2, we report the test results obtained by our algorithm. In this table, we provide the confusion matrix for the test set, indicating the number of samples for which the `reject` action is taken. These results are obtained when `REWARD` and `PENALTY` values are selected to be 100 and 10000, respectively. For comparison, in Table 3, we also report the confusion matrix for the test set when all features are used in classification; here, we also use a decision tree classifier (herein referred to as *all-feature-classifier*). Tables 2 and 3 demonstrate that, compared to the *all-feature-classifier*, our algorithm yields the same number of correct classifications for hypothyroid and hyperthyroid classes. Moreover, for these classes, our algorithm does not lead to any misclassification. For the samples misclassified by the *all-feature-classifier*, our algorithm takes the `reject` action, reducing the overall misclassification cost. Furthermore, for normal class, our algorithm yields a larger number of correct classifications. For the selected parameters, the decrease in the overall feature extraction cost is 47.61%. This demonstrates that the proposed algorithm significantly decreases the overall feature extraction cost without decreasing the accuracy.

In the proposed algorithm, there are two free model parameters: `REWARD` and `PENALTY`. Next, we investigate the effects of these parameters on the classification accuracy and the reduction in the overall cost of feature extraction. For that, we fix one of these parameters and observe the accuracy and the cost reduction in feature extraction as a function of the other parameter. In Figures 1(a) and 1(b), we present the test set accuracy, for each individual class, and the percentage of the reduction in the overall feature extraction cost as a function of the `PENALTY` value when `REWARD` is set to 100. These figures demonstrate that as the penalty

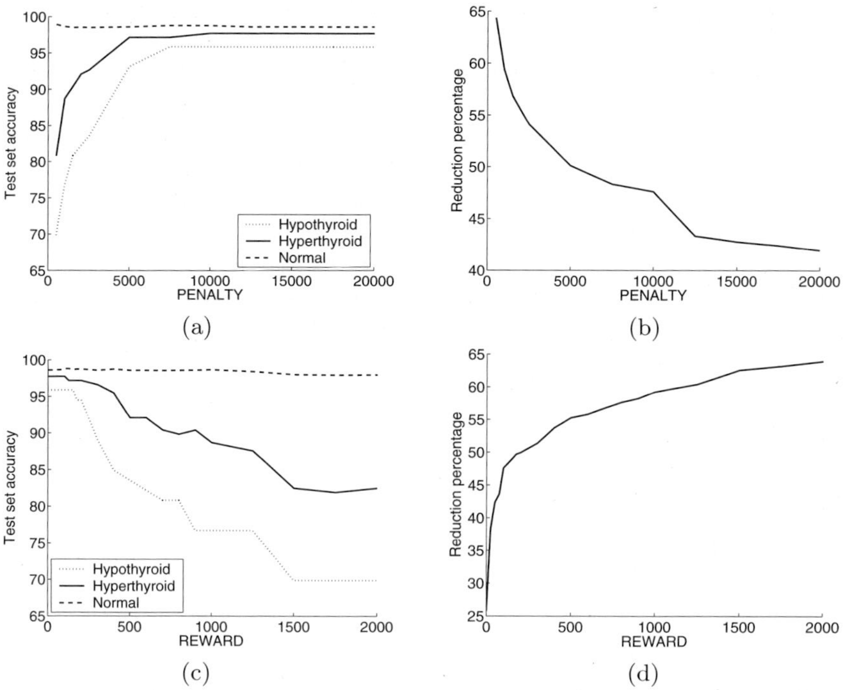

Fig. 1. For our test-cost sensitive classification algorithm, (a)-(b) the test set accuracy and the percentage of the cost reduction as a function of PENALTY when REWARD is set to 100, and (c)-(d) the test set accuracy and the percentage of the cost reduction as a function of REWARD when PENALTY is set to 10000.

of misclassifications and selecting the `reject` action increases, the number of correctly classified samples, for especially hypothyroid and hyperthyroid classes, increases too. With the increasing `PENALTY` value, the algorithm tends to extract more number of features not to misclassify the samples, leading to the decrease in the cost reduction. Similarly, in Figures 1(c) and 1(d), we present the test set accuracy and the percentage of the cost reduction as a function of the `REWARD` value when `PENALTY` is set to 10000. These figures demonstrate that the test set accuracy for hypothyroid and hyperthyroid classes decreases with the increasing `REWARD` value. As shown in Equations 4, 5, and 6, as the `REWARD` value increases, the conditional risks decrease. The factor that affects the conditional risks for all actions is $P(C_{\texttt{curr}})$. While this decrease is proportional to $P(C_{\texttt{curr}})$ for the `classify` action, it is proportional to $[1-P(C_{\texttt{curr}})]$ for the $\texttt{extract}_k$ and `reject` actions. This indicates that when $P(C_{\texttt{curr}})$ is just slightly larger than $[1-P(C_{\texttt{curr}})]$ (e.g., 0.51), the decrease in the conditional risk for the `classify` action is larger. Thus, as the `REWARD` value increases, the algorithm tends to classify the samples without extracting additional features. While this decreases the classification accuracy, it increases the cost reduction.

4 Conclusion

This work introduces a novel Bayesian decision theoretical framework to incorporate the cost of feature extraction into the cost of misclassification errors utilizing the consistency behavior for the first time. In this framework, the loss function is conditioned with the current decision and the estimated decisions that are to be taken after the feature extraction as well as the consistency among the current and the estimated decisions. By using this framework, we propose a new test-cost sensitive learning algorithm that selects a subset of features, dynamically for each instance. The experiments on a medical diagnosis dataset demonstrate that the proposed algorithm leads to a significant decrease (47.61%) in the feature extraction cost without decreasing the classification accuracy.

References

1. Turney, P.D.: Types of cost in inductive concept learning. In: Workshop on Cost-Sensitive Learning. ICML 2000, Stanford, CA (2000)
2. Duda, O.R., Hart, E.P., Stork, G.D.: Pattern Classification. Wiley-Interscience, New York (2001)
3. Turney, P.D.: Low size-complexity inductive logic programming: The East-West Challenge considered as a problem in cost-sensitive classification. In: ILP 1995 (1995)
4. Demir, C., Alpaydin, E.: Cost-conscious classifier ensembles. Pattern Recognit Lett. 26, 2206–2214 (2005)
5. Norton, S.W.: Generating better decision trees. In: IJCAI 1989, Detroit, MI (1989)
6. Nunez, M.: The use of background knowledge in decision tree induction. Mach. Learn. 6, 231–250 (1991)
7. Tan, M.: Cost-sensitive learning of classification knowledge and its applications in robotics. Mach. Learn. 13, 7–33 (1993)
8. Turney, P.D.: Cost-sensitive classification: Empirical evaluation of a hybrid genetic decision tree induction algorithm. J. Artif. Intell. Res. 2, 369–409 (1995)
9. Davis, J.V., Ha, J., Rossbach, C.J., Ramadan, H.E., Witchel, E.: Cost-sensitive decision tree learning for forensic classification. In: Fürnkranz, J., Scheffer, T., Spiliopoulou, M. (eds.) ECML 2006. LNCS (LNAI), vol. 4212, Springer, Heidelberg (2006)
10. Yang, Q., Ling, C., Chai, X., Pan, R.: Test-cost sensitive classification on data missing values. IEEE T Knowl. Data. En. 18, 626–638 (2006)
11. Zhang, Y., Ji, Q.: Active and dynamic information fusion for multisensor systems with dynamic Bayesian networks. IEEE T. Syst. Man. Cy. B 36 (2006)
12. Gunduz, C.: Value of representation in pattern recognition. M.S. thesis, Bogazici University, Istanbul, Turkey (2001)
13. Greiner, R., Grove, A.J., Roth, D.: Learning cost-sensitive active classifiers. Artif. Intell. 139, 137–174 (2002)
14. Zubek, V.B., Dietterich, T.G.: Pruning improves heuristic search for cost-sensitive learning. In: ICML 2002, San Francisco, CA (2002)
15. Ji, S., Carin, L.: Cost-sensitive feature acquisition and classification. Pattern Recogn 40, 1474–1485 (2007)
16. Blake, C.L., Merz, C.J.: UCI Repository of machine learning databases (1998), Available at http://www.ics.uci.edu/~mlearn/MLRepository.html

Probabilistic Models for Action-Based Chinese Dependency Parsing

Xiangyu Duan, Jun Zhao, and Bo Xu

Institute of Automation, Chinese Academy of Sciences, Beijing, China
{xyduan,jzhao}@nlpr.ia.ac.cn, xubo@hitic.ia.ac.cn

Abstract. Action-based dependency parsing, also known as deterministic dependency parsing, has often been regarded as a time efficient parsing algorithm while its parsing accuracy is a little lower than the best results reported by more complex parsing models. In this paper, we compare action-based dependency parsers with complex parsing methods such as all-pairs parsers on Penn Chinese Treebank. For Chinese dependency parsing, action-based parsers outperform all-pairs parsers. But action-based parsers do not compute the probability of the whole dependency tree. They only determine parsing actions stepwisely by a trained classifier. To globally model parsing actions of all steps that are taken on the input sentence, we propose two kinds of probabilistic parsing action models that can compute the probability of the whole dependency tree. Results show that our probabilistic parsing action models perform better than the original action-based parsers, and our best result improves much over them.

Keywords: probabilistic, action-based, Chinese dependency parsing.

1 Introduction

Syntactic parsing is one of the most important tasks in Natural Language Processing (NLP). The mainstream of syntactic parsing is the statistical method that often focuses on generative and discriminative models. These models use different optimization objects for parameter training, and use non-deterministic parsing techniques, usually employing some kind of dynamic programming, to compute the probability of the candidate trees. The tree with the highest probability is outputted. If reranking is used, n-best trees are outputted and a different ranking scheme is adopted to rerank these trees.

All these methods perform well while the time complexity is very high due to the computation of candidate trees. Action-based parsers, also known as deterministic parsers, emerge as efficient algorithms that take parsing actions stepwisely on the input sentence, and reduce the time complexity to linear or quadratic with the sentence's length. Action-based parsers were firstly proposed for dependency parsing [1, 2, 3, 4]. Later, Sagae and Lavie [5] and Wang et al. [6] applied deterministic parsing for phrase structure parsing.

On the standard data set of Penn English Treebank, action-based parsers show great efficiency in terms of time, offering accuracy just below the state-of-the-art

J.N. Kok et al. (Eds.): ECML 2007, LNAI 4701, pp. 559–566, 2007.

parsing methods. In this paper, for Chinese dependency parsing, we use action-based algorithms [2, 4] and compare them with state-of-the-art parsing methods such as a generative constituent parser [7] and a discriminative all-pairs dependency parser (MSTParser version 0.2) [8, 9] on Penn Chinese Treebank version 5.0 [10]. The comparison has never been done before. Contrary to English parsing, we get the result that action-based parsers perform much better than the generative constituent parser and the discriminative all-pairs dependency parser.

Furthermore, we observe that original action-based parsers are greedy. They do not score the entire dependency tree, and only stepwisely choose the most probable parsing action. To avoid greedy property and further enhance the performance of the original action-based parsers, we propose two kinds of probabilistic models of parsing actions at all steps. Results show that our two probabilistic models perform better than the original action-based dependency parsers. Our best dependency parser improves much over them and gets the state-of-the-art performance.

This paper is organized as follows. Section 2 introduces the action-based dependency parsers that are basic components of our models. In section 3, we present our two probabilistic models for the modeling of parsing actions. Experiments and results are presented in section 4. We get a conclusion in section 5.

2 Introduction of Action-Based Dependency Parsing

There are two representative action-based dependency parsing algorithms which are proposed respectively by Yamada and Matsumoto [2], Nivre [3]. Action-based parsing algorithms regard parsing as a sequence of parsing actions that are taken step by step on the input sentence. Parsing actions construct dependency relations between words. A classifier is trained to classify parsing actions. During testing, parsing actions are determined by the trained classifier.

Next we briefly describe Yamada and Matsumoto's method as an illustration of action-based dependency parsing. The other representative method of Nivre also parses sentences in a similar deterministic manner except different data structure and parsing actions.

Figure 1 illustrates the parsing process of Yamada and Matsumoto's method. The example sentence is "Work achieves remarkable success." There are three kinds of parsing actions used to construct the dependency relation between two focus words. In figure 1, the two focus words are in black bold boxes. Every parsing action results in a new parsing state, which includes all elements of the current partially built tree. In the training phase, features extracted from current parsing state and corresponding parsing actions compose the training data. In the testing phase, the classifier determines which parsing action should be taken based on the features. The parsing algorithm ends when there is no further dependency relation can be made on the whole sentence. The details of the three parsing actions are as follows:

***LEFT*:** it constructs the dependency that the right focus word depends on the left focus word.

***RIGHT*:** it constructs the dependency that the left focus word depends on the right focus word.

***SHIFT*:** it does not construct dependency, just moves the parsing focus.

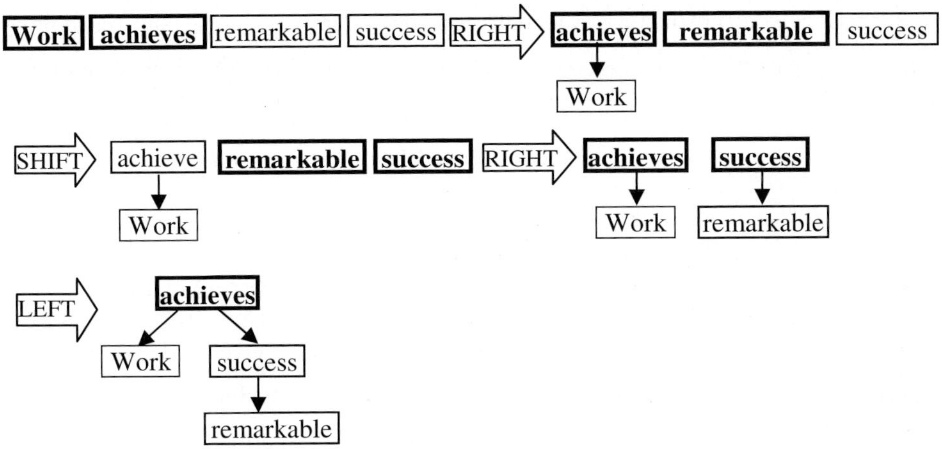

Fig. 1. The example of parsing process of the method of Yamada and Matsumoto

3 Probabilistic Models of Parsing Actions

Action-based dependency parsing introduced in section 2 is greedy. They only choose the most probable parsing action at every parsing step. To overcome this shortsightedness, we propose two kinds of probabilistic models of parsing actions to compute the probability of whole dependency tree. The two models are different from sequential and structural learning models in a way that is explained at the end of section 3.1.

3.1 Parsing Action Chain Model (PACM)

The parsing process can be viewed as a Markov Chain. At every parsing step, there are several candidate parsing actions. The object of this model is to find the right sequence of parsing actions that constructs the dependency tree. As shown in figure 1, the action sequence "***RIGHT*** -> ***SHIFT*** -> ***RIGHT*** -> ***LEFT***" is the right sequence.

Firstly, we should define the probability of the dependency tree conditioned on the input sentence.

$$P(T \mid S) = \prod_{i=1...n} P(d_i \mid d_0 ... d_{i-1}, S) . \quad (1)$$

where T denotes the dependency tree, S denotes the original input sentence, d_i denotes the parsing action at time step i. We add an artificial parsing action d_0 as initial action.

We introduce a variable $context_{d_i}$ to denote the resulting parsing state when the action d_i is taken on $context_{d_{i-1}}$. $context_{d_0}$ is the original input sentence.

Suppose $d_0 ... d_n$ are taken sequentially on the input sentence *S*, and result in a sequence of parsing states $context_{d_0} ... context_{d_n}$, then *P*(*T*|*S*) defined in equation (1) becomes as below:

$$\prod_{i=1...n} P(context_{d_i} \mid context_{d_0}, ..., context_{d_{i-1}}) \approx \prod_{i=1...n} P(context_{d_i} \mid context_{d_{i-1}}) \\ = \prod_{i=1...n} P(d_i \mid context_{d_{i-1}}) . \tag{2}$$

In equation (2), the second formula comes from the first formula by obeying the Markov assumption. Note that the third formula is about the classifier of parsing actions. It denotes the probability of the parsing action d_i given the parsing state $context_{d_{i-1}}$. If we train a classifier that can predict with probability output, then we can compute *P(T|S)* by computing the product of the probabilities of parsing actions. The classifier we use throughout this paper is Libsvm [11], which can train multi-class classifier and support training and predicting with probability output.

For this model, the object is to choose the parsing action sequence that constructs the dependency tree with the maximal probability.

$$\max P(T \mid S) = \max_{d_1 ... d_n} \prod_{i=1...n} P(d_i \mid context_{d_{i-1}}) . \tag{3}$$

Because this model chooses the most probable sequence, not the most probable parsing action at only one step, it avoids the greedy property of the original parsers.

Note that probabilistic models of parsing actions decompose parsing problem into actions. This is the main difference between them and traditional structural learning models, which decompose parsing problem into dependency pairs solely over graphs (dependency trees). PACM is related with Searn [14], which also decomposes structural learning into incremental decisions. But Searn uses policy iterations to find the optimal decision sequence.

At each step, although there are same candidate parsing actions, the parsing states are variant. This property makes exact inference like Viterbi unsuitable for the decoding. Best-first search is the appropriate one. Considering efficiency, we use beam search for the decoding of this model. *m* is used to denote the beam size. At every parsing step, all parsing states are ordered (or partially *m* ordered) according to their probabilities. Probability of a parsing state is determined by multiplying the probabilities of actions that generate that state. Then we choose *m* best parsing states for this step, and next parsing step only consider these *m* best parsing states. Parsing terminates when the first entire dependency tree is constructed.

3.2 Parsing Action Phrase Model (PAPM)

In the Parsing Action Chain Model (PACM), actions are competing at every parsing step. That is, only *m* best parsing states resulted by the corresponding actions are kept at every step. But for the parsing problem, it is reasonable that actions are competing for which next phrase should be built. This is the motivation of Parsing Action Phrase Model (PAPM). For dependency syntax, one phrase consists of the head word and all its dependents. The key question is when the next phrase is built. This can be solved by dividing parsing actions into two classes: constructing action and shifting action.

If a phrase is built after an action is performed, the action is called constructing action. In Yamada and Matsumoto's algorithm, constructing actions are ***LEFT*** and ***RIGHT***. For example, if ***LEFT*** is taken, the right focus word has found all its dependents and becomes the head of this new phrase. Note that one word with no dependents can also be viewed as a phrase if its dependence on other word is constructed. Nivre's method has the similar constructing actions.

If no phrase is built after an action is performed, the action is called shifting action. Such action is ***SHIFT*** in both Yamada and Matsumoto's method and Nivre's method.

We introduce a new concept: parsing action phrase. It is denoted by A_i, the *i*th parsing action phrase. It can be expanded as $A_i \rightarrow b_{j-k}...b_{j-1}a_j$, where a is constructing action and b is shifting action, j indexes the time step. That is, parsing action phrase A_i is a sequence of parsing actions, which consists a constructing action at last step and all its preceding shifting actions. It is this action sequence that constructs the next syntactic phrase.

For example, consider the parsing process in figure 1, A_1 is "***RIGHT***", A_2 is "***SHIFT***, ***RIGHT***", A_3 is "***LEFT***".

The probability of the dependency tree given the input sentence is redefined as:

$$P(T \mid S) = \prod_{i=1...n} P(A_i \mid A_1...A_{i-1}, S) = \prod_{i=1...n} P(A_i \mid context_{A_{i-1}}) . \tag{4}$$

where $context_{A_i}$ is the parsing state resulted by a sequence of actions taken on $context_{A_{i-1}}$. The object in this model is to find the most probable sequence of parsing action phrases.

Similar with Parsing Action Chain Model (PACM), we use beam search for the decoding of Parsing Action Phrase Model (PAPM). The difference is that PAPM do not keep m best parsing states at every parsing step. Instead, PAPM keep m best states which are corresponding to m best current parsing action phrases (several steps of ***SHIFT*** and the last step of a constructing action).

Table 1. The division of CHTB data set.

	CHTB files	word num
Train set	001-815, 1001-1136	434,936
Development set	886-931, 1148-1151	21,595
Test set	816-885, 1137-1147	50,319

4 Experiments and Results

4.1 Experimental Setup

The data set for the experiments is taken from Penn Chinese Treebank (CHTB) version 5.0 [10], consisting of 500k words mostly from different resources of Xinhua newswire, Sinorama news magazine and Hongkong news. To balance each resource in train set, development set and test set, we split the data set as in table 1. We use head rules reported in Sun and Jurafsky's work [12] to convert constituent structure to dependency structure

We implement Yamada and Matsumo's method, and the optimal size of the feature context window is six, which consists of left two sub trees, two focus words and right two sub trees. Nivre's method is also implemented, and the optimal feature template is the same with the work [4].

The following metrics are used for evaluation:

Dependency accuracy (DA): The proportion of non-root words (excluding punctuations) that are assigned the correct head.

Root accuracy (RA): The proportion of root words that are correctly found.

Complete match (CM): The proportion of sentences whose dependency structures are completely correct.

4.2 Comparison of Action-Based Parsers with Generative Constituent Parser and Discriminative All-Pairs Parser

For the comparison, we use dbparser, a generative constituent parser implemented by Daniel M. Bikel [7], and MSTParser version 0.2, a discriminative dependency parser implemented by Ryan Mcdonald [8, 9]. The dbparser is an emulating version of Collins parser [13]. We use the same head rules as that used in this paper for both training and testing of dbparser. We present both first-order ($MSTParser_1$) and second-order ($MSTParser_2$) performances of MSTParser. The comparison of these parsers is presented in part of table 2.

Table 2. Performances of different Parsers

	DA	RA	CM
dbparser	79.84	69.03	27.56
$MSTParser_1$	80.83	68.20	25.72
$MSTParser_2$	82.26	69.36	28.23
Nivre	82.52	68.19	29.82
Yamada	82.82	70.13	30.39
PACM	84.05	73.49	32.34
PAPM	**84.36**	**73.70**	**32.70**

From table 2, we can see that action-based parsers perform better than both dbparser and MSTParser. It is interesting that Wang etc. [6] got the similar results of Chinese constituent parsing on Penn Chinese Treebank. Their experiments showed that action-based parser outperform state-of-the-art parsers. This observation is contrary as to English parsing.

4.3 The Performances of Parsers Based on Action Modeling

Due to the simplicity and comparable performance of Yamada and Matsumoto's method, only their method is adopted in parsers which are based on action modeling.

The performances of these parsers are presented in part of table 2. We can see that the two probabilistic models (PACM and PAPM) all perform much better than the original action-based parsers. Parsing action phrase model (PAPM) gets the highest performance with 9% error reduction over Yamada and Matsumoto's method considering DA, 12% error reduction over MSTParser's second-order model, 22% error reduction over dbparser. It shows the great effectiveness in avoiding greediness when we save *m*-best parses at each parsing step, and the promising tree can possibly rank first at the end of parsing.

We also do the experiments of outputting n-best parses by using Parsing Action Chain Model (PACM) and Parsing Action Phrase Model (PAPM) respectively. The performance is listed in table 3, which presents the performance of a "perfect" parser that magically picks the best parse tree from the top *n* trees. The best parse tree has the highest average accuracy when compared to the Treebank. In terms of outputting n-best parses, PAPM is superior to PACM by a large margin and shows its propriety for reranking research which appears to be a promising work to improve the performance.

Table 3. The performance of a "perfect" parser that picks best among 20-best trees

	DA	RA	CM
PACM	88.64	84.78	46.35
PAPM	**91.30**	**86.88**	**54.59**

5 Conclusion

This paper compares the original action-based dependency parsers with state-of-the-art parsing methods such as a generative constituent parser and a discriminative all-pairs dependency parser for Chinese dependency parsing. The results show that original action-based dependency parsers perform best. Based on the observation that original action-based parsers are greedy, we propose two kinds of probabilistic models of the parsing actions for Chinese dependency parsing. The results show that our probabilistic parsing action models improve much over original action-based parsers.

Acknowledgements

This work was supported by Hi-tech Research and Development Program of China under grant No. 2006AA01Z144, the Natural Sciences Foundation of China under grant No. 60673042, and the Natural Science Foundation of Beijing under grant No. 4052027, 4073043.

References

1. Kudo, T., Matsumoto, Y.: Japanese dependency analysis using cascaded chunking. In: Proceedings of the Sixth Conference on ComputationalLanguage Learning (CoNLL) (2002)
2. Yamada, H., Matsumoto, Y.: Statistical dependency analysis with support vector machines. In: Proceedings of the 8th International Workshop on Parsing Technologies (IWPT) (2003)
3. Nivre, J.: An efficient algorithm for projective dependency parsing. In: Proceedings of the 8th International Workshop on Parsing Technologies (IWPT) (2003)
4. Nivre, J., Scholz, M.: Deterministic dependency parsing of English text. In: Proceedings of the 20th International Conference on Computational Linguistics (COLING) (2004)
5. Sagae, K., Lavie, A.: A classifier-based parser with linear run-time complexity. In: Proceedings of the 9th International Workshop on Parsing Technologies (IWPT) (2005)
6. Wang, M., Sagae, K., Mitamura, T.: A fast, accurate deterministic parser for Chinese. In: Proceedings of the 44th AnnualMeeting of the Association for ComputationalLinguistics (ACL) (2006)
7. Daniel, M.: Bikel, On the Parameter Space of Generative Lexicalized Statistical Parsing Models. Ph.D. thesis, University of Pennsylvania (2004)
8. McDonald, R., Crammer, K., Pereira, F.: Online Large-margin Training of Dependency Parsers. In: Proceedings of the 43rd AnnualMeeting of the Association for Computational Linguistics (ACL) (2005)
9. McDonald, R., Pereira, F.: Online Learning of Approximate Dependency Parsing Algorithms. In: Proceedings of the 11th European Chapter of the Association for Computational Linguistics (EACL) (2006)
10. Xue, N., Xia, F., Chiou, F.-D., Palmer, M.: The Penn Chinese Treebank: Phrase structure annotation of a large corpus. Natural Language Engineering (2005)
11. Chang, C.-C., Lin, C.-J.: LIBSVM: A library for support vector machines (2005)
12. Sun, H., Jurafsky, D.: Shallow semantic parsing of Chinese. In: Proceedings of the HLT/NAACL '04 (2004)
13. Collins, M.: Head-Driven Statistical Models for Natural Language Parsing. Ph.D. thesis, University of Pennsylvania (1999)
14. Daum‘e III, H., Langford, I.J., Marcu, D.: Search-based structured prediction, 2006 (Submission)

Learning Directed Probabilistic Logical Models: Ordering-Search Versus Structure-Search

Daan Fierens, Jan Ramon, Maurice Bruynooghe, and Hendrik Blockeel

K.U.Leuven, Dept. of Computer Science, Celestijnenlaan 200A, 3001 Heverlee, Belgium
{Daan.Fierens,Jan.Ramon,Maurice.Bruynooghe,
Hendrik.Blockeel}@cs.kuleuven.be

Abstract. We discuss how to learn non-recursive directed probabilistic logical models from relational data. This problem has been tackled before by upgrading the structure-search algorithm initially proposed for Bayesian networks. In this paper we propose to upgrade another algorithm, namely ordering-search, since for Bayesian networks this was found to work better than structure-search. We experimentally compare the two upgraded algorithms on two relational domains. We conclude that there is no significant difference between the two algorithms in terms of quality of the learnt models while ordering-search is significantly faster.

Keywords: statistical relational learning, probabilistic logical models, inductive logic programming, Bayesian networks, probability trees, structure learning.

1 Introduction

A Bayesian network is a compact specification of a joint probability distribution on a set of random variables under the form of a directed acyclic graph (the *structure*) and a set of conditional probability distributions (CPDs). When learning from data the goal is usually to find the structure and CPDs that maximize a certain scoring criterion. The most traditional approach to learning Bayesian networks is *structure-search* [5]. Recently, an alternative algorithm called *ordering-search* was introduced that was found to perform at least as good as structure-search while usually being faster [9].

The past few years a variety of formalisms has been introduced to describe probabilistic logical models. Many of these formalisms deal with directed models that are upgrades of Bayesian networks to the relational case. Learning algorithms have been developed for several such formalisms [4,6,7]. Most of these algorithms are essentially upgrades of the structure-search algorithm for Bayesian networks. In this paper we investigate how ordering-search can be upgraded to the relational case.

The contributions of this paper are two-fold. First, we upgrade the ordering-search algorithm towards learning non-recursive directed probabilistic logical models. Second, we experimentally compare the resulting algorithm with the upgraded structure-search algorithm on two relational domains. We use the formalism Logical Bayesian Networks but the proposed approach is also valid for related formalisms such as Probabilistic Relational Models, Bayesian Logic Programs and Relational Bayesian Networks [1].

This paper is structured as follows. We review Logical Bayesian Networks in Section 2. We discuss learning in Section 3 and show experimental results in Section 4. We conclude in Section 5. More details about Sections 2 to 4 are given in the full paper [3].

J.N. Kok et al. (Eds.): ECML 2007, LNAI 4701, pp. 567–574, 2007.

2 Logical Bayesian Networks

We now briefly review Logical Bayesian Networks. For details and formal semantics we refer to the full papers [1,3]. A Logical Bayesian Network or LBN is essentially a specification of a Bayesian network conditioned on some logical input predicates describing the domain of discourse. For instance, when modelling the well-known 'university' domain [4], we would use predicates $student/1$, $course/1$, $prof/1$, $teaches/2$ and $takes/2$ with their obvious meanings. The semantics of an LBN is that, given an interpretation of these logical predicates, the LBN induces a particular Bayesian network.

In LBNs random variables are represented as ground atoms built from certain special predicates, the *probabilistic predicates*. For instance, if $intelligence/1$ is a probabilistic predicate then the atom $intelligence(ann)$ is called a probabilistic atom and represents a random variable. Which random variables exist for a particular interpretation of the logical predicates is determined by a set of random variable declarations [1]. An LBN contains two parts that are typically to be learned: a set of dependency clauses and a set of logical CPDs. We now illustrate this for the university domain.

The dependency clauses for the university domain are the following.

```
grade(S,C) | intelligence(S).
grade(S,C) | difficulty(C).
ranking(S) | grade(S,C).
satisfaction(S,C) | grade(S,C).
satisfaction(S,C) | ability(P) <- teaches(P,C).
rating(C) | satisfaction(S,C).
popularity(P) | rating(C) <- teaches(P,C).
```

Informally, the first clause should be read as "the grade of a student S for a course C depends on the intelligence of S" and the last clause as "the popularity of a professor P depends on the rating of a course C if P teaches C". In this clause, $popularity(P)$ is called the head, $rating(C)$ the body and $teaches(P, C)$ the context of the clause.

To quantify the dependencies specified by the dependency clauses, LBNs associate with each probabilistic predicate a so-called logical CPD. In this work we represent logical CPDs under the form of logical probability trees [2]. The internal nodes in the tree for a probabilistic atom p_{target} can contain a) tests on the values of probabilistic atoms that are parents of p_{target} according to the dependency clauses, b) conjunctions of logical literals, and c) combinations of the two. Leaves contain probability distributions on the values of p_{target}. An example of such a tree is shown in Figure 1.

3 Learning Non-recursive Logical Bayesian Networks

The dependency clauses and the logical CPDs in an LBN can be learned from a dataset of examples where each example consists of two parts: an interpretation of the logical predicates and an assignment of values to all ground random variables (as determined by the random variable declarations). The goal of learning is to find the clauses and logical CPDs that maximize the scoring criterion. In this paper we only deal with learning *non-recursive* LBNs, i.e. LBNs with non-recursive dependency clauses. For a discussion on the relation to learning recursive LBNs we refer to the full paper [3].

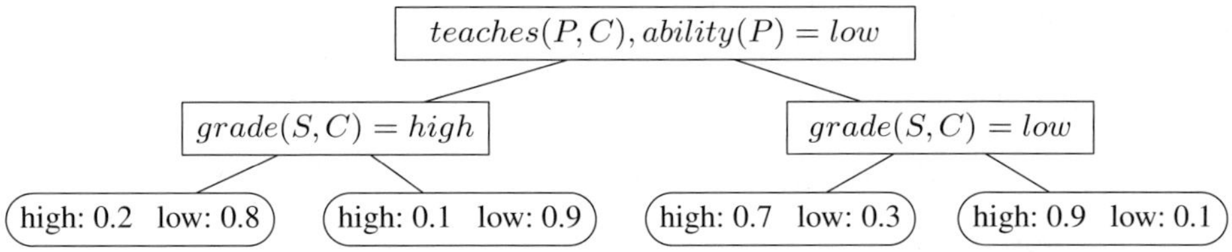

Fig. 1. Example of a logical CPD for $satisfaction(S, C)$. Tests in internal nodes are binary. When a test succeeds the left branch is taken, when it fails the right branch is taken.

Next we discuss a generic hillclimbing algorithm for learning non-recursive LBNs and give two instantiations of this generic algorithm. The first is the upgraded ordering-search algorithm that we introduce in this paper. The second is the existing upgraded structure-search algorithm. To stress the difference with Logical Bayesian Networks we will refer to ordinary Bayesian networks as 'propositional' Bayesian networks.

3.1 A Generic Hillclimbing Algorithm for Learning Logical Bayesian Networks

For LBNs, as for propositional Bayesian networks, there exists a generic learning algorithm of which the structure-search and ordering-search algorithms are specific instantiations. The idea is to perform hillclimbing-search through a space of solutions. In the case of structure-search a *solution* is a structure (a set of dependency clauses), while in the case of ordering-search it is an ordering on the set of probabilistic predicates. The generic algorithm is shown in Figure 2. The *neighbourhood* of the current solution is the set of solutions that can be obtained by making a small change to the current solution. The score of a solution is computed as the product of the scores of the logical CPDs for that solution. In this work we learn logical CPDs under the form of logical probability trees (like the tree in Figure 1). Which probabilistic predicates can be used as input for the tree is determined by the particular solution. We use the standard probability tree algorithms in the TILDE learner and score trees using the Bayesian Information Criterion (BIC) for logical probability trees [2]. Since BIC is a decomposable scoring criterion, the above algorithm can be implemented quite efficiently [3,5].

To use the generic algorithm of Figure 2 with a specific kind of solutions (structures, orderings, ...) one has to determine a) how to obtain an initial random solution[1], b) how to define the neighbourhood of a solution, and c) how to extract the dependency clauses from the learned solution. We will explain each of these issues for ordering-search in Section 3.2 and for structure-search in Section 3.3.

3.2 Ordering-Search

First we discuss the propositional case, then we discuss case of LBNs.

[1] The initial solution might influence the final result since the algorithm only converges to a local optimum. Hence, we experimented with multiple runs with different initial solutions but we found this not to be significantly better than a single run.

% find a good solution:
$Sol_{current}$ = random solution
repeat until convergence
  for each $Sol_{cand} \in neighbourhood(Sol_{current})$
    compute $\Delta score(Sol_{cand}) = score(Sol_{cand}) - score(Sol_{current})$
  end for
  $Sol_{current} = argmax(\Delta score(Sol_{cand}))$
end repeat
% extract the dependency clauses from the final solution:
for each probabilistic predicate p
  extract the dependency clauses for p from $Sol_{current}$
end for

Fig. 2. Generic hillclimbing algorithm for learning LBNs. In the two instantiations of this generic algorithm that we consider, a solution Sol corresponds to respectively a structure or an ordering.

Ordering-Search for Propositional Bayesian Networks. Ordering-search is based on the fact that it is relatively easy to learn a Bayesian network if an ordering on the set of random variables is given [9]. Such an ordering eliminates the possibility of cycles. This makes it possible to decide for each variable X separately which variables, from all variables preceding it in the ordering, are its parents. This can simply be done by learning a CPD for X under the assumption that 'selective' CPDs are used , i.e. CPDs that select from all candidate inputs the relevant inputs (for instance conditional probability tables with a bound on the number of effective inputs [9]). However, the score of the Bayesian network that is learned in this way depends heavily on the quality of the ordering that is used. Hence, the idea of ordering-search is to perform hillclimbing through the space of possible orderings, in each step applying the above procedure.

Teyssier and Koller [9] experimentally compared structure-search and ordering-search and found that ordering-search is always at least as good as structure-search and usually faster. As an explanation they note that the space of orderings is smaller than the space of structures and that ordering-search has no costly acyclicity checks.

Ordering-Search for Logical Bayesian Networks. Until now ordering-search has not yet been upgraded to the case of non-recursive directed probabilistic logical models. The above conclusions from the propositional case motivated us to investigate this. We now show how to upgrade ordering-search towards learning non-recursive LBNs.

Similar to the case of propositional Bayesian networks, it is easy to learn an LBN if an *ordering on the set of probabilistic predicates* is given. We can then learn an LBN simply by learning for each probabilistic predicate p a logical probability tree with as inputs all predicates preceding p in the ordering. Ordering-search corresponds to applying the generic algorithm of Figure 2 with orderings as solutions, this is basically hillclimbing-search through the space of orderings. The neighbourhood of an ordering O is defined as the set of orderings that can be obtained by swapping a pair of adjacent predicates in O. As an initial ordering we use a random ordering.

Apart from using orderings on the set of predicates instead of on the set of random variables, there are two major differences between our algorithm and the propositional algorithm. First, we use logical probability trees instead of simple conditional probability tables. Second, in the case of LBNs once we found the optimal ordering and the logical CPDs for this ordering, we still need an extra step to extract the dependency clauses from these logical CPDs. We now discuss the latter in more detail.

Extracting the Dependency Clauses from the Logical CPDs. Below we explain how to extract the clauses from a logical probability tree. The goal is to find the most specific set of clauses that is 'consistent' with the tree [3]. To obtain an LBN, this procedure has to be applied to the probability tree for each probabilistic predicate.

When extracting clauses from a tree, we create a clause for each test on a probabilistic atom in a node of the tree. Call the atom that is tested p_{test}, the node N and the target atom of the tree p_{target}. In the most general case, apart from the test on p_{test}, the node N can contain a number of tests on other probabilistic atoms and a conjunction of logical literals. Call this conjunction l. We then create a clause of the form $p_{target} \mid p_{test} \leftarrow l, path(N)$, where $path(N)$ is a conjunction of logical literals that describes the path from the root to N. Each node on this path can contribute a number of logical literals to $path(N)$. A succeeded node contributes all logical literals that it contains. A failed node that does not contain any tests on probabilistic atoms contributes the negation of all its logical literals. All other failed nodes do not contribute to the path.

As an example, consider the probability tree in Figure 1. For this tree, p_{target} is $satisfaction(S, C)$. For the root node, p_{test} is $ability(P)$, l is $teaches(P, C)$ and the path is empty. For the internal node below the root to the left, p_{test} is $grade(S, C)$, l is empty and the path is $teaches(P, C)$. For the node below the root to the right, p_{test} is $grade(S, C)$ and l and the path are both empty. The three resulting clauses for these nodes are respectively the following.

```
satisfaction(S,C) | ability(P) <- teaches(P,C).
satisfaction(S,C) | grade(S,C) <- teaches(P,C).
satisfaction(S,C) | grade(S,C).
```

The second clause is redundant (it is a special case of the third) and can be dropped.

3.3 Structure-Search

Structure-search is the most traditional and most straightforward approach for learning propositional Bayesian networks [5]. It is essentially hillclimbing through the space of possible structures. The neighbourhood of the current structure typically consists of all acyclic structures that can be obtained by adding, deleting or reversing an edge.

The structure-search algorithm for propositional Bayesian networks has already been upgraded to the relational case for several formalisms [4,6,7]. The algorithm that we use for LBNs is very similar to these existing upgrades. The main difference is that we use logical probability trees instead of combining rules [6,7] or aggregates [4].

To derive a concrete structure-search algorithm for LBNs from the generic algorithm of Figure 2, we have to define the notion of a neighbourhood and define how an initial structure is obtained (note that the final step in the generic algorithm, extracting clauses from the solution, is not needed for structure-search since a solution is already a set of dependency clauses). We define the neighbourhood of the current structure as the set of all non-recursive structures that can be obtained by adding a dependency clause, deleting a clause or swapping the head and body of a clause in the current structure. To find an initial set of clauses we borrow some elements from the ordering-search algorithm. Specifically, we generate a random ordering, learn logical CPDs for this ordering and apply the procedure for extracting dependency clauses from logical CPDs. As a consequence, in our experiments ordering-search and structure-search always start from the same point. This ensures that an experimental comparison of both algorithms effectively evaluates the search process itself and not the starting point of the search.

4 Experiments

We first discuss the datasets and the experimental setup. Then we discuss our results.

4.1 Datasets and Experimental Setup

We perform experiments on two relational domains. First, we generate synthetic datasets of varying size from the given LBN for the university domain (see Section 2). We use 5, 10, 15, 31, 62, 125 and 250 examples. Each example corresponds to 230 random variables (describing 20 students, 10 courses and 5 professors) and examples are mutually independent. Second, we use the UWCSE dataset, a real-world dataset constructed by extracting information about graduate students, professors and courses from the web pages of a computer science department [8]. Since in this dataset relations are of special importance[2], we model them as probabilistic predicates, leading to what Getoor et al. call “relational uncertainty” [4]. This dataset consists of 5 disjoint subsets (each corresponding to a specific research area) and contains 9607 random variables in total (describing 140 students, 132 courses and 52 professors).

For all experiments we performed 5-fold cross validation. For the university domain, examples were assigned to folds randomly. For UWCSE, each fold corresponds to a research area. We report the average results over the folds and use two-tailed paired t-tests (with α=0.05) to assess the significance of differences between two algorithms.

We use six evaluation criteria. The first four criteria measure characteristics of the learned LBN: *normalized test log-likelihood* (the log-likelihood on the test data divided by the number of examples), *normalized train score* (the score on the training data divided by the number of examples; while not important in itself, this gives some additional insight into the results), *number of dependency clauses learned* (smaller is usually better because of ease of interpretation) and *number of correct dependency clauses learned* (we can only report this for the synthetic university domain since there we know the correct dependency clauses). The other two criteria measure the efficiency of the learning process: *runtime* and *average time per iteration* (in terms of the generic algorithm in Figure 2, one iteration is one step in the repeat loop; while not important in itself, this time gives an idea about the size of a neighbourhood and how efficiently all elements in a neighbourhood can be scored and hence helps to explain runtime).

[2] For supervised learning, for instance, the ‘advised by’ relation is often the target [8].

4.2 Results

The results for ordering-search (OS) and structure-search (SS) are shown in Table 1.

Table 1. Experimental results on various datasets. If the result for one of the two algorithms (OS or SS) is significantly better than the result for the other, the best result is indicated in bold.

Dataset	Method	LogLik(Test)	Score(Train)	#Clauses	#CorrectClauses	Time	TimePerIter
Univ5	OS	-1.3789	-1.3485	9.0	2.0	**27s**	**6s**
Univ5	SS	-1.3750	-1.3365	9.8	3.6	130s	17s
Univ5	empty	-1.4799	-1.4989	-	-	-	-
Univ10	OS	-1.3669	-1.3524	9.8	4.2	**33s**	11s
Univ10	SS	-1.3461	-1.3410	9.4	5.0	126s	20s
Univ10	empty	-1.4722	-1.4880	-	-	-	-
Univ15	OS	-1.3444	-1.3415	8.6	3.2	**42s**	**8s**
Univ15	SS	-1.3328	-1.3305	9.6	**3.8**	155s	20s
Univ15	empty	-1.4697	-1.4792	-	-	-	-
Univ31	OS	-1.3083	-1.3135	8.8	5.0	**43s**	**12s**
Univ31	SS	-1.3023	-1.3060	9.6	6.4	158s	24s
Univ31	empty	-1.4575	-1.4647	-	-	-	-
Univ62	OS	-1.3051	-1.3097	11.2	4.8	**63s**	**13s**
Univ62	SS	-1.2973	-1.3012	10.4	6.2	249s	30s
Univ62	empty	-1.4554	-1.4595	-	-	-	-
Univ125	OS	-1.2905	-1.2959	8.8	5.0	**99s**	**19s**
Univ125	SS	-1.2828	-1.2861	8.2	**6.6**	389s	62s
Univ125	empty	-1.4562	-1.4586	-	-	-	-
Univ250	OS	-1.3001	-1.3035	9.8	4.8	**154s**	62s
Univ250	SS	-1.2894	-1.2913	7.6	**6.4**	553s	84s
Univ250	empty	-1.4561	-1.4573	-	-	-	-
UWCSE	OS	-0.4288	-0.3539	15.2	-	**183s**	**43s**
UWCSE	SS	-0.4160	**-0.3489**	14.6	-	586s	93s
UWCSE	empty	-0.4631	-0.3961	-	-	-	-

Table 1 reports the *test log-likelihood* and *train score* for OS and SS and also for the 'empty LBN' as a baseline. With an 'empty LBN' we mean an LBN with no dependency clauses, this is the LBN according to which all random variables are independent. For all datasets OS and SS perform significantly better than the empty LBN on both training and test data (significance is not indicated in the table). The differences between OS and SS are small as compared to the differences with the empty LBN. For none of the datasets there is a significant difference between OS and SS on the test data (although SS is significantly better on training data for UWCSE).

For none of the datasets there is a significant difference between the *number of dependency clauses* learned by OS and by SS. However, the *number of correct dependency clauses* learned is sometimes significantly higher for SS than for OS. The fact that these differences do not lead to a significantly worse likelihood or score for OS indicates that OS learns all dependencies except the very weak ones [3].

On all the datasets *runtime* is significantly lower for OS than for SS (differences range from a factor 3.2 to 4.8). This is explained by the fact that also the *average time per iteration* is lower for OS than for SS. The latter was expected since an iteration basically corresponds to scoring all solutions in the neighbourhood of the current solution and the size of the neighbourhood is typically smaller for OS than for SS (it is linear in the number of probabilistic predicates for OS but quadratic for SS).

5 Conclusion

In this paper we upgraded the ordering-search algorithm for propositional Bayesian networks towards non-recursive directed probabilistic logical models. We experimentally compared the resulting algorithm with the existing upgraded structure-search algorithm on two relational domains. The results show that ordering-search is competitive with structure-search in terms of quality of the learned models but is significantly faster than structure-search. We conclude that ordering-search is a good alternative to structure-search for learning directed probabilistic logical models.

Acknowledgements. Research supported by the Institute for the Promotion of Innovation by Science and Technology in Flanders (IWT Vlaanderen), Research Foundation-Flanders (FWO Vlaanderen) and GOA 2003/08 "Inductive Knowledge Bases".

References

1. Fierens, D., Blockeel, H., Bruynooghe, M., Ramon, J.: Logical Bayesian networks and their relation to other probabilistic logical models. In: Proceedings of the 15th International Conference on Inductive Logic Programming (ILP), pp. 121–135. Springer, Heidelberg (2005)
2. Fierens, D., Ramon, J., Blockeel, H., Bruynooghe, M.: A comparison of pruning criteria for learning trees. Technical Report CW 488, Department of Computer Science, Katholieke Universiteit Leuven (April 2007)
3. Fierens, D., Ramon, J., Bruynooghe, M., Blockeel, H.: Learning directed probabilistic logical models: ordering-search versus structure-search. Technical Report CW 490, Department of Computer Science, Katholieke Universiteit Leuven (May 2007)
4. Getoor, L., Friedman, N., Koller, D., Pfeffer, A.: Learning Probabilistic Relational Models. In: Relational Data Mining, pp. 307–334. Springer, Heidelberg (2001)
5. Heckerman, D., Geiger, D., Chickering, D.: Learning Bayesian networks: The combination of knowledge and statistical data. Machine Learning 20, 197–243 (1995)
6. Kersting, K., De Raedt, L.: Towards combining inductive logic programming and Bayesian networks. In: Proceedings of the 11th International Conference on Inductive Logic Programming (ILP), pp. 118–131. Springer, Heidelberg (2001)
7. Natarajan, S., Wong, W., Tadepalli, P.: Structure refinement in First Order Conditional Influence Language. In: Proceedings of the workshop on Open Problems in Statistical Relational Learning (SRL) (2006)
8. Richardson, M., Domingos, P.: Markov logic networks. Machine Learning 62(1–2), 107–136 (2006)
9. Teyssier, M., Koller, D.: Ordering-based search: A simple and effective algorithm for learning Bayesian networks. In: Proceedings of the 21st conference on Uncertainty in AI (UAI), pp. 584–590. AUAI Press (2005)

A Simple Lexicographic Ranker and Probability Estimator

Peter Flach[1] and Edson Takashi Matsubara[2]

[1] Department of Computer Science, University of Bristol, United Kingdom
Peter.Flach@bristol.ac.uk
[2] Instituto de Ciências e Matemáticas e de Computação, Universidade de São Paulo
edsontm@icmc.usp.br

Abstract. Given a binary classification task, a ranker sorts a set of instances from highest to lowest expectation that the instance is positive. We propose a lexicographic ranker, *LexRank*, whose rankings are derived not from scores, but from a simple ranking of attribute values obtained from the training data. When using the odds ratio to rank the attribute values we obtain a restricted version of the naive Bayes ranker. We systematically develop the relationships and differences between classification, ranking, and probability estimation, which leads to a novel connection between the Brier score and ROC curves. Combining *LexRank* with isotonic regression, which derives probability estimates from the ROC convex hull, results in the lexicographic probability estimator *LexProb*. Both *LexRank* and *LexProb* are empirically evaluated on a range of data sets, and shown to be highly effective.

1 Introduction

ROC analysis is increasingly being employed in machine learning. It has brought with it a welcome shift in attention from classification to ranking. There are a number of reasons why it is desirable to have a good ranker, rather than a good classifier or a good probability estimator. One of the main reasons is that accuracy requires a fixed score threshold, whereas it may be necessary to change the threshold in response to changing class or cost distributions. Furthermore, good performance in both classification and probability estimation is easily and trivially obtained if one class is much more prevalent than the other, but this wouldn't be reflected in ranking performance.

In this paper we show that, even if one is primarily interested in probability estimation, it is both advantageous and feasible to first construct a ranker. We demonstrate this by proposing a very simple non-scoring ranker, which is based on a linear preference ordering on attributes, which is then used lexicographically. We can obtain calibrated probability estimates from its ROC convex hull, which is in fact equivalent to isotonic regression [1], as noted independently by [2]. In extensive experiments we demonstrate that both our lexicographic ranker and our lexicographic probability estimator perform comparably with models employing a much weaker bias.

The outline of the paper is as follows. In Section 2 we compare and contrast the notions of classification, ranking, and probability estimation, and discuss how to assess

J.N. Kok et al. (Eds.): ECML 2007, LNAI 4701, pp. 575–582, 2007.

performance in each of these cases. In Section 3 we uncover the fundamental relationship between ROC curves and the Brier score or mean squared error of the probability estimates. Section 4 defines lexicographic ranking and the *LexRank* algorithm, which can easily be turned into the lexicographic probability estimator *LexProb* by means of constructing its ROC convex hull. In Section 5 we report on an extensive set of experiments, and Section 6 concludes.

2 Classification, Ranking, and Probability Estimation

Let $X = A_1 \times \ldots \times A_n$ be the instance space over the set of discrete attributes $A_1, \ldots, A_n$. A *classifier* is a mapping $\hat{c} : X \rightarrow C$, where C is a set of labels. For a binary classifier, $C = \{+,-\}$. A *ranker* orders the instance space X, expressing an expectation that some instances are more likely to be positive than others. The ranking is a total order, possibly with ties. The latter are represented by an equivalence relation over X, so the total order is on those equivalence classes; we call them *segments* in this paper. For notational convenience we represent a ranker as a function $\hat{r} : X \times X \rightarrow \{>,=,<\}$, deciding for any pair of instances whether the first is more likely ($>$), equally likely ($=$), or less likely ($<$) to be positive than the second. (By a slight abuse of notation, we also use $>$ and $<$ for the total order on the segments of X). If $X_1, X_2 \subseteq X$ are segments such that $X_1 > X_2$, and there is no segment X_3 such that $X_1 > X_3 > X_2$, we say that X_1 and X_2 are *adjacent*. We can turn a ranker into a binary classifier by splitting the ranking between two adjacent segments. Furthermore, given a ranker $\hat{r}$, we can construct another ranker $\hat{r}'$ by joining two adjacent segments X_1 and X_2, and removing $X_1 > X_2$ from the total order. We say that $\hat{r}'$ is *coarser* than $\hat{r}$, or equivalently, that the latter is *finer* than the former.

A *scoring classifier* is a mapping $\hat{s} : X \rightarrow \mathbb{R}$, assigning a numerical score $\hat{s}(x)$ to each instance x. We will use the convention that higher scores express more preference for the positive class. A *probability estimator* is a scoring classifier that assigns probabilities, i.e., a mapping $\hat{p} : X \rightarrow [0,1]$. $\hat{p}(x)$ is taken to be an estimate of the posterior $p(+|x)$, i.e., the true probability that a random instance with attribute-value vector x belongs to the positive class. Clearly, given a scoring classifier $\hat{s}$ (or a probability estimator) we can construct a ranker $\hat{r}$ that orders instances on decreasing scores. Furthermore, we can turn a scoring classifier into a classifier by turning the associated ranker into a classifier as described above, or equivalently, by setting a threshold $t \in \mathbb{R}$ and assigning all instances x such that $\hat{s}(x) \geq t$ to the positive class and the remaining instances to the negative class.

We illustrate the above on decision trees. [3] and [4] showed that decision trees can be used as probability estimators and hence as rankers. We obtain a probability estimator from a decision tree by considering the numbers of positive (n_i^+) and negative (n_i^-) training examples belonging to the i-th leaf. The estimated posterior odds in $leaf_i$ is then $\frac{P(+|leaf_i)}{P(-|leaf_i)} = \frac{n_i^+}{n_i^-}$ (or $\frac{n_i^+ + 1}{n_i^- + 1}$ if we apply Laplace correction, as recommended by [4]). The corresponding ranker is obtained by ordering the leaves on decreasing posterior odds. A classifier is obtained by labelling the first k^+ leaves in the ordering positive and the remaining k^- leaves negative. Figure 1 shows a small example.

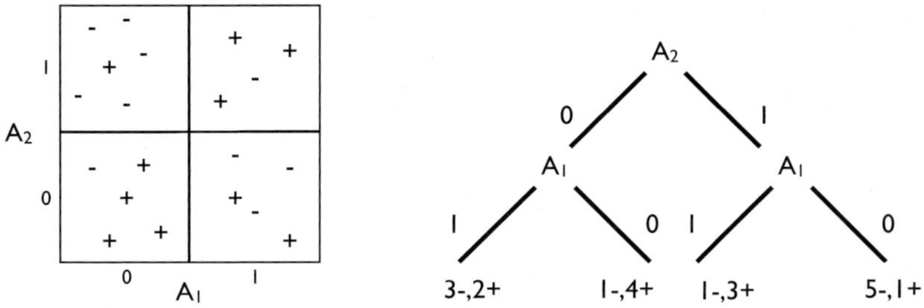

Fig. 1. A data set, and an induced decision tree. Instead of leaf labellings, the class distributions of training instances are indicated for each leaf, which can be used to obtain the ranking leaf 2 – leaf 3 – leaf 1 – leaf 4.

The performance of a binary classifier can be assessed by tabulating its predictions on a test set with known labels in a contingency table, from which true and false positive rates can be calculated. An ROC plot plots true positive rate on the Y-axis against false positive rate on the X-axis; a single contingency table corresponds to a single point in an ROC plot. The performance of a ranker can be assessed by drawing a piecewise linear ROC curve. Each segment of the curve corresponds to one of the segments induced by the ranker; the order of the ROC segments corresponds to the total ordering on the ranking segments. If the i-th segment contains n_i^+ out of a total of n^+ positives and n_i^- out of n^- negatives, the segment's vertical length is n_i^+/n^+, its horizontal width is n_i^-/n^- and its slope is $l_i = \frac{n_i^+}{n_i^-}c^{-1}$, where $c = n^+/n^-$ is the prior odds. We will denote the proportion of positives in a segment as $p_i = \frac{n_i^+}{n_i^+ + n_i^-} = \frac{l_i}{l_i + 1/c}$. We will call these *empirical probabilities*; they allow us to turn a ranker into a probability estimator , as we will show later. The area under the ROC curve or *AUC* estimates the probability that a randomly selected positive is ranked before a randomly selected negative, and is a widely used measure of ranking performance. An ROC curve is *convex* if the slopes l_i are monotonically non-increasing when moving along the curve from $(0,0)$ to $(1,1)$. A concavity in an ROC curve, i.e., two or more adjacent segments with increasing slopes, indicates a locally worse than random ranking. In this case, we would get better ranking performance by joining the segments involved in the concavity, thus creating a coarser classifier.

The performance of a scoring classifier can be assessed in the same way as a ranker. Alternatively, if we know the true scores $s(x)$ we can calculate a loss function such as *mean squared error* $\frac{1}{|T|}\sum_{x \in T}(\hat{s}(x) - s(x))^2$, where T is the test set. In particular, for a probabilistic classifier we may take $s(x) = 1$ for a positive instance and $s(x) = 0$ for a negative; in that case, mean squared error is also known as the *Brier score* [5]. Note that the Brier score takes probability estimates into account but ignores the rankings (it does not require sorting the estimates). Conversely, ROC curves take rankings into account but ignore the probability estimates. Brier score and AUC thus measure different things and are not directly comparable.

3 ROC Curves, the Brier Score, and Calibration

In this section we demonstrate a fundamental and novel relationship between Brier score and ROC curves. We do this by means of a decomposition of the Brier score in terms of calibration loss and refinement loss. A very similar decomposition is well-known in forecasting theory (see, e.g., [6]), but requires a discretisation of the probability estimates and is therefore approximate. Our decomposition uses the segments induced by the ranking and is therefore exact.

Theorem 1. *Given an ROC curve produced by a ranker on a test set T, let $\hat{p}_i$ be the predicted probability in the i-th segment of the ROC curve. The Brier score is equal to* $BS = \frac{1}{|T|}\sum_i n_i(\hat{p}_i - p_i)^2 + \frac{1}{|T|}\sum_i n_i p_i(1-p_i)$.

Proof. $BS = \frac{1}{|T|}\sum_{x\in X}(\hat{p}(x)-p(x))^2 = \frac{1}{|T|}\sum_i [n_i^+(\hat{p}_i-1)^2 + n_i^-\hat{p}_i^2] = \frac{1}{|T|}\sum_i [n_i\hat{p}_i^2 - 2n_i^+\hat{p}_i + n_i^+] = \frac{1}{|T|}\sum_i [n_i(\hat{p}_i - \frac{n_i^+}{n_i})^2 + n_i^+(1-\frac{n_i^+}{n_i})] = \frac{1}{|T|}\sum_i n_i(\hat{p}_i - p_i)^2 + \frac{1}{|T|}\sum_i n_i p_i(1-p_i)$.

Both terms in this decomposition are computed by taking a weighted average over all segments of the ROC curve. The first term, the *calibration loss*, averages the squared prediction error in each segment. It is important to note that the error is taken relative to p_i, which is the proportion of positives in the segment *and thus not necessarily 0 or 1*. In other words, the calibration loss as defined above relates the predicted probabilities to the empirical probabilities obtained from the slopes of the segments of the ROC curve. The second term in the Brier score decomposition is called *refinement loss*. This term is 0 if and only if all ROC segments are either horizontal or vertical, which is the case if all segments are singletons. Consequently, refinement loss is related to the coarseness of the ranker, hence its name. For instance, refinement loss is maximal (0.25) for the ranker which ties all test instances. Notice that refinement loss only takes empirical probabilities into account, not predicted probabilities. It is therefore a quantity that can be evaluated for any ranker, not just for probability estimators. Notice also that, while the Brier score itself does not require ranking the probability estimates, its decomposition into calibration loss and refinement loss does. As an illustration, the decision tree from Figure 1 has 0 calibration loss on the training set (if Laplace correction is not used) and refinement loss $(5\cdot 4/5\cdot 1/5 + 4\cdot 3/4\cdot 1/4 + 5\cdot 2/5\cdot 3/5 + 6\cdot 1/6\cdot 5/6)/20 = 0.18$.

Theorem 2. *The calibration loss is 0 only if the ROC curve is convex.*

Proof. Suppose the ROC curve is not convex, then there are two adjacent segments such that $\hat{p}_i > \hat{p}_j$ but $l_i < l_j$. From the latter it follows that $p_i < p_j$, and thus at least one of the error terms $(\hat{p}_i - p_i)^2$ and $(\hat{p}_j - p_j)^2$ is non-zero.

Theorem 3. *Let $\hat{p}$ be a probability estimator with a convex ROC curve but a non-zero calibration loss. Let $\hat{p}'$ be derived from $\hat{p}$ by predicting p_i rather than $\hat{p}_i$ in each segment. Then $\hat{p}'$ has the same AUC as $\hat{p}$ but a lower Brier score.*

Proof. $\hat{p}'$ may be coarser than $\hat{p}$ because it may merge adjacent segments with $\hat{p}_i > \hat{p}_j$ but $p_i = p_j$. But this will not affect the shape of the ROC curve, nor the AUC. We thus have that the slopes of all segments remain the same, hence the p_i; but since $\hat{p}'$ has zero calibration loss the Brier score is decreased.

Many models do not guarantee convex training set ROC curves. For such models, the above suggests a straightforward procedure to obtain calibrated probabilities, by constructing the *convex hull* of the ROC curve [7]. This can be understood as creating a coarser ranking, by joining adjacent segments that are in the wrong order. Clearly, joining segments results in additional refinement loss, but this is compensated by setting the probability estimates equal to the empirical probabilities, hence obtaining zero calibration loss (although in practice we don't achieve zero calibration loss because we apply the Laplace correction in order to avoid overfitting). This procedure can be shown to be equivalent to isotonic regression [1]; a proof can be found in [2].

4 Lexicographic Ranking

While a ranker is commonly obtained by sorting the scores of a scoring classifier as indicated in Section 2, it is possible to define a ranker without scores. Probably the simplest way to do so is to assume a preference order on attribute values, and to use that ordering to rank instances lexicographically. In the rest of this paper, we will show that such a simple ranker, and the probability estimates derived from it, can perform competitively with less biased models such as decision trees and naive Bayes.

For notational convenience we will assume that all attributes are binary; since a nominal attribute with k values can be converted into k binary attributes, this doesn't represent a loss of generality.

Definition 1 (Lexicographic ranking). *Let $A_1,\ldots,A_n$ be a set of boolean attributes, such that the index represents a preference order. Let v_{i+} denote the preferred value of attribute A_i. The* lexicographic ranker *corresponding to the preference order on attributes and attribute values is defined as follows:*

$$\hat{r}_{lex}(x_1,x_2) = \begin{cases} > \text{ if } A_j(x_1) = v_{j+} \\ < \text{ if } A_j(x_1) \neq v_{j+} \end{cases}$$

where j denotes the lowest attribute index for which x_1 and x_2 have different values (if no such index exists, the two instances are tied).

A lexicographic ranker can be represented as an unlabelled binary decision tree with the following properties: (1) the only attribute occurring at depth i is A_i – i.e., along each path from root to leaf the attributes occur in the preference order; (2) in each split, v_{i+} is the left branch. Consequently, the ranking order is represented by the left-to-right order of the leaves. We call such a tree a *lexicographic ranking tree*. The decision tree shown in Figure 1 is also a lexicographic ranking tree, representing that A_2 is preferred to A_1, 1 is the preferred value of A_1, and 0 the preferred value of A_2. However, as a lexicographic ranking tree, its leaves are ranked left-to-right, which results in a non-convex ROC curve. Clearly, decision trees are much more expressive than lexicographic ranking trees.

We can also draw a connection between lexicographic ranking and the naive Bayes classifier, as we will now show. The naive Bayes ranker obtained from the data from Fig. 1 is as follows. Using $LR(\cdot)$ to denoted the likelihood ratio estimated from the data, we have $LR(A_1=0)=\frac{p(A_1=0|+)}{p(A_1=0|-)}=5/6$, $LR(A_1=1)=\frac{p(A_1=1|+)}{p(A_1=1|-)}=5/4$, $LR(A_2=0)=\frac{p(A_2=0|+)}{p(A_2=0|-)}=6/4$, and $LR(A_2=1)=\frac{p(A_2=1|+)}{p(A_2=1|-)}=4/6$. The prior odds doesn't affect the ranking, and so we can just use the products of these marginal likelihood ratios to determine the ranking: $LR(A_1=1)LR(A_2=0)=30/16 > LR(A_1=0)LR(A_2=0)=30/24 > LR(A_1=1)LR(A_2=1)=20/24 > LR(A_1=0)LR(A_2=1)=20/36$. This is a lexicographic ranking, which is equivalent to the lexicographic ranking tree in Fig. 1.

Definition 2. *LexRank is the lexicographic ranker which uses the following preference criteria. The preferred value v_{i+} for attribute A_i is defined as the one which has $LR(A_i=v_{i+})>1$ (if there is no such value then the attribute doesn't express preference and can be discarded). The preference order on attributes is defined by sorting them on decreasing* odds ratio $OR(A_i)=\frac{LR(A_i=v_{i+})}{LR(A_i=v_{i-})}$, *where v_{i-} denotes the non-preferred value.*

Theorem 4. *For every LexRank ranker over a given set of binary attributes, there exists a data set such that LexRank and naive Bayes, trained on that data set, result in equivalent rankers.*

Proof. Assuming without loss of generality that $A_1,\ldots,A_n$ are already sorted on decreasing odds ratio and that 0 is the preferred value of each attribute, then the leaves of the lexicographic ranking tree can be interpreted as integers in binary representation that are ordered from 0 to 2^n. The naive Bayes ranker will respect this ordering, *unless* there is an i such that $OR(A_i) < \prod_{j>i} OR(A_j)$, as this would reverse any ranking decision for instances differing not just in A_i but also in attributes ranked lower than A_i.

For instance, if $OR(A_1)=5$, $OR(A_2)=3$ and $OR(A_3)=2$, then *LexRank* will rank 011 before 100, whereas naive Bayes will reverse the ranking, since $A_2=0 \wedge A_3=0$ outweighs $A_1=0$.

We conclude that *LexRank* exhibits a much stronger bias than naive Bayes, but as we show in the next section this added bias does not result in a loss of ranking performance. We can turn *LexRank* into a calibrated probability estimator by deriving probability estimates from its convex hull. The resulting lexicographic probability estimator is called *LexProb*.

5 Experimental Evaluation

Our experiments were conducted on 27 data sets from the UCI repository [8] using the Weka toolbox. Continuous attributes were discretised using unsupervised ten-bin discretisation; non-binary k-valued attributes were replaced with k binary-valued attributes. We compared the following algorithms: *LexRank* and *LexProb*, the algorithms proposed in this paper; *NB* and *J48*, naive Bayes and decision tree learners as implemented in Weka; and *CaliNB*, which uses the same wrapper to calibrate probability estimates as *LexRank*, but applied to *NB*. We ran *J48* without pruning and with Laplace correction, to get good ranking performance. We evaluated both ranking performance by means of AUC, and probability estimation performance by means of the Brier score. We used 10-fold cross-validation for all data sets except the ones with less than 270 instances where we used 5-fold cross-validation to ensure the folds contained enough instances for the tests to be meaningful. Table 1 shows the results of all pairwise counts of wins/ties/losses (row vs. column) using AUC (lower triangle) and BS (upper triangle). Most of these counts are not significant according to a sign test (critical value at 0.05 confidence level is 20.7). For illustrative purposes we included *LexRank* in the Brier score results, by calculating scores based on the binary representation of the ranking; these scores are clearly not meaningful as probabilities, resulting in four out of five of the significant counts.

Table 1. Counts of wins/ties/losses using AUC (lower triangle) and BS (upper triangle). Counts in **bold face** are significant according to a sign test at 0.05 confidence level.

set	LexRank	LexProb	NB	CaliNB	J48
LexRank	-	1 0 **26**	4 0 **23**	2 0 **25**	4 0 **23**
LexProb	12 2 13	-	17 0 10	10 0 17	17 0 10
NB	18 3 6	17 2 8	-	3 0 **24**	11 0 16
CaliNB	16 1 10	16 1 10	9 2 16	-	17 0 10
J48	12 1 14	14 2 11	11 2 14	9 2 16	-

The Friedman test uses average ranks of each algorithm over all data sets. From the AUC results, the average ranks are 2.407 for *NB*, 2.926 for *CaliNB*, and 3.222 for *J48*, *LexRank*, and *LexProb*, resulting in an F-statistic of 1.38. The critical value of the F-statistics with 4 and 104 degrees of freedom and at 95 percentile is 2.46. According to the Friedman test, the null-hypothesis that all algorithms have similar ranking performance should not be rejected. The average ranks on the basis of the Brier scores, on the other hand, result in an F-statistic of 17.20, and we proceed to a post-hoc analysis.

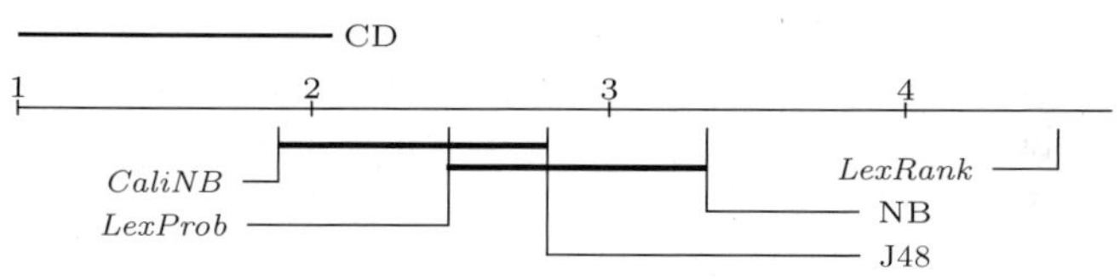

Fig. 2. Critical Difference diagram

According to the Bonferroni-Dunn statistic, the Critical Difference (CD) for comparing the mean-ranking of an algorithm to a control at 95 percentile is 1.07. Mean-ranking differences above this value are significant. Following [9], we can now plot the average ranks in a CD diagram (Figure 2). In this diagram, we connect algorithms that are not significantly different. We also show the CD above the main axis. The analysis reveals that *CaliNB* performs significantly better than *NB*. This demonstrates that isotonic regression can significantly improve the probability estimates of naive Bayes. *LexProb* is connected with – i.e., has comparable performance with – *CaliNB*, *J48* and *NB*.

Finally, we report some runtime results. A single train and test run over all 27 data sets without cross-validation takes 46.72 seconds for *LexRank* against 49.50 seconds for *NB*, and 94.14 seconds for *LexProb* against 100.99 seconds for *CaliNB*.

6 Conclusions

In this paper we have made a number of contributions. First of all, we have clearly defined the relationship and differences between classification, ranking and probability estimation. Secondly, we have defined the notion of lexicographic ranking, which simply employs a linear preference order on attributes. To the best of our knowledge, this is the first ranker that doesn't base its ranking on numerical scores. Thirdly, we have shown that using the odds ratio for ranking attributes results in a lexicographic ranker, called *LexRank*, which is a restricted version of naive Bayes. Fourthly, we have demonstrated a close and fundamental connection between ROC curves and the Brier score, linking in particular the calibration of probability estimates to the convexity of the ROC curve. Experimental results show that lexicographic ranking, and the probability estimates derived from it using isotonic regression, perform comparably to decision trees and naive Bayes.

Acknowledgments. We thank the anonymous reviewers for their constructive comments and the Brazilian Research Council CAPES (Proc.N. 2662060).

References

1. Zadrozny, B., Elkan, C.: Obtaining calibrated probability estimates from decision trees and naive Bayesian classifiers. In: Brodley, C.E., Danyluk, A.P. (eds.) Proceedings of the Eigteenth International Conference on Machine Learning (ICML 2001), pp. 609–616. Morgan Kaufmann, San Francisco (2001)
2. Fawcett, T., Niculescu-Mizil, A.: PAV and the ROC convex hull. Machine Learning 68(1), 97–106 (2007)
3. Ferri, C., Flach, P.A., Hernández-Orallo, J.: Learning decision trees using the area under the ROC curve. In: Sammut, C., Hoffmann, A.G. (eds.) Proceedings of the Nineteenth International Conference (ICML 2002), pp. 139–146. Morgan Kaufmann, San Francisco (2002)
4. Provost, F., Domingos, P.: Tree induction for probability-based ranking. Machine Learning 52(3), 199–215 (2003)
5. Brier, G.: Verification of forecasts expressed in terms of probabilities. Monthly Weather Review 78, 1–3 (1950)
6. Cohen, I., Goldszmidt, M.: Properties and benefits of calibrated classifiers. In: Boulicaut, J.-F., Esposito, F., Giannotti, F., Pedreschi, D. (eds.) PKDD 2004. LNCS (LNAI), vol. 3202, pp. 125–136. Springer, Heidelberg (2004)
7. Provost, F., Fawcett, T.: Robust classification for imprecise environments. Machine Learning 42(3), 203–231 (2001)
8. Newman, D., Hettich, S., Blake, C., Merz, C.: UCI repository of machine learning databases (1998)
9. Demšar, J.: Statistical comparisons of classifiers over multiple data sets. Journal of Machine Learning Research 7, 1–30 (2006)

On Minimizing the Position Error in Label Ranking

Eyke Hüllermeier[1] and Johannes Fürnkranz[2]

[1] Department of Mathematics and Computer Science, Marburg University
eyke@mathematik.uni-marburg.de
[2] Department of Computer Science, TU Darmstadt
juffi@informatik.tu-darmstadt.de

Abstract. Conventional classification learning allows a classifier to make a one shot decision in order to identify the correct label. However, in many practical applications, the problem is not to give a single estimation, but to make repeated suggestions until the correct target label has been identified. Thus, the learner has to deliver a label ranking, that is, a ranking of all possible alternatives. In this paper, we discuss a loss function, called the position error, which is suitable for evaluating the performance of a label ranking algorithm in this setting. Moreover, we introduce "ranking through iterated choice", a general strategy for extending any multi-class classifier to this scenario, and propose an efficient implementation of this method by means of pairwise decomposition techniques.

1 Introduction

The main interest in the context of classification learning typically concerns the correctness of a prediction: A prediction is either correct or not and, correspondingly, is rewarded in the former and punished in the latter case. The arguably best-known loss function reflecting this problem conception is the misclassification or error rate of a classifier, that is, the probability of making an incorrect prediction. In this paper, we are interested in another scenario which motivates a generalization of the misclassification rate. As an illustration, consider a fault detection problem which consists of identifying the cause for the malfunctioning of a technical system. Suppose that a classifier has been trained to predict the true cause, e.g., on the basis of certain sensor measurements serving as input attributes (see, e.g., [1] for an application of that type). Now, if it turned out that a predicted cause is not correct, one cannot simply say that the classification process terminated with a failure. Instead, since the cause must eventually be found, alternative candidates must be tried until the problem is fixed.

What is needed in applications of this type is not only a prediction in the form of a single class label but instead a *ranking* of all candidate labels. In fact, a ranking suggests a simple (trial and error) search process, which successively tests the candidates, one by one, until the correct cause is found. An obvious measure of the quality of a predicted ranking is a loss function that counts the number of futile trials made before the target label is identified.

J.N. Kok et al. (Eds.): ECML 2007, LNAI 4701, pp. 583–590, 2007.

Apart from a suitable loss function, one needs a learner that produces label rankings as outputs. In this regard, the most obvious idea is to use a scoring classifier which outputs a score for each label, which is then used for sorting the labels. In particular, one may use a probabilistic classifier that estimates, for every candidate label λ, the conditional probability of λ given the input $\boldsymbol{x}$. Intuitively, *probabilistic ranking* (PR), i.e., ordering the labels according to their respective probabilities of being the target label, appears to be a reasonable approach.

In Section 3, we show that this approach is indeed optimal in a particular sense. Despite this theoretical optimality, however, an implementation of the approach turns out to be intricate in practice, mainly because estimating conditional probabilities is a difficult problem. In fact, it is well-known that most classification algorithms commonly used in the field of machine learning do not produce accurate probability estimates, even though they may have a strong hit rate. This motivates an alternative approach, to be introduced in Section 3.1, that we call *ranking through iterated choice* (RIC). The idea of this method is to employ a (multi-class) classifier as a choice function which, given a set of candidate labels and related training data, selects the most promising among these candidates. Roughly speaking, a label ranking is then obtained by repeated classification: In every iteration, the learning algorithm removes this label, and retrains a classifier for the remaining labels. Due to the retraining, RIC obviously comes along with an increased complexity. To overcome this problem, an efficient implementation of this approach, which is based on pairwise decomposition techniques, is proposed in Section 3.2. Experimental results, showing that RIC does indeed improve accuracy in comparison with PR, are presented in Section 4.

2 Label Ranking and Position Error

We consider a learning problem which involves an input space $\mathcal{X}$ and an output set $\mathcal{L} = \{\lambda_1 \dots \lambda_m\}$ consisting of a finite number of class labels. Assuming $\mathcal{X} \times \mathcal{L}$ to be endowed with a probability measure, one can associate a vector

$$p_{\boldsymbol{x}} = (\mathbb{P}(\lambda_1 \,|\, \boldsymbol{x}) \dots \mathbb{P}(\lambda_m \,|\, \boldsymbol{x})) \tag{1}$$

of conditional class probabilities with every input $\boldsymbol{x} \in \mathcal{X}$, where $\mathbb{P}(\lambda_i \,|\, \boldsymbol{x}) = \mathbb{P}(\lambda_i = \lambda_{\boldsymbol{x}})$ denotes the probability that $\boldsymbol{x}$ belongs to class λ_i.

Given a set of training examples $\mathcal{D} = \{(\boldsymbol{x}_1, \lambda_{\boldsymbol{x}_1}) \dots (\boldsymbol{x}_n, \lambda_{\boldsymbol{x}_n})\} \subset (\mathcal{X} \times \mathcal{L})^n$, the learning problem is to induce a "label ranker", which is a function that maps any input $\boldsymbol{x}$ to a total order of the class labels, i.e., a complete, transitive, and asymmetric relation $\succ_{\boldsymbol{x}}$ on $\mathcal{L}$; here, $\lambda_i \succ_{\boldsymbol{x}} \lambda_j$ means that λ_i precedes λ_j in the ranking associated with $\boldsymbol{x}$. Formally, a ranking $\succ_{\boldsymbol{x}}$ can be identified with a permutation $\tau_{\boldsymbol{x}}$ of $\{1 \dots m\}$, e.g., the permutation $\tau_{\boldsymbol{x}}$ satisfying $\lambda_{\tau_{\boldsymbol{x}}^{-1}(1)} \succ_{\boldsymbol{x}} \lambda_{\tau_{\boldsymbol{x}}^{-1}(2)} \succ_{\boldsymbol{x}} \dots \succ_{\boldsymbol{x}} \lambda_{\tau_{\boldsymbol{x}}^{-1}(m)}$. Here, $\tau_{\boldsymbol{x}}(i) = \tau_{\boldsymbol{x}}(\lambda_i)$ is the position of label λ_i in the ranking.

In hitherto existing approaches to label ranking [4,3], the quality of a prediction is measured in terms of a similarity or distance measure for rankings; for example, a commonly used measure for comparing a predicted ranking (permutation) $\tau_{\boldsymbol{x}}$ and a true ranking $\tau_{\boldsymbol{x}}^*$ is the Spearman rank correlation. Measures of that type take the position of *all* labels into account, which means, e.g., that swapping the positions of the two bottom labels is as bad as swapping the positions of the two top labels.

Measures such as Spearman rank correlation quantify, say, the *ranking error* of a prediction [5]. In this paper, we are interested in an alternative type of measure, which is especially motivated by practical performance tasks where a prediction is used in order to support the search for a true target label. As outlined in the introduction, an obvious loss function in this context is the number of labels preceding that label in the predicted ranking. Subsequently, a deviation of the predicted target label's position from the top-rank will be called a *position error*. Note that, while a ranking error relates to the comparison of two complete label rankings $\tau_{\boldsymbol{x}}$ and $\tau_{\boldsymbol{x}}^*$, the position error refers to the comparison of a label ranking $\tau_{\boldsymbol{x}}$ and a true class $\lambda_{\boldsymbol{x}}$. More specifically, we define the position error of a prediction $\tau_{\boldsymbol{x}}$ as $\mathrm{PE}(\tau_{\boldsymbol{x}}, \lambda_{\boldsymbol{x}}) \stackrel{\mathrm{df}}{=} \tau_{\boldsymbol{x}}(\lambda_{\boldsymbol{x}})$, i.e., by the position of the target label $\lambda_{\boldsymbol{x}}$ in the ranking $\tau_{\boldsymbol{x}}$. To compare the quality of rankings of different problems, it is useful to normalize the position error for the number of labels. This *normalized position error* is defined as

$$\mathrm{NPE}(\tau_{\boldsymbol{x}}, \lambda_{\boldsymbol{x}}) \stackrel{\mathrm{df}}{=} \frac{\tau_{\boldsymbol{x}}(\lambda_{\boldsymbol{x}}) - 1}{m - 1} \in \{0, 1/(m-1) \ldots 1\}. \tag{2}$$

The position error of a label ranker is the *expected* position error of its predictions, where the expectation is taken with respect to the underlying probability measure on $\mathcal{X} \times \mathcal{L}$.

Compared with the conventional misclassification rate, the position error differentiates between "bad" predictions in a more subtle way: In the case of a correct classification, both measures coincide. In the case of a wrong top label, however, the misclassification rate is 1, while the position error assumes values between 1 and m, depending on how "far away" the true target label is.

Like most performance measures, the position error is a simple scalar index. To characterize a label ranking algorithm in a more elaborate way, an interesting alternative is to look at the mapping $C : \{1 \ldots m\} \to \mathbb{R}$ such that $C(k) = \mathbb{P}\left(\tau_{\boldsymbol{x}}(\lambda_{\boldsymbol{x}}) \leq k\right)$, i.e., $C(k)$ is the probability that the target label is among the top k labels in the predicted ranking. Of course, on the basis of this distribution, only a partial order can be defined on a class of learning algorithms: Two learners are incomparable in the case of intersecting C-distributions.

3 Minimizing the Position Error

What kind of ranking procedure should be used in order to minimize the risk of a predicted ranking with respect to the position error as a loss function? As mentioned before, an intuitively plausible idea is to order the candidate labels λ

according to their probability $\mathbb{P}(\lambda = \lambda_{\boldsymbol{x}})$ of being the target label. In fact, this idea is not only plausible but also provably correct. Even though the result is quite obvious, we state it formally as a theorem.

Theorem 1. *Given a query instance $\boldsymbol{x} \in \mathcal{X}$, ranking the labels $\lambda \in \mathcal{L}$ according to their (conditional) probabilities of being the target class $\lambda_{\boldsymbol{x}}$ yields a risk minimizing prediction with respect to the position error (2) as a loss function. That is, the expected loss $\mathbb{E}(\tau_{\boldsymbol{x}}) = \frac{1}{m-1}\sum_{i=1}^{m}(i-1)\cdot\mathbb{P}\left(\tau_{\boldsymbol{x}}(\lambda_{\boldsymbol{x}}) = i\right)$ becomes minimal for any ranking $\succ_{\boldsymbol{x}}$ such that $\mathbb{P}(\lambda_i = \lambda_{\boldsymbol{x}}) > \mathbb{P}(\lambda_j = \lambda_{\boldsymbol{x}})$ implies $\lambda_i \succ_{\boldsymbol{x}} \lambda_j$.*

According to the above result, the top rank (first position) should be given to the label $\lambda_\top$ for which the estimated probability is maximal. Regarding the second rank, recall the fault detection metaphor, where the second hypothesis for the cause of the fault is only tested in case the first one turned out to be wrong. Thus, for the next choice, one has obtained additional information, namely that *$\lambda_\top$ is not the correct label.* Taking this information into account, the second rank should not simply be given to the label with the second highest probability according to the original probability measure, say, $\mathbb{P}_1(\cdot) = \mathbb{P}(\cdot)$, but instead to the label that maximizes the *conditional* probability $\mathbb{P}_2(\cdot) = \mathbb{P}(\cdot \,|\, \lambda_{\boldsymbol{x}} \neq \lambda_\top)$ of being the target label given that the first proposal was incorrect.

At first sight, passing from $\mathbb{P}_1(\cdot)$ to $\mathbb{P}_2(\cdot)$ may appear meaningless from a ranking point of view, since standard probabilistic conditioning yields

$$\mathbb{P}_2(\lambda) = \frac{1 - \mathbb{P}_1(\lambda)}{\mathbb{P}_1(\lambda_\top)} \propto \mathbb{P}_1(\lambda) \tag{3}$$

for $\lambda \neq \lambda_\top$, and therefore does not change the order of the remaining labels. And indeed, in case the original $\mathbb{P}(\cdot)$ is a proper probability measure and conditioning is performed according to (3), the predicted ranking will not change at all.

3.1 Empirical Conditioning

One should realize, however, that standard conditioning is not an incontestable updating procedure in our context, simply because $\mathbb{P}_1(\cdot)$ is not a "true" probability measure over the class labels. Rather, it is only an estimated measure coming from a learning algorithm, perhaps one which is not a good probability estimator. In fact, it is well-known that most machine learning algorithms for classification perform rather poorly in probability estimation, even though they may produce good classifiers. Thus, it seems sensible to perform "conditioning" not on the measure itself, but rather on the learner that produced the measure. What we mean by this is that the learner should be retrained on the original data without the $\lambda_\top$-examples, an idea that could be paraphrased as "empirical conditioning".

This type of conditioning depends on the data $\mathcal{D}$ and the model assumptions, that is, the hypothesis space $\mathcal{H}$ from which the classifier is taken. To emphasize this dependence and, moreover, to indicate that it concerns an *estimated* ("hat") probability, the conditional measure $\mathbb{P}_2(\cdot)$ could be written more explicitly as

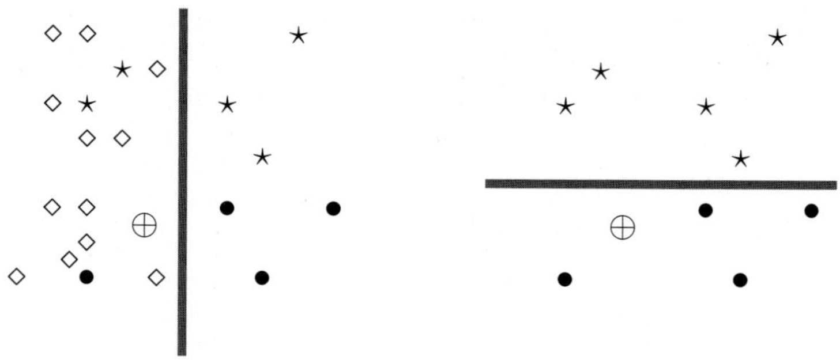

Fig. 1. Example of empirical conditioning: The optimal model (decision stump) for the complete training data (left) and the data omitting the examples of the top label ($\diamond$)

$\mathbb{P}_2(\cdot) = \widehat{\mathbb{P}}(\cdot \,|\, \lambda_{\boldsymbol{x}} \neq \lambda_{\top}, \mathcal{D}, \mathcal{H})$. To motivate the idea of empirical conditioning, consider the simple example in Fig. 1, where the hypothesis space $\mathcal{H}$ is given by the class of decision stumps (univariate decision trees with only one inner node, i.e., axis-parallel splits in the case of numerical attributes). Given the examples from three classes (represented, respectively, by the symbols $\diamond$, $\star$, and $\bullet$), the best model corresponds to the split shown in the left picture. By estimating probabilities through relative frequencies in the leaf nodes of the decision stump, one derives the following estimates for the query instance, which is marked by a $\oplus$ symbol: $\widehat{\mathbb{P}}(\diamond \,|\, \oplus) = 12/15$, $\widehat{\mathbb{P}}(\star \,|\, \oplus) = 2/15$, $\widehat{\mathbb{P}}(\bullet \,|\, \oplus) = 1/15$; thus, the induced ranking is given by $\diamond \succ \star \succ \bullet$. Now, suppose that the top label $\diamond$ turned out to be an incorrect prediction. According to the above ranking (and probabilistic conditioning), the next label to be tested would be $\star$. However, when fitting a new model to the training data without the $\diamond$-examples, the preference between $\star$ and $\bullet$ is reversed, because the query instance is now located "on the $\bullet$-side" of the decision boundary. Roughly speaking, conditioning by "taking a different look" at the data, namely a look that suppresses the $\diamond$ examples, gives a quite different picture (shown on the right-hand side of Fig. 1) of the situation. In fact, one should realize that, in the first model, the preference between $\star$ and $\bullet$ is strongly biased by the $\diamond$-examples: The first decision boundary is optimal only because it classifies all $\diamond$-examples correctly, a property that looses importance once it turned out that $\diamond$ is not the true label of the query.

According to the above idea, a classifier is used as a *choice function*: Given a set of potential labels with corresponding training data (and a new query instance $\boldsymbol{x}$), it selects the most likely candidate among these labels. We refer to the process of successively selecting alternatives by estimating top-labels from (conditional) probability measures $\mathbb{P}_1(\cdot), \mathbb{P}_2(\cdot) \ldots \mathbb{P}_m(\cdot)$ as *ranking through iterated choice* (RIC). As an important advantage, note that this approach can be used to turn any multi-class classifier into a label ranker. In principle, it is not required that a corresponding classifier outputs a score, or even a real probability, for every label. In fact, since only a simple decision in favor of a single label has to be made in each iteration, any classifier is good enough. In this regard, let us note that, for the ease of exposition, the term "probability" will subsequently be used in a rather informal manner.

Regarding its effect on label ranking accuracy, one may expect the idea of RIC to produce two opposite effects: (1) *Information loss:* In each iteration, the size of the data set to learn from becomes smaller. (2) *Simplification:* Due to the reduced number of classes, the learning problems become simpler in each iteration. The first effect will clearly have a negative influence on generalization performance, as a reduction of data comes along with a loss of information. In contrast to this, the second effect will have a positive influence: The classifiers will become increasingly simple, because it can be expected that the decision boundary for separating m classes is more complex than the decision boundary for separating $m' < m$ classes of the same problem. The hope is that, in practice, the second (positive) effect will dominate the first one.

3.2 Efficient Implementation

An obvious disadvantage of RIC concerns its computational complexity. In fact, since empirical conditioning essentially means classifying on a subset of $\mathcal{L}$, the number of models needed is (potentially) of the order $2^{|\mathcal{L}|}$. To overcome this problem, we propose the use of pairwise decomposition techniques.

The idea of pairwise learning is well-known in the context of classification [2], where it allows one to transform a polychotomous classification problem, i.e., a problem involving $m > 2$ classes $\mathcal{L} = \{\lambda_1 \ldots \lambda_m\}$, into a number of *binary* problems. To this end, a separate model (base learner) $\mathcal{M}_{ij}$ is trained for each *pair* of labels $(\lambda_i, \lambda_j) \in \mathcal{L}$, $1 \leq i < j \leq m$; thus, a total number of $m(m-1)/2$ models is needed. $\mathcal{M}_{ij}$ is intended to separate the objects with label λ_i from those having label λ_j. Depending on the classifier used, an output $\mathcal{M}_{ij}(\boldsymbol{x})$ can be interpreted, e.g., as the conditional probability $p_{ij} = \mathbb{P}(\lambda_{\boldsymbol{x}} = \lambda_i \,|\, \lambda_{\boldsymbol{x}} \in \{\lambda_i, \lambda_j\}, \boldsymbol{x})$. In a second step, an estimation of the probability vector (1), i.e., of the individual probabilities $p_i = \mathbb{P}(\lambda_{\boldsymbol{x}} = \lambda_i \,|\, \boldsymbol{x})$, has to be derived from these pairwise probabilities. To this end, different techniques have been developed. Here, we resorted to the approach proposed in [7], which derives the p_i as a solution of a system of linear equations, S, that includes one equation for every label.

RIC can then be realized as follows: First, the aforementioned system of linear equations is solved, and the label λ_i with maximal probability p_i is chosen as the top-label $\lambda_\top$. This label is then removed, i.e., the corresponding variable p_i and its associated equation are deleted from S. To find the second best label, the same procedure is then applied to the reduced system S' thus obtained, i.e., by solving a system of $m-1$ linear equations and $m-1$ variables. This process is iterated until a full ranking has been constructed.

This approach reduces the training effort from an exponential to a quadratic number of models. Roughly speaking, a classifier on a subset $\mathcal{L}' \subseteq \mathcal{L}$ of classes is efficiently assembled "on the fly" from the corresponding subset of pairwise models $\{\mathcal{M}_{ij} \,|\, \lambda_i, \lambda_j \in \mathcal{L}'\}$. Or, stated differently, the *training* of classifiers is replaced by the *combination* of associated binary classifiers.

The hope that empirical conditioning improves accuracy in comparison with conventional probabilistic conditioning is essentially justified by the aforementioned *simplification effect* of RIC. Note that this simplification effect is also inherently present in pairwise learning. Here, the simplification due to a reduction of class labels is already achieved at the very beginning and, by decomposing the original problem into *binary* problems, carried to the extreme. Thus, if the simplification effect is indeed beneficial in the original version of RIC, it should also have a positive influence in the pairwise implementation (RIC-P). These are exactly the two conjectures to be investigated empirically in the next section: (i) Empirical conditioning (RIC) pays off with respect to accuracy, and (ii) the increased efficiency of the pairwise implementation, RIC-P, is achieved without sacrificing this gain in accuracy.

4 Empirical Results

In order to investigate the practical usefulness of empirical conditioning and the related RIC procedure, we compare the corresponding strategy to the most obvious alternative, namely ordering the class labels right away according to the respective probabilities produced by a multi-class classifier (probabilistic ranking, PR). So, given any multi-class classifier, capable of producing such probabilities, as a base learner, we consider the following three learning strategies: **PR:** A ranking is produced by applying the base learner to the complete data set only once and ordering the class labels according to their probabilities. **RIC:** This version refers to the *ranking through iterated choice* procedure outlined in Section 3.1, using the multi-class classifier as a base learner. **RIC-P:** This is the pairwise implementation of RIC as introduced in Section 3.2 (again using as base learners the same classifiers as RIC and PR). In cases of non-unique top-labels, we always break ties by coin flipping.

For 18 benchmark data sets from the UCI repository and the StatLib archive[1] we estimated the mean (absolute) position error of each method using leave-one-out cross validation, using two widely known machine learning algorithms as base learners: C4.5 and Ripper. For comparison purpose, we also derived results for the naive Bayes (NB) classifier, as this is one of the most commonly used "true" probabilistic classifiers. Note that, since conditional probabilities in NB are estimated individually for each class, empirical conditioning is essentially the same as conventional conditioning, i.e., RIC is equivalent to PR.

From the win-loss statistics for NB in comparison with PR using, respectively, C4.5 (10/8) and Ripper (10/8), there is no visible difference between these multi-class classifiers in terms of label ranking accuracy. Important are the win-loss statistics summarized in Table 1 (detailed results had to be omitted here due to space restrictions but can be found in an extended version of this paper [6]). These results perfectly support the two conjectures raised above. First, RIC significantly outperforms PR: According to a simple sign test for the win-loss statistic, the results are significant at a level of 2%. Second, RIP-P is fully

[1] `http://www.ics.uci.edu/~mlearn`, `http://stat.cmu.edu/`

Table 1. Win/loss statistics for each pair of methods, using C4.5 (left) and Ripper (right) as base learners

	PR	RIC	RIC-P	PR	RIC	RIC-P
PR	—	3/13	4/13	—	3/13	3/12
RI	13/3	—	7/8	13/3	—	2/13
RIC-P	13/4	8/7	—	12/3	13/2	—

competitive to RIC (and actually shows a better performance in the case of Ripper as a base learner).

5 Concluding Remarks

In the context of the label ranking problem, we have discussed the position error as an alternative loss function. To minimize this loss function, we proposed *ranking through iterated choice* (RPC), a strategy that essentially reduces label ranking to repeated classification. In each iteration, RPC performs *empirical conditioning*, which in turn requires the retraining of classifiers. To avoid the need for training a potentially large number of models, we used a pairwise implementation in which retraining is done implicitly, namely by combining the outputs of certain pairwise models. In an experimental study, RPC was compared to standard probabilistic ranking, where the class labels are ranked according to the originally estimated probabilities. Our results suggest that retraining (empirical conditioning) does indeed reduce the expected loss when using standard multi-class classifiers as base learners, and that this gain in accuracy is preserved by the pairwise implementation.

References

1. Alonso, C., Rodríguez, J.J., Pulido, B.: Enhancing consistency based diagnosis with machine learning techniques. In: Conejo, R., Urretavizcaya, M., Pérez-de-la-Cruz, J.-L. (eds.) Current Topics in Artificial Intelligence. LNCS (LNAI), vol. 3040, pp. 312–321. Springer, Heidelberg (2004)
2. Fürnkranz, J.: Round robin classification. J. of Mach. Learn. Res. 2, 721–747 (2002)
3. Fürnkranz, J., Hüllermeier, E.: Pairwise preference learning and ranking. In: Lavrač, N., Gamberger, D., Todorovski, L., Blockeel, H. (eds.) ECML 2003. LNCS (LNAI), vol. 2837, Springer, Heidelberg (2003)
4. Har-Peled, S., Roth, D., Zimak, D.: Constraint classification: a new approach to multiclass classification. In: Cesa-Bianchi, N., Numao, M., Reischuk, R. (eds.) ALT 2002. LNCS (LNAI), vol. 2533, pp. 365–379. Springer, Heidelberg (2002)
5. Hüllermeier, E., Fürnkranz, J.: Learning label preferences: Ranking error versus position error. In: Famili, A.F., Kok, J.N., Peña, J.M., Siebes, A., Feelders, A. (eds.) IDA 2005. LNCS, vol. 3646, Springer, Heidelberg (2005)
6. Hüllermeier, E., Fürnkranz, J.: On minimizing the position error in label ranking. Technical Report TUD-KE-2007-04, TU Darmstadt (2007)
7. Wu, T.F., Lin, C.J., Weng, R.C.: Probability estimates for multi-class classification by pairwise coupling. J. Machine Learning Res. 5, 975–1005 (2004)

On Phase Transitions in Learning Sparse Networks

Goele Hollanders[1], Geert Jan Bex[1], Marc Gyssens[1],
Ronald L. Westra[2], and Karl Tuyls[2]

[1] Department of Mathematics, Physics, and Computer Science,
Hasselt University and Transnational University of Limburg,
Hasselt, Belgium
goele.hollanders@uhasselt.be
[2] Department of Mathematics and Computer Science,
Maastricht University and Transnational University of Limburg,
Maastricht, the Netherlands

Abstract. In this paper we study the identification of sparse interaction networks as a machine learning problem. Sparsity means that we are provided with a small data set and a high number of unknown components of the system, most of which are zero. Under these circumstances, a model needs to be learned that fits the underlying system, capable of generalization. This corresponds to the student-teacher setting in machine learning. In the first part of this paper we introduce a learning algorithm, based on L_1-minimization, to identify interaction networks from poor data and analyze its dynamics with respect to phase transitions. The efficiency of the algorithm is measured by the generalization error, which represents the probability that the student is a good fit to the teacher. In the second part of this paper we show that from a system with a specific system size value the generalization error of other system sizes can be estimated. A comparison with a set of simulation experiments show a very good fit.

Keywords: machine learning, sparse network reconstruction, feature identification.

1 Introduction and Motivation

In this paper we consider the problem of identifying interaction networks from a given set of observations. An example of such a network is a sparse gene-protein interaction network, for more details see [1,5,2,7,10,11].

In some engineering applications, the number of measurements M available for system identification and model validation is much smaller than the system order N, which represents the number of components. This substantial lack of data can give rise to an identifiability problem, in which case a larger subset of the model class is entirely consistent with the observed data so that no unique model can be proposed. Since conventional techniques for system identification are not well suited to deal with such situations, it thus becomes important to work around this by exploiting as much additional information as possible about the underlying system. In particular, we are interested in the relation between the number of measurements and the number of components, the sparsity of the regulatory network and the influence of noise.

J.N. Kok et al. (Eds.): ECML 2007, LNAI 4701, pp. 591–599, 2007.

In this setting, it is natural to link network identification to feature selection. Only very few components influence the expression level of any given component, so one can restate the problem as selecting exactly those few among the large amount of components under consideration. Hence the results presented here will not only be applicable to network identification, but more generally to feature selection as well.

In Section 2, we will introduce the definitions of several concepts we use. Section 3 summarizes five research questions we will answer on experimental results. A brief discussion and our conclusions will be presented in Section 4.

2 Definitions and Algorithm

In the first paragraph we translate the problem of network identification formally into machine learning terminology [6]. In the next paragraph we introduce and elucidate the learning algorithm. Then we elaborate on the relation to feature selection. Finally, we discuss the issue of noisy data.

Terminology: Data and Teacher. In order to formalize the problem stated in the previous section we now introduce the model which we will consider more rigorously below. We assume that a *training set* of M input/output pairs $\chi_{\mathrm{tr}} = \{(x_m, \dot{x}_m) \mid m : 1, \ldots, M\}$ is given, where $x_m, \dot{x}_m \in \mathbb{R}^N$. The components of the input vectors x_m are independently and identically distributed so that they are linearly independent. Since the data is assumed to be generated by some interaction network, this network will be denoted by $T = (A^T, B^T)$ where $A^T \in \mathbb{R}^{N \times N}$ and $B^T \in \mathbb{R}^N$. In this context, we refer to T as the unknown *teacher*. For each $(x_m, \dot{x}_m) \in \chi_{\mathrm{tr}}$, $\dot{x}_m = A^T \cdot x_m + B^T$, i.e., $\dot{x}_m$ is the output produced by the teacher T on input x_m. In general, the teacher's output $\dot{x}$ on some input x is computed as follows: $\dot{x} = T(x) \equiv A^T \cdot x + B^T$. Moreover, we consider sparse networks, for each row of the matrix A^T, only K_T components are non-zero. Since the latter models the interactions in the network, a non-zero value of $A^T_{i,j}$ indicates that component i of input x influences component j of the output $\dot{x}$. So the sparsity constraint implies that each component of the output is determined by exactly K_T components of the input.

Learning Algorithm. The learning algorithm should return a network $S = (A^S, B^S)$, referred to as the *student*, with $A^S \in \mathbb{R}^{N \times N}$ and $B^S \in \mathbb{R}^N$, that reproduces the training set χ_{tr}: $\dot{x}_m = A^S \cdot x_m + B^S$ for $m : 1, \ldots, M$. More importantly however, the student should also perform well on input that was not used by the algorithm, i.e., the algorithm should be able to generalize beyond the training set χ_{tr}. To test the student's generalization ability, we use a validation set $\chi_{\mathrm{v}} = \{(x_v, \dot{x}_v) \mid v : 1, \ldots, V\}$ such that $\dot{x}_v = A^T \cdot x_v + B^T$ for each $v : 1, \ldots, V$. The *generalization error* $\varepsilon_{\mathrm{gen}}$ is defined as the ratio of the number of tuples in χ_{v} that is not reproduced by the student to the total number of tuples. More formally, it is the fraction of the patterns in χ_{v} for which $|\dot{x}_v - A^S \cdot x_v - B^S|/|\dot{x}_v| > \varepsilon_{\mathrm{err}}$, where $\varepsilon_{\mathrm{err}}$ is the maximum deviation from zero that is considered insignificant. The learning task can now be formulated as follows: *the algorithm should produce a student S given χ_{tr} such that $\varepsilon_{\mathrm{gen}}$ is minimal.*

The algorithm we use is a reformulation of the problem in terms of linear programming: the objective is to minimize $||A^S||_1$ subject to the M constraints $\dot{x}_m = A^S \cdot x_m + B^S$.

In the target function, $||C||_1$ denotes the 1-norm of the matrix C, i.e., $||C||_1 = \sum_{i,j} |C_{i,j}|$. This choice is motivated by the sparsity constraint on the networks to be identified. If the student S reproduces the teacher T, it will be sparse, hence we prefer solutions with as few non-zero components as possible. It is known from the literature [3,4] that the 1-norm is an acceptable approximation for the 0-norm. Since the latter can only be computed by explicit enumeration, it is unsuitable in practice due to the ensuing combinatorial explosion. For more details about this technique, see [8] and [9].

The constraints can be written more explicitly as:

$$\sum_{i=1}^{N} A^S_{i,j} x_{m,j} + B^S_i = \dot{x}_{m,i}, \quad j : 1, \ldots, N; \; m : 1, \ldots, M. \tag{1}$$

Hence each row of A and B is a solution to a set of M equations and can be determined independently, an observation to which we will return later on. For $M \leq N$, infinitely many solutions can be found, from which linear programming will select the most sparse. Trivially, for $M = N + 1$ the set of equations will have a unique solution: the teacher T. This implies that one can expect a generalization error $\varepsilon_{\text{gen}} \approx 1$ for very small training sets, i.e., $M \ll N$, while $\varepsilon_{\text{gen}} \approx 0$ for $M \approx N$. We may conclude that ε_{gen} will be a function of the training set size M. By convention, the number of patterns such that $\varepsilon_{\text{gen}} = 1/2$ is denoted by M_{gen}, the *generalization threshold*.

Although the generalization error is a good measure to evaluate the student's quality, it will nevertheless be useful to consider a measure to compare the student's structure to that of the teacher. Since our setting is that of identifying interaction networks, the presence or absence of such an interaction in the inferred model S is important. This can be characterized by the following three quantities: (1) n_{fneg}, the number of *false negatives*, i.e., interactions that are modeled by T, but not by S; (2) n_{fpos}, the number of *false positives*, i.e., interaction modeled by S, but not by T; and (3) n_{corr} the number of *correlation errors*, i.e., those components of S and T that are significantly non-zero, but have opposite sign. These three quantities measure the quality of the identification process. By definition, $0 \leq n_{\text{fneg}} \leq NK_T$, $0 \leq n_{\text{fpos}} \leq N(N - K_T)$ and $0 \leq n_{\text{corr}} \leq NK_T$. Note that these error measures can all be zero, even if the student does not generalize well, i.e., $\varepsilon_{\text{gen}} > 0$. Also notice that $0 \leq n_{\text{fneg}} + n_{\text{fpos}} + n_{\text{corr}} \leq N^2$. Therefore, we aggregate these three measures into the operator $S \odot T = (N^2 - n_{\text{fneg}} - n_{\text{fpos}} - n_{\text{corr}})/N^2$ that measures the quality of the identification.

Relation to Feature Selection. From Eq. (1), it is clear that the problem of identifying the interactions within a network modeled by the matrix A^T can be decomposed into identifying the N rows of that matrix. Since, apart from the sparsity constraint, interactions in the teacher are completely random, these rows can be determined independently. Hence we can reformulate the original problem in terms of N simpler ones: given an input vector $x \in \mathbb{R}^N$, which of the N components of x will effectively contribute to the output $\dot{x} \in \mathbb{R}$? This can be viewed as a feature selection problem, since the sparsity of the teacher implies that only very few components will contribute. As for network identification, we can define the generalization error for feature selection $\varepsilon^{\text{fs}}_{\text{gen}}$. At this point, it is useful to note that the generalization error can be interpreted as the probability that the student will not compute the correct output on a random input. The probability that N independent feature selection problems will *all* compute the correct answer is thus given by $(1-\varepsilon_{\text{gen}}^{\text{fs}})^N$, which allows us to compute the generalization error for network identification ε_{gen} from that for feature selection $\varepsilon_{\text{gen}}^{\text{fs}}$ as follows:

$$\varepsilon_{\text{gen}} = 1 - (1 - \varepsilon_{\text{gen}}^{\text{fs}})^N \tag{2}$$

Noisy data. Until now, we have considered an ideal situation in the sense that the data χ_{tr} used to identify the network was noise-free. Obviously, the quality of real world data is typically far from ideal and an algorithm can only be used effectively in practice if it is robust to noise. To model this situation, we will consider a training set with noise: $\chi_{\text{tr}} = \{(x_m, \dot{x}_m + \delta_m) \mid m : 1, \ldots, M\}$ where $\delta_m \in \mathbb{R}^N$. The δ_m are identically and independently distributed and randomly drawn from a normal distribution with zero mean and standard deviation σ_{noise}. To quantify the quality of a student derived from a noisy training set, we introduce the *output deviation*, defined as $\delta\dot{x} = \sum_{x\in\chi_{\text{v}}} |T(x) - S(x)|/|T(x)|$.

3 Experiments

In this section, we will consecutively address the following research questions:

1. Is it possible to identify T with a training set that contains less than $N + 1$ input-output pairs? If so, what is the value of the generalization error ε_{gen} as a function of the training set size?
2. Does the generalization error ε_{gen} depend on the teacher's sparsity?
3. What is the evolution of the student when compared with the teacher as a function of the training set size?
4. Is the algorithm robust against noise?
5. How does the generalization error ε_{gen} scale with the system size N?

All experiments have been carried out using the algebra package Maple 9.5 on a Pentium-M class processor of 1.73 GHz and 1 GB of RAM. The standard implementation of linear programming in Maple is used, which is very convenient since it allows to specify the objective function and the constraints symbolically.

To facilitate the discussion, we first introduce some convenient notation. The ratio of the training set size to the system size is denoted by $\alpha = M/N$. In particular, $\alpha_{\text{gen}} = M_{\text{gen}}/N$. The fraction of non-zero components per row of a system is denoted by $\kappa = K/N$. In particular, $\kappa_T = K_T/N$. The amplitude of the noise should be considered relative to the amplitude of the signal, i.e., we define $\sigma = \sigma_{\text{noise}}/\sigma_{\dot{x}}$, where $\sigma_{\dot{x}}$ is the standard deviation of the output vectors' components $\dot{x}_{m,i}$. The components of the teacher A^T, B^T and of the input x_m are drawn from an uniform distribution over $]-1, 1[$.

Generalization error. To determine the generalization error, we randomly generate a set of M input vectors and a random teacher system so that we can compute the output to obtain a training set χ_{tr}. The algorithm produces a student, for which we calculate the generalization error. Since its value depends on the particular selection of input and teacher, we independently repeat this procedure many times to compute the average. Fig. 1 shows the observed generalization error as a function of the training set size α.

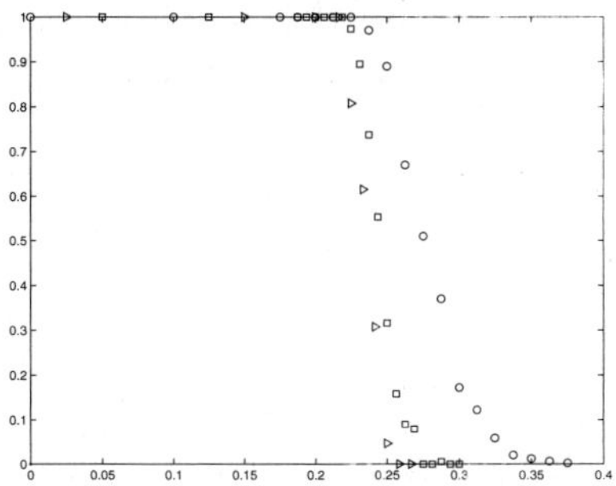

Fig. 1. The generalization error ε_{gen} as a function of the training set size α for $N = 100$ (○), $N = 160$ (□) and $N = 300$ (▷) for $\kappa_T \approx 0.03$

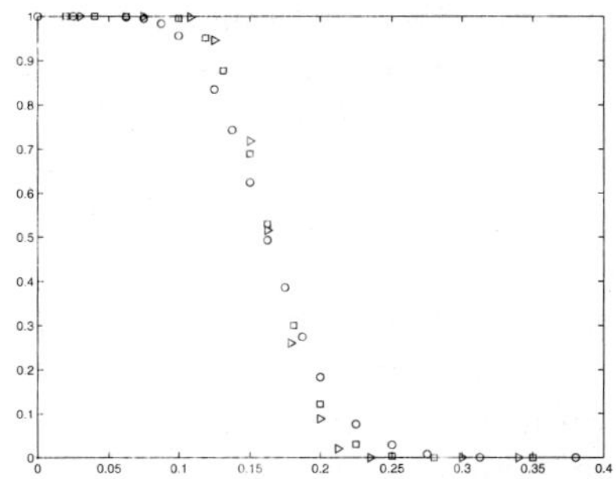

Fig. 2. The generalization error for feature selection ε_{gen}^{fs} as a function of the training set size α for $N = 100$ (○), $N = 160$ (□) and $N = 300$ (▷) for $\kappa_T \approx 0.03$

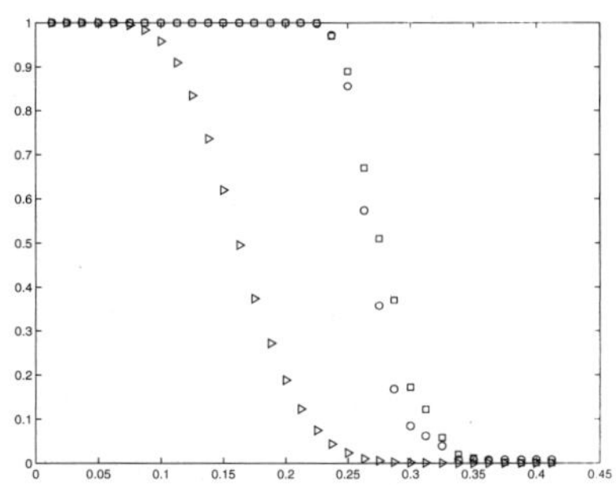

Fig. 3. The observed (□) versus the computed (○) generalization error ε_{gen} as a function of α for $N = 80$, $\kappa_T \approx 0.03$. The curve representing ε_{gen}^{fs} (▷) is given as reference.

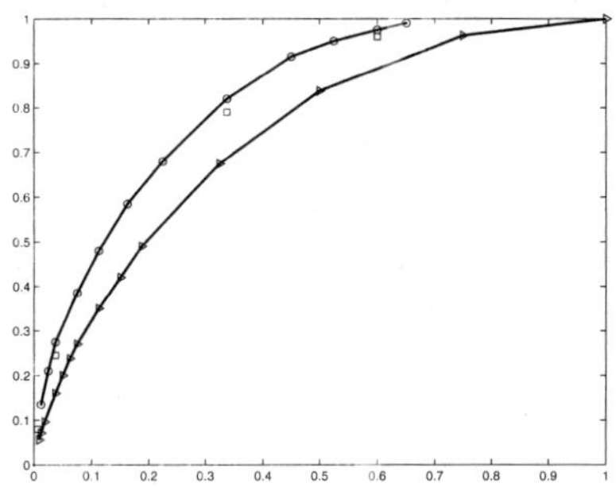

Fig. 4. The generalization threshold α_{gen} as a function of the sparsity κ_T for $N = 80$ (○) and a few values for $N = 160$ (□). The generalization threshold for feature selection α_{gen}^{fs} (▷) is given as reference.

This result is surprising in two respects: (1) the generalization error decreases to zero for a training set size $\alpha < 1$ and (2) the transition towards generalization is quite abrupt. It is also clear from Fig. 1 that the transition is increasingly abrupt for increasing system size N. It is instructive to relate the generalization error ε_{gen} for network identification to that for feature selection ε_{gen}^{fs} in Fig. 2. The latter figure illustrates that α_{gen}^{fs}, the training set size α for $\varepsilon_{gen}^{fs} = 1/2$, is independent of the system size N and that the ε_{gen}^{fs} converges to a step-function for $N \to \infty$. Hence we observe a first order phase transition between a regime for $\alpha < \alpha_{gen}^{fs}$ where the student simply reproduces the training set, and another regime for $\alpha > \alpha_{gen}^{fs}$ where he is able to reproduce the teacher's output perfectly.

The relation between the generalization error for the network identification problem ε_{gen} and that for feature selection ε_{gen}^{fs}, given by Eq. (2), is illustrated in Fig. 3. It is clear that ε_{gen} for the network identification problem can reliably be estimated from ε_{gen}^{fs} for the feature selection problem. Values beyond α_{gen} are less reliable since inaccuracies for $\varepsilon_{\text{gen}}^{\text{fs}}$ are amplified considerably due to the mathematical form of Eq. (2).

Sparsity. The next question concerns the relation between the sparsity of the teacher and the generalization threshold. For a non-sparse teacher, i.e., $\kappa_T \approx 1$, one would need a training set of size $\alpha \approx 1$ since each of the $N(N+1)$ components has to be determined. However, as Fig. 1 illustrated, the fact that the teacher is sparse simplifies the identification process considerably. Fig. 4 shows the generalization threshold α_{gen} for network identification as a function of κ_T. It is clear that training sets of increasing size α are required to facilitate the transition to the generalization regime as κ_T increases, i.e., as the sparsity decreases. As expected, for $\kappa_T \approx 1$, $\alpha_{\text{gen}} \approx 1$. It is clear that the advantage sparsity offers to the efficiency of the learning algorithm virtually vanishes for $\kappa_T \approx 0.5$. However, it is very pronounced for $\kappa_T < 0.2$. As before, these results have been obtained for many independent instances of the training set and teacher.

Learning process. To gain a better understanding of the learning process, i.e., the evolution of the student with respect to the teacher as a function of the training set size we first consider a fixed training set and teacher. Define a sequence of training sets χ_m for $m : 1, \ldots, M$ such that $\chi_m \subset \chi_{m+1}$ and $|\chi_{m+1}| = |\chi_m| + 1$. These sets are used to determine a sequence of students S_m for $m : 1, \ldots, M$. Fig. 5 shows $S_{\alpha N} \odot T$ as a function of the training set size α. For $\alpha N = 1$, the number of false negatives is $N^2\kappa_T$ and the number of false positives is 0. For increasing α, the number of false positives increases approximately linearly with α, while the number of false negatives decreases very slowly. The plot illustrates clearly that the transition to generalization is very sudden: at α_{gen}, $S_{\alpha_{\text{gen}}N} \odot T = 1$. Fig. 6 and 7 confirm that the scenario sketched above is indeed the typical behavior when it is averaged over many independent training sets and teachers. The latter plot illustrates the explanation given above for the behavior of $S_{\alpha N} \odot T$.

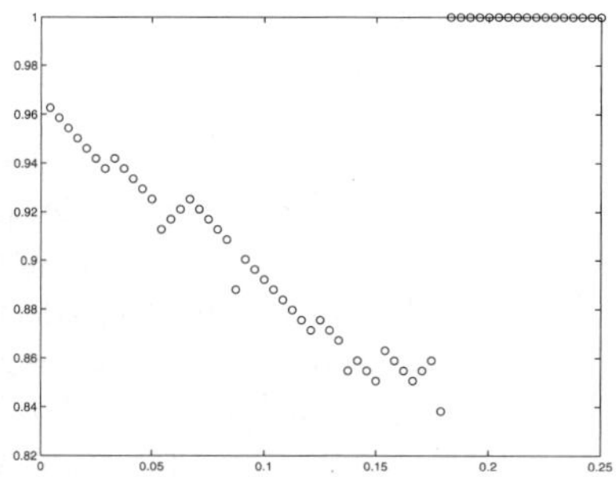

Fig. 5. The learning process characterized by $S_m \odot T$ as a function of the size of the training set m/N for an individual run

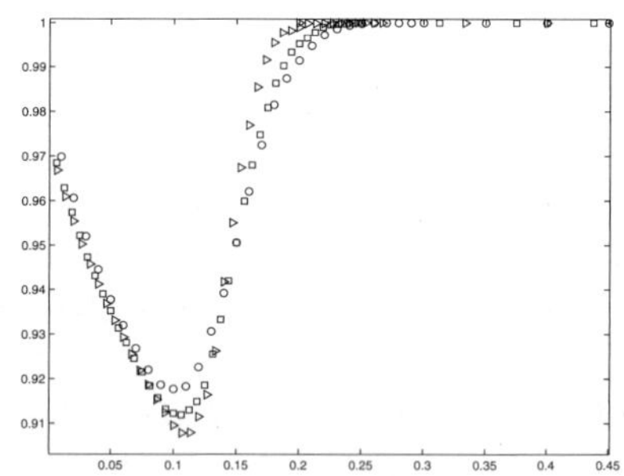

Fig. 6. The learning process characterized by $S_m \odot T$ as a function of the size of the training set m/N, system sizes $N = 100$ (○), $N = 160$ (□) and $N = 300$ (▷) for $\kappa_T \approx 0.03$

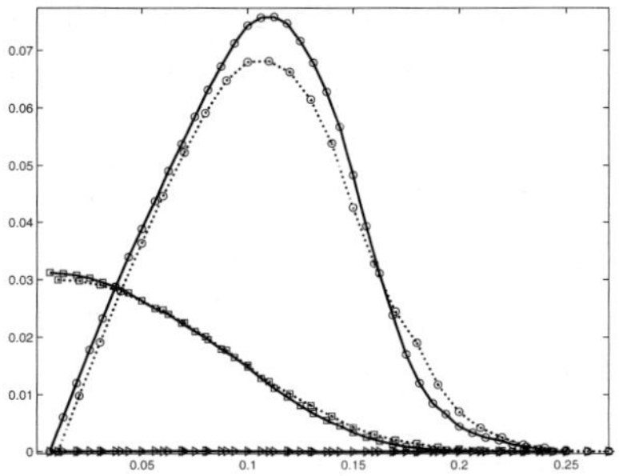

Fig. 7. Measures n_{fneg} (□, $N = 100$ dotted line, $N = 160$ solid line), n_{fpos} (○, $N = 100$ dotted line, $N = 160$ solid line) and n_{corr} (▹, $N = 100$ dotted line, $N = 160$ solid line) as a function of the training set size α for $\kappa_T \approx 0.03$

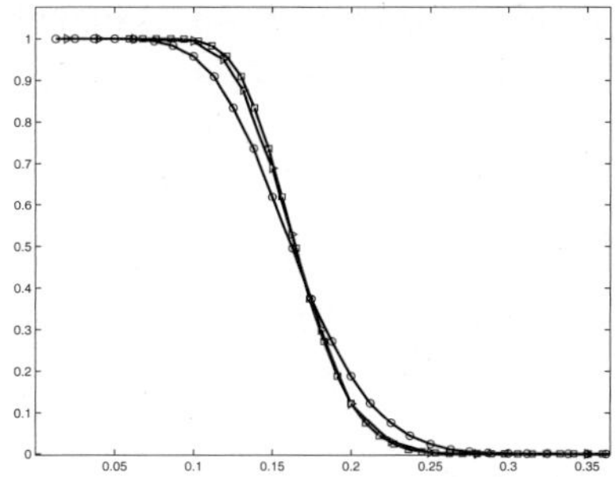

Fig. 8. Fig. 2 using Eq. (3) for $N = 100$ (○), $N = 160$ (□) computed, $N = 160$ observed (▹), $\kappa_T \approx 0.03$

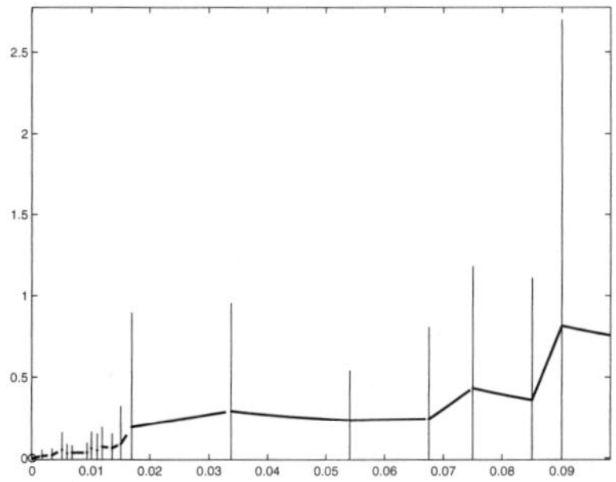

Fig. 9. Deviation of the student and teacher output $\delta\dot{x}$ as a function of the noise level σ on the training set

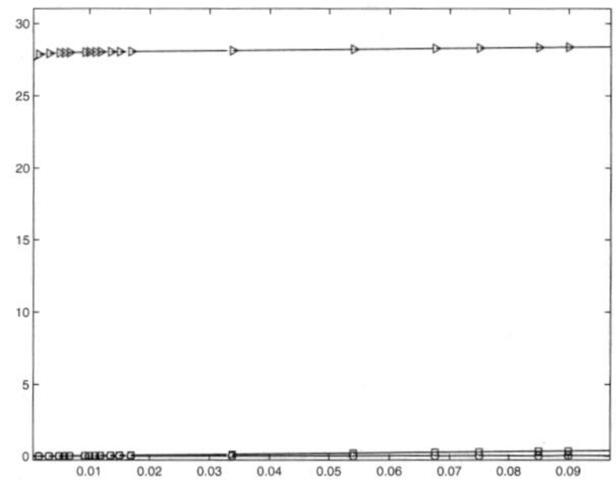

Fig. 10. n_{fneg} (□), n_{fpos} (▹) and n_{corr} (○) as a function of the noise level σ for $N = 100$, $\kappa_T \approx 0.03$

Noisy data. Noise is ubiquitous in real world applications, hence it is mandatory to test the algorithm's robustness. Fig. 9 shows the relative deviation of the respective output of student and teacher $\delta\dot{x}$ as a function of the noise level σ. As can be expected for a linear system, the quality is acceptable for low noise levels only. In particular, $\sigma < 0.01$ still yields a reasonably accurate output. The breakdown for higher noise levels is explained by Fig. 10 which shows a very large increase in the number of false positives n_{fpos} for an increasing noise level σ. Although these components are very small, they nevertheless preclude perfect identification of the network.

Scaling with system size. How the system scales with the system size has already been illustrated in Fig. 1, 4, 6 and 7. However, it is Fig. 2 that provides the most insight. It turns out that the generalization error curves for various system sizes can be computed by applying the correct scaling on the system size α. Suppose we have a curve for $\varepsilon_{\text{gen}}^{\text{fs}}$ versus α for N_0, then the curve for system size N can be obtained by scaling

$$\alpha(N) = \alpha_{\text{gen}}^{\text{fs}} + \sqrt{N_0/N}\,(\alpha(N_0) - \alpha_{\text{gen}}^{\text{fs}}) \tag{3}$$

The result is shown in Fig. 8 for system sizes $N = 100$ and $N = 160$ with sparsity $\kappa_T = 0.03$. The curve computed for $N = 160$ from that for $N = 100$ is in very good agreement with the one observed for that system size.

4 Discussion and Conclusions

It is quite remarkable that a simple model such as the one considered here exhibits so many interesting features. With respect to the research questions addressed, we may conclude that the algorithm identifies a network with $N(N+1)$ interactions using a training set of considerably smaller size. This turns out to be a consequence of the teacher's sparsity. Moreover, a first order phase transition occurs during the learning process. The system shows a sudden transition to perfect generalization during the learning process. The latter can be explained by considering the geometric interpretation of linear programming. Adding an additional constraint in the form of an input-output pair can lead to abrupt changes of the minimal values that can be attained by the objective function when its domain is further restricted. The relation between the feature selection problem and the network identification task is of note, especially since the generalization behavior of the latter can be derived from the former's. Moreover, the scaling properties of feature selection have been demonstrated: given the generalization curve for a certain size and a fixed sparsity, one can compute the generalization curve for a system of any size with that sparsity. Unfortunately, the algorithm's robustness to noise is fairly limited. This is to be expected given the nature of linear programming as mentioned above. This is definitely an area for future research.

References

1. de Jong, H.: Modeling and simulation of genetic regulatory systems: A literature review. Comp. Biol. 9, 67–103 (2002)
2. Jong, H.d., et al.: Qualitative simulation of genetic regulatory networks using piecewise-linear models. Bulletin of Mathematical Biology 66(2), 301–340 (2004)
3. Fuchs, J.: More on sparse representations in arbitrary bases. In: Proc. 13th IFAC Symp. on System Identification, pp. 1357–1362 (2003)
4. Fuchs, J.: On sparse representations in arbitrary redundant bases. IEEE Trans. Infor. Theory 50(6), 1341–1344 (2004)
5. Glass, L., Kauffman, S.: The logical analysis of continuous non-linear biochemical control networks. J. Theor. Biol. 39(1), 103–129 (1973)
6. Mitchell, T.M.: Machine Learning. McGraw-Hill, New York (1997)
7. Novak, B., Tyson, J.: Modeling the control of dna replication in fission yeast. PNAS 94, 9147–9152 (1997)
8. Peeters, R.L.M., Westra, R.L.: On the identification of sparse gene regulatory networks. In: Proc. of the 16th Intern. Symp. on Math. Theory of Networks and Systems (2004)

9. Westra, R.L.: Piecewise linear dynamic modeling and identification of gene-protein interaction networks. In: Nisis/JCB Workshop Reverse Engineering (2005)
10. Westra, R.L., Hollanders, G., Bex, G., Gyssens, M., Tuyls, K.: The identification of dynamic gene-protein networks. In: Tuyls, K., Westra, R., Saeys, Y., Nowé, A. (eds.) KDECB 2006. LNCS (LNBI), vol. 4366, pp. 157–170. Springer, Heidelberg (2007)
11. Yeung, M.K.S., Tegnér, J., Collins, J.: Reverse engineering gene networks using singular value decomposition and robust regression. PNAS 99(9), 6163–6168 (2002)

Semi-supervised Collaborative Text Classification

Rong Jin[1], Ming Wu, and Rahul Sukthankar[2]

[1] Michigan State University, East Lansing MI 48823, USA
rongjin@cse.msu.edu
[2] Intel Research Pittsburgh and Carnegie Mellon University, USA
rahuls@cs.cmu.edu

Abstract. Most text categorization methods require text content of documents that is often difficult to obtain. We consider "Collaborative Text Categorization", where each document is represented by the feedback from a large number of users. Our study focuses on the semi-supervised case in which one key challenge is that a significant number of users have not rated any labeled document. To address this problem, we examine several semi-supervised learning methods and our empirical study shows that collaborative text categorization is more effective than content-based text categorization and the manifold regularization is more effective than other state-of-the-art semi-supervised learning methods.

1 Introduction

Most studies of text categorization are based on the textual contents of documents. The most common approach for text categorization is to first represent each document by a vector of term frequency, often called the bag-of-words representation, and then to apply classification algorithms based on term frequency vectors. The classification accuracy often heavily depends on the quality of textual contents of documents.

This paper focuses on the case where the textual contents of documents are either inaccurate or difficult to acquire, which makes it difficult to apply the standard text categorization methods. To this end, we propose **Collaborative Text Categorization** (as opposed to content-based text categorization) which classifies documents using the users' feedback such as ratings and click-through data. The underlying assumption is that two documents are likely to be in one category if they share similar feedback from a large number of users.

A straightforward approach toward collaborative text categorization is to represent each document by a vector of users' feedback. The problem arises when the number of labeled documents is small, which we refer to as "*semi-supervised collaborative text categorization*". Given a small number of labeled documents, the feedback from users who gave no feedback for *any* of the labeled documents will not be incorporated into the classification model. We refer to this problem as the "*missing user*" problem. This paper focuses on how to address the missing user problem in semi-supervised collaborative text categorization by exploiting

J.N. Kok et al. (Eds.): ECML 2007, LNAI 4701, pp. 600–607, 2007.

the unlabeled documents. We will examine four semi-supervised approaches including *label propagation*, *user clustering*, the *kernel* approach, and *manifold regularization*.

The remainder of this paper is organized as follows: Section 2 briefly reviews the previous work on text categorization as well as the studies on exploiting collaborative feedback for information retrieval; Section 3 describes the problem of collaborative text categorization and the four semi-supervised approaches for the missing user problem; Section 4 presents our empirical study with movie classification; Section 5 concludes this paper with the future work.

2 Related Work

This work is closely related to previous studies on exploiting user feedback information for information retrieval [5, 8, 11]. Unlike the previous studies in information retrieval, this study utilizes the user feedback information for text categorization. Our work also differs from the previous studies on adaptive information filtering (e.g., [10]) in that the adaptive information filtering employs the feedback as a class label while our work uses feedback as part of the document representation.

Our work is related to the previous research on text categorization, including decision trees [2], logistic regression [12], and support vector machines (SVM) reported as the best [7]. A number of studies have also been devoted to using semi-supervised learning techniques for text categorization, including transductive support vector machine [9], graph-based approaches [13, 1] and Bayesian classifiers [4]. Our work differs from earlier research in that it uses the users' feedback, rather than the textual content, for classification and it focuses on exploiting the unlabeled documents to alleviate the missing user problem.

3 Semi-supervised Collaborative Text Categorization

We describe the semi-supervised collaborative text categorization problem, and then present four semi-supervised learning approaches that can potentially alleviate the missing user problem in semi-supervised collaborative text categorization.

3.1 Problem Description

Let $\mathcal{D} = (\mathbf{d}_1, \mathbf{d}_2, \ldots, \mathbf{d}_n)$ denote the document collection; the first n_l documents are labeled, $\bar{\mathbf{y}}_l = (\bar{y}_1, \bar{y}_2, \ldots, \bar{y}_{n_l})$, where each $\bar{y}_i \in \{-1, +1\}$. Let $\mathcal{U} = (u_1, u_2, \ldots, u_m)$ denote the m users who provided feedback on $\mathcal{D}$. Let $F \in \mathbb{R}^{m \times n}$ be the user feedback matrix. $F_{i,j}$ indicates the feedback of the user u_i for the document d_j. It can be a binary number, i.e., either $+1$ or -1, for binary relevance judgments, or a categorical number, such as $1, 2, 3, \ldots$, for user rating information. $F_{i,j} = 0$ if no feedback is provided by u_i for d_j. The goal of collaborative text categorization is to exploit the feedback information encoded in F to classify the documents in the document collection $\mathcal{D}$.

A straightforward approach is to first represent each document $\mathbf{d}_i$ by its user feedback $\mathbf{d}_i = (F_{1,i}, F_{2,i}, \ldots, F_{n,i})$ and then apply standard supervised learning methods using the feedback information. The underlying assumption is that two documents are likely to share the same category if their user feedbacks are similar, which we refer to as the "**user feedback assumption**". We examine this assumption using the movie rating data in Sect. 4. The important challenge in collaborative text categorization is the "*missing user*" problem. For users who have not provided feedback for any labeled document, their feedback information cannot be exploited in standard supervised learning and therefore will be completely wasted. We refer to the users who provide no feedback for any labeled documents as the *missing users*.

3.2 Semi-supervised Learning Approaches

We discuss four semi-supervised approaches for collaborative text categorization.

Label Propagation. One difficulty from the missing user problem is that the feedback of the missing users cannot be used to assess the similarity between the labeled and unlabeled documents. To alleviate this problem, we can employ the label propagation approach. The key idea behind label propagation is to propagate the class labels of documents to neighbors that share similar feedback ratings from a large number of users. Thus, given two documents d_i and d_j sharing no common users, we may still be able to infer the category of d_j from d_i if there is a sequence of documents $d_i, d_{p_1}, d_{p_2}, \ldots, d_{p_l}, d_j$ such that every two consecutive documents in the sequence share large similarity. A potential problem with label propagation is that there may be a sequence of consecutively-similar documents for two documents with completely opposite user feedback. This issue becomes more serious when the similarity information is sparse, as is often the case in collaborative text categorization.

User Clustering. The second approach toward the missing user problem is to reduce the number of distinct users. We can cluster a large number of users into a relatively small number of user clusters and then represent each document by the aggregated feedback from each user cluster. In this study, we choose the probabilistic spectral clustering algorithm [6] because of its effectiveness and *soft* cluster membership assignments that is better for capturing the feedback of users with mixed interests. One difficulty in the user clustering approach is how to determine the number of clusters. A small number of user clusters may not capture the diversity of user interests while a large number of user clusters may not alleviate the missing user problem sufficiently. Cross validation may be employed, but it is unlikely that cross validation will reliably identify the optimal number with the small number of labeled documents.

The Kernel Method. The key idea of the kernel method is to improve the estimation of document similarity by exploiting the user similarity. Two documents d_i and d_j that share no common users may have zero similarity computed as $S^d_{i,j} = \mathbf{d}_i^\top \mathbf{d}_j$. Based on the intuition that d_i and d_j are similar if the two sets of users who provided feedback for d_i and d_j have similar feedback, we can improve document similarity by a kernel similarity measure as $\tilde{S}^d_{i,j} = \mathbf{d}_i^\top S^u \mathbf{d}_j$ with the user similarity matrix S^u. We refer to $\tilde{S}^d_{i,j}$ as the "*transformed document similarity*" as opposed to standard S^d. Such a kernel can then be incorporated into a support vector machine for document classification. A potential problem with the proposed kernel is the overestimated document similarities. This problem could be partially addressed by the user clustering approach, which unfortunately has its own significant weaknesses as described above.

Manifold Regularization. In a linear classifier, the most important parameters are the weights $\mathbf{w} = (w_1, w_2, \ldots, w_m)$ assigned to the m users. Given the limited number of labeled documents, a typical algorithm for maximum margin classification (e.g., SVM) would assign zero weights to these missing users and lead to a classifier that ignores the feedback from these missing users. Given the labeled documents $\mathbf{d}_1, \mathbf{d}_2, \ldots, \mathbf{d}_{n_l}$, a standard support vector machine is formulated as:

$$\begin{aligned}&\min_{\mathbf{w},\varepsilon} \frac{1}{2}\sum_{k=1}^{m} w_k^2 + C\sum_{i=1}^{n_l}\varepsilon_i\\ &\text{s. t. } y_i(\mathbf{w}^\top \mathbf{d}_i - b) \geq 1 - \varepsilon_i,\ \varepsilon_i \geq 0,\ i = 1, 2, \ldots, n_l\ .\end{aligned}$$

Clearly, zero weights are assigned to the missing users because the conventional regularizer, $l(\mathbf{w}) = \sum_{k=1}^{m} w_k^2$, encourages w_k to be set to zero whenever possible.

Based on manifold regularization [3], our approach alleviates the missing user problem by replacing $l(\mathbf{w})$ with $l_m(\mathbf{w}) = \sum_{i,j=1}^{m} S^u_{i,j}(w_i - w_j)^2 = \mathbf{w}^\top L^u \mathbf{w}$ where the graph Laplacian $L^u = D^u - S^u$ and the diagonal matrix D^u has $D^u_{i,i} = \sum_{j=1}^{n} S^u_{i,j}$. The regularizer $l_m(\mathbf{w})$ measures the inconsistency between $\mathbf{w}$ and S^u. By minimizing $l_m(\mathbf{w})$, we enforce similar weights for those users sharing a large similarity in their interests. Hence, the missing users can still be assigned significant weights if they share large similarity with the users who did provide feedback for the labeled documents. $l_m(\mathbf{w})$ leads to the following problem:

$$\begin{aligned}&\min_{\mathbf{w},\varepsilon} \frac{1}{2}\mathbf{w}^\top L^u \mathbf{w} + C\sum_{i=1}^{n_l}\varepsilon_i\\ &\text{s. t. } y_i(\mathbf{w}^\top \mathbf{d}_i - b) \geq 1 - \varepsilon_i,\ \varepsilon_i \geq 0,\ i = 1, 2, \ldots, n_l\ . \qquad (1)\end{aligned}$$

It is not difficult to compute the dual form of the above problem, i.e.,

$$\begin{aligned}&\max_{\alpha} \sum_{i=1}^{n_l}\alpha_i - \frac{1}{2}\alpha^\top X^\top [L^u]^{-1} X\alpha\\ &\text{s. t. } \sum_{i=1}^{n_l}\alpha_i y_i = 0,\ 0 \leq \alpha_i \leq C,\ i = 1, 2, \ldots, n_l\ . \qquad (2)\end{aligned}$$

where $X = (\mathbf{d}_1, \mathbf{d}_2, \ldots, \mathbf{d}_n)$ represents the document collection. We make the transformation $\mathbf{d}_i \leftarrow [L^u]^{-1/2}\mathbf{d}_i$ $(i = 1, 2, \ldots, n_l)$ which turns the dual formulism in (2) into the dual form of the standard SVM. We add a small identity matrix $\delta I_{n_l \times n_l}$ $(\delta \ll 1)$ to L^u to avoid a singularity graph Laplacian.

4 Experiments

We evaluate four methods for semi-supervised collaborative text categorization and address two questions: (1) How effective is collaborative text categorization in comparison to content-based approaches? (2) How effective are the various proposed algorithms in the study?

We employ the MovieRating dataset[1] which consists of 1682 movies in 19 categories rated by 943 users with the integer ratings ranging from 1 (worst) to 5 (best) or 0 for unavailable ratings. We select the four most popular categories: "Action", "Comedy", "Drama", and "Thriller". The resulting dataset has 1422 movies each represented by a vector of ratings from 943 users. We also download the movie keywords from the online movie database[2] resulting in 10116 unique words for 1422 movies. We use the linear SVM as the baseline implemented in SVM-light[3]. For every category, we compute the $F1$ metric by averaging $F1$ scores over 40 independent trials. We compute both the movie similarity matrix S^d and the user similarity matrix S^u by the linear kernel similarity.

4.1 Effectiveness of Collaborative Text Categorization

The number of unique movie keywords is significantly greater than the number of users who rated the movies. This raises the concern that the user feedback representation may be less rich than the keyword representation and thus collaborative text categorization may not be as effective as content-based text categorization. We summarize in Table 1 the $F1$ results for both collaborative text categorization and content-based text categorization. In all cases, collaborative text categorization is considerably more effective.

We then verify the "user feedback assumption", which is that two documents tend to be in the same category if they have similar user ratings. Figure 1 shows the distribution of the probability for two movies to share the same category w.r.t the pairwise movie similarity based on user ratings. The high end of the distribution appears to be spiky because few document pairs are able to achieve a similarity score greater than 0.6. The overall trend proves that our assumption is reasonable for document categorization.

4.2 Semi-supervised Collaborative Text Categorization

To study the effectiveness of semi-supervised collaborative approaches, we randomly select 10, 20, 30, and 40 movies for training. To avoid a skewed number

[1] `http://www.cs.usyd.edu.au/~irena/movie_data.zip`
[2] `http://us.imdb.com/`
[3] `http://svmlight.joachims.org/`

Table 1. F1 scores of collaborative and content-based categorization

Cat.	Classif.	# Training examples 20	40	80	100
Act.	collab.	0.291	0.337	0.353	0.344
	content	0.170	0.229	0.346	0.343
Com.	collab.	0.349	0.399	0.436	0.459
	content	0.321	0.345	0.363	0.374
Dra.	collab.	0.509	0.603	0.645	0.665
	content	0.398	0.416	0.546	0.575
Thri.	collab.	0.159	0.184	0.209	0.207
	content	0.118	0.131	0.153	0.165

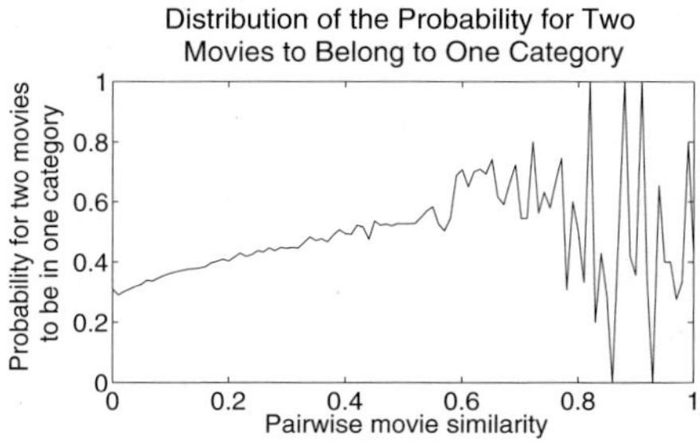

Fig. 1. Distribution of the probability that two movies are in one category

Table 2. The fraction of "missing users" in four categories

Category	# Training examples 10	20	30	40
Action	60.8%	42.2%	34.2%	20.4%
Comedy	57.4%	41.1%	33.2%	23.0%
Drama	57.0%	44.9%	34.9%	22.5%
Thriller	61.4%	41.3%	31.3%	21.1%

Table 3. F1 scores of user clustering with 10 training examples

# Clu.	Action	Comedy	Drama	Thriller
5	0.140	0.329	0.431	0.120
10	0.117	0.308	0.396	0.121
30	0.113	0.311	0.427	0.120
50	0.119	0.290	0.436	0.112
100	0.121	0.319	0.427	0.118

of positively-labeled examples, we set the number of positively-labeled examples to be same as the number of negatively-labeled examples. We first examine the missing user problem. Table 2 shows the percentage of users who did not rate any of the labeled movies (i.e., the fraction of *missing users*). Clearly the missing user problem can be significant when the number of labeled examples is small.

We then examine the classification accuracy of the four discussed methods. Tables 4(a) to 4(d) summarize the $F1$ results of the four methods and linear SVM for the chosen categories. Our implementation of label propagation is based on [13]. We set the number of user clusters to be 5 for the user clustering approach. From the results in Tables 4(a) to 4(d), we first observe that among the four approaches, the manifold regularization approach is the *only* one that consistently improves the performance of the linear SVM. For a number of cases, manifold regularization yields considerable improvements.

The second observation drawn from Tables 4(a) to 4(d) is that the other three methods: user clustering, the kernel method, and label propagation, all perform significantly worse than the linear SVM for all categories but Comedy. The failure of *label propagation* may be attributed to a sparse similarity matrix in which more than 2/3 of the pairwise similarity is less than 0.1 and only 0.5% percentage of the pairwise similarity is significantly large (i.e., > 0.5). Such a sparse similarity matrix is unlikely to reveal any clustering structure of movies. One major problem with the *user clustering* method is the difficulty in determining the appropriate number of clusters. Table 3 shows the F1 scores of

Table 4. F1 measure of the four semi-supervised learning methods for chosen categories

(a) Action Category

	# Training examples			
Classifier	10	20	30	40
SVM	0.219	0.291	0.308	0.344
Manifold Reg.	0.264	0.341	0.375	0.381
User Cluster.	0.140	0.140	0.140	0.140
Kernel	0.146	0.178	0.204	0.207
Label Prop.	0.155	0.147	0.142	0.135

(b) Comedy category

	# Training examples			
Classifier	10	20	30	40
SVM	0.308	0.349	0.394	0.400
Manifold Reg.	0.338	0.370	0.421	0.423
User Cluster.	0.329	0.339	0.343	0.350
Kernel	0.322	0.351	0.355	0.386
Label Prop.	0.300	0.296	0.296	0.295

(c) Drama Category

	# Training examples			
Classifier	10	20	30	40
SVM	0.507	0.509	0.562	0.603
Manifold Reg.	0.519	0.568	0.589	0.643
User Cluster.	0.431	0.484	0.493	0.534
Kernel	0.354	0.496	0.530	0.537
Label Prop.	0.353	0.353	0.360	0.353

(d) Thriller Category

	# Training examples			
Classifier	10	20	30	40
SVM	0.144	0.159	0.171	0.184
Manifold Reg.	0.161	0.169	0.196	0.201
User Cluster.	0.120	0.121	0.122	0.127
Kernel	0.124	0.125	0.125	0.126
Label Prop.	0.136	0.129	0.125	0.129

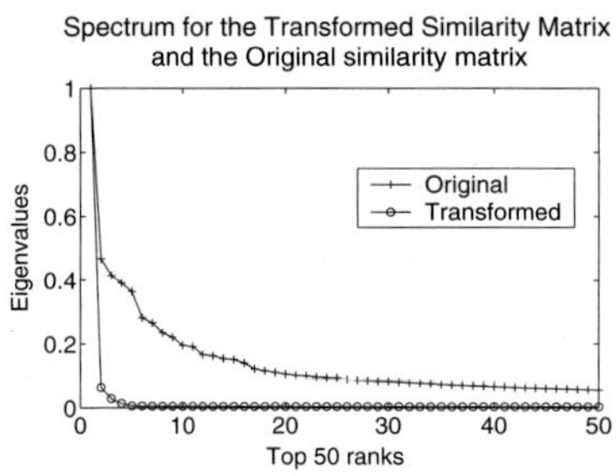

Fig. 2. Spectrum of the original and transformed movie similarity matrix

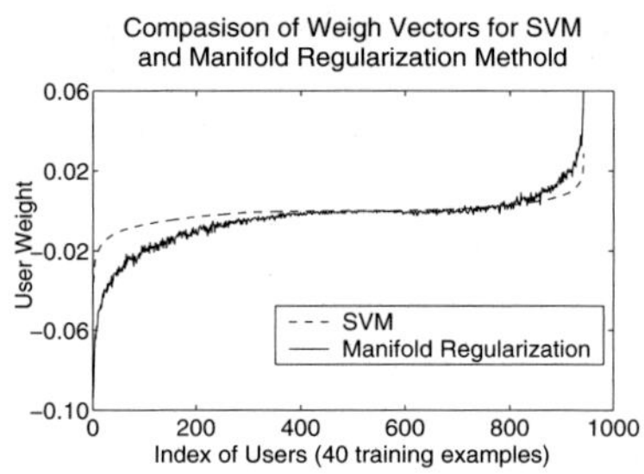

Fig. 3. User weights by linear SVM and manifold regularization

user clustering with different cluster numbers. Regardless of cluster numbers, the algorithm is unable to consistently outperform the linear SVM model. The failure of *the kernel method* may be explained by the overestimated movie similarity which can lead to the skewed spectrum of the similarity matrix. Figure 2 shows the top 100 eigenvalues of the transformed similarity matrix and the original similarity matrix. Clearly the spectrum of the original similarity matrix is much flatter than the transformed one. This is consistent with our hypothesis.

Finally, we examine the missing user problem. Figure 3 shows the weights of 943 users computed by the linear SVM and the manifold regularization method. The horizontal axis (i.e., the user index) is sorted in the ascending order of their weights that are computed by the linear SVM. Evidently most users are assigned zero weights by the linear SVM because of the missing user problem while most users are assigned non-zeros weights by the manifold regularization method which is more effective in alleviating the missing user problem.

5 Conclusions

In this paper, we study the problem of collaborative text categorization by using user feedback as the basis for classifying documents. Our experiments validate the basic assumption behind collaborative text categorization. Moreover, this work evaluated four algorithms for semi-supervised collaborative text categorization and our empirical finding is that manifold regularization is the most effective among the four competitors and is a considerable improvement over traditional content-based categorization.

References

1. Angelova, R., Weikum, G.: Graph-based text classification: learn from your neighbors. In: Proceedings of SIGIR (2006)
2. Apte, C., Damerau, F., Weiss, S.: Automated Learning of Decision Rulesfor Text Categorization. ACM Transactions on Information Systems 12(3) (1994)
3. Belkin, M., Niyogi, P., Sindhwani, V.: Manifold Regularization: a Geometric Framework for Learning from Examples. Technical Report (2004)
4. Dayanik, A., Lewis, D., Madigan, D., Menkov, V., Genkin, A.: Constructing informative prior distributions from domain knowledge in text classification. In: SIGIR'06 (2006)
5. Hoi, C.H., Lyu, M.R.: A novel log-based relevance feedback technique in content-based image retrieval. In: Proceedings of ACM Multimedia, ACM Press, New York (2004)
6. Jin, R., Ding, C., Kang, F.: A Probabilistic Approach for Optimizing Spectral Clustering. In: Advances in NIPS, vol. 18 (2006)
7. Joachims, T.: Text categorization with support vector machines: learning with many relevant features. In: Proceedings European Conference on Machine Learning (1998)
8. Joachims, T.: Optimizing search engines using clickthrough data. In: Proceedings of the eighth ACM SIGKDD, ACM Press, New York (2002)
9. Joachims, T.: Transductive Inference for Text Classification using Support Vector Machines. In: Proceedings of ICML (1999)
10. Robertson, S., Callan, J.: Routing and filtering. In: TREC: Experiment and Evaluation In Information Retrieval, MIT Press, Cambridge (2006)
11. Xue, G., Zeng, H., Chen, Z., Ma, W., Zhang, H., Lu, C.: Implicit link analysis for small web search. In: Proceedings of SIGIR (2003)
12. Zhang, J., Jin, R., Yang, Y., Hauptmann, A.: Modified Logistic Regression: An Approximation to SVM and its Applications in Large-Scale Text Categorization. In: Proceedings of ICML (2003)
13. Zhu, X., Gharahmani, Z., Lafferty, J.: Semi-supervised learning using Gaussian fields and harmonic functions. In: Proceedings of ICML (2003)

Learning from Relevant Tasks Only

Samuel Kaski and Jaakko Peltonen*

Laboratory of Computer and Information Science, Helsinki University of Technology, P.O. Box 5400, FI-02015 TKK, Finland
{samuel.kaski,jaakko.peltonen}@tkk.fi

Abstract. We introduce a problem called relevant subtask learning, a variant of multi-task learning. The goal is to build a classifier for a task-of-interest having too little data. We also have data for other tasks but only some are relevant, meaning they contain samples classified in the same way as in the task-of-interest. The problem is how to utilize this "background data" to improve the classifier in the task-of-interest. We show how to solve the problem for logistic regression classifiers, and show that the solution works better than a comparable multi-task learning model. The key is to assume that data of all tasks are mixtures of relevant and irrelevant samples, and model the irrelevant part with a sufficiently flexible model such that it does not distort the model of relevant data.

Keywords: multi-task learning, relevant subtask learning.

1 Introduction

All too often in classification tasks there is too little training data to estimate sufficiently powerful models. This problem is ubiquitous in bioinformatics; it appears also in image classification from few examples, finding of relevant texts, etc. Possible solutions are to restrict the classifier complexity by prior knowledge, or to gather more data. However, prior knowledge may be insufficient or may not exist, measuring new data may be too expensive, and there may not exist more samples of *representative* data. Most classifiers assume that learning data are representative, that is, they come from the same distribution as test data.

Often, *partially representative* data is available; e.g., in bioinformatics there are databases full of data measured for different tasks, conditions or contexts; for texts there is the web. They can be seen as training data from a (partly) different distribution as the test data. Assuming we have several sets, each potentially having some portion of relevant data, our research problem is, *can we use the partially relevant data sets to build a better classifier for the test data?*

This is a special type of multi-task learning problem. In multi-task learning [1], where learning a classifier for one data set is called a task, models have mainly been symmetrical, and transfer to new tasks is done by using the posterior from other tasks as a prior (e.g. [2,3]). By contrast, our problem is fundamentally asymmetric and more structured: test data fits one task, the "*task-of-interest*," and other tasks may contain *subtasks* relevant for the task-of-interest, but no

* The authors contributed equally to the work.

J.N. Kok et al. (Eds.): ECML 2007, LNAI 4701, pp. 608–615, 2007.

other task needs to be wholly relevant. Our models are better suited in the task-of-interest yet have the same order of complexity as earlier multi-task models.

Previous work. The problem is partly related to several other learning problems: transfer learning, multi-task learning, and semisupervised learning.

A common multi-task learning approach is to build a hierarchical (Bayesian) model of all tasks, with constrained priors favoring similar parameters across tasks. Tasks may be learned together [4,5,6] or a new task can use a prior learned from previous tasks [2,3]. Both approaches model all tasks symmetrically. Support vector machines (SVMs) have been used in symmetric hierarchical modeling as well (e.g. [7]). We study an asymmetric situation with a specific task-of-interest for which only some tasks, or parts thereof, are relevant.

In some multi-task solutions all tasks are not relevant for all others. In [8] tasks are assumed to come in clusters, and tasks in the same cluster are generated with the same parameters. Tasks are also clustered or gated in [9], and based on SVMs in [7]. In all these approaches all tasks are equally important with respect to the clustering so there is no specific task-of-interest.

In some interesting partly heuristic approaches a single task-of-interest is assumed. In [10] a global parameter controls the weight of auxiliary samples in nonparametric classification, or background data are used as support vectors or constraints in SVMs. In [11] extra variables are used to artificially improve the log-likelihood of undesirable samples of auxiliary data, and a constraint on the use of the extra variables forces the model to seek useful auxiliary samples.

2 Relevant Subtask Learning

Consider a set of classification tasks indexed by $S = 1, ..., M$. Each task S has a training data set $D_S = \{\mathbf{x}_i, c_i\}_{i=1}^{N_S}$ where $\mathbf{x}_i \in \mathbb{R}^d$ are d-dimensional input features, c_i are class labels, and N_S is the number of samples for that task. For simplicity, in this paper we assume all tasks are two-class classification tasks (c_i is +1 or -1) with the same d, but the process that generates the classes is different in each task. One task, with index U, is the *task-of-interest*. The other tasks are *supplementary* tasks; in each, some portion (0-100%) of the samples are assumed to come from the same distribution as the task-of-interest. The rest come from another distribution, potentially different for each supplementary task.

We wish to learn to predict classes well for data coming from the task-of-interest. We are not interested in the other tasks except as a source of information for the task-of-interest. There are no paired samples between tasks; the only connections between tasks are possible similarities in their underlying distributions.

The relevant subtask learning problem is to build a classifier, more specifically a model for the class density $p(c|\mathbf{x}, U)$ in task U, because test data is known to come from this distribution. In addition to data $D_U = \{(c_i, \mathbf{x}_i)\}_{i=1}^{N_U}$ of task U, data D_S from other tasks S are available. The assumption is that some samples of each D_S may come from the distribution $p(c|\mathbf{x}, U)$ but the rest do not.

As usual, the analyst chooses a model family for the task-of-interest, by prior knowledge, or resorting to a nonparametric or semiparametric model. Particular models are denoted by $p(c|\mathbf{x}, U; \mathbf{w}_U)$, where the parameter values $\mathbf{w}_U$ identify the model. The interesting question is how to model the relationships between the task-of-interest and the other tasks, which we discuss next.

For each supplementary task S we assume part of the samples come from the same distribution $p(c|\mathbf{x}, U; \mathbf{w}_U)$, part from a different one. Only the former are relevant for modeling the task-of-interest. The analyst must specify a model for the non-relevant samples as well; typically a nonparametric or semiparametric model would be used to avoid collecting prior infomation about all tasks. Denote the model for the non-relevant samples of subtask S by $p_{\text{nonrelevant}}(c|\mathbf{x}, S; \mathbf{w}_S)$. Since task S is a mix of relevant and nonrelevant data, its model should be

$$p(c|\mathbf{x}, S; \boldsymbol{\theta}) = (1 - \pi_S) p(c|\mathbf{x}, U; \mathbf{w}_U) + \pi_S p_{\text{nonrelevant}}(c|\mathbf{x}, S; \mathbf{w}_S) \ , \tag{1}$$

where $\pi_S \in [0, 1]$ is a parameter modeling the mixture proportion of irrelevant samples in task S and $\boldsymbol{\theta}$ denotes all parameters of all tasks. Note that this model reduces to $p(c|\mathbf{x}, U; \mathbf{w}_U)$ for the task-of-interest (where $\pi_S = 0$).

The solution is to use (1) to model the data. The idea behind the functional form is that a flexible enough model for $p_{\text{nonrelevant}}$ "explains away" irrelevant data in the auxiliary subtasks, and hence $p(c|\mathbf{x}, U; \mathbf{w}_U)$ learns only on the relevant data. By forcing one of the subtasks to use the same parameters in all tasks, we force the model to find from the other tasks the common part that is useful for the task of interest. The tradeoff is that to improve performance on the task-of-interest, we spend much computational time to model data of the supplementary tasks too. This is sensible when the bottleneck is the amount of data in the task-of-interest. We call this method *Relevant Subtask Model* (RSM).

We introduce our solution with a simple parametric model; it can easily be generalized to more general parametric or semiparametric models. We model the task-of-interest U with logistic regression, $p(c|\mathbf{x}, U; \boldsymbol{\theta}) = (1 + \exp(-c\mathbf{w}_U^T \mathbf{x}))^{-1}$. We include the bias in the weights $\mathbf{w}_U$, yielding standard logistic regression when one element in the inputs $\mathbf{x}$ is constant.

We model the non-relevant data in the other tasks with logistic regression models as well. Each supplementary task S has a different regression model, having its own parameters: $p_{\text{nonrelevant}}(c|\mathbf{x}, S; \boldsymbol{\theta}) = (1 + \exp(-c\mathbf{w}_S^T \mathbf{x}))^{-1}$, where $\mathbf{w}_S$ is the weight vector. Hence the supplementary tasks are each generated from a mixture of two logistic regression models (with mixture weight π_S):

$$p(c|\mathbf{x}, S; \boldsymbol{\theta}) = (1 - \pi_S)/(1 + \exp(-c\mathbf{w}_U^T \mathbf{x})) + \pi_S/(1 + \exp(-c\mathbf{w}_S^T \mathbf{x})) \ . \tag{2}$$

In this first paper we use simple optimization and spend effort in designing controlled experiments. More advanced methods will be added in later papers.

Since the task is to model the distribution of classes given data, the objective function is the conditional log-likelihood $L_{\text{RSM}} = \sum_S \sum_{i \in D_S} \log p(c_i|\mathbf{x}_i, S; \boldsymbol{\theta})$ where S goes over all tasks including the task-of-interest, and $p(c_i|\mathbf{x}_i, S; \boldsymbol{\theta})$ is given in (2). To optimize RSM, we use standard conjugate gradient to maximize

L_{RSM} with respect to the parameters ($\mathbf{w}_U$, the $\mathbf{w}_S$, and the π_S). The computational cost per iteration is linear with respect to both dimensionality and number of samples.

3 Comparison Methods

As a proof-of-concept we compare RSM to three standard approaches, which assume progressively stronger relationships between tasks, using simple but comparable models, all optimized by maximizing the (conditional) likelihood with a conjugate gradient. More advanced versions will be compared in later work.

One of the most promising multi-task strategies is to assume tasks come from task clusters, and parameters of tasks are shared within each cluster [8]. We implement a simplified maximum likelihood-based clustering comparable to the other methods. Generality is not reduced: all approaches can in principle be given a state-of-the-art full-Bayesian treatment.

Assume there is a fixed number K of task clusters. To keep complexity comparable to RSM, each cluster k is a mixture of two logistic regression models[1]: $p(c|\mathbf{x}, k; \boldsymbol{\theta}) = \pi_k/(1 + \exp(-c\mathbf{w}_{k,1}^T\mathbf{x})) + (1 - \pi_k)/(1 + \exp(-c\mathbf{w}_{k,2}^T\mathbf{x}))$ where the weight vectors $\mathbf{w}_{k,1}$ and $\mathbf{w}_{k,2}$ and the mixing weight π_k are the parameters of cluster k. Each task is fully generated by one cluster but it is unknown which. The class probability of task S is $p_S(\boldsymbol{\theta}) = \sum_{k=1}^{K} \gamma_{k|S} \prod_{i\in D_S} p(c_i|\mathbf{x}_i, k; \boldsymbol{\theta})$ where the parameter $\gamma_{k|S}$ models the probability that task S comes from cluster k.

The parameters are optimized by maximizing the conditional class likelihood $L_{\mathrm{TCM}} = \sum_S \log p_S(\boldsymbol{\theta})$. We call this model "Task Clustering Model" (TCM). It is meant to be a maximum likelihood version of [8], but having a more complex model per cluster (mixture of two instead of one logistic regression model).

We try two naive models. "Single-task learning" uses data of the given task, but does not exploit other tasks. This may work well if there is a lot of data, otherwise it will overfit. It is also good if the other tasks are known to be very different. We simply used a single logistic regression model for single-task learning. The "extreme" multi-task strategy, here called "all together", is: learn as if all data from all tasks came from the task-of-interest. This may work well if tasks are very similar, otherwise the mixture will hide the features of the task-of-interest. This strategy is essentially TCM with a single cluster.

4 Experiments

We have three experimental settings. In the first two we study how RSM and TCM tolerate deviations from their assumptions. We then study news classification according to the interest of one user, when classifications from other users are available. A note on terminology: A multi-task problem has several tasks, each with its own data. The multi-task problem comes from a *domain* specifying the data distribution in each task, and the relationships of the tasks.

[1] We have checked that RSM outperforms a regular one-submodel clustering.

Experiment 1: When Task Clustering Fails. Here we created a continuum of multi-task domains where the relationship between the task-of-interest and the other tasks changes. The continuum was set up so the tasks always follow the assumptions of RSM but the assumption of underlying task clusters in TCM starts to fail. The setting is explained in a schematic diagram in Fig. 1 (left). We created 10 domains and generated 40 learning problems from each. Each problem had 10 tasks; the task-of-interest had less samples than others. Inputs $\mathbf{x}_i$ were Gaussian and labels c_i were from a task-dependent mixture of two logistic regression models, with weight vectors chosen differently in each domain, so the domains form a continuum progressively worse for TCM. We lastly added some Gaussian noise to the $\mathbf{x}_i$.[2]

Fig. 1 (right) shows average results for all domains. RSM maintains high performance, close to the upper limit.[3] TCM worsens as tasks become less clustered, as expected. The number of clusters in TCM was set to the correct value used when generating the data, to give some advantage to TCM. The naive methods perform poorly. "All together" places all data together which introduces noise as well as useful information. For single-task learning, poor performance and large variance are due to overfitting to the small "proper" training data.

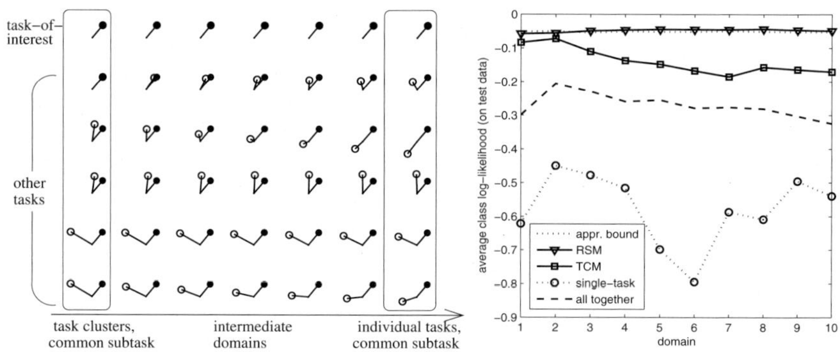

Fig. 1. Comparing methods on domains progressively less suited for TCM. **Left**: conceptual illustration; columns are domains and rows are tasks within a domain. Tasks (data sets) are generated from a mixture of two logistic regression models (weight vectors shown as lines). One subtask (line with closed ball) corresponds to the task-of-interest and appears in all tasks. The other subtask (line with open ball) is common to task clusters in the leftmost domain; in the rightmost domain it differs for each task. **Right**: Results, averaged over 40 problems for each domain. RSM performs well; TCM worsens progressively. The difference at right is significant (Wilcoxon signed rank test).

Experiment 2: When Relevant Subtask Modeling Fails. Above we showed that when the assumptions of RSM hold better it outperforms TCM. Now we show what happens when the assumptions of RSM go wrong. The setting is similar

[2] More details about all experiments can be found in [12].

[3] The bound was computed by using the parameters with which the data was generated. It is approximate because noise has been added to the inputs.

to experiment 1 and is explained in Fig. 2 (left). Domains were set up so that assumptions of TCM hold but those of RSM become progressively worse: neither of the two logistic regression models needs to be common to all tasks.

The results are shown in Fig. 2 (middle). TCM has high performance for all domains, as expected because the tasks always come from task clusters. RSM starts equally good but worsens as its assumptions begin to fail; however, it remains better than the naive methods which behave as in the first experiment.

So far the task-of-interest had less data than the others, meaning that RSM tries to retrieve relevant tasks with little information for the "query." When the task-of-interest has a comparable amount of data[4] RSM performs well for all domains (Fig. 2 (right)). It locates relevant tasks (ones from the same task cluster as the task-of-interest). RSM does not overfit to the other tasks; it models them mostly with the task-specific model. This demonstrates successful "information retrieval" of relevant tasks.

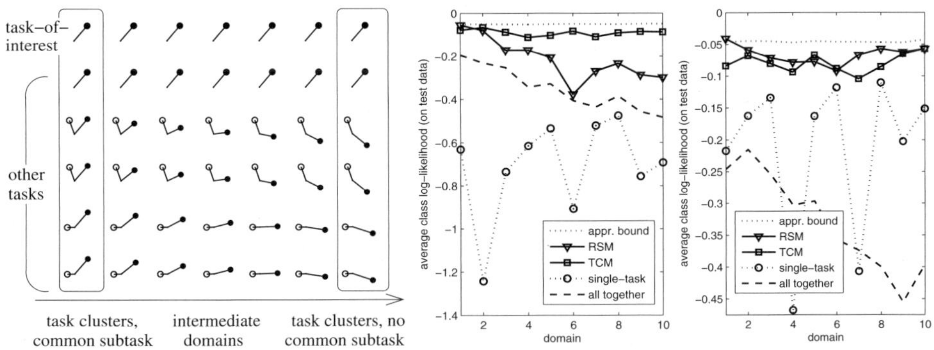

Fig. 2. Comparison of methods on domains progressively less suited for RSM. **Left**: conceptual illustration. Tasks are always clustered; tasks in a cluster are generated with the same model. In the leftmost domain, one subtask (equaling the task-of-interest) is the same in all clusters. In the rightmost domain, clusters are completely different. All domains can be learned by TCM; RSM fits the leftmost domain well but not the rightmost one. **Middle**: Results for a continuum of 10 domains (10 tasks in each; results are averages over 40 replicates); only little data in the task-of-interest. **Right**: Results when the amount of data in the task-of-interest is comparable to the other tasks.

Experiment 3: Predicting Document Relevance. Here we have real news from the Reuters-21578 collection but simulated users to control the problem domain. Each "user" classifies articles as interesting or not. The goal is to learn to predict interestingness for a "user-of-interest," who labels news interesting if they belong to the category "acq." The other users are interested in "acq" part of the time, but otherwise they are interested in another category specific to each user. The problem can be seen as combining collaborative filtering and content-based prediction. Earlier work includes e.g. [13] (partly heuristic kernel combination)

[4] A similar increase in the data amount does not help TCM in experiment 1.

and [14] (naive Bayes imputation followed by collaborative filtering). Note that RSM is more general than [13] which needs samples rated by several users (to estimate meaningful correlation kernels) whereas RSM requires none.

We used a simplistic feature extraction, including stopword removal etc., vector representation, selecting most "informative" words, discarding too sparse documents, and dimensionality reduction by linear discriminant analysis; see [12] for details. As a design parameter we varied how often the other users labeled according to "acq" on average. The user-of-interest had less data than others; test data were left-out documents from the user-of-interest. We repeated the experiment 10 times to reduce variation due to initializations and small datasets.

Results are shown in Fig. 3. RSM performs best. Since there is little data for the user-of-interest, single-task learning overfits badly. TCM[5] and "all together" perform about equally here. At the extreme where all data begins to be relevant, performances of RSM, TCM and "all together" naturally converge.

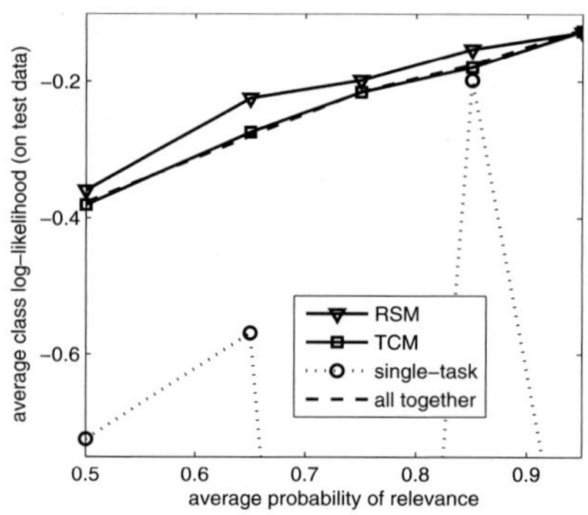

Fig. 3. Comparison of RSM to TCM and two naive methods on Reuters data. Average results over 10 generated problems are shown, as a function of one design parameter, the average probability that a sample is relevant to the task-of-interest. RSM performs the best. Performance of single-task learning varies highly due to overlearning; the worst results (at design parameter values 0.75 and 0.95) do not fit in the figure.

5 Conclusions

We introduced a new problem, *relevant subtask learning*, where multiple background tasks are used to learn one task-of-interest. We showed how a carefully constructed but generally applicable graphical model solves the problem; the idea is to model relevant parts of other tasks with a shared mixture component, and nonrelevant parts by (at least equally) flexible models, to avoid a performance tradeoff between the task-of-interest and the other tasks. Using logistic regression as an example, we showed that the resulting "Relevant Subtask Model"

[5] We used $K = 6$ clusters to have roughly equally many parameters in RSM and TCM.

(RSM) outperforms a comparable traditional multi-task learning model and two naive alternatives, on toy domains and on more realistic text classification.

The method is not restricted to logistic regression or to supervised learning. Here we used simple maximum conditional likelihood estimators, which will be generalized to full-Bayesian treatments of more general models in the next stage.

Acknowledgments. The authors belong to Helsinki Institute for Information Technology and the Adaptive Informatics Research Centre. They were supported by the Academy of Finland, decision numbers 108515 and 207467. This work was also supported in part by the IST Programme of the European Community, PASCAL Network of Excellence, IST-2002-506778. This publication only reflects the authors' views.

References

1. Caruana, R.: Multitask learning. Mach. Learn. 28, 41–75 (1997)
2. Marx, Z., Rosenstein, M.T., Kaelbling, L.P.: Transfer learning with an ensemble of background tasks. In: Inductive Transfer: 10 Years Later, NIPS workshop (2005)
3. Raina, R., Ng, A.Y., Koller, D.: Transfer learning by constructing informative priors. In: Inductive Transfer: 10 Years Later, NIPS workshop (2005)
4. Niculescu-Mizil, A., Caruana, R.: Inductive transfer for Bayesian network structure learning. In: Proceedings of AISTATS. Electronic proceedings (2007)
5. Rosenstein, M.T., Marx, Z., Kaelbling, L.P.: To transfer or not to transfer. In: Inductive Transfer: 10 Years Later, NIPS workshop (2005)
6. Yu, K., Tresp, V., Schwaighofer, A.: Learning Gaussian processes from multiple tasks. In: Proceedings of ICML 2005, pp. 1012–1019. ACM Press, New York (2005)
7. Evgeniou, T., Micchelli, C.A., Pontil, M.: Learning multiple tasks with kernel methods. J. Mach. Learn. Res. 6, 615–637 (2005)
8. Xue, Y., Liao, X., Carin, L., Krishnapuram, B.: Multi-task learning for classification with Dirichlet process priors. J. Mach. Learn. Res. 8, 35–63 (2007)
9. Bakker, B., Heskes, T.: Task clustering and gating for Bayesian multitask learning. J. Mach. Learn. Res. 4, 83–99 (2003)
10. Wu, P., Dietterich, T.G.: Improving SVM accuracy by training on auxiliary data sources. In: Proceedings of ICML 2004, pp. 871–878. Omnipress, Madison, WI (2004)
11. Liao, X., Xue, Y., Carin, L.: Logistic regression with an auxiliary data source. In: Proceedings of ICML 2005, pp. 505–512. Omnipress, Madison, WI (2005)
12. Kaski, S., Peltonen, J.: Learning from relevant tasks only. Technical Report E11, Helsinki University of Technology, Lab. of Comp. and Information Science (2007)
13. Basilico, J., Hofmann, T.: Unifying collaborative and content-based filtering. In: Proceedings of ICML 2004, pp. 65–72. Omnipress, Madison, WI (2004)
14. Melville, P., Mooney, R.J., Nagarajan, R.: Content-boosted collaborative filtering for improved recommendations. In: Proceedings of AAAI-2002, pp. 187–192. AAAI Press (2002)

An Unsupervised Learning Algorithm for Rank Aggregation

Alexandre Klementiev, Dan Roth, and Kevin Small

Department of Computer Science
University of Illinois at Urbana-Champaign
201 N. Goodwin Avenue, Urbana, IL 61801, USA
{klementi,danr,ksmall}@uiuc.edu

Abstract. Many applications in information retrieval, natural language processing, data mining, and related fields require a ranking of instances with respect to a specified criteria as opposed to a classification. Furthermore, for many such problems, multiple established ranking models have been well studied and it is desirable to combine their results into a joint ranking, a formalism denoted as *rank aggregation*. This work presents a novel *unsupervised* learning algorithm for rank aggregation (ULARA) which returns a linear combination of the individual ranking functions based on the principle of rewarding ordering agreement between the rankers. In addition to presenting ULARA, we demonstrate its effectiveness on a data fusion task across ad hoc retrieval systems.

1 Introduction

Ranking items is a fundamental computer and information sciences problem. Most closely associated with information retrieval [1], ranking has recently attracted significant attention from the machine learning [2,3,4,5] and natural language processing [6,7,8] communities. While classification is the standard task of inductive learning, many applications require the expressivity of ranking. A related, but less thoroughly studied problem is *rank aggregation*, where multiple existing rankings of an item set are combined into a joint ranking. In the information retrieval community, this is the *data fusion* problem [9,10] and corresponds to deriving a document ranking based on the input of multiple retrieval systems. For domains where ranking algorithms exist which utilize different modalities or views over the data, rank aggregation is particularly appealing as these views are difficult to combine into a single model.

From a machine learning perspective, this work is most ostensibly related to [2] which extends ideas regarding expert ensembles [11] and boosting [12] to ranking. In addition to a different model representation, the fundamental difference is that our algorithm is an unsupervised learning algorithm. Another related vein is the study of deriving voting policies which satisfy specified axiomatic properties [13] (e.g. the *independence of irrelevant alternatives* [14]). Our

J.N. Kok et al. (Eds.): ECML 2007, LNAI 4701, pp. 616–623, 2007.

algorithm is similar in that the input is a set of ranking functions and no supervised training is required. However, our work adaptively learns a parameterized linear combination to optimize the relative influence of individual rankers.

In the data fusion domain, one widely cited set of approaches is [15]. These solutions are deterministic functions which mix rankings heuristically, differing from our work in that we learn the mixing parameters. One data fusion approach which has learned parameters measuring the reliability of ranking functions is ProbFuse [9], where probabilities that specific rankers return relevant documents are combined to determine the rank ordering. A second supervised approach presented by [10] also resembles our approach in that they use a linear combination of ranking functions to determine the joint ranking. However, unlike both methods, we present an unsupervised learning algorithm.

This paper presents an *unsupervised* learning algorithm for rank aggregation (ULARA) based on a linear combination of ranking functions, guided by the simple but effective principle that the relative contribution of an individual ordering to the joint ranking should be determined by its tendency to agree with other members of the expert pool. To the best of our knowledge, ULARA prescribes the first method for learning a parameterized rank aggregation without supervision. The remainder of the paper proceeds as follows. In addition to deriving ULARA in section 2, we also demonstrate specific properties on synthetic data. Section 3 proceeds by presenting experimental results for a data fusion task. Finally, we conclude and describe future work in section 4.

2 Rank Aggregation Framework

Let $x \in \mathcal{X}$ denote an item (e.g. document) in the instance space and $\mathbf{x}$ represent a set of items (e.g. corpus) to be ranked relative to each other. Furthermore, let $q \in \mathcal{Q}$ represent a query and $r : \mathcal{Q} \times \mathcal{X} \rightarrow \mathbb{N}$ represent a ranking function (e.g. retrieval system) where the output represents the item position in the ranked list such that $r(q, x) < r(q, x')$ specifies that x is ranked higher than x' with respect to q. We use the notation $r_u \succ_{\mathcal{E}} r_v$ to signify that r_u is a better ranking function than r_v with respect to the application specific evaluation criteria $\mathcal{E}$. Examples of $\mathcal{E}$ include Spearman's rank correlation coefficient [16] for general ranking problems or F1 measure for information retrieval.

Given a set of ranking functions $\{r_i\}_{i=1}^{N}$, we desire an aggregate ranking function $R : \mathcal{Q} \times \mathcal{X} \rightarrow \mathbb{N}$ such that $R \succ_{\mathcal{E}} r_i$ for $i = 1, \ldots, N$. This work studies aggregation based on the functional form $R'(q, x) = \sum_{i=1}^{N} w_i \cdot r_i(q, x)$, where w_i are the linear combination parameters, noting that R' is the expected value of the rank if $\mathbf{w}$ is a probability distribution (i.e. $0 \leq w_i \leq 1$ for all i and $\sum_{i=1}^{N} w_i = 1$). This representation has been shown successful in supervised situations [10], which we look to extend to the unsupervised case. Our specific approach derives a surrogate supervision signal in the absence of labeled data, referred to as an *incidental supervision signal*. Given this seting, the technical goals are three-fold: (1) derive an incidental supervision signal, (2) develop a corresponding unsupervised learning algorithm to learn the parameters of R', and

(3) demonstrate that this incidental supervision signal works well for multiple evaluation criteria $\mathcal{E}$.

2.1 Incidental Supervision Based on Ranker Agreement

The fundamental intuition for our incidental supervision signal is that in non-adversarial situations, accurate ranking functions will rank items according to a similar conditional distribution while poor ranking functions will tend towards a more uniformly random ranking distribution. For our representation, rankers that tend to agree with the plurality of rankers will be given large relative weight, while rankers that tend to disagree will be given small relative weight. Let $\mu(q,x) = \frac{\sum_{i=1}^{N_x} r_i(q,x)}{N_x}$ signify the mean ranking where $N_x = \sum_{i=1}^{N} [\![r_i(q,x) \leq \kappa_i]\!]$[1] (i.e. the number of ranking functions which return a ranking higher than a threshold κ_i for x). For each item to be ranked, each ranker will return a value $r_i(q,x)$ which is used to measure agreement using the variance-like measure $\sigma_i(q,x) = [r_i(q,x) - \mu(q,x)]^2$. If this value is small for a given item ranking, the corresponding ranker agrees with other rankers for this item and should be given a large weight and vice versa. Therefore, if we use a scaled variance-like measure $\delta_i(q,x) = w_i \cdot \sigma_i(q,x)$ and sum this value across all $\{query, item, ranker\}$ triples, this statement leads to an optimization problem that minimizes the weighted variance of the aggregate ranking function over the component rankings,

$$\operatorname*{argmin}_{\mathbf{w}} \sum_{q \in Q} \sum_{x \in \mathbf{x}} \sum_{i=1}^{N} \delta_i(q,x) \tag{1}$$

$$\text{s.t. } \sum_{i=1}^{N} w_i = 1; \forall i, w_i \geq 0. \tag{2}$$

2.2 Unsupervised Learning Algorithm for Rank Aggregation

As opposed to optimizing this problem of section 2.1 directly, ULARA uses iterative gradient descent [17] to derive an effective online learning algorithm. Observing that $\delta(q,x)$ is linear in w, the gradient for equation 1 with respect to a single weight w_i is $\nabla = \sum_{q \in Q} \sum_{x \in \mathbf{x}} \sigma_i(q,x)$. To derive an update rule, we are interested in the gradient of the utility function components, $\delta_i(q,x)$, stated as

$$\nabla_i = \frac{\partial \delta_i(q,x)}{\partial w_i} = [r_i(q,x) - \mu(q,x)]^2 \tag{3}$$

and resulting in algorithm 1. ULARA takes as input a set of ranking functions $\{r_i\}_{i=1}^{N}$ along with the associated ranking function threshold values κ_i, a learning rate λ, and a significance threshold value θ, all discussed in greater detail below. Also, ULARA takes a set of queries Q of which we do not know the true ranking. In general, for each item x and query q, the expert ranking for each of the N rankers are determined using $r_i(q,x)$, the mean is calculated (line 8), the gradient is determined (line 11), and the weight update is made (line 14/15). Once all of these updates are completed, the weight vector is normalized (line

[1] $[\![p]\!] = 1$ if the predicate p is true; else $[\![p]\!] = 0$.

Algorithm 1 ULARA - Training

1: **Input:** $Q, \{r_i, \kappa_i\}_{i=1}^{N}, \lambda, \theta$
2: $\mathbf{w} \leftarrow \mathbf{0}$ {additive}
3: $\mathbf{w} \leftarrow \frac{\mathbf{1}}{\mathbf{N}}$ {exponentiated}
4: $t \leftarrow 1$
5: **for all** $q \in Q$ **do**
6:   **for all** $x \in \mathbf{x}$ **do**
7:     **if** $N_x \geq \theta$ **then**
8:       $\mu(q_q, x) = \frac{\sum_{i=1}^{N_x} r_i(q,x)}{N_x}$
9:       **for** $i \leftarrow 1, \ldots, N$ **do**
10:         **if** $r_i(x) \leq \kappa_i$ **then**
11:           $\nabla_i \leftarrow [r_i(q,x) - \mu(q,x)]^2$
12:         **else**
13:           $\nabla_i \leftarrow [\kappa_i + 1 - \mu(q,x)]^2$
14:         $w_i^t \leftarrow w_i^{t-1} + \lambda \cdot \nabla_i$ {additive}
15:         $w_i^t \leftarrow \frac{w_i^{t-1} e^{-\lambda \nabla_i}}{\sum_{j=1}^{N} w_j^{t-1} e^{-\lambda \nabla_i}}$ {exp.}
16:       $t \leftarrow t + 1$
17: NORMALIZE(w) {additive}
18: **Output:** $\mathbf{w} \in [0,1]^N$

Algorithm 2 ULARA - Evaluation

1: **Input:** $q, \mathbf{w}, \{r_i, \kappa_i\}_{i=1}^{N}$
2: **for all** $x \in \mathbf{x}$ **do**
3:   $R_x \leftarrow 0$
4:   **for** $i \leftarrow 1, \ldots, N$ **do**
5:     **if** $r_i(q,x) \leq \kappa_i$ **then**
6:       $R_x \leftarrow R_x + w_i \cdot r_i(q,x)$
7:     **else**
8:       $R_x \leftarrow R_x + w_i \cdot (\kappa_i + 1)$
9: ARGSORTASCENDING(R_x)
10: $R(q,x) \leftarrow$ RANKING(R_x)
11: **Output:** $R : \mathcal{Q} \times \mathcal{X} \rightarrow \mathbb{N}$

Fig. 1. An Unsupervised Learning Algorithm for Rank Aggregation (ULARA). Note that lines 2, 14, and 17 are only used in the case of additive updates and lines 3 and 15 are only used in the case of exponentiated updates.

17) to generate a probability vector for evaluation in algorithm 2. The remaining discussion entails algorithmic details to accommodate practical situations:

- Additive vs. Exponentiated Updates - Two methods for gradient descent are additive and exponentiated updates [17], each with specific properties that will be explored. If using additive updates, lines 3 and 15 should be removed. If using exponentiated updates, lines 2, 14, and 17 should be removed noting that normalization is not necessary.
- Missing Rankings (κ_i) - For most settings, there are more items in the instance space than the individual ranking functions will return. For data fusion, systems return rankings for a fixed set of documents and most corpus documents remain unranked. We denote this threshold value as κ_i, noting that ranking functions may have different thresholds. If a ranking is not returned by a specific ranker, we substitute $\kappa_i + 1$ for update calculations (line 13), assuming unranked items are ranked just below the last ranked item.
- Learning Rate (λ) - For ULARA$_{\text{add}}$, $\lambda = 1$ was used for all experiments. For ULARA$_{\text{exp}}$, λ was set proportional to κ^{-2}.
- Variable Number of Rankers (θ) - For some items, only a small fraction of the ranking functions return a valid rank. If less than θ rankers, as defined by the user, return a valid rank for an item, the information is deemed untrustworthy and no updates are made for this item (line 7).

Studying ULARA Via Controlled Experiments. We first explore ULARA on synthetic data to: (1) examine robustness (2) compare additive and exponentiated updates. We begin by generating $M = 1000$ items with rank designated as $r_\star(x) = \{1, 2, \ldots, 1000\}$. We then specify $N = 14$ ranking functions $r_i(x)$ with varying degrees of perturbation from the true ranking by perturbing $r_\star(x)$ by a random sample from the discrete uniform distribution with window size ω. Formally, $r_i(x) \sim \mathcal{U}\left[\max\left(0, r_\star(x) - \frac{\omega}{2} - \epsilon\right), \min\left(r_\star(x) + \frac{\omega}{2} + \epsilon, M\right)\right]$ where $\epsilon \geq 0$ is the amount necessary to maintain window size ω. Ties are broken with the policy that all tied items receive an the average rank of the item positions as per [16]. $|Q| = 50$ queries were generated for $N = 14$ ranking function with two $r_i(x)$ where $\omega = 200$, two $r_i(x)$ where $\omega = 600$, and 10 $r_i(x)$ where $\omega = 1000$.

Figure 2 displays performance of both ULARA$_{\text{add}}$ and ULARA$_{\text{exp}}$ on the synthetic data. As a baseline, we modify the *CombMNZ* [15] to use rank information as opposed to the underlying real-valued score since we do not have this information in our task; $CombMNZ_{rank} \leftarrow \sum_{i=1}^{N} r_i(q, x) \cdot N_x$. We use a modified *CombMNZ* as it is unsupervised (albeit without learning) and widely used for data fusion. For evaluation, we use Spearman's rank correlation coefficient, $\rho \in [-1, 1]$ [16]. ULARA$_{\text{exp}}$ achieves an increase of 0.28 (39% relative increase) in ρ relative to $CombMNZ_{rank}$ after 40 queries and ULARA$_{\text{add}}$ achieves an increase of 0.24 (35% relative increase) in ρ after only 5 queries, demonstrating that ULARA can effectively weigh rankers without explicit supervision.

The second result is presented in figure 3, showing the average weights associated with the rankers in the three groups ($\omega = 200$, 600, and 1000) during training. ULARA assigns the most weight to the best ranking functions, some weight to the reasonable ranking functions, and almost no weight to the worst ranking functions. In accordance with theory [17], ULARA$_{\text{exp}}$ tends to select the best ranking functions by assigning all of the weight to these rankers. Conversely, ULARA$_{\text{add}}$ tends to mix the ranking functions relative to their performance, which proves beneficial in cases where many reasonable rankers exist and can complement each other in different areas of the item distribution.

3 Data Fusion

The real-world task we study empirically is data fusion [9], utilizing data from the ad hoc retrieval shared task of the TREC-3 conference. For this task, each group of $N = 40$ shared task participants was provided with a set of documents and $|Q| = 50$ of queries, returning the $\kappa = 1000$ documents for which the expected relevance is greatest for each query. ULARA was used to combine the rankings of the individual research groups into an aggregate ranking function R. Performance is quantified by the precision/recall curves and mean average precision metric as provided by the software (`trec_eval`) from the TREC conference series [18].

Figure 4 shows the results of the top individual submissions, $CombMNZ_{rank}$, and ULARA for the data fusion task. We observe that ULARA outperforms

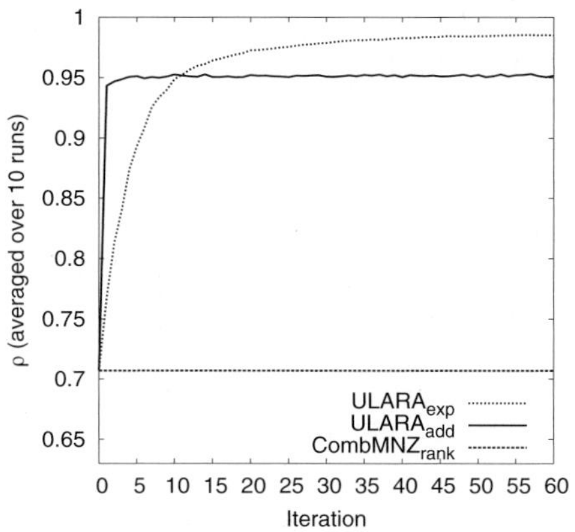

Fig. 2. Experimental results on synthetic data comparing ULARA to $CombMNZ_{rank}$. Exponentiated updates achieve a 39% relative increase compared to $CombMNZ_{rank}$ in the Spearman's ranking coefficient with only 40 queries, while additive updates achieve a 35% relative increase in only 5 queries.

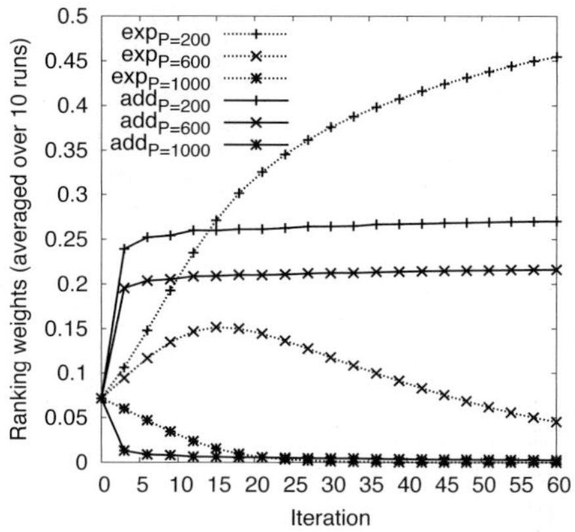

Fig. 3. ULARA ranker weights throughout training on synthetic data, noting the best rankers are weighted the highest, while the poorest rankers have negligible weight. Furthermore, exponentiated updates tends to select the best rankers while additive updates mix rankers relative to their performance.

all component ranking functions as well as $CombMNZ_{rank}$. More significantly, while $CombMNZ_{rank}$ performs slightly better than the top system, ULARA$_{\text{add}}$ achieves a relative increase in average precision of 4.0% at the top ranking, 6.4% at 0.1 recall, and 6.0% at 0.2 recall over $CombMNZ_{rank}$. ULARA$_{\text{exp}}$ achieves a relative increase in average precision of 4.3% at the top ranking, 7.7% at 0.1 recall, and 8.1% at 0.2 recall over $CombMNZ_{rank}$. These results are significant in that they demonstrate that ULARA can not only distinguish good ranking functions from bad as in the synthetic data task, but in practice can generate a joint ranking function superior to its best components on the data fusion task.

The second experiment demonstrates the robustness properties of ULARA by looking not at the situation where we are working with world-class retrieval systems, but at the hypothetical situation where many of the ranking systems were poor. Specifically, we replaced a specified number of the $N = 40$ systems with a rankings drawn uniformly from all documents returned by all systems for a given query, denoted as *random rankings*. As figure 5 shows, the mean average precision of ULARA versus $CombMNZ_{rank}$ is consistently superior, becoming more pronounced as the number of random rankings is increased. To further explore this effect, we varied θ and observe that as more noise is added, θ must be lowered to accommodate the lack of agreement between rankers. However, even under relatively extreme cicumstances, ULARA returns a joint ranking function competitive with a noise free system. This experiment demonstrates that ULARA is capable of discounting bad rankers in a real-world setting such that they are not detrimental to the aggregate ranking function R.

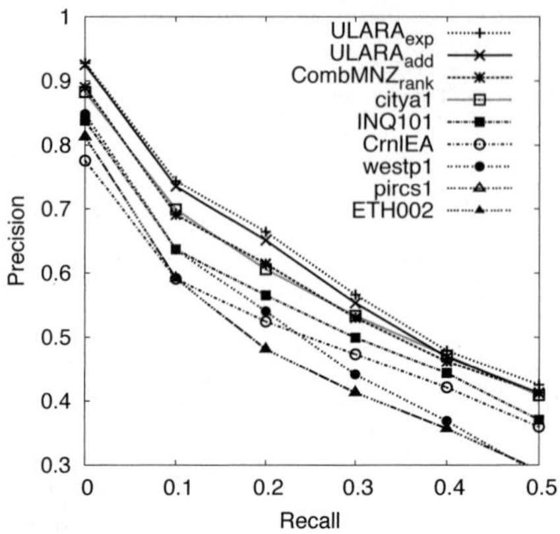

Fig. 4. Experimental results for data fusion of the retrieval systems submitted to the TREC-3 shared task. While $CombMNZ_{rank}$ only negligibly outperforms the top system, ULARA performs significantly better than any component system at multiple recall levels.

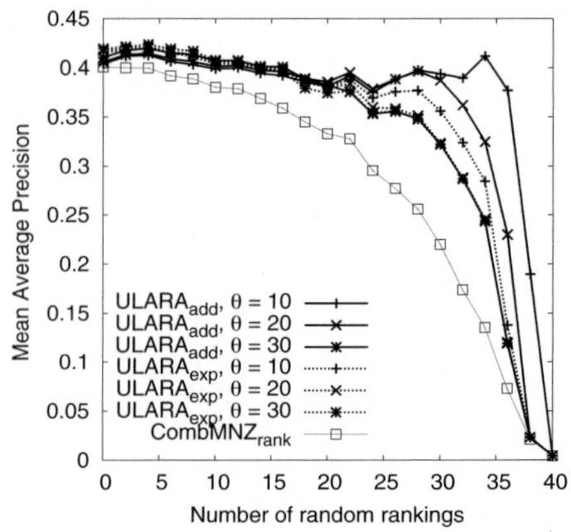

Fig. 5. Experimental results where a number of TREC-3 systems are replaced with random rankings, demonstrating robustness of ULARA. While the performance of the $CombMNZ_{rank}$ algorithm deteriorates rapidly, ULARA performs well even when more than half of the systems are replaced.

4 Conclusions and Future Work

We have presented a novel approach to the rank aggregation problem by specifying an optimization problem to learn a linear combination of ranking functions which maximizes agreement. Secondly, we introduce an unsupervised learning algorithm, ULARA, to solve this problem. This criteria is driven by the assumption that correctly ranked instances will possess a similar position in multiple ranking functions, allowing us to assign a high weight to rankers that tend to agree with the expert pool and reduce the influence of those rankers which tend to disagree. We have successfully demonstrated the effectiveness of our algorithm in two diverse experimental settings which each use a different evaluation function: on synthetic data which quantifies performance with Spearman's rank correlation coefficient and an information retrieval data fusion task which quantifies performance using precision/recall. For future work, we have already generated preliminary results extending ULARA to generalize a reranking approach [6] to named entity discovery [8], which we expect to pursue further.

Acknowledgments

This work is supported by NSF grant NSF ITR IIS-0428472 and by MIAS, a DHS Institute of Discrete Science Center for Multimodal Information Access and Synthesis.

References

1. Baeza-Yates, R.A., Ribeiro-Neto, B.A.: Modern Information Retrieval. ACM Press / Addison-Wesley (1999)
2. Cohen, W.W., Schapire, R.E., Singer, Y.: Learning to order things. Journal of Artificial Intelligence Research 10, 243–270 (1999)
3. Agarwal, S., Roth, D.: Learnability of bipartite ranking functions. In: Proc. of the Annual ACM Workshop on Computational Learning Theory (COLT), pp. 16–31 (2005)
4. Clémençon, S., Lugosi, G., Vayatis, N.: Ranking and scoring using empirical risk minimization. In: Proc. of the Annual ACM Workshop on Computational Learning Theory (COLT), pp. 1–15 (2005)
5. Rudin, C., Cortes, C., Mohri, M., Schapire, R.E.: Margin-based ranking and boosting meet in the middle. In: Proc. of the Annual ACM Workshop on Computational Learning Theory (COLT), pp. 63–78 (2005)
6. Collins, M., Koo, T.: Discriminative reranking for natural language parsing. In: Proc. of the International Conference on Machine Learning (ICML), pp. 175–182 (2000)
7. Li, H., Rudin, C., Grishman, R.: Re-ranking algorithms for name tagging. In: HLT/NAACL Workshop on Joint Inference (2006)
8. Klementiev, A., Roth, D.: Weakly supervised named entity transliteration and discovery from multilingual comparable corpora. In: Proc. of the Annual Meeting of the Association for Computational Linguistics (ACL), pp. 817–824 (2006)
9. Lillis, D., Toolan, F., Collier, R., Dunnion, J.: Probfuse: A probabilistic approach to data fusion. In: Proc. of the International ACM SIGIR Conference on Research and Development in Information Retrieval, pp. 139–146 (2006)
10. Vogt, C.C., Cottrell, G.W.: Fusion via a linear combination of scores. Information Retrieval 1(3), 151–173 (1999)
11. Cesa-Bianchi, N., Freund, Y., Helmbold, D.P., Haussler, D., Schapire, R.E., Warmuth, M.K.: How to use expert advice. Journal of the Association for Computing Machinery 44(3), 427–485 (1997)
12. Freund, Y., Schapire, R.E.: A decision-theoretic generalization of on-line learning and an application to boosting. Journal of Computer and System Sciences 55(1), 119–139 (1997)
13. Conitzer, V.: Computational Aspects of Preference Aggregation. PhD thesis, Carnegie Mellon University (2006)
14. Arrow, K.: Social Choice and Individual Values, 2nd edn. Cowles Foundation, New Haven (1963)
15. Shaw, J.A., Fox, E.A.: Combination of multiple searches. In: Text REtrieval Conference (TREC), pp. 243–252 (1994)
16. Kendall, M., Gibbons, J.D.: Rank Correlation Methods, 5th edn. Edward Arnold, London (1990)
17. Kivinen, J., Warmuth, M.K.: Additive versus exponentiated gradient updates for linear prediction. In: Proc, of the Annual ACM Symposium on Theory of Computing, pp. 209–218 (1995)
18. Voorhees, E.M., Buckland, L.P. (eds.): The Fourteenth Text REtrieval Conference Proceedings (TREC) (2005)

Ensembles of Multi-Objective Decision Trees

Dragi Kocev[1], Celine Vens[2], Jan Struyf[2], and Sašo Džeroski[1]

[1] Department of Knowledge Technologies, Jožef Stefan Institute,
Jamova 39, 1000 Ljubljana, Slovenia
{dragi.kocev,saso.dzeroski}@ijs.si

[2] Department of Computer Science, Katholieke Universiteit Leuven,
Celestijnenlaan 200A, 3001 Leuven, Belgium
{celine.vens,jan.struyf}@cs.kuleuven.be

Abstract. Ensemble methods are able to improve the predictive performance of many base classifiers. Up till now, they have been applied to classifiers that predict a single target attribute. Given the non-trivial interactions that may occur among the different targets in multi-objective prediction tasks, it is unclear whether ensemble methods also improve the performance in this setting. In this paper, we consider two ensemble learning techniques, bagging and random forests, and apply them to multi-objective decision trees (MODTs), which are decision trees that predict multiple target attributes at once. We empirically investigate the performance of ensembles of MODTs. Our most important conclusions are: (1) ensembles of MODTs yield better predictive performance than MODTs, and (2) ensembles of MODTs are equally good, or better than ensembles of single-objective decision trees, i.e., a set of ensembles for each target. Moreover, ensembles of MODTs have smaller model size and are faster to learn than ensembles of single-objective decision trees.

1 Introduction

In this work, we concentrate on the task of predicting multiple attributes. Examples thus take the form $(\mathbf{x_i}, \mathbf{y_i})$ where $\mathbf{x_i} = (x_{i1}, \ldots, x_{ik})$ is a vector of k input attributes and $\mathbf{y_i} = (y_{i1}, \ldots, y_{it})$ is a vector of t target attributes. This task is known under the name of multi-objective prediction. Existing learning techniques have been extended to address this task by learning to predict all target attributes at once [1,2,3,4]. This has two main advantages over building a separate model for each target: first, a multi-objective model is usually much smaller than the total size of the individual models for all target attributes, and second, such a multi-objective model explicates dependencies between the different target attributes. Moreover, the cited literature reports similar or slightly improved predictive performance results for the multi-objective models.

The goal of this paper is to investigate whether ensemble methods [5] can be applied to multi-objective prediction problems in order to achieve better performance. Ensemble methods construct a set of classifiers for a given prediction task and classify new data instances by taking a vote over their predictions. Ensemble methods typically improve the predictive performance of their base classifier [6].

J.N. Kok et al. (Eds.): ECML 2007, LNAI 4701, pp. 624–631, 2007.

Up till now, they have only been applied to single-objective prediction, i.e., predicting one target attribute. Given the non-trivial interactions between the target attributes in a multi-objective domain, it is unclear whether ensembles are also able to improve predictive performance in this non-standard setting. A positive answer would stimulate further research towards multi-objective problems, which are present in many real world applications [1,7,8,9,10,11,12].

In this paper, we use decision trees as base classifiers. The ensemble methods that we investigate are bagging [6] and random forests [13]. More precisely, the main questions we want to answer are (1) does building ensembles of multi-objective decision trees improve predictive performance, and (2) how do ensembles of multi-objective decision trees compare to ensembles of single-objective decision trees, i.e., a set of separate ensembles for each target attribute. The last comparison is made along three dimensions: predictive performance, model size, and running times.

The paper is organized as follows. In Section 2, we briefly discuss ensemble methods. Section 3 explains multi-objective decision trees in more detail. Section 4 presents a detailed experimental evaluation. Conclusions and some ideas for further work are presented in Section 5.

2 Ensemble Methods

An ensemble is a set of classifiers constructed with a given algorithm. Each new example is classified by combining the predictions of every classifier from the ensemble. These predictions can be combined by taking the average (for regression tasks) or the majority vote (for classification tasks), as described by Breiman [6], or by taking more complex combinations [17,18].

A necessary condition for an ensemble to be more accurate than any of its individual members, is that the classifiers are accurate and diverse [14]. An accurate classifier does better than random guessing on new examples. Two classifiers are diverse if they make different errors on new examples. There are several ways to introduce diversity: by manipulating the training set (by changing the weight of the examples [6,15] or by changing the attribute values of the examples [16]), or by manipulating the learning algorithm itself [5].

In this paper, we consider two ensemble learning techniques that have primarily been used in the context of decision trees: bagging and random forests.

2.1 Bagging

Bagging [6] is an ensemble method that constructs the different classifiers by making bootstrap replicates of the training set and using each of these replicates to construct one classifier. Each bootstrap sample is obtained by randomly sampling training instances, with replacement, from the original training set, until an equal number of instances is obtained.

Breiman [6] has shown that bagging can give substantial gains in predictive performance, when applied to an unstable learner (i.e., a learner for which small

Table 1. The top-down induction algorithm for PCTs

procedure PCT(E) **returns** tree	**procedure** BestTest(E)
1: $(t^*, h^*, \mathcal{P}^*) = \text{BestTest}(E)$	1: $(t^*, h^*, \mathcal{P}^*) = (none, 0, \emptyset)$
2: **if** $t^* \neq none$ **then**	2: **for each** possible test t **do**
3: **for each** $E_k \in \mathcal{P}^*$ **do**	3: $\mathcal{P}$ = partition induced by t on E
4: $tree_k = \text{PCT}(E_k)$	4: $h = Var(E) - \sum_{E_k \in \mathcal{P}} \frac{\lvert E_k \rvert}{\lvert E \rvert} Var(E_k)$
5: **return** node(t^*, $\bigcup_k \{tree_k\}$)	5: **if** $(h > h^*) \wedge \text{Acceptable}(t, \mathcal{P})$ **then**
6: **else**	6: $(t^*, h^*, \mathcal{P}^*) = (t, h, \mathcal{P})$
7: **return** leaf(Prototype(E))	7: **return** $(t^*, h^*, \mathcal{P}^*)$

changes in the training set result in large changes in the predictions), such as classification and regression tree learners.

2.2 Random Forests

A random forest [13] is an ensemble of trees, where diversity among the predictors is obtained by using bagging, and additionally by changing the feature set during learning. More precisely, at each node in the decision trees, a random subset of the input attributes is taken, and the best feature is selected from this subset. The number of attributes that are retained is given by a function f of the total number of input attributes x (e.g., $f(x) = 1$, $f(x) = \sqrt{x}$, $f(x) = \lfloor log_2(x) + 1 \rfloor \ldots$). By setting $f(x) = x$, we obtain the bagging procedure.

3 Multi-Objective Decision Trees

Multi-objective decision trees (MODTs) [2] are decision trees capable of predicting multiple target attributes at once. They are an instantiation of predictive clustering trees (PCTs) [2] that are used for multi-objective prediction. In the PCT framework, a tree is viewed as a hierarchy of clusters: the top-node corresponds to one cluster containing all data, which is recursively partitioned into smaller clusters while moving down the tree.

PCTs can be constructed with a standard "top-down induction of decision trees" (TDIDT) algorithm [19]. The algorithm is shown in Table 1. The heuristic that is used for selecting the tests is the reduction in variance caused by partitioning the instances (see line 4 of BestTest). Maximizing the variance reduction maximizes cluster homogeneity and improves predictive performance.

The main difference between the algorithm for learning PCTs and a standard decision tree learner is that the former treats the variance function and the prototype function that computes a label for each leaf as parameters that can be instantiated for a given learning task. In order to construct MODTs, these functions have been instantiated towards multiple target attributes [2,20]. For the classification case, the variance function is computed as the sum of the entropies of class variables, i.e., $Var(E) = \sum_{i=1}^{t} Entropy(E, y_i)$ (this definition has also been used in the context of multi-label prediction [21]), and the prototype function returns a vector containing the majority class for each target attribute.

For multi-objective regression trees, the sum of the variances of the targets is used, i.e., $Var(E) = \sum_{i=1}^{t} Var(y_i)$, and each leaf's prototype is the vector mean of the target vectors of it's training examples.

The PCT framework is implemented in the TILDE [2] and CLUS [22,4] systems. In this work we use CLUS. More information about PCTs and CLUS can be found at `http://www.cs.kuleuven.be/~dtai/clus`.

4 Experimental Evaluation

In this section, we empirically evaluate the application of bagging and random forests to multi-objective decision trees. We describe the experimental methodology, the datasets, and the obtained results.

4.1 Ensembles for Multi-Objective Decision Trees

In order to apply bagging to MODTs, the procedure $PCT(E_i)$ (Table 1) is used as a base classifier. For applying random forests, the same approach is followed, changing the procedure BestTest (Table 1, right) to take a random subset of size $f(x)$ of all possible attributes.

In order to combine the predictions output by the base classifiers, we take the average for regression, and apply a probability distribution vote instead of a simple majority vote for classification, as suggested by Bauer and Kohavi [23]. These combining functions generalize trivially to the multi-objective case. Each ensemble consists of 100 trees, which are unpruned [23]. For building random forests, the parameter $f(x)$ was set to $\lfloor log_2(x) + 1 \rfloor$ as in Breiman [13].

4.2 Datasets

Table 2 lists the datasets that we use, together with their properties. Most datasets are of ecological nature. Each dataset represents a multi-objective prediction problem. Of the 13 listed datasets, 8 are used both for multi-objective regression and for multi-objective classification (after discretizing the target attributes), resulting in 21 datasets in total.

4.3 Results

We assess the predictive performance of the algorithms comparing the accuracy for classification, and RRMSE (relative root mean squared error) for regression. The results are obtained by a 10-fold cross validation procedure[1], using the same folds for all experiments.

Here, we discuss the results along two dimensions of interest: comparing ensembles of MODTs to single multi-objective decision trees, and to ensembles of single-objective decision trees. Afterwards, we investigate ensembles of MODTs

[1] When using bagging or random forests, one could also use the out-of-bag error measure [13]. In order to obtain a fairer comparison with the (non-ensemble) decision tree methods, we instead used 10-fold cross validation.

Table 2. Dataset properties: domain name, number of instances (N), number of input attributes ($Attr$), number of target attributes (T), and whether used as multi-objective classification ($Class$) or regression ($Regr$) dataset

	Domain	Task	N	$Attr$	T	$Class$	$Regr$
E_1	Bridges [24]		85	7	5	√	
E_2	EDM - 1 [7]		154	16	2	√	√
E_3	Monks [24]		432	6	3	√	
E_4	Sigmea real [8]	with coordinates	817	6	2	√	√
E_5		without coordinates	817	4	2	√	√
E_6	Sigmea simulated [9]		10368	11	2	√	√
E_7	Soil quality 1 [10]	Acari/Coll./Biodiv.	1944	142	3		√
E_8	Solar-flare 1 [24]		323	10	3	√	√
E_9	Solar-flare 2 [24]		1066	10	3		√
E_{10}	Thyroid [24]		9172	29	7	√	
E_{11}	Water quality [11,12]	Plants	1060	16	7	√	√
E_{12}		Animals	1060	16	7	√	√
E_{13}		Plants & Animals	1060	16	14	√	√

Table 3. Wilcoxon test outcomes (**SO** Single-Objective, **MO** Multi-Objective; **DT** Decision Tree, **Bag** Bagging, **RF** Random Forest)

Classification	Regression	Classification	Regression
MOBag > MODT $p = 5.14 * 10^{-6}$	MOBag > MODT $p = 2.44 * 10^{-3}$	MOBag > SOBag $p = 0.301$	MOBag > SOBag $p = 1.28 * 10^{-6}$
MORF > MODT $p = 6.61 * 10^{-7}$	MORF > MODT $p = 2.03 * 10^{-5}$	MORF > SORF $p = 0.451$	MORF > SORF $p = 0.094$

in more detail, and compare bagging and random forests in the multi-objective setting. For testing whether the difference in predictive performance between different methods is statistically significant over all datasets and all targets, we use the Wilcoxon test [25]. The results are summarized in Table 3. In the results, $A > B$ means that method A has a better predictive performance than method B. The significance is reported by the corresponding p-value.

Ensembles of Multi-Objective Decision Trees versus Multi-Objective Decision Trees. The left part of Table 3 shows the outcome of the Wilcoxon test comparing ensembles of MODTs to MODTs. The results show that the predictive performance of ensembles of MODTs is better than MODTs, which is the same as for ensembles in the single-objective setting.

A preliminary empirical evaluation of boosting of multi-objective regression trees has been performed by Sain and Carmack [26]. Experimental results on a single dataset yielded the same conclusion.

Ensembles of Multi-Objective Decision Trees versus Ensembles of Single-Objective Decision Trees. Ensembles of single-objective decision trees are ensembles that predict one target attribute. Results of the Wilcoxon

Table 4. Total model size (number of nodes) for the different methods (**SO** Single-Objective, **MO** Multi-Objective; **Bag** Bagging, **RF** Random Forest)

	Classification				Regression			
	MOBag	SOBag	MORF	SORF	MOBag	SOBag	MORF	SORF
E_1	4344	6996	4614	8910				
E_2	4102	4916	5014	5930	4780	5900	5746	7390
E_3	18580	20360	17222	22362				
E_4	29586	37906	30360	38988	46482	70896	46866	71842
E_5	29936	38082	29422	38312	46816	71660	44896	69928
E_6	6184	6544	13104	13990	153994	192038	164814	203416
E_7					53586	160506	24722	73356
E_8	5158	7742	4364	6588	9330	15562	7840	13842
E_9					23196	33264	15248	24018
E_{10}	55454	77244	83506	126916				
E_{11}	68560	137860	71258	163948	78310	221832	79606	257122
E_{12}	69484	137514	72590	164484	80034	229990	81122	267364
E_{13}	80804	275374	81568	328432	82842	451822	83036	524486

test comparing a ensemble of MODTs to building ensembles for each target attribute separately are presented in the right part of Table 3. For regression, ensembles of MODTs are significantly better than ensembles of single-objective decision trees in case of bagging, and, to a lesser extent, in the case of random forests. For classification, the two methods perform comparably.

In addition, we have compared the total sizes of ensembles of multi-objective and single-objective decision trees. While the number of trees will be smaller for ensembles of MODTs (with a factor equal to the number of targets), the effect on the total number of nodes of all trees is less obvious. Table 4 presents the results. We see that ensembles of MODTs yield smaller models, with an increased difference in the presence of many target attributes.

We have also compared the running times of the different methods. Except for dataset E_1, the multi-objective ensemble method is always faster to learn than its single-objective counterpart, with an average speed-up ratio of 2.03.

Multi-Objective Bagging versus Multi-Objective Random Forests. We compared the performance of the two multi-objective ensemble methods. The test concludes that multi-objective random forests have a better predictive performance than multi-objective bagging (p-values of 0.025 for classification and 0.060 for regression). Note that, also in terms of efficiency, random forests are to be preferred, since they are faster to learn.

The obtained results are similar to results obtained in single-objective setting. In their experimental comparison, Banfield et al. [27] obtain significantly better results for random forests on 8 of 57 datasets. Also for our datasets, random forests perform better than bagging in the single-objective case (p-values of 0.047 for classification and $2.37 * 10^{-5}$ for regression).

5 Conclusions and Further Work

In this paper, an empirical study is presented on applying ensemble methods to multi-objective decision trees. As such, the interaction between two dimensions (multi-objective learning and ensemble learning) was investigated. The results can be summarized as follows. First, the performance of a multi-objective tree learner is significantly improved by learning an ensemble (using bagging or random forests) of multi-objective trees. This suggests that the non-trivial relations that may be present between the different target attributes are preserved when combining predictions of several classifiers or when injecting some source of randomness in the learning algorithm. Second, ensembles of MODTs perform equally good as or significantly better than single-objective ones. In addition, ensembles of MODTs are faster to learn and reduce the total model size. Third, multi-objective random forests are significantly better than multi-objective bagging, which is consistent with results in the single-objective context.

As future work, we plan to extend the empirical evaluation along two dimensions: (a) to other ensemble methods, such as boosting; one research question here is how to adapt boosting's reweightening scheme to the multi-objective case; and (b) to multi-objective datasets with mixed nominal and numeric targets.

A different line of work that we consider is to develop methods for directly controlling the model diversity of predictive clustering trees. Model diversity improves the predictive performance of ensemble methods [14]. In particular, Kocev et al. [28] show that beam search with a heuristic that explicitly incorporates the diversity of the trees can be used to this end. We plan to investigate if beam search can yield more accurate ensembles than bagging or random forests.

Acknowledgements. This work was supported by the EU FET IST project "Inductive Querying", contract number FP6-516169. Jan Struyf is a post-doctoral fellow of the Research Foundation - Flanders (FWO-Vlaanderen). The authors would like to thank Hendrik Blockeel for providing valuable suggestions.

References

1. Caruana, R.: Multitask learning. Machine Learning 28, 41–75 (1997)
2. Blockeel, H., De Raedt, L., Ramon, J.: Top-down induction of clustering trees. In: Proc. of the 15th ICML, pp. 55–63 (1998)
3. Suzuki, E., Gotoh, M., Choki, Y.: Bloomy decision trees for multi-objective classification. In: Siebes, A., De Raedt, L. (eds.) PKDD 2001. LNCS (LNAI), vol. 2168, Springer, Heidelberg (2001)
4. Ženko, B., Džeroski, S., Struyf, J.: Learning predictive clustering rules. In: Proc. of the Workshop on KDID at the 16th ECML (2005)
5. Dietterich, T.: Ensemble methods in machine learning. In: Kittler, J., Roli, F. (eds.) MCS 2000. LNCS, vol. 1857, pp. 1–15. Springer, Heidelberg (2000)
6. Breiman, L.: Bagging predictors. Machine Learning 24(2), 123–140 (1996)
7. Karalič, A., Bratko, I.: First order regression. Machine Learning 26, 147–176 (1997)
8. Demšar, D., Debeljak, M., Lavigne, C.: Džeroski, S.: Modelling pollen dispersal of genetically modified oilseed rape within the field. In: The Annual Meeting of the Ecological Society of America (2005)

9. Džeroski, S., Colbach, N., Messean, A.: Analysing the effect of field characteristics on gene flow between oilseed rape varieties and volunteers with regression trees. In: Proc.of the 2nd Int'l Conference on Co-existence between GM and non-GM based agricultural supply chains (2005)
10. Demšar, D., Džeroski, S., Larsen, T., Struyf, J., Axelsen, J., Pedersen, M., Krogh, P.: Using multi-objective classification to model communities of soil microarthropods. Ecological Modelling 191(1), 131–143 (2006)
11. Blockeel, H., Džeroski, S., Grbović, J.: Simultaneous prediction of multiple chemical parameters of river water quality with Tilde. In: Żytkow, J.M., Rauch, J. (eds.) Principles of Data Mining and Knowledge Discovery. LNCS (LNAI), vol. 1704, pp. 32–40. Springer, Heidelberg (1999)
12. Džeroski, S., Demšar, D., Grbović, J.: Predicting chemical parameters of river water quality from bioindicator data. Applied Intelligence 13(1), 7–17 (2000)
13. Breiman, L.: Random forests. Machine Learning 45(1), 5–32 (2001)
14. Hansen, L., Salamon, P.: Neural network ensembles. IEEE Trans. on Pattern Anal. and Mach. Intell. 12, 993–1001 (1990)
15. Freund, Y., Schapire, R.E.: Experiments with a new boosting algorithm. In: Proc. of the 13th ICML, pp. 148–156. Morgan Kaufmann, San Francisco (1996)
16. Breiman, L.: Using adaptive bagging to debias regressions. Technical report, Statistics Department, University of California, Berkeley (1999)
17. Ho, T., Hull, J., Srihari, S.: Decision combination in multiple classifier systems. IEEE Trans. on Pattern Anal. and Mach. Intell. 16(1), 66–75 (1994)
18. Kittler, J., Hatef, M., Duin, R., Matas, J.: On combining classifiers. IEEE Trans. on Pattern Anal. and Mach. Intell. 20(3), 226–239 (1998)
19. Breiman, L., Friedman, J., Olshen, R., Stone, C.: Classification and Regression Trees. Wadsworth, Belmont (1984)
20. Blockeel, H., Schietgat, L., Struyf, J., Džeroski, S., Clare, A.: Decision trees for hierarchical multilabel classification: A case study in functional genomics. In: Fürnkranz, J., Scheffer, T., Spiliopoulou, M. (eds.) PKDD 2006. LNCS (LNAI), vol. 4213, Springer, Heidelberg (2006)
21. Clare, A., King, R.: Knowledge discovery in multi-label phenotype data. In: Siebes, A., De Raedt, L. (eds.) PKDD 2001. LNCS (LNAI), vol. 2168, Springer, Heidelberg (2001)
22. Struyf, J., Džeroski, S.: Constraint based induction of multi-objective regression trees. In: Bonchi, F., Boulicaut, J.-F. (eds.) KDID 2005. LNCS, vol. 3933, pp. 222–233. Springer, Heidelberg (2006)
23. Bauer, E., Kohavi, R.: An empirical comparison of voting classification algorithms: Bagging, boosting, and variants. Machine Learning 36, 105 (1999)
24. Hettich, S., Blake, C.L., Merz, C.J.: UCI repository of machine learning databases (1998)
25. Wilcoxon, F.: Individual comparisons by ranking methods. Biometrics 1 (1945)
26. Sain, R.S., Carmack, P.S.: Boosting multi-objective regression trees. Computing Science and Statistics 34, 232–241 (2002)
27. Banfield, R., Hall, L., Bowyer, K., Kegelmeyer, W.: A comparison of decision tree ensemble creation techniques. IEEE Trans. on Pattern Anal. and Mach. Intell. 29(1), 173–180 (2007)
28. Kocev, D., Džeroski, S., Struyf, J.: Beam search induction and similarity constraints for predictive clustering trees. In: 5th Int'l Workshop on KDID: Revised Selected and Invited Papers (to appear, 2007)

Kernel-Based Grouping of Histogram Data

Tilman Lange and Joachim M. Buhmann

Institue of Computational Science
ETH Zurich
8092 Zurich, Switzerland
{langet,jbuhmann}@inf.ethz.ch

Abstract. Organizing objects into groups based on their co-occurrence with a second, relevance variable has been widely studied with the Information Bottleneck (IB) as one of the most prominent representatives. We present a kernel-based approach to pairwise clustering of discrete histograms using the Jensen-Shannon (JS) divergence, which can be seen as a *two-sample* test. This yields a cost criterion with a solid information-theoretic justification, which can be approximated in polynomial time with arbitrary precision. In addition to that, a relation to optimal hard clustering IB solutions can be established. To our knowledge, we are the first to devise algorithms for the IB with provable approximation guaranties. In practice, one obtains convincing results in the context of image segmentation using fast optimization heuristics.

1 Introduction

Data clustering plays a central role in exploratory data analysis. Formally, one aims at finding a k-partition $C\colon [n] \to [k]$ [1] of a finite set $\mathcal{X} = \{x_1, \ldots, x_n\}$. Often, objects X are characterized by their *joint occurrence* with an additional variable Y, $Y \in \mathcal{Y} = \{y_1, \ldots, y_b\}$: E.g., text documents can be characterized by the words they contain. Image sites may be characterized by colors. In document categorization or image segmentation, this data can be summarized in a table of *counts* – each entry containing the number of *joint occurrences* of object (e.g. pixel or document) x and variable (e.g. word or gray value) y. By normalization, one obtains the Maximum Likelihood (ML) estimate of the joint distribution $p(x, y)$. In clustering, one tries to organize the objects into classes based on the co-occurrence patterns. To this end, the *normalized histograms* $\hat{p}(y|x)$ are usually considered to characterize the objects $x \in \mathcal{X}$. Hence, clustering aims at determining the group structure such that empirically estimated distributions, that might have arisen from the same source, are grouped together. In this work, we introduce the Jensen-Shannon (JS) divergence as a kernel (sec. 2) and use it as distance for pairwise clustering of histograms (sec. 3). This clustering model is motivated by the observation that the JS divergence is a test for the *two-sample problem* [5]. As it is bounded, it has less pathologies in a pairwise setting than the classical Kullback-Leibler (KL) or the Jeffrey divergence.

[1] We use $[n]$ as a shorthand for the set $\{i \mid 1 \le i \le n\}$ throughout this work.

J.N. Kok et al. (Eds.): ECML 2007, LNAI 4701, pp. 632–639, 2007.

A principled approach to address the problem of grouping histogram data represents the *Information-Bottleneck (IB)* introduced in [15] with the *Histogram Clustering Model (HCM)* [12] as a special case. The idea of the IB approach is to find a compact representation of the variable X while preserving as much information as possible about a second (*relevance*) variable Y – given the joint distribution $p(x, y)$. The mutual information, I, is here the performance measure of interest: the IB problem consists of finding cluster assignment probabilities $p(\nu|x)$ such that the functional $\mathcal{L} = \frac{1}{\beta} I(X, C) - I(Y, C)$ is minimized, where $\beta \geq 0$ is a Lagrange parameter. As the IB is intimately related to the JS divergence, we can develop a relationship to the IB for $\beta \to \infty$. Following [13], we use Euclidean embeddings to restate the pairwise as a k-means problem. Thereby, we can devise polynomial time approximation algorithms for pairwise clustering with JS divergences. We establish a relationship to the IB for the HCM case allowing us to extend the approximation results to the IB in the $\beta \to \infty$ limit – which is known to be $\mathcal{NP}$-hard. These are the first rigorous approximation results for such clustering models. We also discuss optimization heuristics allowing quick operation in practice. In the experimental section, the applicability to image segmentation problems is demonstrated. We also show the possibility of simple data fusion in combination with kernel PCA-based de-noising leading to competitive solutions in comparison with HCM (sec. 4).

2 The Jensen-Shannon-Kernel

Let $\mathbf{p} = (p(y)) \in \mathbb{M}(\mathcal{Y})$ and $\mathbf{q} = (q(y)) \in \mathbb{M}(\mathcal{Y})$ be distributions over a discrete domain $\mathcal{Y}$ with $\mathbb{M}(\mathcal{Y})$ the set of distributions on $\mathcal{Y}$. The JS divergence is a symmetrized version of the KL divergence d_{KL}:

$$\mathbb{R}_{\geq 0} \ni d_{\mathrm{JS}}(\mathbf{p}\|\mathbf{q}) := \frac{1}{2} d_{\mathrm{KL}}(\mathbf{p}\|\mathbf{m}) + \frac{1}{2} d_{\mathrm{KL}}(\mathbf{q}\|\mathbf{m}) \tag{1}$$

with $\mathbf{m} = \frac{1}{2}\mathbf{p} + \frac{1}{2}\mathbf{q}$. Clearly, d_{JS} is symmetric, > 0 *iff* $\mathbf{p} \neq \mathbf{q}$, and the square of a metric [6]. In fact, d_{JS} represents a conditionally negative semi-definite kernel function [8]. An outline of the proof and a discussion of the issue of embeddings into vector spaces follows. Let k be a conditionally positive definite (cpd) kernel. Then, k can be transformed into a positive definite kernel function and there is a Hilbert space $\mathcal{H}$, such that $-k$ corresponds to squared 2-norm distances $\mathcal{H}$ [14]. Hence, we show that $k = -d_{\mathrm{JS}}$ is cpd.

Definition 1 (e.g. in [14]). *A symmetric function k on $\mathbb{M}(\mathcal{Y}) \times \mathbb{M}(\mathcal{Y})$ is called* conditionally positive definite (cpd) kernel *if it is a positive semi-definite kernel for all $m \in \mathbb{N}$ and all $c_i \in \mathbb{R}$ with*

$$\sum_{i \in [m]} c_i = 0. \tag{2}$$

Thus, we show that d_{JS} obeys $\sum_{i,j} c_i c_j d_{\mathrm{JS}}(\mathbf{p}_i \| \mathbf{p}_j) \leq 0.$ for all c_i, c_j fulfilling eq. 2 and for all $\mathbf{p}_i, \mathbf{p}_j \in \mathbb{M}(\mathcal{Y})$ (c.f. [1]). Now, note that

$$d_{\mathrm{JS}}(\mathbf{p}\|\mathbf{q}) = \frac{1}{2} \sum_{y \in \mathcal{Y}} \left[p(y) \log \left(\frac{2p(y)}{p(y)+q(y)} \right) + q(y) \log \left(\frac{2q(y)}{p(y)+q(y)} \right) \right] \tag{3}$$

and, hence, if each summand is negative definite, then d_{JS} is. By expansion

$$\underbrace{\sum_{i,j} c_i c_j p_i(y) \log(2p_i(y))}_{=0} + \underbrace{\sum_{i,j} c_i c_j q_j(y) \log(2q_j(y))}_{=0} - \sum_{i,j} c_i c_j (p_i(y) + q_j(y)) \log(p_i(y) + q_j(y)), \tag{4}$$

since $\sum_i c_i = 0$. Because $-z \log z$ is negative definite for $z \in \mathbb{R}_+$, $-d_{\mathrm{JS}}$ is cpd (see e.g. [1],p. 89 & pp. 218-19). Next, we discuss how an embedding can be found using the empirical kernel map.

Let $\mathbf{I}_n$ be the $n \times n$ identity matrix and $\mathbf{e}_n = (1, \ldots, 1)^\top$. Let $\mathbf{Q}_n := \mathbf{I}_n - \frac{1}{n}\mathbf{e}_n\mathbf{e}_n^\top$ be the centering matrix. The centered matrix $\tilde{\mathbf{K}} = -\frac{1}{2}\mathbf{Q}_n \mathbf{D}_{\mathrm{JS}} \mathbf{Q}_n$, with $\mathbf{D}_{\mathrm{JS}} = (d_{\mathrm{JS}}(\mathbf{p}_i\|\mathbf{p}_j))_{1 \leq i,j \leq n}$, is positive definite (prop. 8 in [14]), since $\mathbf{K} = -\mathbf{D}_{\mathrm{JS}}$ is cpd, and, hence, $\mathbf{D}_{\mathrm{JS}}$ must derive from squared Euclidean distances (thm. 1 in [13]). Kernel Principal Component Analysis (kPCA) can be used to find a $(n-1)$-dimensional, *isometric* embedding in $(\mathbb{R}^{n-1}, \|\cdot\|)$ (cf. [13]): Let $\tilde{\mathbf{K}} = \mathbf{U}\mathbf{\Lambda}\mathbf{U}^\top$ be an eigen-decomposition of $\tilde{\mathbf{K}}$ with $\mathbf{U} = (u_1, \ldots, u_n)$ and $\mathbf{\Lambda} = \mathrm{diag}(\lambda_1, \ldots, \lambda_n)$, $\lambda_i \geq \lambda_j$, for $i \leq j$. Then, a d-dimensional embedding, $d \leq n-1$, can be found by $\mathbf{X} := \mathbf{U}_d(\mathbf{\Lambda}_d)^{1/2}$ with $\mathbf{U}_d = (u_1, \ldots, u_d)$ and $\mathbf{\Lambda}_d = \mathrm{diag}(\lambda_1, \ldots, \lambda_d)$. Taking $d < n-1$ comes at the expense of distorting the inter-point distances in the embedding space. However, de-noising of the original data can be achieved this way which can be advantageous for clustering [13]. For $d = n-1$, using kPCA an $(n-1)$-dimensional, isometric embedding into real vector space can be found such that squared Euclidean distances in the embedding space correspond to JS divergences in $\mathbb{M}(\mathcal{Y})$.

3 Pairwise Clustering with the JS-Kernel

The problem of *Pairwise Clustering* [9] can be stated as follows: Given an $n \times n$ matrix $\mathbf{D} = (D_{ij})$ of pairwise dissimilarities between objects i and j, find an assignment $C \colon [n] \to [k]$ of objects to classes such that

$$h^{\mathrm{pw}}(\mathbf{D}; C) = \frac{1}{2} \sum_{\nu \in [k]} \frac{1}{n_\nu} \sum_{i,j \in C^{-1}(\nu)} D_{ij} \tag{5}$$

is minimized where $n_\nu := |C^{-1}(\nu)|$ with $C^{-1}(\nu) = \{i \in [n] | C(i) = \nu\}$. h^{pw} measures the avg. within-cluster dissimilarity and aims at finding *compact* clusters.

In histogram grouping, a problem instance consists of n empirical distributions $\mathbf{p}_x = (\hat{p}(y|x))_{y \in \mathcal{Y}}$ assuming $p(x) = \frac{1}{n}$, $x \in \mathcal{X}$. Here, d_{JS} represents a natural measure for testing if two empirical distributions $\mathbf{p}$ and $\mathbf{q}$ might have arisen from the *same* source: the authors of [5] quantified the probability that the (sequence of) measurements for objects x_i and x_j were drawn from the same distribution by the method of types [3]. Using the JS divergence as dissimilarity $D_{ij} = d_{\mathrm{JS}}(\mathbf{p}_{x_i} \| \mathbf{p}_{x_j})$ for pairwise histogram grouping is, hence, natural, as objects are grouped together that are likely to have the same origin.

The pairwise clustering criterion h^{pw} can be rephrased as a k-means problem (cf. [13]) if pairwise dissimilarities correspond to squared Euclidean distances. We exploit this to get approximation guaranties for pairwise grouping with JS divergences. The results are extended to the first approximation guaranties for the IB in the literature.

Approximation Results: JS divergences correspond to squared distances in a real Hilbert space (cf. sec. 2). Thus, there is a function ϕ mapping distributions $\mathbf{p}$ to $\phi(\mathbf{p})$ in that space. Hence, one obtains for h^{km} and h^{pw} (cf. [13]):

$$h^{\text{pw-js}} = \sum_{\nu,i,j} \frac{1}{2n_\nu} \overbrace{\|\phi(\mathbf{p}_{x_i}) - \phi(\mathbf{p}_{x_j})\|^2}^{=d_{\mathrm{JS}}(\mathbf{p}_{x_i} \| \mathbf{p}_{x_j})} = h^{\mathrm{km}} = \sum_{i \in [n]} \|\phi(\mathbf{p}_{x_i}) - \mathbf{z}_{C(i)}\|^2, \tag{6}$$

where $\mathbf{z}_\nu = \frac{1}{n_\nu} \sum_{i \in C^{-1}(\nu)} \phi(\mathbf{p}_{x_i})$ is the *centroid* in feature space. An isometric embedding into a real vector space based on the empirical kernel map can be computed by the procedure discussed in sec. 2 (cf. [13]). Optimizing h^{pw} with pairwise JS divergences and minimizing h^{km} on the embedded data are, thus, equivalent problems. Hence, every approximation algorithm for h^{km} is one for $h^{\text{pw-js}}$. There is, e.g., a *polynomial time approximation scheme (PTAS)* for the k-means objective function [11]. Hence, one can get ϵ-close, $\forall \epsilon > 1$, to the optimal solution of h^{km} in running time polynomial in n. A 2-approximation can also be obtained by a k-dimensional embedding (via kPCA) of the data: an optimal solution in the k-dimensional subspace is known to yield a 2-approximation for the $(n-1)$-dimensional problem [4]. Finding the optimal solution by enumerating all Voronoi partitions in $\mathbb{R}^k$ takes $O(n^{k^2+1})$ steps (cf. [10]), and, hence, one obtains a polynomial time 2-approximation algorithm.

Theorem 2. *If* $\mathbf{D}_{JS}$ *is a matrix of pairwise JS divergences, there is a PTAS for* $h^{pw}(\mathbf{D}_{JS}; C)$. *Using kPCA, there is also a 2-approximation for* $h^{pw}(\mathbf{D}_{JS}; C)$.

Relation to the Information Bottleneck*:* One motivation for studying the JS kernel for clustering stems from its close relationship to the *Information Bottleneck (IB)* in its hard clustering version, i.e. the *Histogram Clustering Model (HCM)* (cf. [12]). Here, we develop a connection between hard-clustering IB/HCM and Pairwise Clustering with the JS kernel yielding approximation guaranties for the hard-clustering IB case.

The HCM cost function is related to the IB as follows: Suppose, $C\colon [n] \to [k]$ is a hard clustering, then $I(X, C) = H(C)$ holds, since $p(\nu|x) \in \{0, 1\}$, for $\nu \in [k]$.

Now consider $I(Y,C)$: With $\mathbf{q}_\nu = (p(y|\nu))_{y\in\mathcal{Y}}$, where $p(y|\nu) = \sum_x p(y|x)p(x|\nu)$ one obtains for the second term of the IB functional

$$I(Y,C) = -\sum_{\nu,i} p(x_i,\nu) d_{\mathrm{KL}}(\mathbf{p}_{x_i}\|\mathbf{q}_\nu) + \text{const.} \tag{7}$$

with the second term being a data-dependent constant. Assuming that $p(x) = 1/n$ and $p(\nu|x) \in \{0,1\}$, one gets in the $\beta \to \infty$-limit after dropping the constant the HCM cost function:

$$h^{\mathrm{hcm}}(\{\mathbf{p}_{x_i} \mid i \in [n]\}; C) := \frac{1}{n}\sum_{\nu\in[k]}\sum_{i\in C^{-1}(\nu)} d_{\mathrm{KL}}(\mathbf{p}_{x_i}\|\mathbf{q}_\nu). \tag{8}$$

A relationship between h^{hcm} and $h^{\mathrm{pw\text{-}js}}$ is now established. First note, that we have $d_{\mathrm{JS}} \le \frac{1}{2}d_{\mathrm{KL}}$ (eq. (9) in [16]). Consider now

$$h^{\mathrm{cjs}}(\{\mathbf{p}_{x_i} \mid i \in [n]\}; C) = \frac{1}{n}\sum_{\nu\in[k]}\sum_{i\in C^{-1}(\nu)} d_{\mathrm{JS}}(\mathbf{p}_{x_i}\|\mathbf{q}_\nu) \tag{9}$$

obtained by replacing d_{KL} with d_{JS} in h^{hcm}. Clearly, $h^{\mathrm{cjs}} \le \frac{1}{2}h^{\mathrm{hcm}}$ and $nh^{\mathrm{cjs}} \le 2h^{\mathrm{pw\text{-}js}}$ holds, by the joint convexity of the JS divergence [2]. Also from [16]:

$$2h^{\mathrm{pw\text{-}js}} - nh^{\mathrm{cjs}} = \frac{n}{2}h^{\mathrm{hcm}} - \alpha \ge 0 \Leftrightarrow 2h^{\mathrm{pw\text{-}js}} - \frac{n}{2}h^{\mathrm{hcm}} + \alpha = nh^{\mathrm{cjs}} \ge 0 \tag{10}$$

for some $\alpha \ge 0$. Hence, we finally arrive at a **lower bound** on h^{hcm} in terms of $h^{\mathrm{pw\text{-}js}}$:

$$h^{\mathrm{cjs}} \le \frac{1}{2}h^{\mathrm{hcm}} \Rightarrow h^{\mathrm{pw\text{-}js}} \le \frac{n}{2}h^{\mathrm{hcm}}. \tag{11}$$

We now look for an **upper bound**: At first, we note that for any two distributions $\mathbf{p}$ and $\mathbf{q}$, we have

$$d_{\mathrm{KL}}(\mathbf{p}\|\mathbf{q}) \le 2d_{\mathrm{JS}}(\mathbf{p}\|\mathbf{q}) + \log(\frac{1}{2}(1+\gamma)), \tag{12}$$

where $\gamma = \max_y \frac{p(y)}{q(y)}$ (thm. 4 in [16]). For any solution of h^{hcm}, assuming $p(y|\nu) = 1/n_\nu \sum_{i\in C^{-1}(\nu)} \hat{p}(y|x_i)$: γ is bounded for $d_{\mathrm{KL}}(\mathbf{p}_{x_i}\|\mathbf{q}_\nu)$ if only quotients with $p(y|\nu) \ne 0$ are considered. We can neglect the other case because if $p(y|\nu) = 0$, then $\hat{p}(y|x_i) = 0$ and, thus, $0\log\frac{0}{0} = 0$. Let $\bar{\gamma} := \max_\nu \max_{i\in C^{-1}(\nu)} \log(\frac{1}{2}(1 + \max_y\{\frac{\hat{p}(y|x_i)}{p(y|\nu)} \mid p(y|\nu) \ne 0\}))$. Clearly, $\bar{\gamma}$ is also finite. Then,

$$\frac{2}{n}h^{\mathrm{pw\text{-}js}} \le h^{\mathrm{hcm}} \le 2h^{\mathrm{cjs}} + \bar{\gamma} \le 4\frac{h^{\mathrm{pw\text{-}js}}}{n} + \bar{\gamma}. \tag{13}$$

Intuitively, it is clear that an optimal solution for h^{hcm} minimizes $\bar{\gamma}$, since a large $\bar{\gamma}$ corresponds to a large cost contribution. Thereby, we arrive at the following

Theorem 3. *Let $\{\mathbf{p}_{x_i} \mid i \in [n]\}$ be a fixed instance and let C^* be an optimal solution for h^{hcm}. Then, if C is an ϵ-approximate solution for $h^{pw\text{-}js}$, the costs w.r.t. h^{hcm} can be bounded from above by $2\varepsilon h^{hcm}(C^*) + \bar{\gamma} \ge h^{hcm}(C)$.*

Thus, by efficiently approximating $h^{\text{pw-js}}$, we find a good approximate solution to the hard clustering IB / HCM cost function. To the knowledge of the authors, this is the first approximation guaranty for HCM in the literature.

Heuristic Optimization: Although it is pleasing to derive an algorithm that produces results of guaranteed quality, such algorithms still might be impractical since they may require unacceptable computation time, especially for large k. We, thus, resort to the classical k-means algorithm applied to the data embedded into $\mathbb{R}^k$ using kPCA. The embedding represents a major computational burden, as it requires the computation of an eigenbasis usually taking $O(n^3)$ steps. In practice, this can be significantly sped up by first selecting $m \ll n$ randomly sampled objects to compute an approximate eigenbasis and then use this basis to get a representation of the full data set in the embedding space. This is achieved using the technique in [13] which is the *Nyström extension* that has been successfully applied in the spectral clustering context (see [7]). [2] The running time for the embedding step can be reduced from $O(n^3)$ to $O(m^2 n)$ being *linear* in n if m = const. In total, one gets a running time of $O(m^2 n + snk^2)$ (s = # iterations needed by k-means). This is linear in the number of objects in each iteration for constant k and m.

4 Experimental Results

We provide experimental evidence for the usefulness of $h^{\text{pw-js}}$ and compare our results with those obtained with HCM. For the optimization of $h^{\text{pw-js}}$, we used k-means on the data embedded in a k-dimensional subspace. The required eigenbasis has been computed on a random sub-sample of size $m = 500$ (less than 10% of the full data set) and the Nyström extension technique was employed to embed the whole data. For HCM, a multi-scale annealing implementation was used. The number of classes was set to $k = 5$ for the toy image and to $k = 3$ for the real world image. We extracted 12-bin gray-value histograms from the image data on a grid of 128×128 image sites. *Gabor feature histograms* (with 12 bins/channel) for 4 orientations and 3 different scales of the Gabor wavelet were computed. The Gabor feature histograms were then stacked into a single histogram consisting of 144 bins. By suitable re-normalization one obtains empirical probability distributions.

A Toy Example: On the left side of fig. 1(a), an artificial image is shown with 5 segments: 3 segments are characterized by their texture while 2 of the segments are characterized by intensity. We added Gaussian noise to the image to make the segmentation task more difficult. All 5 classes cannot be separated based on either only gray-value or texture information. The information contained in

[2] Let $\mathbf{D}_{\text{JS}}$ be the matrix for which the embedding was computed and $\mathbf{D}_{\text{JS}}^{\text{new}}$ be the $n - m \times m$ matrix with JS divergences between new and already known objects. Set $\tilde{\mathbf{K}}^{\text{new}} := -\frac{1}{2}(\mathbf{D}_{\text{JS}}^{\text{new}}\mathbf{Q}_m - \frac{1}{m}\mathbf{e}_{n-m}\mathbf{e}_m^\top \mathbf{D}_{\text{JS}}\mathbf{Q}_m)$. Then the embedding in d dimensions can be obtained by $\mathbf{X}^{\text{new}} = \tilde{\mathbf{K}}^{\text{new}}\mathbf{U}_d(\mathbf{\Lambda}_d)^{-1/2}$.

the gray-value and in the Gabor histograms was, thus, combined by averaging the JS divergences obtained from both information sources. As the sum of two kernels is a kernel, the algorithms mentioned above can still be applied to perform segmentation (a trace normalization was also applied to the matrices). On the right of figure 1(a) the result for $k = 5$ on this data set is shown, which identifies all segments correctly. A similar combination can be obtained with HCM as well but proves itself to be less efficient. The HCM segmentation, given in the middle of fig. 1(a), was obtained by treating all channels independently, i.e. the costs $\frac{1}{ln}\sum_{j\in[l]}\sum_{\nu\in[k]}\sum_{i\in C^{-1}(\nu)} d_{\mathrm{KL}}(\mathbf{p}_{x_i}^{(j)}\|\mathbf{q}_{\nu}^{(j)})$ were considered, where j runs over the $l = 12 + 1$ different (one intensity and 12 texture) channels. This strategy obviously produces poorer results.[3]

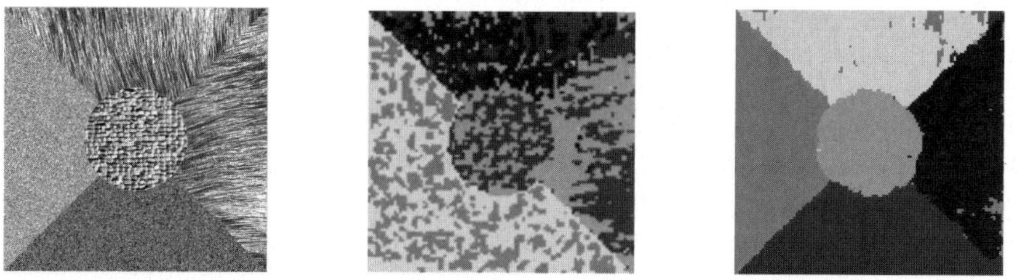

(a) Toy Image Data: (left) Original Image, (middle) segmentation by HCM, (right) JS Pairwise Clustering

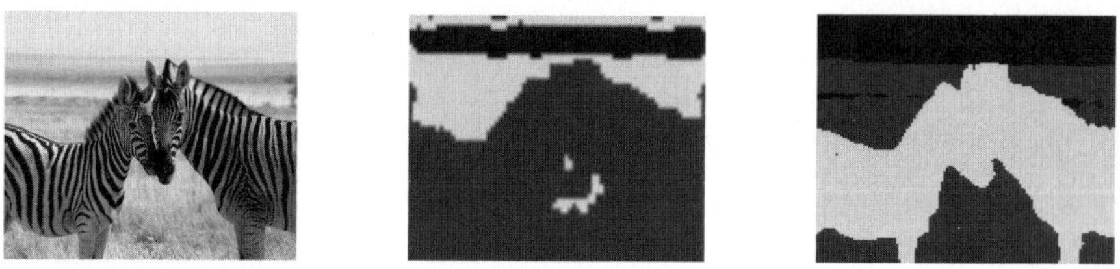

(b) A real world example: Toy Image Data: (left) Original Image, (middle) Segmentation by HCM, (right) JS Kernel Clustering

Fig. 1. Experimental results on the image data

Segmentation of Real World Images: On the left of figure 1(b) a real word image depicting two zebras is shown. Again, HCM and Pairwise Clustering with d_{JS} were used. Obviously, segmentations obtained with JS divergences on the combined data are smoother than those of HCM. In contrast to the HCM result, the segmentation based on $h^{\mathrm{pw\text{-}js}}$ nicely separates the zebras from the two background classes. The use of kPCA for de-noising turned out to be an important component as it emphasizes the group structure in this example.

[3] In principle one could resort to a distribution for the joint occurrence of a gray value and a certain Gabor response. However, this implies a severe estimation problem.

5 Conclusions

This work discussed the grouping of histogram data using pairwise clustering with JS divergences. Theoretical results demonstrate that the JS kernel renders the pairwise clustering problem tractable: efficient approximation algorithms can be devised and fast heuristics exist. A connection to HCM as a special case of IB was established. The experimental section demonstrated that our approach can be useful in image segmentation: Segmentations obtained with $h^{\text{pw-js}}$ were more meaningful than those generated using h^{hcm}. Particularly noteworthy is the possibility to fuse data in a straightforward way allowing for better segmentation results in practice.

References

1. Berg, C., Christensen, J.P.R., Ressel, P.: Harmonic Analysis on Semigroups. Springer, Heidelberg (1984)
2. Burbea, J., Rao, C.R.: On the convexity of some divergence measures based on entropy functions. IEEE T-IT 28(3) (1982)
3. Cover, T.M., Thomas, J.A.: Elements of Information Theory. Wiley Series in Telecommunications. John Wiley & Sons, New York (1991)
4. Drineas, P., Frize, A., Kannan, R., Vempala, S., Vinay, V.: Clustering in large graphs and matrices. Technical report, Yale University (1999)
5. El-Yaniv, R., Fine, S., Tishby, N.: Agnostic classification of markovian sequences. In: NIPS 10 (1998)
6. Endres, D., Schindelin, J.: A new metric for probability distributions. IEEE T-IT 49, 1858–1860 (2003)
7. Fowlkes, C., Belongie, S., Chung, F., Malik, J.: Spectral grouping using the nyström method. IEEE T-PAMI 26, 214–225 (2004)
8. Fuglede, B., Topsœ, F.: Jensen-shannon divergence and hilbert space embedding. In: Proc. ISIT (2004)
9. Hofmann, T., Buhmann, J.M.: Pairwise data clustering by deterministic annealing. IEEE T-PAMI 19 (1997)
10. Inaba, M., Katoh, N., Ima, H.: Applications of weighted voronoi diagrams and randomization to variance-based k-clustering. In: 10th Computational Geometry (1994)
11. Ostrovsky, R., Rabani, Y.: Polynomial time approximation schemes for geometric min-sum median clustering. JACM 49, 139–156 (2002)
12. Pereira, F., Tishby, N., Lee, L.: Distributional clustering of English words. In: 31st ACL (1993)
13. Roth, V., Laub, J., Kawanabe, M., Buhmann, J.M.: Optimal cluster preserving embedding of nonmetric proximity data. IEEE T-PAMI 25, 1540–1551 (2003)
14. Schölkopf, B.: The kernel trick for distances. In: NIPS 12 (2000)
15. Tishby, N., Pereira, F.C., Bialek, W.: The information bottleneck method. In: 37th ACL (1999)
16. Topsøe, F.: Some inequalities for information divergence and related measures of discrimination. IEEE T-IT 46, 1602–1609 (2000)

Active Class Selection

R. Lomasky[1], C.E. Brodley[1], M. Aernecke[2], D. Walt[2], and M. Friedl[3]

[1] Computer Science Department, Tufts University, Medford, MA
{rlomas01,brodley}@cs.tufts.edu
[2] Chemistry Department, Tufts University, Medford, MA
{matthew.aernecke,david.walt}@tufts.edu
[3] Dept. of Geography, Boston University, Boston, MA
friedl@bu.edu

Abstract. This paper presents *Active Class Selection* (ACS), a new class of problems for multi-class supervised learning. If one can control the classes from which training data is generated, utilizing feedback during learning to guide the generation of new training data will yield better performance than learning from any *a priori* fixed class distribution. ACS is the process of iteratively selecting class proportions for data generation. In this paper we present several methods for ACS. In an empirical evaluation, we show that for a fixed number of training instances, methods based on increasing class stability outperform methods that seek to maximize class accuracy or that use random sampling. Finally we present results of a deployed system for our motivating application: training an artificial nose to discriminate vapors.

1 Introduction

Active Class Selection (ACS) addresses the question: if one can collect n additional training instances, how should they be distributed with respect to class? We recognized this new class of supervised learning problems when working with chemists to train an artificial nose. In this domain, creating more data requires chemists to conduct experiments where vapors are passed over a sensor (the nose). Thus, the new data is labeled at the same time as it is generated. This is in contrast to a domain, such as the Reuters articles [15], in which data can be collected independent of the labeling process.

One might assume that ACS is a subclass of active learning rather than its complement [5]. Both iteratively grow the training data. However, active learning requests labels for *existing* instances [1] or explicitly queries the feature space by creating instances for an expert to label [5]. ACS requests that instances be *generated* for a particular class.

Successful methods for ACS can be grounded by recent results in stability and generalization [3,13,10], which show that one can predict expected error based on empirical error with a stable learning algorithm that satisfies certain constraints [13]. The goal of ACS is to minimize the number of new training examples needed in order to maximize learning performance. In our case, given the ability to choose class proportions for data collection we are interested in

J.N. Kok et al. (Eds.): ECML 2007, LNAI 4701, pp. 640–647, 2007.

assessing for each class whether empirical error is converging to expected error; i.e., to determine when we can do no better for this class. Uniform sampling works best if the error rates of all classes are converging at the same rate. If this is not the case, then one heuristic is to sample in proportion to the inverse of the convergence rates for each class. Using this intuition, we propose two methods for ACS that base class proportions on heuristic assessments of class stability. We compare these two methods to uniform and random sampling (sampling in proportion to the distribution specified as best by the domain expert), and to a method that uses error rate directly.

Section 2 outlines five methods for ACS. Section 3 presents a comparison of methods for ACS on both a land cover task and on the motivating problem of this research, building an artificial nose, including results of ACS deployed in the laboratory. In Section 4 we discuss the relationship of ACS to active learning and instance weighting methods. Finally, in Section 5 we conclude with a discussion of the open problems in this new research area.

2 ACS Methods

In this section, we present several methods for determining the class proportions for the generation of new training instances. We assume there are no limits on generating instances of a particular class. All of our methods begin with a small set of labeled training data T_1 of size $b[1]$, where $b[r]$ is the number of instances to add in round r. The choice of $b[1]$ and the class proportions of T_1 are domain specific issues. We perform a f-fold cross validation (CV) over T_1 (in our experiments, f=10). From the CV, we obtain class predictions for T_1. Our methods differ in how they use these predictions to specify the class proportions ($P_r[c]$, $c \in classes$) for the next round of data generation. Specifically, on round r, we generate a new set of examples, T_{new}, a set of $b[r]$ examples generated using the class proportions $P_r[c]$. We add this data to the existing data to create a new set $T_r := T_{r-1} + T_{new}$. We next describe five methods for generating $P_r[c]$ followed by a discussion of the choice of batch size and stopping criteria.

1) Uniform: Sample uniformly from all classes. $P_r[c] := \frac{1}{|classes|} * b[r]$

2) Inverse: Select class proportions $P_r[c]$ inversely proportional to their CV accuracy on round $r-1$. Thus, we obtain more instances from classes on which we have a low accuracy. This method relies on the assumption that poor class accuracy is due to not having observed sufficient training data. Although this may be true initially, our results show that this method does not perform well. $P_r[c] := \frac{\frac{1}{acc[c]}}{\sum_{i=1}^{|classes|} \frac{1}{acc[i]}} * b[r]$

3) Original Proportion: Sample in proportion to the class proportions in T_1. The idea is that domain knowledge led to these proportions, perhaps because they are the true underlying class distribution or because of the creator's intuition as to which classes are more difficult. $P_r[c] := n_c * b[r]$, where n_c is the proportion of class c found in the collected data T_r.

4) Accuracy Improvement: Sample in proportion to each classes' change in accuracy from the last round. If the change for class c is ≤ 0, then $P_r[c] = 0$. The intuition is the accuracy of classes that have been learned as well as possible will not change with the addition of new data and thus we should focus on classes that *can* be improved. This method looks for stability in the empirical error of each class. $P_r[c] := max(0, \frac{currAcc[c]-lastAcc[c]}{\sum_{i=1}^{|classes|} currAcc[i]-lastAcc[i]} * b[r])$

5) Redistricting: The idea behind redistricting is that instances from T_{r-1} whose classification changes when classified by a new classifier trained on $T_{r-1} \cup T_{new}$ are near volatile boundaries. Thus, we strive to assess which classes are near volatile boundaries in order to sample from these these "unstable" classes. The pseudocode is shown in Algorithm 1. We begin with a CV over T_1, the initial sample of the data. We obtain a prediction for each $x_i \in T_1$. In the second round, we collect T_2 of size $b[2]$. We next perform a CV over *all* of the data collected thus far and create a classifier for each fold. Note that on subsequent iterations, we keep the data from T_{r-1} in the same folds, and stratify only the newly generated data T_{new} into the existing folds. For each fold f, we compare the classification results of $C_{r,f}$ and $C_{r-1,f}$ on each instance $x_i \in T_{r-1}$. If the labels are different, then the counter for the class specified by the true label y_i, $redistricted[y_i]$ is incremented. We conclude by generating predictions of the new batch of data T_{new} and increment r.

After the second round we add instances using the formula in Step 12, where c is a class from the set of all classes in the dataset, $P_r[c]$ is the number of instances of c to add, n_c is the proportion of c in T_{r-1} and $b[r]$ is the number of new training instances. We divide $redistricted[c]$ by n_c to keep small classes from being ignored and large classes from being overemphasized.

We note the special cases here rather than in pseudocode. First, for any round r the next batch is added uniformly if instances were not redistricted in round $r-1$. Second, if instances of class c have not been redistricted, then instances of c will not be generated in the next round. Thus, resources are not wasted generating instances of a class in which the accuracy is not changing. Redistricting may temporarily blacklist c, but request c later. Empirical results show a class may be removed from the blacklist upon adding instances of neighboring classes.

Because redistricting seeks to measure stability of the class boundaries, it cares whether the prediction for instances are different than prediction in the previous iteration, not whether it is correct. Ideally, we would like new instances to be near the volatile class boundary. However, for many domains, there is no control over whether data from a particular class is near a classification boundary.

Before moving to our experimental section, we discuss the issues of batch size and stopping criteria. Batch size depends on the cost of generating instances. If too few instances are added, the method may be impractical for domains in which data is generated in large batches. If the batch size is too large, then potentially less instructive training data may be gathered. Note that a different batch size can be specified for each round. Stopping criteria depend on domain-based constraints. Data collection terminates if the accuracy is acceptable to the

Algorithm 1. Redistricting Algorithm (b)

```
Require: b, array of the number of instances to add in round r
Generate a sample T_1 of size b[1]
Divide T_1 into 10 stratified folds T_{1,1}, T_{1,2}....T_{1,10}
for f = 1 to 10 do
   Build Classifier C_{1,f} from {T_1 − T_{1,f}}
   for all instances x_i in T_{1,f} do label_1[x_i] := C_{1,f}(x_i) end for
end for
r := 2
while instance creation resources exist and stopping criteria not met do
   if r = 2 then
      T_new := "random" sample of size b[2]
   else
      T_new := sample of size b[r] where the number of instances for class c is com-
      puted as: P_r[c] = (redistricted[c]/n_c) / (Σ_{i=1}^{|classes|} redistricted[i]/n_c) * b[r]
   end if
   T_r := T_{r−1} + T_new
   Initialize redistricted[c], ∀c ∈ classes
   Divide T_new into 10 stratified folds T_{new,1},T_{new,2}....T_{new,10}
   for f = 1 to 10 do
      T_{r,f} := T_{r−1,f} ∪ T_{new,f}
      Build Classifier C_{r,f} from {T_r − T_{r,f}}
      for all instances x_i in T_{r−1,f} do
         label_r[x_i] := C_{r,f}(x_i)
         if label_r[x_i] ≠ label_{r−1}[x_i] then
            redistricted[y_i]++ /* y_i is the true label of x_i */
         end if
      end for
      for all instances x_i in T_{new,f} do label_r[x_i] := C_{r,f}(x_i) end for
   end for
   r++
end while
```

domain expert, data generation resources are exhausted, or given the available features one is unable to wring more accuracy from the data. Investigation of stopping criteria is an open problem.

3 Experiments

Our experiments compare the proposed methods on two domains for which ACS is applicable. ACS can be applied with any supervised learning algorithm. In our experiments, we report results run with (SVMs)[1] and k-NN.

[1] We used the SMO [12] with pair-wise classification to assess accuracy [7]. Using the default parameters in Weka [21], the complexity parameter is set to one, and we use a linear kernel.

Experimental Method for Static Datasets: We simulate ACS using pre-existing static datasets. We used a uniform distribution for the test set because it is the default choice without knowledge of the class distribution of the underlying population. We performed experiments where T_1 had the same class distribution as the entire dataset, but found no significant difference in any method and thus present the results for T_1 collected uniformly. Because the data are pre-existing static datasets, we may run out of instances from a particular class. In this case, we make the large classes uniform and include all instances from the smaller classes. Similarly, when running the proposed ACS methods, we may not have sufficient data of class c on round r as dictated by the proportion $P_r[c]$. In such cases, we sample the remainder of T_{new} uniformly with respect to the classes that still contain data. In our experiments, we used a 5-fold CV to assess accuracy. This is distinct from the 10-fold CV that redistricting uses on training data.

Artificial Nose Dataset: Gathered in the Walt Laboratory at Tufts University [19], the "artificial nose" dataset consists of experiments in which vapors were passed over an array of sensors (the nose) [2]. The nose is a general purpose device that can be trained to discriminate the k vapors of interest. The accuracy is a function of how well the sensors can differentiate among the vapors. We first present results on a static dataset, and then at the end of this section, we present results from deploying redistricting in the lab.

Prior to our collaboration, the chemists on our team generated a dataset of sixteen classes[2]. The dataset is not uniformly distributed according to class because the chemists used their intuition to collect data from "needed" classes. The nose software currently uses 3-NN and we continued this practice. We repeated the experiments using SVMs, with no significant difference in the results. We started with 100 instances because the chemists believe it is sufficient to to make the initial redistricting decisions. We then add ten instances at a time. As more data is added, all methods have seen the same data, and the results converge.

Figure 1(a) shows the results for the nose. The x-axis represents the number of instances collected and the y-axis shows accuracy. We see that redistricting rivals the scientists' intuitions ("proportion" in the graph), and performs over 10% better than uniform sampling for parts of the graph. The reason that proportion performs comparably to redistricting for this data set is because it was collected before we began to work with the chemists. Prior to our collaboration, the chemists were performing ACS by manually examining the results after each new data collection to see where they were doing poorly and which classes were confused. Inverse performs poorly because as mentioned in Section 2, it skews data collection to favor classes that are "less learnable." Results for "Improvement" for this dataset are inconclusive because this method tends to focus on just a few classes at a time, improving their accuracy, and then moving on to

[2] Toluene, Dimethylmethlphosponate, ethanol, heptane, p-cymene, Isopropenyl acetate, combinations of these vapors, water, and air For some vapor classification problems, the artificial nose can achieve almost 100% accuracy [2].

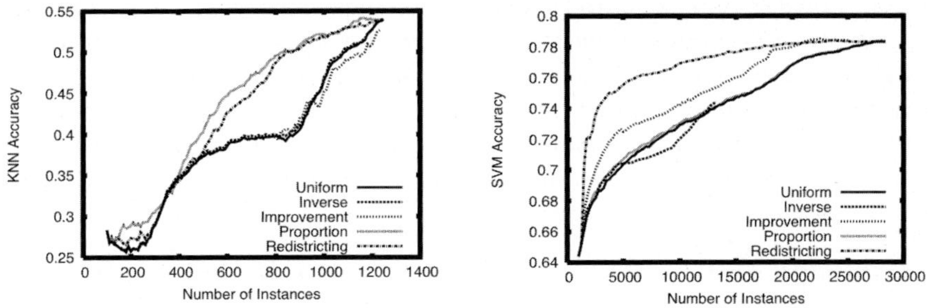

(a) Nose (b) Land Cover

Fig. 1. Results show that the stability-based method, Redistricting, outperforms other methods of ACS

the next set of classes. The small number of instances in the dataset does not allow the full cycle.

Land Cover Data: The land cover dataset consists of a time series of globally distributed satellite observations of the Earth's surface [4]. ACS is applicable because geographers know where on the Earth's surface one can expect to find a given land cover type. We used an existing static dataset to illustrate the benefits of ACS for this domain. Figure 1(b) shows the results for the land cover data. The x-axis represents the number of training instances. The y-axis is the accuracy obtained by applying a set of pair-wise SVMs on the test data that vote based on the confidence assigned by the SVMs. T_1=5000 and $b[r]$=250, a reasonable number to be hand-labeled at one sitting. We exhaust the entire static dataset, causing the same ultimate accuracies for all of the methods because each method has seen the entire dataset. This is a function of the experimental method, not redistricting or ACS, nor limitations in the land cover types of the Earth. Redistricting outperforms uniform, inverse and proportional (for land cover, class proportions are dictated by the geographers' intuition, which is a highly skewed distribution). Accuracy improvement outperforms inverse, proportional and uniform, but is worse than redistricting. We conjecture this is because it looks only for *improvements* in accuracy rather than stability.

ACS in the Field: We deployed our software in the Walt Laboratory and the chemists have begun gathering data guided by redistricting. An initial dataset was gathered using the chemists' intuition of the eight vapors of interest[3]. We compute accuracy using k-NN with k=3 and 5-fold CV. Because of time limitations in the lab, we only deployed uniform and redistricting.

The CV accuracy on the initial 168 instances was 74%. On each iteration, we collected 49 additional instances. After one iteration, uniform achieves an

[3] The vapors are benzaldehyde, benzene, butyraldehyde, chloroform, decanol, ethyl propionate, and n-butanol.

accuracy of 74% and redistricting leads to an accuracy of 83%. The second iteration gives 85% and 86% accuracy, respectively. On the second iteration, both uniform sampling and redistricting obtain similar performance. We conjecture that we are close to the maximum obtainable accuracy for this set of vapors and beads. To test this conjecture we re-ran the k-NN with all of the data (325 instances in total) and obtained an accuracy of 86%, supporting our conjecture.

4 Related Work: Active Learning and Instance Selection

Little attention has been paid to determining whether more accuracy can be achieved when a practitioner can select the classes from which to generate training data. One notable exception is Jo and Japkowicz's method for collecting more examples of the minority class with the goal of increasing accuracy [9].

Active learning, like ACS, adds training examples to the dataset after examining properties of the classifier learned thus far. However, it assumes an existing set of unlabeled data or that one can query the feature space explicitly [14,11]. For active learning, requesting more data is actually requesting a label [18]. ACS does not draw from unlabeled data, rather it guides the generation of new data. Indeed, situations in which both ACS and active learning are applicable translate into situations where both the features' values and the labels exist. In this case, instance selection or weighting are applicable.

ACS is similar to methods for constructing a training set, either by instance selection [17,11], or by weighting methods such as boosting [8]. Instance selection methods focus on removing instances from a dataset that hinder classification accuracy, e.g. [17,4,20,16]. Other methods change the training set's class distribution by sampling or instance replication to handle misclassification costs or minority class issues (see [8] for an overview).

5 Conclusion

This paper identified a new class of problems called *Active Class Section.* ACS answers the question: If given the opportunity, from which classes should you generate additional training data? We evaluated several methods for ACS, each of which can be applied in conjunction with any supervised learning algorithm. We deployed redistricting as part of a real-world system in the Walt Laboratory.

Many open problems remain. First, a deeper analysis of the relationship between the proposed methods and results on stability may lead to even better methods. Second, determining when all of the available "structure" has been learned from the data, and additional learning will lead to over-fitting, is a critical objective for any learning problem. Thus, a more thorough analysis of stopping criteria is needed.

References

1. Baram, Y., El-Yaniv, R., Luz, K.: Online choice of active learning algorithms. JMLR 5, 255–291 (2004)
2. Bencic-Nagale, S., Walt, D.: Extending the longevity of fluorescence-based sensor arrays using adaptive exposure. Anal. Chem. 77(19), 6155–6162 (2005)
3. Bousquet, O., Elisseeff, A.: Stability and generalization. JMLR 2, 499–526 (2002)
4. Brodley, C., Friedl, M.: Identifying and eliminating mislabeled training instances. JAIR 11, 131–167 (1999)
5. Cohn, D.A., Ghahramani, Z., Jordan, M.l.: Active learning with statistical models. In: Advances in NIPS vol. 7, pp. 705–712 (1995)
6. Freund, Y., Schapire, R.: Experiments with a new boosting algorithm. In: ICML, pp. 148–156 (1996)
7. Hastie, T., Tibshirani, R.: Classification by pairwise coupling. In: NIPS, pp. 507–513 (1998)
8. Japkowicz, N., Stephen, S.: The class imbalance problem: A systematic study. Intel. Data Anal. 6(5), 429–449 (2002)
9. Jo, T., Japkowicz, N.: Class imbalances versus small disjuncts. In: KDD, pp. 40–49 (2004)
10. Kearns, M., Ron, D.: Algorithmic stability and sanity-check bounds for leave-one-out cross-validation. In: COLT, pp. 152–162 (1997)
11. Lewis, D.: A sequential algorithm for training text classifiers: Corrigendum and additional data. SIGIR 29(2), 13–19 (1995)
12. Platt, J.: Fast Training of Support Vector Machines Using Sequential Minimal Optimization. MIT Press, Cambridge, MA, USA (1999)
13. Poggio, T., Rifkin, R., Mukherjee, S., Niyogi, P.: General conditions for predictivity in learning theory. Nature 428(6981), 419–422 (2004)
14. Raskutti, B., Ferra, H., Kowalczyk, A.: Combining clustering and co-training to enhance text classification using unlabelled data. In: KDD, pp. 620–625 (2002)
15. Sanderson, M.: Reuters Test Collection. In: BSC IRSG (1994)
16. Sebban, M., Nock, R., Lallich, S.: Stopping criterion for boosting-based data reduction techniques: From binary to multiclass problem. JMLR 3, 863–885 (2003)
17. Srinivasan, A., Muggleton, S., Bain, M.: Distinguishing exceptions from noise in non-monotonic learning. In: Int. Workshop on ILP (1992)
18. Tong, S., Chang, E.: Support vector machine active learning for image retrieval. Multimedia, 107–118 (2001)
19. Optical sensing arrays. White paper, Tufts University (2006), `ase.tufts.edu/chemistry/walt/research/projects/artificialnosepage.htm`
20. Wilson, D., Martinez, T.: An integrated instance-based learning algorithm. Comp. Intel. 16(1), 1–28 (2000)
21. Witten, I., Frank, E., Trigg, L., Hall, M., Holmes, G., Cunningham, S.: Weka: Practical machine learning tools and techniques with java implementations (1999)

Sequence Labeling with Reinforcement Learning and Ranking Algorithms

Francis Maes, Ludovic Denoyer, and Patrick Gallinari

LIP6 - University of Paris 6

Abstract. Many problems in areas such as Natural Language Processing, Information Retrieval, or Bioinformatic involve the generic task of sequence labeling. In many cases, the aim is to assign a label to each element in a sequence. Until now, this problem has mainly been addressed with Markov models and Dynamic Programming.

We propose a new approach where the sequence labeling task is seen as a sequential decision process. This method is shown to be very fast with good generalization accuracy. Instead of searching for a globally optimal label sequence, we learn to construct this optimal sequence directly in a greedy fashion. First, we show that sequence labeling can be modelled using Markov Decision Processes, so that several Reinforcement Learning (RL) algorithms can be used for this task. Second, we introduce a new RL algorithm which is based on the ranking of local labeling decisions.

1 Introduction

Sequence labeling is the generic task of assigning labels to the elements of a sequence. This task corresponds to a wide range of real world problems (*e.g.* character recognition, user modeling, bioinformatic, or information extraction). We consider here supervised sequence labeling where a user provides a training set of labeled sequences and wants to learn a model able to label new unseen sequences. Training examples consist of pairs (X, Y), where $X \in \mathcal{X}$ is an input sequence of elements $(x_1, \ldots x_T)$ and $Y \in \mathcal{Y}$ is the corresponding sequence of labels $(y_1, \ldots y_T)$. Each y_t is the label that corresponds to element x_t and y_t belongs to the label dictionary denoted $\mathcal{L}$. For example in handwritten recognition, X is a written word (an image for example) and $\mathcal{Y}$ is the corresponding recognized word, with characters in $\mathcal{L}$.

The sequence labeling problem has mainly been addressed with models that are based on first-order Markov dependencies assumptions upon the label sequence. For example, the basic *Hidden Markov Models* model considers that a label y_t only depends on the previous label y_{t-1} and the corresponding input element x_t. This assumption allows us to use Dynamic Programming algorithms – typically the Viterbi algorithm [1] – for computing the best sequence of labels knowing an input sequence. We would like to point out two important limitations of this approach. At first, such models exclude the use of long-term output dependencies and particularly the use of features defined globally on the whole label sequence. NLP offers many examples of such long-term dependencies

J.N. Kok et al. (Eds.): ECML 2007, LNAI 4701, pp. 648–657, 2007.

(*e.g.* is there yet any verb in the sentence?) that cannot be handled by classical Markovian models such as *Hidden Markov Models* (HMM) or *Conditional Random Fields* (CRF). A second important issue is that some sequence labeling tasks consider that labels are structured data, *e.g* a label may represent a set of features, or a relation to another element. For example, for the *dependency parsing* task, the aim is to identify relations between words. For these problems, the complexity of Viterbi based inference may be prohibitive. These two points motivate a need to develop fast inference methods for sequence labeling.

Contribution: Recently, a promising new approach has been proposed and has been instantiated in two systems named LaSO [2] and Searn [3] (see part 5 for more details). This approach does not try to model joint or posterior probabilities of sequences, but rather attempts at directly modeling the process of *inferring* the ideal label sequence. Using the same type of idea, we have developed a new method that builds the label sequence sequentially from any input sequence. It is based on *Reinforcement Learning* (RL) models and allows us to obtain nice performances with a very low complexity. The contributions of this paper are then threefold:

- First, we formalize the sequence labeling task as a *Markov Decision Process* (MDP) and then we cast the problem of learning as a Reinforcement Learning problem. This idea will make possible the use of different RL methods for sequence labeling and is new up to our knowledge. In the paper, we will use a specific RL method, namely SARSA, to evaluate this idea. This straightforward application of the MDP/ RL framework to sequence labeling incrementally builds the desired label sequence in a sequential order starting from the first element of the sequence. We also propose an alternative method where labels can be predicted in any order. The idea is that labels with stronger confidence should be decided first so that an enriched contextual information could help to reduce the ambiguities when deciding for labels with smaller confidence. Since the method can take into account non local contexts, the more decisions there are, the more informative the context is for future decisions.
- Second, we propose a new RL algorithm based on a ranking method. Current RL algorithms use classification or regression frameworks for estimating the next "optimal" action. However all that is needed here is an ordering of these potential actions which will allow us to choose the best one. This is closer to a ranking problem than it is to regression or classification one. The new algorithm relies on the idea of learning to rank possible labeling actions at each step of the inference process. This approach will be shown to have performances comparable to state-of-the-art sequence labeling models while keeping a much lower complexity.
- Third, our MDP view allows us to compare methods like LaSO or Searn with standard RL algorithms and with our ranking based method. We especially discuss the *Sampling strategy* of these methods, focussing on ideas from the field of RL that could help for the structured prediction community.

The paper is organized as follows: general background on MDPs and RL algorithms is provided in section 2, section 3 presents our MDP-based models for *label sequence building.* Section 4 describes our new ranking based approach for learning in these MDP-models. Section 5 describes related work in sequence labeling. The efficiency of the proposed RL approach is demonstrated on three standard datasets in section 6. Last, in section 7, we compare the different methods discussed in the paper.

2 Background

Markov Decision Processes [4] provide a mathematical framework for modeling sequential decision-making problems. They are used in a variety of areas, including robotics, automated control, economics and manufacturing. A MDP is defined by a set of states S, a set of actions A, a transition function δ, a scalar *reward* function in $\Re$. It describes an environment in which *agents* can evolve. At any time t, an agent is in a given state $s_t \in S$. In each state s, it can choose between several actions $A_s \subseteq A$. Once the agent has chosen one of those actions a_t, the transition function computes a new state s_{t+1} and the agent receives the immediate reward $r_t \in \Re$. An agent relies on a *policy* π which is a function that maps states to action probabilities. *Reinforcement Learning* (RL) algorithms attempt to find the policy that maximizes the cumulative reward which corresponds to the total amount of reward the agent receives in the long run. Such a policy is called an *optimal policy.*

Many RL algorithms consider a *value function* of each state-action pair given a policy. Informally, this Q-function corresponds to *how good* it is to select a given action in a given state. In this paper, we approximate the action value function using a linear function [5] :

$$Q_\theta(s,a) \stackrel{approx}{=} \tilde{Q}_\theta(\phi(s,a)) =< \theta, \phi(s,a) > \tag{1}$$

where $< .,. >$ is the classical dot product, θ is a vector of parameters and ϕ is feature function $\phi : S \times A \rightarrow \Re^n$ that transforms state-action pairs into vectors. $\tilde{Q}_\theta : \Re^n \rightarrow \Re$ is called the *action value prediction function.* Note that this function could also use non-linear models. In order to demonstrate the straightforward application of RL algorithms to the task of sequence labeling, we used the standard approximate-SARSA(0) algorithm [6], for learning $\tilde{Q}$ which defines the sequence labeling policy.

3 MDPs for Sequence Labeling

In this section, we develop models of incremental sequence labeling using the MDP formalism. We consider that the sequence labeling task is solved by an agent that, knowing the input sequence X, incrementally builds the corresponding output label sequence Y. The MDP defines the environment of this agent.

We first propose, in part 3.1, a model where the agent labels the sequence starting from the first element and then sequentially chooses the label of the next element. In part 3.2, we propose an original approach to sequence labeling, where the agent will label the elements of the input sequence in an *order-free* manner.

3.1 Left to Right Labeling

In order to show how sequence labeling can be modeled using MDPs, we first present the idea of predicting labels from left to right. In *Left to Right* labeling, initial states correspond to unlabeled element sequences. At each step $t \in [1, T]$ of the process, where T is the length of the input sequence, the agent selects a label y_t corresponding to element x_t. The process finishes at time T when the whole label sequence has been built. In order to express this with an MDP, we define the state space S, the set of actions A, the transition function δ, and the rewards.

State space. Since labels can depend on the whole input sequence X and on other labels, our states include both the current X and the current partially labeled sequence $\hat{Y}$. Partially labeled sequences are composed of labels in $\mathcal{L} \cup \{\perp\}$ where $\perp$ means that the corresponding element has not been labeled yet. There is one initial state per input sequence X: $s_{\perp X} = (X, (\perp, \ldots, \perp))$.

Action space and transitions. At time t, in state s_t, we want our agent to select a label for y_t. The possible actions A_{s_t} are simply the possible labels for y_t given by $\mathcal{L}$. When such an action is performed, the transition function of the MDP returns the new state of the agent. In our case, the transition consists in adding the selected label y_t to the already built partial sequence $\hat{Y}$.

Rewards. Sequence labeling is often evaluated using the Hamming loss which counts the number of wrong labels. Since each action corresponds to a single label prediction, we can directly decompose the Hamming Loss over individual actions. Each time the agent fails to predict the correct label it receives a penalty of 1. Since reward should be maximized, a penalty of 1 corresponds to a reward of -1. With this reward, maximizing the total amount of reward is equivalent to minimizing the Hamming loss. Sequence labeling can be evaluated with other loss functions, which eventually are not additively decomposable (*e.g.* F1-scores). In order to enable learning with any loss, the generic solution is to give the whole reward (the opposite of the loss) at the end of the episode. This corresponds to a more traditional RL configuration where the whole sequence of actions leads to a single reward.

Complexity. The *Left to Right* (LR) sequence labeling MDP is illustrated in figure 1 (a). Since inference is greedy, its complexity is the number of steps times the complexity of one step. One step requires to evaluate all actions available in A_s. The complexity of inference in the LR labeling is thus $O(T|\mathcal{L}|)$ where $|\mathcal{L}|$ is the number of possible labels. This complexity is lower than the usual Viterbi complexity $O(T|\mathcal{L}|^2)$.

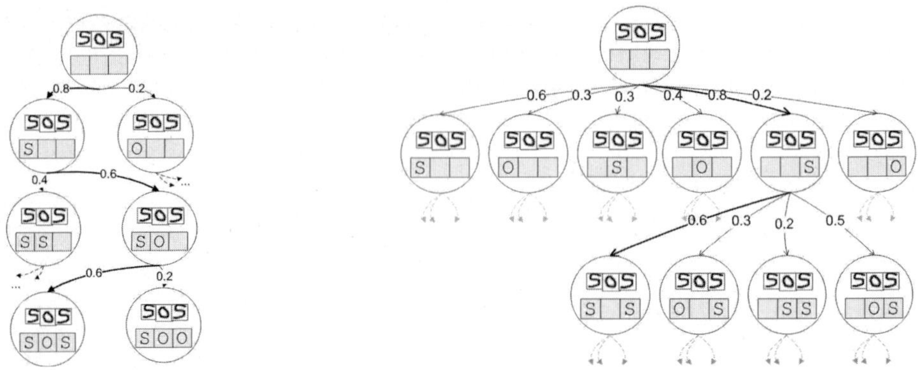

(a) Left to Right (b) Order Free

Fig. 1. This figure illustrates the *Left to Right* and *Order Free* Sequence Labeling MDPs. Each node is a state, which includes both the input sequence X and the partially labeled output sequence $\hat{Y}$. Each edge corresponds to an action and leads to a new state. We have illustrated here, a possible value function $Q(s, a)$ and the corresponding greedy trajectories (bold edges).

3.2 Order Free Labeling

Instead of labeling from left to right (or equivalently from right to left), we consider here a model that is able to label in any order. The underyling idea is that it may be easier to first label elements with a high confidence and then to label elements with lower confidence given the labels already chosen. For example, in a handwritten recognition task, some letters may be very noisy whereas others are clear and easy to recognize. If the agent begins to recognize the letters with a high confidence, it then will be able to use these labels, as additional context, to decide how to label the remaining letters. In order to enable order free labeling, an action will consist of both the position p and the label of an element. The action set A_s of this new MDP is the cartesian product between $\mathcal{L}$ and the set of unlabeled element positions in s. The *Order Free* (OF) sequence labeling MDP is illustrated in figure 1 (b).

Order Free sequence labeling is an original and attracting solution, but it comes with a cost: the number of possible actions per step is much higher than in LR labeling. The inference complexity of OF labeling is $O(T^2|\mathcal{L}|)$. This should be contrasted with the fact that, when the description function ϕ only takes into account local dependencies (as with Markov models), a majority of actions remains unchanged when performing one step and their scores do not need to be re-computed at the next step. An efficient implementation could rely on this idea in order to reduce the inference complexity of OF.

4 Ranking Approach

In this section, we introduce a new ranking based method for learning the optimal policy in MDPs, such as those presented above. This method will be shown to outperform SARSA on the sequence labeling tasks in section 6. Many RL approximate algorithms rely on the idea of modeling the action value function $Q(s, a)$. During inference – the greedy execution of a policy – this value function is used to sort actions and to pick the best one at each step. Since inference only uses an *order* information in Q, we propose here to directly *learn to rank* actions instead of learning to approximate the value function. This is done by learning an action *utility* function which defines an order over the set of possible actions.

Algorithm 1. Ranking Based Algorithm

1: $\theta \leftarrow$ initial value of parameters (*e.g.* $\mathbf{0}$)
2: **repeat** ▷ For all episodes
3:     $s \leftarrow$ sample an initial state
4:     **while** not isStateFinal(s) **do** ▷ For all states
5:         **for** each action $a \in A_s$ **do**
6:             $a^* \leftarrow$ ImproveAction(s, a)
7:             **if** $a^* \neq a$ **then**
8:                 **Learn** $\tilde{Q}_\theta(\phi(s, a)) \ll \tilde{Q}_\theta(\phi(s, a^*))$ ▷ Learning step
9:             **end if**
10:         **end for**
11:         $a \leftarrow$ SampleAction(s, θ) ▷ Sampling step
12:         Take action a and observe new state s'
13:         $s \leftarrow s'$
14:     **end while**
15: **until** convergence of θ
16: **return** θ

The proposed algorithm (algorithm 1) samples the state-action space in the same way as most RL algorithms do (*e.g.* with ϵ-greedy sampling, which most of time selects the action with best score, and sometimes selects a random exploratory action). For learning, the algorithm makes the assumption that it can, for any action a, get a better action a^*. This better action is provided through the improvement function `ImproveAction`(a) (line 6). In models such as LR and OF with Hamming loss, the improvement function is easy to construct: it simply gives the action that provides the best label. In more general situations, the improvement function can be implemented on the basis of simulation using rollout algorithms. We refer the interested reader to [6] and [7] for more information.

For each visited state, the algorithm considers all available actions. For each of those actions a, it computes the action a^* =`ImproveAction`(a) and builds a ranking pair (a, a^*). This pair is then used to update the ranking model (line 9 where the $\ll$ symbol means that utility $\tilde{Q}_\theta(\phi(s, a))$ should be made lower than utility $\tilde{Q}_\theta(\phi(s, a^*))$). Note that any ranking method can be used within algorithm 1. In our experiments, we used a linear utilty function, updated with the online τ-perceptron rule, which is a method close to the standard perceptron update rule that offers better empirical results [8].

5 Related Work

In this part we present state-of-the-art models for sequence labeling. Some of these models will be used as baselines in the experiments part. Many sequence labeling models based on a Markov assumption over labels have been proposed such as Hidden Markov Models and Conditional Random Fields [9] (CRFs). In such models, a label y_t only interacts with the input sequence and its neighborhood labels y_{t-1} and y_{t+1}. This enables Dynamic Programming based inference. CRFs model the conditional probability of the label sequence knowing the input sequence, by using the Maximum Entropy principle. Some recent works suggest the use of discriminant training, such as Hidden Markov Support Vector Machine [10] which have been generalized to different structured learning tasks through the SVM^{struct} model [11]

An other family of methods based on the idea of learning the *label sequence building* process has started to be explored recently in the structured learning community. The *Learning as Search Optimization* [2] (LaSO) model learns a scoring function associated to *building states*. This function is then used to prioritize states using a beam-search procedure. Choosing a beam size of 1 leads to greedy learning and inference methods, which are close to ours. More recently, the same authors have proposed the Searn – Search-Learn – algorithm [3] which reduces the building process to a standard classification task. Searn starts with a good initial policy defined over training examples. The algorithms slowly transforms this initial policy into a fully learned policy able to generalize to new examples. Each learning iteration follows the current policy in order to create a classification example per visited state. These examples are then used to learn a standard classifier. A new policy, which is a linear mixture of the current one and of the new classifier, is then defined for the next iteration. At the end of learning, the initial policy – which only works on training examples – has no more influence on the learned policy. Searn is shown to perform better than LaSO, and also gives better theoretical bounds. See section 7 and [12] for comparison of our approach, LaSO and Searn.

6 Experiments

Baseline Models. We have used three baseline methods in order to compare our models: CRFs, SVM^{struct} and Searn. For CRFs, we used the FlexCRFs implementation[1] with default parameters. We compared with discriminant training of the SVM^{struct} approach, thanks to the implementation given by the authors: SVM^{hmm2}. For each dataset, we tried three values of the C parameter: 0.01, 1, and 100, and kept only the best results. Our last baseline is a simple implementation of Searn provided by the authors. This implementation is limited to sequence labeling with Hamming loss and works with an averaged perceptron as base learner. The implementation does not give access to many parameters, so

[1] http://flexcrfs.sourceforge.net

[2] http://svmlight.joachims.org/svm_struct.html

few tuning was performed. It should be noted that the authors reports better results than those we present here, when using a Support Vector Machine as base learner.

Data Sets. We performed our experiments on three standard sequence labeling datasets corresponding to three tasks: Spanish Named Entity Recognition (NER[3]: 9 labels, 10,000 sentences of 50 words), Natural Language Chunking (Chunk[4]: 3 labels, 250,000 tokens) and Handwritten Recognition (HandWritten [13]: 26 labels, 6,000 words of 5-10 letters). These data sets correspond to the experiments performed in [3] and [11]. We used two train/test splits for NER and HandWritten. In the *Large* split, we used 90% for training and 10% for testing and *Small* is the inverted data set.

Feature Descriptions. All the models we compare rely on a feature function that allows us to jointly describe an $(X, \hat{Y})$ pair. Our approach can use any **non-Markovian features** but, in order to compare the different methods, we decided to use the same feature information. Due to a lack of space, we do not detail here the features that have been used. The features are described in [12] and are the same than the ones in [3].

	SARSA		Ranking		Baselines		
	Left Right	Order Free	Left Right	Order Free	CRF	SVM^{struct}	Simple Searn (LR)
NER-small	91.90	91.28	**93.67**	93.35	91.86	93.45	**93.8**
NER-large	96.31	96.32	**96.94**	96.75	**96.96**	-	96.3
HandWritten-small	68.41	70.63	74.01	73.57	66.86	**76.94**	64.1
HandWritten-large	80.33	79.59	83.80	**84.08**	75.45	-	73.5
Chunk	96.08	96.17	96.22	**96.54**	**96.71**	-	95.0
NER-large	$\approx$ 35min	$\approx$ 11h	$\approx$ 25min	$\approx$ 8h	$\approx$ 8h	$>$ 3 days	$\approx$ 6h
HandWritten-large	$\approx$ 15min	$\approx$ 6h	$\approx$ 12min	$\approx$ 4h	$\approx$ 2h	$>$ 3 days	$\approx$ 3h

Results. We compared the LR and OF approaches using both a SARSA learning algorithm and our new ranking algorithm. We also give results of the three baselines described above. We use ϵ-greedy sampling where ϵ decreases exponentially with the number of iterations. The discount rate in SARSA was tuned manually. Learning rate in both SARSA and our Ranking algorithm decreases linearly. It is not clear whether the OF model helps for better predictions on these datasets. It has been previously shown that first-order dependencies on labels in the NER task do not help much. This could explain why OF and LR are not significantly different on these tasks. In HandWritten and Chunk, OF seams to help a little bit, at the price of a much larger learning time. The ranking approach always perform better than its SARSA counterpart. The idea of ranking actions directly, instead of learning to approximate the value function, leads in our experiments to better generalization. The results demonstrate that our approaches are very competitive for the task of sequence labeling. One can

[3] http://www.cnts.ua.ac.be/conll2002/ner

[4] http://www.cnts.ua.ac.be/conll2000/chunking

choose between the fast method: LR, or the method which suffers much less from local ambiguities: OF.

7 Discussion

LaSO, Searn, SARSA (and most RL algorithms) or our ranking algorithm are tightly related one to the others. We propose a comparison in [12] which is based on four key points: the *sampling strategy*, the *base learning problem*, the *feature description strategy* and the *main learning assumptions* each method is based on. We focus here on one major point: the *sampling strategy* which is the way the actions of the MDPs are chosen during learning. Note that this comparison concerns the use of these methods on general structured prediction tasks and is not specific to sequence labeling.

LaSO: *Optimal Sampling.* The *optimal* strategy corresponds to an algorithm that only chooses correct actions. This leads to optimal trajectories: each visited state corresponds to a perfect partial solution. The problem with such trajectories is that the learner is not trained to recover from previous errors. This is very undesirable, since when generalizing, the action chooser will probably do some prediction errors.

Searn: *Optimal → Predicted Sampling.* The *Predicted Sampling* means that the learner always chooses the action that is predicted by itself at that point. With this kind of sampling, if an error occurs, the learner will be trained to recover from this error. Searn works by moving away from the optimal trajectories toward the predicted trajectories. This has proved to be much more robust than a pure optimal strategy.

Most RL algorithms, Sarsa and Ranking: *Predicted + noise Sampling.* The *Predicted + noise* strategy corresponds to a strategy where the agent follows its predicted actions, corrupted with some noise (*e.g.* with ϵ-greedy or Gibbs sampling). The quantity of noise can be controlled and is generally a decreasing parameter. We believe that this idea from the field of RL should be looked at more closely in the structured prediction community. We believe that this kind of exploration in the state-space leads to more robust learning, especially in the case of few training examples.

8 Conclusion

In this paper, we have proposed a new sequence labeling method based on the RL formalism (MDP and SARSA). The key idea proposed here is to model the *label sequence building* process using a Markov Decision Process. This led us to an original sequence labeling method in which labels can be chosen in any order. We then introduced a Ranking based algorithm in order to efficiently learn how to label a new sequence. Our approach is shown to be competitive with state-of-the-art sequence labeling methods while being simpler and much faster. Finally, on the basis of the link with MDP and RL algorithms, we discussed sampling strategies in LaSO, Searn and RL approaches such as the one we proposed.

We believe that our work is also of general interest for the RL community since it develops an original application of RL algorithms. In order to solve sequence labeling, we construct very large MDPs, where states and actions are formed of structured data. We use a high dimensional feature description of states and actions and present a large scale application of RL which is shown to be competitive with domain specific methods. Furthermore, our application is a successful example of the generalization capability of RL methods.

References

1. Forney, G.D.: The viterbi algorithm. Proceedings of The IEEE 61(3), 268–278 (1973)
2. Daumé III, H., Marcu, D.: Learning as search optimization: Approximate large margin methods for structured prediction. In: ICML, Bonn, Germany, ACM Press, New York (2005)
3. Daumé III, H., Langford, J., Marcu, D.: Search-based structured prediction (2006)
4. Howard, R.A.: Dynamic Programming and Markov Processes. Technology Press-Wiley, Cambridge, Massachusetts (1960)
5. J. Si, A. G. Barto, W.B., P., W.II., D.: Handbook of Learning and Approximate Dynamic Programming. Wiley&Sons, INC., Publications (2004)
6. Sutton, R., Barto, A.: Reinforcement learning: an introduction. MIT Press, Cambridge (1998)
7. Bertsekas, D.P: Rollout agorithms: an overview. In: Decision and Control, pp. 448–449 (1999)
8. Tsampouka, P., Shawe-Taylor, J.: Perceptron-like large margin classifiers (2005)
9. Lafferty, J., McCallum, A., Pereira, F.: Conditional random fields: Probabilistic models for segmenting and labeling sequence data. In: ICML, pp. 282–289. Morgan Kaufmann, San Francisco, CA (2001)
10. Altun, Y., Tsochantaridis, I., Hofmann, T.: Hidden markov support vector machines. In: ICML, pp. 3–10. ACM Press, New York (2003)
11. Tsochantaridis, I., Hofmann, T., Joachims, T., Altun, Y.: Support vector machine learning for interdependent and structured output spaces. In: ICML, ACM Press, New York (2004)
12. Maes, F., Denoyer, L., Gallinari, P.: Sequence labeling with reinforcement learning and ranking algorithms. Technical report, LIP6 - University of Paris 6 (2007)
13. Kassel, R.H.: A comparison of approaches to on-line handwritten character recognition. PhD thesis, Cambridge, MA, USA (1995)

Efficient Pairwise Classification

Sang-Hyeun Park and Johannes Fürnkranz

TU Darmstadt, Knowledge Engineering Group,
D-64289 Darmstadt, Germany
{park,juffi}@ke.informatik.tu-darmstadt.de

Abstract. Pairwise classification is a class binarization procedure that converts a multi-class problem into a series of two-class problems, one problem for each pair of classes. While it can be shown that for training, this procedure is more efficient than the more commonly used one-against-all approach, it still has to evaluate a quadratic number of classifiers when computing the predicted class for a given example. In this paper, we propose a method that allows a faster computation of the predicted class when weighted or unweighted voting are used for combining the predictions of the individual classifiers. While its worst-case complexity is still quadratic in the number of classes, we show that even in the case of completely random base classifiers, our method still outperforms the conventional pairwise classifier. For the more practical case of well-trained base classifiers, its asymptotic computational complexity seems to be almost linear.

1 Introduction

Many learning algorithms can only deal with two-class problems. For multi-class problems, they have to rely on *class binarization* procedures that transform the original learning problem into a series of binary learning problems. A standard solution for this problem is the *one-against-all* approach, which constructs one binary classifier for each class, where the positive training examples are those belonging to this class and the negative training examples are formed by the union of all other classes. An alternative approach, known as *pairwise classification* or *round robin classification* has recently gained attention [3,12]. Its basic idea is to transform a c-class problem into $c(c-1)/2$ binary problems, one for each pair of classes. This approach has been shown to produce more accurate results than the one-against-all approach for a wide variety of learning algorithms such as support vector machines [7] or rule learning algorithms [3]. Moreover, Fürnkranz [3] has also proved that despite the fact that its complexity is quadratic in the number of classes, the algorithm can in fact be *trained* faster than the conventional one-against-all technique.[1] However, in order to obtain a final prediction, we still have to combine the predictions of all $c(c-1)/2$ classifiers, which can be very inefficient for large values of c.

[1] It is easy to see this, if one considers that in the one-against-all case each training example is used c times (namely in each of the c binary problems), while in the round robin approach each example is only used $c-1$ times, namely only in those binary problems, when its own class is paired against one of the other $c-1$ classes.

J.N. Kok et al. (Eds.): ECML 2007, LNAI 4701, pp. 658–665, 2007.

The main contribution of this paper is a novel solution for this problem. Unlike previous proposals (such as [10]; cf. Section 3.2) our approach is not heuristic but is guaranteed to produce exactly the same prediction as the full pairwise classifier, which in turn has been shown to optimize the Spearman rank correlation with the target labels [8]. In essence, the algorithm selects and evaluates iterative pairwise classifiers using a simple heuristic to minimize the number of used pairwise classifiers that are needed to determine the correct *top rank* class of the complete (weighted) voting. We will describe and evaluate this algorithm in Section 3.

2 Pairwise Classification

In the following, we assume that a multi-class problem has c classes, which we denote with $c_1, \ldots, c_c$. A pairwise or round robin classifier trains a set of $c(c-1)/2$ *binary classifiers* $C_{i,j}$, one for each pair of classes $(c_i, c_j), i < j$. We will refer to the learning algorithm that is used to train the classifiers $C_{i,j}$ as the *base classifier*. Each binary classifier is only trained on the subset of training examples that belong to the classes c_i and c_j, all other examples are ignored for the training of $C_{i,j}$. Typically, the binary classifiers are class-symmetric, i.e., the classifiers $C_{i,j}$ and $C_{j,i}$ are identical. However, for some types of classifiers this does not hold. For example, rule learning algorithms will always learn rules for the positive class, and classify all uncovered examples as negative. Thus, the predictions may depend on whether class c_i or class c_j has been used as the positive class. As has been noted in [3], a simple method for solving this problem is to average the predictions of $C_{i,j}$ and $C_{j,i}$, which basically amounts to the use of a so-called *double round robin* procedure, where we have two classifiers for each pair of classes. We will use this procedure for our results with Ripper. At classification time, each binary classifier $C_{i,j}$ is queried and issues a vote (a prediction for either c_i or c_j) for the given example. This can be compared with sports and games tournaments, in which all players play each other once. In each game, the winner receives a point, and the player with the maximum number of points is the winner of the tournament. In our case, the class with the maximum number of votes is predicted (ties are broken arbitrarily for the larger class). In this paper, we will assume binary classifiers that return class probabilities $p(c_i|c_i \vee c_j)$ and $p(c_j|c_i \vee c_j)$. These can be used for *weighted voting*, i.e., we predict the class that receives the maximum number of votes:

$$c' = \arg\max_{i=1\ldots c} \sum_{j=1}^{c} p(c_i|c_i \vee c_j)$$

This procedure optimizes the Spearman rank correlation with the target ranking [8]. Other algorithms for combining votes exist (cf. *pairwise coupling* [5,12]), but are not subject of this paper.

Note that weighted or unweighted voting produce a *ranking* of all classes. For prediction problems, one is typically only interested in the *top ranked class*, but in some applications one might also be interested in the complete ranking of classes. Due to space restrictions we will focus here only on classification. However, the extended version of this paper [9] deals also with the problem of efficiently predicting a full class ranking. We propose for this case the so-called *Swiss-System*, a common scheme for conducting multi-round chess tournaments. Our results show that this algorithm offers a good trade-off between the number of evaluated classifiers and the quality of the approximation of the complete ranking.

3 Efficient Pairwise Classification

3.1 The Quick Weighted Voting (QWEIGHTED) Algorithm

Weighted or unweighted voting predicts the top rank class by returning the class with the highest accumulated voting mass after evaluation of all pairwise classifiers. During such a procedure there exist many situations where particular classes can be excluded from the set of possible top rank classes, even if they reach the maximal voting mass in the remaining evaluations. Consider following simple example: Given c classes with $c > j$, if class a has received more than $c - j$ votes and class b lost j votings, it is impossible for b to achieve a higher total voting mass than a. Thus further evaluations with b can be safely ignored. To increase the reduction of evaluations we are interested in obtaining such exploitable situations frequently. Pairwise classifiers will be selected depending on a *loss* value, which is the amount of potential voting mass that a class has *not* received. More specifically, the loss l_i of a class i is defined as $l_i := p_i - v_i$, where p_i is the number of evaluated incident classifiers of i and v_i is the current vote amount of i. Obviously, the loss will begin with a value of zero and is monotonically increasing.[2] The class with the current minimal loss is one of the top candidates for the top rank class. First the pairwise classifier $C_{a,b}$ will be selected for which the losses l_a

Algorithm 1. QWEIGHTED

```
while c_top not determined do
    c_a ← class c_i ∈ K with minimal l_i;
    c_b ← class c_j ∈ K\{c_a} with minimal l_j & classifier C_{a,b} not yet evaluated;
    if no c_b exists then
        c_top ← c_a;
    else
        v_ab ← Evaluate(C_{a,b});
        l_a ← l_a + (1 − v_ab);
        l_b ← l_b + v_ab;
```

and l_b of the relevant classes c_a and c_b are minimal, provided that the classifier $C_{a,b}$ has not yet been evaluated. In the case of multiple classes that have the same minimal loss, there exists no further distinction, and we select a class randomly from this set. Then, the losses l_a and l_b will be updated based on the evaluation returned by $C_{a,b}$ (recall that v_{ab} is interpreted as the amount of the voting mass of the classifier $C_{a,b}$ that goes

[2] This loss is essentially identical to the voting-against principle introduced by [1,2], which we will discuss later on in Section 3.2.

to class c_a and $1 - v_{ab}$ is the amount that goes to class c_b). These two steps will be repeated until all classifiers for the class c_m with the minimal loss has been evaluated. Thus the current loss l_m is the correct loss for this class. As all other classes already have a greater loss, c_m is the correct *top rank* class. Theoretically, a minimal number of comparisons of $c - 1$ is possible (*best case*). Assuming that the incident classifiers of the correct top rank c_{top} always returns the maximum voting amount ($l_{top} = 0$), c_{top} is always in the set $\{c_j \in K | l_j = \min_{c_i \in K} l_i\}$. In addition, c_{top} should be selected as the first class in step 1 of the algorithm among the classes with the minimal loss value. It follows that exactly $c - 1$ comparisons will be evaluated, more precisely all incident classifiers of c_{top}. The algorithm terminates and returns c_{top} as the correct top rank. The *worst case*, on the other hand, is still $c(c-1)/2$ comparisons, which can, e.g., occur if all pairwise classifiers classify randomly with a probability of 0.5. In practice, the number of comparisons will be somewhere between these two extremes, depending on the nature of the problem. The next section will evaluate this trade-off.

3.2 Related Work

Cutzu [1,2] recognized the importance of the voting-against principle and observed that it allows to reliably conclude a class when not all of the pairwise classifiers are present. For example, Cutzu claims that using the voting-against rule one could correctly predict class i even if none of the pairwise classifiers C_{ik} ($k = 1 \ldots c, k \neq i$) are used. However, this argument is based on the assumption that all base classifiers classify correctly. Moreover, if there is a second class j that should ideally receive $c - 2$ votes, voting-against could only conclude a tie between classes i and j, as long as the vote of classifier C_{ij} is not known. The main contribution of his work, however, is a method for computing posterior class probabilities in the voting-against scenario. Our approach builds upon the same ideas as Cutzu's, but our contribution is the algorithm that exploits the voting-against principle to effectively increase the prediction efficiency of pairwise classifiers without changing the predicted results. The voting-against principle was already used earlier in the form of DDAGs [10], which organize the binary base classifiers in a decision graph. Each node represents a binary decision that rules out the class that is not predicted by the corresponding binary classifier. At classification time, only the classifiers on the path from the root to a leaf of the tree (at most $c - 1$ classifiers) are consulted. While the authors empirically show that the method does not lose accuracy on three benchmark problems, it does not have the guarantee of our method, which will always predict the same class as the full pairwise classifier. Intuitively, one would also presume that a fixed evaluation routine that uses only $c-1$ of the $c(c-1)/2$ base classifiers will sacrifice one of the main strengths of the pairwise approach, namely that the influence of a single incorrectly trained binary classifier is diminished in large ensemble of classifiers [4].

3.3 Evaluation

We compare the QWEIGHTED algorithm with the full pairwise classifier and with DDAGs [10] on seven arbitrarily selected multi-class datasets from the UCI database of machine learning databases [6]. We used four commonly used learning algorithms

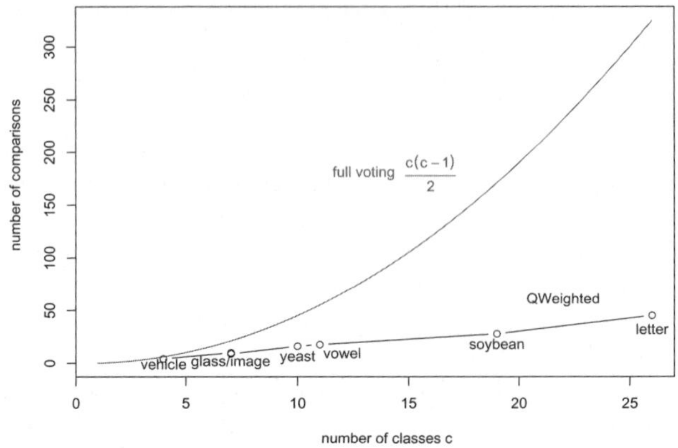

Fig. 1. Efficiency of QWEIGHTED in comparison to a full pairwise classifier

as base learners (the rule learner RIPPER, a Naive Bayes algorithm, the C4.5 decision tree learner, and a support vector machine) all in their implementations in the WEKA machine learning library [11]. Each algorithm was used as a base classifier for QWEIGHTED, and the combination was run on each of the datasets. As QWEIGHTED is guaranteed to return the same predictions as the full pairwise classifier, we are only interested in the number of comparisons needed for determining the winning class.[3] These are measured for all examples of each dataset via a 10-fold cross-validation except for *letter*, where the supplied testset was used. Table 1 shows the results. With respect to accuracy, there is only one case in a total of 28 experiments (4 base classifiers $\times$ 7 datasets) where DDAGs outperformed the QWEIGHTED, which, as we have noted above, optimizes the Spearman rank correlation. This and the fact that, to the best of our knowledge, it is not known what loss function is optimized by DDAGs, confirm our intuition that QWEIGHTED is a more principled approach than DDAGs. It can also be seen that the average number of comparisons needed by QWEIGHTED is much closer to the best case than to the worst case. Next to the absolute numbers, we show the trade-off between best and worst case (in brackets). A value of 0 indicates that the average number of comparisons is $c-1$, a value of 1 indicates that the value is $c(c-1)/2$ (the value in the last column). As we have ordered the datasets by their respective number of classes, we can observe that this value has a clear tendency to decrease with the number of the classes. For example, for the 19-class *soybean* and the 26-class *letter* datasets, only about $6-7\%$ of the possible number of additional pairwise classifiers are used, i.e., the total number of comparisons seems to grow only linearly with the number of classes. This can also be seen from Fig. 1, which plots the datasets with their respective number of classes together with a curve that indicates the performance of the full pairwise classifier. Finally, we note that the results are qualitatively the same for all base classifiers. QWEIGHTED does not seem to depend on a choice of base classifiers.

[3] As mentioned above, we used a double round robin for Ripper for both, the full pairwise classifier and for QWEIGHTED. In order to be comparable to the other results, we, in this case, divide the observed number of comparisons by two.

Table 1. Comparison of QWEIGHTED and DDAGs with different base learners on seven multi-class datasets. Next to the average numbers of comparisons for QWEIGHTED we show their trade-off $\frac{n-(c-1)}{\max -(c-1)}$ between best and worst case (in brackets).

			Accuracy		∅ Comparisons		
dataset	c	learner	QWeighted	DDAG	QWeighted	DDAG	full
vehicle	4	NB	45.39	44.92	4.27 (*0.423*)	3	6
		SMO	75.06	75.06	3.64 (*0.213*)		
		J48	71.99	70.92	3.96 (*0.320*)		
		JRip	73.88	72.46	3.98 (*0.327*)		
glass	7	NB	49.07	49.07	9.58 (*0.238*)	6	21
		SMO	57.01	57.94	9.92 (*0.261*)		
		J48	71.50	69.16	9.69 (*0.246*)		
		JRip	74.77	74.30	9.75 (*0.250*)		
image	7	NB	80.09	80.09	9.03 (*0.202*)	6	21
		SMO	93.51	93.51	8.29 (*0.153*)		
		J48	96.93	96.75	8.55 (*0.170*)		
		JRip	96.62	96.41	8.75 (*0.183*)		
yeast	10	NB	57.55	57.21	15.86 (*0.191*)	9	45
		SMO	57.68	57.41	15.52 (*0.181*)		
		J48	58.56	57.75	15.48 (*0.180*)		
		JRip	58.96	58.09	15.87 (*0.191*)		
vowel	11	NB	63.84	63.64	17.09 (*0.158*)	10	55
		SMO	81.92	81.52	15.28 (*0.117*)		
		J48	82.93	78.28	17.13 (*0.158*)		
		JRip	82.42	76.67	17.42 (*0.165*)		
soybean	19	NB	92.97	92.97	27.70 (*0.063*)	18	171
		SMO	94.14	93.41	28.36 (*0.068*)		
		J48	93.56	91.80	29.45 (*0.075*)		
		JRip	94.00	93.56	27.65 (*0.063*)		
letter	26	NB	63.08	63.00	44.40 (*0.065*)	25	325
		SMO	83.80	82.58	42.26 (*0.058*)		
		J48	91.50	86.15	47.77 (*0.076*)		
		JRip	92.33	88.33	45.01 (*0.068*)		

For a more systematic investigation of the complexity of the algorithm, we performed a simulation experiment. We assume classes in the form of numbers from $1 \ldots c$, and, without loss of generality, 1 is always the correct class. We further assume pairwise base pseudo-classifiers $i \prec_\epsilon j$, which, for two numbers $i < j$, return *true* with a probability $1 - \epsilon$ and *false* with a probability ϵ. For each example, the QWEIGHTED algorithm is applied to compute a prediction based on these pseudo-classifiers. The setting $\epsilon = 0$ (or $\epsilon = 1$) corresponds to a pairwise classifier where all predictions are consistent with a total order of the possible class labels, and $\epsilon = 0.5$ corresponds to the case where the predictions of the base classifiers are entirely random.

Table 2 shows the results for various numbers of classes ($c = 5, 10, 25, 50, 100$) and settings of the error parameter ($\epsilon = 0.0, 0.05, 0.1, 0.2, 0.3, 0.5$). Each data point is

Table 2. Average number n of pairwise comparisons for various number of classes and different error probabilities ϵ of the pairwise classifiers, and the full pairwise classifier. Below, we show their trade-off $\frac{n-(c-1)}{\max-(c-1)}$ between the best and worst case, and an estimate of the growth ratio $\frac{\log(n_2/n_1)}{\log(c_2/c_1)}$ of successive values of n.

c	$\epsilon = 0.0$		$\epsilon = 0.05$		$\epsilon = 0.1$		$\epsilon = 0.2$		$\epsilon = 0.3$		$\epsilon = 0.5$		full
5	5.43		5.72		6.07		6.45		6.90		7.12		10
	0.238	—	*0.287*	—	*0.345*	—	*0.408*	—	*0.483*	—	*0.520*	—	
10	14.11		16.19		18.34		21.90		25.39		28.74		45
	0.142	**1.378**	*0.200*	**1.501**	*0.259*	**1.595**	*0.358*	**1.764**	*0.455*	**1.880**	*0.548*	**2.013**	
25	42.45		60.01		76.82		113.75		151.19		198.51		300
	0.067	**1.202**	*0.130*	**1.430**	*0.191*	**1.563**	*0.325*	**1.798**	*0.461*	**1.974**	*0.632*	**2.109**	
50	91.04		171.53		251.18		422.58		606.74		868.25		1225
	0.036	**1.101**	*0.104*	**1.515**	*0.172*	**1.709**	*0.318*	**1.893**	*0.474*	**2.005**	*0.697*	**2.129**	
100	189.51		530.17		900.29		1684.21		2504.54		3772.45		4950
	0.019	**1.058**	*0.089*	**1.628**	*0.165*	**1.842**	*0.327*	**1.995**	*0.496*	**2.045**	*0.757*	**2.119**	

the average outcome of 1000 trials with the corresponding parameter settings. We can see that even for entirely random data, our algorithm can still save about $1/4$ of the pairwise comparisons that would be needed for the entire ensemble. For cases with a total order and error-free base classifiers, the number of needed comparisons approaches the number of classes, i.e., the growth appears to be linear. To shed more light on this, we provide two more measures below each average: the lower left number (in italics) shows the trade-off between best and worst case, as defined above. The result confirms that for a reasonable performance of the base classifiers (up to about $\epsilon = 0.2$), the fraction of additional work reduces with the number of classes. Above that, we observe a growth. The reason for this is that with a low number of classes, there is still a good chance that the random base classifiers produce a reasonably ordered class structure, while this chance is decreasing with increasing numbers of classes. On the other hand, the influence of each individual false prediction of a base classifier decreases with an increasing number of classes, so that the true class ordering is still clearly visible and can be better exploited by QWEIGHTED. We tried to directly estimate the exponent of the growth function of the number of comparisons of QWEIGHTED, based on the number of classes c. The resulting exponents, based on two successive measure points, are shown in bold font below the absolute numbers. For example, the exponent of the growth function between $c = 5$ and $c = 10$ is estimated (for $\epsilon = 0$) as $\frac{\log(14.11/5.43)}{\log(10/5)} \approx 1.378$. We can see that the growth rate starts almost linearly (for a high number of classes and no errors in the base classifiers) and approaches a quadratic growth when the error rate increases.

In summary, our results indicate that QWEIGHTED always increases the efficiency of the pairwise classifier: for high error rates in the base classifiers, we can only expect improvements by a constant factor, whereas for the practical case of low error rates we can also expect a significant reduction in the asymptotic algorithmic complexity.

4 Conclusions

In this paper, we have proposed a novel algorithm that allows to speed up the prediction phase for pairwise classifiers. QWEIGHTED will always predict the same class as the full pairwise classifier, but the algorithm is close to linear in the number of classes, in particular for large numbers of classes, where the problem is most stringent. For very hard problems, where the performance of the binary classifiers reduces to random guessing, its worst-case performance is still quadratic in the number of classes, but even there practical gains can be expected. A restriction of our approach is that it is only applicable to combining predictions via voting or weighted voting. There are various other proposals for combining the class probability estimates of the base classifiers into an overall class probability distribution (this is also known as *pairwise coupling* [5,12]). Nevertheless, efficient alternatives for other pairwise coupling techniques are an interesting topic for further research.

Acknowledgments

This research was supported by the *German Science Foundation (DFG).*

References

1. Cutzu, F.: How to do multi-way classification with two-way classifiers. In: Kaynak, O., Alpaydın, E., Oja, E., Xu, L. (eds.) ICANN 2003 and ICONIP 2003. LNCS, vol. 2714, pp. 375–384. Springer, Heidelberg (2003a)
2. Cutzu, F.: Polychotomous classification with pairwise classifiers: A new voting principle. In: Proceedings of the 4th International Workshop on Multiple Classifier Systems, pp. 115–124. Springer, Berlin (2003b)
3. Fürnkranz, J.: Round robin classification. Journal of Machine Learning Research 2, 721–747 (2002)
4. Fürnkranz, J.: Round robin ensembles. Intelligent Data Analysis 7, 385–404 (2003)
5. Hastie, T., Tibshirani, R.: Classification by pairwise coupling. In: Advances in Neural Information Processing Systems 10 (NIPS-97), pp. 507–513. MIT Press, Cambridge (1998)
6. Hettich, S., Blake, C.L., Merz, C.J.: UCI repository of machine learning databases. Department of Information and Computer Science, University of California at Irvine, Irvine CA (1998), http://www.ics.uci.edu/~mlearn/MLRepository.html
7. Hsu, C.-W., Lin, C.-J.: A comparison of methods for multi-class support vector machines. IEEE Transactions on Neural Networks 13, 415–425 (2002)
8. Hüllermeier, E., Fürnkranz, J.: Ranking by pairwise comparison: A note on risk minimization. In: Proceedings of the IEEE International Conference on Fuzzy Systems (FUZZ-IEEE-04), Budapest, Hungary (2004)
9. Park, S.-H., Fürnkranz, J.: Efficient Pairwise Classification and Ranking. Technical Report TUD-KE-2007-3. Knowledge Engineering Group, TU Darmstadt (2007)
10. Platt, J.C., Cristianini, N., Shawe-Taylor, J.: Large margin DAGs for multiclass classification. In: Advances in Neural Information Processing Systems 12 (NIPS-99), pp. 547–553. MIT Press, Cambridge (2000)
11. Witten, I.H., Frank, E.: Data mining — practical machine learning tools and techniques with Java implementations, 2nd edn. Morgan Kaufmann Publishers, San Francisco (2005)
12. Wu, T.-F., Lin, C.-J., Weng, R.C.: Probability estimates for multi-class classification by pairwise coupling. Journal of Machine Learning Research 5, 975–1005 (2004)

Scale-Space Based Weak Regressors for Boosting

Jin-Hyeong Park[1] and Chandan K. Reddy[2]

[1] Integrated Data Systems Department, Siemens Corporate Research, Princeton, NJ-08540, USA
jin-hyeong.park@siemens.com
[2] Department of Computer Science, Wayne State University, Detroit, MI-48202, USA
reddy@cs.wayne.edu

Abstract. Boosting is a simple yet powerful modeling technique that is used in many machine learning and data mining related applications. In this paper, we propose a novel scale-space based boosting framework which applies scale-space theory for choosing the optimal regressors during the various iterations of the boosting algorithm. In other words, the data is considered at different resolutions for each iteration in the boosting algorithm. Our framework chooses the weak regressors for the boosting algorithm that can best fit the current resolution and as the iterations progress, the resolution of the data is increased. The amount of increase in the resolution follows from the wavelet decomposition methods. For regression modeling, we use logitboost update equations based on first derivative of the loss function. We clearly manifest the advantages of using this scale-space based framework for regression problems and show results on different real-world regression datasets.

1 Introduction

In statistical machine learning, boosting techniques have been proven to be effective for not only improving the classification/regression accuracies but also in reducing the bias and variance of the estimated classifier. The most popular variant of boosting, namely the AdaBoost (Adaptive Boosting) in combination with trees has been described as the "best off-the-shelf classifier in the world" [1]. In simple terms, boosting algorithms build multiple models from a dataset, using some learning algorithm that need not be a strong learner. Boosting algorithms are generally viewed as functional gradient descent schemes and obtain the optimal updates based on the global minimum of the error function [2]. In spite of its great success, boosting algorithms still suffer from a few open-ended problems such as the choice of the parameters for the weak regressor.

In this paper, we propose a novel boosting framework for regression problems using the concepts of scale-space theory. In the scale-space based approach to boosting, the weak regressors are determined by analyzing the data over a range of scales (or resolutions). Our algorithm provides the flexibility of choosing the weak regressor dynamically compared to static weak regressor with certain

J.N. Kok et al. (Eds.): ECML 2007, LNAI 4701, pp. 666–673, 2007.

pre-specified parameters. For every iteration during the boosting process, the resolution is either maintained or doubled and a weak regressor is used for fitting the data. This method of manipulating different resolutions and modeling them accurately looks similar to wavelet decomposition methods for multi-resolution signal analysis. Throughout this paper, we used a Gaussian kernel as an approximate (or weak) regressor for every iteration during boosting. The data is modeled at multiple resolutions and the final boosted (or additive) model will combine the weak models obtained at various resolutions. In this way, we propose a hierarchical (or scale-space) approach for modeling the data using Gaussian kernels. This approach is similar to decomposing a signal using wavelets. Basically, the low frequency components in wavelet decomposition correspond to fitting a Gaussian for the entire dataset and the high frequency components correspond to fitting fewer data points. We formulate this scale-space based boosting regressor using logitboost with exponential L_2 norm loss function. Though our method can be potentially applied with any base regressor, we chose to have Gaussian model because of its nice theoretical scale-space properties [3].

The rest of this paper is organized as follows: Section 2 gives some relevant background on various boosting techniques. It also gives the problem formulation in detail and discusses the concepts necessary to comprehend our algorithm. Section 3 describes our scale-space based boosting algorithm for regression problems. Section 4 gives the experimental results of our algorithm on different real-world datasets. Finally, Section 5 concludes our discussion with future research directions.

2 Background

Ensemble learning is one of the fundamental data mining operations that has become popular in recent years. As opposed to other popular ensemble learning techniques like bagging [4], boosting methods reduce the bias and the variance simultaneously. A comprehensive study on boosting algorithms and their theoretical properties are given in [5]. One main advantage of boosting methods is that the weak learner can be a black-box which can deliver only the result in terms of accuracy and can potentially be any model [2]. The additive model provides a reasonable flexibility in choosing the optimal weak learners for a desired task. Various extensions for the original adaboost algorithm had also been proposed in the literature [6,7,8]. A detailed study on L_2 norm based classification and regression is given in [9].

In this paper, we propose a novel scale-space based scheme for choosing optimal weak regressors during the iterations in boosting regression problems. The scale-space concept allows for effective modeling of the dataset at a given resolution. The theory of scale-space for discrete signals was first discussed in [10]. Data clustering is one of the most successful applications of the scale-space based techniques [11]. Gaussian kernels have been extensively studied in this scale-space framework [3]. The scale-space based weak regressors will allow systematic hierarchical modeling of the regression function. They also provide more flexibility and can avoid overfitting problem by allowing the user to stop modeling after a certain resolution.

2.1 Problem Specification

Let us consider N i.i.d. training samples with d features $\mathcal{D} = (\mathcal{X}, \mathcal{Y})$ consisting of samples $(\mathcal{X}, \mathcal{Y}) = (x_1, y_1), (x_2, y_2), .., (x_N, y_N)$ where $\mathcal{X} \in \mathbb{R}^{N \times d}$ and $\mathcal{Y} \in \mathbb{R}^{N \times 1}$. Let us denote $x_i \in \mathbb{R}^{N \times d}$ as i^{th} data point in the d-dimensional feature space. For the case of binary classification problems, we have $y_i \in \{-1, +1\}$ and for regression problems, y_i takes any arbitrary real value. In other words, the univariate response $\mathcal{Y}$ is continuous for regression problems and discrete for classification problems. The goal of a regression problem is to obtain the function $F(\mathcal{X})$ that can approximate $\mathcal{Y}$.

The basic idea of boosting is to repeatedly apply the weak learner to modified versions of the data, thereby producing a sequence of weak regressors $f^{(t)}(x)$ for $t = 1, 2, .., T$ where T denotes predefined number of iterations. Each boosting iteration performs the following three steps: (1) Computes response and weights for every data point. (2) Fits a weak learner to the weighted training samples and (3) Computes the error and updates the final model. In this way, the final model obtained by boosting algorithm is a linear combination of several weak learning models. It was also proved that boosting algorithms are stage-wise estimation procedures for fitting an additive logistic regression model [5]. We derive the scale-space boosting algorithm based on this spirit.

2.2 Boosting for Regression

In the case of regression problems, the penalty function is given by:

$$L(y_i, F^{(t)}(x_i)) = \|y_i - F^{(t)}(x_i)\|_p \tag{1}$$

where $\|\cdot\|_p$ indicates the L_p norm. We will consider $p = 2$ namely the Euclidean norm in this paper.

Proposition 1 *[5]. The Adaboost algorithm fits an additive logistic regression model by using quasi-Newton method using the analytical Hessian matrix updates for minimizing the expected value of the loss function.*

Let us consider the following exponential loss function

$$J(f) = exp(\| y - F - f \|^2) \tag{2}$$

Let us now define the residual r as the absolute difference between $\mathcal{Y}$ and F. We chose to use first derivative updates (for faster convergence) by choosing the weak regressor using the residual $(f = r)$.

2.3 Scale-Space Kernels

Let us consider the general regression problem which is a continuous mapping $p(x) : \mathbb{R}^d \to \mathbb{R}$. In scale-space theory, $p(x)$ is embedded into a continuous family $P(x, \sigma)$. Our method starts with an approximation of the entire dataset with Gaussian kernel of $\sigma = 0$. As the resolution (or scale) increases, the sigma value is reduced and eventually converges to zero. In our case, the highest frequency (or resolution) corresponds to fitting every data point with a Gaussian kernel. In simple terms, one can write the new kernel $p(x, \sigma)$ as a convolution of $p(x)$ with a Gaussian kernel $g(x, \sigma)$. As described earlier, choosing optimal σ value during every iteration of boosting becomes a challenging task. In other words, one cannot predetermine the reduction in the σ value. We choose to reduce it by halves using the concepts of wavelet decomposition methods. In signal processing applications, wavelet transformation constructs a family of hierarchically organized decompositions [12]. The frequencies in the wavelet domain correspond to resolutions in our scale-space based algorithm. The original target function ($\mathcal{Y}$) is decomposed using weak regressors(f) and residuals(r). The final regression model at any given resolution is obtained by a weighted linear combination of the weak regressors obtained so far.

3 Scale-Space Based Framework

Algorithm 1 describes our scale-space based approach for boosting regression problems. The initial regressor is set to the mean value of the target values. The main program runs for a predefined number (T) of iterations. To make the problem simpler, 1) we control the resolution of the kernel using the number of data samples; 2) we fit the target values, $\mathcal{Y}$, only using one feature, $\mathcal{X}_i, i \in [1, d]$, at a time. Initially, the number of data points to be modeled is set to the total number of samples in the dataset. $\mathcal{X}_i$'s are sorted independently by column-wise and the indices corresponding to each column are stored. This will facilitate the Gaussian based regression modeling that will be performed later on. For every iteration, the best kernel is fit to the data based on a single feature, $\mathcal{X}_i, i \in [1, d]$, at a particular resolution. The procedure *bestkernelfit* performs this task for a resolution corresponding to n data points. We used Gaussian weak regressors as our kernels since the Gaussian kernels are one of the most popular choice for scale-space kernel. The basic idea is to slide a Gaussian window across all the sorted data points corresponding to each feature, $\mathcal{X}_i, i \in [1, d]$, at a given resolution.

As the iterations progress, the number of data points considered for fitting the weak regressor is retained or halved depending on the error of the model. In other words, depending on the error at a given iteration, the resolution of the data is maintained or increased for the next iteration. For every iteration, the residual r is set to the absolute difference between the target value ($\mathcal{Y}$) and the final regressor (F). By equating the first derivative of the loss function to zero, we will set the residual as the data to be modeled during the next iteration using another weak regressor. The main reason for retaining the resolution in the next iteration is that sometimes there might be more than one significant component at that particular resolution. One iteration can model only one of these components. In order to model the other components, one has to perform another iteration of obtaining the best Gaussian regressor at the same resolution. Increasing the resolution for the next iteration in this case might fail to model the component accurately. Only after ensuring that there are no more significant components at a given resolution, our algorithm will increase the resolution for the next iteration. Hence, the best Gaussian regressor corresponding to n or $n/2$ data points is obtained at every iteration and the model with the least error added to the final regressor. The main aspect of our algorithm, which is the scale-space, can be seen from the fact that the resolution of the data to be modeled is either maintained or increased as the number of iterations increase. Hence, the algorithm proposed here can be more generally termed as "*scale-space based Boosting*" that can model any arbitrary function using the boosting scheme with scale-space based weak regressors. Our algorithm obtains the weak regressors and models the data in a more systematic (hierarchical) manner. Most importantly, the change in resolution is monotonically non-decreasing, i.e. the resolution either remains the same or increased.

Algorithm 1. Scale-space Boosting

Input: Data ($\mathcal{D}$), No. of samples (N), No. of iterations (T).
Output: Final Regressor (F)
Algorithm:
set $n = N, \quad F = \emptyset$
for $i = 1 : d$ **do**
  $[\hat{\mathcal{X}}, idx(:, i)] = \text{sort}(\mathcal{X}(:, i))$
end for
for $t = 1 : T$ **do**
  $r = |\mathcal{Y} - F|$
  $[\hat{f}_0, err_0] = bestkernelfit(\hat{\mathcal{X}}, r, N, d, n, idx)$
  $[\hat{f}_1, err_1] = bestkernelfit(\hat{\mathcal{X}}, r, N, d, n/2, idx)$
  if $err_0 < err_1$ **then**
    $F = F + \hat{f}_0$
  else
    $F = F + \hat{f}_1$
    $n = n/2$
  end if
end for
return F

4 Experimental Results

We performed experiments using two non-linear regression datasets from NIST StRD (Statistics Reference Datasets [13]). We selected two datasets : (1) *Gauss3* from the category of average level of difficulty containing 250 samples with 1 predictor variable (x) and 1 response variable (y). (2) *Thurber* from the category of high level of difficulty containing 37 samples with 1 predictor variable (x) and 1 response variable (y). Figure 1 shows experimental results on these two datasets using the proposed scale-space boosting algorithm after 1, 5, 10 and 50 iterations

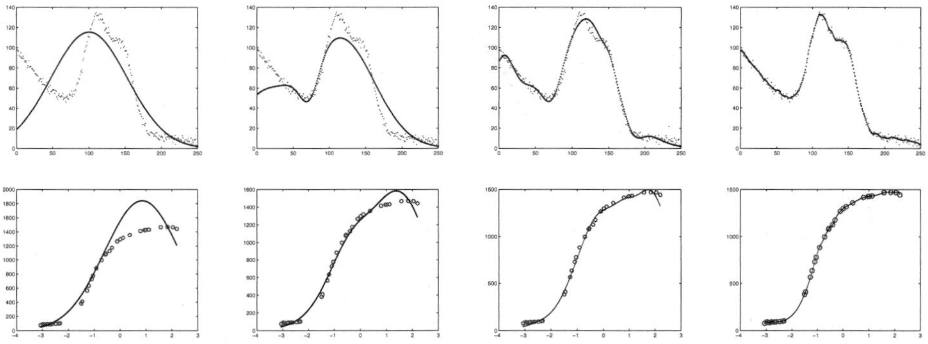

(a) Iteration 1 (b) Iteration 5 (c) Iteration 10 (d) Iteration 50

Fig. 1. Experimental results for *Gauss3* (first row) and *Thurber* (second row) datasets after 1,5,10 and 50 iterations

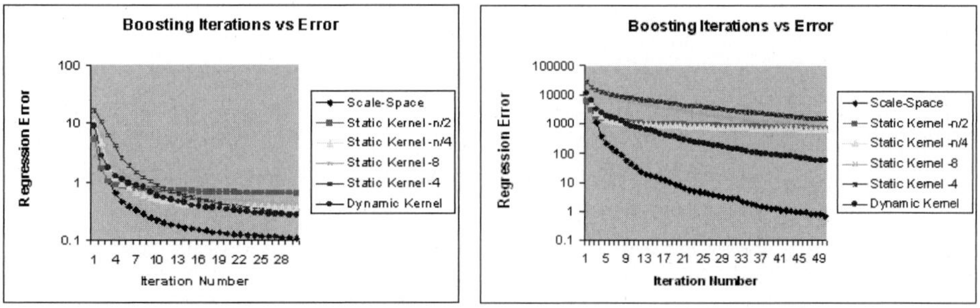

(a) Diabetes (b) Ozone

Fig. 2. Convergence of the regression error during the boosting procedure (training phase) using scale-space kernel and other static and dynamic kernels of various widths

are shown. We also ran our experiments on the following more complicated real world datasets:

- **Diabetes** [14] dataset contains 43 samples with 2 predictor variables.
- **Ozone** [1] dataset contains 330 samples with 8 predictor variables.
- **Abalone** [15] dataset contains 4177 samples with 8 predictor variables.

4.1 Discussion

The scale-space boosting algorithm is very effective in reducing the error quickly in the first few iterations. Significant reduction in the training error occurs within first 10 boosting iterations. By using scale-space kernels, one can achieve the optimal point (point where the over-fitting starts) within this first few iterations. Usually this point is obtained after at least 40 boosting iterations in the case of

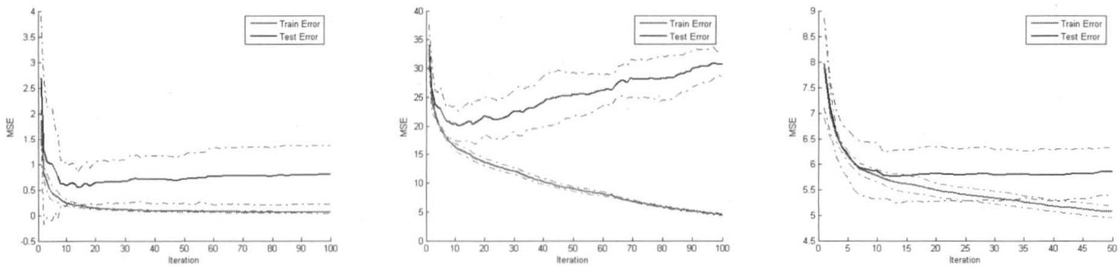

(a) Diabetes (b) Ozone (c) Abalone

Fig. 3. Results of training and test error on different datasets using 5-fold cross validation. The solid lines indicate the mean of the error and the dashed lines indicate the standard deviation in the errors.

static kernels as shown in Fig. 2, which gives the convergence of the regression error during the boosting iterations. Clearly the behavior of the convergence is similar to static kernels of very less width but the error is much lesser in the case of scale-space kernel. The main reason for using the scale-space framework is for faster convergence of the results by *dynamically choosing the weak regressors* during the boosting procedure. One can also see the comparison between the convergence behaviour of a randomly chosen dynamic kernel versus the scale-space kernel. Choosing an optimal weak regressor by exploring all possibilities might yield a better result, but it will be computationally inefficient and infeasible for most of the practical problems. For such problems, scale-space kernels will give the users with a great flexibility of adaptive kernel scheme at a very low computational effort (also considering the fact of speedy convergence). To the best of our knowledge, this is the first attempt to use the concepts of scale-space theory and wavelet decomposition in the context of boosting algorithms for any regression modeling.

We also demonstrate that the scale-space framework does not suffer from the over-fitting problem. Fig. 3 shows the train and test errors during the boosting iterations along with the standard deviation using 5-fold cross validation scheme for the different datasets. For improving the computational efficiency, the sliding window kernel in the $bestkernelfit$ procedure is moved in steps of multiple data points rather than individual data points. One other advantage of using the scale-space based boosting approach is that it obtains smooth regression functions (approximators) at different level of accuracies as shown in our results. This cannot be achieved by using a decision tree or a boosting stump though they might yield lower RMSE values for prediction. Hence, our comparisons were specifically made with other smooth kernels that were used in the literature.

5 Conclusions and Future Research

Recently, boosting have received great attention from several researchers. Choosing optimal weak regressors and setting their parameters during the boosting iterations have been a challenging task. In this paper, we proposed a novel boosting algorithm that uses scale-space theory to obtain the optimal weak regressor at every iteration. We demonstrated our results for logitboost based regression problems on several real-world datasets. Similarities and differences of our method compared to other popular models proposed in the literature are also described. Extensions to Adaboost framework and use of scale-space kernels in classification problems are yet to be investigated. Effects of different loss functions in this scale-space boosting framework will also be studied in the future.

References

1. Breiman, L.: Arcing classifiers. The Annals of Statistics 26(3), 801–849 (1998)
2. Hastie, T., Tibshirani, R., Friedman, J.: Boosting and Additive Trees. In: The Elements of Statistical Learning. Data Mining, Inference, and Prediction, Springer, Heidelberg (2001)
3. Sporring, J., Nielsen, M., Florack, L., Johansen, P.: Gaussian Scale-Space Theory. Kluwer Academic Publishers, Dordrecht (1997)
4. Breiman, L.: Bagging predictors. Machine Learning 24(2), 123–140 (1996)
5. Friedman, J.H., Hastie, T., Tibshirani, R.: Additive logistic regression: A statistical view of boosting. Annals of Statistics 28(2), 337–407 (2000)
6. Zemel, R.S., Pitassi, T.: A gradient-based boosting algorithm for regression problems. Neural Information Processing Systems, 696–702 (2000)
7. Schapire, R.E., Singer, Y.: Improved boosting using confidence-rated predictions. Machine Learning 37(3), 297–336 (1999)
8. Zhu, J., Rosset, S., Zou, H., Hastie, T.: Multi-class adaboost. Technical Report 430, Department of Statistics, University of Michigan (2005)
9. Buhlmann, P., Yu, B.: Boosting with the l2 loss: Regression and classification. Journal of American Statistical Association 98(462), 324–339 (2003)
10. Lindeberg, T.: Scale-space for discrete signals. IEEE Transactions on Pattern Analysis Machine Intelligence 12(3), 234–254 (1990)
11. Leung, Y., Zhang, J., Xu, Z.: Clustering by scale-space filtering. IEEE Transactions on Pattern Analysis Machine Intelligence 22(12), 1396–1410 (2000)
12. Mallat, S.: A theory for multiresolution signal decomposition: the wavelet representation. IEEE Transaction on Pattern Analysis and Machine Intelligence 11, 674–693 (1989)
13. Information Technology Laboratory, N.I.o.S. (NIST), T.: Nist strd (statistics reference datasets), `http://www.itl.nist.gov/div898/strd/`
14. Hastie, T., Tibshirani, R.: Generalized additive models. p. 304. Chapman and Hall, London (1990)
15. Blake, C., Merz, C.: UCI repository of machine learning databases. University of California, Irvine, Dept. of Information and Computer Sciences (1998), `http://www.ics.uci.edu/~mlearn/MLRepository.html`

K-Means with Large and Noisy Constraint Sets

Dan Pelleg and Dorit Baras

IBM Haifa Labs
dpelleg@il.ibm.com, doritb@il.ibm.com

Abstract. We focus on the problem of clustering with soft instance-level constraints. Recently, the CVQE algorithm was proposed in this context. It modifies the objective function of traditional K-means to include penalties for violated constraints. CVQE was shown to efficiently produce high-quality clustering of UCI data. In this work, we examine the properties of CVQE and propose a modification that results in a more intuitive objective function, with lower computational complexity. We present our extensive experimentation, which provides insight into CVQE and shows that our new variant can dramatically improve clustering quality while reducing run time. We show its superiority in a large-scale surveillance scenario with noisy constraints.

1 Introduction

Recently, a growing interest in utilizing side-information in clustering led to a variety of new clustering techniques. The side information is used to encode a tacit bias to counter that of the original clustering algorithm. In this sense, the new algorithm can be thought of as supervised. But in contrast to traditional supervision, the ground truth labels need not be explicitly present in the input.

Typically, the side information is in the form of pairwise instance-level constraints. Constraints of this type come in two flavors: a *must-link (ML)* constraint, to indicate that a pair of input points need to be in the same output cluster, and a *cannot-link (CL)* constraint, to indicate the opposite. These types of constraints were thoroughly investigated and have been shown to improve results in different application areas. Some of these areas include GPS lane finding [1], video and image indexing [2,3], robot navigation [4], image segmentation [5], and text categorization [6,7]. The constraints are considered to increase cluster purity, decrease convergence time, and reduce error [8].

The method in which the constraints are acquired depends on the application itself. For example, spatial or temporal proximity of observations may be used to induce constraints, or user feedback on a clustering result may be used in an active-learning or semi-supervised setting. In experimentation, it is also popular to use the ground truth labels to induce constraints.

In general, existing methods fall into one of two categories: constraint-driven and distance-driven. The first type tries to directly satisfy the constraints. There are hard and soft versions of these, which vary in their ability to ignore some

J.N. Kok et al. (Eds.): ECML 2007, LNAI 4701, pp. 674–682, 2007.

constraints. The second type learns a distance metric from the constraints, and it is later used in a constraint-agnostic clustering algorithm.

This work is motivated by a surveillance application. In this setting, a sensor (e.g., a video camera), or a network of such sensors, is located in a public area. The sensor can locate objects in a 2-D or 3-D space. It can also track their movement over a short period of time. For example, if object locations are recorded every minute, the sensor may also identify that the same object that was at location P at time t, is at location P' at time $t+1$. Noise in the measurements may come in the form of false tracking due to objects or agents leaving and entering the scene, occlusion, etc. The goal of the application is to perform long-term tracking of objects. That is, cluster the observation points such that each cluster corresponds to a single object. This naturally gives rise to the constrained clustering problem with the following characteristics: 1) The number of data points and constraints is large (thousands or more, depending on the monitoring period and frequency). 2) The constraints are mostly ML. 3) The constraints are noisy.

This paper explores solutions to such problems. From the description above, some required properties for such solutions emerge: scalability, efficiency, and resilience to constraint noise. The latter immediately precludes hard satisfaction algorithms. Of the soft variants, algorithms based on K-means are a natural fit to the scalability requirement, since they are potentially linear in the number of points, dimensions, constraints and clusters.

We also note the common practice of augmenting the constraint set by transitive and entailed constraints. This is a widely-used heuristic [9], but unfortunately, it cannot be used in our scenario for two reasons. First, the noise may introduce ML constraints between some members of different clusters. When the number of constraints is large, the probability of such an event is high, and the result would be the complete— and useless— clique in the ML graph. Second, the size of the augmented set is huge. In one experiment with around 20000 points and constraints, this kind of pre-processing generated approximately half a million constraints.

Davidson et al. [10] propose using a black-box method to evaluate the usefulness of constraints. Two measurements are defined on constraint sets: *informativeness* and *coherence*. Informativeness represents the tacit bias, due to the constraints, that is different from the algorithm's own bias. Coherence is the disparity between ML and CL pairs. These measures can be used to evaluate a given constraint set. In a convincing experiment, an extremely small constraint set is shown to dramatically enhance clustering results. Taking this idea further, the authors suggest using the same measures to filter constraint sets before feeding them to a constrained clustering algorithm. The benefit would be smaller and cleaner sets, resulting in faster operation and increased accuracy. This approach seems like a viable alternative to our scalable algorithms. We look forward to the bridging of the gap between this idea and a working embodiment, enabling us to directly compare the two approaches.

2 The CVQE Algorithm

The unconstrained clustering problem is defined on instances $S_i, i = 1, ...n$ and a parameter K for the number of clusters. Let C_j be the centroid representing cluster j. Denote by Q_j the set of instances that are closest to C_j. The K-means algorithm uses the following update rule: $C_j = \frac{1}{|Q_j|} \sum_{s_i \in Q_j} s_i$, where after every centroid update, each instance is reassigned to the cluster of its closest centroid (i.e., the groups Q_j are recalculated). This update rule is derived from minimization of the vector quantization error function, $VQE = \frac{1}{2} \sum_{j=1}^{K} \sum_{s_i \in Q_j} (C_j - s_i)^2$.

The Constrained Vector Quantization Error(CVQE) algorithm [4] generalizes K-means to handle constraints. It does so by modifying the error function to penalize violated constraints. In the original notation, there are r must-link and s cannot-link constraints, $\{(s_1(i), s_2(i))\}_{i=1}^{s+r}$. Let Q_j be the set of instances assigned to the j-th cluster, and C_j be the centroid corresponding to the j-th cluster. Define $M(x) = \{j \,|x \in Q_j\}$, and let $g(i) = M(s_1(i))$ and $g'(i) = M(s_2(i))$. Further, let $h(i)$ be the cluster index whose centroid is closest to C_i. As in Davidson et al. [4], in the case of violation, $s_2(i)$ is associated with the violation. Finally, $v(i)$ indicates whether the i-th constraint is violated. Namely, for $i = 1, ..., r$, $v(i) = 1 \leftrightarrow g(i) \neq g'(i)$ and for $i = r+1, ..., s+r$, $v(i) = 1 \leftrightarrow g(i) = g'(i)$, and $v(i) = 0$ in all other cases. The update rule is as follows:

$$C_j = \frac{1}{N_j} \left\{ \sum_{s_i \in Q_j} (s_i) + \sum_{l=1, g(l)=j}^{r} v(l) \cdot C_{g'(l)} + \sum_{l=r+1, g(l)=j}^{s+r} v(l) \cdot C_{h(g'(l))} \right\}$$

And $N_j = |Q_j| + \sum_{l=1, g(l)=j}^{r+s} v(l)$. Intuitively, in violations of ML constraints, one of the two affected centroids is moved towards the other, wheres CL violations move one of the points towards its next-closest centroid. Similarly to K-means, after each iteration, each instance is reassigned to minimize the error function (described below). Hence unlike K-means, Q_j can contain instances where C_j is not their closest centroid. This update rule minimizes the error function $CVQE = \sum_{j=1}^{K} CVQE_j$, where

$$CVQE_j = \frac{1}{2} \sum_{s_i \in Q_j} T_{j,1} + \frac{1}{2} \sum_{l=1, g(l)=j}^{r} T_{j,2} + \frac{1}{2} \sum_{l=r+1, g(l)=j}^{r+s} T_{j,3} \qquad (1)$$

where $T_{j,1} = (C_j - s_i)^2$, $T_{j,2} = \left[(C_j - C_{g'(l)})^2 \cdot v(l) \right]$, and $T_{j,3} = \left[(C_j - C_{h(g'(l))})^2 \cdot v(l) \right]$.

In each step of the CVQE algorithm, each pair of instances that form a constraint are assigned such that the CVQE error function is minimized. The rest of the algorithm (initialization and termination) is the same as K-means.

We now discuss some properties of CVQE. First, the order of the points in a constraint is significant. Consider a violated constraint generated by the instances $(s_1(l), s_2(l))$ such that $s_1(l) \in Q_{g(l)}$, $s_2(l) \in Q_{g'(l)}$. Only $C_{g(l)}$ is affected

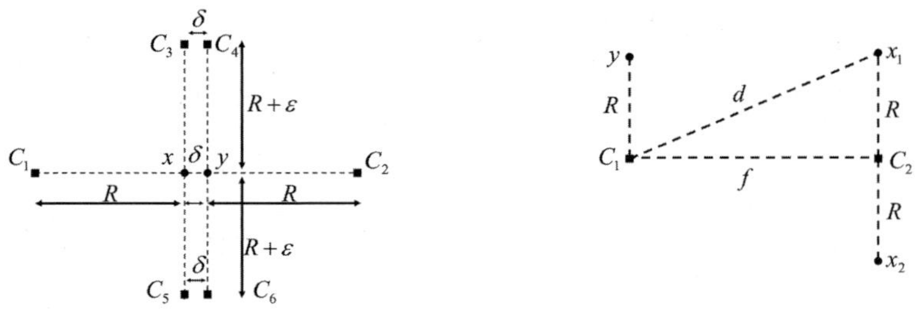

Fig. 1. CVQE examples

by violation of this link, while $C_{g'(l)}$ is not affected at all. This observation holds in both the ML and CL cases.

Second, determining the assignment that minimizes the error function requires $O(K^2)$ calculations for every constraint, which can be expensive when dealing with large numbers of either constraints or clusters. It is also not possible to prune out any possibility (other than the trivial $s_1(l) \in Q_{g'(l)}, s_2(l) \in Q_{g(l)}$) from the calculation. To see this, consider Figure 1(a). The pair (x, y) is ML and the current centroids are $C_i, i = 1, ..., 6$. The distances are shown in the figure. Depending on the values of R, δ, and ϵ, points may be assigned to any of the pairs (C_1, C_2), (C_3, C_4), or (C_5, C_6). Hence, all K^2 options must be checked for every constraint.

Another issue arises from the fact that the penalty for violated links depends on the distance between the corresponding centroids, but the locations of the instances are not taken into account. Consider the two clustering problems shown in Figure 1(b). In both, the initial centroids are C_1, C_2. One problem includes the ML (x_1, y), while the other includes ML (x_2, y). Table 1 summarizes the available assignments in each case and the CVQE value. Note that, regardless of d and f, both problems always have the same solution, although our intuition says that violating (x_1, y) is "worse" than violating (x_2, y). Furthermore, the corrective action in both cases is the same: move C_1 along the line connecting it to C_2, completely ignoring the relative orientation of the offending instance.

3 The LCVQE Algorithm

Our modification of CVQE follows. The proposed algorithm minimizes a target function composed of the vector quantization error as well as a penalty for violated constraints, in the style of CVQE. For each constraint assignment, the LCVQE algorithm considers at most two naturally chosen clusters, hence its complexity is independent of K. Informally, violated ML constraints update each centroid toward the opposite instance, hence they are symmetric in instance order. For violated CL constraints, the instance that is farther from the cluster

Table 1. CVQE values for Figure 1

Algorithm	Constraint	$y \in Q_1, x_i \in Q_2$	$x_i, y \in Q_1$	$x_i, y \in Q_2$
CVQE	(x_1, y)	$R^2 + R^2 + f^2$	$R^2 + d^2$	$R^2 + d^2$
CVQE	(x_2, y)	$R^2 + R^2 + f^2$	$R^2 + d^2$	$R^2 + d^2$
LCVQE	(x_1, y)	$(d^2 + d^2)/2$	d^2	d^2
LCVQE	(x_2, y)	$(d^2 + d^2)/2$	d^2	d^2

centroid is determined and the closest centroid to that instance (other than the current centroid) is moved towards it.

To formalize the algorithm, we define two new functions. $R_j(l)$ returns the instance among $s_1(l), s_2(l)$ whose distance to C_j is larger. $\mathrm{MM}(s)$ returns the centroid which is the closest to s, other than $C_{M(s)}$. The LCVQE update rule is given by:

$$C_j = \frac{1}{N_j}\Bigg\{ \sum_{s_i \in Q_j} s_i + \frac{1}{2} \sum_{l=1, g(l)=j}^{r} v(l) \cdot s_2(l) + \frac{1}{2} \sum_{l=1, g'(l)=j}^{r} v(l) \cdot s_1(l) \tag{2}$$

$$+ \sum_{l=r+1, j=\mathrm{MM}(R_{M(s_1(l))}(l))}^{s+r} v(l) \cdot R_{M(s_1(l))}(l) \Bigg\}$$

$N_j = |Q_j| + \frac{1}{2}\sum_{l=1,g(l)=j}^{r} v(l) + \frac{1}{2}\sum_{l=1,g'(l)=j}^{r} v(l) + \sum_{l=r+1,j=\mathrm{MM}(R_{M(s_1(l))}(l))}^{s+r} v(l)$.

This update rule minimizes the error function:

$$E_j = \frac{1}{2} \sum_{s_i \in Q_j} T_{j,1} + \frac{1}{2} \sum_{l=1, g(l)=j}^{r} T_{j,2} + \frac{1}{2} \sum_{l=1, g'(l)=j}^{r} T_{j,3}$$

$$+ \frac{1}{2} \sum_{l=r+1, j=\mathrm{MM}(R_{M(s_1(l))}(l))}^{s+r} T_{j,4}$$

Here,

$$T_{j,1} = (C_j - s_i)^2 \qquad T_{j,2} = \left[\tfrac{1}{2}(C_j - s_2(l))^2 \cdot v(l)\right]$$

$$T_{j,3} = \left[\tfrac{1}{2}(C_j - s_1(l))^2 \cdot v(l)\right] \qquad T_{j,4} = \left[(C_j - R_{M(s_1(l))}(l)))^2 \cdot v(l)\right]$$

Detailed pseudo-code is in [11]. The LCVQE algorithm requires $O(d)$ operations (for d dimensions) in each step because only three possible assignments are checked, regardless of K. Hence, this algorithm is faster and efficient for problems having large numbers of constraints or clusters. Another benefit of the algorithm is that the constraints are symmetric and that the centroid that is updated depends on the exact setting of both instances rather than the violating instance alone.

Finally, our algorithm does a better job of handling the example shown in Figure 1(b). Table 1 summarizes the available assignments in each case and the

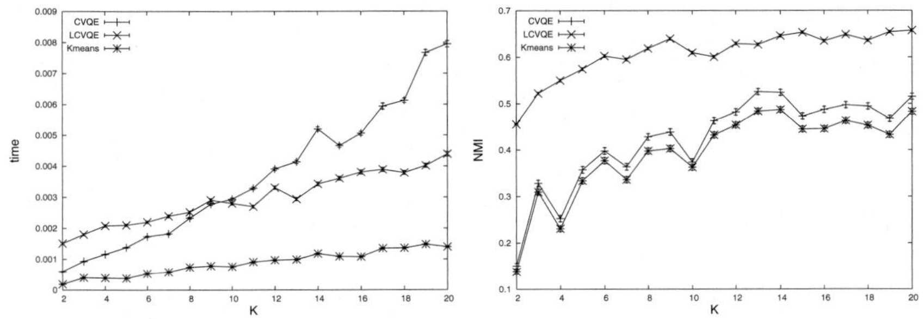

Fig. 2. Performance on Iris

LCVQE values. Assume that the assignment in both problems is $x_i \in Q_2, y \in Q_1$. In the case of (x_1, y), the centroid is updated as follows: $C_1 = (y + \frac{1}{2}x_1)/1.5$. In the case of (x_2, y), the centroid is updated as follows: $C_1 = (y + \frac{1}{2}x_2)/1.5$, which is intuitively better (because the centroid is moving toward the mean of the instances rather then toward the other centroid).

4 Experiments

We first compare the performance of LCVQE and CVQE on UCI data. We implemented both, as well as K-means, in C, and used a $3.6GHz$ Pentium 4 machine for testing. Times in the plots are all in seconds.

We drew random data pairs to generate constraints. Noise was inserted with probability $p = 1\%$ by changing the labels in a pair to labels drawn uniformly from the set of classes. Afterwards, the labels were compared to generate either an ML or a CL constraint. In each case 25 ML and 25 CL constraints were generated.

We generated the augmented set of transitive and entailed constraints in pre-processing, which did not contribute towards the measured run time of any algorithm. To measure clustering performance, we used NMI [7]. Figure 2 shows NMI and run time values averaged over 100 runs over the Iris dataset. Data for the other UCI datasets can be found in [11]. Accuracy is increased dramatically for all values of K in the Iris and Glass datasets, and is significantly better for most values of K for Ionosphere, Wine, and Pima, and at par for E-coli and Breast. Note that for the Glass and Wine datasets, CVQE is substantially worse than unconstrained K-means, a phenomenon we did not observe for LCVQE.

For run times, the quadratic growth in K is clearly visible for CVQE, whereas LCVQE (and, as expected, K-means), are linear in K. At the same time, there are cases where LCVQE is slower, especially at the low end of K. We explore this point below.

Recall that, for each constraint, LCVQE searches over a space that includes just two centroids, whereas CVQE performs the search over all K centroids. This reduction in search space movement has the potential to make each change in

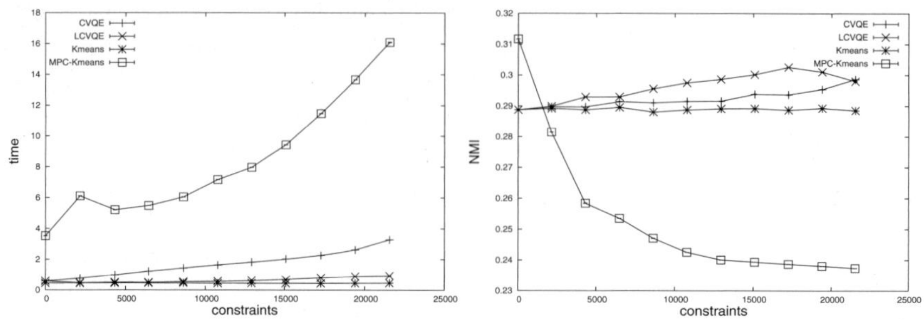

Fig. 3. Performance on tracking data, $k = 10$

centroids smaller. We tested this hypothesis, and conclude that that LCVQE does tend to iterate longer than CVQE, which explains the longer run times for low values of K. See [11] for details.

We also examined the dependence of run time on the size of the input. Here we added to the mix the MPC-Kmeans algorithm [12], which is an efficient hybrid of the distance-learning and constraint-satisfaction approaches[1]. Results are omitted due to lack of space, and can be found in [11]. They show that the K-means variants are linear in the number of constraints, whereas MPC-Kmeans is super-linear. Here, too, the entailed constraints were generated by the wrapper script, and MPC-Kmeans was instructed not to run its own entailment code.

Our final experiment tests performance on surveillance data from a realistic arena. In it, ten uncontrolled agents move in a 2-D space and interact among themselves and with the surroundings. Each minute, a snapshot is taken, and the location and true identity of each agent are recorded. We generate raw data that corresponds to the locations of agents, and ML constraints between each agent's location and its location at the previous time step. In a sense, this is a version of the famous GPS lane finding data but with greater freedom of movement for the agents. Noise was added as above. Here we did not augment the constraint set (nor did MPC-Kmeans run its own augmentation routine). Because of the long chains in the ML graph, the transitive closure becomes huge and mostly uninformative. See Figure 3. We observe that LCVQE produces better or equivalent results to CVQE, while running much faster. In particular, the performance of MPC-Kmeans degrades very quickly when the number of constraints increases. We can speculate that this could be the effect of noise. Another possible reason is the absence of the connected-component heuristic — published work on MPC-Kmeans did not explore any of these scenarios.

5 Conclusion

Having emerged as a new technology a few short years ago, constrained clustering methods are now transitioning to the status of established practice.

[1] In terms of NMI, it outperforms LCVQE on the small UCI datasets.

Consequently, the question of constraint acquisition is increasing in importance. Without automatic constraint generation, plugging in a constrained method in place of a traditional unsupervised method is impossible. We hypothesize that, in many realistic scenarios, the graphs of generated constraints will look very different from the label-based constraint sets that are traditionally used to evaluate new algorithms. In particular, the graphs of ML constraints are likely to contain long chains rather than (dense or sparse) cliques. An interesting avenue of research is to explore the effect of graph structure and noise on the qualities and desired properties of constrained clustering algorithms, in the spirit of Davidson et al. [13]. We explore this issue in a forthcoming paper.

In this light, we discuss a real-world tracking scenario where data points and constraints are plentiful and possibly noisy. This notion alone breaks the consistency assumption central to many of the existing constrained clustering algorithms, resulting in poor performance. We propose a scalable and robust algorithm, based on the CVQE framework, capable of operating in this kind of environment. We show extensive experimental results that shed light on the relative performance of both algorithms and compare them to a distance-learning algorithm.

Acknowledgments

We thank Ian Davidson for helpful comments and discussion.

References

1. Wagstaff, K., Cardie, C., Rogers, S., Schroedl, S.: Constrained k-means clustering with background knowledge. In: Brodley, C., Danyluk, A. (eds.) Proceeding of the 17th International Conference on Machine Learning, Morgan Kaufmann, San Francisco (2001)
2. Lin, W.-H., Hauptmann, A.: Structuring continuous video recordings of everyday life using time-constrained clustering. In: IS&T/SPIE Symposium on Electronic Imaging, San Jose, CA (January 2006)
3. Hertz, T., Shental, N., Bar-Hillel, A., Weinshall, D.: Enhancing image and video retrieval: Learning via equivalence constraints. In: Proc. of IEEE Conference on Computer Vision and Pattern Recognition, IEEE Computer Society Press, Los Alamitos (2003)
4. Davidson, I., Ravi, S.S.: Clustering with constraints: Feasibility issues and the k-means algorithm. In: 5th SIAM Data Mining Conference (2005)
5. Yu, S.X., Shi, J.: Grouping with directed relationships. In: Figueiredo, M., Zerubia, J., Jain, A.K. (eds.) EMMCVPR 2001. LNCS, vol. 2134, Springer, Heidelberg (2001)
6. Cohn, D., Caruana, R., McCallum, A.: Semi-supervised clustering with user feedback. Technical report, Cornell University, TR2003-1892 (2003)
7. Basu, S., Bilenko, M., Mooney, R.J.: A probabilistic framework for semi-supervised clustering. In: Kim, W., Kohavi, R., Gehrke, J., DuMouchel, W. (eds.) Proceedings of the Tenth ACM SIGKDD International Conference on Knowledge Discovery and Data Mining, Seattle, WA, pp. 59–68. ACM Press, New York (2004)

8. Basu, S., Davidson, I.: Clustering with constraints: Theory and practice. In: Online Proceedings of a KDD tutorial (2006), `http://www.ai.sri.com/~basu/kdd-tutorial-2006/`
9. Davidson, I., Ravi, S.S.: Identifying and generating easy sets of constraints for clustering. In: AAAI, AAAI Press (2006)
10. Davidson, I., Wagstaff, K., Basu, S.: Measuring constraint-set utility for partitional clustering algorithms. In: Fürnkranz, J., Scheffer, T., Spiliopoulou, M. (eds.) PKDD 2006. LNCS (LNAI), vol. 4213, pp. 115–126. Springer, Heidelberg (2006)
11. Pelleg, D., Baras, D.: k-means with large and noisy constraint sets. Technical Report H-0253, IBM (2007)
12. Bilenko, M., Basu, S., Mooney, R.J.: Integrating constraints and metric learning in semi-supervised clustering. In: Brodley, C.E. (ed.) ICML, ACM, New York (2004)
13. Davidson, I., Ravi, S.S.: Intractability and clustering with constraints. In: ICML (2007)

Towards 'Interactive' Active Learning in Multi-view Feature Sets for Information Extraction

Katharina Probst and Rayid Ghani

Accenture Technology Labs, Chicago, IL, USA
katharina.a.probst@accenture.com, rayid.ghani@accenture.com

Abstract. Research in multi-view active learning has typically focused on algorithms for selecting the next example to label. This is often at the cost of lengthy wait-times for the user between each query iteration. We deal with a real-world information extraction task, extracting attribute-value pairs from product descriptions, where the learning system needs to be interactive and the users time needs to be used efficiently. The first step uses coEM with naive Bayes as the semi-supervised algorithm. This paper focuses on the second step which is an interactive active learning phase. We present an approximation to coEM with naive Bayes that can incorporate user feedback almost instantly and can use any sample-selection strategy for active learning. Our experimental results show high levels of accuracy while being orders of magnitude faster than using the standard coEM with naive Bayes, making our IE system practical by optimizing user time.

1 Introduction

There has been a lot of recent research in semi-supervised learning algorithms for multi-view feature sets that deal with learning problems where each example is described by two distinct sets of features, either of which is sufficient to approximate the function; that is, they fit the cotraining problem setting [1,3,8]. These approaches have been applied to several domains such as Named Entity Recognition, Information Extraction, Text Classification, and Speech Recognition. The major motivation behind this work has been to exploit the multiple feature sets in order to reduce the number of labeled examples required to learn by making use of the abundance and cheapness of unlabeled data.

Active learning is a closely related field of research that seeks to make efficient use of a trainer's time by intelligently selecting examples to label based on the anticipated value of that label to the learner. Because of the effectiveness of multi-view semi-supervised algorithms, several techniques have been proposed to combine semi-supervised learning with active learning. [7] proposed Co-EMT which interleaves semi-supervised coEM (with naive Bayes) and co-Testing. [6] propose active learning with multiple feature sets and experiment with various selection strategies. Both of these contributions show the efficacy of using unlabeled data by combining multi-view semi-supervised learning with active learning.

However, the focus, as in most other active learning research, has mostly been on improving algorithms and measures for selecting the next example to be labeled by the user. This has often been at the cost of increased time between iterations of active

J.N. Kok et al. (Eds.): ECML 2007, LNAI 4701, pp. 683–690, 2007.

learning feedback which in practice results in lengthy wait times between interactions for the user. Here, we address the 'interactive' aspect of active learning which is one of the major motivations for this line of research - making the most efficient use of the trainer's time. Our motivation comes from a real-world information extraction task: extracting attribute-value pairs from free-text product descriptions [9]. The work presented in this paper aims at making the process of extracting attribute-value pairs from product descriptions more efficient and cheaper by developing an interactive tool.

Our system consists of two parts. The first part is a semi-supervised (non-interactive) classifier (coEM with naive Bayes) that results in a set of attribute-value pairs described in earlier work [9]. The focus of this paper is the next step where the user works with our tool to provide feedback in order to improve the extraction accuracy. When coEM is interleaved in the active learning phase as the underlying semi-supervised classifier (as in [7], [6]), we get good extraction accuracy but the wait time for the user becomes extremely long. In order to make this active learning phase faster while achieving comparable accuracy, we developed a fast approximation to coEM with naive Bayes that can incorporate user feedback almost instantly and can work with any sample-selection strategy for active learning. Our experimental results, on a real world data set of sports products, show high levels of accuracy while being orders of magnitude faster than using the standard coEM with naive Bayes, making our system practical by minimizing user wait time between feedback iterations.

2 Attribute Extraction

Before we discuss our contributions in active learning, we briefly describe the larger system we are building. Our goal is to take natural language product descriptions (such as those on retail catalogs or websites) and extract sets of attribute-value pairs. The products can then be represented in a structured way, which enables a number of business applications, e.g., product recommendations, assortment optimization, and pricing.Since there are no off-the-shelf tools available to extract these attribute-value pairs, it is mostly being done manually which makes the process very expensive. Our system automates the extraction and then learns incrementally from user feedback.

3 Making coEM with Naive Bayes Fast

In this paper, we focus on developing a fast semi-supervised learning algorithm in the context of an active learning system that is *interactive*. Since the semi-supervised learning algorithm needs to be retrained at every iteration of active learning, it commonly leads to long spans when the user sits idle waiting for the system, something we want to avoid.

Our main contribution is a fast approximation to coEM with naive Bayes which is used in active learning in order to make our system interactive. The sections below describe coEM with naive Bayes (our initial approach which was accurate but slow), an approximation to coEM with naive Bayes, and the fast version of that approximation.

Our initial system uses coEM with naive Bayes since that has been previously shown to outperform other semi-supervised algorithms for text learning and information tasks

[4,5,7]. When we incorporate this algorithm in our active learning setting, we get high extraction accuracy but the training time at each iteration is too slow. Thus, we developed an approximation that uses relative frequencies and devise a fast version of it by formulating coEM as a matrix multiplication algorithm. This fast approximation to coEM with naive Bayes is able to retrain and incorporate new labeled data instantly, making our attribute extraction system practical by minimizing user wait time. The sections below describe each of these three algorithms: coEM with naive Bayes (our initial approach which was accurate but slow), approximation to coEM with naive Bayes, and the fast version of that approximation.

3.1 coEM

For the initial (batch) learning phase, our system uses coEM [8] which has been shown to outperform other semi-supervised algorithms for several text learning tasks [4,5,7].

To express the data in two views, each word is expressed in *view1* by the stemmed word itself, plus the part of speech as assigned by the Brill tagger [2]. The *view2* for this data item is a context of window size 8, i.e. up to 4 words (plus parts of speech) before and up to 4 words (plus parts of speech) after the word or phrase in *view1*. We are currently experimenting with adding additional features (such as syntactic features, spelling features, etc.) to measure whether they can significantly enhance performance. By default, all words are processed into *view1* as single words. Sequences of words with high correlation scores (Yule's Q, χ^2, and pointwise mutual information) are treated as phrasal entities and thus as a single $view1$ data item. Co-EM uses the initial labels to label all training examples in $view1$. These labels are then used to probabilistically label all $view2$ elements [9]. The $view2$ labels are in turn used to relabel $view1$, etc.

3.2 Simpler Version of Co-EM with Naive Bayes

When we use coEM with naive Bayes as the semi-supervised algorithm in our active learning setting, the wait time between interactions is unacceptable[1]. To make our tool *interactive*, we propose an approximation to coEM with naive Bayes that does not compromise much on accuracy but is orders of magnitude faster. We briefly describe the algorithm here, and give the fast version of it in the next section. The algorithm works as follows (following [5]): Suppose we want to determine a distribution over all possible labels for each training element, both in $view1$ and $view2$. In our case, the possible labels are *unassigned (the default before learning), attribute, value, neither* (all items default to *unassigned* at the beginning). Denote these labels as $p(1|\langle view1, view2\rangle)$, $\ldots$, $p(4|\langle view1, view2\rangle)$. The goal of the algorithm is to assign these probabilities to each item. In each iteration, however, we label $view1$ and $view2$ separately as follows. Using the initial labeled data, we assign all labeled $view1$ items to their respective class (attribute, value, or neither) as the initial labeling. The next step is to relabel all $view2$ data items using the $view1$ labels. The label distribution of a *view2* element $v2_{i2}$, $1 \leq i2 \leq n2$, where $n2$ is the number of distinct $v2$ elements, is obtained from the *view1* elements $v1_{i1}$, $1 \leq i1 \leq n1$, where $n1$ is the number of distinct $v1$ elements,

[1] See section 4 for more details.

it aligns with, weighted by the number of times the *v1* and *v2* elements align. Denote $cooc(v1_{i1}, v2_{i2})$ as the number of times $v1_{i1}$ and $v2_{i2}$ align to each other. Then:

$$p(1|v2_{i2}) = \frac{\sum_{i1=1}^{n1} cooc(v2_{i2}, v1_{i1}) * p(1|v1_{i1})}{\sum_{i1=1}^{n1} cooc(v2_{i2}, v1_{i1})} \tag{1}$$

Similarly for $p(2|v2_{i2})$, $p(3|v2_{i2})$, and $p(4|v2_{i2})$. Re-estimation of all $view1$ elements follows in the reverse way. However, for those $v1_{i1}$ that are found in the initial labels, there is no re-estimation.The re-estimation steps are repeated until convergence or for a fixed number of iterations. The final probabilities for a data item in its context is finally assigned by averaging $p(j|v1_{i1})$ and $p(j|v2_{i2})$ for $1 \leq j \leq 4$.

3.3 Fast Incremental Approximation of coEM with Naive Bayes

We will now reformulate a fast, incremental variation of the above algorithm that compromises little on accuracy but is orders of magnitude faster. The first insight is that the re-estimation can essentially be viewed as a matrix multiplication: Let A_1 be the probability matrix of $view1$ that is obtained by the initial labeling of all $view1$ elements using the labeled data. A_1 is of size n_1x4. Denote each $view1$ data element as $v1_i, 1 \leq i \leq n1$, where $n1$ is the number of $view1$ data elements. Denote the classes $c_j, 1 \leq j \leq 4$, where the classes are as described above. This matrix will have the following form:

$$A_1 = \begin{bmatrix} p(c_1|v1_1) & p(c_2|v1_1) & p(c_3|v1_1) & p(c_4|v1_1) \\ p(c_1|v1_2) & p(c_2|v1_2) & p(c_3|v1_2) & p(c_4|v1_2) \\ \dots & \dots & \dots & \dots \\ p(c_1|v1_{n1}) & p(c_2|v1_{n1}) & p(c_3|v1_{n1}) & p(c_4|v1_{n1}) \end{bmatrix}$$

Let A_2 be the n_2x4 probability matrix of $view2$, defined in the same ways as A_1. Further, let $B_{1,2}$ be the $(n_1 x n_2)$ transition matrix from $view1$ to $view2$. This transition matrix is a sparse matrix that stores for every $view1$ entry all the $view2$ data elements that it co-occurs with, along with the count of how often the $view1$ and $view2$ co-occur. The transition matrices are *normalized* by the total number of co-occurrences for each data element. This matrix will take the following form:

$$B_{1,2} = \begin{bmatrix} p(v2_1|v1_1) & p(v2_2|v1_1) & \dots & p(v2_{n2}|v1_1) \\ p(v2_1|v1_2) & p(v2_2|v1_2) & \dots & p(v2_{n2}|v1_2) \\ \dots & \dots & \dots & \dots \\ p(v2_1|v1_{n1}) & p(v2_2|v1_{n1}) & \dots & p(v2_{n2}|v1_{n1}) \end{bmatrix} \quad Where$$

$$p(v2_{i2}|v1_{i1}) = \frac{cooc(v2_{i2}, v1_{i1})}{\sum_{i2=1}^{n2} cooc(v2_{i2}, v1_{i1})}. \tag{2}$$

$B_{2,1}$ is defined in an analogous way. Each iteration of the coEM algorithm can then be seen as a matrix multiplication:

$$A_2' = B_{2,1} * A_1, Similarly: A_1' = B_{1,2} * A_2' \tag{3}$$

This multiplication is equivalent to the above iterative algorithm for those items that are not in the initial training data: each cell (i,j) in the resulting matrix will be the result of the sum of all the probabilities for column j (the class label) for all the data items in the other view with which i has a non-zero transition probability, weighted by this transition probability. Note also that these multiplications are the first iteration of the coEM algorithm. Further iterations proceed by the same principle, e.g., $A_2'' = B_{2,1} * A_1'$. This computation is recursive, and the following holds:

$$\begin{aligned} A_2'' &= B_{2,1} * A_1' = B_{2,1} * (B_{1,2} * A_2') \\ &= B_{2,1} * (B_{1,2} * (B_{2,1} * A_1)) = (B_{2,1} * B_{1,2} * B_{2,1}) * A_1 \end{aligned} \tag{4}$$

Similarly for further iterations. The modified probability matrix of each view is computed by multiplying the *original* probability matrix of the other view by a product of transition matrices, where the number of factors is a function of the number of desired coEM iterations. Thus, coEM can either be run iteratively as described in the previous section, or by multiplying the original A_1 by the transition matrices.

When recomputing A_2, we will have a product of transition matrices that is different from the one used for recomputing A_1: A_1 will be recomputed as follows:

$$A_1^n = (B_{1,2} * \cdots * B_{1,2} * B_{2,1}) * A_1 = T_{1,1} * A_1 \tag{5}$$

whereas A_2 will be recomputed with:

$$A_2^n = (B_{2,1} * \cdots * B_{1,2} * B_{2,1}) * A_1 = T_{2,1} * A_1 \tag{6}$$

$T_{1,1}$ and $T_{2,1}$ are the products of transition probabilities. Their interpretation is as follows: each cell (i,j) in the matrix $T_{1,1}$ represents the influence $view1$ data element j has on $view1$ data element i after n iterations; similarly for $T_{2,1}$.

So far, we have described the base algorithm, and how it can be expressed as a set of matrix multiplications. However, as laid out in the iterative algorithm, re-estimation as described here only applies to the cases where a data item is not already known from the original labeled data. For known examples, the iterative algorithm will proceed by simply not relabeling $view1$ elements in any of the iterations. The computation of $T_{1,1}$ and $T_{2,1}$ as described above did not take this into account. Rather, in such cases, the transition matrix should reflect that the $view1$ element is known. To see how this can be accomplished, note again that the transition matrices capture how much impact one data element has on another. Known data items receive the same probability distribution in each iteration, i.e., they should not be updated from other data items. This is done by setting all transition probabilities in $T_{1,1}$ *into* the data item to 0 except the transition from itself, i.e., the row for data item $v1_{i1}$ is all 0s except for the cell $T_{1,1}(i1, i1)$.

Although we have now reformulated the coEM algorithm, we have not yet dealt with user feedback. How can this be done efficiently? *Note that new labeled examples do not modify the transition matrix, but rather only the current probability matrix*, i.e., A_1. This is because the transition matrix *only* captures the cooccurrence counts, and says nothing about the labels for either the $view1$ or the $view2$ element. For this reason, a user interaction will not have any impact on the transition matrix products $T_{1,1}$ and $T_{2,1}$, and we can therefore *precompute* the transition matrix products. The interactive algorithm will now proceed as follows: in an offline step, we precompute the matrices $T_{1,1}$ and $T_{2,1}$. When the user provides feedback, we simply modify A_1, recompute A_1 and A_2 by multiplication with the transition matrices. Final probabilities are then assigned as in the iterative algorithm (i.e., by averaging the $view1$ and $view2$ probabilities).

4 Experimental Results

For the experiments reported in this paper, we crawled the web site of a sporting goods retailer[2], concentrating on the domain of tennis. The crawler gives us a set of product descriptions, which we use as unlabeled training data. Some examples are:

4 rolls white athletic tape
Audio/Video Input Jack
Vulcanized latex outsole construction is lightweight and flexible

For more details on the dataset, please refer to [9]. The experiments reported here were run on 3194 product descriptions. The results were then compared to 620 randomly selected descriptions that were manually labeled with the correct pairs. Below, we show a sample of extracted attribute-value pairs:

⟨*val*⟩ *1 1/2-inch*⟨*/val*⟩ ⟨*att*⟩*polycotton blend tape*⟨*/att*⟩
⟨*val*⟩*1 roll*⟨*/val*⟩ ⟨*att*⟩*underwrap*⟨*/att*⟩
Synthetic ⟨*val*⟩*leather*⟨*val*⟩ ⟨*att*⟩*upper*⟨*/att*⟩
⟨*val*⟩*adiWear tough*⟨*/val*⟩ ⟨*att*⟩*rubber outsole*⟨*att*⟩

We provide results comparing the performance of the fast approximation to coEM with naive Bayes. The first set of results demonstrates that the approximation yields comparable performance to coEM with naive Bayes. We compare three sample selection methods over 25 user interaction iterations: the first method randomly selects the next example to present to the user. Another method, density-based sample selection, selects the most frequent data elements. Finally, KL-divergence is a method that selects those examples that the algorithm is most uncertain about. We measure uncertainty by the KL-divergence between the *view1* and *view2* probability distributions for each data element. The KL-divergences are weighted by frequency. For precision (figure 1a), we report only fully correct pairs, because almost all (around 96%) of the extracted pairs are at least partially correct in the baseline system. We further report recall (figure 1b), i.e., how many of the manually extracted pairs were at least partially extracted by the system. Finally, we report the f-measure (figure 1c).

The results, as in previous active learning studies, show that density and KL-divergence sample selection outperform random sample selection consistently. More importantly to this paper, the results also show that the proposed algorithm is an effective approximation of the coEM algorithm with naive Bayes for our task. Moreover, this statement holds true for all the sample selection methods that are commonly used in this

[2] www.dickssportinggoods.com

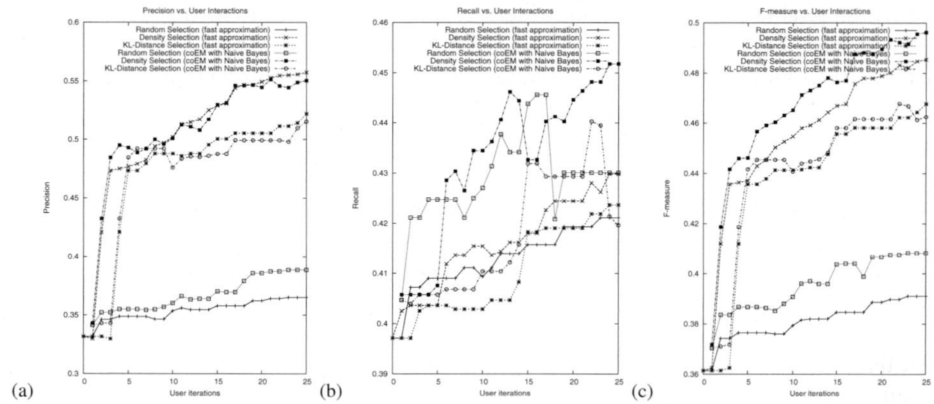

Fig. 1. Precision, Recall, and F-measure for fast algorithm compared to coEM with naive Bayes. The y-value for k indicates the recall, precision, and F-measure after the kth user interaction

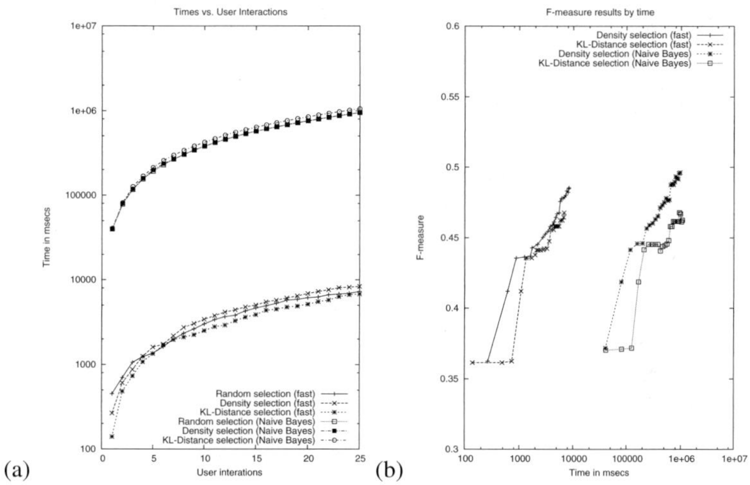

Fig. 2. Time comparison between Fast algorithm and coEM with naive Bayes. The y-value for k indicates the time the user needed to wait until the kth user interaction.

setting. We then compare the fast approximation algorithm and coEM with naive Bayes in terms of user time. The time reported is the time that a user has to wait between interactions (iterations). We show that the fast approximation algorithm performs about two orders of magnitude faster than the coEM algorithm with naive Bayes (figure 2a). The time is plotted on a log scale to enable plotting in one figure. We plot the *cumulative* times for user interactions. The results show that the interaction with the fast approximation algorithm is almost instantaneous, which was the goal of our work, whereas coEM with naive Bayes will require long user idle times. We finally combine the accuracy and time performance results to show that the fast approximation algorithm can yield comparable performance, but orders of magnitude faster (figure 2b). In fact, the performance after 25 user interactions was reached by the fast approximation algorithm before coEM with naive Bayes had finished even one user interaction iteration.

5 Conclusions

We addressed interactivity, an important issue that has not received much attention when combining active learning and semi-supervised learning for multi-view feature sets. Most research in multi-view active learning has focused on algorithms for selecting the next example to label. This is often at the cost of long wait-times for the user between each query iteration. We were motivated by a practical task, attribute-value extraction from product descriptions, where the learning system needs to be interactive and the user's time needs to be used efficiently. We use coEM with naive Bayes, a state-of-the art multi-view semi-supervised algorithm, which yields good extraction accuracy but is too slow to be interactives. We present an effective method for interactively incorporating user feedback in real-time with a fast approximation to coEM with naive Bayes where the bulk of computation can be done offline, before the user gets involved. Our approach can take any sample selection metric; we show experimental results with random, density-based and KL-divergence based metrics. Our experiments show that our algorithm gives comparable performance (precision, recall, and F1) to the original coEM with naive Bayes algorithm *but is orders of magnitude faster*. This results in our information extraction system being practical and minimizing user wait time. We believe that the combination of active learning and semi-supervised learning has enormous practical implications but the issue of long wait times can be a hinderance in many real applications. The work presented in this paper is a step towards building practical systems and will hopefully drive further research in this direction.

References

1. Blum, A., Mitchell, T.: Combining labeled and unlabeled data with co-training. In: COLT (1998)
2. Brill, E.: Transformation-based error-driven learning and natural language processing: A case study in part of speech tagging. Computational Linguistics (1995)
3. Collins, M., Singer, Y.: Unsupervised models for named entity classification. In: Joint SIGDAT Conference on EMNLP and VLC (1999)
4. Ghani, R., Jones, R.: A comparison of efficacy of bootstrapping algorithms for information extraction. In: LREC 2002 Workshop on Linguistic Knowledge Acquisition (2002)
5. Jones, R.: Learning to extract entities from labeled and unlabeled text. Ph.D. Thesis (2005)
6. Jones, R., Ghani, R., Mitchell, T., Riloff, E.: Active learning for information extraction with multiple view feature sets. In: Lavrač, N., Gamberger, D., Todorovski, L., Blockeel, H. (eds.) ECML 2003. LNCS (LNAI), vol. 2837, Springer, Heidelberg (2003)
7. Muslea, I., Minton, S., Knoblock, C.A.: Active + Semi-supervised Learning = Robust Multi-View Learning. In: ICML (2002)
8. Nigam, K., Ghani, R.: Analyzing the effectiveness and applicability of co-training. In: CIKM (2000)
9. Probst, K., Ghani, R., Krema, M., Fano, A., Liu, Y.: Semi-supervised learning of attribute-value pairs from product descriptions. In: IJCAI (2007)

Principal Component Analysis for Large Scale Problems with Lots of Missing Values

Tapani Raiko, Alexander Ilin, and Juha Karhunen

Adaptive Informatics Research Center, Helsinki Univ. of Technology
P.O. Box 5400, FI-02015 TKK, Finland
{Tapani.Raiko,Alexander.Ilin,Juha.Karhunen}@tkk.fi
http://www.cis.hut.fi/projects/bayes/

Abstract. Principal component analysis (PCA) is a well-known classical data analysis technique. There are a number of algorithms for solving the problem, some scaling better than others to problems with high dimensionality. They also differ in their ability to handle missing values in the data. We study a case where the data are high-dimensional and a majority of the values are missing. In case of very sparse data, overfitting becomes a severe problem even in simple linear models such as PCA. We propose an algorithm based on speeding up a simple principal subspace rule, and extend it to use regularization and variational Bayesian (VB) learning. The experiments with Netflix data confirm that the proposed algorithm is much faster than any of the compared methods, and that VB-PCA method provides more accurate predictions for new data than traditional PCA or regularized PCA.

1 Introduction

Principal component analysis (PCA) [1,2,3] is a classic technique in data analysis. It can be used for compressing higher dimensional data sets to lower dimensional ones for data analysis, visualization, feature extraction, or data compression.

PCA can be derived from a number of starting points and optimization criteria [3,4,2]. The most important of these are minimization of the mean-square error in data compression, finding mutually orthogonal directions in the data having maximal variances, and decorrelation of the data using orthogonal transformations [5].

In this paper, we study PCA in the case that most of the data values are missing (or unknown). Common algorithms for solving PCA prove to be inadequate in this case, and we thus propose a new algorithm. The problem of overfitting is also studied and solutions given.

We make the typical assumption that values are missing at random, that is, the missingness does not depend on the unobserved data. An example where the assumption does not hold is when out-of-scale measurements are marked missing.

J.N. Kok et al. (Eds.): ECML 2007, LNAI 4701, pp. 691–698, 2007.

2 Principal Component Analysis

Assume that we have n d-dimensional data vectors $\mathbf{x}_1, \mathbf{x}_2, \ldots, \mathbf{x}_n$, which form the $d \times n$ data matrix $\mathbf{X} = [\mathbf{x}_1, \mathbf{x}_2, \ldots, \mathbf{x}_n]$. The matrix $\mathbf{X}$ is decomposed into $\mathbf{X} \approx \mathbf{AS}$, where $\mathbf{A}$ is a $d \times c$ matrix, $\mathbf{S}$ is a $c \times n$ matrix and $c \leq d \leq n$. Principal subspace methods [6,4] find such $\mathbf{A}$ and $\mathbf{S}$ that the reconstruction error

$$C = \|\mathbf{X} - \mathbf{AS}\|_F^2 = \sum_{i=1}^{d} \sum_{j=1}^{n} (x_{ij} - \sum_{k=1}^{c} a_{ik} s_{kj})^2 , \tag{1}$$

is minimized. Typically the row-wise mean is removed from $\mathbf{X}$ as a preprocessing step. Without any further constraints, there exist infinitely many ways to perform such a decomposition. PCA constraints the solution by further requiring that the column vectors of $\mathbf{A}$ are of unit norm and mutually orthogonal and the row vectors of $\mathbf{S}$ are also mutually orthogonal [3,4,2,5].

There are many ways to solve PCA [6,4,2]. We will concentrate on the subspace learning algorithm that can be easily adapted for the case of missing values and further extended.

Subspace Learning Algorithm. Works by applying gradient descent to the reconstruction error (1) directly yielding the update rules

$$\mathbf{A} \leftarrow \mathbf{A} + \gamma(\mathbf{X} - \mathbf{AS})\mathbf{S}^T , \qquad \mathbf{S} \leftarrow \mathbf{S} + \gamma \mathbf{A}^T(\mathbf{X} - \mathbf{AS}) . \tag{2}$$

Note that with $\mathbf{S} = \mathbf{A}^T\mathbf{X}$ the update rule for $\mathbf{A}$ is a batch version of Oja's subspace rule [7]. The algorithm finds a basis in the subspace of the largest principal components. If needed, the end result can be transformed into the PCA solution by proper orthogonalization of $\mathbf{A}$ and $\mathbf{S}$.

3 Principal Component Analysis with Missing Values

Let us consider the same problem when the data matrix has missing entries. We would like to find $\mathbf{A}$ and $\mathbf{S}$ such that $\mathbf{X} \approx \mathbf{AS}$ for the observed data samples. The rest of the product $\mathbf{AS}$ represents the reconstruction of missing values.

The subspace learning algorithm works in a straightforward manner also in the presence of missing values. We just take the sum over only those indices i and j for which the data entry x_{ij} (the ijth element of $\mathbf{X}$) is observed, in short $(i, j) \in O$. The cost function is

$$C = \sum_{(i,j) \in O} e_{ij}^2 , \qquad \text{with} \qquad e_{ij} = x_{ij} - \sum_{k=1}^{c} a_{ik} s_{kj} , \tag{3}$$

and its partial derivatives are

$$\frac{\partial C}{\partial a_{il}} = -2 \sum_{j|(i,j) \in O} e_{ij} s_{lj} , \qquad \frac{\partial C}{\partial s_{lj}} = -2 \sum_{i|(i,j) \in O} e_{ij} a_{il} . \tag{4}$$

We propose to use a speed-up to the gradient descent algorithm. In Newton's method for optimization, the gradient is multiplied by the inverse of the Hessian matrix. Newton's method is known to be fast-converging, but using the full Hessian is computationally costly in high-dimensional problems ($d \gg 1$). Here we use only the diagonal part of the Hessian matrix, and include a control parameter α that allows the learning algorithm to vary from the standard gradient descent ($\alpha = 0$) to the diagonal Newton's method ($\alpha = 1$). The final learning rules then take the form

$$a_{il} \leftarrow a_{il} - \gamma' \left(\frac{\partial^2 C}{\partial a_{il}^2} \right)^{-\alpha} \frac{\partial C}{\partial a_{il}} = a_{il} + \gamma \frac{\sum_{j|(i,j)\in O} e_{ij} s_{lj}}{\left(\sum_{j|(i,j)\in O} s_{lj}^2 \right)^{\alpha}} , \tag{5}$$

$$s_{lj} \leftarrow s_{lj} - \gamma' \left(\frac{\partial^2 C}{\partial s_{lj}^2} \right)^{-\alpha} \frac{\partial C}{\partial s_{lj}} = s_{lj} + \gamma \frac{\sum_{i|(i,j)\in O} e_{ij} a_{il}}{\left(\sum_{i|(i,j)\in O} a_{il}^2 \right)^{\alpha}} . \tag{6}$$

For comparison, we also consider two alternative PCA methods that can be adapted for missing values.

Imputation Algorithm. Another option is to complete the data matrix by iteratively imputing the missing values (see, e.g., [8]). Initially, the missing values can be replaced by zeroes. With completed data, PCA can be solved by eigenvalue decomposition of the covariance matrix. Now, the missing values are replaced using the product $\mathbf{AS}$, PCA is applied again, and this process is iterated until convergence. This approach requires the use of the complete data matrix, and therefore it is computationally very expensive if a large part of the data matrix is missing.

EM Algorithm. Grung and Manne [9] studied the EM-like algorithm for PCA in the case of missing values.[1] In the E-step, $\mathbf{A}$ is fixed and $\mathbf{S}$ is solved as a least squares problem. In the M-step, $\mathbf{S}$ is fixed and $\mathbf{A}$ is solved again as a least squares problem. Computations are a lot heavier than in the fully observed case, but still, experiments in [9] showed a faster convergence compared to the iterative imputation algorithm.

4 Overfitting in PCA

A trained PCA model can be used for reconstructing missing values by $\hat{x}_{ij} = \sum_{k=1}^{c} a_{ik} s_{kj}$. Although PCA performs a linear transformation of data, overfitting is a serious problem for large-scale datasets with lots of missing values. This happens when the cost value (3) is small for training data but the quality of prediction $\hat{x}_{ij}$ is poor for new data. This effect is illustrated using the following toy example.

[1] The procedure studied in [9] can be seen as the zero-noise limit of the EM algorithm for a probabilistic PCA model [8].

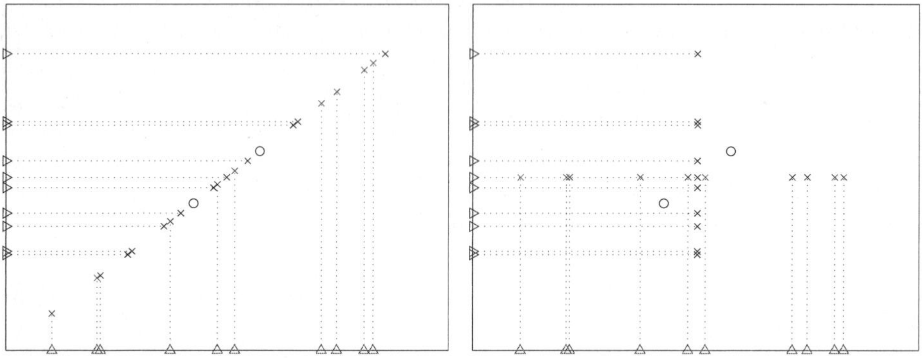

Fig. 1. An artificial example where all but two data points have one of the two components missing. On the left, the correlation between the components is determined by these two samples, giving a badly overfitted solution. On the right, the desired solution where the correlation is not trusted as much (the reconstruction is obtained using the VB algorithm explained in Section 4).

Assume that the observation space is $d = 2$-dimensional, and most of the data are only partly observed, that is either x_{1j} or x_{2j} is unknown for most js. These observations are represented by triangles placed on the two axes in Fig. 1. There are only two full observations (x_{1j}, x_{2j}) which are shown on the plot by circles. A solution which minimizes the cost function (3) to zero is defined by a line that passes through the two fully observed data points (see the left subfigure). The missing values are then reconstructed by points lying on the line.

In this example, the solution is defined by only two points and the model is clearly overfitted: There is very little evidence in the data that there exists a significant correlation between the two dimensions. The overfitting problem is even more severe in high-dimensional problems because it is likely that there exist many such pairs of directions in which the evidence of correlation is represented by only a few samples. The right subfigure of Fig. 1 shows a regularized solution that is not overfitted. The correlation is not trusted and the missing values are reconstructed close to the row-wise means. Note that in regularized PCA, the reconstructions are no longer projections to the underlying subspace.

Another way to examine overfitting is to compare the number of model parameters to the number of observed values in data. A rule of thumb is that the latter should be at least tenfold to avoid overfitting. Consider the subproblem of finding the jth column vector of $\mathbf{S}$ given jth column vector of $\mathbf{X}$ while regarding $\mathbf{A}$ a constant. Here, c parameters are determined by the observed values of the jth column vector of $\mathbf{X}$. If the column has fewer than $10c$ observations, it is likely to suffer from overfitting, and if it has fewer than c observations, the subproblem is underdetermined.

Regularization. A popular way to regularize ill-posed problems is penalizing the use of large parameter values by adding a proper penalty term into the cost function. This can be obtained using a probabilistic formulation with (independent) Gaussian priors and a Gaussian noise model:

$$p(x_{ij} \mid \mathbf{A}, \mathbf{S}) = \mathcal{N}\left(x_{ij}; \sum_{k=1}^{c} a_{ik} s_{kj}, v_x\right) \tag{7}$$

$$p(\mathbf{A}) = \prod_{i=1}^{d} \prod_{k=1}^{c} \mathcal{N}\left(a_{ik}; 0, 1\right), \quad p(\mathbf{S}) = \prod_{k=1}^{c} \prod_{j=1}^{n} \mathcal{N}\left(s_{kj}; 0, v_{sk}\right). \tag{8}$$

The cost function (ignoring constants) is minus logarithm of the posterior of the unknown parameters:

$$C_{\mathrm{BR}} = \sum_{(i,j) \in O} \left(e_{ij}^2 / v_x + \ln v_x\right) + \sum_{i=1}^{d} \sum_{k=1}^{c} a_{ik}^2 + \sum_{k=1}^{c} \sum_{j=1}^{n} \left(s_{kj}^2 / v_{sk} + \ln v_{sk}\right). \tag{9}$$

The cost function can be minimized using a gradient-based approach as described in Section 3. The corresponding update rules are similar to (5)–(6) except for the extra terms which come from the prior. Note that in case of joint optimization of C_{BR} w.r.t. a_{ik}, s_{kj}, v_{sk}, and v_x, the cost function (9) has a trivial minimum with $s_{kj} = 0$, $v_{sk} \to 0$. We try to avoid this minimum by using an orthogonalized solution provided by unregularized PCA for initialization. Note also that setting v_{sk} to small values for some components k is equivalent to removal of irrelevant components from the model. This allows for automatic determination of the proper dimensionality c instead of discrete model comparison (see, e.g., [10]).

Variational Bayesian Learning. Variational Bayesian (VB) learning provides even stronger tools against overfitting. VB version of PCA [10] approximates the joint posterior of the unknown quantities using a simple multivariate distribution. Each model parameter is described *a posteriori* using independent Gaussian distributions: $q(a_{ik}) = \mathcal{N}(a_{ik}; \overline{a}_{ik}, \widetilde{a}_{ik})$ and $q(s_{kj}) = \mathcal{N}(s_{kj}; \overline{s}_{kj}, \widetilde{s}_{kj})$, where $\overline{a}_{ik}$ and $\overline{s}_{kj}$ denote the mean of the solution and $\widetilde{a}_{ik}$ and $\widetilde{s}_{kj}$ denote the variance of each parameter. The means $\overline{a}_{ik}$, $\overline{s}_{kj}$ can then be used as point estimates of the parameters while the variances $\widetilde{a}_{ik}$, $\widetilde{s}_{kj}$ define the reliability of the estimates (or credible regions). The direct extension of the method in [10] to missing values can be computationally very demanding. VB-PCA has been used to reconstruct missing values in [11,12] with algorithms that complete the data matrix, which is also very inefficient in case a large part of data is missing. In this article, we implement VB learning using a gradient-based procedure similar to the subspace learning algorithm described in Section 3.

By applying the framework described in [12] to the model in Eqs. (7–8), the cost function becomes:

$$C_{\mathrm{KL}} = \mathrm{E}_q\left\{\ln \frac{q(\mathbf{A}, \mathbf{S})}{p(\mathbf{X}, \mathbf{A}, \mathbf{S})}\right\} = \sum_{(i,j) \in O} C_{xij} + \sum_{i=1}^{d} \sum_{k=1}^{c} C_{aik} + \sum_{k=1}^{c} \sum_{j=1}^{n} C_{skj}, \tag{10}$$

where individual terms are

$$C_{xij} = \frac{(x_{ij} - \sum_{k=1}^{c} \overline{a}_{ik}\overline{s}_{kj})^2 + \sum_{k=1}^{c} \left(\widetilde{a}_{ik}\overline{s}_{kj}^2 + \overline{a}_{ik}^2\widetilde{s}_{kj} + \widetilde{a}_{ik}\widetilde{s}_{kj}\right)}{2v_x} + \frac{\ln 2\pi v_x}{2},$$

$$C_{aik} = \frac{\overline{a}_{ik}^2 + \widetilde{a}_{ik}}{2} - \frac{1}{2}\ln \widetilde{a}_{ik} - \frac{1}{2}, \quad C_{skj} = \frac{\overline{s}_{kj}^2 + \widetilde{s}_{kj}}{2v_{sk}} - \frac{1}{2}\ln \frac{\widetilde{s}_{kj}}{v_{sk}} - \frac{1}{2}.$$

We update $\widetilde{a}$ and $\widetilde{s}$ to minimize the cost by setting the gradient of the cost function to zero:

$$\widetilde{a}_{ik} \leftarrow \left[1 + \sum_{j|(i,j)\in O} \frac{\overline{s}_{kj}^2 + \widetilde{s}_{kj}}{v_x}\right]^{-1}, \quad \widetilde{s}_{kj} \leftarrow \left[\frac{1}{v_{sk}} + \sum_{i|(i,j)\in O} \frac{\overline{a}_{ik}^2 + \widetilde{a}_{ik}}{v_x}\right]^{-1}. \tag{11}$$

The gradients for learning $\overline{a}$ and $\overline{s}$ are somewhat similar to (4):

$$\frac{\partial C_{\mathrm{KL}}}{\partial \overline{a}_{il}} = \overline{a}_{il} + \sum_{j|(i,j)\in O} \frac{-\left(x_{ij} - \sum_{k=1}^{c} \overline{a}_{ik}\overline{s}_{kj}\right)\overline{s}_{lj} + \overline{a}_{il}\widetilde{s}_{lj}}{v_x}, \tag{12}$$

$$\frac{\partial C_{\mathrm{KL}}}{\partial \overline{s}_{lj}} = \frac{\overline{s}_{lj}}{v_{sk}} + \sum_{i|(i,j)\in O} \frac{-\left(x_{ij} - \sum_{k=1}^{c} \overline{a}_{ik}\overline{s}_{kj}\right)\overline{a}_{il} + \widetilde{a}_{il}\overline{s}_{lj}}{v_x}. \tag{13}$$

We can use the speed-up described in Section 3 by computing the second derivatives. These derivatives happen to coincide with the inverse of the updated variances given in (11): $\partial^2 C_{\mathrm{KL}}/\partial \overline{a}_{il}^2 = \widetilde{a}_{il}^{-1}$ and $\partial^2 C_{\mathrm{KL}}/\partial \overline{s}_{lj}^2 = \widetilde{s}_{lj}^{-1}$. The v_x and v_s parameters are updated to minimize the cost C_{KL} assuming all the other parameters fixed. The complete algorithm works by alternating four update steps: $\{\widetilde{a}\}$, $\{\widetilde{s}\}$, $\{\overline{a}, \overline{s}\}$, and $\{v_x, v_s\}$.

5 Experiments

Collaborative filtering is the task of predicting preferences (or producing personal recommendations) by using other people's preferences. The Netflix problem [13] is such a task. It consists of movie ratings given by $n = 480189$ customers to $d = 17770$ movies. There are $N = 100480507$ ratings from 1 to 5 given, and the task is to predict 2817131 other ratings among the same group of customers and movies. 1408395 of the ratings are reserved for validation (or probing). Note that the 98.8% of the values are thus missing. We tried to find $c = 15$ principal components from the data using a number of methods.[2] The mean rating was subtracted for each movie and robust estimation of the mean was used for the movies with few ratings.

[2] The PCA approach has been considered by other Netflix contestants as well (see, e.g., [14,15]).

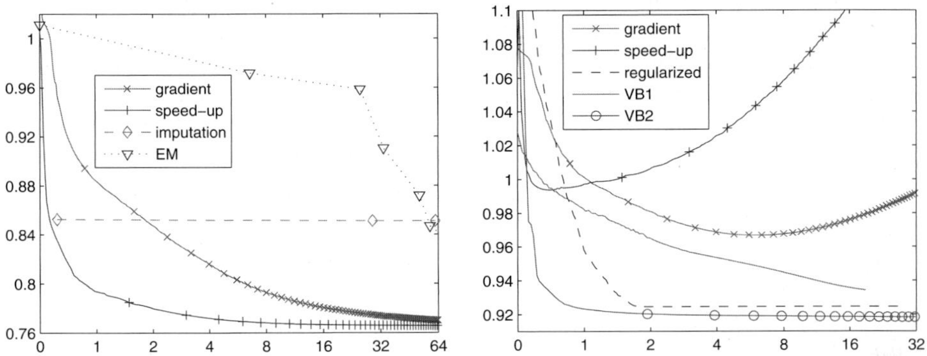

Fig. 2. *Left:* Learning curves for unregularized PCA (Section 3) applied to the Netflix data: Root mean square error on the training data is plotted against computation time in hours. Runs are given for two values of the speed-up parameter α and marks are plotted after every 50 iterations. For comparison, the training errors for the imputation algorithm and the EM algorithm are shown. The time scale is linear below 1 and logarithmic above 1. *Right:* The root mean square error on the validation data from the Netflix problem during runs of several algorithms: basic PCA (Section 3) with two values of α, regularized PCA (Section 4) and VB (Section 4). VB1 has v_{sk} fixed to large values while VB2 updates all the parameters. The curves clearly reveal overlearning for unregularized PCA.

Computational Performance. In the first set of experiments we compared the computational performance of different algorithms for PCA with missing values. The root mean square (rms) error is measured on the training data, that is, the observed values in the training set. All experiments were run on a dual cpu AMD Opteron SE 2220.

The comparison methods, the imputation algoritm and the EM algorithm, were very slow, except for the first iteration of the imputation algorithm due to the complete data matrix being sparse. Fig. 2 (left) shows the learning curves. The closer a curve is to the origin, the faster the algorithm minimizes the cost function.

We also tested the subspace learning algorithm described in Section 3 with and without the proposed speed-up, starting from the same random starting point. The learning rate γ was adapted such that if an update decreased the cost function, γ was multiplied by 1.1. Each time an update would increase the cost, the update was canceled and γ was divided by 2. The best α seemed to be around 0.6 to 0.7, the curve shown in Fig. 2 is for $\alpha = 5/8$. It gave a more than tenfold speed-up compared to the gradient descent algorithm even if one iteration took on average 97 seconds against the gradient descent's 57 seconds.

Overfitting. We compared PCA (Section 3), regularized PCA (Section 4) and VB-PCA (Section 4) by computing the root mean square reconstruction error for the validation set, that is, ratings that were not used for training. We tested

VB-PCA by firstly fixing v_{sk} to large values (this run is marked as VB1 in Fig. 2) and secondly by adapting them (marked as VB2) to isolate the effects of the two types of regularization. We initialized regularized PCA and VB1 using unregularized subspace learning algorithm with $\alpha = 0.625$ transformed into the PCA solution. VB2 was initialized using VB1. The parameter α was set to 2/3.

Fig. 2 (right) shows the results. The performance of unregularized PCA starts to degrade after a while of learning, especially with large values of α. This effect, known as overlearning, did not appear with VB. Regularization helped a lot and the best results were obtained using VB2: The final validation rms error was 0.9180 and the training rms error was 0.7826 which is naturally a bit larger than the unregularized 0.7657.

Acknowledgments. This work was supported in part by the Academy of Finland under its Centers for Excellence in Research Program, and the IST Program of the European Community, under the PASCAL Network of Excellence, IST-2002-506778. This publication only reflects the authors' views. We would like to thank Netflix [13] for providing the data.

References

1. Pearson, K.: On lines and planes of closest fit to systems of points in space. Philosophical Magazine 2(6), 559–572 (1901)
2. Jolliffe, I.: Principal Component Analysis. Springer, Heidelberg (1986)
3. Bishop, C.: Pattern Recognition and Machine Learning. Springer, Heidelberg (2006)
4. Diamantaras, K., Kung, S.: Principal Component Neural Networks - Theory and Application. Wiley, Chichester (1996)
5. Haykin, S.: Modern Filters. Macmillan (1989)
6. Cichocki, A., Amari, S.: Adaptive Blind Signal and Image Processing - Learning Algorithms and Applications. Wiley, Chichester (2002)
7. Oja, E.: Neural networks, principal components, and subspaces. International Journal of Neural Systems 1(1), 61–68 (1989)
8. Tipping, M., Bishop, C.: Probabilistic principal component analysis. Journal of the Royal Statistical Society: Series B (Statistical Methodology) 61(3), 611–622 (1999)
9. Grung, B., Manne, R.: Missing values in principal components analysis. Chemometrics and Intelligent Laboratory Systems 42(1), 125–139 (1998)
10. Bishop, C.: Variational principal components. In: Proc. 9th Int. Conf. on Artificial Neural Networks (ICANN99), pp. 509–514 (1999)
11. Oba, S., Sato, M., Takemasa, I., Monden, M., Matsubara, K., Ishii, S.: A Bayesian missing value estimation method for gene expression profile data. Bioinformatics 19(16), 2088–2096 (2003)
12. Raiko, T., Valpola, H., Harva, M., Karhunen, J.: Building blocks for variational Bayesian learning of latent variable models. Journal of Machine Learning Research 8(January), 155–201 (2007)
13. Netflix: Netflix prize webpage (2007), `http://www.netflixprize.com/`
14. Funk, S.: Netflix update: Try this at home (December 2006), Available at `http://sifter.org/~simon/journal/20061211.html`
15. Salakhutdinov, R., Mnih, A., Hinton, G.: Restricted Boltzmann machines for collaborative filtering. In: Proc. Int. Conf. on Machine Learning (to appear, 2007)

Transfer Learning in Reinforcement Learning Problems Through Partial Policy Recycling*

Jan Ramon, Kurt Driessens, and Tom Croonenborghs

K.U. Leuven, Dept. of Computer Science, Celestijnenlaan 200A, B-3001 Leuven

Abstract. We investigate the relation between transfer learning in reinforcement learning with function approximation and supervised learning with concept drift. We present a new incremental relational regression tree algorithm that is capable of dealing with concept drift through tree restructuring and show that it enables a Q-learner to transfer knowledge from one task to another by recycling those parts of the generalized Q-function that still hold interesting information for the new task. We illustrate the performance of the algorithm in several experiments.

1 Introduction

Inductive transfer or transfer learning is concerned with the connection between learning in different but related contexts, e.g. learning to drive a bus after having learned to drive a car. In a machine learning context, transfer learning is concerned with the added benefits that learning one task can have on a different, but related task. More specifically, in a reinforcement learning (RL) context, the added effects of transfer learning can help the learning agent to learn a new (but related) task faster, i.e., with a smaller amount of training experience.

Concept drift [14] refers to changes over time in the concept under consideration. Examples include socioeconomic phenomena such as fashion, but also more technical subjects such as computer-fraud and -intrusion. In a machine learning context, concept drift is usually seen as an added difficulty in a learning task and has given rise to the field of theory revision.

In principle, the two notions of transfer learning and concept drift are very similar. Both deal with a change in the target hypothesis, but both also assume that there will be large similarities between the old and the new target concept. The biggest difference between the two problem definitions is that for transfer learning, it is usually known when the context change takes place. For concept drift, this change is usually unannounced.

In this paper, we investigate the possibility of using methods from theory revision in a transfer learning context. While reinforcement learning, we will try to recycle from one task, those parts of a learned policy that still hold relevant information for a new, related task. We do this by introducing a new incremental

* Research supported by Research Foundation-Flanders (FWO-Vlaanderen), by the Institute for the Promotion of Innovation through Science and Technology in Flanders (IWT-Vlaanderen) and by GOA 2003/08 "Inductive Knowledge Bases".

J.N. Kok et al. (Eds.): ECML 2007, LNAI 4701, pp. 699–707, 2007.

relational regression tree algorithm that uses a number of tree restructuring operators that are suited for first-order regression trees. The algorithm does not store past training experience but instead stores statistical information about past experience that allows it to decide when to use which operator. We will illustrate the performance both on a relational task with concept drift and for transfer learning in relational reinforcement learning tasks.

2 Transfer Learning and Theory Revision

Most current work in transfer learning does not incorporate ideas from theory revision. A lot of transfer learning approaches use a mapping to relate the new task to the task for which a policy was already learned. Some approaches use the learned knowledge to aid exploration in the new task [7,9]. Although guided exploration is well suited to overcome the problem of sparse rewards, we believe that a lot of knowledge is lost if one only uses earlier experience to steer exploration. In the context of concept drift or theory revision it is common to try to use knowledge learned previously to facilitate learning the new concept.

The approach of Torrey et al. [12] incorporates knowledge about the Q-values of the first task into the construction of the Q-function of the new task as soft-constraints to the linear optimization problem that approximates the Q-function. However, we feel that a lot of knowledge about the structure of the Q-function is lost. Taylor et al. [11] take a first step into this direction by reusing policies represented by neural networks. In a general game playing context, there is the approach of Banerjee and Stone [1] where game independent features that encode search knowledge are learned that can be used in new tasks.

However, we would like to re-use partial policies to a larger extend. As is common in theory revision approaches, we will conserve structures in the target function that were discovered for the first task when they apply to the second and expand on them or, if necessary delete them from the learned model. Building an adapted model of the target concept based on already discovered structural knowledge about related tasks should facilitate learning and thus create a new form of transfer learning for reinforcement learning.

3 Incremental Tree Learning and Restructuring

We will be using logical decision trees as our target models. Because we will be re-using learned models from related but different tasks, we need to be able to learn models that generalize well over tasks which share some properties. For this, relational or first-order representations are very well suited. We will use decision trees because the built-in modularity of trees allows easy access to different parts of the learned theory.

Chapman and Kaelbling [3] proposed an incremental regression tree algorithm designed with reinforcement learning in mind. On a high level, the G-algorithm stores the current decision tree and, for each leaf, statistics for all tests that can be used to split that leaf further. Except for the leaf-splitting, i.e. building the tree incrementally, no tree-restructuring operators are used. TG [5] upgrades the G-algorithm to a first-order context and uses a similar approach to build first-order decision trees. A first-order decision tree is a binary decision tree in which internal nodes contain tests which are a conjunction of first-order literals. A constraint placed on the first-order literals is that a variable that is introduced in a node (i.e., it does not occur in higher nodes) does not occur in the right subtree of the node. This constraint stems from the fact that variables in the tests of internal nodes are existentially quantified. Suppose a node introduces a new variable X. Where the left subtree of a node corresponds to the fact that a substitution for X has been found to make the conjunction true, the right side corresponds to the situation where no substitution for X exists, i.e., there is no such X. Therefore, it makes no sense to refer to X in the right subtree.

Probably the best known tree-restructuring algorithm is the ITI-algorithm [13]. It stores statistics about the performance of all splitting criteria for all the nodes in the tree and incorporates operators for tree-restructuring such as tree-transposition or slewing cut-points for numerical attributes. The tree-transposition operator switches tests between parent and child nodes and copies the statistical information from the original tree to the restructured one. Recursive tree-transpositioning can be used to install a designated test at any internal node of a propositional tree. Recently, Dabney and McGovern [4] developed relational UTrees (which incorporate relational tests in nodes) and an ITI-based incremental learner. However, this system has several drawbacks. First, it requires all training examples to be remembered. Second, the performance of nodes is measured by a set of randomly generated trees, which are of limited depth and whose generation is computationally expensive.

We will introduce the TGR algorithm, an incremental relational decision tree algorithm that employs tree restructuring operators and does not need to store all past learning experience. It extends the TG algorithm mentioned above, the difference being the availability of four tree-restructuring operators:

Splitting a leaf. This operator splits a leaf into two subleafs, using the best suited test. This is the only operator used by standard (non-restructuring) top down induction of decision trees (TDIDT) algorithms such as TG .

Pruning a leaf. This is the inverse operator of the first. When predictions made in two sibling-leafs (leafs connected to the same node) become similar, it will join the two leafs and remove the internal node.

Revising an internal node. This is a bit more complex than the two previous ones. It is illustrated on the left side of Figure 1. When it turns out that a different test from the one originally chosen at an internal node becomes significantly better, the dependencies between tests in first-order trees make it impossible to make a straightforward swap of the two tests. Instead, we construct a new node with the new test and repeat on both sides the original tree (Figure 1). This avoids any information loss, and it can be hoped that redundant nodes will be further pruned away by the other operators.

Pruning a subtree. This operator is related to the previous one, but will shrink the tree instead of enlarging it. It is illustrated at the right side

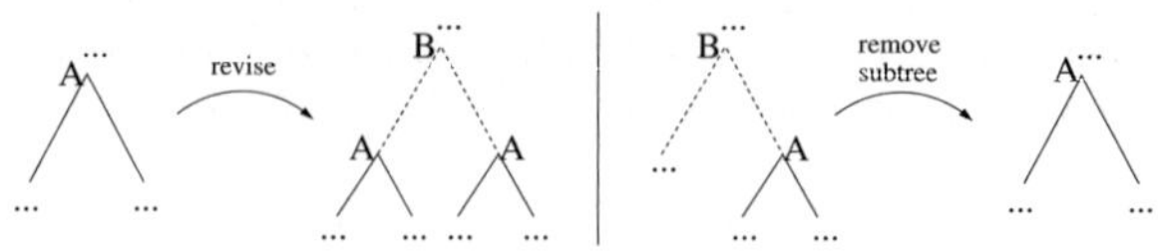

Fig. 1. Revising a test (left) and pruning a subtree (right)

of Figure 1. This operator is used when a node can (or should) be deleted. Because of the dependencies between tests in a first-order tree, the choice of subtrees to replace the original tree starting at the deleted node is limited to the right-side one. As before, the left subtree can contain references to variables introduced by the test used in the deleted node (e.g. B in Figure 1).

Although these restructuring operators differ from those used in ITI, the resulting trees are quite similar. One difference is that the recursive application of the transposition operator changes the bottom most tests in the tree and our revision operator does not. Just like the TG algorithm, TGR will not store learning examples, but discard them after the update of the statistics in the tree. The major difference between the two is that TGR stores the statistics that TG only stores in the leafs for all the nodes in the tree. On top of this, to be able to use the pruning operator, TGR stores the predictive performance of both the entire subtree and just the right subtree for each node in the tree.

4 Experimental Evaluation

4.1 Bongard Problems with Concept Drift

In a first series of experiments we will use Bongard problems [2] to evaluate the performance in the context of concept drift. One Bongard learning example consists of a (varying) number of objects and relations between them. For our experiments, we created a dataset of Bongard examples (with every example having randomly 0-4 circles, 0-4 triangles and a number of $in/2$ relations depending on the concept) and feed them to the learner one by one, together with the classification (positive or negative) for a chosen concept. After a certain number of learning examples, we change the concept. We will show the predictive accuracy (tested on 500 examples) for both TG and TGR on all problems. The results are averaged over 10 runs, evaluated once per 500 training examples.

In the first experiment we interleave two target concepts. We start with the concept "Is there a triangle inside a circle?" (A) for 2000 learning examples, then change it to "Is there a circle inside a triangle?" (B) and alternate the two in an $ABABAB$ fashion every 5000 learning examples with in the end 5000 examples extra to show further convergence. Figure 2 (left) shows that TGR is able to keep up with the concept changes while TG adapts much more slowly. In Figure 2 (right), one can see that although the tree size of the theory built by TGR can grow suddenly when TGR decides to swap one of the topmost tests in the tree using the third revision operator and thereby almost doubling the size

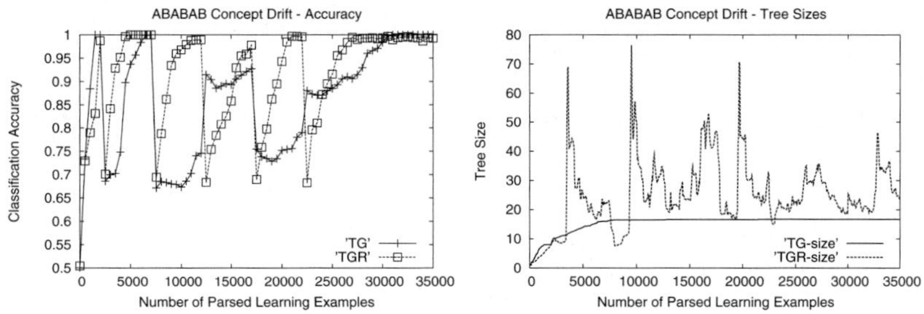

Fig. 2. Bongard problem with $ABABABB$ concept drift

of the tree, TGR usually recovers quickly by deleting appropriate parts of the tree. The tree does however stay larger than the TG one most of the time. This experiment also shows the independence of the TGR algorithm to the number of already processed examples.

In a second experiment, we increase the difficulty of the concept change during the experiment. We again start with concept A and change it into concept B after 5000 learning examples, but after 10 000 examples we change it into "Is there a circle in a circle?" and after 20 000 learning examples into "Is there a triangle in a triangle?". The concept changes are ordered by difficulty, i.e. by the size of the subtree that will have to be changed. Between the first two concepts, there is only a change in the relationship of the two objects involved. The built tree will still have to verify the existence of both a circle and a triangle, but will have to change the test on the $in/2$ relation. The second change will require the change of both the $in/2$ relation and one of the existence checks. The last step changes the entire concept.

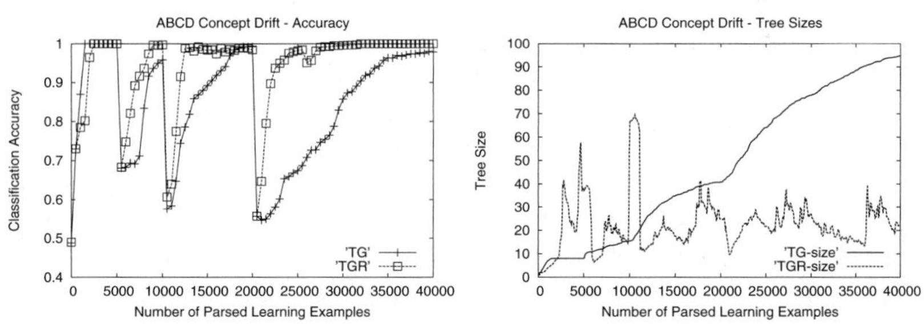

Fig. 3. Bongard problem with increasingly difficult concept changes

Figure 3 shows that TGR adapts to concept changes better and faster than the TG algorithm. TG quickly starts to slow down and, after a while, is not able to react to the concept changes within a reasonable amount of learning examples. The right graph clearly shows the advantage of TGR with respect to the size of the resulting theory. Although this is difficult to show, TGR succeeds

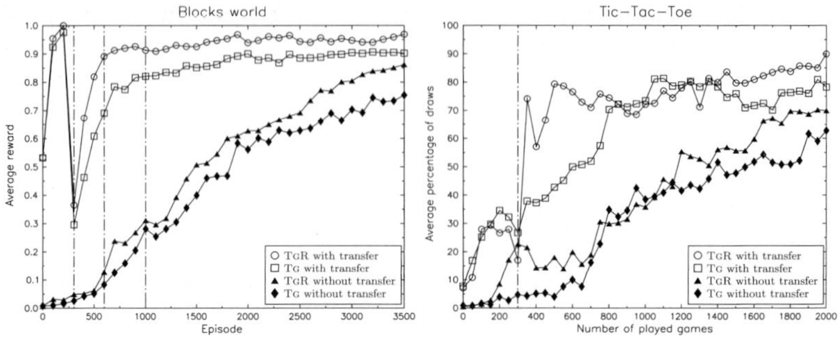

Fig. 4. The performance of RRL with and without inductive transfer

in transferring the usable part of its tree through the concept changes. The dip in performance that can be seen for TGR is largely caused by the time it takes TGR to actually notice the concept change, before it starts rebuilding its model. The fact that the second and especially the last concept change require more changes in the tree cause TGR to take a bit more time before the new concepts are learned, but the differences are minimal compared to TG.

4.2 Relational Reinforcement Learning with Transfer of Knowledge

We also present experiments with inductive transfer for relational reinforcement learning problems. In relational reinforcement learning as presented by Džeroski et al. [6], a relational regression algorithm is used to learn a generalized Q-function. We performed experiments in the blocks world [10], an often used test bed for relational reinforcement learning and in the tic-tac-toe game as an example application from the general game playing challenge [8]. In the experiments, we use two versions of the RRL system, one that uses TG as a regression algorithm to approximate the Q-function and one that uses the new TGR algorithm. We will refer to these two systems with RRL-TG and RRL-TGR respectively.

Blocks World. In the blocks world experiments, we added transfer learning to the regular blocks world setting by allowing the agent to train in worlds with easier goal-concepts before learning the target task. The agent only receives a reward when it reaches the desired goal in the minimal number of steps. If the goal is not reached in that time, the episode ends without any rewards.

We consider the $on(A, B)$-goal, i.e. block A needs to be directly on top of block B, as target task in a blocks world with 13 blocks. In the setting with inductive transfer, the agent's goal in the first 300 episodes is to clear a certain block ($clear(A)$) in a world with 4 blocks, then the goal is changed so that the agent only receives a reward iff 2 target blocks are clear at the same time ($clear(A), clear(B)$) in a world with 7 blocks. In episode 600 the goal is changed to $on(A, B)$ with 10 blocks and finally to the target goal-concept of $on(A, B)$ in an environment with 13 blocks at episode 1000. For both RRL-TG and RRL-TGR we use a language bias similar to previously reported experiments performed with RRL-TG in the blocks world [5].

Figure 4 shows the learning graph for RRL-TG and RRL-TGR both with and without transfer of knowledge. The shown received reward was obtained by freezing the Q-function approximation and testing its policy on 100 test-episodes, every 100 episodes. The results are averaged over 10 runs. The horizontal lines indicate where the goal-concept is changed. Hence the reader should compare the performance in the target task for the experiment without transfer with that for the experiment with transfer, starting after 1000 training episodes.

The performance without transfer is tested on the target goal from the start. In this setting the learning behavior of RRL-TGR is slightly better than that of RRL-TG since concept drift is by nature unavoidable in reinforcement learning. As the learning agent explores more of the world and gets a better idea of the optimal strategy, the utility (e.g. Q)-values that it computes will automatically increase and earlier underestimates should be forgotten. In the setting with inductive transfer, a good policy for the target task is learned a lot faster. Although inductive transfer also helps RRL-TG , the concept changes make it harder to learn an optimal policy.

Making a direct comparison of the RRL-TGR system to the Relational UTrees of [4] is difficult, both because they did not perform any experiments involving changing goals and because they only report results obtained by an ϵ-greedy policy on the $on(A, B)$ task in a blocks world with three blocks. We can state however that on $on(A, B)$ in a world with three blocks, RRL-TGR clearly learns much faster (converging to an optimal policy after 200-300 learning episodes with a maximum length of 3 steps) than the results reported in [4] where an "epsilon-optimal" policy is only reached after learning on 20.000 (state,action)-pairs.

Tic-tac-toe. We also present an experiment using tic-tac-toe, an application from the general game playing challenge. This is a well known two player game. If both players play optimally it results in a draw. The game is very asymmetric and although it is relatively easy to learn to draw against an optimal player using reinforcement learning when one is allowed to start the game, it becomes really hard to do this when the opposing player is allowed to act first. In fact, against a starting player that optimizes his game strategy against a random player, the probability of playing a draw with a random strategy is only 0.52%. This sparsity of the reward makes it very hard to build a good policy starting from scratch against an optimal player. We therefor devised an experiment which allowed RRL to start playing against a starting player which performs 1-step-look-ahead and transfer the learned knowledge when learning against the optimal player. The 1-step-look-ahead player will play winning moves if they exist and counter winning moves of the opponent. However, in states where neither exists, it will play randomly and therefor will not be immune to the generation of forks.

The language used by TG and TGR includes both non-game-specific knowledge (e.g. search related features) and game-specific features that can be automatically extracted from the specification of the game in the general game description language as used in the general game playing challenge.

Figure 4 shows the percentage of draws (the optimal result) RRL achieves against an optimal player both with and without inductive transfer averaged over 10 runs. In the experiment without transfer, RRL-TGR does slightly better than RRL-TG . In the case where the agent can start learning against an easier player and transfer the learned knowledge, it learns to draw much faster against the optimal player. For these experiments we let RRL practice against the 1-step-look-ahead player for the first 300 games. The first seven reported results in the graph are draws against the 1-step-look-ahead player. In fact, RRL-TGR learned to win against that player in 76% of its games after 300 training games (56% for RRL-TG). After game 300, RRL is allowed to train against the optimal player and using the results from the first 300 games, learns to achieve draws against the optimal player a lot faster. In this setting, RRL-TGR can adapt his policy a lot faster while RRL-TG needs more time to adjust its policy to the new player.

5 Conclusions and Future Work

We introduced inductive transfer in reinforcement learning through partial re-use of previously learned policies, by using an incremental learner capable of dealing with concept drift. We designed a first-order decision tree algorithm that uses four tree-restructuring operators suited for first-order decision trees to adapt its theory to changes in the target concept. These operators take the dependencies that occur between the tests in different nodes in first-order trees into account and can be applied without the need to store the entire past training experience.

Experimental results from a Bongard learning problem with concept drift showed that the resulting algorithm is indeed capable of dealing with changes in the target concept using partial theory revision. Experiments with relational reinforcement learning show both that the new algorithm allows the RRL system to react to goal changes more rapidly and to benefit from the re-use of parts of previously learned policies when the learning task becomes more difficult.

The TGR algorithm currently does not know when the agent changes to a new task. Exploiting this knowledge is an important direction for future work.

References

1. Banerjee, B., Stone, P.: General game learning using knowledge transfer. In: The 20th International Joint Conference on Artificial Intelligence, pp. 672–677 (2007)
2. Bongard, M.: Pattern Recognition. Spartan Books (1970)
3. Chapman, D., Kaelbling, L.: Input generalization in delayed reinforcement learning: An algorithm and performance comparisons. In: Proceedings of the 12th International Joint Conference on Artificial Intelligence, pp. 726–731 (1991)
4. Dabney, W., McGovern, A.: Utile distinctions for relational reinforcement learning. In: Proc. of IJCAI'07, pp. 738–743 (2007)
5. Driessens, K., Ramon, J., Blockeel, H.: Speeding up relational reinforcement learning through the use of an incremental first order decision tree learner. In: Flach, P.A., De Raedt, L. (eds.) ECML 2001. LNCS (LNAI), vol. 2167, pp. 97–108. Springer, Heidelberg (2001)

6. Džeroski, S., De Raedt, L., Driessens, K.: Relational reinforcement learning. Machine Learning 43, 7–52 (2001)
7. Fernández, F., Veloso, M.: Probabilistic policy reuse in a reinforcement learning agent. In: AAMAS '06: Proceedings of the fifth international joint conference on Autonomous agents and multiagent systems, pp. 720–727. ACM Press, New York (2006)
8. Genesereth, M., Love, N.: General game playing: Overview of the AAAI competition. AI Magazine 26(2), 62–72 (2005)
9. Madden, M., Howley, T.: Transfer of Experience Between Reinforcement Learning Environments with Progressive Difficulty. AI Rev. 21(3-4), 375–398 (2004)
10. Slaney, J., Thiébaux, S.: Blocks world revisited. AI Jour. 125(1-2), 119–153 (2001)
11. Taylor, M., Whiteson, S., Stone, P.: Transfer via inter-task mappings in policy search reinforcement learning. In: AAMAS'07 (2007)
12. Torrey, L., Shavlik, J., Walker, T., Maclin, R.: Skill acquisition via transfer learning and advice taking. In: Fürnkranz, J., Scheffer, T., Spiliopoulou, M. (eds.) ECML 2006. LNCS (LNAI), vol. 4212, pp. 425–436. Springer, Heidelberg (2006)
13. Utgoff, P.: Decision tree induction based on efficient tree restructuring. Machine Learning 29(1), 5–44 (1997)
14. Widmer, G., Kubat, M.: Learning in the presence of concept drift and hidden contexts. Machine Learning 23(2), 69–101 (1996)

Class Noise Mitigation Through Instance Weighting

Umaa Rebbapragada and Carla E. Brodley

Dept. of Computer Science, Tufts University
161 College Ave., Medford, MA 02155, USA
{urebbapr,brodley}@cs.tufts.edu

Abstract. We describe a novel framework for class noise mitigation that assigns a vector of class membership probabilities to each training instance, and uses the confidence on the current label as a weight during training. The probability vector should be calculated such that clean instances have a high confidence on its current label, while mislabeled instances have a low confidence on its current label and a high confidence on its correct label. Past research focuses on techniques that either discard or correct instances. This paper proposes that discarding and correcting are special cases of instance weighting, and thus, part of this framework. We propose a method that uses clustering to calculate a probability distribution over the class labels for each instance. We demonstrate that our method improves classifier accuracy over the original training set. We also demonstrate that instance weighting can outperform discarding.

1 Introduction

Cleaning training data of mislabeled instances improves a classifier's accuracy. Past research has focused on cleaning the training data by either discarding or correcting mislabeled instances. This paper proposes a different approach: assign a probability vector of class membership to each training instance, and use the confidence on the current label as a weight during training. Correcting and discarding techniques can also make use of this probability vector, and indeed, are special cases of instance weighting. A technique that discards is effectively assigning a 0 to the current label of an instance it discards and a 1 to the label of an instance it keeps. Similarly, a correcting technique assigns a confidence of 1 to the new class label, and 0 to all others.

An objective then is to find an accurate method for assigning confidences such that incorrect labels receive a low confidence and correct labels receive a high confidence. This paper presents pair-wise expectation maximization (PWEM), a confidence-labeling technique that clusters instances from pairs of classes and assigns to each instance a probability distribution over the class labels. We use the EM [3] algorithm to perform the clustering because it conveniently outputs the probability distribution of the instance's cluster membership, but our approach can be used with any partitioning clustering technique.

J.N. Kok et al. (Eds.): ECML 2007, LNAI 4701, pp. 708–715, 2007.

We validate our method on three data sets in which we introduce both random and rule-based noise of up to 40%. Our experiments demonstrate that PWEM correctly assigns a low confidence to the mislabeled examples. We discuss limitations on PWEM to generate accurate confidences caused by noise level and class separability. We demonstrate that these confidences can be used to implement instance discarding and weighting, and show empirical evidence in favor of instance weighting over discarding. Finally, we demonstrate that PWEM in conjunction with instance weighting can significantly improve the accuracy of a classifier over the original mislabeled training set.

2 Instance Weighting

Instance weighting may be preferable to discarding when class noise mitigation techniques make errors. Discarding can lead to two types of errors: 1) discarding a clean instance and 2) retaining a mislabeled instance. Another disadvantage of discarding is that it reduces the training set's size. If valuable minority class instances are mislabeled or erroneously identified as noise and discarded, the resulting classifier will not generalize well for examples of those classes. Correcting methods retain the full data set, but have the potential to maintain or introduce more noise into the labeling process via three types of errors: 1) changing the label on a clean instance, 2) retaining the label of a mislabeled instance, and 3) changing the label of a mislabeled instance to another incorrect label.

Instance weighting via confidences on the current label may be preferable over 0|1 weights because the full data set is retained and the penalty for making errors may be smaller. Let $P(l|x)$ be the confidence associated with instance x's current label l. The error associated with the instance is $P(l|x)$ if the instance is mislabeled, and $1 - P(l|x)$ if the instance is clean.

Consider a discarding technique that bases its decision on an instance's confidence. One can synthetically assign these confidences to any discarding algorithm such that each instance it discards has a confidence below a threshold T and each instance it keeps has a confidence greater than T. As a best case scenario for instance weighting in comparison to discarding, imagine that both make mistakes on the same set of mislabeled and clean instances. Given a training set composed of a set of mislabeled instances M and a set of clean instances C (where x_i is an instance), and assuming all other confidences are correct, instance weighting errors are bounded by:

$$\sum_{i=1}^{|M'|} P(l|x_i) \leq |M'| \text{ where } M' = \{P(l|x_i) > T | \forall x_i \in M\}$$

$$\sum_{i=1}^{|C'|} (1 - P(l|x_i)) \leq |C'| \text{ where } C' = \{P(l|x_i) \leq T | \forall x_i \in C\}$$

Thus, in terms of error, instance weighting is penalized less for making mistakes on the same instances because the loss is not 0|1. Of course, instance weighting incurs a penalty on correct decisions while discarding does not. However, our hypothesis is that weighting's error gain on correct decisions is more than offset by its error reduction on mistakes. We defer an analytical proof of this hypothesis to future work. Meanwhile, Section 4 presents empirical evidence that weighting outperforms discarding. A similar argument applies for correcting versus weighting. The skew in error is even more pronounced under correcting as it is capable of three types of error rather than two. We defer both our analytical and empirical analysis of weighting versus correcting to future work.

3 Computing Confidence on the Class Labels

Instance weighting is only as effective as the quality of the confidences associated with each instance. PWEM is our method for assigning a probability distribution over the class labels to each instance. For each instance x, PWEM outputs the confidence $P(l|x)$ that the label of x is $l \in L$, where L is the set of class labels. In this section, we describe how we use clustering to find $P(l|x)$.

Intuitively, one expects instances from the same class to cluster together. We can use clustering to create a set of class probability vectors by having each instance inherit the distribution of classes within its assigned cluster. The drawback of this method is that there is no guarantee that a multi-class data set will cluster perfectly along class lines. Feature selection may improve class separability, but it is possible that two or more classes may not separate under any circumstances because their distributions overlap.

We improve class separability by clustering pairs of classes, and leave feature selection as an area of future work. For each of the $\binom{|L|}{2}$ pairs of classes, we cluster only those instances assigned a label in that pair. Thus, each instance belongs to only $|L-1|$ clusterings. If an instance's label has a low confidence in one clustering due to class inseparability, it may still receive a high confidence in its other clusterings if its assigned class separates well from others.

Our method, called PWEM, uses the EM algorithm to perform clustering.[1] Given a set of $L-1$ clusterings for instance x, we calculate the probability that x belongs to class l as follows:

$$P(l|x) = \sum_{\theta} P(\theta)P(l|x,\theta) = \sum_{\theta} P(\theta) \sum_{c=1}^{k} P(l|c,\theta)P(c|x,\theta) \quad (1)$$

where l is a class label, x is an instance, c is a cluster, k is the number of clusters (determined by the Bayesian Information Criterion [9]), and θ is the given clustering model. $P(l|x)$ represents the probability that instance x should have class label l. $P(l|x,\theta)$ represents the probability that x should have label l given the clustering θ. This probability is calculated by summing the probability that x belongs to cluster c (as calculated by EM) times the probability that c should be labeled as l. Summing over all clusters results in the probability that x should be labeled l. If $P(l|c,\theta)$ and $P(c|x,\theta)$ form probability distributions, it

[1] Our implementation of EM estimates both the mean and variance of a finite mixture of Gaussians.

is trivial to show that $P(l|x)$ also forms a probability distribution over the class labels. We assume each clustering (θ) is equally likely. Thus, $P(\theta)$ is $\frac{1}{L-1}$. Each $P(l|x)$ acts as a confidence on the class label l for instance x.

4 Experiments

Our experimental goals are to 1) assess the quality of the confidences produced by PWEM, 2) demonstrate that PWEM in conjunction with instance weighting improves classifier accuracy over the mislabeled data set and 3) show empirical evidence in favor of instance weighting over discarding as a technique for class noise mitigation.

4.1 Data

We perform experiments on three data sets, refered to as segmentation (or segm), road, and modis. These are multi-class data sets with 2310, 2056 and 3398 instances and 7, 9 and 11 classes respectively. Segmentation has an even distribution of classes, while road and modis do not. For detailed descriptions, we refer the reader to Brodley & Friedl (1999) [1].

We perform ten runs of each experiment. For each run we randomly shuffle the data set and reserve 2/3 for training and 1/3 for testing. Both test and training sets are stratified samplings. Copies of the training set are mislabeled to have up to 30% random and 40% rule-based noise. Our experiments use Weka's [13] implementation of the C4.5 classifier, which allows the input of instance weights.

Random noise is introduced by randomly flipping $n\%$ instances of the training set, with noise introduced in proportion to class distribution. The new label is chosen uniformly among the other classes. We denote random noise levels of 10, 20, and 30% as MA10, MA20, and MA30.

Rule-based noise is introduced with the assistance of rules provided by a domain expert for each data set. These rules reflect the natural confusions that exist between classes. We use the rules outlined in Brodley & Friedl (1999) [1]. Each instance has a $n\%$ chance of being flipped according to its rule. Thus, the data set potentially has $n\%$ noise. The actual noise level is usually less than $n\%$. Mislabeling to ensure $n\%$ noise in the data can create pathological mislabeling among minority classes in cases where minority classes have mislabeling rules and majority classes do not. For rule-based noise, MU10, MU20, MU30 and MU40 indicate the potential noise levels of 10, 20, 30 and 40%. Table 2 provides the mean actual noise levels. In this paper, the unqualified use of the word 'noise' refers to potential noise. Only under rule-based noise is potential noise not equal to actual noise.

4.2 Quality of Confidences

To assess the efficacy of PWEM, we examine the confidences associated with the current label of the clean (C) and mislabeled (M) instances. For PWEM to

Table 1. Mean and standard deviation on the confidence of the current class label for clean (C) and mislabeled (M) instances for random (MA) and rule-based (MU) noise

DATA	M/C	MA10	MA20	MA30	MU10	MU20	MU30	MU40
segm	M	.45 ± .22	.46 ± .19	.47 ± .15	.39 ± .18	.45 ± .16	.53 ± .17	.58 ± .17
segm	C	.82 ± .11	.77 ± .11	.73 ± .11	.83 ± .12	.78 ± .11	.74 ± .11	.72 ± .11
road	M	.47 ± .15	.46 ± .13	.47 ± .12	.62 ± .16	.63 ± .15	.65 ± .13	.65 ± .13
road	C	.85 ± .16	.83 ± .16	.81 ± .15	.86 ± .15	.84 ± .15	.82 ± .15	.80 ± .15
modis	M	.46 ± .19	.47 ± .16	.47 ± .13	.70 ± .17	.72 ± .16	.75 ± .15	.78 ± .14
modis	C	.86 ± .13	.83 ± .13	.79 ± .14	.90 ± .11	.89 ± .11	.88 ± .11	.87 ± .12

work effectively with instance weighting, there must be a separation between the means of the C and M instances.

Table 1 shows average confidences on the current label of clean and mislabeled instances. There are several observable trends in the results. First, as the level of noise increases, the separation between the confidences decreases. At best, that separation is approximately 0.4 (modis, MA10), and at worst it is 0.09 (segmentation, MU40). As class noise increases, it becomes more difficult for PWEM to assign high and low confidences to the clean and mislabeled data respectively. PWEM also has more difficulty separating confidences under rule-based noise than random noise. This is an expected result, as rule-based noise is a tougher problem. However, in all cases, the mean confidences of the mislabeled instances are always lower than the mean confidences of the clean instances. This will downweight the effect of the mislabeled instances in relation to clean ones.

PWEM currently does a poor job at assigning a high confidence to the true labels of mislabeled instances, rendering it ineffective as a label correction method. We leave label correction as an area of future work.

4.3 Weighting Versus Discarding

We now compare the accuracy of classifiers on training sets created by discarding and weighting instances. First, we establish two baselines for classifier accuracy. The first, MK, is the accuracy of a classifier trained from the mislabeled training set (MK stands for mislabeled kept). The second, MD, is the accuracy of a classifier trained from only the clean instances of the training set (MD stands for mislabeled discarded). This is the accuracy achieved under perfect discarding or perfect confidences. We discard instances (DIST(T)) whose confidence on their assigned class label is less than a user-specified threshold T. We weight instances (WGHT) according to the confidence on their assigned labels.

Table 2 shows our accuracy results. Each cell of the table shows the mean and standard deviation of the accuracy for a method at the noise level indicated. Our results show that, in general, instance weighting achieves a better classifier accuracy than discarding (with a sole exception at MA10 in segmentation). Indeed, in all cases, instance weighting achieves accuracy within three percentage points of the MD upper limit. For all potential noise levels greater than 20, weighting improves accuracy significantly over the original mislabeled data (MK).

Table 2. Accuracy on segmentation, road and modis using random (MA) and rule-based (MU) noise. The MISL column shows potential noise while ACT reports the actual noise. Results compare instance weighting (WGHT) and discarding (DISC) at thresholds 0.2, 0.5 and 0.8.

DATA	MISL	ACT	MK	MD	DISC(.2)	DISC(.5)	DISC(.8)	WGHT
segm	MA10	10.0	94.1 ± 0.9	95.7 ± 0.8	94.8 ± 0.9	94.1 ± 0.8	70.3 ± 5.4	94.4 ± 0.8
segm	MA20	20.0	91.1 ± 1.2	95.3 ± 0.4	91.4 ± 1.3	91.7 ± 0.8	36.9 ± 9.6	93.4 ± 0.8
segm	MA30	30.0	82.2 ± 2.6	95.0 ± 1.0	82.9 ± 3.2	89.6 ± 1.8	21.3 ± 7.4	92.4 ± 1.5
segm	MU10	5.8	95.2 ± 0.7	95.9 ± 0.8	95.3 ± 0.7	94.9 ± 1.5	72.1 ± 6.4	95.3 ± 1.3
segm	MU20	11.4	93.5 ± 1.5	95.9 ± 0.9	94.0 ± 1.4	93.1 ± 1.3	56.0 ± 10.7	94.8 ± 1.2
segm	MU30	17.2	89.6 ± 1.9	95.9 ± 1.2	90.1 ± 1.8	91.8 ± 1.7	30.6 ± 10.7	94.8 ± 1.0
segm	MU40	22.9	84.9 ± 2.9	95.4 ± 1.0	84.7 ± 3.1	86.7 ± 4.3	25.6 ± 11.8	93.0 ± 1.6
road	MA10	10.0	78.5 ± 0.8	80.5 ± 2.0	78.3 ± 1.0	78.8 ± 1.5	78.4 ± 0.8	80.2 ± 1.3
road	MA20	20.0	76.9 ± 1.7	80.7 ± 1.4	76.9 ± 1.7	77.9 ± 1.1	74.2 ± 4.2	79.9 ± 0.5
road	MA30	30.0	69.6 ± 4.8	80.5 ± 1.8	69.6 ± 4.8	77.3 ± 1.2	71.1 ± 2.7	79.9 ± 1.0
road	MU10	9.7	79.1 ± 1.3	80.2 ± 1.2	79.2 ± 1.4	78.6 ± 1.5	77.1 ± 1.6	80.8 ± 1.0
road	MU20	19.2	76.3 ± 2.9	80.7 ± 1.3	76.7 ± 2.8	76.0 ± 2.4	76.2 ± 3.2	80.7 ± 1.1
road	MU30	30.0	67.5 ± 2.6	80.1 ± 1.4	67.7 ± 2.5	68.3 ± 2.8	72.3 ± 3.3	80.3 ± 0.7
road	MU40	39.6	59.7 ± 4.8	80.0 ± 1.2	60.8 ± 4.8	59.6 ± 4.6	71.0 ± 2.3	79.6 ± 0.8
modis	MA10	10.0	84.0 ± 0.9	85.5 ± 0.9	84.0 ± 0.9	84.6 ± 0.9	77.2 ± 1.8	85.4 ± 0.8
modis	MA20	20.0	80.5 ± 1.2	84.7 ± 1.0	80.5 ± 1.2	83.3 ± 1.5	65.7 ± 2.4	83.9 ± 1.4
modis	MA30	30.0	75.9 ± 2.4	84.5 ± 1.3	75.9 ± 2.4	81.9 ± 1.6	56.6 ± 5.5	83.7 ± 1.3
modis	MU10	6.6	84.4 ± 0.6	85.6 ± 0.8	84.4 ± 0.6	85.1 ± 1.1	81.3 ± 1.0	84.9 ± 0.7
modis	MU20	13.4	81.5 ± 1.4	85.1 ± 0.9	81.6 ± 1.6	82.4 ± 1.1	80.1 ± 1.3	84.2 ± 1.0
modis	MU30	19.5	79.1 ± 2.1	85.5 ± 1.0	79.3 ± 2.2	78.6 ± 1.4	76.9 ± 2.4	82.6 ± 1.8
modis	MU40	26.6	74.2 ± 2.7	84.5 ± 0.9	74.3 ± 2.8	75.1 ± 1.9	68.6 ± 2.5	77.9 ± 1.9

For space reasons, Table 2 shows discard thresholds of 0.2, 0.5 and 0.8 only. However, we performed experiments with discard thresholds $0.1, 0.2, \ldots, 0.9$. Our results show that weighting results in a higher classifier accuracy than discarding at all nine threshold levels. Discarding performs better than the original mislabeled training set (MK) up until a certain threshold. This point is generally just below the mean confidence value for clean instances. At this point, too many clean instances have been discarded and classifier performance deteriorates. Table 2 shows that weighting never falls below MK, and of the two methods, is the more reliable class mitigation technique.

5 Related Work

With the exception of Lawrence and Schölkopf [7], existing methods discard [15,5,4,2,1,11,12,16], correct [14,10] or are capable of both [8,6]. The majority of existing work in class noise mitigation evaluates their methods on random-noise only. As demonstrated by our results, and discussed in Brodley and Friedl [1] and Zhu et al. [16], rule-based noise is more difficult to eliminate than random noise.

Our approach differs from existing work by introducing instance weighting as a technique for class noise mitigation. We also experiment on both types of noise.

Methods for discarding differ in how they determine which instances are mislabeled. Using a n-fold CV, Brodley and Friedl discard instances that fail to get either a majority or consensus vote from the ensemble that matches their label. Verbaeten [11,12] builds ensembles on different subsets of the data (e.g., via bagging) and identifies mislabeled instances as those that receive high weights by boosting. Zhu et al. [16] propose an iterative algorithm that partitions the data set and creates rules for each subset. A set of "good rules" are used to classify an instance as noise by either majority vote or consensus. The noisy instances along with a small set of good examples are then set aside as the method repeats on the reduced data set until a stopping criterion is met. Gamberger et al. [5,4] use compression-based measures to eliminate noise from the training set. A training instance is discarded if its elimination reduces the complexity of the hypothesis on the training set. This process iterates until a user-specified noise-sensitivity threshold is reached. Zeng and Martinez [14,15] calculate a probability distribution over the class labels for each instance, which they use to discard or correct instances. One could adapt their method to use instances weights. Our hypothesis is their accuracy results will improve. Whether their method provides better confidences than PWEM is an open question to be addressed in the future.

Lawrence and Schölkopf's [7] method for two class problems learns the conditional probabilities that a class label is flipped. These probabilities are learned at the class level rather than the instance level. The method uses a kernel Fisher discriminant in conjunction with the EM algorithm to iteratively estimate class conditional probabilities that indicate mislabeling.

Finally, class noise mitigation is closely related to instance selection techniques, which were designed either to improve computational efficiency or improve classification accuracy by discarding the data (see [14] for a good overview).

6 Conclusion and Future Work

This paper presents a new technique that reduces the effects of class noise. PWEM clusters pairs of classes to gain insight into the true class labels of the training set. We present empirical evidence that PWEM in conjunction with instance weighting significantly improves classifier accuracy close to the theoretical best on all noise levels. In cases where it does not, weighting significantly improves classifier accuracy over the original mislabeled set.

An area of future work is to improve PWEM's ability to calculate the probability distribution over the class labels. In particular, improvement of PWEM's ability to predict the true class label of a mislabeled instance will enable it to be used as a correcting technique. Other ideas to improve PWEM include weighting the influence of the each clustering according to its class separability and size, and incorporating feature selection. Finally, we will investigate a wider range of weighting techniques that use the full probability vector, rather than the confidence on the current label only.

References

1. Brodley, C.E., Friedl, M.A.: Identifying mislabeled training data. JAIR 11, 131–167 (1999)
2. Brodley, C.E., Friedl, M.A.: Identifying and eliminating mislabeled training instances. In: Proc. of the 13th National Conference on Artificial Intelligence, pp. 799–805 (1996)
3. Dempster, A.P., Laird, N.M., Rubin, D.B.: Maximum likelihood from incomplete data via the EM algorithm. Journal of the Royal Statistical Society 39, 1–38 (1977)
4. Gamberger, D., Lavrač, N., Grošelj, C.: Experiments with noise filtering in a medical domain. In: Proc. of the 16th ICML, pp. 143–151 (1999)
5. Gamberger, D., Lavrač, N., Džeroski, S.: Noise elimination in inductive concept learning: a case study in medical diagnosis. In: 7th Int. Wkshp. on Algorithmic Learning Theory, pp. 199–212 (1996)
6. Lallich, S., Muhlenbach, F., Zighed, D.A.: Improving classification by removing or relabeling mislabeled instances. In: Proc. of the 13th Int. Symp. on the Foundations of Intelligent Systems, pp. 5–15 (2002)
7. Lawrence, N.D., Schölkopf, B.: Estimating a Kernel Fisher Discriminant in the presence of label noise. In: Proc. of the 18th ICML, pp. 306–313 (2001)
8. Muhlenbach, F., Lallich, S., Zighed, D.A.: Identifying and handling mislabelled instances. Journal of Intelligent Information Systems 22, 89–109 (2004)
9. Pelleg, D., Moore, A.: X-means: extending K-means with efficient estimation of the number of clusters. In: Proc. of the 17th ICML, pp. 727–734 (2000)
10. Teng, C.: Correcting noisy data. In: Proc. of the 16th ICML, pp. 239–248 (1999)
11. Verbaeten, S.: Identifying mislabeled training examples in ILP classification problems. In: Proc. of the Machine Learning Conference of Belgium (2002)
12. Verbaeten, S., Van Assche, A.: Ensemble methods for noise elimination in classification problems. In: Multiple Classifier Systems, 4th International Workshop (2003)
13. Witten, I.H., Frank, E.: Data mining: practical machine learning tools and techniques, 2nd edn. Morgan Kaufmann, San Francisco (2005)
14. Zeng, X., Martinez, T.: An algorithm for correcting mislabeled data. Intelligent Data Analysis 5 (2001)
15. Zeng, X., Martinez, T.: A noise filtering method using neural networks. In: Proc. of the Int. Wkshp. of Soft Computing Techniques in Instrumentation, Measurement and Related Applications (2003)
16. Zhu, X., Wu, X., Chen, S.: Eliminating class noise in large datasets. In: Proc. of the 20th ICML, pp. 920–927 (2003)

Optimizing Feature Sets for Structured Data

Ulrich Rückert and Stefan Kramer

Institut für Informatik/I12, Technische Universität München, Boltzmannstr. 3, D-85748 Garching b. München, Germany
{rueckert,kramer}@in.tum.de

Abstract. Choosing a suitable feature representation for structured data is a non-trivial task due to the vast number of potential candidates. Ideally, one would like to pick a small, but informative set of structural features, each providing complementary information about the instances. We frame the search for a suitable feature set as a combinatorial optimization problem. For this purpose, we define a scoring function that favors features that are as dissimilar as possible to all other features. The score is used in a stochastic local search (SLS) procedure to maximize the diversity of a feature set. In experiments on small molecule data, we investigate the effectiveness of a forward selection approach with two different linear classification schemes.

1 Introduction

Feature generation and selection for structured data is complicated by the vast number of possible candidate features. In graph classification, for instance, the number of ways to describe a graph is virtually unlimited, and often expert knowledge is necessary to identify relevant aspects of a graph. A popular choice is to represent a graph by features that specify whether or not a subgraph is present. If there is only limited expert knowledge available about relevant subgraph features in an application, the learning algorithm needs to generate meaningful features on its own. Unfortunately, the number of subgraphs grows exponentially with the size of the graphs, so it is clearly infeasible to use all possible subgraphs as features. Therefore, many approaches restrict the set of subgraph features to frequently occurring, frequent closed, or class-correlated subgraphs [3,2]. In all of these cases, however, there is no guarantee that the resulting feature sets have sufficient coverage over all instances of a dataset. Moreover, the resulting features may be only slight alterations of a few subgraphs. As a consequence, the number of features required to reach some level of performance may be unnecessarily high, potentially harming comprehensibility and efficiency. While we focus on graph classification in this paper, the same problems occur with other forms of structured data, for instance, in logic-based representations.

Instead of generating a bulk of features and obtaining a well-balanced coverage only incidentally, it may be worthwhile to actively construct favorable structural features in the first place. One way to minimize the number of features required

J.N. Kok et al. (Eds.): ECML 2007, LNAI 4701, pp. 716–723, 2007.

is to explicitly maximize the diversity of subgraph features. Thus, we frame the search for diverse, complementary sets of subgraph features as an optimization problem. We define a scoring function measuring the diversity of a feature set and present a stochastic local search (SLS) procedure to find subgraphs optimizing that score. Stochastic local search is motivated by the NP-hardness of the problem of finding a perfectly complementary subgraph given a set of graphs and optimal features so far. To focus the search for useful structural features even further, it is possible to extend the scoring function by balancing diversity with class correlation. The resulting feature sets are used in linear classifiers. The effectiveness of the method and its dependence on variations are tested in experiments on three small molecule datasets from cheminformatics.

2 Background and Motivation

We deal with the problem of *feature generation* for linear classifiers. In this setting, the instances are arbitrary objects and we need to find features that extract meaningful information from the objects. In particular, we are interested in features that are well suited for use by a learning algorithm to construct a predictive classifier. Information theory gives us the tools to quantify what constitutes a feature set that is informative about the target class: Let $X \in \{-1,1\}^{m \times n}$ be the training matrix containing m instances $x_1, \ldots, x_m$, where each instance $x_i = (x_i(1), \ldots, x_i(n))$ ranges over n features. X_i denotes the ith column of the training matrix, that is, the instantiation of the ith feature. Assuming a binary classification problem, we denote the class labels of the instances by $Y \in \{-1,1\}^m$. Then we are aiming at features $X_1, \ldots, X_n$ with high mutual information $I(X;Y) = I(X_1, \ldots, X_n; Y)$ between features and target class. We can write the mutual information as the difference between the entropy of X and the conditional entropy of X given Y: $I(X;Y) = H(X) - H(X|Y)$. Thus, in order to obtain highly informative features, we need to maximize $H(X) := H(X_1, \ldots, X_n)$ and to minimize $H(X|Y) := H(X_1, \ldots, X_n|Y)$. This leads to the following three criteria:

- *High correlation with the class.* Since we would like to minimize $H(X|Y)$, we are looking for features that are highly correlated with Y. This is the criterion that is most prominently applied in most traditional multi-relational learning systems. Theoretically, a single feature X_i agreeing with Y on all instances would be enough to ensure $H(X_i|Y) = 0$. In practice it is rarely possible to find such a perfect feature and often there is only a small number of features with high correlation. In such a setting, the learning algorithm also needs to consider features with comparably low correlation and the two other criteria below become relevant for optimal feature construction.
- *High feature entropy.* The joint entropy can be upper-bounded by the sum of single features: $H(X) = \sum_{i=1}^{n} H(X_i|X_{i-1}, \ldots, X_1) \leq \sum_{i=1}^{n} H(X_i)$. Thus, in order to maximize $H(X)$ we need to maximize the entropy of each single feature. For Boolean features this means that each feature should divide the training instances in two parts of preferably equal size, so that it assigns -1

to roughly the same number of objects as $+1$. This is intuitively intriguing: a set of k features that assign $+1$ to only one training instance and -1 to the others can discriminate only between k different instances, whereas a set of features that divide the instances into two equal-sized parts can discriminate between up to 2^k bins of instances.

- *High inter-feature entropy.* Even if all single features have maximal entropy, it could be the case that the features are highly correlated to each other. In the most extreme case, it could be that all features assign the same labels to all instances $X_1 = \ldots = X_n$. Clearly, we need to ensure that the features complement each other and do not provide the same information all over again. In terms of information theory one can write $H(X) = \sum_{i=1}^{n} H(X_i|X_{i-1}, \ldots, X_1) \leq \sum_{i=1}^{n} H(X_i|X_{i-1})$. Thus we need to maximize $H(X_i|X_{i-1})$ for all $1 < i \leq n$. Since the features can be ordered arbitrarily, this essentially means we need to maximize $H(X_i|X_j)$ for each pair of features.

The first criterion has been dealt with to great extent in the existing literature on relational learning, the second is sometimes addressed by putting minimum frequency constraints on the features, and the third is usually not considered or included only implicitly. This is a problem in particular in the graph learning setting, where a feature indicates the occurrence or absence of a substructure in a graph. Typically, it is easy to construct substructures that appear in only a very small number of graphs, so the entropy of single features tends to be low. To avoid this, one often selects substructures that appear only with a certain minimal frequency in the graph database. Unfortunately, the resulting substructure's instantiations are often very similar to each other so that inter-feature entropy is low. For instance, mining all subgraphs that appear in at least six percent of the NCTRER dataset (see section 4) yields 83,537 frequent subgraphs. However, when comparing the instantiation X_i with X_j for all pairs of subgraphs (i, j), it turns out, that in 19% of the pairs $X_i = X_j$ and in 77% of the pairs X_i differs from X_j on less than ten instances. Hence, training matrices based on minimum frequency mining tend to be large and exhibit an unnecessarily large degree of redundancy.

On the other hand, it is easy to see that *Hadamard matrices* constitute optimal training matrices with regard to the latter two criteria, because any two columns are orthogonal (so $H(X_i, X_j) = 2$ is maximal for all $i \neq j$), and the number of ones is equal to the number of minus ones in each column (so $H(X_i) = 1$ is maximal for all i). Hadamard matrices of order 2^i can be generated using Sylvester's recursive construction:

$$H_1 = \begin{pmatrix} 1 & 1 \\ 1 & -1 \end{pmatrix}, \quad H_i = \begin{pmatrix} H_{i-1} & H_{i-1} \\ H_{i-1} & -H_{i-1} \end{pmatrix}.$$

Hadamard matrices are also well suited for linear classifiers, because they have full rank. One can show that a matrix of rank d leads to 2^d different linear classifiers, so a large-rank matrix allows the linear learner to choose from a larger amount of different hypotheses. In the following we propose a method that optimizes the second and third criterion for *linear classifiers* on subgraph features.

While a Hadamard matrix would be optimal for learning, it is certainly impossible to find subgraphs whose instantiations give rise to it. Instead, we are faced with the problem of finding subgraphs that approximate a Hadamard matrix as good as possible. In the following, we assume a forward selection setting and frame the problem as an iterative combinatorial optimization problem: Let $D = \{g_1, \ldots, g_m\}$ be a set of graphs (the instances), and $F = \{f_1, \ldots, f_n\}$ be a set of subgraphs (the already included features), and denote by s_i the instantiation vector of the ith subgraph f_i with regard to D, i.e., the vector whose jth component is 1 if f_i is a subgraph of g_j and -1 otherwise. We are then looking for a new subgraph f_{n+1} whose instantiation vector s_{n+1} optimizes some score quantifying the criteria explained above. For the experiments in section 4, we use what we call a *dispersion score* in the remainder of the paper:[1] $d(s_{n+1}) := \sum_{i=1}^{n}(s_i^T s_{n+1})^2$. Minimizing this score directly addresses the third criterion: if s_{n+1} and some s_i agree on many instances, the square of their dot product is large. Thus, summing up over all squared dot products essentially penalizes features that are similar to existing ones. One can show that it promotes features that discriminate between instances that have not been separated well by the existing features. It also implicitly optimizes the second criterion, because it aims at features that agree with existing features on half of the instances and disagree on the other half, thus leading on average to features which assign +1 to approximately the same number of instances as -1. Finally, the score reaches the global optimum zero precisely for the Hadamard matrix. Of course, the dispersion score does not aim at finding features that correlate well with the target. In order to also incorporate the first criterion, we extend it to not only penalize features that are similar to the existing features s_i, but also to reward features that are similar to the target class vector t: $d'(s_{n+1}) := \sum_{i=1}^{n}(s_i^T s_{n+1})^2 - n(t^T s_{n+1})^2$. The modified *class-correlated dispersion score* is designed to value dispersion to the same extent as similarity with the target. In the following section we describe our algorithmic approach to optimizing the dispersion score.

3 Stochastic Local Search for Optimal Dispersion Features

The dispersion score provides a practical way to formulate the search for features with large discriminative power as a combinatorial optimization problem. Unfortunately, due to the complexity inherent in graph operations, the problem can be extremely difficult to solve. It is clear that computing the instantiation vector for an arbitrary graph involves the repeated computation of solutions to NP-complete graph isomorphism problems. Even if one avoids these subgraph isomorphism tests, the problem can be shown to be NP-hard:

[1] In principle one could also apply mutual information instead of the dispersion score, but experiments have shown that this is not effective for the datasets in section 4.

Theorem 1. *The problem of deciding whether there exists a graph, that achieves a dispersion score of zero on a given training matrix and a given graph database is NP-hard.*

(Proof omitted)

There is no generally applicable approach to solving such a combinatorial optimization problem. However, in recent years stochastic local search (SLS) algorithms have been applied with remarkable success on similar NP-hard combinatorial problems. In particular, they are among the best algorithms available to solve hard satisfiability problems. SLS can be described as a randomized greedy walk in the space of solution candidates. More precisely, an SLS algorithm starts by generating a random solution candidate. It then iterates in a loop over two steps: in the first step, it calculates "neighboring" solution candidates according to some predefined neighborhood relation. For each neighbor, it computes a score indicating to which degree the candidate is optimal. In the second step, it randomly selects a new candidate among the neighbors with the best score. As such a pure greedy algorithm can easily be trapped in local optima, the second step is from time to time (i.e., with a predefined noise probability p) replaced by a step, where a completely random neighbor is selected as new candidate. Finally, the algorithm keeps track of the best candidate found so far and outputs this candidate as a solution after a maximum number of iterations. While modern SLS algorithms often use more sophisticated decision functions, the basic principle has been shown to be effective on a range of NP-hard problems, see e.g. [8] for an generic SLS algorithm and applications.

The SLS framework can be easily adjusted to the optimization problem presented in this paper. A solution candidate is simply a graph, and the scoring function is the dispersion score explained in the preceding section. For the neighborhood relation we generate two different kinds of neighbors: more *specific neighbors* are built by extending the current candidate graph with an edge so that the resulting subgraph occurs in at least one graph of the graph database. This avoids generating neighbors that do not occur in the database at all. More *general neighbors* are built by removing one edge from the current candidate. If the removal of the edge separates the graph into two unconnected components, we keep the larger of the two as neighbor and discard the smaller one.

It is crucial for the effectivity of an SLS algorithm that the calculation of the score function and the neighbors is as fast as possible. Unfortunately, both tasks are exceptionally expensive in our case. To compute the dispersion score and to determine more specific neighbors, one needs to identify the instantiation vector and that implies a subgraph isomorphism test with each graph in the database. To overcome this performance bottleneck, we pre-compute an index structure that stores all subgraphs up to a maximum size that occur in the database. The calculation of a candidate's instantiation vector and more specific neighbors is then just a lookup or a limited search operation in the index structure. As there is a huge number of subgraphs in a typical database, it is important to design the index structure to be space efficient, yet fast to access. We achieve this by associating each (sub-)graph with a *canonical code string*, i.e., a string that uniquely determines the graph, and storing those canonical strings in a trie. We follow the breadth-first-search scheme [1] to compute the canonical code strings of all subgraphs with less than a user-defined number of edges. The strings are then stored in a trie structure, so that the SLS procedure can simply look up which of the database graphs contain a specific subgraph.

4 Experiments

In order to evaluate the approach, we implemented the dispersion optimizing SLS algorithm and applied it to three data sets. The NCTRER dataset [4] deals with the binding activity of small molecules at the estrogen receptor, the Yoshida dataset [10] classifies molecules according to their bio-availability, and the blood-barr dataset [7] deals with the degree to which a molecule can cross the blood-brain barrier. For the experiments, we set the noise probability of taking a purely random step in the SLS loop to 0.2, the maximum size of subgraphs stored in the graph trie to fifteen edges and the maximal number of iterations for the SLS loop to 2000. The resulting feature sets are processed by a SVM with the C parameter set to 1 and Margin Minus Variance (MMV) optimization [9] with the p parameter set to 2. To keep the induced linear model comprehensible, we build it in an iterative fashion: we start with an empty feature set and then add the features one by one according to the optimal dispersion criterion. Whenever the number of features exceeds one hundred, we compute the linear classifier and remove the feature with the smallest weight before adding a new feature. The time to generate the trie is typically a few minutes. As it is generated once per dataset (like an index structure in a database), it does not influence the runtimes of subsequent SLS runs.

For the first experiment, we investigate to what extent SLS with dispersion and the class-correlated dispersion are able to generate training sets that are well suited for classification. To do so, we apply SLS with the two scores to construct four feature sets containing 25, 50, 150 and 300 features. We report the training set and test accuracies of SVM and MMV as estimated by tenfold cross-validation in the first four columns of table 1. The results point out some interesting insights. First of all, dispersion with class correlation is on average able to obtain a better *training accuracy* than the pure dispersion score, in particular with larger feature sets. This is expected as the pure dispersion score does not consider the class labels. However, the improvement in training accuracy does not always translate to an improvement in predictive accuracy. It does so for small feature sets up to 50 features, but for larger feature sets the difference in predictive accuracy is small even though the training accuracy is way larger for the class-correlated dispersion score. Also, MMV tends to perform better with regard to predictive accuracy than the SVM, even though its training accuracy is generally inferior to that of the SVM. Overall, MMV with the class-correlated dispersion score achieves good predictive performance for all feature set sizes.

As the SLS-based method should be particularly well-suited for obtaining small (e.g., size 25 or 50) useful feature sets, we set up an experiment comparing

Table 1. Results: percentage of correct classifications of four feature generation methods on training and test set according to tenfold cross validation

Dataset & Nr. Features		SLS (Dispersion)				SLS (Class Corr.)				MinFreq (Sorted by Size)				MinFreq (Sorted by Corr.)			
		MMV		SVM		MMV		SVM		MMV		SVM		MMV		SVM	
		Trg	Tst	Trg	Tst	Trg	Tst	Trg	Tst	Trg	Tst	Trg	Tst	Trg	Tst	Trg	Tst
	25	70.1	61.5	72.4	60.0	75.3	65.3	76.7	60.0	65.7	58.5	68.6	60.0	70.9	61.9	71.2	60.0
yo-	50	75.6	64.5	79.2	62.3	78.0	67.2	80.5	66.4	67.7	57.0	73.4	60.0	72.2	60.4	73.1	60.0
shida	150	76.6	67.2	81.5	62.3	78.8	68.3	81.7	64.2	80.8	66.4	91.3	68.7	73.5	64.9	76.4	60.0
	300	77.2	66.4	81.5	63.8	85.9	66.4	96.1	65.7	85.8	66.8	96.4	68.7	76.4	66.8	83.4	63.4
	25	84.2	82.8	83.1	77.6	82.6	81.5	82.9	76.3	80.2	76.3	80.7	59.9	79.2	78.4	79.6	59.9
NCT	50	84.1	81.9	85.2	78.4	83.8	82.3	84.5	78.0	83.4	79.7	84.2	69.4	80.6	80.2	79.3	59.9
RER	150	84.2	81.0	84.5	77.2	84.3	82.3	86.1	82.8	87.1	82.3	91.3	78.0	80.8	79.7	82.2	79.3
	300	84.4	80.2	84.5	77.2	88.6	81.5	96.5	78.4	87.6	80.6	92.5	75.9	81.1	79.7	82.5	77.6
	25	72.7	69.6	76.8	66.5	77.1	72.5	78.2	68.2	72.9	70.4	73.6	66.5	76.2	73.7	77.3	67.5
blood	50	77.5	71.3	80.0	67.2	77.5	73.5	79.5	68.4	76.8	71.3	81.0	70.4	76.7	74.2	79.7	67.5
barr	150	77.3	69.9	81.1	69.9	78.0	74.9	80.8	68.0	83.2	75.7	90.0	75.9	78.4	72.0	85.6	70.1
	300	77.7	71.1	81.2	70.4	84.7	73.7	95.2	74.5	85.7	75.2	95.1	74.2	81.3	73.7	87.9	74.0

it to minimum-frequency and class-correlation feature generation within this range and beyond (size 150 and 300). First, we apply a subgraph mining tool to identify all subgraphs that occur in more than six percent of the dataset's graphs. Then, we sort the subgraphs by size (i.e. number of edges) or by the correlation with the target according to a χ^2 test on the 2x2 contingency table. Finally we derive four feature sets with 25, 50, 150 and 300 features from those two sorted feature sequences. Hence, the first sorting order is essentially an unsupervised propositionalization approach (similar to the one by Deshpande *et al.* [3]), while the second resembles the class-correlation based approach by Bringmann *et al.* [2]. The third and fourth column of table 1 give the training and test accuracies for MMV and the SVM. On feature sets with 150 and 300 features, the differences between dispersion-based and minimum frequency approaches are only marginal. However, in the target range of small feature sets, the SLS optimization of dispersion outperforms other approaches on two of the three datasets (Yoshida and NCTRER) in almost all pairwise comparisons.

We also compared our approach with the published accuracies (as estimated by tenfold cross validation) of two recently proposed learning systems for structured data. On the Yoshida dataset, an SVM with optimal assignment kernel [5] had 67.8% accuracy, a bit more than the dispersion-based SVM (65.7%), but less than dispersion-based MMV (68.3%). On bloodbarr, the dispersion-based approaches featured 74.9% (MMV) and 74.5% (SVM), outperforming the OA kernel SVM with 57.97% by a large margin. On the NCTRER dataset, kFOIL, an extension of FOIL incorporating an SVM in a novel evaluation function [6], had 77.6% accuracy, while the presented system yields 82.3% (MMV) and 82.8% (SVM), a significant improvement.

5 Conclusion

On structured data, a small set of strong features is vital for comprehensibility and efficiency of computation. In the paper, we framed the search for a suitable set of structural features as a combinatorial optimization problem. We proposed a scoring function fostering the diversity of feature sets and an optimization scheme based on stochastic local search (SLS) to maximize that score. The choice of SLS is motivated by the NP-hardness of finding an optimally complementary subgraph feature. In our experiments on small molecule data, we found that the optimization of dispersion pays particularly when aiming for small feature sets. Unlike many other approaches to feature selection (e.g. [11]), we can take advantage of the structure of features, intertwining structure search and feature selection. In principle, the basic approach is more general than presented here. First, it is not restricted to graphs, but could be extended to more expressive representations such as first-order logic. Second, it is not restricted to the forward selection procedure tested in section 4, since a variant of the dispersion score and SLS could be used for the optimization of fixed-size feature sets as well.

References

1. Borgelt, C.: On canonical forms for frequent graph mining. In: Proc. 3rd Int. Workshop on Mining Graphs, Trees, and Sequences, pp. 1–12 (2005)
2. Bringmann, B., Zimmermann, A., De Raedt, L., Nijssen, S.: Don't be afraid of simpler patterns. In: Fürnkranz, J., Scheffer, T., Spiliopoulou, M. (eds.) PKDD 2006. LNCS (LNAI), vol. 4213, pp. 55–66. Springer, Heidelberg (2006)
3. Deshpande, M., Kuramochi, M., Wale, N., Karypis, G.: Frequent substructure-based approaches for classifying chemical compounds. IEEE Transactions on Knowledge and Data Engineering 17(8), 1036–1050 (2005)
4. Fang, H., Tong, W., Shi, L.M., Blair, R., Perkins, R., Branham, W., Hass, B.S., Xie, Q., Dial, S.L., Moland, C.L., Sheehan, D.M.: Structure-activity relationships for a large diverse set of natural, synthetic, and environmental estrogens. Chemical Research in Toxicology 14(3), 280–294 (2001)
5. Fröhlich, H., Wegner, J.K., Sieker, F., Zell, A.: Optimal assignment kernels for attributed molecular graphs. In: Proceedings of the 22nd ICML, pp. 225–232. ACM Press, New York (2005)
6. Landwehr, N., Passerini, A., De Raedt, L., Frasconi, P.: kFOIL: Learning simple relational kernels. In: AAAI, AAAI Press (2006)
7. Li, H., Yap, C.W., Ung, C.Y., Xue, Y., Cao, Z.W., Chen, Y.Z.: Effect of selection of molecular descriptors on the prediction of blood-brain barrier penetrating and nonpenetrating agents by statistical learning methods. Journal of Chemical Information and Modeling 45(5), 1376–1384 (2005)
8. Rückert, U., Kramer, S.: Stochastic local search in k-term DNF learning. In: Proceedings of the 20th ICML, pp. 648–655. AAAI Press (2003)
9. Rückert, U., Kramer, S.: A statistical approach to rule learning. In: Proceedings of the 23rd ICML, pp. 785–792. ACM Press, New York (2006)
10. Yoshida, F., Topliss, J.: QSAR model for drug human oral bioavailability. J. Med. Chem. 43, 2575–2585 (2000)
11. Yu, L., Liu, H.: Efficient feature selection via analysis of relevance and redundancy. J. Mach. Learn. Res. 5, 1205–1224 (2004)

Roulette Sampling for Cost-Sensitive Learning

Victor S. Sheng and Charles X. Ling

Department of Computer Science, University of Western Ontario,
London, Ontario, Canada N6A 5B7
{ssheng,cling}@csd.uwo.ca

Abstract. In this paper, we propose a new and general preprocessor algorithm, called *CSRoulette*, which converts any cost-insensitive classification algorithms into cost-sensitive ones. *CSRoulette* is based on cost proportional roulette sampling technique (called *CPRS* in short). *CSRoulette* is closely related to Costing, another cost-sensitive meta-learning algorithm, which is based on rejection sampling. Unlike rejection sampling which produces smaller samples, *CPRS* can generate different size samples. To further improve its performance, we apply ensemble (bagging) on *CPRS*; the resulting algorithm is called *CSRoulette*. Our experiments show that *CSRoulette* outperforms Costing and other meta-learning methods in most datasets tested. In addition, we investigate the effect of various sample sizes and conclude that reduced sample sizes (as in rejection sampling) cannot be compensated by increasing the number of bagging iterations.

Keywords: meta-learning, cost-sensitive learning, decision trees, classification, data mining, machine learning.

1 Introduction

Classification is a primary task of inductive learning in machine learning. However, most original classification algorithms ignore different misclassification errors; or they implicitly assume that all misclassification errors cost equally. In many real-world applications, this assumption is not true. For example, in medical diagnosis, misdiagnosing a cancer patient as non-cancer is very serious than the other way around; the patient could die because of the delay in treatment.

Cost-sensitive classification [11, 5, 8, 10, 12] has received much attention in recent years. Many works have been done; and they can be categorized into two groups. One is to design cost-sensitive learning algorithms directly [11 4, 7]. Another is to make wrappers that convert existing cost-insensitive inductive learning algorithms into cost-sensitive ones. This method is called cost-sensitive meta-learning, such as MetaCost [3], Costing [14], and CostSensitiveClassifier [13]. Section 2 provides a more complete review of cost-sensitive meta-learning approaches.

These cost-sensitive meta-learning techniques are useful because they let us reuse existing inductive learning algorithms and their related improvements. *CSRoulette* (see Section 3 and 4) is another effective cost-sensitive meta-learning algorithm. *CSRoulette* is very similar to Costing, as they both are based on sampling. Costing is

J. N. Kok et al. (Eds.): ECML 2007, LNAI 4701, pp. 724–731, 2007.

based on rejection sampling [14]. The weakness of rejection sampling is that the size of resampled training set is reduced dramatically, and much useful information is thrown away in the preprocessing procedure.

To overcome this weakness, *CSRoulette* is based on a cost-sensitive sampling technique – cost proportionate roulette sampling (CPRS in short). CPRS is an improvement of the advanced sampling. It can generate samples of any sizes from the original dataset. By default it generates samples with the same size as the original dataset (details in Section 3).

We compare *CSRoulette* with Costing and other cost-sensitive meta-learning methods. The experimental results show that *CSRoulette* outperforms others (see Section 5.1). Furthermore, we investigate the effect of various sample sizes, and conclude that reduced sample sizes cannot be compensated by increasing the number of iterations in ensemble learning (see Section 5.2).

2 Related Work

Cost-sensitive meta-learning converts existing cost-insensitive learning algorithms into cost-sensitive ones without modifying them. Thus, all the cost-sensitive meta-learning techniques become middleware components that pre-process the training data for a cost-insensitive learning algorithm or post-process the output of a cost-insensitive learning algorithm.

Currently, cost-sensitive meta-learning techniques fall into three categories. The first is *relabeling* the classes of instances, by applying the minimum expected cost criterion [3]. This approach can be further divided into two branches: relabeling training instances and relabeling test instances. MetaCost [3] belongs to the former branch. CostSensitiveClassifier (called CSC in short) [13] belongs to the latter branch. The second category is *Weighting* [10]. It assigns a certain weight to each instance in terms of its class, according to the misclassification costs, such that the learning algorithm is in favor of the class with high weight/cost. The Third is *sampling*, which changes the distribution of the training data according to their costs. Both Costing [14] and *CSRoulette* belong to this category. Thus, we provide a detailed comparison between them in Section 5.

Costing [14] uses the advanced sampling - rejection sampling - to change the distribution of the training set according to the misclassification costs shown in a cost matrix $C(i,j)$. More specifically, each example in the original training set is drawn once, and accepted into the sample with the accepting probability $C(i)/Z$, where $C(i)$ is the misclassification cost of class i, and Z is an arbitrary constant chosen with the condition $max C(i) \leq Z$. However, we notice that rejection sampling has a shortcoming. The sample S' produced by rejection sampling is much smaller than the original training set S (i.e. $|S'| << |S|$); even the constant Z is set as $Z = max C(i)$ to maximize the size of the sample $|S'|$, if the misclassification costs are not equal or the dataset is imbalanced. The learning model built on the reduced samples is not stable (see Section 5.1). Apparently to reduce the instability, Costing [14] applies bagging [2] to the rejection sampling.

However, cost proportionate roulette sampling can generate samples with any size. If it generates samples with the same size as the original training set, it uses more available information in the training set. Thus, it can be expected that cost proportionate roulette sampling outperform rejection sampling.

3 Cost Proportionate Roulette Sampling (CPRS)

Roulette sampling is a stochastic sampling with replacement [6]. The training examples are mapped into segments of a line. The size of each segment is equal to the weight of the corresponding examples. The weight of each example is assigned according to the misclassification costs. To simplify this issue, we discuss binary classification here.

For binary classes, we assume we have the misclassification costs false positive (*FP*, the cost of misclassifying a negative instance into positive) and false negative (*FN*, the cost of misclassifying a positive instance into negative), and the cost of correct classification is zero. We simply assign *FP* as the weight to each negative instance, and assign *FN* as the weight to each positive instance. That is, the weight ratio of a positive instance to a negative instance is proportional to *FN/FP* [5].

In the cost proportional roulette sampling, we normalize their weights such that the sum of them equals to the number of instances. If we have a training set with *P* positive instances and *N* negative instances, then the weight of each negative instance is $\frac{FP\times(P+N)}{P\times FN+N\times FP}$, and the weight of each positive instance is $\frac{FN\times(P+N)}{P\times FN+N\times FP}$. Thus, the sum of the weights is $P+N$. That is, the length of the mapped line is $P+N$.

One of the important steps of roulette sampling is to select an example. Each time, roulette sampling generates a random number within the range of the length of the line. Then the example whose segment spans the random number is selected. The selection process does not stop until the total number of examples is reached. That is, users can indicate the size of samples generated by roulette sampling.

Like rejection sampling, roulette sampling makes use of the misclassification cost information. However, unlike rejection sampling, which draws examples independently from the distribution of the original training set, roulette sampling takes the distribution of original training set into consideration. In sum, roulette sampling integrates the effect of misclassification cost, the distribution of original training set, and the size of samples.

4 CPRS with Aggregation (CSRoulette)

Many researchers have shown that bagging (bootstrap aggregating) [2] can reliably improve base classifiers. Bagging is a voting process, which counts the votes from the base classifiers trained on different bootstrap samples. The bootstrap samples are generated from the original training set by uniformly sampling with replacement. In order to improve the performance of rejection sampling, Zadrozny et al. [14] take advantage of a voting algorithm, i.e., Costing, a procedure that is similar to bagging. Instead of using uniformly sampling with replacement, Costing uses rejection sampling to generate multiple samples and build a classifier on each sample.

Algorithm: *CSRoulette(T, B, C, I, x)*
Input: cost proportional roulette sampling (*CPRS*), training set *T*, based-classifier *B*, cost matrix *C*, a testing example *x*, and integer *I* (number of iterations of bootstrap).
For $r = 1$ to I do //build I classifiers
  $S' = CPRS\ (T, C)$
  Let $h_r = B(S')$
Output $h(x) = sign\ (\sum_{r=1}^{I} h_r(x))$

Fig. 1. Pseudo-code of *CSRoulette*

In the same way that Zadrozny et al. apply bagging to rejection sampling to become Costing, we also apply bagging on cost proportional roulette sampling. That is, we repeatedly perform cost proportional roulette sampling to generate multiple set $S'_1, \ldots, S'_i$ from the original training set *T*, and learn a classifier from each sampled set. The resulting method is called *CSRoulette*. The procedure of *CSRoulette* is shown in Figure 1.

5 Empirical Comparisons

To compare *CSRoulette* with Costing and other existing cost-sensitive meta-learning algorithms, we choose seventeen datasets (Breast-cancer, Breast-w, Car, Credit-g, Cylinder-bands, Diabetes, Heart-c, Heart-statlog, Hepatitis, Ionosphere, Labor, Molecular, Sick, Sonar, Spect, Spectf, and Tic-tac-toe) from the UCI Machine Learning Repository [1]. Since misclassification costs are not available for the datasets in the UCI Machine Learning Repository, we reasonably assign their values that are inversely proportional to the ratio of the number of class instances in the experiments. For each dataset in experiments, we set the misclassification cost ratio is inversely proportional to the number of positive/negative instances.

We choose C4.5 [9] as the base learning algorithm with Laplace correction. We first conduct experiments to compare *CSRoulette* with MetaCost, CSC, Weighting, and Costing. In order to maximize the size of the sample produced by rejection sampling in Costing, we set the constant $Z = maxC(i)$ in all following experiments. Furthermore, we also conduct experiments to investigate the effect of various sample sizes in *CPRS*.

5.1 Average Cost

The average cost is an ultimate measure for the performance of a cost-sensitive learning algorithm. It is the average misclassification cost of testing examples. In this section, we conduct experiments to compare *CSRoulette* (under default sample sizes) with Costing, MetaCost, CSC, and Weighting measured by the average cost. To be comparable with *CSRoulette* and Costing, we also apply bagging on MetaCost, CSC, and Weighting. The results are presented in terms of the average of the misclassification cost per test example via 10 runs over ten-fold cross-validation shown in Figure 2. The vertical axis represents the average cost, and the horizontal axis represents the number of iterations. The legends of the first dataset are shared by others.

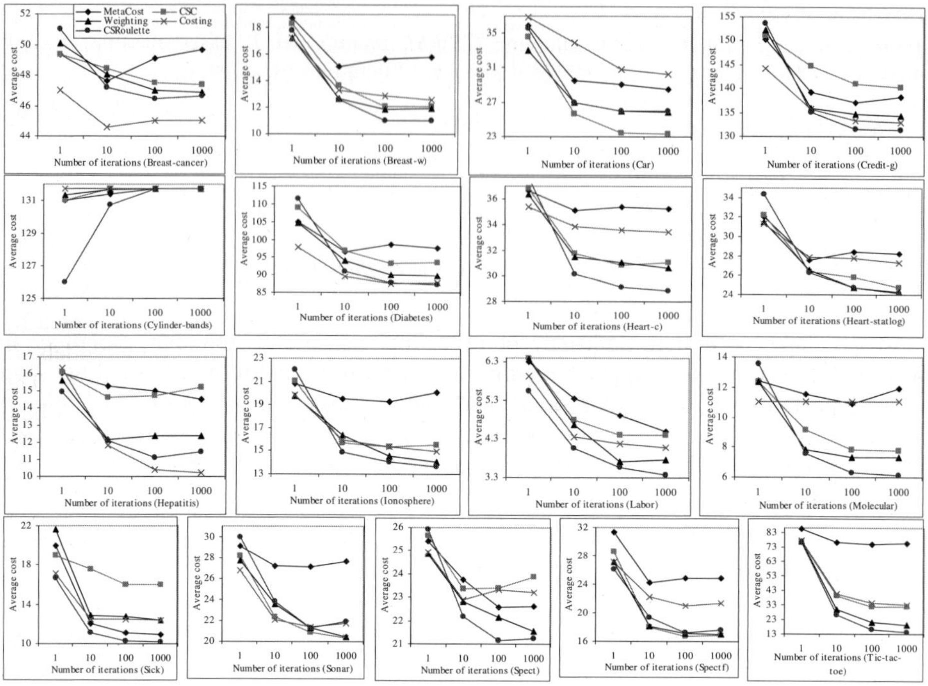

Fig. 2. Average cost of each dataset (the lower, the better)

We can draw the following interesting conclusions from the results shown in Figure 2. First of all, MetaCost is almost always the worst (twelve out of seventeen datasets). Bagging does improve its performance. However, the improvement is not as significant as bagging applied on *CSRoulette*, Costing, CSC, and Weighting. Second, CSC performs better than Costing on nine datasets. In other datasets, it is similar or worse. Third, only in three datasets (Car, Sick and Sonar) is CSC better than Weighting. In all other datasets, it is similar or worse. Fourth, overall, *CSRoulette* and Weighting perform better than MetaCost, Costing, and CSC. However, *CSRoulette* performs better than Weighting in thirteen out of seventeen datasets. In others, it is similar to Weighting in three datasets (Car, Heart-statlog and Spectf). It per-forms worse only in the dataset Sonar.

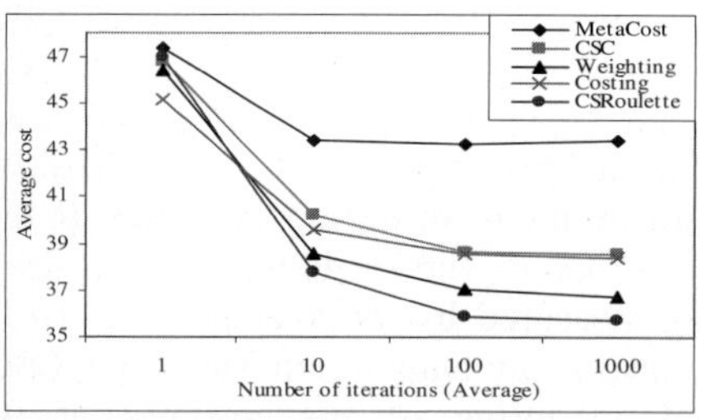

Fig. 3. The average cost over the seventeen datasets of meta-learning algorithms (the lower, the better)

From above individual analysis for the seventeen datasets in our experiments, we can conclude that *CSRoulette* performs better than Weighting, Weighting does better than CSC and Costing, and CSC and Costing do better than MetaCost.

We further summarize the experimental results in average over all the datasets represented in Figure 3. The results in Figure 3 agree with our conclusion made from the analysis for all seventeen datasets in previous paragraphy and show quantitively that *CSRoulette* is the best, followed by Weighing and followed by CSC and Costing. MetaCost is the worst.

5.2 Sample Size vs. Number of Bagging

We further investigate the effect of the size of the sample on the cost-sensitive sampling techniques between *CSRoulette* and Costing. *CPRS* (cost proportional roulette sampling) can generate any sample sizes according to the size indicated by users. Thus, *CSRoulette* can use the various sizes samples to build learning models. In Costing, we use maximum sample size generated by rejection sampling. The maximum sample size for each dataset is listed in the following table (Table 1), where $k = |S'| / |S|$, where $|S'|$ is the maximum sample size, and $|S|$ is the size of the original data. For *CSRoulette*, we generate samples under four different sizes indicated ($0.2\times|S|$, $0.5\times|S|$, $1\times|S|$, $2\times|S|$, and $5\times|S|$). Note that when $k=0.5$, the size of the sample generated by *CPRS* is similar to the maximum size of most samples generated by rejection sampling (see Table 1).

Table 1. The ratio of the maximum sample size of the *i*th dataset shown in Figure 2 over its original size with the rejection sampling. The 12th dataset (Molecular) is absolute balanced.

1	2	3	4	5	6	7	8	9	10	11	12	13	14	15	16	17
0.59	0.69	0.60	0.60	0.84	0.70	0.91	0.89	0.41	0.72	0.70	1.00	0.12	0.93	0.41	0.54	0.69

From the above table, we can see that the maximum sample size generated by rejection sampling of each dataset is less than the original training set, particularly in the dataset Sick. This is one of reasons why *CSRoulette* performs much better than Costing in Section 5.1. That is, the sample size affects the quality of the cost-sensitive classifier, as *CPRS* generates samples with the same size of the dataset. Does the original training set size is optimum for the sample generated? Or does each dataset have its own optimal sample size for cost sensitive sampling techniques (such as cost proportional roulette sampling used in *CSRoulette*)? Can we compensate the effect of reduced sample sizes by increasing the number of iterations in bagging? To investigate this question we conduct experiments controlling the number of iterations for different sample sizes to make the total training size equal. The total training size is defined as the sample size multiples the number of iterations. To be specific, if we have i iterations for the sample size $|S|$, the total training size is $i\times|S|$. Thus, for the sample size $0.5\times|S|$, we have to iterate $2i$ times to make its total training size as $i\times|S|$. We compare Costing (with its maximum sample size) and *CSRoulette* (with five different sample sizes). The detail experimental results could not be shown here as the limited space.

Generally, our experimental results show that bagging could not compensate the effect of small sample sizes. In eleven out of seventeen datasets (Breast-w, Car, Cylinder-bands, Hepatitis, Ionosphere, Labor, Sick, Sonar, Spect, Spectf, and Tic-tac-toe), bagging could not compensate the effect of the small sample sizes. For these datasets, larger sample sizes are preferred. Although in six out of seventeen datasets (such as Breast-cancer, Credit-g, Diabetes, Heart-c, Heart-statlog, and Molecular), *CSRoulette* prefers small sample sizes with more iterations of bagging.

CSRoulette outperforms Costing in most cases. *CSRoulette* can generate samples with different sizes. For most sample sizes, *CSRoulette* have a lower average cost compared to Costing. Even when the sample size of *CSRoulette* is similar (when k=0.5) to the sample size of Costing, *CSRoulette* still performs better than Costing.

We further summarize the experimental results in average in Figure 4. Its vertical axis represents the average cost (the lower, the better), and its horizontal axis represents the total training size. The results are represented in terms of the average of misclassification cost per test example of 10 runs over ten-fold cross validation. There are five curves in each figure, one for Costing, and four for *CSRoulette* (with size $k \times |S|$, where $k=0.2$, 0.5, 1.0, 2.0, and 5.0 respectively).

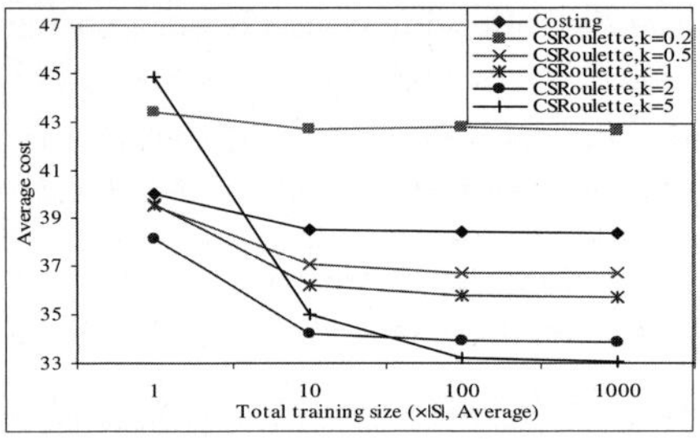

Fig. 4. The average cost over all seventeen datasets of Costing and *CSRoulette* under different cases (the lower, the better)

From Figure 4, we can see that *CSRoulette* and Costing perform better when the total training size increases. Under the same total training size, *CSRoulette* performs better when the sample size increases. However, when the sample size increases from twice to five times of the sizes of original training sets, *CSRoulette* performs similarly. We can also see that *CSRoulette* performs badly without bagging (i.e., bagging iteration is 1) when the sample size is five times (i.e., the curve of *CSRoulette, k=5*) of that of original training set. When we further increase the iterations, the average costs of all curves do not further go down. Thus, we can conclude that bagging is useful, but it could not compensate the effect of small sample sizes.

6 Conclusions and Future Work

In this paper, we propose a new cost-sensitive meta-learning algorithm *CSRoulette*. It is based on the cost proportional roulette sampling technique, called *CPRS*. It overcomes the shortcomings of rejection sampling. Rejection sampling reduces significantly the sample size of an original training set. *CPRS* can generate different size samples according to users' indication. If it generates samples with the same size as the original training set by default, it makes better use of the available information in the training set.

Similar to Costing, *CSRoulette* takes advantage of ensemble learning to further improve the performance of cost proportional roulette sampling. The experimental results show that *CSRoulette* outperforms Costing in most cases. Comparing with other cost-sensitive meta-learning algorithms (MetaCost, CSC, and Weighting), *CSRoulette* also performs better. In general, we can conclude that *CSRoulette* is the best, followed by Weighting, followed by CSC and Costing. MetaCost is the worst

Our experiment results indicate that the best sample size is a characteristic of a dataset. The effect of small sample size could not be compensated by increasing the iterations of bagging, although bagging is useful to improve the performance of all the meta-learning cost-sensitive algorithms.

In our future work, we will further investigate the performance of *CSRoulette* by searching its best sample size for each dataset and compare it with other cost-sensitive learning algorithms under different cost ratios.

References

1. Blake, C.L., Merz, C.J.: UCI Repository of machine learning databases (website). University of California, Department of Information and Computer Science, Irvine, CA (1998)
2. Breiman, L.: Bagging predictors. Machine Learning 24, 123–140 (1996)
3. Domingos, P.: MetaCost: A general method for making classifiers cost-sensitive. In: Proceedings of the Fifth International Conference on Knowledge Discovery and Data Mining, pp. 155–164. ACM Press, New York (1999)
4. Drummond, C., Holte, R.: Exploiting the cost (in)sensitivity of decision tree splitting criteria. In: Proceedings of the 17th International Conference on Machine Learning, pp. 239–246 (2000)
5. Elkan, C.: The foundations of cost-sensitive learning. In: Proceedings of the Seventeenth International Joint Conference of Artificial Intelligence, pp. 973–978. Morgan Kaufmann, Seattle, Washington (2001)
6. Goldberg, D.E.: Genetic Algorithm in Search, Optimization and Machine Learning. Addison-Wesley Publishing Company, Inc., Reading, Massachusetts (1989)
7. Ling, C.X., Yang, Q., Wang, J., Zhang, S.: Decision trees with minimal costs. In: Proceedings of the Twenty-First International Conference on Machine Learning, Morgan Kaufmann, Banff, Alberta (2004)
8. Lizotte, D., Madani, O., Greiner, R.: Budgeted learning of naïve-Bayes classifiers. In: Proceedings of the Nineteenth Conference on Uncertainty in Artificial Intelligence, Morgan Kaufmann, Acapulco, Mexico (2003)
9. Quinlan, J.R. (ed.): C4.5: Programs for Machine Learning. Morgan Kaufmann, San Francisco (1993)
10. Ting, K.M.: Inducing cost-sensitive trees via instance weighting. In: Proceedings of the Second European Symposium on Principles of Data Mining and Knowledge Discovery, pp. 23–26. Springer, Heidelberg (1998)
11. Turney, P.D.: Cost-sensitive classification: empirical evaluation of a hybrid genetic decision tree induction algorithm. Journal of Artificial Intelligence Research 2, 369–409 (1995)
12. Weiss, G., Provost, F.: Learning when training data are costly: the effect of class distribution on tree induction. Journal of Artificial Intelligence Research 19, 315–354 (2003)
13. Witten, I.H., Frank, E.: Data Mining – Practical Machine Learning Tools and Techniques with Java Implementations. Morgan Kaufmann Publishers, San Francisco (2005)
14. Zadrozny, B., Langford, J., Abe, N.: Cost-sensitive learning by cost-proportionate instance weighting. In: Proceedings of the 3th International Conference on Data Mining (2003)

Modeling Highway Traffic Volumes

Tomáš Šingliar and Miloš Hauskrecht

Computer Science Dept, University of Pittsburgh, Pittsburgh, PA 15260
{tomas,milos}@cs.pitt.edu

Abstract. Most traffic management and optimization tasks, such as accident detection or optimal vehicle routing, require an ability to adequately model, reason about and predict irregular and stochastic behavior. Our goal is to create a probabilistic model of traffic flows on highway networks that is realistic from the point of applications and at the same time supports efficient learning and inference. We study several multivariate probabilistic models and analyze their respective strengths. To balance accuracy and efficiency, we propose a novel learning model, mixture of Gaussian trees, and show its advantages in learning and inference. All models are evaluated on real-world traffic flow data from highways of the Pittsburgh area.

1 Introduction

The importance of road transportation systems to our daily lives can hardly be overstated. To facilitate monitoring and management of their complexities, sensors collecting traffic information (such as traffic volumes and speeds) are installed on many roads. Today, coverage is good for major highways in many metropolitan areas and traffic sensor deployment is rapidly increasing worldwide.

Road networks exhibit strong interaction patterns among traffic variables and traffic is subject to stochastic fluctuations. The ability to adequately model, reason about and predict stochastic behavior is crucial to computational support of many traffic management tasks, such as traffic routing, congestion analysis and accident detection. The objective of our work is to develop models of large multivariate continuous probability distributions describing vehicular traffic. We require that the models be compactly parameterized and admit efficient inference and learning algorithms.

The quantities of primary interest in this paper are traffic flows. Traffic flow is defined as the number of vehicles passing a point on a highway in a unit of time. Traffic flows in the highway network are typically modeled with Gaussian densities [1]. An assumption very often made in stochastic analysis of a network system is that the components of the system behave independently. The multivariate probabilistic model of the network then factorizes to a product of univariate distributions that are easy to learn and reason with. Unfortunately, the assumption of full independence is unrealistic and ignores strong interaction patterns between traffic variables observable in real data. On the other hand, the full-covariance model is too complex to learn reliably from limited data.

J.N. Kok et al. (Eds.): ECML 2007, LNAI 4701, pp. 732–739, 2007.

Consequently, we seek models between the two extremes that provide the right balance between model complexity and accuracy. The ideal model captures the important dependencies and at the same time remains tractable.

Intuitively, vehicles on distant roadways do not interact and the dependency patterns must be "local" and closely tied to the topology of the physical road network. In this work we study two models that attempt to capture only the key local interactions: the *conditional autoregressive (CAR) model* [2], and our novel approach with *mixture of Gaussian trees.*

We analyze and compare all models on real-world traffic data collected at 75 sensor locations on major highways in the Pittsburgh metropolitan region. We demonstrate that the new model represents the sought middle ground for Pittsburgh traffic network data.

2 Gaussian Models

The Gaussian probability distribution appears to be particularly suitable for modeling traffic volumes [1]. The number of cars passing during a given interval can be thought of as a result of a stochastic process in which drivers choose to take the particular segment with a probability, resulting in a binomial distribution of the number of observed cars. The binomial distribution, for large N, is well approximated by the computationally favorable Gaussian. The multivariate Gaussian model is characterized by its mean $\boldsymbol{\mu}$ and covariance matrix $\boldsymbol{\Sigma}$. The parameters are usually learned from observed traffic data using maximum-likelihood estimates. The estimate quality depends on the number N of datapoints available. The number of free parameters in the covariance matrix grows quadratically with the number of sensors, adversely impacting the variance of the parameter estimates.

The model-complexity problem of the full multivariate Gaussian model is often avoided by assuming that all variables are independent, i.e. the covariance matrix is restricted to be diagonal. As a result, the learning problem decomposes to D univariate learning problems, where D is the dimensionality of the data. The advantage of the approach is that the number of free parameters is linear in the number of sensors. The drawback is that ignoring all interactions is unrealistic for traffic networks that exhibit strong correlation between readings of neighboring sensors.

3 The Conditional Autoregressive Model

Traffic flows at places not directly adjacent will not influence each other except via the situation on a road segment(s) connecting them. In other words, the Markov property [3] holds. The popular conditional autoregressive (CAR) model [2] embodies this intuition about locality. The model assumes that the volume y observed at location s obeys:

$$y(s) = \epsilon_s + \sum_{r \in N(s)} \theta_r^s y(r), \tag{1}$$

where $N(s)$ denotes the neighborhood of s and $\epsilon_s \sim \mathcal{N}(0, \sigma_s^2)$ is additive noise. We fit the model parameters $\boldsymbol{\theta}$ using a ridge-regression procedure [4].

The limitation of the CAR model is that the conditional probabilities need not define a proper probabilistic model [5]. Even if it exists, the joint distribution may be intractable and the most natural way to obtain proper probabilities from the CAR model is Gibbs sampling [6].

4 Mixture of Gaussian Trees

Bayesian networks [7] are an elegant formalism for capturing probabilistic dependencies. A Bayesian network consists of a directed *acyclic* graph and a probability specification. In the directed graph, each node corresponds to a random variable, while edges define the decomposition of the represented joint probability distribution:

$$p(X) = \prod_{i=1}^{D} p(x_i|pa(x_i)),$$

where $pa(X_i)$ are the parents of X_i in the graph. The probability specification is the set of conditional distributions $p(X_i|pa(X_i))$, $i = 1, \ldots, D$. Intuitively (but not exactly), an edge in a Bayesian network represents a causal influence of the parent on the child. However, traffic congestions are subject to cyclic interaction patterns (e.g., gridlocking) that cannot be directly modeled with a Bayesian network.

One way to address the problem of cyclic interactions is to approximate the underlying distribution with a simpler dependence structure that permits both efficient learning and inference. Having the maximum number of edges without introducing cycles, tree structures are a natural choice. By committing to a single tree, we capture the maximum number of dependencies without introducing a cycle; but inevitably, some dependencies will be ignored. In the *mixture of trees* model [8], the missed dependencies may be accounted for by the remaining mixture components.

Meilă developed the model in a discrete variable setting. In this work we propose the *mixture of Gaussian trees (MGT)* model where Gaussian instead of discrete variables are used. The mixture of Gaussian trees consists of:

- a collection of m trees with identical vertex sets $T_1 = (X, E_1), \ldots, T_m = (X, E_m)$, where each node $v \in V_k$ with parent x_u has a conditional probability function such that $x_v \sim \mathcal{N}(\mu + c_v x_u, \sigma_v)$. Note that it is always possible to orient a tree so that each node has at most one parent.
- mixture weights $\boldsymbol{\lambda} = (\lambda_1, \ldots, \lambda_m)$ such that $\sum_{k=1}^{m} \lambda_i = 1$.

Let $T_k(\mathbf{x})$ denote the probability of $\mathbf{x}$ under the distribution implied by the tree Bayesian network T_k. The joint probability for the mixture model is then:

$$p(x) = \sum_{k=1}^{m} \lambda_k T_k(x). \tag{2}$$

4.1 Inference in the MGT Model

Any probabilistic query in the form $p(\mathbf{y}|\mathbf{e})$ can be answered from the joint distribution (Equation 2) by taking:

$$p(\mathbf{y}|\mathbf{e}) = \frac{p(\mathbf{y},\mathbf{e})}{p(\mathbf{e})} = \frac{\sum_i \lambda_i T_i(\mathbf{y},\mathbf{e})}{\sum_i \lambda_i T_i(\mathbf{e})} \tag{3}$$

Both the numerator and denominator represent m instances of inference in tree Gaussian networks, which is a linear-complexity problem [9].

4.2 Learning in the MGT Model

The maximum likelihood parameters for the MGT model can be obtained by the EM algorithm. Three quantities must be estimated in each M-step: (1) the structure of trees that constitute the mixture components, (2) their parameterization and (3) the mixture proportions. Let $\gamma_k(n)$ denote the posterior mixture proportion:

$$\gamma_k(n) = \frac{\lambda_k T_k(\mathbf{x}^n)}{\sum_i \lambda_i T_i(\mathbf{x}^n)}.$$

The $\gamma_k(n)$s can be interpreted as "responsibility" of tree k for the n-th datapoint. Computing $\gamma_k(n)$s constitutes the E-step. The quantity $\Gamma_k = \sum_{n=1}^{N} \gamma_k(n)$ takes on the meaning of the expected count of datapoints that T_k is responsible for generating. Let us also define the distribution P_k associated with T_k over the set of datapoints by $P_k(x^n) = \frac{\gamma_k(n)}{\Gamma_k}$.

In the M-step, we need to update three quantities: the tree structures, their parameters and the mixture proportions.

The **tree structures** are selected using a variant of the Chow-Liu procedure [10]. The Chow-Liu procedure selects a tree model T such that the KL-divergence (or equivalently, the cross-entropy) between the responsibilities computed in the E-step and the tree distribution is minimized:

$$T_k^{new} = \operatorname*{argmax}_{T_k} \sum_{i=1}^{N} P_k(x^i) \log T_k(x^i). \tag{4}$$

This is accomplished by finding a Maximum Weight Spanning Tree (MWST), where the edges are weighted by the mutual information between variables they connect. The structure update for the tree T_k requires that we compute the mutual information between all variables $x_u, x_v \in X$. In the continuous case, this is computationally infeasible without making a distributional assumption. We therefore treat $P_k(x^i)$ as a sample from a Gaussian and compute the mutual information in closed form:

$$I_k(x_u, x_v) = -\frac{1}{2} \log(|\hat{\Sigma}_k|/(\sigma_u^2 \sigma_v^2)), \tag{5}$$

where $\hat{\Sigma}_k$ is the maximum likelihood estimate of the 2×2 covariance matrix and σ_u^2 and σ_v^2 are its diagonal elements. After we have determined the optimal structure, we orient the tree by picking a vertex at random and directing all the edges away from it. In this manner we achieve that every vertex has at most one parent. Mutual information is symmetrical, which means that any orientation of edges yields an optimal spanning tree.

Parameter learning. It is unsurprising to derive that the M-step update for $\boldsymbol{\lambda}$ is to match the expected empirical marginal: $\lambda_k = \frac{\Gamma_k}{N}$.

Consider an arc $u \rightarrow v$ and recall that $x_v \sim N(\mu_v + c_v x_u, \sigma_v)$. We have data in the form $D_{uv} = \{(x_u^{(i)}, x_v^{(i)}, w^{(i)})\}_{i=1}^N$, where the weight $w^{(i)}$ corresponds to $P_k(x^i)$ computed in the E-step. We can update the parameters of v, denoted $\theta_v = \{\mu_v, c_v, \sigma_v\}$, by maximizing the likelihood of the data $P(D_{uv}|\theta_v)$. We obtain that the update of μ_v and c_v is the solution of the following linear system:

$$\left(\begin{array}{cc|c} \sum_{n=1}^N w_v^{(i)} & \sum_{i=1}^N x_u^{(i)} w_v^{(i)} & \sum_{i=1}^N x_v^{(i)} w_v^{(i)} \\ \sum_{i=1}^N x_u^{(i)} w_v^{(i)} & \sum_{i=1}^N x_u^{(i)} x_u^{(i)} w_v^{(i)} & \sum_{i=1}^N x_v^{(i)} x_u^{(i)} w_v^{(i)} \end{array}\right). \tag{6}$$

Knowing μ_v and c_v we can estimate σ^2:

$$\sigma_v^2 = \left(\sum_{n=1}^N w_v^{(i)}\right)^{-1} \sum_{i=1}^N (x_v^{(i)} - \mu_v - c_v x_u^{(i)})^2 w_v^{(i)} \tag{7}$$

E- and M- step are alternated until the expected complete log-likelihood stabilizes.

Model selection. The parameter that remains to be chosen is the number of mixture components (trees). We propose that the search be performed by learning the model with increasing number of components until the Bayesian Information Criterion (BIC) no longer decreases. The BIC is defined as an approximation to the integrated likelihood [11]:

$$BIC(k) = -2 \ln p(\mathcal{D}|k, \hat{\theta}_k) + \psi_k \ln N \tag{8}$$

where $\hat{\theta}_k$ is the ML estimate of parameters and ψ_k is the number of free parameters in model with k components.

5 Experimental Evaluation

The data was collected by 75 sensors monitoring Pittsburgh highways. Each datapoint is thus a vector consisting of the numbers of vehicles passing the respective sensors during a five-minute interval. The dataset contains all measurements at a fixed time of all workdays throughout one year. The correlations between sensors are high and we expect that this will be a challenging dataset for the structure search algorithms, causing them to capture spurious correlations.

5.1 Evaluation Metrics

In order to assess the quality of distribution modeling, we use three metrics: a log-likelihood score, relative error and coefficient of determination. The complexity of the model is accounted for by also reporting the BIC score obtained in training of the model. The data is divided into the training and testing set. After the model is trained on the training set, some variables in each datapoint of the testing set are chosen to be hidden; they will be denoted by $h^{(n)}$, while the remaining – observed variables will be denoted by $e^{(n)}$. Denote the set of hidden variables by H.

We compute the log-likelihood score

$$LLS(H|\theta_M) = \sum_{n=1}^{N} \log p(h^{(n)}|e^{(n)}, \theta_M) \tag{9}$$

This score reflects how well the model predicts the set of chosen values, given the remaining observations. As this measure is computed on a subset of the unseen test set and the sample space of observables in all models is the same, it is not skewed by the different complexity of the models.

The coefficient of determination is a classical measure of predictor quality and can be interpreted as the proportion of the data variance explained by the model. It is obtained as $1 - RSS/TSS$. Denoting the actually observed value of the hidden variable h by $x(h)$ and the model's prediction by $y(h)$, the residual sum of squares is $RSS = \sum_{h \in H}(x(h) - y(h))^2$. The prediction given by model M is defined to be the mean of $p(h^{(n)}|e^{(n)}, M, \theta_M)$. The total sum of squares is defined as $TSS = \sum\limits_{h \in H} (y(h) - E(y(h)))^2$.

The relative error is defined naturally as $e_{rel} = |x(h) - y(h)|/x(h)$.

We argue that multivariate metrics such as the LLS, which considers all hidden values in a particular datapoint jointly, reflect the model prediction quality better and should be given more weight than the univariate scores such as the coefficient of determination, which look at each missing value in isolation.

5.2 Experiment Setup and Parameters

The product of univariate Gaussians is learned using the ML estimate of mean and variance for each dimension separately. Conditioning is trivial for the model: $p(h^{(n)}|e^{(n)}, \mu, \sigma) = p(h^{(n)}|\mu, \sigma)$.

The full covariance Gaussians are parameterized from the data by the maximum likelihood estimates. Conditionals are obtained as $p(h^{(n)}|e^{(n)} = f, \boldsymbol{\mu}, \boldsymbol{\Sigma}) = \mathcal{N}(\overline{\boldsymbol{\mu}}, \overline{\boldsymbol{\Sigma}})$, where $\overline{\boldsymbol{\mu}} = \boldsymbol{\mu}_h - \boldsymbol{\Sigma}_{he}\boldsymbol{\Sigma}_{ee}^{-1}(\boldsymbol{\mu}_e - f)$, $\overline{\boldsymbol{\Sigma}} = \boldsymbol{\Sigma}_{hh} - \boldsymbol{\Sigma}_{he}\boldsymbol{\Sigma}_{ee}^{-1}\boldsymbol{\Sigma}_{eh}$ and $\boldsymbol{\Sigma}_{..}$ are the respective block submatrices of $\boldsymbol{\Sigma}$.

Since the CAR model may not define a proper distribution, we obtain a large number (10^6) of samples with the Gibbs sampler and fit a multivariate Gaussian to compute the likelihood.

Table 1. The likelihood scores (larger is better), and BIC scores (smaller is better), relative errors (smaller is better) and coefficients of determination (larger is better). The parenthesized numbers are the standard deviations across test splits.

Method	# prms	LLS	BIC	Relat err	Coef of det
$N(\mu, \boldsymbol{\Sigma})$	2,925	$-8,448(664.2)$	186,910 (6,751)	0.039(0.0022)	0.889(0.012)
$N(\mu, \text{diag}(\boldsymbol{\sigma}))$	150	$-13,314(1,036.3)$	197,910 (7,361)	0.073(0.0050)	0.638(0.019)
CAR	1,277	$-8,162(598.3)$	203,126 (5,970)	0.037(0.0023)	0.868(0.016)
SingleTree	224	$-8,282(616.6)$	13,667 (784.1)	0.057(0.0056)	0.765(0.050)
MixTrees(2)	449	$-8,176(638.6)$	17,159 (4,299)	0.053(0.0050)	0.766(0.052)
MixTrees(3)	674	$-8,158(632.0)$	24,562 (12,995)	0.055(0.0141)	0.704(0.176)
MixTrees(5)	1,124	$-8,226(624.2)$	67,787 (32,787)	0.197(0.4567)	0.305(0.341)

We learn the Mixture of Gaussian Trees (MGT) model using the EM algorithm described in Section 4, using 1,2,3 and 5 mixture components. The LL score is computed by conditional inference as described in Section 4.1.

In the reported experiment, 20% of the values are omitted at random from the testing set; the values omitted are fixed across the methods so that each method encounters the same set of missing data. This ensures comparability of the quality metrics across the methods. The statistics from 20 train/test splits are shown in Table 1.

5.3 Results

Evaluation results show that the mixture-of-trees model performed the best. The 3-component MGT yielded the best score, closely followed by the conditional autoregressive model. However, the MT model achieves this performance with much fewer parameters. The difference is reflected in the BIC complexity penalty. The BIC suggests that even a single-tree model might be appropriate, although the likelihood is lower for mixtures of 2 and 3 trees. Further in favor of the mixture model, the MGT model also has an embedded structure-learning component, while the CAR model operates with informed pre-defined neighborhoods. Therefore MGT achieves this performance with less prior information. MGT is very good at modeling the training data, yielding low BIC scores. This can lead to some amount of overfitting: the 5-component MGT shows signs of testing performance deterioration.

The relative error results confirm our original intuition that the MGT stands between the full and independent Gaussian in performance and complexity.

We note the disproportionately high BIC scores of the full-Gaussian, independent Gaussian and CAR models. In the independent Gaussian case, this is caused by poor modeling of the dependencies in data. On the other hand, the full Gaussian and CAR models suffer a high complexity penalty.

This cautions us that normally we do not have the data to fit a full covariance Gaussian. A variety of factors is observable in traffic networks, of which the most obvious is the variability with the time of day. The correct way to deal with observable factors is to condition on them, which cuts down the training data severely. The full covariance Gaussian will likely meet scaling-up problems in such context.

6 Conclusions

We developed and presented a new mixture of Gaussian trees model that provides a middle ground in between the data-hungry full covariance and the unrealistic all-independent Gaussian models. We have explored several other methods for modeling traffic density and used a predictive likelihood measure to compare their performance. If data are plentiful, the full-covariance Gaussian can be estimated with a high accuracy. However, in the more realistic case when data is scarce, our mixture-of-trees model, with a number of parameters that increases linearly with the dimension of the dataset, offers itself as the method of choice.

Many interesting research issues remain open. For example, when learning from small sample-size datasets, it would be advantageous to generalize the Bayesian version of the MT learning algorithm [12] to handle the distributions in the exponential family (including Gaussians that we used here). Automatic model complexity selection and greater resistance to overfit are among the expected benefits of applying the Bayesian framework.

References

1. Belomestny, D., Jentsch, V., Schreckenberg, M.: Completion and continuation of nonlinear traffic time series: a probabilistic approach. Journal of Physics A: Math. Gen. 36, 11369–11383 (2003)
2. Besag, J., York, J., Mollie, A.: Bayesian Image Restoration With Two Applications In Spatial Statistics. Annals of the Institute of Statistical Mathematics 43(1), 1–59 (1991)
3. Lauritzen, S.L.: Graphical Models. Oxford University Press (1996)
4. Hastie, T., Tibshirani, R., Friedman, J.: Elements of Statistical Learning. Springer, Heidelberg (2001)
5. Chellappa, R., Jain, A. (eds.): Markov Random Fields - Theory and Applications. Academic Press, London (1993)
6. Doucet, A., de Freitas, N., Gordon, N.: Sequential Monte Carlo Methods in Practice. Springer, New York (2001)
7. Jensen, F.V.: An Introduction to Bayesian Networks. Springer, New York (1996)
8. Meilă-Predoviciu, M.: Learning with mixtures of trees. PhD thesis, MIT (1999)
9. Shachter, R., Kenley, R.: Gaussian influence diagrams. Management Science 35(5), 527–550 (1989)
10. Chow, C.J.K., Liu, C.N.: Approximating discrete probability distributions with dependence trees. IEEE Trans. on Inf. Theory 14(3), 462–467 (1968)
11. Schwarz, G.: Estimating the dimension of a model. Annals of Statistics 6, 461–464 (1978)
12. Meilă, M., Jaakkola, T.: Tractable Bayesian learning of tree belief networks. Technical Report CMU–RI–TR–00–15, Carnegie Mellon University Robotics Institute (2000)

Undercomplete Blind Subspace Deconvolution Via Linear Prediction

Zoltán Szabó, Barnabás Póczos, and András Lőrincz

Department of Information Systems, Eötvös Loránd University,
Pázmány P. sétány 1/C, Budapest H-1117, Hungary
szzoli@cs.elte.hu, pbarn@cs.elte.hu, andras.lorincz@elte.hu

Abstract. We present a novel solution technique for the blind subspace deconvolution (BSSD) problem, where temporal convolution of multidimensional hidden independent components is observed and the task is to uncover the hidden components using the observation only. We carry out this task for the undercomplete case (uBSSD): we reduce the original uBSSD task via linear prediction to independent subspace analysis (ISA), which we can solve. As it has been shown recently, applying temporal concatenation can also reduce uBSSD to ISA, but the associated ISA problem can easily become 'high dimensional' [1]. The new reduction method circumvents this dimensionality problem. We perform detailed studies on the efficiency of the proposed technique by means of numerical simulations. We have found several advantages: our method can achieve high quality estimations for smaller number of samples and it can cope with deeper temporal convolutions.

1 Introduction

There is a growing interest in independent component analysis (ICA) and blind source deconvolution (BSD) for signal processing and hidden component searches. For recent reviews on ICA and BSD see [2] and [3], respectively. The traditional example of ICA is the so-called *cocktail-party problem*, where there are D pieces of *one-dimensional* sound sources and D microphones and the task is to separate the original sources from the observed mixed signals. Clearly, applications where not all, but only certain groups of the sources are independent may have high relevance in practice. For example, there could be *independent rock bands* playing at a party. This is the independent subspace analysis (ISA) extension of ICA [4]. Strenuous efforts have been made to develop ISA algorithms, where the theoretical problems concern mostly (i) the estimation of the entropy or of the mutual information, or (ii) joint block diagonalization. A recent list of possible ISA solution techniques can be found in [1].

Another extension of the original ICA task is the BSD problem [3], where the observation is a temporal mixture of the hidden components (*echoic cocktail party*). A novel task, the blind subspace deconvolution (BSSD) [1] arises if we combine the ISA and the BSD assumptions. One can think of this task as the separation problem of the pieces played simultaneously by independent rock

J.N. Kok et al. (Eds.): ECML 2007, LNAI 4701, pp. 740–747, 2007.

bands in an echoic stadium. One of the most stringent applications of BSSD could be the analysis of EEG or fMRI signals. The ICA assumptions could be highly problematic here, because some sources may depend on each other, so an ISA model seems better. Furthermore, the passing of information from one area to another and the related delayed and transformed activities may be modeled as echoes. Thus, one can argue that BSSD may fit this important problem domain better than ICA or even ISA. It has been shown in [1] that the undercomplete BSSD task (uBSSD)—where in terms of the cocktail-party problem there are more microphones than acoustic sources—can be reduced to ISA by means of temporal concatenation. However, the reduction technique may lead to 'high dimensions' in the associated ISA problem. Here, an alternative reduction method is introduced for uBSSD and this solution avoids the increase of ISA dimensions. Namely, we show that one can apply linear prediction to reduce the uBSSD task to ISA such that the dimension of the associated ISA problem equals to the dimension of the original hidden sources. As an additional advantage, we shall see that this reduction principle is more efficient on problems with deeper temporal convolutions.

The paper is built as follows: Section 2 formulates the problem domain. Section 3 shows how to reduce the uBSSD task to an ISA problem. Section 4 contains the numerical illustrations. Section 5 contains a short summary.

2 The BSSD Model

We define the BSSD task in Section 2.1. Earlier BSSD reduction principles are reviewed in Section 2.2.

2.1 The BSSD Equations

Here, we define the BSSD task. Assume that we have M hidden, independent, multidimensional *components* (random variables). Suppose also that only their casual FIR filtered mixture is available for observation:

$$\mathbf{x}(t) = \sum_{l=0}^{L} \mathbf{H}_l \mathbf{s}(t-l), \tag{1}$$

where $\mathbf{s}(t) = \left[\mathbf{s}^1(t); \ldots; \mathbf{s}^M(t)\right] \in \mathbb{R}^{Md}$ is a vector concatenated of components $\mathbf{s}^m(t) \in \mathbb{R}^d$. Here, for the sake of notational simplicity we used identical dimension for each component. For a given m, $\mathbf{s}^m(t)$ is i.i.d. (independent and identically distributed) in time t, there is at most a single Gaussian component in $\mathbf{s}^m$s, and $I(\mathbf{s}^1, \ldots, \mathbf{s}^M) = 0$, where I stands for the mutual information of the arguments. The total dimension of the components is $D_s := Md$, the dimension of the observation $\mathbf{x}$ is D_x. Matrices $\mathbf{H}_l \in \mathbb{R}^{D_x \times D_s}$ $(l = 0, \ldots, L)$ describe the convolutive mixing. Without any loss of generality it may be assumed that $E[\mathbf{s}] = \mathbf{0}$, where E denotes the expectation value. Then $E[\mathbf{x}] = \mathbf{0}$ holds, as well. The goal of the BSSD problem is to estimate the original source $\mathbf{s}(t)$ by using observations $\mathbf{x}(t)$ only. The case $L = 0$ corresponds to the ISA task, and if $d = 1$ also holds then the ICA task is recovered. In the BSD task $d = 1$ and L is a non-negative integer. $D_x > D_s$ is the *undercomplete*, $D_x = D_s$ is the *complete*, and $D_x < D_s$ is the *overcomplete* task. Here, we treat the undercomplete BSSD (uBSSD) problem.

For consecutive reductional steps we rewrite the BSSD model using operators. Let $\mathbf{H}[z] := \sum_{l=0}^{L} \mathbf{H}_l z^{-l} \in \mathbb{R}[z]^{D_x \times D_s}$ denote the $D_x \times D_s$ polynomial matrix corresponding to the convolutive mixing, in a one-to-one manner, where z is the time-shift operation. Now, the BSSD equation (1) can be written as $\mathbf{x} = \mathbf{H}[z]\mathbf{s}$. In the uBSSD task it is assumed that $\mathbf{H}[z]$ has a polynomial matrix left inverse: there exists polynomial matrix $\mathbf{W}[z] \in \mathbb{R}[z]^{D_s \times D_x}$ such that $\mathbf{W}[z]\mathbf{H}[z]$ is the identity mapping. It can be shown [5] that for $D_x > D_s$ such a left inverse exists with probability 1, under mild conditions: coefficients of polynomial matrix $\mathbf{H}[z]$, that is, the random matrix $[\mathbf{H}_0; \ldots; \mathbf{H}_L]$ is drawn from a continuous distribution. For the ISA task it is supposed that mixing matrix $\mathbf{H}_0 \in \mathbb{R}^{D_x \times D_s}$ has full column rank, i.e., its rank is D_s.

2.2 Existing Decomposition Principles in the BSSD Problem Family

There are numerous reduction methods for the BSSD problem in the literature. For example, its special case, the undercomplete BSD task can be reduced (i) to ISA by temporal concatenation of the observations [6], or (ii) to ICA by means of either spatio-temporal decorrelation [7], or by linear prediction (autoregressive (AR) estimation), see e.g., [8]. As it was shown in [1], the uBSSD task can also be reduced to ISA by temporal concatenation. In Section 3, we show another route and describe how linear prediction can help to transcribe the uBSSD task to ISA. According to the ISA Separation Theorem [9, 1], under certain conditions, the solution of the ISA task requires an ICA preprocessing step followed by a suitable permutation of the ICA elements. This principle was conjectured in [4] on basis of numerical simulations. Only sufficient conditions are available in [9,1] for the ISA Separation Theorem.

3 Reduction of uBSSD to ISA by Linear Prediction

Below, we reduce the uBSSD task to ISA by means of linear prediction. The procedure is similar to that of [8], where it was applied for undercomplete BSD (i.e., for $d = 1$).

Theorem. *In the uBSSD task, observation process* $\mathbf{x}(t)$ *is autoregressive and its innovation* $\tilde{\mathbf{x}}(t) := \mathbf{x}(t) - E[\mathbf{x}(t)|\mathbf{x}(t-1), \mathbf{x}(t-2), \ldots]$ *is* $\mathbf{H}_0\mathbf{s}(t)$*, where* $E[\cdot|\cdot]$ *denotes the conditional expectation value. Consequently, there is a polynomial matrix* $\mathbf{W}_{\mathrm{AR}}[z] \in \mathbb{R}[z]^{D_x \times D_x}$ *such that* $\mathbf{W}_{\mathrm{AR}}[z]\mathbf{x} = \mathbf{H}_0\mathbf{s}$.

Proof. We assumed that $\mathbf{H}[z]$ has left inverse, thus the hidden $\mathbf{s}$ can be expressed from observation $\mathbf{x}$ by causal FIR filtering, i.e., $\mathbf{s} = \mathbf{H}^{-1}[z]\mathbf{x}$, where $\mathbf{H}^{-1}[z] = \sum_{n=0}^{N} \mathbf{M}_n z^{-n} \in \mathbb{R}[z]^{D_s \times D_x}$ and N denotes the degree of the $\mathbf{H}^{-1}[z]$

polynomial. Thus, terms in observation $\mathbf{x}$ that differ from $\mathbf{H}_0\mathbf{s}(t)$ in (1) belong to the linear hull of the finite history of $\mathbf{x}$: $\mathbf{x}(t) = \mathbf{H}_0\mathbf{s}(t) + \sum_{l=1}^{L} \mathbf{H}_l(\mathbf{H}^{-1}[z]\mathbf{x})(t - l) \in \mathbf{H}_0\mathbf{s}(t) + \langle \mathbf{x}(t-1), \mathbf{x}(t-2), \ldots, \mathbf{x}(t-L+N) \rangle$. Because $\mathbf{s}(t)$ is independent of $\langle \mathbf{x}(t-1), \mathbf{x}(t-2), \ldots, \mathbf{x}(t-L+N) \rangle$, we have that observation process $\mathbf{x}(t)$ is autoregressive with innovation $\mathbf{H}_0\mathbf{s}(t)$.

Thus, the AR fit of $\mathbf{x}(t)$ can be used for the estimation of $\mathbf{H}_0\mathbf{s}(t)$. This innovation corresponds to the observation of an undercomplete ISA model[1], which can be reduced to a complete ISA model using principal component analysis (PCA). Finally, the solution can be finished by any ISA procedure. We will call the above uBSSD method linear predictive approximation (LPA). The LPA pseudocode is given in Table 1. The reduction procedure implies that hidden components $\mathbf{s}^m$ can be recovered only up to the ambiguities of the ISA task [10]: that is, assuming (without any loss of generality) that both the hidden source ($\mathbf{s}$) and the observation are white – their expectation values are zeroes and the covariance matrices are identities – the $\mathbf{s}^m$ components are determined up to permutation and orthogonal transformation.

Table 1. Linear predictive approximation (LPA): Pseudocode

Input of the algorithm
Observation: $\{\mathbf{x}(t)\}_{t=1,\ldots,T}$
Optimization
AR fit: for observation $\mathbf{x}$ estimate $\hat{\mathbf{W}}_{\mathrm{AR}}[z]$
Estimate innovation: $\tilde{\mathbf{x}} = \hat{\mathbf{W}}_{\mathrm{AR}}[z]\mathbf{x}$
Reduce uISA to ISA and whiten: $\tilde{\mathbf{x}}' = \hat{\mathbf{W}}_{\mathrm{PCA}}\tilde{\mathbf{x}}$
Apply ISA for $\tilde{\mathbf{x}}'$: separation matrix is $\hat{\mathbf{W}}_{\mathrm{ISA}}$
Estimation
$\hat{\mathbf{W}}_{\mathrm{uBSSD}}[z] = \hat{\mathbf{W}}_{\mathrm{ISA}}\hat{\mathbf{W}}_{\mathrm{PCA}}\hat{\mathbf{W}}_{\mathrm{AR}}[z]$
$\hat{\mathbf{s}} = \hat{\mathbf{W}}_{\mathrm{uBSSD}}[z]\mathbf{x}$

4 Illustrations

We show the results of our studies concerning the efficiency of the algorithm of Table 1.[2] We compare the LPA procedure with the uBSSD method described in [1], where temporal concatenation was applied to transform the uBSSD task to a 'high-dimensional' ISA task. We shall refer to that method as the method of temporal concatenation, or TCC for short. Test problems are introduced in Section 4.1. The performance index that we use to measure the quality of the solutions is detailed in Section 4.2. Numerical results are presented in Section 4.3.

[1] Assumptions made for $\mathbf{H}[z]$ in the uBSSD task implies that $\mathbf{H}_0$ is of full column rank and thus the resulting ISA task is well defined.

[2] Further details can be found in our accompanying technical report [11].

4.1 Databases

We define four databases (s) to study our LPA algorithm[3]. These are the databases used in [1], too. In the *3D-geom*, *celebrities* and *letters* data sets, the d-dimensional hidden components $\mathbf{s}^m$ are 3,2,2-dimensional random variables, respectively. They are distributed (a) uniformly on geometric forms, (b) according to pixel intensities on cartoons of celebrities, and (c) uniformly on images of letters A and B. We have $M = 6, 10, 2$ components, thus the dimension of the hidden source $\mathbf{s}$ is $D_s = 18, 20, 4$. Databases are illustrated in Figs. 1(a)-(c). Our *Beatles* database is a non-i.i.d. example. Here, hidden sources are stereo Beatles songs. 8 kHz sampled portions of two songs (A Hard Day's Night, Can't Buy Me Love) made the hidden $\mathbf{s}^m$s ($d = 2, M = 2, D_s = 4$). In the *letters* and *Beatles* test the number of components and their dimensions were minimal ($d = 2$, $M = 2$).

Fig. 1. Illustration of the (a) *3D-geom*, (b) *celebrities* and (c) *letters* databases

4.2 The Amari-Index

According to Section 3, in the ideal case, the product of matrix $\hat{\mathbf{W}}_{\text{ISA}}\hat{\mathbf{W}}_{\text{PCA}}$ and matrix $\mathbf{H}_0$, that is matrix $\mathbf{G} := \hat{\mathbf{W}}_{\text{ISA}}\hat{\mathbf{W}}_{\text{PCA}}\mathbf{H}_0 \in \mathbb{R}^{D_s \times D_s}$ is a block-permutation matrix made of $d \times d$ blocks. To measure this block-permutation property, the Amari-error adapted to the ISA task [12] was normalized [9] to take values in $[0, 1]$ *independently from* d *and* D_s. This performance measure, the Amari-index, was used to compare the TCC and LPA techniques.

4.3 Simulations

The experimental studies concern two questions: (i) the TCC and the LPA methods are compared on uBSSD tasks, (ii) the performance as a function of convolution length is studied for the LPA technique.

We studied the $D_x = 2D_s$ case, like in [1]. Both the TCC and the LPA method reduce the uBSSD task to ISA problems and we use the Amari-index (Section 4.2) to measure and compare their performances. For all values of the parameters (sample number: T, convolution length: $L + 1$), we have averaged the performances upon 50 random initializations of $\mathbf{s}$ and $\mathbf{H}[z]$. The coordinates of matrices $\mathbf{H}_l$ were chosen independently from standard normal distribution. We

[3] *Smiley*: http://www.smileyworld.com, *Beatles*: http://rock.mididb.com/beatles/ .

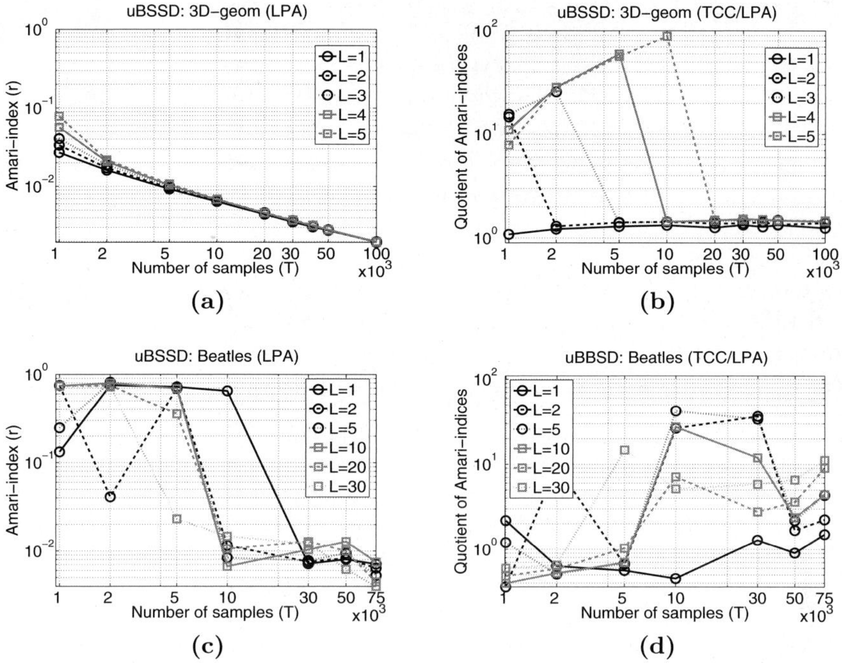

Fig. 2. Estimation error of the LPA method and comparisons with the TCC method for the *3D-geom* and *Beatles* databases. Scales are 'log log' plots. Data correspond to different convolution lengths $(L+1)$. (a) and (c): Amari-index as a function of the sample number. (b) and (d): Quotients of the Amari-indices of the TCC and the LPA methods: for quotient value $q > 1$, the LPA method is q times more precise than the TCC method. In the *celebrities* and *letters* tests, we found similar results as on the *3D-geom* data set.

used the Schwarz's Bayesian Criterion to determine the optimal order of the AR process. The criterion was constrained: the order Q of the estimated AR process (see Table 1) was limited from above, the upper limit was set to twice the length of the convolution, i.e., $Q \leq 2(L+1)$. The AR process and the ISA subtask of TCC and LPA were estimated by the method detailed in [13], and by joint f-decorrelation (JFD) [14], respectively.

We studied the dependence of the precision versus the sample number. In the *3D-geom* and *celebrities* (*letters* and *Beatles*) tests, the sample number T varied between $1,000$ and $100,000$ ($1,000$ and $75,000$), the length of the convolution $(L+1)$ changed between 2 and 6 (2 and 31). Comparison with the TCC method and the estimations of the LPA technique are illustrated in Figs. 2(a)-(b) (Figs. 2(c)-(d)) on the *3D-geom* (*Beatles*) database. According to Fig. 2(a), the LPA algorithm is able to uncover the hidden components with high precisions on the *3D-geom* database. We found that the Amari-index r decreases according to power law $r(T) \propto T^{-c}$ $(c > 0)$ for sample numbers $T > 2000$. The power law is manifested by straight lines on log log scales. According to

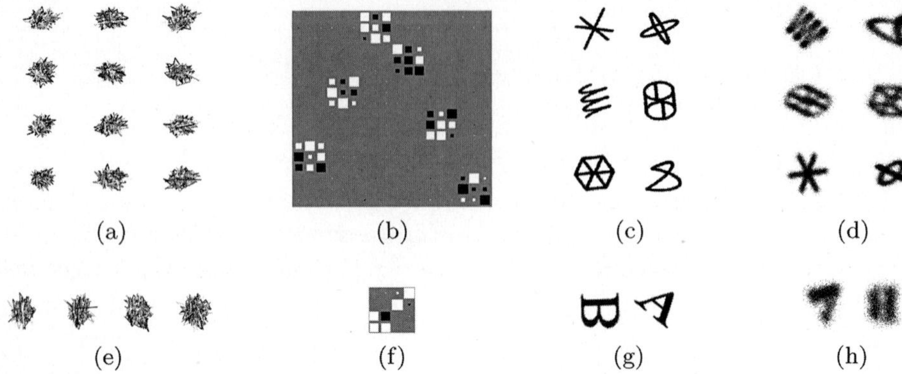

Fig. 3. Illustration of the LPA method on the uBSSD task for the *3D-geom* (*letters*) database. (a)-(c) [(e)-(g)]: sample number $T = 100,000$ [75,000], convolution length $L+1=6$ [31]. (a), (e): observed convolved signals $\mathbf{x}(t)$. (b) [(f)]: Hinton-diagram of $\mathbf{G}$, ideally block-permutation matrix with 3×3 [2×2] blocks. (c) [(g)]: estimated components ($\hat{\mathbf{s}}^m$), Amari-index: 0.2% [0.3%]. (d) [(h)]: estimation of hidden components ($\hat{\mathbf{s}}^m$) for sample number $T = 20,000$ [15,000] and convolution parameter $L = 20$ [230].

Fig. 2(b) the LPA method is superior to the TCC method (i) for all sample numbers $1,000 \leq T \leq 100,000$, moreover (ii) LPA can provide reasonable estimates for much smaller sample numbers. on the *3D-geom* database. This behavior is manifested by the initial steady increase of the quotients of the Amari indices of the TCC and LPA methods as a function of sample number followed by a sudden drop when the sample number enables reasonable TCC estimations, too. Similar results were found on the *celebrities* and the *letters* databases, too. The LPA method resulted in $1.1-88$, $1.0-87$, $1.2-110$-times increase of precision for the *3D-geom*, *celebrities* and *letters* database, respectively. For the *3D-geom* (*celebrities*, *letters*) dataset the Amari-index for sample number $T = 100,000$ ($T = 100,000$, $T = 75,000$) is $0.19-0.20\%$ ($0.33-0.34\%$, $0.30-0.36\%$) with small $0.01-0.02$ (0.02, $0.11-0.15$) standard deviations.

Visual inspection of Fig. 2(c) shows that on the *Beatles* database the LPA method found the hidden components for sample number $T \geq 30,000$. The TCC method gave reliable solutions for sample number $T = 50,000$ or so. According to Fig. 2(d) the LPA method is more precise than TCC for $T \geq 30,000$. The increase in precision becomes more pronounced for larger convolution parameter L. Namely, for sample number 75,000 and for $L = 1,2,5,10,20,30$ the ratios of precision are $1.50, 2.24, 4.33, 4.42, 9.03, 11.13$, respectively on the average. For sample number $T = 75,000$ the Amari-index stays below 1% on average ($0.4-0.71\%$) and has $0.02-0.08$ standard deviation for the *Beatles* test.

According to our simulations, the LPA method may provide acceptable estimations for sample number $T = 20,000$ ($T = 15,000$) up to convolution length $L = 20$ ($L = 230$) for the *3D-geom* and *celebrities* (*letters* and *Beatles*) datasets. Such estimations are shown in Fig. 3(d) and Fig. 3(h) for the *3D-geom* and *letters* tests, respectively.

5 Summary

We presented a novel solution method for the undercomplete case of the blind subspace deconvolution (uBSSD) task. We used a stepwise decomposition principle and reduced the problem with linear prediction to independent subspace analysis (ISA) task. We illustrated the method on different tests. Our method supersedes the temporal concatenation based uBSSD method, because (i) it gives rise to a smaller dimensional ISA task, (ii) it produces similar estimation errors at considerably smaller sample numbers, and (iii) it can treat deeper temporal convolutions.

References

1. Szabó, Z., Póczos, B., Lőrincz, A.: Undercomplete blind subspace deconvolution. Journal of Machine Learning Research 8, 1063–1095 (2007)
2. Cichocki, A., Amari, S.: Adaptive blind signal and image processing. John Wiley & Sons, Chichester (2002)
3. Pedersen, M.S., Larsen, J., Kjems, U., Parra, L.C.: A survey of convolutive blind source separation methods. In: Springer Handbook of Speech, Springer, Heidelberg (to appear, 2007), `http://www2.imm.dtu.dk/pubdb/p.php?4924`
4. Cardoso, J.: Multidimensional independent component analysis. In: ICASSP '98, vol. 4, pp. 1941–1944 (1998)
5. Rajagopal, R., Potter, L.C.: Multivariate MIMO FIR inverses. IEEE Transactions on Image Processing 12, 458–465 (2003)
6. Févotte, C., Doncarli, C.: A unified presentation of blind source separation for convolutive mixtures using block-diagonalization. In: ICA '03, pp. 349–354 (2003)
7. Choi, S., Cichocki, A.: Blind signal deconvolution by spatio-temporal decorrelation and demixing. Neural Networks for Signal Processing 7, 426–435 (1997)
8. Gorokhov, A., Loubaton, P.: Blind identification of MIMO-FIR systems: A generalized linear prediction approach. Signal Processing 73, 105–124 (1999)
9. Szabó, Z., Póczos, B., Lőrincz, A.: Cross-entropy optimization for independent process analysis. In: Rosca, J., Erdogmus, D., Príncipe, J.C., Haykin, S. (eds.) ICA 2006. LNCS, vol. 3889, pp. 909–916. Springer, Heidelberg (2006)
10. Theis, F.J.: Uniqueness of complex and multidimensional independent component analysis. Signal Processing 84, 951–956 (2004)
11. Szabó, Z., Póczos, B., Lőrincz, A.: Undercomplete blind subspace deconvolution via linear prediction. Technical report, Eötvös Loránd University, Budapest (2007), `http://arxiv.org/abs/0706.3435`
12. Theis, F.J.: Blind signal separation into groups of dependent signals using joint block diagonalization. In: ISCAS '05, pp. 5878–5881 (2005)
13. Neumaier, A., Schneider, T.: Estimation of parameters and eigenmodes of multivariate AR models. ACM Trans. on Mathematical Software 27, 27–57 (2001)
14. Szabó, Z., Lőrincz, A.: Real and complex independent subspace analysis by generalized variance. In: ICARN '06, pp. 85–88 (2006)

Learning an Outlier-Robust Kalman Filter

Jo-Anne Ting[1], Evangelos Theodorou[1], and Stefan Schaal[1,2]

[1] University of Southern California, Los Angeles, CA 90089
[2] ATR Computational Neuroscience Laboratories, Kyoto, Japan
{joanneti,etheodor,sschaal}@usc.edu

Abstract. We introduce a modified Kalman filter that performs robust, real-time outlier detection, without the need for manual parameter tuning by the user. Systems that rely on high quality sensory data (for instance, robotic systems) can be sensitive to data containing outliers. The standard Kalman filter is not robust to outliers, and other variations of the Kalman filter have been proposed to overcome this issue. However, these methods may require manual parameter tuning, use of heuristics or complicated parameter estimation procedures. Our Kalman filter uses a weighted least squares-like approach by introducing weights for each data sample. A data sample with a smaller weight has a weaker contribution when estimating the current time step's state. Using an incremental variational Expectation-Maximization framework, we learn the weights and system dynamics. We evaluate our Kalman filter algorithm on data from a robotic dog.

1 Introduction

Systems that rely on high quality sensory data are often sensitive to data containing outliers. While data from sensors such as potentiometers and optical encoders are easily interpretable in their noise characteristics, other sensors such as visual systems, GPS devices and sonar sensors often provide measurements populated with outliers. As a result, robust, reliable detection and removal of outliers is essential in order to process these kinds of data. For example, in the application domain of robotics, legged locomotion is vulnerable to sensory data of poor quality, since one undetected outlier can disturb the balance controller to the point that the robot loses stability.

An outlier is generally defined as an observation that "lies outside some overall pattern of distribution" [1]. Outliers may originate from sensor noise (producing values that fall outside a valid range), from temporary sensor failures, or from unanticipated disturbances in the environment (e.g., a brief change of lighting conditions for a visual sensor). Note that some prior knowledge about the observed data's properties must be known. Otherwise, it is impossible to discern if a data sample that lies some distance away from the data cloud is truly an outlier or simply part of the data's structure.

For real-time applications, storing data samples may not be a viable option due to the high frequency of sensory data and insufficient memory resources. In

J.N. Kok et al. (Eds.): ECML 2007, LNAI 4701, pp. 748–756, 2007.

this scenario, sensor data are made available one at a time and must be discarded once they have been observed. Hence, techniques that require access to the entire set of data samples, such as the Kalman smoother [2] are not applicable. Instead, the Kalman filter [3] is a more suitable method, since it assumes that only data samples up to the current time step have been observed.

The Kalman filter is a widely used tool for estimating the state of a dynamic system, given noisy measurement data. It is the optimal *linear* estimator for linear Gaussian systems, giving the minimum mean squared error [4]. Using state estimates, the filter can also estimate what the corresponding (output) data are. However, the performance of the Kalman filter degrades when the observed data contains outliers.

To address this, previous work has tried to make the Kalman filter more robust to outliers by addressing the sensitivity of the squared error criterion to outliers [5,6] and by considering non-Gaussian, heavy-tailed distributions for random variables (e.g., [7,8]) or for observation and state noise, e.g., [9]. However, the resulting estimation of parameters may be quite complicated for systems with transient disturbances, and these filters may be more difficult to implement. Other approaches use resampling techniques or numerical integration, e.g., [10], that are not suitable for real-time applications.

Yet another class of methods uses a weighted least squares approach, as done in robust least squares [11], where each data sample is assigned a weight that indicates its contribution to the hidden state estimate at each time step, e.g., [12]. These methods model the weights as some heuristic function of the data (e.g., the Huber function [11]) and often require manual tuning of threshold parameters for optimal performance. Using incorrect or inaccurate estimates for the weights may lead to deteriorated performance, so special care is necessary with these techniques.

In this paper, we are interested in making the Kalman filter more robust to the outliers in the observations (i.e. the filter should identify and eliminate possible outliers as it tracks observed data). Identifying outliers in the state is a different problem, left for another paper. We introduce a modified Kalman filter that can detect outliers in the observed data without the need for manual parameter tuning or use of heuristic methods. For ease of analytical computation, we assume Gaussian distributions for variables and states. We illustrate the performance of this robust Kalman filter on robotic data, comparing it with other robust Kalman filter methods and demonstrating its effectiveness at detecting outliers in the observations.

2 Outlier Detection in the Kalman Filter

Let us assume we have data observed over N time steps, $\{\mathbf{z}_k\}_{k=1}^N$, and the corresponding hidden states as $\{\boldsymbol{\theta}_k\}_{k=1}^N$ (where $\boldsymbol{\theta}_k \in \Re^{d_2 \times 1}, \mathbf{z}_k \in \Re^{d_1 \times 1}$). The Kalman filter system equations are:

$$
\begin{aligned}
\mathbf{z}_k &= \mathbf{C}\boldsymbol{\theta}_k + \mathbf{v}_k \\
\boldsymbol{\theta}_k &= \mathbf{A}\boldsymbol{\theta}_{k-1} + \mathbf{s}_k
\end{aligned}
\tag{1}
$$

where $\mathbf{C} \in \Re^{d_1 \times d_2}$ is the observation matrix, $\mathbf{A} \in \Re^{d_2 \times d_2}$ is the state transition matrix, $\mathbf{v}_k \in \Re^{d_1 \times 1}$ is the observation noise at time step k, and $\mathbf{s}_k \in \Re^{d_2 \times 1}$ is the state noise at time step k. We assume $\mathbf{v}_k \sim \text{Normal}(0, \mathbf{R})$, $\mathbf{s}_k \sim \text{Normal}(0, \mathbf{Q})$, where $\mathbf{R} \in \Re^{d_1 \times d_1}$ and $\mathbf{Q} \in \Re^{d_2 \times d_2}$ are diagonal covariance matrices (with vectors $\mathbf{r}$ and $\mathbf{q}$ on their diagonals) for the observation and state noise, respectively. The corresponding filter propagation and update equations are, for $k = 1, .., N$:

Propagation:

$$\boldsymbol{\theta}'_k = \mathbf{A} \langle \boldsymbol{\theta}_{k-1} \rangle \tag{2}$$

$$\boldsymbol{\Sigma}'_k = \mathbf{A} \boldsymbol{\Sigma}_{k-1} \mathbf{A}^T + \mathbf{Q} \tag{3}$$

Update:

$$\mathbf{S}'_k = \left(\mathbf{C} \boldsymbol{\Sigma}'_k \mathbf{C}^T + \mathbf{R} \right)^{-1} \tag{4}$$

$$K'_k = \boldsymbol{\Sigma}'_k \mathbf{C}^T \mathbf{S}'_k \tag{5}$$

$$\langle \boldsymbol{\theta}_k \rangle = \boldsymbol{\theta}'_k + K'_k \left(\mathbf{z}_k - \mathbf{C} \boldsymbol{\theta}'_k \right) \tag{6}$$

$$\boldsymbol{\Sigma}_k = \left(\mathbf{I} - K'_k \mathbf{C} \right) \boldsymbol{\Sigma}'_k \tag{7}$$

where $\langle \boldsymbol{\theta}_k \rangle$[1] is the posterior mean vector of the state $\boldsymbol{\theta}_k$, $\boldsymbol{\Sigma}_k$ is the posterior covariance matrix of $\boldsymbol{\theta}_k$, and $\mathbf{S}'_k$ is the covariance matrix of the residual prediction error—all at time step k. The system dynamics ($\mathbf{C}$, $\mathbf{A}$, $\mathbf{R}$ and $\mathbf{Q}$) are unknown, and we can use a maximum likelihood framework to estimate these parameter values [13]. Unfortunately, the standard Kalman filter is not robust to outliers.

2.1 Robust Kalman Filtering with Bayesian Weights

To overcome this limitation, we introduce a scalar weight w_k for each observed data sample $\mathbf{z}_k$ such that the variance of $\mathbf{z}_k$ is weighted with w_k, as done in [14]. [14] considers a weighted least squares regression model and assumes that the weights are known and given. We place a Gamma prior distribution over the the weights to ensure they remain positive, as done previously in [15]. Additionally, we learn estimates for the system dynamics at each time step. The prior distributions of our model are:

$$\begin{aligned} \mathbf{z}_k | \boldsymbol{\theta}_k, w_k &\sim \text{Normal}\left(\mathbf{C} \boldsymbol{\theta}_k, \mathbf{R}/w_k \right) \\ \boldsymbol{\theta}_k | \boldsymbol{\theta}_{k-1} &\sim \text{Normal}\left(\mathbf{A} \boldsymbol{\theta}_{k-1}, \mathbf{Q} \right) \\ w_k &\sim \text{Gamma}\left(a_{w_k}, b_{w_k} \right) \end{aligned} \tag{8}$$

We can treat this problem as an Expectation-Minimization-like (EM) learning problem [16, 17] and maximize the log likelihood $\log p(\boldsymbol{\theta}_{1:N})$. Due to analytical issues, we only have access to a lower bound of this measure. This lower bound is based on an expected value of the "complete" data likelihood $\langle \log p\left(\boldsymbol{\theta}_{1:N}, \mathbf{z}_{1:N}, \mathbf{w} \right) \rangle$, formulated over all variables of the learning problem. Since we are considering a real-time problem, we will have observed only data samples $\mathbf{z}_{1:k}$ at time step k. Consequently, we should consider the log evidence

[1] Note that $\langle \rangle$ denotes the expectation operator.

of only the data samples observed to date, i.e., $\log p(\boldsymbol{\theta}_{1:k}, \mathbf{z}_{1:k}, \mathbf{w}_{1:k})$, when estimating the posterior distributions of random variables at time step k.

The expectation of the complete data likelihood should be taken with respect to the true posterior distribution of all hidden variables $Q(\mathbf{w}, \boldsymbol{\theta})$. Since this is an analytically intractable expression, we use a technique from variational calculus to construct a lower bound and make a factorial approximation of the true posterior as follows: $Q(\mathbf{w}, \boldsymbol{\theta}) = \prod_{i=1}^{N} Q(w_i) \prod_{i=1}^{N} Q(\boldsymbol{\theta}_i|\boldsymbol{\theta}_{i-1}) Q(\boldsymbol{\theta}_0)$ (e.g., [17]). This factorization of $\boldsymbol{\theta}$ conserves the Markov property that Kalman filters, by definition, have and makes the resulting posterior distributions over hidden variables analytically tractable. The factorial approximation was chosen purposely so that $Q(w_k)$ is independent from $Q(\boldsymbol{\theta}_k)$; performing joint inference of w_k and $\boldsymbol{\theta}_k$ does not make sense in the context of our generative model. The final EM update equations for time step k are:

E-step:

$$\boldsymbol{\Sigma}_k = \left(\langle w_k \rangle \mathbf{C}_k^T \mathbf{R}_k^{-1} \mathbf{C}_k + \mathbf{Q}_k^{-1} \right)^{-1} \tag{9}$$

$$\langle \boldsymbol{\theta}_k \rangle = \boldsymbol{\Sigma}_k \left(\mathbf{Q}_k^{-1} \mathbf{A}_k \langle \boldsymbol{\theta}_{k-1} \rangle + \langle w_k \rangle \mathbf{C}_k^T \mathbf{R}_k^{-1} \mathbf{z}_k \right) \tag{10}$$

$$\langle w_k \rangle = \frac{a_{w_k,0} + \frac{1}{2}}{b_{w_k,0} + \left\langle (\mathbf{z}_k - \mathbf{C}_k \boldsymbol{\theta}_k)^T \mathbf{R}_k^{-1} (\mathbf{z}_k - \mathbf{C}_k \boldsymbol{\theta}_k) \right\rangle} \tag{11}$$

M-step:

$$\mathbf{C}_k = \left(\sum_{i=1}^{k} \langle w_i \rangle \mathbf{z}_i \langle \boldsymbol{\theta}_i \rangle^T \right) \left(\sum_{i=1}^{k} \langle w_i \rangle \langle \boldsymbol{\theta}_i \boldsymbol{\theta}_i^T \rangle \right)^{-1} \tag{12}$$

$$\mathbf{A}_k = \left(\sum_{i=1}^{k} \langle \boldsymbol{\theta}_i \rangle \langle \boldsymbol{\theta}_{i-1} \rangle^T \right) \left(\sum_{i=1}^{k} \langle \boldsymbol{\theta}_{i-1} \boldsymbol{\theta}_{i-1}^T \rangle \right)^{-1} \tag{13}$$

$$r_{km} = \tfrac{1}{k} \sum_{i=1}^{k} \langle w_i \rangle \left\langle (\mathbf{z}_{im} - \mathbf{C}_k(m,:)\boldsymbol{\theta}_i)^2 \right\rangle \tag{14}$$

$$q_{kn} = \tfrac{1}{k} \sum_{i=1}^{k} \left\langle (\boldsymbol{\theta}_{in} - \mathbf{A}_k(n,:)\boldsymbol{\theta}_{i-1})^2 \right\rangle \tag{15}$$

where $m = 1,..,d_1$, $n = 1,..,d_2$; r_{km} is the mth coefficient of the vector $\mathbf{r}_k$; q_{kn} is the nth coefficient of the vector $\mathbf{q}_k$; $\mathbf{C}_k(m,:)$ is the mth row of the matrix $\mathbf{C}_k$; $\mathbf{A}_k(n,:)$ is the nth row of the matrix $\mathbf{A}_k$; and $a_{w_k,0}$ and $b_{w_k,0}$ are prior scale parameters for the weight w_k. Equations (9) to (15) should be computed once for each time step k (e.g., [18]) when the data sample $\mathbf{z}_k$ becomes available.

Since storing sensor data is not possible in real-time applications, (12) to (15)—which require access to all observed data samples up to time step k—need to be re-written using only values observed, calculated or used in the current time step k. We can do this by collecting sufficient statistics in (12) to (15) and rewriting them as:

$$\mathbf{C}_k = \mathrm{sum}_k^{\mathbf{wz}\boldsymbol{\theta}^T} \left(\mathrm{sum}_k^{\mathbf{w}\boldsymbol{\theta}\boldsymbol{\theta}^T} \right)^{-1} \tag{16}$$

$$\mathbf{A}_k = \mathrm{sum}_k^{\boldsymbol{\theta}\boldsymbol{\theta}'} \left(\mathrm{sum}_k^{\boldsymbol{\theta}'\boldsymbol{\theta}'} \right)^{-1} \tag{17}$$

$$r_{km} = \tfrac{1}{k} \left[\mathrm{sum}_{km}^{\mathbf{w}zz} - 2\mathbf{C}_k(m,:)\mathrm{sum}_{km}^{\mathbf{w}z\boldsymbol{\theta}} + \mathrm{diag}\left\{ \mathbf{C}_k(m,:)\mathrm{sum}_k^{\mathbf{w}\boldsymbol{\theta}\boldsymbol{\theta}^T} \mathbf{C}_k(m,:)^T \right\} \right] \tag{18}$$

$$q_{kn} = \tfrac{1}{k} \left[\mathrm{sum}_{kn}^{\theta^2} - 2\mathbf{A}_k(n,:)\mathrm{sum}_{kn}^{\boldsymbol{\theta}\boldsymbol{\theta}'} + \mathrm{diag}\left\{ \mathbf{A}_k(n,:)\mathrm{sum}_k^{\boldsymbol{\theta}'\boldsymbol{\theta}'} \mathbf{A}_k(n,:)^T \right\} \right] \tag{19}$$

where $m = 1, .., d_1$, $n = 1, .., d_2$, and the sufficient statistics are:

$$\mathrm{sum}_k^{\mathbf{wz}\boldsymbol{\theta}^T} = \langle w_k \rangle \mathbf{z}_k \langle \boldsymbol{\theta}_k \rangle^T + \mathrm{sum}_{k-1}^{\mathbf{wz}\boldsymbol{\theta}^T} \qquad \mathrm{sum}_k^{\mathbf{w}\boldsymbol{\theta}\boldsymbol{\theta}^T} = \langle w_k \rangle \langle \boldsymbol{\theta}_k \boldsymbol{\theta}_k^T \rangle + \mathrm{sum}_{k-1}^{\mathbf{w}\boldsymbol{\theta}\boldsymbol{\theta}^T}$$

$$\mathrm{sum}_k^{\boldsymbol{\theta}\boldsymbol{\theta}'} = \langle \boldsymbol{\theta}_k \rangle \langle \boldsymbol{\theta}_{k-1} \rangle^T + \mathrm{sum}_{k-1}^{\boldsymbol{\theta}\boldsymbol{\theta}'} \qquad \mathrm{sum}_k^{\boldsymbol{\theta}'\boldsymbol{\theta}'} = \langle \boldsymbol{\theta}_{k-1} \boldsymbol{\theta}_{k-1}^T \rangle + \mathrm{sum}_{k-1}^{\boldsymbol{\theta}'\boldsymbol{\theta}'}$$

$$\mathrm{sum}_{km}^{\mathbf{w}zz} = \langle w_k \rangle z_{km}^2 + \mathrm{sum}_{k-1}^{\mathbf{w}zz} \qquad \mathrm{sum}_{km}^{\mathbf{w}z\boldsymbol{\theta}} = \langle w_k \rangle z_{km} \boldsymbol{\theta}_k + \mathrm{sum}_{k-1,m}^{\mathbf{w}z\boldsymbol{\theta}}$$

$$\mathrm{sum}_{kn}^{\theta^2} = \langle \theta_{kn}^2 \rangle + \mathrm{sum}_{k-1,n}^{\theta^2} \qquad \mathrm{sum}_{kn}^{\theta\boldsymbol{\theta}'} = \langle \theta_{kn} \rangle \langle \boldsymbol{\theta}_{k-1} \rangle + \mathrm{sum}_{kn}^{\theta\boldsymbol{\theta}'}$$

A few remarks should be made regarding the initialization of priors used in (9) to (11), (16) to (19). In particular, the prior scale parameters $a_{w_k,0}$ and $b_{w_k,0}$ should be selected so that the weights $\langle w_k \rangle$ are 1 with some confidence, i.e., the algorithm starts by assuming most data samples are inliers. We set $a_{w_k,0} = 1$ and $b_{w_k,0} = 1$ so that $\langle w_k \rangle$ has a prior mean of $a_{w_k,0}/b_{w_k,0} = 1$ with a variance of $a_{w_k,0}/b_{w_k,0}^2 = 1$. This set of values is generally valid for any data set and/or application and does not need to be modified, unless the user has good reason to insert strong biases towards particular parameter values. Since prior knowledge about the observed data's properties must be known in order to distinguish if a data sample is an outlier or part of the data's structure, this Bayesian approach provides a natural framework to incorporate this information.

Secondly, the algorithm is relatively insensitive to the the initialization of $\mathbf{A}$ and $\mathbf{C}$ and will always converge to the same final solution, regardless of these values. For our experiments, we initialize $\mathbf{C} = \mathbf{A} = \mathbf{I}$, where $\mathbf{I}$ is the identity matrix. The initial values of $\mathbf{R}$ and $\mathbf{Q}$ should be set based on the user's initial estimate of how noisy the observed data is (e.g., $\mathbf{R} = \mathbf{Q} = 0.01\mathbf{I}$ for noisy data, $\mathbf{R} = \mathbf{Q} = 10^{-4}\mathbf{I}$ for less noisy data [19]).

2.2 Relationship to the Kalman Filter

If we substitute (2) and (3) into (4) to (7), we reach recursive expressions for $\langle \boldsymbol{\theta}_k \rangle$ and $\boldsymbol{\Sigma}_k$, proving that our model is a variant of the Kalman filter. By applying this sequence of algebraic manipulations in reverse order to (9) and (10), we arrive at the following:

Propagation:

$$\boldsymbol{\theta}_k' = \mathbf{A}_k \langle \boldsymbol{\theta}_{k-1} \rangle \tag{20}$$

$$\boldsymbol{\Sigma}_k' = \mathbf{Q}_k \tag{21}$$

Update:

$$\mathbf{S}_k' = \left(\mathbf{C}_k \boldsymbol{\Sigma}_k' \mathbf{C}_k^T + \frac{1}{\langle w_k \rangle} \mathbf{R}_k \right)^{-1} \tag{22}$$

$$K_k' = \boldsymbol{\Sigma}_k' \mathbf{C}_k^T \mathbf{S}_k' \tag{23}$$

$$\langle \boldsymbol{\theta}_k \rangle = \boldsymbol{\theta}_k' + K_k' \left(\mathbf{z}_k - \mathbf{C}_k \boldsymbol{\theta}_k' \right) \tag{24}$$

$$\boldsymbol{\Sigma}_k = \left(\mathbf{I} - K_k' \mathbf{C}_k \right) \boldsymbol{\Sigma}_k' \tag{25}$$

Close examination of the above equations show that (9) and (10) in the Bayesian model correspond to standard Kalman filter equations, with modified expressions for $\boldsymbol{\Sigma}_k'$ and $\mathbf{S}_k'$ and time-varying system dynamics. $\boldsymbol{\Sigma}_k'$ is no longer *explicitly* dependent on $\boldsymbol{\Sigma}_{k-1}$, since $\boldsymbol{\Sigma}_{k-1}$ does not appear in (21). However, the current state's covariance $\boldsymbol{\Sigma}_k$ is still dependent on the previous state's covariance $\boldsymbol{\Sigma}_{k-1}$ (through parameters K' and $\mathbf{C}_k$).

Additionally, the term $\mathbf{R}_k$ in $\mathbf{S}_k'$ is now weighted. Equation (11) reveals that if the prediction error in $\mathbf{z}_k$ is so large that it dominates the denominator, then the weight $\langle w_k \rangle$ of that data sample will be very small. If $\mathbf{z}_k$ has a very small weight $\langle w_k \rangle$, then $\mathbf{S}_k'$, the posterior covariance of the residual prediction error, will be very small, leading to a very small Kalman gain K_k'. In short, the influence of the data sample $\mathbf{z}_k$ will be downweighted when predicting $\boldsymbol{\theta}_k$, the hidden state at time step k. The resulting Bayesian algorithm has a computational complexity on the same order as that of a standard Kalman filter, since matrix inversions are still needed, as in the standard Kalman filter. In comparison to other Kalman filters that use heuristics or require more involved computation/implementation, this outlier-robust Kalman filter is principled and easy to implement.

3 Experimental Results

We evaluated our weighted robust Kalman filter on data collected from a a robotic dog, LittleDog, manufactured by Boston Dynamics Inc. (Cambridge, MA), and compared it with two other filters. We omitted the filter of [12], since we had difficulty implementing it. Instead, we used a hand-tuned thresholded Kalman filter to serve as a baseline comparison. The two other filters consist of the standard Kalman filter and a Kalman filter where outliers are determined by thresholding on the Mahalanobis distance. If the Mahalanobis distance exceeds a certain threshold value, the associated data sample is considered an outlier and ignored. If we have a priori access to the entire data set and are able to *manually hand-tune* this threshold value accordingly, the thresholded Kalman filter gives *near-optimal* performance. Recall that we are interested in the Kalman filter's prediction of the observed data and detection of outliers in the observations. Estimation of the system dynamics for the purpose of parameter identification is a different problem, and more details can be found in [20].

3.1 LittleDog Robot

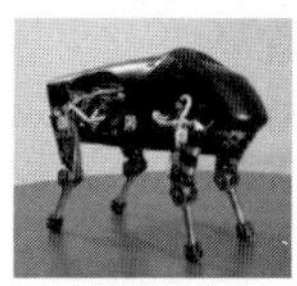

Fig. 1. LittleDog

We evaluated all filters on a 12 degree-of-freedom robotic dog, LittleDog, shown in Fig. 1. The robot dog has two sources that measure its orientation: a motion capture (MOCAP) system and an on-board inertia measurement unit (IMU). Both provide a quaternion q of the robot's orientation: q_{MOCAP} from the MOCAP and q_{IMU} from the IMU. q_{IMU} drifts over time, since the IMU cannot provide stable orientation estimation but its signal is clean. In contrast, q_{MOCAP} has outliers and noise, but no drift. We would like to estimate the offset between q_{MOCAP} and q_{IMU}, and this offset is a *noisy slowly drifting signal containing outliers*. Depending on the quality of estimate desired, we can estimate it with a straight line, as done in [15]. Alternatively, if we want to estimate the signal more accurately, we can use the proposed outlier-robust Kalman filter to track it. For optimal performance, we manually tuned **C**, **A**, **R** and **Q** for the standard Kalman filter—a tricky and time-consuming process. The system dynamics of the thresholded Kalman filter were learnt using a maximum likelihood framework. Its threshold parameter was manually tuned for best performance on this data set.

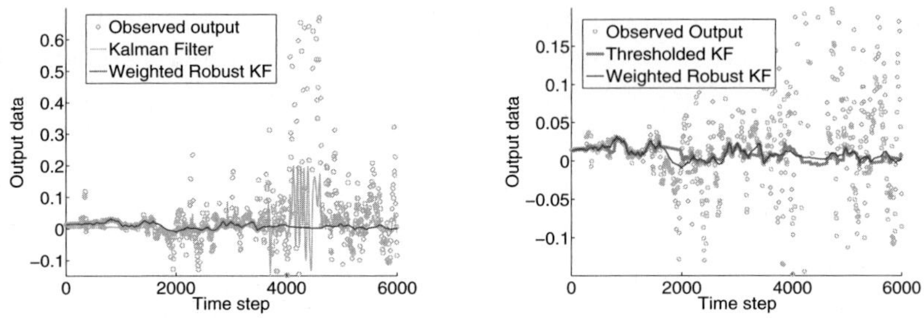

(a) Predicted data for the standard and weighted robust KFs

(b) Predicted data for the thresholded and weighted robust KFs

Fig. 2. Observed vs. predicted data from LittleDog robot shown for all Kalman filters (KF), over 6000 samples

Figure 2 shows the offset data (in gray circles) between q_{MOCAP} and q_{IMU} for one of the four quaternion coefficients, collected over 6000 data samples, at 1 sample/time step. Figure 2(a) shows that the standard Kalman filter fails to detect outliers occurring between the 4000th and 5000th sample. Figure 2(b) shows that the thresholded Kalman filter does not react as violently as the standard Kalman filter to outliers and, in fact, appears to perform similarly to the weighted robust Kalman filter. This is to be expected, given we hand-tuned the threshold parameter for optimal performance.

4 Conclusions

We derived an outlier-robust Kalman filter by introducing weights for each data sample. This Kalman filter learns the weights and the system dynamics, without the need for any manual parameter tuning by the user, heuristics or sampling. It performs as well as a hand-tuned Kalman filter (that required prior knowledge of the data) on robotic data. It provides an easy-to-use competitive alternative for robust tracking of sensor data and offers a simple outlier detection mechanism that can potentially be applied to more complex, nonlinear filters.

Acknowledgments

This research was supported in part by National Science Foundation grants ECS-0325383, IIS-0312802, IIS-0082995, ECS-0326095, ANI-0224419, a NASA grant AC#98−516, an AFOSR grant on Intelligent Control, the ERATO Kawato Dynamic Brain Project funded by the Japanese Science and Technology Agency, and the ATR Computational Neuroscience Laboratories.

References

1. Moore, D.S., McCabe, G.P.: Introduction to the Practice of Statistics. W.H. Freeman & Company (1999)
2. Jazwinski, A.H.: Stochastic Processes and Filtering Theory. Academic Press, London (1970)
3. Kalman, R.E.: A new approach to linear filtering and prediction problems. Transactions of the ASME - Journal of Basic Engineering 183, 35–45 (1960)
4. Morris, J.M.: The Kalman filter: A robust estimator for some classes of linear quadratic problems. IEEE Transactions on Information Theory 22, 526–534 (1976)
5. Tukey, J.W.: A survey of sampling from contaminated distributions. In: Olkin, I. (ed.) Contributions to Probability and Statistics, pp. 448–485. Stanford University Press (1960)
6. Huber, P.J.: Robust estimation of a location parameter. Annals of Mathematical Statistics 35, 73–101 (1964)
7. West, M.: Robust sequential approximate Bayesian estimation. Journal of the Royal Statistical Society, Series B 43, 157–166 (1981)
8. Meinhold, R.J., Singpurwalla, N.D.: Robustification of Kalman filter models. Journal of the American Statistical Association, 479–486 (1989)
9. Masreliez, C.: Approximate non-Gaussian filtering with linear state and observation relations. IEEE Transactions on Automatic Control 20, 107–110 (1975)
10. Kitagawa, G., Gersch, W.: Smoothness priors analysis of time series. In: Lecture Notes in Statistics, Springer, Heidelberg (1996)
11. Huber, P.J.: Robust Statistics. Wiley, Chichester (1973)
12. Chan, S.C., Zhang, Z.G., Tse, K.W.: A new robust Kalman filter algorithm under outliers and system uncertainties. In: IEEE International Symposium on Circuits and Systems, pp. 4317–4320. IEEE Computer Society Press, Los Alamitos (2005)
13. Myers, K.A., Tapley, B.D.: Adaptive sequential estimation with unknown noise statistics. IEEE Transactions on Automatic Control 21, 520–523 (1976)
14. Gelman, A., Carlin, J., Stern, H., Rubin, D.: Bayesian Data Analysis. Chapman and Hall (2000)
15. Ting, J., D'Souza, A., Schaal, S.: Automatic outlier detection: A Bayesian approach. In: IEEE International Conference on Robotics and Automation, IEEE Computer Society Press, Los Alamitos (2007)
16. Dempster, A., Laird, N., Rubin, D.: Maximum likelihood from incomplete data via the EM algorithm. Journal of Royal Statistical Society. Series B 39(1), 1–38 (1977)
17. Ghahramani, Z., Beal, M.J.: Graphical models and variational methods. In: Saad, D., Opper, M. (eds.) Advanced Mean Field Methods - Theory and Practice, MIT Press, Cambridge (2000)

18. Neal, R.M., Hinton, G.E.: A view of the EM algorithm that justifies incremental, sparse, and other variants. In: Jordan, M.I. (ed.) Learning in Graphical Models, pp. 355–368. MIT Press, Cambridge (1999)
19. Maybeck, P.S.: Stochastic models, estimation, and control. Mathematics in Science and Engineering, vol. 141. Academic Press, London (1979)
20. Ting, J., D'Souza, A., Schaal, S.: Bayesian regression with input noise for high dimensional data. In: Proceedings of the 23rd International Conference on Machine Learning, pp. 937–944. ACM Press, New York (2006)

Imitation Learning Using Graphical Models

Deepak Verma and Rajesh P.N. Rao

Dept. of Computer Science & Engineering
University of Washington
Seattle, WA, USA
{deepak,rao}@cs.washington.edu
http://neural.cs.washington.edu/

Abstract. Imitation-based learning is a general mechanism for rapid acquisition of new behaviors in autonomous agents and robots. In this paper, we propose a new approach to learning by imitation based on parameter learning in probabilistic graphical models. Graphical models are used not only to model an agent's own dynamics but also the dynamics of an observed teacher. Parameter tying between the agent-teacher models ensures consistency and facilitates learning. Given only observations of the teacher's states, we use the expectation-maximization (EM) algorithm to learn both dynamics and policies within graphical models. We present results demonstrating that EM-based imitation learning outperforms pure exploration-based learning on a benchmark problem (the FlagWorld domain). We additionally show that the graphical model representation can be leveraged to incorporate domain knowledge (e.g., state space factoring) to achieve significant speed-up in learning.

1 Introduction

Learning by imitation is a general mechanism for rapidly acquiring new skills or behaviors in humans and robots. Several approaches to imitation have previously been proposed (e.g., [1,2]). Many of these treat the problem of imitation as trajectory-following where the goal is to follow the teacher's trajectory as best as possible. However, imitation often involves the need to infer intentions and goals which introduces considerable uncertainty into the problem, besides the uncertainty already existing in the observation process and in the environment. Previous models of imitation have typically not been probabilistic and are therefore not geared towards handling uncertainty. There have been some recent efforts in modeling goal-based imitation [3] but these either assume that the dynamics of environment are given or need to learn the dynamics using a time-consuming exploration stage.

A different approach to imitation is based on ideas from the field of Reinforcement Learning (RL) [4]. In reinforcement learning, the agent is assumed to receive rewards in certain states and the agent's goal is to learn a state-to-action mapping ("policy") that maximizes the total future expected reward. The computational challenge of solving RL problem is hard for a variety of reasons: (1) the state space is often exponential in the number of attributes, and (2) for

J.N. Kok et al. (Eds.): ECML 2007, LNAI 4701, pp. 757–764, 2007.

uncertain environments with large state spaces, the agent needs to perform a large amount of exploration to learn a model of the environment before learning a good policy. These problems can be ameliorated by using imitation [5] (or "apprenticeship" [6]) where a teacher exhibits the optimal behavior that is observed by the student or the teacher guides the student to the most important states for exploration. Price and Boutilier formulate this in the RL framework as *Implicit Imitation* [7], in which the student learns the dynamics of the environment by passively observing the teacher without any explicit communication regarding what actions to take. This speeds up the learning of policies. However, these approaches rely on knowing or inferring an explicit reward function in the environment, which may not always be available or easy to infer.

In this paper, we propose a new approach to imitation that is based on probabilistic Graphical Models (GMs). We pose the problem of imitation learning as learning the *parameters* of the underlying GM for the mentor's and observer's behavior (we use the terms mentor/teacher (and observer/student) interchangeably in the paper). To facilitate the transfer of knowledge from mentor to observer we tie the parameters of dynamics for the mentor with that of the observer, and update the observer's policy using the learned mentor policy. Parameters are learned using the expectation-maximization (EM) algorithm for learning in GMs from partial data. Our approach provides a principled approach to imitation based *completely* on an internal GM representation, allowing us to leverage the growing number of efficient inference and learning techniques for GMs.

2 Graphical Models for Imitation

Notation: We use capital letters for variables and small case letters to denote specific instances. We assume there are two agents, the observer $\mathcal{A}^o$ and the mentor $\mathcal{A}^m$ operating in the environment[1]. Let Ω_S be the set of states in the environment and Ω_A the set of all possible actions available to the agent[2] (both finite). At time t, the agent is in state S_t and executes action A_t. The agent's state changes in a stochastic manner given by the transition probability $P(S_{t+1} \mid S_t, A_t)$, which is assumed to be independent of t, i.e., $P(S_{t+1} = s' \mid S_t = s, A_t = a) = \tau_{s'sa}$. When obvious from context, we use s for $S_t = s$ and a for $A_t = a$, etc. For each state s and action a, there is a real valued reward $\mathcal{R}^m(s,a)$ for the mentor ($\mathcal{R}^o(s,a)$ for the observer) associated with being in state s and executing the action a (with negative values denoting undesirable states or the cost of the action). The parameters described above define a Markov Decision Process (MDP) [9]. Solving an MDP typically involves computing an optimal *policy* $a = \pi(s)$ that maximizes total expected future reward (either a finite

[1] We use the superscript to distinguish the two agents and omit it for common variables (e.g., dynamics of the environment).

[2] For simplicity of exposition, we assume that agents operate (non-interactively) in the *same* environment. However, as discussed in [8], this assumption is not essential and one can apply the techniques discussed here to the more general setting where observer and mentor(s) have different action and state spaces.

horizon cumulative reward or discounted infinite horizon cumulative reward) when action a is executed in state s.

In a typical Reinforcement Learning problem, the dynamics and the reward function are not known, and one cannot therefore compute an optimal policy directly. One can learn both these functions by exploration but this requires the agent to execute a large number of exploration steps before an optimal policy can be computed. Learning can be greatly sped up via *implicit imitation* [7] which involves an agent (the observer) observing another agent (mentor) who has similar goals. . The main idea is to allow the agent to quickly learn the parameters in the relevant portion of the state space, thereby cutting down on the exploration required to compute a near-optimal policy.

We assume that the mentor follows a stationary policy $\pi^m(s)$ which defines its behavior completely. The observer is only able to observe the sequence of states that mentor has been in ($S^m_{1:t}$) and *not the actions*: this is important because some of the most useful forms of imitation learning are those in which the teacher's actions are not available, e.g., when a robot must learn by watching a human – in such a scenario, the robot can observe body poses but has no access to the human's actions (muscle or motor commands). The task of the observer is then to compute the best estimate of the dynamics $\hat{\tau}$ and mentor policy $\hat{\pi}^m$, given its own history $S^o_{1:t}, A^o_{1:t}$ and the mentor's state history $S^m_{1:t}$. Note that π^m can be completely independent of the observer's reward function $\mathcal{R}^o$: in fact, the problem as formulated above does not require the introduction of a reward function at all. The goal is simply to imitate the mentor by estimating and executing the mentor's policy. In the special case where the mentor is optimizing the same reward function as the observer, π^m becomes the optimal MDP policy. Note that since the observer cannot see actions that the mentor took and the transition parameters are not given, the problem is different from other approaches which speed up RL via imitation [6,10].

2.1 Generative Graphical Model

Both the mentor and the observer are solving an MDP. One key observation we make is that *given* the mentor policy the action choice and dynamics can be modeled easily using a *generative model* based on the well-known graphical model for MDP shown in Fig. 1(a). One does not need to know the mentor's reward model as π^m completely explains the mentor state sequence observed. The figure shows the 2-slice representation of the *Dynamic Bayesian Network* (DBN) used to model the imitation problem. Since we are assuming that the two agents are operating in the same environment, they have the same transition parameters ($\tau^m{=}\tau^o{=}\tau$). Note that the two graphical models (for the mentor and observer respectively) are disconnected as the two agents are non-interacting. The mentor's actions are guided by the optimal mentor policy $P(A^m_t = a|S^m_t = s) = \pi^m(a|s)$ and the observer's actions by the policy $P(A^o_t = a|S^m_t = s) = \pi^o_t(a|s)$. Unlike the mentor, the observer updates its policy over time (hence the subscript t on π^o). We require only the mentor to have a stationary policy. The mentor observations $s^m_{1:T}$ are generated by "sampling" the DBN. In our

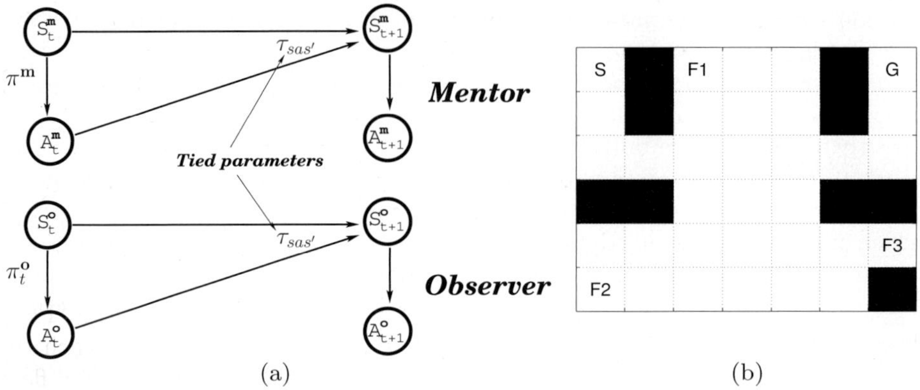

Fig. 1. Model and Domain for Imitation. (a) Graphical Model Representation for Imitation. (b) FlagWorld Domain.

experiments, when a goal state is reached, we jump to the start state in the next step. T thus represents the total number of steps taken by agent, which could span multiple "episodes" of reaching a goal state.

3 Imitation Via Parameter Learning

Our approach to imitation is based on estimating the unknown parameters $\theta = (\tau, \pi^m)$ of the graphical model in Fig. 1(a) given observed data as "evidence," i.e., $\hat{\theta} = (\hat{\tau}, \hat{\pi}^m) = \underset{\theta}{\text{argmax}}\, P(\theta | s^m_{1:T}, s^o_{1:T}, a^o_{1:T})$. Note that the evidence does *not* include mentor actions $A^m_{1:T}$. This means that the data is "incomplete" as not all nodes of the graphical model are observed. A well-known approach to learning the parameters of a GM from incomplete data [11] is to use the expectation-maximization (EM) algorithm [12]. Although any parameter learning method could be used, we use EM in the present study since it is a general-purpose, well-understood algorithm widely used in machine learning.

The EM algorithm involves starting with an initial estimate θ^0 (chosen randomly or incorporating any prior knowledge) which is then iteratively improved by performing the following two steps:

Expectation: The current set of parameters θ^i is used to compute a distribution (expectation) over the hidden nodes: $h(A^m_{1:T}) = P(A^m_{1:T} | \theta^i, s^m_{1:T}, s^o_{1:T}, a^o_{1:T})$. This allows the *expected sufficient statistics* to be computed for the complete data set.

Maximization: The distribution h is then used to compute the new parameters θ^{i+1} which maximize the (expected) log-likelihood of evidence:

$$\theta^{i+1} = \underset{\theta}{\text{argmax}} \sum_{a_{1:T}} h(a^m_{1:T}) \log(P(s^m_{1:T}, a^m_{1:T}, s^o_{1:T}, a^o_{1:T} | \theta))$$

When states and actions are discrete, the new estimate can be computed by simply using the expected counts. The two steps above are performed alternatively until convergence. The method is guaranteed to improve performance in each iteration in that the incomplete log likelihood of data ($\log P(s^m_{1:T}, s^o_{1:T}, a^o_{1:T}|\theta^i)$) is guaranteed to increase in every iteration and converge to a local maximum [12]. We then use the estimate for $\hat{\theta}$ to control the observer. In particular, the observer combines the learned mentor policy $\hat{\pi}^m$ with an exploration strategy to arrive at the policy π^o_t.

3.1 Parameter Learning Results

Domain: We tested our results on a benchmark problem known as the "Flag-World" domain [13] shown in Fig. 1(b). The agent's objective is to reach the goal state G starting from the state S and pick up a subset of the three flags located at states $F1$, $F2$ and $F3$. It receives a reward of 1 point for each flag picked up but rewards are discounted by a factor of $\gamma = 0.99$ at each time step until the goal is reached; the latter constraint favors shortest paths to goal. The environment is a standard maze environment used in RL [4] in that each action (N,E,S,W) takes the agent to the intended state with a high probability (0.9) and to a state perpendicular to the intended state with a small probability (0.1). The probability mass going into the wall or outside the maze is assigned to the state in which action taken. This domain is interesting in that there are 264 states (33 locations, augmented with a boolean attribute for each flag picked), resulting in a large number of parameters that needs to be learned (264×4 state action pairs for which $\tau(s, a, :)$ and $\pi^m(a|s)$ needs to be learned). However, the optimal policy path is sparse and hence only a small subset of parameters needs to be learned to compute a near-optimal policy, thereby making it ideal for demonstrating the utility of imitation as a medium to speed up RL.

Exploration versus Exploitation: We used the $\epsilon-$greedy method to trade-off exploration of the domain with exploitation of the current learned policy: a random action is chosen with probability ϵ, with ϵ gradually decreased over time to favor exploration initially and exploitation of the learned policy in later time steps.

Results: The results of EM-based learning are shown in Fig 2(a) (averaged over 50 runs). The parameters were learned in a "batch" mode where T was increased from 0 to 5000 in steps of 200 and reward in the last 200 steps was reported. Average reward received is shown in top right corner. Also shown are the Error in parameters (mean absolute difference w.r.t. true parameters[3]), the log-likelihood of the learned parameters and value function of start state under the current estimate for observer policy $V_{\hat{\pi}^o}(S)$ w.r.t the true transition parameters. The results show that the observer is able to learn the mentor policy to a high degree of accuracy, though not perfectly. The uncertain dynamics of the environment leads it to collect less rewards than the mentor as the optimal policy is not learned everywhere. An important point to note is that the error in

[3] The error between uniformly random parameters and true parameters is 1.5 for π^m and $\approx$1.75 for τ.

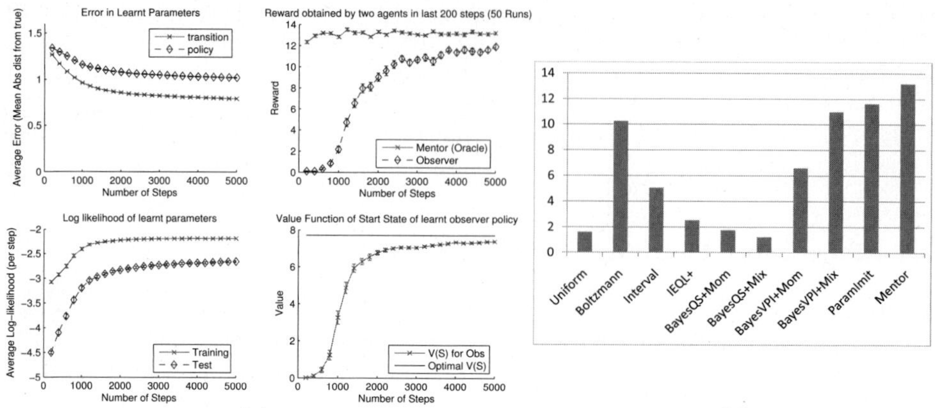

(a) (b)

Fig. 2. Imitation Learning Results for FlagWorld Domain. (a) (Clockwise) Error in parameters (mean absolute difference w.r.t. true parameters), average reward received, the log-likelihood of the learned parameters, and value function of start state $V_{\hat{\pi}^o}(S)$ w.r.t the true transition parameters. (b) Comparison of learned policy (ParamImit) with some popular exploration techniques (measured in terms of average discounted reward obtained per 200 steps). ParamImit outperforms all the pure exploration-based methods.

parameters is still quite high even when observer policy is quite good, thereby confirming the intuition that only a small (relevant) subset of parameters needs to be learned well before the agent can start exploiting a learned policy.

Figure 2(b) compares the relative quality of the learned policy with a number of pure exploration-based techniques used in [13]. The bars represent the average discounted reward obtained per 200 steps in the 2nd stage, i.e., obtained in next 20,000 steps after an initial 1st stage of exploration consisting of 20,000 steps. For ParamImit (our algorithm) the average is taken after only 4000 steps of exploration. The rightmost bar is the Mentor value. As can be seen, ParamImit outperforms all the exploration strategies with far less experience.

3.2 Factored Graphical Model

A major advantage of using a graphical models-based approach to imitation is the ability to leverage domain knowledge to speed up learning. For example, the number of true parameters in the FlagWorld is actually much less than the number that was learned in the previous section since there are only 33 locations for which the transition parameters need to be learned: the dynamics are the same irrespective of which flags have been picked up. To reflect this fact, we can *factor* the mentor state S_t^m into location L_t^m and flag status variable “Picked Flag” PF_t^m as shown in Fig. 3(a) (and similarly for the observer). This reduces the number of transition parameters significantly (from $\tau_{sas'}$ to $\tau_{lal'}$).

We can incorporate domain knowledge about the flags by defining the CPT $P(PF_{t+1}|L_{t+1}, PF_t)$ as the ,

$$\begin{aligned} P(PF_{t+1}|L_{t+1}, PF_t) &= \delta(PF_{t+1}, pf(PF_t, i)) \quad \text{if } L_{t+1} = Fi \\ &= \delta(PF_{t+1}, PF_t) \quad \text{otherwise} \end{aligned}$$

where $pf(PF_t, i)$ is the *determinstic* function[4] which maps the old value of PF_t to one in which the ith flag is picked up.

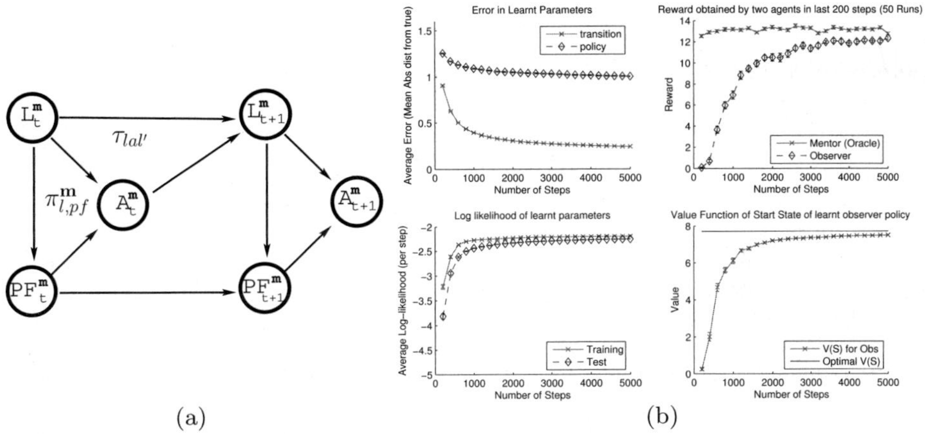

Fig. 3. Fast Learning using Factored Graphical Models. (a) Factored model for FlagWorld (only the mentor model is shown). (b) Results using factored model. Note the speed-up in learning w.r.t. the unfactored case (Fig. 2(a)).

The results of EM-based parameter learning for the factored graphical model are shown in Fig. 3(b). As expected, the error in transition parameters goes down much more rapidly than in the unfactored case (compare with Fig. 2(a)).

4 Conclusion

This paper introduces a new framework for learning by imitation based on modeling the imitation process in terms of probabilistic graphical models. Imitative policies are learned in a principled manner using the expectation-maximization (EM) algorithm. The model achieves transfer of knowledge by tying the parameters for the mentor's dynamics with those of the observer. Our results[5] demonstrate that the mentor's policy can be estimated directly from observations of

[4] This is a common trick used in GMs to encode *deterministic* domain knowledge.

[5] Additional results are presented in the extended version of the paper available at `http://neural.cs.washington.edu/`. In particular, we show how learning can be further sped up by incorporating reward information collected on the way. Also, we demonstrate the generality of parameter learning by extending the graphical model to learn task-oriented policies.

the mentor's state sequences and that significant speed-up in learning can be achieved by exploiting the graphical models framework to factor the state space in accordance with domain knowledge. Our current work is focused on testing the approach more exhaustively, especially in the context of robotic imitation. Not only do Graphical Models provide a computationally efficient framework for general imitation, they are also being used for modeling behavior [14]. An exciting prospect of using graphical models for imitation is the ease of extension to models with more abstraction, including partially observable, hierarchical, and relational models.

Acknowledgments

This material is based upon work supported by ONR, the Packard Foundation, and NSF Grants 0413335 and 0622252.

References

1. Schaal, S.: Is imitation learning the route to humanoid robots? Trends in Cognitive Sciences 3, 233–242 (1999)
2. Dautenhahn, K., Nehaniv, C.: Imitation in Animals and Artifacts. MIT Press, Cambridge, MA (2002)
3. Verma, D., Rao, R.P.N.: Goal-based imitation as probabilistic inference over graphical models. In: NIPS 18 (2006)
4. Sutton, R.S., Barto, A.: Reinforcement Learning: An Introduction. MIT Press, Cambridge, MA (1998)
5. Atkeson, C.G., Schaal, S.: Robot learning from demonstration. In: Proc. 14th ICML, pp. 12–20 (1997)
6. Abbeel, P., Ng, A.Y.: Apprenticeship learning via inverse reinforcement learning. In: ICML '04, pp. 1–8 (2004)
7. Price, B., Boutilier, C.: Accelerating reinforcement learning through implicit imitation. JAIR 19, 569–629 (2003)
8. Price, B., Boutilier, C.: A bayesian approach to imitation in reinforcement learning. In: IJCAI, pp. 712–720 (2003)
9. Boutilier, C., Dean, T., Hanks, S.: Decision-theoretic planning: Structural assumptions and computational leverage. JAIR 11, 1–94 (1999)
10. Ratliff, N.D., Bagnell, J.A., Zinkevich, M.A.: Maximum margin planning. In: ICML06, pp. 729–736 (2006)
11. Heckerman, D.: A tutorial on learning with bayesian networks. Technical report, Microsoft Research, Redmond, Washington (1995)
12. Dempster, A.P., Laird, N.M., Rubin, D.B.: Maximum likelihood from incomplete data via the EM algorithm. Journal of the Royal Statistical Society, Series B 39, 1–38 (1977)
13. Dearden, R., Friedman, N., Andre, D.: Model-based Bayesian Exploration. In: UAI-99, San Francisco, CA, pp. 150–159 (1999)
14. Griffiths, T.L., Tenenbaum, J.B.: Structure and strength in causal induction. Cognitive Psychology 51(4), 334–384 (2005)

Nondeterministic Discretization of Weights Improves Accuracy of Neural Networks

Marcin Wojnarski

Warsaw University, Faculty of Mathematics, Informatics and Mechanics
ul. Banacha 2, 02-097 Warszawa, Poland
mwojnars@ns.onet.pl

Abstract. The paper investigates modification of backpropagation algorithm, consisting of discretization of neural network weights after each training cycle. This modification, aimed at overfitting reduction, restricts the set of possible values of weights to a discrete subset of real numbers, leading to much better generalization abilities of the network. This, in turn, leads to higher accuracy and a decrease in error rate by over 50% in extreme cases (when overfitting is high).

Discretization is performed nondeterministically, so as to keep expected value of discretized weight equal to original value. In this way, global behavior of original algorithm is preserved. The presented method of discretization is general and may be applied to other machine-learning algorithms. It is also an example of how an algorithm for continuous optimization can be successfully applied to optimization over discrete spaces. The method was evaluated experimentally in WEKA environment using two real-world data sets from UCI repository.

Keywords: Generalization, Overtraining, Overfitting, Regularization.

1 Introduction

Multi-layer artificial neural networks [1,2] are well-established tools in machine learning, with proven effectiveness in many real-world problems. However, there are still many tasks in which they perform worse than other machine-learning systems [3]. One of the reasons is that neural networks contain usually thousands of real-valued adaptive parameters, and so they have strong tendency to get *overtrained* (*overfitted*), especially when the size of the training set is not large enough. Thus, methods to improve generalization abilities of neural networks are necessary.

Several such methods have been already proposed: early stopping [2] – the simplest and most commonly used – which consists of finishing the training process when the error on a validation set starts increasing; regularization [4,5,6] based on adding a regularization term to the error function; pruning [4,7], i.e. removing unnecessary weights or neurons during or after training; training with noise [5,8,9], i.e. disturbing training instances in a random way; weight sharing [10].

This paper introduces a novel method based on discretization of weights. The method is easy to implement and potentially more versatile than existing

J.N. Kok et al. (Eds.): ECML 2007, LNAI 4701, pp. 765–772, 2007.

ones, yet it can lead to significant improvement in generalization abilities and accuracy of the neural network. It can be also used in conjunction with the above-mentioned algorithms.

Motivation which underlies the presented method is described in Sect. 2. It is followed by presentation of the algorithm in Sect. 3 and its experimental assessment in Sect. 4. Finally, Sect. 5 recaps main points of the paper and presents conclusions.

2 Motivation

Discretization of weights means restricting the set of possible values of neuron weights to a small discrete subset of real numbers. In this way, the decision model represented by a neural network gets simpler and can be described using fewer number of bits, since every weight may be represented, for instance, by a single byte instead of four or eight bytes. This in turn leads to better generalization abilities.

Theoretical justification of the method is provided by Rissanen's Minimum Description Length (MDL) Principle [11,12] which states that the best way to capture regularities in data and avoid overfitting is to choose a model that has short description. Thus, a neural network which uses only one byte to represent a weight value is better than a network requiring 4-byte-long description of every weight, even if the latter has slightly higher accuracy on training data than the former.

A more intuitive justification might be given by considering a system whose accuracy (measured during training on a training set) abruptly decreases when some weight is slightly disturbed, e.g. by 0.01. High accuracy of such a system is probably accidental and will not recur on test data. A system which is insensitive to such small perturbations of weight values would be much more trustworthy.

3 The Algorithm

Let us denote by Ω, $\Omega \subset \mathbb{R}$, the set of *permitted values* of weights. Assume that Ω is discrete (and usually $0 \in \Omega$). There is a training algorithm $\mathcal{A}$ given, e.g. backpropagation, which searches through a family $\mathcal{F}$ of models to find the one that achieves (approximately) minimum error rate on training data. Let us denote by $\mathcal{F}_\Omega$ the family of models from $\mathcal{F}$ whose weights belong to Ω (so $\mathcal{F}_\Omega \subset \mathcal{F}$). The goal is to create a discretized variant of algorithm $\mathcal{A}$, which finds a model in $\mathcal{F}_\Omega$ that minimizes the error rate over $\mathcal{F}_\Omega$.

The easiest way to do this is to discretize weights of the model found by algorithm $\mathcal{A}$, by simply rounding them to the closest values from Ω. This procedure is very simple, but it does not provide any control over the accuracy of the discretized model, so it cannot be beneficial for accuracy of the final model.

A better method is to interlace discretization with training process $\mathcal{A}$ by rounding weights every time they are updated. In this case, the process of searching for the best model is restricted to $\mathcal{F}_\Omega$ from the beginning, so it is directed by accuracy of *discretized* models and thus is able to find a better model than the previous method.

However, there is still another problem if the process of searching guided by algorithm $\mathcal{A}$ moves slowly through the space $\mathcal{F}$, which happens for example in backpropagation algorithm when the *learning rate* [1] is small. In this case, simple discretization – meant as deterministic rounding of every weight to the nearest value in Ω – may turn values of all updated weights back to the values from before the update. Consequently, the searching process guided by discrete variant of $\mathcal{A}$ may easily get stuck in some point of $\mathcal{F}_\Omega$ which is neither global nor even local minimum of error function.

This can be avoided by performing discretization in a *nondeterministic* way.

Let v denote the weight value to be discretized; $L_\Omega(v)$ is the greatest value in Ω not greater than v; $G_\Omega(v)$ is the least value in Ω not less than v. Value v is discretized by replacing it nondeterministically with either $L_\Omega(v)$ or $G_\Omega(v)$, according to the formula:

$$D_\Omega(v) = \begin{cases} L_\Omega(v) & \text{with probability } (G_\Omega(v) - v)/R_\Omega(v) \\ G_\Omega(v) & \text{with probability } (v - L_\Omega(v))/R_\Omega(v) \end{cases} , \qquad (1)$$

where $D_\Omega(v)$ denotes discretized value of v and $R_\Omega(v) = G_\Omega(v) - L_\Omega(v)$. The above choice of probabilities makes the following important property hold:

$$\mathbb{E}(D_\Omega(v)) = v , \qquad (2)$$

i.e. expected value of discretized weight is equal to the original value. In this way, discretization may be viewed as adding some zero-mean random fluctuations to weight values, without disturbing global behavior of the original algorithm. Note, however, that discretization is *not* equivalent to adding random fluctuations to weight values. General structure of the training algorithm which performs discretization of weights is presented in Figure 1.

```
for cycle := 1 to number of training cycles do
   pattern := GetNextPattern();
   CalculateResponse(network, pattern);
   UpdateWeights(network);   /* standard algorithm, e.g. backpropagation */
   for each weight in network do
      w := ValueOf(weight);
      d := D_Ω(w);   /* nondeterministic discretization of w, Eq. (1) */
      ValueOf(weight) := d;
   end
end
```

Fig. 1. Outline of the neural network training algorithm with discretization of weights

Some attention should be paid to the question of what set of permitted values Ω to use. Simple yet efficient choice is to take a set of evenly-spaced numbers containing zero:

$$\Omega = \{k\gamma : k \in \mathbb{Z}\} , \tag{3}$$

where $\gamma \in \mathbb{R}$ is a parameter that controls *granularity* of discretization.

4 Experimental Results

The presented modification was applied to standard backpropagation algorithm [2,1] used for training of multilayer neural networks. The modified algorithm was compared with the standard one on two real-world datasets from the UCI [13] machine-learning repository: *Labor* and *Image Segmentation*. Experiments were conducted in WEKA [14] environment, whose implementation of backpropagation algorithm was extended by the author to handle discretization of weights.

To enable thorough analysis and reliable comparison of the algorithms, different numbers of hidden neurons were tested: 5, 10, 20, 30, 50, 70, 100, 150, 200 and 250. In this way, it was possible to draw final conclusions that were independent from specific choice of training parameters.

To obtain plausible results, 20 networks were trained for each algorithm and size of hidden layer, using different (random) split of data into training and test sets each time (percentage split: $50+50\%$ for *Labor* data; $25+75\%$ of training and test instances respectively for *Image Segmentation* data). Thus, 20 estimates of error rate on test set were obtained for each algorithm and size of hidden layer. Mean and standard deviation of these 20 values formed the basis of subsequent analysis.

Throughout all experiments, the learning rate [1] of neural networks (which controls magnitude of updates) was set to 0.1 and each network underwent 20 epochs of training. In discrete variant of the algorithm, all weights of networks – both in hidden and output layers – were discretized in the same way, with granularity $\gamma = 0.1$.

4.1 *Labor* Data

Labor data set[1] [13,15,16] contains information on final settlements in labor negotiations in Canadian industry. It is composed of 57 instances described by 16 attributes – mixed symbolic and numeric. In the experiment, symbolic attributes were turned into binary, which resulted in a data set described by 26 numeric or binary attributes. Then, all attributes were normalized. There were two classes with 37 and 20 instances respectively. Neural networks created during the experiment consisted of two layers of sigmoidal neurons: hidden one, of different size; and output one, containing two neurons, one for each class. Results of experiments are listed in Table 1 and presented graphically in Figure 2.

The results show that discretization substantially improves accuracy of neural networks trained on *Labor* data. The lowest error rate obtained with discretized

[1] ftp://ftp.ics.uci.edu/pub/machine-learning-databases/labor-negotiations .

Table 1. Error rates [%] and their standard deviations for neural networks trained with either standard or discrete backpropagation algorithm, evaluated on *Labor* data

No. of hidden neurons	Discrete backpropagation	Standard backpropagation
5	22.55 ± 9.83	35.10 ± 0.63
10	15.25 ± 7.93	35.10 ± 0.63
20	10.17 ± 5.42	34.06 ± 2.28
30	9.49 ± 4.99	28.08 ± 5.61
50	8.25 ± 5.37	26.00 ± 9.45
70	7.54 ± 4.98	22.62 ± 9.30
100	7.37 ± 3.94	18.26 ± 8.48
150	7.20 ± 3.33	21.39 ± 9.29
200	7.72 ± 4.37	21.25 ± 10.85
250	7.91 ± 4.11	21.96 ± 11.67

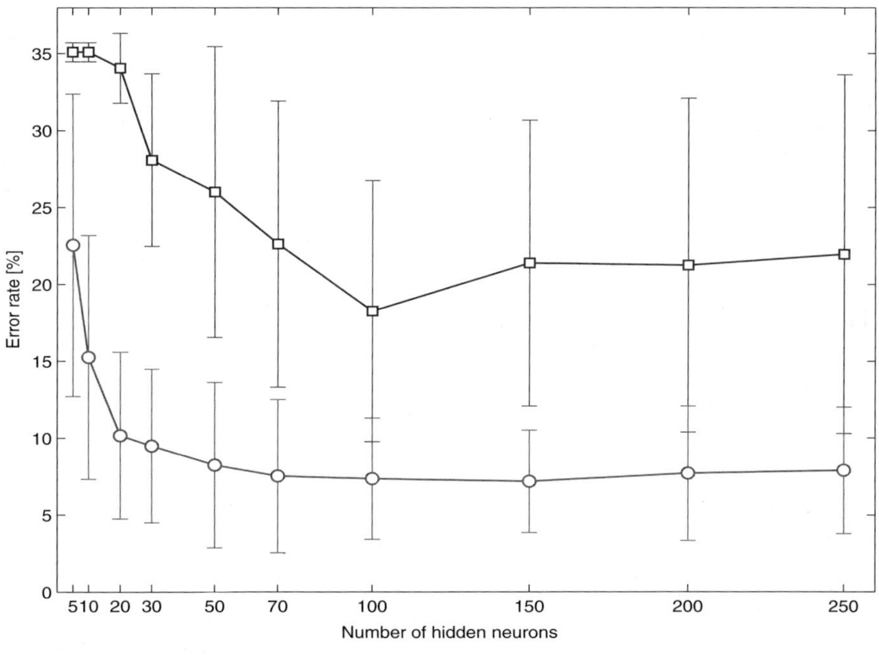

Fig. 2. Error rates [%] and their standard deviations (vertical bars) for neural networks trained with either standard (squares) or discrete (circles) backpropagation algorithm, evaluated on *Labor* data. Networks with different number of hidden neurons (horizontal axis) were checked.

algorithm (7.20%) is by 60% smaller than with standard algorithm (18.26%), which is a huge difference. Moreover, standard deviation of the error rate among networks with the same size of hidden layer is also significantly lower when

Table 2. Error rates [%] and their standard deviations for neural networks trained with either standard or discrete backpropagation algorithm, evaluated on *Image Segmentation* data

No. of hidden neurons	Discrete backpropagation	Standard backpropagation
5	24.41 ± 3.84	37.72 ± 5.94
10	15.18 ± 3.02	27.88 ± 3.94
20	12.12 ± 1.43	19.94 ± 2.26
30	11.15 ± 1.12	19.61 ± 2.10
50	10.91 ± 1.25	17.45 ± 1.50
70	10.34 ± 0.97	16.59 ± 1.21
100	10.24 ± 0.99	16.24 ± 1.29
150	10.87 ± 1.40	16.24 ± 1.68
200	10.77 ± 1.75	16.76 ± 2.11
250	10.63 ± 1.90	17.04 ± 2.41

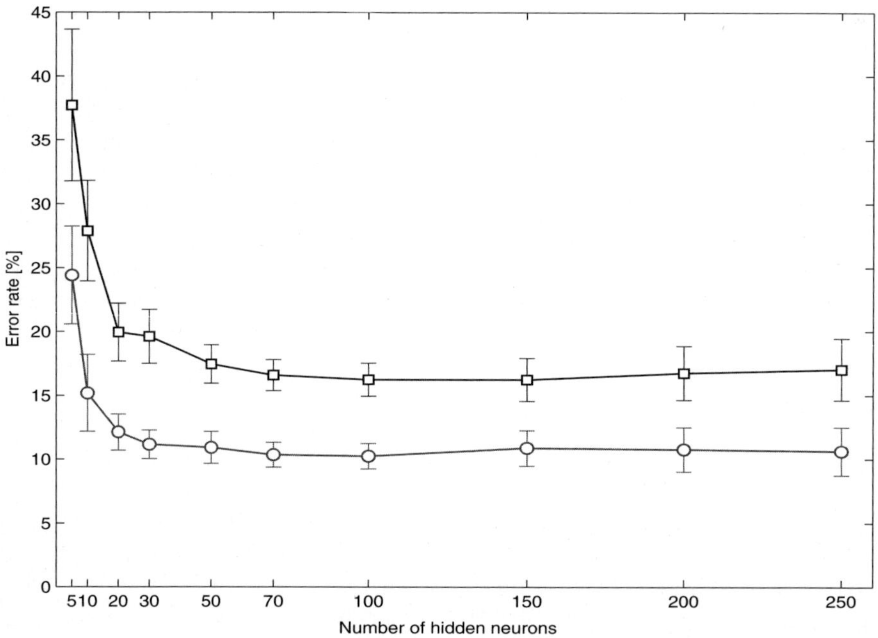

Fig. 3. Error rates [%] and their standard deviations (vertical bars) for neural networks trained with either standard (squares) or discrete (circles) backpropagation algorithm, evaluated on *Image Segmentation* data. Networks with different number of hidden neurons (horizontal axis) were checked.

discretization is used. These large differences indicate that standard backpropagation highly overtrains on *Labor* data and discretization of weights is an efficient way to reduce this overtraining.

4.2 *Image Segmentation* Data

Image Segmentation data set[2] [13,3] contains 2310 instances, described by 19 numeric attributes and uniformly distributed in 7 classes. The attributes were normalized before training. Neural networks created during the experiment consisted two layers of sigmoidal neurons: hidden one, of different size; and output one, containing 7 neurons, one for each class. Results of experiments are listed in Table 2 and presented graphically in Figure 3.

As in the case of *Labor* data, also for *Image Segmentation* data the performance of neural networks can be improved by discretization of weights. The best result achieved with discretization (10.24% error rate) is by 37% better than the best result of standard algorithm (16.24%). The improvement is smaller than for *Labor* data, probably due to significantly bigger size of the training set and thus smaller degree of overfitting.

5 Conclusions

A novel method that reduces overfitting of neural networks has been presented. The method is based on non-deterministic discretization of weights after every training cycle, which restricts the set of possible weight values to a discrete subset of real numbers and enables much shorter description of the network. This, in turn, improves generalization abilities and performance of the system, according to Minimum Description Length principle. Thanks to non-determinism, there is no risk that discretization would force the training process to stop in some far-from-optimal point of parameter space. The method was evaluated on two real-world data sets from UCI repository, exhibiting high effectiveness in preventing neural network from overfitting: the use of discretization enabled decrease in error rate by 60% and 37% respectively. Importantly, it was better to use discretization than to decrease the number of hidden neurons, so discretization appeared to be more effective than the most straightforward method of avoiding overtraining.

It should be emphasized that the presented method is potentially very versatile. Although the paper covers only neural networks and backpropagation algorithm, discretization of parameters of a model could be applied to many other algorithms and systems, as different as evolutionary algorithms, Bayesian networks or Gaussian mixture models, to name just a few.

There are also two more general conclusions which follow from the presented study. They may seem strange at first sight but have deep consequences. Firstly, it appears that methods of continuous optimization – like gradient descend, which lies in the basis of backpropagation algorithm – can be successfully applied to optimization over *dis*continuous (e.g. discrete) spaces, as well.

Secondly, all decision systems built from data and described by real-valued parameters might probably benefit from some kind of restriction imposed on possible parameter values.

These conclusions definitely need more investigation.

---

[2] ftp://ftp.ics.uci.edu/pub/machine-learning-databases/image

Acknowledgement

The author thanks anonymous reviewers for their helpful remarks.

References

1. Russell, S., Norvig, P.: Artificial Intelligence: A Modern Approach. Prentice-Hall, Englewood Cliffs (1995)
2. Ripley, B.D.: Pattern recognition and neural networks. Cambridge University Press, Cambridge (1996)
3. Michie, D., Spiegelhalter, D.J., Taylor, C.C.: Machine Learning, Neural and Statistical Classification. Elis Horwood, London (1994)
4. Rychetsky, M., Ortmann, S., Glesner, M.: Pruning and regularization techniques for feed forward nets applied on a real world data base. In: Heiss, M. (ed.) International Symposium on Neural Computation, pp. 603–609 (1998)
5. Bishop, C.M.: Training with noise is equivalent to Tikhonov regularization. Neural Computation 7(1), 108–116 (1995)
6. Burger, M., Neubauer, A.: Analysis of tikhonov regularization for function approximation by neural networks. Neural Networks 16(1), 79–90 (2003)
7. Wojnarski, M.: LTF-C: Architecture, training algorithm and applications of new neural classifier. Fundamenta Informaticae 54(1), 89–105 (2003)
8. Sietsma, J., Dow, R.J.F.: Creating artifical neural networks that generalize. Neural Networks 4(1), 67–79 (1991)
9. Holmström, L., Koistinen, P.: Using additive noise in back-propagation training. IEEE Transactions on Neural Networks 3(1), 24–38 (1992)
10. LeCun, Y., Bottou, L., Bengio, Y., Haffner, P.: Gradient-based learning applied to document recognition. Proceedings of the IEEE 86(11), 2278–2324 (1998)
11. Rissanen, J.: Modeling by shortest data description. Automatica 14, 465–471 (1978)
12. Grünwald, P., Myung, I.J., Pitt, M.: Advances in Minimum Description Length. MIT Press, Cambridge (2005)
13. Newman, D.J., Hettich, S., Merz, C.B.: UCI repository of machine learning databases (1998)
14. Witten, I.H., Frank, E.: Data Mining: Practical Machine Learning Tools and Techniques, 2nd edn. Morgan Kaufmann, San Francisco (2005)
15. Bergadano, F., Matwin, S., Michalski, R.S., Zhang, J.: Measuring quality of concept descriptions. In: EWSL, pp. 1–14 (1988)
16. Bergadano, F., Matwin, S., Michalski, R.S., Zhang, J.: Representing and acquiring imprecise and context-dependent concepts in knowledge-based systems. In: ISMIS, pp. 270–280 (1988)

Semi-definite Manifold Alignment

Liang Xiong, Fei Wang, and Changshui Zhang

Dept. Automation, Tsinghua University,
Beijing, China
{xiongl,feiwang03}@mails.tsinghua.edu.cn,
zcs@mail.tsinghua.edu.cn

Abstract. We study the problem of *manifold alignment*, which aims at "aligning" different data sets that share a similar intrinsic manifold provided some supervision. Unlike traditional methods that rely on pairwise correspondences between the two data sets, our method only needs some relative comparison information like "A is more similar to B than A is to C". This method provides a more flexible way to acquire the prior knowledge for alignment, thus is able to handle situations where corresponding pairs are hard or impossible to identify. We optimize our objective based on the graphs that give discrete approximations of the manifold. Further, the problem is formulated as a *semi-definite programming* (SDP) problem which can readily be solved. Finally, experimental results are presented to show the effectiveness of our method.

1 Introduction

In machine learning, we are often faced with data with very high dimensionality. Directly dealing with these data is usually intractable due to the computational cost and *the curse of dimensionality*. In recent years, researchers have realized that in many situations the samples are confined to a low-dimensional manifold embedded in the feature space [1,2]. This intrinsic structure is of great value to facilitate the analysis and learning. Consequently, many methods have been developed to reveal data manifolds, such as *Locally Linear Embedding* [2], *Laplacian Eigenmaps* [3] and *Maximum Variance Unfolding* [4]. However, all these algorithms are *unsupervised*. Therefore, their results usually fail to reflect samples' underlying parameters (*e.g.* the pose parameters for head images). Fortunately, provided some *supervised* information, we are able to develop methods that can reveal these parameters.

In this paper, we will focus on the problem of *manifold alignment*. More concretely, given some data sets sharing the same manifold structure, we seek to learn the correspondences between samples from different data sets (*e.g.* Finding different persons' face images with the same pose). Besides its usage in data analysis and visualization, this problem also have wide range of applications. For instance, in *facial expression recognition*, one may have a set of labeled images with known expressions. Then we can recognize the expressions of another person by aligning his/her facial images to the standard image set. One can refer to [5] for more details.

J.N. Kok et al. (Eds.): ECML 2007, LNAI 4701, pp. 773–781, 2007.

Fig. 1. An example of data sharing the same manifold. Above are facial expressions from *JAFFE* [6]. The top and bottom rows show pairs with the same underlying facial expression.

(a) (b) (c)

Fig. 2. Three facial expression images. (a) and (c) is *surprised* and (b) is *neutral.* It is hard to make a confident decision that (a) and (c) have the same expression. However, it is obvious that (c) is more similar to (a) than (b) is.

There have already been some methods to align manifolds in a *semi-supervised* way [7,8,5,9,10]. Specifically, they assume that some pairwise correspondences of samples between data sets are known, and then use those information to guide the alignment. However, in practice it might be difficult to obtain and use such information since:

1. The sizes of data sets can be very large, then finding high-quality correspondences between them can be very time consuming and even intractable.
2. There may exist some ambiguities in the images (see Fig. 2 for an example), which makes explicit matching a hard task. Brutally determine and enforce these unreliable constraints may lead to poor results;
3. There may not exist exact correspondences. For example, this situation may happen when the data is restricted and users can only access a small subset.

To solve these problems, we propose to apply another type of supervision to guide manifold alignment. In particular, we consider a relative and qualitative supervision of the form "*A is closer to B than A is to C*". We believe that this type of information is more easily available than traditional correspondence information. With this information, we show that the manifold alignment problem can be formulated as a *Quadratically Constrained Quadratic Programming* (*QCQP*) [11] problem. To make the solution tractable, we further relax it to a *Semi-Definite Programming* (*SDP*) [11] problem, which can be readily solved. Besides, under this formulation we can incorporate both relative relations and correspondences to align manifolds in a very flexible way. Finally experimental results are presented to show the effectiveness of our method.

The rest of this paper is organized as follows. Section 2 will introduce some basic notations and related works. The detailed algorithm will be presented in section 3. The experimental results will be provided in section 4, followed by the discussions in section 5 and conclusions in section 6.

2 Notations and Related Works

We study the problem of *aligning* different data sets that share the same underlying manifold. For the convenience of presentation, first let us consider the case of two data sets $\mathcal{X}$ and $\mathcal{Y}$ in high-dimensional vector spaces

$$\mathcal{X} = \{\mathbf{x}_1, \mathbf{x}_2, \cdots, \mathbf{x}_N\} \subset \mathbb{R}^{d_x}, \ \ \mathcal{Y} = \{\mathbf{y}_1, \mathbf{y}_2, \cdots, \mathbf{y}_N\} \subset \mathbb{R}^{d_y}. \tag{1}$$

Manifold learning methods such as *Laplacian eigenmaps* [3] can learn the low-dimensional embeddings by constructing an *undirected weighted graph* that captures the local structure of data. For example, for $\mathcal{X}$ we can construct a graph $\mathcal{G}_\mathcal{X} = (\mathcal{V}_\mathcal{X}, \mathcal{E}_\mathcal{X})$, where $\mathcal{V}_\mathcal{X} = \mathcal{X}$ are the vertices and $\mathcal{E}_\mathcal{X}$ are the edges. Generally there is a nonnegative weight W_{ij} associated with each edge $e_{ij} \in \mathcal{E}_\mathcal{X}$, and all the edge weights form an $N \times N$ *weight matrix* $\mathbf{W}_\mathcal{X}$ with its (i,j)-th entry $\mathbf{W}_\mathcal{X}(i,j) = W_{ij}$. The *degree matrix* $\mathbf{D}_\mathcal{X}$ is an $N \times N$ diagonal matrix with the i-th diagonal entry $\mathbf{D}_\mathcal{X}(i,i) = \sum_j W_{ij}$, and the *combinatorial graph Laplacian* is defined as $\mathbf{L}_\mathcal{X} = \mathbf{D}_\mathcal{X} - \mathbf{W}_\mathcal{X}$.

The low-dimensional embeddings of the data in $\mathcal{X}$, say $\mathbf{F} = [\mathbf{f}_1, \mathbf{f}_2, \cdots, \mathbf{f}_N] \in \mathbb{R}^{d \times N}$ $(d \ll d_\mathcal{X})$ can be achieved by minimizing the criterion $\mathcal{S}_\mathcal{X} = tr(\mathbf{F}\mathbf{L}_\mathcal{X}\mathbf{F}^T)$, where $tr(\cdot)$ represents the trace of a matrix. According to [3], $\mathcal{S}_\mathcal{X}$ measures the smoothness of the embeddings of $\mathcal{X}$ over the its underlying manifold. Similarly, we can define a graph $\mathcal{G}_\mathcal{Y} = (\mathcal{V}_\mathcal{Y}, \mathcal{E}_\mathcal{Y})$ for $\mathcal{Y}$ with its combinatorial graph Laplacian $\mathbf{L}_\mathcal{Y} = \mathbf{D}_\mathcal{Y} - \mathbf{W}_\mathcal{Y}$. And the low-dimensional embeddings of $\mathcal{Y}$, say $\mathbf{G} = [\mathbf{g}_1, \mathbf{g}_2, \cdots, \mathbf{g}_N] \in \mathbb{R}^{d \times N}$ can also be achieved by minimizing $\mathcal{S}_\mathcal{Y} = tr(\mathbf{G}\mathbf{L}_\mathcal{Y}\mathbf{G})^T$. Moreover, we can minimize the following combined criterion to achieve the common embeddings of both $\mathcal{X}$ and $\mathcal{Y}$

$$\mathcal{S} = tr(\mathbf{F}\mathbf{L}_\mathcal{X}\mathbf{F}^T) + tr(\mathbf{G}\mathbf{L}_\mathcal{Y}\mathbf{G}^T). \tag{2}$$

Now let's return to our *manifold alignment* problem. Assuming that we have known some pairwise correspondences $\{\mathbf{x}_i, \mathbf{y}_i\}_{i=1}^l$, we can align $\mathcal{X}$ and $\mathcal{Y}$ in a common low-dimensional space by minimizing [8]

$$\mathcal{J} = \mu \sum\nolimits_{i=1}^{l} \|\mathbf{f}_i - \mathbf{g}_i\|^2 + tr(\mathbf{F}\mathbf{L}_\mathcal{X}\mathbf{F}^T) + tr(\mathbf{G}\mathbf{L}_\mathcal{Y}\mathbf{G}^T), \tag{3}$$

where μ is a regularization parameter to balance the embedding smoothness and the matching precision. When $\mu = \infty$, the pairwise correspondences will become hard constraints which impose $\mathbf{f}_i = \mathbf{g}_i$ after embedding [7,10]. However, as we explained in the introduction, it may be difficult to obtain the pairwise correspondences. Hence we propose a novel scheme for manifold alignment in this paper, which is based on relative comparisons among the data points.

3 Manifold Alignment Via Semi-definite Programming

3.1 The Quadratic Formulation

In this section we show how to correctly embed the data from different data sets into a common low-dimensional space with the guidance of supervised information.

Co-embedding Without Prior Knowledge. Following [8], we adopt the graph based criterion as our optimization objective. We construct weighted undirected graphs $\mathcal{G}_{\mathcal{X}}, \mathcal{G}_{\mathcal{Y}}$ for data sets $\mathcal{X}$ and $\mathcal{Y}$ respectively, and then seek a embedding which minimize Eq.(2). To avoid the illness of this problem, we impose the scale and translational invariance constraints. Then the *co-embedding* problem can be formulated as

$$\begin{aligned} \min_{\mathbf{F},\mathbf{G}} \ & tr(\mathbf{F}\mathbf{L}_{\mathcal{X}}\mathbf{F}^T) + tr(\mathbf{G}\mathbf{L}_{\mathcal{Y}}\mathbf{G}^T) \\ s.t. \ & tr(\mathbf{F}\mathbf{F}^T) = 1, tr(\mathbf{G}\mathbf{G}^T) = 1 \\ & \mathbf{F}\mathbf{e} = \mathbf{0}, \mathbf{G}\mathbf{e} = \mathbf{0} \end{aligned} \tag{4}$$

which is a co-dimensionality reduction problem without any prior knowledge about the relationship between $\mathcal{X}$ and $\mathcal{Y}$. For the choice of the *Laplacian* matrices $\mathbf{L}_{\mathcal{X}}$ and $\mathbf{L}_{\mathcal{Y}}$, we use the *iterated Laplacian* [3] $\mathbf{M}_{\mathcal{X}} = (\mathbf{I} - \mathbf{Q}_{\mathcal{X}})^T(\mathbf{I} - \mathbf{Q}_{\mathcal{X}})$, where $\mathbf{Q}_{\mathcal{X}}$ is an $N \times N$ matrix with its (i,j)-th entry q_{ij} being calculated by optimizing

$$\min_{q_{ij}} \left\| \mathbf{x}_i - \sum\nolimits_{\mathbf{x}_j \in \mathcal{N}(\mathbf{x}_i)} q_{ij}\mathbf{x}_j \right\|^2 \ s.t. \sum\nolimits_j q_{ij} = 1,$$

where $\mathcal{N}(\mathbf{x}_i)$ is the neighborhood of $\mathbf{x}_i$ (*e.g. k-nearest neighborhood* or ε*-ball neighborhood*), and for $\mathbf{x}_j \notin \mathcal{N}(\mathbf{x}_i)$, $q_{ij} = 0$. Similarly, we can define the iterated Laplacian $\mathbf{M}_{\mathcal{Y}}$ for data set $\mathcal{Y}$.

Manifold Alignment by Incorporating the Prior Knowledge. Now let's take the relative comparison constraints into account. As we have introduced in section 2, the knowledge "$\mathbf{y}_i$ *is closer to* $\mathbf{x}_j$ *than* $\mathbf{x}_k$" can be translated into the relative distance constraint

$$\|\mathbf{g}_i - \mathbf{f}_j\|^2 \leq \|\mathbf{g}_i - \mathbf{f}_k\|^2 \tag{5}$$

in the embedded space. In the rest of this paper, for notational convenience, we will denote the constraint shown in Eq.(5) as an ordered 3-tuple $t_c = \{\mathbf{y}_i, \mathbf{x}_j, \mathbf{x}_k\}$. We use $\mathcal{T} = \{t_c\}_{c=1}^C$ to denote the set of constraints. Let $\mathbf{H} = [\mathbf{F}, \mathbf{G}]$, $\mathbf{M} = \begin{bmatrix} \mathbf{M}_{\mathcal{X}} & \mathbf{0} \\ \mathbf{0} & \mathbf{M}_{\mathcal{Y}} \end{bmatrix}$. By incorporating those constraints, our optimization problem (4) can be formulated as

$$\begin{aligned} \min_{\mathbf{H}} \ & tr(\mathbf{H}\mathbf{M}\mathbf{H}^T) \\ s.t. \ & \forall \{\mathbf{y}_i, \mathbf{x}_j, \mathbf{x}_k\} \in \mathcal{T}, \|\mathbf{h}_{i+N} - \mathbf{h}_j\|^2 \leq \|\mathbf{h}_{i+N} - \mathbf{h}_k\|^2 \\ & tr(\mathbf{H}_F\mathbf{H}_F^T) = 1, tr(\mathbf{H}_G\mathbf{H}_G^T) = 1 \\ & \mathbf{H}_{\mathbf{F}}\mathbf{e} = \mathbf{0}, \mathbf{H}_{\mathbf{G}}\mathbf{e} = \mathbf{0}, \end{aligned} \tag{6}$$

where $\mathbf{H}_F$ and $\mathbf{H}_G$ are the sub-matrices of $\mathbf{H}$ corresponding to $\mathbf{F}$ and $\mathbf{G}$.

Now we have formulated our tuple-constrained optimization as a *Quadratically Constrained Quadratic Programming* (*QCQP*) [11] problem. However, since the relative distance constraints in Eq.(6) is not *convex*, then 1) computationally the solution is difficult to derive and 2) the solution is trapped in local minima. Therefore, a reformulation is needed to make this problem tractable.

3.2 A Semi-definite Approach

Now we present how to relax the QCQP problem Eq.(6) to a SDP problem. Note that

$$\|\mathbf{h}_{i+N} - \mathbf{h}_j\|^2 \leq \|\mathbf{h}_{i+N} - \mathbf{h}_k\|^2 \Leftrightarrow 2\mathbf{h}_{i+N}^T\mathbf{h}_j + 2\mathbf{h}_{i+N}^T\mathbf{h}_k + \mathbf{h}_j^T\mathbf{h}_j - \mathbf{h}_k^T\mathbf{h}_k \leq 0$$
$$tr(\mathbf{HMH}^T) = tr(\mathbf{MH}^T\mathbf{H}).$$

These two facts motivate us to deal with the *Gram matrix* of data instead, which is defined as $\mathbf{K} = \mathbf{H}^T\mathbf{H}$. $\mathbf{K}$ can be divided into four blocks as

$$\mathbf{K} = \begin{bmatrix} \mathbf{F}^T\mathbf{F} & \mathbf{F}^T\mathbf{G} \\ \mathbf{G}^T\mathbf{F} & \mathbf{G}^T\mathbf{G} \end{bmatrix} = \begin{bmatrix} \mathbf{K}^{FF} & \mathbf{K}^{FG} \\ \mathbf{K}^{GF} & \mathbf{K}^{GG} \end{bmatrix}. \tag{7}$$

Using $\mathbf{K}$, we are able to convert the formulas in Eq.(6) into linear forms as follows:

– **The objective function** is

$$\min_{\mathbf{K}} tr(\mathbf{MK}). \tag{8}$$

– **The relative distance constraints** is

$$\forall\{\mathbf{y}_i, \mathbf{x}_j, \mathbf{x}_k\} \in \mathcal{T}, -2\mathbf{K}_{i+N,j} + 2\mathbf{K}_{i+N,k} + \mathbf{K}_{j,j} - \mathbf{K}_{k,k} \leq 0. \tag{9}$$

– **The scale invariance** is achieved by constraining the traces of $\mathbf{K}^{FF}$ and $\mathbf{K}^{GG}$ *i.e.*

$$trace(\mathbf{FF}^T) = trace(\mathbf{K}^{FF}) = 1, trace(\mathbf{GG}^T) = trace(\mathbf{K}^{GG}) = 1. \tag{10}$$

– **The translation invariance** is achieved by constraints

$$\sum_{i,j} \mathbf{K}_{i,j}^{FF} = 0, \sum_{i,j} \mathbf{K}_{i,j}^{GG} = 0. \tag{11}$$

To see this, consider the following fact for $\mathbf{F}$ (and similar for $\mathbf{G}$)

$$\sum_i \mathbf{f}_i = 0 \Leftrightarrow \left|\sum_i \mathbf{f}_i\right|^2 = \sum_{i,j} \mathbf{f}_i^T\mathbf{f}_j = \sum_{i,j} \mathbf{K}_{ij}^{FF} = 0 \tag{12}$$

Finally, $\mathbf{K}$ must be *positive semi-definite i.e.* $\mathbf{K} \succeq 0$ to be a valid Gram matrix. And to avoid the case of empty feasible set and to encourage the influence of prior knowledge, we introduce slack variables $\mathcal{E} = \{\varepsilon_c\}_{c=1}^C$ and write the problem as:

$$\begin{aligned}
\min_{\mathbf{K},\varepsilon}\ & tr(\mathbf{MK}) + \alpha\sum_{c=1}^{C}\varepsilon_c \\
s.t.\ \ & \forall\{\mathbf{y}_i, \mathbf{x}_j, \mathbf{x}_k\} \in \mathcal{T}, -2\mathbf{K}_{i+N,j} + 2\mathbf{K}_{i+N,k} + \mathbf{K}_{j,j} - \mathbf{K}_{k,k} \leq \varepsilon_c \\
& trace(\mathbf{K}^{FF}) = 1, trace(\mathbf{K}^{GG}) = 1, \\
& \sum_{i,j} \mathbf{K}_{i,j}^{FF} = 0, \sum_{i,j} \mathbf{K}_{i,j}^{GG} = 0, \\
& \mathbf{K} \succeq 0, \\
& \forall\varepsilon_c \in \mathcal{E},\ \varepsilon_c \leq 0,
\end{aligned} \tag{13}$$

where α is a parameter to balance between the data's structure and the supervision.

Since Eq.(13) is a *Semi-Definite Programming* (*SDP*) problem [11], we call our method *Semi-Definite Manifold Alignment* (*SDMA*). Clearly, Eq.(13) is convex and thus is free of local minima. Besides, various software packages are available for efficient solutions, and we have preferred the *Sedumi* [12] package in this paper. When the Gram matrix $\mathbf{K}$ is solved, the embedded coordinates $\mathbf{F}, \mathbf{G}$ can be recovered from $\mathbf{K}^{FF}$ and $\mathbf{K}^{\mathbf{GG}}$'s dominant eigenvectors.

We emphasize that SDMA can serve as a very flexible framework for manifold alignment and embedding. More concretely, Eq.(13) can be generalized (or degenerated) in the following ways. 1) Flexible supervision. First, the form of tuple constraints can be changed from $t_c = \{\mathbf{y}_i, \mathbf{x}_j, \mathbf{x}_k\}$ to $t_c = \{\mathbf{h}_i, \mathbf{h}_j, \mathbf{h}_k\}$. This means that SDMA can accept relative distance constraints between *any* three samples (*e.g.* all from the same manifold, or from 3 different manifolds). Moreover, our formulation is able to incorporate the traditional correspondence information by adding constraints "$\mathbf{K}_{i,i} = \mathbf{K}_{i,j} = \mathbf{K}_{j,j}$". 2) Multi-manifold alignment. This can be done straightforwardly by adding more manifold components into $\mathbf{H}$ and $\mathbf{M}$ along with corresponding constraints. 3) Semi-supervised embedding. When there is only one manifold component, SDMA provides a way to embed it with the guide of flexible supervision.

4 Experiments

4.1 Data and Settings

- **Head pose** [13]. This data set contains head images of 15 sets, each of which has 2 series of 93 images of the same person at 93 different poses.
- **Facial expression** [6]. This data set contains 213 images of 7 facial expressions posed by 10 Japanese female models. The underlying parameters are unknown.

The relative distance constraints $\mathcal{T}$ are obtained as follows. First, samples are randomly drawn to form a tuple $T = \{\mathbf{y}_i, \mathbf{x}_j, \mathbf{x}_k\}$ meaning that "$\mathbf{y}_i$ *is more similar to* $\mathbf{x}_j$ *than to* $\mathbf{x}_k$". Then let a user judge if this tuple is valid based on relative similarity. Finally, valid tuples are collected into $\mathcal{T}$. Since only "yes/no" questions are involved, this procedure is very easy for the users. Specifically, for the head pose data, similarity is determined by the sum of horizontal and vertical angle differences. For the facial expression data, if y_i and x_j have the same expression that is different from x_j, then T is valid. This strategy gives a conservative yet reliable supervision.

The parameter α tunes the strength of relative distance constraints. In our experiments it is chosen manually from the grid $\{10^{-5}, \cdots, 10^{-1}, 1\}$.

4.2 Results

Figure 3 shows the experimental result of SDMA on head pose data. We construct the graph using neighborhood size 7, and use 500 tuples, $\alpha = 10^{-3}$. 130 samples from 2 subjects are embedded onto a 2-D plane. It can be seen that both of the underlying manifold parameters are successfully captured and aligned.

Figure 4 shows the alignment of facial expression data. The graph is constructed with neighborhood size 5, and 50 tuples are used. Since its manifold structure is not evident,

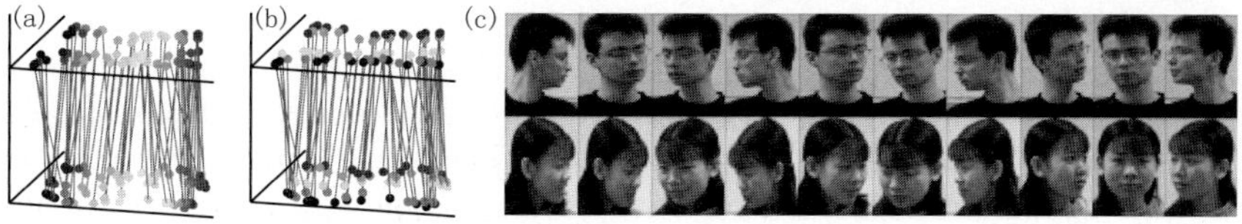

Fig. 3. Alignment of head pose images. (a) and (b) shows the embedding by SDMA and the correspondences found. Points are colored according to horizontal angles in (a) and vertical angles in (b). (c) shows some samples of matched pairs.

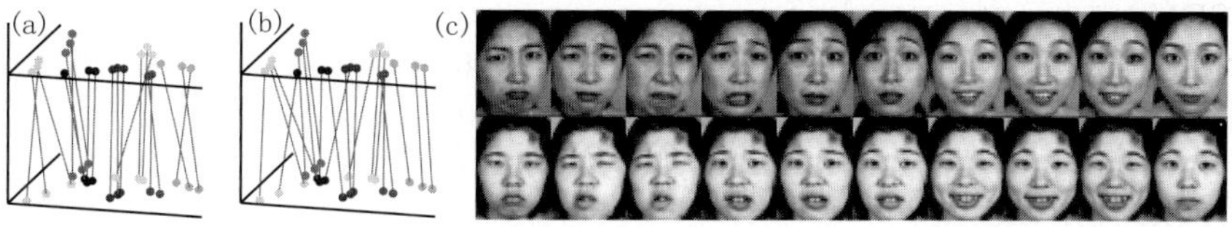

Fig. 4. Alignment of facial expression images. (a) and (b) shows the embedding, with points colored according to the true expressions. (a) shows the true correspondences, while (b) shows those found by SDMA. (c) shows some matched pairs.

we set $\alpha = 10^{-1}$ to strengthen the influence of relative distance constraints. 40 samples are embedded onto a 2-D plane since only two eigenvalues of $\mathbf{K}$ are not zero.

5 Discussions

The idea of learning with relative comparisons has also been used in other problems. [14] treat relative distance relations as the character of data, and use *AdaBoost* to seek for an embedding where this character is preserved. However, they did not utilize the data's intrinsic structure. [15] and [16] propose to learn distance metrics from relative comparisons. They both seek a distance measure $d(\mathbf{x}, \mathbf{y}) = \sqrt{(\mathbf{x}-\mathbf{y})^T \mathbf{A}(\mathbf{x}-\mathbf{y})}$ and use the relative relations to constrain the feasible region of $\mathbf{A}$ through *mathematical programming*. In spirit, our method is similar to [15]. They learn a distance measure that preserves global distance relations, and we learn an embedding that preserves local manifold structures.

SDMA are closely related to *kernel* methods. By the semi-definite relaxation, we first derive the data's Gram matrix (*a.k.a. Kernel matrix*), and then calculate the low-dimensional coordinates by eigen-decomposition. This procedure is similar to *kernel principal component analysis* (KPCA) [17] except that our kernel matrix is learnt by aligning manifolds. Therefore, SDMA can be considered a *kernel learning* method. From this perspective, SDMA is similar to [18]. The difference is that they only use a single manifold's structure, while we exploit multiple manifolds and their correspondences.

One drawback of SDMA is that its computational cost is high when dealing with large data sets. Although the semi-definite relaxation makes the problem tractable, it inevitably increases the number of variables. In the future we are aiming at finding more efficient solutions.

6 Conclusion

Traditional align algorithms rely on the knowledge of high-quality pairwise correspondence, which is difficult to acquire in many situations. In this paper, we study a new way of aligning manifold based on the smoothness on graphs. To achieve maximum applicability and minimum user effort, we introduce the novel *relative distance constraint* to guide the alignment. Alignment using this type of prior knowledge is first formulized as a *quadratically constrained quadratic programming* (QCQP) problem. Further, by manipulating the *Gram matrix* of data instead of the coordinates, we relax this problem to a *semi-definite programming* (SDP) problem, which can be solved readily. Besides, we show that this semi-definite formulation can serve as a general framework for semi-supervised manifold alignment and embedding. Experiments on aligning various data demonstrate the effectiveness of our method.

Acknowledgement

Funded by Basic Research Foundation of Tsinghua National Laboratory for Information Science and Technology (TNList).

References

1. Seung, H.S., Lee, D.D.: The manifold ways of perception. Science 290, 2268–2269 (2000)
2. Roweis, S.T., Saul, L.K.: Nonlinear dimensionality reduction by locally linear embedding. Science 290, 2323–2326 (2000)
3. Belkin, M., Niyogi, P.: Laplacian eigenmaps for dimensionality reduction and data representation. Neural Computation 15, 1373–1396 (2003)
4. Weinberger, K.Q., Saul, L.K.: Unsupervised learning of image manifolds by semidefinite programming. International Journal of Computer Vision 70(1), 77–90 (2006)
5. Ham, J., Ahn, I., Lee, D.: Learning a manifold-constrained map between image sets: Applications to matching and pose estimation. In: CVPR-06 (2006)
6. Lyons, M.J., Kamachi, M., Gyoba, J., Akamatsu, S.: Coding facial expressions with gabor wavelets. In: Procedings of the 3rd IEEE Aut. Face and Gesture Recog., IEEE Computer Society Press, Los Alamitos (1998)
7. Ham, J., Lee, D., Saul, L.: Learning high dimensional correspondence from low dimensional manifolds. In: Workshop on The Continuum from Labeled to Unlabeled Data in Machine Learning and Data Mining, ICML-03 (2003)
8. Ham, J., Lee, D., Saul, L.: Semisupervised alignment of manifolds. In: Proceedings of the 8th International Workshop on Artificial Intelligence and Statics (*AISTATS 2005*) (2005)
9. Verbeek, J., Roweis, S., Vlassis, N.: Non-linear cca and pca by alignment of local models. In: Advances in NIPS-04 (2004)
10. Verbeek, J., Vlassis, N.: Gaussian fields for semi-supervised regression and correspondence learning. Pattern Recognition 39(10), 1864–1875 (2006)
11. Boyd, S.P., Vandenberghe, L.: Convex Optimization. Cambridge, UK (2004)
12. Sturm, J.F.: Using sedumi 1.02, a matlab toolbox for optimization overy symmetric cones. Optimization Methods and Software 11-12, 625–653 (1999)
13. Gourier, N., Hall, D., Crowley, J.L.: Estimating face orientation from robust detection of salient facial features. In: Proceedings of Pointing 2004, ICPR, International Workshop on Visual Observation of Deictic Gestures, Cambridge, UK (2004)

14. Athitsos, V., Alon, J., Sclaroff, S., Kollios, G.: Boostmap: A method for efficient approximate similarity rankings. In: CVPR-04 (2004)
15. Schultz, M., Joachims, T.: Learning a distance metric from relative comparisons. In: Advances in NIPS-03 (2003)
16. Rosales, R., Fung, G.: Learning sparse metrics via linear programming. In: KDD-06 (2006)
17. Schölkopf, B., Smola, A., Müller, K.-R.: Nonlinear component analysis as a kernel eigenvalue problem. Neural Computation 10, 1299–1319 (1998)
18. Weinberger, K., Fei, S., Saul, L.K.: Learning a kernel matrix for nonlinear dimensionality reduction. In: ICML-04 (2004)

General Solution for Supervised Graph Embedding

Qubo You, Nanning Zheng, Shaoyi Du, and Yang Wu

Institute of Artificial Intelligence and Robotics, Xi'an Jiaotong University, Xi'an,Shaanxi Province 710049 P.R. China
youqubo@gmail.com, nnzheng@mail.xjtu.edu.cn, sydu@aiar.xjtu.edu.cn, ywu@aiar.xjtu.edu.cn

Abstract. Recently, Graph Embedding Framework has been proposed for feature extraction. However, it is an open issue that how to compute the robust discriminant transformation. In this paper, we first show that supervised graph embedding algorithms share a general criterion (Generalized Rayleigh Quotient). Through novel perspective to Generalized Rayleigh Quotient, we propose a general solution, called *General Solution for Supervised Graph Embedding (GSSGE)*, for extracting the robust discriminant transformation of Supervised Graph Embedding. Finally, extensive experiments on real-world data are performed to demonstrate the effectiveness and robustness of our proposed GSSGE.

1 Introduction

Distance metric learning plays an important role in the field of machine learning. Actually, learning a robust distance metric is equivalent to looking for a robust transformation which transforms the original space into the feature space. Hence, those traditional methods for feature extraction can be viewed as metric learning algorithms, such as Linear Discriminant Analysis (LDA) [1], Local Discriminant Embedding (LDE) [2] and Locality Sensitive Discriminant Analysis (LSDA) [3]. In 2007, Yan et al. [4] presented a general framework (Graph Embedding) to unify the above algorithms. In this framework, however, it is an open issue that how to compute the robust discriminant transformation. Since this framework uses a general criterion, it is natural that a general solution can be used for extracting the robust discriminant transformation. Unfortunately, most of algorithms don't thoroughly consider the problem that how to compute the robust discriminant transformation. Similar to classical LDA [1], LDE and LSDA first use Principal Component Analysis (PCA) to reduce dimension for dealing with small sample size problem (SSS) where the data dimension is much larger than the sample size. However, this method may result in the loss of important discriminative information [5]. In the literature of LDA, different variations have been proposed to deal with the SSS problem [6,7,8,9]; however, they aim at LDA.

In this paper, we focus on the problem that how to compute the robust discriminant transformation of Supervised Graph Embedding. We first show that supervised graph embedding algorithms share a general criterion (Generalized

J.N. Kok et al. (Eds.): ECML 2007, LNAI 4701, pp. 782–789, 2007.

Rayleigh Quotient). Then, we propose a general solution, called *General Solution for Supervised Graph Embedding (GSSGE)*, to extract the robust discriminant transformation. Finally, experimental results on real-world data demonstrate the robustness of GSSGE.

The rest of the paper is organized as follows: Supervised Graph Embedding framework is briefly reviewed in Section 2. In Section 3, General Solution for Supervised Graph Embedding (GSSGE) is described. Extensive experiments are performed to demonstrate the effectiveness and robustness of our proposed GSSGE in Section 4. Finally, conclusions are summarized in Section 5.

2 Supervised Graph Embedding

For the convenience of understanding, in the following, the small *italic* letters denote scalars, such as a, b, c; the small **bold** non-italic letters denote vectors, such as **a**, **b**, **c**; and the capital **bold** non-italic letters denote matrices, such as **A**, **B**, **C**. Let we have n samples $\{\mathbf{x}_i | \mathbf{x}_i \in \mathbb{R}^d\}_{i=1}^n$ belonging to c classes.

Let $\mathbf{G} = \{\mathbf{X}, \mathbf{W}\}$ be an undirected weight graph with vertex set $\mathbf{X} = [\mathbf{x}_1, \mathbf{x}_2, \cdots, \mathbf{x}_n]$ and the similarity matrix $\mathbf{W} \in \mathbb{R}^{n \times n}$. The element of similarity matrix $\mathbf{W}$ measures the similarity of the vertex pair. Graph Embedding is to extract the optimal low dimensional vector representation for each vertex of the graph $\mathbf{G}$. Assume that the low dimensional vector representation of each vertex can be obtained from linear projections. For simplicity, we consider the one dimensional case. It is easy to extend to multi-dimensional cases. Let $\mathbf{q} \in \mathbb{R}^{d \times 1}$ be the linear mapping from the d-dimensional space to a line, and $\{y_i = \mathbf{q}^T \mathbf{x}_i\}_{i=1}^n$ are the low dimensional representation of the vertex set $\mathbf{X}$. In order to preserve the similarity of the graph $\mathbf{G}$, we should minimize the *graph preserving criterion* as follows [4]:

$$\mathbf{q}^* = \arg \min_{\substack{\mathbf{q} \\ \mathbf{q}^T \mathbf{X}\mathbf{B}\mathbf{X}^T \mathbf{q} = c}} \mathbf{q}^T \mathbf{X}\mathbf{L}\mathbf{X}^T \mathbf{q} \tag{1}$$

where c is a constant, $\mathbf{B}$ is the constraint matrix and $\mathbf{L} = \mathbf{D} - \mathbf{W}$ is the Laplacian matrix. $\mathbf{D}$ is the diagonal matrix with diagonal element $\mathbf{D}_{ii} = \sum_{j \neq i} \mathbf{W}_{ij} \forall i$.

In supervised learning problem, Supervised Graph Embedding is to extract the graph embeddings which best characterize the compactness of the intra-class graph and the separability of the inter-class graph. Therefore, in order to provide the robust graph embeddings, we should maximize the following criterion:

$$\mathbf{q}^* = \arg \max_{\mathbf{q}} \frac{\mathbf{q}^T \mathbf{X}\mathbf{L}^b \mathbf{X}^T \mathbf{q}}{\mathbf{q}^T \mathbf{X}\mathbf{L}^w \mathbf{X}^T \mathbf{q}} \tag{2}$$

where $\mathbf{L}^b = \mathbf{D}^b - \mathbf{W}^b$ and $\mathbf{L}^w = \mathbf{D}^w - \mathbf{W}^w$ are the Laplacian matrices of the *inter-class graph* $\mathbf{G}^b$ and the *intra-class graph* $\mathbf{G}^w$ respectively. Both $\mathbf{D}^b$ and $\mathbf{D}^w$ are the diagonal matrices with diagonal element $\mathbf{D}^b_{ii} = \sum_{j \neq i} \mathbf{W}^b_{ij} \forall i$ and $\mathbf{D}^w_{ii} = \sum_{j \neq i} \mathbf{W}^w_{ij} \forall i$ respectively.

3 General Solution for Supervised Graph Embedding

As we know in Section 2, the criterion of Supervised Graph Embedding is:

$$\mathrm{J}(\mathbf{q}) = \frac{\mathbf{q}^T\mathbf{X}\mathbf{L}^b\mathbf{X}^T\mathbf{q}}{\mathbf{q}^T\mathbf{X}\mathbf{L}^w\mathbf{X}^T\mathbf{q}} \tag{3}$$

Thus, the optimal vector is $\mathbf{q}^* = \arg\max_{\mathbf{q}} \mathrm{J}(\mathbf{q})$. From Eq. (3), we can find that the criterion of Supervised Graph Embedding is a Generalized Rayleigh Quotient. The optimal $\mathbf{q}^*$ is the top eigenvector of the generalized eigenvalue problem

$$(\mathbf{X}\mathbf{L}^b\mathbf{X}^T)\mathbf{q} = \lambda(\mathbf{X}\mathbf{L}^w\mathbf{X}^T)\mathbf{q} \tag{4}$$

For the convenience of description, we define that $\mathbf{M}_b = \mathbf{X}\mathbf{L}^b\mathbf{X}^T$, $\mathbf{M}_w = \mathbf{X}\mathbf{L}^w\mathbf{X}^T$ and $\mathbf{M}_t = \mathbf{M}_b + \mathbf{M}_w$. Since both $\mathbf{L}^b$ and $\mathbf{L}^w$ are the Laplacian matrices, $\mathbf{M}_b$, $\mathbf{M}_w$ and $\mathbf{M}_t$ are symmetric positive semi-definite.

Since the null space of $\mathbf{M}_t = \mathbf{M}_b + \mathbf{M}_w$ is the intersection of the null space of $\mathbf{M}_b$ and the null space of $\mathbf{M}_w$, the samples are projected onto the range space of $\mathbf{M}_t$ without loss of any discriminant information. Therefore, the criterion of Supervised Graph Embedding can be changed to:

$$\mathrm{J}_1(\mathbf{p}) = \frac{\mathbf{p}^T\tilde{\mathbf{M}}_b\mathbf{p}}{\mathbf{p}^T\tilde{\mathbf{M}}_w\mathbf{p}} \tag{5}$$

where $\tilde{\mathbf{M}}_b = \mathbf{U}_t^T\mathbf{M}_b\mathbf{U}_t$, $\tilde{\mathbf{M}}_w = \mathbf{U}_t^T\mathbf{M}_w\mathbf{U}_t$ and $\mathbf{U}_t$ is the set of eigenvectors, corresponding to all the nonzero eigenvalues, of $\mathbf{M}_t$. Then, the optimal discriminant transformation vector is $\mathbf{q}^* = \mathbf{U}_t\mathbf{p}^*$ where $\mathbf{p}^* = \arg\max_{\mathbf{p}} \mathrm{J}_1(\mathbf{p})$.

Let λ_i^t and $\mathbf{u}_i^t$ be the ith eigenvalue and the corresponding eigenvector of $\mathbf{M}_t$, $\lambda_1^t \geq \cdots \geq \lambda_{\ell_1^t}^t$, $\mathbf{\Sigma}_t = diag(\lambda_1^t, \cdots, \lambda_{\ell_1^t}^t)$, $\mathbf{U}_t = [\mathbf{u}_1^t, \cdots, \mathbf{u}_{\ell_1^t}^t]$ and $\ell_1^t = rank(\mathbf{M}_t)$. Then, $\tilde{\mathbf{M}}_t = \mathbf{U}_t^T\mathbf{M}_t\mathbf{U}_t = \mathbf{\Sigma}_t$. Let $\bar{\lambda}_i^b$ and $\bar{\mathbf{u}}_i^b$ be the ith eigenvalue and the corresponding eigenvector of $\mathbf{\Sigma}_t^{-1/2}\tilde{\mathbf{M}}_b\mathbf{\Sigma}_t^{-1/2}$, $\bar{\lambda}_1^b \geq \cdots \geq \bar{\lambda}_{\ell_1^t}^b \geq 0$, $\bar{\mathbf{\Sigma}}_b = diag(\bar{\lambda}_1^b, \cdots, \bar{\lambda}_{\ell_1^t}^b)$ and $\bar{\mathbf{U}}_b = [\bar{\mathbf{u}}_1^b, \cdots, \bar{\mathbf{u}}_{\ell_1^t}^b]$.

Theorem 1. $\mathbf{\Sigma}_t^{-1/2}\bar{\mathbf{U}}_b$ *simultaneously diagonalizes* $\tilde{\mathbf{M}}_b$, $\tilde{\mathbf{M}}_w$ *and* $\tilde{\mathbf{M}}_t$.

Proof. Due to $\bar{\mathbf{U}}_b^T\bar{\mathbf{U}}_b = \mathbf{I}$, we can obtain

$$(\mathbf{\Sigma}_t^{-1/2}\bar{\mathbf{U}}_b)^T\tilde{\mathbf{M}}_t\mathbf{\Sigma}_t^{-1/2}\bar{\mathbf{U}}_b = \bar{\mathbf{U}}_b^T\bar{\mathbf{U}}_b = \mathbf{I} \tag{6}$$

Because of $\tilde{\mathbf{M}}_t = \tilde{\mathbf{M}}_b + \tilde{\mathbf{M}}_w$, we can rewrite Eq. (6) as:

$$(\mathbf{\Sigma}_t^{-1/2}\bar{\mathbf{U}}_b)^T\tilde{\mathbf{M}}_t\mathbf{\Sigma}_t^{-1/2}\bar{\mathbf{U}}_b = \bar{\mathbf{\Sigma}}_b + (\mathbf{\Sigma}_t^{-1/2}\bar{\mathbf{U}}_b)^T\tilde{\mathbf{M}}_w\mathbf{\Sigma}_t^{-1/2}\bar{\mathbf{U}}_b = \mathbf{I}$$

Then, we can obtain

$$(\mathbf{\Sigma}_t^{-1/2}\bar{\mathbf{U}}_b)^T\tilde{\mathbf{M}}_w\mathbf{\Sigma}_t^{-1/2}\bar{\mathbf{U}}_b = \mathbf{I} - \bar{\mathbf{\Sigma}}_b = \bar{\mathbf{\Sigma}}_w \tag{7}$$

where $\bar{\mathbf{\Sigma}}_w = diag(\bar{\lambda}_1^w, \cdots, \bar{\lambda}_{\ell_1^t}^w)$. Due to $\mathbf{I} - \bar{\mathbf{\Sigma}}_b = \bar{\mathbf{\Sigma}}_w$, we can find that $\bar{\mathbf{\Sigma}}_w = diag(1 - \bar{\lambda}_1^b, \cdots, 1 - \bar{\lambda}_{\ell_1^t}^b)$, $1 \geq \bar{\lambda}_i^b, \bar{\lambda}_i^w \geq 0$ and $\bar{\lambda}_1^w \leq \cdots \leq \bar{\lambda}_{\ell_1^t}^w$. □

Theorem 2. $\Sigma_t^{-1/2}\bar{\mathbf{U}}_b$ *is the optimal discriminant transformation which maximizes the following criterion:*

$$\mathrm{J}_2(\mathbf{p}) = \frac{\mathbf{p}^T\tilde{\mathbf{M}}_b\mathbf{p}}{\mathbf{p}^T\tilde{\mathbf{M}}_t\mathbf{p}} \tag{8}$$

Proof. From Eq. (8), we can find that the optimal $\mathbf{p}^*$, maximizing J_2, is the top eigenvector of the eigenvalue problem

$$\tilde{\mathbf{M}}_b\mathbf{p} = \lambda\tilde{\mathbf{M}}_t\mathbf{p} \overset{\tilde{\mathbf{M}}_t=\Sigma_t}{\Rightarrow} \Sigma_t^{-1/2}\tilde{\mathbf{M}}_b\mathbf{p} = \lambda\Sigma_t^{1/2}\mathbf{p} \tag{9}$$

Let $\mathbf{p}' = \Sigma_t^{1/2}\mathbf{p}$, we can obtain

$$\Sigma_t^{-1/2}\tilde{\mathbf{M}}_b\Sigma_t^{-1/2}\mathbf{p}' = \lambda\mathbf{p}' \tag{10}$$

Since $\bar{\lambda}_i^b$ and $\bar{\mathbf{u}}_i^b$ are the ith eigenvalue and the corresponding eigenvector of Eq. (10), $\Sigma_t^{-1/2}\bar{\mathbf{U}}_b$ maximizes the criterion J_2. □

Theorem 3. *When* $\tilde{\mathbf{M}}_w$ *is nonsingular,* $\Sigma_t^{-1/2}\bar{\mathbf{U}}_b$ *is the optimal discriminant transformation which maximizes the criterion* J_1 *in Eq. (5).*

Proof. From Eq. (5), we can find that the optimal $\mathbf{p}^*$, maximizing J_1, is the top eigenvector of the eigenvalue problem

$$\tilde{\mathbf{M}}_b\mathbf{p} = \lambda\tilde{\mathbf{M}}_w\mathbf{p} \tag{11}$$

Adding both sides of Eq. (11) by $\lambda\tilde{\mathbf{M}}_b\mathbf{p}$, we can find

$$\tilde{\mathbf{M}}_b\mathbf{p} = \frac{\lambda}{1+\lambda}\tilde{\mathbf{M}}_t\mathbf{p} = \mu\tilde{\mathbf{M}}_t\mathbf{p} \tag{12}$$

Since both $\tilde{\mathbf{M}}_w$ and $\tilde{\mathbf{M}}_t$ are nonsingular, we can find that Eq. (11) and Eq. (12) share the same eigenvector with different eigenvalues. Therefore, the optimal discriminant transformation, maximizing the criterion J_1, is $\Sigma_t^{-1/2}\bar{\mathbf{U}}_b$. □

Since $\tilde{\mathbf{M}}_w$ is singular in the case of the SSS problem, we can't directly computed the eigenvector $\mathbf{v}$ in the following generalized eigenvalue problem

$$\tilde{\mathbf{M}}_b\mathbf{v} = \lambda\tilde{\mathbf{M}}_w\mathbf{v} \tag{13}$$

Theorem 4. *When* $\tilde{\mathbf{M}}_w$ *is singular,* $\lambda_i = \bar{\lambda}_i^b/\bar{\lambda}_i^w$ *and* $\Sigma_t^{-1/2}\bar{\mathbf{u}}_i^b$ *are the ith eigenvalue and the corresponding eigenvector in Eq. (13).*

Proof. Let $rank(\tilde{\mathbf{M}}_w) = \ell_1^w < \ell_1^t$, $\ell_2^w = \ell_1^t - \ell_1^w$, $rank(\tilde{\mathbf{M}}_b) = \ell_1^b \le \ell_1^t$ and $\ell_2^b = \ell_1^t - \ell_1^b$. According to **Theorem** 1, $\bar{\Sigma}_w$ and $\bar{\Sigma}_b$ can be rewritten as

$$\bar{\Sigma}_w = diag(\bar{\lambda}_1^w, \bar{\lambda}_2^w, \cdots, \bar{\lambda}_{\ell_1^t}^w) = \begin{bmatrix} \mathbf{0}_w & \mathbf{0} & \mathbf{0} \\ \mathbf{0} & \mathbf{D}_w & \mathbf{0} \\ \mathbf{0} & \mathbf{0} & \mathbf{I}_w \end{bmatrix}$$

$$\bar{\mathbf{\Sigma}}_b = \mathbf{I} - \bar{\mathbf{\Sigma}}_w = diag(\bar{\lambda}_1^b, \bar{\lambda}_2^b, \cdots, \bar{\lambda}_{\ell_1^t}^b) = \begin{bmatrix} \mathbf{I}_b & \mathbf{0} & \mathbf{0} \\ \mathbf{0} & \mathbf{D}_b & \mathbf{0} \\ \mathbf{0} & \mathbf{0} & \mathbf{0}_b \end{bmatrix}$$

where $\mathbf{0}_w \in \mathbb{R}^{\ell_2^w \times \ell_2^w}$ and $\mathbf{0}_b \in \mathbb{R}^{\ell_2^b \times \ell_2^b}$ are zero matrices, $\mathbf{I}_w \in \mathbb{R}^{\ell_2^b \times \ell_2^b}$ and $\mathbf{I}_b \in \mathbb{R}^{\ell_2^w \times \ell_2^w}$ are identity matrices, $\mathbf{D}_w = diag\left(\bar{\lambda}_{\ell_2^w+1}^w, \bar{\lambda}_{\ell_2^w+2}^w, \cdots, \bar{\lambda}_{\ell_1^b}^w\right)$ and $\mathbf{D}_b = diag\left(\bar{\lambda}_{\ell_2^w+1}^b, \bar{\lambda}_{\ell_2^w+2}^b, \cdots, \bar{\lambda}_{\ell_1^b}^b\right)$ are diagonal matrices, $0 < \bar{\lambda}_{\ell_2^w+1}^w \leq \bar{\lambda}_{\ell_2^w+2}^w \leq \cdots \leq \bar{\lambda}_{\ell_1^b}^w < 1$ and $1 > \bar{\lambda}_{\ell_2^w+1}^b \geq \bar{\lambda}_{\ell_2^w+2}^b \geq \cdots \geq \bar{\lambda}_{\ell_1^b}^b > 0$.

Let $\mathbf{V} = \mathbf{\Sigma}_t^{-1/2}\bar{\mathbf{U}}_b = [\mathbf{v}_1, \mathbf{v}_2, \cdots, \mathbf{v}_{\ell_1^t}]$. According to **Theorem** 1, $\mathbf{V}^T\tilde{\mathbf{M}}_w\mathbf{V} = \bar{\mathbf{\Sigma}}_w$ and $\mathbf{V}^T\tilde{\mathbf{M}}_b\mathbf{V} = \bar{\mathbf{\Sigma}}_b$. Then, $\tilde{\mathbf{M}}_w\mathbf{V} = (\mathbf{V}^{-1})^T\bar{\mathbf{\Sigma}}_w$ and $\tilde{\mathbf{M}}_b\mathbf{V} = (\mathbf{V}^{-1})^T\bar{\mathbf{\Sigma}}_b$. Let $\mathbf{V}' = (\mathbf{V}^{-1})^T = [\mathbf{v}'_1, \mathbf{v}'_2, \cdots, \mathbf{v}'_{\ell_1^t}]$, we can find, for $i = 1, \cdots, \ell_1^t$

$$\tilde{\mathbf{M}}_w\mathbf{v}_i = \bar{\lambda}_i^w\mathbf{v}'_i \tag{14}$$

$$\tilde{\mathbf{M}}_b\mathbf{v}_i = \bar{\lambda}_i^b\mathbf{v}'_i \tag{15}$$

$$\bar{\lambda}_i^w\tilde{\mathbf{M}}_b\mathbf{v}_i = \bar{\lambda}_i^b\tilde{\mathbf{M}}_w\mathbf{v}_i \tag{16}$$

Then, $\tilde{\mathbf{M}}_b\mathbf{v}_i = (\bar{\lambda}_i^b/\bar{\lambda}_i^w)\tilde{\mathbf{M}}_w\mathbf{v}_i$. Thus, $\lambda_i = \bar{\lambda}_i^b/\bar{\lambda}_i^w$ and $\mathbf{\Sigma}_t^{-1/2}\bar{\mathbf{u}}_i^b$ are the ith eigenvalue and the corresponding eigenvector in Eq. (13). □

Since $\tilde{\mathbf{M}}_w$ is symmetric positive semi-definite and $\bar{\lambda}_1^w = \cdots = \bar{\lambda}_{\ell_2^w}^w = 0$, $\mathbf{v}_i$ lies in the null space of $\tilde{\mathbf{M}}_w$ for $i = 1, \cdots, \ell_2^w$ according to Eq. (14). Due to $0 < \bar{\lambda}_{\ell_2^w+1}^w \leq \cdots \leq \bar{\lambda}_{\ell_1^b}^w < 1$, $\mathbf{v}_i$ doesn't lie in the null space of $\tilde{\mathbf{M}}_w$ for $i = \ell_2^w + 1, \cdots, \ell_1^b$. According to the definition of λ_i, we can find that $\lambda_i = +\infty$ for $i = 1, \cdots, \ell_2^w$, $0 < \lambda_i < +\infty$ for $i = \ell_2^w + 1, \cdots, \ell_1^b$ and $\lambda_{\ell_2^w+1} \geq \cdots \geq \lambda_{\ell_1^b} > 0$. Due to $\mathrm{J}_1(\mathbf{v}_i) = \lambda_i$, the robust discriminant transformation vectors can be first extracted from the null space of $\tilde{\mathbf{M}}_w$, and then from the range space of $\tilde{\mathbf{M}}_w$.

When transformation vector $\tilde{\mathbf{v}}$ lies in the null space of $\tilde{\mathbf{M}}_w$ not in the null space of $\tilde{\mathbf{M}}_b$, $\mathrm{J}_1(\tilde{\mathbf{v}}) = +\infty$, which means that the null space of $\tilde{\mathbf{M}}_w$ is an effective discriminant space with respect to the criterion J_1. Assume that both $\tilde{\mathbf{v}}_1$ and $\tilde{\mathbf{v}}_2$ lie in the null space of $\tilde{\mathbf{M}}_w$, $\tilde{\mathbf{v}}_1^T\tilde{\mathbf{M}}_b\tilde{\mathbf{v}}_1 > 0$ and $\tilde{\mathbf{v}}_2^T\tilde{\mathbf{M}}_b\tilde{\mathbf{v}}_2 > 0$; however, $\mathrm{J}_1(\tilde{\mathbf{v}}_1) = \mathrm{J}_1(\tilde{\mathbf{v}}_2) = +\infty$. That means every vector, lying in the null space of $\tilde{\mathbf{M}}_w$ not in the null space of $\tilde{\mathbf{M}}_b$, can make J_1 infinite. In this case, the criterion J_1 can't characterize the separability of the inter-class graph. Therefore, we should replace J_1. In this paper, we extract the robust discriminant transformation vectors from the null space of $\tilde{\mathbf{M}}_w$ based on the following criterion:

$$\mathrm{J}_3(\mathbf{p}) = \frac{\mathbf{p}^T\tilde{\mathbf{M}}_b\mathbf{p}}{\mathbf{p}^T\mathbf{p}} \tag{17}$$

where $\mathbf{p}^T\mathbf{p}$ normalizes $\mathbf{p}^T\tilde{\mathbf{M}}_b\mathbf{p}$ so that the optimal vector can't be selected randomly. Therefore, the optimal discriminant transformation vector $\mathbf{p}^*$ is

$$\mathbf{p}^* = \arg \max_{\substack{\mathbf{p} \\ \mathbf{p}^T\tilde{\mathbf{M}}_w\mathbf{p}=0}} \mathrm{J}_3(\mathbf{p}) \tag{18}$$

Let $\tilde{\lambda}_i^w$ and $\tilde{\mathbf{u}}_i^w$ be the ith eigenvalue and the corresponding eigenvector of $\tilde{\mathbf{M}}_w$, $0 \leq \tilde{\lambda}_1^w \leq \cdots \leq \tilde{\lambda}_{\ell_1^t}^w$. We define $\tilde{\mathbf{U}}_w^a = [\tilde{\mathbf{u}}_1^w, \cdots, \tilde{\mathbf{u}}_{\ell_2^w}^w]$ and $\tilde{\mathbf{U}}_w^b = [\tilde{\mathbf{u}}_{\ell_2^w+1}^w, \cdots, \tilde{\mathbf{u}}_{\ell_1^t}^w]$.

Since the vector $\mathbf{p}$ in Eq. (18) lies in the null space of $\tilde{\mathbf{M}}_w$, let $\mathbf{p} = \tilde{\mathbf{U}}_w^a \mathbf{z}$. Therefore, the objective function in Eq. (18) can be changed to

$$\mathbf{z}^* = \arg\max_{\mathbf{z}} \frac{\mathbf{z}^T (\tilde{\mathbf{U}}_w^a)^T \tilde{\mathbf{M}}_b \tilde{\mathbf{U}}_w^a \mathbf{z}}{\mathbf{z}^T \mathbf{z}} \tag{19}$$

Thus, the optimal $\mathbf{z}^*$ is the top eigenvector of the eigenvalue problem $(\tilde{\mathbf{U}}_w^a)^T \tilde{\mathbf{M}}_b \tilde{\mathbf{U}}_w^a$. Let the column vectors $\mathbf{z}_1, \mathbf{z}_2, \cdots, \mathbf{z}_{\ell_2^w}$ be the leading eigenvectors of the eigenvalue problem $(\tilde{\mathbf{U}}_w^a)^T \tilde{\mathbf{M}}_b \tilde{\mathbf{U}}_w^a$. Thus, the optimal discriminant transformation of J_3 in Eq. (17) is $\mathbf{P}_1^* = \tilde{\mathbf{U}}_w^a [\mathbf{z}_1, \mathbf{z}_2, \cdots, \mathbf{z}_{\ell_2^w}]$.

When the extracted transformation vector lies in the range of $\tilde{\mathbf{M}}_w$, the objective function is

$$\max_{\substack{\mathbf{p} \\ \mathbf{p}^T \tilde{\mathbf{M}}_w \mathbf{p} \neq 0}} \frac{\mathbf{p}^T \tilde{\mathbf{M}}_b \mathbf{p}}{\mathbf{p}^T \tilde{\mathbf{M}}_w \mathbf{p}} \tag{20}$$

Since the vector $\mathbf{p}$ in Eq. (20) lies in the range space of $\tilde{\mathbf{M}}_w$, let $\mathbf{p} = \tilde{\mathbf{U}}_w^b \mathbf{z}'$. Therefore, Eq. (20) can be rewritten as:

$$\max_{\substack{\mathbf{z}' \\ \mathbf{z}'^T (\tilde{\mathbf{U}}_w^b)^T \tilde{\mathbf{M}}_w \tilde{\mathbf{U}}_w^b \mathbf{z}' \neq 0}} \frac{\mathbf{z}'^T (\tilde{\mathbf{U}}_w^b)^T \tilde{\mathbf{M}}_b \tilde{\mathbf{U}}_w^b \mathbf{z}'}{\mathbf{z}'^T (\tilde{\mathbf{U}}_w^b)^T \tilde{\mathbf{M}}_w \tilde{\mathbf{U}}_w^b \mathbf{z}'} \tag{21}$$

Due to $(\tilde{\mathbf{U}}_w^b)^T \tilde{\mathbf{M}}_w \tilde{\mathbf{U}}_w^b = diag(\tilde{\lambda}_{\ell_2^w+1}^w, \cdots, \tilde{\lambda}_{\ell_1^t}^w)$ where $0 < \tilde{\lambda}_{\ell_2^w+1}^w \leq \cdots \leq \tilde{\lambda}_{\ell_1^t}^w$, $(\tilde{\mathbf{U}}_w^b)^T \tilde{\mathbf{M}}_w \tilde{\mathbf{U}}_w^b$ is nonsingular. Therefore, the optimal $\mathbf{z}'^*$ is the top eigenvector of $((\tilde{\mathbf{U}}_w^b)^T \tilde{\mathbf{M}}_w \tilde{\mathbf{U}}_w^b)^{-1} (\tilde{\mathbf{U}}_w^b)^T \tilde{\mathbf{M}}_b \tilde{\mathbf{U}}_w^b$. Let the column vectors $\mathbf{z}'_1, \mathbf{z}'_2, \cdots, \mathbf{z}'_{\ell_1^w}$ be the leading eigenvectors of the eigenvalue problem $((\tilde{\mathbf{U}}_w^b)^T \tilde{\mathbf{M}}_w \tilde{\mathbf{U}}_w^b)^{-1} (\tilde{\mathbf{U}}_w^b)^T \tilde{\mathbf{M}}_b \tilde{\mathbf{U}}_w^b$. Thus, the optimal discriminant transformation of the objective function in Eq. (20) is $\mathbf{P}_2^* = \tilde{\mathbf{U}}_w^b [\mathbf{z}'_1, \mathbf{z}'_2, \cdots, \mathbf{z}'_{\ell_1^w}]$.

Based on the analysis of Eq. (16), we have known that the robust discriminant transformation vectors can be first extracted from the null space of $\tilde{\mathbf{M}}_w$, and then from the range space of $\tilde{\mathbf{M}}_w$. Therefore, the robust discriminant transformation of Supervised Graph Embedding is $\mathbf{Q} = \mathbf{U}_t [\mathbf{P}_1^*, \mathbf{P}_2^*]$ when $\tilde{\mathbf{M}}_w$ is singular.

4 Experiments

In order to validate GSSGE, we apply GSSGE for computing the discriminant transformation of Local Discriminant Embedding (LDE) [2]. Extensive experiments on FERET [10] are performed to demonstrate the effectiveness and robustness of GSSGE. Since ULDA/GSVD [6], Exact Algorithm [7], LDA/FKT [8] and LDA/GSVD [9] are essentially equivalent, we only compare ULDA/GSVD with other algorithms without loss of generality. Therefore, the system performance of GSSGE is compared to the ones of classical LDA [1], ULDA/GSVD, LDE [2] and LSDA [3]. Since the dimension of the facial image is often very high,

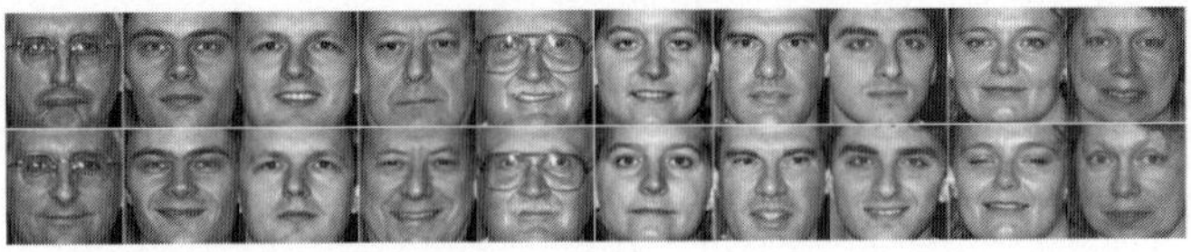

Fig. 1. Twenty facial images of ten individuals in the FERET database

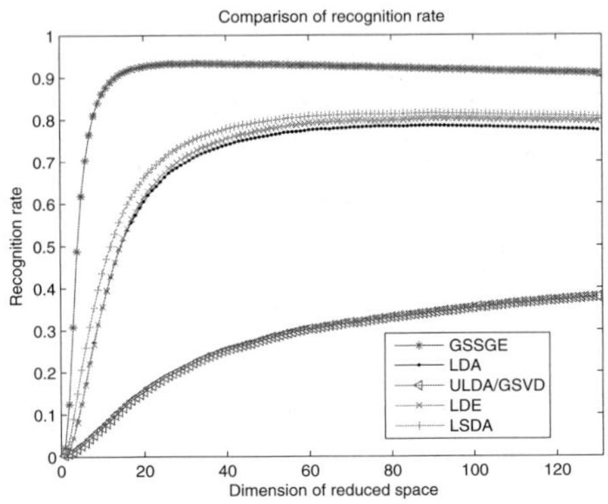

Fig. 2. Recognition rate versus dimension m of reduced space

which can result in the SSS problem, the experimental results can demonstrate the robustness of each method for dealing with the SSS problem.

This dataset consists of all the 1195 people from the FERET Fa/Fb data set. There are two face images for each person. We preprocessed these original images by aligning transformation and scaling transformation so that the two eyes were aligned at the same position. Then, the facial areas were cropped into the resulting images. The size of each cropped image is 64×64, with 256 grey levels per pixel. We didn't perform further preprocessing. Fig. 1 shows the twenty facial images of ten individuals from this dataset.

We selected randomly 495 people for training and used the remaining 700 people as testing. For each testing people, one face image is in the gallery and the other is for probe. Thus, this dataset has no overlap between the training set and gallery/probe set, which results in the requirement of generalizable ability from known objects in the training set to unknown objects in the gallery/probe set for each method. Therefore, the result on the dataset from the FERET database is convincing to evaluate the robustness of each method. We performed 50 times to choose randomly the training set. The final result is the average recognition rate over 50 random training sets. Fig. 2 illustrates the plot of recognition rate versus the dimension m of reduced space for LDA, ULDA/GSVD, LDE, LSDA and GSSGE. From the experimental results, we can find that GSSGE is superior to the other methods. However, it is obvious that ULDA/GSVD works badly.

5 Conclusions

In this paper, we first show that supervised graph embedding algorithms share a general criterion (Generalized Rayleigh Quotient). Through thorough perspective to Generalized Rayleigh Quotient, we propose a general solution, called *General Solution for Supervised Graph Embedding (GSSGE)*, to extract the robust discriminant transformation. Experimental results on FERET database demonstrate the effectiveness and robustness of GSSGE. Furthermore, because our proposed GSSGE is a general solution for Supervised Graph Embedding, GSSGE can be used to extract the robust discriminant transformation of Supervised Graph Embedding algorithms, such as LDA [1] and LSDA [3], and so on.

Acknowledgments. This work was supported by the National High-Tech Research and Development Plan of China under Grant No. 20060101Z1059, and the National Basic Research Program of China under Grant No. 2006CB708303.

References

1. Belhumeur, P.N., Hepanha, J.P., Kriegman, D.J.: Eigenfaces vs. Fisherfaces: recognition using class specific linear projection. IEEE Trans. Pattern Anal. Machine Intell. 19(7), 711–720 (1997)
2. Chen, H.-T., Chang, H.-W., Liu, T.-L.: Local discriminant embedding and its variants. In: Proceedings of the IEEE Computer Society Conference on Computer Vision and Pattern Recognition, vol. 2, pp. 846–853 (2005)
3. Cai, D., He, X., Zhou, K., Han, J., Bao, H.: Locality Sensitive Discriminant Analysis. In: Proceedings of the Twentieth International Joint Conference on Artificial Intelligence (2007)
4. Yan, S., Xu, D., Zhang, B., Zhang, H.-J., Yang, Q., Lin, S.: Graph Embedding and Extensions: A General Framework for Dimensionality Reduction. IEEE Trans. Pattern Anal. Machine Intell. 29(1), 40–51 (2007)
5. You, Q., Zheng, N., Du, S., Wu, Y.: Neighborhood Discriminant Projection for Face Recognition. In: Proceedings of the International Conference on Pattern Recognition, vol. 2, pp. 532–535 (2006)
6. Ye, J., Janardan, R., Li, Q., Park, H.: Feature Reduction via Generalized Uncorrelated Linear Discriminant Analysis. IEEE Trans. Knowledge Data Eng. 18(10), 1312–1322 (2006)
7. Ye, J., Janardan, R., Park, C.H., Park, H.: An optimization criterion for generalized discriminant analysis on undersampled problems. IEEE Trans. Pattern Anal. Machine Intell. 26(8), 982–994 (2004)
8. Zheng, S., Sim, T.: When Fisher meets Fukunage-Koontz: A New Look at Linear Discriminant. In: Proceedings of the IEEE Computer Society Conference on Computer Vision and Pattern Recognition, vol. 1, pp. 323–329 (2006)
9. Howland, P., Park, H.: Generalizing discriminant analysis using the generalized singular value decomposition. IEEE Trans. Pattern Anal. Machine Intell. 26(8), 995–1006 (2004)
10. Phillips, P.J., Moon, H., Rizvi, S.A., Rauss, P.J.: The FERET evaluation methodology for face-recognition algorithms. IEEE Trans. Pattern Anal. Machine Intell. 22(10), 1090–1104 (2000)

Multi-objective Genetic Programming for Multiple Instance Learning

Amelia Zafra and Sebastián Ventura

Department of Computer Science and Numerical Analysis,
University of Córdoba
{azafra,sventura}@uco.es

Abstract. This paper introduces the use of multi-objective evolutionary algorithms in multiple instance learning. In order to achieve this purpose, a multi-objective grammar-guided genetic programming algorithm (MOG3P-MI) has been designed. This algorithm has been evaluated and compared to other existing multiple instance learning algorithms. Research on the performance of our algorithm is carried out on two well-known drug activity prediction problems, Musk and Mutagenesis, both problems being considered typical benchmarks in multiple instance problems. Computational experiments indicate that the application of the MOG3P-MI algorithm improves accuracy and decreases computational cost with respect to other techniques.

1 Introduction

Multiple instance learning, or multi-instance learning (MIL) introduced by Dietterich et al. [1] is a recent learning framework which has stirred interest in the machine learning community. In this paradigm, instances are organized in bags (i.e., multisets) and it is the bags, instead of individual instances, that are labeled for training. Multiple instance learners assume that every instance in a bag labeled negative is actually negative, whereas at least one instance in a bag labeled positive is actually positive. Note that a positive bag may contain negative instances.

Since its introduction, a wide range of tasks have been formulated as multi-instance problems. Among these tasks, we can cite content-based image retrieval [2] and annotation [3], text categorization [4], web index page recommendation [5,6] and drug activity prediction [7,8]. Also, a variety of algorithms have been introduced to learn in the multi-instance setting. Some of them are algorithms designed from scratch [1,7,8], while others [4,9,10,11,12,13,14] are based on well-known supervised learning algorithms. In this sense, the work of Zhou [15] is relevant in that it shows a general way in which supervised learners can be turned into multi-instance learners by shifting their focus from a discrimination on instances to the discrimination on the bags.

In this paper, we introduce a multi-objective grammar guided genetic programming algorithm designed to handle MIL problems. Our main motivations with this are: (a) genetic programming that allows a rule based classifier to be

J.N. Kok et al. (Eds.): ECML 2007, LNAI 4701, pp. 790–797, 2007.

generated (well known are the exceptional properties of these systems with respect to the comprehensibility and clarity of the knowledge being discovered) and (b) multi-objective strategy solutions that represent a tradeoff between different rule quality measurements, which is more interesting than maximising one individual measurement. As we will see, our algorithm (MOG3P-MI) generates a simple rule based classifier that increases generalization ability and includes interpretability and clarity in the knowledge discovered. Experiments are carried out by solving two well-known examples of drug activity prediction, Musk and Mutagenesis, which have been extensively used as benchmarks in evaluating and comparing MIL methods. Results show that this approach improves accuracy considerably with respect to existing techniques used to date.

The rest of this paper is organized as follows. Section 2 describes the proposed MOG3P-MI algorithm. Section 3 reports on experimental results. Finally, section 4 presents the conclusions and future work.

2 Multi-objective Genetic Programming for Multiple-Instance Learning

In this section we specify different aspects which have been taken into account in the design of the MOG3P-MI algorithm: individual representation, genetic operators and fitness function. With regard to the evolutionary process, our algorithm is based on the well-known Strength Pareto Evolutionary Algorithm 2 (SPEA2) [16] and, for this reason, no explanation about how it works is included.

2.1 Individual Representation

An individual consists of two components, a *genotype* which is encoded as tree structures with limitations in tree depth to avoid too large a size, and a *phenotype* which represents the full rule with antecedents and consequences. The antecedent consists of tree structures and represents a rule which can contain multiple comparisons attached by conjunction or disjunction, while the consequence specifies the class for the instance that satisfies all the conditions of the antecedent. To carry out the classification of the bags of instances, we use the formal definition of multi-instance coverage given by [15]. We consider that the possible value of the consequence is always the positive class, that is, all individuals are classified in the positive class and all examples that do not satisfy the individuals rule set are implicitly classified as belonging to the negative class.

We use a grammar to enforce syntactic constrains and satisfy the closure property (see Figure 1). This grammar mantains syntactical and semantic constraints in both the generation of individuals in the initial population and the production of new individuals via crossover.

2.2 Genetic Operators

The elements of the next population are generated by means of two operators: mutation and crossover.

```
antecedent ->                comparison
                           | OR comparison antecedent
                           | AND comparison antecedent

comparison ->              comparatorNumerical valuesToCompare
                           comparatorCategorical valuesToCompare

comparatorNumerical ->         <
                             | ≥

comparatorCategorical ->     | CONTAIN
                             | NOT_CONTAIN

valuesToCompare ->  attribute  value
```

Fig. 1. Grammar used for individual representation

Mutation. The mutation operator can be applied to either a function node or a terminal node. A node in the tree is randomly selected. If the chosen node is a terminal it is simply replaced by another terminal. If it is a function, there are two possibilities with the same likelihood: (a) the function is replaced by a new function with the same arity and, (b) a new function node (not necessarily with the same arity) is chosen, and the original node together with its relative sub-tree is substituted by a new randomly generated sub-tree. If the new offspring is too large, it will be eliminated to avoid having invalid individuals.

Crossover. The crossover is performed by swapping the sub-trees of two parents between two compatible points randomly selected in each parent. Two tree nodes are compatible if their operators can be swapped without producing an invalid individual according to the defined grammar. If any of the two offspring is too large, they will be replaced by one of their parents.

2.3 Fitness Function

The fitness function evaluates the quality of each individual according to two indices that are normally used to evaluate the accuracy of algorithms in classification problems [17,18]. These are sensitivity and specificity. Sensitivity is the proportion of cases correctly identified as meeting a certain condition and specificity is the proportion of cases correctly identified as not meeting a certain condition. A value of 1 in both measures represents a perfect classification.

$$specificity = \frac{tn}{tn + fp}, \qquad sensitivity = \frac{tp}{tp + fn} \tag{1}$$

Where tp is the number of positive bags correctly predicted, tn is the number of negative bags correctly predicted, fp is the number of positive bags incorrectly predicted and fn is the number of negative bags incorrectly predicted.

Our fitness function combines these two indicators and the goal is to maximize them at same time. These measures are relationed, that is, there is a tradeoff between sensitivity and specificity (any increase in sensitivity will be accompanied by a decrease in specificity).

3 Experiments and Results

Our experiments are aimed to evaluate our proposed algorithm as compared to other classification techniques. Experimental results were estimated by 5 runs of 10-fold cross-validation with five different seeds for each partition and the average values of accuracy are reported in the next sections.

3.1 Datasets and Running Parameters

Experiments have been made on a drug activity prediction problem which is the most famous application for MIL. We discuss two datasets, Musk and Mutagenesis which are available at *http://www.cs.waikato.ac.nz/ml/milk*. The key properties of these datasets are shown in Table 1.

Table 1. Characteristics of the Musk and Mutagenesis datasets

	Musk		Mutagenesis	
Data Set	Musk1	Musk2	Easy	Hard
Number of bags	92	102	188	42
Number of positive bags	47	39	125	13
Number of negative bags	45	63	63	29
Number of instances	476	6598	10486	2132

These datasets are the most popular ones in the MIL domain, especially Musk. Every MIL algorithm developed so far has been tested using this problem. Therefore, we evaluated our algorithm based on these datasets.

The parameters used in all MOG3P-MI runs were: population size: 1000, external population size: 50, generations: 100, crossover probability: 95%, mutation probability: 15%, selection method for both parents: binary tournament selection with replacement, maximum tree depth: 15. The initial population was generated using the ramped-half-and-half method. The algorithm has been implemented in the JCLEC framework [19].

3.2 Comparison with Other Algorithms

Solving the Musk Problem. Comparisons are made with previous algorithms that include the ones specially designed for attacking the multiple-instance problem, as ITERATED-DISCRIM-APR which is the best of the four APR algorithms reported in [1], TILDE which is a top-down induction system for learning first order logical decision tree [20], CITATION-KNN [11] which is a variant of k nearest neighbour algorithm, RIPPER and RIPPERMI [21] which are a generic

Table 2. Summary results for Musk dataset

	Musk1	Musk2
Algorithm	Acc	Acc
MOG3P-MI	**0.93**	**0.93**
ITERATED-DISCRIM-APR	0.92	0.89
CITATION-KNN	0.92	0.86
DIVERSE DENSITY	0.89	0.82
RIPPERMI	0.88	0.77
NAIVE-RIPPERMI	0.88	0.77
TILDE	0.87	0.79
SVM	0.87	0.83

extension to propositional rule learners to handle multiple-instance data, Diverse Density [22] which is one of the most popular algorithms and MI-SVM [4] which is the best approach of support vectorial machines for MIL.

Table 2 shows a summary with the average values obtained by the different algorithms for each association of datasets. The results of the different algorithms are taken from [4] and [21].

In the Musk1 dataset, the hypotheses generated by MOG3P-MI contain an average of eight literals. These results are more accurate than those of other techniques which also generate interpretable knowledge. Moreover, the results are better than models which are not directly interpretable and have been specifically designed for this learning task, as ITERATED-DISCRIM-APR algorithm. The following is an example of rules generated by our algorithm.

IF (*(f10 > -220.3815)* $\wedge$ *(f7 > 35.2688)* $\wedge$ *(f163 ≤ 199.6827)*
$\wedge$ *(f55 > -84.9990)* $\wedge$ *(f134 > -216.0463)* $\wedge$ *(f34 > -216.1496)*
$\wedge$ *((f128 ≤ 18.1158)* $\vee$ *(f140 > 13.6820)* $\vee$ *(f136 > -78.2625))*)
THEN *Molecules have a musky smell.*
ELSE *Molecules have not a musky smell.*

In the Musk2 dataset, MOG3P-MI obtains an accuracy of 93%, which is far from the results found with the other techniques. This dataset has more bags and more instances by bags than in Musk1. However, our algorithm is not affected by these characteristics, and again it obtains the best results with respect to the rest of the techniques, these being comparable to those obtained in Musk1.

Solving the Mutagenesis Problem. The results of MOG3P-MI are compared to learners able to generate comprehensible hypotheses like PROGOL [23], FOIL and TILDE [20]. Also, we compare them to propositional rule learners, RIPPERMI [21] and NAIVE-RIPPERMI [21]. Table 3 displays the accuracy of MOG3P-MI, as well as the accuracy of five popular learners explained previously. The results of the different algorithms are taken from [21].

The best accuracy was obtained using Mutagenesis-hard which uses individual atoms and global molecular features that are highly correlated with the activity

Table 3. Summary results for Mutagenesis dataset

	Mutagenesis-easy	Mutagenesis-hard
Algorithm	Acc	Acc
MOG3P-MI	**0.84**	**1.00**
RIPPERMI	0.82	0.91
NAIVE-RIPPERMI	0.78	0.91
TILDE	0.77	0.86
PROGOL	0.76	0.86
FOIL	0.61	0.83

of the molecule. For this dataset, the other techniques obtain a good performance, but the best results are obtained by MOG3P-MI which obtains a perfect classification.

In a Mutagenesis-easy dataset, the accuracy of all the techniques fell. Nevertheless, our algorithm got the best results on the other ones. Thus, we can say that MOG3P-MI is competitive in terms of predictive accuracy, with respect to other learners. In addition, the induced hypotheses are concise, they contain an average of seven literals. The following is an example of the rule generated by our algorithm.

IF ($(element2 = 7.0) \wedge (charge1 > -0.4862) \wedge (charge2 \leq -0.5673) \wedge$
$((quanta1 \neq 9.0) \vee (charge2 > -0.3719)))$
THEN *Molecules have mutagenic activity.*
ELSE *Molecules do not have a mutagenic activity.*

4 Conclusion and Future Work

The problem of MIL is a learning problem which has raised interest in the machine learning community. This problem is encountered in contexts where an object may have several alternative vectors to describe its different possible configurations.

In this paper, we describe the first attempt to apply multi-objective grammar guided genetic programming for multiple instance learning. MOG3P-MI is derived from the traditional G3P method and the SPEA2 multiobjective algorithm. Experiments on the Musk and Mutagenesis datasets show that our approach obtains the best results in terms of accuracy in the rest of the existing learning algorithm. Added to this are the benefits of interpretability and clarity in the knowledge discovered which provides a rule based system. The experimental study shows the success of our approach. However, further optimization is possible: issues such as the stopping criterion, the pruning strategy, and introduction of a third objective to improve the simplicity of obtaining easier rules would be an interesting issue for future work.

Acknowledgment

This work has been financed in part by the TIN2005-08386-C05-02 project of the Spanish Inter-Ministerial Commission of Science and Technology (CICYT) and FEDER funds.

References

1. Dietterich, T.G., Lathrop, R.H., Lozano-Perez, T.: Solving the multiple instance problem with axis-parallel rectangles. Artifical Intelligence 89(1-2), 31–71 (1997)
2. Yang, C., Lozano-Perez, T.: Image database retrieval with multiple-instance learning techniques. In: ICDE '00: Proceedings of the 16th International Conference on Data Engineering, p. 233. IEEE Computer Society Press, Washington (2000)
3. Qi, X., Han, Y.: Incorporating multiple svms for automatic image annotation. Pattern Recognition 40(2), 728–741 (2007)
4. Andrews, S., Tsochantaridis, I., Hofmann, T.: Support vector machines for multiple-instance learning. In: NIPS'02: Proceedings of Neural Information Processing System, pp. 561–568 (2002)
5. Zhou, Z.H., Jiang, K., Li, M.: Multi-instance learning based web mining. Applied Intelligence 22(2), 135–147 (2005)
6. Xue, X., Han, J., Jiang, Y., Zhou, Z.: Link recommendation in web index page based on multi-instance learning techniques. Jisuanji Yanjiu yu Fazhan/Computer Research and Development 44(3), 406–411 (2007)
7. Maron, O., Lozano-Pérez, T.: A framework for multiple-instance learning. In: NIPS'97: Proceedings of Neural Information Processing System 10, pp. 570–576. MIT Press, Cambridge (1997)
8. Zhang, Q., Goldman, S.: EM-DD: An improved multiple-instance learning technique. In: NIPS'01: Proceedings of Neural Information Processing System, pp. 1073–1080 (2001)
9. Zucker, J.D., Chevaleyre, Y.: Solving multiple-instance and multiple-part learning problems with decision trees and decision rules. Application to the mutagenesis problem. In: Proceedings of the 14th Canadian Conference on Artificial Intelligence, Lecture Notes in Artificial Intelligence, Ottawa, Canada, pp. 204–214 (2000)
10. Ruffo, G.: Learning single and multiple instance decision tree for computer security applications. PhD thesis, Department of Computer Science. University of Turin, Torino, Italy (2000)
11. Wang, J., Zucker, J.D.: Solving the multiple-instance problem: A lazy learning approach. In: ICML'00: Proceedings of the Seventeenth International Conference on Machine Learning, pp. 1119–1126. Morgan Kaufmann Inc., San Francisco (2000)
12. Tao, Q., Scott, S., Vinodchandran, N.V., Osugi, T.T.: SVM-based generalized multiple-instance learning via approximate box counting. In: ICML'04: Proceedings of the twenty-first international conference on Machine learning, pp. 799–806. ACM Press, New York (2004)
13. Zhang, M.L., Zhou, Z.H.: Ensembles of multi-instance neural networks. In: Intelligent information processing II, vol. 163, pp. 471–474. Springer Boston, London, UK (2005)
14. Zhang, M.L., Zhou, Z.H.: Adapting RBF neural networks to multi-instance learning. Neural Processing Letters 23(1), 1–26 (2006)

15. Zhou, Z.H.: Multi-instance learning from supervised view. Journal Computer Science and Technology 21(5), 800–809 (2006)
16. Zitzler, E., Laumanns, M., Thiele, L.: SPEA2: Improving the Strength Pareto Evolutionary Algorithm. Technical Report 103, Gloriastrasse 35, CH-8092 Zurich, Switzerland (2001)
17. Bojarczuk, C.C., Lopes, H.S., Freitas, A.A.: Genetic programming for knowledge discovery in chest-pain diagnosis. IEEE Engineering in Medicine and Biology Magazine 19(4), 38–44 (2000)
18. Tan, K.C., Tay, Lee, A., Heng, T.H., C.M.: Mining multiple comprehensible classification rules using genetic programming. In: CEC'02: Proceedings of the Congress on Evolutionary Computation. Honolulu, HI, USA, vol. 2, pp. 1302–1307(2002)
19. Ventura, S., Romero, C., Zafra, A., Delgado, J.A., Hervás, C.: JCLEC: A java framework for evolutionary computation soft computing. Soft Computing (2007) ((in Press)
20. Blockeel, H., Raedt, L.D., Jacobs, N., Demoen, B.: Scaling up inductive logic programming by learning from interpretations. Data Mining Knowledge Discovery 3(1), 59–93 (1999)
21. Chevaleyre, Y., Zucker, J.D.: A framework for learning rules from multiple instance data. In: Flach, P.A., De Raedt, L. (eds.) ECML 2001. LNCS (LNAI), vol. 2167, pp. 49–60. Springer, Heidelberg (2001)
22. Maron, O., Ratan, A.L.: Multiple-instance learning for natural scene classification. In: ICML '98: Proceedings of the Fifteenth International Conference on Machine Learning, pp. 341–349. Morgan Kaufmann Publishers Inc., San Francisco (1998)
23. Srinivasan, A., Muggleton, S.: Comparing the use of background knowledge by inductive logic programming systems. In: ILP '95: Proceedings of International Workshop on Inductive Logic Programming (1995)

Exploiting Term, Predicate, and Feature Taxonomies in Propositionalization and Propositional Rule Learning

Monika Žáková and Filip Železný

Czech Technical University
Technická 2, 16627 Prague 6, Czech Republic
zakovm1@fel.cvut.cz, zelezny@fel.cvut.cz

Abstract. Knowledge representations using semantic web technologies often provide information which translates to explicit term and predicate taxonomies in relational learning. We show how to speed up the propositionalization by orders of magnitude, by exploiting such taxonomies through a novel refinement operator used in the construction of conjunctive relational features. Moreover, we accelerate the subsequent propositional search using feature generality taxonomy, determined from the initial term and predicate taxonomies and θ-subsumption between features. This enables the propositional rule learner to prevent the exploration of conjunctions containing a feature together with any of its subsumees and to specialize a rule by replacing a feature by its subsumee. We investigate our approach with a deterministic top-down propositional rule learner, and propositional rule learner based on stochastic local search.

1 Introduction

With the development of semantic web technologies and knowledge management using ontologies, increasing amounts of expert knowledge in important knowledge-intensive domains such as bioinformatics is becoming available in the form of ontologies and semantic annotations. However, semantic representation is becoming popular even in industrial use [13] for sharing and efficient searching of information in production enterprises. Knowledge representation formalisms used to capture ontologies and semantic annotations are based on description logics, which have convenient properties with regard to complexity and decidability of reasoning [1].

Inductive logic programming (ILP) aims at learning a theory in a subset of first-order logic from given examples, taking background knowledge into account. It has been considerably successful in various knowledge discovery problems such as in bioinformatics [4]. Standard ILP techniques cannot efficiently exploit explicit taxonomies on concepts and relations, which are typically available in semantic knowledge representations [13]. While in principle, any taxonomy can be encoded in background knowledge, there is good reason to view ontologies

J.N. Kok et al. (Eds.): ECML 2007, LNAI 4701, pp. 798–805, 2007.

as meta-information, which can be directly exploited to guide the refinement operator used to search through the space of first-order rules.

Recently, effort has been exerted to utilize the information available in ontologies out of the scope of the traditional ILP settings. There are 3 main approaches to this problem: introduce learning mechanisms into description logics [1], [3], hybrid languages integrating Horn logic and description logics [7], [10] and learning in a more expressive formalism [9]. Learning in description logics is useful mainly for the refinement of existing description hierarchies; however, here we are constrained to limitations of description logic and therefore e.g. unable to express formulas with a free variable. Therefore the works investigating learning in description logics are valuable especially in their results on dealing with the open-world assumption in learning and in transformations of description logics into some other subset of the first-order logic. Reasoning and learning in hybrid languages attempts to loosely couple descriptions of concept hierarchies in description logics with rules expressed in function-free Horn logic. Learning in hybrid languages is often split into two phases, each utilizing well-known algorithms particular to each of the respective formalisms. Reasoning in hybrid languages is more complex than reasoning in both its constituent formalisms. E.g. even if reasoning in the chosen subsets of both DL and HL formalisms separately is decidable, reasoning in the corresponding hybrid formalism may be undecidable [6]. A growth in computational complexity is obviously also a deficiency of approaches using representation formalisms with expressivity exceeding that of first-order logic.

This paper concentrates on the problem of exploiting taxonomies in the framework of propositionalization of relational data by constructing relational features and subsequent learning from the propositionalized representation. We exploit the term and predicate taxonomies in the process of relational feature construction, by adopting the formalism of sorted logic for feature representation and by adapting a refinement operator for first-order features to be co-guided by the taxonomies. In contrast to state-of-the-art logic-based propositionalization systems [5], we explicitly store the information that a feature has been obtained by specializing another feature. The propositional algorithm utilizes the resulting feature taxonomy to prevent the exploration of a conjunction containing a feature together with any of its subsumees and to specialize a rule by replacing a feature by its subsumee. Since the feature taxonomy is determined partly by θ-subsumption, it can be exploited whether or not relation and term taxonomies were available.

2 Sorted Logic

Our approach to propositionalization is based on RSD system [14]. In RSD, a predicate declaration assigns a type symbol to each argument, from a finite set of type symbols. The present approach replaces the notion of type with that of *sort* borrowed from the formalism of sorted logic, which is suitable for encoding term taxonomies. We shall introduce sorted logic and its use by an example. The Gene Function Ontology declares a concept `binding` and its subconcept protein_binding. Such concepts are reflected by terms in ILP. It is possible to declare in background knowledge e.g.

```
subclass(binding, protein_binding).
geneFunction(G, F1) :- geneFunction(G, F2), subclassTC(F1, F2).
```

(where subclassTC/2 is defined as the transitive closure of subclass/2). Unfortunately, in such an approach, for the following two exemplary clauses (hypotheses)

$C =$ activeGene(G):- geneFuction(G, binding).
$D =$ activeGene(G):- geneFuction(G, protein_binding).

it does not hold $C\theta \subseteq D$, so clause D is not obtained by applying a specialization refinement operator onto clause C. Similar reasoning applies to taxonomies on relations (predicates).

Sorted logic contains in addition to predicate and function symbols also a disjoint set of sort symbols. A sort symbol denotes a subset of the domain called a sort [2]. A *sorted variable* is a pair, $x\!:\!\tau$, where x is a variable name and τ is a sort symbol. Semantically, a sorted variable ranges over only the subset of the domain denoted by its sort symbol. The semantics of universally-quantified sorted formulas can be defined in terms of their equivalence to ordinary formulas: $\forall x\!:\!\tau\ \phi$ is logically equivalent to $\forall x : \neg\tau(x) \vee \phi^{'}$ where $\phi^{'}$ is the result of substituting x for all free occurrences of $x\!:\!\tau \in \phi$.

A *sort theory* Σ is a finite set of formulas containing function formulas and subsort formulas. A *function formula* has the form

$$\forall x_1, \ldots, x_n \tau_1(x_1) \wedge \ldots \wedge \tau_n(x_n) \rightarrow \tau(f(x_1, \ldots, x_n)) \quad (1)$$

where, in this paper, we constrain ourselves to $n = 0$, thus reducing function formulas to the form $\tau(f)$ reflecting that constant f is of sort τ. A *subsort formula* has the form

$$\forall x \tau_1(x) \rightarrow \tau_2(x) \quad (2)$$

reflecting that τ_1 is a direct subsort of τ_2. It is required that the directed graph corresponding to the subsort theory is acyclic and has a single root denoted *univ*.

For a sort theory Σ, a *Σ-sorted substitution* is a mapping from variables to terms such that for every variable $x\!:\!\tau$, it holds that $\Sigma \models \forall\tau(t)$ where t is $(x\!:\!\tau)\theta$, where θ is the sorted substitution. Informally, this is a substitution that does not violate the sort theory.

In the present propositionalization approach, terms in features are constants or sorted variables. Background knowledge consists of an ordinary first-order theory and a sort theory Σ. A *declaration* for a predicate of symbol π and arity n has the form

$$\pi(m_1\tau_1, \ldots, m_n\tau_n)$$

where $m_i \in \{+, -\}$ denotes whether i-th argument is an input (+) or an output (-). Besides the constraints imposed on features in RSD, correct features must respect the sort relationships. Formally, a literal *Lit* may appear in a feature only if there is a declaration $\pi(m_1\tau_1, \ldots, m_n\tau_n)$ and a Σ-sorted substitution θ such that $\pi(\tau_1, \ldots, \tau_n)\theta = Lit$. Next we turn attention to the refinement operator through which features are constructed.

3 Feature Construction and Adaptation of Learning

We have adapted the *sorted downward refinement* from [2], which accounts for term taxonomies, to further account for the earlier defined feature constraints and predicate declarations used in propositionalization, and for a further kind of taxonomy – the *predicate taxonomy* – often available in ontology data. This taxonomy is encoded through meta-predicates in the form

`subrelation(`$pred_1/n$`, `$pred_2/n$`).`

providing the explicit meta-information that goal $pred_1(Arg_1, \ldots, Arg_n)$ succeeds whenever goal $pred_2(Arg_1, \ldots, Arg_n)$ succeeds, i.e. $pred_1$ is more general. The directed graph corresponding to the entire set of the `subrelation/2` statements (where direction is such that edges start in the more general goal) is assumed to be a forest. The set of its roots is exactly the set of predicates declared through the predicate declarations defined in the previous section. It is assumed that the non-root predicates inherit the argument declarations from their respective roots.

As feature heads are fixed in our propositionalization framework, we are concerned with refinement of their bodies, i.e. conjunctions. We will use the notion of an *elementary Σ-substitution.* Its general definition can be found in [2], however, adapted to our framework, the definition simplifies.

An elementary Σ-substitution for a sorted conjunction C is $\{x : \tau_1\} \rightarrow \{x : \tau_2\}$ where $\{x : \tau_1\}$ occurs in C and Σ contains the subsort formula $\forall\psi\tau_2(\psi) \rightarrow \tau_1(\psi)$ for some variable ψ. If $\{x : \tau_2\}$ already occurs in C, then x is deterministically renamed[1] to a variable not occurring in C. Unlike in [2], we can disregard the case of substituting a sorted variable by a function (as we work with function-free features) and, similarly to RSD [14], we neither allow to unify two distinct variables (an equality theory can be defined instead in background knowledge).

Let C be a conjunction of non-negated atoms where any term is either a constant or a sorted variable, Σ be a sort theory, and Δ a set of predicate declarations. We define the *downward Δ, Σ-refinement*, written $\rho_{\Delta,\Sigma}(C)$, as the smallest set such that:

1. For each θ that is an elementary Σ-substitution for C, $\rho_{\Delta,\Sigma}(C)$ contains $C\theta$.
2. Let $\pi(m_1\tau_1, \ldots, m_n\tau_n)$ be a declaration in Δ such that for each i for which $m_i = +$, C contains a variable (denote it x_i) of sort τ_i' which equals or is a subsort of τ_i. Let further $\{x_i | m_i = -\}$ be a set of distinct variables not appearing in C. Then $\rho_{\Delta,\Sigma}(C)$ contains $C \wedge \pi(x_1 : \upsilon_1, ..., x_n : \upsilon_n)$, where $\upsilon_i = \tau_i'$ if $m_i = +$ and $\upsilon_i = \tau_i$ otherwise.

[1] That is, we do not allow several elementary substitutions differing only in the chosen renaming.

3. Let C contain a literal $pred_1(x_1\tau_1,\ldots,x_n\tau_n)$ and let $pred_2$ be a direct subrelation of $pred_1$. Then $\rho_{\Delta,\Sigma}(C)$ contains C', which is acquired by replacing $pred_1(x_1\tau_1,\ldots,x_n\tau_n)$ with $pred_2(x_1\tau_1,\ldots,x_n\tau_n)$ in C.

Confined to 8 pages, we skip the proof that, under very general assumptions on Δ, the defined refinement operator is (i) finite, (ii) complete, in that all correct features (as defined in [14] and Section 2) up to variable renaming are enumerated by its recursive closure, whenever the initial C in the recursive application of $\rho_{\Delta,\Sigma}(C)$ is true, and also (iii) non-redundant, in that $\rho_{\Delta,\Sigma}(C_1)\cap\rho_{\Delta,\Sigma}(C_2) = \{\}$ if $C_1 \neq C_2$. However, the operator is not necessarily correct, in that all its products would be correct feature bodies. In particular, it may produce a conjunction violating the undecomposability condition defined in [14].

During the recursive application of the refinement operator, a feature generality taxonomy becomes explicit. For purposes of enhancing the performance of the propositional learning algorithm applied subsequently on the propositionalized data, we pass the feature taxonomy information to the learner through two Boolean matrices.[2] Assume that features $f_1,\ldots f_n$ have been generated with corresponding conjunctive bodies $b_1,\ldots b_n$. The *elementary subsumption matrix* $\mathbf{E}$ of n rows and n columns is defined such that $\mathbf{E}_{i,j} = 1$ whenever $b_i \in \rho_{\Delta,\Sigma}(b_j)$ and $\mathbf{E}_{i,j} = 0$ otherwise. The *exclusion matrix* $\mathbf{X}$ of n rows and n columns is defined such that $\mathbf{X}_{i,j} = 1$ whenever $i = j$ or $b_i \in \rho_{\Delta,\Sigma}(\rho_{\Delta,\Sigma}(\ldots\rho_{\Delta,\Sigma}(b_j)\ldots))$ and $\mathbf{X}_{i,j} = 0$ otherwise.

A skeleton of the propositionalization algorithm is shown in Fig. 1. The algorithm is a depth-first search generally similar to the feature constructor of RSD [14]. The main difference lies in using the novel sorted refinement operator $\rho_{\Delta,\Sigma}$ and also in creating the matrices $\mathbf{E}$ and $\mathbf{X}$ storing the generality taxonomy of constructed features. The **Undecomposable** procedure checks whether a feature is not a conjunction of already generated features, through a method used in RSD and detailed in [14]. The **AddFeatureHead** forms a feature clause by formally attaching a head to the body, which consists of the constructed conjunction *Curr*. The **Coverage** procedure verifies the truth value of a conjunction for all examples in E returning a vector of Boolean values. The verification is done by a transformation of the sorted conjunction *Curr* to an ordinary first-order conjunction as explained in Sec. 2 and then using a standard resolution procedure against a Prolog database consisting of B and Σ. For efficiency, the procedure obtains the coverage $\mathbf{A}_{Parent,1\ldots l}$ of the closest ancestor (subsuming) conjunction whose coverage was tested: any example i such that $\mathbf{A}_{Parent,i}$ is false can be left out of testing as it makes the current conjunction necessarily false as well. The **Closure** procedure computes the transitive closure of the elementary subsumption relation captured in $\mathbf{E}$ in the manner described above, and represents the closed relation analogically in matrix $\mathbf{X}$, in which it further sets $\mathbf{X}_{i,i} = 1$ for all $1 \leq i \leq n$.

[2] While alternative data structures are of course possible for this sake, the elected binary matrix form requires modest space for encoding (our implementation uses one byte for each 8 matrix elements) and also is conveniently processed in the propositional algorithm implementation.

Propositionalize$(\Delta, B, \Sigma, E, l)$: **Given**, a set Δ of predicate declarations, a first-order theory (background knowledge) B, a sort theory Σ, a set of unary ground facts (examples) $E = \{e_1, \ldots, e_m\}$ and a natural number l; **returns** a set $\{f_1, \ldots, f_n\}$ of constructed features, each with at most l atoms in the body, an elementary subsumption matrix $\mathbf{E}$, an exclusion matrix $\mathbf{X}$, and an attribute-value matrix $\mathbf{A}$ where $\mathbf{A}_{i,j} = 1$ whenever f_i is true for e_j and $\mathbf{A}_{i,j} = 0$ otherwise.

1. $n = 0$; $Agenda$ = a single element list $[(C, 0)]$, where C = true;
2. If $Agenda = []$: go to 10
3. $(Curr, Parent) :=$ **Head**$(Agenda)$; $Tail :=$ **Tail**$(Agenda)$
4. If **Nonempty**$(Curr)$ and **Undecomposable**$(Curr)$:
5. $\quad n := n + 1$; $f_n =$ **AddFeatureHead**$(Curr)$;
6. $\quad \mathbf{E}_{n,Parent} = 1$; $Parent = n$;
7. $\quad \mathbf{A}_{n,1\ldots l} =$**Coverage**$(Curr, E, B, \Sigma, \mathbf{A}_{Parent,1\ldots l})$
8. $Rfs := \rho_{\Delta,\Sigma}(Curr)$; $Rfs := \{(Cnj, Parent) | Cnj \in Rfs, |Cnj| \leq l\}$
9. $Agenda :=$ **Append**(Rfs, Tail); go to 2
10. $\mathbf{X} =$ **Closure**$(\mathbf{E})$
11. **Return** $f_1, \ldots, f_n$, **E**, **X**, **A**

Fig. 1. A skeleton of the algorithm for propositionalization through relational feature construction using the sorted refinement operator $\rho_{\Delta,\Sigma}$

We have adapted two rule learning algorithms to account for the feature taxonomy information provided by the propositionalization algorithm. The first algorithm stems from the rule inducer of RSD [14]. It is based on a heuristic general-to-specific deterministic beam search for the induction of a single propositional conjunctive rule for a given target class, and a cover-set wrapper for the induction of the entire rule set for the class. Given a set of features $F = \{f_1, \ldots f_n\}$, the standard algorithm refines a conjunction C of features into the set $\{C \wedge f_i | f_i \in F, f_i \notin C\}$. In our enhanced version, the algorithm is provided with the elementary subsumption matrix $\mathbf{E}$ and the exclusion matrix $\mathbf{X}$. Using these matrices it can prevent the useless combination of a feature and its subsumee within the conjunction, and specialize a conjunction by replacing a feature with its elementary (direct) subsumee. Furthermore, we have similarly enhanced the stochastic local DNF search algorithm introduced in [11] and later transferred into the propositionalization framework by [8]. This algorithm conducts search in the space of DNF formulas, i.e. it refines entire propositional rule sets. Refinement is done by local, non-deterministic DNF term changes detailed in [11]. In our version, the $\mathbf{X}$ matrix is used to prevent the combination of a feature and its subsumee within a DNF term.

4 Experimental Results

We designed experiments to assess the runtime impact of (i) the novel taxonomy-aware refinement operator in propositionalization, and (ii) the exploitation of the feature-taxonomy in subsequent propositional learning. We conducted tests in two domains. The first concerns genomics, where we used data and language

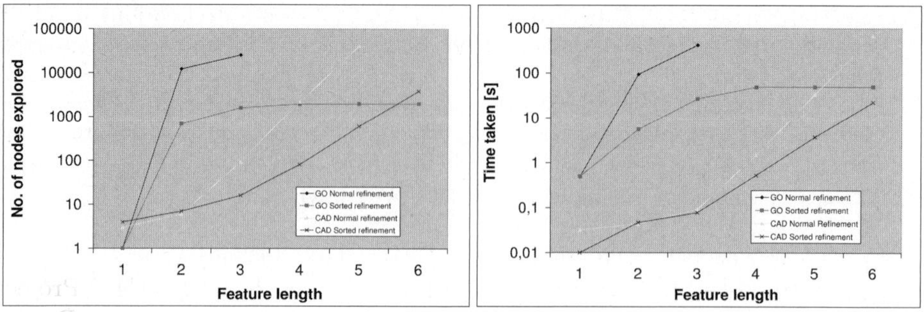

Fig. 2. Sorted refinement vs. standard refinement on CAD and Genomic data. Left: Nodes explored Right: Time taken. (Experiments exceeding 1000s were discarded).

Table 1. Propositional rule learning from CAD and Genomic data

Domain	CAD data		Genomic data	
Algorithm	Time taken	Predict. acc.	Time taken	Predict. acc.
Top-down	0.22 ± 0.08	0.66 ± 0.21	0.99 ± 0.65	0.79 ± 0.13
Top-down, FT	0.06 ± 0.02	0.66 ± 0.22	0.34 ± 0.19	0.76 ± 0.07
SLS	0.63 ± 1.45	0.62 ± 0.18	3.00 ± 2.59	0.79 ± 0.13
SLS, FT	0.28 ± 0.83	0.61 ± 0.19	1.90 ± 1.69	0.76 ± 0.07

declarations from [12]. The second is concerned with learning from product design data. Here the examples are semantically annotated CAD documents. We used the same learning setting and ontology data as in [13].

Figure 2 illustrates on log scale the number of conjunctions searched (left) and the time spent on search (right) to enumerate all conjunctions true for at least 80% examples, for increasing maximum conjunction size l. Here, we distinguish the sorted refinement operator using a special sort theory Σ encoding the taxonomy information, against the standard refinement operator, which treats the taxonomy information only as part of background knowledge. While in both cases exactly the same set of conjunctions is produced, an order-of-magnitude runtime improvement is observed for the 'taxonomy-aware' operator.

Table 1 shows the runtime spent of inducing a rule set by two algorithms (top-down and stochastic) through 10-fold cross validation in two scenarios: in the first, no feature taxonomy information is used by the algorithms, in the second, feature taxonomy is exploited. A significant speedup is observed when feature taxonomy is used without compromising the predictive accuracy.

5 Conclusions

In this work we have proposed principled methods to exploit term, predicate and feature taxonomies to increase the performance of propositionalization and subsequent propositional learning. The significance of our work is supported by three factors: (i) order-of-magnitude runtime improvements with no sacrifice in predictive accuracy, (ii) the practical value and common use [5] of the propositionalization strategy, which was the target of our methodological enhancements, and (iii) the increasing volumes of semantic knowledge representations providing explicit taxonomies. In future work, we plan to extend the scope of meta-information exploitable by refinement operators beyond taxonomy information including e.g. "relation R is a function" or "binary relation R is symmetrical."

Acknowledgements. This research was supported by the FP6-027473 Project SEVENPRO. The authors would like to thank Peter Flach and Simon Rawles for valuable advice concerning term taxonomies in ILP.

References

1. Badea, L., Neinhuys-Cheng, S.-W.: A Refinement Operator for Descriptionn Logics. In: Cussens, J., Frisch, A.M. (eds.) ILP 2000. LNCS (LNAI), vol. 1866, pp. 40–59. Springer, Heidelberg (2000)
2. Frisch, A.: Sorted downward refinement: Building background knowledge into a refinement operator for ILP. In: Džeroski, S., Flach, P.A. (eds.) Inductive Logic Programming. LNCS (LNAI), vol. 1634, pp. 104–115. Springer, Heidelberg (1999)
3. Kietz, J.-U.: Learnability of Description Logic Programs. In: Matwin, S., Sammut, C. (eds.) ILP 2002. LNCS (LNAI), vol. 2583, Springer, Heidelberg (2003)
4. King, R.D., et al.: Functional genomic hypothesis generation and experimentation by a robot scientist. Nature 427, 247–252 (2004)
5. Krogel, M.-A., Rawles, S., et al.: Comparative evaluation of approaches to propositionalization. In: Horváth, T., Yamamoto, A. (eds.) ILP 2003. LNCS (LNAI), vol. 2835, pp. 197–214. Springer, Heidelberg (2003)
6. Levy, A.Y., Rousset, M.-C.: The Limits on Combining Recursive Horn Rules with Description Logics. In: AAAI/IAAI, vol. 1, pp. 577–584 (1996)
7. Lisi, F.A.: Principles of Inductive Reasoning on the Semantic Web: A Framework for Learning in AL-log. In: Fages, F., Soliman, S. (eds.) PPSWR 2005. LNCS, vol. 3703, pp. 118–132. Springer, Heidelberg (2005)
8. Paes, A., Zaverucha, G., Železný, F., et al.: ILP through Propositionalization and k-Term DNF Learning. In: Proc. of the 16th Conference on ILP, Springer, Heidelberg (2007)
9. Popelínský, L.: Inductive inference to support object-oriented analysis and design. Frontiers in Artificial Intelligence and Applications 48, IOS Press (1998)
10. Rouveirol, C., Ventos, V.: Towards learning in CARIN-ALN. In: Cussens, J., Frisch, A.M. (eds.) ILP 2000. LNCS (LNAI), vol. 1866, pp. 191–208. Springer, Heidelberg (2000)
11. Rückert, U., Kramer, S.: Stochastic local search in k-term dnf learning. In: Proc. of the 20th ICML, pp. 648–655 (2003)
12. Trajkovski, I., et al.: Relational Subgroup Discovery for Descriptive Analysis of Microarray Data. In: Proc. of CompLife 06, Springer, Heidelberg (2006)
13. Žáková, M., Železný, F., et al.: Relational Data Mining Applied to Virtual Engineering of Product Designs. In: Proc. of ILP 06, Springer, Heidelberg (2007)
14. Železný, F., Lavrač, N.: Propositionalization-based relational subgroup discovery with RSD. Machine Learning 62, 33–63 (2006)

Author Index

Printing: Mercedes-Druck, Berlin
Binding: Stein+Lehmann, Berlin

Lecture Notes in Artificial Intelligence (LNAI)

Vol. 4733: R. Basili, M.T. Pazienza (Eds.), AI*IA 2007: Artificial Intelligence and Human-Oriented Computing. XVII, 858 pages. 2007.

Vol. 4720: B. Konev, F. Wolter (Eds.), Frontiers of Combining Systems. X, 283 pages. 2007.

Vol. 4702: J.N. Kok, J. Koronacki, R. Lopez de Mantaras, S. Matwin, D. Mladenič, A. Skowron (Eds.), Knowledge Discovery in Databases: PKDD 2007. XXIV, 640 pages. 2007.

Vol. 4701: J.N. Kok, J. Koronacki, R.Lopez de Mantaras, S. Matwin, D. Mladenič, A. Skowron (Eds.), Machine Learning: ECML 2007. XXIV, 809 pages. 2007.

Vol. 4694: B. Apolloni, R.J. Howlett, L. Jain (Eds.), Knowledge-Based Intelligent Information and Engineering Systems, Part III. XXIX, 1126 pages. 2007.

Vol. 4693: B. Apolloni, R.J. Howlett, L. Jain (Eds.), Knowledge-Based Intelligent Information and Engineering Systems, Part II. XXXII, 1380 pages. 2007.

Vol. 4692: B. Apolloni, R.J. Howlett, L. Jain (Eds.), Knowledge-Based Intelligent Information and Engineering Systems, Part I. LV, 882 pages. 2007.

Vol. 4682: D.-S. Huang, L. Heutte, M. Loog (Eds.), Advanced Intelligent Computing Theories and Applications. XXVII, 1373 pages. 2007.

Vol. 4676: M. Klusch, K. Hindriks, M.P. Papazoglou, L. Sterling (Eds.), Cooperative Information Agents XI. XI, 361 pages. 2007.

Vol. 4667: J. Hertzberg, M. Beetz, R. Englert (Eds.), KI 2007: Advances in Artificial Intelligence. IX, 516 pages. 2007.

Vol. 4660: S. Džeroski, J. Todorovski (Eds.), Computational Discovery of Scientific Knowledge. X, 327 pages. 2007.

Vol. 4659: V. Mařík, V. Vyatkin, A.W. Colombo (Eds.), Holonic and Multi-Agent Systems for Manufacturing. VIII, 456 pages. 2007.

Vol. 4651: F. Azevedo, P. Barahona, F. Fages, F. Rossi (Eds.), Recent Advances in Constraints. VIII, 185 pages. 2007.

Vol. 4648: F. Almeida e Costa, L.M. Rocha, E. Costa, I. Harvey, A. Coutinho (Eds.), Advances in Artificial Life. XVIII, 1215 pages. 2007.

Vol. 4635: B. Kokinov, D.C. Richardson, T.R. Roth-Berghofer, L. Vieu (Eds.), Modeling and Using Context. XIV, 574 pages. 2007.

Vol. 4632: R. Alhajj, H. Gao, X. Li, J. Li, O.R. Zaïane (Eds.), Advanced Data Mining and Applications. XV, 634 pages. 2007.

Vol. 4629: V. Matoušek, P. Mautner (Eds.), Text, Speech and Dialogue. XVII, 663 pages. 2007.

Vol. 4626: R.O. Weber, M.M. Richter (Eds.), Case-Based Reasoning Research and Development. XIII, 534 pages. 2007.

Vol. 4617: V. Torra, Y. Narukawa, Y. Yoshida (Eds.), Modeling Decisions for Artificial Intelligence. XII, 502 pages. 2007.

Vol. 4612: I. Miguel, W. Ruml (Eds.), Abstraction, Reformulation, and Approximation. XI, 418 pages. 2007.

Vol. 4604: U. Priss, S. Polovina, R. Hill (Eds.), Conceptual Structures: Knowledge Architectures for Smart Applications. XII, 514 pages. 2007.

Vol. 4603: F. Pfenning (Ed.), Automated Deduction – CADE-21. XII, 522 pages. 2007.

Vol. 4597: P. Perner (Ed.), Advances in Data Mining. XI, 353 pages. 2007.

Vol. 4594: R. Bellazzi, A. Abu-Hanna, J. Hunter (Eds.), Artificial Intelligence in Medicine. XVI, 509 pages. 2007.

Vol. 4585: M. Kryszkiewicz, J.F. Peters, H. Rybinski, A. Skowron (Eds.), Rough Sets and Intelligent Systems Paradigms. XIX, 836 pages. 2007.

Vol. 4578: F. Masulli, S. Mitra, G. Pasi (Eds.), Applications of Fuzzy Sets Theory. XVIII, 693 pages. 2007.

Vol. 4573: M. Kauers, M. Kerber, R. Miner, W. Windsteiger (Eds.), Towards Mechanized Mathematical Assistants. XIII, 407 pages. 2007.

Vol. 4571: P. Perner (Ed.), Machine Learning and Data Mining in Pattern Recognition. XIV, 913 pages. 2007.

Vol. 4570: H.G. Okuno, M. Ali (Eds.), New Trends in Applied Artificial Intelligence. XXI, 1194 pages. 2007.

Vol. 4565: D.D. Schmorrow, L.M. Reeves (Eds.), Foundations of Augmented Cognition. XIX, 450 pages. 2007.

Vol. 4562: D. Harris (Ed.), Engineering Psychology and Cognitive Ergonomics. XXIII, 879 pages. 2007.

Vol. 4548: N. Olivetti (Ed.), Automated Reasoning with Analytic Tableaux and Related Methods. X, 245 pages. 2007.

Vol. 4539: N.H. Bshouty, C. Gentile (Eds.), Learning Theory. XII, 634 pages. 2007.

Vol. 4529: P. Melin, O. Castillo, L.T. Aguilar, J. Kacprzyk, W. Pedrycz (Eds.), Foundations of Fuzzy Logic and Soft Computing. XIX, 830 pages. 2007.

Vol. 4520: M.V. Butz, O. Sigaud, G. Pezzulo, G. Baldassarre (Eds.), Anticipatory Behavior in Adaptive Learning Systems. X, 379 pages. 2007.

Vol. 4511: C. Conati, K. McCoy, G. Paliouras (Eds.), User Modeling 2007. XVI, 487 pages. 2007.

Vol. 4509: Z. Kobti, D. Wu (Eds.), Advances in Artificial Intelligence. XII, 552 pages. 2007.

Vol. 4496: N.T. Nguyen, A. Grzech, R.J. Howlett, L.C. Jain (Eds.), Agent and Multi-Agent Systems: Technologies and Applications. XXI, 1046 pages. 2007.

Vol. 4483: C. Baral, G. Brewka, J. Schlipf (Eds.), Logic Programming and Nonmonotonic Reasoning. IX, 327 pages. 2007.

Vol. 4482: A. An, J. Stefanowski, S. Ramanna, C.J. Butz, W. Pedrycz, G. Wang (Eds.), Rough Sets, Fuzzy Sets, Data Mining and Granular Computing. XIV, 585 pages. 2007.

Vol. 4481: J. Yao, P. Lingras, W.-Z. Wu, M. Szczuka, N.J. Cercone, D. Ślęzak (Eds.), Rough Sets and Knowledge Technology. XIV, 576 pages. 2007.

Vol. 4476: V. Gorodetsky, C. Zhang, V.A. Skormin, L. Cao (Eds.), Autonomous Intelligent Systems: Multi-Agents and Data Mining. XIII, 323 pages. 2007.

Vol. 4456: Y. Wang, Y.-m. Cheung, H. Liu (Eds.), Computational Intelligence and Security. XXIII, 1118 pages. 2007.

Vol. 4455: S. Muggleton, R. Otero, A. Tamaddoni-Nezhad (Eds.), Inductive Logic Programming. XII, 456 pages. 2007.

Vol. 4452: M. Fasli, O. Shehory (Eds.), Agent-Mediated Electronic Commerce. VIII, 249 pages. 2007.

Vol. 4451: T.S. Huang, A. Nijholt, M. Pantic, A. Pentland (Eds.), Artifical Intelligence for Human Computing. XVI, 359 pages. 2007.

Vol. 4441: C. Müller (Ed.), Speaker Classification. X, 309 pages. 2007.

Vol. 4438: L. Maicher, A. Sigel, L.M. Garshol (Eds.), Leveraging the Semantics of Topic Maps. X, 257 pages. 2007.

Vol. 4434: G. Lakemeyer, E. Sklar, D.G. Sorrenti, T. Takahashi (Eds.), RoboCup 2006: Robot Soccer World Cup X. XIII, 566 pages. 2007.

Vol. 4429: R. Lu, J.H. Siekmann, C. Ullrich (Eds.), Cognitive Systems. X, 161 pages. 2007.

Vol. 4428: S. Edelkamp, A. Lomuscio (Eds.), Model Checking and Artificial Intelligence. IX, 185 pages. 2007.

Vol. 4426: Z.-H. Zhou, H. Li, Q. Yang (Eds.), Advances in Knowledge Discovery and Data Mining. XXV, 1161 pages. 2007.

Vol. 4411: R.H. Bordini, M. Dastani, J. Dix, A.E.F. Seghrouchni (Eds.), Programming Multi-Agent Systems. XIV, 249 pages. 2007.

Vol. 4410: A. Branco (Ed.), Anaphora: Analysis, Algorithms and Applications. X, 191 pages. 2007.

Vol. 4399: T. Kovacs, X. Llorà, K. Takadama, P.L. Lanzi, W. Stolzmann, S.W. Wilson (Eds.), Learning Classifier Systems. XII, 345 pages. 2007.

Vol. 4390: S.O. Kuznetsov, S. Schmidt (Eds.), Formal Concept Analysis. X, 329 pages. 2007.

Vol. 4389: D. Weyns, H.V.D. Parunak, F. Michel (Eds.), Environments for Multi-Agent Systems III. X, 273 pages. 2007.

Vol. 4386: P. Noriega, J. Vázquez-Salceda, G. Boella, O. Boissier, V. Dignum, N. Fornara, E. Matson (Eds.), Coordination, Organizations, Institutions, and Norms in Agent Systems II. XI, 373 pages. 2007.

Vol. 4384: T. Washio, K. Satoh, H. Takeda, A. Inokuchi (Eds.), New Frontiers in Artificial Intelligence. IX, 401 pages. 2007.

Vol. 4371: K. Inoue, K. Satoh, F. Toni (Eds.), Computational Logic in Multi-Agent Systems. X, 315 pages. 2007.

Vol. 4369: M. Umeda, A. Wolf, O. Bartenstein, U. Geske, D. Seipel, O. Takata (Eds.), Declarative Programming for Knowledge Management. X, 229 pages. 2006.

Vol. 4343: C. Müller (Ed.), Speaker Classification I. X, 355 pages. 2007.

Vol. 4342: H. de Swart, E. Orłowska, G. Schmidt, M. Roubens (Eds.), Theory and Applications of Relational Structures as Knowledge Instruments II. X, 373 pages. 2006.

Vol. 4335: S.A. Brueckner, S. Hassas, M. Jelasity, D. Yamins (Eds.), Engineering Self-Organising Systems. XII, 212 pages. 2007.

Vol. 4334: B. Beckert, R. Hähnle, P.H. Schmitt (Eds.), Verification of Object-Oriented Software. XXIX, 658 pages. 2007.

Vol. 4333: U. Reimer, D. Karagiannis (Eds.), Practical Aspects of Knowledge Management. XII, 338 pages. 2006.

Vol. 4327: M. Baldoni, U. Endriss (Eds.), Declarative Agent Languages and Technologies IV. VIII, 257 pages. 2006.

Vol. 4314: C. Freksa, M. Kohlhase, K. Schill (Eds.), KI 2006: Advances in Artificial Intelligence. XII, 458 pages. 2007.

Vol. 4304: A. Sattar, B.-h. Kang (Eds.), AI 2006: Advances in Artificial Intelligence. XXVII, 1303 pages. 2006.

Vol. 4303: A. Hoffmann, B.-h. Kang, D. Richards, S. Tsumoto (Eds.), Advances in Knowledge Acquisition and Management. XI, 259 pages. 2006.

Vol. 4293: A. Gelbukh, C.A. Reyes-Garcia (Eds.), MICAI 2006: Advances in Artificial Intelligence. XXVIII, 1232 pages. 2006.

Vol. 4289: M. Ackermann, B. Berendt, M. Grobelnik, A. Hotho, D. Mladenič, G. Semeraro, M. Spiliopoulou, G. Stumme, V. Svátek, M. van Someren (Eds.), Semantics, Web and Mining. X, 197 pages. 2006.

Vol. 4285: Y. Matsumoto, R.W. Sproat, K.-F. Wong, M. Zhang (Eds.), Computer Processing of Oriental Languages. XVII, 544 pages. 2006.

Vol. 4274: Q. Huo, B. Ma, E.-S. Chng, H. Li (Eds.), Chinese Spoken Language Processing. XXIV, 805 pages. 2006.

Vol. 4265: L. Todorovski, N. Lavrač, K.P. Jantke (Eds.), Discovery Science. XIV, 384 pages. 2006.

Vol. 4264: J.L. Balcázar, P.M. Long, F. Stephan (Eds.), Algorithmic Learning Theory. XIII, 393 pages. 2006.